The 1997 Good Hotel Guide

The 1997 Good Hotel Guide

To Britain and Europe

Editor: Hilary Rubinstein

Deputy Editor and Editor for the British Isles:
Caroline Raphael

Continental Editor:
John Ardagh

Contributing Editor:
Emily Read

VERMILION
LONDON

Please send reports on hotels to
The Good Hotel Guide
61 Clarendon Road, London W11 4JE
or (posted in UK only) Freepost, London W11 4BR
Tel/fax: (0171) 221 5291

This edition first published in 1996 by Vermilion,
an imprint of Ebury Press,
Random House, 20 Vauxhall Bridge Road,
London SW1V 2SA

1 3 5 7 9 10 8 6 4 2

Text editor: Sarah Thomas
Managing editor for Ebury Press: Alison Wormleighton
Editorial assistants: Katinka Ardagh, Anne Gray

A catalogue for this book may be found in the British Library.

ISBN 0 09 178714 9

Typeset from author's disks by
SX Composing DTP, Rayleigh, Essex
Printed and bound in Great Britain by
BPC Paperbacks Ltd
A member of
The British Printing Company Ltd

Contents

A note for new readers vii
Introduction ix
The 1997 César awards xvi
Special hotels xix
How we choose our hotels xxvii
How to read the entries xxix

PART ONE
Great Britain and Ireland
England 3
Wales 227
Scotland 249
Channel Islands 303
Northern Ireland 309
Republic of Ireland 313

PART TWO
The Continent
Austria 349
Belgium 365
The Czech Republic 379
Denmark 385
France 391
Germany 561
Greece 599
Hungary 609
Italy 613
Luxembourg 675
Malta 679

The Netherlands 681
Norway 689
Portugal (including Madeira) 695
Slovenia 709
Spain (including The Balearics and The Canaries) 715
Sweden 755
Switzerland (including Liechtenstein) 761

The Heart of an Innkeeper 781
Entente Cordiale 783
Alphabetical list of hotels 785
Maps 801
Exchange rates 832
Champagne winners and hotel reports 833
Hotel report forms 835

A note for new readers

This is an annual guide to hotels, guest houses and inns in the British Isles and on the Continent of Europe that are of unusual character and quality. It is completely independent. No cash changes hands at any point; contributors are not rewarded for writing to us; hotels do not pay for their entries; the editor and his staff accept no free hospitality.

The entries are based on reports from readers who write to us when they come across an establishment which has given them out-of-the-ordinary satisfaction, and who send us their comments, critical or appreciative, when they visit places already included in the *Guide*. We verify and collate the reports, making inspections where necessary, and select those hotels which we consider make the grade.

We do not attempt to be comprehensive. There are many blank areas on our maps, and even major cities lack a single entry. We see no point in lowering our standards in order to recommend an indifferent establishment as "the best available". But of course we are particularly glad to receive nominations for hotels in a town or a region that is poorly represented. If you can help to plug our gaps, please do so.

Most of our entries, especially in rural areas, are for small establishments (but never with fewer than three rooms) in the hands of resident owners. We don't have any *prima facie* objection to large hotels or those run by managers, except that, in our experience, they often fail to provide the welcome and care for guests' comforts that can be found in the best of the small individually owned hostelries. And this failure is particularly evident in the case of hotels owned by a chain, which explains why there are few chain hotels in these pages.

The entries in this book cover a wide range. People want different things from a hotel depending on whether they are making a single-night stop or spending a whole holiday in one place, whether they have young children with them, whether they are visiting a city or staying in the remote countryside, and according to their age and means. Many *Guide* establishments are distinctly unhotel-like. Some are very small; many do not have the kind of facilities which are normal in chain hotels. We try to convey the flavour of each place. We make no claims of universal compatibility, but hope that our descriptions will help you to find hotels that suit your tastes, needs and purse. If an entry has misled you, please use one of the report forms at the back of the book and tell us, so that we can do better next time. We hope also that you will write to us if a hotel has fulfilled your expectations. Both endorsement and criticism are essential if the *Guide* is to achieve its purpose. A hotel is dropped unless we get a positive feedback.

We should emphasise that this is a thoroughly personal work. We started the *Guide* 20 years ago because we wanted a book that would tell us honestly what to expect when we make a reservation. Brochures help, but are often deceptive. Travel agents can be useful if they specialise in particular localities, but they often know at recent first-hand only a fraction of the hotels on their books. *Michelin* is an invaluable touring companion, but its conventional signs, useful though they are, do not convey the flavour of a place. For many, the most reliable way to choose a hotel is by word-of-mouth recommendation. One way to describe this work is to say that it is the word of mouth in print.

The book's aim is to reflect the discriminating taste of its readers. From the first edition, we have depended on the generosity of those who write to us about the hotels they visit. We could not function without this continuous blood transfusion. We appreciate even the briefest endorsement or comment; but it is of course the stylish, witty, perceptive reports that help to give the *Guide* its special character. We are always grateful, too, for suggestions as to how to make the *Guide* more useful.

Inevitably, the book is full of personal prejudices and preferences, including the editor's. We loathe big anonymous hotels where we might as well be in Los Angeles or Lisbon as in London. We avoid, if we can, boring establishments which lack individuality in their decor and warmth in their welcome. We care about good food, but decry pretentiousness in cooking. We cherish the dedicated hotelier who, like a monk, has a vocation for his work.

Introduction

Our twentieth edition. Not a long span by the standards of *Baedeker* or *Michelin* perhaps, but still a milestone birthday and something to celebrate.

"If I had to offer a single reason why I have embarked on this risky undertaking," I wrote in 1977, "it is in the hope that the *Guide* can help the dedicated individual hotelier to survive and flourish against the formidable opposition of the big battalions, with all the resources and economies of scale which they are able to deploy. I loathe the safe, boring, homogenised hotel that insulates its guests from their environment. I treasure the personal and idiosyncratic establishment that is waging a fight against entropy."

Twenty years on, I still subscribe to that code. How far have these worthwhile aspirations been realised? I am happy to say that, notwithstanding the looming presence of Big Brothers, mostly engaged in fighting their siblings, small personal hotels continue to be launched and find their niche. No one would call them an endangered species. Our first edition offered a paltry 250 hotels. Over the years, the number of entries has multiplied some six times, despite annual culling of hotels that go out of business or lower their standards. I would be happy to stay in any of the 1,500 houses described on the following pages. Being eclectic in my taste, I would expect to enjoy equally those dream palaces catering for the seriously rich and the more modest Budgets which can be quite as enticing in their own way and often offer staggering value for money.

I am still surprised that no one else had the idea before I did. *The Good Food Guide* had been garnering gourmet *vox pop* from its readers since 1951, and had become a national institution. It seemed a reasonable bet that the same technique of selecting and collating contributions from members of the public would work as well for hotels. My first step was to ask the then editor of the *GFG*, Christopher Driver, what he thought of my plan. In the nicest way, he told me I needed my head examining. But he didn't succeed in putting me off.

The *Good Hotel Guide*, though covering the whole of Western Europe, not just the UK, was from its inception a transparent spin-off of the *GFG*, so much so that Consumers' Association, the publishers of *The Good Food Guide*, considered trying to stop my book on the grounds of passing off. I am glad they thought better of it! In a note at the front of the first edition, I disclaimed any connection between my guide and CA, but acknowledged that the book was a descendant, even if through the natural line, of the *GFG*'s founder, Raymond Postgate.

Our first edition got off to a rousing start, thanks in part to sponsorship by *The Observer*. Travel editors on other papers also supported the cause, and Derek Cooper, doyen of food broadcasters, gave me generous airspace to propagate the enterprise. After the second edition, I was chuffed to be asked by Consumers' Association if they could become my publishers, alongside the *GFG*, *The Good Pub Guide* and *The Which? Wine Guide*, on the "if you can't beat 'em, join 'em" principle.

For ten years, CA were my publishers, but then a new director decided that the Association should henceforth own the copyright in all its publications. I was invited to sell, but declined – as did Alasdair Aird of *The Good Pub Guide*. We both valued our independence and were sceptical that our guides could retain their personal, not to say idiosyncratic, styles once they were owned by a large corporation, even one as high-minded as CA.

I am glad to say that the *GHG* continues to flourish as an independent enterprise, eschewing all advertising and kick-backs – as *The Guardian* put it: "squeaky clean". In the intervening years, we have been flattered by the number of look-alike guides that have been launched in our slipstream. Notwithstanding the competition, we sold more copies in the trade in 1996 than ever before, and our sights are set still higher. We have more entries this year than ever before, and have enfranchised two new countries in Central Europe. And I am particularly delighted that Alasdair and I, while still doing our individual thing in our own way, are once again stable mates, this time with Ebury Press.

Winds of Change?

I am not a natural Cassandra, but for several years past my introductory comments have made gloomy reading. In Britain we have had five lean years, but at long last in 1996 there appear to be prospects, even if somewhat patchy, of an economic upturn for hoteliers. In February we were glad to read that the number of overseas visitors to the UK had risen by 4% in 1995, and that the money spent by 21.9 million visitors was 9% up on the previous year. Not only were more visitors coming from abroad, attracted from the Continent by the Channel Tunnel, and from all quarters of the globe by the weak pound, but the hot summer of 1995 helped to remind the British of the neglected delights of holidays at home. The lure of France had lessened as the franc rose in value.

London is the hive where tourists swarm most busily. Unfortunately, the end of the long recession has caught the London Tourist Board on the hop: there has been a grave shortage of beds in 1996 at every price range. One consequence has been an instant rise in the value of hotels, both the chains and the independents. Hoteliers, especially owners of the ever more fashionable town house establishments, who had no thought of selling, are liable to be destabilised by fancy offers that sound more like lottery money. We hear a rumour that such-and-such a hotel is on the market. We ring up to confirm. "Absolutely not." But after a bit of probing, they confess that, yes, they have had some attractive offers – and, yes, they might find themselves cashing in on their good fortune if something really irresistible turns up. All of which is a prelude to warning readers that they should be prepared for unanticipated changes of ownership.

We don't blame hotels for being reticent about their plans before they are fully hatched, and, as we go to press, were given a good illustration of the pitfalls of coming clean prematurely. *Plas Bodegroes*, Chris Chown's *Michelin*-starred restaurant-with-rooms in Pwllheli, which won a César in 1992, was omitted last year because we were told that it was up for sale. The sale never came off, but sadly news of this reached us only when it was too late to reinstate the entry. Chris Chown is kicking himself for being too honest, but we continue to hope and expect that hoteliers will level with us about possible plans for moving.

In the meantime, one hotel story beyond all others has commanded the column inches in British papers – namely, Granada's hostile bid for the Forte Empire. In our Introduction to the 1996 edition, under the heading "Forte Towers", we commented on the fierce competition to conventional hotels from the new budget-priced purpose-built chain hotels, most notably Forte's Posthouses and Travelodges, that were reproducing themselves promiscuously along major routes throughout the British Isles. Do you imagine that there will be any benefit to the consumer from the fact that these lodgings, and most other enterprises formerly listed on the Forte inventory, will henceforth be subsumed under an even larger corporation? We doubt it, and were not reassured by a statement put out by Charles Allen, Granada's chief operating officer, shortly after victory had been achieved. "All the changes we make will be focused on the customer," he declared. "In the longer term, staff at the base of operations will be increased, but above that the structure will be flattened." At the time of writing, far from there being any signs of improvement for the customer, prices at Travelodges have risen as Granada no longer needs to worry about competition from its former rival. And spare a thought for those flattened folk – and all the other culled victims of takeovers or rationalisations, mergers or privatisations in the past decade. Can you think of a single case where, after the event, the customer has been better served?

Plus ça change

Six years after our first edition, we made a survey of readers' most frequently recurring complaints. Facilities in hotels have of course improved enormously in the past two decades, and we welcome the advent of more imaginative menus but in other respects very little has changed for the better. Our 1984 catalogue of pet hates is reproduced below. A 1997 whinge-list would be much the same.

Bedrooms Cramped, cold, noisy, dirty, damp. Not enough storage space. Inadequate bedside lighting. Cheap furnishings. Lumpy mattress. Lingering smell of cigarettes.

Bathrooms Inadequate hot water, lighting, mirror. Noisy malodorous plumbing. Small, poor-quality towels. No shelf for toilet accessories.

Public rooms Inadequate heating, lighting. Over-crowded when hotel full or busy with non-resident diners. Smoky. Muzak.

Breakfasts Disappointing in contrast to evening meal. Poor coffee. Teabags. Packet or tinned fruit juice. No home-made jam. Wrapped butter. Cold limp toast. Greasy fry-ups.

Lunch and Dinner Pretentious menu. Menu doesn't change. No, or insufficient, choice for vegetarians. Mediocre cooking. Microwave cooking. Portions too large or too small. Service too slow or too hustling. Made to wait and order in bar. Tables too close together. Too much noise. Residents squeezed out by outsiders. Frozen vegetables. Wine over-priced. Limited or no choice of half bottles. Stale bread. Elderly cheeseboard. Only very rich desserts. Smoking permitted. Muzak.

Service Cool, rude, haughty, offhand, obsequious, over-matey, inquisitive, amateurish.

General Letters requesting bookings not answered. Rooms specially requested not provided (eg, asked for quiet room, given noisy one; booked a double bed, given twins). No one in reception when required. No help with luggage. Check-out time inconveniently early. Slow in producing bills. Too many extras. Being given inferior rooms when better ones are free.

Farewell to alms?

In our 1984 survey of the things that annoyed readers most about hotels, we noticed an anomaly: no one was complaining about the arbitrary, antiquated and discreditable practice of imposing a service charge or touting for tips that was common throughout the restaurant and catering trades. Yet as soon as we raised the subject in general conversation, everyone – except those deriving a direct benefit from these impositions – agreed that they loathed having a service charge added to their bill, whether dubbed "optional" or not, and/or a blank space on their credit card voucher marked "tip" or "gratuity". No other service industry, unless you count hairdressing, countenanced these extortions.

In a campaign to give the issue greater prominence, we asked hoteliers the following year, when filling up their annual questionnaire, to tell us what their policy was on this topic, and we printed the answer at the end of their entry. Many ignored the question or side-stepped it with a bland "left to guests' discretion". But we were encouraged by the number of leading hoteliers, including Brian Sack of *Sharrow Bay* and Grete Hobbs of *Inverlochy Castle,* who warmly supported our initiative. Our impression is that there is nowadays far less nudging for tips in hotels, and that guests settling their bills by credit card are rarely confronted with a so-called optional service charge or any other form of moral blackmail.

Would that one could say the same about UK restaurants where, increasingly, the credit card voucher is left open, with or without a reference to the fact that "service is not included". We welcomed the Earl of Bradford's Bill to outlaw such practices, but perhaps predictably, the lobbies for the catering industry rallied to support their staff's handouts, and the Bill was wrecked in the Lords even before, as was widely expected, it was clobbered in the Commons.

As Lord Nolan discovered, it isn't easy to alter bad old habits. Despite some claptrap in the press about "the graceful custom of tipping", we know which way most consumers would vote on this issue, but it may take government legislation to achieve a change.

When is a freebie not a freebie?

Hotels these days, even quite modest ones, provide a range of toiletries, known colloquially as "freebies", implying that guests can help themselves. Where do you draw the line? Little bottles of hair-conditioner, shower-caps and unused packets of soap OK, but clearly not face flannels and books, let alone hair-dryers – though in fact the last are quite often filched because guests forget that the appliance isn't their own. We hate "captive" coat-hangers which can't be removed from the wardrobe, but recognise that congenital pilfering of such objects is an expensive annoyance to hoteliers. And there are borderline cases. A guest at *Gidleigh Park* this year took offence at finding the tops removed from bottles of shampoo and bath lotions. She assumed that it was to stop her stealing them, but she could have been mistaken.

It isn't always easy to spot light-fingered guests. Brian Sack of *Sharrow Bay* likes to tell of a lady to whom he was saying good-bye. She happened to open her handbag to take out a handkerchief and inadvertently revealed three of the hotel's ashtrays. Sack relates that he nonchalantly took out two, saying: "I think one is acceptable, but three is just a bit greedy." The lady, not at all put out, protested that she always helped herself to souvenir ashtrays. "Yes, madam," Sack replied, "but I doubt whether they are all Royal Worcester."

Richard Sherwood of *Ashwick Park,* Dulverton, has devised an ingenious method for minimising his losses, putting in rooms the following notice:

"We hope you appreciate all the small touches which we have added around the hotel. Unfortunately, not everybody leaves things for future guests to enjoy. The favourite items which go missing: scallop-shaped soap dishes, hand-made toilet-roll holders, Laura Ashley sewing kits, napkin rings, hair-dryers, torches, telephones and hot-water bottles.

"'Superior' rooms have a mini-bar. We have learnt that you need a razor blade to cut the seal around a mini vodka bottle. You can then drink the contents and fill it up with water. For whisky and rum it is a little more difficult, but if you order early morning tea, you can fill the bottles with unmilked tea. It has happened in this hotel."

We would be interested to hear from other hoteliers their own stories of audacious kleptomaniacs and the techniques they have evolved for foiling them.

What's new in 1997

Regular readers of the *Guide* will notice a few changes this year. In 1992, following the collapse of the USSR, we expressed our keenness that in due course the *Guide* should include all the countries of central and eastern Europe. In the following year we made a start with a Hungarian section, but lost our Yugoslav chapter. This year we are delighted to be offering fully-fledged, if small, sections on the Czech Republic and Slovenia. We like to think that by the millennium we shall have a fully comprehensive European guide. In the meantime, please help this worthy cause by letting us know if you come across more than merely acceptable accommodation in the wilderness of the East.

For some years past, we have mentioned in the text if a hotel is a member of the Wolsey Lodge consortium or a Relais du Silence or a Romantik Hotel. This year, for the first time, we say if a hotel belongs to the Relais & Châteaux consortium. There are a lot of other international consortia which some might feel deserve a mention – Small Luxury Hotels of the World, Leading Hotels of the World and, in the UK, Pride of Britain at the posh end of the market, for instance, and Best Western lower down the price scale. Why make an exception for the Relais group? Because "Relais" is a useful shorthand for an independently owned hotel of the grander sort whose individuality is coloured by the Relais connection. We don't hold any brief to promote these hotels. It's true that, with only one exception, we have entries for all the British Relais hotels. But in Ireland, only seven out of ten qualify. And in France, Relais hotels often seem to us to be snooty and overpriced. Still, Relais does convey a good deal in one brief word, so we have overcome our inhibitions about mentioning their name.

One of our César winners last year was Graeme Jameson of the *Wykeham Arms* in Winchester. We were so struck by his skills in combining under one roof three quite different establishments – an admirable restaurant, a charming small hotel and a busy city inn – that we invited him to tell us the secret of his success. We recommend his essay, "The Heart of an Innkeeper", printed as an appendix, not just to our lay readers, but to all hoteliers everywhere.

This year we acquire a partner in collaborative promotion – namely, the small but distinguished champagne house of Joseph Perrier. The name of Joseph Perrier did in fact feature inconspicuously on page 830 of last year's *Guide* (the arrangements were made shortly before we went to press) as co-hosting our reception launch and providing a distinctly superior champagne for the dozen winners of our Report Competition. We are glad to say that our association has strengthened in the past twelve months. If you would like to know more about the house of Joseph Perrier, please turn to page 783.

As some of you know, the *Guide* is published in the States as *Europe's Wonderful Little Hotels & Inns*. Attentive regulars may also spot that we no longer mention our sibling guide in the US, *America's Wonderful Little Hotels & Inns*. *America's Wonderful* was almost as old as we are – it first appeared in 1979 – but its editor has now decided to change the character of the book by accepting fees from innkeepers. So we have negotiated a divorce, and henceforth Sandra Soule's book will have a different title. Perhaps at some future date it will be possible for us to revive an equivalent to the *Guide* in the States – but, sadly, not for the time being.

And, finally, our customary exhortation

At charity gatherings, guests are invited at the end of the evening to bring out their cheque books and give generously to the cause. We are just as keen on generous contributions, though not of the pecuniary sort. We are insatiably eager to have feedback from our readers – endorsements or reservations, bouquets or brickbats, they are all grist to our mill. When you have stayed in a *Guide* hotel, we urge you to fill in our Report form while the details of your visit are still fresh. We groan when we meet people who tell us that they love the *Guide* and use it regularly, but have never bothered to send us a report. "We always mean to. . . ." If you are one of these laggards, please make a resolution to do better this year.

Enjoy your hotel visits, and please don't forget to write.

HILARY RUBINSTEIN
JULY 1996

The 1997 César awards

Since 1984, as a way of demonstrating our appreciation for different kinds of excellence among hotels in Britain and Ireland, we have made annual awards called Césars, after the most celebrated of all hoteliers, César Ritz. Hotels of the grandest sort, like the finest restaurants, rarely lack public attention, but there are many more modest establishments that are supremely good in their own way. Their owners are dedicated to their vocation and commonly work from seven in the morning till one the next morning. Their contribution to innkeeping deserves to be recognised and honoured along with that of the professionals at the top of the ladder.

This year, as previously, we have bestowed ten laurel wreaths on a heterogeneous selection of hotels, inns and guest houses, each of which we consider to be outstanding in its own class. Previous César winners, provided the establishments are still in the same hands and as good as ever, are indicated in the text by the symbol of a smaller laurel wreath.

AWARD	WINNER
Country house hotel of the year	Hartwell House Aylesbury The epitome of an English country seat at its opulent best. *Hartwell House* has all the trappings of grandeur – parklands, spectacular decor, magnificent rooms, distinguished cooking – while happily eschewing the stuffiness that spoils the pleasures of so many posh country hotels.
Newcomer of the year	Romney Bay House New Romney This splendid Clough Williams-Ellis house, beach in front, golf course behind, has been given a hotelier's kiss of life by Helmut and Jennifer Gorlich. Its proximity to the Channel Tunnel is an incidental bonus.

Scottish hotel of the year — Kilcamb Lodge, Strontian

An incomparable location in isolated splendour on the Ardnamurchan peninsula gives *Kilcamb Lodge* a head-start in the César stakes. The Blakeway family's comprehensive concern for their guests' comfort wins them the top Scottish accolade.

Unpressured home hospitality in perfect p. and q. — Boscundle Manor, St Austell

A peaceful setting, a fine 18th-century manor house, lovingly furnished rooms, the really acceptable kind of home cooking – many country house hotels could claim the same. What makes guests return to *Boscundle Manor*, year after year, is Andrew and Mary Flint's relaxed, sympathetic warmth. This year, like the *Guide*, they celebrate their 20th year. Long may they flourish!

The prince of Welsh hotels — Ynyshir Hall, Eglwysfach

In a part of Wales poorly endowed with good hotels, *Ynyshir Hall* is a shining beacon. Rob and Joan Reen are dedicated to excellence in all departments. Both the house and its decor, and the garden are a visual delight. The kitchen is no let-down. And their proximity to the Ynyshir Bird Reserve is an added excuse for a visit.

The best of Lakeland hospitality — Ivy House, Braithwaite

Nick and Wendy Shill, in their cosseting 17th-century Lakeland village hotel, live up to the boast in their brochure: "affordable comfort amid breathtaking scenery". The tariff is low; standards are impeccably high.

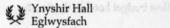

Best restaurant-with-rooms, Irish style

Aherne's
Youghal

Aherne's Seafood Bar, in this showplace old walled port at the mouth of the Blackwater River, has long been a mecca for fish-loving gourmets. The Fitzgibbon family's joyous establishment is every bit as much of a draw in its new incarnation as a restaurant-with-rooms. "Wonderful, extremely Irish hospitality," as one enthusiast put it.

Best budget hotel in the North

The Coach House
Crookham

Lynne Anderson's home near the Scottish border is an unashamed guest house, but of the most caring kind. And unlike some sophisticated guest houses, you can be as sociable or as private as you wish. The disabled have an additional reason to appreciate the *Coach House*'s facilities.

Best budget hotel in the South

Hancocks Farmhouse
Cranbrook

Bridget and Robin Oaten have only three rooms in their 16th-century timber-framed house amid the oast houses and orchards of Kent, but their attention to every detail of their guests' well-being is as professional as that offered by any grand hotel.

For utterly acceptable mild eccentricity

Frogg Manor
Broxton

Last year we were dismayed not to be able to award a César for enjoyable mild eccentricity. We are glad to find John Sykes, self-styled Chief Frog, a true successor to our long line of maverick hoteliers. Wall-to-wall frogs may be OTT for some, but they are a diverting treat for others. And the needs of Sykes's customers are properly addressed in this refreshingly different establishment.

Special hotels

City hotels with luxury and/or grandeur

England

Royal Crescent, Bath
42 The Calls, Leeds
Cadogan, London
Capital, London
Connaught, London
Goring, London
22 Jermyn Street, London
Middlethorpe Hall, York

Scotland

One Devonshire Gardens, Glasgow

Belgium

Snippe, Bruges

Czech Republic

Hoffmeister, Prague

Denmark

Angleterre, Copenhagen

France

Europe, Avignon
Tour Rose, Lyon

Hungary

Gellért, Budapest
Hilton, Budapest

Italy

Villa Cipriani, Asolo
Certosa di Maggiano, Siena

Netherlands

Europe, Amsterdam

Norway

Continental, Oslo

Spain

Parador, Granada

Town and city hotels of character and/or value

England

Bridge House, Beaminster
Collin House, Broadway
Evesham, Evesham
Lansdowne, Leamington Spa
D'Isney Place, Lincoln
Basil Street, London
Beaufort, London
Hazlitt's, London
Swiss Cottage, London
Hodgkinson's, Matlock Bath
Angel, Midhurst
Old Parsonage, Oxford
Abbey, Penzance
Mansion House, Poole
Jeake's House, Rye
George, Stamford
Castle, Taunton
Du Vin, Winchester
Wykeham Arms, Winchester
Feathers, Woodstock
Mount Royale, York

Scotland

Malmaison, Edinburgh
Babbity Bowster, Glasgow
Malmaison, Glasgow
Clifton House, Nairn

Northern Ireland

Ash-Rowan, Belfast

Belgium

Adornes, Bruges

Denmark

Ascot, Copenhagen

France

Chaîne d'Or, Les Andelys
Parc des Maréchaux, Auxerre
Thermes, Bourbon-l'Archambault
Angleterre, Châlons-en-Champagne
Diderot, Chinon
Bourgogne, Cluny
Armes de Champagne, l'Épine
Rivage, Gien
Midi, Lamastre
Vieux Puits, Pont-Audemer
Tour du Roy, Vervins
Prieuré, Villeneuve-lès-Avignon

Lucarne aux Chouettes, Villeneuve-sur-Yonne

Germany

Abtei, Hamburg
Hanseatic, Hamburg
Petrisberg, Trier

Italy

Loggiato dei Serviti, Florence
Monna Lisa, Florence
Morandi alla Crocetta, Florence
Campo de' Fiori, Rome
Belvedere, Taormina

The Netherlands

Ambassade, Amsterdam

Portugal

Quinta da Penha de França, Funchal
Caçador, Macedo de Cavaleiros

Spain

Parador, Carmona
América, Granada
Residencia Rector, Salamanca
Altamira, Santillana del Mar
Doña María, Seville
Cardenal, Toledo
Parador, Úbeda

Sweden

Lady Hamilton, Stockholm
Victory, Stockholm

Rural charm and character in the luxury class

England

Hartwell House, Aylesbury
Mallory Court, Bishop's Tachbrook
Lygon Arms, Broadway
Buckland Manor, Buckland
Brockencote Hall, Chaddesley Corbett
Gidleigh Park, Chagford
Gravetye Manor, East Grinstead
Summer Lodge, Evershot
Stock Hill House, Gillingham
Manoir aux Quat'Saisons, Great Milton
Hambleton Hall, Hambleton
Hintlesham Hall, Hintlesham
Chewton Glen, New Milton
Ston Easton Park, Ston Easton
Cliveden, Taplow
Thornbury Castle, Thornbury
Sharrow Bay, Ullswater

Wales

Bodysgallen, Llandudno
Llangoed Hall, Llyswen

Scotland

Arisaig House, Arisaig
Kinnaird, Dunkeld
Inverlochy Castle, Fort William
Ardanaiseig, Kilchrenan
Cromlix House, Kinbuck

Channel Islands

Longueville Manor, St Saviour

Republic of Ireland

Marlfield House, Gorey
Park, Kenmare

Denmark

Falsled Kro, Millinge

France

Moulin de l'Abbaye, Brantôme
Moulin du Roc, Champagnac-de-Belair
Manoir d'Hautegente, Coly
Beau Rivage, Condrieu
Crillon le Brave, Crillon-le-Brave
Régalido, Fontvieille
Magdeleine, Gémenos
Cagnard, Haut-de-Cagnes
Pont de l'Ouysse, Lacave
Hostellerie de Levernois, Levernois
Moulin, Lourmarin
Château d'Adoménil, Lunéville
Château de Madières, Madières
Frênes, Montfavet
Château de Nieuil, Nieuil
Clos Saint Vincent, Ribeauvillé
Moulin de la Gorce, La Roche-l'Abeille
Rochecotte, St-Patrice
Prés du Lac, Talloires

Germany

Pflaums, Pegnitz

Italy

Principessa, Lucca
Borgo Paraelios, Poggio Catino
San Domenico Palace, Taormina

Spain

Residencia, Deyá

Switzerland

Casa Berno, Ascona
Paradies, Ftan

Rural charm and character at medium price

England

Rothay Manor, Ambleside
Wateredge, Ambleside
Amerdale House, Arncliffe
Callow Hall, Ashbourne
Little Barwick House, Barwick
Cavendish, Baslow
Netherfield Place, Battle
Lindeth Fell, Bowness
Linthwaite House, Bowness
Woolley Grange, Bradford-on-Avon
Farlam Hall, Brampton
Danescombe Valley, Calstock
Aynsome Manor, Cartmel
Uplands, Cartmel
Chedington Court, Chedington
Highbullen, Chittlehamholt
Ashwick House, Dulverton
Congham Hall, Grimston
Highfield House, Hawkshead
Heddon's Gate, Heddon's Mouth
At the Sign of the Angel, Lacock
Langley House, Langley Marsh
Lastingham Grange, Lastingham
Hope End, Ledbury
Lewtrenchard Manor, Lewdown
Morston Hall, Morston
Beetle and Wedge, Moulsford-on-Thames
Pear Tree, Purton
Stone House, Rushlake Green
Boscundle Manor, St Austell
Whitechapel Manor, South Molton
Plumber Manor, Sturminster Newton
Calcot Manor, Tetbury
Priory, Wareham
Woodhayes, Whimple
White House, Williton

Wales

Gliffaes, Crickhowell
Ynyshir Hall, Eglwysfach
Tyddyn Llan, Llandrillo
Lake, Llangammarch Wells
Portmeirion, Portmeirion
Maes-y-Neuadd, Talsarnau

Scotland

Farleyer House, Aberfeldy
Old Mansion House, Auchterhouse
Banchory Lodge, Banchory
Old Manse, Bridge of Marnoch
Kinnaird, Dunkeld
Minmore House, Glenlivet
Dunain Park, Inverness
Knockie Lodge, Whitebridge

Channel Islands

Château La Chaire, Rozel Bay

Republic of Ireland

Caragh Lodge, Caragh Lake
Hilton Park, Clones
Doyle's Townhouse, Dingle
Assolas, Kanturk
Currarevagh House, Oughterard
Coopershill, Riverstown
Ballymaloe House, Shanagarry

Austria

Walkner, Seeham

France

Vieux Pont, Belcastel
Petit Castel, Beuzeville
Touron, Carsac-Aillac
Clairefontaine, Chonas-l'Amballon
Cuq en Terrasses, Cuq-le-Château
Esplanade, Domme
Glycines, Eyzies-de-Tayac
Moulin, Flagy
Orée du Bois, Futeau
Florets, Gigondas
Tirel-Guérin, La Gouesnière
Val d'Or, Mercurey
Grenouillère, Montreuil
Madone, Peillon
Hospitaliers, Poët-Laval
Belle Gasconne, Poudenas
Hameau, St-Paul-de-Vence
Bois St-Georges, Saintes

Germany

Stein, Bayreuth-Seulbitz
Schlosshotel, Daun
Historische Schlossmühle, Horbruch im Hunsrück

Schindlerhof, Nuremberg-Boxdorf
Schönburg, Oberwesel

Italy

Cannero, Cannero Riviera
Tenuta di Ricavo, Castellina in Chianti
Castello, Gargonza
Fragsburg, Merano
Sangiovese, Panzano
Stella d'Italia, San Mamete
Bastiglia, Spello

Norway

Mundal, Fjærland
Utne, Utne

Portugal

Quinta da Capela, Sintra

Spain

Es Molí, Deyá
Peñalba, Figueras del Mar
Posada, Gualchos
Rectoral, Taramundi

Sweden

Åkerblads, Tällberg

Switzerland

Rothorn, Schwanden
Soglina, Soglio
Beau Rivage, Weggis
Alpenrose, Wengen

Rural charm, simple style

England

Frog Street Farm, Beercrocombe
Parrock Head, Slaidburn
Howtown, Ullswater

Republic of Ireland

Temple House, Ballymote
Ballymakeigh House, Killeagh

France

Poste, Brioude
Hermitage, Buzançais
Renaudière, Chenonceaux
Lozerette, Cocurès
Halle, Givry
Alisiers, Lapoutroie
Vieux Logis, Lestelle-Bétharram
Montagnes, Pailherols
Rostaing, Passenans
Mistou, Pontempeyrat
Poids Public, St-Félix-Lauragais
Midi-Papillon, St-Jean-du-Bruel
Ferme du Vert, Wierre-Effroy

Germany

Lipmann, Beilstein

Italy

Belvedere, Argegno
Giardinetto, Pettenasco

Spain

Tahona, Besnes-Alles
Pousada O Almacén, Cervo

Sweden

Grythyttans, Grythyttan

Switzerland

Bergsonne, Rigi-Kaltbad

Hotels by the sea, luxury style

England

Island, Tresco

Channel Islands

Atlantic, St Brelade

Denmark

Sønderho Kro, Sønderho

France

Grand, Cabourg

Greece

Elounda Mare, Elounda
Kivotos Clubhotel, Mykonos
Akti Myrina, Myrina

Italy

Pellicano, Porto Ercole

Hotels by the sea, medium-priced or simple

England

Burgh Island, Bigbury-on-Sea
Budock Vean, Budock Vean
Treglos, Constantine Bay
Crantock Bay, Crantock
Boscundle Manor, St Austell
Garrack, St Ives
Tides Reach, Salcombe

Seaview, Seaview
Soar Mill Cove, Soar Mill Cove
Talland Bay, Talland-by-Looe
Trebrea Lodge, Tintagel
Nare, Veryan

Wales

St Tudno, Llandudno

Scotland

Summer Isles, Achiltibuie
Loch Melfort, Arduaine
Balcary Bay, Auchencairn
Crinan, Crinan
Enmore, Dunoon
Baile-na-Cille, Timsgarry

Republic of Ireland

Zetland House, Cashel Bay
Rosturk Woods, Mulrany

France

Treizain, Gassin
Plage, Ste-Anne-la-Palud
Ti al Lannec, Trébeurden

Italy

Arathena Rocks, Giardini-Naxos
Ottone, Ottone

Spain

Aigua Blava, Bagur
Mar i Vent, Bañalbufar
Parador, Gomera

Skiing, walking or mountain hotels

England

Grey Friar Lodge, Ambleside
Appletree Holme Farm, Blawith
Seatoller House, Borrowdale
Ivy House, Braithwaite
Mill, Mungrisdale
Swinside Lodge, Newlands
Howtown, Ullswater
Wasdale Head, Wasdale Head

Wales

Pen-y-Gwryd, Nantgwynant

Scotland

Summer Isles, Achiltibuie
Knockie Lodge, Whitebridge

Austria

Madrisa, Gargellen

France

Bérangère, Les Deux-Alpes

Norway

Dr Holms, Geilo
Alexandra, Loen

Sweden

Fryksås, Orsa

Switzerland

Flüela, Davos
Metropol, Zermatt

Fishing hotels

England

Callow Hall, Ashbourne
Mill End, Chagford
Highbullen, Chittlehamholt
Tarr Steps, Hawkridge
Arundell Arms, Lifton

Wales

Gliffaes, Crickhowell
Tyddyn Llan, Llandrillo
Lake, Llangammarch Wells
Penmaenuchaf Hall, Penmaenpool

Scotland

Banchory Lodge, Banchory
Coul House, Contin
Kinnaird, Dunkeld
Taychreggan, Kilchrenan
Cromlix House, Kinbuck
Ballathie House, Kinclaven
Dryburgh Abbey, St Boswells
Knockie Lodge, Whitebridge

Republic of Ireland

Ballylickey Manor, Ballylickey
Caragh Lodge, Caragh Lake
Enniscoe House, Crossmolina
Sheen Falls Lodge, Kenmare
Delphi Lodge, Leenane
Longueville Manor, Mallow
Newport House, Newport
Currarevagh House, Oughterard

Hotels for gourmets

England

Fischer's Baslow Hall, Baslow

Mallory Court, Bishop's Tachbrook
Restaurant Nineteen, Bradford
Waterside Inn, Bray
Buckland Manor, Buckland
Gidleigh Park, Chagford
White Moss House, Grasmere
Manoir aux Quat'Saisons, Great Milton
Hambleton Hall, Hambleton
Hintlesham Hall, Hintlesham
Langley House, Langley Marsh
Capital, London
Connaught, London
Halkin, London
Morston Hall, Morston
Beetle and Wedge, Moulsford-on-Thames
Chewton Glen, New Milton
Seafood Restaurant, Padstow
McCoy's, Staddlebridge
Castle, Taunton
Sharrow Bay, Ullswater
Miller Howe, Windermere
Winteringham Fields, Winteringham

Wales

Old Rectory, Llansanffraid Glan Conwy
Carlton House, Llanwrtyd Wells

Scotland

Inverlochy Castle, Fort William
The Cross, Kingussie
Airds, Port Appin
Knockinaam Lodge, Portpatrick
Altnaharrie, Ullapool

Channel Islands

Longueville Manor, St Saviour

Republic of Ireland

Doyle's Townhouse, Dingle
Marlfield House, Gorey
Park, Kenmare
Ballymaloe House, Shanagarry
Aherne's, Youghal

Belgium

Scholteshof, Hasselt-Stevoort

France

Lameloise, Chagny
Prés d'Eugénie, Eugénie-les-Bains
Berges, Illhaeusern
Côte St-Jacques, Joigny
Michel Bras, Laguiole
Alain Chapel, Mionnay
Aubergade, Puymirol
Bretagne, Questembert
Troisgros, Roanne
Lion d'Or, Romorantin-Lanthenay
Espérance, Vézelay
Georges Blanc, Vonnas

Germany

Heinz Winkler, Aschau in Chiemgau

Italy

Albareta, Erbusco
Sole, Ranco

The Netherlands

Kaatje bij de Sluis, Blokzijl

Switzerland

Gare, Le Noirmont

Friendly informality/hotel run like a private house

England

Chapel House, Atherstone
Little Hemingfold, Battle
Frog Street Farm, Beercrocombe
Little Hodgeham, Bethersden
Appletree Holme Farm, Blawith
Bourne Eau House, Bourne
Chilvester Hill House, Calne
Hancocks Farmhouse, Cranbrook
Coach House, Crookham
Upper Court, Kemerton
Bowerfield House, Otley
Stratton House, Swaffham
Thomas Luny House, Teignmouth

Wales

Ty-Isaf, Llanfachreth
Old Rectory, Llansanffraid Glan Conwy

Scotland

Glenfeochan, Kilmore
Viewfield House, Portree
Baile-na-Cille, Timsgarry

Republic of Ireland

Temple House, Ballymote
Tullanisk, Birr

Hilton Park, Clones
Delphi Lodge, Leenane
Roundwood House, Mountrath

Austria

Burg Bernstein, Bernstein

France

La Daille, Florimont-Gaumiers
Château de Poitevinière, Huismes
Château de Boussac, Target

Italy

Monte Solare, Fontignano
Rucellai, Prato
Castel San Gregorio, San Gregorio

Norway

Trugstad Gård, Holter
Utne, Utne

Spain

Molina del Santo, Benaoján
Finca Listonero, Turre

Hotels in the UK and Ireland that welcome children

England

Rothay Manor, Ambleside
Cavendish, Baslow
Eagle House, Bathford
Little Hemingfold, Battle
Blakeney, Blakeney
Woolley Grange, Bradford-on-Avon
Dove, Brighton
Crantock Bay, Crantock
Evesham, Evesham
Manoir aux Quat'Saisons, Great Milton
Highfield House, Hawkshead
Lastingham Grange, Lastingham
Great House, Lavenham
Arundell Arms, Lifton
Old Bell, Malmesbury
Beetle and Wedge, Moulsford-on-Thames
Boscundle Manor, St Austell
Seaview, Seaview
Soar Mill Cove, Soar Mill Cove
Cliveden, Taplow
Island, Tresco
Nare, Veryan
Wallett's Court, West Cliffe

Wales

Porth Tocyn, Abersoch
St Tudno, Llandudno

Scotland

Loch Melfort, Arduaine
Kirkton House, Cardross
Enmore, Dunoon
Creebridge House, Newton Stewart
Cringletie House, Peebles
Baile-na-Cille, Timsgarry

Republic of Ireland

Coopershill, Riverstown
Ballymaloe House, Shanagarry

No-smoking hotels

England

Abbey House, Abbotsbury
Haydon House, Bath
Holly Lodge, Bath
Somerset House, Bath
Frog Street Farm, Beercrocombe
Crit Hall, Benenden
Appletree Holme Farm, Blawith
Bradford Old Windmill, Bradford-on-Avon
Cokerhurst Farm, Bridgwater
Twelve Angel Hill, Bury St Edmunds
Pickett Howe, Buttermere
Cross Keys, Cautley
Cleeve Hill Hotel, Cleeve Hill
Manor Farm, Crackington Haven
Hancocks Farmhouse, Cranbrook
Tamhorn Park Farmhouse, Fisherwick
Ashfield House, Grassington
Northleigh House, Hatton
Old Bank House, Hayfield
Windrush House, Hazleton
Old Rectory, Hopesay
New House Farm, Lorton
Swinside Lodge, Newlands
Newstead Grange, Norton
Bowerfield House, Otley
Cotswold House, Oxford
Mizzards Farm, Rogate
Hazel Bank, Rosthwaite
Nanscawen House, St Blazey
Stratford Lodge, Salisbury
Upper Green Farm, Towersey
Old Millfloor, Trebarwith Strand

Old Parsonage, West Dean
Bales Mead, West Porlock
Archway, Windermere

Wales

Dol-llyn-wydd, Builth Wells
Gilfach Goch, Fishguard

Scotland

Torbeag House, Banavie
Brook Linn, Callander
Drummond House, Edinburgh
17 Abercromby Place, Edinburgh
Sibbet House, Edinburgh
Crolinnhe, Fort William
Skirling House, Skirling
Altnaharrie, Ullapool
Grange House, Whiting Bay

Republic of Ireland

Bow Hall, Castletownshend

Austria

Römischer Kaiser, Vienna

France

Château de Poitevinière, Huismes

Sweden

Åby Gård, Knivsta

Hotels with facilities for disabled

England

Rothay Manor, Ambleside
Callow Hall, Ashbourne
Hartwell House, Aylesbury
The Coach House, Crookham
Old Manor, Cropredy
Casterbridge, Dorchester
Croft, Great Longstone
West Lodge Park, Hadley Wood
Northill House, Horton
Knightsbridge Green, London
Rookery Hall, Nantwich
The Beeches, Norwich
Garrack, St Ives
Albright Hussey, Shrewsbury
Leeming House, Watermillock
Old Vicarage, Worfield

Wales

Penbontbren Farm, Glynarthen

Scotland

Roman Camp, Callander
Dryburgh Abbey, St Boswells

Northern Ireland

Tullylagan, Cookstown

Republic of Ireland

Milltown House, Dingle
Hibernian, Dublin
Rosturk Woods, Mulrany

Czech Republic

Harmony, Prague

France

Manoir du Lys, Bagnoles-de-l'Orne
Hostellerie des Clos, Chablis
Aigle Noir, Fontainebleau
Vieux Logis, Lestelle-Bétharram
Mougins, Mougins
Val d'Orbieu, Ornaisons
Montrachet, Puligny-Montrachet
Ile de la Lagune, St-Cyprien-Sud
Pen'Roc, St-Didier
Château St-Saturnin, St-Saturnin
Carayon, St-Sernin-sur-Rance
Beaucour, Strasbourg
Tour du Roy, Vervins
Val de Vienne, Le Vigeant

Germany

Hecker's, Berlin
Martha Hospiz, Dresden
Pannonia, Gotha

Hungary

Hilton, Budapest

Italy

Fonte della Galletta, Alpe Faggeto
Chiostro, Pienza
Emilia, Portonovo
Villa Campestri, Vicchio

Norway

Mølla, Lillehammer

Spain

Casa de Carmona, Carmona
Can Boix, Peramola

Switzerland

Castle, Blitzingen
Chesa Mulin, Pontresina

How we choose our hotels

We are often asked about our principles of selection and rejection. This is a fair question, since the hotels included in the *Guide* cater for a wide spectrum of ages, incomes, tastes and prejudices, and have been nominated by a miscellaneous collection of individuals, whose own predilections and standards of judgment cannot be known to us. How then can there be any coherent standard behind our choices?

There clearly is no single standard. Our own tastes are eclectic, and the only thing which all these hotels have in common is that the editor would be happy to stay in them himself. Nevertheless the process of selection is by no means arbitrary. Among the factors which assist us are the following:

- The consensus of recent reports on a hotel that already has an entry in the *Guide*, and the tone of the nominating letter in the case of a candidate for first-time selection. If someone whose judgment we know and trust tells us of an exciting new find or that a particular hotel does not deserve its entry, he or she obviously carries more weight than a nominator or complainant out of the blue.
- The hotel's brochure. Its pitch will usually reveal the kind of custom it is hoping to attract, and its photographs or drawings, while no doubt always aiming to beguile, may indicate instantly that this one is not for us.
- Menus. Very instructive in subtle as well as in obvious ways.
- Hoteliers' responses to our questionnaire. We invite them to expand on their answers by telling us what sort of custom they hope to attract; relatively few take the trouble; the replies of those who do are of great help to us.
- Whether and how a hotel features in other guides.
- Inspections. In cases of doubt (due to unconvincing or ambivalent reports), in the UK we arrange an anonymous inspection. We have a limited inspection budget, but a number of readers have generously volunteered to do unreimbursed inspections for us, which is particularly useful on the Continent.

Of course, such a pragmatic system is open to error, but the fact that we get far more endorsements than blackballs encourages us to think that we are on the right lines.

Hotels are dropped when it is clear that there has been a fall in standards or – a tricky question this – when we feel that they are no longer offering value for money. We also omit a hotel after a change of ownership or management, if we do not have enough evidence that the new regime is maintaining previous standards. And hotels are dropped – often unfairly – when we have had inadequate feedback. We are used to getting a spate of letters asking: "Why on earth have you left out — ?" If the case is well made, we reinstate the place in the next edition. As we have said *ad nauseam*, we wish that readers who find the *Guide* useful would make a habit of sending reports after staying in a *Guide* hotel.

A common practice is for hotels to give departing guests a report form and invite them to send us an "unsolicited" recommendation. Sometimes we receive a rash of fulsome reports on a particular establishment, all from people who have never written to us before. Our report forms are paginated, and frequently these inspired tributes arrive in faithful sequence. Some hotels photocopy our report forms, and, having prevailed on their guests to fill them in, post them to us in a batch. One hotel designed a special postcard for the purpose. The owners of a French hotel once asked their English customers to fill in a special questionnaire which they then posted to us. They did not take the trouble to read these first, or else their English was not up to the job; many of the so-called reports contained more insults than compliments. We wish that hoteliers would desist from these collusive and counter-effective practices.

How to read the entries

The long and the short of it Entries vary in length. A long entry need not necessarily imply an especially good hotel, nor a short one a marginal case. Sometimes it takes a lot of words to convey a hotel's special flavour, and sometimes we can't resist quoting at length from an amusing report since we aim to be entertaining as well as informative. In general, city hotels get less space than country ones because the ambience of a hotel matters less in towns, and also because it is often helpful, when a hotel is in a relatively remote or little-known area, for the entry to comment on the location.

Names The names in a citation are those of people who have nominated that hotel or endorsed the entry that appeared in a previous edition. We don't give the names of writers of adverse reports, though their contributions are every bit as important as the laudatory ones.

Maps and index You will find these at the end of the book. The *Guide* lists hotels country by country under the name of the town or village. If you remember the hotel's name but not its precise location you should consult the alphabetical list of hotels.

Nuts and bolts The factual material varies in length. Some hotels have lots of facilities, others few. If a hotel fails to return our detailed questionnaire or send us a brochure, we don't always know what it has to offer. All hotels in Part One have completed our questionnaire, but around a quarter of those in Part Two have either ignored it or will return it months after the *Guide* has gone to press. In these cases, the information is not always as full or as accurate as we would like. The fact that no lounge or bar is mentioned in an entry doesn't mean that a hotel lacks public rooms, but only that we can't be sure. The same applies to parking, which we mention in the case of town and city hotels. We don't give detailed information about bedroom facilities. Most hotel bedrooms nowadays have telephone, TV and *en suite* bathroom; in the UK many have tea-making facilities. If any of these is vital to your comfort you should discuss it with the hotel at the time of booking. A "double room" may be double- or twin-bedded; you should mention which you prefer when booking. We aim to provide accurate information about opening times, but hotels, particularly small ones, do sometimes close on the spur of the moment. And hotels on the Continent often close one day a week, but don't always tell us which day that is. Finally, hotels don't always give us reliable information about whether they take credit cards or which ones; please check with the hotel if this is vital to you.

Italic entries These describe hotels which are worth considering but which we feel, for various reasons – inadequate information, lack of feedback, ambivalent reports – do not at the moment deserve a full entry. Reports on these hotels are particularly welcome.

Symbols This is an unashamedly wordy guide. We are against providing a lot of information in complicated hieroglyphic form. Days and months are abbreviated; "B&B" means bed and breakfast, "D,B&B" means dinner, bed and breakfast, and "alc" is *à la carte*. The "full alc" price is the hotel's estimate per person for a three-course meal and a half-bottle of modest wine, including service and taxes; "alc" indicates the price excluding the wine. We say: "Unsuitable for ♿", when hotels tell us that, and we list under "Special hotels", places which claim to have full facilities for the disabled; but it is vital that you check details with the hotel. We have a "New" label for hotels making their debut in the *Guide* or being readmitted after an absence, and a "Budget" label for hotels which offer dinner, bed and breakfast at around £50 (or its foreign currency equivalent) per person, or B&B for about £30 and dinner for about £20. ***V*** indicates hotels in the UK and Ireland which have agreed to take part in our Voucher scheme.

Vouchers Once again we offer our readers an opportunity to obtain discounts at many British and Irish *Guide* hotels. On the tear-out card in the centre of the book, you will find four vouchers which may be used at any hotel in the UK or Ireland with ***V*** at the end of its entry. A voucher will entitle you to a discount of 25 per cent from the normal price for bed and breakfast (or the price of a room in the case of hotels that charge for breakfast separately). It won't apply if you are already on a bargain break or special deal, and you will be expected to pay the full price for all other services. The discount will apply whether you use the voucher for one night or for a longer visit, and is for one room. You must produce two vouchers if you are booking two rooms. The vouchers remain valid till the publication of the 1998 edition in the autumn of 1997. *Important*: you must request a voucher booking at the time of reservation, and participating hotels may refuse a voucher reservation or accept the voucher for one night only if they expect to be fully booked at the full room price at that time.

Tariffs Terms are regrettably complicated. Some hotels have a standard rate for all rooms regardless of season and length of stay, but many operate a complicated system which varies from low season to high (some have a medium-high season as well), and according to length of stay, whether there is a bathroom *en suite* and, in the case of most British hotels, whether the room is in single or double occupancy. To complicate matters further, most British hotels offer breaks of one kind or another, but rarely of the same kind. When figures are given without mention of single or double rooms they indicate the range of tariffs per person; otherwise we give a room rate. Lowest rates are what you pay for the simplest room, sharing a double, or out of season, or both; highest rates are for the "best" rooms, and for the high season if the hotel has one. Meal prices are per person.

One crucial point must be emphasised with regard to the tariffs: their relative unreliability. We ask hotels when they complete our questionnaire in the spring of one year to make an informed guess at their tariffs for the following year. This is a difficult exercise. Many prefer to quote their current rates. Please *don't* rely on the figures printed. You should *always* check at the time of booking and not blame the hotel or the *Guide* if prices are different from those printed.

Special offers If you wish to spend two days or more at a hotel in the British Isles, it is worth asking about special offers. The bargain terms can be amazing value, and may apply throughout the year. And the voucher scheme mentioned on the previous page should help you to find accommodation at cheaper rates.

We end with our customary exhortation, imploring readers to tell us of any errors of omission or commission in both the descriptive and the informative parts of the entries. Our entries are written in good faith, but we can't guarantee that, after we have gone to press, a hotel won't close or change its owners. We make constant efforts to improve our information under Location, especially with out-of-the-way places, and would like to hear from readers who have found our directions inadequate. We recognise what an imposition it is to ask readers to write us letters or fill in report forms, but it is essential that people let us know their views if the *Guide* is to continue to meet consumer needs as well as it can.

Part one

England
Wales
Scotland
Channel Islands
Northern Ireland
Republic of Ireland

England

Hartwell House, Aylesbury

Most of our hotels in the UK and Ireland, like those on the Continent, are independently owned and run. There are a few exceptions: large hotels, especially those in cities, may well be in the hands of managers, and there is a small number of hoteliers in the *Guide* who own more than one establishment. You will also find the occasional maverick hotel belonging to one of the big chains – an establishment which miraculously has escaped the soullessness usually associated with members of a major hotel conglomerate.

Many *Guide* hotels, however, belong to a consortium for the purposes of marketing and promotion, and it may be useful to identify the more important of these groupings. The most famous, also the most expensive, is Relais & Châteaux, French-owned but world-wide. This year, for the first time, we mention in the text if a hotel belongs to Relais. All Relais establishments, be they grand castles, lush country houses or gourmet restaurants, are privately owned. But so strong is the Relais brand image that they are sometimes mistaken for a chain. Some well-heeled folk, who like to be assured of the acme of luxury when they travel abroad, use the Relais booklet extensively or exclusively. Others steer clear, not caring for the swank – and sometimes the snootiness – which they detect in these posh places, and feel they are being asked to pay too high a price for the grand trappings. In the past we have been critical of certain British members, which we felt were living off their reputation and failing to maintain standards. Over the last two decades, however, these weaker members seem to have been eased out. The present Relais contingent in the UK are in general an impressive lot, more dependable in our view than their associates across the Channel, where you may well find rip-offs and snobbery.

Pride of Britain, a similar consortium, is exclusively British. It was formed originally by a breakaway group from Relais who resented the French domination of the latter, and the high prices they were being asked to pay for the privilege of membership. Not all Pride of Britain establishments are independent entities – they include a Hebridean Cruise company and the Royal Scotsman. About two-thirds of their members have an entry in the *Guide*.

A third group you may come across, world-wide like Relais but strongest in the US, is Best Western. It too insists on independence for its members, but they are less homogeneous than those of the two groups mentioned above. In the US, Best Western hotels are often motels; in the UK they are mostly what in the old AA parlance would be called two- or three-star establishments. There are only a few British Best Westerns in the *Guide*; most of them cater for a market very different from ours.

There are other consortia you may come across, such as Welsh Rarebits or A Taste of Scotland. There are some fine hotels or guest houses in these associations, but for a variety of reasons not many of their members would merit an entry in these pages.

Apart from Relais, there are two other consortia which we mention in the text. The first is the self-explanatory Relais du Silence, long established on the Continent, but now actively recruiting in the UK. Finally, there are Wolsey Lodges. The group was launched in 1981, when a Lodge was defined as "an Englishman's home where you are welcome to stay as a guest for a night or more". Today it has more than 200 members scattered throughout the UK, as well as half a dozen on the Continent – though none in Ireland. They aren't strictly speaking hotels, although a few achieve an entry in *Michelin*. They are private guest houses catering for travellers who like to socialise with their hosts and enjoy the lottery of eating, dinner party style, with fellow guests. Many have only two bedrooms and are therefore too small to qualify for a *Guide* entry. There are some splendid examples of the species scattered through these pages, as well as many other similar sophisticated guest houses that might well qualify for Wolsey Lodge membership if they cared to apply. They are not for everyone: you have to take pot luck with the cooking as well as the company. But there is a sufficient family resemblance between them to justify our mentioning that connection.

Prominent on the façade of many British hotels is the red, white and blue plaque of the British Tourist Authority, displaying a row of between one and five crowns. But few *Guide* hotels sport these plaques. As we explain in the Introduction, most would not demean themselves by applying for registration. You will find no reference to crowns in these pages.

As usual, if a hotel or a restaurant-with-rooms has a *Michelin* star, or a red "Meals" for a good meal at a moderate price, we mention this in the text. We also add, where appropriate, the name of our sibling publication, *The Good Pub Guide*, indicating a hotel or inn that has won its approval too.

ABBOTSBURY Dorset **Map 1**

Abbey House BUDGET *Tel* (01305) 871330
Church Street *Fax* (01305) 871088
Abbotsbury DT3 4JJ

Guest house in lovely old village near Weymouth, with stone houses, swannery, excellent coastal walks nearby (Chesil Bank 15 mins' walk). Beautiful part-15th-century building, once infirmary of St Peter's Abbey. 1½-acre grounds with largest tithe barn in England and unique Benedictine water mill. Charming owners, Jonathan and Maureen Cooke. No smoking. Unsuitable for ♿. *No dogs. 1 family suite, 4 double bedrooms, "perfect and spacious", all with facilities* en suite. *Evening meal available in peak season; lunch, cream teas served from Easter. Good breakfasts. Credit cards not accepted. B&B £27–£30. Set lunch/dinner £7–£15. Children under 13 half-price when sharing with parents. House parties welcomed. 1-night bookings sometimes refused in high season. More reports, please.*

ALSTON Cumbria **Map 4**

Lovelady Shield *Tel* (01434) 381203
Nenthead Road *Fax* (01434) 381515
nr Alston CA9 3LF

"Warm and sheltered in the bleak midwinter. Log fires inside, frozen river and blizzards on the moors." "Relaxed atmosphere. No piped music, no organised entertainment; a place to 'get away from it all'." Kenneth and Margaret Lyons' handsome white 19th-century house is in a remote setting in the High Pennines, at the foot of majestic fells. It is reached up a long tree-lined drive; the river Nent borders its grounds. It makes a good base for visiting Hadrian's Wall and touring the border country. The bedrooms (two are quite small) were recently redecorated. Chef Barrie Garton's quite ambitious cooking on a daily-changing menu is mainly English in style and served in generous portions; there's always a hot dessert. Plenty of half bottles of wine. Breakfast includes freshly squeezed orange juice, home-made marmalade, kedgeree and mixed grills. (*Mr and Mrs WA Pedder*) More reports, please.

Open 2 Feb–4 Jan.
Rooms 10 double, 2 single.
Facilities Drawing room, library, bar, restaurant. 4-acre grounds: tennis, croquet. Fishing, shooting, riding nearby. Unsuitable for ♿.
Location 2½ miles E of Alston. Take A689 to Nenthead. 2 miles on left, at junction with B6294.
Restrictions No smoking: drawing room, restaurant. No children under 5 at dinner. No dogs in public rooms.
Credit cards All major cards accepted.
Terms [1996] B&B £47–£57; D,B&B £71.50–£81.50. Set lunch £13.50, dinner £24.95. Christmas, New Year, winter, spring breaks. *V*

AMBERLEY West Sussex **Map 2**

Amberley Castle NEW *Tel* (01798) 831992
Amberley, nr Arundel BN18 9ND *Fax* (01798) 831998

12th-century castle in village 4 miles N of Arundel. In prime condition, offering "absolute privacy, comfort and security". Serene garden behind portcullis. Glorious views from battlements. Cosy reception rooms, decorated with flair. 15 luxurious bedrooms, in manor house, tower and castle wall; all with jacuzzi. "No effort spared by resident owners, Joy and Martin Cummings, to make your stay memorable." Meals, some based on 12th-century recipes, served in barrel-vaulted, lancet-windowed restaurant (no smoking). 12-acre grounds. Unsuitable for ♿. No children under 10. No dogs. All major credit cards accepted. B&B: single £100, double £130–£275. Set lunch £19.50, dinner £29.50; full alc £45. New manager, new chef, in 1996. More reports, please.

AMBLESIDE Cumbria **Map 4**

Grey Friar Lodge BUDGET *Tel/Fax* (0153 94) 33158
Clappersgate
Ambleside LA22 9NE

"Marvellous value for money." "A very well-run business." This former vicarage, built in traditional Lakeland stone, is set well back from a fairly busy road, in sloping gardens on the wooded flanks of Loughrigg Fell, with lovely views over the Brathay River Valley. It is "pleasantly home-like, with antiques and interesting pictures and curios". Bedrooms, some with four-poster, have pine furniture, flowery fabrics, lots of storage space, and good views. The gregarious hosts, Tony and Sheila Sutton, run it informally; first names tend to be used. "Hard to single out one aspect for special praise," writes a recent visitor. "The friendliness of the owners, their sense of humour, their willingness to explain how they cook things, the excellent but healthy food, the immaculate housekeeping. . . ." Dinner, "a blend of traditional English and mildly exotic", is at 7.30. "It is frequently capped by a brilliant old-fashioned hot pudding. No choice, but they will provide alternative dishes." (*Jane Barry, and others*) "Probably most enjoyable when not at full stretch," runs one caveat. "The dining room is small, and the tables are too close together for confidences with one's dining partner."

Open Easter–end Oct; weekends Feb, Mar. Dining room closed for lunch and to non-residents.
Rooms 8 double. No telephone.
Facilities 2 lounges, dining room. 1-acre garden: patio, sun terrace. River, fishing 500 yds; Lake Windermere 1 mile. Golf, pony trekking, cycling nearby. Unsuitable for ♿.
Location 1½ miles SW of Ambleside on A593.
Restrictions Smoking in 1 lounge only. No children under 10. No dogs.
Credit cards None accepted.
Terms B&B £21.50–£32; D,B&B £37–£47.50. Special breaks; winter weekend tariffs. 1-night bookings refused if too far in advance.

If you find details of a hotel's location inadequate, let us know.

Rothay Manor *Tel* (0153 94) 33605
Rothay Bridge, Ambleside LA22 0EH *Fax* (0153 94) 33607
César award in 1992

A handsome Georgian house, "full of English atmosphere", with many original architectural features. It stands in lovingly tended gardens half a mile from Lake Windermere, in a valley surrounded by fine mountain scenery. It is run by the Nixon brothers, Nigel and Stephen; their wives, Jane and Colette, are in charge of the restaurant. "Reception warm and friendly," writes a 1996 visitor. "The food thoroughly deserves its high reputation." There are "plenty of lounges to relax in", with deep carpets, flowers, books and magazines. Most bedrooms are spacious; best ones lead off an imposing first-floor veranda with cast iron railings. At dinner, served by candlelight on polished wooden tables, with heavy glass and tableware, there's the option of two to five courses; cooking is a mixture of English and French, served in generous portions. There's an excellent wine list. Breakfast is "copious and excellent". Children are welcomed: there are family rooms, free cots, baby-listening, and a children's tea which is not confined to fish fingers. One suite is adapted for disabled guests. There's a busy one-way traffic system close by, but rooms have double-glazing. (*John Rowlands*)

Open All year, except 3 Jan–7 Feb.
Rooms 3 suites (in annexe, 20 yds: 1 honeymoon; 2 family, 1 with ♿ access), 13 double, 2 single.
Facilities Ramps. 3 lounges, 2 dining rooms. 1-acre garden: croquet. Free use of nearby leisure club. Near river Rothay and Lake Windermere: sailing, water-skiing, fishing, riding, golf.
Location On A593 to Coniston, SW of Ambleside. Garden-facing rooms are quietest.
Restrictions No smoking: dining rooms, 1 lounge. No very young children in the restaurant at night. No dogs.
Credit cards All major cards accepted.
Terms B&B: single £78, double £118–£132, suite £165; D,B&B: single £105, double £172–£186, suite £219. Set lunch £14, dinner (2–3-course) £25–£30. Off-season breaks. Reductions for children. Christmas, New Year programmes. 1-night bookings sometimes refused Sat.

Wateredge Hotel *Tel* (0153 94) 32332
Borrans Road *Fax* (0153 94) 31878
Waterhead, Ambleside LA22 0EP

"Another delightful visit. We booked for our next when we left," writes a devoted fan of this family hotel, run by Mr and Mrs Cowap and their two sons, daughter and daughter-in-law. The house has undergone numerous conversions down the centuries, "resulting in interesting nooks and crannies". Bedrooms in the old part are sometimes an odd shape; those in the newer part are larger and more conventional; most have a view of the lake. The furniture is eclectic, "with the nonchalant juxtaposition of styles and periods a family house tends to acquire over the years. The tiny cocktail bar, in the oldest part, is a particular delight." There are two small lounges and a large one with picture windows overlooking the lake. Housekeeping is meticulous: "Everywhere is well furnished and shining clean. Bathroom towels are changed frequently; beds are made during breakfast. The food is interesting and beautifully presented. Five courses for dinner, followed, if you can manage it, by cheese. Portions not overlarge. Croissants, good brown bread, and the best muesli we know, for breakfast. The Cowaps are always there, in the background; the staff, mainly young, are competent and friendly." (*Margaret Box, and others*)

Open Early Feb–mid-Dec.
Rooms 5 suites (across small courtyard), 15 double, 3 single.
Facilities 3 lounges, TV room, bar, restaurant; patio. ½-acre grounds: lake frontage, private jetty, rowing boat, fishing, bathing. Access to nearby leisure club with swimming pool, sauna etc. Unsuitable for ♿.
Location ½ mile S of town; off A591 Kendal–Keswick at Waterhead (roadside rooms can be noisy).
Restrictions No smoking in restaurant. No children under 7. Dogs by arrangement; not in suites, public rooms.
Credit cards Access, Visa.
Terms [1996] B&B £31–£63; D,B&B £51–£83. Set dinner £26.90. Winter breaks. 1-night bookings sometimes refused Sat.

APPLETHWAITE Cumbria — Map 4

Underscar Manor — *Tel* (0176 87) 75000
Applethwaite, nr Keswick CA12 4PH — *Fax* (0176 87) 74904

A grey stone italianate Victorian house standing amid formal gardens, parkland and woods, with red squirrels, guinea fowl and deer. It has "phenomenal" views across Keswick to Derwent Water, and immediate access to the Lake District National Park. It is co-owned with Gordon Evans by Pauline and Derek Harrison, who also own and run the *Moss Nook*, near Manchester Airport, "arguably that city's best restaurant". Pauline's brother, Robert Thornton, is head chef. The decor is ornate (a bit much for some tastes), with lavish fabrics and antiques in public rooms and bedrooms. The restaurant, partly housed in a magnificent original conservatory, with large tables elegantly set, is "luxurious and stylish", and serves "very good" classic/modern food to match; at night a pianist plays a grand piano. "Cunning lighting gives the house and gardens a fabulous aspect. Breakfast up to standard, with freshly squeezed orange juice, and various combinations of the English breakfast; locally cured ham and Cumberland sausages were particularly good." Extras can be pricey. More reports, please.

Open All year.
Rooms 11 double.
Facilities 2 lounges, 2 dining rooms; meeting room. 40-acre grounds: formal garden, woodland. Fishing, golf, pony-trekking, sailing nearby. Unsuitable for ♿.
Location M6 exit 40; A66 towards Workington for 17 miles. At large roundabout take 3rd exit; turn immediately right up lane signposted Underscar.
Restrictions No smoking in restaurant. No children under 12. No dogs.
Credit cards Access, Amex, Visa.
Terms D,B&B: single £85–£125, double £150–£250. Set lunch £18.50, dinner £29.50; full alc £38. 1-night bookings sometimes refused.

> The length of an entry need not reflect the merit of a hotel. The more interesting the report or the more unusual or controversial the hotel, the longer the entry.

ARNCLIFFE North Yorkshire Map 4

Amerdale House *Tel/Fax* (01756) 770250
Arncliffe, Littondale
Skipton BD23 5QE

César award in 1995

Nigel and Paula Crapper's Victorian manor is in a tiny unspoilt hamlet amid the spectacularly beautiful countryside of one of the quietest dales, "with the sound of curlews, lambs grazing in green fields with huge trees, parkland to gaze upon while dining, tranquil fields and hills to calm and restore as one walks". As ever, there's plenty of praise: "We arrived to a tremendously warm welcome, and were instantly made to feel at home. Lovely comfortable public rooms with log fires and books. Delicious dinner, chosen from a small menu. A heavenly location for walkers and birdwatchers. Good value." "Service friendly but not intrusive. No false attempt at bonhomie or house party atmosphere. Bedroom basic but comfortable." "Wonderful breakfast: fresh orange juice, good brown toast, nice croissants, excellent grill." "The wine list is wide-ranging and fairly priced." (*Anne Abel Smith, R and A Baxter, Mr and Mrs T Nash; also Lt. Col Pugh, and others*) Not many rooms have a dale view, and some are small. Some niggles: "Tiny bath, with no shower, which made hair-washing awkward." "Vegetables undercooked." One complaint about a room with poor insulation and disturbance from milking machinery on a nearby farm.

Open Mid-Mar–mid-Nov. Dining room closed for lunch.
Rooms 2 suites, 9 double. 1 on ground floor in converted stables.
Facilities Lounge, library, bar, restaurant. 2-acre grounds. Unsuitable for ♿.
Location 17 miles N of Skipton; fork left off B6160 to Arncliffe.
Restrictions No smoking: restaurant, library. No dogs in house.
Credit cards Access, Visa.
Terms [1996] D,B&B £54.50–£59.50. Set dinner £25. Special breaks: 4 nights for the price of 3. 1-night bookings refused bank holidays, high-season weekends.

ASHBOURNE Derbyshire Map 3

Callow Hall *Tel* (01335) 343403
Mappleton Road *Fax* (01335) 343624
Ashbourne DE6 2AA

A large Victorian house, quietly set up a tree-lined drive in large grounds on the edge of the Peak National Park. It has fine fireplaces and moulded ceilings, antique and period furniture, flowered fabrics, and potted plants and flowers. The dining room is strikingly decorated in shades of red and pink. Best bedrooms are high-ceilinged and bay-windowed, and "ornately decorated, with massive furniture": "Our wardrobe was big enough to be let as a single room. The bathroom was large and luxurious." Some rooms are quite small; one is equipped for disabled visitors. Despite the house's grandeur, David and Dorothy Spencer are unpretentious hosts and, with their long-serving staff, create a caring atmosphere. Son Anthony is co-chef with his father. Their "consistently good" cooking is mostly traditional, based on high-quality materials: meat is home-produced, much garden produce is home-grown; bread is home-baked, and there's a good selection of fresh fish. "Breakfast, served in a charming room, decorated in springtime colours, was a great spread, with a generous buffet and a huge choice of cooked items. We were most impressed by the staff, who went out of their way to look after two families with babies." There is good fishing, for trout and grayling, on a private stretch of the Bentley Brook, a main tributary of the river Dove. (*P Flynn, and others*)

Open All year, except Christmas, possibly 1 week Feb. Restaurant closed midday Mon–Sat, evening Sun to non-residents.
Rooms 1 suite, 15 double. 1 on ground floor, equipped for ♿.
Facilities Lounge, bar, 3 dining rooms; function/conference facilities. 42-acre grounds: garden, woodland, farm, stables, fishing (tuition available).
Location ¾ mile from Ashbourne: A515 to Buxton; sharp left at top of first hill by *Bowling Green* pub, first right to Mappleton; cross bridge; drive is on right.
Restrictions No smoking in restaurant. No dogs in public rooms.
Credit cards All major cards accepted.
Terms B&B: single £65–£85, double £95–£120, suite £140; D,B&B: single £95–£115, double £155–£180; suite £200. Set Sun lunch £15.50, dinner £30; full alc £35. Weekend, midweek breaks. *V*

ATHERSTONE Warwickshire — Map 3

Chapel House BUDGET
Friar's Gate
Atherstone CV9 1EY
Tel (01827) 718949
Fax (01827) 717702

David and Pat Roberts's small white-painted Georgian dower house – "a delightful oasis in the Birmingham triangle" – abuts a large sandstone church (whose bell chimes hourly). It is in a pleasant backwater just off the square of an old market town, only two miles from the A5. Bedrooms are small (some with sloping ceiling) but agreeably furnished, with lots of extras: pot-pourri, dried flowers, shoe-cleaning materials, etc. Public rooms are decorated with a profusion of lace, doilies and dried flower arrangements. The conservatory overlooks a pretty walled garden with two ornamental ponds teeming with goldfish. The popular restaurant serves good traditional and modern cooking, attractively presented, with friendly service. There is a decent selection of half bottles of wine. The English breakfast is generous, with a wide range of preserves and honey. Snacks, tea, coffee and drinks are available "at reasonable times". There is plenty of interesting sightseeing nearby, and the National Exhibition Centre is within easy reach. (*Jan Morris*)

Open All year, except 25/26 Dec. Restaurant closed Sun evening; snacks available.
Rooms 7 double, 6 single.
Facilities Lounge, restaurant, conservatory. ¼-acre garden. Unsuitable for ♿.
Location Off market square, by church. From S bear right at Nationwide Building Society, then right at T-junction. First right into Friar's Gate. Parking directly outside.
Restrictions No children under 10 in restaurant. No dogs.
Credit cards All major cards accepted.
Terms B&B: single £45–£55, double £55–£65. Set Sun lunch £14.95; full alc £30. Weekend rates.

Hotels are dropped if we lack positive feedback. If you can endorse an entry, we urge you to do so.

AYLESBURY Buckinghamshire — Map 2

Hartwell House
Oxford Road
Aylesbury HP17 8NL

Tel (01296) 747444
Fax (01296) 747450

César award: country house hotel of the year

A serene country mansion, with Jacobean and Georgian façades, in lush parkland with a trout lake, a ruined church and lots of statuary, all immaculately maintained. It was restored to its original splendour by Historic House Hotels Ltd (see also *The Cadogan*, London, *Middlethorpe Hall*, York, and *Bodysgallen Hall*, Llandudno). It is as impressive inside as out, with fine paintings and plasterwork, antiques, a Jacobean central staircase, a spectacular 18th-century great hall, a fine library, "and a maze of corridors, corners and different levels". Bedrooms are spacious, some huge; some have magnificent panelling and a four-poster. Visitors "feel like guests in a stately home", but owing to the friendliness of the manager, Jonathan Thompson, and his mainly young staff, it is not intimidating. Chef Alan Maw's menu is "refreshingly straightforward", and his English cooking much admired: "Unusual fish dishes, deliciously sauced, and some quite exceptional meat. Puddings were nectar, and light. Wide choice of wine by the glass." In the spa, "the agreeable buttery serves tasty, reasonably priced light meals". The champagne breaks are "superb value". There are extensive conference facilities, well away from the private guests.

Open All year.
Rooms 13 suites, 32 double, 1 single. Some in stable block. Some on ground floor. 1 equipped for ♿.
Facilities Lift, ramp. Great hall, morning room, drawing room, library, bar, buttery, restaurant; conference facilities; spa: indoor swimming pool, whirlpool, saunas, beauty salon, bar/buttery. 90-acre grounds: croquet, lake (fishing), woodlands.
Location 2 miles S of Aylesbury on A418 towards Oxford; hotel on right.
Restrictions No smoking: dining rooms, first-floor bedrooms. No children under 8. No dogs in public rooms.
Credit cards Access, Amex, Visa.
Terms Rooms: single £105–£160, double £160–£220, suite £260–£450. Breakfast: continental £9.50, English £13.50. Set lunch (2–4 courses) £18.45–£24.90, dinner £39.90; full alc £47. 2-night breaks: D,B&B from £107 per person per night.

BARWICK Somerset — Map 2

Little Barwick House
Barwick, nr Yeovil BA22 9TD

Tel (01935) 423902
Fax (01935) 420908

A welcoming "country house restaurant-with-rooms", offering "really good value for money". It is a lovingly cared-for Georgian dower house in a secluded corner of a tiny village near Yeovil, "in a delightful, peaceful garden, Matisse-like with stripey deck chairs". Christopher Colley is "front-of-house, waiter, wine waiter and ambassador"; his wife Veronica, "with that special gift which distinguishes inspiration from competence", cooks mainly British dishes using local ingredients. "There's nothing phony or pretentious; the dining room is not a temple, service is not patronising – just first-class. Meals are balanced, steamed vegetables crunchy, puddings indulgent." There are choices at each stage of the four-course set menu; you can opt for two and pay less. The lounge is small, so are some bedrooms, but they are quiet and well equipped, with comfortable chairs and good lights. "Proper" breakfasts include good toast, no packet butters, ample coffee. Afternoon tea with crumpets is free. Winter breaks are excellent value. For architectural enthusiasts there's a folly-hunting package. (*JD Crosland; also PE Carter, DA O'Bryen, and others*) "All new beds!" write the Colleys in answer to last year's caveat. One moan this year: "With such high culinary standards, packet orange juice was a surprise."

Open All year, except Christmas, New Year. Restaurant closed midday, to non-residents Sun.
Rooms 6 double.
Facilities Lounge, bar, restaurant. 3½-acre garden. Unsuitable for ♿.
Location Left off A37 Yeovil–Dorchester at *Red House* pub. Hotel ¼ mile on left.
Restrictions No smoking: dining room, bedrooms. No dogs in public rooms.
Credit cards Access, Amex, Visa.
Terms [1996] B&B: single £49, double £78; D,B&B: single £69, double £118. Set dinner (2–4-course): £18.90–£24.90. Reductions for 2 nights or more. Winter breaks Oct–Apr. 1-night bookings sometimes refused Sun off-season. Children accommodated free in parents' room. *V*

BASLOW Derbyshire — Map 3

The Cavendish *Tel* (01246) 582311
Baslow DE45 1SP *Fax* (01246) 582312

A hotel of character in a lovely position on the edge of Chatsworth Park. Owned by the Duke and Duchess of Devonshire, it has been run since 1975 by Eric Marsh. All the bedrooms overlook the park; some, in the Mitford wing, are named for members of the Duchess's famous family. Smart public rooms have log fires, impressive flower arrangements, antiques and fine paintings (some from Chatsworth House). In the main restaurant, Nick Buckingham's highly praised cooking, ranging from traditional to sophisticated, is served by knowledgeable waitresses. The wine list is "intelligently arranged, with a fair mark-up". For £40 a head you can eat in the kitchen, watching the chef at work. Simpler and less expensive meals, from late breakfast and *plats du jour*, to soups and sandwiches – "designer" or "regular" – are served in the Garden Room between 11 am and 11 pm. In winter, if you book for Friday and Saturday nights you can stay for Sunday night at no extra charge, paying only for meals. Children are welcomed here. "Lovely in every way," was one recent accolade. Another went further in hyperbole: "The nearest thing to paradise I know. The only problem is coming back to earth when you return home." (*JS Rutter, and others*) One gourmet correspondent was ambivalent about some of the cooking – "better on robust than on delicate flavours," was his summing up.

Open All year.
Rooms 1 suite, 23 double.
Facilities Lounge with bar, 2 restaurants; private dining room, conference room. 2-acre grounds: putting green; fishing in river Derwent. Unsuitable for ♿.
Location On A619 in Chatsworth grounds. M1 exit 29.
Restrictions No smoking in restaurant. No dogs.
Credit cards All major cards accepted.
Terms Rooms: single £79–£94, double £99–£114, suite £135. Alc breakfast from

£4.95; full English £9.20. Light meals in Garden Room. Main restaurant: set lunch / dinner £28.75; kitchen table £40; full alc £45. Winter bonus weekends.

Fischer's Baslow Hall *Tel* (01246) 583259
Calver Road *Fax* (01246) 583818
Baslow DE45 1RR

In their Edwardian manor, up a tree-lined drive in a village on the edge of the Chatsworth estate, Max and Susan Fischer run a *Michelin*-starred restaurant-with-rooms alongside a less formal café. The house is furnished in personal style, with Victorian and country pine furniture, bold colours, and fabrics of quality; fresh flowers, plants and bowls of pot-pourri abound. The bedrooms are up a splendid carved oak staircase; some are quite small, and priced accordingly. Some bathrooms are agreeably old-fashioned, with an Edwardian bath, and a loo with a wooden seat and a pull-chain. The hotel's lounge, formerly the entrance hall, can get crowded, as it serves non-resident diners as well as residents. In the restaurant, which has a fine plaster ceiling, Max Fischer's cooking is modern and eclectic; fish is a speciality. Service is by knowledgeable waitresses in attractive long skirts, long cardigans, and pretty bows at the neck. The wine list is "interesting, though not large"; local mineral water included in the price. "Delicious home-made bread." Oven-fresh brioches and croissants accompany the cooked breakfast.

Open All year, except 25/26 Dec. Restaurant closed to non-residents Sun evening. Café closed Sat evening / midday Sun.
Rooms 1 suite, 5 double.
Facilities Lounge / bar, breakfast room, restaurant, bistro. 5-acre grounds. Fishing 3 miles. Unsuitable for ♿.
Location Take A623 Baslow–Stockport. Last entrance on right within village boundary.
Restrictions No smoking in restaurant. No children under 12 in restaurant after 7 pm. Guide dogs only.
Credit cards All major cards accepted.
Terms B&B: single £75–£90, double £95–£120. Set lunch £19.50, dinner £38.50; full alc (café) £20. 2-night packages; weekend breaks. 1-night bookings sometimes refused.

BATH Somerset **Map 2**

Dukes Hotel NEW/BUDGET *Tel* (01225) 463512
Great Pulteney Street *Fax* (01225) 483733
Bath BA2 4DN

Grade I listed Georgian house in one of the town's premier streets, just across river from Abbey (quietest rooms at rear). Many original features, including fine staircase (no lift). Exceptionally kind American owners, Tim and Rosalind Forester. Unpretentious regional English cooking, well prepared and served, in no-smoking basement restaurant. Garage, unrestricted street parking. Closed Christmas; restaurant closed Sun evening. 22 rooms (5 family). Unsuitable for ♿. No dogs in public rooms. All major credit cards accepted. B&B: single £50–£70, double £60–£90; D,B&B single £60–£80, double £80–£110. Set dinner (2–3-course) £13.50–£17.50. V*

Haydon House BUDGET *Tel/Fax* (01225) 427351 and 444919
9 Bloomfield Park
Bath BA2 2BY

"B&B at its best. Everything immaculate. Spacious bedroom with amenities galore: sherry, shortbread, iron; bathroom with good-sized tub and power shower. Breakfast an elegant affair, with good china, silver and crystal." "Hosts just as nice as could be. Tray of tea and home-made shortbread on arrival. Well-kept garden, colourful even in February, with statues, lit up at night. Help with dinner reservations." Recent endorsements for Magdalene Ashman-Marr's semi-detached Edwardian house in a quiet residential area, a stiff walk up from the centre of Bath (no parking problems). It has a terrace for summer drinks, and a chintzy lounge crammed with family photos, ornaments and dried flowers. Bedrooms have flowery wallpapers and fabrics and many knick-knacks; one has a four-poster; a spacious one at the top is suitable for a family. The cooked breakfast is served communally at flexible times by the gregarious Gordon Marr. It includes whisky or rum porridge, scrambled eggs with smoked salmon, eggs Benedict, and home-made mango and orange marmalade. A generous continental one can be taken in the bedrooms. (*Larissa and Michael Milne, D and PH; also Jill McLaren, and others*) "Strictly speaking, we are not equipped for disabled guests," write the owners, "but we do our best if warned in advance." In low season, guests who book for two nights may stay free for a third, except Friday.

Open All year.
Rooms 5 double.
Facilities Sitting room, study, breakfast room; sun terrace. ½-acre garden. Sports/leisure centre nearby. Not really suitable for ♿.
Location From centre take A367 (to Exeter) *c.* ½ mile up Wells Rd. Right into shopping area (*Bear* pub on right). At end of short dual carriageway fork right into Bloomfield Rd; Bloomfield Pk 2nd right. Street parking.
Restrictions No smoking. Children by arrangement. No dogs.
Credit cards Access, Amex, Visa.
Terms B&B: single £45–£55, double £60–£75. 3 nights for price of 2 (except Fri/Sat) Nov–Mar. 1-night bookings occasionally refused weekends. *V*

Holly Lodge *Tel* (01225) 424042
8 Upper Oldfield Park *Fax* (01225) 481138
Bath BA2 3JZ

A no-smoking B&B in a large Victorian house, high above Bath with a fine view of the city. Sadly the co-owner, Carrolle Sellick, died in 1995, but her husband, George Hall, continues to run it, and a regular visitor reports that "rooms, housekeeping, and food are all still of the highest standard". "It was beautifully quiet," writes another guest. "The bedrooms are delightful, and sumptuously decorated; ours had views of the city and the immaculate terraced garden. The bathroom was large and well appointed, with plenty of everything. Breakfast, served in a Mediterranean-style sun room, was a feast, with masses of fresh fruit, including strawberries, mangoes and passion fruit, freshly baked croissants, a vast variety of teas and coffees, and a choice of cooked dishes to satisfy the hungriest and fussiest of guests. The sitting room is delightful, with newspapers and glossy magazines." It takes about ten minutes to walk to the centre; there are local minibuses for the return journey. (*KK, Christina Sausman*)

Open All year.
Rooms 5 double, 1 single. 1 on ground floor.
Facilities Lounge, breakfast room. ½-acre garden: gazebo.
Location ½ mile SW of centre. 1st right off Wells Rd (A367). Private parking.
Restrictions No smoking. No dogs.
Credit cards All major cards accepted.
Terms B&B: single £46–£48, double £75–£90. 2-night breaks Jan–Mar.

The Priory *Tel* (01225) 331922
Weston Road *Fax* (01225) 448276
Bath BA1 2XT

A 19th-century Gothic-style house, Grade II listed, in large grounds on the edge of the town – it's an easy walk through a park to the centre. It has a country house decor, and an atmosphere "of quiet good taste": antiques, splendid flower arrangements, log fires. The hotel recently underwent a complete refurbishment, and a leisure centre was added. The owner (since 1994), Andrew Brownsword, has kept on the admirable managing director, Tom Conboy, and the long-serving chef, Mike Collom. There are two restaurants: the formal Gothic Room, serving classical French and traditional English cooking, and the brasserie-style Garden Room, leading on to an orangery. Room-service meals are available. "Warm hospitality, coupled with excellent food, accommodation and service." "Beautiful bedroom; everything of the highest quality. Splendid bathroom, naturally lit. Private parking a boon, too." (*Roland English, Alan Greenwood*) "Young children are welcome, provided they are accompanied by well-behaved parents," writes Mr Conboy. By 1997 there will be nine new bedrooms, the garden will have been extended, and the outdoor pool refurbished.

Open All year.
Rooms 4 suites, 14 double, 1 single. 2 on ground floor. 9 more planned for 1997.
Facilities Drawing room, lounge, 2 restaurants; function facilities; leisure centre: swimming pool, gym, sauna. 2-acre grounds: swimming pool, croquet. Tennis, riding, fishing, golf nearby.
Location 1 mile W of centre, off A4 to Bristol. Carpark.
Restrictions No smoking in restaurants. No dogs.
Credit cards All major cards accepted.
Terms [1996] B&B (continental): single £85, double £155–£190, suite £225; D,B&B: single £120, double £195–£225, suite £260. English breakfast £5. Set lunch £14.50, dinner £33.50. Winter breaks. *V*

The Queensberry *Tel* (01225) 447928
Russel Street *Fax* (01225) 446065
Bath BA1 2QF

Stephen and Penny Ross's upmarket small hotel is in a residential street not far from the Assembly Rooms. The house was designed by John Wood for the Marquis of Queensberry in 1772, and its decor complements the 18th-century stucco ceilings, cornices and panelling. There's a cream-coloured drawing room where teas are served, a small bar, and a patio garden. Best bedrooms, on the first floor, are large; top ones are smaller, and priced accordingly. Mixed reports this year. One reader found both the hotel and the basement restaurant, *The Olive*

Tree (popular for Stephen Ross's modern British cooking) "first class", but others have been critical of the restaurant, "and the breakfast orange juice seemed to be commercially squeezed". Some bedrooms are said to be in need of redecoration, and there are also mutterings about value for money. More reports, please.

Open All year, except 1 week Christmas.
Rooms 22 double.
Facilities Drawing room, bar, restaurant; meeting room. Courtyard garden. Unsuitable for ♿.
Location Central. Take Bennett St left off Lansdown Rd, then 1st right. Street parking.
Restrictions No smoking in restaurant. Guide dogs only.
Credit cards Access, Visa.
Terms B&B: single £70–£120, double £70–£175. English breakfast £7.50. D,B&B: single £95–£145, double £120–£225. Set lunch £10.50–£12.50, dinner £19; full alc £30. Extra bed for child £10. 2-night winter breaks. **V***

Royal Crescent Hotel NEW
The Royal Crescent
Bath BA1 2LS

Tel (01225) 739955
Fax (01225) 339401

A luxurious hotel, right in the middle of Bath's most glorious crescent, its entrance discreetly marked by bay trees. It was skilfully created from two adjoining Georgian houses; many period features have been retained. There are antiques and fine paintings in the grand public rooms. The suites, too, are grand, with "everything you could possibly want: bottled water, fresh flowers, bathrobes in the luxurious bathroom"; most doubles too, are large; the single is "quite small, but adequate, if rather cluttered". The restaurant, the bar, and further bedrooms are in the Dower House, Pavilion and Garden Villa, across the peaceful garden. The hotel is chain-owned (by Queen's Moat) but well managed, and unintimidating despite its grandeur. "The staff are most friendly and helpful," writes a 1996 visitor. "It was pleasant to find old-fashioned services such as porterage and shoe-cleaning. The *nouvelle cuisine* food was beautifully served, though the choice was quite limited." "Breakfast very good, with a wide-ranging menu. Expensive, but good value for money." (*Mr and Mrs TI Frith, Francis Aglionby, and others*)

Open All year.
Rooms 15 suites, 30 double, 1 single. In 5 separate buildings.
Facilities 3 lounges (1 with bar), restaurant; function facilities. 1-acre garden: plunge pool, croquet. Unsuitable for ♿.
Location ½-mile from centre. Valet parking.
Restriction No smoking in restaurant.
Credit cards All major cards accepted.
Terms Rooms: single £85–£105, double £140–£165, suite £250–£395. Breakfast: continental £9.50, English £12.50. Set lunch £18.50, dinner £35; full alc £49.

Somerset House NEW/BUDGET
35 Bathwick Hill
Bath BA2 6LD

Tel (01225) 466451
Fax (01225) 317188

A handsome listed Regency mansion, a short drive or bus ride, or a stiffish walk uphill, from the centre. It has been run for many years by Jean and Malcolm Seymour with son Jonathan (the chef). Polly, the parrot by the door "adds to the friendly atmosphere". There is a flowery garden with a large Judas tree. The bedrooms retain their original dimensions (one double and the single are small), but each has a bathroom or shower. The restaurant is open to the public. Dinner, served at 7 pm (7.30 on Saturday; two or three choices for each course) is traditional English family cooking, with occasional ethnic or "themed" menus. The hotel was dropped from the *Guide* some years back, but many visitors have written to urge its reinstatement. "A truly family atmosphere. Bedrooms, named for George III's children, with every comfort. Breakfast is an experience: sideboard laden with cereals, home-made muesli, bread, jams, marmalades; every cooked dish one can expect. Superb, imaginative dinners." "In two weeks not a single dish was repeated on the menu." "An exceptionally warm welcome. We particularly enjoyed the meals themed to suit the composer of the opera weekends." "Informality the trademark." "The friendly gathering of guests before dinner is a great start to the evening." (*Mary Kerensky, Richard Herz, Mr and Mrs V Forster, Mrs G Willy, JM Chandler, and others*) No smoking.

Open All year. Restaurant closed Sun evening.
Rooms 9 double, 1 single. 2 on ground floor. 3 with TV.
Facilities 2 lounges, restaurant, conservatory. 1-acre garden: miniature railway. Kennet and Avon Canal, fishing, boat trips close by.
Location ¾ mile from centre. Junction of Bathwick Hill (leading to university) and Cleveland Walk. Carpark.
Restrictions No smoking. No dogs in public rooms.
Credit cards Access, Amex, Visa.
Terms B&B: single £20.50–£32, double £41–£64; D,B&B: single £43–£51, double £79.50–£102. Set lunch £11, dinner £19. Midweek bargain breaks. Opera, Brunel, canal weekends in low season. Christmas, New Year house party. *V*

BATHFORD Somerset **Map 2**

Eagle House BUDGET *Tel/Fax* (01225) 859946
Church Street
Bathford BA1 7RS

Bathford, a pretty conservation village spread up a steep hill, three miles east of Bath, makes a pleasant alternative to staying in the city; you can avoid parking problems there by taking a bus. This B&B is a listed Georgian building by John Wood the Elder, quietly set in a large garden (complete with treehouse, sandpit, swing and grass tennis court). It has a handsome drawing room with a fine marble fireplace and moulded ceiling, and "old family furniture – good, but not too smart". It is informally run by "charming but not intrusive" hosts, John and Rosamund Napier. "I have rarely stayed in a hotel with such a nice atmosphere," runs a recent encomium. "We were in a large party, with five children. The welcome could not have been friendlier. Our rooms were large and pretty, with beautiful views. Everything had been thought of, down to fresh milk in a thermos for tea-making. The bathrooms were great. Breakfast was plentiful, with a ridiculously small extra charge for cooked dishes. The children loved the garden. We enjoyed every minute." Bedrooms are mostly spacious; two are in a cottage with its own walled garden and kitchen. Breakfast is until 10 am on weekdays, 10.30 on Sunday. "Even the dog and cat are hospitable." (*Caroline Thomson, and others*)

Open All year, except 20–31 Dec.
Rooms 1 family, 6 double, 1 single. 2 double in cottage with sitting room, kitchen, walled garden.
Facilities Drawing room, breakfast room. 2½-acre garden: tennis, croquet, sandpit, treehouse, swings. Unsuitable for ♿.
Location First right off Bathford Hill; 200 yds on right behind high stone wall and wrought iron gates (conservation area; no sign permitted). Ample parking.
Restrictions No smoking in 1 bedroom. Generally no dogs in public rooms.
Credit cards Access, Visa.
Terms B&B: single £34–£45, double £46–£72, suite £72–£98. Cooked breakfast £2.95 added. Winter breaks. 1-night bookings sometimes refused Sat, bank holidays. Children accommodated free in parents' room. *V*

The Lodge *Tel* (01225) 858467 and 858575
Bathford Hill *Fax* (01225) 858172
Bathford BA1 7SL

Keith and Mary Johnson's B&B "exudes a feeling of peace and quiet. The stylishly furnished, spacious bedrooms add to the relaxed atmosphere. Service is excellent, without being overbearing." The English breakfast is "a feast, including a large buffet of fresh fruit, yogurt, and an array of cereals". In the lounge, visitors may browse through the papers over tea or a complimentary sherry. In the award-winning landscaped garden (with a sheltered swimming pool) they may socialise with the owners' friendly dogs and cats. The Johnsons own a narrow boat, which guests may hire, on the Kennet and Avon canal. They specialise in house parties. The *Crown* pub, just down the road, is recommended for an evening meal. (*Michael Sprunck, and others*)

Open All year, except Christmas/New Year.
Rooms 1 suite, 4 double. 1 on ground floor.
Facilities Lounge, breakfast room. 3-acre garden: swimming pool (heated May–Oct).
Location Up Bathford Hill, on right, 100 yds after *Crown* inn.
Restriction No dogs in public rooms.
Credit cards Access, Visa.
Terms B&B: single £50–£90, double £65–£110. Weekend breaks "negotiable". Children under 5 accommodated free in parents' room. 1-night bookings sometimes refused bank holidays.

BATTLE East Sussex Map 2

Little Hemingfold *Tel* (01424) 774338
Telham, Battle TN33 0TT *Fax* (01424) 775351

An informal hideaway in a "glorious rural setting", yet only 40 minutes' drive from the Newhaven ferry. Popular for its friendly hosts, Paul and Allison Slater, and the "home-from-home surroundings", it is a higgledy-piggledy, not very *soigné* mixture of old buildings up a bumpy track ("not recommended to the proud owner of a new and expensive car"), in a bucolic position by a lake. There's a grass tennis court, plenty for children to do, and good walking, "with two labradors for those needing an incentive". The guests' lounges are large, with big windows overlooking lovely countryside. Bedrooms, some with a small wood-burning stove, are spacious; though simple, and plainly furnished, they have telephone, TV, and electric blanket. Dinner, "no-frills cooking, using fresh produce from the garden, and served by charming young students", is at 7.30, with some choice; vegetarians are catered for. Communal eating is the norm, but you can ask for a separate table. "Nothing chi-chi. Good value." (*George Hope*)

Open All year. Lunch not served.
Rooms 12 double. 10 with bath. 9 in adjoining coach house.
Facilities 2 lounges, bar, dining room. 40-acre grounds: tennis, woods, lake: swimming, fishing, boating. Unsuitable for ♿.
Location 1½ miles S of Battle off A2100; blue hotel sign on left by road sign indicating sharp bend.
Restrictions No smoking: dining room, 1 lounge. No dogs in public rooms.
Credit cards All major cards accepted.
Terms B&B £34–£38; D,B&B £54–£56. Set dinner £20.50. Children under 4 accommodated free in parents' room. Special breaks; house parties; Christmas, New Year packages. 1-night bookings sometimes refused.

Netherfield Place *Tel* (01424) 774455
Battle TN33 9PP *Fax* (01424) 774024

"A lovely hotel, comfortable and welcoming. I have stayed many times." A recent endorsement for Michael and Helen Collier's Georgian-style 1920s country house. It is set up a long drive in extensive, well-kept grounds, with plenty to do (see below). Its decor is traditional, with antiques and repro furniture. Bedrooms, with light colours and flowery fabrics, vary in size and are well supplied with flowers, fresh fruit, chocolates etc; their old-fashioned carpeted bathrooms have capacious (if "well-worn") towels and bathrobes, and good toiletries. The food, served in a "very attractive" panelled dining room (popular locally), is modern, not *haute cuisine*, but freshly prepared, using ingredients from the large kitchen garden. There's a "particularly good vegetarian menu". Staff are "kind, attentive and thoughtful". (*Judy Rothenburg, Paul Jackson*) Room maintenance and lighting have been criticised.

Open All year, except Christmas–early Jan.
Rooms 10 double, 4 single.
Facilities Lounge, bar, restaurant; conference facilities. 30-acre grounds: gardens, tennis, putting, croquet, clay pigeon-shooting, woodland walks. Golf, fishing, riding nearby. Sea 8 miles. Unsuitable for ♿.
Location 2 miles NW of Battle. Turn left towards Netherfield off A2100. Hotel is 1½ miles on.
Restriction Dogs by arrangement, in bedrooms only.
Credit cards All major cards accepted.
Terms [1996] B&B: single £60, double £100–£140; D,B&B: single £90, double £150–£170. Set lunch £13.95, dinner £24.50; full alc £34. 2-night breaks. 1-night bookings refused Sat Apr–Nov. *V*

Powder Mills NEW *Tel* (01424) 775511
Powdermill Lane *Fax* (01424) 774540
Battle TN33 0SP

Listed 18th-century house (Mediterranean feel: Doric columns, Greek statues) in 150-acre park and woodlands, up lane opposite Battle railway station. 4 lakes (trout fishing), unheated swimming pool. Informal style; country atmosphere. Antiques, log fires, books in public rooms. Light lunches and snacks available in library. Orangery restaurant (closed Sun evening Jan/Feb) serves acceptable modern cooking: elegant atmosphere, professional service; dinner-dance on Fri in autumn/winter. Splendid breakfast buffet. 35 rooms; best in main house, 12 in annexes, 5 on ground floor. No smoking: restaurant, some bedrooms. All major credit cards accepted. B&B: single £55, double £80, suite £120–£150. D,B&B: single £70, double £115, suite £155–£185. Venue for weddings, conferences, etc. Routiers *Hotel of the Year, 1996. More reports, please.*

BEAMINSTER Dorset **Map 1**

Bridge House *Tel* (01308) 862200
3 Prout Bridge *Fax* (01308) 863700
Beaminster DT8 3AY

"A super, good-value break. Atmosphere that of a visit to attentive friends; proprietor and staff there when needed. Tea by a fire on a winter afternoon. Dinner menu just what we like: not too ambitious, nor too long to be believably fresh, using largely local produce. Enormous, enjoyable breakfast – smoked salmon and scrambled eggs adding a touch of glamour at 9.30 am." "Large, well-lit bedroom with beautiful decor, upmarket tea bags and fresh milk. Extremely good service. Wine list excellent." This 13th-century house, with mullioned windows, old beams and inglenook fireplaces, is in a pretty walled garden in an old country town in the west Dorset hills (the heart of Hardy country – Beaminster is Emminster in *Tess of the D'Urbervilles*). Bedrooms are in the main house, converted stables and a new wing. The candlelit restaurant serves fairly traditional English/international cooking by the proprietor/chef Peter Pinkster with Jacky Rae. Breakfast, including a good selection of both uncooked and cooked items and home-made preserves, is served in a "delightful garden room". (*Bernard and Elizabeth Biggs, and others*) Only caveat: "The china did not add the grace note the food deserved."

Open All year.
Rooms 13 double, 1 single. 4 in coach house. 5 on ground floor.
Facilities Lounge/bar, sitting room, sun room, restaurant, conservatory; patio. ½-acre walled garden. Unsuitable for ♿.
Location 2 mins' walk from centre. Windows on road double-glazed. Private carpark.
Restrictions No smoking: restaurant, conservatory. No dogs in public rooms or alone in bedrooms.
Credit cards All major cards accepted.
Terms B&B: single from £56, double from £78; D,B&B (min. 2 days): single £72, double £113. Snack lunches available. Set lunch £11.95–£13.95, dinner £18.95. Winter breaks; Christmas, New Year packages. 1-night bookings sometimes refused weekends. *V*

BECKINGTON Somerset **Map 2**

The Woolpack Inn *Tel* (01373) 831244
Beckington, nr Bath BA3 6SP *Fax* (01373) 831223

The "imaginative and well-prepared food, with informed service by local waitresses" is one of the many attractions of this award-winning 16th-century coaching inn in the centre of a pleasant village near Bath. Chef David Woolfall's modern English/French cooking, which has an enthusiastic *Good Food Guide* entry, was much liked by our inspectors, who also praised the "reasonably priced, eclectic wine list" and the "down-to-earth, lively, ambience". The small public rooms "give a sense of cosy intimacy". Bedrooms, too, are on the small side, "with nice repro furniture, and good reading lights". One, at the top, is "tiny, but well organised, with low beams and a small shower for contortionists – a hoot". There are two small patios at the back for summer dining. The flag-stoned bar, popular with locals, serves "very good" snacks. "Breakfast pretty good too." (*J and S Chute, and others*)

Open All year.
Rooms 12 double.
Facilities Lounge, bar, garden room, dining room; courtyard. ¼-acre garden. Unsuitable for ♿.
Location In village off A36, 10 miles SE of Bath. Carpark.
Restrictions No smoking in dining room. No children under 5. No dogs in public rooms.
Credit card Access.
Terms B&B: single £54.50, double £64.50–£84.50. Full alc £25–£30. Christmas package.

BEERCROCOMBE Somerset — Map 1

Frog Street Farm BUDGET — *Tel* (01823) 480430
Beercrocombe, Taunton TA3 6AF

César award in 1988

"One of the best small-scale establishments we have come across recently. What made it special was Veronica Cole's jolly personality, and the excellence of her cooking – straightforward English at its best. Ingredients, almost all locally produced, were as fresh as is possible, with vegetables more flavoursome and meat more tender than one generally gets nowadays. Our bedroom was spacious and pleasantly decorated. Downstairs there are three delightful lounges. Henry Cole is a racehorse trainer of some note; his horses add interest to the fields around." "Mrs Cole is a real charmer, dedicated to looking after her guests." "Such peace combined with such generosity! Superb breakfasts." This unpretentious listed 15th-century farmhouse is on a large working farm, deep in rural Somerset, with fields and woods on one side, orchards on the other, and a heated pool under cherry trees. It has beams, panelling, inglenook fireplaces, "and furnishings and fittings appropriate to its style". There are never more than six guests. Dinners, by arrangement, are generally served at separate tables, but guests may eat together if they prefer. The menus include traditional roasts, wild salmon and pheasant, and "wicked" desserts. No licence: bring your own wine. The north and south coasts are about 21 miles away. (*Richard and Cecily Nesbit, Tim Moorey, and others*) No smoking.

Open Apr–Oct.
Rooms 3 double. No telephone/radio/TV.
Facilities 2 lounges, dining room. Garden: swimming pool. On 130-acre working farm with trout stream. Unsuitable for ♿.
Location 7 miles SE of Taunton. M5 exit 25, A358 to Ilminster. In Hatch Beauchamp, at *Hatch Inn*, take Station Rd; left down no through road. Signposted.
Restrictions No smoking. No children under 11. No dogs.
Credit cards None accepted.
Terms B&B £27. Set dinner £16 (unlicensed: bring your own wine). Reductions for 4 or more nights. Weekly rates.

BENENDEN Kent Map 2

Crit Hall BUDGET
Cranbrook Road
Benenden TN17 4EU
Tel (01580) 240609
Fax (01580) 241743

"A delightful Georgian house in a splendid location with magnificent views, where the hosts, John and Sue Bruder, have created a particularly welcoming atmosphere. My large bedroom was extremely comfortable and richly furnished with dramatic fabrics. Dinner was excellent, and unbelievable value." "The Bruders are interested and caring people. Their kind of hospitality attracts the like-minded, and our fellow guests were delightful. No detail is overlooked. Much better than many far pricier places." "I adored the kitchen/breakfast arrangements; when I asked for a light supper, I got what I wanted. Very relaxing." Warm endorsements for this informally run small hotel in the Weald of Kent. It has an open position, surrounded by farmland and good walking country. In the vast kitchen with Aga, garlanded beams and an old dresser, "a divine breakfast is served at a huge pine table groaning with goodies – juices, fruits, compotes, etc". The drawing room has well-stuffed sofas, and books and magazines in abundance. Bedrooms "have all mod cons including colour TV, and *fresh* milk on the tea tray". (*Janet Street-Porter, Joan Prince, Richard Creed; also Helen Harrison*) No smoking.

Open 15 Jan–15 Dec.
Rooms 3 double. No telephone.
Facilities Drawing room, dining room, conservatory. 1-acre garden. Riding, fishing, water sports, golf, nearby. Unsuitable for ♿.
Location NW of Benenden off B2086.
Restrictions No smoking. No children under 10. No dogs.
Credit cards Access, Visa.
Terms B&B £23–£36. Set dinner £17.50. 4-day half-board rates. 1-night bookings sometimes refused weekends. *V*

BETHERSDEN Kent Map 2

Little Hodgeham BUDGET
Smarden Road
Bethersden TN26 3HE
Tel (01233) 850323

César award in 1994

Erica Wallace's half-timbered Tudor cottage is set in a flower-filled garden, with a swimming pool, a pond stocked with carp and tench, and a water garden, in a tiny Kent village. Inside are more ancient beams, fresh flowers, and log fires in cold weather. Both house and garden are lovingly tended. The public rooms are spotless, with shining antique furniture. In the brown dining room, with yellow silk curtains, fine china and good silver, Miss Wallace presides over communal meals ("gourmet cooking beyond most expectation") served by candlelight. Guests are consulted in advance about their likes and dislikes. "Every bedroom is utterly charming and original," one visitor has written, "the four-poster is like something out of *The Princess and the Pea*." Others have praised the "personal touch", and the attention to detail: "A tea basket when you go touring, and the loan of wellies when it rains; a small example of the measure of comfort and satisfaction appreciated by her guests." "This home exudes warmth, concern and also fun and laughter; it attracts congenial company." "Wonderful value for money." (*Francine Walsh; and others*) Full hotel amenities are not on offer.

Open Mid-Mar–1 Sept. Dining room may be closed "when I am exhausted".
Rooms 3 double. No telephone/TV.
Facilities Drawing room, library/TV room, dining room, conservatory. ½-acre garden: swimming pool, pond, water garden. Tennis, golf nearby. Unsuitable for ♿.
Location 10 miles W of Ashford. From Bethersden, at *Bull* pub, take Smarden road for 2 miles.
Restrictions No smoking in dining room. Dogs in barn and garden only.
Credit cards None accepted.
Terms D,B&B £52.50–£59 (£47.50 for 4 nights or more).

BIGBURY-ON-SEA Devon — Map 1

Burgh Island Hotel — *Tel* (01548) 810514
Bigbury-on-Sea TQ7 4BG — *Fax* (01548) 810243

César award in 1993

Tony and Beatrice Porter's lovingly restored Art Deco extravaganza, "a fantasy world of the 1920s", is on a private island in Bigbury Bay. At low tide you walk across the sand; at high water you are carried by a giant sea tractor – "a magical experience". The hotel's splendours include a palm court with peacock dome, a 1920s bar serving exotic cocktails, and a glass sun lounge where residents take tea. Accommodation is in suites with a sitting room and one or two bedrooms; most have a balcony and sea view; there is also a two-bedroomed beach house. Dinner is served in a 1920s ballroom – in deference to its splendour guests are asked to dress formally. "The personal touch of the amiable, caring host made our stay memorable," wrote visitors last year. "The staff's enthusiasm adds to the fun." "A very special hotel. Our suite, with authentic Art Deco decor, was simple, almost stark, with breathtaking views. On Saturday night a crooner entertained us with twenties and thirties songs. Cliff walks also breathtaking, particularly in a high wind." "Faded elegance rather than plush modern furniture; superb breakfast – both the continental and the fry-up." "Excellent dinners." More reports, please.

Open All year, except midweek Jan/Feb.
Rooms 15 suites, 1 room in Beach House 100 yds.
Facilities Lift. Sun lounges, palm court bar, restaurant, breakfast room, ballroom (dinner-dance Sat), games room, billiards; sauna. On 26-acre island: pub, tennis, tidal swimming pool; beach: safe bathing, water sports, cliff walks, bird sanctuary. Unsuitable for ♿.
Location Leave A38 at Modbury exit. Through Modbury to Bigbury-on-Sea (telephone for collection). Lockup garage on mainland.
Restrictions No smoking in breakfast room. No dogs.
Credit cards All major cards accepted.
Terms B&B £84; D,B&B £119. Set lunch £24, dinner £34. Reductions for longer stays. Christmas, New Year, Easter packages. 1-night bookings sometimes refused weekends.

Give the *Guide* positive support. Don't leave feedback to others.

BIGGIN BY HARTINGTON Derbyshire Map 3

Biggin Hall BUDGET

Biggin by Hartington
Buxton SK17 0DH

Tel (01298) 84451
Fax (01298) 84681

A 17th-century house, with stone walls, mullioned windows, old beams and antique furniture, in a peaceful setting in the Peak District National Park. It is a family-run affair with a cheerful atmosphere and a "courteous, gregarious" owner, Mr Moffett, who writes: "Those looking for a posh hotel would be happier elsewhere." Recent *Guide* correspondents have confirmed this: "Relaxed and enjoyable. Traditional food, simple and well cooked. Public rooms can be crowded at busy times." "Catering a bit haphazard, but this creates an unstuffy atmosphere. Breakfasts are far from restful; people jump up to fill cups and bowls; queues form for milk, tea and fruit juice; staff bustle in and out. Friendships start in the queues; guests chat freely between tables." Meals are served in a "charming" dining room, with a fireplace at one end and a picture window at the other. Dinner is at 7 pm, no choice of main course; seconds sometimes offered. Huge slabs of butter are left on the table and you help yourself from a cheeseboard. The continental breakfast "includes every kind of cereal, hot croissants, rolls and toast". Guests not on special breaks pay a small supplement for the cooked one. Most bedrooms are spacious, with old beams and chintz and "beautifully appointed bathroom". Some are in converted outbuildings. There are two sitting rooms and a "splendid" library. Cream teas and packed lunches are available. The winter break is "amazing value". (*Val and Mike Langford, Mrs L Sheppard*)

Open All year.
Rooms 14 double, 2 single. 9 in outbuildings. 3 on ground floor. No telephone.
Facilities Sitting room, TV room/library, dining room; meeting room. 7-acre grounds. River Dove 1½ miles. Not really suitable for ♿.
Location 8 miles N of Ashbourne, ½ mile W of A515.
Restrictions No smoking: dining room, sitting room. No children under 12. No dogs in public rooms.
Credit cards Access, Visa.
Terms B&B £27.50–£49.50; D,B&B £32.50–£59.50. English breakfast £3.50. Set dinner £14.50. Christmas, New Year, winter breaks. 1-night bookings sometimes refused. *V*

BINBROOK Lincolnshire Map 4

Hoe Hill BUDGET

Swinhope, Binbrook LN3 6HX

Tel (01472) 398206

"I arrived after a difficult drive, and have seldom been made to feel more welcome," writes a 1996 visitor. "My bedroom was simple but adequate; the power shower along the landing was tremendous. I now plan to install one at home. The hosts, Erica and Ian Curd, are charming. I shared an excellent dinner (main course roast poussin) with my fellow guests, a music examiner and a circuit judge. We drank the wine I had brought (*Hoe Hill* is unlicensed), and afterwards had some good conversation over coffee. Such experiences make me wonder why anyone would want to stay in a Post House." "Stunning value." This unassuming guest house, 18th-century in origin, is set amid the unspoilt

Lincolnshire Wolds. It was once the home of the local warren bailiff (ie rabbit catcher). The best bedroom, overlooking the garden, has an *en suite* bathroom, with a spa bath and power shower. Breakfast includes home-made muesli, local sausages, eggs, home-made bread and marmalade. A pre-dinner sherry is included in the price of the "plentiful" dinner (by arrangement; no choice of main course). (*Chris Kay, and others*)

Open Mid-Feb–Dec (B&B only Christmas/New Year). Closed during owners' holiday.
Rooms 3 double, 1 with *en suite* bathroom. No telephone/TV.
Facilities Lounge, dining room. 1-acre garden. Unsuitable for ♿.
Location On B1203 1 mile NE of Binbrook (towards Grimsby).
Restrictions No smoking: dining room, bedrooms. No children under 5. No dogs.
Credit cards None accepted.
Terms [1996] B&B £17–£25. Set dinner (by arrangement) £12. Reductions for 3 or more nights.

BIRCH VALE Derbyshire — Map 3

The Waltzing Weasel NEW/BUDGET *Tel* (01663) 743402
New Mills Road
Birch Vale SK12 5BT

An upmarket pub, "in some of the most beautiful countryside Derbyshire has to offer", yet only forty minutes' drive from Manchester. The owner, Michael Atkinson, is a former philosophy lecturer, "which leads to some interesting conversations"; Linda, his wife, is an artist. "They generate a relaxed atmosphere," says an inspector, "and they love antiques, which are plentifully scattered in all the rooms. Our bedroom was generous in size, and decorated in soft colours, with Victorian furniture. The combination of a popular local pub and a small, more sophisticated restaurant, works well. The bar is cosy and machine-free, praise be. The dining room has superb views from mullioned windows across to Kinder Scout, one of the highest peaks in the county. We enjoyed our meal, geared towards hearty appetites, though service was a bit speedy. The wine list is reasonably priced. The guests ranged from walkers in stout boots to visitors to local National Trust properties. Only regret: we never saw a weasel, waltzing or otherwise." "Service is obliging and individual; good natural cooking," says the *Good Pub Guide*.

Open All year.
Rooms 7 double, 1 single.
Facilities Bar, restaurant. Small grounds. Shooting, golfing, fishing nearby.
Location On A6015, ½ mile west of Hayfield.
Restriction No children under 7.
Credit cards Access, Amex, Visa.
Terms [1996] B&B: single £45, double £65–£95. Bar meals. Set dinner (2–3-course) £19.50–£23.50; full alc £28. 30% reduction for 2 or more nights. *V*

> British hotels nowadays have private facilities in most bedrooms. And many have TV, baby-listening and tea-making facilities. To save space we do not list all of these; if any is particularly important to you, please discuss with the hotel.

BISHOP'S TACHBROOK Warwickshire — Map 3

Mallory Court — *Tel* (01926) 330214
Harbury Lane, Bishop's Tachbrook — *Fax* (01926) 451714
Leamington Spa CV33 9QB

Jeremy Mort and Allan Holland have been 19 years at their luxurious 1920s mansion (Relais & Châteaux); they have had a *Guide* entry since 1980. It stands "Lutyens-style" in formal gardens with statuary, ponds, croquet lawns, a magnificent box-hedged herb garden, and a stylish swimming pool. The large entrance hall has soft sofas, chesterfields, and quality magazines; a cosy lounge behind looks through small leaded panes on to the garden. The dining room is oak-panelled, with sliding doors to make it large or intimate, depending on numbers. *Michelin* withdrew its star last year, but the modern French cuisine, say our readers, is "as delicious as ever, with modern variations of classic dishes on an interesting new menu". The comprehensive wine list has a sensible mark-up. "Bedrooms, with everything you could want to make the visit delightful: country house decor at its most tasteful; deep plain carpet, thick curtains, discreetly patterned wallpaper, huge double bed. Copious continental breakfast. Staff dedicated, friendly and professional; housekeeping exemplary." Lavish teas are served, on a terrace in fine weather. Despite its rural setting, *Mallory Court* is close to Birmingham and Stratford-upon-Avon; it arranges trips to the Royal Shakespeare Theatre. (*Pat and Jeremy Temple, FW, and others*)

Open All year, except 2–9 Jan.
Rooms 1 suite, 10 double.
Facilities Lounge, drawing room, garden room, restaurant. 10-acre gardens: swimming pool (unheated), tennis, squash, croquet. Balloon trips, riding, golf nearby. Unsuitable for ♿.
Location 2 miles S of Leamington Spa. Turn left off B4087 towards Harbury.
Restrictions No smoking in restaurant. No children under 9. No dogs (kennels nearby).
Credit cards All major cards accepted.
Terms B&B: single £115–£145, double £170–£230, suite £375. Set lunch £25, dinner £30; full alc £57. 2/3-day winter breaks. *V*

BLAKENEY Norfolk — Map 2

The Blakeney Hotel — *Tel* (01263) 740797
Blakeney, nr Holt NR25 7NE — *Fax* (01263) 740795

"Our two young daughters enjoyed themselves tremendously (as did we) at this good, solid traditional hotel. The position on the quay is wonderful, and the view from the attractive bar and dining room across the estuary (excellent for children at low tide) is splendid. The dinners are on the whole good if you choose the simpler items. Breakfasts decent also. Our bedrooms were reasonably well appointed, if a little on the small side. The staff were helpful and friendly." A recent report on a conventional hotel – a bit stuffy for some – in an area of outstanding beauty owned by the National Trust. It welcomes families ("we expect parents to ensure that they do not spoil the enjoyment of others"), providing cots, high chairs, and good meals for small children. Its decor is simple. Bedrooms vary greatly in style; some are quite basic and priced accordingly. There are spacious ones in a modern annexe, some with a private patio. Other visitors have praised the staff's caring behaviour towards the elderly and the disabled, the "lovely rear garden", and the cream teas. (*NM Mackintosh, Prof. Sir Alan Cook, CRA Jackson*) Things can go wrong at busy times, and one reader this year was severely critical of the restaurant. Others have murmured about maintenance, but "the location and views make up for any small defects".

Open All year.
Rooms 50 double, 10 single. 10 in annexe across drive. Some on ground floor.
Facilities Lift, ramp. Lounge, sun lounge, cocktail bar, games room, restaurant; function facilities; indoor swimming pool, spa bath, sauna. Small gardens: table-tennis, swings.
Location On quay. Off A149 coast road between Cromer and Wells-next-the-Sea.
Restrictions No smoking: restaurant, sun lounge. No dogs in public rooms.
Credit cards All major cards accepted.
Terms B&B £52–£87; D,B&B £57–£98. Light lunches Mon–Sat. Set lunch (Sun) £10, dinner £16; full alc £30. 1-night bookings sometimes refused Fri/Sat. 4/7-day breaks. Midweek breaks for senior citizens. Christmas, New Year house parties.

BLANCHLAND Co. Durham — Map 4

The Lord Crewe Arms — *Tel* (01434) 675251
Blanchland, nr Consett DH8 9SP — *Fax* (01434) 675337

An ancient building "with slightly eccentric rooms and furnishings", in the heart of a picturesque village in a remote position on the river Derwent. It is set in lovely gardens, and surrounded by moors, fields, forests and a lake. The trio of owners: Alec Todd, Peter Gingell and Ian Press (the chef), run it with a friendly young staff, "who made us feel at home in a quiet sort of way". Formerly the abbot's lodgings, guest house and kitchen of Blanchland Abbey (named for its monks' white robes), it is redolent of the past, with beams, stone-flagged floors, coats of armour, huge wood fires and well-upholstered settles. Bedrooms, of various sizes, "with everything one could need", are serviced during dinner. Some of the best are in the annexe, *The Angel*, an old inn across the village square. Guests may eat in the restaurant overlooking the garden, or in the less formal bar, formerly the crypt. The cooking is traditional English, sometimes found a trifle over-elaborate. This year the breakfast was considered a great letdown. "Similar to THF in buffet style, the hot items pre-cooked; and the bar meals offered little choice." (*GPG*) Conferences sometimes change the atmosphere. Several readers have complained of poor room maintenance.

Open All year.
Rooms 20 double. 10 in *Angel Inn* 30 yds.
Facilities 3 lounges, bar, restaurant; conference facilities. 1-acre walled garden. Derwent reservoir 1 mile. Unsuitable for ♿.
Location On B6306, 10 miles S of Hexham.
Restriction No dogs in restaurant.
Credit cards All major cards accepted.
Terms B&B: single £75, double £105; D,B&B (min. 2 nights): single £83, double £126. Bar meals; set Sun lunch £14.50; full alc £33. Children under 14 accommodated free in parents' room. *V*

BLAWITH Cumbria — Map 4

Appletree Holme Farm *Tel* (01229) 885618
Blawith, nr Ulverston LA12 8EL

"I have travelled widely for 30 years, and have never had a better experience than a few days here. The owners are charming and highly professional, striking just the right balance between formality and informality. The facilities are excellent, the food is varied and delicious, the wine list splendid and reasonably priced." A recent accolade for Roy and Shirley Carlsen's old stone farmhouse in a remote corner of the south-western part of the Lake District. It "nestles idyllically in the fellside" amid carefully tended gardens and orchard; the immediate surroundings are a designated site of special interest, where flora and fauna are protected. All the bedrooms have a fell view and private facilities (one bathroom is across a corridor). The suite, on two floors, has a large bed/sitting room upstairs, a bathroom with a "sybaritic" double bath downstairs, and a private patio and separate entrance. There's a "home-like" lounge, with log fire, brasses, silver and paintings, and a well-stocked library. The Carlsens do not offer hotel-style facilities – one of the attractions in the eyes of its devotees: no reception; visitors are asked not to arrive between 2 and 5 pm without prior arrangement. The food is traditional British, with Mediterranean influences; no choice on the menu, preferences discussed in advance. No smoking. (*Prof. Ian Gust*)

Open All year. Dining room closed for lunch (picnics/light lunches available).
Rooms 1 suite (adjacent to main building), 3 double.
Facilities Sitting room, library, dining room. 5-acre grounds: gardens, orchards. Lake, tarn, swimming, fishing, boating nearby. Unsuitable for ♿.
Location M6 exit 36; A590 to Greenwood; A5084 to Blawith church; up lane opposite church; right after farm; left 1 mile, at sign.
Restrictions No smoking. Small children by arrangement. No dogs in house.
Credit cards Access, Visa.
Terms [1996] D,B&B £59–£63. Set dinner £23. £3 reduction for 2 or more nights (except bank holidays).

****

Traveller's tale We were amazed by the unbelievably garish bright bubble-gum pink-and-white exterior; it should have warned us that we were entering the territory of a true eccentric. The interior is stuffed with paper flowers in fairground hues, augmented by as many grey and long-dead dried flowers, and sagged drapes hanging in mad confusion everywhere – often with the aforementioned dead or paper flowers attached. There were books and magazines like Foyle's after bombing; pots and pans; gew-gaws, and enough bric-à-brac to rival Caledonian Road; not a chair without a heap of something on it; not a square inch of table without books, magazines, photo-frames, scent bottles, vases and the like. The table where, Madame announced, we should take breakfast, was impossible to imagine in that role, so laden was it with personal mementos and, let me be frank, junk.

****

BOLTON ABBEY North Yorkshire — Map 4

The Devonshire Arms — *Tel* (01756) 710441
Bolton Abbey, nr Skipton BD23 6AJ — *Fax* (01756) 710564

"A jewel in a gorgeous setting – the grounds, and the nearby moors and ruins are so spectacular it could have been constructed by a Hollywood set designer," write American visitors. "There's a real country home feel about this lovely hotel. Staff are helpful yet unobtrusive. Public rooms are cosy, and bedrooms well provisioned (many are themed). Altogether a memorable experience." The Duke and Duchess of Devonshire own this smart former coaching inn, set back from the road in large, well-kept grounds in glorious Wharfedale. Many antiques and pictures come from nearby Chatsworth. Best bedrooms are in the main house; those in the newer wing have less character. The *Burlington Restaurant* serves traditional and modern English dishes, including game in season; informal meals are available in the bar, lounges or bedrooms. Guests have free membership of the health club (see next page). "How delightful to find a hotel totally lacking in airs and graces." "Restaurant service knowledgeable, enthusiastic and humorous. Free newspaper, free use of wellington boots for riverside walks." (*Dr and Mrs Viola, and others*) One caveat about the cooking: "Some of the entrées relied more on presentation than appeal to the palate, and the menu did not change during our three-night visit." At times, the hotel is busy with conferences and functions.

Open All year.
Rooms 1 suite, 40 double. 2 suitable for ♿, 2 for lady executives.
Facilities 3 lounges, 3 bars, restaurant; function/conference facilities; health club: swimming pool, sauna, gym, beauty treatments, tennis court. 12-acre grounds: croquet, helipad. River fishing 200 yds.
Location On B6160 to Bolton Abbey, 250 yds from roundabout with A59 Skipton–Harrogate.
Restrictions No smoking: restaurant, 13 bedrooms. No children under 12 in restaurant.
Credit cards All major cards accepted.
Terms B&B: single £100–£110, double £140–£165, suite £225–£250; D,B&B: single £110–£118, double £170–£185. Set lunch £18.95, dinner £32.50; full alc £45. Special breaks: active, romantic, etc. *V*

BONCHURCH Isle of Wight — Map 2

Winterbourne — *Tel* (01983) 852535
Bonchurch, nr Ventnor PO38 1RQ — *Fax* (01983) 853056

Mr and Mrs O'Connor's pretty creepered house, not far from Ventnor, has a quiet setting near a tiny church. Its delightful terraced gardens, with a stream, pools, waterfalls, a sheltered swimming pool and sea views, slope down a hillside. A gate at the bottom leads to the path to the shore. "The prettiest place I ever saw in my life, at home or abroad," wrote Charles Dickens, who worked here on *David Copperfield*. A recent visitor, who stayed a week, was very comfortable: "Staff pleasant, though not what one might describe as professional, probably the right approach for this place. Ambitious home cooking, with only one disappointment, but a poor wine list." Others have praised the "atmosphere of happiness, elegance and charm", the ample breakfasts, and the Victorian decor in the public rooms. Bedrooms, most with a sea view, vary greatly in style; the singles are said to be "quite basic"; the garden suites are good for families. (*Esme Scott, and others*)

Open Mar–Nov.
Rooms 2 family (in annexe), 8 double, 3 single.
Facilities Lounge, restaurant; patio. 4-acre grounds: gardens, swimming pool (heated Apr–Oct), stream. Shingle/sand beach, riding, fishing, golf, tennis, bowls nearby. Unsuitable for ♿.
Location 1 mile NE of Ventnor. Right off A3055 into Bonchurch Shute; sharp left at bottom of road.
Restrictions No smoking in restaurant. No dogs in restaurant.
Credit cards All major cards accepted.
Terms [1996] D,B&B: single £44–£53, double £88–£144, suite £106–£124. Light lunch available. 1-night bookings sometimes refused.

BORROWDALE Cumbria — Map 4

Seatoller House BUDGET — *Tel* (0176 87) 77218
Borrowdale, Keswick CA12 5XN

César award in 1984

"After more than ten visits we still keep going back. It is comfortable, warm and friendly, with excellent housekeeping." "The manager, Ann Pepper, is exceptionally pleasant and efficient; the atmosphere is unique." Typical encomiums for an unpretentious establishment in a glorious setting at the head of the Borrowdale valley, near the start of many spectacular fell walks. Over 300 years old, it has been a guest house for more than a century. Its many regulars love the "warmth of welcome, the mixture of 'low-key-ness' and style", and the home-like atmosphere and food, which includes "particularly delicious soups and puddings, and an excellent cheeseboard". Meals are served at two long oak tables, breakfast at 8.30 am and dinner (no choice) at 7 pm. There's a well-chosen wine list. No TV; socialising and board games are the order of the evening. Bedrooms, some quite large, are simple, but spotless and sympathetically decorated; all have a private bathroom, but not always *en suite*. No special concessions (high tea, games room, etc) are made to children, "but they fit in very well and respond to the civilised atmosphere". (*RL Galloway, M Kershaw*)

Open Mar–Nov. Dining room closed for lunch, Tues dinner.
Rooms 9 double. 1 in garden annexe, 2 on ground floor. No telephone/tea-making facilities, etc.
Facilities Lounge, library, dining room, tea room; drying room. 2-acre grounds: pond. Unsuitable for severely ♿.
Location 8 miles S of Keswick on B5289. Regular bus service.
Restrictions Smoking in library only. No children under 5. No dogs in public rooms.
Credit cards None accepted.
Terms B&B £26–£27; D,B&B £36–£37. Packed lunches available. Weekly rates. Children under 12 half-price in parents' room. 1-night bookings sometimes refused.

BOSHAM West Sussex **Map 2**

The Millstream *Tel* (01243) 573234
Bosham Lane *Fax* (01243) 573459
Bosham, nr Chichester PO18 8HL

"We were delighted. Service was friendly, the menu interesting, and the food very good. The charming setting added an extra dimension to the outing." Composed of a small manor and an 18th-century malt house cottage, this hotel is set in tranquil gardens, on a stream complete with ducks, in an old fishing and sailing village near Chichester. The public rooms and bedrooms have a pretty, unfussy decor, with pale colours, antique and period furniture, potted plants and unexceptional pictures. It is popular with non-residents for bar lunches and teas (served outdoors in summer), and for dinners in the restaurant overlooking the garden, where traditional English/French dishes are served on a daily-changing menu. Other reporters have praised the restaurant manager, "who brings together charm, humour and efficiency, adding to one's sense of well-being", and the "excellent wine cellar". Breakfasts are "delicious, served promptly and hot". A pianist performs in the lounge on Friday and Saturday evenings. (*Joyce Beagarie, and others*) Chichester theatre-goers may order a late supper. The hotel is licensed for weddings.

Open All year.
Rooms 1 suite, 23 double, 5 single. Some on ground floor.
Facilities Lounge, bar, restaurant; conference room. 1½-acre garden.
Location In village 3½ miles W of Chichester. Follow signs for Bosham Quay. Carpark.
Restrictions No smoking: dining room, 5 bedrooms. No dogs in public rooms.
Credit cards All major cards accepted.
Terms B&B: single £65–£71, double £105–£111, suite £117–£123; D,B&B (min. 2 nights): single £62–£71, double £124–£142, suite £136–£154. Set lunch £12.95, dinner £19.90. 3-day breaks. Falconry, murder/mystery packages, Christmas, New Year breaks. 1-night bookings refused Sat. *V*

BOUGHTON MONCHELSEA Kent **Map 2**

Tanyard *Tel* (01622) 744705
Wierton Hill, Boughton Monchelsea *Fax* (01622) 741998
Maidstone ME17 4JT

"Highly individual", this beautiful, carefully restored medieval yeoman's house is peacefully set on a sheltered hillside, amid orchards in the Weald of Kent; there is good walking all around. It has landscaped grounds with a pond and stream, and "very pleasing views". Inside, the feel is intimate, with ancient beams, open-hearth fireplaces, antiques, designer pastels and chintzes. A narrow staircase, quite awkward, leads to the "charming" bedrooms; some are small, and sound insulation is not always perfect, but the suite, with far-reaching views and bathroom with spa bath, occupies the entire top floor. The restaurant is in the beamed former kitchen. Here the owner/chef Jan Davies serves classical English/French cooking on a menu "both short and wide-ranging" (four choices for each course). "The ingredients are excellent, the sauces finely flavoured. There is a fine selection of British cheeses. Service can be slow when the restaurant is busy. For breakfast (served until 9.30) we had delicious 'Kentish Korker' sausages." (*JC and GM*) More reports, please.

Open All year, except 24 Dec–mid-Jan. Restaurant open for lunch Wed, Thurs, Fri, Sun only, for pre-booked groups of 6 or more.
Rooms 1 suite, 4 double, 1 single.
Facilities Reception/hall, lounge, bar, restaurant. 10-acre grounds: garden, pond, stream. Unsuitable for ♿.
Location From B2163 at Boughton Monchelsea, turn opposite *Cock* into Park La; right into Wierton Rd, right again for *Tanyard*.
Restrictions No smoking in restaurant. No children under 6. No dogs.
Credit cards All major cards accepted (Amex, Diners *with surcharge*).
Terms [1996] B&B: single £60–£80, double £90–£95, suite £125. Set lunch £20; dinner £25. 1-night bookings generally refused Sat.

BOURNE Lincolnshire — Map 2

Bourne Eau House BUDGET *Tel* (01778) 423621
30 South Street
Bourne PE10 9LY

"Difficult to imagine a more delectable place," was our impressed inspector's verdict on this Wolsey Lodge. It is a listed Elizabethan/Georgian house, set in a lovely garden, in a conservation area of a small market town, and separated from a Norman abbey and the ruins of Hereward the Wake's castle by the winding Bourne Eau, complete with swans and ducks. "The public rooms are light and pretty, with period furniture. There is a music room with a concert piano. Dr and Mrs Bishop are an interesting couple; he was with UNESCO, and is the author of several books. Dinner, at 7.30, was served at a long refectory table with candles, and silver and cut glass glinting in the light of a huge log fire. It was well cooked, if not gourmet or exciting, served by the Bishops in the nicest way, with all our dietary quirks catered for. Couples are split up, to encourage conversation. Our bedroom was pretty and bright; we had the sole use of an enormous bathroom next door. Breakfast was excellent, with fresh grapefruit, cereals, and very good cooked items if required." "Perfect; a home from home," runs an endorsement.

Open All year, except Christmas, New Year, Easter. Lunch not served.
Rooms 3 double. 2 with bathroom *en suite*.
Facilities Drawing room, music room, breakfast room, dining room. 1-acre garden. Unsuitable for ♿.
Location 200 yds from traffic lights in centre; concealed entrance opposite cenotaph in park. Courtyard parking.
Restrictions No smoking in dining room. No dogs.
Credit cards None accepted.
Terms B&B £30–£35. Set dinner £18 (including wine).

> Hotels often book you into their most expensive rooms or suites unless you specify otherwise. Even if all room prices are the same, hotels may give you a less good room in the hope of selling their better rooms to late customers. It always pays to discuss accommodation in detail when making a reservation and to ask for a free upgrade on arrival if the hotel isn't full.

BOWNESS-ON-WINDERMERE Cumbria — Map 4

Lindeth Fell — *Tel* (0153 94) 43286
Lyth Valley Road — *Fax* (0153 94) 47455
Bowness-on-Windermere LA23 3JP

A turn-of-the-century Lakeland house reached by a tree-lined drive, tranquilly set above Bowness – "one of the most beautifully situated hotels in Lakeland". Its large grounds have rhododendrons and azaleas, lawns for tennis, putting and croquet, and a small tarn with trout. Family photographs, books and log fires add to the home-like atmosphere in the lounges. One has a beautiful plaster ceiling and large windows looking over the treetops towards distant Windermere. Bedrooms ("charmingly furnished") vary in size; some have a lake view. The atmosphere "is cheerful and relaxed", thanks to the "outgoing personalities" of the owners, Pat Kennedy (ex-RAF) and his wife Diana, and their highly motivated young staff. "They showed every kindness to my elderly and ailing parents," wrote one visitor. "The food struck just the right balance of interest and home cooking, which made a week's stay a culinary pleasure. Portions just right." Breakfast is "copious, with particularly good porridge". "Very reasonable prices for such high standards." (*Clare Carr-Archer, and others*) New this year is head chef, Emma Sharman. We'd be glad of reports from the kitchen front.

Open Mar–Nov.
Rooms 12 double, 2 single. 1 on ground floor.
Facilities 2 lounges, 2 dining rooms. 7-acre grounds: gardens, tennis, croquet, putting, tarn with fishing. Lake Windermere 1 mile.
Location 1 mile S of Bowness on A5074.
Restrictions No smoking in dining rooms. No children under 7. Dogs in grounds only.
Credit cards Access, Visa.
Terms [Until Easter 1997] B&B: single £47–£60, double £94–£106; D,B&B: single £57–£70, double £114–£127.50. Set lunch £10, dinner £21. 1-night bookings sometimes refused bank holidays.

Linthwaite House — *Tel* (0153 94) 88600
Crook Road — *Fax* (0153 94) 88601
Bowness-on-Windermere LA23 3JA

In an exceptionally tranquil position overlooking Lake Windermere, this Edwardian stone house stands in large grounds with immaculate gardens, woods, and a trout-stocked tarn. It has an unstuffy owner, Michael Bevans, a convivial air, and a stylish decor: modern furniture and strong-coloured fabrics combine with an interesting collection of antiques and memorabilia. The bedrooms vary in size; best ones have a king-size bed and a lake view. The candlelit, mahogany-tabled restaurant serves original but unpretentious modern cooking by Ian Bravey. The four-course menu, with plenty of choice, always includes an unusual vegetarian dish and a hot traditional pudding; rolls are home-baked. The cheeseboard won an Egon Ronay award in 1996. The hotel has won other awards also, including (twice) one from the AA for care and courtesy. *Guide* readers, too, have been enthusiastic. "Lovely setting. Public rooms very appealing. Meals immensely enjoyable." "Professional but unpretentious service." "Good wine list; good breakfast."

Open All year.
Rooms 1 suite, 16 double, 1 single. 5 on ground floor.
Facilities Lounge, bar, restaurant, conservatory; function facilities. 14-acre grounds: garden, woods, tarn (fishing), croquet, golf practice; guests have access to nearby leisure spa.
Location ¾ mile S of Bowness, off B5284, on left past Windermere Golf Club.
Restrictions No smoking: restaurant, some bedrooms. No children under 7 in restaurant (early meal provided). No dogs in house.
Credit cards Access, Amex, Visa
Terms B&B: single £90–£100, double £100–£170, suite £140–£195; D,B&B £69–£125 per person. Set lunch: main dish from £6; dinner £29.50. Weekend, midweek, romantic, Christmas, New Year, Easter breaks. 10% reduction on 7-nights stay. 1-night bookings usually refused weekends. V*

BRADFIELD COMBUST Suffolk Map 2

Bradfield House *Tel* (01284) 386301
Bradfield Combust *Fax* (01284) 386177
Bury St Edmunds IP30 0LR

The Green family's restaurant-with-rooms is an old house, 17th-century in origin, in a hamlet near Bury St Edmunds. Pale pink, with a fine half-timbered façade, it stands in a well-tended garden, with yew hedges, listed trees and a summer house. Its interior is a mixture of periods, "with a home-like feeling": eclectic furniture, mostly Edwardian and Victorian, old French wood-burning stoves, lots of pictures. Best bedrooms overlook the garden; roadside ones are double-glazed. Cooking by owner / chef, Douglas Green is "innovative and delicious"; there's an "excellent, reasonably priced" wine list. "Very good croissants for breakfast, and the full cooked works if wanted." (*BC Kay; also JJ Edwards*)

Open All year. Restaurant closed Sun evening / Mon.
Rooms 3 double, 1 single.
Facilities Lounge, bar, 2 dining rooms. 1½-acre garden. Golf, shooting, riding nearby. Unsuitable for ♿.
Location 5 miles S of Bury St Edmunds on A134 to Sudbury (front windows double glazed).
Restrictions No smoking: restaurant, bedrooms.
Credit cards Access, Diners, Visa.
Terms B&B: single £50, double £70–£85. Set lunch £8.50, £17.50, £21.50, dinner £17.50, £19.50. 2-day breaks. V*

BRADFORD West Yorkshire Map 4

Restaurant Nineteen *Tel* (01274) 492559
North Park Road *Fax* (01274) 483827
Heaton, Bradford BD9 4NT

A "charming, unpretentious place", this restaurant-with-rooms is a substantial stone house in a leafy suburb, quietly overlooking Lister Park. It has a relaxed atmosphere, smartly set, well-spaced tables, and a *Michelin* star for Stephen Smith's original modern British cooking, "with strong and direct flavours". The fairly priced wine list ranges the world. The sitting room, recently redecorated, is "impressive, with plaster ceiling, lavish fabrics, good lighting and upholstered chairs". Bedrooms are named for works by Sir William Russell Flint, much in evidence: "Best ones are high ceilinged, with a large bed, antiques, decent lighting, and a good-size bathroom equipped with everything from toiletries and bathrobes to loud-speaker for listening to TV while wallowing. Breakfast, with fresh orange juice, real bacon, moist scrambled eggs, granary bread and home-made jams, is excellent. The co-owner, Robert Barbour, who is front-of-house, is reserved and pleasant." (*David and Kate Wooff*)

Open All year, except 1 week Christmas, 2 weeks Aug/Sept. Restaurant closed midday, Sun/Mon.
Rooms 4 double.
Facilities Lounge, restaurant. Unsuitable for ♿.
Location 2 miles N of centre. Take A650 Manningham La. Left at park gates (just before school), 1st right on to North Park Rd. Parking.
Restrictions No children under 8. No dogs.
Credit cards Access, Amex, Visa.
Terms Room: single £70, double £85. Breakfast £7.50. Set dinner £28.

Victoria Hotel *Tel* (01274) 728706
Bridge Street *Fax* (01274) 736358
Bradford BD1 1JX

A traditional Victorian station hotel, recently revamped throughout in great style by Jonathan Wix, owner of *42 The Calls*, Leeds (*qv*). "The character of the old building has been retained," wrote the nominators. "Cavernous entrance lobby, high ceilings and tall sash windows, but the architectural purity has been updated into a cool 1990s operation. It aims to appeal to those who value comfort and design over porterage, all-night room service, etc. Stephen Smith, co-owner of the *Michelin*-starred *Restaurant Nineteen* [above], acts as food consultant, aiming for the same mix of quality and value. The large brasserie-style restaurant, *Vic and Bert's*, is informal, with white linen-dressed tables, well-designed glassware and cutlery, and ceiling fans. Its menu includes pasta, grills from a wood-burning grill, and salads. Our bedroom, large and high-ceilinged, had a vast bed, a plethora of sound systems, and a smart modern bathroom. Breakfast had an impressive buffet, and was excellent. On weekdays the hotel is geared to business folk. The weekend rate made it the bargain of the year." (*David and Kate Wooff*) The hotel's pub, *The Pie Eyed Parrot*, has dark-painted woodwork and plaster ceiling, a remarkable old juke box "and the feel of a Paris bistro"; it is a popular meeting place for the local *beau monde*, and serves snacks and salads. More reports, please.

Open All year, except Christmas.
Rooms 3 suites, 57 double.
Facilities Ramp. Lounge, bar, pub, restaurant; ballroom; gym, sauna.
Location Central, opposite new law courts (rooms double-glazed). Entrance on Exchange Square. Large carpark adjacent.
Restrictions Smoking discouraged in restaurant, banned in 20 bedrooms. No dogs in public rooms.
Credit cards All major cards accepted.
Terms [1996] Room: single £69–£89, double £79–£89, suite £89–£99. Breakfast: continental £6.95, English £10. Set lunch £7.95, dinner £9.95; full alc £27.50. Special breaks. Weekend reductions: double room £35; D,B&B £39–£54. *V*

BRADFORD-ON-AVON Wiltshire **Map 2**

Bradford Old Windmill *Tel* (01225) 866842
4 Masons Lane *Fax* (01225) 866648
Bradford-on-Avon BA15 1QN

In a "glorious, quiet setting", this converted mill, "full of atmosphere", stands in a small garden on a steepish hill overlooking Bradford-on-Avon. Peter and Priscilla Roberts have filled it with old pine furniture, and an eclectic collection of *objets trouvés* acquired during their travels around the world. Bedrooms, with patchwork quilts and books about local flora and fauna, come in varying shapes and sizes: one has a round bed, another a water bed. The Wallower Room is suitable for families; children are accommodated in a minstrels' gallery up a ladder. Priscilla Roberts sometimes cooks vegetarian/ethnic dinners by arrangement. A "bread and soup tray" is also available for £6. Breakfast, communally served (outdoors in fine weather), offers alternatives "to suit carnivores, vegetarians, vegans, healthy and unhealthy eaters". "Charming and unusual; delightfully run." "Relaxed atmosphere and cosmopolitan hosts. They go to great lengths to make you feel part of their lives." (*IK Mathieson, and others*) No smoking. Unlicensed: bring your own wine.

Open Mar–Nov. Evening meal by arrangement, Mon, Thurs, Sat.
Rooms 3 double, 1 single. No telephone.
Facilities Lounge, dining room. Small garden. 5 mins' walk to river Avon. Unsuitable for ♿.
Location Entering town on A363 from N find *Castle* pub; go down hill towards centre. Left after 100 yds into private drive immediately before first roadside house.
Restrictions No smoking. No children under 6. No dogs.
Credit cards (*With commission charge*) Access, Amex, Visa.
Terms (*Not VAT-rated*) B&B: single £45–£65, double £55–£75; D,B&B: single £64–£84, double £92–£112. Set dinner £18. Child in family room £15. Honeymoon package. *V*

Burghope Manor *Tel* (01225) 723557
Winsley *Fax* (01225) 723113
nr Bradford-on-Avon BA15 2LA

In village near Bradford-on-Avon, beautiful house, "exuding history", part Tudor, gabled and creepered, with family portraits and antiques. The ancestral home of John Denning; he and his wife, Elizabeth, "welcome guests as friends". 8 large bedrooms, all with sofa, easy chairs, plenty of storage space and bathroom en suite. *English breakfast at flexible times; evening meal by arrangement, dinner party style; two recommended local eateries:* Seven Stars *pub, and* Nightingales *(Italian). Set back, in large garden, from trafficky road – bypass due to open end 1996. Closed Christmas/New Year. No smoking: dining room, bedrooms. No children under 10. No dogs. Access, Amex, Visa accepted. B&B: single £50–£55, double £65–£75. No recent reports; we'd like some, please.*

We need feedback on all hotels: big and small, far and near, famous and first-timers.

Priory Steps BUDGET Tel (01225) 862230
Newtown, Bradford-on-Avon BA15 1NQ Fax (01225) 866248

Wolsey Lodge: 6 converted 17th-century weavers' cottages perched on hill in terraced garden above town; wonderful views. 3 mins' walk from centre. Period furniture, well-stocked library/lounge. Informal owners, Carey and Diana Chapman. 5 good-sized, well-equipped bedrooms. Good breakfast, served at flexible times; home-made jams and marmalades. Home-cooked communal dinner, by candlelight, at 7.30. Closed Christmas; occasionally other times. Unsuitable for ♿. Children "not encouraged". No dogs. Access, Visa accepted. B&B: single £45–£48, double £58–£64. Set dinner £17 [1996]. No recent reports; we'd like some, please.

Woolley Grange Tel (01225) 864705
Woolley Green Fax (01225) 864059
Bradford-on-Avon BA15 1TX E-mail woolley@cityscape.co.uk

César award in 1992

"An extremely well-run hotel. Friendly young staff. Relaxed atmosphere. Bedroom comfortable and individual. Informal antiques and amusing primitive paintings adorn the landings and dining rooms. Cosy panelled hall with every imaginable newspaper and magazine. Food of a high standard, with daily-changing multi-choice menu. Superior cheese selection. Splendid cooked breakfasts. Our two daughters had a fantastic time in the Woolley Bears' Den – only the Vietnamese pot-bellied pig could tempt them out. Wonderful gardens and grounds, with just the right degree of informality. Beautifully situated swimming pool. All manner of bicycles for adult and child use." A 1996 encomium for Nigel and Heather Chapman's mainly Jacobean manor, geared to give children a good time while providing sophisticated comforts for their parents. They supply reliable babysitting in the evening, a nanny, and supervised children's meals ("good basic fare"); there's an outdoor play area, and a children's vegetable and flower garden. Bedrooms, with beams, windows in odd places, and, for some, a gas log fire, have been fitted into the old structure; some are spacious, others "very small, but cleverly designed". Parents pay by the bedroom, squeezing in as many children as they can tolerate. Peter Stott runs the kitchens, and the flexible pricing policy of meals is admired. "We offer anything from a casual but amazing club sandwich to a gourmet blowout," write the Chapmans. For visitors without children there are honeymoon packages and local activity holidays. (*NM Mackintosh, and others*) The Chapmans' new hotel, the *Old Bell*, Malmesbury, run on similar lines, makes its *Guide* debut this year.

Open All year.
Rooms 4 suites, 17 double, 1 single. 8 in outbuildings round courtyard. Some on ground floor.
Facilities 4 lounges, dining room, dining terrace, conservatory; children's playroom/nursery, games room. 14-acre grounds: gardens, swimming pool, tennis, badminton, croquet, children's play area. Cycling, riding, golf, fishing, hot-air ballooning nearby.
Location 1 mile NE of Bradford-on-Avon on B3105.
Restrictions No smoking in restaurant. No dogs in restaurant.
Credit cards Access, Visa.

Terms B&B: single £85, double £99–£180, suite £155–£210. Alc lunch weekdays; set Sun lunch £18, dinner £29. Off-season reductions; Christmas, New Year packages. 1-night bookings refused weekends. Children accommodated free in parents' room.

BRAITHWAITE Cumbria — Map 4

Ivy House BUDGET — *Tel* (0176 87) 78338
Braithwaite, Keswick CA12 5SY — *Fax* (0176 87) 78113

César award: the best of Lakeland hospitality

A small village hotel, 17th-century in origin, with a dark green exterior and a traditional decor. It has a beamed lounge, with log fires at each end, and a candlelit galleried restaurant where dinner is served on fine linen with silver, crystal and good china. Bedrooms vary in size; one is small. No garden, but there are good walks from the door. "Affordable comfort amid breathtaking beauty," says the brochure, and *Guide* readers agree: "Wonderful value; the perfect place to return to at the end of a good day's walking." "It cannot be faulted." "The hosts, Nick and Wendy Shill, were charming and the staff very friendly. There was a lot of laughter around. Our spacious room was well equipped. The dinners were wonderful. There is plenty of choice on the menu, but many dishes were so delicious we wanted to have them more than once; one of us had the duck four times." There is a comprehensive wine list. (*Jon and Sherry Beere, Mr and Mrs C Redman, UJ and LK*) Guests may now use the leisure facilities at a nearby club.

Open All year, except Jan. Lunch not served.
Rooms 10 double, 2 single.
Facilities Lounge, bar, dining room. Use of leisure facilities at nearby club. Unsuitable for ♿.
Location 2½ miles W of Keswick. Take B5292 off A66; turn left down narrow road by *Royal Oak* inn; hotel straight ahead. Private carpark.
Restrictions No smoking in dining room. Dogs by arrangement; not in public rooms.
Credit cards All major cards accepted.
Terms [1996] B&B: single £27–£40, double £54–£66; D,B&B: single £43.95–£56.95, double £87.90–£99.90. Set dinner £18.95. 3-night midweek breaks Feb–Apr; Christmas package. 1-night bookings sometimes refused Fri/Sat. *V* (1 Nov–Easter, except Christmas week, Feb half term).

BRAMPTON Cumbria — Map 4

Farlam Hall — *Tel* (0169 77) 46234
Brampton CA8 2NG — *Fax* (0169 77) 46683

A cosseting country hotel (Relais & Châteaux) "with a real feeling of quality", not far from Hadrian's Wall. "It is a mellow building surrounded by pretty gardens with huge trees, a lake and waterfowl." It is a true family affair (a rarity in Britain), run by Alan and Joan Quinion, their son Barry (the chef), their daughter Helen and her husband, Alastair Stevenson. The public rooms are Victorian and ornate, with dark wallpaper, heavy furniture, and lots of trimmings and ornaments. Bedrooms vary considerably in size and shape and are priced accordingly; they have high-quality linen, good lighting, and lots of extras. Best ones have a whirlpool bath. Drinks are served in the lounge (no bar). Dinner is formal, starting punctually at 8. The four-course menu, country house cooking based on local produce, changes daily. Recent praise: "You could not have a more friendly welcome. Kindness from everyone." "Unpretentious outside; family atmosphere within – informal without being matey." "Breakfast particularly good." (*P Flynn, and others*) Bedrooms on the road hear traffic, but there's effective double-glazing. Some visitors find the whole *Farlam* experience a little OTT.

Open 31 Dec 1996–24 Dec 1997. Restaurant closed for lunch (light meals for residents by arrangement).
Rooms 12 double. 1 in converted stable block. 2 on ground floor.
Facilities 2 lounges, restaurant. 12-acre grounds: croquet. Golf nearby. Unsuitable for ♿.
Location On A689, 2½ miles SE of Brampton (*not* in Farlam village). Rooms double-glazed.
Restriction No children under 5.
Credit cards Access, Amex, Visa.
Terms D,B&B £95–£120. Light and packed lunches by arrangement. Set dinner £29.50. Winter, spring breaks; New Year package.

BRANSCOMBE Devon **Map 1**

The Look Out *Tel* (01297) 680262
Branscombe EX12 3DP *Fax* (01297) 680272

"A beautiful house in a stunning position, decorated and furnished in excellent taste, offering peace, solitude and relaxation." A recent endorsement for Peter and Dodie Leach's skilful conversion of six coastguard cottages. It stands on a small hill at the end of "one of the prettiest villages imaginable", scattered along a valley – much of it belongs to the National Trust. The downstairs decor is sophisticated; the long beamed lounge has oriental rugs on a flagstone floor, antiques, comfortable chairs and sofas, flowers, books and magazines, and a fire. Bedrooms, overlooking the sea, are simple and on the small side, but pretty and light; their bathrooms are *en suite* or opposite. Dinners are formally served. The French chef, Eric Coulon, cooks traditional English and French dishes, which some praise highly, but others find over-elaborate. You pay according to whether you choose two or three courses. Breakfast is "generous and good". The small gardens are beautifully maintained, with ample outdoor seating. Excellent walks and climbs nearby. (*Helen Hancock; also Michael Owens, and others*) Some have found the atmosphere too formal.

Open All year, except 4 days at Christmas. Restaurant closed midday, Mon evening.
Rooms 5 double.
Facilities Lounge, restaurant. 1½-acre garden; direct access to beach. Fishing, boating, golf nearby. Unsuitable for ♿.
Location ½ mile beyond village centre; follow signs to beach.
Restrictions Smoking banned in dining room, discouraged in bedrooms. No children under 8. No dogs in public rooms.
Credit cards None accepted.
Terms [1996] B&B: single £48–£58, double £82–£89; D,B&B: single £60, double £110. Set dinner (2/3 courses) £18/£23; full alc £29.50. 1-night bookings refused high season, holiday weekends. Discounts for 7-night stays.

All our inspections are carried out anonymously.

BRAY Berkshire **Map 2**

The Waterside Inn NEW *Tel* (01628) 20691
Ferry Road *Fax* (01628) 784710
Bray SL6 2AT

"A must for the *Guide*," writes the enthusiastic nominator of Michel Roux's renowned *restaurant-avec-chambres* on the banks of the Thames ("the ducks must be the best fed in the country"). A Relais & Châteaux member, with three *Michelin* stars and four crossed spoon-and-forks, it is "expensive, but wonderful value": "Dinner was superb, every course immaculately presented and delicious. Our perfect room opened on to a terrace overlooking the river, perfect for breakfast – and what a breakfast!" Another visitor wrote: "Setting idyllic; service faultless; housekeeping excellent." (*Tim and Pam Moorey, and others*) But, warns an inspector, some of the cheaper rooms are very small. "Le Nid Jaune, dominated by an iron-framed bed, has a bathroom designed for the slim, only one chair, and no table, so the tray with a rather indifferent continental breakfast had to be perched on the bed. Very noisy plumbing." There are kitchen facilities on each landing where drinks may be made. Maidenhead station is a short taxi ride away.

Open All year, except 26 Dec–31 Jan. Restaurant closed bank holidays, Mon; also Sun evening, Tues lunch mid-Oct–mid-Apr.
Rooms 1 suite (in cottage, 30 yds), 6 double.
Facilities Restaurant. Private dining room in cottage. Unsuitable for ♿.
Location On Thames, just SE of Maidenhead. M4 exit 8/9 towards Maidenhead Central. At 2nd roundabout follow sign to Windsor/Bray. Left after ½ mile on to B3028. In Bray 2nd right into Ferry Rd; hotel on left.
Restrictions No children under 12. No dogs.
Credit cards All major cards accepted.
Terms B&B: single/double £130–£160, suite £205. Set lunch £28.50 weekdays, £42.50 weekend, dinner £66.50; full alc £70.

BRIDGWATER Somerset **Map 1**

Cokerhurst Farm BUDGET *Tel* (01278) 422330
87 Wembdon Hill
Bridgwater TA6 7QA

Derrick and Diana Chappell's unpretentious no-smoking B&B, in 16th-century farmhouse on 100-acre farm on fringe of Quantocks, 1½ miles W of Bridgwater. Peaceful setting overlooking lake; sheltered walled garden; unheated swimming pool. Interesting collection of "bygones": polyphon, barrel organ, pennyfarthing bicycle. "Amazing value. Bedroom well up to Guide *standard. First-class breakfast. No dinners, but good pub meals nearby. Very friendly, helpful owners." Pick your own strawberries and raspberries in season. Closed Christmas. 3 bedrooms, 1 with facilities* en suite. *Unsuitable for ♿. Dogs in cars only. Credit cards not accepted. B&B double £34 (without bath), £45. "As good as ever," writes revisiting nominator.*

In your own interest, always check latest tariffs with a hotel when you make your booking.

BRIGHTON East Sussex Map 2

The Dove BUDGET
18 Regency Square
Brighton BN1 2FG
Tel (01273) 779222
Fax (01273) 746912

"First-class people in a first-class hotel. We took our 18-month-old son and a group of friends. The Kalinkes went a long way to create a relaxed atmosphere and to cope with our different needs." "Peter Kalinke is always so eager to help." "We were amazed to be telephoned by him before arrival to discuss our needs in detail." This Grade II listed building has a prime location, opposite West Pier. The decor is simple, with bright clear colours, "flowers all over the place", and an uncluttered feel. There is a bar where drinks and snacks are served, and a lounge with TV and videos. A home-cooked evening meal is available by arrangement ("usually served to classical music, but they turn it off if you wish"). Breakfast, "including spectacularly good scrambled eggs, superb mushrooms and lovely Greek yogurt", is served between 7.30 and 10 am. If brought to the room, it comes in two stages so cooked dishes don't get cold. There's no lift; the bedrooms are priced according to size and position: singles are small. Four large front rooms are suitable for families, and children are welcomed; babysitters are available, and there is a supply of toys. (*Mr C Kerridge, and others*)

Open All year.
Rooms 7 double, 3 single. 3 on ground floor.
Facilities Lounge, bar/dining room. Small courtyard.
Location 200 yds from centre, opposite West Pier, but quiet. NCP carpark nearby.
Restrictions No smoking in dining room. No dogs.
Credit cards All major cards accepted.
Terms [1996] B&B: single £28–£35, double £45–£78, family £55–£78; D,B&B: single £35–£72, double £58–£106. Set lunch £8, dinner £14; full alc £18. 10% discount for 2 nights. Long-stay midweek rates, family rates. 1-night bookings sometimes refused. *V*

Topps
17 Regency Square
Brighton BN1 2FG
Tel (01273) 729334
Fax (01273) 203679

"I was delighted with everything: courteous telephone manner and welcome, large bedroom, well-equipped bathroom. Breakfast, brought to the room each day for no extra charge, beautifully cooked and presented. Fresh milk in the well-stocked fridge. As 'home from home' as a hotel could be." "Helpful staff; superb attention to detail." Paul and Pauline Collins's small hotel is a block away from the sea. A conversion of two Regency terrace houses opposite a small green square, it is eclectically furnished, and decorated in soft colours. The only public room acts as reception, library and meeting place. Bedrooms are warm (11 have a gas fire), and well lit. The best one is spacious and high-ceilinged, with a huge bay window, a small balcony, and a four-poster. Bathrooms have large towels, dressing gowns, and generous toiletries. In the pretty basement restaurant, bistro-type dinners are cooked by Mrs Collins. Meals can be served in the bedroom when the restaurant is closed. (*Jean Hampton, JC Field*) One dissenting report of an unsatisfactory room-service dinner and a poorly maintained bedroom.

Open All year. Restaurant closed Sun, Mon, Tues, all Jan.
Rooms 13 double, 2 single. Some on ground floor.
Facilities Lift. Reception/lounge, restaurant. Near sea; safe bathing. Unsuitable for ♿.
Location 200 yds from centre, opposite West Pier, but quiet. NCP carpark nearby.
Restriction No dogs.
Credit cards All major cards accepted.
Terms B&B: single £45, double £79–£109. Set dinner £19.95. Reductions for 2 nights or more; weekly rates. Children accommodated free in parents' room. 1-night bookings sometimes refused Sat.

BRISTOL — Map 2

Berkeley Square Hotel — *Tel* (0117) 925 4000
15 Berkeley Square — *Fax* (0117) 925 2970
Clifton BS8 1HB

The flagship of a group of four hotels in the Clifton area of Bristol is close to the university, museum and art gallery. It is a conversion of two houses in a sedate Georgian square, and is popular with business visitors, having an unusually large number of single rooms. A reporter last year found it "welcoming and comforting". Another described her bedroom: "Well planned and well lit, with a pleasant if anodyne decor." A 1996 report, however, was critical of reception and room maintenance. The grey and dark red pillared restaurant, predictably called *Nightingales*, has a new chef, Joe Mifsud, who specialises in Creole and Cajun cooking. We'd be grateful for comments on the food. No residents' lounge, but guests may sit in the conference room when it is not in use. There's a busy bar in the basement.

Open All year. Restaurant closed Sun evening; room service available.
Rooms 1 suite, 17 double, 25 single.
Facilities Reception, bar, restaurant; conference facilities. Access to square garden. Unsuitable for ♿.
Location 10 mins' walk (½ mile) from centre. Garage.
Restrictions No smoking in 12 bedrooms. No dogs in public rooms.
Credit cards All major cards accepted.
Terms Rooms: single £78–£84, double £102–£110, suite £115–£130. Full alc from £20. Weekend, Christmas discounts. **V** (weekends only)

BROADWAY Hereford and Worcester — Map 3

Collin House — *Tel* (01386) 858354
Collin Lane
Broadway WR12 7PB

An unpretentious Cotswold stone house, run by John Mills and a helpful staff. "Neither too posh nor too casual", it has mullioned windows, beams, fine fireplaces, lots of antique furniture and china, and interesting prints and pictures. It stands amid trees, lawn and gardens, in a picturesque setting near this famous showplace village. The bedrooms, with flowery fabrics and wallpaper, vary in size and style; some, particularly the single, are small. Lunches are served in a lounge bar with pews and settees, or in the garden. Evening meals are taken in the oak-beamed candlelit dining room; there is a *carte* with plenty of choice, priced according to the main course, and a simpler supper menu (not available on Saturday). Cooking is dependable traditional English, served in generous portions, with old-style puddings; local produce is used, and fresh fish is delivered daily. Breakfasts, too, are generous. *Collin House* does not have extensive facilities for small children. "But," says Mr Mills, "they are very welcome provided parents control them and accept certain modest limitations." More reports, please.

Open All year, except 24–28 Dec.
Rooms 6 double, 1 single. No telephone; TV on request.
Facilities Lounge, lounge bar, restaurant. 3-acre grounds: swimming pool (unheated). Riding, golf nearby. Only bar, restaurant suitable for ♿.
Location 1 mile NW of Broadway on A44. Turn right down Collin La.
Restrictions No smoking in restaurant. Children under 7 by agreement. No dogs.
Credit cards Access, Visa.
Terms B&B: single £45, double £87; D,B&B (min. 2 nights) £55 per person (including £16 towards dinner). Bar lunches. Set lunch £16.50, dinner £16.50–£24; full alc £24. 1-night bookings sometimes refused Sat. Child sharing parents' room: B&B £20. *V*

The Lygon Arms *Tel* (01386) 852255
High Street *Fax* (01386) 858611
Broadway WR12 7DU

A historic, handsome building in the centre of *the* showplace Cotswold village (crowded in summer). It is owned by the Savoy Group; Kirk Ritchie is managing director. It has beamed ceilings, panelled public rooms, fine fireplaces, polished stone floors and antique and period furniture. Traditional bedrooms, some with four-poster, are in the main building; modern ones are in rear extensions; some overlook the carpark. B&B terms include the *Daily Telegraph*. An eclectic menu is served in the great hall, which has a barrel ceiling, a minstrels' gallery, stags' heads and a heraldic frieze. Less formal meals may be taken in the wine bar. The hotel has a pretty walled garden, and good leisure facilities (see below). Recent visitors have enthused: "Bedroom full of character, with flowers, champagne, chocolates, good modern bathroom. Lots of little lounges, most with fire; you could happily sit in your own nook. Staff universally nice." "Our party of 11 (18 months to 80) all made most welcome. Splendid for a special occasion, providing value for money." "Excellent breakfast." (*Heather Sharland, SA Nash, JW Gibbon; also Judy Rothenburg*) The leisure centre can be crowded with outside visitors. The hotel is a popular venue for conferences, "but not at all corporate or commercial".

Open All year.
Rooms 5 suites, 57 double, 3 single. Some on ground floor.
Facilities 5 lounges, cocktail bar, wine bar, restaurant; function facilities. 3½-acre grounds: tennis, croquet; Country Club: swimming pool, spa bath, sauna, solarium, fitness room, beauty salon, light meals. Fishing, golf, riding, hunting etc, nearby.
Location Central (front rooms double-glazed; quietest ones at rear). Garage, large carpark.
Restrictions Smoking discouraged in restaurant. No dogs in restaurant/bar.
Credit cards All major cards accepted.

Terms [1996] B&B: single £95–£122, double £147–£215, suite £225–£305. Cooked breakfast £8.75. Set lunch £21.75, dinner £34; full alc £44. Weekend, midweek breaks; Shakespeare, Christmas package.

BROMSGROVE Hereford and Worcester — Map 3

Grafton Manor
Grafton Lane
Bromsgrove B61 7HA

Tel (01527) 579007
Fax (01527) 575221

Morris family's historic manor, 16th-century, with later additions, in lovely 11-acre grounds with large lake (fishing), fine herb garden. 9 bedrooms, "with many touches to make the stay memorable". Beautiful, romantic smoke-free restaurant, popular locally; balanced meals, imaginative, but not fussy, on short menu; good wine list. Adequate breakfast – "tasty home-made bread". Young, enthusiastic staff, but some housekeeping shortcomings; also, it is "set amid urban sprawl – some rooms overlook (and hear, despite double-glazing) the M5 motorway". Unsuitable for ♿. No dogs. All major credit cards accepted. B&B: single £85, double £105–£125. Set lunch £20.50, dinner £24.95–£31.50 [1996].

BROXTED Essex — Map 2

Whitehall
Church End
Broxted CM6 2BZ

Tel (01279) 850603
Fax (01279) 850385

The Keane family's gabled black-and-white Tudor manor stands on a hill by the old church on the edge of a village, overlooking rolling Essex countryside. It has beautifully maintained grounds, with an Elizabethan walled garden, a terrace for early evening drinks, a good-sized swimming pool, and a hard tennis court. The peace is broken only by the occasional flight to or from Stansted airport, conveniently nearby. The old interior, with beams and rough plaster walls, has been sympathetically renovated; some bedrooms are in a modern extension. Most are large and well furnished. "Consistently first class, and very fair value for money, with faultless service by the young staff, especially room service," a regular visitor has written. The timber-vaulted restaurant serves "highly professional" modern British cooking by Stuart Townsend, with the option of a six-course surprise menu in the evening. Some diners have lamented the absence of a no-smoking area. The hotel does a considerable business trade, but functions are held in a separate building, a converted barn. One visitor this year criticised room maintenance. More reports, please.

Open All year, except 26 Dec–1 Jan.
Rooms 25 double. 2 on ground floor.
Facilities 2 lounges, 2 bars, restaurant; function facilities. 7-acre grounds: tennis, swimming pool (unheated).
Location M11 exit 8. Take new road to Stansted airport; at third roundabout (Coopers End), by new terminal building, take last exit; follow signs to Broxted. Hotel is on edge of village, past turn to Great Easton.
Restriction No dogs.
Credit cards All major cards accepted.
Terms [1996] B&B single £80, double £110–£140. Set lunch/dinner (2–3-course) £13.50–£16.50; menu surprise (dinner only) £37.50; full alc £32. Weekend breaks.

BROXTON Cheshire **Map 3**

Frogg Manor NEW
Nantwich Road, Fullers Moor
Broxton, Chester CH3 9JH

Tel (01829) 782629
Fax (01829) 782238

César award: for utterly acceptable mild eccentricity

As enjoyably eccentric a hotel as any we have come across in a score of years. In his white Georgian manor near Chester, John Sykes styles himself "chief frog". He offers an unlikely combination of plush surroundings, old-time music and over 100 frogs (ceramic, straw, brass, etc), ubiquitously scattered around among a plethora of *objets*. Our inspectors found him in reception in stockinged feet, but he tends to greet his guests wearing a frock coat, and to deliver a champagne breakfast to the honeymoon suite wearing a tall top hat. All this may sound OTT, but the nominator was beguiled: "One of the most enjoyable nights in a hotel that I can recall – like staying in the home of a genial and mildly eccentric relative. Bedrooms are lavish, and the honeymoon suite (entered through the bookcase in the sitting room!) is worth getting married for – especially its amazing bathroom. There is a charming dining room, and the sitting room has wall-to-wall frogs of every shape and form. But what really stands out is the owner's obvious pleasure in having guests." Other visitors, too, have enjoyed the cheerful atmosphere and the generosity of spirit, and the garden, romantically floodlit at night. Cooking is "unfussy, but modern", writes Mr Sykes. "We like to know in advance when to expect you; dinner is served between 7 and 10 pm, but a light supper at any time may be arranged for late arrivals." Breakfast is served round the clock Monday to Saturday, and 9 to 10.30 am on Sunday. (*Michael Freeman, and others*) As with other establishments of this kind, you should be prepared for minor hiccups – and, our inspectors warn, an excess of not-too-fragrant air-freshening devices.

Open All year. Restaurant closed 1 Jan.
Rooms 1 suite, 5 double.
Facilities Lounge, restaurant. 10-acre grounds: tennis. Unsuitable for ♿.
Location 15 miles SE of Chester. From A41, take A534 to Nantwich. Hotel on right.
Restriction No dogs in public rooms.
Credit cards All major cards accepted.
Terms Rooms: single £45–£95, double £55–£80, suite £100. Breakfast alc from *c.* £3.50. Set lunch £15, dinner £25; full alc £30. Discounts for 2 or more nights (except Christmas, New Year). *V* (room only)

BUCKLAND Hereford and Worcester **Map 3**

Buckland Manor
Buckland, nr Broadway WR12 7LY

Tel (01386) 852626
Fax (01386) 853557

"A lovely hotel. Staff attentive. Food excellent. Good value for money." A 1996 endorsement for this beautiful 13th-century manor (Relais & Châteaux), in a harmonious Cotswold village. Much gabled, it stands in large grounds, with formal flowery gardens, a stream, and a swimming pool. Other visitors found it "well nigh flawless. Superb house, all of a period, without obvious renovation, beautifully quiet. We were upgraded to the Oak Room, with lots of panelling and chintz, and a gorgeous view of the landscaped and water-cascaded terraced garden. No key, which gave us a curious sense of security. We liked the welcoming public rooms, the clutter of antique furniture, the flower displays, and the light coming through the mullioned windows, crying out to be photographed. It is remarkably relaxed, unfussy and unpretentious [but jacket and tie are expected of male guests at night]. Even that dreaded event, pre-dinner drinks, was animated. Dinner, admirably, was *à la carte*, each course served on a plate with a different design. Martyn Pearn's cooking well deserves its *Michelin* star. Much pleasure, too, could be derived from the wine list. The charming manager, Nigel Power, subsequently took us on a tour of the cellars." The English breakfast is also praised. Only church bells at 9 am on Sunday interrupt the peace. An early supper may be served for visitors to the Royal Shakespeare Theatre, Stratford-upon-Avon, 16 miles away. (*Denis W Tate, AT, and others*) Rooms vary in size from "spacious" to "quite small". Some complaints about the price of extras.

Open All year.
Rooms 14 double. Some on ground floor.
Facilities Ramp. 2 lounges, restaurant. 10-acre grounds: gardens, stream, waterfalls, tennis, putting, swimming pool, croquet. Golf, riding nearby.
Location Centre of quiet village off B4632, 2 miles SW of Broadway.
Restrictions No smoking in restaurant. No children under 12. No dogs.
Credit cards All major cards accepted.
Terms [1996] B&B: single £165–£315, double £175–£325. Set lunch £28.50; full alc £55–£60. Winter breaks; Christmas package. 1-night bookings refused Sat.

BUDOCK VEAN Cornwall — Map 1

Budock Vean Hotel — *Tel* (01326) 250288
Mawnan Smith, Falmouth TR11 5LG — *Fax* (01326) 250892

A "golf and country house hotel" in huge grounds with sub-tropical gardens and woodland, in a designated area of outstanding natural beauty. It has a private waterfront on the Helford Passage ("super views"). Its large swimming pool opens on to a terrace in summer; in winter it is enclosed, and has a log fire. The golf course is "not championship, but in excellent order, and a challenge, due to the terrain". The hotel is now fully owned by the Barlows of the César-winning *Treglos*, Constantine Bay (*qv*). They have refurbished extensively, and acquired a licence for weddings. There are good amenities for children, and plenty of activities for the sportingly inclined (see below); special arrangements are offered for families during school holidays and half term; under-sixes are free at certain times. The food is traditional, on a varied five-course dinner menu; seafood, local lobsters and oysters are often available; portions are generous, wines reasonably priced. Visitors in early 1996 enjoyed the meals and found the staff "most friendly", but one felt the hotel "lacked the presence of an owner/manager, and the dining service could be improved". A new manager, Allan Tookey, arrived shortly after, and we'd be grateful for more reports.

Open All year, except 3 Jan–12 Feb.
Rooms 3 suites, 45 double, 7 single. 3 self-catering cottages.
Facilities Lift. 3 lounges, 2 bars, restaurant; pianist 5 nights a week; children's playroom. 65-acre grounds: garden, 9-hole golf course, tennis, croquet, archery, river frontage, fishing, water sports, etc; riding nearby. Not really suitable for &.

Location 5 miles S of Falmouth. A39 to Hillhead roundabout; right to Mawnan Smith. Follow brown signs to Trebah Gardens; hotel ¼ mile after gardens.
Restrictions No smoking: dining room, 1 lounge. No children under 7 in dining room for dinner. No dogs in public rooms.
Credit cards Access, Diners (*2% surcharge*), Visa.
Terms B&B £28–£73; D,B&B £38–£83. Set dinner £18.50; full alc £29. Christmas, Easter tariffs; golf breaks. Children under 14 accommodated free in parents' room; free holidays for children under 6 at Easter, half term. *V* (room only)

BURFORD Oxfordshire **Map 3**

The Lamb *Tel* (01993) 823155
Sheep Street *Fax* (01993) 822228
Burford OX18 4LR

"Quite magical." "A combination of old-fashioned elegance and character with an easy-going, friendly feel." "Service without exception friendly and attentive, never intrusive." "Particularly good public rooms, with wood fires day and night." "Tea in the garden on a summer's day everything it should be." This lovely 15th-century Cotswold inn, breathing tradition, stands just off the main street of a showpiece village. Restored with taste by the resident owners, Richard and Caroline de Wolf, it has stone-flagged or oak floors, antiques, fresh flowers and open fireplaces in the lounges. Bedrooms vary in size; the best are "lovely, with antiques (not too glossy), and an efficient bathroom". There's an idyllic walled garden with deck chairs on a lawn surrounded by flowers. Good lunches are served in the stylish public bar, with old elm tables and leather-backed settees. But opinion remains divided about the meals in the formal candlelit dining room. "Stupendous, with hearty, delicious main course and pudding, excellent house wine," was one report; others have found the cooking "pretentious", "over-rich – too many concentrated tastes on the same plate" – and "too expensive". Some have criticised the buffet breakfast, though this is generally liked. (*Sarah Dallas, Good Pub Guide, Alice Goodman, William G Hall*). Other caveats: "The small carpark is a nightmare to manoeuvre in and out of. The garden furniture tends to tip without warning."

Open All year, except 25/26 Dec.
Rooms 15 double.
Facilities 3 lounges, bar, restaurant. 1½-acre walled garden. Unsuitable for ♿.
Location From roundabout (junction of A40 and A361) go down High St; Sheep St 1st left.
Restrictions No smoking in restaurant. No dogs in restaurant.
Credit cards Access, Visa.
Terms [1996] B&B £45–£57.50 midweek, £50–£75 weekend; D,B&B £65–£75 midweek, £70–£95 weekend. Bar lunches except Sun; set Sun lunch £17.50, dinner £24. 3 nights for price of 2 in winter.

BURNHAM MARKET Norfolk **Map 2**

The Hoste Arms *Tel* (01328) 738777
The Green *Fax* (01328) 730103
Burnham Market PE31 8HD

Paul Whittome's cheerful pub, winner of several Pub of the Year awards in 1995, dates from the 17th century, and is named for a *protégé* of Lord Nelson, a local. It is on the green of a lovely Georgian village. Even in low season it buzzes. Live jazz and picture exhibitions reflect the owner's interests; the first floor houses a fine shell collection. There's a nautical flavour to the bar decor. Bedrooms vary from "stylish, with old features preserved and period furniture", to "small, with shower too small for comfort". The staff, from Australia, South Africa, etc, are "extremely helpful and friendly". "Dinner, in a dining room full of character – red walls, wooden floors and panels – was near faultless; well-presented, simple wine list with a comprehensive range," writes a recent visitor. Others have thought the food variable, and breakfast, in the conservatory, can be disorganised. But all agree about the place's friendly atmosphere and "generous spirit". (*CRA Jackson, GPG, and others*)

Open All year.
Rooms 1 family, 4 suites, 16 double. Some on ground floor.
Facilities 2 lounges, bar, restaurant with conservatory, art gallery, music room (live jazz weekly); conference facilities. Walled garden. Sea, golf, bird sanctuaries nearby.
Location Central. Large carpark.
Restrictions No smoking in conservatory. No dogs in restaurant.
Credit cards Access, Visa.
Terms B&B: single £60, double £96, suite £108. Bar meals; full alc £27.50. Child 2–14 sharing parents' room £15. Short breaks all year.

BURY ST EDMUNDS Suffolk — Map 2

Ounce House BUDGET — *Tel* (01284) 761779
Northgate Street — *Fax* (01284) 768315
Bury St Edmunds IP33 1HP

"Highly civilised, yet utterly unpretentious. Delightfully furnished bedroom overlooking the garden, beautifully quiet at night. Breakfast perfectly cooked and presented." "Simon and Jenny Pott are absolutely charming. Lovely warm house, with an air of quiet, expensive elegance. Spacious bedrooms, huge chests of drawers, lashings of hot water. No stinting anywhere." "Mrs Pott sets the tone of the welcoming family atmosphere. The dinner menu was well chosen and the food beautifully cooked and presented." "First-rate fabrics, antiques, pictures and prints of superior quality, inviting colour schemes, fresh flowers. The off-street parking is a huge attraction." This merchant's house, "a model of Victorian elegance", is in a street of handsome buildings just north of the Abbey Gardens, a short walk from the centre. Traditional English dinners (by arrangement) are served communally round a large table. Light sleepers might be disturbed by traffic noise in the front rooms. (*E and A Thin, and others*)

Open All year.
Rooms 3 double, 1 single.
Facilities Drawing room, snug, bar/library, dining room. ¾-acre walled garden. Unsuitable for ♿.
Location Central. Leave A14 (formerly A45) at 2nd Bury exit. Left at 1st roundabout into Northgate St; house at top of hill. Private parking.
Restrictions Smoking in bar/library only. No dogs.
Credit cards Access, Visa.
Terms B&B: single £35–£40, double £64–£75. Set dinner (by arrangement) £18–£20. Reductions for weekends/3 or more nights.

Twelve Angel Hill *Tel* (01284) 704088
12 Angel Hill *Fax* (01284) 725549
Bury St Edmunds IP33 1UZ

This no-smoking B&B, a Georgian house with Tudor origins, stands on the north side of Bury's main square, near the abbey ruins and the cathedral. Its bedrooms are named after wines, Claret, Chablis, etc, and have colour schemes to match, and a bath or shower *en suite*. Some have a large four-poster. The chatty owners, Bernadette and John Clarke, "are excellent hosts," writes a 1996 visitor, "with an inexhaustible knowledge of local eating places, many of which offer discounts to the Clarkes' guests." Breakfast – "a silver service experience" – includes freshly squeezed fruit juice, fruit salad, cereals, an "enticing" variety of hot dishes, cooked to order, "and delicious home-made marmalade". "High standard of service and amenities." (*Ian Cunningham, Geoff Johnstone, and others*)

Open All year, except Jan.
Rooms 6 double.
Facilities Lounge, bar, breakfast room; meeting room. Small walled garden. Unsuitable for ♿.
Location Central, on main square (front rooms double-glazed). Private parking at rear.
Restrictions No smoking. No children under 16. No dogs.
Credit cards All major cards accepted.
Terms [1996] B&B £45, double £65–£75. Weekend breaks.

BUTTERMERE Cumbria Map 4

Pickett Howe *Tel* (01900) 85444
Buttermere CA13 9UY *Fax* (01900) 85209

"The best hotel, by a long way, during a week's holiday," writes a regular *Guide* correspondent. "Small and cosy, personal and romantic, it recently won awards for conservation and 'England for Excellence'. The bedrooms are rather small, with lots of low beams, tiny windows, sprigged wallpaper, fine china teapot and cups, home-made biscuits, fresh fruit. The immaculate bathrooms have a jacuzzi bath or a power shower. The food, cooked to order, is real and excellent. Dinners, by candlelight, with good crystal and silver on oak tables, are semi-communal (two tables for four). Very more-ish truffles with coffee in the lounge or garden afterwards. David and Dani Edwards (she is chef) were most helpful, and full of suggestions about what to do. Excellent value." This farmhouse hotel is on a hillside in an untouristy Lakeland setting. You approach down a rough track through trees. Inside are slate floors, mullioned windows, antique furniture, and all manner of comforts. Other visitors, too, have praised the well-balanced, eclectic dinner menu, which draws on English, French and Mediterranean styles, and features local cheeses and Cumbrian puddings: "A treat for both eyes and palate, with unobtrusive service. The only sounds were gentle classical music in the background, and the hoot of an owl at night." There's a huge choice at breakfast, including a plentiful Cumbrian cooked affair and home-made preserves. You can walk straight out on to open hillside or fields. (*Kate Kelly, and others*) No smoking.

Open Mar–Nov.
Rooms 4 double.
Facilities Lounge, study / reading room, dining room. 15-acre grounds: garden; direct access to hills. Boat for hire on Crummock Water. Unsuitable for ♿.
Location From Lorton, follow signs to Buttermere, going south on B5289. Track on right about ⅓ mile after turning to Buttermere.
Restrictions No smoking. No children under 10. No dogs in house.
Credit cards Access, Visa.
Terms B&B £36. Set dinner £21. 1-night bookings sometimes refused.

BUXTON Derbyshire — Map 3

Brookfield on Longhill — *Tel* (01298) 24151
Long Hill, Buxton SK17 6SU — *Fax* (01298) 72231

This "comfortable, well-run establishment" is a brown stone Victorian family house, peacefully set in large grounds amid gardens and trees, in beautiful countryside on the edge of town. It is owned by Roger Handley and Brian Brooke, who run it with their families and friends. Visitors this year found it "charming": "There are many thoughtful touches, eg, a glass of fresh orange juice and a newspaper (no charge) with the early morning tea. Excellent food. Ideally situated for touring, and a paradise for walkers." Other praise: "It is delightfully decorated, and offers exceptional value. Our children were made very welcome. We appreciated the lack of extra charges for tea, coffee, etc. The huge breakfast obviated the need for lunch." "A delightful alternative to the cooked breakfast was a large plate of fresh fruit, with a small dish of yogurt on the side." "Spacious bedroom, with gas coal fire and enormous bathroom. Service willing and thoughtful at all times." There is plenty of choice on the eclectic menu, portions are generous. (*Elizabeth and Eric Price, and others*) In response to last year's caveat, the owners have invested in "larger and better bath towels". One visitor would have liked to see more half bottles on the wine list.

Open All year.
Rooms 8 double.
Facilities Ramp. Drawing room, library, balcony room, restaurant, conservatory; function facilities. 10-acre grounds: gardens, woods, stables. Walking, sailing, riding nearby. Only restaurant suitable for ♿.
Location 1½ miles NW of Buxton, on A5004.
Restrictions No smoking in restaurant. No dogs in restaurant.
Credit cards Access, Visa.
Terms [1996] B&B: single £47.50, double £75. Set Sun lunch £14.50, dinner £18.50; full alc £26. Discounts for 2 or more nights. Christmas, New Year, opera festival programmes. V

CALNE Wiltshire — Map 2

Chilvester Hill House BUDGET — *Tel* (01249) 813981 and 815785
Calne SN11 0LP — *Fax* (01249) 814217

César award in 1992

"Fabulous. John and Gill Dilley are lovely. Though one stays in their home, one never feels on top of them. Combines the best elements of a B&B and a fine small hotel." "The most relaxing stay I can remember." "Very good value." Recent tributes to this Wolsey Lodge member, a spacious Victorian house, "filled with fascinating antiques and mementos of a lifetime". It stands in a large garden amid fields. No brochure; enquirers get a friendly letter describing the facilities, and discussing dietary requirements. The guest bedrooms are "huge, with a lovely view" and generously kitted out. The *en suite* bathrooms have a hand-held shower, and a large shower room is available (bathrobes provided). Cooked-to-order breakfasts – "what you want, when you want" – are "as generous as the rest". The Dilleys join their guests for pre-dinner drinks or coffee, and occasionally for the four-course no-choice dinner ("honest English fare", with home-grown vegetables) served round one splendidly set table (couples may be invited to split up to keep the conversation going). Light meals can sometimes be arranged. There's no obligation to dine in; the Dilleys will help with reservations at local eating places. Dr Dilley has an encyclopaedic knowledge of local sights. (*Ayelet and Michael Chabon, WK Moulding*)

Open All year, except 1 week off-season (autumn or spring).
Rooms 3 double. No telephone.
Facilities Drawing room, sitting room with TV, dining room. 2½-acre grounds (also 5 acres used for cattle). Golf, riding locally. Unsuitable for ♿.
Location From Calne, A4 towards Chippenham. Right after ½ mile to Bremhill; drive immediately on right (gateposts with stone lions).
Restrictions No smoking in dining room. Generally no children under 12. No dogs.
Credit cards All major cards accepted.
Terms B&B: single £40–£50, double £60–£75, triple £81–£96. Packed or snack lunches. Set dinner £18–£22. 10% reductions for B&B for a week or longer.

CALSTOCK Cornwall — Map 1

Danescombe Valley Hotel — *Tel* (01822) 832414
Lower Kelly, Calstock PL18 9RY — *Fax* (01822) 832446
E-mail 101447.775@compuserve.com

"After many visits, still our favourite place to stay in England." Martin and Anna Smith's Victorian villa is set against a steep wooded slope on a meander of the river Tamar, in a designated area of natural beauty. Its grounds adjoin those of Cotehele House, a rewarding National Trust property 15 minutes' walk away. There are lovely views up and down the river from the veranda and most bedrooms. The house is filled with *objets d'art*, books and paintings. The airy bedrooms have antique and traditional furniture, and an *en suite* or adjacent private bathroom. The charms of the tranquil setting are enhanced by the absence of TV, the "warm and personal welcome" (first names tend to be used), and the excellent food. Anna Smith's cooking, modern British with an Italian bias (red "Meals" in *Michelin*), makes abundant use of local suppliers. Dinner (no choice) is at 7.30 for 8, and ends with a huge choice of British cheeses. The wine list offers excellent, robust, mainly Italian wines, with a modest mark-up. The simple breakfast – juice, muesli, yogurt, etc – is a leisurely affair. Prices include morning coffee, afternoon tea, mineral water, etc. (*Dr and Mrs James Stewart; also J and D Jennings*)

Open Apr–Oct, Christmas.
Rooms 5 double. No telephone/TV. 1 self-catering cottage down lane.
Facilities Lounge, bar, restaurant. 5 acres steep woodland; steps to river Tamar: moorings, fishing, walking. Golf, riding nearby. Unsuitable for ♿.

Location ½ mile W of Calstock village. Go under viaduct, past Methodist church, sharp right; follow road parallel to river for ½ mile.
Restrictions No smoking in dining room. No children under 12. No dogs.
Credit cards All major cards accepted (*3% surcharge*).
Terms B&B: single by arrangement, double £125. Set dinner £30. 1-night bookings sometimes refused weekends. 4-night Christmas break.

CAMPSEA ASHE Suffolk — Map 2

The Old Rectory BUDGET — *Tel/Fax* (01728) 746524
Campsea Ashe, nr Woodbridge IP13 0PU
César award in 1992

This restaurant-with-rooms, a Wolsey Lodge member, is a spacious Georgian rectory in a large garden with statuary. It has high ceilings, grandiose antiques, and "a wealth of interesting books in the large drawing room, where guests help themselves from the honesty bar and quickly get to know each other". Its *César* was awarded for "utterly acceptable mild eccentricity"; it is run in laid-back style by proprietor/chef Stewart Bassett. "He is like a favourite uncle," writes an Irish hotelier who stayed on her own. "I was warmly welcomed, and well fed." "Well up/down to expectations," runs a more wry endorsement. "Attic room where we bumped into things. Good dinner party food, kindly adapted to our dietary restrictions." Dinner (no choice) is at 7.30. The food is the foil to the outstanding, reasonably priced wines. The place is too casual for some, but not for a reporter last year who stayed for almost two months, while on business locally: "I slept in four of the bedrooms, ranging from the wonderful four-poster room overlooking the garden to the 'au pair's room', which is used *in extremis*. All were comfortable. I dined at least 35 times. Every meal was a pleasure. Not once was a course repeated. Stewart Bassett prided himself on remembering everything we had eaten, without making notes. The service was enjoyably idiosyncratic. A haven of peace." Children are welcomed (high tea by arrangement). (*Lady Levinge, Brian Knox, AL*) Bedrooms vary in size; the one above the kitchen can be noisy.

Open All year, except Christmas, and sometimes New Year. Closed Sun.
Rooms 8 double, 1 single. No telephone/radio/TV.
Facilities Lounge/TV room, bar, restaurant; function facilities. 4-acre garden: croquet. Unsuitable for ♿.
Location In village 1½ miles E of A12 on B1078. Next to church.
Restrictions No smoking: restaurant, bedrooms. No dogs in public rooms.
Credit cards All major cards accepted.
Terms [1996] B&B: single £35, double £50–£60; D,B&B: single £51, double £82–£92. Set dinner £16.50 (£19.20 to non-residents). Half board obligatory on Sat. Winter mid-week breaks; Easter/bank holiday breaks; house parties. Children under 3 accommodated free in parents' room.

> The *V* sign at the end of an entry indicates hotels in the UK and Ireland that have agreed to take part in our Voucher scheme and to give *Guide* readers a 25% discount on their room rates, subject to the conditions explained in *How to read the entries* and listed on the backs of the vouchers.

CARLISLE Cumbria — Map 4

Avondale BUDGET — *Tel* (01228) 23012
3 St Aidan's Road
Carlisle CA1 1LT

Michael and Angela Hayes' civilised guest house, "spruce and clean, and run in an uncommercial, helpful manner", is a large Edwardian building in a quiet road in a residential area, ten minutes' walk from the centre. It has many original features – fireplaces, stained glass, elaborate ceilings, even door handles – and an agreeably unostentatious decor. Only three bedrooms; the largest, overlooking the garden, has a private bathroom. There's "a good choice for breakfast"; everything is freshly cooked. A simple evening meal is available by arrangement – traditional dishes, served in generous portions (unlicensed: bring your own wine). (*Mrs PJ Broadhurst; also DG Presland*)

Open All year, except Christmas.
Rooms 3. 1 with bathroom *en suite*. No telephone.
Facilities Lounge, dining room. Small garden. Unsuitable for ♿.
Location Central; near bus and railway stations. Parking.
Restrictions Not really suitable for small children. No dogs.
Credit cards None accepted.
Terms (*Not VAT-rated*) B&B £18–£20; evening meal £8.

CARTMEL Cumbria — Map 4

Aynsome Manor BUDGET — *Tel* (0153 95) 36653
Cartmel LA11 6HH — *Fax* (0153 95) 36016

"Price extremely reasonable. Staff friendly and helpful. Food above average. Rooms well equipped. House-keeping impeccable." "Personal service. Excellent in every way." Recent encomiums for this handsome 16th-century house in a cobbled courtyard, run by two generations of the Varley family, Tony, Margaret, Chris and Andrea. It has a pastoral setting in a picturesque village on the edge of the Lake District, well away from the busy holiday resorts but near enough for a visit. From the small garden there is a "soothing" view across meadows with sheep and cows, towards the 12th-century priory. The decor is cheerful and traditional. There are two spacious, well-lit lounges; the one upstairs has a fine old marble fireplace. The oak-panelled restaurant, with large bay windows, moulded plaster ceiling and distinctive oil paintings, serves four- or five-course dinners, unpretentious English cooking, with choice, generally at 7. On Sunday there is a traditional lunch and a generous supper (soup, cold buffet, etc). The wine list is long, "and should suit most pockets". The bedrooms vary in size; some are suitable for a family; there is a heavily beamed one, with sloping ceilings, on the top floor; two are in a cottage with a sitting room, across the courtyard. (*Dr John Rowlands, and others*)

Open All year, except 2–24 Jan. Lunch served Sun only.
Rooms 12 double. 2 in cottage across courtyard.
Facilities 2 lounges, bar, restaurant. ¾-acre garden. Outdoor swimming pool 2 miles, Windermere 8 miles, golf nearby. Unsuitable for ♿.
Location Leave A590 at Cartmel sign. 12 miles from M6 exit 36. Hotel on right, ½ mile before village.
Restrictions No smoking in restaurant. No children under 5 in restaurant

for dinner (high tea 5–6 pm). No dogs in public rooms, or unsupervised in bedrooms.
Credit cards Access, Amex, Visa.
Terms D,B&B £44–£60. Set Sun lunch £11.50, dinner from £16.50. Weekend, midweek, Christmas breaks; bonus breaks for returning guests. 1-night bookings occasionally refused. *V*

Uplands *Tel* (0153 95) 36248
Haggs Lane *Fax* (0153 95) 36848
Cartmel LA11 6HD

A mustard-coloured pebble-dash house perched on a hillside with fine views over Morecambe Bay. Tom and Diana Peter (he in the kitchen, she – "very jolly" – front-of-house) co-own it with John Tovey of *Miller Howe*, Windermere (*qv*). It is run "in the *Miller Howe* manner", but is less grand, less theatrical and less pricey. Mealtimes are more flexible than at the parent hotel. The walls of the pink and grey dining room are crammed with Impressionist prints from the Metropolitan Museum of Art, New York. There is limited choice on the four-course fixed-price dinner menu (modern English cooking). Bedrooms are simply furnished, comfortable if not spacious; three have a small shower room, the others a bathroom; two enjoy the view. "Delicious food, immaculately served, with just the right delay between courses," ran a recent report. "Wonderful breakfast, with toaster at table; superb home-made bread. The young staff seemed genuinely to enjoy their work. Gardens a delight, reinforcing the feel of care and attention to detail. Extremely good value." Also commended, "a pair of gorgeous marmalade cats, on which to stroke away the tension of a long journey". (*JE Borron, Ron and Eve Jones*) One dissenter was less enthusiastic about the food, and would have preferred smaller servings.

Open Mar–end Dec. Restaurant closed Mon, midday Tues, midday Wed.
Rooms 5 double.
Facilities Lounge, restaurant. 2-acre garden. Golf nearby. Unsuitable for ♿.
Location In Cartmel, opposite *Pig & Whistle*, take road to Grange-over-Sands for 1 mile; hotel on left. Private parking.
Restrictions No smoking in dining room. No children under 8. No dogs in public rooms.
Credit cards Access, Amex.
Terms D,B&B £48–£78. Set lunch £14.50, dinner £26. Reductions for 2 or more nights Nov–Apr. Christmas package. 1-night bookings occasionally refused. *V*

CASTLE CARY Somerset Map 1

Bond's BUDGET *Tel/Fax* (01963) 350464
Ansford Hill
Castle Cary BA7 7JP

A listed, creeper-covered Georgian former coaching inn, in an agreeable mid-Somerset town, with kindly hosts, Kevin and Yvonne Bond. It has a period feel, "with William Morris wallpaper in the dining room, an open fire in the bar, antique furniture, and nice knick-knacks dotted around". Mrs Bond cooks imaginative English dishes on the reasonably priced, constantly changing menu. Cheese is a special feature. The short wine list includes some excellent bottles at moderate prices. Breakfast is generous and varied: continental, traditional, healthy etc. . . . "Bedrooms are small, but delightful – attractively furnished, with lots of towels in the bathroom. Mr Bond is a punctilious, informative host; he will gladly show you his immaculate classic cars and charming garden. High standard of service from quiet, friendly local staff. All very good and comforting." Some traffic noise in front rooms.

Open All year, except 1 week Christmas.
Rooms 7 double.
Facilities Lounge/bar, restaurant. Small garden. Unsuitable for ♿.
Location ½ mile N of Castle Cary, on A371, 300 yds from station. Large carpark.
Restrictions No children under 8, except babes in arms. No dogs.
Credit cards Access, Visa
Terms B&B £30–£51; D,B&B £48–£69. Light lunch £4. Set dinner £12.50–£19.75; full alc £25. 2-day breaks. *V*

CAUTLEY Cumbria — Map 4

Cross Keys NEW/BUDGET — *Tel* (0153 96) 20284
Cautley, Sedbergh LA10 5NE

"An inn of character in the Yorkshire Dales National Park. It has a magnificent, remote setting, in a corner of the Howgill Fells, at the foot of Cautley Spout, the highest single drop waterfall in England. The building was donated to the National Trust on condition that it be run as a temperance hotel, but you may take your own drinks; corkage is not charged. Frank and Lesley Hart, who run it informally, without a staff, are walkers and climbers, familiar with most of the highland areas of Britain." The Trust has preserved many original features of the building: low beamed ceilings, flag-stone floors, spiral stone stairs, mullioned windows, period furniture and open fires. No TV, "but books to read, a piano to play, people to talk to". All the food, including bread, biscuits, preserves, and ice cream, is prepared by Lesley Hart; meals are not normally served to more than 12 people, and 24 hours' notice is needed. "The menu changes every night," she writes. "I do not serve food with fancy descriptions and silly decorations. I keep a register of all guests and ensure that they do not get the same meal for at least three years. We offer peace and quiet. If you behave well you may come again; most of our visitors do, year after year. If your behaviour is not up to standard, we do not want you. We are too quiet and boring for the noisy young. We accept but do not encourage children." No smoking. (*Daniel Johnson*)

Open 21 Mar–6 Jan. Possibly other times too.
Rooms 1 with bath/shower, 3 double, 1 single. No telephone, TV, etc.
Facilities Lounge, dining room, conservatory. Small grounds. River fishing, riding nearby.
Location 4 miles NE of Sedbergh on A463 towards Kirkby Stephen, on left.
Restrictions No smoking. Guide dogs only.
Credit cards None accepted.
Terms (*Not VAT-rated*) B&B £26–£31; D,B&B £45–£51. £5 supplement for single occupant of double room. Light lunch available. *V*

If you think we have over-praised a hotel or done it an injustice, please let us know.

CHADDESLEY CORBETT Hereford and Worcester Map 3

Brockencote Hall *Tel* (01562) 777876
Chaddesley Corbett *Fax* (01562) 777872
nr Kidderminster DY10 4PY

"A flawless stay. Alison and Joseph Petitjean could give a course on hotel management. Our last-minute booking and bedraggled appearance in the immaculate entry hall did nothing to diminish the warmth of welcome. Our bedroom was full of grace and light, with fresh flowers and fruit, excellent sherry, up-to-date magazines, immaculate bathroom. A spirit of generosity pervades: delicious bites accompanied our drinks; coffee and petits fours are included in the dinner price. Didier Philipot's cooking deserves a *Michelin* star. You can mix and match between the menus. Breakfast, served at hours reflecting the accommodating spirit of the staff, was perfect, too, with home-made marmalade and jam, flavourful Cumberland sausages, perfectly cooked eggs." "I have never eaten a meal here that I do not remember with pleasure. The food suited all our party, from children wanting simple dishes, to those for whom nothing is too rich or strange. The Petitjeans were much in evidence, and the staff helpful and kind – never in the way, never out of the way. Very good for a family; excellent value." This engaging Anglo-French establishment is a serene turn-of-the-century mansion, set by a lake in large grounds outside a village not far from Birmingham. The interior is airy, with well-proportioned rooms, honey-coloured panelling, open fires, potted plants, and a "restrained country house decor". Spacious bedrooms radiate the same discreet luxury; some have views of the Malvern hills. (*Ruth and Derek Tilsley, Alice Goodman and Geoffrey Hill; also KE Woolley*)

Open All year. Restaurant closed for lunch Sat.
Rooms 17 double. 1 on ground floor.
Facilities Lift, ramps. Lounges, restaurant, conservatory. 70-acre grounds: gardens, lake, croquet.
Location On A448 between Kidderminster and Bromsgrove. M42 exit 1; M5 exit 4.
Restrictions No smoking in restaurant. No dogs.
Credit cards All major cards accepted.
Terms B&B: single £85, double £115–£140. Set lunch £18.50, dinner £23.50–£38.50. Weekend breaks; aromatherapy, shooting, golfing breaks. Christmas, Easter, Whitsun packages. Children under 12 accommodated free in parents' room. *V*

CHAGFORD Devon Map 1

Easton Court NEW *Tel/Fax* (01647) 433469
Easton Cross, Chagford TQ13 8JL

Grade II listed thatched Tudor house on A382 Whiddon Down–Moretonhampstead; 1½ miles E of Chagford, on edge of Dartmoor. Granite walls, exposed beams, inglenook, large library; literary connections: Evelyn and Alec Waugh and Patrick Leigh Fermor stayed and worked here. Enthusiastic new owners in 1996, Gordon and Judy Parker, have extensively refurbished "in good taste". Delicious dinners; breakfast "well up to standard". Dogs welcomed. Open Feb–Dec. 8 bedrooms (rear ones quietest), 2 on ground floor. No smoking: dining room, library. No children under 12. No dogs in public rooms. Access, Amex, Visa accepted. B&B £40–£48; D,B&B £58–£64 [1996]. More reports, please. *V*

Gidleigh Park *Tel* (01647) 432367 and 432225
Chagford TQ13 8HH *Fax* (01647) 432574
E-mail gidleighpark@cityscape.co.uk

César award in 1989

"We had thought it might be OTT, but it was simply superb. Beautiful setting, beautiful gardens and grounds, beautiful public rooms and sumptuously comfortable bedroom. The service was impeccable, friendly, attentive, but not overly so. The house was deliciously and more-or-less evenly warm, and there was oodles of very hot water." "Visual impact of restrained opulence. The rooms are filled with rich fabrics in vibrant colours, good antiques, and exquisite water colours, mainly of Dartmoor. Michael Caines cooks with *élan* and enthusiasm, underpinned by classical technique – meals for hedonists." "Quite the best hotel we've visited in England." Paul Henderson's mock-Tudor hotel, a Relais & Châteaux member "committed to pleasing affluent connoisseurs", is in a remote setting on the edge of Dartmoor. The North Teign river runs through its grounds, which have carefully-laid-out woodland walks, a water garden, a tennis court, four croquet lawns and a "golf garden" (or "upmarket putting green"). Bedrooms are priced by size and view; courtyard-facing ones are cheapest. The *Michelin*-starred restaurant has a "marvellously interesting wine list, with a sensible pricing policy". The staff, ably led by manageress Catherine Endacott, is noted for kindness to babies, children and dogs. (*Carol Heaton, Padi and John Howard, J and D Jennings*) One reader had a few niggles: "At these prices one expects perfection. Breakfast was second-rate, with poor cooked dishes, cold toast, and dainty tea-cups instead of proper-sized breakfast cups. The shower was under-powered."

Open All year.
Rooms 2 suites, 12 double. Also 3-roomed cottage.
Facilities Hall, lounge, bar, 2 dining rooms. 45-acre grounds: gardens, croquet, tennis, bowls, putting green, walks. Fishing, riding nearby. Unsuitable for ♿.
Location Approach from Chagford, *not* Gidleigh. From main square, facing Webbers with Lloyds Bank on right, turn right into Mill St. After 150 yds fork right; downhill to Factory Crossroad; straight across into Holy St; follow lane 1½ miles to end.
Restrictions No smoking in restaurant. No dogs in public rooms.
Credit cards All major cards accepted.
Terms D,B&B: single £200–£340, double £285–£390, suite £335–£390. Set lunch £29–£35, dinner £55. Winter discounts; walking holidays, shooting weekends. 1-night bookings sometimes refused.

Mill End Hotel BUDGET *Tel* (01647) 432282
Sandy Park, Chagford TQ13 8JN *Fax* (01647) 433106

Nicholas and Hazel Craddock's white converted mill, overlooked by Castle Drogo, is by the river Teign on the edge of Dartmoor. The wheel still turns in the courtyard. There is excellent walking on footpaths from the grounds; many outdoor activities are available locally (see below). The hotel is well run and unpretentious, with a friendly staff, and a home-like rather than elegant decor. The walls are hung with watercolours and old maps. Bedrooms vary in size; they are well endowed with "practical comforts". Those on the ground floor have a stone-flagged patio leading on to the garden. The older ones have an old-fashioned, chintzy decor; newer ones are more contemporary in style. The food, served in a low-ceilinged, beamed restaurant, is mainly traditional English – "varied, with some sophistication and a good choice". There's an extensive wine list. Wine and food weekends are held regularly. "Good breakfasts." Children and dogs are welcomed. (*Endorsed this year by Mrs J Ekins-Daukes*)

Open All year, except 7–18 Dec, 6–17 Jan.
Rooms 15 double, 1 single. 3 on ground floor.
Facilities Lounge, TV lounge, bar lounge, restaurant. 1½-acre grounds: river, fishing; hunting, clay pigeon-shooting, pony-trekking, hot-air ballooning by arrangement. Golf nearby.
Location In hamlet 4 miles NW of Moretonhampstead. Turn S from A382 at Whiddon Down (do *not* go into Chagford). Hotel is at Dog Marsh Bridge.
Restrictions No smoking in restaurant while others are eating. No dogs in public rooms.
Credit cards All major cards accepted.
Terms [1996] B&B: single £35–£60, double £79–£90; D,B&B £53–£80 per person. Set lunch £14.50, dinner £17.50; full alc £29. 2-day breaks; winter wine and food weekends; fishing packages. Christmas, New Year packages. Children accommodated free in parents' room.

CHARINGWORTH Gloucestershire — Map 3

Charingworth Manor NEW
Charingworth
nr Chipping Campden GL55 6NS
Tel (01386) 593555
Fax (01386) 593353

A beautiful house, early 14th-century with Jacobean additions, with mullioned windows, oak beams, log fires, flowers and "nice pieces of furniture". It is set in beautiful gardens amid a huge Cotswold estate (lovely views), and has a leisure centre with "the warmest pool we have bathed in since the Indian Ocean". The best bedrooms are in the main building (so are some less good attic ones); cheaper, modern ones, "well appointed and spacious but lacking character, and with no view", are in converted stables. There was a change of owner in 1995, and visitors since then have been pleased: "warm and comfortable sitting rooms – nice for dozing in front of a fire on a rainy day"; "furnishing not luxurious, but adequate; we liked the faded atmosphere and the laid-back approach of the staff." The food is thought "good, if a little pretentious" (but the dining room was cold in winter). "Very good breakfast brought to the bedroom." (*Jane Bailey, Mrs E Yentob; also Judy Schiller*) Some caveats: "Drinks absurdly expensive." "Creaking floorboards." "Stable block rooms sometimes noisy." "Can be draughty in winter."

Open All year.
Rooms 3 suites, 23 double.
Facilities 3 lounges, billiard room, restaurant; function facilities; leisure spa (indoor pool, sauna, etc). 50-acre grounds: tennis. Unsuitable for ♿.
Location 2½ m E of Chipping Campden, on B4035.
Restriction No smoking in restaurant.
Credit cards All major cards accepted.

Terms B&B: single from £95, double from £132, suite £239; D,B&B: single from £125, double from £189, suite £296. Set lunch from £15.95, dinner from £32.25. 1-night bookings sometimes refused. Weekend and midweek breaks. *V*

CHARMOUTH Dorset **Map 1**

The White House *Tel* (01297) 560411
2 Hillside, The Street *Fax* (01297) 560702
Charmouth DT6 6PJ

John and Mollie Belfry's modest guest house, in group of Regency houses on hilly main street of village. Small garden with pergola. Private parking. Pristine inside and out. Simple decor, but finely proportioned public rooms: unusual curved walls, bow doors, full-length windows, original cornices. 11 cheerful bedrooms, some small, 3 in adjacent cottage; generous extras. Family atmosphere. Traditional West Country cooking; interesting wine list. Beach 5 mins' walk; spectacular National Trust coastal walks close by. Open Feb–Nov. Unsuitable for ♿. No smoking: dining room, bar. No children under 14. No dogs in public rooms. All major credit cards accepted. B&B £36–£56; D,B&B £53–£70. Set lunch £14.50, dinner £18.50; full alc £25.20. More reports badly needed. *V*.

CHEDINGTON Dorset **Map 1**

Chedington Court *Tel* (01935) 891265
Chedington, nr Beaminster DT8 3HY *Fax* (01935) 891442

"There is an old wooden seat tucked into the corner of the porch where, in the last warmth of the sun, looking over the beautiful balustraded flowery terrace, I sat with a pre-dinner drink and listened to the sound of a grand piano, drifting through the hall doors. This was as close as I have ever come to contentment in a hotel. The building is lovely; we specially enjoyed the tranquil atmosphere of the library. The gardens are large and well cared for. Our spacious bedroom had a four-poster – the real thing – and a huge bathroom." "Perfect surroundings for a truly peaceful break. The owners went out of their way to accommodate our needs. Staff work amazingly quietly. True country house atmosphere." "A very special place." Tributes to this handsome Jacobean-style manor, high up in the Dorset hills, with panoramic views. Philip and Hilary Chapman run a "splendidly understated establishment, very much a private house" – "we never claim to be elegant," they write. The decor is traditional; some solid pieces of furniture came from staterooms of the liner, *Queen Mary*. Mealtimes are flexible. The breakfast menu is oral: you can have "pretty much anything – within reason". No hidden extras: coffee, tea, newspapers (except on Sunday) are included in the price. The hotel has an 18-hole golf course, open to the public, which guests may use free of charge on weekdays. (*Kay Hickman, Christina Baron and Alan Butt Philip, Richard Graham, and others*) There have been some criticisms this year of decor, maintenance and food –"it promised more than it delivered."

Open Early Feb 1997–2 Jan 1998. Dining room closed for lunch.
Rooms 10 double.
Facilities Drawing room, library, billiard room, dining room, conservatory.

10-acre grounds: garden, putting, croquet, golf course. Fishing nearby; coast 10 miles. Unsuitable for ♿.
Location 4 miles SE of Crewkerne, just off A356 at Winyard's Gap.
Restrictions No children under 9 in dining room at night. No dogs in public rooms.
Credit cards Access, Amex, Visa.
Terms B&B: single £65.60–£81.60, double £115.20–£147.20; D,B&B: single £82–£102, double £144–£184. Set dinner £27.50. Reductions for 2 or more nights. Christmas package. 1-night bookings sometimes refused. *V*

CHELTENHAM Gloucestershire — Map 3

Hotel on the Park — *Tel* (01242) 518898
38 Evesham Road — *Fax* (01242) 511526
Cheltenham GL52 2AH

A handsome white-painted 1830s house opposite Pittville Park, an agreeable short walk from the centre of a delectable Regency town. The decor is sumptuous, with swagged and draped chintz, strong colours, and many antiques. The coral-and-cream drawing room and the dignified library have French windows overlooking the secluded garden. The high-ceilinged restaurant, pale green, with striped fabrics, is run as a concession by Graham Mairs. Bedrooms and bathrooms are large, and as chic as the rest. Recent visitors were "impressed by the friendly welcome from the owner, Darryl Gregory, and by the personal atmosphere and the universally high standards, and found the meals "beautifully presented, and the ingredients fresh and interesting". Others enjoyed sitting by the fire in the library, "where lilies in every vase spread their wonderful aroma", and praised the hearty English breakfast. (*Mr and Mrs TR Manderson, Mr S Horne*)

Open All year, except 1 week Jan.
Rooms 2 suites, 10 double.
Facilities Lounge with bar, library, restaurant. Small garden.
Location 5 mins' walk from centre. On A435 towards Evesham (front rooms double-glazed). Carpark.
Restrictions No smoking in restaurant. No children under 8. No dogs in public rooms.
Credit cards All major cards accepted.
Terms Rooms: single £74.50, double from £89.50, suite from £119.50. Breakfast: continental £6, English £8.25. Set lunch £14.95, dinner £21.50; full alc £35. Weekend rates.

CHELWOOD Somerset — Map 2

Chelwood House — *Tel/Fax* (01761) 490730
Chelwood, nr Bristol BS18 4NH

"Jill and Rudolf Birk went out of their way to extend warm hospitality. I needed extra help due to an injured foot, and this was given cheerfully. Dinner, cooked by Mr Birk, was excellent." "Comfortable and well decorated. Makes a good base for exploring the lovely countryside of Avon, Somerset and Wiltshire." This 17th-century dower house is in a village on the A37, almost equidistant from Bath, Bristol and Wells. Its upper rooms have far-reaching views over meadows to the Mendip Hills. Public rooms are well proportioned, and filled with period furniture, knick-knacks, antiques, and elaborate flower arrangements. Best bedrooms, on the first floor, have armchairs, a settee, and a spacious bathroom; there are three four-posters in different styles – French, Victorian and Chinese. English/Bavarian cooking ("with good, fresh ingredients, and interesting vegetables") is served in the "enchanting" conservatory dining room, with murals, a fountain, and trailing greenery. (*Niles E Helmboldt, Ann and Norman Leece*)

Open All year, except Christmas evening, New Year. Restaurant closed for lunch weekdays, Christmas.
Rooms 10 double. 2 on ground floor.
Facilities 2 lounges, restaurant. 1½-acre grounds: croquet. Fishing, golf nearby. Unsuitable for ♿.
Location On A37 7 miles S of Bristol (front rooms double-glazed; back rooms quietest).
Restrictions No smoking in restaurant. No dogs.
Credit cards All major cards accepted.
Terms B&B: single £49–£55, double £69–£95. Set lunch £14.50; full alc £30. Weekend, midweek breaks. *V*

CHIPPING CAMPDEN Gloucestershire — Map 3

Cotswold House *Tel* (01386) 840330
The Square *Fax* (01386) 840310
Chipping Campden GL55 6AN

A fine Regency house (Relais du Silence) overlooking a little square in the centre of this showplace Cotswold town. It has a particularly noble central staircase, and is filled with oriental rugs, antiques, works of art, and impressive flower arrangements. The airy dining room has a *trompe l'oeil* view of an imaginary garden at its entrance, echoing the real view through ceiling-high french. There is a brasserie for simpler meals. In summer, guests take drinks and meals in a willow-shaded courtyard; there's an old-fashioned walled garden (floodlit at night) with clipped yew hedges. New owners, Christopher and Louise Forbes, arrived in mid-1995, but the chef, Raymond Boreham, has stayed. Recent visitors have praised the staff, "friendly, attentive, yet discreet"; the modern British cooking, "beautifully presented, with a good selection of vegetables, perfectly cooked"; and the wide-ranging wine list. "Our bedroom, not large, was warm and comfortable (but the duvet kept us almost too warm). Breakfast very good indeed, with wide choice." (*Brian and Mary Trump, and others*) Some caveats: "The owners were there, but didn't take the time to introduce themselves to their guests; limited choice (two choices for each of three courses) on the menu included in the midweek break; the chef seemed to be on a tight budget."

Open All year, except 3 days over Christmas
Rooms 12 double, 3 single.
Facilities Sitting room, hall/lounge, restaurant, brasserie; private dining/conference room; courtyard. 1¾-acre grounds: croquet. Unsuitable for ♿.
Location Central (front rooms sound-proofed). Private parking.
Restrictions Smoking banned in restaurant, discouraged in bedrooms. No children under 6. Guide dogs only.
Credit cards All major cards accepted.
Terms [1996] B&B: £50–£80; D,B&B £63–£97. Restaurant: set Sun lunch £15.75, dinner £17; full alc £27. Brasserie: alc from £12. Weekend, midweek, off-season breaks. 1-night bookings sometimes refused weekends Apr–Oct.

CHITTLEHAMHOLT Devon — Map 1

Highbullen Hotel
Chittlehamholt, Umberleigh EX37 9HD
Tel (01769) 540561
Fax (01769) 540492

César award in 1991

"A winner." "Hospitality experienced, kindly and friendly. They coped with a full house over New Year without a hitch. Marvellous value." More praise this year for Hugh and Pam Neil's idiosyncratic Victorian mansion, set in large, immaculate grounds. The many amenities, sporting and other (see below), most free to residents, make it ideal for a family holiday. The loyal clientele love it for the tranquillity, the "mixture of relaxed informality and good service when it is needed", and "the many small generosities". It is "a splendid place to unwind; you are left to your own devices. The slight shabbiness makes one feel at home." Bedrooms in the main house are traditional, many large, "with glorious view"; those in the outbuildings are modern; a four-bedroom house with a kitchen has an "idyllic" riverside setting. Food, on an eclectic menu, is "good home-entertaining cooking of the ambitious kind" (the Neils' daughter, Colette Potter, is chef). There's an "excellent" wine list; drinks are fairly priced. "Delightful breakfasts in a sunny room." "Good bar snacks." (*K and B McCann, Nick and Myriam Whalley, and others*) One family was miffed to find the swimming pool out of action: "We felt we should have been warned when we booked." And: "Help-yourself tea and coffee at breakfast meant you had to keep getting up and down".

Open All year.
Rooms 36 double, 1 single. 24 in converted outbuildings. Some on ground floor.
Facilities 3 sitting rooms (2 in annexes), library, bar, billiard room, breakfast room, restaurant; steam room, sunbed, exercise room, table-tennis, squash. 200-acre grounds: 85-acre woodland, garden, croquet, putting, swimming pool, 18-hole golf course, tennis (golf and tennis tuition), 10 miles river fishing (ghillie available).
Location M5 exit 27. A361 to South Molton. B3226 for 5 miles, up hill to Chittlehamholt; through village, ½ mile to hotel.
Restrictions No smoking: restaurant, breakfast room. No children under 8. No dogs.
Credit cards Access, Visa.
Terms D,B&B: single £60–£75, double £100–£160. Cooked breakfast: £2.50–£4. Snack lunches £5. Set dinner £18.50. Off-season breaks. Midweek reductions.

CHURCH STRETTON Shropshire — Map 3

Mynd House BUDGET
Little Stretton
Church Stretton SY6 6RB
Tel (01694) 722212
Fax (01694) 724180

"Attentive service and excellent cooking. Janet and Robert Hill do a first-class job of looking after their guests." A 1996 encomium for the Hills's red brick Edwardian house on a hillside in a hamlet in the Marches, the western strip of Cheshire, Shropshire, Worcestershire and Herefordshire that borders on Wales. There is good walking from the door. No enforced socialising here; guests may sit peacefully in the two small lounges or the cosy bar (with original stained glass). Bedrooms in the original house have the most character; those in the new wing are simple but carefully thought out, with a compact bathroom (but the walls are thin). One suite has a four-poster and spa bath. The restaurant serves local country dishes, such as hoggit pie and cherry pottage, and also regional recipes from Italy and France. The wine list is a veritable tome, with over 200 half-bottles. Ranging across the world, it includes English country fruit wines, eg, gooseberry, dandelion and parsnip. Mrs Hill cooks, her husband serves in the bar and waits at table, with impeccable timing. "Like a stage army, one minute he emerges from the kitchen with plates of food, the next he appears through the opposite door, ushering guests to their table. Good breakfasts, promptly served, with excellent wholemeal bread and satisfying 'Make for the hills' mixed grill." Children are welcomed. (*John Rae, A and CR; also John and Joan Wyatt*) One visitor, arriving at 1.30 pm, was coolly received. Another would have wished for larger bath towels.

Open All year, except Christmas, New Year, Jan, 2 weeks in summer. Restaurant closed for lunch.
Rooms 2 suites, 5 double, 1 single.
Facilities 2 lounges, bar, restaurant. 3½-acre garden. Unsuitable for ♿.
Location In hamlet 1½ miles SW of Church Stretton; take B4370 to Ludlow.
Restrictions Smoking in bar only. No dogs in public rooms.
Credit cards Access, Amex, Visa.
Terms B&B: single £38–£45, double £50–£70, suite £100–£120; D,B&B £50–£80 per person. Set dinner (4–5-course) £22–£26. Themed breaks: local history, Go Green, etc. *V*

CLEEVE HILL Gloucestershire — Map 3

Cleeve Hill Hotel — *Tel* (01242) 672052
Cleeve Hill, Cheltenham GL52 3PR

"We loved it," runs this year's endorsement for John and Marian Enstone's friendly, informal, no-smoking B&B. It is just ten minutes from the centre of Cheltenham, and has glorious views across a valley to the Malvern hills or over Cleeve Common. Others have praised the bedrooms: "large, comfortable, clean, and equipped with all one could require"; the lounge, "decorated in excellent taste", which has a licensed bar; and the kindness and thoughtfulness of the proprietors. "Superb breakfasts, after which you can't eat all day", are served in a conservatory-style room, overlooking the pretty garden. Behind the hotel are fields with sheep and horses; there is direct access to the Cotswold Way. *Wesley House* in nearby Winchcombe, which makes its *Guide* debut this year, is recommended for meals. (*Ann and Fred Hammer; also P Esposito*)

Open All year, except Christmas, New Year.
Rooms 2 suites, 6 double, 2 single.
Facilities Lounge, lounge bar, breakfast room; patio. ¼-acre garden. Riding, golf nearby. Unsuitable for ♿.
Location 2½ miles NE of Cheltenham.
Restrictions No smoking. No children under 8. No dogs.
Credit cards Access, Amex, Visa.
Terms B&B: single £45, double £60–£70, suite £75. 10% discount off season for 2 or more nights. 1-night bookings sometimes refused.

Report forms (Freepost in UK) are at the end of the *Guide*.

CLIMPING West Sussex **Map 2**

Bailiffscourt *Tel* (01903) 723511
Climping BN17 5RW *Fax* (01903) 723107

A 1920s "medieval" house in style of 12th-century bailiff monks' courthouse, recently expensively refurbished by owners Sandy and Anne Goodman. In "magnificently peaceful" 22-acre grounds (with tennis, croquet, golf practice, unheated swimming pool, peacocks) on beautiful beach, 3 miles S of Arundel. "Romantic, stylish; intimate maze of rooms, corridors and courtyards." 27 bedrooms, 17 in buildings in grounds; 2 with ♿ access. Many have fireplace; some four-posters; lovely views. Elegant restaurant (no smoking); new chef, Chris Colmer, has worked at Michelin-*starred* Troigros, *Roanne. Light lunches available in bar, except Sun. No dogs in public rooms. All major credit cards accepted. B&B: single from £89, double from £140, suite from £195; D,B&B from £110. Set lunch £18, dinner £30. Child in parents' room £25. 1 recent report queries value for money. New manager in 1996. More reports, please.*

COLN ST ALDWYNS Gloucestershire **Map 3**

The New Inn *Tel* (01285) 750651
Coln St Aldwyns *Fax* (01285) 750657
nr Cirencester GL7 5AN

A creeper-clad, flower-bedecked inn (a Relais du Silence) in a "delightfully unspoilt village". "It was old when Wren built St Paul's cathedral," write the owners, Brian and Sandra-Anne Evans. "Queen Elizabeth I decreed that there should be a coaching inn within a day's travel of every major centre of population. Through 20 changes of monarch, neither the purpose nor the fabric of the building has changed." Nowadays modern comforts combine with old beams and inglenook fireplaces; chintzy bedrooms, with floral prints on the walls, have telephone and TV. "We have occupied most of them," write regular visitors. "They are beautifully furnished, and a pleasure to relax and sleep in. Our favourite has a beamed pointed ceiling and a downstairs bathroom *en suite*. Two well-trained labradors will accompany you on walks." Other praise: "The Evanses skilfully combine the needs of locals and residents; few places in the Cotswolds get this right. Superb breakfasts." "The sort of English pub we Americans imagine, but rarely find." "Thoroughly civilised, with a genuinely old-fashioned atmosphere and caring, concerned owners." A new chef, Stephen Morey, arrived from *Gravetye Manor* (*qv*), in March 1996. (*John and Ann Smith, George Hope, Jean Deinhard, Good Pub Guide; also Helen and Jack Thornton*) Only caveat: "Uncomfortable seating in the lounge."

Open All year.
Rooms 1 suite, 9 double, 1 single. 2 in dovecote.
Facilities Lounge, bar, breakfast room, restaurant; function facilities. Small garden. River 100 yds; golf nearby. Unsuitable for ♿.
Location In village 8 miles E of Cirencester, between Bibury and Fairford.
Restrictions No smoking in restaurant. Dogs in bar only.
Credit cards Access, Amex, Visa.
Terms [1996] B&B: single £55, double £70–£79, suite £85–£95; D,B&B £56–£74.50 per person. Bar meals. Set Sun lunch £13.50, dinner £22.50.

CONSTANTINE Cornwall Map 1

Trengilly Wartha BUDGET *Tel/Fax* (01326) 340332
Nancenoy, Constantine
nr Falmouth TR11 5RP

This "place above the trees", a lively pub, is on a country lane in the wooded valley of Polpenwith creek, in a designated area of outstanding natural beauty. Good home-cooked lunches and suppers are served in its popular low-beamed bar and conservatory / family room; there's a tapas menu, accompanied by Spanish sherries and wines. The restaurant, "in the style of a French country hotel", serves local produce, especially fish. "The exception to the Gallic theme," write the owners, Michael and Helen Maguire and Nigel and Isabel Logan, "is the definitely traditional English breakfast." "Excellent food; small but neat bedroom with comfortable bed," wrote the American nominator. "We were concerned about the noise, since our room was over the pub, but the pleasant buzz of conversation lulled us to sleep." Regular festivals – eg sausage, fish, pudding – are held. The pretty landscaped garden has an international-size *piste* for *boules*. (*WH, Good Pub Guide*)

Open All year.
Rooms 6 double. 5 with private facilities.
Facilities Lounge, bar, restaurant, conservatory. 6-acre grounds by small lake. Unsuitable for ♿.
Location 1 mile S of Constantine. Signposted off Port Navas–Constantine and Constantine–Gweek roads.
Restrictions No smoking: at breakfast, in conservatory. No dogs in restaurant.
Credit cards All major cards accepted.
Terms B&B: single £32–£40, double £46–£60; D,B&B: single £59–£61, double £94–£98. Bar meals. Full alc £25. 2-night breaks.

CONSTANTINE BAY Cornwall Map 1

Treglos Hotel BUDGET *Tel* (01841) 520727
Constantine Bay, Padstow PL28 8JH *Fax* (01841) 521163
César award in 1994

"A really well-managed hotel; if only there were more of them around." "Atmosphere relaxed and professional." Recent accolades for the Barlow family's traditional seaside hotel (they have been there for 31 years). "By no means luxurious, but consistent", it has a choice position, overlooking the bay, near a sandy beach and the coastal footpath. Regular visitors enjoy the peaceful atmosphere (no canned music, no entertainment), the excellent service (many of the staff are long-serving) and the old-fashioned courtesies: cleaning shoes, carrying luggage, tidying rooms during dinner. In low season it is a favourite of retired people; the disabled and children are welcome. The decor – brick fireplaces, log fires, chintzy furniture, patterned carpets – is conventional. Bedrooms, many with sea view, some with balcony, have light colour-schemes and white fitted furniture. There is a sheltered sunken garden and a "deliciously warm" indoor pool. The six-course dinner is generally liked; the menu is adaptable, and special diets are catered for. Breakfast and afternoon tea are "particularly good". (*IC Dewey, JB Freeman*) The Barlows also own the *Budock Vean Hotel* (*qv*).

Open 13 Mar–1 Nov.
Rooms 4 suites, 32 double, 8 single. 1 on ground floor. 4 self-catering flats in grounds.
Facilities Lift, ramps. Lounges, bridge/TV room, restaurant; children's den, snooker room; indoor swimming pool, whirlpool. 3-acre grounds: croquet. Sandy beach 400 yds, golf, tennis, riding nearby.
Location 4 miles W of Padstow. Avoid Bodmin and Wadebridge. From cross-roads at St Merryn take B3276.
Restrictions No smoking: dining room, 1 lounge, 10 bedrooms. No under-7s in dining room after 7.30 pm. No dogs in public rooms.
Credit cards Access, Visa (small percentage added).
Terms B&B: single £35–£54, double £70–£108, suite £106–£152; D,B&B: single £47–£71, double £94–£142, suite £130–£186. Bar lunches. Set lunch £11.75, dinner £21.50; full alc £25.50. Weekend and midweek breaks. Bridge, golf packages. Children's tariff during school holidays. *V*

CORSE LAWN Gloucestershire Map 3

Corse Lawn House *Tel* (01452) 780771
Corse Lawn GL19 4LZ *Fax* (01452) 780840

"Well nigh perfect." "Reception attentive and friendly. Baba Hine's warm personality infects the staff." This elegant Grade II listed Queen Anne coaching inn is set back from the green of an unspoiled hamlet in lovely countryside. In front is a large pond (once the coach wash) with assorted wildfowl. Though much extended, it retains its country house atmosphere, and has an agreeably understated decor to match. The owners are Baba and Denis Hine, he ("an imperious character") of the cognac family; son Giles is front-of-house. Bedrooms (some named for brandies) are "large and airy, with high ceiling, king-sized bed, good storage, superb shortbread biscuits, real tea and coffee, and smart bathroom, a mixture of ancient and modern". The restaurant, run by Baba Hine with Tim Earley (recently returned after four years abroad), is popular for its French/English modern-influenced cooking, served on set menus, including an attractive vegetarian one, and a *carte*. The wine list "could make one weep at some of the names and their prices, but there are some first-class choices at a reasonable cost". Snacks and light meals are served in the brightly upholstered, informal bistro where no dish costs more than £10. Breakfast is "worth skipping lunch for, and you can have it in your room until 11 am". (*Mr and Mrs J Williams, HR, N and M Whalley, and others*) One couple visiting in early 1996 had a disappointing meal; another wrote: "Noisy kitchen arguments filtered out into the dining room."

Open All year.
Rooms 2 suites, 16 double, 1 single. 5 on ground floor.
Facilities 2 lounges, bar, bistro, restaurant; small conference facilities. 12-acre grounds: croquet, tennis, swimming pool. Golf, fishing, riding nearby.
Location 5 miles SW of Tewkesbury on B4211.
Restrictions No smoking in restaurant. No dogs in restaurant.
Credit cards All major cards accepted.
Terms B&B: single £70, double £90, suite £125; D,B&B: single £85, double £135, suite £170. Set lunch £15.95, dinner £24.50; full alc £30–£45. 2-day breaks. *V*

Please write and confirm an entry when it is deserved. If you think that a hotel is not as good as we say, write and tell us.

COWAN BRIDGE Lancashire — Map 4

Hipping Hall — *Tel* (0152 42) 71187
Cowan Bridge — *Fax* (0152 42) 72452
Kirkby Lonsdale LA6 2JJ

A fine old house on the Cumbrian border, in well-maintained grounds with a stream with ducks and geese. Named for "hipping" or stepping stones where drovers forded a stream, it is run in house party style by Ian Bryant with Jocelyn Ruffle, who cooks. Guests are introduced at pre-dinner drinks in a pretty conservatory (with parakeets). The communal dinner (no choice) is at 8 pm in the Great Hall, which serves as restaurant and lounge – "a magnificent room, huge and beautifully furnished, with a minstrels' gallery and an enormous fireplace". The host, "a charming man", waits at table, pouring wines selected by himself to match the five-course meal, "which is well balanced, with a host of flavours, and beautifully presented". A traditional breakfast is served at separate tables in another attractive room. Bedrooms are spacious and "furnished with care, with flowery wallpaper, antique furniture, a sofa, fresh flowers, TV, plenty of storage space, excellent lighting, and a large, well-lit bathroom". Two cottages can be rented on a self-catering basis. "Warm, cosy, and imaginatively run," wrote our inspectors. This is endorsed: "We arrived as guests and left as friends." "If you like meeting people from all walks of life in an informal atmosphere, this is for you. If you want a romantic evening *à deux*, don't spoil my dinner – try somewhere else." (*John and Mona Taylor, Dr and Mrs JH Jones*)

Open Mar–Nov, and for private parties in winter (not Christmas).
Rooms 2 cottage suites (with sitting room, kitchen), 5 double.
Facilities Lounge, Great Hall, breakfast room, conservatory; small function facilities; terrace. 3-acre grounds: croquet.
Location On A65, 2 miles E of Kirkby Lonsdale. 8 miles from M6 exit 36.
Restrictions Smoking prohibited in breakfast room, dining area; discouraged in bedrooms. No children under 12. No dogs in public rooms.
Credit cards Access, Amex, Visa.
Terms B&B: single £67, double £84, suite £94; D,B&B: single £89, double £128, suite £148. Set dinner £22 (3-course supper Sun, Mon £15). Reduced half-board rates all year for stays of more than 1 night. 1-night bookings sometimes refused bank holidays. *V*

CRACKINGTON HAVEN Cornwall — Map 1

The Manor Farm BUDGET — *Tel* (01840) 230304
Crackington Haven EX23 0JW

A Domesday-listed manor house, with old beams, log fires and antique furniture, "not a hotel, rather a country house for guests". It has a secluded setting, with extensive views, in landscaped gardens in the middle of farmland ("not working; no smells"); the sea is a mile away. "We don't offer telephones, trouser presses, etc, in the bedrooms," writes the owner, Muriel Knight. "Meals are 'at' rather than 'from'; we are not for the anti-social." "It is attractive in every way," writes its nominator on a re-visit, endorsing his earlier praise: "The house is immaculately maintained inside and out and attractively furnished. No smoking (three cheers!). No choice on the dinner menu (enterprising home cooking) but guests' special requirements are observed." Dinner is a civilised affair, served at 7, with good china, glass and silver; men tend to wear jacket and tie. Wines are modestly priced; there's an honesty bar. A full farmhouse breakfast is served at 8.30 am. (*PE Carter*) The whole place may be booked for a house party.

Open All year, except Christmas.
Rooms 5 double. No telephone/TV.
Facilities 2 lounges, TV room, bar, breakfast room, dining room; games room: snooker, table-tennis, darts. 2-acre garden in 25-acre farmland. Sea 1 mile. Unsuitable for ♿.
Location From Wainhouse Corner on A39 follow signs to Crackington Haven. At beach turn inland, ignoring Highcliff Rd; after 1 mile left into Church Park Rd, then 1st right.
Restrictions No smoking. No children. No dogs in house.
Credit cards None accepted.
Terms B&B £30–£35; D,B&B £45–£50.

CRANBROOK Kent — Map 2

Hancocks Farmhouse BUDGET — *Tel* (01580) 714645
Tilsden Lane
Cranbrook TN17 3PH

César award: best budget hotel in the South

"Excellent in every way. Bridget and Robin Oaten, top-notch people, have thought of everything for their guests' comfort. The house is lovely, with beautiful antiques, and fresh flowers everywhere." "Memorable food, especially the puddings, and the generous English breakfast, complete with freshly squeezed orange juice and croissants." "So welcoming that it would be easy to become the guest who comes for the weekend and stays 20 years." "Generous, elegant hospitality. No charge for early morning trays, generous pots of tea and coffee with biscuits, home-made cakes and crumpets, and sherry before dinner. Lovely walks from the door." "The Oatens are former diplomats, whose interests span a wide range. Their teamwork is effortlessly professional." Many accolades this year and last for this 16th-century Grade II listed timber-framed house. It is quietly situated amid farmland just outside Cranbrook, in pleasant gardens against a background of oast houses and pear orchards. Inside are old beams, low doorways, and an inglenook fireplace. Spacious bedrooms have TV, electric blanket, fruit, a decanter of Madeira, sweets, and a private bathroom (two are *en suite*). Dinner (by arrangement) is traditional English with a French influence, with limited choice. A light supper is available when dinner is not served. Guests may opt to dine communally at a beautiful Georgian table; breakfast is at separate tables. No smoking. (*Mr and Mrs William J McGowan, Dr CP Lawrence, Lady Levinge, Vanessa Beriowits, and others*)

Open All year, except Christmas, occasional unfixed times.
Rooms 1 suite, 2 double. 1 on ground floor. No telephone.
Facilities Drawing room/dining room. ½-acre garden.
Location From Cranbrook take Tenterden road; fork right towards Benenden (Tilsden La). *Hancocks* up first track on left.
Restrictions No smoking. Generally no children under 9 ("but we are flexible"). No dogs in public rooms.
Credit cards None accepted.

Terms B&B £25–£35; D,B&B £44–£54. Set dinner £19–£20; light supper £10–£12. 1-night bookings sometimes refused weekends.

The Old Cloth Hall *Tel/Fax* (01580) 712220
Cranbrook TN17 3NR

"We love this place and its owner." "Perfect for relaxing in peaceful surroundings. Katherine Morgan went out of her way to make us welcome. We felt we'd known her for years. We enjoyed tea with delicious home-made cakes in front of a roaring log fire, and the dinners were superb." A member of the Wolsey Lodge consortium, this Elizabethan house with later extensions has a lovely setting deep in the country. Its large grounds have gardens noted for rhododendrons and azaleas, an unheated swimming pool and a tennis court. Inside are low-ceilinged, panelled public rooms with highly polished floors. Books, magazines and flower arrangements are everywhere, and "a miscellany of relics from a lifetime of journeys, sitting next to mellow antiques, family portraits and personal whimsy objects, all reflecting the originality and strong artistic sense of the owner. The three guest bedrooms are "scattered among those of the hostess and her absent family"; the best has a four-poster. Guests dine with Mrs Morgan by candlelight. Many are regulars who enjoy not just the cooking – "simple dinner party stuff; desserts are the strongest point; second helpings are offered" – but also the "absence of the anonymity of an ordinary hotel". Unlicensed: bring your own wine. (*AR Gilroy, Andrew H Nelson*)

Open All year, except Christmas.
Rooms 3 double. No telephone (portable one available).
Facilities Drawing room, dining room. 13-acre grounds: swimming pool (unheated), tennis, croquet. Sea 25 mins. Unsuitable for ♿.
Location 1 mile SE of Cranbrook on Golford Rd to Tenterden. Private road on right, immediately before cemetery.
Restrictions Smoking in bedrooms discouraged. No dogs.
Credit cards None accepted.
Terms B&B: single £45, double £85–£95. Set dinner £25. 1-night bookings sometimes refused bank holiday Sat.

CRANTOCK Cornwall Map 1

Crantock Bay Hotel BUDGET *Tel* (01637) 830229
Crantock, Newquay TR8 5SE *Fax* (01637) 831111

Excellent facilities and entertainments for children; the Smartie Party was a great favourite. Yet children do not dominate. Comfortable bedroom, with adequate facilities. Glorious sea views from dining room. Lots of locally produced food; friendly, efficient waitresses." "Adaptability combined with total professionalism. Attention to detail unsurpassed." "Delightful host." This unpretentious seaside hotel is near an old village with an ancient church and thatched cottages. It has a stunning, quiet setting on West Pentire headland, facing the Atlantic and a huge sandy beach. The North Cornwall Coastal Path runs through the garden. A large extension houses a warm swimming pool, spa bath, toddlers' pool, sauna and exercise room. Most bedrooms have a sea view (partly obscured, on the first floor, by a large flat roof). Many guests are faithful regulars; the long-serving owners, Brenda and David Eyles, welcome all generations, and dogs too. The food is traditional; lunch is a self-service buffet; excellent scones and home-baked biscuits are served with afternoon tea. Entertainments are organised in season. Special breaks of all kinds are offered. There are six golf courses nearby. (*Linda and Mike Proctor, and others*)

Open End Mar–end Oct, winter weekends, New Year.
Rooms 25 double, 9 single. 1 on ground floor. 1 self-catering cottage.
Facilities 2 lounges, bar lounge, bar, restaurant; games room, indoor swimming pool, exercise room; dances, competitions, children's parties in season. 4½-acre grounds: tennis, croquet, adventure playground. Sea, sandy beach, safe bathing 200 yds. Riding, golf nearby.
Location 5 miles SW of Newquay, 1 mile beyond Crantock. Guests met by arrangement at Newquay and Truro stations.
Restrictions No smoking: dining room, 1 lounge. No dogs in public rooms.
Credit cards All major cards accepted.
Terms [1996] D,B&B £54–£59. Set lunch £8.95, dinner £14.95. 4- and 7-day stays: D,B&B from £47 per person per day; half-term packages. Children under 2 accommodated free in parents' room. *V*

CROOKHAM Northumberland — Map 4

The Coach House at Crookham BUDGET *Tel* (01890) 820293
Crookham, Cornhill-on-Tweed TD12 4TD *Fax* (01890) 820284

César award: best budget hotel in the North

"This place is something else. Visitors are treated as guests in Lynne Anderson's home. She is charming; the staff are sunny. You can be as private as you like, or socialise. Nothing has been forgotten, from small scented soaps in the bathroom, to fridge in cupboard with real milk in jug. It's like staying with an aunt – tapestry cushions, Lloyd's loom tub chairs, etc. Super free tea, with home-made cakes and wide choice of teas, on arrival. Guests meet for pre-dinner drinks (honesty system) in the delightful drawing room. The food is home-cooked; soups, ice-creams, preserves, etc, are home-made. Masses of vegetables; free-range, quality ingredients. Some dishes rather quirky, all distinctive. Mrs Anderson trips around serving gravy (very good) herself. Real table napkins, excellent bed-linen. Pretty surroundings: orchards of damson trees, sheep and goats grazing." "Our small daughter and our dogs were made extremely welcome. Our bedroom was large, with large bathroom, and plainly but pleasantly furnished. Dinner is in two attractive dining rooms, with a variety of antique tables, lovely paintings and large fireplaces. Breakfast delicious with lots of choice. Extremely good value." In an area "with amazing scenery", near the Scottish border, this sympathetic guest house is a complex of venerable farm buildings set well back from the road around a sun-trap courtyard. No regular choice of main course at dinner (at 7.30), but individual tastes and diets are catered for. Very good facilities for the disabled. (*Imogen Mottram, Judith Stringer, and others*)

Open Mid-Mar–mid-Nov.
Rooms 7 double, 2 single. 7 with bath/shower. No telephone; some have TV.
Facilities Lounge with self-service bar, TV lounge, 2 dining rooms; large terrace. 3-acre grounds. Golf, fishing, riding, gliding, birdwatching nearby.
Location On A697, 3½ miles N of Milfield.
Restrictions No smoking in dining rooms. No dogs in public rooms.
Credit cards Access, Visa.
Terms B&B £21–£34; D,B&B £36.50–£49.50.

CROPREDY Oxfordshire Map 2

The Old Manor NEW/BUDGET *Tel* (01295) 750235
Cropredy, nr Banbury OX17 1PS *Fax* (01295) 758479

A mellow manor set amid garden and orchard, in a pretty village, steeped in history, in the Cherwell valley. "Its fields," write the owners, Liz and John Atkins, "border the Oxford canal, and are stocked with Gloucester Old Spot pigs and thoroughbred horses; ducks and geese patrol the moat." It boasts a private motor museum (Silverstone is nearby), and welcomes the disabled. "A lovely spot," says its nominator. "I never tire of looking round the beautiful old rooms. Bedrooms have antiques, books, magazines, sherry, etc, and the Atkinses share the honours with two Airedale dogs and three cats." A full English breakfast is served in the 15th-century dining room, which is filled with antiques, books and clocks. The guests' sitting room (with TV) is stocked with games, local information, and yet more books. (*Linda Brook*)

Open All year, except Christmas / New Year.
Rooms 1 suite (suitable for ♿) in barn, 3 double (2 with private facilities).
Facilities Lounge, breakfast room. 2-acre grounds: moat (coarse fishing), motor museum.
Location 4 miles N of Banbury. M40 exit 11, A361 to Daventry; left, after 2½ miles, to Cropredy. Follow lane to T-junction; B&B sign 25 yds on left.
Restrictions No smoking: breakfast room, bedrooms. No dogs in public rooms.
Credit cards Access, Visa.
Terms [1996] B&B: single £25–£28, double £44–£48; suite £30 per person. Very small children accommodated free. 1-night bookings refused during British Grand Prix. *V*

CROSBY-ON-EDEN Cumbria Map 4

Crosby Lodge *Tel* (01228) 573618
High Crosby, Crosby-on-Eden *Fax* (01228) 573428
nr Carlisle CA6 4QZ

"Comfortable, welcoming and dependable. It makes a good overnight stop on the way to Scotland," write regular visitors to this castellated 18th-century country house not far from the M6. It is set in lovely grounds, overlooking the river Eden. It has been run since 1970 by Michael and Patricia Sedgwick; their son James is co-chef with his father; daughter Pippa is in charge of the wide-ranging wine list (plenty of half bottles). Most bedrooms are in the main house, reached by a carved staircase; two are in converted stables, overlooking the walled garden. "The atmosphere is personal, but never intrusive," wrote an earlier guest. "Much care has been taken with the decor. Our spacious bedroom had a dazzling combination of wallpapers and wonderful drapes. Almost OTT, but it worked. Real fires in the lounge; antiques, fine fabrics, bowls of fruit everywhere. Lots of help when we wanted to plan an outing. There was plenty of choice, and coffee ad lib, for breakfast." The restaurant serves traditional British and continental cooking in generous portions, on set menus and a *carte*; seafood, local game and desserts are a speciality; much is home-made, including the bread. There is a wide range of bar snacks. Good walking nearby. (*John and Helen Wright; also John E Borron*) In reply to last year's lamentation, the Sedgwicks write: "Guests wanting a smaller meal may now order a single course from the set menu."

Open All year, except 24 Dec–20 Jan.
Rooms 10 double, 1 single. 2 in stable block.
Facilities 2 lounges, bar, restaurant. 4-acre grounds. River Eden ½ mile. Unsuitable for ♿.
Location 4½ miles NE of Carlisle, just off A689, on right. (Pass hotel; take right turn just before left bend.)
Restrictions No smoking in restaurant. Dogs by arrangement; not in main house.
Credit cards Access, Amex, Visa. None accepted for weekend breaks.
Terms [1996] B&B: single £68–£72, double £95–£115; D,B&B: single £95.50–£99.50, double £150–£190. Set lunch £16.50 (light lunch available, except Sun), dinner £27.50. Winter weekend breaks.

CROYDE Devon — Map 1

The Whiteleaf at Croyde NEW/BUDGET *Tel* (01271) 890266
Croyde, nr Braunton EX33 1PN

"Magical. Charming, attentive people with real flair for what they are doing. Our bedroom was a delight. So was the sun room, where we ordered our dinner. The food was amazing. cooked with imagination and creativity. Delicious bread. I'm going back." "Great value for money, unpretentious style and exceptional hospitality in this lovely part of Britain." David (the chef) and Flo Wallington's small guest house stands in a large garden, surrounded by bungalows, on the outskirts of a seaside village on the edge of the Exmoor National Park. The beach is a few minutes' walk along a private path across the dunes, and there's immediate access to the North Devon coastal path. Last year the Wallingtons thought of selling, and the entry was dropped, but they are still here, though operating on a slightly lower key. The bedrooms, small but comfortable, have a fridge, novels and games. The lounge has magazines and tapes. In the dining room, where French windows open on to the garden, dinner, at about 8.15 and generally for no more than eight, is a five-course affair. Cooking is "traditional with a modern touch", served in large portions; plenty of choice. The wide-ranging wine list includes many half-bottles. The "exceptional" breakfast, cooked by Mrs Wallington, and served until 10 am, includes devilled kidneys, poppadoms and smoked salmon. "Top marks for lack of background music." Children and dogs are welcome. (*Annie Freud, and others*)

Open Feb–Nov. Closed 1 week Mar, 2 weeks May, July, Oct. Restaurant sometimes closed; please check.
Rooms 1 family, 3 double.
Facilities Lounge, sun lounge, restaurant. ½-acre grounds. ½-mile footpath to beach: surfing, bathing. Unsuitable for ♿.
Location From Saunton/Braunton, on left 300/400 yds before village centre.
Restrictions No smoking in restaurant. No dogs in public rooms.
Credit cards Access, Visa.
Terms B&B £25–£37; D,B&B £45–£57. Set dinner £20. Off-season breaks; 3/7-night rates. 1-night bookings occasionally refused.

We need detailed fresh reports to keep our entries up to date.

DEDHAM Essex Map 2

Maison Talbooth *Tel* (01206) 322367
Stratford Road *Fax* (01206) 322752
Dedham, Colchester CO7 6HN

In the heart of Constable country, two luxurious establishments are run by Gerald Milsom with a friendly staff. *Maison Talbooth* is a Victorian country house in pretty grounds, with a view over Dedham Vale. Accommodation is in large bedrooms and suites: "Nice colour scheme, king-size bed, huge bathroom, and view on to woodland with plenty of animal and bird life. Welcoming sherry, mineral water, bowl of fruit, lots of reading matter. Breakfast is generally served in the bedrooms: excellent scrambled eggs, good bread and pastries, superb coffee. Snacks and drinks are available during the day. There is a beautifully proportioned sitting room with squashy chairs and settees, and a large garden, mainly lawns, with loungers." Dinner is taken at *Le Talbooth*, a half-timbered building ten minutes' walk away (there's also a courtesy car) in a lovely setting on the Stour, by a bridge, with a flowery riverside terrace and swans gliding by. Cooking by Terry Barber is eclectic, on set-price menus and a *carte*. (*P and JT, JS Rutter*) One visitor criticised room maintenance; restaurant service can be pressed at times. We'd like more reports, please.

Open All year. Restaurant closed Sun evening Oct–end May.
Rooms 5 suites, 5 double. Some on ground floor.
Facilities Drawing room; function facilities. 7-acre grounds: giant chess, croquet. Restaurant, 3-acre grounds on banks of Stour, 10 mins' walk (courtesy car provided).
Location 6 miles NE of Colchester, just E of A12.
Restriction No smoking in restaurant. No dogs in hotel.
Credit cards Access, Amex, Visa.
Terms B&B: single £85–£120, double £125–£160. Cooked breakfast £7.50. Set lunch £16, dinner £21; full alc £25–£50. Short breaks; weekend rates. Christmas, Easter packages.

DIDDLEBURY Shropshire Map 3

Delbury Hall NEW *Tel* (01584) 841267
Diddlebury, Craven Arms SY7 9DH *Fax* (01584) 841441

In tiny village 10 minutes' drive from Ludlow, beautiful, dignified 18th-century house: fine plasterwork, striking hall with open-string staircase leading to spectacular gallery. The unpretentious family home of Lucinda and Patrick Wrigley, warmly welcoming. He is former amateur jockey who learned to cook at Leith's, London. Imaginative dinners, immaculately served (communal dining; no menu – meals discussed in advance). 20-acre grounds: flower-filled gardens; lake with ornamental duck; dovecote; tennis; farm. Families welcomed. Closed Christmas. Unsuitable for ♿. No smoking: dining room, bedrooms. No dogs in house (kennels available). 4 bedrooms, all with bathroom. B&B £40–£50; D,B&B £67–£77. Set dinner £27. More reports, please.

Don't keep your favourite hotel to yourself. The *Guide* supports; it doesn't spoil.

DORCHESTER Dorset **Map 1**

Casterbridge Hotel BUDGET
49 High East Street
Dorchester DT1 1HU
Tel (01305) 264043
Fax (01305) 260884

"A clean, comfortable, friendly hotel," write visitors from Texas. "We stayed 11 days; leaving was like parting with family. The breakfast was sumptuous and beautifully presented. Plenty of fruit, yogurt, cereal, toast, muffins; excellent cooked dishes." Others have praised the "convenient location", the "relaxed, essentially English ambience", and the "consistently high standards" of Stuart and Rita Turner's B&B. It is a Georgian house, with period furnishings and original paintings, in the centre of the pleasant town on which Thomas Hardy modelled Casterbridge. Some bedrooms ("quite small – doorways not designed for a six-footer") are in the main house; the four front ones are now double-glazed. The quietest rooms are in a modern annexe across a small courtyard; one has wheelchair access. There is good family accommodation; children are welcome. Breakfast is served in a pretty conservatory with a fountain. No restaurant, but tea and coffee are served all day, and the owners do not object to guests' picnicking in the conservatory. The Turner family also owns *The Priory*, Wareham (*qv*). (*Edward C Cross; also John Mainwaring, and others*)

Open All year, except 25/26 Dec.
Rooms 10 double, 5 single. 6 in modern annexe across courtyard. 3 on ground floor.
Facilities Ramps. Lounge, bar/library, breakfast room, conservatory; small courtyard.
Location Main street, just below town clock (front rooms double-glazed). 2 garages; free overnight parking in public carpark in adjacent street.
Restrictions Smoking discouraged in breakfast room, banned in 11 bedrooms. No dogs.
Credit cards All major cards accepted.
Terms B&B: single £32–£45, double £45–£70. Discounts for extended stays, winter weekends. *V*

Yalbury Cottage
Lower Bockhampton
nr Dorchester DT2 8PZ
Tel (01305) 262382
Fax (01305) 266412

This village just outside Dorchester was immortalised by Thomas Hardy as "Mellstock" in *Under the Greenwood Tree*. Here, two old thatched cottages, with inglenook fireplaces and low, beamed ceilings, have been joined together to make a cottage hotel. Bedrooms are in a discreet modern wing. "Who would have suspected such a clever conversion behind a 300-year-old façade? Everything runs like clockwork. Heather and Derek Furminger, attentive, caring, and full of know-how, don't 'try to please', they do it in the most natural way. My bedroom, which had exceptionally good lighting, looked over a hilly meadow where two horses grazed and the sun rose over the frosty ground. Utter peace and beauty." "Bedrooms are spacious and airy, with pretty bedclothes and much use of pine furniture, adding warmth and naturalness. Nick Larby's cooking uses fresh local ingredients, and is successfully designed to highlight their quality rather than show off the chef's cleverness. Lovely walks through Hardy country, and a sense of rural tranquillity made this a memorable stay." Cream teas are served, in the garden in fine weather. (*Katie Plowden, David Young*)

Open All year, except 30 Dec 1996–31 Jan 1997.
Rooms 8 double.
Facilities Lounge, restaurant. ½-acre garden. River Frome 200 yds. Unsuitable for ♿.
Location In hamlet 2 miles E of Dorchester. Turn E off A35 Bournemouth–Dorchester,
Restrictions No smoking: restaurant, 6 bedrooms. No dogs in public rooms.
Credit cards Access, Visa.
Terms B&B £35–£45; D,B&B £52–£62. Set dinner £18.50. Discounts for 3 or more nights; Christmas package. 1-night bookings occasionally refused. *V*

DORRINGTON Shropshire — Map 3

Country Friends BUDGET — *Tel* (01743) 718707
Dorrington, nr Shrewsbury SY5 7JD

Charles and Pauline Whittaker are the owners and chefs in this restaurant-with-rooms in a hamlet near Shrewsbury. It is a large, half-timbered building, in small grounds above a busy road. The cooking is modern, with an emphasis on local produce. The half board rate includes a breakfast of Bucks Fizz, smoked salmon and scrambled eggs, and toasted home-made bread and marmalade. The three bedrooms over a converted coach house are "simple to the point of being slightly basic", and a bit dark; but they are comfortable, "and provided with useful amenities, such as tea-making facilities". One has a private shower, the others share a bathroom. "Warm welcome, attentive service, lovely food," runs a recent endorsement. There's good walking in the Shropshire hills a few miles away. Could we have some more reports, please?

Open All year, except Sun/Mon, 2 weeks mid-July, 1 week end Oct, 26–30 Dec.
Rooms 3 double. 1 with shower *en suite.* No telephone/TV.
Facilities Lounge, bar, restaurant. ¼-acre grounds. Unsuitable for ♿.
Location 6 miles S of Shrewsbury, on A49. 1 room double-glazed.
Restrictions No smoking in restaurant. No dogs.
Credit cards Access, Amex, Visa.
Terms [1996] D,B&B: single £60, double £98. Set lunch/dinner (2–4-course) £22.50–£28.95.

DOWNTON Wiltshire — Map 2

The Warren BUDGET — *Tel* (01725) 510263
15 High Street
Downton, Salisbury SP5 3PG

Mrs Baxter's grade II listed house, "a B&B in a class of its own", is in part Elizabethan. It is in a delightful village on the river Avon, near Salisbury, and is "generously run by the charming hostess": "No trouble is spared. Everything is in exquisite taste; it is well carpeted throughout, and has beautiful antiques. Good bed-linen too. Breakfast, served in a room with french windows overlooking the walled garden, was ample and delicious." No evening meals, but plenty of restaurants, pubs and cafés nearby. Downton Moot, a historic site with a

Grade I listed house, gardens and statuary, is hard by; concerts are held here in summer. More reports, please.

Open 10 Jan–20 Dec, New Year
Rooms 6 double. 2 with facilities *en suite*. No telephone/TV.
Facilities 2 lounges, TV lounge, breakfast room. ½-acre garden. Unsuitable for ♿.
Location In village 6 miles S of Salisbury; opposite post office. Carpark.
Restrictions No smoking: breakfast room, bathrooms, toilets. No children under 5. No dogs in public rooms.
Credit cards None accepted.
Terms (*Not VAT-rated*) B&B: single £25–£30, double £38–£44. 1-night advance bookings generally refused Easter and bank holiday weekends.

DREWSTEIGNTON Devon — Map 1

Hunts Tor House BUDGET — *Tel* (01647) 281228
Drewsteignton EX6 6QW

An architectural oddity, in a beautiful, tiny village below Castle Drogo, this large 18th-century house encloses a smaller 17th-century one with a low-ceilinged, heavily beamed dining room. The decor is a blend of Art Deco and Art Nouveau ornaments and Victorian and Edwardian furniture. It is run almost single-handed by Chris and Sue (the chef) Harrison. No brochure, no written menu, and hotel-style facilities are not available, but the Harrisons offer a high level of personal service. *Michelin* awards a red "Menu" for the modern cooking "with a tendency to the healthy", which *Guide* readers have found "imaginative, delicious, and well balanced". Dinner (no choice, 24 hours' notice required) is at 7.30 pm; the short wine list is well chosen ("but no half bottles"). Separate tables, but the smallness of the place encourages socialising. Breakfast at 9 am includes freshly squeezed orange juice, home-made croissants and preserves, and scrambled eggs with smoked salmon. On the first floor are four simple, bright bedrooms, with plenty of storage space, good lights and *en suite* bathroom; three have a sitting room with TV. There's good walking from the front door. One couple thought their bathroom cramped and the breakfast "mingy". But one visitor, returning after a five-year gap, was ecstatic in its praise: "Marvellous to come back to somewhere *even* better than you remember. The rest of the world must be odd to go to other, grander places." (*Sarah Curtis*)

Open Probably Mar–Dec (please check). Dining room closed for lunch.
Rooms 3 suites, 1 double. No telephone.
Facilities Lounge, bar/dining room, dining room. River Teign nearby: fishing. Unsuitable for ♿.
Location On square in village 3 miles N of Moretonhampstead.
Restrictions No smoking in restaurant. No children under 10. No dogs in public rooms.
Credit cards None accepted.
Terms [1996] B&B: single £40, double £60, suite £70–£90; D,B&B: single £58–£61, double £96–£102, suite £106–£112. Set dinner (3–4-course) £18–£21. 1-night bookings sometimes refused bank holidays.

> Please make a habit of sending a report if you stay at a *Guide* hotel, even if it's only to endorse the existing entry.

DULVERTON Somerset — Map 1

Ashwick House — *Tel/Fax* (01398) 323868
Dulverton TA22 9QD

César award in 1994

"Words cannot describe its unique atmosphere. Mr Sherwood's restful attitude hides a phenomenal amount of hard work. The weather forecast on the breakfast menu is thoughtful. The handwritten personalised menus at dinner are a delight. The waitress at dinner was warm, friendly, informative. The list of items stolen by previous guests is alarming. Stunning views." "Very personal service from Richard Sherwood. We never ceased to be amused at what he dreamt up. The bedrooms were full of thoughtful items for our comfort. The information folder is a mine of information." "The first night we had a teddy bear hot water-bottle in our bed, the second, Peter Rabbit." "A beguiling experience. The peace and tranquillity are palpable. Extremely good food." This lovingly cared-for small Edwardian house has a magnificent position high up in the Exmoor National Park, overlooking the Barle valley. It has large grounds with sweeping lawns, mature trees, water gardens and lily ponds, and an old-fashioned, colourful decor. The hall, with a long gallery and log fire, has its original William Morris wallpaper. Food is English home cooking "with flair and imagination", based on good local produce, on a four-course menu with limited choice. Guests are expected to dine in. Generous breakfasts (on a sunny terrace in summer) include freshly made apple juice and good brown toast. Upgrading of bedrooms and bathrooms has continued; new touches include binoculars, portable electric heaters and Scrabble. (*Diane E Godfrey, Adam Mather; also Mr and Mrs JP Humphrey, and others*)

Open All year.
Rooms 6 double.
Facilities 2 lounges, library, bar, dining room. 6-acre grounds: water garden, croquet, woodland. Unsuitable for ♿.
Location 2½ miles NW of Dulverton. B3223 to Lynton; drive up steep hill, over 2 cattle grids, signpost on left.
Restrictions No smoking in dining room. No children under 8. No dogs in house.
Terms B&B £47–£61; D,B&B £56–£80. Set lunch £12.25, dinner £21.75. 2/5-day breaks. Christmas package. *V*

DUXFORD Cambridgeshire — Map 2

Duxford Lodge — *Tel* (01223) 836444
Ickleton Road — *Fax* (01223) 832271
Duxford CB2 4RU

Suzanne and Ron Craddock's unpretentious hotel is in a village near Cambridge. The M11 runs nearby, but not within earshot of this square red brick house, set back in a garden. Downstairs walls are hung with pictures of fighter aircraft (the Imperial War Museum's magnificent aircraft collection is close by). Bedrooms are neat and well lit, with flowery fabrics, unexceptional furniture and efficient bathroom. The restaurants, *Le Paradis* and *Le Petit Paradis*, are popular with outside diners and business folk. The chef, Patrick Tweedie, trained at *Le Gavroche*, and recent visitors have enjoyed his modern French/British cooking, though some have reported slow service. There's a fixed-price menu with plenty of choice, and a *carte*. The wine list is keenly priced. The welcome is friendly, "but don't expect luggage carrying or evening bedroom tidying". (*Nick and Myriam Whalley*)

Open 2 Jan–24 Dec. (Bed only Christmas/New Year.)
Rooms 13 double, 2 single. 4, on ground floor, across garden.
Facilities Lounge with TV, bar, 2 restaurants; conference facilities. ½-acre garden.
Location From M11 exit 10, go E on A505; take 1st right to junction, then right fork. Entrance 700 yds on left.
Restriction No dogs in public rooms.
Credit cards All major cards accepted.
Terms B&B: single £40–£70; double £75–£90; D,B&B: single £60–£90, double £115–£130. Set lunch/dinner £20; full alc £30. Weekend discounts: "The more nights you stay, the higher the discount." Bed-only rates also offered.

EAST BUCKLAND Devon Map 1

Lower Pitt Restaurant BUDGET *Tel/Fax* (01598) 760243
East Buckland, Barnstaple EX32 0TD

"Delightful. Very good value. Superb dinner, comfortable room and excellent breakfast. Mr and Mrs Lyons sensibly have not introduced the frills and furbelows so beloved of modern interior decorators and so wholly inappropriate to a country setting." "Perfect hosts, welcoming, yet discreet, with that instinct of all good hoteliers of knowing when a chat would be welcome and when to let people be. We enjoyed eating in the conservatory, enjoyed the copious breakfast, indeed enjoyed everything." Recent praise for Jerome and Suzanne Lyons (she is cook). They have been 19 years at their popular restaurant-with-rooms in a peaceful hamlet set in the fold of a hillside, surrounded by the walled fields of south Exmoor. It is a 16th-century white-washed stone farmhouse, Grade II listed, with low doorways, open fire, old bread-oven in the small sitting room, and books in the cosy bar lounge. The small bedrooms are simple, with pine furniture, duvet, electric blanket, radio, fresh milk in a thermos for tea. In the two dining rooms, one a conservatory, all green and white, residents have the run of the *carte*. Cooking is original but not gimmicky, using local produce and home-grown herbs – "well chosen, balanced and healthy, without being 'food fascist'." There's a good wine list with plenty of half bottles.

Open All year, except Christmas. Restaurant closed to non-residents Sun/Mon. Lunch by arrangement.
Rooms 3 double. 1 with bath, 2 with shower. Mobile telephone available.
Facilities Lounge, lounge/bar, dining room, conservatory dining room; terrace. 2-acre grounds. Unsuitable for ♿.
Location 45 minutes' drive from M5 exit 27. 3 miles NW of South Molton off A361.
Restrictions No smoking: dining rooms, bedrooms. No children under 12. No dogs.
Credit cards Access, Amex, Visa.
Terms D,B&B £47.50–£55. Full alc £26.50. Residents are expected to dine in.

We are particularly keen to have reports on italicised entries.

EAST GRINSTEAD West Sussex Map 2

Gravetye Manor *Tel* (01342) 810567
East Grinstead RH19 4LJ *Fax* (01342) 810080

César award in 1991

Peter Herbert's renowned Elizabethan manor house hotel, "beautiful, refined and supremely comfortable", is set amid a 1,000-acre forest. Its magnificent grounds, designed by William Robinson, pioneer of the English natural garden, include "a delightful trout lake, secluded in a hollow, where wind can rarely interfere with the pleasures of casting". The panelled public rooms have understated fabrics, antiques, good paintings, and beautiful flower arrangements. Bedrooms, some in a new wing imperceptibly melded on to the old house, are decorated in similar style. "Unusual attention to detail. The lighting is excellent. The information folder covers almost any question. Very prompt room service." "What sets it apart is the faultless, never intrusive, service by a predominantly young staff. They provided an elegant picnic for Glyndebourne; we wished we had taken a butler." "Of all the hotels I know, it provides the best traditional country house experience." "Excellent modern cooking (portions not too large)" by Mark Raffan, who returned to the kitchens last year after a spell with King Hussein of Jordan. "We liked being able to choose just one or two items from the *carte*, rather than eat a heavy meal day after day. Superb coffee and croissants at breakfast." "Peter Herbert and his charming wife are model hosts." (*Mary B Dawson, Christina Baron, HR, JS Rutter, Susan B Hanley, and others*) One caveat: "The wine list is impressive, but mark-up ridiculous."

Open All year. Restaurant closed to non-residents Christmas evening.
Rooms 16 double, 2 single.
Facilities 3 sitting rooms, bar, restaurant; private dining room. 30-acre grounds: gardens, croquet, lake: trout-fishing. Unsuitable for ♿.
Location 5 miles SW of East Grinstead, off B2110 to West Hoathly.
Restrictions No smoking in restaurant. No children under 7, except babies. No dogs.
Credit cards Access, Visa.
Terms (*Excluding VAT*) Rooms: single £85–£114, double £115–£226. Continental breakfast £10; English alc. Set lunch £24 (£30 on Sun), dinner £30; full alc £60. Off-season rates. 1-night bookings sometimes refused weekends.

ERPINGHAM Norfolk Map 2

The Ark BUDGET *Tel* (01263) 761535
The Street
Erpingham NR11 7QB

A "tranquil and indulgent" spot, a typical brick-and-flint Norfolk house, with a pretty garden at the back, in the middle of a quiet village. It is a popular restaurant run by Mike and Sheila Kidd, with daughter Becky as chef, and has just three bedrooms. One has large windows leading on to the garden; another is an attic, "charmingly furnished in cottage style, and well equipped, with an excellent bathroom under the eaves". Arriving guests reported a warm welcome, with tea "and exquisite little biscuits", in the slightly formal lounge. Dinner is served by the gregarious Mike. The food is English/French traditional, "imaginative and full of flavour"; many ingredients are organically home-grown; rolls are home-made. There is an extensive wine list, ranging from reasonably priced house wines up to the £80 mark. Breakfast, served at flexible times, includes a good spread of preserved fruits, yogurt, cereals, and excellent home-made marmalade. Endorsed this year by *William Bentsen*: "*Very* friendly staff." There are some wonderful beaches nearby, and a spectacular National Trust house, Blickling Hall.

Open All year, except perhaps Christmas.
Rooms 3 double. 1 on ground floor. No telephone.
Facilities Reception/bar, lounge, restaurant. 1-acre garden: croquet. Sea 8 miles.
Location 4 miles N of Aylsham. Left off A140, just before Alby Centre.
Restrictions No smoking: restaurant, bedrooms. No very young children in restaurant at night. Dogs in garden bedroom only, not in public rooms.
Credit cards None accepted.
Terms D,B&B: single £60–£70, double £100–£115. Set Sun lunch £13.25. dinner £21.50; full alc £26.50. Off-season breaks. *V*

EVERSHOT Dorset — Map 1

Summer Lodge — *Tel* (01935) 83424
Evershot DT2 0JR — *Fax* (01935) 83005

César award in 1985

Nigel and Margaret Corbett are in their 18th year at their ever-popular dower house in a quiet Dorset village. It has had a *Guide* entry since 1981. Although it has become smarter (it is now a Relais & Châteaux member), and there have been many changes of chef, the caring welcome and personal attention remain undiminished, as countless regulars bear witness: "We have watched this little paradise grow for 14 years. It is one of the most friendly, well-run hotels we visit, so obviously loved by the owners and their welcoming and willing staff." "Perfection all round." "A truly family atmosphere, congenial, warm, yet always professional." "Flower arrangements as magnificent and ubiquitous as ever. The new chef, Timothy Ford, uses only the finest and freshest of ingredients, giving them the best and most appropriate treatment, so that everything tastes as it should. Presentation is exquisite." "Picturesque and tranquil setting. The prices include morning and afternoon tea (a lavish affair) and a newspaper; we thought it good value." Bedroom extras include home-made shortbread and fresh milk for tea-making, replenished twice daily; car windscreens are cleaned during breakfast. There's excellent walking in the nearby deerpark. "The gardens are currently being done up under the watchful eye of Penelope Hobhouse," writes Mr Corbett. (*Eve Webb, AS-M, Peter and Susan Ranft; also Heather Sharland, and many others*) Some rooms in the coach house are poorly insulated. One complaint about poor coffee, at both dinner and breakfast.

Open All year.
Rooms 14 double, 3 single. 6 (3 on ground floor, 2 with private terrace) in coach house 20 yds.
Facilities Ramps. 2 lounges, bar, dining room. 5-acre garden: swimming pool, croquet, tennis. Golf, fishing nearby.
Location 10 miles N of Dorchester. Cars must turn left at village entrance, into Summer Lane, then right into drive.

Restrictions No smoking in dining room. No dogs in public rooms.
Credit cards All major cards accepted.
Terms B&B: single £105, double £135–£225; D,B&B: single £82–£145, double £125–£295. Set lunch £12.50, dinner £32.50. Christmas, New Year packages. 1-night bookings occasionally refused Sat.

EVESHAM Hereford and Worcester **Map 3**

The Evesham Hotel
Cooper's Lane, off Waterside
Evesham WR11 6DA

Tel (01386) 765566
Fax (01386) 765443
Freephone (0800) 716969
(reservations only)

César award in 1990

"A life-enhancing place. We loved it. John Jenkinson is very much in evidence, joking and jollying all parties, while keeping a vigilant eye on the show. The buffet lunch was wonderful value." "We have visited regularly since 1981. Service is excellent. Bedrooms of a high standard: comfortable beds, good lighting, coffee, bubble bath, etc in large jars (no horrid sachets). Consistently good food, and the chef will adapt dishes if asked." "Very good vegetarian meals." Recent praise for this friendly hotel (its César was for "utterly acceptable mild eccentricity") in a secluded setting a short walk from the town centre. Run for the past 21 years by the Jenkinson family, with a long-serving staff, it is genuinely welcoming to children. Under-twelves are charged £1.50 for each year of their age; items on the children's menu are charged according to size of portion and age of child. The convivial sitting room is well supplied with board games. The jokey style includes a wise-cracking brochure and menu, countless teddy bears, toy ducks and boats in the baths, and a huge wine list devoid of French vintages. Behind this is genuine professionalism and will to please. The popular restaurant, overlooking a large garden with a huge old cedar of Lebanon, offers exotic dishes from around the world (with some startling combinations), as well as plain grills; at lunchtime there is also a 50-dish buffet. (*HR, C Golding, D Drury*)

Open All year, except 25/26 Dec.
Rooms 1 family, 33 double, 6 single. 10 on ground floor. Some no-smoking.
Facilities Bar, lounge, restaurant; small indoor swimming pool. 2½-acre grounds: croquet, putting. "Though not officially suitable for ♿, we manage to cope."
Location Off Riverside Rd. 5 mins' walk from town centre, across river. Parking.
Restriction No dogs in public rooms.
Credit cards All major cards accepted.
Terms B&B: single £57–£65, double £74–£90, suite £110–£115; D,B&B £47–£60 per person. Buffet lunch £6.85; full alc £25. Off-season breaks. 1-night bookings sometimes refused. Children under 12 charged £1.50 for each year of their age.

EYTON Hereford and Worcester **Map 3**

The Marsh
Eyton, Leominster HR6 0AG

Tel (01568) 613952

A 14th-century timbered house, in a "delightful isolated position", handy for exploring the English and Welsh border country. It is set in a peaceful garden with a stream and a lily pond. "The mixture of finesse and friendliness which Jacqueline and Martin Gilleland offer is hard to beat," writes a returning visitor. "The house is sensitively restored and furnished, but has a lived-in feel. We were welcomed with tea and lemon cake in the stone-flagged, two-storey-high medieval hall. Our bedroom had an attractive, individual decor, with unintimidating antique furniture. The food is delicious – imaginative dishes, exquisitely presented, with fresh ingredients from trusted suppliers and from the Gillelands' herb and vegetable garden. Residents on half board get a choice of starters and desserts and a fixed main course: Herefordshire duck so tender that the memory still lingers; lots of delicious fish, straight from Cornwall. In ten days we never had the same dish twice. The delightful garden is designed in a series of 'rooms', each with a different character, and a great sense of colour. Martin Gilleland's enthusiasm for the local wildlife is infectious." "Large, comfortable bedroom with fresh fruit replenished daily. Well-stocked library. Extensive wine list with reasonable mark-up. Helpful owners." "Wonderful choice at breakfast, beautifully executed." For non-residents there is a *table d'hôte* with choices of each course. (*Brenda and Michael Peover, J Rudd, T Peter Wall, HR; and others*) Extras can make the bill mount up.

Open All year, except Christmas, 4–31 Jan.
Rooms 3 double.
Facilities Medieval hall, sitting room, solar, bar dining room. 1½-acre garden: croquet. Unsuitable for ♿.
Location 2 miles NW of Leominster. From A49 by-pass, take B4361 to Richards Castle; left after ¾ mile towards Eyton/Lucton. Continue along lane to common; hotel on right.
Restrictions No smoking: dining room, bedrooms. No children under 8. No dogs.
Credit cards All major cards accepted.
Terms [1996] B&B: single £80, double £112. Set Sun lunch £19.95, dinner £22.50. Off-season breaks.

FALMOUTH Cornwall **Map 1**

Penmere Manor
Mongleath Road
Falmouth TR11 4PN

Tel (01326) 211411
Fax (01326) 317588

Unpretentious family hotel SW of town centre, owned by Pope family for many years; run by Andrew Pope and Elizabeth Rose. "Happy atmosphere; courteous staff." 5-acre grounds: sub-tropical gardens, woodland walks, fitness trail, swimming pool, adventure playground, practice golf, giant chess and draughts, croquet. Sandy beach, golf, tennis nearby. Well-equipped leisure centre, with fine swimming pool, and bar serving informal meals 10 am to 9.30 pm. 38 bedrooms, best ones, with lounge area, in garden wing; cheaper ones ("very ordinary") in main house. Traditional dinners in Bolitho's Restaurant *(pianist most evenings); lobster often available. Closed Christmas. No smoking: restaurant, some bedrooms. No dogs in public rooms, unattended in bedrooms. All major credit cards accepted. B&B £41–£52.50; D,B&B (min. 2 nights) £58–£71.50. Set dinner £20; full alc £30 [1996].* **V**

Don't let old favourites down. Entries are dropped when there is no endorsement.

FISHERWICK Staffordshire Map 3

Tamhorn Park Farmhouse BUDGET *Tel* (01543) 432241
Fisherwick, nr Whittington *Fax* (01543) 433499
Lichfield WS14 9JJ

Anne and David Adams' B&B in a small village near Lichfield, handy for Birmingham's NEC, 30 minutes' drive away, is a Grade II listed early Georgian farmhouse, once owned by Sir Robert Peel, in grounds adjoining the Birmingham and Fazeley Canal. "It has been exquisitely renovated," wrote the nominator. "You can enjoy its period feel with none of the inconveniences. The lounge has a wood-burning stove and satellite TV; there's a snooker room with a full-size billiard table. Our bedroom, complete with fresh flowers, fruit, current magazines, and proper bath sheets, was perfect. Breakfast was a delight, both visually and gastronomically. The charming family go out of their way to make you feel at home." "We are very flexible," writes Mrs Adams. "Breakfast falls into the 'farmhouse cooking' category, erring on the low-fat side; the eggs are from our own hens. Ten minutes away is Tamworth's 'real snow' Snow Dome for skiers of all levels." (*CK, endorsed this year by Jeremy Canney*) Evening meals no longer on offer.

Open Feb–Nov.
Rooms 3 double, 1 with shower. No telephone/TV.
Facilities Lounge with TV, snooker room, dining room. 1-acre garden, patio; canal adjoining. Unsuitable for &.
Location 4 miles NW of Tamworth. From Lichfield take A51 towards Tamworth; left to Whittington ¼ mile past *Horse and Jockey* pub. Drive c. 3 miles on right, ¼ mile after level crossing.
Restrictions No smoking. Dogs by arrangement.
Credit cards None accepted.
Terms B&B: single £26, double £40.

FOWEY Cornwall Map 1

Carnethic House BUDGET *Tel/Fax* (01726) 833336
Lambs Barn, Fowey PL23 1HQ

A Regency house in the countryside near Fowey, with peaceful, award-winning gardens, a heated swimming pool, ample parking for cars and boats, and a loyal following. It has an extrovert host, David Hogg, "the most attentive we've ever had". He welcomes guests, makes introductions, takes them to and collects them from various walks, and organises games and quizzes in the evening. "Some of the happiest times of my life; he breaks down the British reserve in newcomers, persuading even snooty Londoners to join in," says one devotee. "Intimate and friendly," writes another, "with good decor and furnishing. Food of extremely high quality; the varied menu always includes local fish. The Hoggs don't just run the place as a business; they take pleasure in what they are doing. All ages are made welcome." The wine list "offers excellent value for money". "No white-tied waiters or deferential doormen here; we aim to provide a carefree holiday at a reasonable cost," say the Hoggs. (*G and J Cooke, Mr and Mrs G Jarrett; also J and D Knight*)

Open 1 Feb–30 Nov.
Rooms 7 double, 1 single. Some on ground floor.

Facilities Lounge/bar, dining room. 2-acre grounds: swimming pool, tennis, putting, croquet. Sandy beach 1 mile.
Location ½ mile from centre. Off A3082 St Blazey–Fowey, opposite "Welcome to Fowey" sign.
Restrictions No smoking: dining room, 2 bedrooms. Dogs in bar only (by agreement with other guests).
Credit cards All major cards accepted.
Terms B&B £23–£40; D,B&B £33–£50. Set dinner £14. 2–5-day breaks. Winter house parties. ***V***

FRANT Kent — Map 2

The Old Parsonage **NEW/BUDGET** *Tel* (01892) 750773
Church Lane
Frant, nr Tunbridge Wells TN3 9DX

An unassuming B&B in a quiet village near Tunbridge Wells. "This spacious Georgian house served as a rectory until 1989. It is beautifully furnished with antiques, and tastefully decorated. A lovely, huge terrace leads to the well-kept garden. The bedrooms, two with a four-poster, have TV and a luxuriously equipped bathroom. There's a large lounge and a sunny conservatory. Breakfast is continental, with ham, cheese and croissants, or English, with a choice of eggs, bacon, etc, or kedgeree. A simple evening meal is available by arrangement; there are good restaurants and pubs nearby. The hostess, Mrs Dakin, is a charming, hospitable young woman." (*Uli Lloyd Pack*)

Open All year. Dining room open for dinner by arrangement (groups only).
Rooms 3 double. No telephone.
Facilities Drawing room, conservatory, dining room. 3-acre grounds: terrace, lawns, croquet. Lake, trout fishing 3 miles; reservoir, leisure facilities 5 miles. Unsuitable for ♿.
Location By church in village 300 yds off A267, 2 miles S of Tunbridge Wells.
Restrictions Smoking in conservatory only. No dogs in public rooms.
Credit cards Access, Visa.
Terms B&B: single £35–£45, double £55–£65. Set dinner £16.50. 1-night bookings sometimes refused weekends in season.

GATESHEAD Tyne and Wear — Map 4

Eslington Villa *Tel* (0191) 4876017 and 4200666
8 Station Road *Fax* (0191) 48200667
Low Fell, Gateshead NE9 6DR

On south bank of Tyne opposite Newcastle, in quiet residential area of Gateshead (not a particularly prepossessing setting), Mr and Mrs Tulip's Edwardian country house is "an oasis". Friendly atmosphere; caring, dedicated staff. Good public rooms, with some original features. Agreeably furnished bedrooms, well-planned bathrooms. English/French traditional food in smart, popular restaurant; good cooked dishes at breakfast. Mainly business visitors on weekdays; weekend reductions. 12 bedrooms, some on ground floor. 1½-acre grounds. Closed bank holidays. No smoking in restaurant. No dogs in public rooms. Access, Amex, Visa accepted. B&B: single £44.50–£54.50 (weekends £34.50–£44.50), double £64.50 (weekends £54.50). Set lunch £15.95, dinner £21.95 [1996]. More reports, please. ***V***

GILLAN Cornwall Map 1

Tregildry BUDGET *Tel* (01326) 231378
Gillan, Manaccan *Fax* (01326) 231561
nr Helston TR12 6HG

A small hotel in glorious setting on a peninsula in a designated area of outstanding natural beauty. It has magnificent views over Gillan Bay. A private path leads down to a small stony cove. The coastal path is nearby. It was bought in mid-1995 from the Norton family by Lynne and Huw Phillips, whose former hotel, *Quarry Garth*, Windermere, was popular with *Guide* readers for its personal atmosphere and high standards of decor and food. They have refurbished the public areas. The bedrooms (some are small) will be brought up to scratch during the winter of 1996. "Relaxing atmosphere," wrote a 1996 visitor. "Public rooms decorated in excellent taste. Interesting and delicious food on a daily changing menu." (*Mrs EA Stephens*) Another visitor this year was more cautious in her praise of the cooking: "imaginative and sometimes unusual, but often too ambitious." And one complaint of a cold house in May, "admittedly the coldest May in memory".

Open Mar–Nov.
Rooms 10 double.
Facilities 2 lounges, bar, restaurant. 4-acre grounds. Private path to beach: bathing, sailing, fishing, windsurfing. Golf nearby. Unsuitable for ♿.
Location 12 miles E of Helston. Take A3083 towards the Lizard. 1st left for St Keverne; follow signs for Manaccan and Gillan.
Restrictions No smoking: 1 lounge, restaurant, bedrooms. No dogs in public rooms.
Credit cards Access, Visa
Terms D,B&B £50–£55. Set dinner £19.50. 1-night bookings sometimes refused Sat in season, bank holidays. Special breaks for 3 nights and more. *V*

GILLINGHAM Dorset Map 2

Stock Hill House *Tel* (01747) 823626
Stock Hill, Gillingham SP8 5NR *Fax* (01747) 825628

César award in 1991

Peter and Nita Hauser's *César* was for "dedicated hotelmanship" – "still well deserved". They are exuberant and gregarious hosts. Their Victorian manor (Relais & Châteaux) is quietly situated in parkland and gardens, with a stream, a fountain, old and rare trees and lots of wildlife. It is "shining clean and sumptuously if somewhat eccentrically decorated", with heavy drapes, elaborate chandeliers, and *objets d'art* (eg, Indian horses, immense Siamese cats, buddhas). Bedrooms, in similar style, vary in size. Dinner is an occasion, for which guests are expected to dress, and leisurely. Using locally produced ingredients and home-grown herbs and vegetables, Peter Hauser, "an artist in the kitchen", cooks a mixture of English and Austrian dishes, served in generous portions; Viennese-style desserts are particularly good. There is plenty of choice; wines are reasonably priced. "It is the house for perfectionists," one guest has written. "I was even offered help with unpacking and packing. Every meal tray brought to the room had a miniature vase of fresh flowers." Others have praised the "charming, very professional staff". Breakfasts are "excellent, if rather protracted, with eggs from the Hausers' ultra-free-range hens". When he has the time, Mr Hauser will play the zither for his guests.

Open All year. Restaurant closed Mon midday.
Rooms 1 suite, 9 double, 1 single. 3 in coach house.
Facilities Foyer, small bar, lounge, breakfast room, restaurant. 10-acre grounds: croquet, tennis, putting, stream, lake (fishing), wildlife. Unsuitable for ♿.
Location On B3081 1½ miles W of Gillingham, 3 miles S of A303.
Restrictions Smoking banned in dining room, breakfast room; discouraged in bedrooms. No children under 6. No dogs (kennels nearby).
Credit cards All major cards accepted.
Terms D,B&B: single £95–£145, double £200–£280. Set lunch £22, dinner £30. Winter breaks. Wine and food weekends. 1-night bookings sometimes refused. *V* (31 Oct–1 Mar, except Christmas)

GLEWSTONE Hereford and Worcester **Map 3**

Glewstone Court NEW *Tel* (01989) 770367
Glewstone, nr Ross-on-Wye HR9 6AW *Fax* (01989) 770282

A listed building set amid orchards, in a garden with an ancient cedar of Lebanon. Its bar and restaurant are popular locally – the New Year brunch is "well known". "It is informally run by Bill Reeve-Tucker and his wife, Christine (the chef), with a friendly local staff. Lovely lounge, with log fires and comfortable chairs and sofas. Large well-furnished bedrooms with TV, and warm bathroom with his and hers towelling robes. Leisurely breakfasts – the best we have eaten this year, wonderful bacon, thick granary toast – served up to 10 am. Excellent bar lunches. The dinner menu didn't change during the four days we were there, but there was plenty of choice. Children and dogs are made to feel most welcome." Good walking; plenty of activities available locally (see below). "This is our family home, not a pretentious, overstuffed 'Country House Hotel'," write the owners. (*Janice Carrera*) More reports, please.

Open All year, except 25–27 Dec.
Rooms 6 double, 1 single.
Facilities Lounge hall, drawing room bar, restaurant, bistro; private dining room. 3½-acre grounds: garden, croquet. River Wye ½ mile: fishing, canoeing; riding, golf, tennis, hot-air ballooning nearby. Unsuitable for ♿.
Location 3 miles SW of Ross-on-Wye. Signposted from A40, A4137 and A49.
Restriction No dogs in dining rooms.
Credit cards Access, Amex, Visa.
Terms B&B: single £40–£65, double £60–£95. Bar lunches. Set dinner £24. 2-day break all year, except bank holidays, New Year's Eve, Cheltenham race week. *V*

GRANGE-IN-BORROWDALE Cumbria **Map 4**

The Borrowdale Gates *Tel* (0176 87) 77204
Grange-in-Borrowdale *Fax* (0176 87) 77254
Keswick CA12 5UQ

"We have only praise for this hotel and its management. It is quietly situated, with superb views of the fells. The dinners are of exceptional standard and value. Delightful bedrooms." "Excellent rapport between management and staff." Recent praise for Terry and Christine

Parkinson's traditional hotel, a Victorian house on the edge of an ancient hamlet in the Borrowdale valley, not far from Derwentwater. It is set in wooded grounds, and well placed for walking, climbing and touring. It has "attractive, thoughtfully planned" lounges, with antique and period furniture, fresh flowers, roaring fires in winter, and good views. In the dining room, with picture windows, the traditional cooking is "outstanding in quality and presentation", with plenty of choice; lush puddings or local cheeses to finish. The wine list is "wide-ranging in country and price". Some bedrooms are in the main building; larger, if less characterful, ones are in a modern wing; best views are from those at the back. (*Joan A Powell, John and Margaret Myring, Mr and Mrs Wittenberg; also Michael Crick*)

Open 31 Jan–7 Dec, 19 Dec–1 Jan.
Rooms 2 family, 16 double, 4 single. 6 on ground floor.
Facilities Ramps. 3 lounges, bar, restaurant. 2-acre grounds. Derwent Water 1 mile.
Location From Keswick take B5289. After 4 miles right into Grange over hump-backed bridge; hotel 400 yds on right.
Restrictions No smoking in restaurant. No children under 5 in restaurant. No dogs.
Credit cards Access, Amex, Visa.
Terms B&B: single £43.50–£62.50, double £80–£120; D,B&B: single £56–£75, double £105–£145. Set Sun lunch £13.50, dinner £23.50. Weekend and midweek breaks, off-season rates; Christmas, New Year programmes. 1-night bookings sometimes refused weekends.

GRASMERE Cumbria — Map 4

Michael's Nook — *Tel* (0153 94) 35496
Grasmere LA22 9RP — *Fax* (0153 94) 35645

Standing on a hill well back from the A591, in large landscaped gardens, is this hotel "with more than a touch of eccentricity" which, say recent guests, "deserves all the praise it can get". "Very friendly, helpful staff." The owner since 1969, Reg Gifford, is a former antiques dealer and there's plenty of evidence in the decor of his collector's eye for furniture, rugs, prints and porcelain. A grand piano in the lounge, a spinet in the hall, "flower displays several feet high", potted plants, great danes and exotic cats add to the atmosphere. A fine mahogany staircase leads up to bedrooms of varying sizes, all "beautifully furnished and decorated, with a smart bathroom". The dining room, with deep red walls and white cornices, has a collection of antique tables and a log fire. The chef, Mark Treasure, was *sous-chef* at London's *Michelin*-starred *Capital Hotel (qv)*; his cooking is "modern, with a European influence". There is plenty of choice on the set-price menu, and there are many half bottles on the wide-ranging wine list. Sadly, the parrot that used to greet arriving guests is no more.

Open All year.
Rooms 2 suites, 12 double.
Facilities Lounge/hall, lounge, bar, 2 dining rooms; conference room. 3-acre garden adjoining 10-acre woodland: croquet. Guests have access to leisure facilities at *The Wordsworth*, under the same management. River Rothay, free river and lake fishing nearby. Unsuitable for ♿.
Location Turn up between *Swan* hotel and its carpark on A591 just N of village. Hotel 400 yds on right.
Restrictions No smoking in restaurant. No dogs.

Credit cards All major cards accepted.
Terms D,B&B: single £120–£140, double £160–£280, suite £300–£390. Set lunch £28.50, dinner £39.50 and £48. Midweek, weekend breaks off-season. Christmas, New Year house parties. 1-night bookings sometimes refused Sat, bank holidays in high-season. *V* (not on discounted winter rates)

White Moss House *Tel* (0153 94) 35295
Rydal Water, Grasmere LA22 9SE *Fax* (0153 94) 35516

A grey stone, creepered Lakeland house, in a little garden above the A591 looking across to Rydal Water. It is a long-established restaurant-with-rooms – "over 21 years in the *Good Food Guide,* and deservedly so" – run "with a personal touch" by Peter (the chef) and Susan Dixon. Its small lounge is conducive to after-dinner socialising. Bedrooms (with numerous extras) are also small, with tiny bathrooms. Five are in the main house; two (let as a unit) are in a "delightful" late 18th-century cottage up the hill, with spectacular fell views: "The final approach up an unmetalled track might upset fastidious car-owners, but it's easily reached on foot in daylight, ten minutes up, five minutes down." Dinner, five-courses, no choice until dessert, is at 7.30 for 8. "The cooking is extraordinary in quality and consistency, and you can stay a week without feeling bloated. The meal is well paced, with a welcome pause after the main course. This is one of the few restaurants in the country where one can drink like a prince on little more than a decent professional salary. Breakfasts include a wide choice of starters and the full cooked works, artfully bringing the principles of *nouvelle cuisine* to the great British fry-up. The packed lunches are ideal for walkers: inexpensive, and light to carry. Service by well-trained local girls. Owners friendly but never intrusive." Guests may row on Rydal Water in the hotel's old wooden rowing boat. (*Mr and Mrs RO, and others*)

Open Mar–Dec. Restaurant closed midday, Sun.
Rooms 5 double. 2-room cottage on hillside (10 mins' drive or direct footpath).
Facilities Lounge, dining room; terrace. 2-acre garden. Near Rydal Water and river Rothay: swimming, fishing, boating. Free use of nearby leisure club: swimming pool, sauna, gym, etc. Unsuitable for ♿.
Location 1 mile S of Grasmere on A591 (heavy lorries banned; double-glazing); cottage rooms quietest.
Restrictions No smoking in dining room. No toddlers. No dogs.
Credit cards Access, Visa.
Terms [1996] D,B&B £67–£87. Set dinner £28. Special breaks Nov, Dec, Mar, Apr. 1-night bookings sometimes refused bank holiday weekends.

GRASSINGTON North Yorkshire Map 4

Ashfield House BUDGET *Tel* (01756) 752584
Grassington, nr Skipton BD23 5AE

"A friendly, warm little hotel, remarkably insulated from the bustle, despite its position just off the busy village square. My compact room looked over the very pretty garden. Hard-working hosts. Highly recommended for value for money, and niceness of other guests." "Cottagey, cosy and relaxed. Bedroom clean and comfortable, with gorgeously tiled little shower room. Excellent, unpretentious dinner, everything freshly cooked. Generous breakfast, with fine scrambled eggs." This creeper-covered 17th-century stone house is tucked away from the centre of the principal village in Upper Wharfedale, which can be tourist-ridden in summer. It is informally run by Linda and Keith Harrison, "with two equally friendly cats". The decor is simple: old oak and pine furniture, modern fabrics, log fires. Seasonal produce, and vegetables from the garden are used in the traditional English dishes on the four-course menu, served punctually at 7 pm. "There is very little choice – much preferable to a long menu, always ominous in a small place. Second helpings are offered. The wine list is short, but very acceptable." No smoking. (*Trevor Lockwood, Kate Kelly; also Charles Moncreiffe, and others*)

Open All year, except Christmas, Jan/early Feb, 1 week May.
Rooms 7 double. No telephone (payphone for guests).
Facilities 2 lounges (1 with small bar), dining room; drying room. ½-acre garden. Access to local leisure centre 10 am–4 pm weekdays. River, fishing ¼ mile. Unsuitable for ♿.
Location Village centre. Private parking.
Restrictions No smoking. No children under 5. No dogs.
Credit cards Access, Visa.
Terms B&B £24.50–£38.50; D,B&B £37–£53. Set dinner £12.50–£14.50. Spring breaks; Dickensian festivities in Dec. 1-night bookings refused bank holidays, some Sats.

GREAT DUNMOW Essex — Map 2

The Starr — *Tel* (01371) 874321
Market Place — *Fax* (01371) 876337
Great Dunmow CM6 1AX

An old inn, black-and-white and beamed, now a smart restaurant-with-rooms, with "caring owners, Brian and Vanessa Jones, and an enthusiastic and charming staff". It stands in the village's old market place, where two roads converge. The no-smoking bedrooms, with names such as Rose, Poppy, Pine and Blue, and decor to match, are in converted stables in a rear courtyard; four are above bays where guests may park their car. They are well supplied with local information, books, magazines, mineral water, etc. Some have antique or period furniture; one has a freestanding, curtainless bath in the middle ("you can relax in it and watch TV") as well as a conventional shower room. Beds include four-posters and ones with brass or wooden heads. The daily-changing menu is "English with a French accent". Fish is a speciality. "Cooked breakfast is anything you want – splendid scrambled eggs." Stansted airport is only 15 minutes away. Some noise from passing traffic. (*Pat and Jeremy Temple*)

Open All year, except 1 week beginning Jan.
Rooms 8 double, all in rear courtyard. 2 on ground floor.
Facilities Reception/bar, restaurant; function/conference facilities.
Location Central (some traffic noise). Courtyard parking.
Restrictions No smoking: restaurant, bedrooms. No dogs in public rooms.
Credit cards Access, Amex, Visa.
Terms [1996] B&B: single £55, double £90–£100. Alc lunch £34; set dinner £21.50 and £32.50. Weekend rate for diners. **V**

For details of the Voucher scheme see page xxx.

GREAT LONGSTONE Derbyshire Map 3

The Croft *Tel* (01629) 640278
Great Longstone
nr Bakewell DE45 1TF

A Victorian house in secluded, slightly wild grounds in the heart of the Peak District, an area of outstanding natural beauty. It is run by Allan and Lynne Macaskill (he is front-of-house, she is chef), supported by a huge black labrador and some cats. Its most remarkable feature is the imposing two-storey main hall, with a lantern ceiling, a galleried landing off which the pretty bedrooms lead, and rose-pink walls hung with a collection of watercolour landscapes. Guests are welcomed with tea and biscuits. Home-cooked dinners are served at 7.30. No choice of main course; guests are asked to select the first two courses in the late afternoon. "The atmosphere is warm and friendly," write 1996 inspectors. "With caring hosts and staff. Dinner was mostly good, though there were some odd combinations of flavours. Service, by waitresses with white blouses and black skirts, was charming. Everyone was having a good time. But banal country / pop piped music detracted from the atmosphere; it was as out of character as the processed orange juice and packaged butter and jams at breakfast. The bedside lights were hopeless, and the bath towels small. If these minor matters were put right, this could be a first-rate hotel." More reports, please.

Open 7 Feb–31 Dec. Restaurant closed for lunch.
Rooms 8 double, 1 single. 1 accessible for ♿. No telephone.
Facilities Lift. 2 lounges, bar, restaurant. 3½-acre grounds: croquet, pitch-and-put. Fishing nearby.
Location 3 miles N of Bakewell. Take A6; right after 1¾ miles on to A6020: left after ¾ mile.
Restrictions No smoking in restaurant. Guide dogs only.
Credit cards Access, Visa.
Terms B&B: single £60, double £97; D,B&B: single £81.50, double £140. Set dinner £21.50. 2-day, Christmas, New Year packages. 1-night bookings sometimes refused far in advance. *V*

GREAT MILTON Oxfordshire Map 2

Le Manoir aux Quat'Saisons *Tel* (01844) 278881
Great Milton OX44 7PD *Fax* (01844) 278847

César award in 1985

This celebrated manor (Relais & Châteaux), with two *Michelin* stars for Raymond Blanc's inimitable cooking, stands by the church in a peaceful village near Oxford. Its immaculate gardens have statue-dotted lawns, an "exquisite selection of plants and trees, and luscious vegetable and herb gardens". Inside, fine fabrics, and antique and period furniture abound. The bedrooms "contain every luxury imaginable". Some, in the main house, face the front and the carpark; those in the extension have a private terrace; there's a romantic round one in a converted dovecote. Children are genuinely welcomed; they have their own menu, devoid of fish fingers. The eulogies continue: "Perfect. It could be pretentious and stuffy, but the staff are outstandingly relaxed and friendly." "A paradigm of the English country house hotel for the nineties, more innovative and less stuffy than some of the older generation. We were awestruck by the quality of everything we ate." "I do not remember such charm and natural grace in any other hotel. The superb *sommelier* is a judge of both pocket and taste." (*David and Kate Wooff, HR, and others*) Richard Branson is a partner in *Le Manoir*, but Raymond Blanc is in control. A health spa, created jointly with the fashion house Givenchy, is due to open in 1997. Some caveats: Extras can mount up. "More than enough staff at most times, but not at breakfast." "It is an international bolt hole, and difficult to get into at short notice."

Open All year.
Rooms 3 suites, 16 double. 9 in garden extension. Some on ground floor.
Facilities 2 lounges, restaurant; function room. 27-acre grounds: gardens, swimming pool, croquet, tennis, lake, fishing.
Location 7 miles SE of Oxford. From London: M40 exit 7, 1 mile, 2nd right. From Oxford: A40, A329 at Milton Common towards Wallingford, 2nd right. Coach service from *The Lanesborough Hotel*, Hyde Park Corner, London (11 am and 6 pm; £35 return).
Restrictions No smoking in 1 dining room. No dogs in house (free kennels).
Credit cards All major cards accepted.
Terms [1996] No single rates. Double room £185–£285, suite £345–£395. Breakfast: continental £9.50, cooked £14.50. Midweek breaks. Set lunch Mon–Sat £29.50; *menu gourmand* (lunch and dinner) £69; full alc £75. Child's menu £12. Cooking courses.

GREAT SNORING Norfolk — Map 2

The Old Rectory — *Tel* (01328) 820597
Barsham Road — *Fax* (01328) 820048
Great Snoring, Fakenham NR21 0HP

Old manor, Elizabethan in origin with Victorian additions, idyllically set in large walled garden by church in unspoilt village. Polished floor tiles, dark wood furniture; dining room with mullioned windows, heavy oak beams, good silver, plate and glass. 6 bedrooms: comfortable rather than luxurious; some quite small, others spacious, with good antiques. Courteous welcome, excellent service. Substantial English dinners (no choice of main course). Closed 24–27 Dec. Unsuitable for ♿*. No smoking in dining room. Children by arrangement. No dogs. All major credit cards accepted. B&B: single £68, double £89–£91. Set dinner £22.50. More reports, please.*

GRIMSTON Norfolk — Map 2

Congham Hall — *Tel* (01485) 600250
Lynn Road — *Fax* (01485) 601191
Grimston, King's Lynn PE32 1AH

César award in 1994

"My mother and I (born 1909 and 1935 respectively) regard *Congham* as outstanding in comfort, service and cuisine. We were shown the utmost courtesy throughout our stay. The staff were not effusive, but kind, charming and thoughtful. We fully endorse *Michelin*'s accolade for the food [red 'Menu'], and welcomed the opportunity to eat in moderation rather than surfeit. Our two-day break offered rare pleasure and rare value for money." "Trevor and Christine Forecast's personal touch makes all the difference." "Represents everything one longs for in an English country house hotel and rarely finds." The Forecasts' handsome Georgian manor has large, manicured grounds with a colourful country garden, a fine herb garden, cricket pitch, swimming pool and tennis court. Fragrant home-grown flowers and baskets of pot-pourri fill the house. There's a beautiful drawing room and a formal orangery-style dining room, where modern British cooking "with a light touch" is served by chef Jonathan Nicholson. All appetites are catered for: there are two- and three-course fixed-price dinner menus with choice; also bar snacks, light room-service meals, and a flexible *carte* for lunch, which is served alfresco in fine weather. The bedrooms vary in size; some are small; impressive suites have luxurious bathrooms. (*Richard Sachs, RM Everett, and others*) Answering last year's cavil, Mr Forecast writes: "Each dish now has its own selection of vegetables."

Open All year.
Rooms 2 suites, 11 double, 1 single.
Facilities Lounge, bar, restaurant; boardroom; room service (£2 per person). 40-acre grounds: swimming pool, jacuzzi, tennis, cricket, parklands, orchards, stables. Coast, sandy beaches 10 miles; nature reserves, fishing, golf, riding nearby. Unsuitable for ♿.
Location 6 miles NE of King's Lynn. Right towards Grimston off A148; hotel 2½ miles on left. Do not go to Congham.
Restrictions No smoking in restaurant. No children under 12. Dogs in kennels only.
Credit cards All major cards accepted.
Terms [1996] B&B: single £69–£120, double £120–£135, suite £170–£189. Light lunch from *c.* £5; 2–3-course set lunch £25–£32. Weekend breaks all year; racing, shooting, Christmas breaks.

GULWORTHY Devon — Map 1

The Horn of Plenty

Tel/Fax (01822) 832528
Gulworthy, Tavistock PL19 8JD

Ian and Elaine Gatehouse's popular restaurant-with-rooms is in the foothills of Dartmoor, near Tavistock. It has a peaceful setting amid gardens and orchards, and wonderful views down to the Tamar valley. The simple, modern bedrooms are in converted stables, a few yards from the wisteria-clad Georgian main house. Each has a large balcony, where breakfast can be served, and a well-stocked mini-bar. In the restaurant, with picture windows and matching flowery wallpaper and curtains, chef Peter Gorton serves modern cooking with oriental influences on a fixed-price menu. High-quality local produce, game and fish ("specially good") are used; the desserts have won prizes. On Monday there's a cheaper three-course "pot luck" menu. The wine list is "interesting, with some expensive bottles, and a good selection of house wines of quality and value". "Welcoming and caring." "Impeccable attention to detail, lovely flowers everywhere, exquisite food." Breakfasts have been described as "decadent". (*M Horne, and others*) One visitor felt that tea-bags at breakfast let the side down.

Open All year, except Christmas. Restaurant closed for lunch Mon.
Rooms 7. 6 in coach house. Some on ground floor.
Facilities Ramps. Drawing room, bar area, restaurant; function room. 4-acre grounds: garden, orchards. Golf, riding, fishing, walking, sailing nearby.
Location 3 miles W of Tavistock. Right at Gulworthy Cross; 1st left.

Restrictions No smoking: restaurant, 2 bedrooms. No children under 13 (except Sun lunch). No dogs in public rooms.
Credit cards Access, Amex, Visa.
Terms [1996] B&B: single £63–£78, double £83–£98. English breakfast £7.50. Set lunch £10.50–£17.50, dinner £29.50 (Mon £19.50). 2-day breaks. V*

HADLEY WOOD Hertfordshire — Map 2

West Lodge Park NEW
Cockfosters Road
Hadley Wood EN4 0PY

Tel (0181) 440 8311
Fax (0181) 449 3698

Our only entry outside London within the M25 orbital. Owned by Beale family: William IV mansion, on A111, 1 mile S of M25, junction 24. 35-acre park with arboretum, lake, boating, croquet, etc; guests may use nearby health centre (free taxi ride). "Beautifully decorated" country house-style public rooms; fine collection of Stuart portraits, some by Beale ancestress, Mary. Winter classical music concerts. Well decorated and equipped bedrooms, with good bathroom. Modern/traditional cooking by award-winning chef, Peter Leggat, in modern split-level Cedar Restaurant (sometimes with pianist). Polite staff. Conference/business facilities. 32 double rooms, 13 single. 1 adapted for ♿. No smoking: restaurant, 19 bedrooms. No dogs. Access, Amex, Visa accepted. Rooms: single £77.50, double £110–£140. Breakfast (included at weekends) £10.50. Set lunch £23.50, dinner £29.50. More reports, please.

HAMBLETON Rutland — Map 2

Hambleton Hall
Hambleton, Oakham LE15 8TH

Tel (01572) 756991
Fax (01572) 724721

César award in 1985

Tim and Stefa Hart's grand Victorian mansion (Relais & Châteaux) has a "sublime setting" in manicured gardens with mature trees, on a peninsula in Rutland Water. Some of Britain's greatest treasure houses, Burghley, Belton, Boughton and Belvoir, are nearby. The house is decorated in sophisticated country house style: fine fabrics, good antiques and paintings; flowers everywhere. *Michelin* awards a star for the modern British cuisine of Aaron Patterson: "The cooking is very accomplished, with first-class ingredients; the food tastes as it should, though the presentation is sometimes a little florid. The staff are outstandingly pleasant and friendly throughout, from receptionists (well informed on returning guests by an efficient database) to the knowledgeable restaurant staff (with a strong French contingent). They all took time to exchange pleasantries with guests. Breakfasts are impeccable, though the continental one, included in the room rate, is fairly basic." "Exceptionally high standards in every department. Breakfast on a terrace overlooking Rutland Water, everything superbly laid out. Literate guide book in the bedroom (written by the owner)." "Seriously expensive, but luxury and panache never come cheaply." (*David and Kate Wooff, Eric Kellerman and Keiko Yoshioka, and others*) Guests paying top prices expect perfection. But mishaps do occur, even in the garden of Eden. A 1996 correspondent told us of several disappointments in one celebration weekend. An isolated fall from grace? We hope so.

Open All year.
Rooms 15 double.
Facilities Lift, ramp. Hall, drawing room, bar, dining room; small conference facilities, 2 private dining rooms. 17-acre grounds: swimming pool, tennis; lake with trout-fishing, windsurfing, sailing. Riding, shooting by arrangement.
Location 2 miles E of Oakham. Follow the Hambleton sign off A606 to Stamford.
Restriction Dogs by arrangement; not in public rooms, alone in bedrooms.
Credit cards All major cards accepted.
Terms B&B: single £125–£130, double £155–£285. English breakfast £12. Set lunch (2-course) £14.50, dinner (3-course) £37.50; full alc £45. 2-day break any time: D,B&B (for 2) £370. Winter rates. 1-night bookings sometimes refused Sat.

HARVINGTON Hereford and Worcester Map 3

The Mill at Harvington *Tel/Fax* (01386) 870688
Anchor Lane
Harvington, nr Evesham WR11 5NR

A Georgian house and red brick mill (with original features, eg cast iron bakery doors and wooden beams) in a peaceful setting. Its large garden (with hard tennis court, and swimming pool) runs down to the river Avon, where guests may fish for chub, roach, dace and barbel, and moor their boats. The hotel is owned and run by Simon and Jane Greenhalgh, with partners Richard and Sue Yeomans, and makes a useful base for visiting Stratford-upon-Avon, only ten miles away, and touring the Cotswolds. The bedrooms ("not enormous, but well equipped") enjoy the view of the river. The restaurant and lounge, with log fire in winter, overlook the garden. Cooking is a mixture of English and French, modern and traditional. "Exemplary" breakfasts include excellent wholemeal toast. "So consistent, I rarely go elsewhere for fear of being disappointed," ran a report last year. "The atmosphere is not grand or pompous; we feel valued, but never overwhelmed. Every member of staff is friendly and helpful. There is a wide choice on the menu, but dishes are willingly adapted for those who prefer plainer food or smaller portions; we never feel uncomfortable about asking. The wine list is excellent, with many half bottles, and the three-day breaks are fabulous value." (*Adam Mather; endorsed this year by Christina Baron*) Poor sound insulation in some bedrooms; and their lighting has been criticised.

Open All year, except 24–29 Dec.
Rooms 15 double. 3 on ground floor.
Facilities Ramp. Lounge, restaurant; private dining room. 8-acre grounds: swimming pool, tennis, 200 yds river frontage, fishing.
Location Turn S off B439 down Anchor La (coming from Stratford do not go in to Harvington).
Restrictions No smoking in restaurant. No children under 10. No dogs.
Credit cards All major cards accepted.
Terms B&B: single £50–£56, double £80–£88; D,B&B: single £69–£74, double £99–£110. Set lunch £14.25, dinner £22; full alc £28.75. 3-night breaks. 1-night bookings sometimes refused. *V*

> Important reminder: terms printed must be regarded as no more than a rough guide to the size of the bill to be expected at the end of your stay. For latest tariffs, it is vital that you check when booking.

HARWICH Essex **Map 2**

The Pier at Harwich NEW/BUDGET *Tel* (01225) 241212
The Quay *Fax* (01225) 551922
Harwich CO12 3HH

Handsome Victorian building (built for passengers on packet boats to Holland), overlooking busy harbour. Now owned (with Richard Wheeler) by Gerald Milsom of Maison Talbooth, *Dedham* (qv), *and housing renowned fish restaurant and 6 neat bedrooms. Nautical decor, fine collection of railway posters. "Charming, helpful management and staff; food exceptional by any standard." Parking. Closed 24–26 Dec. Unsuitable for ♿. No dogs. All major credit cards accepted. B&B: single £45, double £62.50–£72.50. English breakfast £4. Set lunch £13.50, dinner £17.50* (plus 10% service) *[1996]. More reports, please.*

HATCH BEAUCHAMP Somerset **Map 1**

Farthings BUDGET *Tel* (01823) 480664
Hatch Beauchamp, nr Taunton TA3 6SG *Fax* (01823) 481118

An elegant white-painted Georgian house in a secluded setting in a quiet old village, well placed for exploring Somerset, Devon and Dorset, but only three miles from the M5. The owners, David and Marie Barker, returned recently from the Far East, bringing furniture, china, fabrics, and "the decor is a pleasure to the eye". "The most pleasant, freshest stay for some time in a middle-price hotel," ran a report last year. "Mr Barker has loads of energy and steady enthusiasm which he imparts to his staff, all loyal and sincerely helpful. Good wine list." Bedrooms, some with a sitting area, are "artistically but unpretentiously decorated" and light, with an efficient bathroom. We'd be grateful for reports on the modern English cooking of the new chef, Jason Harmer.

Open All year. Restaurant closed Sun midday.
Rooms 9 double.
Facilities Lounge, reading room, bar, restaurant. 3-acre grounds: croquet. Golf nearby. Unsuitable for ♿.
Location Centre of village 5 miles SE of Taunton, signposted from A358 Taunton–Ilminster.
Restrictions No smoking: reading room. No dogs in public rooms.
Credit cards All major cards accepted.
Terms B&B: single £45–£60, double £55–£80; D,B&B £42.50–£75 per person. Alc lunch from £8, set dinner £18.50–£20. Short breaks from £42.50 per person per night; Christmas, New Year breaks. V*

HATTON Warwickshire **Map 3**

Northleigh House BUDGET *Tel* (01926) 484203
Five Ways Road *Fax* (01926) 484006
Hatton, Warwick CV35 7HZ

Sylvia Fenwick's no-smoking B&B, formerly her family home, is in a rural setting near Warwick, but only 30 minutes' drive from Birmingham. She is an enthusiastic decorator. Each bedroom has a different theme. The Blue Room (the priciest) has a bed in a blue curtained alcove, blue couches, pine furniture, a bamboo coffee table, a kitchenette, and a huge *en suite* bathroom "with masses of hot water, big soft towels, etc". Others include the Chinese Room, the Gold Room, Victoria, Poppy and the Studio Room. A hearty English breakfast (with a toaster at each table) is served in the pretty dining room overlooking the garden. The panelled lounge has a wood-burning stove, books and original paintings. A home-cooked evening meal or a supper tray can be arranged; there are pubs and restaurants nearby. "Friendly welcome, attractive room, service attentive but not fussy. Superb value," was a recent comment. More reports, please.

Open Feb–mid-Dec. Evening meals by arrangement.
Rooms 6 double, 1 single. 1 with kitchenette. 2 on ground floor. Pay-phone for guests.
Facilities Sitting room, dining room. Small garden; access to fields. Unsuitable for ♿.
Location 5 miles NW of Warwick. From A4177 at Five Ways roundabout take Shrewley turning for ½ mile.
Restrictions No smoking. No dogs in public rooms.
Credit card Access.
Terms B&B: single £28–£38, double £38–£55. Supper tray from £6.50; dinner £14.50.

HAWES North Yorkshire — Map 4

Stone House BUDGET
Sedbusk, nr Hawes
Wensleydale DL8 3PT
Tel (01969) 667571
Fax (01969) 667720

A turn-of-the-century house, owned and run by the Taplin family. It has a glorious, peaceful setting, just outside the market town of Hawes, overlooking the Wensleydale valley. Some bedrooms have their own conservatory, opening on to the garden. The Taplins' collections of antique thimbles, teapots, old Dinky toys, and vintage slot machines add interest to the public rooms. Substantial Yorkshire meals are accompanied by "for once, drinkable" house wines on a short list. "Welcome genuinely warm; delightful, helpful owners," wrote our inspector. "Bedroom with pink decor and wonderfully light (if not very private) conservatory, with bamboo chairs and oak table. Poor sound insulation, however, and the bathroom was not cosy. Blissful bar with roaring log fire. Nice oak-beamed dining room. Dinner for the most part fine – good plain cooking, served with care. Adequate breakfast." Dogs are welcome. All manner of special breaks are on offer.

Literary footnote The Taplins write: "The original owner of *Stone House* employed a gardener surnamed Jeeves. PG Wodehouse, while looking for a name for the butler character in his new novel, was watching a local cricket match. In to bat went Jeeves. Problem solved!"

Open Feb–end Dec.
Rooms 3 suites, 15 double, 1 single. 4 in coach house. 5 on ground floor.
Facilities Ramp. Lounge, library, billiard room, bar, dining room. 1-acre grounds: tennis, croquet. River Ure ¼ mile, fishing.
Location ¾ mile N of Hawes by Muker road. Over bridge, up steep hill, right towards Sedbusk; hotel 500 yds on left.
Restrictions No smoking in dining room. No dogs in dining room.
Credit cards Access, Visa.
Terms B&B £27.50–£39; D,B&B £44–£55.50. Set dinner £16.95. Christmas, New

Year house parties. Bargain breaks Oct–end Apr; specialist courses: photography, sheepdog training, bridge, flower arranging, landscape painting. *V*

HAWKRIDGE Somerset — Map 1

Tarr Steps Hotel — *Tel* (01643) 851293
Hawkridge, Dulverton TA22 9PY — *Fax* (01643) 851218

This Georgian ex-rectory is named for the rough stone Cyclopean bridge, owned by the National Trust, across the river Barle nearby. Approached by switchback country roads, it is peacefully set above the river valley, and is a sporting hotel *par excellence,* with six miles of salmon- and trout-fishing (and tuition for beginners), stabling for guests' horses, rough and formal shooting, and hunting. It was taken over in October 1995 by Sue and Shaun Blackmore, local people, who have carried out extensive repairs and redecoration (much needed). Visitors in early 1996 were well pleased: "A splendid five-day stay in beautiful countryside. Excellent welcome from very friendly, practical hosts. Pleasant bedroom. Jolly bar with deer and fox heads on the wall. In the drawing room, with open fire, games, local history books, you can be private or convivial. Decent and varied food. No sound at night except river and owls. Delightful atmosphere." Bedrooms "are blissfully free of telephones and TV". Children and dogs are welcomed – there is a two-bedroom cottage annexe that would be good for a family. The bar lunch menu has been much extended. Tea is included in the half board rate.

Open All year.
Rooms 10 double, 3 single. 2 in cottage annexe. 1 on ground floor. No telephone, TV, etc.
Facilities Lounge, bar, 2 dining rooms. 11-acre grounds: garden, stables and paddocks for guests' horses, dog kennels, 6 miles river fishing, 500 acres rough shooting. Hunting, tennis, squash, golf nearby.
Location 7 miles NW of Dulverton. Go to Hawkridge, then follow signs to Tarr Steps. Do *not* follow earlier signs to Tarr Steps; they lead to wrong side of river.
Restrictions No smoking in dining room. No dogs in lounge, dining room.
Credit cards Access, Visa.
Terms [1996] B&B: single £30–£45, double £70–£90; D,B&B: single £55–£59.50, double £105–£119. Snack lunch from £2; set dinner £25. Painting, fishing, rest and relaxation courses. Discount for 5 or more nights. Christmas, New Year packages. *V*

HAWKSHEAD Cumbria — Map 4

Highfield House — *Tel* (0153 94) 36344
Hawkshead Hill — *Fax* (0153 94) 36793
Hawkshead LA22 0PN

"A perfect stay: peace and quiet, supreme cleanliness and wonderful food," writes a honeymoon couple of Pauline and Jim Bennett's unpretentious Lakeland stone house. Others, too, have praised this "most excellent small hotel": "Terrific value for money, with the best ever breakfasts: superb Loch Fyne kippers and wonderful fried bread." Just outside a showplace village on the road to Coniston, it stands on high ground in large gardens with fine trees and shrubs and a glorious view. "The bar is small but attractive, the lounge well supplied with books and local information, and the bedrooms well thought out," ran an earlier report. "But most important is the welcome given by the Bennetts. They are accommodating, and interested in their guests without being intrusive." Washing and drying facilities are available. Children of all ages are welcomed: cots, baby seats, high teas, are provided. In the restaurant, open to outside diners, cooking is English with continental influences, with choices for each course, including a vegetarian option. (*Mr and Mrs N Mullis*) One reader would have liked subtler lighting in the dining room, and was put off by a "bizarre combination of flavours" in her dinner.

Open New Year, Feb–Dec.
Rooms 9 double, 2 single. No telephone.
Facilities Lounge, bar, restaurant; laundry facilities, drying room. 2½-acre garden. Free use of nearby leisure club. Fishing nearby. Unsuitable for ♿.
Location ¾ mile W of Hawkshead on B5285 to Coniston.
Restrictions No smoking in restaurant. No dogs in public rooms.
Credit cards Access, Visa.
Terms B&B £35–£40; D,B&B £51–£56. Set dinner £17. Snacks and packed lunches available. Winter breaks. No 1-night bookings New Year, Easter. Children under 2 free; 2–12 sharing with parents: B&B £12.50.

Rough Close BUDGET *Tel* (0153 94) 36370
Hawkshead LA22 0QF

An unassuming small hotel, "sparkling with warmth and friendliness", and "great value for money". It is just outside Hawkshead, overlooking Esthwaite Water. There is good walking from the grounds. Many visitors are regulars, who sing the praise of the owners, Tony and Marylin Gibson, "a charming couple, genuinely interested in their visitors", and the food: "English at its best, with a wide choice of vegetables and mouthwatering home-made puddings." Dinner is at 7 pm – five courses, with no choice except alternative desserts. Helpings are generous; nothing is over-elaborate. Mr Gibson serves, acting also as wine waiter (each menu suggests a wine to match the food). Coffee is taken round the fire in the sitting room; later guests may adjourn to the small bar. Substantial breakfasts, between 8.45 and 9.15 am, "set you up for the day". All the bedrooms have private facilities, but one bathroom is not *en suite*. (*Shaun and Sandra Tobin, and others*)

Open Late Mar–early Nov. Lunch not served.
Rooms 5 double. No telephone/TV.
Facilities Lounge, bar, dining room. 1-acre garden: *boules*. Lake, boating, fishing nearby. Unsuitable for ♿.
Location 1¼ miles S of Hawkshead on Newby Bridge road.
Restrictions No smoking: dining room, bedrooms. No children under 12. Dogs in bar only.
Credit cards Access, Visa.
Terms [1996] B&B £25–£27.50; D,B&B £35.50–£39.50. Set dinner £12 (£14 to non-residents). Reductions for long stays.

If you have had recent experience of a good hotel that ought to be in the *Guide*, please write to us at once. Report forms are to be found at the back of the book. Procrastination is the thief of the next edition.

HAWORTH West Yorkshire — Map 4

Weaver's BUDGET — *Tel* (01535) 643822
15 West Lane — *Fax* (01535) 644832
Haworth BD22 8DU

A restaurant-with-rooms composed of three adjoining traditional cottages on the cobbled main street of the Brontes' village. "Altogether an excellent place," writes a regular visitor. "It offers comfort, friendliness and super food in a beautiful location – fine moorland scenery all around. The decor is a delight: old photographs, modern paintings, antiques, bric-à-brac, and mementoes of the Yorkshire spinners' craft. Nothing that intrudes or obstructs. The bedrooms, up a narrow staircase, are all different, all beautifully furnished, and supplied with tea, fresh milk and satellite TV. The bar and lounge can be crowded in a friendly sort of way. The young staff are without exception willing and pleasant. Colin Rushworth is an archetypal bluff Yorkshireman, an excellent host who fulfils the front-of-house role perfectly, but has little tolerance of pretension. Jane Rushworth is a talented chef. The food, northern cooking with a light touch, is difficult to fault, particularly at these prices. Everything from bread to ice-cream is made on the premises. Always a couple of vegetarian options. There's a wide selection of wines, some quite unusual, with a low mark-up, and honestly priced half bottles. Music is unobtrusive, an interesting mixture of jazz, blues, opera – no 'easy listening', thank goodness." There's a reduced-price menu on weekdays if you order by 7.15 pm. English breakfast is served at flexible times. (*BCK*)

Open All year, Tues–Sat from 6.45 pm, except 2 weeks after Christmas, 2 weeks midsummer, Sun lunch in winter.
Rooms 2 double, 2 single.
Facilities Lounge, bar, restaurant. Unsuitable for ♿.
Location By Bronte Parsonage Museum: use its pay and display carpark. Ignore sign for Bronte village/Tourist Information.
Restrictions No smoking in restaurant. No dogs.
Credit cards All major cards accepted.
Terms B&B: single £49.50, double £69.50. Set menu (6.45–7.15 pm, Sun lunch) £12.50; full alc £25. *V*

HAYFIELD Derbyshire — Map 4

The Old Bank House BUDGET — *Tel* (01663) 747354
Market Street
Hayfield SK12 5EP

Welcoming guest house ("everything about it is good") in listed Georgian building with many original features. By river in pretty village, W of Buxton; set back from traffic. Caring hostess, Mrs Sheila Collier – guests "leave as friends". 4 beautiful, spacious bedrooms: 1 family, 1 with four-poster and William Morris wallpaper, 1 with brass bed; separate bathroom, shower room (bathrobes provided). Unsuitable for ♿. No smoking. Credit cards not accepted. B&B: single £20, double £38. Evening meal by arrangement £12. More reports, please.

HAYLING ISLAND Hampshire — Map 2

Cockle Warren Cottage
36 Seafront
Hayling Island PO11 9HL

Tel (01705) 464961
Fax (01705) 464838

Hayling Island, reached by a bridge from the mainland, is in Chichester and Langstone harbours on the Hampshire/Sussex border, and is known for its warm climate. Here, on the seafront, is David and Diane Skelton's tile-hung cottage hotel, bedecked in summer with geraniums. In winter a log fire burns in the lounge which has antique furniture, magazines and games. A conservatory dining room overlooks the heated swimming pool (lit at night). Bedrooms are decorated in country style; each has a trouser press, an iron, playing cards and a carafe of Madeira; two have a sea view and a four-poster. Last year's nominator was enthusiastic about Mrs Skelton's English/continental cooking, served in generous portions. No choice at dinner except for dessert, but prior discussion is encouraged. "Breads and brioches are home-made. There is a small but inexpensive wine list. Bell pushes at table summon the next course." One account of a booking muddle and a lack of welcome. More reports, please.

Open All year.
Rooms 1 suite, 5 double. 2 in barn annexe. Some on ground floor.
Facilities Lounge, conservatory restaurant. ⅓-acre garden: swimming pool. Sea, sandy beach 70 yds: bathing, fishing, sailing. Golf nearby.
Location Over bridge, S to seafront, turn left; *c.* 1 mile on left. Carpark.
Restrictions No smoking: restaurant, bedrooms. No children under 12. No dogs in public rooms.
Credit cards Access, Amex, Visa.
Terms B&B: single £45–£65, double £68–£96; D,B&B: single £60–£91.50, double £121–£149. Cooked breakfast £3.50–£9.50. Set dinner £26.50. 1-night bookings sometimes refused. *V*

HAZLETON Gloucestershire — Map 3

Windrush House BUDGET
Hazleton, nr Cheltenham GL54 4EB

Tel (01451) 860364

Mrs Sydney Harrison's modern stone-built guest house, in quiet setting on edge of hamlet in heart of the North Cotswolds. Wonderful views. "Cosy and appealing." Modest accommodation. "Food which puts many plusher establishments to shame: soft dark home-made bread, tender young vegetables, flavoursome meat and delicious sweets. Breakfasts excellent too." Small garden. 4 bedrooms, 2 with shower; 2 on ground floor. Unsuitable for ♿. Closed mid-Dec–mid-Jan approx. No smoking. No dogs. B&B: single £22–£25, double £40–£44. Light supper from £10, set dinner £18.75–£20. Endorsed this year: "Dinner a gourmet delight, excellent breakfast, rooms attractively furnished" – but we'd be glad of fuller reports.

> Our italicised entries indicate hotels which are worth considering but which, for various reasons – inadequate information, lack of feedback, ambivalent reports – do not at the moment warrant a full entry. We particularly welcome comments on these hotels.

HEADLAM Durham — Map 4

Headlam Hall — *Tel* (01325) 730238
Headlam, Gainford — *Fax* (01325) 730790
Darlington DL2 3HA

"Beautiful surroundings and excellent facilities." "Courteous, considerate staff. The three-day break was excellent value." Recent endorsements for the Robinson family's creeper-covered manor, part Jacobean, part Georgian. It is peacefully set in mature gardens within its own large farm, in a hamlet in lower Teesdale. "It has been furnished quietly and sympathetically with the sort of furniture folk acquire in their homes over the century," wrote the nominator. "Local people dine here, and it is a restful place for a country holiday. The public rooms are warm, with huge log fires. Bar drinks are of good quality, and the wine list is not long, but well chosen and not horribly expensive. In the pretty dining room, with immaculately set tables, the cooking is traditional English, with plenty of choice." Recent opinions of the dinners vary: "Good, though slightly repetitive, with lots of cream in sauces." "Unexciting in choice and average in execution, but good breakfast." The best bedrooms are well furnished, with thick fitted carpets, but one couple's room was small and stuffy. The hotel's conference and banqueting trade is kept well away from residents. (*Charles Sommer, John and Helen Bennett*)

Open All year, except Christmas Day.
Rooms 2 suites, 24 double. 3 on ground floor. 9 in coach house 20 yds.
Facilities Lounge, 2 bars, restaurant, conservatory; ballroom, conference facilities; snooker room; indoor swimming pool. 100-acre farm: 4-acre garden, trout lake, fishing, croquet, tennis.
Location 7 miles W of Darlington. 1 mile N of Gainford off A67 to Barnard Castle.
Restriction No dogs in bedrooms, public rooms.
Credit cards All major cards accepted.
Terms B&B: single £55–£65, double £70–£80, suite £95. Set lunch £12; full alc £27. 2-night breaks: D,B&B £49–£54 per person per night.

HEDDON'S MOUTH Devon — Map 1

Heddon's Gate Hotel BUDGET — *Tel* (01598) 763313
Heddon's Mouth, Parracombe — *Fax* (01598) 763363
Barnstaple EX31 4PZ

César award in 1990

"We've been coming for almost 20 years, and regard it almost as a second home. It is quietly situated in some of the finest walking country in England. To spend a good day out, after an excellent breakfast, and return to be cosseted in unpretentious style is a real treat." "Food one of the main attractions: inventive but not outlandish; attractively served." Recent tributes to this turn-of-the-century Swiss/Victorian lodge, in large grounds with steeply terraced gardens and lovely views, on the edge of Exmoor. Here, proprietor/chef for 28 years, Robert Deville, aided by front-of-house manager, Heather Hurrell, and a long-serving staff, "dispenses quiet hospitality". The faithful clientele appreciate the "real generosity, eg, fresh fruit in the bedroom *every* day", the "wonderful location", and the "high standard of comfort". Bedrooms, named for their original use, eg, Grandmama's Room, the Servants' Quarters, vary greatly in size, style and view, and are priced accordingly. The Indian Room and its bathroom are particularly liked. There is an "excellent" library, and a large dining room where dinner with limited choice is served promptly at 8. A generous afternoon tea is included in the rates. The sitting room has been redecorated: "It is now more Victorian than Edwardian," writes Mr Deville, "with large French tapestries depicting the four seasons." The two-bedroomed cottages in the grounds are "good for guests with dogs". (*SC and PM Glover, JP Berryman; also PE Carter, Linda Gillinson, and others*)

Open End Mar–1st week Nov.
Rooms 4 suites (3 in cottages with access for ♿), 9 double, 1 single.
Facilities Lounge, library, piano room, bar, dining room; table-tennis room. 20-acre grounds. Near sea; river, fishing, riding, pony-trekking nearby.
Location 6 miles W of Lynton. From A39, after 3 miles, take road to Martinhoe/Woody Bay; follow signs for Hunter's Inn; hotel drive on right.
Restrictions No smoking in dining room. Children "must be old enough to dine at 8pm". No dogs in dining room.
Credit cards Access, Amex, Visa.
Terms D,B&B £47.50–£67.70. Set dinner £25. 3-day breaks. 1-night bookings occasionally refused. Children accommodated in parents' room 50% reduction.

HELSTON Cornwall — Map 1

Nansloe Manor BUDGET
Meneage Road
Helston TR13 0SB
Tel (01326) 574691
Fax (01326) 564680

A "delightful" Grade II listed Georgian manor with Victorian additions, in a secluded valley on the edge of Helston. It is set down a long drive, in wooded grounds surrounded by farmland. The welcoming owners, John and Wendy Pyatt, "work incredibly hard, and seem to be always at hand". Bedrooms enjoy "a soothing country view". The main one, No 3, has a large seating area. The others are fairly small. "But the ambience of care and competence more than compensates. The housekeeping is immaculate." In the large lounge are fresh flowers, watercolours by local artists, and games and cards for rainy days. Breakfasts include yogurt, proper toast, and dishes of marmalade and honey – "nothing packaged". The food on the long dinner menu is English in style, using fresh local produce: "Very reliable, with excellent fish dishes. All desserts come with clotted cream. The short wine list is eclectic and reasonable value." Portions are over-large for some. "An air of efficiency and attention to detail pervades the place; members of staff contribute to a marvellously relaxed atmosphere. An ideal centre for exploring the Lizard peninsula and west Cornwall." (*Richard Creed, Ian and Dorothy Young; also David B Gerden*) Occasional disturbances may be expected from the Culdrose Naval Air Station nearby.

Open All year, except Christmas/New Year.
Rooms 6 double, 1 single.
Facilities Lounge with bar, dining room. 4½-acre grounds: walled garden, croquet. Sea 1 mile. Unsuitable for ♿.
Location 1 mile S of town. Signposted off A394. Details on brochure.
Restrictions No smoking in restaurant. No children under 12. Dogs in cars only.
Credit cards Access, Visa.
Terms B&B £37–£54; D,B&B £48–£68. Set Sun lunch £12.50; full alc £26.50. Spring and autumn breaks.

HENLEY-ON-THAMES Oxfordshire — Map 2

The Red Lion — *Tel* (01491) 572161
Hart Street — *Fax* (01491) 410039
Henley-on-Thames RG9 2AR

Wisteria-clad 16th-century red brick inn, owned by Miller family of Durrants, *London (qv), on Thames at crossroads by bridge at end of Royal Regatta course (some traffic noise). Antique panelling in public rooms, flagstones and rowing memorabilia in bar. French Mediterranean cooking, "with a light touch", in riverside restaurant. Bedrooms have antique and reproduction furniture, flowery fabrics, marble-tiled bathrooms. New manager (Mr Buswell, formerly of the* Swan, *Bibury) and new chef in 1996. Earlier visitors praised warm atmosphere, kind, professional staff and food; we'd like reports on the recent developments, please. 26 rooms. Large carpark. Unsuitable for ♿. Smoking in bedrooms discouraged. No dogs. Access, Amex, Visa accepted. Room: single £79, double £99. Breakfast: continental £5.95, English £8.95. D,B&B: single £95.50; double £125. Set lunch/dinner £17.50; full alc £24.50.* *V*

HINTLESHAM Suffolk — Map 2

Hintlesham Hall — *Tel* (01473) 652268
Hintlesham, Ipswich IP8 3NS — *Fax* (01473) 652463

A stunning country house, "classy, welcoming and comfortable", Tudor in origin, with a Georgian façade. Its interior is sumptuous, with beautiful panelling and mouldings, fine fabrics and antiques. The bedrooms vary in size and style; some are huge and opulent; some have a gas log fire, some the real thing. Guests' accommodation is upgraded at no extra cost when possible. In its vast grounds there is an 18-hole championship golf course, well hidden by trees; its clubhouse is an agreeable place for a light lunch. Many other outdoor pursuits are available (see below). "Everything continues as beautifully as ever," write regular visitors. "We were particularly impressed by the quality of the service. Breakfasts are impeccable." "Extremely well managed by Tim Sunderland. His staff are charming and efficient." Chef Alan Ford cooks meals "in elegant country house style", with first-class raw materials. "They are lighter nowadays – a welcome development – with a slightly Mediterranean influence." The wine list is "superb – the house recommendations are always worth trying". The breaks are "good value". (*Kate and David Wooff, Pat and Jeremy Temple*)

Open All year.
Rooms 4 suites, 29 double. 11 in courtyard wing 20 yds. 8 on ground floor.
Facilities 4 lounges, 3 dining rooms; conference/function facilities; snooker room. 175-acre grounds: 18-hole golf course with club house, swimming pool, tennis, croquet, trout lake, fishing, riding, shooting. Unsuitable for ♿.
Location 5 miles W of Ipswich on A1071 to Sudbury.
Restrictions No smoking in dining rooms. "Good children and good dogs welcomed", but no dogs in house.
Credit cards All major cards accepted.
Terms B&B: single from £89, double from £110, suite from £210. English breakfast £7.50. Set lunch £19.50, dinner £25; full alc £37. 2-day breaks; golf breaks; Christmas package. 1-night bookings refused bank holidays. Child accommodated in parents' room £10.

HINTON CHARTERHOUSE Somerset Map 2

Homewood Park
Hinton Charterhouse
nr Bath BA3 6BB

Tel (01225) 723731
Fax (01225) 723820

Frank and Sara Gueuning's mainly 18th-century house, with skilful later additions, is set in lovely grounds in a village on the edge of the Limpley Stoke valley, near Bath. The decor is "fresh, warm and country house-ish", with antiques, oriental rugs, and works by local artists on display; log fires warm the lounge and bar in winter. Bedrooms are spacious and luxurious; most overlook the well-cared-for garden. There are two new suites this year, (one sponsored by Marks and Spencer). A new chef, too, Gary Jones, who has worked at the *Manoir aux Quat'Saisons*, Great Milton (*qv*), and the *Waterside*, Bray (*qv*). A Californian visitor in 1996 was impressed: "Total excellence and professionalism, yet relaxed and friendly, a rare mix. The owners were in evidence, but not pushy. The bedrooms were the best of our trip, and the food was better than excellent." Others have thought it "pricey, but worth every penny". (*Tom Rulley, and others*)

Open All year.
Rooms 2 suites, 19 double.
Facilities 2 lounges, bar, restaurant; private dining room, conference room. 14-acre grounds: tennis, swimming pool, croquet, parkland.
Location 6 miles SE of Bath opposite Hinton Priory. Left off A36 at Freshford. Some traffic noise; rooms double-glazed.
Restrictions No smoking: restaurant, some bedrooms. No dogs.
Credit cards All major cards accepted.
Terms B&B: single £95–£215, double £98–£190, suite £250; D,B&B: single £125–£245, double £160–£255, suite £315. Set lunch £19.50, dinner £37; full alc £50. Winter breaks; Christmas package.

HOCKLEY HEATH Warwickshire Map 3

Nuthurst Grange
Nuthurst Grange Lane
Hockley Heath B94 5NL

Tel (01564) 783972
Fax (01564) 783919

An Edwardian house, approached by an immaculate drive through well-maintained, spacious grounds (superb views). It has "a genuine country house feel", congenial owners, David (the chef) and Darryl Randolph, very much in evidence, and a helpful staff. The decor is traditional, "comfortable, but not showy", with lavish use of fabrics, and stylish flower arrangements. Two light sitting rooms overlook the garden. The restaurant is set out in a string of rooms, with well-spaced tables. Cooking is "English in the light French style", and generally liked by *Guide* readers. Desserts are particularly praised; there is an impressive wine list. The bedrooms are spacious, with a sitting area, "and the sort of extras one really needs". "Suitable for children who are well behaved," says the brochure. The hotel is only five miles from Birmingham airport (there's some traffic noise from the M40 half a mile away). One couple this year criticised the restaurant service and the English breakfast. More reports, please.

Open All year.
Rooms 1 suite, 15 double. 2 on ground floor.

Facilities Ramp. 2 lounges, restaurant; 2 private dining rooms, function room. 7½-acre grounds: croquet, helipad. Riding, hunting, tennis, golf, clay pigeon-shooting, canal boating nearby.
Location Off A3400 ½ mile S of Hockley Heath. Turn right at hotel sign.
Restrictions No smoking: restaurant, 1 lounge. No dogs.
Credit cards All major cards accepted.
Terms [1996] B&B: single £95, double £115–£130, suite £140. English breakfast £9.90. Set lunch £16.90–£24.90, dinner £24.90–£42.50. Weekend breaks.

HOLDENBY Northamptonshire — Map 2

Lynton House — *Tel/Fax* (01604) 770777
Holdenby Road
Holdenby NN6 8DJ

Restaurant-with-rooms, Victorian former rectory, in open country 5 miles NW of Northampton. Engaging Italian owner, Carlo Bertozzi. His English wife, Carol, serves good classic and modern Italian cooking in smart bay-windowed restaurant; plenty of choice; reasonable prices. Excellent breakfast in conservatory. 5 good-sized bedrooms, with shower, overlook pretty garden or surrounding fields. Closed Sun, midday Mon/Sat, Christmas, 2 weeks summer. Unsuitable for ♿. No smoking: conservatory, 1 bedroom. No children under 5/6. No dogs. Access, Amex, Visa accepted. B&B: single £53, double £65. English breakfast £7.50. Set lunch from £14.25, dinner £23.75. More reports, please. *V*

HOPESAY Shropshire — Map 3

The Old Rectory BUDGET — *Tel* (01588) 660245
Hopesay, Craven Arms SY7 8HD

"Not really a hotel, but a private house in which we felt entirely at home, and like family friends after only two days. Roma Villar is a superb cook and Michael Villar is justly proud of his breakfasts." "A lovely house, beautifully decorated and equipped. Very good wines." "A real tonic for jaded townees." "Charming, courteous owners." Recent accolades for this Wolsey Lodge member, a 17th-century ex-rectory. It stands in landscaped gardens by a 12th-century church in a hamlet in the Clun valley – the heart of Housman country. It has antique and period furniture, and books and a fine stone fireplace in the lounge. The spacious bedrooms, all with *en suite* bathroom, have TV, armchairs, and many extras; two have an emperor-size bed. Breakfast includes home-made yogurt and preserves, fruit salad, home-baked bread, and traditional cooked items. The Aga-cooked dinners (no choice until dessert) are served at 8 pm, generally communally. "I try to use food in season and adjust menus to suit individual tastes and also weather conditions," writes Mrs Villar. (*M Kershaw, Roger and Jytte Hardisty, Bruce and Pat Orman*) Good birdwatching; there are RSPB bird hides nearby. Light sleepers should ask for a room out of earshot of the church bells. No smoking.

Open All year, except Christmas. Occasionally at other times.
Rooms 1 suite, 2 double. No telephone.
Facilities Drawing room, dining room. 2-acre grounds. Unsuitable for ♿.
Location 3 miles W of Craven Arms. B4368 to Clun. At Aston-on-Clun turn right over humpback bridge to Hopesay. Hotel 1½ miles, by church.

Restrictions No smoking. No children under 12. No dogs.
Credit cards None accepted.
Terms B&B £32; D,B&B £50.

HORLEY Surrey Map 2

Langshott Manor *Tel* (01293) 786680
Langshott, Horley RH6 9LN *Fax* (01293) 783905

"To slide into the finest bedlinen on the most comfortable beds we know, after a delicious candlelit dinner, and awake to the birdsong which abounds in the lush gardens – this is the only way to begin or end a holiday." Thus an American visitor to this refuge from nearby Gatwick (not on a flight path), with "dedicated hosts", New Zealand-born Geoffrey, Rish and Christopher Noble. Reached down a quiet country lane, it is a Grade II Elizabethan manor in a traditional English garden ("always improving") with roses, herbaceous borders and a lake. It cossets travellers in every way: airport collection/delivery service in the house Jaguar; traditional evening meals by an inglenook fire; early morning tea with newspapers and shortbread. Breakfasts include fresh fruit, a variety of compotes, and excellent cooked dishes. Reasonably priced snacks are also available. It has spacious reception rooms with log fires, and large bedrooms "with nice touches everywhere: books, magazines, sewing basket, bath salts in large jar, plants and flowers". One is the old nursery at the top: "Comforting and homelike as a nursery should be; its bathroom has a freestanding, clawfooted bath, Victorian-style loo, and lots of humorous touches." (*Romney Bathurst, David and Jennifer Williams*) Guests may leave their car here for up to two weeks while they are abroad.

Open All year, except 25–30 Dec.
Rooms 8 double. 1 in mews 50 yds. 1, on ground floor, with ♿ access.
Facilities Sitting room, morning room/bar, 2 dining rooms; conference/private dining room. 3-acre garden. 2 weeks' free parking; courtesy car to Gatwick (2½ miles).
Location From A23 in Horley take Ladbroke Rd (*Chequers* hotel roundabout) to Langshott. Hotel ¾ mile on right.
Restrictions No smoking: restaurant, bedrooms. No dogs.
Credit cards All major cards accepted.
Terms B&B: single £91–£95, double £114–£130. Set lunch £24, dinner £26. 2-day breaks Oct–end Apr.

HORTON Dorset Map 2

Northill House BUDGET *Tel* (01258) 840407
Horton, Wimborne Minster BH21 7HL

"Thoroughly recommended for an unpretentious country weekend." This 19th-century red brick former farmhouse is set in well-kept grounds, adjoining a farm in an isolated situation ("no sound to disturb you until the birds are up"). The owners, Courtney and Joy Garnsworthy, and son Brendan, are "welcoming, nice and characterful without being overly present". The decor, with Victorian wallpaper, old pine furniture, log fires in winter, and fresh flowers, is in keeping with the house. Plenty of accolades this year: "Courteous, thoughtful service. One of the best hotel beds we've slept in. We felt really rested when we left." "Good reading light over the bed (quite rare); lots of thoughtful touches, such as fresh milk for bedroom tea-making." "Pleasing public rooms, with a wonderful selection of interesting books, and some nice paintings." "Splendid" breakfasts, served in a large conservatory, include freshly squeezed orange juice, home-made preserves and toasted home-made bread. Dinner, at 7.30, is "plain English cooking" (no choice of starter or main course, but guests are consulted in advance), and is enjoyed. "But it is not a gastronomic experience, and the standard is variable; they seem to operate a rota for cooking." Some guests have rung the changes, dining at *Moonacre*, a *Good Food Guide*-rated restaurant in nearby Alderholt, run by the Garnsworthys' daughter, Barbara. The hotel has won an award for its facilities for the disabled. (*Sholto Cross, Ann Lawson Lucas, Mrs JR Bainbridge, and others*)

Open Mid-Feb–20 Dec.
Rooms 9 double. 1 equipped for ♿. 4 in adjoining annexe.
Facilities Lounge, bar, dining room, conservatory. 2-acre grounds. Golf, fishing, riding nearby.
Location 7 miles N of Wimborne Minster, ½ mile from B3078.
Restrictions No smoking in dining room. No children under 8. No pets.
Credit cards Access, Amex, Visa.
Terms B&B: single £39, double £68. Snack lunches. Set dinner £14. 3- and 7-night breaks. **V**

HOVINGHAM North Yorkshire — Map 4

The Worsley Arms — *Tel* (01653) 628234
Hovingham YO6 4LA — *Fax* (01653) 628130

Old coaching inn overlooking green of unspoilt village 17 miles N of York. Traditional decor: chintz, antiques, hunting and cricketing prints. Nice touches in comfortable bedrooms: champagne, mineral water, bathroom goodies. Bar, bistro, pleasant dining room; new chef in 1996, Andrew Jones, serves modern British cooking. Good breakfasts. Willing staff. ½-acre garden. Unsuitable for ♿. No dogs in public rooms. 19 bedrooms, some in cottages. Access, Amex, Visa accepted. B&B: single £55–£60, double £75–£80; D,B&B: single £75–£80, double £115–£125. Set lunch £15–£16, dinner £23.50. More reports, please.

HUNTSHAM Devon — Map 1

Huntsham Court — *Tel* (01398) 361365
Huntsham Valley — *Fax* (01398) 361456
nr Tiverton EX16 7NA

César award in 1988

This unique establishment, in a secluded Devon setting, received its *César* for "utterly acceptable mild eccentricity". Run in laid-back style by Mogens and Andrea Bolwig, it is a choice example of high-Victorian architecture, with huge rooms, massive fireplaces, impressive panelling and marble pillars. It is often taken over by private parties. Dinner (good home-cooking) is communal; there's no menu, but an "amazing wine cellar". The house is eclectically furnished, and dedicated to music. There are pianos everywhere – a grand in the hall, uprights in the drawing room and bar, and a pianola in the dining room, and there is a vast collection of records and cassettes. The bedrooms (no locks on doors, no telephone or TV) are named after composers, and have a pre-war radio. Beethoven has a log fire, a seven-foot-wide bed, a baby grand piano, and two free-standing old bathtubs, with silver claws, side by side in its bathroom (most bathrooms are huge). Breakfast is served until noon; free tea and coffee is available all day in the butler's pantry. *Huntsham*'s motto is *Dulce nihil facere*. It is too casual for some; others find it "addictive".

Open All year.
Rooms 3 suites, 11 double.
Facilities Drawing room, music room, bar, great hall/dining room, library/snooker room; mini-gym, sauna. 8-acre grounds: tennis, croquet, lake (fishing), bicycles. Golf, shooting, riding nearby.
Location From M5 exit 27, sharp right on bridge in Sampford Peverell, 2 miles to Uplowman, then 4 miles to Huntsham.
Restriction No dogs.
Credit cards Access, Visa.
Terms B&B: single £85, double £115, suite £135. Set dinner: £30. House parties; midweek breaks. *V*

IPSWICH Suffolk — Map 2

The Marlborough NEW — *Tel* (01473) 257677
73 Henley Road — *Fax* (01473) 226927
Ipswich IP1 3SP

A hotel which dropped from the *Guide* during a rocky period returns, supported by a visitor who knows it well: "Robert Gough has got his act together, and has some extremely good staff. He is always welcoming. Public rooms and bedrooms are attractive, and room service is excellent. The delightful restaurant, with well-spaced tables, and impeccable napery and flowers, overlooks the pretty garden. The food is excellent, particularly the starters and fish dishes, and service is deft and speedy. Breakfast includes tender kidneys, and especially good marmalade." The Victorian building is in a quiet residential area near Christchurch Park. Its decor is traditional, with pastel colours and antique or period furniture. There's a patio for outdoor meals in fine weather. Weekend breaks are "splendid value". (*Moira Jarrett*) Mr Gough's mother, Mary, owns the *Angel*, Bury St Edmunds, which fell from the *Guide* last year. We'd be grateful for readers' views on it.

Open All year.
Rooms 1 suite, 15 double, 6 single. Some on ground floor.
Facilities Ramps. Lounge, study, bar, restaurant; private dining/conference room. ⅓-acre garden.
Location N of Christchurch Park; turn S off A1214. Private parking.
Restriction No smoking in restaurant.
Credit cards All major cards accepted.
Terms [1996] B&B: single £68, double £78, suite £85. Set lunch £10–£15, dinner £11–£18. Weekend breaks: D,B&B £51.50–£53.50 per person per day.

Most hotels have reduced rates out of season and for children, and offer "mini-break" rates throughout the year. It is always worth asking about special terms.

KEMERTON Gloucestershire — Map 3

Upper Court — *Tel* (01386) 725351
Kemerton, nr Tewkesbury GL20 7HY — *Fax* (01386) 725472

Bill and Diana Herford's beautiful Georgian manor, an informally run Wolsey Lodge, is in a lovely village on Bredon Hill. It stands in show-piece gardens with the ruins of a Domesday-old water mill, a lake with two islands, rainbow trout and water fowl, and a sheltered swimming pool and tennis court. The decor is traditional, with antiques, oriental rugs, porcelain, etc, in the public rooms. The chintzy guest bedrooms in the main house, twin-bedded or with four-poster, are in similar style. Others, in cottages and stables, can be self catering. The Herfords have an antiques and interior decorating business; something is always for sale, and they can offer advice about other dealers in the area. A home-cooked dinner is served by arrangement, generally communally; guests' requirements are discussed in advance. *Guide* readers have enjoyed the food: "Ingredients always good and fresh; lots of home-grown vegetables". Wine is reasonably priced. Breakfast is flexibly served, "in bed, in the conservatory, even by the pool in mid-summer". *Upper Court* is often taken over by house parties, small conferences, etc. More reports, please.

Open All year. Dinner by arrangement (not always available).
Rooms 3 suites, 1 double. 9 more in cottages/converted stables (can be self-catering). 1, with ramp, on ground floor. No telephone.
Facilities 2 drawing rooms, dining room, conservatory. 15-acre grounds: walled garden, swimming pool (heated May–Sept), tennis, croquet, archery, lake: fishing, boating. Riding, clay pigeon-shooting, good walking nearby.
Location From Cheltenham N on A435/B4079; right to Kemerton 1 mile past junction with A438. Turn off main road at war memorial; house behind church.
Restrictions No smoking: some bedrooms; dining room, 1 lounge if requested. Dogs in outbuildings, garden room only.
Credit card Access.
Terms [1996] B&B: single £50–£65, double £75–£95, suite £115. Set dinner £27. 1-night bookings sometimes refused summer weekends.

KIRKBYMOORSIDE North Yorkshire — Map 4

The George and Dragon BUDGET — *Tel/Fax* (01751) 433334
Market Place
Kirkbymoorside YO6 6AA

This "particularly civilised" old coaching inn is on the main street of an attractive small market town in the Vale of Pickering. It is handy for the moors, and a good staging point on the journey to Scotland. The "charming" owners, Stephen and Frances Colling, spent some time in France, and "the bedroom decor and wine list benefit from this connection". They are much in evidence, and the mostly young staff are cheerful and efficient. The lively pub, with much gleaming woodwork, log fires, newspapers, fresh flowers, and the owners' collection of sporting memorabilia, has a bistro blackboard menu. Traditional meals, "imaginative and highly enjoyable", with the emphasis on simple flavours and fresh local ingredients, are served in the restaurant (formerly the brewhouse). Bedrooms, some large, are in a converted corn mill and old vicarage across a courtyard, well away from the pub.

They are well furnished, "with plenty of DIY refreshments, and lots of freebies". Some have a garden view. (*Good Pub Guide, John and Joan Wyatt, John and Helen Bennett*)

Open All year.
Rooms 2 family, 15 double, 2 single. In 2 separate buildings, at rear. 5 on ground floor.
Facilities Residents' lounge, bar/bistro, restaurant. ¼-acre walled garden. Golf nearby.
Location Town centre. Carpark.
Restrictions No smoking in restaurant. No dogs in public rooms.
Credit cards Access, Visa.
Terms B&B: single £45–£49, double £69–£83; D,B&B (2 nights min.): single £59–£63, double £89–£113. Bar meals. Full alc £20. 2/4-day breaks. Activity breaks: microlight, gliding, golfing, riding, etc; Christmas, New Year programmes. Children accommodated free in parents' room. *V*

LACOCK Wiltshire — Map 2

At the Sign of the Angel BUDGET — *Tel* (01249) 730230
6 Church Street — *Fax* (01249) 730527
Lacock, Chippenham SN15 2LA

César award in 1989

Lacock is a lovely old wool village preserved in its entirety by the National Trust. It is famous for its abbey and the Fox-Talbot Museum of Photography, and is beloved by film-makers (it had a starring role in *Pride and Prejudice* in 1996). The Levis family have owned its quintessentially English 14th-century half-timbered inn – low doorways and beams, oak panelling, antique furniture, open fires, and squeaky floorboards – for over 40 years. It is run by chef/*patronne* Lorna Levis and manager/*sous chef* George Hardy, and has simple, pretty bedrooms with *en suite* facilities, some compact – "not the most modern, but none the worse for that". Grand-hotel trimmings are not offered, but the hotel continues to be liked for its "no-frills style and intimacy", and the "friendly but not gushing" service. "Some wear and tear," wrote one fan, "but the overall atmosphere is one of calm and peace, ideal for relaxation. It is beautifully warm, with lovely log fires. Breakfasts are wonderful." "Robustly satisfying English cooking, using excellent local produce." Inevitably there's imperfect sound insulation between some rooms.

Open All year. Restaurant closed midday Mon, except bank holidays.
Rooms 9 double. 3 in garden cottage. 1 on ground floor.
Facilities Lounge, 3 dining rooms. Small garden: stream.
Location 7 miles S of M4 exit 17; E of A350 Chippenham–Melksham. Garages, off-street parking.
Restriction No dogs in public rooms.
Credit cards Access, Amex, Visa.
Terms [1996] B&B: single £55–£70, double £75–£93. Light or full lunch £5–£20; full alc dinner £22.50. Winter, summer breaks.

> There are many expensive hotels in the *Guide*. We are keen to increase our coverage at the other end of the scale. If you know of a simple place giving simple satisfaction, please write and tell us.

LANGAR Nottinghamshire — Map 2

Langar Hall
Langar NG13 9HG

Tel (01949) 860559
Fax (01949) 861045

This lovely Regency house "has a pleasant seat". It nestles by a venerable village church, in large grounds with parkland and ornamental fish ponds, overlooking the Vale of Belvoir. "All very dreamlike," wrote enchanted visitors, captivated by the hostess, Imogen Skirving (whose family home this is), and the informal atmosphere. Others have found the staff "charming" and "thoughtful", the bedrooms "warm and comfortable", the dinners "excellent", and have written: "Eccentric, yes. Where else would you find a cat asleep in a huge bowl of pot-pourri in the study?" There is after-dinner entertainment on last Friday of the month by local professional singers and actors. Bedrooms vary in size; best ones are in the main house, newer ones are off a courtyard; all have a desk; some are suitable for people on business in nearby Nottingham. The hotel caters for weddings and parties, which could disturb the peace at times. It recently underwent an extensive refurbishment. One couple was worried: "Mrs Skirving is improving procedures by employing a hotel management consultant. If things go too smoothly, will it retain its charm?" More reports, please. (*HR, Sarah Chrisp, Michael Forrest, Jerome and Suzanne Lyons, and others*)

Open All year, except Christmas.
Rooms 10. 3 in new wing.
Facilities Drawing room, study, dining room; monthly entertainment; function facilities. 30-acre grounds, gardens, ponds, fishing. Unsuitable for ♿.
Location By church, in village 12 miles SE of Nottingham.
Restriction No smoking in bedrooms.
Credit cards All major cards accepted.
Terms B&B: single £50–£85, double £75–£135. Set lunch/dinner £17.50; full alc £30. 2-day breaks. V*

LANGHO Lancashire — Map 4

Northcote Manor
Northcote Road
Langho, nr Blackburn BB6 8BE

Tel (01254) 240555
Fax (01254) 246568

Michelin awarded a star in 1996 to this restaurant-with-rooms, owned by Craig Bancroft and Nigel Haworth (the chef). It is a late-Victorian manor in pretty countryside on the edge of the Ribble Valley, just 15 minutes from the M6. There's some traffic noise from the A59 nearby, but bedrooms are double-glazed. The interior is comfortable rather than designerish, beamed and oak-panelled, with deep leather armchairs and real fires in the public rooms, and a handsome staircase. Bedrooms, of varying sizes, are "well furnished, with good-quality fabrics, antique and period furniture, knick-knacks and games". The British cooking has robust regional overtones – black pudding ("the best ever"), braised brisket, and jam roly poly feature on the menu alongside more "modern" items. There is an extensive wine list. Breakfasts are "exceptional and generous". The staff are "always ready to help". The atmosphere is too casual for some. More reports, please.

Open All year.
Rooms 1 suite, 13 double. Some on ground floor.

Facilities Ramps. 2 lounges, bar, restaurant; private dining/meeting room. 2-acre grounds. Shooting, hunting, fishing, golf nearby.
Location From M6 exit 31 take A59 to Clitheroe for 9½ miles; turn left immediately before large roundabout at Langho.
Restrictions Smoking discouraged in dining room. No dogs.
Credit cards All major cards accepted.
Terms B&B: single £75–£85, double £95–£110, suite £110–£130. Set lunch £15; dinner £35; full alc £40. 1–2-night gourmet breaks.

LANGLEY MARSH Somerset — Map 1

Langley House — *Tel* (01984) 623318
Langley Marsh, Wiveliscombe TA4 2UF — *Fax* (01984) 624573

"Absolute perfection. One feels like the most pampered guest in a private home with a model hostess. Delicious food. Fantastic breakfast obviated the need for lunch." "A really lovely country hotel; friendly, relaxed and efficient." Peter and Anne Wilson's Grade II listed house is set amid the Brendon Hills, in "some of the most magnificent countryside in the south-west". A handsome gold grasshopper sign marks the entrance to the gravel drive. "The gardens are a delight, with a pond, tiny stream, and walled vegetable and herb garden, all surrounded by soft hills dotted with sheep. The decor, with emphasis on comfort as well as elegance, has been done with flair, with vibrant colours, antique furniture and rich fabrics; dainty ornaments and fresh and dried flowers abound. Bedrooms, up a curved staircase, are of medium size, with floral fabrics, flowers, books, magazines and excellent bedside lighting. We heard owls in the garden at night and awoke to the sound of sheep, lambs and birdsong." Dinner, at 8.30, in the small beamed pink and green dining room, consists of three or four courses on weekdays, and five at weekends; no choice until dessert or cheese. Peter Wilson's "beautifully presented" modern English cooking has earned a *Michelin* red "Meals". (*Hillary de Ste Croix, Jean Taylor, and others*) Extra charges, for after-dinner coffee and chocolates, morning tea and newspapers, etc, can bump up the bill. In winter 1995–96 some guests felt cold in the dining room, "but the rest of the house was lovely and warm".

Open All year.
Rooms 1 suite, 6 double, 1 single.
Facilities 2 drawing rooms, bar, restaurant, conservatory. 4½-acre garden: croquet. Unsuitable for ♿.
Location ½ mile N of Wiveliscombe. Turn left at town centre.
Restrictions No smoking: restaurant, some bedrooms. No dogs in public rooms.
Credit cards Access, Amex, Visa.
Terms B&B: single £64.50–£72.50, double £83–£120, suite £125–£145. Set dinner: 3-course £25. 4-course £30.50. Discount all year for 2 or more nights. 1-night bookings sometimes refused weekends.

LANGLEY-ON-TYNE Northumberland — Map 4

Langley Castle — *Tel* (01434) 688888
Langley-on-Tyne, Hexham NE47 5LU — *Fax* (01434) 684019

Authentic 600-year-old castle overlooking Tyne valley. On A686, 1½ miles S of Haydon Bridge, in forest of tall trees. 7-foot-thick walls, well-preserved architectural details; turrets reaching towards the sky. Lots of stairs –

unsuitable for ♿. Drawing room in former hall; beamed dining room (no smoking). Log fires, some antiques, but decor mostly simple. 16 bedrooms; no "pampering extras", but some have spa bath, sauna, half-tester bed. Traditional English/French cooking, "good if slightly gimmicky, with pretentious descriptions". 11-acre grounds. All major credit cards accepted. B&B £37.50–£90. Set lunch £12.50, dinner £21.95. Good-value breaks. Entry endorsed, but with reservations about service –"friendly, but lacking supervision" – and bedroom decor. More reports, please. *V*

LASTINGHAM North Yorkshire — Map 4

Lastingham Grange — *Tel* (01751) 417345 and 417402
Lastingham YO6 6TH

César award in 1991

"A haven of peace and care, with an excellent staff." This unpretentious, well-run hotel, with hosts Dennis and Jane Wood, was given its *César* for "preserving traditional values of country hospitality". It is in a "charming" village in the heart of the North York Moors National Park. There is wonderful walking from the door. Started in 1946 by the father of the present proprietor, it has had a *Guide* entry since the first edition. It is an old creeper-covered house in large grounds, with beautifully kept gardens, fine old trees, and fields. The decor is thoroughly traditional. The food "is wholesome; and there is plenty of it. The wine list is straightforward and reasonably priced." Newspapers, morning coffee, afternoon tea and shoe-cleaning are included in the rates. "The Woods treat you like valued house guests," ran a report last year. "Babies are listened for in the evening; children have their own playground and ponies, teens are treated with respect that elicits adult behaviour." Visitors in 1996 were intrigued: "Owls everywhere: inside as figurines, and outside, alive and hooting. A benign phantom hand ensures that every lampshade lists to port or starboard; if straightened, they return to the tilt within half a day. Mr Wood has a slightly butlerish air, which made for some pleasant exchanges." (*RV, Nicholas and Myriam Whalley, KW*) Only caveats: "The beds have served more than a reasonable lifetime, and with such wonderful meat available, it was a pity about the breakfast sausages."

Open Mar–end Nov.
Rooms 10 double, 2 single.
Facilities Hall, lounge, dining room; laundry facilities. 10-acre grounds: garden, adventure playground. In National Park, near moors and dales; riding, golf, swimming nearby. Unsuitable for ♿.
Location Off A170, 5 miles NE of Kirkbymoorside. Turn N towards Appleton-le-Moor 2 miles E of Kirkbymoorside.
Restrictions No smoking in dining room. No dogs in public rooms.
Credit cards None accepted.
Terms [1996] B&B: single £64.50–£70.50, double £119.75–£131.25; D,B&B: single £77.75–£91.75, double £144.75–£167.25. Set lunch £14.75, dinner £25.50. Light and picnic lunches available. Reductions for long stays; winter breaks. Children accommodated free in parents' room.

Please never tell a hotel you intend to send a report to the *Guide*. Anonymity is essential for objectivity.

LAVENHAM Suffolk — Map 2

The Great House BUDGET
Market Place
Lavenham CO10 9QZ
Tel (01787) 247431
Fax (01787) 248007

Quintessentially French, not least in its welcoming attitude towards children, this restaurant with four suites (a Logis of Great Britain) is in the centre of a quintessentially English medieval town. Once the home of Stephen Spender, it is a "splendid" 15th-century building with a Georgian façade. "Without doubt, one for Francophiles," wrote its nominator. "You could be in Normandy." Other correspondents have praised the kind proprietors and the courteous all-French staff, and thought the place "jolly good value". There's a little sitting room/bar, and a pretty leafy rear garden where tea can be served. The suites have a lounge or sitting area, individually controlled heating, and a "homey" decor – floral fabrics, antiques, old beams. Windows may be on the small side and hard to shut tight; sloping floors with squeaking floorboards are another period feature. Chef/*patron* Regis Crepy serves traditional French dishes in the oak-beamed, candlelit dining room, with its original inglenook fireplace. The *carte* can be pricey, but the *prix fixe* offers plenty of choice. (*Adrian Wright, and others*) Some visitors have praised the meals; others have found them variable, particularly when the owners are away. The dining room "tends to be stretched at weekends".

Open All year, but sometimes closed Sun night/Mon (open bank holidays).
Rooms 4 suites.
Facilities Lounge/bar, restaurant; patio. ½-acre garden with swings. Unsuitable for ♿.
Location Behind Market Cross, near Guildhall. Carpark.
Restrictions Smoking discouraged in restaurant. No dogs in public rooms.
Credit cards Access, Amex, Visa.
Terms [1996] B&B: single £50–£75, double £68–£88; D,B&B: single £56.45, double £83.90. Set lunch £9.95–£12.95, dinner £16.95; full alc: lunch £17.45, dinner £28. Midweek breaks; off-season rates. Children under 3 accommodated free in parents' room; 4–12 £10. *V*

LEAMINGTON SPA Warwickshire — Map 3

The Lansdowne BUDGET
87 Clarendon Street
Leamington Spa CV32 4PF
Tel (01926) 450505
Fax (01926) 421313

César award in 1989

A green-painted Regency town house, fronted by a monkey-puzzle tree, near the centre of this once fashionable, still delightful, watering place, convenient for Warwick Castle, the National Exhibition Centre (25 minutes by car) and the National Agricultural Centre (10 minutes). It has "most welcoming, attentive" proprietors, David and Gillian Allen, and a willing staff. "The atmosphere is excellent," wrote recent visitors. "The food was simple, beautifully cooked, and excellent value. The wines were well chosen, with plenty of half bottles, and good value too." Public rooms are not large, but "delightfully done, with period pieces". Bedrooms, some very small, have pine furniture, spriggy fabrics and "every facility: alarm clock, fresh milk offered, etc", though storage space can be limited. They are well insulated against traffic noise (the hotel stands at a busy crossroads). "Jolly good breakfasts." The small garden won the "Britain in Bloom" award in 1995. More reports, please.

Open All year, except 24/25 Dec.
Rooms 10 double, 5 single. 2 on ground floor.
Facilities Lounge, bar, restaurant. Small garden. Discounts for local attractions. Not really suitable for ♿.
Location Central, on A425 (rear rooms quietest). Small private carpark.
Restrictions No smoking in restaurant. Preferably no children under 5. No dogs.
Credit cards Access, Visa.
Terms B&B: single £29.85–£49.95, double £39.90–£61.70; D,B&B £37.90–£67.90 per person. Set lunch (by arrangement) 2–3-courses: £14.95–£17.95, dinner £16.95; full alc £22.90. 2- and 5-day breaks.

LECK Lancashire — Map 4

Cobwebs — *Tel/Fax* (0152 42) 72141
Leck, Cowan Bridge
nr Kirkby Lonsdale LA6 2HZ

In hamlet in isolated position amid fields with sheep, 2 miles SE of Kirkby Lonsdale, idiosyncratic restaurant-with-rooms. Excellent modern cooking by kindly hostess, Yvonne Thompson, served in light dining room. Intimate atmosphere (only 16 covers); Paul Kelly is an informal host. "Stunning home-made breads; remarkable wine list." Delicious breakfast with huge choice. 5 bedrooms: hectic decor, with much pink ("but not a cobweb"); some bathrooms are tiny. 4-acre grounds. Open mid-Mar–end Dec. Unsuitable for ♿. No smoking in restaurant. No children under 12. No dogs. Access, Visa accepted. B&B: single £45, double £60. Set dinner £28 [1996]. *V*

LEDBURY Hereford and Worcester — Map 3

Hope End — *Tel* (01531) 633613
Ledbury HR8 1JQ — *Fax* (01531) 636366

César award in 1992

John and Patricia Hegarty's idiosyncratic hotel (Relais du Silence) was once the home of Elizabeth Barrett Browning. It has a lovely setting in a hidden valley, amid romantic, quite wild gardens with rambling roses, walled courtyards, gothic temples and a grotto. A vast walled organic vegetable and fruit garden supplies ingredients for Mrs Hegarty's much-admired cooking "in English country tradition, with balanced, clear flavours, and clever use of herbs" on a three-course menu with choice at each stage. The decor is of upmarket simplicity: wood-burning stoves, polished floors, modern pine, woven fabrics, autumn colours, books everywhere. Breakfast includes a good choice of fresh fruits and yogurt and "an excellent mixed grill". Returning fans are warm in their praise: "After 18 years, the standards are as impeccable as ever. I have only praise for the Hegartys' avoidance of the false effusiveness found nowadays in many establishments. They love their work, and this is apparent in every way, not least in their choice of staff. Everything is produced unobtrusively where and when you want it. The food is outstanding; John Hegarty is as wise about wine as any *sommelier*." "No TV, no radio. Absolute bliss." "Must be the most peaceful hotel in England. If some of your readers find Mr Hegarty self-righteous, that's their problem. If he can create a place as wonderful as this, he has plenty to be self-righteous about." (*Alan Blyth, DW Tate, Peter McLeod*) Not for those in search of conventional hotel facilities and a gushing welcome. One couple thought their small bedroom overpriced.

Open Feb–mid-Dec. Lunch not served.
Rooms 8 double. 1 in cottage 200 yds, 1 in minaret.
Facilities 3 lounges, dining room. 40-acre grounds: garden, walled garden, parkland. Unsuitable for ♿.
Location 2 miles N of Ledbury, just beyond Wellington Heath; signposted after railway station.
Restrictions No smoking in restaurant. No children under 12. Dogs in car only.
Credit cards Access, Visa.
Terms [1996] B&B: single £85–£108, double £120–£140. Set dinner £30. Single occupancy: £12 reduction on room rate. Reductions for 2 or more nights; off-season breaks. 1-night bookings sometimes refused Sat.

LEEDS West Yorkshire **Map 4**

---

42 The Calls *Tel* (0113) 244 0099
42 The Calls *Fax* (0113) 234 4100
Leeds LS2 7EW
César award in 1995

Jonathan Wix's luxurious riverside warehouse conversion, with stunning ultra-modern decor, is in an up-and-coming area of central Leeds. "We loved the cityscape view from our window," one couple has written. Rooms are "all different, all wonderful"; one is black – "very dramatic". They have original pictures, desk, CD player, satellite TV, *three* telephones, a lavish bathroom, and jokey touches, eg frog soaps, smarties on pillows, wooden animal for keyring. Continental breakfast is delivered via a hatch "so you are not caught half dressed – brilliant". Downstairs there's an impressive breakfast buffet and an enticing selection of cooked items. Michael Gill's adjacent restaurant, *Pool Court at 42*, serving "*haute cuisine* with an Italian influence", has regained the *Michelin* star lost when it moved from Poole-in-Wharfedale, and earned three red crossed spoon-and-forks. Its riverside terrace is pleasant for a drink in summer; its wine list "covers the globe". Gill also runs the popular *Brasserie 44*, with swings for bar seats, tables close together, and loud taped jazz. The hotel is business-orientated during the week, but offers generous weekend reductions. Plenty of praise this year: "Jaded from nights in characterless, expensive business hotels, I branched out, and could not have done better. Immaculate bedroom overlooking the river, extremely quiet, with (joy of joys) windows that open." "I was enchanted. On a winter afternoon they greet you with a glass of warm cider." "Staff well trained but unaffected; they seem genuinely pleased to see you." (*Katharine Lyall, Geraldine Terry, Pat and Jeremy Temple, David and Kate Wooff*) Mr Wix also owns the *Victoria Hotel*, Bradford (*qv*), less glitzy and less quirky.

Open All year, except Christmas. Restaurants closed Sat lunch/Sun, bank holidays.
Rooms 3 suites, 32 double, 6 single. 1 suitable for ♿.

Facilities Lift. Lounge, bar, breakfast room, 2 restaurants; conference facilities.
Location Central, near Corn Exchange (quiet rooms overlook river, others triple-glazed). Hard to find; ask hotel for directions. Private and street parking.
Restrictions No smoking in 6 bedrooms. "Small, well-behaved dogs only"; not in public rooms.
Credit cards All major cards accepted.
Terms Rooms: single £135 (£65 weekend), double £140 (£65 weekend), suite £220 (£115 weekend). Breakfast: continental £6.95, English £10. Cot for child £5. Restaurant: set lunch £17.50, dinner £22.50; full alc £35; *Brasserie 44*: set lunch £7.95; full alc £24. *V*

Haley's *Tel* (0113) 278 4446
Shire Oak Road *Fax* (0113) 275 3342
Headingley, Leeds LS6 2DE

"Quiet surroundings. Warm welcome. Relatively small dinner menu, but we found plenty to tempt us. Well-trained young staff." "No sycophancy; real friendliness." John Appleyard's unusual turreted building, in a quiet road near the university, is named after a master stonemason prominent in Leeds at the turn of the century. Though "country house" in style, it is only two miles from the city centre and eight miles from the airport. Carefully restored to its original Victorian splendour, it has a large hall, a bay-windowed drawing room, a fine staircase, open fires, period furniture, lavish drapes, and pictures everywhere, many with a cricketing theme in tribute to the famous cricket ground nearby. "Beautifully decorated bedrooms" (some quite small) have a smart tiled bathroom and many extras, including two telephones. The restaurant, with a striking modern decor, serves "light modern cooking with a classical base" by Jon Vennell. Breakfast (Yorkshire or continental) is "a generous repast". (*SC Whitbread; also Tim Moorey*) One visitor thought the food "pretentious, and a bit ordinary". We'd like more reports, please. *Haley's* is licensed for civil weddings.

Open All year, except 26–30 Dec. Restaurant closed evening Sun to non-residents, midday, except Sun.
Rooms 2 interconnecting, 14 double, 8 single.
Facilities Lounge, lounge/bar, restaurant; function room. Small front lawn. Unsuitable for ♿.
Location 2 miles N of centre. Turn off A660 Leeds–Otley between Yorkshire and Midland banks in Headingley. Private parking.
Restrictions No smoking in restaurant. No dogs.
Credit cards All major cards accepted.
Terms [1996] B&B: single £95 (£55 weekend), double £112 (£75 weekend). Set Sun lunch £14.50; full alc £30. Weekend break (2 nights min.) D,B&B double £130. Children accommodated free in parents' room. *V*

LEONARD STANLEY Gloucestershire Map 3

The Grey Cottage BUDGET *Tel/Fax* (01453) 822515
Bath Road
Leonard Stanley, Stonehouse GL10 3LU

"I've never been better looked after. Mr and Mrs Reeves are real professionals. Service was unobtrusive, though warm." "They have worked hard to restore their 1807 Cotswold stone cottage, retaining many original features and adding modern comforts and tasteful furnishing. Everything is of high quality, down to beautiful china, silver and crystal, and bed-linen and towels which are changed daily. The bedrooms have a large selection of hot drinks, biscuits, chocolates, fruit, fresh flowers, magazines, local information, dressing gowns, an assortment of medications, even ear plugs in case of early-morning tractors in summer." "Breakfast better than in many five-star hotels." Meals are taken at a polished dining table in front of a log fire, or in a sunny conservatory. Dinner – "good and varied home-cooking" – is by prior arrangement; preferences are discussed at the time of booking. No licence; guests may bring their drinks, and there is an honesty bar. "The perfect way to finish the evening is in front of the sitting room fire; if you wish, the Reeves will join you for a drink and a chat; their knowledge of the area is fascinating. The cottage is set on top of a hill overlooking fields, and is perfectly located for exploring the area on foot." Advance booking essential. (*Matthew Crampton, Mrs SV Smith, Susan E Seed, Jenny Broom, Glenn Sneddon*)

Open All year, except Christmas and occasionally at other times.
Rooms 2 double, 1 single.
Facilities Sitting room, honesty bar, dining room. ¼-acre garden. Unsuitable for ♿.
Location 3 miles W of Stroud. 1 mile S of A419, between King's Stanley and Leonard Stanley.
Restrictions No smoking: dining room, bedrooms. No dogs.
Credit cards Credit cards not accepted.
Terms [1996] B&B: single £25–£29, double £46–£49; D,B&B: single £39–£45, double £74–£82. Reductions for 2/3 nights. *V* (Mon–Thurs, min. 3 nights)

LEWDOWN Devon **Map 1**

Lewtrenchard Manor *Tel* (01566) 783256 and 783222
Lewdown, nr Okehampton EX20 4PN *Fax* (01566) 783332

"A beautiful house in lovely, slightly neglected gardens, which added to its *Secret Garden*-ish charms. It is furnished with taste and slight eccentricity. Service in the restaurant was charming, and the breakfasts particularly good. The hotel has its own spring, and the water is glorious." Sue and James Murray are the "genteel, sociable" proprietors of this grey stone manor, run on house party lines. Elizabethan in origin, with mullioned windows and a dovecote, it stands near a church in a peaceful Devon valley. It was once the home of the Revd Sabine Baring-Gould, author of the hymn "Onward Christian Soldiers". His renovations have given it a predominantly Victorian interior: ornate plaster ceilings, dark oak panelling, large fireplaces with log fires; there are portraits everywhere, knick-knacks, gleaming brass door-handles and locks, and cats and dogs. Bedrooms are on the first floor off a long gallery, reached by an impressive staircase. It is worth paying extra for a garden-facing one. No key, but you can bolt yourself in. A new chef, Jason Buck, arrived as we went to press; we'd be grateful for comments on the cooking. Not everyone agrees with the political views of the owners, aired in the bar after dinner.

Open All year.
Rooms 1 suite, 7 double. 1 more room planned for late 1996.
Facilities Stair lift. 2 lounges, bar lounge, 2 dining rooms; ballroom. 11-acre grounds: garden, croquet, fishing lake, clay pigeon-shooting. River fishing nearby; sea 4 miles.

Location Off A30 between Okehampton and Launceton. Follow signs for Lewtrenchard.
Restrictions No smoking in dining rooms. No children under 8. No dogs in public rooms.
Credit cards All major cards accepted.
Terms [1996] B&B: single £75–£95, double £85–£130, suite £119–£140. Set lunch £16, dinner £26–£30. Off-season discounts, Christmas house party. 1-night bookings refused bank holidays.

LEWES East Sussex **Map 2**

Berkeley House BUDGET *Tel/Fax* (01273) 476057
2 Albion Street
Lewes BN7 2ND

Small B&B in elegant Georgian terrace in quiet street near centre of historic county town, handy for Glyndebourne. Caring owner, Roy Patten provides "thoroughly pleasant stay at modest cost, with breakfast to last you the day". South-facing roof terrace. 6 rooms including family suite, 5 with shower. 2 spaces in carpark opposite. Closed Christmas. No smoking: breakfast room, 1 bedroom. Unsuitable for ♿. No dogs. Access, Amex, Visa accepted. B&B: single £30–£45, double £45–£50 [1996]. Special breaks: 25% discount. More reports, please. *V* (Oct–Mar)

LIFTON Devon **Map 1**

The Arundell Arms *Tel* (01566) 784666
Lifton PL16 0AA *Fax* (01566) 784494

In a small Devon town, a traditional creeper-covered coaching inn with a pretty terraced garden, complete with one of the few remaining cockpits in England, at the rear. The owner since 1961, Ann Voss-Bark, a keen fly fisher, presides "with the air of a benign headmistress". It is popular with fishing folk, having 20 miles of trout-, sea trout- and salmon-fishing on the river Tamar and four of its tributaries, and a three-acre stocked lake. It has full-time fishing instructors, and offers courses of all kinds, sending fisherfolk off for the day with a packed lunch in a wicker basket. There is good shooting, too. The hotel also welcomes the non-sporting, including families. Chef Philip Burgess has been here 14 years, and his "modern English cooking, with a traditional French influence", is much admired. There is a wide selection, of wines, reasonably priced. Unusually sophisticated bar meals are served. Service is "polite, never pompous or stuffy". Bedrooms vary; some are spacious, some plain; quietest ones are at the back. There's a variety of off-season packages; functions and conferences are also catered for. (*A and CR*)

Open All year, except 3 days over Christmas (restaurant open for Christmas lunch).
Rooms 19 double, 10 single. 5 more, cottagey in style, in annexe opposite.
Facilities Ramp. Lounge, cocktail bar, public bar, 2 dining rooms; conference/meeting rooms; games room, skittle alley. ½-acre garden. 20 miles fishing rights on river Tamar and tributaries, 3-acre stocked lake, fishing school for beginners. Only restaurant suitable for ♿.
Location 3 miles E of Launceston, ½ mile off A30. Road-facing rooms double-glazed.
Restrictions No smoking in restaurant. No dogs in restaurant.

Credit cards All major cards accepted.
Terms B&B: £40–£64; D,B&B (min. 2 nights) £59–£79. Bar meals. Set meals (2–3 courses): lunch £14–£17.50, dinner £26–£32. 2–6-night breaks all year; off-season breaks: sporting, gourmet, etc. Children under 16 accommodated free in parents' room.

LINCOLN Lincolnshire — Map 2

D'Isney Place Hotel — *Tel* (01522) 538881
Eastgate — *Fax* (01522) 511321
Lincoln LN2 4AA

David and Judy Payne's Georgian B&B, with Victorian extensions, is in the heart of the city; the wall of the cathedral close forms the southern boundary of its garden. It has no public rooms. A "first-class" breakfast (English or continental) is served in the bedrooms, which vary greatly in size and style: some are quite basic, others "charming, with a spacious bathroom"; one has a four-poster; three have a jacuzzi. Some rooms get traffic noise, others are praised for their quietness. Reports to the *Guide* therefore tend to be mixed, but those who are fortunate with their accommodation write with enthusiasm: "Quite excellent." "Beautifully warm on a freezing day." "Unpretentious, pretty, comfortable and superbly clean. Fresh flowers in bedrooms, corridors *and* on breakfast tray. Service unobtrusive but solicitous. Weekend bargain break excellent value." The *Wig and Mitre* and *The Jew's House* are recommended for meals. *(Will Camp, JP Marland, and others)*

Open All year.
Rooms 1 suite (2 rooms), 14 double, 2 single. 2 in cottage annexe with sitting room, kitchen, dining room. Some on ground floor.
Facilities Ramps. 1-acre garden adjoining cathedral.
Location By cathedral. Front rooms double-glazed; back ones quietest. Limited private parking. Street parking after 6 pm.
Restriction No smoking in 9 bedrooms.
Credit cards All major cards accepted.
Terms [1996] B&B: single £52.50, double £66, suite £105–£132. Weekend breaks. *V*

LITTLE MALVERN Hereford and Worcester — Map 3

Holdfast Cottage — *Tel* (01684) 310288
Little Malvern WR13 6NA — *Fax* (01684) 311117

"Excellent in every way." "One of the best small hotels we know." "Stephen and Jane Knowles (she is chef) combine professional expertise with a charming, caring manner, and make their guests feel thoroughly welcome. Food is original without being pretentious. Sweets particularly delicious. Breakfast in the best English tradition; no plastic containers here. Service exemplary." Recent tributes to this 17th-century cottage with Victorian extensions, pretty, long and low, in a pleasant country setting amid trees and farmland. Gloucester, Worcester, Hereford and Tewkesbury are all within easy reach. The small public rooms include a conservatory entrance, a beamed hall, and a diminutive bar opening on to a wisteria-covered terrace with lovely views of the Malvern Hills. The blue-and-white dining room is larger, and pretty, with candles, flowers, knick-knacks on tables, prints on walls. Here home-cooked dinners are served, with three choices for each course. Rolls are home-baked, ice-creams home-made, herbs home-grown. "Odd little staircases abound, leading to small, pretty bedrooms; teddy bear on chair, duck and small boat in well-equipped bathroom. Warm throughout." "Very good value." Children are welcomed. (*C Hepburne Scott, Mrs W Barratt, Margaret Dixon, and others*)

Open All year.
Rooms 7 double, 1 single.
Facilities Lounge, conservatory, bar, restaurant. 2-acre grounds: small wood, croquet. Unsuitable for ♿.
Location On A4104 midway between Welland and Little Malvern.
Restriction No smoking: dining room, bedrooms.
Credit cards Access, Visa.
Terms [1996] B&B: single £42–£44, double £74–£82; D,B&B £52–£61 per person. Set dinner £17–£18. Short breaks all year; 10% reduction for weekly stays. *V*

LITTLE SINGLETON Lancashire **Map 4**

Mains Hall NEW *Tel* (01253) 885130
86 Mains Lane, Little Singleton *Fax* (01253) 894132
nr Blackpool FY6 7LE

Handy for those who cannot stand the rigours of staying in nearby Blackpool, this house, overlooking the river Wyre, was once the home of Maria Fitzherbert. Here, in the 18th century, she was courted and married by Prince George, later George IV. And, since the change in the marriage laws, 20th-century couples, too, may marry in *Mains Hall*'s marquee-style conservatory and be photographed in its sheltered gardens, with orchards, walnut trees and a fountain. "What a breath of fresh air," writes the nominator. "Roger Yeomans is a lovely chap and will look after your every need. Helpful staff, convivial atmosphere, a little like a weekend country house party. The restaurant is beautiful, and the food is *nouvelle cuisine*, but with local flavour and proper helpings. The wine list is extensive, with tastes and prices to suit all pockets." Decor is in keeping with the date of the house; bedrooms are stocked with mineral water and fresh fruit; some have a four-poster or half-tester bed. (*David Pook*)

Open All year.
Rooms 10 double.
Facilities Garden room, library, bar, 2 dining rooms, conservatory. 5-acre garden: river frontage.
Location 6 miles NE of Blackpool. From M55 exit 3, follow signs for Fleetwood (A585) for 5 miles. Hotel is ½ mile past 2nd set of traffic lights, on right.
Restrictions No smoking: restaurant, some bedrooms. No dogs in public rooms.
Credit cards Access, Amex, Diners.
Terms B&B: single £40–£70, double £50–£100. Set lunch £15, dinner £20–£25; full alc £30.

****

Traveller's tale The girl at reception asked four times in a five-minute conversation: "How was your journey?" I appreciate the need to make guests feel at home, but this was ridiculous and irritating. May I suggest other suitable subjects: the weather; the hotel's facilities; is the visit business or pleasure?

****

LITTLEBURY GREEN Essex **Map 2**

Elmdon Lee BUDGET *Tel/Fax* (01763) 838237
Littlebury Green
nr Saffron Walden CB11 4XB

Large 18th-century farmhouse, a Wolsey Lodge, in 900-acre working farm. On outskirts of village 4 miles W of Saffron Walden, 16 miles from Cambridge; handy for M11. Large drawing room. Light, well-equipped bedrooms (3 double, 1 single), all with en suite *or private facilities. Lovely views. Dinner by arrangement (country farmhouse cooking) at 7.30* en famille *with Diana Duke, "a relaxed hostess". 1-acre garden. Unsuitable for ♿. Closed Christmas. No children. No dogs. Access, Diners, Visa accepted. B&B: single £30–£35, double £55–£60. Set dinner £17. Recently endorsed, but we'd like more reports, please.*

LODDISWELL Devon **Map 1**

Hazelwood House BUDGET *Tel* (01548) 821232
Loddiswell, nr Kingsbridge TQ7 4EB London office: (0171) 538 5633
Fax (01548) 821318

"The sense of peace and friendliness has to be experienced to be appreciated fully," writes a seasoned traveller. "It won't suit everyone, but it worked for me." A trio: Jane Bowman, Gillian Kean and Anabel Watson, own this "graceful, unimposing early Victorian house". It is set in huge, rambling grounds, above a valley sweeping down to the river Avon, opposite a magnificent wooded hill. "You need to be a reasonably confident driver to negotiate the track to the house. The welcome, including that by the soft labrador, the 'outside concierge', could not be faulted. Inside, it feels more like a commune than a hotel." There's a "delightful mix" of simple furniture and antiques and paintings. Bedrooms, though quite small, are "clean and fresh". "Deliciously simple" meals, with little choice, are prepared in the enormous Victorian kitchen. Organically grown vegetables and meat are served, accompanied by the house's own spring water, and "excellent" organic wines, one red, one white. Mealtimes are flexible. The staff "is endowed with a marvellous sense of fun". The house runs a varied programme of cultural events: concerts by the Medici Quartet, Indian music, jazz, blues, painting, life drawing, etc. Sandy beaches, fishing and moorland walks are nearby. (*Chris Kay, Maryly La Follette, Michael Crick*) One couple felt out of place in the "rather puritanical New Age atmosphere".

Open All year.
Rooms 1 suite, 11 double, 4 single. 1 with bath, 1 with shower. 1 on ground floor. No telephone/TV. 4 self-catering cottages.
Facilities Lounge, reading room (with payphone), TV room, dining room. 67-acre grounds. Cultural events and courses.
Location 4 miles E of Loddiswell. From California Cross on B3207 Dartmouth–Modbury take road to Kingsbridge/Loddiswell. Left after *c.* ¾ mile to Hazelwood. Gate with stone pillars on right.
Restrictions No smoking: bedrooms, public rooms sometimes. Dogs by arrangement.
Credit cards None accepted.

Terms B&B £20–£40; D,B&B from £30, full board from £35. Set lunch £6.50–£8.50, dinner £12; alc £15–£18 (excluding wine). Children 4–12 half price. Negotiable rates for parties, groups, etc. *V*

LONDON Map 2

Basil Street Hotel *Tel* (0171) 581 3311
8 Basil Street, SW3 1AH *Fax* (0171) 581 3693
César award in 1993

Privately owned by one family for 84 years, this Edwardian hotel is convenient for Hyde Park and Knightsbridge. Despite its location, in a busy one-way street off Sloane Street, it is "reminiscent of a fine old country house". Regulars love its old-fashioned style and the civilised public rooms with antiques, oriental rugs, mirrors and paintings. Women have their own domain, the Parrot Club. Service is "impeccable". "Most of the staff have been there for years and treat you with the utmost accommodation and warmth." Bedrooms vary greatly. Some are spacious, with a large bathroom; some have noise from traffic, a nearby fire station or neighbouring bedrooms ("but a note offers earplugs"); others are surprisingly quiet. A few singles lack private facilities – "a real bargain for the intrepid". Stephen Korany, the much-admired manager, retired in 1995 after 42 years in harness, to be succeeded by David Brockett, ex-*Chewton Glen*. He has tackled the restaurant, often regarded as the hotel's Achilles' heel; first reports from this front are encouraging. As to other changes. . . . "It would break our hearts," write *aficionados*, "to find that the old-fashioned delights had given way to their modern counterparts: early morning tea no longer brought to the room, for instance, but an electric kettle installed. We have always felt at home here, as in no other city hotel, precisely because it has never bowed the knee to the Baal of the Age of Commerce." No sign of that. Meanwhile, a regular writes: "As reliable as ever, but with a marked improvement in the style and quality of service in the dining room. The mafia have finally been ousted – and about time too." (*Richard Creed*)

Open All year.
Rooms 4 family, 41 double, 45 single. 80 with facilities *en suite*.
Facilities Lift. Lounge bar, ladies' club, restaurant; function facilities. Unsuitable for ♿.
Location Central; public carpark nearby. (Underground: Knightsbridge.)
Restriction No dogs in public rooms.
Credit cards All major cards accepted.
Terms [1996] Rooms: single £130, double £165–£185; family £260. Extra bed £15. Breakfast: continental £8.50, English £12.50. Set lunch £14–£17, dinner £18–£24. Concessions to regular visitors; special rates Aug, winter; weekend rates; long-stay rates. *V*

The Beaufort *Tel* (0171) 584 5252
33 Beaufort Gardens, SW3 1PP *Fax* (0171) 589 2834

A small town house hotel on a quiet Knightsbridge square, owned by Diana Wallis. It has a pretty decor, recently extensively renovated, a fine collection of original English floral watercolours, a mainly female staff, and a large cat, Harry. No reception formalities; arriving guests are given a front-door key. Pricey, but you get quite a lot for your money. Bedrooms, of varying sizes, have sherry, chocolates, flowers, biscuits, personal fax/answering system, video, bathroom scales, jogging map, a teddy bear.... Free champagne is available 24 hours a day; generous afternoon cream teas, too, are free. Room service offers anything from soup and sandwiches to a full meal. For breakfast there are home-made croissants, jams and marmalade, served on fine Wedgwood china. Some guests have praised the "excellent" service and "charming" staff, and welcomed the "no tipping" policy, but one potential visitor was put off by a curt response when attempting to discuss a weekend rate. More reports, please.

Open All year.
Rooms 5 suites, 17 double, 6 single. Some on ground floor.
Facilities Lift. Lounge with honour bar. Air conditioning. Guests have automatic membership of nearby health club.
Location Central, near Harrods. Meter parking; public carpark nearby. (Underground: Knightsbridge.)
Credit cards All major cards accepted.
Terms [1996] (*Excluding VAT*) Rooms: single £110, double from £150, suite £240. Breakfast £6.50. Weekend reductions. Children in cot free, on sofa-bed £25. *V*

The Cadogan NEW *Tel* (0171) 235 7141
75 Sloane Street, SW1X 9SG *Fax* (0171) 245 0994

In a prime position, handy for smart shops, restaurants, museums and Hyde Park, this has been a distinguished hotel for over 100 years. Lily Langtry (mistress of King Edward VII) was a visitor; Oscar Wilde was arrested while staying here, an event immortalised in a poem by John Betjeman: "... the door of the bedroom swung open / And TWO PLAIN-CLOTHES POLICEMEN came in: / 'Mr Woilde, we 'ave come for tew take yew / Where felons and criminals dwell: / We must ask yew tew leave with us quoietly / For this is the *Cadogan Hotel*.'" In 1990 it was taken over by Historic House Hotels Ltd, which exists to conserve buildings of historical and architectural interest (see also *Hartwell House*, Aylesbury, *Middlethorpe Hall*, York, and *Bodysgallen Hall*, Llandudno). Their meticulous renovation will be complete by 1997. "It has a nice clubby atmosphere," writes the nominator, an expert in such things, "and a pleasant staff. The lounge is agreeable for reading newspapers and taking coffee or tea. Bedrooms are well designed and comfortable, without being OTT. Good value for London." The Edwardian-style restaurant serves traditional English cooking. (*Paul Henderson*)

Open All year. Restaurant closed Sat midday.
Rooms 5 suites, 56 double, 4 single. Some air-conditioned.
Facilities Drawing room, bar, restaurant; function facilities. Access to Cadogan Square gardens opposite: tennis. Unsuitable for ♿.
Location Central (rear rooms quietest). Meter parking; NCP carpark opposite. (Underground: Sloane Square, Knightsbridge.)
Restrictions No smoking in 20 bedrooms. Dogs by arrangement only.
Credit cards Access, Amex, Visa.
Terms Rooms: single £135–£155, double £165–£190, suite £275. Breakfast: continental £9.50, English £13.50. Set lunch £16.90, dinner £23.90; full alc £45. Weekend rates; theatre packages.

If you are recommending a bed-and-breakfast hotel and know of a good restaurant nearby, do mention it in your report.

The Capital *Tel* (0171) 589 5171
22–24 Basil Street, SW3 1AT *Fax* (0171) 225 0011

David and Margaret Levin's "grand hotel in miniature" is in a narrow but busy side street near Harrods. In the *Michelin*-starred restaurant, with its impressive chandeliers, Philip Britten's French-inspired cooking is "of a very high standard, and immaculately served, with a personal style". Bedrooms, with patterned wallpaper and heavy drapes, vary in size and style. They have original paintings, double-glazing and air-conditioning, 24-hour room service, etc. Some are quite dark. Compact bathrooms are lavishly marbled and comprehensively equipped. There's a small lounge (where tea may be served) and a cosy bar. The Levins also own *L'Hotel*, next door but one, at 28 Basil Street: *Tel* (0171) 589 6286; *fax* (0171) 225 0011. This is cheaper and simpler than the *Capital* (no porterage, room service, bathroom extras, etc). Its bedrooms, recently refurbished, have a country-style decor, and a kettle, crockery and a fridge. A busy basement wine bar, the *Metro*, serves good-value meals to all comers, and breakfast to *L'Hotel*'s residents. We'd be grateful for reports on all three establishments.

Open All year.
Rooms 8 suites, 28 double, 12 single.
Facilities Lift. Lounge, bar, restaurant; 2 private dining rooms, business facilities.
Location Central. Rooms double-glazed; rear ones quietest. Garage for 12 cars (£20 per night). (Underground: Knightsbridge.)
Restriction Dogs at management's discretion, not in public rooms.
Credit cards All major cards accepted.
Terms (*Excluding VAT on accommodation*) Rooms: single £167, double £197, suite £290. Breakfast £12.50. Set lunch £25, dinner £55 and £75; full alc £60. Weekend rates.

The Connaught *Tel* (0171) 499 7070
Carlos Place, W1Y 6AL *Fax* (0171) 495 3262

One of London's most exclusive hotels, in the heart of Mayfair. Owned by the Savoy Group, and overseen by the vigilant manager, Paolo Zago, and his German wife, it offers "a standard of discreet service almost unknown these days, without a hint of pretension". Guests' privacy is jealously guarded, bedrooms are often booked months in advance. Public rooms are panelled and staid, with formal, fragrant flower arrangements; there's a splendid mahogany staircase. "We have been visiting the *Connaught* for over 15 years, and consider it the best hotel in the world," write a couple of veteran hoteliers. "The restaurant manager, M. Chevallier, is the most courteous, considerate and efficient we have ever encountered." The *Michelin*-starred kitchen serves both the restaurant, with its gleaming panels, arched windows and glittering chandeliers, and the more intimate green-walled Grill Room. On Michel Bourdin's wide-ranging *carte*, classic French dishes rub shoulders with traditional English fare. There is also a small daily-changing *table d'hôte* menu for lunch in both restaurants, and for dinner in the Grill Room. Formal dress *de rigueur* in both. "There seemed to be as many waiters as diners, all busy – carving the joint on the trolley, flambéeing dishes at the table, pouring wine; no rush, no delays." "One of the most *home-like* hotels we have ever stayed at. Staff are friendly and warm. Arriving with our ten-month-old baby, we were upgraded to a magnificent suite – high-ceilinged, with good lighting, and immaculate marble bathroom." "Top-class breakfast." A sign of the times: notices everywhere asking visitors not to use their mobile telephones. (*Francis Coulson and Brian Sack, and others*)

Open All year. Grill Room closed midday Sat/Sun.
Rooms 24 suites, 36 double, 30 single.
Facilities Lift. 2 lounges, cocktail bar, Grill Room, restaurant; private dining room.
Location Central. Limited private parking. (Underground: Bond St.)
Restrictions Guests asked to refrain from smoking in restaurants. No dogs.
Credit cards All major cards accepted.
Terms [1996] (*Excluding VAT on accommodation*) Rooms: single £198, double £265–£285, suite £495–£600. Breakfast: continental £12 (*plus 15% service*); English alc. Set lunch £25 (Sun £30), dinner £35; full alc £48.20.

Durrants *Tel* (0171) 935 8131
George Street, W1H 6BJ *Fax* (0171) 487 3510

Traditional and "firmly English in character", this is one of the city's oldest privately owned hotels; it has been run by the Miller family since 1921. Composed of a row of terraced houses, it has a quaint and rambling interior, with small panelled lounges leading off a corridor. Bedrooms vary greatly (some are extremely small): rear ones are quietest; front ones are larger and lighter. A report on a visit when many things went wrong (messages not delivered, wake-up calls forgotten, room service muddles) led to the hotel's demotion to italics last year. Now a frequent visitor leaps to the defence: "I have stayed often, for several weeks at a time, and frequently lunched and dined here. I cannot speak too highly of the kindly reception I have always received. The food is of high quality, and one receives perfect attention in the restaurant." This is endorsed: "Delightful and well maintained. Lounges and bar a pleasure. Good breakfast. Good concierge. Good value." Oxford, Harley and Baker streets and the Wallace Collection are close by. (*Iris, Lady Inverforth, DW, and others*)

Open All year.
Rooms 95 bedrooms, most with bath and/or shower. Some on ground floor. Some air-conditioned.
Facilities 3 lounges, bar, restaurant; function facilities.
Location Central (rear rooms quietest). Public carpark 5 mins' walk. (Underground: Bond St.)
Restrictions Smoking discouraged in dining room. No dogs.
Credit cards Access, Amex, Visa.
Terms Rooms: single £85–£87.50, double £105–£110, suite £150-£210. Breakfast: continental £6.25, English £9.25. Set lunch/dinner £17; full alc £25 (*plus 12½% "optional" service charge*).

Egerton House *Tel* (0171) 589 2412
Egerton Terrace, SW3 2BX *Fax* (0171) 584 6540

A smart little Knightsbridge hotel, with an international clientele "who know a good thing when they find it". It is tucked away on a residential side-street, "and remarkably quiet for London". "We were delighted," writes a visitor from Vancouver. "Smiling faces everywhere. Nothing is too much trouble. Eleven out of ten." And the original nominators, on a return visit, thought it "still a shining example of good London hotel-keeping". It is a red brick Victorian house on four floors, with a town house decor: good antique furniture and pictures and "luscious fabrics". Bedrooms and bathrooms vary in size; most overlook private gardens to which guests have access. "Impeccable" breakfasts are taken in the bedrooms or in a pretty basement room. Afternoon tea is served in the sitting rooms; there is an honesty bar ("pricey"), and an extensive room-service menu, ranging from snacks to full meals. Shoe-cleaning and a newspaper are included in the rates. Accommodation is upgraded when possible. The *Egerton*'s owner, David Naylor-Leyland, also owns the *Franklin*, nearby, and *Duke's Hotel*, St James's. (*David Lodge, David and Kate Wooff*)

Open All year.
Rooms 1 suite, 17 double, 10 single. All air-conditioned.
Facilities Lifts. Drawing room, bar, breakfast room. 24-hour room service. Access to private gardens. Unsuitable for ♿.
Location Central. Valet parking. (Underground: South Kensington.)
Restrictions No smoking in breakfast room. No children under 8. No dogs.
Credit cards All major cards accepted.
Terms [1996] (*Excluding VAT*) Rooms: single £125, double £155–£190, suite £250. Breakfast: continental £9, English £14. Light meals; full alc (*c.* £25).

The Goring *Tel* (0171) 396 9000
Beeston Place *Fax* (0171) 834 4393
Grosvenor Gardens, SW1W 0JW

César award in 1994

"A great hotel." "Friendly, able staff. Bedrooms – even the singles – attractive: pretty mouldings, striped wallpaper, handsome chintz curtains, writing desk and easy chairs. Smashing bathrooms, with pink marble and dark wood." Satisfied American visitors to a traditional establishment in a quiet small street near Victoria, handy for Buckingham Palace and Westminster. Unique among London hotels, it has been a family fief for over 85 years. It was built in 1910 by the grandfather of the present Mr Goring, George the Third, who was born in Room 114. The staff are long-serving – William Cowpe has been general manager for 26 years. Many bedrooms face the pretty private garden (not accessible to guests); some have a balcony. Guests tend to be upgraded when better rooms than booked are available. Meals in the restaurant, accompanied at night by a pianist, are traditional English, "good and well served"; there's an "exceptional, fairly priced" wine list. Bar lunches ("my egg sandwich was virtually a salad") and teas are served in the impressive lounge. (*Alfred Knopf Jr, Carolyn Mathiasen, Richard Creed*) In the past the breakfast has been admired, but there's one comprehensive thumbs-down in 1996; both food and service "quite out of character with the rest".

Open All year.
Rooms 4 suites, 51 double, 21 single.
Facilities Lifts, ramps. Lounge with bar, restaurant; function facilities. Free use of nearby health club.
Location Central, by Buckingham Palace (front rooms double-glazed). Garage and mews parking. (Underground: Victoria.)
Restriction No dogs.
Credit cards All major cards accepted.
Terms Rooms (*excluding VAT*): single £115–£145, double £155–£180, suite £235–£260. Breakfast: continental £10, English £13.50. Bar meals. Set meals (*excluding 12½% service charge*): lunch (2–3 courses) £20–£24, dinner £30. Christmas, Easter, weekend breaks.

Halkin Hotel *Tel* (0171) 333 1000
Halkin Street, SW1X 7DJ *Fax* (0171) 333 1100

A "remarkable" hotel in a residential street in Belgravia, near Hyde Park Corner. It has a striking ultra-modern Italian decor, a *Michelin*-starred Italian restaurant, overlooking a private garden, and a show-biz/business clientele. "Perfection at a price," wrote its nominator. "The unbridled technology takes some getting used to, but after several visits I am completely hooked. The staff are *all* charming. The interior design is supremely functional, and the food is superb, if expensive, with the best bread basket at breakfast I have encountered." (*JW*) There is a Reuters area supplying up-to-date financial news. Bedrooms have a sitting area, fax, video, two telephone lines, and 24-hour room service. More reports, please.

Open All year. Restaurant closed 25/26 Dec, 1 Jan.
Rooms 11 suites, 30 double.
Facilities Lounge, cocktail bar, restaurant. Live harp/guitar at night. Only restaurant suitable for ♿.
Location Central (double-glazing). (Underground: Hyde Park Corner.)
Restriction Guide dogs only.
Credit cards All major cards accepted.
Terms [1996] (*Excluding VAT on meals*) Room: single £220–£245, double £220–£275, suite £350–£450. Breakfast: continental £9.50, cooked £13. Set lunch £18.50; full alc £50–£60. Weekend rates.

Hazlitt's *Tel* (0171) 434 1771
6 Frith Street, W1V 5TZ *Fax* (0171) 439 1524

A conversion of three 18th-century terrace houses in the heart of Soho, within easy walking distance of theatres, museums and countless restaurants. It is named after the essayist, who died here in 1830. "A bountiful clutter of antiques gives a Victorian atmosphere to the whole building." Bedrooms, named after other famous residents and visitors to the house, are well cared for, and generally light and airy; back ones are quietest, though some have a gloomy outlook on to the inner court-yard. Top ones are quite small, lower ones have high ceilings; all have agreeable prints and plants, 18th- and 19th-century beds (many a four-poster or half-tester), and decent linen. Furnishings are mahogany, oak and pine. Some bathrooms have a free-standing bath. An "excellent continental breakfast" is brought to the bedroom; light refreshments and cream teas are available in the lounge. As it's a listed building, there's no lift. The staff are friendly, if a bit too informal for some. More reports, please.

Open All year, except Christmas.
Rooms 1 suite, 17 double, 5 single. 3 on ground floor.
Facility Lounge. Unsuitable for ♿.
Location Central. NCP nearby. (Underground: Tottenham Court Rd.)
Credit cards All major cards accepted.
Terms [1996] (*Excluding VAT*) Rooms: single £108, double £138, suite £185. Continental breakfast £6.25.

There is a greater danger than usual this year that some London hotels may change hands (see page xi of the Introduction). *Caveat emptor*!

Knightsbridge Green Hotel *Tel* (0171) 584 6274
159 Knightsbridge, SW1X 7PD *Fax* (0171) 225 1635

Owned by the Marler family for 30 years, managed by Ann Thomson for ten, and with a devoted clientele from around the world, this unassuming hotel is on Knightsbridge, and handy for Hyde Park. Accommodation is mainly in suites; most are large, and each has a double bedroom, sitting room and bathroom. A "very good" breakfast is brought to the room. The only public room, on the first floor, provides free tea and coffee all day. "It is more like a home than a hotel," writes one regular visitor. "The staff are always friendly and smiling, the service quick and efficient. We usually travel in a big group with children; everyone is well looked after." Another is "warmly enthusiastic about the comfort and consistently high standards of this exceptional small hotel", concluding: "Splendid value for money." A major renovation was recently completed: the entrance has been embellished, bedrooms and bathrooms have been redecorated; there is now air-conditioning and double-glazing throughout. "But," the Marlers say, "the hotel's character has not changed." Comprehensive services are not available; the reception desk and switchboard operate from 8 am to 10.30 pm; direct-dial telephone facilities are available by arrangement. (*P Buranastidporn, SB*)

Open All year (closed 24–27 Dec 1996).
Rooms 12 suites, 8 double, 5 single. All air-conditioned. 1 with ♿ access.
Facilities Lift. Club Room with complimentary refreshments.
Location Central (rooms double-glazed; quietest ones at rear). NCP carpark nearby. (Underground: Knightsbridge.)
Restriction No dogs.
Credit cards All major cards accepted.
Terms [Until Mar 1997] Rooms: single £85, double £120, suite £135. Breakfast: continental £6, English £9.50. *V* (1st night only)

Langorf Hotel *Tel* (0171) 794 4483
20 Frognal *Fax* (0171) 435 9055
Hampstead, NW3 6AG

Edwardian house with leafy walled garden. In residential area in southern part of Hampstead, 3 mins' walk from Finchley Rd tube station with quick transport to centre. Street parking. Good value. Decor simple but tasteful. Helpful staff. Generous continental breakfast buffet in airy no-smoking room. 24-hour bar and light meal service. Nearby Italian restaurant, Mama Rosa, *warmly recommended. 31 bedrooms, including family accommodation; some on ground floor; also 5 serviced apartments. Lift. Unsuitable for ♿. No dogs. All major credit cards accepted. B&B: single £62–£75, double £80–£95, suite £105 [1996]. More reports, please.*

The Leonard NEW *Tel* (0171) 935 2010
15 Seymour Street, W1H 5AA *Fax* (0171) 935 6700

Smart, pricey new town house hotel (opened Feb 1996) off Portman Square, near Marble Arch. "All the comfort and luxury one could want." Antiques, fine fabrics, paintings, plants, flowers. Bedrooms (some no-smoking, all double-glazed) have video, hi-fi; suites have dedicated line for fax or modem. Lounges, café/bar; 24-hour room service menu. Lift, ramp. Exercise room. NCP 2 mins' walk. No dogs. All major credit cards accepted. 20 spacious suites (1 or 2 bedrooms) from £225; 6 doubles from £165; 2 singles £115 (excluding VAT). *Breakfast: continental £9, English £13.50.*

Number Sixteen NEW *Tel* (0171) 589 5232
16 Sumner Place, SW7 3EG *Fax* (0171) 584 8615

Conversion of four late-Victorian town houses in residential street near South Kensington station. Recently refurbished. Traditional decor. Lift, lounges, conservatory (tea and breakfast service), flowery garden with fountain and fishpond. 36 bedrooms (quietest overlook garden), some on ground floor. Access to nearby health and fitness club. Paid parking 5 mins' walk. No children under 8. No dogs. All major credit cards accepted. B&B: single £80–£105, double £140–£170, suite £180 [1996]. English breakfast £8. More reports, please.

Pembridge Court *Tel* (0171) 229 9977
34 Pembridge Gardens, W2 4DX *Fax* (0171) 727 4982

"Thoroughly civilised" town house, in quiet setting near Notting Hill Gate. Handy for travel to centre. "Neither dauntingly luxurious nor vastly expensive." 20 stylish bedrooms, ranging from large to rather poky, some on ground floor. Pretty lounge. Basement restaurant serves snacks (residents only). Recently sold by long-time owner Paul Capra, but Valerie Gilliat, general manager, and most of the "lovely" long-serving staff have stayed. Special rates at nearby health club. Unsuitable for ♿. No dogs in public rooms. All major credit cards accepted. B&B: single £100–£125, double £125–£165. More reports, please. V* *(1 night only)*

Sandringham Hotel *Tel* (0171) 435 1569
3 Holford Road, NW3 1AD *Fax* (0171) 431 5932

This four-storeyed Victorian town house is in a quiet residential street, and handy for Hampstead Heath and for the tube station. It had a *Guide* entry for over ten years when it was run as a modest B&B by the friendly Dreyer family. After Mr Dreyer's death and a period in the doldrums, it was bought by an American couple, Michael and Jill von Grey. They have extensively redecorated, in smart country house style. The public rooms have "voluptuous curtains, striped wallpaper, and an overall impression of warmth and good taste". Bedrooms are good-sized to small, depending on their position in the house, "and attractive, with flowers, sherry, mineral water and good toiletries". Some overlook the pretty garden, with a goldfish pond, benches among flower borders, and a view of a nearby church steeple. Breakfast "is very good, with attentive service, no packets, and a wide selection of cooked dishes". The "Sunday Baroque Brunch" is accompanied by chamber music. Afternoon teas and room service evening meals are served. "The place has charm and a helpful proprietor," says a recent report, "but my bathroom was minute and gimcrack, and the room was cold until I asked for a heater. Good value, though." (*BB, and others*) Late news: the hotel is up for sale, though no immediate change of owner is expected.

Open All year.
Rooms 2 suites, 11 double, 4 single. 2 on ground floor.
Facilities Lounge, dining/function room. Small garden.

Location 15 mins by underground from central London. Private parking. (Underground: Hampstead.)
Restrictions No smoking: dining room, bedrooms. No children under 7. No dogs.
Credit cards Access, Amex (*£5 surcharge*), Visa.
Terms B&B: single £68–£98, double £110–£130, suite £145. Cooked breakfast: £3.50 added.

Swiss Cottage Hotel *Tel* (0171) 722 2281
4 Adamson Road, NW3 3HP *Fax* (0171) 483 4588

An idiosyncratic establishment in a residential area, convenient for transport to the centre, and generally considered good value for money. Its decor is Victorian; public rooms have antiques, oriental rugs "and 'real' though sometimes strange paintings". Bedrooms vary greatly in size and comfort; some have a sitting room overlooking the small walled garden. There are some inexpensive singles with shared shower. The hotel's wayward charms have always drawn mixed reports, and this year is no exception: "We stay there regularly and recommend it to all our friends," says a fan. Another adds: "Staff of a cheerfulness and helpfulness unusual for a city hotel. Furnishings attractive, if sometimes in need of repair." One dissenter thought that the accommodation was "perfectly adequate", but that breakfast was "a disaster", while another was critical of room maintenance. (*Dr David H Clark, JD, and others*) There is a 24-hour snack service. More reports, please.

Open All year.
Rooms 47 double, 16 single, most with bath/shower. Some on ground floor. Also 17 self-catering apartments.
Facilities Lift. Lounge, bar, breakfast room; function facilities. Walled garden. Unsuitable for ♿.
Location 2 mins' walk from Swiss Cottage Underground (Eton Avenue exit). Small carpark; street parking (comparatively easy).
Restrictions No smoking in breakfast room. No dogs.
Credit cards All major cards accepted.
Terms [1996] B&B: single £75–£130, double £85–£140. Children under 8 accommodated free in parents' room.

Tophams Ebury Court *Tel* (0171) 730 8147
28 Ebury Street, SW1W 0LU *Fax* (0171) 823 5966

Family-owned for over 55 years, this hotel rambles through five adjoining houses near Victoria Station. The bedrooms are mostly small; not all have facilities *en suite*, but bathrobes are provided for the trip down the corridor. Rear ones are quietest. It has small public rooms, too; there's a pleasant basement bar, open to all, and a restaurant, recently revamped, serving a *table d'hôte* lunch and dinner *à la carte*. The hotel is now run by Marianne Kingsford, of the third generation of Tophams, with her husband, Nicholas, "both much in evidence". Many of the staff are long-serving. "Though they have modernised to some necessary degree," writes a regular visitor, "it retains much of its old-fashioned style." An American, who stayed for ten days, thought it "a gem": "Impeccably clean. with a calm country house atmosphere, and a competent staff." "Friendly atmosphere. Good breakfast served by nice ladies," writes a regular visitor from the Netherlands. (*RAL Ogston, Nancy T Elmer, CC Ten Hallers*)

Open All year, except Christmas, New Year. Restaurant closed 2 weeks Aug.
Rooms 26 double, 14 single. 22 with private facilities. Some on ground floor.
Facilities Sitting room, bar, restaurant; private dining/function room.
Location Central (front rooms double-glazed). Meter parking. (Underground: Victoria.)
Restriction No dogs.
Credit cards All major cards accepted.
Terms [1996] B&B: single £70–£100, double £95–£135. Set lunch £10.50; full alc £24.

---

22 Jermyn Street *Tel* (0171) 734 2353
22 Jermyn Street, SW1Y 6HL *Fax* (0171) 734 0750
E-mail 100445.1627@compuserve.com

César award in 1996

"A gem of understated elegance. The staff go out of their way to make guests welcome, but they are never intrusive." A 1996 endorsement for a small hotel in a prime position in St James's. Owned by the same family since 1915, it is currently run by Henry Togna. West End theatres and shops, and many good restaurants, are nearby. No public rooms; accommodation is in spacious suites and studios; the decor is an appealing blend of contemporary furniture and fabrics with antiques, potted plants and flowers. The bathrooms are "marvellously luxurious". "Information folder the best I have seen in any hotel." Mr Togna is a fitness fanatic: guests may use the sporting facilities at a luxurious club nearby, or borrow a mountain or a racing bike. The able manager, Annette Foster, will accompany guests on an early-morning three-park jog. Mr Togna, a technology buff, "is continually adding 'information super-highway services' for his guests". "Check-in procedure simple and friendly. Acceptably quiet for such a central location." Light room-service meals are available. Children are made welcome: there are games and videos, teddy-bear dressing gowns, a special menu, and a newsletter listing local attractions and child-friendly eating places. (*AA van Straubenzee, and others*)

Open All year.
Rooms 13 suites, 5 double.
Facilities Lift. Small conference facilities. Access to pool, gym, squash courts at nearby club.
Location Central. Valet parking. (Underground: Piccadilly Circus.)
Restriction No dogs.
Credit cards All major cards accepted.
Terms (*Excluding VAT*) Room £185, suite £235–£270. Extra bed £30. Continental breakfast £12.

The Wilbraham *Tel* (0171) 730 8296
1 Wilbraham Place *Fax* (0171) 730 6815
Sloane Street, SW1X 9AE

A long-established privately owned hotel, "useful but not luxurious", remarkably reasonable in price for its prime position near Sloane Square. "The epitome of an old London house, generally quiet and warm, with agreeable public rooms, nice pictures, pretty wallpaper. Several staircases; you have to remember which is yours. Good breakfast, with brown bread and scones, brought to the room." Some bedrooms are "large and handsome", others are small; the bathrooms, both private and shared, can at best be called "dowdy". It has always aroused mixed emotions. Those in favour praise the "old-fashioned service – porter available to carry bags"; the "warmth of welcome, no charm school here"; and the "lovely cotton sheets and luscious towels". But housekeeping is "patchy at best", the meals in the bar/buttery are nothing to write home about, and one would-be visitor had an abrasive telephone exchange when booking.

Open All year. Bar/buttery closed Sun, bank holidays.
Rooms 4 suites, 33 double, 14 single. 45 with private facilities.
Facilities 2 lifts. Residents' lounge, bar/buttery. 24-hour room service. Unsuitable for ♿.
Location Central, near Sloane Square. Public garage nearby. (Underground: Sloane Square.)
Restriction No dogs.
Credit cards None accepted.
Terms [1996] (*Excluding VAT*) Rooms: single £39–£54, double £66–£72. Breakfast: continental from £3.50, English from £5.50. Alc (excluding wine): lunch from £5, dinner from £10. *V*

LONGHORSLEY Northumberland — Map 4

Linden Hall

Longhorsley, Morpeth NE65 8XF

Tel (01670) 516611
Fax (01670) 788544

An impressive ivy-covered Georgian country house near Morpeth, "with an atmosphere of quiet grandeur and luxury". It is set in huge well-kept grounds, with formal gardens: "A pleasure to walk in; no road sounds can be heard, just birdsong." There is a health and beauty spa, "with a superb swimming pool and jacuzzi, which greatly enhances the pleasure of a visit". Bedrooms are "elegantly decorated, comfortable and immaculately clean, with an excellent bathroom, full of treats"; best ones are in the original house. Public rooms are spacious and grand. "Quality is value for money," wrote a devotee last year, "and it would be easy to blanch at the price, but we consider it fair for the level of service, and the attitude of staff. We were hooked 11 years ago. The spell has not worn off. If we came without our children (four and seven on our first visit) we would not be forgiven." Others praise the porters, "who create an excellent first impression". In the "rather grand" *Dobson* restaurant (jacket and tie rule strictly enforced), Anglo-French cooking by chef Keith Marshall is "served with polish". Those who prefer less formal surroundings can eat in the *Granary* restaurant in the pub in the grounds. (*NB, and others*) The hotel is company-owned and goes in for functions and conferences, which can diminish the pleasure of private guests. There is a £5 charge for room-service meals.

Open All year.
Rooms 3 suites, 45 double, 2 single. 1 adapted for ♿.
Facilities Lift, ramps. Reception room, drawing room, bar, billiard room, restaurant, conservatory; conference/function facilities; *Linden* pub with restaurant; health spa: swimming pool, jacuzzi, beauty treatments, etc. 450-acre park: croquet, tennis, putting, fishing, jogging, clay pigeon-shooting, mountain bikes for hire; 18-hole golf course to open Apr 1997.
Location On A697, 1 mile N of Longhorsley.
Restrictions No smoking: restaurant, spa lounge. No dogs in public rooms.
Credit cards All major cards accepted.
Terms B&B: single £97.50–£102, double £125–£195, suite £195. Pub meals from £5. Set dinner £25; full alc £30. Christmas, New Year breaks.

LORTON Cumbria Map 4

New House Farm BUDGET *Tel/Fax* (01900) 85404
Lorton, Cockermouth CA13 9UU

Neither new nor a farm, Hazel and John Hatch's no-smoking 17th-century guest house has 15-acre grounds with garden, fields, woodland and stream. In beautiful, unspoilt area, off B5289 S of Lorton; easy access to Loweswater, Crummere, Buttermere. "Warm, friendly atmosphere, cosy lounge with open fire." Traditional English dinners (no choice of main course); short, intelligent wine list. Lunch ("above average") and tea served in old barn alongside. 3 spacious bedrooms, all with private facilities (no TV*). Unsuitable for* ♿*. No children under 12. No dogs in public rooms. Credit cards not accepted. Double room: B&B £60–£70, D,B&B £100–£106. Recently endorsed, but we'd like more reports, please.*

LOWER BEEDING West Sussex Map 2

South Lodge *Tel* (01403) 891711
Brighton Road, Lower Beeding *Fax* (01403) 891766
nr Horsham RH13 6PS

An impressive wisteria-clad mansion in the Sussex Downs, peaceful, but handy for Gatwick airport. It was originally the home of Frederick Ducane Godman, a Victorian explorer and botanist who planted rare trees and shrubs, including some magnificent rhododendrons, in its vast and lovely grounds. There are lots of outdoor pursuits (see below). The interior is elegant, with wooden floors, panelling, moulded ceilings, chandeliers, antiques, and luxurious bedrooms, some with wonderful views of the Sussex Downs. The hotel goes in for conferences, and is not personally owned, but our correspondents have found it welcoming and good value: "We'd booked the least expensive rooms; they were quiet and huge, with all the goodies one expects of a luxury hotel, but packaged in a homely way, eg, cotton buds in pretty Thai pottery. Excellent lighting. Lavish marble bathrooms. Cooking by chef Timothy Neal was a sort of revisited English *cuisine*, extremely good, served in a room with lovely views. Breakfast also good, with nice bread." "The staff were genuinely concerned that we should have exactly what we wanted, particularly during meals." "Afternoon tea one of the finest ever." (*GD, and others*) Guests have members' rights at Mannings Heath Golf Club nearby, under the same management.

Open All year.
Rooms 4 suites, 33 double, 2 single. 1 on ground floor.
Facilities Ramp. Lounge (pianist Fri/Sat evening), bar, restaurant; conference/function facilities. 93-acre park: gardens, tennis, croquet, *pétanque*, clay pigeon-shooting; shooting, archery by arrangement. Golf, coarse fishing, riding nearby.
Location On A281, 5 miles S of Horsham.
Restrictions No smoking in restaurant. No dogs.
Credit cards All major cards accepted.
Terms [1996] Rooms: single from £110, double from £135, suite from £205. Breakfast: continental £8, English £10. Set lunch from £16, dinner from £25; full alc from £47. *V* (Aug only; 2 nights max.)

LOWER BOCKHAMPTON Dorset — Map 2

See Dorchester

LOWER SLAUGHTER Gloucestershire — Map 3

Lower Slaughter Manor — *Tel* (01451) 820456
Lower Slaughter GL54 2HP — *Fax* (01451) 822150

By the church on the edge of an unspoilt Cotswold village, a Grade II listed manor, recently refurbished, set in large grounds with manicured lawns, a flowery walled garden and an ancient dovecote. It has a fine interior with a country house decor: superb plaster ceilings and chimney pieces, open fires, fine oak staircase, galleried landing, antiques, smart soft furnishings, family photographs, impressive flower arrangements. Bedrooms are well stocked with sherry, home-made shortbread, etc; some have a four-poster. There's a pretty indoor swimming pool, with arched French windows leading on to the garden. Another new chef, Alan Dann, arrived in April 1996. He has worked at the *Waterside*, Bray (*qv*) and spent some time in France. Visitors shortly after his arrival thought his modern French cooking "excellent", adding: "The restaurant is efficient and comfortable, with charming French waiters. Our bedroom was large and stylish." Others enjoyed the atmosphere: "More home than hotel: no reception desk; owners, Audrey and Peter Marks, very much in evidence. Staff pleasant and attentive." Breakfast is continental or cooked. Half board only. (*Pat and Jeremy Temple, and others*) One couple were strongly critical of their room in the coach house, and thought the place over-managed. The restaurant can be busy with non-residents at the weekend. Some eyebrows are raised at the "upper-bracket Cotswold" prices.

Open All year, except 2–9 Jan.
Rooms 2 suites, 12 double. 4 in separate buildings.
Facilities 3 lounges, restaurant; function facilities; indoor swimming pool, sauna. 4-acre grounds: tennis, croquet, putting. Fishing nearby. Unsuitable for ♿.
Location By church in village, off A429 (direction The Slaughters) 3 miles SW of Stow-on-the-Wold.
Restrictions No smoking in restaurant. No children under 10. No dogs.
Credit cards Access, Amex, Visa.
Terms [1996] D,B&B: single £145–£220, double £190–£300, suite £320. Set lunch £18.95, dinner £32.50. 2-night breaks Nov–Mar; Christmas, New Year house parties. 1-night bookings sometimes refused weekends.

LUDLOW Shropshire — Map 3

Dinham Hall NEW — *Tel* (01584) 876464
Dinham, Ludlow SY8 1EJ — *Fax* (01584) 876019

A handsome 18th-century house in a quiet street near the castle of this historic town – "a perfect position". It was recently bought by the Mifsuds of *The Lake*, Llangammarch Wells (*qv*), and is run by manager James Warlow. Redecoration was still in progress at the time of writing. "The young staff are charming," wrote our inspector, "and it has the advantages of a country hotel – total silence, and views of fields –

without the feeling of isolation. There is an agreeable garden. Our room at the top was sunny, spacious, bright and clean, with good views. The restaurant, with pastel colours and gas lighting, serves modern English/French cooking; we thought the main courses over-ambitious, with odd combinations of flavours, but the puddings were delicious. Breakfast was good, with butter and marmalade in pots, and very good coffee." The hotel is within walking distance of Shaun Hill's *Michelin*-starred *Merchant House* restaurant, and would make a good base for Ludlow's annual festival, during which Shakespeare is produced in the castle.

Open All year.
Rooms 10 double, 2 single.
Facilities 2 lounges, dining room; 2 private dining rooms; gym, sauna. ½-acre garden. Fishing, riding, golf nearby. Only public rooms suitable for ♿.
Location By castle. Private parking.
Restrictions No smoking in dining room. No dogs in public rooms.
Credit cards All major cards accepted.
Terms B&B: single £62, double £89–£120; D,B&B £60–£73 per person. Set lunch £13.50, dinner £23.50; full alc £29.40. Winter, Christmas breaks *V*

LYME REGIS Dorset — Map 1

Hotel Alexandra BUDGET
Pound Street
Lyme Regis DT7 3HZ
Tel (01297) 442010
Fax (01297) 443229

In this most attractive town, Mr and Mrs Haskins' large white hotel enjoys a superb position looking over the sea and the famous Cobb harbour. It has a lovely, well-kept garden, where cream teas and snacks are served in fine weather. It is a Georgian dower house, with later additions (it became a hotel in 1901), and has many flights of stairs, and long corridors. Bedrooms vary greatly in size and quality. "No 12, one of the best, is a stunner, very large with a marvellous bay window looking over the garden to the sea. It was cleaned whilst we breakfasted, and serviced while we dined." Other rooms have been called "small, but charmingly decorated", but one recent visitor experienced thin walls and poor-quality furnishings. The restaurant serves good traditional English cooking; there is a comprehensive, fairly priced wine list. Breakfast is "excellent, with an extensive buffet; the cooked dishes included particularly good fish". "Rather old-fashioned; good value for money. Helpful staff. Nice lounge, with lots of games and current magazines." Children are welcomed. Some meals have been spoiled by smokers; there's only a partial smoking ban in the restaurant.

Open All year, except Dec–mid-Jan.
Rooms 25 double, 2 single. 3 on ground floor. 1 on garden, with private patio.
Facilities Lounge, conservatory, bar, restaurant. 1½-acre garden. Beach 300 yds; fishing, tennis, golf, riding, nearby.
Location 200 yds from centre. Courtyard parking.
Restrictions No very young children at dinner. No dogs in public rooms, unattended in bedrooms.
Credit cards All major cards accepted.
Terms [1996] B&B: single £25–£45, double £45–£108; D,B&B: single £40–£60, double £75–£138. Bar lunches. Set lunch £12.50 (Sun £10.50), dinner £18.50; full alc £30. 7 nights for the price of 6. Off-season breaks.

LYNMOUTH Devon — Map 1

The Rising Sun

Lynmouth EX35 6EQ
Tel (01598) 753223
Fax (01598) 753480

A picturesque hostelry on the harbourside. "All crooked beamed ceilings, winding passages, uneven creaky floors, leaded windows, and mind-your-head notices", it is composed of a 14th-century inn and a row of thatched cottages. The poet Shelley honeymooned with Harriet Westbrook in one of these; it is now a suite with a four-poster. A charming terraced garden has been cut into the hill at the back. Bedrooms and bathrooms are pretty, "with extra comforts to compensate for lack of size", though some have thought them over-priced. The oak-panelled, beamed dining room is small too, with tables close together. It serves traditional dishes, using locally caught fish and shellfish and Exmoor game, with simple, freshly cooked vegetables. Staff are "mostly Antipodean – young, friendly and efficient". "The host, Hugo Jeune, is genuinely interested in his guests; we could have chatted with him for hours." (*Linda K Dwyer; also Barbara Hill, Good Pub Guide*) The D,B&B rate gives residents a £21.50 allowance towards dishes from the *carte* which, one couple felt, was "not enough for a proper dinner, unless you chose the cheapest items".

Open All year.
Rooms 1 suite (in cottage), 13 double, 2 single. 4 in annexes.
Facilities Lounge, bar, restaurant. Small terraced garden. Rock beach; sea fishing. Salmon-fishing ¼ mile. Unsuitable for ♿.
Location On harbourside. Public carpark nearby.
Restrictions No smoking: dining room, 6 bedrooms. No children under 8. No dogs.
Credit cards All major cards accepted.
Terms B&B £41.50–£61; D,B&B £59–£82. Bar lunches. Full alc £29. 2–5-day breaks except Aug, Sept, bank holidays. Christmas, New Year packages. 1-night bookings sometimes refused. V

LYNTON Devon — Map 1

Old Rectory

Martinhoe, nr Lynton EX31 4QT
Tel (01598) 763368
Fax (01598) 763567

An unpretentious small hotel set in tranquil gardens in a Domesday-old hamlet just outside Lynton, on the edge of Exmoor. "John and Suzanne Bradbury are lovely hosts, friendly, but not too friendly, and thoroughly professional. The food is based on the best possible materials, all cooked perfectly in the Jane Grigson tradition, and served in generous portions. The wine list is carefully selected, with a modest mark-up. No charge for morning coffee and afternoon tea with home-made cake. All details are carefully attended to: elegant table settings, fresh flowers and fruit in bedrooms, beds turned down at night. There are beautiful walks close by, and two bays with good swimming within walking/driving distance." "Spacious bedrooms. Never a hint of 'hotel style' in the decor." Much of the furniture is made by the Bradburys' talented cabinet-maker son, Daniel, who also waits at table. There's an agreeable vinery for tea and drinks. The North Devon Coastal Path is close by. (*Sir Arnold and Lady Burgen; also Prof. Malcolm D Lilly, and others*) The hotel is now completely smoke-free.

Open Easter–end Oct. Lunch not served.
Rooms 1 suite, 7 double. 2 on ground floor. No telephone.
Facilities 2 lounges, dining room, vinery. 3½-acre garden. Sea 1½ miles. Sea and game fishing, riding, golf nearby.
Location From M5 exit 27 take A361; by-pass South Molton, right on to A399 for Blackmore Gate; right on to A39 for Parracombe/Lynton, bypass Parracombe; at Martinhoe cross, 3rd unclassified road on left for Woody Bay/Martinhoe.
Restrictions No smoking. No children under 14. No dogs.
Credit cards None accepted.
Terms [1996] B&B £38–£45; D,B&B £50–£65. Set dinner £22.

MALMESBURY Wiltshire — Map 3

The Old Bell NEW
Abbey Row
Malmesbury SN16 0AG

Tel (01666) 822344
Fax (01666) 825145

This old inn, in a pretty town "with marvellous views", was built in the 12th century for visitors to the library of the abbey next door; some original features have survived. It was recently taken over and refurbished by Nigel Chapman of *Woolley Grange* (*qv*) and Nicholas Dickinson, formerly managing director of *Le Manoir aux Quat'Saisons* (*qv*). It aims, as does *Woolley Grange*, to provide civilised comforts for adults while happily accommodating their children. "It's a rambling building, much extended over the years," wrote our inspectors. "Good atmosphere. Attractive decor: antiques, interesting pictures and artefacts, plants and flowers. The oldest part, the 'Great Hall' (now, in fact, a jumble of small rooms), serves light lunches, teas, and evening snacks. A twisting corridor leads to two lounges with comfortable chairs and sofas, books, magazines, newspapers and games. Our smallish front bedroom had some traffic noise by day, but was quiet at night. It was adequate, but without 'extras'. Children may be left all day with trained nursemaids (no charge) in the Den, with a huge TV screen with nintendo, and lots of games; they have their own supper. Parents dine quietly later, when the sophisticated listening system takes over. The attractive Edwardian-style dining room is large and high-ceilinged, with huge mirrors and old oil paintings. Good, straightforward British cooking was marred by amateurish service, Surprisingly, smoking is allowed. Breakfast was poor, with long delays. Reception was casual, and there were some housekeeping lapses. If these teething troubles are sorted out, it could be an excellent hotel. There are an attractive garden and terrace, with tables, chairs and swings, at the rear." Subsequent visitors have been more impressed with the restaurant: "Four distinct hits and only one miss on the £18.50 menu, which changes daily. Excellent service, generous portions." (*HR, Godfrey Smith*)

Open All year.
Rooms 2 suites, 25 double, 4 single. 14 in coach house, 6 on ground floor.
Facilities 2 lounges, Great Hall (for drinks and snacks), children's playroom (supervised 10 am–6 pm), dining room. Small garden. Riding, tennis, golf, gliding, dry skiing, water-sports, cycling nearby.
Location Central, by abbey. Carpark.
Restriction No dogs in dining room.
Credit cards All major cards accepted.
Terms [1996] B&B: single £60–£70, double £85–£130, suite £150. Set lunch £15, dinner £18.50–£24. Children accommodated free in parents' room. Special interest breaks; off-season breaks. 1-night bookings generally refused Sat.

MALVERN WELLS Hereford and Worcester — Map 3

The Cottage in the Wood — *Tel* (01684) 575859
Holywell Road — *Fax* (01684) 560662
Malvern Wells WR14 4LG

A Georgian dower house high on the slopes of the Malvern Hills, amid woods and shrubbery. It has a stunning view over the Severn valley to the distant Cotswolds, and is in a designated area of outstanding natural beauty. From its grounds you can follow a sign, "To the Hills", and walk straight out to a nine-mile range of the Malverns and more than a hundred miles of tracks. The hotel is a family concern, run by the resident owners, John and Sue Pattin ("genial hosts"), with daughter Maria as manager; son Dominic is *sous chef*, and his wife Romy is housekeeper. Public rooms have fine antique furniture "and the kind of magazines that aid digestion". Bedrooms in the main house (some small) are decorated in traditional style, "with the traveller's every possible requirement, including lovely home-made shortbread and plenty of local information". Others (modern, smallish but with huge picture-windows and terrace or balcony) are in a converted coach house, or else (cottagey) in Beech Cottage. The restaurant, serving modern English cooking on the large menu, is "very pretty", and one couple thought the dinners "of a high quality"; others have been less satisfied. The light lunches and the breakfasts are enjoyed. (*Ruth and Derek Tilsley, and others*)

Open All year.
Rooms 20 double. 4 in Beech Cottage (70 yds), 8 in Coach House 100 yds.
Facilities Lounge, lounge bar, restaurant; function facilities. 7-acre grounds leading to Malvern Hills. Golf, squash nearby. Unsuitable for ♿.
Location Off A449 to Ledbury, 3 miles S of Malvern; turn right opposite Gulf/Rover petrol station. Do not approach from S end of Holywell Rd.
Restrictions No smoking in dining room. No dogs in main house.
Credit cards Access, Amex, Visa.
Terms B&B: single £68–£74, double £89–£135; D,B&B (min. 2 nights) £50–£77 per person. Set lunch: £11 Mon–Sat, £14 Sun; full alc £33. Bargain breaks all year. Christmas, New Year packages. 1-night bookings sometimes refused Fri/Sat. **V**

MATLOCK BATH Derbyshire — Map 3

Hodgkinson's Hotel BUDGET — *Tel* (01629) 582170
150 South Parade — *Fax* (01629) 584891
Matlock Bath DE4 3NR

César award in 1994

The first hotel to be built in the spa, in 1698. The original oval hotel sign still hangs outside, and much of the ground floor has not changed greatly since this time. It has been lovingly restored by Malcolm Archer, who has a hairdressing salon on the first floor, and Nigel Shelley, an interior designer. It won its *César* for the enjoyably eccentric atmosphere and decor behind its plain façade. It is a collector's treasure trove, unashamedly dedicated to Victoriana. William Morris wallpaper, Victorian prints, and Staffordshire china adorn the public rooms. Fox furs, hats, gloves, shoes, Dinky toys, Minton china, figurines, Art Nouveau relics, dress-maker's dummy, birdcages, old shoes and exotic paintings enliven the climb up the stairs – four floors, no lift. The owners share the cooking "which is as eclectic and imaginative as the rest, with impeccable vegetables and succulent desserts". The bedrooms are priced according to size; some are spacious, and there are some splendid beds. Service is "willing", breakfast "excellent". Only snag: the hotel stands on a busy thoroughfare; front rooms are subject to noise from passers-by and from traffic.

Open All year. Dining room closed midday, to non-residents Sun.
Rooms 7 double.
Facilities 2 lounges, restaurant. ¼-acre garden. By river Derwent: fishing. Unsuitable for ♿.
Location Central (2 quiet rooms at rear). Private carpark.
Restriction No dogs in public rooms.
Credit cards Access, Amex, Visa.
Terms [1996] B&B: single £30–£60, double £50–£90. Set dinner £19.50, £24.50. 1-night bookings sometimes refused weekends.

MEMBURY Devon **Map 1**

Lea Hill Hotel NEW/BUDGET *Tel* (01404) 881881
Membury, nr Axminster EX13 7AQ

"A comfortable family-run hotel, providing excellent value for money," writes the nominator of this 14th-century thatched longhouse. It is in large grounds in a designated area of outstanding natural beauty, and has ancient beams, flagstone floors, inglenook fireplaces and a pretty decor. "Reached by narrow lanes, it is high up, with stunning views. The owners, Hilary and Jim Reaney, new to the hotel trade, are easy and welcoming. They greeted us with tea and biscuits, and help with luggage. Most bedrooms are in smartly converted barns; most have a private garden or patio. Ours had quality fabrics, nice prints, good china for tea, excellent lighting, and modern bathroom with lots of goodies. Public rooms have old furniture, copper, brass, flowers, etc. There's a pub-like bar, with leather furniture. The dining room has a cottagey feel; Mrs Reaney cooks good dinner-party food; there is a set menu with no choice of main course, or they make an allowance of £12.95 towards dishes from the *carte*. Small, inexpensive wine list. Good breakfasts, with fruit, wide choice of cooked items, bowls of marmalade and jam. Duvets on beds, but you can ask for blankets." Children are welcomed; two suites are suitable for a family. (*Heather Sharland*)

Open Feb–Dec.
Rooms 2 suites, 8 double, 1 single. 9 in converted barns. Most with private patio or garden. 3 on ground floor.
Facilities Lounge, bar, study, restaurant. 8-acre grounds: croquet. Riding, hunting, fishing nearby; sea, safe beaches 10 miles.
Location 2½ miles NW of Axminster. A35 towards Honiton; turn right opposite *Old Inn*, Kilmington, to Stockland; following signs to Membury, cross Yarty River, turn left at T-junction. Driveway on left, after ½ mile. If you reach Membury you have gone too far. From Membury: ¾ miles S; ¼ mile after trout farm.
Restrictions No smoking, except in bar. No dogs, except in bar, 2 bedrooms.
Credit cards Access, Amex, Visa.
Terms B&B £35–£47; D,B&B £47–£59. Set lunch £14.95, dinner £16.95; full alc £23.95. 3-night breaks; Christmas, New Year breaks; wine-tasting, walking, painting weekends.

MIDDLECOMBE Somerset — Map 1

Periton Park — *Tel/Fax* (01643) 706885
Middlecombe, nr Minehead TA24 8SW

Richard and Angela Hunt's Victorian house in peaceful setting in 4-acre grounds 1½ miles from Minehead, on edge of Exmoor National Park. Large, attractive lounge. Good country house cooking in panelled dining room, sunny at breakfast, candlelit at night (no-smoking). Riding, shooting, fishing, golf available. Open Feb–Dec. 8 smart bedrooms, 3 no-smoking, 1 on ground floor. No children under 12. No dogs in public rooms. Access, Amex, Visa accepted. B&B: single £56, double £92; D,B&B: single £73, double £126 [1996]. More reports, please.

MIDDLEHAM North Yorkshire — Map 4

The Miller's House — *Tel* (01969) 622630
Middleham DL8 4NR — *Fax* (01969) 623570

Middleham is a small, peaceful village in the heart of the Yorkshire dales, and a major racehorse-training centre. Just off its cobbled market square, in an elevated position overlooking an impressive ruined castle, is Judith and Crossley Sunderland's small grey stone Georgian house. They run it "with a great staff, as helpful and friendly as their employers". It is decorated "with lavish use of fabrics, and lots of attention to detail". Bedrooms, some beamed, are "stylish"; one has a four-poster and a free-standing Victorian roll-top bath in the room. Some bathrooms are small. There is plenty of choice on the menu, which includes such exotica as ostrich, kangaroo and crocodile, alongside less startling dishes. Fresh local produce and home-grown vegetables, herbs and fruit are used, and vegetarians are catered for. There's an award-winning wine list, competitively priced. Most *Guide* reporters have liked the food, but one couple this year was critical and thought the dining room "lacked atmosphere".

Open All year, except Jan.
Rooms 6 double, 1 single.
Facilities Lounge with bar, dining room, conservatory. Small garden. Fishing nearby. Unsuitable for ♿.
Location Centre of small, quiet village.
Restrictions No smoking: dining room, conservatory. No children under 10. No dogs.
Credit cards Access, Visa.
Terms [1996] B&B from £36.50; D,B&B from £54. Set dinner £19.50. Special breaks: wine-tasting, racing, romantic, autumn, spring, Christmas. *V*

Waterford House — *Tel* (01969) 622090
19 Kirkgate — *Fax* (01969) 624020
Middleham DL8 4PG

A restaurant-with-rooms in a Grade II listed house crammed with antiques and knick-knacks, in the heart of the village. It is owned by Brian and Everyl Madell "warmly welcoming" (she is chef). Entrance is through a paved garden ablaze in summer with colourful flowers in pots. Bedrooms are warm, quite spacious, and eclectically and lovingly decorated. "Much thought had gone into the comforts provided:

fruit, sherry, chocolates . . .," wrote our inspectors. "In the cosy lounge, with grand piano, blazing log fire, huge pine dresser and interesting pictures, our genial host, Brian Madell, silver wine-taster adorning ample chest, showed us his astonishing wine list, with many bottles dating from the fifties, sixties and seventies, some very pricey. For pre-dinner drinking, we ordered a relatively humble wine, which he sampled with a flourish before pouring. The restaurant, with large bay windows, was attractively furnished, with smart napery and crockery. The *carte* was interesting, and the food delicious, served in generous portions, and accompanied by a bottle of Beaune, which Mr Madell tasted with panache and declared to be in fine condition. Breakfast had a good buffet, a wide choice of cooked dishes, quality preserves and thick slices of toast. High standards of food and hospitality. Only caveat: we weren't too keen on the cats, particularly Tripod, who rather sinisterly has only three legs." More reports please.

Open All year.
Rooms 5 double.
Facilities 2 lounge/bars, 2 dining rooms. Walled garden. Fishing nearby. Unsuitable for ♿.
Location Centre of small, quiet village. Parking.
Restriction No smoking: restaurant, 1 lounge. No dogs in public rooms.
Credit cards Access, Diners, Visa.
Terms [1996] B&B: single £40–£55, double £65–£75; D,B&B: single £59.50–£80, double £104–£125. Set lunch £17.50, dinner £19.50; full alc £27.50. Wine weekends, private parties. Christmas, New Year, bank holiday breaks. *V*

MIDHURST West Sussex — Map 2

The Angel
North Street
Midhurst GU29 9DN
Tel (01730) 812421
Fax (01730) 815928

César award in 1995

An old coaching inn, which has sprawled in all directions behind its Georgian front. Owner Peter Crawford-Rolt has extensively renovated, retaining the original atmosphere while adding "sophistication without gimmicks". Situated in the main street of an historic West Sussex town, with the ruins of Cowdray House and the famous polo lawns behind, it caters for all tastes and pockets, and is popular with "the polo crowd". Locals call in for a drink, or tea or coffee. The brasserie is casual, with simple wooden tables and chairs, fresh seafood on display and a daily changing menu, with a good choice of char-grilled meat and fish. The smart restaurant, the spacious and handsome *Cowdray Room*, serves modern British and French cooking – fairly simple dishes, deftly handled and well presented (*Michelin* red "Meals"). There's a quiet rear garden. The bedrooms are in harmony with the age of the house; some are large, with good lighting, quality fabrics and pictures, and antiques. The service has been described as "sympathetically amateurish". A new manager, William Older, arrived recently. Goodwood House and its horse racing are nearby; so are some particularly fine National Trust properties, Uppark and Petworth; there is good walking on the South Downs.

Open All year.
Rooms 2 suites, 16 double, 3 single. 4 across courtyard (2 on ground floor; 1 with facilities for ♿).

Facilities 2 residents' lounges, bar, brasserie, restaurant (pianist Sat night); 2 function rooms. 1½-acre walled garden.
Location Town centre (Union Jack flying). Front rooms double-glazed. Carpark. Taxis from Haslemere/Petersfield stations.
Restrictions No smoking in 2 bedrooms. No dogs (kennels nearby).
Credit cards All major cards accepted.
Terms B&B: single £75, double £80–£140, suite £130–£140; D,B&B from £99 per person. Set lunch £15.50, dinner £18.50; full alc £35. 2-night breaks. Christmas, Easter packages. 1-night bookings sometimes refused. *V*

MORSTON Norfolk — Map 2

Morston Hall — *Tel* (01263) 741041
Morston, Holt NR25 7AA — *Fax* (01263) 740419

A small flint-walled Georgian house owned by Galton Blackiston (the chef), his wife Tracy, and Justin Fraser, all trained in the business by John Tovey at *Miller Howe* (*qv*). It is in a hamlet on the Norfolk coast near Blakeney, in gardens with a lily pond and fountain, roses, a croquet lawn, and a sunny terrace. Inside are two small lounges, one with a lovely old fireplace. Bedrooms are spacious and quiet. The centre of the operation is the restaurant, with garden views and well-spaced tables, running the width of the house. *Michelin*'s red "Meals" is endorsed by *Guide* readers: "Faultless cooking." "The finest ingredients, prepared to near perfection, consoled one for the slight sense of regimentation of having to eat at an appointed time [7.30 for 8] with no choice of dishes [until dessert]." "The local staff are delightful." Some excellent half bottles on the well-chosen wine list. Admirers "cannot praise the hotel enough": "The owners have everything under control, with the minimum of fuss." "Accommodation well up to the rest." But criticisms have surfaced recently: "Proprietors, apart from the chef, not much in evidence"; "waiting sometimes unprofessional, particularly at breakfast"; "noisy hoovering disturbed our breakfast"; "with the emphasis on food, the accommodation has become neglected"; "insufficient hot water"; "we've had nicer rooms for less money".

Open 14 Feb–1 Jan. Restaurant closed for lunch, except Sun.
Rooms 6 double.
Facilities 2 lounges, restaurant, conservatory. 3-acre garden: large pond, croquet. Sailing, birdwatching nearby. Unsuitable for ♿.
Location On A149 coast road, 2 miles W of Blakeney. Private parking.
Restrictions No smoking in restaurant. No dogs in public rooms.
Credit cards Access, Amex, Visa.
Terms D,B&B £75–£100. Set Sun lunch £15, dinner £26. Children accommodated free in parents' room. 3-night bargain breaks. Christmas package. Cookery courses. 1-night bookings sometimes refused Sat.

MOULSFORD-ON-THAMES Oxfordshire — Map 2

The Beetle and Wedge — *Tel* (01491) 651381
Ferry Lane — *Fax* (01491) 651376
Moulsford-on-Thames OX10 9JF

César award in 1993

A much refurbished old ferry inn on a lovely stretch of the Thames. It has a charming water garden, where summer meals are served, and a smart conservatory-style dining room serving proprietor / chef Richard Smith's sophisticated, if pricey, cooking (*Michelin* red "Meals"). The informal restaurant, the beamed *Boathouse*, open seven days a week, serves grills from an open charcoal fire, salads, casseroles, traditional puddings, etc. "Wonderful" wine list; no half bottles, but you can drink only half a bottle and pay for this plus a surcharge of £1.25. Bedrooms, though not large, are agreeably furnished and have gleaming bathrooms; most have a river view. Kate Smith, a welcoming hostess, leads a helpful staff. "Twenty-four hours of relaxed pleasure," write satisfied customers. "We liked the trusting feel. They did not ask for a deposit, they upgraded us to a lovely riverside room, and when we asked about hiring a boat, they lent us theirs. Breakfast was lovely, with fresh orange juice, fruit, and a good choice of cooked dishes." (*Mary Lawrence*) But it is at times the victim of its own success; long waits can occur at mealtimes, and the food sometimes disappoints. One diner wrote: "The view of the river was obscured by large cabin cruisers moored in front of the hotel." One bedroom was "seriously overheated because hot pipes run under its floor".

Open All year. Dining room closed 25 Dec, Sun evening / Mon.
Rooms 10 double. 4 in adjacent cottage. 2 on ground floor.
Facilities Lounge, bars, dining room, *Boathouse* restaurant; function facilities. ½-acre grounds on river: water garden, boating, fishing, mooring.
Location From M4 junction 12 take A4 S; at 2nd roundabout take A340 Pangbourne / Streatley / Moulsford. In village turn to river on Ferry La. Parking.
Restrictions No smoking: dining room, bedrooms. No dogs.
Credit cards All major cards accepted.
Terms [1996] B&B: single £80–£100, double £105–£125, suite £125. Bar meals. Set lunch £21.50, dinner £35 (dining room); full alc (*Boathouse*) £32.50. Champagne weekends; cooking tutorials, etc. *V*

MUNGRISDALE Cumbria — Map 4

The Mill Hotel BUDGET

Mungrisdale, Penrith CA11 0XR
Tel (0176 87) 79659
Fax (0176 87) 79155

César award in 1993

"We treasure our visits here as to no other *Guide* hotel. The approach and the setting, in sweeping north lakes countryside, are appropriate preparation for the warm and relaxed comfort that greet you. Richard Quinlan is an excellent host, genuinely interested in his guests. He caters to their wants with quiet charm and a delightful sense of humour. Dinners always delight and satisfy. If we want to transport ourselves back here, we say: 'Manchester pudding' and have a moment of silent recollection. High standards in every department." "We were touched by the warm welcome to our children." The Quinlan's hotel, simple but civilised, is a former mill cottage in a lovely, quiet setting at the foot of the fells, with millrace, waterfall and trout stream, and excellent walking from the door. Public rooms are small, and crowded at busy times. Bedrooms are immaculate and warm; some are very small. Two, with a shared sitting room, are in the old mill itself – "bright and airy, with sloping ceiling and skylight; you can lie in bed looking at the stars while listening to the stream". Dinner, cooked by Mrs Quinlan, and served by her husband at 7 pm, is traditional, with some choice, accompanied by a short, carefully selected wine list. Breakfasts are "first class". (*Margaret and Alan Clarke,*

Mrs JJ Carr, Prof. J Mandelstam, and others) The Penrith exit of the M6 is only 12 miles away.

NB Not to be mistaken for the *Mill Inn*, with which it confusingly shares an entrance.

Open Feb–Nov. Dining room closed for lunch.
Rooms 9 double. Some on ground floor. No telephone.
Facilities 3 lounges, dining room; drying room. 2-acre grounds: millrace, waterfall, trout stream. Ullswater 5 miles, fishing, sailing. Unsuitable for ♿.
Location 2 miles N of A66 Penrith–Keswick. M6 exit 40.
Restrictions No smoking in restaurant. Dogs at proprietors' discretion, not in public rooms.
Credit cards None accepted.
Terms B&B: single £30–£42, double £56–£78; D,B&B £49–£65 per person. Set dinner £22.50. Weekly rates. *V*

MURSLEY Buckinghamshire — Map 2

Richmond Lodge BUDGET — *Tel* (01296) 720275
Mursley, nr Milton Keynes MK17 0LE

"Remarkably pleasant" no-smoking B&B; sedate Edwardian house in rural setting, just outside village 12 miles S of Milton Keynes; handy for Silverstone. "Delightfully personal" reception from kind hosts, Mr and Mrs Abbey. 3 charming, spotless bedrooms, 1 with facilities en suite. *"Delicious" breakfast (on flowery terrace in summer). 3½-acre "rather dreamy" garden with lily pond, croquet, lawn tennis. Closed Christmas; open New Year by arrangement. No children under 6, except babies. Dogs in cars only. Credit cards not accepted. B&B: single from £25, double £40–£45. Light evening meal at 7 pm (by arrangement, residents only) £14.50; unlicensed: bring your own wine.*

NANTWICH Cheshire — Map 3

Rookery Hall — *Tel* (01270) 610016
Worleston, Nantwich CW5 6DQ — *Fax* (01270) 626027

This "quietly luxurious" hotel is set amid gardens and pastures on a large estate bordering the river Weaver. It has an impressive baronial-style interior, with moulded ceilings, chandeliers, fine paintings, antiques, impressive flower arrangements, and spacious bedrooms, many decorated in similar style. It started life in 1816 as the home of a wealthy landowner. Fifty years later it was bought by a Bavarian banker, who added a *schloss*-style tower "to remind him of home". It became a hotel in 1978, but has been in receivership for the past four years. It is now ably managed for the creditors by Jeremy Rata, and the oak-panelled restaurant with a magnificent ceiling and lovely views has become a magnet for local gourmets, attracted by David Alton's modern British cooking. "A marvellous hotel," writes one of this year's enthusiastic correspondents. "Elegant lounges, sumptuously furnished bedroom, excellent food, quiet but friendly service." The hotel goes in for conferences, but these are in converted stables, away from the main house. (*Prof. and Mrs FA Holland; also JA Vincent, and others*)

Open All year.
Rooms 16 suites, 29 double. 15 in coach house. 6 on ground floor (1 suitable for ♿).

Facilities Salon, drawing room, bar, restaurant; private dining room, conference/function facilities. 200-acre estate: 15-acre gardens, tennis, croquet, putting, woodland, river (fishing), clay pigeon-shooting, falconry.
Location 2 miles N of Nantwich, off B5074.
Restrictions No smoking in restaurant. Dogs by arrangement; not in bedrooms.
Credit cards All major cards accepted.
Terms [1996] B&B: single £98.50, double £180, suite £215–£265. Set lunch from £8.50, dinner £37.50. 2-night breaks. *V*

NEAR SAWREY, Cumbria — Map 4

Ees Wyke — *Tel/Fax* (0153 94) 36393
Near Sawrey, nr Ambleside LA22 0JZ

John and Margaret Williams's Georgian country house, with colonnaded doorway, white walls and black window frames, was once the holiday home of Beatrix Potter, whose farmhouse, Hill Top, is just up the road. It has a tranquil setting with wonderful views of Esthwaite Water, mountains, forests, fells and sheep – and "spectacular sunsets". The atmosphere is cheerful. Guests assemble for drinks at 7 (on a terrace in warm weather); dinner is at 7.30. "The Williamses do everything themselves, with great good humour and lightness of touch. Margaret jollies guests along, making sure everyone is included in the repartee. John's cooking is first rate, if a little robust for those who haven't climbed Great Gable or Helvellyn earlier in the day. But we learned to ask for small portions, so as to do justice to the perfect vegetables." "Straightforward, competent cooking. Modest, reasonably priced wine list." "Amazing breakfast: five or six cereals, wonderful choice of fruit; and having produced eggs and bacon, Margaret appears with a large platter with mushrooms, tomato, three sorts of sausage, fried bread, black pudding, etc." Bedrooms, all but one with a lake view, are good-sized and "nicely decorated, with compact but charming bathrooms"; each is named for its colour scheme. (*Iris Johnson, SA Cheetham, Heather Kirk*) Only let-down: prepackaged butter and marge at breakfast, and UHT cream on the bedroom tray.

Open Mar–Dec.
Rooms 8 double. 1 on ground floor. No telephone.
Facilities 2 lounges, dining room. 2-acre garden. Access to lake; fishing. Unsuitable for ♿.
Location SE of Hawkshead on road to Windermere ferry; on edge of village.
Restrictions No smoking in dining room. No children under 8. No dogs in public rooms.
Credit card Amex.
Terms B&B £42–£52; D,B&B £54–£64. Set dinner £12 (£18 to non-residents). 3-day breaks Mar, Nov; 4-day Christmas house party.

NEW MILTON Hampshire — Map 2

Chewton Glen — *Tel* (01425) 275341
Christchurch Road — *Fax* (01425) 272310
New Milton BH25 6QS

An internationally famous 18th-century mansion, large and luxurious, in huge grounds, with parkland, woodland, lawns and gardens, on the southern fringe of the New Forest. The sea is a short walk away, along a footpath. *Chewton Glen* has been owned for over 29 years by Martin

Skan, who runs it with an "unfailingly courteous staff". The decor is lush; lounges are large and light, with antiques and fine fabrics. Suites and bedrooms, some vast, are equally lavish, and have fruit, sherry, biscuits, plentiful toiletries, huge towels, bathrobes, etc. Some have a balcony or terrace. Almost all of the outstanding health and sporting facilities (see below) are free to residents. The restaurant, named for Captain Marryat, who wrote *The Children of the New Forest* here, has a pretty conservatory extension, and a *Michelin* star for Pierre Chevillard's modern cooking. "It is difficult to fault; the food is exquisite, the waiters are great fun and professional." The young new *sommelier*, Mark Walter, "does an excellent job with the wines, which are memorable". "Superb" breakfasts offer a wide choice of cooked and uncooked dishes. "Extremely expensive, but worth it," is the general view. (*JS Rutter, and others*)

Open All year.
Rooms 16 suites (2 in grounds), 37 double. Some on ground floor.
Facilities Ramps. 3 lounges, bar, 4 dining rooms; function rooms; snooker room; health club: indoor tennis, swimming pool, gymnasium, beauty salon. 70-acre grounds: lake, tennis, croquet, 9-hole golf course, jogging course, swimming pool, helipad; bicycle hire. Beach, fishing, sailing, riding nearby. Chauffeur service.
Location From A35 *don't* follow New Milton signs; turn off to Walkford and Highcliffe; through Walkford, 4th left (Chewton Farm road). Entrance on right.
Restrictions No smoking in restaurant. No children under 7. No dogs (kennels nearby).
Credit cards All major cards accepted.
Terms [Until end Mar 1997] Double room £195–£300, suite £300–£395. Breakfast: continental £9.50, English £16. Set lunch £23.50, dinner £42. 5-night breaks; healthy breaks; golfing, Christmas, Easter packages. 2-night bookings preferred weekends.

NEW ROMNEY Kent — Map 2

Romney Bay House NEW — *Tel* (01797) 364747
Coast Road — *Fax* (01797) 367156
Littlestone, New Romney TN28 8QY

César award: newcomer of the year

An enticing newcomer, enthusiastically nominated by several readers: "A jewel." "A real find." "Unique." Owned by Helmut and Jennifer Gorlich, this white-walled, red-roofed house stands on its own with the sea in front and a golf course behind. It was built in the 1920s for the American actress and journalist Hedda Hopper, by Sir Clough Williams-Ellis, of Portmeirion fame. "It has had love lavished on it in every nook and cranny. The aim is to make you feel you are in someone's home. Help-yourself bar, breakfast (sumptuous, continental or English) whenever you like. Little public rooms. My room had everything you could need: flowers, hot-water bottle, bathrobe, etc. Service from a covey of young women. Tennis, croquet on the lawn. Everything is bijou and friendly." "Jennifer Gorlich is an interior designer and the whole house reflects her taste: antiques, interesting decorative items, wonderful pictures. There is always something interesting to look at." "Excellent dinners (no choice), home-cooked and beautifully presented. We enjoyed everything we ate. Interesting wine list. Helmut Gorlich enjoys playing host, and does it with style and wit." Cream teas are served, on the terrace in fine weather. The Channel Tunnel is just 20 minutes' drive away. (*Braham Murray, Bridget and Robin Oaten, Mrs S Plant*)

Open All year, except 24–30 Dec. Restaurant closed *c.*2 weeks mid-June, some evenings in winter.
Rooms 8 double, 2 single.
Facilities 2 sitting rooms, bar, 2 dining rooms; small function facilities. 1½-acre garden: tennis, croquet, *boules*. Sea, golf course. Unsuitable for ♿.
Location From New Romney, follow signs to Littlestone; at sea, turn left. Continue as far as possible. Hotel alone, opposite sea, on left.
Restrictions No smoking except main lounge, bar. No children. No dogs.
Credit cards Access, Diners, Visa.
Terms [1996] B&B £40, double £65–£95. Snack lunch from £6.50; set dinner £25. 1-night bookings sometimes refused on weekends. Off-season and mid-week breaks.

NEWCASTLE UPON TYNE Tyne and Wear — Map 4

Horton Grange — *Tel* (01661) 860686
Seaton Burn — *Fax* (01661) 860308
Newcastle upon Tyne NE13 6BU

Though only six miles from the city centre, Sue and Andrew Shilton's hotel stands in open farm country, and is "blissfully quiet at night". *Michelin* recognises the quality of the restaurant with a red "Meals" and two red crossed spoon-and-forks. Our readers, with one exception, continue to be pleased: "The Shiltons are assiduous hosts, hard-working, thoroughly professional, and responsive. For a modest price, they provide everything we value in a hotel. Rooms (which are serviced in the evening), are not luxurious, but pleasantly furnished with antiques; beds are comfortable, with crisp cotton bedding. There is always a small vase of flowers from the garden. Bathrooms are reasonably supplied with toiletries; water is reliably hot. The sitting room is a beauty with two fires, comfortable sofas and chairs arranged to provide privacy, attractive lighting from table lamps, and arrangements of flowers and foliage. The serious restaurant provides safe but competent modern British cooking. Breakfasts, especially the cooked ones, continue to be excellent, apart from the orange juice." "The Shiltons have mastered that difficult task of supplying perfect hospitality without ever being intrusive. Delicious tea with freshly baked biscuits in front of the fire specially lit for us on a miserable day." (*David and Kate Wooff, Mrs William H Crook*) The single suites in a garden annexe have a desk, and the airport is nearby.

Open All year, except 25/26 Dec.
Rooms 4 single suites (on ground floor in garden annexe, ♿ access), 5 double.
Facilities Ramps. Lounge, restaurant. 3-acre grounds. Lake, fishing 10 mins' walk.
Location 6 miles N of centre. From A1 western by-pass take A19 Ashington/Tyne Tunnel exit. At roundabout take 1st exit; left after 1 mile to Dinnington/Ponteland/Airport. Hotel 2 miles on right. Large carpark.
Restrictions No smoking in restaurant. No dogs.
Credit cards Access, Amex, Visa.
Terms B&B: single £50–£59, double £70–£80; D,B&B £75 per person. Set dinner £32.

NEWLANDS Cumbria — Map 4

Swinside Lodge *Tel/Fax* (0176 87) 72948
Grange Road
Newlands, nr Keswick CA12 5UE

César award in 1996

"Everything you could ask for in a small hotel. Graham Taylor's desire to please is evident from the moment one arrives, to be greeted by help with cases, and tea with home-made biscuits." "We enjoyed every moment. Sensitive attention to every detail." "Thoroughly deserves its *César*. Every meal outstanding, with an adventurous menu; it was a pleasure to match one's own wines [the hotel is unlicensed] to such wonderful food." "My fifth visit. Perfection." "Caring but never intrusive service. Amazing cleanness and freshness everywhere. Delightful bedroom, with abundant small luxuries. The dining room is charming and the staff attentive." "A soothing atmosphere of cosy sophistication." "Outstanding value." Praise this year and last for one of the *Guide*'s most popular small hotels, peacefully set at the foot of Catbells. This year *Michelin* awards a red "Meals" for Chris Astley's cooking, on a no-choice-until-dessert menu. Packed lunches are "memorable". Cumbrian breakfasts include fresh orange juice and "delicious" croissants. No hidden extras. (*Mr and Mrs Austin Gibbons, Dr and Mrs RR Evans, Peter Rudd, AT Tulloch, and many others*) No smoking.

Open Mid-Feb–Dec. Dining room closed midday.
Rooms 7 double. No telephone.
Facilities 2 sitting rooms, dining room. ¾-acre garden. Derwent Water 5 mins' walk: shingle beach, safe bathing. Unsuitable for ♿.
Location 3 miles SW of Keswick. A66 for Cockermouth; left at Portinscale; follow road to Grange and Lingholm Gardens (do *not* turn off at Swinside sign).
Restrictions No smoking. No children under 12. No dogs.
Credit cards None accepted.
Terms B&B: single £43–£52, double £70–£100; D,B&B: single £69–£78, double £122–£152. Packed lunches. Set dinner £26–£29. Off-season rates, Christmas package. 1-night bookings sometimes refused.

NORTH BOVEY Devon — Map 1

Blackaller Hotel BUDGET *Tel/Fax* (01647) 440322
North Bovey
nr Newton Abbot TQ13 8QY

A "special, peaceful place" – a converted woollen mill on the outskirts of a lovely village in the Dartmoor National Park, with a "gentle, genial host", Peter Hunt (who also keeps bees and plays the sitar), and a "jolly hostess", Hazel Phillips – "a wonderful cook". Long, low and white, it nestles at the end of a long lane. Its well-kept garden has a smooth lawn running down to the river, and garden furniture dotted about. Here cream teas are served in fine weather. The public rooms are "restful and unpretentious, with antiques, china and family photos – more like a home than a hotel". There are flowers everywhere. Bedrooms, some up a steep staircase, have a simple decor, with oak beams and quality fabrics, and a clean, bright bathroom. In the pretty candlelit dining room, dinners are "well balanced, with excellent sauces and vegetables", accompanied by reasonably priced wines on a predominantly New World list. "One of the most enjoyable meals I have eaten this year. Breakfast just as I like it, with toast to die for (a real test)." "Despite its simple appearance, this is a sophisticated operation. There's glorious walking nearby." (*Jeffrey and Jane Mallinson, Alan and Philippa Daniels, Mike Hutton; also MA Stockton, and others*)

Open Mar–Dec.
Rooms 4 double, 1 single. No telephone.
Facilities Lounge, bar, restaurant. 3-acre garden on river: coarse fishing. Unsuitable for ♿.
Location From Moretonhampstead follow sign to North Bovey. Hotel sign on wall at edge of village.
Restrictions Smoking in bar only. No children under 12. No dogs in public rooms.
Credit cards None accepted.
Terms B&B £28–£35; D,B&B £47.50–£54.50. Week, weekend, Christmas, New Year breaks. *V*

NORTH HUISH Devon — Map 1

Brookdale House BUDGET — *Tel* (01548) 821661
North Huish, South Brent TQ10 9NR — *Fax* (01548) 821606

Listed Tudor-style Victorian rectory with fine moulded ceilings, marble fireplaces, traditional decor: antiques, country house furnishings, light colours. In 4½-acre wooded grounds, with brook and waterfall, in remote Devon valley 7 m SW of Totnes. Dartmoor 10 mins' drive, beaches 15 mins. "Wonderful hosts", managers Mike and Gill Mikkelsen (he is chef). Traditional dishes ("with hint of Scandinavian"): organic vegetables and meat, freshly caught fish; generous portions; extensive wine list. Small conference/function facilities. 8 bedrooms, 3 no-smoking, 2 in cottage 25 yds. Unsuitable for ♿. "Children not encouraged." Dogs in cottages only. Access, Amex, Visa accepted. B&B: single £45–£55, double £60–£90. Set lunch £9.50, dinner (2–3-course) £15.95–£18.95 [1996]. Recently warmly endorsed: "5 perfect days" – but we'd like more reports, please.

NORTON North Yorkshire — Map 4

Newstead Grange BUDGET — *Tel* (01653) 692502
Norton, nr Malton YO17 9PJ — *Fax* (01653) 696951

Pat and Paul Williams's old stone Georgian house is on a road just outside the ancient market town of Malton, amid beautiful countryside: dramatic moors to the north, softer wolds further south. It is set peacefully in a large, mature garden, with glimpses of fields beyond. It has a period decor, with old features retained, and antiques, comfortable chairs, settees and chandeliers. There are open fires in the sitting rooms; one has a grand piano. Bedrooms, in similar style, are pretty, "with beautifully appointed bathrooms". The dining room is spacious, with lace table-cloths and Victorian chairs. This is a friendly place, where guests enjoy socialising in the evening. Dinners, cooked by Mrs Williams (no choice), are "well balanced and wholesome, with lovely soups and beautifully presented puddings". Some of the fruit and vegetables are organically home-grown. "Excellent, old-fashioned breakfasts, too." "Genuinely welcoming hosts. A real home from home." (*V and M Langford, J Wiggins, and others*)

Open Mid-Feb–late Nov.
Rooms 8 double. No telephone.
Facilities 2 lounges, dining room. 2½-acre garden. Unsuitable for ♿.
Location 1½ miles SE of Malton. Follow signs to Beverley. Hotel on B1248 ½ mile beyond last houses, at junction with road to Settrington.
Restrictions No smoking. Children under 10 by arrangement. No dogs in house.
Credit cards Access, Visa.
Terms B&B £30–£42. Set dinner £15.50. 2-night breaks (min. 2 nights): D,B&B from £40 per person. *V* (end Sept–end Apr)

NORWICH Norfolk — Map 2

The Beeches BUDGET — *Tel* (01603) 621167
4–6 Earlham Road — *Fax* (01603) 620151
Norwich NR2 3DB

10 minutes' stroll west of historic city centre, on B1108, 2 listed Victorian mansions, carefully renovated. One has a later extension; quietest rooms in the other (more imposing). Sloping wooded 3-acre italianate garden, once sadly neglected, now being brought back to life by a trust. Friendly resident owners, the Hill family. 26 bedrooms of varying sizes, 4 no-smoking, 1 designed for ♿. Quite simple decor but all mod cons. Good breakfasts. Informal bistro-style restaurant (dinners only). Ample parking. No dogs. Closed 23 Dec–1 Jan. All major credit cards accepted. B&B: single £43–£46, double £54.50–£59, suite £64–£69. Full alc £17 [1996]. Recently endorsed, but we'd like more reports, please. *V*

OAKAMOOR Staffordshire — Map 3

Bank House NEW/BUDGET — *Tel/Fax* (01538) 702810
Farley Lane, Oakamoor
nr Stoke-on-Trent ST10 3BD

"Enticing guest house, grandly decorated, yet exuding warmth and comfort." 1 mile from Alton Towers, in lovely Churnet valley, within Staffordshire moorlands, on edge of Peak National Park. Excellent walks from door. Run on house party lines by welcoming hosts, Muriel and John Egerton-Orme, with 2 friendly dogs. 1-acre garden in 4 acres woodland. Pastoral views. Tranquil atmosphere. Elegant home-cooked dinners (no choice). 4 charming bedrooms, packed with "goodies". Good family accommodation. Closed Christmas. Unsuitable for ♿. No smoking: dining room, library, bedrooms. Dogs by arrangement. Access, Visa accepted. B&B: single £40, double £50–£70. Set dinner £20 [1996]. More reports, please. *V*

OTLEY Suffolk — Map 2

Bowerfield House BUDGET — *Tel* (01473) 890742
Helmingham Road — *Fax* (01473) 890059
Otley, nr Ipswich IP6 9NR

Lise and Michael Hilton's listed 17th-century barn and stable conversion is set well back from the road, overlooking fields, in a village in the heart of rural Suffolk. It is run on Wolsey Lodge lines. The decor is home-style, with antiques, and a wood fire in the sitting room, where guests may play the grand piano. There's a billiard room with a fine table. Michael Hilton will give guests a game of snooker, or play croquet with them on the manicured lawn. The spacious bedrooms have antiques, too, and fresh flowers, TV, etc; the bathrooms are well endowed with toiletries and medicaments. An "excellent" dinner, cooked by Mrs Hilton, and "impeccably served", is available on weekdays by arrangement. She is Danish, and this is often reflected in the menu. It is communally served at an elegantly appointed table in the beamed dining room; the Hiltons sometimes eat with their guests. No licence: guests bring their own wine. "Delicious breakfast," wrote our inspector, "with thick Danish bacon, some of the best we have tasted, proper brown bread, home-made marmalade and strong coffee. There's a terrace, and a pond with koi carp and golden orf. The house has been restored with taste and imagination; the Hiltons have long-term professional skills, and are welcoming hosts. Altogether remarkable value." "Meals and accommodation of a style that 'great' hotels might emulate," runs a recent endorsement. (*Andrew Wilson; also Colin Mabey*)

Open Mar–Oct. Dining room closed for lunch, Sat/Sun.
Rooms 3 double. 2 in carriage house across courtyard. 2 on ground floor.
Facilities Drawing room, billiard room, dining room. 2-acre grounds: pond, croquet. Golf, fishing, riding nearby. Unsuitable for ♿.
Location On B1079, in village 6 miles NW of Woodbridge. Hotel 6th house on right after post office.
Restrictions No smoking. No children under 12. Dogs in cars only.
Credit cards None accepted.
Terms B&B: single £34–£36, double £42–£46. Set dinner £17. 1-night bookings sometimes refused weekends.

OXFORD Oxfordshire — Map 2

Cotswold House BUDGET — *Tel/Fax* (01865) 310558
363 Banbury Road
Oxford OX2 7PL

As ever, plenty of praise for this modest, welcoming B&B, a double-fronted Cotswold stone house, with flower baskets hung all around. It is in the leafy environs of North Oxford, an easy two-mile bus ride from the city centre. "Jim and Anne O'Kane's constant but unobtrusive attention to details and their guests' special needs is without equal. Large, spotless bedroom; substantial, delectable breakfast. On a rainy day Mr O'Kane drove us into the city centre." "An excellent base, and a haven of peace and quiet at the end of the day. We were given maps and detailed instructions about how to get the most out of Oxford." Bedrooms are modern, furnished in pastel linens with flounces; they have TV, a fridge, fruit, masses of hot water, "and the odd pious tome by the bed, which adds to the atmosphere". Duvet or blankets at your choice; traditional or vegetarian breakfast. Guests have access to the well-kept garden at the rear. (*Daniel and Susan Davidson; also Paul Sellars, and others*) One single room is very small; one visitor found the music played at breakfast "creepy".

Open All year, except Christmas/New Year.
Rooms 5 double, 2 single, all with shower. 1 on ground floor. No telephone.
Facilities Lounge, breakfast room. Small garden. Unsuitable for ♿.
Location 2 miles N of centre, just inside ring road (A40), on A423. Carpark.
Restrictions No smoking. No children under 5. No dogs.

Credit cards None accepted.
Terms B&B: single £37–£39, double £54–£57.

Old Parsonage
1 Banbury Road
Oxford OX2 6NN
Tel (01865) 310210
Fax (01865) 311262

"A delight. One of the best hotels I've visited in England in the past few years. The nicest staff. The prettiest rooms, with all creature comforts. Great food." A 1996 endorsement for Jeremy Mogford's sophisticated hotel, a venerable creeper-clad 17th-century parsonage, perfectly placed for university sightseeing. Others, too, have praised the "beautifully finished modern bedrooms with excellent bathrooms" (some are small), the "quiet, professional, and charming staff", and the "wonderful breakfasts". "No hidden extras." The locally popular large bar, "a friendly place, with masses of pictures and comfortable seating", serves snacks and imaginative, informal meals all day from a short menu, ranging from soups and salads to steak and chips; there's a fairly priced wine list. In fine weather, residents can sit in the courtyard or the roof garden, and take alfresco meals, including breakfast, on a terrace. They may also eat at two restaurants under the same management: the conservatory-style *Gee's*, five minutes' walk away, or the "excellent" bistro-style *Brown's*, close by. The hotel has its own punt and provides picnics. Some bedrooms face the carpark. The road can be noisy. (*Jean Deinhard; also Richard Stuart-Price, and others*)

Open All year, except 25/26 Dec.
Rooms 4 suites, 25 double, 1 single. 10 on ground floor.
Facilities Small lounge, bar/restaurant; terrace, roof garden. Walled garden. Unsuitable for ♿.
Location N end of St Giles (some traffic noise). Parking for 16 cars.
Restriction Dogs by arrangement, not in public rooms.
Credit cards All major cards accepted.
Terms B&B: single £115–£120, double £155, suite £195. Full alc £30. 2-night breaks.

PADSTOW Cornwall — Map 1

The Seafood Restaurant and St Petroc's House BUDGET
Riverside, Padstow PL28 8BY
Tel (01841) 532485 and 532700
Fax (01841) 533344

César award in 1995

"The food, oh, the food! The signature fish soup, the mouclade to die for, the superb fresh plain grilled plaice, and let us not forget the breakfast kipper. Bliss." "Jill Stein presides over the restaurant with charm and professionalism." "Delicious continental breakfast in the bedroom, prettily set on a wicker tray." Recent accolades for Rick Stein's seafood restaurant (red "Meals", two red spoon-and-forks in *Michelin*). It has a ringside view of the harbour of this attractive fishing village, a "buzzy atmosphere", and "acceptably matey waitresses". The decor is cheerful: white walls, lots of plants, modern pictures, cane chairs; tables somewhat packed. There are generally two sittings for dinner, at 7.30 and 9.30; state your preference when booking. Pre-dinner drinks are in a "delightful conservatory". Above the restaurant are pleasant bedrooms, on the expensive side, priced according to size and view, with a modern decor and a stylish bathroom; two have a balcony. (*M and JB, HR; also JD Crosland, and others*) Cheaper rooms and a bistro (a new chef this year, Warwick Brown) are in *St Petroc's House*, just up the hill, one of the oldest buildings in Padstow. There are also three inexpensive bedrooms let on a B&B basis above the Steins' coffee shop, the *Middle Street Café*. Some visitors this year thought the bedrooms needed attention; one guest was miffed to find his party allocated rooms other than those reserved, and another, who complained of offhand service, felt that the set-up was geared to the restaurant at the expense of residents.

Open All year, except Christmas. Restaurant closed 1 May.
Rooms 25 double, 1 single. 8 in *St Petroc's*, 3 above coffee shop.
Facilities *Seafood*: conservatory bar, restaurant. *St Petroc's*: lounge, bar, bistro. Sandy beaches ¼ mile. Unsuitable for ♿.
Location Central: *Seafood* on harbour; *St Petroc's* in New St (150 yds). Garage, parking.
Restriction No smoking in restaurant.
Credit cards Access, Visa.
Terms B&B: single £25, double £62–£120; D,B&B £50–£80 per person. Set meals: bistro £16.95; restaurant: lunch £23.05, dinner £30.80; full alc £50. 2-day breaks in low season. Children under 6 accommodated free in parents' room.

PAINSWICK Gloucestershire — Map 3

Painswick Hotel — *Tel* (01452) 812160
Kemps Lane — *Fax* (01452) 814059
Painswick GL6 6YB

Somerset and Hélène Moore's lovely Palladian-style ex-vicarage (Relais du Silence) behind church in picture-postcard Cotswold village. Lovely views. Elegant private-home decor: antiques, fine fabrics, objets d'art. *20 well-equipped bedrooms, some with four-poster. Panelled restaurant specialising in local game and seafood, including oysters and lobster from its sea-water tank. Garden, with croquet. Not for the infirm – lots of steps. No dogs in public rooms. Access, Amex, Visa accepted. B&B: single £65–£95, double £98–£130. Set lunch £14.75, dinner £24.50. New managers, Caroline and Nick Benson (he is also chef). Recently endorsed, but we'd like some more reports, please.*

PAULERSPURY Northamptonshire — Map 2

The Vine House — *Tel* (01327) 811267
100 High Street — *Fax* (01327) 811309
Paulerspury, nr Towcester NN12 7NA

A restaurant-with-rooms in a 300-year-old limestone house and adjoining cottage, with many original features carefully preserved. It is in a village handy for Milton Keynes, Stowe and Silverstone, and has a large cottage garden. Inside, there is a tiny bar and a residents' lounge; the dining rooms have low ceiling, beams and a light decor. *Michelin* awards a red "Meals" for chef/proprietor Marcus Springett's traditional English cooking "with a modern twist", which a recent guest, on two "very pleasant" visits, found "difficult to fault", with "a high standard" of presentation. "Julie Springett, front of house, is efficient and very friendly. The wine list is fairly comprehensive, not overpriced, and with a decent selection of half bottles. All the bedrooms are named after grapes; mine, Syrah, was not large, but well equipped. Its tiny shower room had one of the best showers I have ever encountered. Though the room overlooked the high street, it was quiet." "All our food is home-made," write the Springetts, "from bread to petits fours." Their lemonade and ginger beer are also admired. (*Chris Kay, and others*)

Open All year, except 24 Dec–6 Jan. Lunch served Tues–Fri; dinner Mon–Sat.
Rooms 5 double, 1 single.
Facilities Lounge bar, 2 dining rooms. Unsuitable for ♿.
Location In village 3½ miles SE of Towcester. Rear carpark.
Restrictions No smoking in restaurant. No dogs.
Credit cards Access, Visa.
Terms [1996] B&B: single £38.78, double £61.10. Set lunch £13.95, dinner £21.50.

PENZANCE Cornwall — Map 1

The Abbey Hotel — *Tel* (01736) 66906
Abbey Street — *Fax* (01736) 51163
Penzance TR18 4AR

César award in 1985

This 17th-century house, painted turquoise, and with Gothic windows, stands in one of the narrow streets that run down from the centre of Penzance towards the sea. "A Victorian collector's dream", it is crammed with curios, oriental rugs, paintings and photographs, magazines, books and flowers. The drawing room is "inviting, with flowered sofas, a fire, and a window looking on to a lovely garden". Some bedrooms look towards the harbour, others towards the garden; some are quite small, with a small shower room. Room 1 is huge, with antiques and a working fireplace; "using the wood-surrounded bath in its large bathroom is a memorable experience". There's a "light, airy suite with an enormous living area". In the pretty white-panelled dining room, the menu has three choices at each stage; there is always a vegetarian main course. The hotel is run in laid-back style – its *César* was for "utterly acceptable mild eccentricity" – and readers' reports have always ranged from ecstatic to thumbs-down. This year is no exception. "The friendliest of welcomes," writes an enthusiast. "The staff could not have been more helpful – to three octogenarians. We felt like guests in a private home. The house is delightfully furnished throughout. Dinner was excellent and wine very good; both reasonably priced." "Altogether lovely." (*Barbara Blake, and others*) But sightings of the owners, Jean and Michael Cox, are irregular, and though most visitors have been ably looked after by manager/chef/factotum Glyn Green, the welcome can be "non-existent" when he is away, leading to snorts of "grossly over-rated". The decor of some bedrooms has been criticised; some get noise from the street.

Open All year, except 2 weeks at Christmas. Dining room closed for lunch.
Rooms 1 2-bedroom suite (in adjoining building), 4 double, 2 single. No telephone.
Facilities Drawing room, dining room. Small walled garden. Sandy beach ¼ mile. Unsuitable for ♿.
Location Take road marked Sea Front; pass carpark on left; right after 300 yds, just before bridge, then left, up slipway, to hotel. Courtyard parking for 7 cars.

Restrictions No smoking in 1 bedroom. No dogs in public rooms.
Credit cards Access, Amex, Visa.
Terms B&B: single £55–£120, double £85–£130, suite £130–£180. Set dinner (2–3-course) £17.50–£23.50. Weekend breaks; winter rates. 1-night bookings sometimes refused bank holidays. *V*

PICKHILL North Yorkshire — Map 4

The Nags Head NEW/BUDGET — *Tel* (01845) 567391
Pickhill, nr Thirsk YO7 4JG — *Fax* (01845) 567212

Welcoming village inn, run, for 25 years, by Boynton brothers, Raymond and Edward. 9 miles W of Thirsk, 1 mile E of A1; a useful stop on way to or from Scotland. 15 comfortable bedrooms, 7 in annexe, 3 on ground floor, all with en suite *facilities. Excellent English/European meals (generous portions) in traditional bar (with necktie collection) and smart restaurant – food award in* Good Pub Guide. *Small lounge. Beer garden. Handy for Jervaulx, Rievaulx and Fountains abbeys. Golf, shooting, hunting, fishing, hang-gliding, gliding, swimming nearby. Closed 25 Dec. No smoking: restaurant, some bedrooms. No dogs in public rooms. Access, Amex, Visa accepted. B&B: single £34, double £48. Set lunch £10, dinner £16. "The best, and friendliest small hotel I know in England," writes nominator. More reports, please.*

POOLE Dorset — Map 2

The Mansion House — *Tel* (01202) 685666
Thames Street, Poole BH15 1JN — *Fax* (01202) 665709

"A charming hotel; the whole ambience is welcoming; staff very much in evidence, and ready to help with any problem." "The remarkable manageress, Jackie Godden, runs the place in the most efficient way. Her husband Gerry, the chef, produces outstanding food." "Wonderful value, and a good stopover for the ferry." Recent encomiums for a handsome Georgian town house in a quiet cul-de-sac near the town's old parish church and bustling quay. Its finest architectural feature is a grand sweeping staircase leading up from the entrance hall to a stylish residents' lounge. The panelled restaurant is a fashionable dining club, of which residents are temporary members; they may also eat in the bar/bistro. "The menu in both is extensive and reasonably priced." Cooking is traditional and modern English. Vegetarian dinners are "unusually good"; on Saturday evening and at Sunday lunch there is a "fantastic" hors d'oeuvre table. Most bedrooms are good-sized and luxurious, "with fresh fruit, thermos with ice, even a telephone in the bathroom", but singles can be small. No charge for room service. (*RCJ Gordon, PG Horrocks*) One guest was put out: "On arrival we found that the restaurant was fully booked for a private function; we were unceremoniously shunted off to the bistro – good value, but not on a par with what we'd expected, and extremely slow service."

Open All year. Restaurant closed for lunch Sat, bank holidays, Sun dinner.
Rooms 1 suite, 19 double, 9 single.
Facilities Lounge, bar/bistro, restaurant; private dining room. Poole Quay 100 yds: fishing, boating, sailing. Unsuitable for ♿.
Location Follow signs to channel ferry. Left at Poole Bridge, then 1st left, signposted to parish church. 2 private carparks.
Restrictions No children under 5 in restaurant. No dogs in public rooms.

Credit cards All major cards accepted.
Terms B&B: single £52–£77, double £85–£122, suite £130–£150. Set lunch £9.75 (£11.25 to non-members), dinner £19.50 (£22.50 to non-members). Weekend rates. *V*

PORTSCATHO Cornwall — Map 1

Roseland House NEW/BUDGET — *Tel* (01872) 580644
Rosevine, nr Portscatho TR2 5EW — *Fax* (01872) 580801

A period house with modern extensions, set high on a cliff, with wonderful views over Gerrans Bay. It is in a quiet position in the lovely Roseland peninsula. A path leads through its sloping grounds to a private beach. There is excellent walking from the door. "The lounge, bar and dining room are informal and comfortable," writes the nominator. "The bedrooms are quite simply, but attractively, furnished; almost all have splendid sea views. The proprietors, Mr and Mrs Hindley, are experienced and innovative chefs and provide a wide range of first-rate dishes at the five-course dinner [traditional English/French cooking, served between 7.30 and 8]. Staff are courteous, efficient and unobtrusive." Picnic lunches and cream teas are available. (*JF Thompson; also P and P Mishcon*)

Open All year.
Rooms 2 family, 8 double. 1 on ground floor. Also self-catering chalet and bungalow.
Facilities 2 lounges, bar, restaurant, conservatory. 6½-acre grounds: private beach, safe bathing. Sailing, golf, nearby.
Location N side of Portscatho. On A3078 to St Mawes, look for hotel sign on right, two miles after Ruan High Lanes.
Restrictions No smoking: restaurant, 1 lounge, bedrooms. No dogs in house.
Credit cards Access, Amex, Visa.
Terms [1996] D,B&B £36–£54 (single supplement at peak times). 3-day breaks. Children 14 and under half-price in parents' room. *V*

POSTBRIDGE Devon — Map 1

Lydgate House BUDGET — *Tel* (01822) 880209
Postbridge, Yelverton PL20 6TJ — *Fax* (01882) 880202

"Charming; relaxed and friendly. Hilary Townsend and Judy Gordon Jones are congenial hosts who have thought of everything to make their guests comfortable." "They were wonderfully kind to the two old ladies in our party." "Wholesome, plentiful food made up for lack of atmosphere in the dining room. Vegetables cooked to a T. Very acceptable wine list." "Excellent value." This "magical place" is set in its own wild Dartmoor valley, rough and boulder-strewn; the river Dart (with bathing and fishing) runs through the grounds, as does a bridle path. Beautiful views. You can walk straight on to the moor, and Postbridge, with a village shop, is accessible by foot along the river. The sitting room, with a log-burning stove, magazines and games, is comfortable, warm and airy, "and conversation tends to embrace anyone who cares to join in". Guests on their own are welcomed. The bedrooms, "pleasantly though sparsely decorated", vary in size; all have a private bath (most *en suite*). The short dinner menu, served at 7.30, has two choices for each course, with a vegetarian alternative to the main dish.

(*Elizabeth Neame, Caroline Horne, Ann and John Smith*) Only caveats: "Dinner a bit rushed." "Small towels."

Open Mar–1st week Jan.

Rooms 7 double, 1 single. 1 on ground floor.

Facilities Sitting room with bar, dining room/conservatory. 37-acre grounds: river, fishing, bathing. Unsuitable for ♿.

Location Small turning off B3212 in village, between humpback bridge and *East Dart* pub.

Restrictions Smoking banned in dining room, discouraged elsewhere. No dogs in dining room (or sitting room if other guests object).

Credit card Access.

Terms B&B: single £29.50, double £49–£59. Packed lunches £4.50. Set dinner £15.50. Weekly rates. Christmas, New Year packages.

POUNDSGATE Devon — Map 1

Leusdon Lodge NEW
Poundsgate, nr Ashburton
Newton Abbot TQ13 7PE
Tel (01364) 631304 and 631573
Fax (01364) 631599

"Outstanding in every way. The best small hotel I have found anywhere in Britain. The owners, Ivor and Miranda Russell, are intensely civilised, and the furniture and pictures are far nicer than is usual in this sort of place. Everything is in the best possible taste. Our bedroom had a delightful bay window with a sofa and armchairs, in which we sat in front of as fine a view as you can get in this country. The Russells are very professional. They will talk if you want to talk, but respect your privacy if that is what you want." This accolade restores to the *Guide* a hotel which had an entry in the eighties, with different owners, and in a simpler incarnation. It has a wonderful position, high in a hamlet on the eastern slopes of Dartmoor, overlooking the Dart valley. There's marvellous walking from the door. The restaurant is popular locally. "Food is taken seriously here," write the proprietors, "we are both very greedy." "Mrs Russell's cooking is as good as her husband's welcome," say the nominators. "Unfussy, using excellent ingredients, with delicious desserts." There's a wide-ranging wine list. (*Dr EDA Hay, and others*)

Open All year, except Christmas, mid-Jan–end Feb.

Rooms 1 suite, 6 double. 1 on ground floor.

Facilities Lounge, bar, restaurant. 2-acre grounds. River Dart 1 mile, fishing.

Location Leave A38 at Ashburton (Peartree Cross) exit. Take Princetown/Two Bridges road to Poundsgate (*c*. 5 miles). ½ mile after Poundsgate, take first turn right to Leusdon; after 600 metres fork right to Leusdon church. Turn right at small T-junction at end of small common. Hotel down hill on right.

Restrictions No smoking: restaurant, some bedrooms. No children under 12. No dogs in public rooms.

Credit cards Access, Visa.

Terms B&B: single £40–£54, double £60–£88; D,B&B: single £64–£78, double £108–£136. Set lunch £17.50, dinner £25. Children under 15 accommodated free in parents' room. 1-night bookings sometimes refused in season. V

> Don't trust out-of-date editions of the *Guide*. Hotels change hands, deteriorate or go out of business. Many hotels are dropped and new ones added every year.

POWBURN Northumberland — Map 4

Breamish House — *Tel* (01665) 578266
Powburn, nr Alnwick NE66 4LL — *Fax* (01665) 578500

Doreen and Alan Johnson's Georgian-style former hunting lodge is in a village at the foot of the Cheviot hills. It is set at the end of a long avenue of trees, amid gardens and woodland, with a stream. It has well-proportioned, airy public rooms, filled with home-grown flowers, and warmed all day in winter by log fires. The decor is "appropriate and not too *House Beautiful* for comfort". "It is a haven of peace," writes a regular visitor. "The standards are impeccable. The bedrooms are superbly equipped, and have the best hotel beds I have ever experienced; they are unobtrusively tidied during meals. I could take you to places with more exotic food, but the cooking here is varied and of a high quality, and you could stay for a week without being overcome." Others, too, were impressed by the dinners: "Choice relatively limited, but the cooking and presentation were of a consistently high standard; excellent selection of vegetables. Our bedroom was light and very comfortable, with a good view of the hills. Service was immaculate." (*Geoffrey Yates, HH Liesner*)

Open Mid-Feb–30 Dec.
Rooms 10 double, 1 single. Some in cottage over coach house.
Facilities 2 drawing rooms, dining room. 5-acre grounds: stream. Sea, beaches 15 miles. Only restaurant suitable for ♿.
Location From Morpeth, turn left off main street of village, by sharp bend.
Restrictions No smoking in dining room. Children under 12 by arrangement. No dogs in public rooms.
Credit cards Access, Visa.
Terms [Until Apr 1997] B&B £34–£56; D,B&B £55–£77. Set lunch £13.50, dinner £23.50. Special breaks. Christmas package. **V** (low season; not on discounted rates)

PRESTBURY Cheshire — Map 3

The White House Manor and Restaurant — *Tel* (01625) 829376 — *Fax* (01625) 828627
The Village, Prestbury SK10 4HP

"A highly enjoyable place to stay. The young, cheerful staff are most welcoming. The rooms are maintained to a high standard, full of interesting knick-knacks, and quiet." A recent endorsement from regular visitors to Ryland and Judith Wakeham's restaurant-with-rooms-just-down-the-road. The restaurant is in a listed white building in "one of Cheshire's prettiest villages", handy for Manchester. It has a high reputation locally for its contemporary British cooking, served amid silk, lace and greenery. Bedrooms, in a redbrick manor a short walk away, are themed: Trafalgar is military in style, Glyndebourne has a sophisticated music centre, Earl Grey has a blue and yellow decor and a vast range of teas and tisanes, Minerva, with an accent on sport and health, has a Turkish steam room and a collection of antique sporting equipment. "This may sound twee," wrote one nominator last year, "but it worked." Another "could find no fault: exquisite and stylish: quality linen, good antiques, well-thought-out bathroom." Breakfast (continental with fresh orange juice, muffins, croissants, etc, or "full

Cheshire") is served "properly laid out" in the bedrooms, or in a small conservatory (the manor's only public room). (*Peter and Susan Ranft, also ULP, and others*)

Open All year, except 25 Dec.
Rooms 6 double, 3 single.
Facilities Lounge/conservatory with honesty bar, restaurant; function rooms. ½-acre garden. Unsuitable for ♿.
Location Edge of village 2 miles N of Macclesfield.
Restriction No dogs in public rooms.
Credit cards All major cards accepted.
Terms Rooms: single £65, double £95–£110. Breakfast: continental £5, English £8.50. Set lunch £12.50, dinner £16.95; full alc £30.

PURTON Wiltshire — Map 3

The Pear Tree at Purton — *Tel* (01793) 772100
Church End — *Fax* (01793) 772369
Purton, nr Swindon SN5 9ED

A Cotswold stone house, once a rectory, in a peaceful village amid rolling Wiltshire farmland, but only four miles from the M4. It has "very pleasant" hosts, Francis and Anne Young, and a "delightful" staff. The decor "is distinctly pink and rather feminine". Bedrooms, well endowed with sherry, bottled water, biscuits, etc, are named after characters associated with the village. Some overlook the unusual twin-towered parish church and beautiful manor house, newer ones ("slightly soulless") are built round a galleried atrium; some bathrooms have a jacuzzi. The large grounds include a traditional Victorian garden, where herbs are grown for the modern British dishes served in the pretty conservatory restaurant by chef Catherine Berry. There's plenty of choice on the fixed-price menu which, at lunch, includes a traditional pudding, eg, spotted dick. Some find the food "excellent", others think it "a bit hit-and-miss", and one reader has written: "I like vegetables *al dente*, but some of these had barely been heated, and one yellow object (a swede?) proved impenetrable." Breakfast has been pronounced "splendid". The clientele tends to be business-oriented during the week; weekend rates are excellent value. A "let off steam" package enables guests to learn to drive a steam locomotive and enjoy a traditional railwayman's lunch. (*Larissa and Michael Milne, and others*) Bedroom lighting has been criticised.

Open All year. Restaurant closed for lunch Sat.
Rooms 2 suites, 15 double, 1 single. Some on ground floor.
Facilities Ramps. Lounge bar, library, conservatory restaurant; function facilities. 7½-acre grounds: croquet.
Location 5 miles NW of Swindon. From M4 exit 16 follow signs to Purton; through village, right at Spar grocer.
Restriction No dogs in public rooms.
Credit cards All major cards accepted.
Terms B&B: single/double £80–£100, suite £100. Children in parents' room £10. Set lunch £19.50, dinner £29.50; full alc £35.50. Weekend breaks. *V*

> Always let a hotel know if you have to cancel a booking, whether you have paid a deposit or not. Hotels sustain huge losses due to "no-shows".

RASKELF North Yorkshire **Map 4**

Old Farmhouse BUDGET *Tel* (01347) 821971
Raskelf YO6 3LF *Fax* (01347) 822392

Unpretentious small hotel and restaurant with friendly owners, Bill and Jenny Frost. In main street of quiet village NW of York, 2½ miles W of Easingwold. Small garden, patio. Lounge "a jumble of furniture; pleasant in an old-fashioned way". Substantial home-cooked four-course dinners, with surprising amount of choice, "interesting and well prepared, good value for money"; good cheeseboard; extensive wine list. Substantial Yorkshire breakfast. 10 straightforward bedrooms with personal touches, eg, home-made shortbread replenished daily. But some are small, some are poorly insulated, some have thin curtains. Open Feb–mid-Dec. Unsuitable for ♿. No smoking in restaurant. Credit cards not accepted. B&B: single £25–£29, double £44–£54; D,B&B (obligatory in season): single £41–£44, double £76–£84. (Endorsed in 1996, but fuller reports welcome)

REETH North Yorkshire **Map 4**

The Burgoyne BUDGET *Tel/Fax* (01748) 884292
On the Green
Reeth, nr Richmond DL11 6SN

"A perfect hotel. The attention to detail is meticulous, even to the clipping of the hedges to allow those seated in the restaurant to see the stone roofs of the village and a view of the hills, but not the cars parked on the green. The proprietors, Derek Hickson and Peter Carwardine (also chef), are friendly and amusing. Very good food; each meal was perfectly balanced." This fine, Grade II listed Regency house stands on the large green of a picturesque Dales village. It has glorious views of Swaledale; there is good walking all around. The decor is "charming, especially in the spacious lounge, with log fire, books and magazines", and furniture is a pleasing blend of antique and modern. Most bedrooms are large; three have their bathroom across a corridor (bathrobes and slippers are provided). In the candlelit dining room, green with pink touches, the menu is "encouragingly short, with the emphasis broadly on English cooking". There is a good wine list with plenty of half bottles, and you can order a bottle of the house wine and pay only for what is consumed. "Excellent breakfast – large grill, beautiful cold ham, unlimited coffee." "Very good value." (*Norman Waterman, and others*)

Open Feb–Dec. Restaurant closed midday.
Rooms 9 double. 1 on ground floor, suitable for partially ♿.
Facilities 2 lounges, restaurant. ⅓-acre grounds. Fishing rights on river Swale.
Location Centre of village, 10 miles W of Richmond. Parking.
Restrictions No smoking: 1 lounge, dining room, bedrooms. No children under 7 in dining room at night. No dogs in dining room.
Credit card Access.
Terms [1996] B&B: single £57.50–£80, double £67.50–£90; D,B&B: single £78.50–£101, double £109.50–£132. Set dinner £21. Child in parents' room £15. Off-season breaks, grouse shooting parties. 1-night bookings refused Christmas, New Year, Easter.

ROGATE Hampshire Map 2

Mizzards Farm BUDGET
Rogate, Petersfield GU31 5HS

Tel (01730) 821656
Fax (01730) 821655

"A small upmarket B&B, with delightfully appointed rooms overlooking an imaginative, mature garden and the best of unspoiled Hampshire countryside. The house revolves around a quite substantial central hall, with a staircase rising to a gallery. There is much hewn woodwork. Tea and coffee are served in the first-floor conservatory at any reasonable time. This is very much a family home, and life discreetly goes on around the guests. The bedrooms are charming and well equipped; they vary in size. The showpiece is a remarkable suite of opulent design, which would have a natural home in Venice or Vienna. Helpful hosts, accommodating in every way." Julian and Harriet Francis's 16th-century farmhouse, formerly owned by a pop star, has landscaped gardens on the river Rother, with a lake and a covered swimming pool. It is in a designated area of outstanding natural beauty; nearby are excellent walks on the South Downs and in the Wealden country. The "splendid" traditional breakfasts, served at separate tables in an impressive vaulted room, include kedgeree, kippers, home-produced honey and jam. (*Jeremy and Anthea Larken*) No smoking.

Open All year, except Christmas.
Rooms 3 double. No telephone.
Facilities Lounge, conservatory. 2-acre grounds: covered swimming pool, croquet, lake, river. Golf, riding, polo nearby. Unsuitable for ♿.
Location From centre of Rogate go S ½ mile, cross river, then 1st right.
Restrictions No smoking. No children under 7. No dogs.
Credit cards None accepted.
Terms B&B £25–£38. 1-night bookings sometimes refused bank holidays.

ROMALDKIRK Co. Durham Map 4

The Rose and Crown
Romaldkirk
nr Barnard Castle DL12 9EB

Tel (01833) 650213
Fax (01833) 650828

A civilised old coaching inn on the green (complete with stocks and water pump) of a quiet Dales village with a beautiful old church. Inside are log fires, panelling, brass and copper, old farming implements, prints, maps and etchings, and fresh flowers; the small lounge is equipped with magazines, books and games. The beamed, traditional bar, with old-fashioned seats facing a log fire, is popular with locals. The restaurant has earned a *Good Food Guide* entry for proprietor/chef Christopher Davy's cooking (English, with modern and regional influences). There are limited choices on the dinner menu, "always beautifully cooked and presented"; puddings are "delicious and never pretentious"; portions are generous, "but not embarrassingly so". Alison Davy "expertly oversees a local staff". "The welcome is always friendly, and a room upgrade seems to be standard when they are not busy." Best bedrooms are in the courtyard annexe. Christopher Davy is knowledgeable about local attractions. Good birdwatching and some of Britain's finest grouse moors are nearby. (*HH Liesner, JC Ford; also Good Pub Guide*)

Open All year, except Christmas. Restaurant closed Sun evening to non-residents.
Rooms 2 suites, 10 double. 5 in courtyard annexe. Some on ground floor.
Facilities Lounge, lounge bar, Crown Room (bar meals), restaurant. Fishing, grouse-shooting, birdwatching nearby.
Location Village green, 6 miles NW of Barnard Castle on B6277. Ample parking.
Restrictions No smoking in restaurant. Dogs in lounge bar only.
Credit cards Access, Visa. (Not accepted for special breaks.)
Terms [1996] B&B: single £56, double £78, suite £86. Set lunch £11.95, dinner £22.50. Special breaks all year. *V*

ROSTHWAITE Cumbria — Map 4

Hazel Bank BUDGET — *Tel* (0176 87) 77248
Rosthwaite, nr Keswick CA12 5XB

Gwen and John Nuttall's pristine Victorian no-smoking guest house is quietly set in large landscaped grounds above the village, with fine views of surrounding mountains and fells. It is popular with walkers and ramblers, to whom it offers efficient drying facilities and abundant hot water. "Friendly, thoughtful owners who welcome us as old friends," write returning visitors. "They are thoroughly professional." "Our spacious bedroom was a delight, with a lovely view and an excellent bathroom. You help yourself to drinks in the lounge before dinner, which is served at 7 pm. At least five vegetables accompany the main course, there are delicious old-fashioned puddings and an excellent cheeseboard. The house wine is reasonably priced. Coffee afterwards in the lounge, where a house-party atmosphere prevails. Breakfast (8.30 to 9 am) is equally delicious, with a self-service buffet followed by cooked items." No choice on the menu until dessert. The Nuttalls write: "We make no apology for providing meals to suit those who spend their days exploring the Lakeland mountains. Whilst food fads come and go, we will continue to use the finest fresh local ingredients to produce home cooking with a traditional British theme." (*Dr Arthur and Mrs Irene Naylor, Hugh and Mary Barkley, Sally Seysell*)

Open Apr–end Oct.
Rooms 5 double, 1 single. 1 self-catering cottage. No telephone.
Facilities Lounge, honour bar, dining room; drying room. 4-acre grounds. Derwentwater 3 miles. Unsuitable for ♿.
Location 6 miles S of Keswick on B5289 to Borrowdale. Just before village turn left over small hump-backed bridge.
Restrictions No smoking. No children under 6. No dogs in public rooms.
Credit card Access.
Terms D,B&B £45. 3-night breaks Mar, Nov. 1-night bookings sometimes refused.

RUSHLAKE GREEN East Sussex — Map 2

Stone House — *Tel* (01435) 830553
Rushlake Green, Heathfield TN21 9QJ — *Fax* (01435) 830726

A beautiful old house, built in 1495, extended in Georgian days, now run on country house lines by Peter Dunn, a descendant of the original owners, and his wife Jane (the chef). It stands in a vast estate on the Kent/Sussex border in a walled garden; plenty of outdoor activities are on offer (see below); picnic dinner hampers for nearby Glyndebourne can be provided. "One of the loveliest places I have ever stayed in," writes a regular *Guide* correspondent. "High standards of old-fashioned service and civility. Nothing hotel-like about it. You are cherished and cosseted from the moment you arrive. Cases vanish upstairs, tea (real tea, exquisite china and silver, home-made fruit cake, moist and crumbly) is served in the drawing room amid antiques, family heirlooms, portraits, photos in silver frames. We occupied two different bedrooms. One was a vision in white, the other had a four-poster with swathes and folds of sprigged materials – sheer comfort and beauty from a bygone age." Others have praised the dinners on a set menu with choices, served in the pleasant small dining room: "Delicious and varied; the *Michelin* red 'Meals' is fully justified." A good traditional breakfast is served downstairs, but the one brought to the bedroom has been called "hopeless". The bedrooms vary; the twin-bedded ones at the back are on the small side. (*Ruth West, Sue and Martin Gates*)

Open All year, except 24 Dec–early Jan, 2 weeks beginning Feb.
Rooms 1 suite, 5 double, 1 single.
Facilities Hall, drawing room, library, billiard room, dining room. 1,000-acre estate: 4½-acre garden, tennis, croquet, archery, off-road driving, shooting, ballooning, pheasant/clay pigeon-shooting, lake, fishing.
Location 4 miles E of Heathfield. Take B2096 towards Battle; 4th right to Rushlake Green. At green turn left; keep green on right; entrance on far left at crossroads.
Restrictions No children under 9. No dogs in public rooms.
Credit cards None accepted.
Terms B&B: single £55–£71.25, double £85–£167.50, suite £130–£167.50. Set lunch £18.95, dinner £26.50. Weekend house parties. "V" (Oct–end Apr)

RYE East Sussex — Map 2

Jeake's House BUDGET — *Tel* (01797) 222828
Mermaid Street — *Fax* (01797) 222623
Rye TN31 7ET

César award in 1992

"Here was a hotel we talked about afterwards, hoping to return. In every way it complements the town. It is in possibly Rye's quaintest, most photogenic street. Step inside, and the character of Rye follows you. Our charming bedroom at the top, with sloping ceiling, beams and dormer window, had a view over the garden to the sea. Its decoration brought out its individuality. We felt we were in a world apart." "Jenny and Francis Hadfield's approach is hands-on, but never officious. Many larger hotels with more resources could take note." "The best value of our holiday." This civilised B&B is composed of two venerable buildings, "congenially furnished with brass or mahogany bedsteads, antiques, old pictures, samplers and lots of books". There's a Victorian parlour with an upright piano complete with period sheet music, and a quiet sitting room with a bar. Breakfast (vegetarian or traditional) is served to soft classical music in a large adjoining galleried room – formerly a Quaker meeting house – with high windows, good paintings and china, books, plants, and a fire on cold days. The writer Conrad Aiken lived here for 23 years. Francis Hadfield owns a laundry, and his "excellent and prompt shirt laundering" is also appreciated. (*Margaret and Alan Clarke, Charles Gorer*)

Open All year.
Rooms 1 suite, 10 double, 1 single. 10 with *en suite* facilities.
Facilities Sitting room, bar/sitting room, breakfast room. Beaches, bird sanctuary nearby. Unsuitable for ♿.
Location Central. Carpark nearby.
Restrictions No smoking in breakfast room. No dogs in public rooms.
Credit cards Access, Visa.
Terms [1996] B&B: single £22.50, double £41–£59, suite £84. Reductions for 4 or more days. 15% midweek reduction Nov–Feb, except Christmas, New Year. 1-night bookings generally refused weekends.

The Old Vicarage NEW/BUDGET *Tel* (01797) 222119
66 Church Square *Fax* (01797) 227466
Rye TN31 7HF

A pink ex-vicarage with literary connections, now a civilised B&B. It was the birthplace of the Elizabethan playwright John Fletcher, and Henry James wrote *The Spoils of Poynton* here before moving to nearby Lamb House. It is "perfectly placed" for exploring Rye: "We had enjoyable morning and evening walks and peaceful nights' sleep." The cheerful bedrooms, with flowery fabrics, drinks tray, TV and magazines, have "a wonderful view of the 15th-century church whose golden cherubs chime on the quarter-hour". In the small bay-windowed room overlooking the walled garden, there's ample choice for breakfast, continental or English. Tea is properly brewed, marmalade is home-made, scones are home-baked, eggs new-laid, sausages award-winning. Paul and Julia Masters, "concerned hosts", help guests to book tables in local restaurants and to plan sightseeing. Tea on arrival, a newspaper, and a glass of sherry are included in the price. (*Mrs L Shepperd*) Only caveat: "The shower room was cramped and cold."

Note: Not to be confused with *The Old Vicarage Hotel* in East Street.

Open All year, except 25–27 Dec.
Rooms 1 suite, 5 double. 5 with *en suite* facilities.
Facilities Lounge, reading room, breakfast room. Walled garden. Tennis, bowling, putting, beach (safe bathing) 2 miles. Unsuitable for ♿.
Location By St Mary's church. Follow signs to town centre. Through Landgate Arch to High St, 3rd left into West St. Private parking nearby.
Restrictions No smoking: breakfast room, bedrooms. No children under 8. No dogs.
Credit cards None accepted.
Terms [1996] B&B £20–£29.50. Winter breaks Nov–Mar; weekly discounts. 2 nights min. Apr–Oct weekends. *V* (Nov–Feb, Sun–Thurs)

ST AUSTELL Cornwall Map 1

Boscundle Manor *Tel* (01726) 813557
Tregrehan, St Austell PL25 3RL *Fax* (01726) 814997
César award: for unpressured home hospitality in perfect p. and q.

Andrew and Mary Flint's manor, part medieval, but mainly 18th-century, is near the sea at Carlyon Bay. Reached up winding stone steps, it has a bosky setting in pretty grounds with lovely views, secluded seats, ponds, a small lake, and a sheltered heated swimming pool, and there are plenty of outdoor activities (see next page). Inside are thick walls, beams, low ceilings, antique furniture and prints, "chosen with loving care", and bedrooms "with comforts ancient and modern aplenty, including a little fridge with fresh milk". Some have a spa bath, some a patio. The garden cottage has the best views. The manor is run on country house lines. Recent eulogies: "A blissful four days. Guests are treated with respect and attention, albeit in a laid-back atmosphere." "Food superbly cooked and presented; wine list probably the best in Cornwall. Charming cottage garden, with a variety of interesting plants in a natural setting." "A divine place, comfortably lived in, done with well-heeled, but uncontrived style." The "dinner party-style cooking" is based on fresh ingredients, on a short menu with choices. Drink "is treated seriously, and if you can't finish your bottle of wine you are charged only for what you consume". Breakfast is in a pretty conservatory. *Boscundle Manor* has "mildly eccentric" characteristics: no formal reception, no bedroom keys (though most rooms have a small safe). A bit informal for some; but its fans enjoy "the combination of easy cordiality and comfort with understated luxury". (*Charles Moncrieffe, JR Quarmby, and others*)

Open End Mar–end Oct. Dining room closed midday, to non-residents Sun.
Rooms 2 suites, 6 double, 2 single. 1 in garden, 2 in cottage (can be self-catering).
Facilities Sitting room, bar, games room, dining room, conservatory; private dining room. 10-acre grounds: garden, swimming pool, exercise room, croquet, golf practice, small lake, ponds, woodlands. Beaches, riding, coastal walks, fishing nearby. Unsuitable for ♿.
Location 2 miles E of St Austell. 200 yds off A390 on road to Tregrehan.
Restrictions No smoking in dining room. No dogs in public rooms.
Credit cards Access, Amex, Visa.
Terms B&B: single £60–£80, double £110–£130, suite £140–£160; D,B&B: single £80–£100, double £150–£170, suite £180–£200. Set dinner £22.50. Reductions for longer stays.

ST BLAZEY Cornwall — Map 1

Nanscawen House NEW — *Tel/Fax* (01726) 814488
Prideaux Road
St Blazey, nr Par PL24 2SR

A no-smoking B&B, with cosseting proprietors Janet and Keith Martin. It is a fine, spacious old country house, wisteria-covered, in secluded grounds with a heated swimming pool and whirlpool spa. Only three bedrooms, all large, with a garden view and a bathroom with a spa bath; one has a four-poster. Breakfast, "a grand display", is taken in a conservatory. There's a small bar in the drawing room. For dinner, the Martins will help guests choose among the many restaurants in nearby Fowey. "A wonderful two days; delightful bedroom; we were superbly looked after." (*David B Gordon*)

Open All year, except Christmas/New Year.
Rooms 3 double.
Facilities Drawing room, conservatory/breakfast room. 5-acre garden: swimming pool (heated Apr–Sept), whirlpool spa. Golf, riding, beaches, fishing nearby. Unsuitable for ♿.
Location 5 miles NW of Fowey. After level-crossing in St Blazey, from A390 turn right opposite Texaco garage into Prideaux Road. *Nanscawen* is ¾ mile on right (row of trees marks foot of drive).
Restrictions No smoking. No children under 12. No pets.
Credit cards Access, Visa.
Terms B&B: single £40–£58, double: £68–£78.

ST IVES Cornwall Map 1

The Garrack
Burthallan Lane
St Ives TR26 3AA

Tel (01736) 796199
Fax (01736) 798955

This traditional seaside hotel (Relais du Silence), offering "warm, heartfelt value for money", has been owned by the Kilby family for about 30 years. It is a stone building with a modern extension, quietly set on a hill above the town, overlooking the spectacular Porthmeor surfing beach. The town and the Tate Gallery are "within short but steep walking distance". The hotel is "most welcoming, catering happily for all ages, and with accommodation for the disabled. "Staff really keen to please. Well-appointed bedroom with lovely view and tea cheerfully brought, rather than DIY. High standards all round." The restaurant, with conservatory extension, attracts outside diners. There is a comprehensive wine cellar, reasonably priced. The set dinner menu is "compact but varied"; there's a large *carte*, with several vegetarian dishes. Breakfasts are generous. Some rooms are in the old house; less characterful ones in the new part have the best views. The small leisure centre has a very warm swimming pool, sauna, solarium, exercise machines described as "cardio-vascular fitness equipment", and an all-day snack bar. (*Derek and Carol Clark, and others*)

Open All year (subject to maintenance).
Rooms 17 double, 1 single. 2 in cottage. 1 designed for ♿.
Facilities Lounge, TV lounge, bar, dining room; conference facilities; leisure centre: small swimming pool, sauna, whirlpool, solarium, fitness room, coffee shop, bar. 2-acre grounds. Beaches 5–10 mins' walk.
Location 1 m from centre. From Penzance on B3311 turn right on to B3306 towards St Ives. Hotel off this, to left.
Restrictions No smoking in leisure centre. No dogs in public rooms.
Credit cards All major cards accepted.
Terms B&B: single £61–£64, double £99–£128; D,B&B: single £70–£83.50, double £131–£167. Snack lunches. Set dinner (2–3-course) £17.50–£19.50; full alc £27. Off-season breaks; Christmas programme.

ST KEYNE Cornwall Map 1

The Well House
St Keyne, Liskeard PL14 4RN

Tel (01579) 342001
Fax (01579) 343891

A Victorian stone house surrounded by an informal garden, with duck-ponds, a tennis court and a swimming pool, in an unspoilt spot in the Looe valley. "A jewel, with an enjoyably idiosyncratic host, Nick Wainford. We ate more good food here at reasonable prices than anywhere else during a three-week trip to England," wrote a correspondent from Seattle. "No skimping: fresh orange juice and real croissants for breakfast; delicious soups for lunch; wonderfully garnished main courses at dinner. Though not obliged to dine in, you'd be mad not to. The dining room is arranged so that every table is private. We had a lovely bay window overlooking the garden. The lounge is what one would expect in someone's home. The bedrooms, none large, but some relatively good-sized, have everything you need, all in working order (but no keys). This is not a full-service hotel; you feel that you are staying with a host who is determined you will be happy; he does a great deal of the work himself, and genuinely likes talking to his guests. Real value for money." Other reporters, too, have praised the balanced modern cooking by the young chef, Wayne Pearson, the "well-furnished sitting room with an amazing array of current glossy magazines", the wine list, "a treat, and only modestly marked up", the helpfulness towards babies, and the "sensible pro-dog policy". (*Susan B Hanley, and others*)

Open All year.
Rooms 7 double.
Facilities Lounge, bar, restaurant. 4-acre grounds: tennis, swimming pool. Walking, fishing, riding, golf nearby; coast 4 miles. Unsuitable for ♿.
Location 3 miles S of Liskeard on B3254. At church fork left to St Keyne Well; hotel ½ mile on left.
Restrictions No children under 8 in restaurant for dinner. No dogs in public rooms.
Credit cards Access, Amex, Visa.
Terms B&B: single £60, double £72–£105. Cooked breakfast £7.50 extra. Set meals: (2–4 courses) £19.95–£29.70. Winter breaks. 1-night bookings refused bank holidays.

ST MARY'S Isles of Scilly — Map 1

Star Castle NEW — *Tel* (01720) 422317 and 423234
St Mary's, Isles of Scilly — *Fax* (01720) 422343
Cornwall TR21 0JA

In a "stunning location" overlooking the town, harbour and surrounding islands (fine sunsets), this 16th-century castle, built in the shape of an eight-pointed star, is surrounded by a dry moat and 18-foot ramparts. Now a modest and welcoming hotel, it has a small lounge, and an atmospheric bar in the former dungeon. The dining room is the former officers' mess. In its grounds there is a wealth of subtropical plants, suntrap lawns enclosed by high hedges, a covered swimming pool, and two modern blocks with large bedrooms, and suites suitable for families. The most characterful rooms are in the main house (two have a four-poster). Three singles are in guard rooms on the battlements. The hotel featured in earlier editions of the *Guide* under previous owners. Now in the hands of Mr and Mrs Nicholls, it is renominated by a visitor with much experience of the hotel trade: "I stayed with my wife and two children, and was impressed. The hands-on owner remembers the names of the guests and makes a point of talking to them at breakfast. He often takes them in the hotel's launch to visit other islands (he is the pilot for large ships visiting the island, and head of the lifeboat service). The staff are very friendly. The food is imaginative, with plenty of choice; there's a reasonable wine list." (*Gary Crossley*)

Open Mid-Mar–mid-Oct.
Rooms 7 suites, 19 double, 5 single. 19 in 2 garden blocks.
Facilities Lounge, conservatory, games room, bar, restaurant. 4-acre grounds: covered swimming pool; private motor launch. Beach 10 mins' walk. Golf, cycle hire, riding, sailing, diving, fishing available. Unsuitable for ♿.
Location ¼ mile from town centre. Boat or scheduled helicopter flight from Penzance (neither on Sun).
Restrictions No smoking in restaurant. No children under 5 in restaurant at night. No dogs in public rooms.
Credit cards Access, Visa.
Terms B&B £40–£49.50; D,B&B £50–£75. Light lunch £2–£5. Set dinner £19.95.

SALCOMBE Devon — Map 1

Tides Reach — *Tel* (01548) 843466
South Sands, Salcombe TQ8 8LJ — *Fax* (01548) 843954

"I have stayed many times. I am a very fussy person, but I cannot fault management, staff or food. Super hotel, super beach, usually super weather." "Consistently courteous and efficient staff, many long serving. Food more than adequate." Praise from two returning visitors to this seaside hotel, which has been owned by the Edwards family for 30 years. It is a mile from the centre of one of Devon's prettiest towns, and can be reached by a passenger ferry as an alternative to the narrow road, which tends to get crowded in season. It faces across an estuary and is surrounded by National Trust land; excellent cliff walks, and a lovely National Trust garden, Sharpitor, are close by. It has a pleasant lounge, full of greenery, large, bright bedrooms, most sea-facing, many with a balcony, and an agreeable dining room, serving modern English/continental food. The leisure centre has a large swimming pool with glass panels which open in summer to let in fresh air. The garden consists mainly of a pond with ducks and moorhens, surrounded by a lawn with loungers, where good snack lunches are served. The bar has a mini-aquarium. There is entertainment by a magician on Saturday nights in season. (*Irene Ketch, RCJ Gordon*)

Open All year, except 22 Dec–10 Feb.
Rooms 3 family suites, 35 double.
Facilities 3 lounges, 2 bars, restaurant; leisure centre: swimming pool, sauna, solarium, spa bath, squash, beauty salon, bar/coffee shop. ⅓-acre grounds: lawns, water garden. Sandy beach opposite. Sailing, fishing, windsurfing, golf, tennis nearby.
Location Through Salcombe: follow signs to South Sands. Carpark.
Restrictions No smoking: restaurant, 1 lounge. No children under 8. No dogs in public rooms.
Credit cards All major cards accepted.
Terms B&B £44–£78; D,B&B £55–£104. Set dinner £25.75; full alc £39. Bargain breaks; winter rates; early booking discount scheme; children's tariffs. 1-night bookings refused bank holiday weekends.

SALISBURY Wiltshire — Map 2

Leena's Guest House BUDGET — *Tel* (01722) 335419
50 Castle Road
Salisbury SP1 3RL

Welcoming B&B in Edwardian house, an enjoyable 10–15-min walk along river from centre. Park, leisure centre, nearby. Welcoming Finnish hostess, Leena Street. 6 simple bedrooms (1 on ground floor), all no-smoking, all with facilities en suite, *"appetising" linen, effective lighting. Good breakfast (English or vegetarian.) On busy road to Amesbury, but windows double-glazed. Parking. Guide dogs only. Credit cards not accepted. B&B: single £18–£24.50, double £33–£39.50. More reports, please.*

Please make a habit of sending in a report as soon as possible after a visit when details are still fresh in your mind. The more you can tell us of your impressions the better.

Stratford Lodge BUDGET *Tel* (01722) 325177
4 Park Lane *Fax* (01722) 412699
Salisbury SP1 3NP

This informal no-smoking guest house, just off the Amesbury road on a quiet lane at the far end of a park, was the family home of the proprietor, Jill Bayly. "The Victorian building is rambling, and furnished with taste," wrote our inspector. "It's generously run, with a home-like feel and a happy atmosphere. My bedroom, overlooking the greenhouse, was tiny, but warm and well lit, with old-fashioned furniture and a small shower room (other rooms are larger, some have a bath). Very good dinner, an eclectic menu with plenty of choice; lots of vegetables, all garden fresh; huge portions. Desserts are home-made; you help yourself to as many as you fancy. Excellent breakfast, in a conservatory, with stewed fruit, ample toast, home-made marmalade and generous cooked items – kedgeree, mushrooms on toast, eggs." No particular facilities for small children, but they are accepted if parents have the necessary equipment. There's a pretty, secluded garden. The city centre is reached by a peaceful riverside walk.

Open All year, except Christmas/New Year.
Rooms 6 double, 2 single. 1 on ground floor.
Facilities Lounge, piano room, breakfast room, dining room. ½-acre garden: covered swimming pool.
Location 1 mile from centre. Turn at post office/store by park on A345. Parking.
Restrictions No smoking. No dogs.
Credit cards Access, Amex, Visa.
Terms [1996] B&B: single £30–£34.50, double £50–£54. Set lunch £12, dinner £19. Winter/spring breaks.

SANDY PARK Devon Map 1

See Chagford

SEAVIEW Isle of Wight Map 2

Seaview Hotel *Tel* (01983) 612711
High Street *Fax* (01983) 613729
Seaview PO34 5EX
César award in 1988

Seaview is an old-fashioned, picturesque sailing village, generally peaceful, but bustling in July and August. This thriving small hotel stands at the foot of the High Street, Union flag flying, and is something of a maritime museum – the proprietors, Nicholas and Nicola Hayward, are collectors of naval prints and things nautical. They welcome children (there's a "wholesome" high tea) and dogs, and number businessfolk and "slightly older couples" among their regular visitors. Traditional English/French cooking by Mrs Hayward and Charles Bartlett on a quite short, but varied, menu is served in the popular restaurant (in two sittings at busy times). "Of necessity tables are quite close together," a visitor wrote last year. "We have had amicable conversations on many occasions." Pretty bedrooms, serviced at night, have good fabrics, antiques and a smart bathroom. They vary in size; rear ones are perhaps the quietest (some overlook the carpark); front ones have a view of the sea ("you can lie in bed watching tankers negotiate the Solent"). Recent praise: "Concerned host, first-rate housekeeping." "Imaginative bar snacks. Highly enjoyable dinner. Service of the highest order." There's a new restaurant/function room this year, and three of the smallest bedrooms have been given a south-facing balcony. More reports, please.

Open All year.
Rooms 3 suites, 13 double. 2 on ground floor.
Facilities Lounge, 2 bars, restaurant, restaurant/function room; patio, courtyard. Sea, sandy beach 50 yds: sailing, fishing, windsurfing.
Location Central. Follow signs for seafront. Small carpark.
Restrictions No smoking: 1 restaurant, lounge. No children under 5 in restaurant at night. No dogs in restaurant.
Credit cards All major cards accepted.
Terms B&B: single £45–£55, double £70–£78, suite £90–£95; D,B&B: single £61.95–£71.95, double £103.90–£111.90, suite £123.90–£128.90. Set lunch (Sun) £10.95; full alc £23. Weekend, midweek, Christmas, New Year, painting breaks. *V*

SEAVINGTON ST MARY Somerset — Map 1

The Pheasant BUDGET — *Tel* (01460) 240502
Water Street, Seavington St Mary — *Fax* (01460) 242388
nr Ilminster TA19 0QH

A 17th-century thatched farmhouse, quietly set amid landscaped gardens and lawns in a pretty village on the Devon/Dorset border. Here an Italian-British couple dispense "excellent food and service". "Edmondo Paoloni sets a high standard in the dining room," wrote its nominator. "His wife, Jacqueline, is charming and efficient. The housekeeping is beyond reproach." The decor is chintzy and traditional, with low beams, a rustic bar, a low-ceilinged restaurant with a large fireplace; and floral fabrics and wallpapers and period furniture in the bedrooms. The eclectic menu includes many varieties of pasta, chargrills, and vegetarian dishes. Good choice of Italian wines. (*DO*)

Open All year. Restaurant closed Sun evening, midday except Sun.
Rooms 8 double. 6 in barn and cottage.
Facilities Lounge, bar, restaurant. 1-acre garden. Unsuitable for ♿.
Location From B3168 turn S at *Volunteer* inn. Hotel on right.
Restriction No dogs in house.
Credit cards All major cards accepted.
Terms B&B: single from £60, double from £90. Full alc £25–£30.

SHEPTON MALLET Somerset — Map 1

Bowlish House BUDGET — *Tel/Fax* (01749) 342022
Wells Road
Shepton Mallet BA4 5JD

Linda and Bob Morley's restaurant with only three bedrooms is a beautiful Palladian house, "not grand, but elegant and comfortable", with some good antique furniture and an intimate sitting room and bar. The panelled dining room is hung with portraits, and has a jungle-like conservatory extension. The reasonably priced three-course menu offers plenty of choice, including a vegetarian main dish. Mrs Morley's modern British cooking (red "Meals" in *Michelin*) is sophisticated and interesting but not over-elaborate. There's a wide-ranging wine list. The generous continental breakfast includes freshly squeezed orange juice, Greek yogurt and muffins; there is a small extra charge for the "wonderful" English breakfast. Recent visitors liked their spacious bedroom: "Excellent beds, TV and lots of interesting reading – newspapers, guides, etc. We could not have been more comfortable. The owners manage to strike just the right note, not too fussy, not too casual; Mr Morley is a mine of local information." (*JC, and others*) The house is on a main road, but its rear garden is peaceful.

Open All year, except 1 week autumn, 1 week spring. Lunch by arrangement.
Rooms 3 double. No telephone.
Facilities Lounge, bar, restaurant, conservatory. ¼-acre garden. Unsuitable for ♿.
Location ¼ mile outside Shepton Mallet, on A371 to Wells.
Restrictions No smoking in restaurant while people are eating. No dogs in public rooms.
Credit cards Access, Amex, Visa.
Terms [1996] B&B double £48. English breakfast £3.50. Set dinner £22.50.

SHERBORNE Dorset — Map 2

The Eastbury NEW/BUDGET — *Tel* (01935) 813131
Long Street — *Fax* (01935) 817296
Sherborne DT9 3BY

Recently taken over and renovated by Mr and Mrs Pickford, this Georgian building stands in a quiet street a short walk from the centre. It retains many original features and is decorated in period style. "It is not often that one finds a pleasant country town hotel where the management and staff are so consistently helpful and cheerful," writes its nominator. "Every request we made was met with total cooperation. Our bedroom was bright and clean, with all facilities. Our son and his family shared a family suite comprising most of the top floor. The dining room, with a conservatory extension, overlooks the pretty walled garden. The food was best traditional English, cooked with a light touch, on a varied *table d'hôte* menu. (*JS Stooke*)

Open All year.
Rooms 9 double, 6 single.
Facilities Lounge, 2 bars, restaurant. 1½-acre garden. Unsuitable for ♿.
Location Near centre; hotel will send directions. Carpark.
Restrictions Smoking discouraged in restaurant. No dogs.
Credit cards Access, Amex, Visa.
Terms B&B: single £50, double £70; D,B&B (min. 2 nights): single £65, double £94. Set lunch £14.50, dinner £19.50.

SHIPTON-UNDER-WYCHWOOD Oxfordshire — Map 3

The Lamb Inn NEW — *Tel* (01993) 830465
Shipton-under-Wychwood OX7 6DQ — *Fax* (01993) 832025

"An extremely nice small hotel," writes its nominator. "Excellent atmosphere, warm welcome. The proprietor, Luciano Valenta, from Trieste, who runs it with his English wife, makes a point of calling his customers by name, and personally seeing to their welfare." Our inspectors, too, greatly liked this trim stone 18th-century building in a quiet setting in a fringe-Cotswold village. "It is intimate, and rather select, with a civilised clientele. There's a patio in front with tables for drinks and snacks. Inside are rough stone walls, wood panelling, polished floors, beamed ceilings, good wooden tables and chairs. Newspapers on sticks in the bar. Log fires in the tiny, cosy lounge. Everything beautifully kept; potted plants and flowers everywhere. The small dining room and the bar serve English dishes, copious and decently cooked. Pleasant young waiters. Excellent breakfasts include salmon kedgeree, smoked kippers and mixed grill. Bedrooms are named after local villages. Ours, Bruern, was white-walled, beamed-ceilinged, and well equipped; the bathroom was medium-sized and adequate, but the water could have been hotter." (*PW Moore, and others; also Good Pub Guide*)

Open All year, except Christmas.
Rooms 5 double.
Facilities Lounge, bar, restaurant. Patio. Unsuitable for ♿.
Location S edge of village, 4 miles NE of Burford. Carpark.
Restrictions No smoking: restaurant, some bedrooms. No dogs.
Credit cards Access, Amex, Visa.
Terms [1996] B&B: single £58, double £75. Set Sun lunch £14.95, dinner £21.

SHREWSBURY Shropshire — Map 3

Albright Hussey *Tel* (01939) 290571
Ellesmere Road *Fax* (01939) 291143
Shrewsbury SY4 3AF

In an area "knee-deep in history", a "strangely wonderful" hybrid moated house, half black-and-white early Tudor, half 17th-century brick and timber. It is owned by Franco, Vera and Paul Subbiani, who also own a restaurant, *Henry's*, in Shrewsbury. It was recently much extended, with the addition of nine bedrooms (some quite small), a new residents' lounge, and a large conference room. Some alterations were still in progress as we went to press, but 1996 visitors were enthusiastic: "The main house will be virtually unchanged, and the pleasant atmosphere should be unaffected. We had the suite, complete with four-poster spa bath, a novel innovation due to constraints in using the half-timbered walls in a listed building. The new chef, Nigel Huxley, has stamped his style on the menu. The three-course *table d'hôte* was so good that we had no need to venture on to the *carte*. It offered a wide choice, and was a feast to the eye as well as the palate. Canapés and coffee were included in the price. Good wine list too – 120 selections and six house wines." The cooking is modern British/French. Earlier visitors have praised the exotic decor, the warm welcome and the attentive service. (*PJ and BA D'Arcy*)

Open All year.
Rooms 1 suite, 13 double. 1, on ground floor, suitable for ♿.
Facilities Lounge, bar, restaurant; large function room. 4-acre grounds.
Location On A528 to Ellesmere, 2 miles N of Shrewsbury,
Restrictions No smoking in restaurant. No children under 3. Dogs by arrangement, not in public rooms.
Credit cards All major cards accepted.
Terms B&B: single £55–£100, double £75–£150, suite £150; D,B&B £50–£110 per person. Set lunch £12.50, dinner £23.50; full alc £30.

SHURDINGTON Gloucestershire — Map 3

The Greenway — *Tel* (01242) 862352
Shurdington, nr Cheltenham GL51 5UG — *Fax* (01242) 862780

A creeper-clad mansion, Elizabethan in origin, just outside Cheltenham, named for the pre-Roman path which runs beside it to the Cotswold Hills beyond (good walking). Owned by David and Valerie White, it is peacefully set in a lovely garden amid parkland. The interior is traditional, with flowery sofas and chairs in the large drawing room. "And," wrote the nominators, "our bedroom was excellent – spacious, with good fabrics, magazines, books, fruit, ice-bucket with champagne, and a well-equipped bathroom. Very good breakfast, with proper fresh orange juice, good toast, delicious scrambled eggs. Enthusiastic, welcoming host, pleasant staff, relaxing atmosphere, good housekeeping." The restaurant is quite formal, with a bright conservatory opening on to a pretty terrace. We'd be grateful for reports on the country house cooking by Peter Fairclough, who recently took over the kitchen, having earlier served here as *sous-chef*. (*P and JT*)

Open All year. Restaurant closed Sat lunch.
Rooms 17 double, 2 single. 8 in coach house. 4 on ground floor (1 suitable for partially ♿).
Facilities Hall, drawing room, bar; function facilities. 7-acre grounds: croquet. Golf, riding, tennis, swimming, clay pigeon-shooting available.
Location 2½ miles SW of Cheltenham, on A46.
Restrictions No smoking in 8 bedrooms. No children under 7. No dogs.
Credit cards All major cards accepted.
Terms [1996] B&B: single £87.50, double £127.50–£180. Set lunch £17.50, dinner £30. Off-season rates; 2-day breaks. *V*

SIMONSBATH Somerset — Map 1

Simonsbath House — *Tel* (01643) 831259
Simonsbath, nr Minehead TA24 7SH — *Fax* (01643) 831557

"A delightful hotel in a magnificent location. Our room was very comfortable. Some of your readers have called the decor 'claustrophobic'; we thought it charming, and in the best of taste." Sue and Mike Burns' 17th-century hunting lodge, long, low and white, is off a small road in the Exmoor National Park. It overlooks the river Barle; excellent walks start from the grounds. It has a panelled lounge, a library bar, and an "exceptionally pretty dining room, with pale green walls, dark red table cloths covered with white, and nice pictures of Exmoor". Here "outstanding food, each dish on the limited menu beautifully cooked and presented", is served by a friendly local staff. "There's plenty of choice on the wine list, including some unusual bottles. Good breakfasts too." (*JR Sargent, Heather Sharland, and others*) Some bathrooms are small. One visitor was less enthusiastic about the food but concluded, nevertheless: "A lovely place to stay when exploring Exmoor."

Open 1 Feb–30 Nov.
Rooms 7 double.
Facilities Lounge, library, dining room. ½-acre grounds. Riding, shooting, fishing in river Barle nearby; coast 10 miles. Unsuitable for ♿.
Location On B3223, 7 miles SE of Lynton. Carpark.

Restrictions No smoking in dining room. No children under 10. No dogs.
Credit cards All major cards accepted.
Terms B&B £40–£64; D,B&B £60–£84.

SLAIDBURN Lancashire — Map 4

Parrock Head BUDGET
Woodhouse Lane
Slaidburn, Clitheroe BB7 3AH
Tel (01200) 446614
Fax (01200) 446313

"Extreme professionalism, combined with a very friendly atmosphere. It is quietly unpretentious, exceedingly comfortable, and good value for money." Praise from a regular visitor to Richard and Vicky Umbers' low, whitewashed 17th-century farmhouse in a remote and beautiful setting amid the fells and pastureland of the Forest of Bowland. It makes an excellent base for touring, walking, and bird-watching. The valley of the river Hodder is nearby. Three spacious bedrooms (the best) are in the main building; the rest are in a garden block. Guests may sit by the fire in the large upstairs sitting room (once the hay loft) or browse over local information in the timbered library with antique furniture. They are encouraged to meet over drinks in the bar and expected to dine in the restaurant (the low-beamed former milking parlour), also open to non-residents. The short, reasonably priced *carte* changes daily. "Mrs Umbers is highly entertaining, and also an excellent cook, using the best ingredients; her husband waits at table. The wine list is not unduly marked up." Breakfast is "substantial and efficiently served". Good packed lunches. (*RAL Ogston, and others*)

Open All year, except Jan.
Rooms 5 double, 2 single. 4 in garden cottages. 3 on ground floor.
Facilities Lounge, library, bar, restaurant; terrace. 1-acre grounds. Fishing, bird-watching nearby.
Location 9 miles N of Clitheroe. 1 mile NW of Slaidburn village.
Restrictions No smoking in dining room. No dogs in public rooms, unattended in bedrooms.
Credit cards All major cards accepted.
Terms B&B: single £40–£45, double £60–£70; D,B&B (min. 2 nights) £48.50–£63.50 per person. Set lunch £14, dinner £19.50. Light and packed lunches available. Winter breaks. Christmas, New Year packages. 1-night bookings sometimes refused weekends. *V*

SLINFOLD West Sussex — Map 2

Random Hall
Stane Street
Slinfold, nr Horsham RH13 7QX
Tel (01403) 790558
Fax (01403) 791046

Nigel and Cathy Evans's old farmhouse, with oak beams, flagstone floors, and a fine inglenook fireplace in its lounge, is "unpretentious yet thoughtful and comforting, and reasonably priced", according to its nominator. "It has a lovely welcoming feeling, friendly but not gushing. It is part 16th-century, so not all that sound-proof. My bedroom was not at all 'country living', but it had good lights, TV, a large, solid desk, plenty of pillows, no silly extras, and I was tremendously comfortable. The bathroom was a dream. I had a good room service supper and slept soundly (there is some traffic noise but it didn't obtrude). Good breakfast, actually with the paper I had ordered, was also brought to the room. No early vacuuming outside the door, as can happen in the best hotels." (*NB*) Meals (traditional/modern British cooking by Jonathan Gettings) are served in the candlelit Tudor-style restaurant or, on warm evenings, on the Vinery Terrace. One 1996 visitor found the cooking disappointing, but others thought it excellent. (*NB, Tony Thomas*).

Open All year, except 27–30 Dec.
Rooms 10 double, 5 single.
Facilities Lounge, bar, restaurant; small conference facilities. terrace. 1-acre grounds: terrace. Golf, ballooning, clay pigeon-shooting nearby. Unsuitable for ♿.
Location 4 miles W of Horsham. Set back from A29 (some traffic noise).
Restrictions No smoking in restaurant. No children under 8. No dogs.
Credit cards Access, Amex, Visa.
Terms Rooms: single £46–£57.50, double £57.50. Breakfast: continental £6.50, English £8.50. D,B&B £56.60–£85.35 per person. Set meals (1–3-course): lunch £12.95–£16.95, dinner £13.95–£19.95. Golf, gardens, Christmas breaks.

SOAR MILL COVE Devon — Map 1

Soar Mill Cove Hotel — *Tel* (01548) 561566
Soar Mill Cove — *Fax* (01548) 561223
nr Salcombe TQ7 3DS

The Makepeace family's purpose-built, single-storey hotel has a "supremely peaceful" setting at the head of an isolated cove surrounded by National Trust land. Wonderful cliff walks start from its grounds; a fine beach is a short walk down the hill. It has two small swimming pools – one, unheated, outdoors; one, very warm, indoors. All ages are welcomed. "It is a fine place to take children, while enjoying adult comforts," writes a regular visitor. "The food was more consistent this time, with particularly good fish dishes. The service had improved too; personal and friendly, but not familiar." Others have thought the meals "imaginative and exciting" (but some "over-saucing" has been reported), and have written of the "warmth of welcome and concern for guests" and of the young staff "all involved in their well-being". The bedroom decor is too florid for some, "but they are supplied with everything, and it's lovely to have doors on to your own patio". "Great consideration" is shown for the disabled, though the hotel is not fully equipped for them. "Well-kept grounds, impeccable housekeeping. Proprietors always around." Excellent laundry facilities too, and a freshly cooked supper for children at 5.30 pm. A car is essential if you want to explore. (*Marion and David Fanthorpe, Alan Rossiter; also Mrs M Box, and others*) A frequent criticism: "The most uncomfortable dining chairs I've ever sat on." And: "Breakfast at 8.45 is too late for families with young children."

Open 7 Feb–end Oct.
Rooms 3 suites, 16 double. All on ground floor.
Facilities 2 lounges, lounge bar, restaurant; indoor swimming pool. 5-acre grounds: Swimming pool (unheated), tennis, putting. Sea 500 yds.
Location 3 miles W of Salcombe. From A381 turn right through Marlborough; follow signs for Soar, then Soar Mill Cove.
Restrictions No smoking in restaurant. No dogs in public rooms.
Credit cards Access, Visa.

Terms B&B £60–£70; D,B&B £82–£94. Set lunch £18, dinner £34. 3-day packages all year. Cookery classes.

SOUTH MOLTON Devon — Map 1

The Park House NEW — *Tel/Fax* (01769) 572610
South Molton EX36 3ED

An "exquisite" house, wisteria-covered, with "friendly and available" owners, Michael and Anne Gornall – "great chatters". "All that a country house should be," writes its nominator, "in lovely countryside, outside the Devon market town. In summer, the garden is a superb setting for cream teas and Pimms. It has comfortable bedrooms and spacious public rooms. The wine list contains some noble bottles." "You approach via a long beech-lined drive through imposing gates," writes an inspector. "Rhododendrons tower on one side; lawns slope down to a pond on the other; horses graze beyond, on paddocks running down to the river Mole. Inside, the original sweeping staircase and marble gallery have been carefully restored. Mementos of Michael Gornall's spell in the army in Africa, and of his wife's interest in horses, abound. Lots of magazines and books, mostly on country pursuits, to read by a log fire in the lounges. Colour schemes are haphazard, giving an uncontrived feel. Bedrooms have every mod con except good lighting. Competent country house cooking (with choices) by Anne Gornall in nice dining room, with ceiling-to-ground bay windows, dark green paint and good china. Rather a lot of extras on the bill." "We attract people wanting to get away from their children, and over-40s who love gardens and country pastimes," write the Gornalls. (*Donald Johnston, and others*)

Open 1 Mar–31 Dec.
Rooms 1 suite, 7 double.
Facilities Lounge, lounge with TV, bar, dining room. 18-acre grounds: 3-acre garden, river with fishing, riding, croquet. Shooting, tennis, golf, nearby. Unsuitable for ♿.
Location Leave A361 at South Molton roundabout; take North Molton road out of town. Hotel on right after 250 yds.
Restrictions No smoking: dining room, 1 lounge. No children under 11. No dogs in bedrooms, public rooms (except bar).
Credit cards All major cards accepted (*3% surcharge*).
Terms B&B £44–£49; D,B&B £60–£65. Alc lunch from £15; set dinner £16. Special breaks. Christmas house party.

Whitechapel Manor — *Tel* (01769) 573377
South Molton EX36 3EG — *Fax* (01769) 573797

Patricia Shapland's Grade I listed Elizabethan manor is in an isolated setting near the Exmoor National Park, with well-maintained gardens and wonderful views; there are good walks in its wooded grounds. It has a magnificent Jacobean carved oak screen in the entrance hall, fine panelling, high ceilings, intricate William and Mary plaster carvings and mouldings, deep recessed windows, and quality furnishings and fabrics. Its Great Hall is the lounge, where cream teas (with fine china) are served, by a fire in cold weather. Bedrooms vary in size. "Ours was delightful," writes a 1996 visitor, "with fresh flowers, good soaps and an exceptionally comfortable bed. The food [a new chef, David

Alexander, arrived in February 1996] was delicious – local meats and vegetables, freshly and flavoursomely cooked; splendid cheeses; the chocolate and orange tart was exceptional. Warm welcome. Eccentric but efficient service." Others have called the service "friendly, but not matey", and admired the "lovely, spotless" bedrooms. Breakfast is a hearty country affair, with home-made breads, croissants and preserves. (*Roland Philipps, and others*) Parking is across the garden; guests who drive to the door will have their car parked for them.

Open All year.
Rooms 2 suites, 6 double, 2 single.
Facilities 2 lounges, bar, dining room; private dining room. 15-acre grounds: croquet. Unsuitable for ♿.
Location From M5 exit 27 go towards Barnstaple. After *c.* 30 mins right at roundabout. Hotel signposted to right.
Restrictions No smoking in dining room. No dogs.
Credit cards All major cards accepted.
Terms [1996] B&B: single £70–£85, double £110–£150, suite £170; D,B&B: single £95–£110, double £160–£200, suite £220. Set lunch / dinner (3–4-course) £34–£40. Easter, Christmas, Lundy Island breaks.

SOUTH ZEAL Devon **Map 1**

The Oxenham Arms BUDGET *Tel* (01837) 840244
South Zeal, Okehampton EX20 2JT *Fax* (01837) 840791

A historic pub on a steep hill in the centre of a peaceful village in undulating countryside on the north edge of Dartmoor. Licensed since the 14th century, it is thought to have been built by lay monks in the 12th century, around a monolith which can be seen in a small room behind the bar. It is now run by the Henry family. Good traditional food is served in the beamed, panelled bar with Stuart fireplaces, and in the fine old dining room. There is a comfortable sitting room with a large open fire. The simple, pretty bedrooms have telephone and TV, and most have *en suite* facilities. "Very friendly service," writes a recent visitor, "tea was brought the moment we arrived." "A fine unhurried atmosphere," adds the *Good Pub Guide*. "Imposing stone steps lead up to the garden, where there is a sloping spread of lawn."

Open All year.
Rooms 8 double.
Facilities Lounge, family room, bar, dining room. ¼-acre garden. Unsuitable for ♿.
Location Centre of village just S of A30, 4 miles E of Okehampton.
Credit cards All major cards accepted.
Terms B&B: single £40–£45, double £50–£60; D,B&B: single £55–£60, double £80–£90. Set lunch £9.50, dinner £16.50. Christmas package, winter breaks. 1-night bookings refused 24 Dec–1 Jan, some holiday weekends.

SOUTHWOLD Suffolk **Map 2**

The Crown BUDGET *Tel* (01502) 722275
High Street *Fax* (01502) 727263
Southwold IP18 6DP

Adnams, the wine merchants ("who have perhaps the best wine warehouse on the east coast"), own most of the hotels in this unspoilt seaside town. The *Crown*, a lively, sophisticated pub, offers decent accommodation in bedrooms which are "small but well appointed, with a reasonably sized bathroom". Public rooms, all with open fire, are "warm and welcoming". The popular bar serves "eclectic dishes with a rustic approach"; a queue builds up for the dinner menu, which appears at 7 pm (no booking). The same interesting menu is offered in the restaurant, where you may book, but this has less local character. There's a new chef, Gary Marsland; we'd like more reports on the food. The wine list "is, of course, superb" (a wide range of wines by the glass). Breakfasts are huge and well cooked. "Good value." "A most enjoyable place to stay." (*Brian Knox, Good Pub Guide, and others*)

Open All year, except 2nd week Jan.
Rooms 1 family, 9 double, 2 single. All with private facilities; 3 not *en suite*.
Facilities Lounge/parlour, bar, public bar, restaurant; private dining room; patio. Sea, pebble beach nearby. Unsuitable for ♿.
Location Central (front rooms might get some traffic noise). Limited private parking.
Restrictions No smoking: restaurant, parlour. Dogs in public bar only.
Credit cards All major cards accepted.
Terms B&B: single £41, double £63, family £87. Bar meals; set meals (2–3 courses): lunch £12.95–£15.50, dinner £17.95–£19.95. Christmas break.

The Swan
Market Place
Southwold IP18 6EG

Tel (01502) 722186
Fax (01502) 724800

"A lovely hotel in a lovely location, with a friendly feel." This stately building, with white-framed windows, iron balconies, and union flag flying, stands by the town hall in the market place. Also owned by Adnams, it is smarter, pricier, and larger than the *Crown*. It has a flagstoned hall, a fine staircase with wrought-iron banisters, and a spacious lounge (with an open fire) where teas are served. The large, stylish dining room, popular locally, serves "good, but not great" food, accompanied, of course, by "superb" wines. There are reasonably priced bar snacks. Service is "excellent of its type, by local people doing a good and careful job". Readers prefer the traditionally furnished bedrooms of varying sizes in the main building, overlooking the square. Smaller, newer ones, called Garden Rooms, surround what was once a bowling green at the back. (*Prof. R Cormack, T Moorey, and others*) Severe criticism this year of decor and maintenance in the Garden Rooms.

Open All year. Restaurant closed for lunch Mon–Fri Jan–Easter.
Rooms 2 suites, 37 double, 6 single. 18 in garden annexe, 5 with access for ♿.
Facilities Lift, ramps. 2 lounges, bar, restaurant; function facilities. Garden. Sea 200 yds.
Location Central. Rear parking.
Restrictions No smoking in restaurant. No under-5s in restaurant after 7 pm. Dogs in garden rooms only.
Credit cards All major cards accepted.
Terms [Until Easter 1997] B&B: single £40–£69, double £84–£118, suite £139–£149; D,B&B £52–£73 per person. Set lunch: weekdays £12.50–£14.95, Sun £14.95–£16.95; set dinner £19.50–£31.50.

For details of the Voucher scheme see page xxx.

STADDLEBRIDGE North Yorkshire Map 4

McCoy's
The Cleveland Tontine
Staddlebridge, Northallerton DL6 3JB
Tel (01609) 882671
Fax (01609) 882660

César award in 1989

"I wanted to stay one night, but it was so enjoyable that I booked a second. When they saw I was tucking gleefully into the oysters, they threw in extra ones on the house. Ditto fresh raspberries. Wonderful breakfast: fresh eggs and dry-cured bacon; real tea; home-made bread. A must for connoisseurs of mild eccentricity coupled with enthusiasm. If only there were more places like this." A recent encomium for this Victorian stone restaurant-with-rooms, exuberantly and idiosyncratically run by the McCoy brothers and a friendly staff. It is at the Cleveland Tontine, where two busy roads converge, but effective double-glazing keeps the bedrooms surprisingly quiet. Their decor is "a curious mixture of homeliness, glitz, and riotous colour". Tea is served in the "junk shop-style" sitting room. Dinner orders are taken in the bar, furnished with pre-war sofas and lamps. Tom McCoy is chef (modern classical cooking with lots of choice on the *carte*). "It is served in semi-darkness in a dining room with bare floorboards, potted palms, good napery and cutlery, and no restraint on smoking. Luxury ingredients abound and prices are high. Peter McCoy stars as front-of-house and prepares breakfast: whatever you want, within reason, served in a peaceful room." "Straightforward but stylish meals with strong sauces and flavours" are served by the third brother, Eugene, in the busy bistro downstairs, with its close-packed tables, blackboard menus and loud rock music. (*Alasdair Riley, DW, and others*) No grounds, but good views. The brochure is a minor classic of humorous writing.

Open All year, except 25/26 Dec, 1 Jan.
Rooms 6 double.
Facilities 2 lounges, breakfast room, bar, bistro, restaurant. Small garden. Unsuitable for ♿.
Location Junction of A19/A172 (rooms double-glazed). 6 miles NE of Northallerton (Staddlebridge not on map).
Restriction No dogs in restaurant, bistro.
Credit cards All major cards accepted.
Terms [1996] B&B: single £79, double £99. Full alc: bistro from £30, restaurant from £35.

STAMFORD Lincolnshire Map 2

The George
71 St Martin's
Stamford PE9 2LB
Tel (01780) 55171 (755171 from 1.1.97)
Fax (01780) 57070 (757070 from 1.1.97)

César award in 1986

"An excellent hotel, full of character and life. High quality food; interesting, reasonably priced wine list. Lovely walled garden." "A perfect example of what such an establishment should be. Marvellous staff. Wine list one of the most interesting in the country, and not too expensive." This busy, historic, creeper-covered coaching inn has a cobbled, flower-tubbed courtyard, mullioned windows, a flagstoned entrance hall, panelled rooms, creaking floorboards, and a rambling nature. Some bedrooms are a considerable walk from reception; they vary greatly in size and shape; best ones are spacious, stylishly decorated and well lit; many have antiques. Meals in the panelled dining room are "very good, if not *haute cuisine*", mainly traditional, with roasts on a silver carving wagon, and cheeses and puddings on trolleys. Light meals and breakfast – "an array of wonderful things" – are served in the "delightful" garden lounge. Stamford is a beautiful, unspoilt old market town, with many fine Georgian buildings; it starred as Middlemarch in the TV adaptation of George Eliot's novel. Burghley House, not to be missed, is on the town's outskirts. (*JE Robbs, CM; also Good Pub Guide, and others*) On busy Saturdays, dinner is sometimes served in two shifts.

Open All year.
Rooms 1 suite, 34 double, 12 single. Some on ground floor.
Facilities Ramps. 2 lounges, 2 bars, 2 restaurants; 4 private dining rooms, business centre. 2-acre grounds: patio, monastery garden, croquet.
Location ¼ mile from town centre (front rooms double-glazed; quietest overlook courtyard). Large carpark.
Restrictions No smoking in some bedrooms. No dogs in restaurant.
Credit cards All major cards accepted.
Terms [1996] B&B: single £72–£78, double £95–£160, suite £125–£160. Light meals in Garden Lounge. Set lunch £13.50–£16.50; full alc dinner £30–£35. Weekend, August breaks; Sunday reductions; Christmas, New Year packages.

STOKE GABRIEL Devon — Map 1

Gabriel Court NEW — *Tel* (01803) 782206
Stoke Gabriel, nr Totnes TQ9 6SF — *Fax* (01803) 782333

In an old village on an inlet of the river Dart, not far from Totnes, stands this pretty white-painted manor. Having been occupied by successive generations of one family from 1487 until 1928, it then became a hotel, and is now owned and run by two generations of the Beacom family. It stands in a terraced Elizabethan garden, with clipped yew arches, magnolias and box hedges, and a swimming pool and a grass tennis court. The hotel dropped from earlier editions of the *Guide* following criticisms, but recent visitors were enthusiastic: "Well worth a detour. Very quiet; no passing traffic. Warm welcome, help with baggage, comfortable bedroom. Polite and friendly service, and general atmosphere of a country house. Dinner the best of traditional English cooking, with satisfying portions and not too many frills, supported by fresh vegetables in quantity. House wines reasonably priced." "Unpretentious food – such a relief. Terrific value for money." Children and dogs are welcomed. Afternoon tea is included in the half-board price. (*Mr and Mrs NE Long, Jean Nicol; also Richard Creed, Mrs A Turner*) Even devotees have some reservations: "Decor boring, but clean."

Open All year. Dining room closed midday, except Sun.
Rooms 17 double, 2 single. 1 self-contained chalet.
Facilities Bar lounge, library, TV/meeting room, dining room. 3-acre grounds: swimming pool, tennis. River Dart, fishing, 300 yds. Golf, riding nearby. Beach 3 miles. Unsuitable for ♿.
Location In village 3 miles SW of Paignton; turn S off A385 to Totnes.
Credit cards All major cards accepted.

Terms B&B £37–£55; D,B&B £59–£79. Packed lunches available. Set Sun lunch £12, dinner £23–£24. Christmas house party.

STON EASTON Somerset — Map 1

Ston Easton Park
Ston Easton, nr Bath BA3 4DF
Tel (01761) 241631
Fax (01761) 241377
César award in 1987

Peter and Christine Smedley's magnificent Palladian mansion (Relais & Châteaux) stands in a large park between Bath and Wells. Its gardens were designed by Humphry Repton in the 18th century; the river Norr flows over his flight of shallow cascades. The sitting rooms and library are grand, with antiques, fine paintings, comfortable sofas, elegant flower arrangements. The dining room, with a modern decor – white-painted panelling, bamboo chairs, flowers and candles – is supplied with fruit, vegetables and herbs from an impressive kitchen garden. Mark Harrington's "light, elegantly presented" cooking is "of a consistently high standard". Meals end with an "expertly described and served" cheeseboard. There's a good selection of not too pricey wines on a wide-ranging list. A lavish afternoon tea is served in the lounge. Breakfast includes "some of the best croissants outside France". Immaculate bedrooms are luxuriously decorated and equipped. Those on the first floor have huge windows and fine proportions; smaller ones are on the floor above; there are two spacious, air-conditioned suites in a garden cottage. "Particularly attentive, caring staff." "Unpretentious and skilful hostess." "Obliging manager Kevin Marchant, unfailingly courteous." "Highly commendable policy of upgrading accommodation whenever possible." Dogs are kennelled in a heated basement and fed and exercised in the morning. Shoes are cleaned, cars are valeted. (*Joy and Raymond Golding, AS-M, and others*)

Open All year.
Rooms 2 suites (in cottage), 19 double.
Facilities Drawing room, salon, library, billiard room, restaurant; private dining room; terrace. 28-acre grounds: tennis, croquet, river, fishing. Only restaurant suitable for ♿.
Location On A37 Bristol–Shepton Mallet.
Restrictions No smoking in restaurant. No children under 7 (except babes in arms). No dogs in house (free kennelling in heated basement).
Credit cards All major cards accepted.
Terms [To March 1997] Room: single £75–£320, double £145–£320, suite £245–£265. Breakfast: continental £8.50, English £12.50. Set lunch £26, dinner £38.50; full alc £48. Christmas programme; winter tariff.

STRATFORD-UPON-AVON Warwickshire — Map 3

Caterham House BUDGET
58/59 Rother Street
Stratford-upon-Avon CV37 6LT
Tel (01789) 267309 and 297070
Fax (01789) 414836

A well-run hotel with a stylish decor, and a French proprietor. "He knows and enjoys his Shakespeare, and speaks his mind with gusto," writes a literary editor, visiting the theatre a brisk four-minutes walk away. "The food is as friendly as the service, with as light or as big a breakfast as you want. Not for those in search of obsequious service." Others have enjoyed the "bright continental atmosphere, with unusual pictures, painted furniture, brass bedsteads, plants and flowers" and add: "Dominique Maury and his English wife, Olive, are superb hosts, not intrusive, but intelligently friendly." (*Tony Thomas, and others*) Pre-theatre suppers may be served to residents. Rooms in the house are preferred to those in the annexe.

Open All year.
Rooms 12 double. 2 in annexe, 2 in cottage.
Facilities Lounge with TV, bar, dining room; small patio. Unsuitable for ♿.
Location Central, opposite police station (some traffic noise possible). Carpark.
Restriction Dogs by arrangement, not unattended in bedrooms, not in public rooms.
Credit cards Access, Visa.
Terms B&B: single £50–£58, double £62–£68. Pre-theatre snack by arrangement. Children under 10 accommodated in parents' room half price.

STRETTON Rutland — Map 2

Ram Jam Inn BUDGET — *Tel* (01780) 410776
Great North Road — *Fax* (01780) 410361
Stretton LE15 7QX

César award in 1993

A popular "motel with a difference" on the Great North Road (A1M), owned by Tim Hart of nearby *Hambleton Hall* (*qv*). "It offers a lot for the money," runs a 1996 endorsement of earlier praise: "Comfort but not luxury, a warm welcome, kindly attention, and food well above average." In the snack bar, guests perch on stools to tuck into home-made soups, giant sandwiches, steaks, pasta, salads and calorific puddings, or breakfast from a *carte*. The restaurant menu is similar, with a short but adequate wine list. Bedrooms are cheerful, simple, spacious and modern, with large bathroom; all but one overlook the garden and apple orchard at the back. The weekend break rate is "marvellous value". (*John Mainwaring*)

Open All year, except 25 Dec.
Rooms 1 family, 6 double.
Facilities Lounge, snack bar, restaurant; conference room. 2-acre grounds. Only restaurant suitable for ♿.
Location W side of A1 9 miles N of Stamford. Travelling S leave A1 on B668 to Oakham; travelling N leave A1 through Texaco garage just past B668 turnoff. Large carpark.
Restrictions No smoking in restaurant. No dogs in public rooms.
Credit cards All major cards accepted.
Terms Rooms: single £41, double £51. Alc breakfast from £2 (full English £4.55). Set lunch £7.95; full alc £23. Weekend breaks.

STURMINSTER NEWTON Dorset — Map 2

Plumber Manor — *Tel* (01258) 472507
Sturminster Newton DT10 2AF — *Fax* (01258) 473370

César award in 1987

This handsome Jacobean house with trout stream, tennis courts, and two labradors in attendance, is set amid pasture in the heart of Hardy countryside. The home of the Prideaux-Brune family since the early 17th century, *Plumber Manor* has a genuine family feel. It has for years been run, informally but highly professionally, as a restaurant with particularly comfortable bedrooms. Six are in the house, off a gallery hung with family portraits; ten larger ones ("supremely comfortable") are in a converted barn. Lavish public rooms and comprehensive cosseting are not on offer, but the manor's consistent standards continue to draw back many regulars. "The personal touch of the jovial proprietor, Richard Prideaux-Brune, makes this a very special experience," one fan has written. "We felt utterly at home and sensed that the other guests did too." The traditional cooking of Brian Prideaux-Brune, Richard's brother, is served in generous portions and "succeeds where more elaborate country house fare sometimes fails by going over the top". The dessert cart has been called "heaven on wheels". The hearty English breakfasts are also admired. (*B and BK, and others*)

Open All year, except Feb. Restaurant closed for lunch, except Sun.
Rooms 16 double. 10 in stable courtyard (2 with ♿ access).
Facilities 2 lounges (1 with bar), gallery, restaurant. 5-acre grounds: garden, tennis, croquet, trout stream; stabling for visiting horses. Golf, swimming, fishing, clay pigeon-shooting nearby.
Location 2 miles SW of Sturminster Newton; turn off A357 to Hazelbury Bryan.
Restrictions Children under 12 by prior arrangement. No dogs (except owners') in public rooms.
Credit cards All major cards accepted.
Terms [1996] B&B: single £65–£80, double £90–£120. Set Sun lunch £17.50, dinner £15–£25 midweek, £20–£27.50 weekend. Off-season reductions.

SWAFFHAM Norfolk — Map 2

Stratton House — *Tel* (01760) 723845
4 Ash Close — *Fax* (01760) 720458
Swaffham PE37 7NH

"A memorable weekend; we felt more like friends than paying guests." "We spent ten days, and were treated to a feast for both eyes and stomach. Beautiful furniture, original pictures, bedrooms full of thoughtfulness: flowers, books, magazines, home-baked biscuits, rubber ducks, *wonderful* beds." "Vanessa's artistic and creative talents spread across the menu: unusual combination of grilled salmon with rhubarb vinaigrette; delicious home-made ice-creams." "We particularly enjoyed the winter fruit salad at breakfast followed by kedgeree." Recent praise for Leslie and Vanessa Scott's Grade II listed Palladian villa with a Victorian wing, and a highly individual decor. Though only a few yards from Swaffham's famous marketplace, its setting is almost rural, in a garden with old trees, near a church. The owners have filled the house with antiques and paintings (some for sale); also cat cushions, china cats, and sometimes two Siamese. Children are welcomed; there's a family room. Traditional English/French meals, which can be leisurely, are served in the pretty rustic dining room. The daily changing menu has a choice of five starters and three main courses. In 1995, Mrs Scott won the BBC's "Family Veggie Cook of the Year" award. The wine list, also prize-winning, is "decorative, informative and well chosen". (*Jeannette and Barry Gowing, George Murphy, Richard and Karyn B ay, and others*)

Open All year, except 24–26 Dec. Lunch by arrangement.
Rooms 6 double, 1 single.
Facilities Drawing room/library, 2 lounges (1 with TV), restaurant; conference facilities. 1-acre garden: patio, croquet. Unsuitable for ♿.
Location Enter Ash Close at N end of Market Place, between estate agent and Express Cleaners. Ample private parking.
Restrictions Smoking in drawing room only. "Well-behaved dogs admitted."
Credit cards Access, Amex, Visa.
Terms B&B: single £58, double £80; D,B&B: single £82, double £128. Set dinner £24.

TALLAND-BY-LOOE Cornwall — Map 1

Talland Bay Hotel — *Tel* (01503) 272667
Talland-by-Looe PL13 2JB — *Fax* (01503) 272940

César award in 1996

Annie and Barry Rosier's hotel, 16th-century in parts, stands high above an unspoilt bay. It has carefully tended sub-tropical gardens, with a swimming pool ("large enough for proper exercise"). The beach is five-minutes' walk away. "It is an archetypal *Guide* hotel. Plenty of atmosphere. Excellent food, thoughtfully served. Lovely quiet room overlooking countryside." "Professionally run, with no pretence that you are staying in a country house. The building is a fascinating architectural mix; our room in the oldest part had walls three feet deep with window seats overlooking the gardens and sea; another was smaller and a little cramped, but charming and functional. The decor is country house style, but not overly feminine or knick-knacked. The food was neither 'gourmet' nor home-cooking; menus were suited for a long stay – different every night, plenty of choice. Very good snack lunches, teas and breakfasts, too. Not for rumbustious teenagers or those who want fast-paced service or an active night life." (*Michael O'Flaherty, Susan B Hanley, and others*) Some cool comments this year about the cooking of vegetables and desserts. Two couples visiting in October 1995 experienced a "frosty" reception. "And why don't they serve freshly squeezed orange juice at breakfast?" (Late news: the Rosiers promise fresh orange juice in 1997!)

Open Mid-Feb–end Dec.
Rooms 1 suite, 12 double, 3 single. 3 in grounds, 1 across lane.
Facilities 2 lounges, bar, restaurant. 2½-acre grounds: patio, garden, swimming pool, sauna, putting, croquet. Beach 5 mins' walk. Unsuitable for ♿.
Location 2½ miles SW of Looe. Left at hotel sign on Looe–Polperro road.
Restrictions No smoking: restaurant, 1 lounge. No under-5s in dining room at night. No dogs in public rooms.
Credit cards All major cards accepted.
Terms B&B: single £40–£74, double £88–£148, suite £90–£120; D,B&B: single £55–£89, double £110–£180, suite £120–£150. Snack lunches; set Sun lunch £10.95, dinner £21; full alc £36.50. Off-season breaks, painting holidays; Christmas, New Year packages. Children accommodated free in parents' room. *V*

> We need feedback on all entries. Often people fail to report on the better-known hotels, assuming that "someone else is sure to".

TAPLOW Buckinghamshire Map 2

Cliveden *Tel* (01628) 668561
Taplow SL6 0JF *Fax* (01628) 661837

César award in 1995

This magnificent stately home, "a wonderful evocation of the Edwardian era" (and a Relais & Châteaux member), stands in huge National Trust grounds (open to the public in summer) on the Thames. Its public rooms are spectacular, with tapestries, armour, fine paintings and glorious views. Bedrooms in the main house are equally grand; newer ones in the wings are attractive if less characterful. There are two dining rooms: the quite formal *Terrace*, serving "English modern and traditional" food, and the smaller, pricier *Waldo's* (*Michelin* star, four red crossed spoon-and-forks), where "inventive modern cooking" by chef Ron Maxfield is served by "knowledgeable and courteous waiters". The many sporting facilities (see below) are included in the room price; so is afternoon tea. Children are welcome. Last year we received some critical reports, but the manager, Stuart Johnson (ex-*Savoy*), is now well established, and recent visitors have been pleased. "With his immaculate style and contagious smile, he presides over a professional young team." "I know a number of country house hotels, but none so much country house and so little hotel in the welcome of its guests." "I stay regularly on my own; despite the sophistication, one feels at home. The staff is quite exceptional. The facilities are wonderful; but without the warmth and care, it would not be the great hotel it is." (*Gerald H David, DE, Lady Napley*) The *Draycott* in London was recently taken over by Cliveden plc; it has been extensively refurbished, and is managed by Michael Holiday, who was *Cliveden*'s butler for 10 years. We'd like to hear from anyone who has stayed there.

Open All year. *Waldo's* closed for lunch, Sun/Mon.
Rooms 10 suites, 27 double. 12 in wings. 9 on ground floor. 6 air-conditioned.
Facilities Lift, ramp. Great hall (pianist each evening), 2 lounges, library, billiard room, club room, breakfast room, 2 restaurants, conservatory (light lunches served); function facilities; crèche; pavilion: swimming pool, sauna, jacuzzi, gym, health and beauty treatments. 375-acre grounds: gardens, swimming pool, tennis, squash, riding, practice golf, fishing, jogging routes; 3 boats for river trips.
Location 10 miles NW of Windsor. M4 exit 7. On B476 opposite *Feathers* pub.
Restrictions No smoking in restaurants. No dogs in restaurants.
Credit cards Access, Diners, Visa.
Terms (*Excluding donation to National Trust*) Rooms: single/double £220, suite £398–£685. English breakfast £16. *Terrace*: set lunch £28, dinner £40; full alc £60. *Waldo's*: set dinner £45–£75. Weekend, fitness, Christmas, New Year packages. Children under 14 accommodated free in parents' room. 1-night bookings sometimes refused.

****

Health assurance The beef choices on this menu all use fillet locally selected for its quality and purity. In our opinion you are more likely to win the lottery twice in succession or, if you are male and over forty, to be bedded by Bridget Fonda or, if female, by Tom Cruise, than to be harmed by the beef supplied by this establishment, not to mention passive smoking, alcohol, motor cars, or sex. *Boast from Frogg Manor, Broxton*

****

TAUNTON Somerset — Map 1

The Castle
Castle Green
Taunton TA1 1NF
Tel (01823) 272671
Fax (01823) 336066

César award in 1987

The Chapman family's 300-year-old hostelry, "reeking history", has "high standards of comfort", and "an aura of happiness". Wisteria-covered and castellated, it stands on the site of Taunton's old castle, with pleasant moated gardens at the back. Reception is "warm and friendly". The public rooms are elegant, with old oak furniture, tapestries and paintings and a fine wrought-iron staircase. Bedrooms, some recently refurbished, vary in size and style; the best and quietest overlook the garden; they are "not too gadget-minded, and well maintained". There is a new penthouse suite and roof garden with far-reaching views. Philip Vickery, "an enthusiastic chef with a delightful personality", presides over the *Michelin*-starred restaurant. His cooking, "exceptionally good, and beautifully presented", is English, traditional and modern, using local suppliers who are given credit on the menus; meal service is "swift and pleasant". The long wine list is "generally good value". Continental breakfast may be served in the bedrooms; there's a good cooked one in the dining room. Numerous special breaks and discounts are offered (see below). (*Eve Webb, and others*) More reports, please.

Open All year.
Rooms 5 suites, 19 double, 12 single.
Facilities Lift, ramp. Lounge, lounge/bar, restaurant; private dining/meeting rooms; roof garden. 1-acre grounds.
Location Central (follow signs for castle). Garages, parking.
Restrictions No smoking in restaurant. Small dogs by arrangement; not in public rooms.
Credit cards All major cards accepted.
Terms [1996] B&B: single £75, double £115, suite £185; D,B&B (2 nights min.) £70–£100 per person. Set lunch from £8.50, dinner £23; full alc from £34. Golf, gardening, West Country, cricket, theatre, fishing, ballooning, golfing breaks; musical weekends; Christmas, New Year packages. Special rates for honeymooners, and old boys and parents from local schools. *V*

TEIGNMOUTH Devon — Map 1

Thomas Luny House BUDGET
Teign Street
Teignmouth TQ14 8EG
Tel (01626) 772976

César award in 1995

"A splendid hotel," runs a warm encomium. "For a week, we were cosseted with discreet charm by John and Alison Allan. There were cups of tea, wedges of morally degenerate chocolate cake, delicious dinners, elegantly served, early morning tea in fine bone china, and unrestrained breakfasts to order. Our room was large, airy, and well-appointed. For those who are drawn towards small hotels where circumstance encourages mutual courtesy among the guests, it would be hard to find anywhere to beat this. Teignmouth may not be the most sophisticated of English watering places, but it has its charms." And a traveller on his own concurs: "Delightful bedroom; superb bathroom. The Allans joined me for pre-dinner drinks and a chat." This Wolsey Lodge member is a beautifully proportioned Georgian house, named for the marine artist who built it. Though central, near the fish quay in the old quarter of town, it is quiet. It is "excellently furnished with antiques and curios". The lounge and dining room, both with open fire, lead through French windows on to a small walled garden. Three bedrooms are spacious, the fourth is smallish; all have fresh flowers, Malvern water, books and magazines. Guests eat together, dinner party style, no choice on the menu; the Allans sometimes join them. There's a short, reasonably priced wine list. The special break is excellent value: early morning tea, newspaper, afternoon tea and after-dinner coffee are included in the price. (*John and Moira Cole, Chris Kay, and others*)

Open 1 Feb–31 Dec. Lunch not served.
Rooms 4 double.
Facilities 2 lounges, dining room. Small walled garden. Sea, sandy beach 5 mins' walk. Unsuitable for ♿.
Location Central. From dual carriageway, follow signs to quay. First left into Teign St. Courtyard parking.
Restrictions No smoking in dining room. No children under 12. No dogs.
Credit cards None accepted.
Terms B&B £35; D,B&B £53.50. 2-night breaks: D,B&B £45 per person per night.

TEMPLE SOWERBY Cumbria — Map 4

Temple Sowerby House — *Tel* (0176 83) 61578
Temple Sowerby, nr Penrith CA10 1RZ — *Fax* (0176 83) 61958

In a quiet village in the Eden Valley, this Cumbrian farmhouse, with Georgian additions, stands in a formal walled garden overlooking Cross Fell, the highest peak in the Pennines. The dramatic landscapes of the Pennines and Lake District lie only a few miles away on either horizon. The hotel changed hands shortly after we went to press last year. Cécile and Geoffrey Temple, who have worked in America and the Virgin Islands, are now the resident owners, with Andrew Walker (regional young chef of the year) in the kitchen. Visitors in 1996 were pleased: "It is run with friendly professionalism. The cooking was of a consistently high standard, and personal whims were cheerfully catered for. If you insisted on very rare lamb it came in baa-ing; well-done beef would arrive satisfactorily incinerated. Geoffrey Temple is knowledgeable about his carefully chosen wines. They showed great charm and flexibility when our plans went awry and we asked at short notice for a late dinner." "Staff some of the most pleasant we've come across. A useful stop on the way north." (*Tony Thomas, Val Ferguson*) The decor in the comfortable sitting rooms is pretty and traditional, with antiques and open fires; dinner is taken in the Rose Room, which has a pink decor, or in a white-panelled, beamed dining room. The tea shop serves light meals all day, and cream teas. Children are welcomed.

Open All year.
Rooms 12 double. 4 in coach house (2 on ground floor).
Facilities Ramps. 2 lounges, bar, restaurant, conservatory; function facilities; tea shop; courtyard, terrace. 2-acre walled garden: croquet. River, fishing 400 yds.
Location On A66, 6 miles NW of Appleby.

Restrictions No smoking in restaurant. No dogs in public rooms.
Credit cards All major cards accepted.
Terms B&B: single £55–£60, double £78–£88; D,B&B: single £80–£85, double £128–£138. Full alc £27.50. 2-day breaks; Christmas, New Year packages. *V*

TETBURY Gloucestershire — Map 3

Calcot Manor
nr Tetbury GL8 8YJ
Tel (01666) 890391
Fax (01666) 890394

A mellow Cotswold manor (a Relais du Silence) "with a country elegance – smart fabrics, nice furniture and bits of china; plenty of sofas and armchairs, and new magazines and old books in the drawing rooms". Some bedrooms are in the main house, others are in a range of venerable outbuildings, complete with beams (some are low). They are spacious, and stocked with shortbread, fruit, toiletries, etc; some have a whirlpool bath. There are family suites with bunk beds. Once quite staid, the manor is now run less formally by Richard Ball, son of the previous owners. "The staff is not an army of uniformed bellmen and waiters, but young professionals who do a bit of everything and grant every request with an indulgent 'of course'. To stay here is to live for a few days in a beautiful, cosy house, with pampering friends all around." "Delicious" breakfasts include fresh orange juice, good coffee, local sausages, etc. The *Gumstool Inn* provides casual meals; the restaurant serves modern English cooking by chef Michael Croft, who has worked at the *Royal Crescent* in Bath (*qv*), and the *Mirabelle* in London. By mid-1997, it will have increased in size and its decor will be "more contemporary". We'd like reports on these developments, please.

Open All year.
Rooms 4 family, 16 double. 10 in courtyards. Some on ground floor.
Facilities Ramps. 2 lounges, pub, restaurant; private dining room, conference facilities. 7-acre grounds: swimming pool, tennis, croquet; bicycles. Golf, fishing, riding nearby.
Location 3 miles W of Tetbury, on intersection of A4135 and A46.
Restrictions No smoking in restaurant. No dogs.
Credit cards All major cards accepted.
Terms B&B: single £75–£90, double £97–£135. English breakfast £5. Pub meals. Set lunch £17, dinner £22; full alc £30. Cotswold breaks.

THORNBURY Somerset — Map 3

Thornbury Castle
Castle Street
Thornbury, Bristol BS12 1HH
Tel (01454) 281182
Fax (01454) 416188

Maurice and Carol Taylor (aka the Baron and Baroness of Porthlethen) own this imposing hotel, carefully created from an unfinished early 16th-century castle. It has baronial public rooms, with huge fireplaces, mullioned windows, antique furniture and tapestries. Some of the bedrooms are equally impressive, with views of the well-tended gardens and large grounds. The singles are small. "It remains for us the quintessential stopping place in this 'treasured isle'," write regular American visitors. "It sets the standard against which we judge all other hotels. None has surpassed it. The staff are its highest achievement, and provide a seamless and perfect experience. There is no stuffiness, but their friendliness and charm in no way detract from the quiet attention to every detail. The strength of the new chef, Steven Black, is evident in superb, subtle sauces. The menu changes daily, affording a delicious anticipation each day of what will come tomorrow." The meals include rack of lamb, sirloin of North American beef (in these days of BSE panic), and traditional British hot puddings, eg, treacle tart and butterscotch pudding. There is an extensive wine list. A note on the menu, to be applauded, reads: "You are entitled to good service – gratuities are not expected." The castle is licensed for civil marriages. (*Dr and Mrs Viola*)

Open All year, except 2 days Jan.
Rooms 1 suite, 15 double, 2 single. 7 across small courtyard.
Facilities Lounge, library, 3 dining rooms. 15-acre grounds: garden, croquet, small farm, vineyard. Unsuitable for ♿.
Location 12 miles N of Bristol. From Thornbury on B4061 continue downhill to monumental water pump; bear left. Entrance to left of parish church 300 yds.
Restrictions No smoking in dining rooms. "No children under 12 unless known." No dogs.
Credit cards All major cards accepted.
Terms B&B: single £75–£95, double £95–£220, suite £175–£210. English breakfast £8.95. Set lunch £20.50, dinner £31. Winter breaks; Christmas house party. 1-night bookings sometimes refused weekends, bank holidays.

THORNTON-LE-FYLDE Lancashire — Map 4

The River House NEW — *Tel* (01253) 883497 and 883087
Skippool Creek, Thornton-le-Fylde — *Fax* (01253) 892083
nr Blackpool FY5 5LF

An 1830s gentleman farmer's house quietly set on a river estuary. Now a restaurant-with-rooms, it offers a refuge in the autumn to wearied attenders of party conferences at Blackpool, 15 minutes' drive away. It delighted a regular *Guide* correspondent: "Gentle, warm welcome from Bill Scott. The four dogs will accompany you on the lovely walk along a well-kept path round the estuary; you see only boats and birds. The house is crammed with well-chosen antiques. Our bedroom had a mahogany bureau with secret drawers, an enormous built-in wardrobe, very comfortable beds with velvet headboards, tea tray with delicate china, and shining new bathroom with upmarket soaps, etc. Carol Scott, very calm, tends the dark, pub-like bar, and waits at table in the pretty restaurant, which has deep green walls, beautiful old mahogany tables, proper cutlery and lace mats. Bill cooks: fresh, light and interesting dishes; my scallops in a delicate creamy sauce were the best I've ever had. Veg out of this world. Full English breakfast if you wish, or make your own toast in an interesting eight-slice toaster. Freshly squeezed orange juice, home-made marmalade; excellent coffee. There is a Victorian conservatory, with basket chairs and glossy magazines." (*Minda Alexander*) The eclectic menu includes ostrich and venison, and "ticky tacky pudding".

Open All year. Restaurant closed Sun.
Rooms 5 double.
Facilities Lounge with TV, bar, conservatory, restaurant. 1-acre garden on river. Clay pigeon/duck-shooting nearby.
Location 5 miles NE of Blackpool. From N: M6 exit 33; A6 S past Garstang, then A586/A585 towards Fleetwood. At roundabout after 3 sets of traffic lights take

3rd exit. Follow signs to Skippool Creek. From S: M6; M55 to exit 3; A585 towards Fleetwood; then as above.
Restriction No dogs in restaurant.
Credit cards Access, Visa.
Terms [1996] B&B: single £65, double £80. Set lunch/dinner £18.50; full alc £36–£40. Weekend breaks: D,B&B £90.

TINTAGEL Cornwall — Map 1

Trebrea Lodge *Tel* (01840) 770410
Trenale, Tintagel PL34 0HR *Fax* (01840) 770092

A pretty Grade II* listed building, 14th-century in origin, with a symmetrical Georgian façade, in a "wonderful position" on a wooded hillside, looking across open country to the sea. "Not a hotel, more a home, it is old-fashioned, leisured and comfortable." The house is only one room deep. There is a smart upstairs drawing room, and a cosier sitting/smoking room with an honesty bar and a log fire. "The quality of decor and housekeeping are high, and the collection of antiques grows by the year," wrote devotees last year. Bedrooms, "full of charm", are of varying shapes and sizes; one has a wooden carved four-poster; a small one with beamed ceiling is reached up a steep stairway; one has a separate entrance. The owners, John Charlick and Sean Devlin (the chef), are "caring, welcoming and highly efficient, but unobtrusive". No choice at dinner ("good private house cooking", preferences discussed in advance), served at 8 pm in the panelled dining room ("ask for a window table"). There's a "small but excellently chosen wine list". "Good breakfast; serve yourself from the sideboard, followed by cooked dishes." Tintagel is an undistinguished village, usually full of tourists, but the ruin-strewn headland is "wonderfully romantic". (*John and Ann Smith, SMB, and others*) One visitor disliked the "intrusive music from the kitchen. Who wants Billie Holiday at dinner and Wagner at breakfast?"

Open All year, except 5 Jan–10 Feb. Dining room closed for lunch.
Rooms 7 double. 1 with separate entrance.
Facilities Lounge, smoking room, dining room. 4½-acre grounds. Sea ½ mile. Unsuitable for ♿.
Location ½ mile SE of Tintagel. From Boscastle road, right by modern Roman Catholic church, right at top of lane. Hotel 300 yds on left.
Restrictions Smoking in smoking room only. No children under 8.
Credit cards Access, Visa.
Terms B&B: single £52.50–£57.50, double £62–£84; D,B&B: single £72–£74.50, double £101–£123. Set dinner £19.50. Special breaks; winter rates. Christmas, New Year packages.

TONBRIDGE Kent — Map 2

Goldhill Mill *Tel* (01732) 851626
Golden Green, Tonbridge TN11 0BA *Fax* (01732) 851881

"A wonderfully civilised B&B." This beautiful old mill house, part Tudor, part Georgian, but dating back to the days of the Norman Conquest, is in large, quiet grounds, with mature trees and ponds, on the edge of a village near Tonbridge. Its mill wheel still turns in the stream, and much of the machinery is in working order. "Shirley and

Vernon Cole are a cultivated couple," wrote our inspector. "They have a real feel for old houses and have restored the mill beautifully. Two of the bedrooms have a jacuzzi; ours, with a four-poster, flowery fabrics and good modern bathroom, had all you could need – TV, hair-dryer, trouser-press, fruit and flowers, etc – and looked over the garden with fruit trees, statuary, and cows mooing. There's an elegant lounge for guests. Breakfast is served communally in the big Tudor-beamed farmhouse kitchen: fruit salad, muesli, etc, followed by a real English spread, with local sausages, scrambled eggs and giant mushrooms, which the Coles prepared while chatting to us; three types of home-made jam. The whole perfectionist operation is supervised by two Burmese cats." No smoking.

Open 1 Jan–15 July, 1 Sept–31 Dec, but closed 25/26 Dec.
Rooms 3 double. Also 2 self-catering cottages.
Facilities Lounge, TV room. 20-acre grounds: river, tennis. Unsuitable for ♿.
Location 4 miles NE of Tonbridge. Take Hadlow road, signposted Maidstone. After *c.* 2 miles turn right on Three Elm La. Drive after 1¼ miles on left, at 30 mph sign.
Restrictions No smoking. No children under 12, except babies. No dogs.
Credit cards Access, Visa.
Terms B&B: single £55–£65, double £69–£75. Extra bed £15. 10% discount for 7 or more days. 1-night bookings sometimes refused Fri/Sat.

TOWERSEY Oxfordshire — Map 2

Upper Green Farm BUDGET — *Tel* (01844) 212496
Manor Road, Towersey OX9 3QR — *Fax* (01844) 260399

Euan and Marjorie Aitken's rural retreat is well placed for both Oxford and London. It is a thatched 15th-century B&B, with a delightful garden, lots of flowers in tubs, a large pond complete with ducks and a skiff, and views towards the Chilterns. Marjorie Aitken was formerly in the antiques business, and country antiques and knick-knacks, lace and patchwork abound. An 18th-century barn, called Paradise, houses a lounge, the beamed breakfast room, and six bedrooms with white walls, good linen, TV, video, fridge and *en suite* facilities. Breakfasts include home-grown fruit, home-made jams, local honey, free-range (often home-laid) eggs, and sausages and black pudding from an award-winning butcher in Thame. Nearby, there are any number of places for eating in the evening, ranging from *Le Manoir aux Quat'Saisons* (*qv*) to the village pub. No smoking.

Open All year, except Christmas/New Year.
Rooms 9 double, 1 single. 6 in converted barn. 2 on ground floor, with access for ♿. No telephone/TV.
Facilities 2 lounges, breakfast room. 7-acre grounds: mini-golf, croquet.
Location Take Towersey road off Thame ring road. Hotel on left just after Towersey Manor.
Restrictions No smoking. No children under 13. No pets.
Credit cards None accepted.
Terms B&B: single £34, double £40–£55. 1-night bookings refused bank holidays, some weekends.

> If you are nominating a hotel, we'd be grateful if you could send us the brochure.

TREBARWITH STRAND Cornwall — Map 1

The Old Millfloor BUDGET — *Tel* (01840) 770234
Trebarwith Strand, Tintagel PL34 0HA

"Quirky and thoroughly individual", with a kind hostess, Janice Waddon-Martyn, this small, "pleasantly old-fashioned" guest house is tranquilly set in a fern-filled glen by a millstream. Inside are light and colour, gleaming wood, fresh flowers and cleverly used fabrics. Bedrooms have white walls, pure white linen, lots of lace, big feather pillows. Dinner, "delicious home cooking" with limited choice, is by candlelight in the small beamed dining room; menus feature home-made soups and ice creams, organic and free-range meat, fresh vegetables, clotted cream. Rolls are freshly baked, as are the scones for tea (no charge). Breakfast is good. No licence, bring your own wine. Not for the disabled or infirm – there is a steep path down from the road (best to take the minimum of luggage), but perfect for families: lots of pets, large grounds; the beach is a short walk away. "The plumbing might not reach the standard expected by some pernickety people," one reporter has written, "but that is part of the charm of the place." "Amazing value" is the consensus. More reports, please.

Open Easter–Nov.
Rooms 3 doubles with wash-basin.
Facilities Restaurant/lounge. 10-acre grounds: garden, orchard, paddocks, stream. Beach 10 mins' walk. Riding nearby. Unsuitable for ♿.
Location 2 miles S of Tintagel.
Restrictions No smoking. No dogs.
Credit cards None accepted.
Terms [1996] (*Not VAT-rated*) B&B £18 (£16.50 for 2 or more days). Dinner £12 (unlicensed: bring your own wine). 1 child accommodated free in parents' room; otherwise half price.

TREGONY Cornwall — Map 1

Tregony House BUDGET — *Tel* (01872) 530671
15 Fore Street
Tregony, Truro TR2 5RN

"Excellent value for little money." Andrew and Catherine Webb's friendly village guest house, part 17th-century, part Victorian. On main street of quiet inland village at entrance to Roseland peninsula, about 6 miles from sea. Pretty walled garden. Small lounge. Plentiful, excellent breakfasts; good traditional dinners with limited choice in beamed, stone-floored dining room. 6 bedrooms: 2 have facilities en suite, *more are planned; no telephone/TV. Open Feb–Nov. No smoking: dining room, bedrooms. Unsuitable for ♿. No children under 7. No dogs. Access, Visa accepted. B&B £18.75–£22; D,B&B £29.75–£33.*

> Hotels often book you into their most expensive rooms or suites unless you specify otherwise. Even if all room prices are the same, hotels may give you a less good room in the hope of selling their better rooms to late customers. It always pays to discuss accommodation in detail when making a reservation and to ask for a free upgrade on arrival if the hotel isn't full.

TRESCO Isles of Scilly — Map 1

The Island Hotel
Tresco, Isles of Scilly
Cornwall TR24 0PU

Tel (01720) 422883
Fax (01720) 423008

Tresco is a private island, two miles by one, renowned for the Abbey Gardens, which are filled with exotic plants from around the world. No cars; there are bicycles for hire. This smart hotel is a modern building in large grounds by the sea, with a private beach, a swimming pool, and beautiful gardens. Public areas are spacious and attractive. A floor-to-ceiling glass wall in the sitting room gives dramatic views of Tresco's rocky coast and other islands. The suite has its own balcony ("great for watching the sun rise"), and the best bedrooms (in the Flower wing), have picture-windows opening on to a private patio, and views over the garden to the sea. "The manager, Ivan Curtis, is thoroughly but unobtrusively in command," wrote recent visitors. "We were impressed by the high standard of service and housekeeping." Others have praised the "friendly and *very* patient staff", and rhapsodised: "A queen of hotels, the best of its kind in the UK." Children are welcomed. (*Alan Greenwood, Rosemary Wright, and others; also Richard Creed*) But while some have praised the food, several others have thought it merely "OK": "Despite excellent ingredients, it suffers from a peculiar combination of blandness and over-elaboration." And several visitors have found fault with the breakfast: "Cheap tea bags, horrible preserves." "Poor cooked dishes." A recent increase in time-share accommodation is lamented by visitors who knew Tresco in earlier days: "It is now like a resort village."

Open 8 Mar–end Oct.
Rooms 2 suites, 33 double, 5 single. 2 on ground floor.
Facilities Lounge, bar, library, restaurant. 8-acre grounds: tennis, croquet, swimming pool, beach. Tresco not really suitable for ♿.
Location From Penzance: boat (via St Mary's) or scheduled helicopter flight (neither on Sun).
Restriction No dogs allowed on Tresco.
Credit cards Access, Amex, Visa.
Terms D,B&B: single £70–£95, double £140–£190, suite £200–£320. Snack lunches; packed lunches. Set dinner £30. Gardeners' holidays.

TROUTBECK Cumbria — Map 4

The Mortal Man BUDGET
Troutbeck, Windermere LA23 1PL

Tel (0153 94) 33193
Fax (0153 94) 31261

Annette and Christopher Poulsom's "most comfortable and well-managed" 300-year-old inn, with oak beams, thick walls and a simple decor, is peacefully set on a hilltop above the Troutbeck valley. It is "a handsome house, beautifully kept" in carefully maintained gardens with lovely views. The residents' lounge (with an open fire, old hunting prints, easy chairs, fresh flowers, gleaming brass-topped tables) is "quite small but arranged so you can converse within your own party, chat to fellow guests, or ignore everyone and read a book". The small bedrooms have very small bathrooms, and "solid, attractive furniture". "Thank heavens nothing much changes here," writes a returning visitor, endorsing last year's praise: "Warm, charming, laid back and amusing

Australian hostess; unfailingly courteous host. A combination of stalwart local staff and a changing group of cheerful young seasonal workers, often Antipodean, provides excellent service." The traditional bar serves good pub food. The restaurant, with a separate kitchen, is popular locally for Sunday lunch, and for dinner. "Varied and interesting food; lots of choice; exceptional sweet trolley. Worth every penny." "Stunning walks nearby. Admirable drying room." Dogs are welcome. (*C Beadle, Anne Sharp; also Good Pub Guide, and others*) As before, there are reports of "too brisk" meal service; and "pretentious" menus; and five courses, with large portions is "too much" for some.

Open Mid-Feb–mid-Nov.
Rooms 10 double, 2 single.
Facilities Residents' lounge, bar, restaurant. 2-acre grounds. Unsuitable for ♿.
Location 3 miles N of Windermere on A592.
Restrictions No smoking in restaurant. No children under 5.
Credit cards None accepted.
Terms [1996] D,B&B £47–£57. Set Sun lunch £13, dinner £21. Bar meals. Reductions for longer stays; off-season rates. *V*

TYNEMOUTH Tyne and Wear — Map 4

Hope House BUDGET — *Tel/Fax* (0191) 257 1989
47 Percy Gardens
Tynemouth NE30 4HH

"An oasis in a desert; thoroughly civilised, and amazingly inexpensive," wrote the nominator of this small guest house overlooking the magnificent beach of a clifftop Victorian village at the mouth of the Tyne. Once a merchant's house, its original features have been carefully retained. "It is beautifully decorated, with bright colours and antiques. The host is a charming Frenchman, Pascal Delin; his English wife, Anna, is the cook. Our large, comfortable room had a marvellous sea view and a small but adequate shower room. Dinner is served communally, normally for residents only. It was delicious, beautifully served, and ended with unlimited coffee." The Delins write: "We never forget that you are our guest, not a room number; we can provide attention and service which many large hotels can no longer afford." Cooking is traditional English / French, with much use of local produce, particularly seafood. (*GH*)

Open All year; dining room closed midday, 2-week annual holiday.
Rooms 3 double (1 with bath, 2 with shower). No telephone.
Facilities Drawing room, dining room. Beach 1 min. Unsuitable for ♿.
Location A1058 to Tynemouth. To seafront, then right for ½ mile. Garages.
Restriction No dogs.
Credit cards All major cards accepted.
Terms B&B: single £35, double £42.50–£55. Set dinner £16.50.

UCKFIELD East Sussex — Map 2

Hooke Hall — *Tel* (01825) 761578
250 High Street — *Fax* (01825) 768025
Uckfield TN22 1EN

Juliet and Alister Percy's Queen Anne house is in the centre of a busy little Sussex town. It has been restored to a high standard (she is an interior designer). Panelled public rooms have designer fabrics, antiques, ancestral paintings and open fires. The pretty bedrooms are named after famous mistresses and lovers, eg, Nell Gwynn and Madame de Pompadour. Attic rooms are small, with sloping ceiling, but well equipped, with good bathroom. In the pink-walled restaurant, *La Scaletta,* chef Michele Pavanello specialises in northern Italian regional cooking from the Veneto and Liguria. Light lunches are served. Juliet Percy will cook (English/French style) for private parties. Good traditional breakfast. "Marvellous decor," wrote recent guests. "Generous, interested hosts. It was like staying in a wonderful home. Courteous, efficient staff. Very good food." (*VN and AB*) More reports, please.

Open All year, except Christmas. Restaurant closed 1 week Feb.
Rooms 2 suites, 7 double.
Facilities Lounge, study, restaurant; function facilities. Unsuitable for ♿.
Location Central (traffic noise in some rooms). Parking adjacent.
Restrictions No smoking in restaurant. No children under 12. No dogs.
Credit cards Access, Amex, Visa
Terms Rooms: single £40–£70, double £55–£70, suite £90–£110. Breakfast: continental £5, English £7. Set lunch £9.95; full alc dinner £22.50. *V*

ULLINGSWICK Hereford and Worcester — Map 3

The Steppes — *Tel* (01432) 820424
Ullingswick, nr Hereford HR1 3JG — *Fax* (01432) 820042

Grade II listed 14th-century house in tiny, quiet Wye valley hamlet off A417. Exposed beams, inglenooks, rustic antiques, Highly personal service from Henry and Tricia Howland. "Excellent value." 6 generously proportioned bedrooms, tastefully furnished, with good en suite *facilities, in converted stable and timber-framed barn. Eclectic candlelit home-cooked dinners "expertly cooked": 4-course set meal;* carte *by arrangement. Generous breakfasts. 1½-acre garden with pond. Closed Dec/Jan, except Christmas, New Year (house parties); also "odd intervals for a rest". Unsuitable for ♿. No smoking: dining room, 4 bedrooms. No children under 10. No dogs in public rooms. Access, Visa accepted. B&B: single £50–£55, double £80–£90; D,B&B: single £65–£70, double £110–£120. More reports, please.* *V*

ULLSWATER Cumbria — Map 4

Howtown Hotel BUDGET — *Tel* (0176 84) 86514
Ullswater, nr Penrith CA10 2ND

César award in 1991

An unsophisticated former farmhouse, set back from a road in a beautiful position on Ullswater's eastern shore. Well placed for yachting, windsurfing and other water sports, it is a favourite of walkers and climbers, too, and so popular that it is often fully booked. It is run on old-fashioned lines by Jacquie Baldry and her son David, the fourth generation of the family to be involved. "The style of our food," writes Mrs Baldry, "hasn't changed over 36 years: home-made soups and puddings, traditional roasts and pies." Furnishings are unpretentious and comfortable. Few bedrooms have private facilities, none has telephone or TV; keys are not given. But early morning tea is brought to the room, and beds are turned down during dinner, which is at 7 pm (tables are quite close together). "Just as a country hotel should be," wrote a visitor last year. "No nonsense, but most attractive and satisfying. Meals unaffectedly excellent. Substantial packed lunches. Walkers come rushing down from the hills for 4 pm tea: perfect scones and cake." Another view is more quizzical: "Meals average to good. Public rooms adequately furnished, but a bit hugger-mugger. When one of us turned in the double bed, the other bounced, and vice versa. But excellent value. The Baldrys and their enchanting dog, Tad, are to be congratulated." (*Mary and Gerald Clark, and others*)

Open End Mar–1 Nov.
Rooms 12 double, 3 single. 3 with bath, 1 with shower. 2 in annexe. 4 self-catering cottages.
Facilities 4 lounges, TV room, 2 bars, dining room. 2-acre grounds. 300 yds from lake: private foreshore. Walking, climbing, riding, golf nearby. Unsuitable for ♿.
Location E shore of lake, 4 miles S of Pooley Bridge.
Restrictions No children under 7. Dogs at management's discretion, not in public rooms.
Credit cards None accepted.
Terms [1996] D,B&B £36–£40. Cold weekday lunch from £6.75, set Sun lunch £8.75, dinner £12.50; cold Sun supper £8.75. 1-night bookings sometimes refused.

Sharrow Bay *Tel* (0176 84) 86301 and 86483
Ullswater, nr Penrith CA10 2LZ *Fax* (0176 84) 86349
César award in 1985

In a lovely setting on the eastern shore of Ullswater stands the first English country house hotel, for many years a Relais & Châteaux member. Now entering its 49th season, it has had a *Guide* entry since our first edition. Supported by co-directors Nigel Lawrence and Nigel Lightburn, and a large, well-trained staff, many long-serving, the founders, Francis Coulson and Brian Sack still preside over this "well-oiled machine". The house is packed with porcelain, flowers, plants, pictures and pot-pourri. Some bedrooms, particularly in the main building, are small; larger ones are in *Bank House*, a mile away (transport provided). In 1996, not before time, *Michelin* awarded a star for the traditional ("but lighter nowadays") British cooking on a famously enormous menu, served in two dining rooms, one with a lake view. Recent praise: "A little paradise, run with amazing consistency. You are utterly pampered. No hint of obsequiousness; everyone is genuinely friendly. Rooms serviced three times a day. The display of puddings – works of art – before dinner is not to be missed." "Splendid bedroom with everything you could want – and more. Pleasant, spacious dining rooms, stuffed with expensive glass and china knick-knacks. Service, like most things, absolutely perfect. Excellent breakfast, apart from the croissants, with lots of choice." "You cannot fault it. There is an air of camaraderie among the guests." At busy times the lounges and restaurant can get crowded, and the whole experience is too much for some tastes, but the majority verdict is: "Expensive, but worth it." (*T Lockwood, Stephanie Sowerby, Heather Sharland, and others*)

Open 21 Feb–24 Nov.
Rooms 6 suites, 25 double, 3 single. 16 in cottages, lodge, and *Bank House*. 3 on ground floor.

Facilities Main house: 3 lounges, 2 dining rooms; *Bank House*: lounge, breakfast room. Extensive grounds: gardens, woodland; ½-mile lake shore, safe (cold) bathing, private jetty, boathouse. Unsuitable for ♿.
Location E shore of Ullswater, 2 miles S of Pooley Bridge. M6 exit 40. Turn on to Howtown La by small church in Pooley Bridge.
Restrictions Smoking banned in dining room, discouraged in lounges, bedrooms. No children under 13 approx. No dogs.
Credit cards None accepted.
Terms D,B&B: single £90–£130, double £200–£320, suite £320–£360. Set lunch £31.75, dinner £41.75. Midweek reductions off season. 1-night bookings sometimes refused weekends. *V* (midweek, Mar, Nov)

UPPER SLAUGHTER Gloucestershire **Map 3**

Lords of the Manor *Tel* (01451) 820243
Upper Slaughter *Fax* (01451) 820696
nr Bourton-on-the-Water GL54 2JD

"Absolute bliss," writes a fellow *Guide* hotelier. "A most welcoming and comfortable hotel. Our smallish room (my wife had to stand in the wardrobe in order to see herself full length in the mirror on the back of the door) was beautifully furnished with antiques and chintzes, all in a calm yellow. Breakfast was one of the best we have had." Other praise: "An indulgent, pampered night. Excellent dinner, exquisitely served by a young, confident and professional staff. Breakfast in bed, followed by a romantic walk along the river." "Idyllic setting, superior service, fine dining." This handsome 17th-century/Victorian former rectory is set in a large park with sweeping lawns and a trout lake, in an unspoilt Cotswold village. It has a pretty walled garden, low ceilings, mullioned windows, narrow passages, and a traditional decor: antiques, family portraits, log fires and flowers. *Michelin* awards a star to the perfectionist young chef, Robert-Clive Dixon, for his "country cooking with modern influence, served in trenchermen's portions, and accompanied by a selection of irresistible breads". Children are welcome. (*Robin Oaten, Marion Fanthorpe, and others*) Rooms in the main house are to be preferred to those overlooking the courtyard. Some readers in spring 1996 found serious hiccups in reception and restaurant service.

Open All year.
Rooms 25 double, 2 single.
Facilities Drawing room, writing room, library, garden room, bar, restaurant, conservatory. 8-acre parkland: gardens, croquet, lake, fishing. Riding, shooting, golf nearby.
Location Village centre. Rear carpark.
Restrictions No smoking in restaurant. No dogs.
Credit cards All major cards accepted.
Terms (*Excluding 12½% service charge on meals*) B&B: single £90, double £120–£145, suite £165–£225; D,B&B £77.50–£140 per person. Set lunch (2–3-course) £16.95–£19.95; set dinner (3-course) £32.50; full alc £50. 1-night bookings sometimes refused weekends. Children accommodated free in parents' room. Winter, summer breaks. *V*

> Many hotels put up their prices in the spring. Tariffs quoted in the text may therefore be more accurate before April/May 1997 than after.

UPPINGHAM Rutland — Map 2

The Lake Isle *Tel/Fax* (01572) 822951
16 High Street East
Uppingham LE15 9PZ

Claire and David Whitfield's small restaurant-with-rooms (he is chef) is on the main street of a delightful small market town, famous for its public school. You approach through a neat yard with hanging flower baskets. The old building has had many uses. Its restaurant was once a barber's shop, known as "Sweeney Todd's", where the schoolboys had their hair cut. It has pine panelled walls and pine furniture, and serves three- to five-course meals on a weekly-changing menu. Cooking is straightforward English / French, with the emphasis on fresh ingredients. There's a pretty pink-walled lounge, and a small garden. Bedrooms, at the back, are named after French wine regions; Dom Pérignon is large, with a whirlpool bath; others are small; two suites are in adjacent cottages. A recent report: "Difficult to reach by car, owing to the one-way system, but it was worth the effort. Reception was efficient, and not too formal. My room was tiny, but well equipped, with sherry, fresh fruit, biscuits, etc. The bathroom was almost the same size, and equally pleasant. Dinner was first class throughout. A small loaf on a breadboard with a good sharp knife was a nice touch. Impressive wine list, with pages of halves. I thoroughly enjoyed all aspects of my stay." Breakfast in the restaurant includes exotic fruits, grilled kidneys, and home-made preserves; a continental one may be delivered to the bedroom. When the restaurant is closed, simple meals are provided for residents. (*Chris Kay*) One reader complained of a cool reception, on arrival and on checking out.

Open All year. Restaurant closed to residents Sun evening / midday Mon.
Rooms 2 suites (in cottage), 9 double, 1 single.
Facilities Lounge, bar, restaurant. Small walled garden. Unsuitable for ♿.
Location Town centre. Entrance at rear of hotel. By foot approach via Reeves Yard, by car via Queen Street. Private parking.
Restriction No dogs in public rooms.
Credit cards All major cards accepted.
Terms [1996] B&B: single £43–£49, double £60–£69, suite £75–£79. Set lunch £9.50–£12.50, dinner £21.50–£24.50. Special breaks.

VELLOW, Somerset — Map 1

Curdon Mill BUDGET *Tel* (01984) 656522
Vellow, Williton TA4 4LS *Fax* (01984) 656197

An old mill, still with its waterwheel, in a quiet hamlet at the foot of the Quantock Hills. It is in a charming garden within a large working farm. "The conversion is a triumph of imagination and execution. There are exposed beams, log fires, and fresh flowers everywhere. The chintzy sitting room is filled with magazines and local information. Bedrooms, though small, are pretty, with everything you need." In the large dining room, "a discriminating and appropriately limited choice of menu ensures the freshness of the food – wholesome, traditional cooking, beautifully presented. It is matched by a short but exceptional wine list, reasonably priced." "The sound of the millstream makes it very relaxing. Richard and Daphne Criddle are welcoming hosts. All very good value." The mill is now licensed for weddings. One reporter loved the house, and would happily return, but thought that the cooking failed to match other aspects of the hotel.

Open All year (for lunch only 25 Dec). Restaurant closed evening Sun, midday except Sun.
Rooms 6 double. No telephone.
Facilities Lounge, bar, restaurant. On 200-acre farm: garden, swimming pool, river, fishing; stabling for visiting horses. Sea, sandy beaches nearby. Unsuitable for ♿.
Location 2 miles SE of Williton. Follow signs for Vellow and Curdon Mill.
Restrictions No smoking: restaurant, bedrooms. No children under 8. No dogs in house.
Credit cards Access, Amex, Visa.
Terms B&B: single £30–£40, double £50–£70; D,B&B £41.50–£46.50 per person. Set Sun lunch £12.50, dinner £16.50–£22.50. Winter package; off-season breaks.

VERYAN Cornwall — Map 1

The Nare
Carne Beach
Veryan, nr Truro TR2 5PF
Tel (01872) 501279
Fax (01872) 501856

"A traditional English hotel in a lovely position, offering first-class service from a professional, yet friendly staff, and a profusion of good fresh food." "Lots of character; fragrant conservatory; two friendly donkeys in the grounds." "Housekeeping impeccable." Surrounded by National Trust land, on the Roseland peninsula, *The Nare* stands in sub-tropical gardens with a swimming pool, a tennis court, secluded corners for sunbathing, and direct access to a safe, sandy beach. For inclement weather, there's a "really warm" indoor pool, heated all year. The "charming" owners, Mr and Mrs Gray, are supported by grandson Toby Ashworth, the fourth generation of a hotel-keeping family. The hotel is decorated in country house style, with antiques, oriental rugs, ornaments and flowers. Bedrooms, many with a balcony or patio, vary in size; best-designed ones are at the back, with sea view. Dinner is a quite formal five-course affair. There's plenty of choice on the breakfast menu. Teas and light lunches are served outdoors in fine weather. Old-fashioned services – shoe-cleaning, room-tidying in the evening, and hot water-bottles in beds – are on offer. Guests of all ages, and people on their own, are pampered. There are inter-communicating bedrooms for families, and a nursery tea for under-sevens. (*Mr and Mrs JC Moulton, Francine Walsh, Dr NB Fintner, and others*)

Open 9 Feb–4 Jan.
Rooms 2 suites, 30 double, 4 single. 5 on ground floor.
Facilities Lift. 4 lounges, 2 bars, billiard room, light lunch/supper room, restaurant, conservatory; drying room; indoor swimming pool, whirlpool spa, sauna, solarium, gym. 5-acre grounds: gardens, swimming pool (heated end May–mid-Sept), tennis, children's play area, safe sandy beach, sailboards, fishing. Concessionary golf at Truro Golf Club.
Location From A390 take B3287 towards Tregony; then A3078 towards St Mawes *c.* 1½ miles. 1st left to Veryan; through village, leaving *New Inn* on left; 1 mile straight towards sea.
Restriction Only guide dogs in public rooms.
Credit cards Access, Visa.
Terms B&B: single £53–£114, double £100–£198, suite £256–£420; D,B&B (min. 3 nights): single £82–£143, double £158–£302, suite £314–£478. Set lunch:

weekdays £13.50, Sun £15.50, dinner £29; full alc £47. Winter, spring, bridge breaks. Christmas, New Year house parties.

WAREHAM Dorset **Map 2**

The Priory *Tel* (01929) 551666
Church Green *Fax* (01929) 554519
Wareham BH20 4ND

César award in 1996

A carefully converted medieval priory, "with the ambience of a manor house", and a decor in tune with its historic past. It has a "wonderful setting in big and beautiful gardens sweeping down to the river Frome, with distant view of the Purbeck hills". Two beamed lounges overlook the grounds; in one a pianist plays on Saturdays and bank holidays. Bedrooms vary greatly in size; most are large and grand; those in the converted boathouse are particularly luxurious; some are "a miracle of compact planning". There are two dining rooms: one in vaulted cellars, the other, used mainly for breakfast and lunch, overlooks the grounds. On fine days lunch is served alfresco. Michael Rust's cooking on a daily-changing menu is based on local and seasonal produce. Last year's *César* award is mostly endorsed: "Truly a remarkable hotel. Courteous service. Meals produced with the minimum of fuss. Outstanding soups each day and, despite the dreaded influence of *nouvelle cuisine*, the main courses were superb and the servings generous." "High quality of service; memorable dinners and breakfasts." There is a wide choice of wines – "some are pricey, but the head waiter happily recommended the less expensive bottles". A full breakfast is served until 10.30 am in the bedrooms or in the dining room. (*Julia de Waal, A and N Leece; also Sheila Parsons, and others*) But there are also criticisms: one report of a poor meal; "unnecessary piped music in the reception area"; "the seating in the lovely drawing room was uncomfortable". The proprietor, Ian Turner, is the brother of Stuart Turner of the *Casterbridge Hotel*, Dorchester (*qv*).

Open All year.
Rooms 2 suites, 16 double, 3 single. 4 in boathouse. Some on ground floor.
Facilities 2 lounges (1 with TV, 1 with pianist, Sat and holiday evenings), bar, 2 dining rooms; 4-acre gardens: river frontage, mooring, fishing. Sea 4 miles.
Location From A351 by-pass at station roundabout, take North Causeway/North St. Left into East St, 1st right into Church St; hotel between church and river.
Restrictions No smoking in dining rooms. Guide dogs only.
Credit cards All major cards accepted.
Terms [1996] B&B: single £65–£105, double £80–£170, suite £195. Light lunches. Set lunch: 2–3-course £12.95–£14.95 (weekdays), £17.95 (Sun), dinner £24.50 (£26.50 on Sat); full alc from £35. Off-season breaks; Christmas package.

WARMINSTER Wiltshire **Map 2**

Bishopstrow House NEW *Tel* (01985) 212312
Boreham Road *Fax* (01985) 216769
Warminster BA12 9HH

This late Georgian country house stands in large grounds (the major part reached through a tunnel under a road), with gardens, ancient trees, temples, and many sporting facilities (see below), and its own stretch of the river Wylye. The hotel was bought in 1995 by Howard Malin, Simon Lowe and Andrew Leeman, the owners of *The Feathers*, Woodstock (*qv*), but the manager, David Dowden, and the chef, Chris Suter, have remained. It has been extensively refurbished; there is now a second restaurant for light meals, and a spa. "Vibrant colours throughout the public rooms," noted our inspector. "Mirrors of gargantuan proportions, heraldic motifs; dramatic red walls in the library, daintier colours in the drawing room. Our bedroom, one of the smallest, at the top (a steep climb), was comfortable, but lacked character; its bathroom could have been more efficient. A generous, but pricey, tea was laid out in the hall. The dinner menu was eclectic and tempting, and the food was excellent – cooked with enthusiasm, with lots of herbs and vegetables. The wine list is good, but priced in the upward direction. Most of the staff were very pleasant. Breakfast, served by jolly ladies, consisted of a self-help buffet and a good choice of cooked dishes. The hotel is genuinely welcoming to children, and though it lacks the hands-on touch of a resident owner, and housekeeping is not always perfect, it has much to recommend it. Dogs are welcomed too." More reports, please.

Open All year.
Rooms 4 suites, 26 double. 6 on ground floor.
Facilities Hall, lounge, library, conservatory, 2 restaurants; function facilities; health spa: swimming pool, sauna, sunbed, tennis, gym, hairdresser. 28-acre grounds: tennis, swimming pool, sauna, solarium, river, fishing. Golf nearby.
Location On B3414, 1½ miles E of Warminster.
Restriction No smoking in restaurant.
Credit cards All major cards accepted.
Terms B&B: single £75, double £110–£130, suite £195–£215. Set lunch £12.30, dinner £26.50; full alc £32. Summer/winter breaks. 1-night bookings sometimes refused Sat.

WASDALE HEAD Cumbria **Map 4**

Wasdale Head Inn BUDGET *Tel* (0194 67) 26229
Wasdale Head, nr Gosforth CA20 1EX *Fax* (0194 67) 26334

An unsophisticated, welcoming old gabled pub, popular for more than a century among walkers and climbers. It is in a magnificent isolated setting at the head of Wasdale, surrounded by steep fells, and is traditional in decor, with solid old furniture and much panelling. The main bar is named after the inn's first landlord, Will Ritson, reputed to be the world's biggest liar – lying competitions are held once a year in his memory. Good, simple bar food is served, and there's "a splendid selection of beers". Traditional *à la carte* English dinners, served in *Abrahams*, the low-ceilinged dining room, end with home-made puddings. A substantial breakfast is announced by a gong at 8 am. There is a comfortably old-fashioned residents' lounge. The pine-panelled bedrooms are small, but clean and well lit, with private facilities, plenty of hot water and lovely views. The atmosphere is relaxed – no dress rules. The owners, Mr and Mrs Hammond, recently appointed a new management and chef, and a visitor who has known the pub for sixty years writes: "It's as good as I have known it; they are wholly eager to give visitors careful attention. Accommodation, food, service all thoroughly satisfying." There are well-equipped self-catering apartments, a large drying room and a simple laundry service. (*Jack and Helen Thornton*)

Open 28 Dec–mid-Nov.
Rooms 6 double, 3 single. No TV. 8 self-catering apartments.
Facilities Residents' lounge, residents' bar, public bar, dining room; drying room; beer garden. 3-acre grounds. Lake 1 mile, sea 12 miles. Unsuitable for ♿.
Location 10 miles from Gosforth and Holmbrook. Follow signs from A595.
Restrictions No smoking in dining room. No dogs in public rooms.
Credit cards Access, Visa.
Terms [1996] B&B £29. Full alc £21.50. Bar meals; packed lunches.

WATER YEAT Cumbria — Map 4

Water Yeat Guest House NEW/BUDGET *Tel* (01229) 885306
Water Yeat, nr Ulverston LA12 8DJ

Pierre and Jill Labat's little guest house at the southern tip of Coniston Water was built in 1660 as a farmhouse. Its simple bedrooms have a floral, chintzy decor, and lovely views of the Crake valley and the fells. "It is a secret closely guarded by a clientele who return again and again," writes its nominator. "I have been coming since they opened in 1984, for the peace, the country air, a little light sailing (Arthur Ransome's Wild Cat Island is halfway down the lake) and the most wonderful food, for which locals come from far and wide. Pierre appears at 7.15 to describe the evening's choice: just two options for the first two courses, plus a vegetarian dish. Even so, decision is agonising. And the real hush comes after the adventurous cheeseboard, when anxiously swivelling eyes scan the pudding trolley, with plenty of sensational offerings, and second helpings offered. The superb ingredients are from local suppliers; Jill is a brilliant cook. Pierre is a perfect host, sensing whether you are feeling sociable or hermit-like, and behaving accordingly. The place is beautifully kept, pretty and spotlessly clean. Arriving here is to shed the troubles of the world. Bliss." The food is "a mixture of hearty French home cooking and modern English". Breakfast includes yogurt, muesli, croissants, and a hearty Cumbrian affair, with oatcakes. (*Christina Hardyment*)

Open Feb–Dec. Closed Sun, except bank holidays.
Rooms 5 double, 2 single. 2 with shower, 1 with bath. No telephone/TV.
Facilities Lounge, dining room. 3-acre garden. Mountain bikes, canoe available. Lake ½ mile. Unsuitable for ♿.
Location S tip of Coniston Water. On A5084, 2½ miles N of Lowick 3 miles S of Torver.
Restrictions No smoking: dining room, bedrooms. No children under 4. No dogs in house.
Credit cards None accepted.
Terms B&B: single £19–£22, double £41–£58; D,B&B: single £35.50–£38.50, double £74–£91. 1-night bookings sometimes refused weekends. Off-season breaks; creative textile courses. *V*

> "Budget" labels indicate hotels offering accommodation for up to about £50 (or its foreign currency equivalent) for dinner, bed and breakfast, or £30 for B&B and £20 for an evening meal. But we would emphasise that this is a rough guide only, and does not always apply to single rooms or in high season.

WATERHOUSES Staffordshire — Map 3

The Old Beams
Leek Road
Waterhouses ST10 3HW
Tel (01538) 308254
Fax (01538) 308157

A restaurant-with-rooms in a hamlet on the edge of the Peak District. "The best in the UK," wrote one *Guide* reader last year. "All the feeling of France, with delightful touches everywhere. Quality abounds in the fixtures, the fittings, and above all in the service." It is run by Nigel Wallis, the chef, his wife Ann ("exuberantly front-of-house"), and son Simon. *Michelin* awards a star for the modern English / French cooking, and two red crossed spoon-and-forks for the attractive beamed dining room, with frescoes of an italianate landscape, and a conservatory extension, overlooking the pretty sloping garden, floodlit at night. Our readers too, with one exception, have enjoyed the food: "Lovingly prepared; the finest ingredients; exciting combinations of flavours and textures; generous portions; exquisite home-made bread; judiciously selected wine list." The bedrooms are across a busy road, in a stone cottage by a millstream – double-glazing mitigates traffic noise, and umbrellas are provided for inclement weather. Some of the bedrooms are small. One couple found theirs claustrophobic, but others have been "enchanted: celestial blue and cream decor, hand-embroidered sheets and duvet cover, excellent home-made biscuits, home-made fudge, books, glossy magazines, smart bathroom." (*Nichola Arditti; also FW, Pat and Jeremy Temple, and others*) A continental breakfast, with home-made croissants, brioches and jam, is included in the B&B rates, but one reader thought cereal or fruit should also be offered, as a supplement is charged for cooked items.

Open All year. Closed Sun evening / Mon; restaurant also closed Sat midday.
Rooms 5 double. All in annexe across road. 1 with ♿ access.
Facilities Small lounge, restaurant with lounge and bar areas; private dining room. ½-acre garden.
Location On A523 Ashbourne–Leek (all rooms double-glazed).
Restrictions No smoking: restaurant, bedrooms. No dogs.
Credit cards All major cards accepted.
Terms [1996] B&B: single £55, double £70–£89.95. English breakfast £5–£6.50. Set lunch £19.50, dinner £37.50. *V*

WATERMILLOCK Cumbria — Map 4

Leeming House
Watermillock, Penrith CA11 0JJ
Tel (0176 84) 86622
Fax (0176 84) 86443

The only *Guide* hotel belonging to the Forte chain. An early Victorian house, it has magnificent grounds, with mature trees, running down to Ullswater, and superb views, particularly from the first-floor bedrooms and the quite formal restaurant. Its "exemplary", long-serving manager, Christopher Curry, "spares himself no effort": "He is there round the clock, and runs a first-class, ever-smiling team." "It is faultless," wrote a recent visitor. "The food is excellent; the service outstanding. My husband would like to live there." Others have agreed about the cooking: "Finely poised between traditional and gourmet, with interesting sauces and generous helpings. The wine list may lack panache but it offers robust and drinkable wines at fairly reasonable prices. The tea trolley groans under the weight of scrumptious cream cakes. Light lunches are served in the bright conservatory. Delicious croissants at breakfast. Bedrooms in the new wing are beyond reproach in both style and comfort; they lack the individuality of those in the main building but are larger, warmer and quieter." (*Mrs EB Burns, FW, and others*) One couple was less pleased with food and service, "and the unwanted complimentary *Daily Telegraph* was delivered to our room anyway – no one told us that our requested *Guardian* (at extra cost) would be waiting at our breakfast table."

Open All year.
Rooms 39 double, 1 single. 10 on ground floor, 1 equipped for ♿.
Facilities Drawing room, sitting room, library, cocktail bar, dining room, conservatory; boardroom. 20-acre grounds: gardens, croquet, arboretum, golf practice, helipad, lake frontage: fishing, sailing, etc.
Location W shore of Ullswater on A592. 8 miles from M6 exit 40.
Restrictions No smoking: dining room, library, 11 bedrooms. No dogs in public rooms.
Credit cards All major cards accepted.
Terms B&B: single £91–£136.50, double £123–£168. Set dinner £30 and £37.50; light lunches; full alc lunch £33. Half board rates (min. 2 days); 5- and 7-night rates. Christmas, New Year packages. Small shooting parties. 1-night bookings sometimes refused. *V* (Nov–Mar, except Christmas/New Year)

The Old Church *Tel* (0176 84) 86204
Watermillock, Penrith CA11 0JN *Fax* (0176 84) 86368

Reached by a long drive through large grounds, this 18th-century house has a beautiful, peaceful position on the shore of Ullswater, with lovely views of the fells. It is informally run by the owners, Kevin and Maureen Whitemore, and their family – "friendly and readily available, but never intrusive". "The service is cheerful and efficient, yet unpretentious," write recent guests. "Don't expect beds to be turned down, and crumbs swept from the table between courses. Everyone was very kind to our young son and our baby, and adaptable about their needs. The food was wholesome, with particularly good fish and vegetables; only one dish disappointed in four days." Others, too, have enjoyed the English home cooking, on a *carte* with ample choice, and the decor, with warm colours, flowers, pot plants, books and magazines, and plenty of evidence of Mrs Whitemore's enthusiasm for soft furnishings (she runs upholstery courses during much of the year). Rooms vary in size and style and are priced accordingly: some have lake views. Breakfasts are "generous and varied enough to satisfy the most demanding of appetites". (*Annie and David Lade and family, and others*)

Open Apr–Oct. Restaurant closed midday, Sun evening.
Rooms 10 double.
Facilities 2 lounges, bar, dining room. 4-acre grounds on lake: mooring, fishing, rowing boat. Unsuitable for ♿.
Location Off A592, 3 miles S of Pooley Bridge; 5 miles from M6 exit 40.
Restrictions No smoking in dining room. No children in dining room or bar after 7 pm. No dogs inside hotel.
Credit cards Access, Amex, Visa.
Terms [1996] B&B £45–£59; D,B&B £75–£84; full alc £25. 1-night bookings sometimes refused. Soft-furnishing courses Mar–Oct.

Rampsbeck NEW
Watermillock, Penrith CA11 0LP

Tel (0176 84) 86442
Fax (0176 84) 86688

A very pretty 18th-century house in a tranquil setting on the shore of Ullswater, warmly nominated by experienced hotel-goers: "It is set in manicured gardens with formal flower beds and precisely trimmed hedges. This welcoming establishment is run by a charming family: Thomas and Marion Gibb and Mrs Gibb's mother, Marguerite MacDowall. The furnishings are slightly old-fashioned, and comfortable, unlike the contrived slickness of so many country house hotels. The huge hall is friendly, with a crackling log fire, and someone always at reception. We took tea in a high-ceilinged lounge with lovely plaster work, Victorian furniture, current newspapers, plants and flowers. Some bedrooms have a private balcony. Ours was exceptionally spacious, well lit, and supplied with fruit, plants etc. In the elegant, spacious dining room the menu was imaginative, the cooking precise, using local ingredients, attractively presented, and the service was well-paced. The wine list is comprehensive and moderately priced." (*Padi and John Howard*)

Open Mid-Feb–beginning Jan, except few days Dec.
Rooms 1 suite, 18 double, 2 single.
Facilities Hall, 2 lounges, bar, dining room. 19-acre grounds: croquet, lake frontage: fishing, sailing, etc; golf, clay pigeon-shooting nearby. Unsuitable for ♿.
Location From M6 exit 40, follow signs for A592 to Ullswater. At T-junction on lake shore turn right. Hotel 1¼ miles.
Restrictions No smoking: dining room, 1 lounge, 2 bedrooms. No children under 5 in dining room at night. No dogs in public rooms.
Credit cards Access, Visa.
Terms B&B: £45–£90; D,B&B £71–£116. Set lunch £22, dinner £26, £36. Mid-week breaks. 1-night bookings sometimes refused bank holidays. V*

WELLAND Hereford and Worcester — Map 3

See Little Malvern

WENLOCK EDGE Shropshire — Map 3

Wenlock Edge Inn BUDGET
Hilltop, Wenlock Edge TF13 6DJ

Tel (01746) 785678
Fax (01768) 785285

Wenlock Edge, of Housman fame, is in a designated area of outstanding natural beauty largely owned by the National Trust, with stunning views to west and south. This "honest old-fashioned inn" is in a fine position, right by the Ippikins Rock viewpoint. It makes an excellent base for walking the extensive National Trust land that runs along the Edge. It is owned by two generations of the Waring family, Harry, Joan, Diane and Stephen, "as chatty and convivial as you could wish". Bedrooms, with beams, sloping ceiling, smallish windows and padded window seat, are "fair-sized and slightly cluttered, with pretty furniture, TV, lots of goodies, spotless shower room with water from the pub's own well" (the plumbing can be noisy at times). One bar has wooden pews, a fine oak counter and an open fire; the other has an inglenook fireplace with a wood-burning stove. The busy little dining room serves "excellent, simple home-cooked dinners", chosen from a blackboard menu; there is a short but adequate selection of wines. After dinner everybody congregates for a good time in the bar, urged on by the Warings. The robust traditional breakfast includes good thick brown toast. "Not at all smart or fancy, but if you want genuine warmth and hospitality, better than average pub food and a simple pretty room, this is it." On the second Monday of the month the pub is host to a story-telling club. "One of the most welcoming pubs we know." (*HR, Good Pub Guide*) Most of the rooms face a quiet B road, but this hasn't bothered our reporters.

Open All year, except 24–26 Dec. No food served to non-residents Mon (except bank holidays).
Rooms 4 double. 1 on ground floor, in adjacent cottage. No telephone.
Facilities Lounge bar, public bar, dining room. Patio, paddock. Walking, riding, fishing, mountain biking nearby; gliding, hang-gliding 9 miles.
Location On B4371, 4 miles W of Much Wenlock.
Restrictions No smoking in dining room. Children under 8 not accommodated. No dogs in dining room, lounge.
Credit cards Access, Amex, Visa.
Terms B&B: single £40–£45, double £55–£65. full alc £16.50 *V*

WEOBLEY Hereford and Worcester — Map 3

Ye Olde Salutation Inn BUDGET — *Tel* (01544) 318443
Market Pitch — *Fax* (01544) 318216
Weobley HR4 8SJ

"Excellent bedroom, looking down quietish picturesque main street to church and hills. Spotlessly clean. Friendly welcome and service. Lots of character." Ancient and timber-framed, this "relaxed, traditional pub, with quiet, comfortable lounges", is in a "gem" of a medieval village. It has "courteous, but not intrusive hosts", Chris and Frances Anthony, and just four bedrooms, all different, all no-smoking. The one with a four-poster is particularly admired: "spacious and beautifully decorated, with a luxurious bathroom"; the others have brass or wooden bedheads and pretty fabrics. The food, too, is liked, particularly the bar meals ("delicious, quickly served and reasonably priced"). Breakfast is "huge, with home-made jam". Following last year's report of noise in the four-poster room, the owners write: "We slept there and realised that it was due to barrels being moved. This is now done only in the morning." Guests arriving between 3 pm and 7 pm, when the bars are closed, have a special point of entry. There's a timbered self-contained cottage across the road, good for families. (*JD Crosland, Good Pub Guide*) One caveat: "The breakfast orange juice should be fresh, or at least 'fresh'."

Open All year, except Christmas Day. Restaurant closed Sun evening/Mon.
Rooms 4 double. 1 self-contained cottage.
Facilities Residents' lounge with TV, lounge bar, public bar, restaurant. Small patio. River Wye 6 miles: fishing. Unsuitable for ♿.
Location Top of main street. Carpark.
Restrictions No smoking: restaurant, bedrooms. No children under 14 except in cottage. Dogs in cottage and public bar only.
Credit cards All major cards accepted.
Terms B&B: single £35, double £60–£65. Bar meals. Full alc £27.

WEST CLIFFE Kent — Map 2

Wallett's Court BUDGET — *Tel* (01304) 852424
West Cliffe, St Margaret's at Cliffe — *Fax* (01304) 853430
Dover CT15 6EW

A Grade II* listed manor house, mentioned in the Domesday Book, developed in the 17th century, and rescued from dereliction 20 years ago by Chris and Lea Oakley. It has exposed brickwork, moulded plaster fireplaces, black wood-burning stoves, antiques, a large, comfortable lounge and "plenty of olde-worlde charm". The setting is rural, but it is handy for the Dover ferries and the Channel Tunnel. The best bedrooms are in the main house (one has an oak-panelled four-poster); others (more austere) are in converted barns. Early leavers may ask for breakfast from 6.30 am, or a continental tray in their room. Those in less of a hurry may enjoy a "very good cooked breakfast in a charming conservatory". The restaurant is popular locally for Chris Oakley's cooking: "English/French with a Jacobean influence". On weekdays there is a quite simple three-course dinner; on Saturday it is a more expensive five-course gourmet affair. "We were impressed," writes a recent guest. "The owners have everything under control with the minimum of fuss. Good food and wine, with prompt service. Relaxed atmosphere. Very good value." "Excellent waiting staff, good housekeeping, friendly part-Siamese cat. They have developed the site very sympathetically." (*Colin Eastaugh; also Dr Arthur and Mrs Irene Naylor, and others*) One warning: "The ancient staircase in the main house should be treated with respect."

Open All year, except Christmas. Restaurant closed midday except Sun, evening Sun.
Rooms 3 suites, 8 double, 1 single, most with facilities *en suite*. 9 in converted barns, 10–40 yds.
Facilities Lounge/bar, 2 dining rooms, conservatory. 4-acre grounds: tennis, croquet, swings, tree house. Unsuitable for ♿.
Location 3 miles N of Dover. From A2, take A258 to Deal. 1st right to West Cliffe; hotel ½ mile on right, opposite church.
Restrictions No smoking in restaurant. No dogs.
Credit cards All major cards accepted.
Terms [1996] B&B: single £40–£60, double £60–£80; D,B&B: single £63–£83, double £106–£126. Set Sun lunch £15, dinner: £23 weekdays, £28 Sat. Extra bed for child £5–£10. Off-season breaks.

WEST DEAN East Sussex — Map 2

The Old Parsonage NEW/BUDGET — *Tel* (01323) 870432
West Dean, nr Seaford BN25 4AL

Medieval house, remarkably well preserved, with Victorian extension. By 12th-century church in quiet hamlet 5 miles W of Eastbourne, in heart of Friston Forest. Thick stone walls, small mullioned windows, beams, stone spiral staircases. Only 3 bedrooms: 1, with 4-poster, in old Hall; 1 in Solar; 1 in Middle Room, between Solar and Crypt. Private facilities (not en suite); no telephone/TV. Friendly owners, Raymond and Angela Woodhams, "very interested in their guests". Excellent breakfasts. 2-acre grounds. Closed Christmas, New Year. No children under 12. No smoking. No dogs. Credit cards not accepted. B&B double £50–£65. No restaurant; Hungry Monk,

Jevington, warmly recommended. "Things ancient and modern combine to make this memorable," writes inspector, "but it was cold in winter." More reports, please.

WEST PORLOCK Somerset — Map 1

Bales Mead NEW/BUDGET — *Tel* ((01643) 862565
West Porlock TA24 8NX

Welcoming B&B in hamlet between Porlock and Porlock Weir, surrounded by Exmoor National Park. Lovely views. "Stunning Edwardian house, with aura of peaceful elegance; decor with 1920/30s feel; high quality fabrics." ½-acre garden. Shingle beach, harbour ½-mile; bathing, fishing, boating. "Charming, helpful" owners, Stephen Blue and Peter Glover (who had 1990 Guide *entry for previous hotel,* Waterloo House, *Lynton). 3 bedrooms, warm and welcoming: excellent beds, sherry and amaretti;* en suite *power shower. Traditional English or generous continental breakfast. Closed Christmas/ New Year. Unsuitable for ♿. No smoking. No children under 14. No dogs. Credit cards not accepted. B&B £25–£35.*

WHIMPLE Devon — Map 1

Woodhayes — *Tel* (01404) 822237
Whimple, nr Exeter EX5 2TD — *Fax* (01404) 822337

A large white Georgian house in a well-tended garden in a peaceful apple-orchard village. Its decor is "smart and home-like, with chintzes, and flowers everywhere – in fresh arrangements, and in delicately painted watercolours, oils and prints". It is run in a generous spirit by the family owners, Katherine and Frank Rendle and their son Michael, "all charm personified". The tariff includes early morning tea delivered to the bedroom, afternoon cream tea, newspapers, full English breakfast, tea and coffee during the day, and light laundry. "The welcome eclipses most hotel receptions, and was maintained throughout the visit. Our room was delightful, furnished with Edwardian pieces, with ample wardrobe accommodation, sofa and comfortable chairs, and an excellent bathroom. At night, Mr Rendle performs in the bar and serves the copious courses very elegantly. Dinner (six courses, no choice) was thoroughly enjoyable, with home-grown fruit and vegetables, home-baked rolls, and a good wine selection, but we were almost defeated by the cheese course. Breakfast was equally good, with a buffet of fresh fruit salad, etc, and an interesting choice of cooked dishes." "If you want peace, and relaxation from a hectic world, here it is. We cannot praise *Woodhayes* too highly." (*Joan Powell, PN Nicholas, and others*) Dartmoor, Exmoor, Exeter and the coast are all within striking distance.

Open All year, except 4 days over Christmas. Lunch served to residents only.
Rooms 6 double.
Facilities 2 lounges, bar, dining room. 4-acre grounds: garden, croquet, paddock. Unsuitable for ♿.
Location 8 miles E of Exeter. ¾ mile off A30, on right just before village.
Restrictions No smoking in dining room. No children under 12. No dogs.
Credit cards Probably all major cards accepted.
Terms B&B: single £70, double £95; D,B&B: single £90, double £140. Set lunch £17.50, dinner £28. Reduced rates for children sharing parents' room.

WHITEWELL Lancashire **Map 4**

The Inn at Whitewell
Forest of Bowland
nr Clitheroe BB7 3AT

Tel (01200) 448222
Fax (01200) 448298

An inn with a difference, dating in part to the 14th century, and run with a touch of eccentricity (jokey tariff, chatty menus, etc) by Richard Bowman. "The civilised atmosphere and individual furnishings make it more like a hospitable country house than a traditional pub." It is a long, low stone building, set in "a marvellous landscape", deep in the Forest of Bowland. It's worth paying extra for one of the rooms with a glorious view over the river Hodder. The inn has an authentically English, old-fashioned feel, with gleaming brass, log fires, fresh flowers and sporting paraphernalia. The bedrooms are sophisticated, with antiques, brass bed, pure cotton sheets, books, and a first-rate sound system, with TV, video and CD player; some have a peat fire. Bathrooms have Edwardian or Victorian fittings. The joint head chefs, Brenda Murphy and Annette Fitzgerald, are from the famous *Ballymaloe* cookery school in Ireland; there is an extensive *à la carte* dinner menu offering "the best ingredients, classically cooked"; unpretentious, generous bar meals are also served. The inn houses a wine merchant (hence the unusually wide range of bottles), and an art gallery. The sheltered garden overlooks the river, on which the pub owns six miles of trout-, sea trout- and salmon-fishing. Children and dogs are welcome. The inn is on a road with little traffic, quiet at night. It is handy for Manchester airport. (*Good Pub Guide, and others*)

Open All year.
Rooms 1 suite, 10 double.
Facilities Lounge, bar, dining room; 2 private dining rooms. 3-acre grounds: garden, river frontage, fishing.
Location 6 miles NW of Clitheroe. Large carpark.
Restriction "Dogs with kind natures are welcome and allowed almost everywhere except the dining room, but no alsatians, rottweilers or moody dogs in public rooms."
Credit cards All major cards accepted.
Terms [1996] B&B: single £49.50–£57, double £68–£78, suite £98. Bar meals. Full alc dinner £26. Weekly rates negotiable.

WHITNEY-ON-WYE Hereford and Worcester **Map 3**

Rhydspence Inn BUDGET
Whitney-on-Wye
Hereford HR3 6EU

Tel (01497) 831262
Fax (01497) 831520

Just in England – the stream in the garden marks the border with Wales – is this attractive, part 14th-century black-and-white timbered inn. It is owned and solicitously run by Peter and Pamela Glover. The bar is "all an English pub should be, with old wooden furniture, gleaming copper, and fresh flowers". "Admirable" traditional food is served in generous portions in the blue-carpeted, pink-tableclothed, candlelit restaurant. The bedrooms, up a narrow staircase, are pretty, with flowery fabrics and simple bathrooms. Good breakfast. (*John E Borron*) Only snag: no residents' lounge.

Open All year, except Christmas.
Rooms 6 double, 1 single. No telephone.
Facilities 2 bars, restaurant, small dining room, family room. ½-acre garden: terrace, patio, stream. Unsuitable for ♿.
Location Just off A438 Hereford–Brecon, 4 miles N of Hay-on-Wye.
Restrictions Smoking discouraged in dining room. No dogs.
Credit cards Access, Amex, Visa.
Terms [1996] B&B £27.50–£37.50. Bar meals; full alc £23. Mid-week breaks. *V*

WICKHAM Hampshire — Map 2

The Old House
The Square
Wickham, nr Fareham PO17 5JG

Tel (01329) 833049
Fax (01329) 833672

Six-foot-six Richard Skipwith and his "stunningly attractive" French wife, Annie, have been 26 years at their red brick, creeper-covered Grade II listed early-Georgian town house. It stands in the picturesque part-medieval, part-Georgian square of an old market town. Inside, it is panelled and beamed, with antique and period furniture. The pretty bedrooms are "full of old-world charm"; most are large; some, on the second floor, have beams, sloping ceiling and flowery wallpaper. There is a French provincial-style bar. The restaurant, once the timber-framed outhouse and stables, looks on to an attractive small garden. "The food was excellent in every way," wrote a recent visitor, "and the wines were magnificent." Others have agreed about the French cooking – "imaginative and well executed" – but thought the wines expensive. Everyone praises the hosts ("friendly but not obsequious") and their helpful staff. "Though professionally run, it retains the atmosphere of a family house." The walk from Wickham down the disused railway line to Alton "is highly recommended after the hearty breakfasts". (*SD, Alan and Sophie Miodownik, and others*)

Open All year, except 2 weeks Christmas, 1 week Easter, 2 weeks August, bank holidays, Sun night. Restaurant closed Sat midday, Sun, Mon.
Rooms 9 double, 3 single. 3 in cottage 50 yds.
Facilities 2 lounges, bar, restaurant; private dining room, function room. ¼-acre grounds. Unsuitable for ♿.
Location Centre of village at junction of A32 and B2177, 3 miles N of Fareham (front rooms double-glazed. Carpark.
Restriction No dogs.
Credit cards All major cards accepted.
Terms Rooms: single £70–£75, double £80–£90. Breakfast: continental £6, English from £10. Set lunch/dinner £30. 2-day breaks.

WILLESLEY Gloucestershire — Map 3

Tavern House NEW
Willesley, nr Tetbury GL8 8QU

Tel (01666) 880444
Fax (01666) 880254

"An excellent B&B in a hamlet on the Tetbury to Bath road. Once a 17th-century coaching inn, it offers the highest degree of luxury and comfort. It is furnished in good taste, with antiques and country furniture. The bedrooms are immaculate. There is a pleasant lounge, a charming breakfast room, and a flowery walled garden. The delightful owners, Janet and Tim Tremellen, are helpful with local know-how. We dined well at the *Rattlebone Inn* in the nearby village of Sherston, which for sheer beauty warrants a visit. There is lovely walking all around. A peaceful base for exploring the Cotswolds." (*Uli Lloyd Pack*)

Open All year.
Rooms 4 double.
Facilities Lounge, breakfast room. ¾-acre garden. Golf, hunting, horse racing, motor-racing nearby. Unsuitable for ♿.
Location 4 miles SW of Tetbury on A433 (quiet at night; rooms double-glazed).
Restrictions No smoking: breakfast room, bedrooms. No children under 10. No dogs.
Credit cards Access, Visa.
Terms B&B £30.50–£55. 2/3-day mini-breaks. 1-night bookings refused Christmas, bank holidays, Badminton horse trials (early May).

WILLITON Somerset — Map 1

The White House — *Tel* (01984) 632306 and 632777
Williton TA4 4QW

César award in 1988

"Delightful. We have visited many times. Dick and Kay Smith are friendly hosts, and in no way intrusive. Hard to improve on the food, yet each time we stay they achieve fresh standards of excellence." The Smiths have run their civilised restaurant-with-rooms for 29 years, and it has appeared in almost every edition of the *Guide*. The cooking is "mainly modern English, with French, Mediterranean and Californian influences". Husband does the hors d'oeuvre and main course, wife the vegetables and puddings. "Difficult to decide who is the more skilled." There is plenty of choice on the menu, a "very good" wine list, with several wines available by the glass, and a wide choice for breakfast. The house is filled with paintings, prints and ceramics, old and modern, chosen with taste. Bedrooms are thoughtfully equipped. Those in the main building are "spacious and lovely; and it is no hardship to stay in the room without *en suite* facilities – the bathroom on the hall is gorgeous, with huge bathtub, thick carpeting and extraordinary large mirrors." Smaller rooms are in converted stables and a coach house in the courtyard. The hotel stands on the main road, but is separated from it by a semi-circle of lawn with tall palm trees; front rooms get traffic noise during the day. (*John and June Astle-Fletcher*)

Open Mid-May–Nov. Restaurant closed for lunch.
Rooms 1 family suite, 11 double, 9 with private facilities. 4 on ground floor, around courtyard.
Facilities Lounge, bar, restaurant. Sea, shingle beaches 2 miles.
Location On A39 in centre of village; rear rooms quietest. Forecourt parking.
Restrictions No smoking in restaurant. No dogs in restaurant.
Credit cards None accepted.
Terms B&B £35–£49; D,B&B £63–£77. Bargain breaks all year. *V*

WILMINGTON East Sussex — Map 2

Crossways Hotel BUDGET — *Tel* (01323) 482455
Lewes Road — *Fax* (01323) 487811
Wilmington BN26 5SG

In a "delightful" village in the South Downs – "all cottage gardens and expensive cars" – this white Georgian house is owned by "very friendly" ex-restaurateurs, David Stott and Clive James. Its garden contains a duckpond, several rabbits and a herb garden. The house is "pleasantly furnished, though the breakfast room might be considered over the top if you are not a cheese dish fan". Recent visitors enjoyed their "lovely big room with a sofa and a balcony". David Stott was a finalist in the *Logis of Great Britain* regional cooking competition in 1993. Many of the ingredients for his "remarkably good food" are locally produced or home-grown; portions are generous. The Long Man of Wilmington is "the largest representation of the human figure in Europe". The whole area is criss-crossed with footpaths. Glyndebourne is 15 minutes' drive away. (*Ayelet and Michael Chabon, and others*) One visitor was critical of the decor and the hotel is on a busy road, "but the double-glazing helps".

Open 21 Jan–20 Dec. Restaurant closed midday, and Sun/Mon.
Rooms 5 double, 2 single.
Facilities Breakfast room, restaurant. 2-acre grounds. Sea 4 miles. Unsuitable for ♿.
Location 6 miles N of Eastbourne on A27 (rooms double-glazed). Large carpark.
Restrictions No smoking in restaurant. No children under 12. No dogs.
Credit cards All major cards accepted.
Terms B&B: single £42–£44, double £66–£72; D,B&B (min. 2 nights) £57.50 per person. Set dinner £27. Gourmet breaks. Special privileged guest scheme Feb/Mar.

WIMBORNE MINSTER Dorset — Map 2

Beechleas — *Tel* (01202) 841684
17 Poole Road — *Fax* (01202) 849344
Wimborne Minster BH21 1QA

Josephine McQuillan's skilfully restored Grade II listed Georgian house on road to Poole in Dorset market town. Pretty sitting room with fire; charming dining room with conservatory extension; Aga-cooked English food, with French influence: organically produced meat, home-grown vegetables; delectable desserts. Short wine list with wide price range. 9 bedrooms with pleasing, restful decor; some in converted coach house and lodge. Small walled garden. Small carpark. Closed 24 Dec–13 Jan; dining room closed midday. Coast 8 miles. Unsuitable for ♿. No smoking: restaurant, bedrooms. No dogs. Access, Amex, Visa accepted. B&B: single £60–£80, double £75–£95. Set dinner £19.75. No recent reports; we'd like some, please. *V*

WINCHCOMBE Gloucestershire — Map 3

Wesley House NEW — *Tel* (01242) 602366
High Street — *Fax* (01242) 602405
Winchcombe GL54 5LJ

This restaurant-with-rooms is a half-timbered 15th-century building, in the main street of a handsome small town, Saxon in origin, near Cheltenham. It is named for the Methodist preacher, who is believed to have stayed here in 1779. "Not an elaborate hotel, but a most welcoming one," writes its enthusiastic nominator. "It offers straightforward comfort and excellent food without pretension. Co-owner Matthew Brown, front of house, is genuinely warm, and could not do enough for us. The ambience is charming. You enter straight into a parlour, with a huge fireplace (blazing fire). The restaurant [three red spoon-and-forks in *Michelin*] is on several levels. Bedrooms, up a steep beamed staircase, are quite small, but tastefully decorated and well equipped: drinks tray with milk in thermos, flowers, huge vases and *objets d'art* in nooks and crannies. Beautifully warm on a bitterly cold December day. Jonathan Lewis's modern cooking was highly enjoyable, and the restaurant service attentive but unintrusive. Breakfast, of similar quality, included freshly squeezed orange juice, basket of warm rolls and croissants, butter and jams in little bowls and excellent cooked dishes." There is some traffic noise; but most rooms are at the rear. The Terrace Bedroom (the best) has panoramic views across the Cotswold edge towards Sudeley Castle. (*Jon Hughes*)

Open 12 Feb 1997–12 Jan 1998.
Rooms 5 double, 1 single.
Facilities Lounge/bar, restaurant, function facilities. Horse-racing, riding, golf nearby. Unsuitable for ♿.
Location High street of town 6 miles NE of Cheltenham (4 rear rooms quietest). Street parking.
Restrictions No smoking: restaurant, bedrooms. No dogs.
Credit cards Access, Amex, Visa.
Terms [1996] D,B&B £45–£63.50. Set lunch £14, dinner £23. 1-night bookings sometimes refused bank holidays.

WINCHESTER Hampshire — Map 2

Hotel du Vin & Bistro
14 Southgate Street
Winchester SO23 9EF

Tel (01962) 841414
Fax (01962) 842458

A Georgian red-brick town house, opened as a hotel in 1994 by two graduates of *Chewton Glen* (*qv*), Robin Hutson, who was its managing director, and moustachioed Gerald Bassett the much-admired *sommelier*. In contrast to their *alma mater*, they aim for "style without frills, at a sensible price". The decor is "in praise of wine": walls are densely hung with vinous pictures, old photographs, labels, menus, etc. Bedrooms, each sponsored by a wine house, are sophisticated – "subtle colours, tasteful fabrics, pristine white linen" – but lack extras. This year there are six new ones. Four are in a purpose-built building in the garden, "less characterful than those in the main house", according to one visitor. The high-ceilinged sitting room has a beautiful *trompe l'oeil* painting, huge sofas and squashy armchairs, but one couple found its lighting too dim for reading; there is a pretty walled garden, where meals are served in summer. The lively bistro, with bare floors, small polished mahogany tables, and festoons around the windows, is pale yellow, softly lit and picture-bedecked. Chef James Martin trained with the renowned restaurateur Antony Worrall Thompson, and his cooking, served in large portions, has a Mediterranean bent. "Good food and excellent wines at reasonable prices," writes a 1996 visitor on a return visit. "Bedrooms clean and comfortable, bathrooms just right, without unnecessary luxury. Staff are always pleased to see you, and look after you without fuss." Some feel that breakfast lets the side down, but others have written: "Memorable pain chocolat." (*Richard Townend, Susan Gillotti, and others*) The house is on a busy road; garden-facing rooms are quietest ("we heard only birdsong and bells"). One couple complained of rushed service at dinner.

Open All year.
Rooms 19 double. 4 in garden. 1 on ground floor with ♿ access.
Facilities Drawing room, bar, bistro. Small walled garden: *boules*.
Location Central (back rooms quietest). Hotel will send directions. Carpark.
Restriction Guide dogs only.
Credit cards All major cards accepted.
Terms Rooms: single/double £69–£105. Breakfast: continental £4, English £8. Full alc £30.

The Wykeham Arms *Tel* (01962) 853834
75 Kingsgate Street *Fax* (01962) 854411
Winchester SO23 9PE

César award in 1996

This popular hostelry is an historic building close by the cathedral and handy for sight-seeing, yet quiet; it's on a road with little through traffic. Its hands-on proprietor, Graeme Jameson, is a great collector. Military memorabilia, hats, tankards, pictures of royalty, framed collections of cigarette cards fill the public rooms. The main bar has old school desks from the college. In a series of intimate eating areas, some no-smoking, traditional cooking is served in generous portions. There's an enticingly long but reasonably priced list of wines, many available by the glass. More enthusiasm this year: "A great place. Lovely bedroom. Friendly, thoughtful service. Wonderful value." "We loved the buzz of the place, and the bonhomie dispensed by Graeme and Anne Jameson." "Very good meal. Though very busy, they did not hurry us." "Fresh local veg in variety, properly cooked. Enterprising starters and comforting puds." The attractive small bedrooms upstairs have a mini-bar with fresh milk for tea-making, hot-water bottles, two single duvets on the double bed to prevent marital strife, and an efficient, well-lit bathroom. Breakfast includes excellent wholemeal toast; nothing is packaged or wrapped. Not for visitors wanting full hotel facilities: no residents' lounge or reception; you go straight into a bar from the street, but "hard to beat for all-round comfort and hospitality". Difficult to find, but confirmations of reservation are accompanied by good instructions, and Mr Jameson has been known to park cars for arriving guests. Frequent concerts in the College and Evensong in the cathedral provide entertainment on the doorstep. (*Joan Hare, HR, Mr and Mrs TR Rowe, and others; also Good Pub Guide*)

Open All year, except 26 Dec. No evening meal 23 Dec–1 Jan.
Rooms 7 double.
Facilities 2 bars, 5 eating areas, breakfast room; sauna. Small garden. Unsuitable for ♿.
Location Central, between college and cathedral; hotel will send directions. Carpark.
Restrictions No smoking in 3 eating areas. No children under 14.
Credit cards Access, Amex, Visa.
Terms B&B: single £67.50–£69.50, double £77.50–£79.50. Full alc: lunch £17, dinner £25.60.

> British hotels nowadays have private facilities in most bedrooms. And many have TV, baby-listening and tea-making facilities. To save space we do not list all of these; if any is particularly important to you, please discuss with the hotel.

WINDERMERE Cumbria **Map 4**

The Archway **BUDGET** *Tel* (0153 94) 45613
13 College Road
Windermere LA23 1BU

"I cannot adequately express how much we valued Anthony and Aurea Greenhalgh's warmth and hospitality; they went out of their way to help us during our visit to the Lake District. The food is fresh beyond the ordinary." A tribute from California for this "aesthetically pleasing" Victorian terrace guest house, filled with antiques, paintings, flowers, books, local maps and guides, "and domestic comfort". It is in a quiet road near the rail and bus stations, and has an open view of green field and trees. The lake, half a mile away, is visible from some top rooms (one overlooks a carpark). The small bedrooms have flowery fabrics, Victorian quilts and duvets, pine furniture, home-made biscuits, hot water-bottles and TV. One has a bath; the others have a shower room – one is large, with a dressing area, the others are compact. Lavish breakfasts include dried fruit, home-made yogurt, bread and marmalade, and a huge choice of cooked dishes. Supper is at 6.45 with no choice – three courses in winter, two in summer: imaginative traditional English cooking, with an emphasis on fresh organic produce, and home-made puddings are a speciality; vegetarians are catered for. The wine list is "brief but good". (*Victoria Cooper; also Natalie Bown, Paul Knight*) No smoking.

Open All year. Dinner not served Wed, Sun.
Rooms 4 double.
Facilities Sitting room, dining room. Small front garden. Lake 15 mins. Unsuitable for ♿.
Location 2 mins' walk from centre; W of Main Road. Parking for 2 cars.
Restrictions No smoking. No children under 10. No dogs.
Credit cards Access, Amex, Visa.
Terms B&B £20–£27. Set dinner £12.50. Bargain breaks; Christmas, New Year breaks. 1-night bookings sometimes refused summer.

Cragwood *Tel* (0153 94) 88177
Ecclerigg, Windermere LA23 1LQ *Fax* (0153 94) 42145

Turn-of-the-century stone house, 2 miles NW of Windermere, on A591, by Brockhole National Park. 16-acre wooded grounds leading to the water, with boathouses and jetties; semi-formal gardens, plenty of wildlife, lovely views. "Ideal for a relaxing stay." Welcoming manager, Philip Hornby, "a man of many waistcoats". Panelling, fine plaster ceilings, open fires, leather chairs in public rooms. Many bedrooms overlook lake. Imaginative dinners: traditional/modern English/French cooking. Breakfast "as English ample or as health conscious as desired". 23 rooms, 4 on ground floor. No smoking: dining rooms, bedrooms. Access, Amex, Visa accepted. B&B £55; D,B&B £75. Set lunch £14.95, dinner £26 [1996]. More reports, please.

Gilpin Lodge *Tel* (0153 94) 88818
Crook Road *Fax* (0153 94) 88058
Windermere LA23 3NE

"John and Christine Cunliffe run this exceptional small hotel with dedication and professionalism," writes a former hotelier. "They are charming hosts, and their kindness to their guests permeates through their staff." This is seconded: "They are perfectionists. Hotel warmth in low season is a real test – they passed with flying colours. The food was wonderful, the ambience relaxing and friendly, but not exaggeratedly so; the decor interesting, but not distracting." This old white Lakeland house is set well back from the road in large grounds with gardens and woodland. It has "large, charming public rooms", with bright colours, stylish Chinese pottery, open fires and flowers. The bedrooms, many spacious and with a sitting area, have lovely views, fine textiles, antiques and original pictures; there are "superb bathrooms with Victorian fittings". Breakfast includes a generous Cumbrian spread. The restaurant, with a conservatory extension, is popular locally for its attractive ambience and "modern English/French cooking" by Christopher Davies, ex-*Connaught Hotel,* London (*qv*). There is plenty of choice on the fixed-price dinner menu; lunches are flexible, ranging from full meals in the dining room to light ones served in the lounge. (*John Donnithorne, Margaret Reid*)

Open All year.
Rooms 11 double.
Facilities 2 lounges, 3 dining rooms. 20-acre grounds: gardens, croquet. Lake Windermere 2 miles. Free access to nearby country club: swimming pool, sauna, squash, badminton, snooker. Only restaurant suitable for ♿.
Location On B5284 Kendal–Bowness. M6 exit 36.
Restrictions No smoking: restaurant, 1 lounge. No children under 7. No dogs.
Credit cards All major cards accepted.
Terms B&B: single £65–£85, double £80–£140; D,B&B: single £80–£100, double £110–£170. Light lunches; full alc lunch £20; set dinner £27.50. Off-season reductions; reductions for longer stays. Christmas, New Year packages.

Holbeck Ghyll — *Tel* (0153 94) 32375
Holbeck Lane — *Fax* (0153 94) 34743
Windermere LA23 1LU

David and Patricia Nicholson's large late-Victorian house is a former hunting lodge, rich in Art Nouveau features such as stained glass in the style of Charles Rennie Macintosh. It stands up a steep drive off the road to Ambleside, and has fine views of Lake Windermere and Langdale Fells. Streams run through the landscaped garden. Public areas have high ceilings, wood panelling, large pieces of antique furniture, mirrors, and good quality curtains and carpets. Bedrooms are similar in style; many are spacious. The "unpretentious good taste", the warm welcome, with tea in front of a log fire, and the "outstanding, cheerful service" by the all-female staff, are all admired. Dinner (English with a French influence) is "cooked with flair and imagination, with many choices"; vegetarians are well served. The wine list is extensive, with a good half bottle range, and reasonably priced. Good breakfasts too. The Nicholsons' labrador enjoys being taken for a walk. A small health spa was due to open in late 1996. More reports, please.

Open All year.
Rooms 3 suites, 11 double.
Facilities 2 lounges, bar area, billiard room, restaurant; function facilities; small health spa: sauna, gym equipment, etc. 7-acre grounds: streams, woods leading to lakeshore. Unsuitable for ♿.
Location 3 miles N of Windermere off road to Ambleside. Pass Brockhole Visitor Centre on left, right turn (Holbeck La) to Troutbeck. Drive ½ mile on left.
Restrictions No smoking in restaurant. No dogs in public rooms.

Credit cards All major cards accepted.
Terms D,B&B £65–£125. Alc lunch £15; set dinner (4–5 courses) £27.50–£30. 10% reduction for 5 or more nights. Off-season, Christmas, New Year breaks. 1-night bookings sometimes refused Sat.

Miller Howe
Rayrigg Road
Windermere LA23 1EY

Tel (0153 94) 42536
Fax (0153 94) 45664

César award in 1986

"I have never enjoyed a stay so much. We were welcomed into a warm, friendly atmosphere. The meals were faultless." "Truly individualistic." Accolades in 1996 for this famously pampering hotel, over which the renowned TV chef, John Tovey, has presided for 26 years, supported by a loyal staff. Perched above Windermere, it overlooks statue-dotted lawns sloping down to the water, and has magnificent views to the great peaks beyond. It is an Edwardian house, with a decor to match: "Its style is a throwback to the seventies, with gold-painted cherubs in the bathroom and a crown above the draped double bed." Bedrooms are "a delight, and unusually well-equipped: stereo, radio, excellent bedside lights, books, binoculars, Backgammon, Scrabble *and* a dictionary". Some have a terrace. The lounges are luxurious, with leather sofas and chairs. Dinner (7.30 for 8; four courses, no choice until dessert) is theatrically served in the two-tier dining room (recently revamped), which has lovely views; lights are dimmed as the meal begins. Chris Blaydes's cooking is modern, "with strong flavours and textures"; five small portions of vegetables accompany the main dish. "Lovely breakfast, with a huge choice, including home-made bread – very more-ish", is preceded by Buck's Fizz in the hall. Light lunches and traditional afternoon teas are available. Lakeland visitors can take advantage of a package consisting of a night each at *Miller Howe* and its two less pricey siblings, *Uplands*, Cartmel (*qv*), and the *Bay Horse Inn*, Ulverston. (*Thelma Wynn, John Rowlands, Minda Alexander*)

Open End Feb–early Dec.
Rooms 12 double.
Facilities 3 lounges, restaurant, conservatory; terrace. 4-acre grounds: landscaped garden. Walking, climbing, tennis, sailing, fishing, water sports nearby. Unsuitable for ♿.
Location On A592 N of Bowness. Lake-facing rooms quietest.
Restrictions No children under 8. No dogs in public rooms.
Credit cards All major cards accepted.
Terms (*Excluding 12½% service charge*) D,B&B: single £90–£100, double £130–£250. Set lunch £12.50, dinner £30. Off-season breaks, cookery courses Mar/Nov. 1-night bookings sometimes refused Sat.

WINTERINGHAM Humberside — Map 4

Winteringham Fields
Winteringham DN15 9PF

Tel (01724) 733096
Fax (01724) 733898

César award in 1996

"Lucky Humberside," say admiring southerners. And *Michelin* bestows a star and four red crossed spoon-and-forks on Germain and Annie Schwab's restaurant-with-rooms ("one of the best in the UK") at a crossroads in a village on the southern bank of the Humber estuary. "What distinguishes it from the norm is the sheer niceness of the Schwabs – he a shy genius in the kitchen, she, front of house, a powerhouse of enthusiasm. Their staff function with great charm and professionalism." "Outstanding food [French and Swiss provincial, with particularly enticing fish dishes using local catches]; impressive *maître d'*; the biggest cheese trolley I have ever seen. Noteworthy breakfast: fresh orange juice, home-baked breads and croissants, and home-made jams. A female travelling alone, I felt most welcome." The house is 16th-century, with exposed beams, low doorways and ceilings, oak panelling and period fireplaces, "cosseting sitting rooms in well-upholstered style", narrow corridors and staircase, Victorian furniture and *objets d'art*. The smart restaurant has large, elegantly dressed tables, ornamental pillars, and an open fire in an antique range. Bedrooms, some small, "are un-designerish, but done with care", and packed with extras – flowers, mineral water, magazines, fine toiletries. In summer, guests enjoy the conservatory and the small but pretty garden. One word of warning: "In winter there isn't a great deal to do in Winteringham, surrounded by mangel-wurzel fields; if you plan to arrive well before dinner you should take a good book." (*Pat and Jeremy Temple, David and Kate Wooff, Lynn Byers*)

Open All year, except Sun, bank holidays, 1st week Aug, 2 weeks Christmas. Lunch served Tues–Fri, dinner Mon–Sat.
Rooms 1 suite, 6 double. 3 in courtyard. 3 on ground floor.
Facilities Lounges, bar, restaurant, conservatory; private dining room. ½-acre grounds. Unsuitable for ♿.
Location Centre of village 4 miles SW of Humber Bridge.
Restrictions No smoking: restaurant, bedrooms. No children under 8, except babies. No dogs.
Credit cards Access, Amex, Visa.
Terms [1996] B&B: single £60–£75, double £80–£100. English breakfast £8. Set lunch £18, dinner £29 and £45; full alc £49.

WITHERSLACK Cumbria — Map 4

The Old Vicarage — *Tel* (0153 95) 52381
Church Road — *Fax* (0153 95) 52373
Witherslack
Grange-over-Sands LA11 6RS

"Civilised, friendly and efficient; the genius of the place is in the fact that the four partners work actively in the day-to-day management." "Altogether an excellent hotel. Well-pitched welcome, neither too effusive, nor too distant. You are left alone if you want this, but the owners welcome conversation if you feel like it." Plaudits this year for this mellow stone house in the unspoilt Winster valley, jointly owned by Roger and Jill Burrington-Brown and Irene and Stanley Reeve. It is set in mature gardens and woodland, with abundant flowers and wildlife. The main house is Victorian in style, with William Morris fabrics, padded armchairs, cane furniture; its bedrooms (some quite small) are in similar style. Larger bedrooms, with a modern decor, are in a "charming farmhouse-style building" in a damson orchard; they have sliding patio doors on to a private terrace, a generously stocked fridge, a CD player, and a well-equipped bathroom. Dinners (four courses with choices) are liked by some visitors – "genuine English cooking of the best kind, with regional dishes" – but others have been mildly disappointed in some of the main courses, and the fixed meal-times don't suit everyone. The "less-than-private *en suite* arrangements" in Room 5 are not to everyone's taste, though the owners insist: "Most people thoroughly enjoy the room, and it has a lovely outlook." (*WA, Dr and Mrs David Rampton; also Sybella Zisman, and others*) Some criticisms this year of housekeeping and breakfasts.

Open All year.
Rooms 14 double. 5 in Orchard House.
Facilities 2 lounges, 2 dining rooms. 5-acre grounds: gardens, tennis, woodlands. Lake Windermere, river fishing nearby. Unsuitable for ♿.
Location M6 exit 36. Take A590 Barrow-in-Furness road. Turn off to Witherslack, then 1st left past phone box. Hotel ½ mile on left.
Restrictions No smoking in dining rooms. No dogs in public rooms.
Credit cards Access, Amex, Visa.
Terms B&B: single £59–£79, double £89–£138; D,B&B: single £75–£90, double £135–£155. Set lunch £13.50, dinner £26.50. 2-day breaks; Christmas package. *V*

WITHYPOOL Somerset — Map 1

Westerclose Country House NEW/BUDGET — *Tel* (01643) 831302
Withypool TA24 7QR — *Fax* (01643) 831307

"A friendly hotel in a wonderful setting." This 1920s hunting lodge is set in paddocks and gardens above the river Barle, in the heart of Exmoor, amid "breathtaking scenery". It is a family concern, informally run by Mrs "Tinker" Foster, and her son, daughter and son-in-law. It specialises in walking weekends, offering "healthy but not too strenuous exercise", which are described as "very well organised" by our nominator. "Mrs Foster is an experienced guide. Packed lunches are brought to the half-way point. On return, there's a stupendous cream tea. Pre-dinner drinks are in a pretty conservatory. At 8 pm a wonderful three-course dinner is served by candlelight, with white starched tablecloths, impeccable napkins and tableware, and bone china. Everything cooked to order. The delicious breakfast includes stewed fruit, yogurt, choice of eggs, bacon, etc. Our bedroom was large, comfortable and very warm. It had a super bathroom with a corner bath. Dogs are welcomed (no charge)." The restaurant is open to non-residents. Cooking is a mixture of English and French, with the emphasis on fresh local ingredients; there's an interesting vegetarian menu (notice needed). The bedrooms vary in size and style; those on the second floor are "cottage-like". The hotel has a close relationship with riding stables in the village. (*Janice Carrera*)

Open 1 Mar–28 Dec.
Rooms 8 double, 2 single. No telephone.
Facilities Lounge/reception, lounge/library, conservatory/bar, restaurant. 9-acre grounds: garden, paddocks; stabling for visiting horses. Riding, fishing nearby. Only restaurant suitable for ♿.
Location N of Dulverton. Take B3223 for 7 miles. Withypool signposted on left. In village turn right at inn, follow hotel signs.
Restriction No smoking in restaurant.
Credit cards Access, Amex, Visa.
Terms B&B: single £29–£34, double £68–£85; D,B&B £46–£60. Set lunch £12.50, dinner (3- to 4-course) £19.75–£22; full alc £19. Reductions depending on length of stay. Walking weekends once a month. Christmas, Easter package. *V*

WOODSTOCK Oxfordshire **Map 2**

The Feathers
Market Street,
Woodstock OX20 1SX

Tel (01993) 812291
Fax (01993) 813158
E-mail http://www.oxlink.co.uk/woodstock/feathers

"Not too grand, but comfortably smart", this "lively, comfortable, well-run hotel", once a coaching inn, is in the centre of the showplace town, a few minutes' stroll from Blenheim Palace. It has expanded over the years into neighbouring buildings. "We enjoyed the way it rambles," wrote an American couple last year. "So many nooks and crannies and interesting places to get lost on the way to your room. The young staff are particularly friendly and enthusiastic." Though the *Feathers* has gone upmarket, it still fulfils the function of a town hotel: drinks and tea are served in the garden, and its bar lunches are popular with locals. It has low beamed ceilings and small lounges with log fires, interesting furniture, books, "and wonderful flower arrangements everywhere". Bedrooms vary in size; the best have a high ceiling and a modern bathroom. In the partly panelled restaurant, with its starched white linen tablecloths, crystal and candles, modern cooking by chef David Lewis, on a daily-changing menu, is "progressive English, with Mediterranean and Californian influences". It is generally thought "excellent and imaginative", but pricey owing to all the extras, including a "suggested gratuity" of 15% – which the hotel says "no one need pay". Children are welcome. (*BK, endorsed this year by Hana Dobias; also Good Pub Guide*) *Bishopstrow House*, Warminster (*qv*), is now under the same management.

Open All year. Bar meals not served weekend evenings.
Rooms 3 suites, 13 double, 1 single.
Facilities 2 lounges, bar, restaurant; courtyard. ¼-acre garden. Unsuitable for ♿.
Location Central (generally quiet at night). Street parking; public carpark nearby.
Restriction No dogs in bar, restaurant.
Credit cards All major cards accepted.
Terms B&B: single £78–£98, double £99–£150, suite £185–£195. Bar meals. 2–3-course lunch/dinner £17.50–£22.50; full alc from £25. 2-day breaks.

WOOLTON HILL Berkshire **Map 2**

Hollington House
Woolton Hill
nr Newbury RG20 9XA

Tel (01635) 255100
Fax (01635) 255075

An Edwardian house in rolling Berkshire countryside, "sybaritic and luxurious", and informally run by Australian owners, John and Penny Guy. It is set in large wooded grounds with gardens designed by Gertrude Jekyll. "From the lovely terrace which runs the length of the house you can see neither buildings, pylons nor poles, nor can you hear traffic." Inside are high-ceilinged, large-windowed lounges, with fires in cold weather, a large panelled hall, an imposing wooden staircase and an interesting mixture of paintings and artefacts. Bedrooms are spacious and elegant. "The owners are charming and unassuming," writes one satisfied customer. "Flower arrangements, cleanliness, attention to detail with unobtrusive service, made for much contentment. Our large bedroom had flowers, fruit, mineral water, books, fine views, a superb bathroom with spa bath, turned-back beds at night, and faultless room service breakfast." In the splendid oak-panelled dining room kangaroo is sometimes served. Christopher Lightfoot's cooking, served with much dome-lifting, is found pretentious by some. The "amazing" wine list is strong on the New World. A pianist plays loudly on Saturday night. Children are welcomed.

Open All year.
Rooms 1 suite, 19 double.
Facilities Lift, ramp. Lounge, 2 dining rooms; 4 meeting rooms; terrace. 25-acre grounds: swimming pool, croquet. River Kennet nearby: fishing.
Location 3 miles SW of Newbury, off A343 to Andover. Turn right to Woolton Hill; hotel next to Hollington Herb Garden.
Restrictions No smoking in 2 bedrooms. No dogs (kennels nearby).
Credit cards All major cards accepted.
Terms [1996] B&B: single £90–£165, double £130–£225, suite £225–£375. Set lunch (2-course) £14.50, dinner (3-course) £30; full alc £45. Children under 7 accommodated free in parents' room. 2-day unwinder break: D,B&B from £90. Christmas, New Year packages.

WORCESTER Hereford and Worcester — Map 3

Diglis House NEW — *Tel* (01905) 353518
Severn Street — *Fax* (01905) 767772
Worcester WR1 2NF

In lovely quiet position near cathedral, on bank of river Severn, 10 mins' walk from centre: 18th-century house, recently refurbished by "charming, stylish" owner, Julia Seymour. Mostly good modern British cooking with fresh ingredients "and lots of cream", served in 2 dining rooms (1 a riverside conservatory). Friendly, if casual atmosphere. Some shortcomings, perhaps teething troubles: service can be amateurish, housekeeping not perfect; piped music in public rooms all day. 11 bedrooms; new building with 12 more (including some with ♿ access) planned for 1997. ½-acre garden. Carpark. No smoking: dining rooms, some bedrooms. No dogs where food is served. Access, Amex, Visa accepted. B&B £36–£60. Light lunch c. *£10; full alc £25–£35 [1996].*

WORFIELD Shropshire — Map 3

The Old Vicarage — *Tel* (01746) 716497
Worfield, Bridgnorth WV15 5JZ — *Fax* (01746) 716552

Peter and Christine Iles's Edwardian parsonage is set amid lovely countryside on the edge of a peaceful village near the Ironbridge Gorge. Its spacious public rooms are "furnished with unpretentious taste: a mixture of antiques and repro, with handsome flower arrangements, and remarkable collections of watercolours and antique clocks". There's a "nice conservatory" for drinks and coffee. Bedrooms are complete with fruit, sweets, mini-bar and books. The best, in a coach house, have a whirlpool bath. Imaginative four-course meals, cooked by John Williams, earn a red "Meals" in *Michelin*. "A shining example of what a small country house hotel should be," is a lawyer's verdict. "Excellent food gracefully served in a small, smart dining room. Lovely bedroom with french windows leading on to a private garden, where we were happily served dinner on warm evenings. Breakfasts unsurpassed." Other visitors concur: "Excellent atmosphere; an oasis in this area. They are happy to provide dishes not on the menu." "Care is the hallmark of the Iles and their local staff. One of the most pleasant away-from-home settings you could find." (*Anthony Berry, J Sparks, Andrew and Mary Barclay; also BA Tycer, Capt. JP Gould, and others*) Some have found the place "cluttered"; more than one visitor has thought the wines expensive (but the long list of half bottles is appreciated); and – a recurring grouse – "extras make the bill mount up".

Open All year, except Christmas, New Year; restaurant closed for lunch, except Sun.
Rooms 1 suite (with facilities for ♿), 13 double (4, with jacuzzi, in coach house).
Facilities Lounge/bar, restaurant, conservatory. 2-acre grounds.
Location 4 miles E of Bridgnorth. 1 mile from A454, by cricket ground.
Restrictions No smoking: restaurant, bedrooms. No dogs in public rooms.
Credit cards All major cards accepted.
Terms [1996] B&B: single £67.50–£87.50, double £95–£130; D,B&B double £143–£190. Set lunch (Sun) £15.50, dinner £24–£29.50. Special breaks, including entrance to Ironbridge Gorge Museum.

YORK North Yorkshire — Map 4

The Grange — *Tel* (01904) 644744
Clifton, York YO3 6AA — *Fax* (01904) 612453

"A lovely, well-kept hotel within walking distance of the minster. Our room was large and luxurious, with all the amenities one could want. Service and food at dinner were impeccable." (*Dr and Mrs Viola*) Jeremy Cassel's Regency town house has a striking period decor, "more private house than hotel", with panelling, smart wallpapers, family portraits, and open fires in the large drawing room and morning room. There's a grand original staircase. The bedrooms have fine fabrics, antiques, good lighting and a smart bathroom, but some are small and on the dark side; numbers 4 and 5, by Reception, are said to be noisy, and the latter "has a poor outlook"; number 20, with a four-poster, is quiet and comfortable. The restaurant, hung with pictures of racehorses, serves traditional English and French cooking by Christopher Falcus. Good food is also available in the brasserie in a vaulted cellar, open from 10 am until late, and a seafood bar recently opened. Breakfast has been thought excellent in the past, but 1996 visitors were dismayed: "It must have been served by a walk-in crew. Items ordered arrived out of sequence and on a delayed schedule. The only glitch in an otherwise noteworthy establishment." The hotel is on a busy road, but front rooms are double-glazed. We'd like further reports, please.

Open All year. Restaurant closed Sun evening; brasserie closed Sun lunch; seafood bar closed Sat/Sun.
Rooms 1 suite, 26 double, 3 single. Some on ground floor.
Facilities Ramps. Drawing room, morning room, library, restaurant, brasserie, seafood bar; conference facilities.
Location 500 yds from city wall, on A19 N to Thirsk (front rooms double-glazed). Carpark.
Restriction No dogs in public rooms.
Credit cards All major cards accepted.

Terms B&B: single £95, double £105–£155, suite £185. Brasserie dishes from £3.50. Seafood bar: set lunch/dinner £10; restaurant: set lunch £14, dinner £23. 2-day breaks; Christmas, New Year breaks.

Hobbits BUDGET *Tel* (01904) 624538 and 642926
9 St Peter's Grove *Fax* (01904) 651765
Clifton, York YO3 6AQ

"It is many years since I stayed here; I found it just as good as ever. Mrs Miller was just as friendly, the bedroom as cosy and immaculate. Delicious breakfast: muesli, yogurt, home-produced stewed gooseberries, home-made jams and good coffee. Easy parking in cul de sac. Excellent value." Praise this year for Rosemary Miller's civilised B&B, an Edwardian house in a quiet, leafy street 15 minutes' walk from the city centre. It is the Millers' family home, complete with children and cats, and a collection of jugs. The spacious bedrooms (some, reached by a winding staircase, are in an attic) have a well-stocked fridge, TV, a writing table, books, etc. Breakfast (full English or vegetarian) is generally served communally, but there is a separate small table for those wanting privacy. (*Caroline Currie; also Barbara Hill*)

Open All year, except Christmas.
Rooms 4 double, 2 single.
Facilities 2 lounges, breakfast room. Small garden. River Ouse 5 mins: fishing, boating. Unsuitable for ♿.
Location Entering York from N on A19, turn left just before footbridge in Clifton. Private and street parking.
Restrictions No smoking: dining room, bedrooms. No dogs in public rooms.
Credit cards Access, Diners, Visa.
Terms B&B £25–£27. *V*

Middlethorpe Hall *Tel* (01904) 641241
Bishopthorpe Road *Fax* (01904) 620176
York YO2 1QB

"Lived up to all the good things we had heard. The whole ambience is highly civilised and welcoming. Our courtyard room was very attractive, with no sound from the main road. The staff were professional, and seemed to enjoy their work. Dinner was excellent and well presented. Altogether a happy experience." "It was as if our names had been stamped on our forehead when registered – we were greeted by name by all the staff throughout our stay, which made us feel very welcome." "Expert porterage and room service, and very good housekeeping." Praise this year and last for this noble Grade II listed William III house. Once the home of the diarist Lady Mary Wortley Montagu, it has imposing façades, and stately public rooms filled with fine furniture, paintings and *objets d'art*. It stands in magnificent large grounds with parkland, a walled garden and a small lake, near York racecourse. Some bedrooms are small, "but pleasant"; the best ones are "thrillingly large, with every creature comfort", including a large sitting room and a walk-in wardrobe, "but not a hint of a designer's hand"; at least one has two bathrooms. In the panelled dining rooms overlooking the garden, the cooking by chef Andrew Wood is traditional English. (*Andrew and Meg Davies, Frances Wright*) The midweek breaks are considered excellent value. One caveat: "It is not geared to teenagers and younger folk." Some walls are thin.

Open All year. Restaurant open for residents only Christmas Day.
Rooms 7 suites, 19 double, 4 single. 19 in courtyard.
Facilities Drawing room, library, bar, restaurant; private dining rooms, function facilities. 26-acre grounds: croquet, walled garden, lake. Racecourse, golf nearby. Unsuitable for ♿.
Location 1½ miles S of city, by racecourse.
Restrictions No smoking in restaurant. No children under 8. No dogs.
Credit cards Access, Amex, Visa.
Terms (until 31.3.97) Rooms: single £89–£108, double £125–£139, suite £160–£199. Breakfast: continental £7.95, English £10.50. Set lunch £12.50, dinner £25.95; full alc £42.95. Champagne breaks Nov–Apr; 2-day summer breaks; Christmas, New Year packages.

Mount Royale *Tel* (01904) 628856
The Mount *Fax* (01904) 611171
York YO2 2DA

A traditional hotel, Gothic in appearance but mainly William IV, with modern extensions and a comfortable decor. It is near the racecourse and Micklegate Bar and three-quarters of a mile from the minster. Run by two generations of the Oxtoby family with a friendly, long-serving staff (friendly cats and dogs, too), it is popular for its un-hotel-like atmosphere and pretty garden (with swimming pool). Best bedrooms, with sitting area and private veranda, are in the garden annexe, connected to the main building by a covered walkway filled with orange trees, figs, and sub-tropical plants. Bathrooms are "stocked with useful goodies". Some rooms in the main house are quite small and old-fashioned; front ones get traffic noise (mitigated by triple-glazing); back ones overlook the garden. Public rooms have antiques and paintings; there is a full-sized snooker table. Traditional English dinners are well prepared and generous. Substantial breakfasts include fresh fruit, fish cakes and crumpets. (*Endorsed this year by PJG Ransom*)

Open All year, except 24–31 Dec.
Rooms 6 suites, 16 double, 1 single. 4 in garden annexe. Some on ground floor.
Facilities 2 lounges (pianist 6 nights a week), bar, restaurant, conservatory; meeting room. 1½-acre grounds: swimming pool (heated May–Oct). Unsuitable for ♿.
Location Past racecourse on A1036 from Tadcaster (front rooms triple-glazed), at junction with Albemarle Rd. Parking.
Credit cards All major cards accepted.
Terms B&B: single £67.50–£85, double £80–£100, suite £90–£130. Full alc £35. 2-day breaks.

Open All year. [illegible]
Rooms [illegible]
Facilities [illegible] walled garden, [illegible]
[illegible]
Location [illegible]
Restrictions [illegible]
Credit cards [illegible] Visa.
Terms [illegible]

Mount Royale Tel (0904) 628856
The Mount Fax (0904) 611171
York YO2 2DA

A traditional [illegible], with modern extensions and a comfortable decor [illegible] by two generations of the [illegible] family [illegible] for its [illegible] swimming pool [illegible] in the garden [illegible] the main building [illegible] sub-tropical plants, but rooms are [illegible] old-fashioned [illegible] traffic noise [illegible] the garden [illegible] traditional English [illegible] the cakes and [illegible]

Open All year except [illegible] Dec.
Rooms [illegible]
Facilities [illegible] swimming pool [illegible]
Location [illegible]
Credit cards All major cards accepted.
Terms [illegible]

Wales

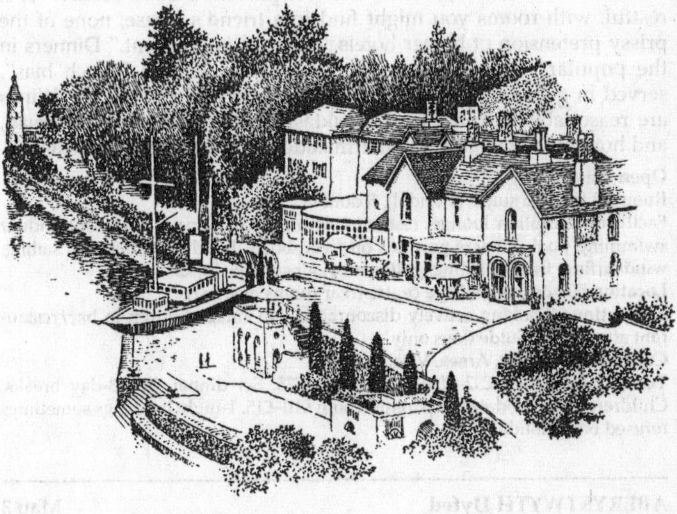

Hotel Portmeirion, Portmeirion

ABERSOCH Gwynedd **Map 3**

Porth Tocyn Hotel *Tel* (01758) 713303
Abersoch LL53 7BU *Fax* (01758) 713538

Traditional hotel, in "perfect setting" on headland 2½ miles S of Abersoch; glorious views of Cardigan Bay and Snowdonia. 20-acre farm; garden, tennis, swimming pool (heated May–Sept); sea 5 mins' walk: safe bathing. Heritage Coastal Walk, water sports, fishing, golf, riding nearby. Popular with, but not exclusively for, families (children's needs discussed at time of booking). Ebullient, ubiquitous host, Nick Fletcher-Brewer, who some find "mercurial"; attentive staff. "Food of the highest quality"; flexible menus; buffet lunch Sun; light lunches weekdays. 17 rooms, with some lounges interconnecting; 3 on ground floor; some in 1960s extension (thinnish walls); many recently renovated. Traditional decor, with country antiques. Some criticisms this year of upkeep and management. Open 1 week before Easter–mid-Nov. No children under 7 in restaurant at night. No dogs in public rooms. Access, Visa accepted. B&B: single £43.50–£56.50, double £67–£104. English breakfast

£4. Sun lunch £16 (£7.50 for children), dinner: 2–5 courses £20–£26.75 [1996]. More reports, please.

Riverside Hotel BUDGET Tel (01758) 712419
Abersoch LL53 7HW Fax (01758) 712671

John and Wendy Bakewell, owner/chefs, have been 28 years at their unpretentious hotel and restaurant in an agreeable position overlooking the harbour of this popular yachting village. Its pretty garden on the river Soch is popular with guests who enjoy "messing about on the river" (there are two rowing boats and a canoe for their use) or watching the abundant wildlife. There is a heated swimming pool in a conservatory. The hotel welcomes families, and has good facilities for children. "A rare find," wrote one well-travelled *Guide* reader. "It is restful, with rooms you might find in a friend's house; none of the prissy pretension of bigger hotels. The food is excellent." Dinners in the popular restaurant are "English with a definite French bias", served in generous portions; vegetarians are well catered for. Wines are reasonably priced. Good breakfasts include home-baked bread, and home-made yogurt and marmalade. (*SL*) More reports, please.

Open Mar–Nov.
Rooms 2 triple, 2 suites (1 bridal), 8 double.
Facilities Reception lounge, residents' lounge, bar lounge, restaurant; indoor swimming pool. 1¼-acre grounds on river, boats. Beach, safe bathing, sailing, windsurfing, fishing, riding, golf nearby. Unsuitable for ♿.
Location 50 yds from village centre (rear rooms quietest).
Restrictions Smoking actively discouraged. No small children in bar/restaurant after 6 pm. Guide dogs only.
Credit cards Access, Amex, Visa.
Terms [1996] B&B £32–£54; D,B&B £53–£75. Set dinner £22. 3-day breaks. Children accommodated in parents' room £10–£15. 1-night bookings sometimes refused bank holidays.

ABERYSTWYTH Dyfed Map 3

Conrah Country House NEW Tel (01970) 617941
Chancery, Aberystwyth SY23 4DF Fax (01970) 624546

Fine country house with 20th-century extensions, up long drive in 22-acre rolling grounds with woods, fine views. Beautiful gardens; vegetables home grown for "memorable" dinners (traditional/modern cooking), with fine cheeseboard. Excellent breakfast, with Welsh delicacies. Impeccable service. 3 attractive lounges. 20 bedrooms of varying size: 11, traditional, in main house; more modern ones, on ground level, round courtyard. Indoor swimming pool, sauna; croquet, table tennis. 3½ miles S of Aberystwyth on A487 coast road. River ½ mile, sea 3½ miles. Closed Christmas week. Unsuitable for ♿. No smoking in restaurant. No children under 5. No dogs. All major credit cards accepted. B&B: single £59, double £88–£108; D,B&B (min. 2 nights): single £76, double £116–£136. Set Sun lunch £15.75, dinner £25.50 [1996]. More reports, please.

> We need feedback on all hotels: big and small, far and near, famous and first-timers.

BRECHFA Dyfed Map 3

Ty-Mawr NEW *Tel* (01267) 202332
Brechfa, nr Carmarthen SA32 7RA *Fax* (01267) 202437

Beryl and Dick Tudhope's small 16th-century house, "beautifully restored and maintained", has a lovely setting by a river in an unspoilt village on the edge of Brechfa forest. The interior is light, with low ceilings, stone walls, oak beams, tiled floors and a log fire in the large sitting room. Bedrooms, some quite small, have flowery wallpaper, pretty fabrics, books, guides, magazines, and a good bathroom. In a candlelit restaurant with well-spaced tables and lace cloths over pastel linen, Mrs Tudhope produces "interesting and delicious" but unpretentious classical and regional dishes, using local produce, particularly fish, lamb, beef and cheeses, and home-grown herbs. Home-baked breads are a speciality; puddings are "refreshing, not too heavy". The traditional breakfast includes porridge, kipper, and smoked haddock. The gregarious Mr Tudhope takes a great interest in his guests. "Very helpful hosts," report recent visitors. "The food was excellent, the wines well chosen and well priced, and the smallness of the place added to the pleasure. The other guests were interesting and international. The setting in the Cardiganshire hills was spectacular." (*Dr and Mrs PM Tattersall, and others*) *Ty-Mawr* was omitted from last year's *Guide* because the Tudhopes were thinking of selling, but they plan to remain for the foreseeable future.

Open All year, except Christmas, 1st week Nov, 1st week Dec, last 2 weeks Jan.
Rooms 4 double, 1 single. No telephone/TV.
Facilities Lounge, bar, restaurant; function facilities. 1-acre riverside garden. Fishing, walking, riding, golf, sandy beaches nearby. Unsuitable for ♿.
Location In village on B4310, 13 miles NE of Carmarthen (turn off A40 at Nantgaredig).
Restrictions No smoking: dining room, bedrooms. No dogs in public rooms.
Credit cards Access, Amex, Visa.
Terms B&B: single £52, double £84; D,B&B: single £68, double £116, Set lunch (Sun) £12.50, dinner £19–£23. Bread-making courses June, Nov.

BUILTH WELLS Powys Map 3

Dol-llyn-wydd NEW/BUDGET *Tel* (01982) 553660
Builth Wells, LD2 3RZ

17th-century farmhouse B&B, in lovely countryside 1 mile S of Builth Wells off B4520; you can walk on to the hills from the door. "Wonderfully welcoming hostess, Biddy Williams; charming decor; plentiful, excellent home-cooked evening meal by arrangement." 4 bedrooms, 1 with bath en suite; *showers available. 20-acre grounds. Fishing, golf, tennis, riding nearby. Open Mar–Dec. No smoking. No children under 14. No dogs in house. Credit cards not accepted. B&B £15–£20; D,B&B £25–£30.*

We quote either prices per room, or else the range of prices per person – the lowest is likely to be for one person sharing a double room out of season, the highest for a single room in the high season.

CRICKHOWELL Powys — Map 3

Gliffaes — *Tel* (01874) 730371
Crickhowell NP8 1RH — *Fax* (01874) 730463

"Goes from strength to strength. Atmosphere relaxed and happy. We have spent 126 nights here in the past 12 years, including six Christmases." So writes a devotee of this imposing italianate mansion, which the Brabner family have run since 1948. It has a beautiful setting in well-tended gardens, above the lovely Usk valley. There's excellent fishing (two stretches of the Usk). The decor is comfortable and traditional – "no hint of interior design". Plenty of places for sitting: a large lounge, a pretty conservatory and a terrace overlooking the valley. The hotel is informally run, but service is friendly and generally efficient, and staff are available when needed. Mealtimes are elastic. Mark Coulton took over the kitchen in mid-1995: "The food is delicious: light first courses, good fish dishes, pretty, delicately flavoured desserts. Breakfast good too, with large self-service buffet and freshly cooked eggs, kippers, etc." Bar lunches range from light snacks, served wherever you want, to a substantial meal, and "you need to go into training for that magnificent institution, the *Gliffaes* tea, laid out in all its glory each afternoon". Bedrooms are priced according to view. (*Col. and Mrs AJW Harvey; A and CR, J and JW, and others*) Housekeeping can be "hit and miss"; one visitor complained about reception; and "because tea at breakfast and in the afternoon is self-help, it tends to get stewed, but they will make a special pot if you ask".

Open All year.
Rooms 22 double. 3 in lodge ¼ mile away.
Facilities 2 sitting rooms, TV room, billiard room, conservatory bar, dining room. 34-acre grounds: gardens, tennis, croquet, putting, fishing. Unsuitable for ♿.
Location 2½ miles W of Crickhowell, 1 mile off A40; follow *Gliffaes* sign.
Restrictions No smoking in dining room. Dogs in lodge only.
Credit cards All major cards accepted.
Terms B&B: single £36, double £72–£107; D,B&B: single £56.50, double £113–£148; full board (2–6 nights): single £66, double £132–£168. Bar lunches. Set Sun lunch £19.75, dinner £21; full alc £26.50. 2–6-night breaks off season; history, cookery courses. *V*

EGLWYSFACH Powys — Map 3

Ynyshir Hall — *Tel* (01654) 781209
Eglwysfach — *Fax* (01654) 781366
nr Machynlleth SY20 8TA

César award: the prince of Welsh hotels

"A gorgeous house with much to delight the eye and cosset the senses: beautiful furniture, oriental rugs, *objets d'art*, spectacular flower arrangements, bold paintings by the owner, Rob Reen. Walking into the dining room is like entering an art gallery of colour and light. Our bedroom had everything we could wish for; its bathroom was yellow and blue, with white clouds floating across the ceiling. The food was of the same high standard, served by candlelight, with gleaming silver and crystal and snow-white china: delicate sauces, ambrosial desserts. In four days we never heard noises of housework. A haven of peace and beauty." "The welcome struck just the right balance: friendly but not oppressive. Food copious and generally good. Extensive wine list, acceptably priced, with good half bottles. Not cheap, but worth it." "The owners are charm itself." Encomiums in 1996 for Rob and Joan Reen's white Georgian longhouse. It has an idyllic setting in large landscaped gardens, surrounded by the 365 acres of the Ynyshir bird reserve, on the southern shore of the Dyfi estuary. Cooking by the young chefs Ian White and Chris Dawson, is modern, using Welsh-produce. Breakfast is a lavish affair, "with delicious home-made marmalade and jams"; afternoon tea comes with home-made scones and jams. (*Ruth West, LV Boobyer, Prof. R Wise; also John and June Astle-Fletcher*)

Open All year.
Rooms 4 suites, 4 double. 1 on ground floor.
Facilities Drawing room, bar lounge, breakfast room, restaurant. 14-acre landscaped gardens in 365-acre bird reserve. Near Dyfi estuary and beaches; sailing, fishing, riding, golf nearby.
Location Just W of A487, 6 miles SW of Machynlleth, 11 miles NE of Aberystwyth.
Restrictions No smoking: drawing room, restaurant, 3 bedrooms. No children under 9. Dogs by arrangement, not in public areas.
Credit cards All major cards accepted.
Terms B&B: single £80–£100, double £110–£150, suite £140–£160. Set lunch from £20, dinner from £30. 1-night bookings sometimes refused high season weekends. Gourmet, bird-watching weekends; Christmas, New Year packages.

FISHGUARD Dyfed — Map 3

Gilfach Goch Farmhouse NEW/BUDGET *Tel/Fax* (01348) 873871
Fishguard SA65 9SR

Simple guest house in Pembrokeshire Coast National Park 2 miles E of Fishguard, S of A487. 18th-century stone farmhouse with original features (beams, inglenook), but modern comforts. In 10-acre grounds with sheep, donkeys, lovely views. Children warmly welcomed. Run by husband-and-wife team, the Devonalds; she cooks, he waits at table. "High standards all round." 6 immaculate bedrooms with TV and good bathroom. Wholesome evening meals (no choice), except Wed. Open Mar–end Oct. No smoking. No dogs. Credit cards not accepted. B&B £22–£24; D,B&B £34–£36. Children half-price in parents' room. 1-night bookings refused July, Aug.

GLYNARTHEN Dyfed — Map 3

Penbontbren Farm BUDGET *Tel* (01239) 810248
Glynarthen, nr Cardigan SA44 6PE *Fax* (01239) 811129

A farmhouse hotel "authentically Welsh", in a lovely, peaceful setting amid fields with grazing sheep. Barrie and Nan Humphreys and their staff speak Welsh; the menus and information are bilingual. The farm has a little countryside museum and a nature trail. The sea and the coastal path are two-and-a-half miles away. Harp music accompanies meals in the locally popular restaurant, which has friendly waitresses and well-spaced tables. It serves reasonably priced dinners in generous portions, on a *carte* with regional specialities and high-cholesterol puddings. Breakfast includes Glamorgan sausages; there's an "appetising" buffet lunch. "Compact but pretty" bedrooms with pine furniture are in outbuildings around the farmyard. The conversion is in no way luxurious, "but all the important elements are there: good lighting, TV, rough but decent-sized towels in spotless bathroom, and generous touches such as sherry, biscuits and fudge". However, service can be casual. One couple, visiting in early 1996, received an off-hand welcome, and were critical of bedroom decor and cooking, and parents with young children felt "there was much emphasis on our leaving the restaurant before the adults arrived". More reports, please.

Open All year, except Christmas.
Rooms 10 double. 2 on ground floor, suitable for ♿.
Facilities Ramp. 2 lounges, games room, bar, restaurant. 90-acre farm: nature trail. Coast 10 mins' drive.
Location Travelling S from Aberystwyth on A487, 1st left at hotel sign, just S of Sarnau; N from Cardigan, 2nd right, 1 mile N of Tan-y-groes.
Restrictions No smoking in restaurant. No dogs in public rooms, unattended in bedrooms.
Credit cards All major cards accepted.
Terms B&B £34–£43; D,B&B £46–£55. Bar lunches £6–£8; full alc £20–£70. 2-night breaks; weekly rates.

GOVILON Gwent — Map 3

Llanwenarth House — *Tel* (01873) 830289
Govilon, nr Abergavenny NP7 9SF — *Fax* (01873) 832199

A fine tall-windowed old manor house, built of warm grey limestone, in the Brecon Beacons National Park. Its grounds, "with well-loved horses", overlook the Usk valley, and border the Brecon and Monmouthshire canal, where boats may be hired by the day – an agreeable way to explore the area. This is the family home of Bruce and Amanda Wetherill, their children and their lurcher dogs. "Bruce and Amanda make a great team. He provides the charm and chat, she the brilliant food. They know the area well, and gave us better advice than the AA's local guide. The bedroom was spacious, and its bathroom adequate, though it lacked a shower." "I have never felt so welcome in a hotel. We were treated like friends and encouraged to relax completely." Pre-dinner drinks are served in the Georgian drawing room. Dinner, by candlelight, is available five days a week, by arrangement. Many of the vegetables are home-grown, so is much of the fruit; honey comes from hives in the orchard. (*WR Dellridge, Lucy Booth*)

Open Late Feb–mid-Jan. No lunches; dinner served 5 nights a week.
Rooms 5 double, 1 on ground floor. No telephone.
Facilities Drawing room, dining room. 10-acre grounds: croquet, canal (boat hire). Fishing, golf, foxhunting nearby.
Location 2 miles W of Abergavenny. From A40 take A465 to Merthyr Tydfil; follow first sign to Govilon; hotel drive ½ mile on right.
Restrictions Smoking banned in dining room, discouraged in bedrooms. No children under 10. No dogs in public rooms.
Credit cards None accepted.
Terms B&B £32–£52. Set dinner £22.50.

> The "New" label is used both for debutants and for hotels which have been readmitted to the *Guide* this year.

KNIGHTON Powys — Map 3

Milebrook House BUDGET — *Tel* (01547) 528632
Milebrook, Knighton LD7 1LT — *Fax* (01547) 520509

18th-century grey stone house in hamlet in Teme valley, 2 miles E of Knighton on A4113, in designated area of outstanding natural beauty. Pretty 3-acre garden leading to river; croquet, fly fishing. Homely feeling; friendly, uneffusive owners, Rodney and Beryl Marsden. 10 pleasant bedrooms; 2 on ground floor. Ramps. Traditional, above-average cooking served in small, smart dining room (closed for lunch Mon). Bar meals too. No smoking: dining room, some bedrooms. No children under 5. No dogs. Access, Amex, Visa accepted. B&B: single £44.80, double £66; D,B&B: single £61.75, double £99.90 [1996]. More reports, please. *V*

LLANDDEINIOLEN Gwynedd — Map 3

Ty'n Rhos BUDGET — *Tel* (01248) 670489
Llanddeiniolen — *Fax* (01248) 670079
nr Caernarfon LL55 3AE

Nigel and Linda Kettle's former farmhouse, "an excellent establishment", is in a "marvellous rural setting" in the plain between Snowdonia and the sea. It has spectacular views towards the beaches of Anglesey and the Menai Strait, two ponds with ducks, an attendant sheepdog, and a "cosy, though not cottagey, atmosphere, with plenty of light". There is a large lounge, with antiques, books and games. The pretty, unfussy bedrooms have pine furniture, fresh flowers, and a hospitality tray. Two, on the ground floor, have a sliding picture window and patio overlooking the garden, and the fields beyond; three new ones are in converted outhouses. In the restaurant, open to the public, local produce and home-grown vegetables are used for the traditional/modern cooking on set menus and a *carte*, priced according to the main course. The cooking has been taken over by Carys Davies, and we'd be grateful for reports on her work. There are kippers and kedgeree for breakfast as well as the usual eggs-and-bacon-plus, and excellent home-made preserves; nothing packaged. The farm, with its carp lake, is separately operated, but open to *Ty'n Rhos*'s guests. (*John and Joan Wyatt, and others*)

Open 1 Jan–23 Dec, except 1 week in Jan. Restaurant closed midday; also Sun/Mon to non-residents.
Rooms 11 double, 3 single. 3 in outhouses. Some on ground floor.
Facilities 2 lounges, restaurant/bar. 72-acre farm: 1-acre garden, carp lake. Sea 9 miles.
Location In hamlet of Seion, off B4366, 1½ miles N of Bethel.
Restrictions No smoking: restaurant, bedrooms. No children under 5. No dogs in house.
Credit cards Access, Amex, Visa.
Terms [1996] B&B: £40–£45, double £60–£80. Set dinner £19; full alc £29. *V*

> Important reminder: terms printed must be regarded as no more than a rough guide to the size of the bill to be expected at the end of your stay. For latest tariffs, it is vital that you check when booking.

LLANDRILLO Clwyd **Map 3**

Tyddyn Llan
Llandrillo, nr Corwen LL21 0ST

Tel (01490) 440264
Fax (01490) 440414

César award in 1989

A grey stone Georgian country house, tranquilly set in the Vale of Edeyrnion. There's lovely walking in the unspoilt surrounding Berwyn mountains; guided walks can be arranged. Excellent fishing, too, particularly for grayling, on the hotel's four-mile stretch of the river Dee. Eric, the ghillie, is a delightful man "who really adds to the pleasure of a day out on the water". The hotel is run "competently and without gush" by the hard-working owners, Peter and Bridget Kindred. It is "laid back in the best sense. Peter Kindred has a delightful dry wit and a considerable artistic talent; his paintings are everywhere. The decor is in quiet good taste, with antique and period furniture, and clever use of colour." The pretty, high-ceilinged restaurant, popular with outside diners, has "charming" waitresses. A new chef arrived in spring 1996. "Excellent," says our first report on the new cuisine. There is a good, reasonably priced wine list. Breakfast is served until 10 am. All bedrooms now have TV. (*Braham Murray, DN, CR, and others*)

Open All year.
Rooms 10 double.
Facilities Lounge, bar, restaurant. 3½-acre grounds: water garden, croquet. River fishing (ghillie available), riding, golf, sailing, walking nearby. Only restaurant suitable for ♿.
Location Through Corwen on A5; take B4401 to Llandrillo.
Restrictions No smoking in restaurant. No dogs in public rooms.
Credit cards All major cards accepted.
Terms B&B: single £46–£63.50; double £92–£102; D,B&B: single £60–£91, double £120–£155. Set lunch £13, dinner £25. Special interest weekends; off-season breaks. Christmas, New Year house parties.

LLANDUDNO Gwynedd **Map 3**

Bodysgallen Hall
Llanrhos, Llandudno LL30 1RS

Tel (01492) 584466
Fax (01492) 582519

César award in 1988

A carefully restored Grade I listed house, mainly 17th-century with skilful later additions, in parkland on a hillside outside the agreeable Victorian seaside resort. Its 17th-century knot garden and 18th-century walled rose garden are much admired, as is its fine interior, with panelled rooms, splendid fireplaces, and stone mullioned windows. It has "an excellent manager, Nigel Taylor, and a super staff". Most bedrooms are spacious and elegant. Some are in cottages grouped around a secluded courtyard (seven new ones this year). "Ours," wrote one enthusiastic visitor, "was a lovely assemblage of two bedrooms, two bathrooms and sitting room with the best tea- and coffee-making facility we have encountered. Our other abiding memory is of the smell of burning logs which greeted us when we entered the hall." Another admired the "relaxing atmosphere (so many nooks and crannies, you could never feel exposed)". Chef Michael Penny's menus, served in the elegant dining room, include traditional and modern dishes, and a five-course gourmet dinner. One complaint about a bathroom: "It was like a closet; is this what they mean by 'Edwardian'?" A leisure centre, with 54-foot swimming pool, sauna, solarium, etc, opened in mid-1996. More reports, please.

Open All year.
Rooms 16 cottage suites, 17 double, 2 single.
Facilities Hall, drawing room, library, bar, 2 dining rooms; conference centre. 250-acre parkland: gardens, tennis, croquet; spa: swimming pool, gym, sauna, beauty treatment, club room (light meals and drinks). Riding, shooting, fishing, sandy beaches nearby.
Location Off A470, 1 mile N of junction with A55.
Restrictions No children under 8. Dogs in cottages/grounds only.
Credit cards Access, Amex, Visa.
Terms [1996] Rooms: single £79–£85, double £115–£130, suite £135–£150; D,B&B £86–£100 per person. Breakfast: continental £6.95, full £9.95. Set lunch £11.50–£13.50, dinner £27.50–£36. Special breaks; Christmas package.

The St Tudno Hotel
The Promenade
Llandudno LL30 2LP

Tel (01492) 874411
Fax (01492) 860407

César award in 1987

Martin and Janette Bland have been 24 years at their Grade II listed building on the seafront of this attractive Victorian seaside resort. It has pleasing Victorian-style lounges with much drapery, potted plants, and patterned wallpaper. Bedrooms have a similar period decor; some are spacious but some are small. There is good family accommodation, and a small indoor swimming pool. "It is a gem of a hotel," writes a 1996 visitor. "Our front bedroom had a wonderful view of the promenade, and nice touches like fresh milk for tea, iced water, and sweets on pillows at night. The vigilant owners were always around. The food was excellent, particularly the seafood." Other readers, too, have praised the "modern British cookery, with Welsh and classic French influences", served in a pretty, garden-style restaurant with plenty of greenery: "It is beautifully cooked and presented." "The Blands' attention to every detail shows, and the staff follow their lead. Well-priced wine list. Breakfast particularly good." (*Dr AM Jenner, and others*) There is harp or piano music in the lounges most Saturdays.

Open All year.
Rooms 19 double, 2 single. 1 on ground floor.
Facilities Lift. Sitting room, coffee lounge, lounge bar, restaurant; small indoor swimming pool; 2 patios. Sandy beach 60 yds. Unsuitable for severely ♿.
Location Central, opposite pier. Secure car park and garaging.
Restrictions No smoking: dining room, sitting room. No children in high chairs in restaurant at night. Small dogs only, not in public rooms/unattended in bedrooms.
Credit cards All major cards accepted.
Terms B&B £42.50–£95; D,B&B £72–£124.50. Set lunch £15.50, dinner £22–£29.50. Bar lunches. Mid-week, weekend, off-season, Christmas, New Year breaks. 1-night bookings occasionally refused bank holidays. V

> If you are nominating a hotel, please tell us enough to convey its character and quality. We can't make good bricks without plenty of straw. We find brochures very helpful.

LLANFACHRETH Gwynedd — Map 3

Ty-Isaf Farmhouse BUDGET *Tel* (01341) 423261
Llanfachreth
nr Dolgellau LL40 2EA

Graham and Diana Silverton's friendly small 17th-century guest house: beams, inglenook, simple country decor. Peaceful 3-acre grounds, with goats, sheep, stream, in secluded hamlet in Snowdonia National Park, 3½ miles NE of Dolgellau. Lovely views. Walking, climbing, riding, fishing, sailing, beaches, castles nearby. 3 bedrooms, "smallish, comfortable, warm". House party atmosphere: free pre-dinner drink; communal dinner. Traditional home cooking, with choices, generous portions. Wines reasonably priced. Generous breakfasts. Closed Christmas. Unsuitable for ♿. No smoking: dining room, bedrooms. No children under 13. Dogs by arrangement; not unattended in bedrooms. Credit cards not accepted. B&B £25–£35; D,B&B £37–£47. No recent reports; we'd like some, please. *V*

LLANFIHANGEL CRUCORNEY Gwent — Map 3

Penyclawdd Court NEW *Tel* (01873) 890719
Llanfihangel Crucorney *Fax* (01873) 890848
nr Abergavenny NP7 7LB

A Wolsey Lodge, full of character, reached up an exceedingly bumpy track at the foot of Bryn Arw mountain, in the Brecon Beacons National Park. It is a Grade II* listed Tudor manor house, "oozing antiquity, with beams, crooked walls, sloping floors". The grounds contain a listed Norman motte and bailey, a traditional herb garden and a knot garden. The quality of the restoration by Julia Horton-Evans has been recognised by awards from the Prince of Wales and others. Heating is beneath the flagstone floor to avoid the need for radiators; there's no electricity in the dining room – dinner and breakfast are served by candlelight. Tudor feasts are sometimes held. Lots of oxblood-red paint in the public areas, which our inspectors found gloomy, "but our bedroom, the Granary, up a steep, winding stone staircase, was a pleasant surprise: cream paint, low beams, beds cleverly contrived from church pews, the prayerbook rests full of books and magazines, TV, and modern bathroom (but no shower). The Oak Room has an open fireplace and a free-standing bath. Dinner, at 8 pm – good home cooking – was communally served; we sat on excruciatingly hard benches; lighting was by candles in a black wrought iron coronet overhead, dripping wax. It was very dark, but we enjoyed talking to our fellow guests. No licence; bring your own wine (no corkage charged). Breakfast was served rather inflexibly 8.30–9 am. Good cooked items, and home-made marmalade, but no fruit, and muesli the only cereal. Friendly owner; all very informal. The setting is deeply peaceful. Wonderful walking all around." More reports, please.

Open All year.
Rooms 3 double. No telephone.
Facilities Lounge, dining room. 6-acre grounds: Norman motte and bailey, herb and knot gardens, maze. Unsuitable for ♿.
Location 4 miles NE of Abergavenny. Turn off A465 on to Old Hereford Road, signed Pantgelli; cross railway line. Drive 2nd right, between Victorian house and modern bungalow (follow B&B sign).

Restrictions No smoking: restaurant, bedrooms. No children under 14. No dogs.
Credit cards Access, Visa.
Terms B&B: single £50, double £70; D,B&B: single £70, double £110. Set dinner £20. 1-night bookings refused Christmas, New Year, most bank holidays.

LLANGAMMARCH WELLS Powys — Map 3

The Lake — *Tel* (01591) 620202
Llangammarch Wells LD4 4BS — *Fax* (01591) 620457

César award in 1992

"Fabulous. Pretty garden. Staff charming and helpful; proprietor vigilant but unobtrusive." Jean-Pierre and Jan Mifsud's large half-timbered turn-of-the century purpose-built hotel is set in large grounds above lawns sloping down to a river. You can walk along the banks by fields with sheep or to the well-stocked lake; there are other rivers with good fishing close by. Bedrooms and suites, though not large, are well insulated and uncluttered, "with nice touches, such as a sherry decanter"; they are serviced during dinner; no tea-making facilities, morning tea is brought up. There's a huge, comfortable lounge, with deep sofas and armchairs, where a lavish afternoon tea is served. In the large dining room, with candlelit tables at night, cooking by Richard Arnold is modern English / French, "of a high standard"; some of the ingredients are organically produced locally; there is plenty of choice. "Very good food, and the young and welcoming staff were happy to serve me dinner when I arrived half an hour after they stopped serving." "The cheeseboard is worth a detour; the wine list is of exceptional variety, quality and value." "Generous Welsh breakfasts, well served, nothing packaged." (*Ben Bradshaw, SR, TT, and others; also Bruce Douglas-Mann*)

Open All year.
Rooms 10 suites, 9 double. 2 on ground floor.
Facilities Ramp. 2 lounges, bar, billiard room, restaurant. 50-acre grounds: lake, river, fishing (tuition available), practice golf, tennis. Riding, pony-trekking, golf nearby.
Location 8 miles SW of Builth Wells, S of A483 to Garth; follow signs to hotel.
Restrictions No smoking: restaurant, some bedrooms. No children under 7 in dining room after 7.30 pm. No dogs in public rooms.
Credit cards All major cards accepted.
Terms B&B: single £78, double £120, suite £162; D,B&B (min. 2 days) £78–£100 per person. Set lunch £16.50, dinner £28.50. Winter breaks; Christmas, New Year breaks. V*

LLANSANFFRAID GLAN CONWY Gwynedd — Map 3

The Old Rectory — *Tel* (01492) 580611
Llanrwst Road — *Fax* (01492) 584555
Llansanffraid Glan Conwy
nr Conwy LL28 5LF

César award in 1994

This sophisticated Georgian house, a member of the Wolsey Lodge consortium, stands in carefully tended grounds up a steep drive, with glorious views over the Conwy estuary to Conwy Castle and

Snowdonia. It is "a lovely old building with superb antique and repro furniture, pictures, family photos, lots of bric-à-brac and beautiful flowers", and very Welsh in atmosphere. The "kindly, thoughtful hosts", Michael and Wendy Vaughan, are knowledgeable about Welsh history and culture, local walks, etc. "They work very hard to achieve a perfect balance," writes a recent guest. "The atmosphere is quiet and calm." Others have admired the "personal touch – the fond farewells were very fond." The bedrooms (some are a little small) are "luxuriously kitted out; fresh fruit and bottled water are renewed each day". This is one of only two establishments in Wales with a red "Meals" in *Michelin*, for the quality of Mrs Vaughan's cooking – "brilliant use of local produce" on a no-choice menu, served at 8 pm. "Good wine list, with a wide selection of half bottles." There are separate tables for those who wish to dine alone. Breakfasts include freshly squeezed orange juice and Welsh rarebit made with Welsh ale. (*Colin Eastaugh, Patrick Jefferson, Andrew and Celia Payne*)

Open 1 Feb–20 Dec. Dining room closed for lunch, occasionally for dinner (guests warned when booking).
Rooms 6 double. 2 on ground floor in coach house.
Facilities Lounge, restaurant. 2½-acre grounds. Sea, safe bathing 2½ miles; fishing, golf, riding, sailing, dry ski-slope nearby. Unsuitable for ♿.
Location On A470, ½ mile S of junction with A55.
Restrictions No children under 5, except babies. Smoking/dogs in coach house only.
Credit cards All major cards accepted.
Terms B&B: single £80–£104, double £89–£119. Set dinner £29.50. 2-day breaks. 1-night bookings refused high season weekends, bank holidays. *V* (Nov, Dec, Feb, Mar)

LLANWRTYD WELLS Powys **Map 3**

Carlton House BUDGET
Dolycoed Road
Llanwrtyd Wells LD5 4RA
Tel (01591) 610248
Fax (01591) 610242

In the centre of the smallest town in Britain, at the foot of the Cambrian mountains amid lovely countryside with lakes, stands Dr and Mrs Gilchrist's bow-windowed Edwardian villa. The exterior is "somewhat stark" but inside the decor is stylish, with strong colours and oriental artefacts. Bedrooms are well equipped, though some are a bit dark; the suite has a view of the Cambrian mountains. The owners, who do everything themselves, "are welcoming without being intrusive". "What makes it stand out is the cooking. No wonder Mary Anne Gilchrist is Mid-Wales Cook of the Year. Fantastic dishes, crying out to be photographed. Succulent meat, sauces which are out of this world in flavour and artistry. The wine list is well chosen, with good-value New World bottles." Breakfast includes home-made breads and marmalade, and local honey. The debate about George, the resident bassett hound, continues: Mrs Gilchrist has banned him from eating fudge these days, "so he is marginally less of a nuisance". Recent guests found him "melancholic but endearing". (*Stephen and Judy Parish, Tony Thomas*) One caveat: "Since being soaked to the skin seems to be the norm here, heated towel rails would have been welcome."

Open All year, except Christmas. Restaurant closed midday.
Rooms 1 suite, 4 double. No telephone.

Facilities Lounge, restaurant. Tiny garden. Golf, pony-trekking, riding, mountain biking, birdwatching nearby. Unsuitable for ♿.
Location Town centre. No private parking.
Restrictions No smoking in restaurant. No dogs in public rooms.
Credit card Access.
Terms B&B: single £35, double £50, suite £59; D,B&B £42.50–£57 per person. Set dinner £18.50; full alc £27.50. 2-night breaks: D,B&B £35; seasonal breaks.

LLYSWEN Powys — Map 3

Llangoed Hall
Llywen, Brecon LD3 0YP — *Tel* (01874) 754525 — *Fax* (01874) 754545
César award in 1990

An impressive 17th-century mansion, redesigned in the 20th century by Sir Clough Williams-Ellis of Portmeirion fame. It is set well back from a main road, in formal gardens. Behind are lovely views across the river Wye to the Black Mountains. Owner Sir Bernard Ashley aims for "the atmosphere of an Edwardian house party"; many country pursuits are available (see below). The public rooms are impressive: great hall with deep sofas and stone fireplace, morning room with piano, library with snooker table. Sir Bernard's magnificent collection of pictures is lavishly distributed throughout; antiques and oriental rugs abound. Bedrooms have high ceilings, period furniture (some four-posters), garden views, sherry, mineral water, fruit, "paperbacks ranging from Sophocles to James Dean, and splendid bathroom with Edwardian-style taps". Ben Davies, the chef since February 1995, has won a *Michelin* star (as he did at *Calcot Manor*, Tetbury) for his cooking – "modern classical with a Provençal feel". Following last year's complaints about the wine mark-up, the manager, Gareth Pugh, writes: "We have reduced many prices and purchased more wines in the £15–£20 range." "Great breakfasts" include local sausages, black pudding and laver bread. Mixed reviews this year: "A lovely hotel, welcoming and wonderfully comfortable." "Staff the best I have ever seen; superbly helpful." But also reports of excessive waits before and during meals, and serious hiccups in the restaurant. One reader wrote of the decor: "The corridors, painted white, look more NHS than CHH." And a woman on her own complained of a frosty welcome and reluctant service. More reports, please.

Open All year.
Rooms 3 suites, 18 double, 2 single.
Facilities Ramps. 2 lounges, garden room, orangery, dining room, billiard room. 17-acre grounds: tennis, croquet. River Wye 200 yds: fishing (ghillie). Riding, golf, gliding, clay pigeon-shooting, canoeing nearby. Only public areas suitable for ♿.
Location On A470, 1 mile N of Llyswen.
Restrictions No smoking in dining room. No children under 8. Dogs in kennels only.
Credit cards All major cards accepted.
Terms [1996] B&B: single £95, double £155–£195, suite £195–£285; D,B&B: £85–£160 per person. Set lunch £16, dinner £29.50; full alc £42.50. 2-day breaks; Christmas, New Year house parties. 1-night bookings refused weekends 1 May–31 Oct. *V*

MUMBLES West Glamorgan Map 3

Hillcrest House BUDGET
1 Higher Lane
Mumbles, Swansea SA3 4NS

Tel (01792) 363700
Fax (01792) 363768

A quirky establishment with a Scottish hostess, Yvonne Scott, and an international flavour, in a "wonderful location overlooking the bay, in a salubrious suburb of Swansea". It is instantly recognisable by the flags on the wall adjoining the carpark. They refer to the "themed" bedrooms, each one related to a country in which the owner has lived. Wales has mining memorabilia, modern "rustic" furniture, and a giant daffodil lamp, Scotland is done in tartan; Navajo, Kraal and Safari are less *outré* than you might expect. Our inspectors found them "charming and original". The dining room decor is based on fruit and food. The cooking, "like the decor, is fresh, if not gourmet; wines are reasonably priced, with some real bargains. Service, by a very young *maître d'* and barmaid, was delightful. The place has panache, and is good value for money." Background music, both jazz and classical. Some rooms overlook a busy road, but there is effective double-glazing. More reports, please.

Open 20 Jan–23 Dec. Restaurant closed Sun.
Rooms 6 double, 1 single.
Facilities Lounge/bar, restaurant; terrace. Small garden. Beaches, golf, tennis nearby. Unsuitable for ♿.
Location 4 miles SW of Swansea centre; off first corner junction of Langland Rd. Carpark.
Restrictions No smoking: restaurant, 5 bedrooms. No dogs.
Credit cards Access, Amex, Visa.
Terms B&B: single £50, double £60–£80. Set dinner: 2–3 courses £16–£18.95. *V*

NANTGWYNANT Gwynedd Map 3

Pen-y-Gwryd Hotel BUDGET
Nantgwynant
Llanberis LL55 4NT

Tel (01286) 870211

César award in 1995

"Wonderful. A step back in time. Charming young staff. In the hot summer, we swam in the natural spring-fed pool (with water lilies) and had delicious cream teas on the lawn. Prices are incredibly low." "Unique hospitality. Brian and Jane Pullee draw you into their family; after dinner, one sits on high-backed settees in the Smoke Room, conversing with like-minded people (there's no TV). Breakfasts (no portion control) set you up for the day." This historic climbers' hotel ("without frills") is in the heart of the Snowdonia National Park. In 1953, Hunt and Hillary and most of the Everest team stayed here before flying to Nepal. It is also well equipped for walkers and fishermen. Bedrooms are adequate and comfortable, and the large games room is good for younger guests. Nine pairs of well-worn climbing boots hang from the ceiling of the public snug – "all no doubt can tell a story". Furnishings in the lounge "are a little spartan, but the blazing log fire compensates". The chef, Lena Jensen, from Jutland, produces five-course dinners – "wholesome, tasty, plentiful and hot" – announced by a gong at 7.30. "Five bedrooms now have *en suite* bathroom," write the Pullees. "We hope this will up the comfort level." There are five public bathrooms; some with a massive old bath, "an experience to use". (*J Woolf, DM Golding; also Beverley Adams and Peter Saberton, Good Pub Guide, and others*)

Open Mar–beginning Nov, New Year, weekends Jan/Feb.
Rooms 15 double, 1 single. 4 with bath, 1 with shower. 1 on ground floor.
Facilities Lounge, bar, smoke room, games room, dining room; sauna. 2-acre grounds: natural swimming pool. River and lake fishing nearby.
Location On A498 Beddgelert–Capel Curig, at junction with A4086.
Restriction Smoking banned in dining room, discouraged in bedrooms.
Credit cards None accepted.
Terms B&B £20–£25. Bar and packed lunches *c.* £3.50. Set dinner £15. 1-night bookings occasionally refused weekends.

NEWPORT Dyfed — Map 3

Cnapan BUDGET — *Tel* (01239) 820575
East Street, Newport — *Fax* (01239) 820878
nr Fishguard SA42 0SY

A pink listed restaurant-with-rooms in an attractive small town (not to be confused with Newport in Gwent) in the Pembrokeshire National Park, and close to the coast. Here, John and Eluned Lloyd and their daughter and son-in-law, Judith and Michael Cooper, dispense "innovative evening meals, accompanied by a good wine list". For a set price, residents choose items from the extensive *carte*, which includes plenty of vegetarian dishes. The place has a homely style: a traditional Welsh dresser, crowded with family treasures, stands in the hall; a woodburning stove burns in the guests' sitting room. Books and local information are everywhere. In summer, drinks and tea are served in the sheltered garden. A typical *Cnapan* evening might be rounded off in the lounge with coffee, an "amazing dessert wine" and a board game. The guest bedrooms "are comfortably cluttered with whatever one might want"; each has a shower; guests wanting a good soak may avail themselves of the "massive" bath along the corridor. "Breakfast, serve yourself as much as you like, with home-made bread, sets you up for the day." "Wonderful value for money; the proprietors get the balance between friendliness and reserve right." There's good coastal path walking nearby. The road in front of the house is busy by day. More reports, please.

Open All year, except Christmas, Feb. Restaurant closed Tues.
Rooms 1 family (with bunk beds in adjoining room), 4 double. No telephone.
Facilities Lounge, bar, restaurant. Small garden. 10 mins' walk to sea; fishing, birdwatching, pony-trekking, golf, boating nearby. Unsuitable for ♿.
Location In centre of small town (but quiet at night). Private parking.
Restrictions Smoking banned in dining room, discouraged in bedrooms. No dogs.
Credit cards Access, Visa.
Terms B&B £25; D,B&B £40. Set dinner £15; full alc £20–£21. 1-night bookings occasionally refused.

We are particularly keen to get more reports on our italicised entries.

PENMAENPOOL Gwynedd — Map 3

Penmaenuchaf Hall *Tel/Fax* (01341) 422129
Penmaenpool
Dolgellau LL40 1YB

A fine old manor house, with "friendly owners, Mark Watson and Lorraine Fielding, and a helpful staff", in a peaceful setting in the foothills of Cader Idris. Its large grounds, with mature woodland, lawns and terraced gardens, overlook the Mawddach estuary. There's excellent walking all around, and many country pursuits are on offer (see below). The decor of the spacious reception rooms and bedrooms combines clear colours, oriental rugs, antiques, good reproduction furniture and quality fabrics, and "pleasant touches, eg, sweets on platter in hall, binoculars by window". Most visitors have enjoyed the modern cooking "with straightforward, attractive presentation", accompanied by an "interesting" wine list. Breakfast includes large bowls of fruit, cereal and yogurt, and generous traditionally cooked Welsh dishes. The hotel has an important bat roost, home to five different species. "They may enter the house on summer evenings," it warns, "but do not be alarmed. It is an honour to be visited by the Lesser Horseshoe. They do not get in people's hair or suck blood. They can see, and will eventually fly away." No *Guide* reader has yet reported a sighting. (*Pat and Jeremy Temple, John and Joan Wyatt, and others*) Some caveats: "Bedside lighting necessitated violent contortions for reading in bed." Some have thought the large dining room "rather bleak", and the dinners "over-elaborate, with slow service".

Open All year, except 2nd week Jan.
Rooms 14 double.
Facilities Hall, morning room, library, bar, snooker room, restaurant; conference facilities. Free salmon/sea trout-fishing on 13 miles of river (ghillies available); birdwatching, clay pigeon-shooting, sailing, trekking, golf nearby; safe sandy beaches 6 miles. Only restaurant accessible to ♿.
Location 2 miles W of Dolgellau. From Dolgellau by-pass (A470) take A493 to Tywyn/Fairbourne. Hotel drive on left after ¾ mile, by sign to Penmaenpool.
Restrictions No smoking: restaurant, morning room, library, 2 bedrooms. No children under 8, except babies. Dogs in entrance hall, gun room only.
Credit cards All major cards accepted.
Terms [1996] B&B: single £50–£95, double £95–£150; D,B&B: single £73–£118, double £141–£196. Set lunch £11.95, dinner £23; full alc £33. Guided walks. Weekend, midweek and long breaks; Christmas/New Year programmes. V*

PORTHKERRY South Glamorgan — Map 3

Egerton Grey *Tel* (01446) 711666
Porthkerry, nr Cardiff CF6 9BZ *Fax* (01446) 711690

A 19th-century rectory, "full of country charm", with ornate mouldings, "acres of beautiful panelling", antiques, porcelain, paintings, and a collection of old clocks. It looks over Porthkerry Park to the sea, and stands in a wooded valley 20 minutes' drive from Cardiff. Though near the airport, it is generally peaceful. It is stylishly run by Anthony and Magda Pitkin, with a courteous staff. The spacious bedrooms have bold colour schemes, antiques, thick carpets, and carefully restored Edwardian bathrooms. One has a tub "about the size of a small swimming pool". A nice touch is the placing of guests' names on their door. Everyone praises the food (there's plenty of choice), though one diner thought it "a little eccentric". Another wrote: "Menu and presentation of dinner rather OTT. But the food was first class. Home-made savoury biscuits came with an excellent cheeseboard which was competently described by the charming and efficient waiter. Decent wine list too." (*CE Beckett, Chris Kay; also TE Reynolds*) An American visitor took umbrage at hand-sprayers in place of fixed showers.

Open All year.
Rooms 2 suites, 7 double, 1 single.
Facilities Drawing room, library, loggia, dining room; private dining room. 7-acre garden: croquet, tennis. Beach 200 yds; golf nearby. Unsuitable for ♿.
Location 10 miles SW of Cardiff. From M4 exit 33 follow signs to airport, by-passing Barry. Left at small roundabout by airport, signposted Porthkerry; after 500 yds left again, down lane between thatched cottages.
Restrictions No smoking in dining room. No dogs in public rooms.
Credit cards All major cards accepted.
Terms [1996] B&B: single £55, double £90, suite £120; D,B&B: single £75, double £125, suite £140. Set lunch/dinner £22. 3-day Christmas break. *V*

PORTMEIRION Gwynedd — Map 3

Hotel Portmeirion — *Tel* (01766) 770228
Portmeirion LL48 6ET — *Fax* (01766) 771331

César award in 1990

Sir Clough Williams-Ellis's italianate fantasy village has a stunning setting on the steep hillside of a sheltered wooded peninsula, above a wide estuary. It is busy with tourists by day, but the hotel's guests are well protected in lovely gardens ("quite Mediterranean in feel") with peacocks and a swimming pool. "One of the pleasures of staying is that you have the village to yourself in the early morning and after dinner." Behind its unpretentious early Victorian exterior, the hotel is exuberantly decorated with bright fabrics, carved panels, and furniture and ornaments imported from Rajasthan. It's also very Welsh, "with bilingual staff, bilingual menus, live Welsh music, lots of animated Welsh conversation". The accommodation ranges from lavish suites in the main house to quite simple rooms ("with old-fashioned bathroom with small water tank") in houses in the village. The food is modern Welsh, "not breathtaking, but often good". And the restaurant is "friendly, with a traditional *maître d'* and a swift and attentive staff". Breakfast includes fresh fruit and a good choice of cooked dishes. (*Mike Hutton, Patrick Jefferson*) A new chef, formerly second chef, was appointed in January 1996. More reports from the kitchen would be appreciated.

Open All year, except 5 Jan–7 Feb. Restaurant closed Mon midday (except bank holidays).
Rooms 13 suites, 24 double. 23 in village. Also self-catering cottages. Some on ground floor.
Facilities Hall, 2 lounges, 2 bars, restaurant, children's supper room; function room. 70-acre grounds: garden, swimming pool (heated May–Sept), tennis, lakes, sandy beach; free golf at Porthmadog Golf Club.
Location SW of Penrhyndeudraeth, SE of Porthmadog, off A487 at Minffordd. Street parking.
Restrictions No smoking: restaurant, lounges, some bedrooms. No dogs.
Credit cards All major cards accepted.

Terms B&B: single £63.50–£123.50, double £82–£142, suite £102–£167. Set lunch £13.50, dinner £25. Christmas, New Year, 2-day breaks.

REYNOLDSTON West Glamorgan — Map 3

Fairyhill NEW — *Tel* (01792) 390139
Reynoldston, nr Swansea SA3 1BS — *Fax* (01792) 391358

An 18th-century house, peacefully set in large grounds, with woodland, a trout stream and a lake with wild ducks, amid lovely scenery near the north coast of the Gower Peninsula. It has a trio of owners: Jane and Peter Camm, Andrew Hetherington, and Paul Davies, the chef. "A real port in a storm. The restaurant is closed on winter Sunday evenings but they served a delicious supper by a roaring fire in the drawing room. Our room had a hi-fi set and we were encouraged to borrow CDs from their collection. Dinners cooked by Paul Davies, and served in a green-and-yellow dining room, "reflect traditional influences with a modern touch". The award-winning wine list includes many reasonably priced bottles. There's a leafy patio for alfresco drinks and tea, and a cosy bar. (*Curzon Tussaud*) Only grouses: "The £5 dog levy – £1 per tail and leg? And the problems of flushing their electric lavatories." More reports, please.

Open All year. Restaurant closed for dinner Sun in winter.
Rooms 8 double.
Facilities Lounge, bar, 2 dining rooms. 24-acre grounds: croquet, woodland, stream, lake. Beaches, water sports nearby. Unsuitable for ♿.
Location 11 miles W of Swansea. M4 exit 47 to Gowerton; then B4295 for 9 miles.
Restrictions No children under 8, except at lunch. No dogs in public rooms.
Credit cards Access, Amex, Visa.
Terms B&B £42–£65. Set lunch from £7.50, dinner £22. 1-night bookings refused Sat in Aug.

ST DAVID'S Dyfed — Map 3

Warpool Court — *Tel* (01437) 720300
St David's SA62 6BN — *Fax* (01437) 720676

The former choir school ("outwardly rather austere") of the awesome St David's cathedral, in a stunning setting near the westernmost tip of Wales. It has panoramic views of St Bride's Bay. The Pembrokeshire Coastal Path is close by. "The gardens and grounds are splendid, with tall hedges, statues, and garden chairs. The decent-size covered swimming pool is warm and scrupulously clean." Inside, there are striking armorial and ornamental tiles, hand-painted by Ada Williams, an earlier owner, and the current owner, Peter Trier, "has put together an interesting collection of prints and watercolours". Bedrooms (opening, institution-fashion, off a long corridor) and bathrooms were recently upgraded. They include good family accommodation. "This hotel genuinely looks after children – splendid high teas. The food was very good: beautifully cooked and sauced local fish, Welsh lamb, game, etc. Enormous selection of fresh vegetables. Superb local cheese." "Interesting wine list, including some Welsh ones, well worth tasting." "Good value bar meals. Warm welcome, staff helpful throughout our stay." (*NM Mackintosh, Michael Schofield, M and S Tattersall Darby*) But there are criticisms: "erratic water supply"; "the manager divided guests into two groups – those worth talking to, and others"; "decor undistinguished for such prices"; and sheets not changed over a week's stay.

Open All year, except Jan.
Rooms 22 double, 3 single.
Facilities Drawing room, summer lounge, bar/lounge, restaurant; conference facilities; excercise room with sauna. 7-acre grounds: tennis, croquet, covered swimming pool (heated Apr–end Oct), children's play area. Cliff path 5 mins' walk; beach 10 mins' walk.
Location Bear left after Cross Sq in St David's, between Midland Bank and *Cartref* restaurant. Left at next road fork; follow hotel signs.
Restrictions No smoking in restaurant. Dogs allowed in some bedrooms (£4); not in public rooms.
Credit cards All major cards accepted.
Terms B&B £53–£80; D,B&B £81–£108. Bar meals. Set lunch £15.95, dinner £28. Special breaks from £69 per person per night. Christmas, New Year packages. *V*

TALSARNAU Gwynedd — Map 3

Maes-y-Neuadd — *Tel* (01766) 780200
Talsarnau LL47 6YA — *Fax* (01766) 780211

"Warm, comfortable, relaxing and welcoming as ever." "Food and service of a very high standard." Praise from returning visitors to this grey granite-and-slate mansion, 14th-century in origin, enlarged in the 16th and 17th. Owned and run by two couples, the Horsfalls and the Slatters, it stands amid lawns, orchards and paddocks, on a wooded hillside with glorious views across to the Snowdonia National Park. You approach by a narrow lane up a one-in-five hill. Inside are oak beams, decorated plasterwork, and good antique and modern furniture; there's a bar with an inglenook fireplace. Bedrooms vary greatly in style and size; some have pine furniture, others antiques; three have a spa bath. Some are in the main house; others in a converted coach house. In the panelled dining room, chef Peter Jackson offers "a mix of sophisticated and simpler meals to suit all tastes and moods"; guests may take between three and five courses. Vegetables and herbs are home-grown; there is an excellent cheeseboard, and an "interesting wine list". "Good breakfasts, cooked and continental." "Dogs as friendly as the owners." (*Mr and Mrs EH Warner, Alan Greenwood, and others*) The Royal St David's golf course, Harlech Castle, and Portmeirion are nearby.

Open All year.
Rooms 1 suite, 14 double, 1 single. 4 in coach house 10 yds. 2 on ground floor.
Facilities Ramps. Lounge, bar, conservatory, 2 dining rooms; terrace. 8-acre grounds: croquet, orchard, paddock. Sea, golf, riding, sailing, fishing, climbing nearby.
Location 3 miles NE of Harlech, signposted off B4573. ½ mile up narrow, steep lane. Guests may be met at Harlech/Blaenau Ffestiniog stations.
Restrictions No smoking in restaurant. No children under 8 in dining room for dinner. Dogs by prior arrangement only; not in public rooms.
Credit cards All major cards accepted.
Terms D,B&B: single £67–£76, double £136–£205, suite £191–£209. Set lunch £12.50, dinner (2–5-course) £23–£29. 2-night breaks all year; 3-day breaks Nov–Mar. Christmas, New Year packages. 1-night bookings sometimes refused bank holidays.

TALYLLYN Gwynedd Map 3

Minffordd Hotel NEW/BUDGET
Talyllyn, Tywyn LL36 9AJ
Tel (01654) 761665
Fax (01654) 761517

A welcome return to the *Guide* of a hotel which won a *César* under its earlier owners, the Pickles. "It is run by Mark Warner and Mary McQuillan with the same solicitous care and attention. They are friendly but not invasive." Though comfortably modernised and spick-and-span, this rambling 300-year-old drovers' inn has retained its old-world atmosphere. It has a glorious setting at the head of the Dysynni valley; flocks of sheep graze in the surrounding fields. The footpath to the top of Cader Idris starts by its front gate. It is not for the misanthrope: the smallness of the public rooms makes socialising inevitable, though the dining room tables are well spaced. Bedrooms, too, are compact, "but spotless, with good bathroom". "Good home-cooked dinners; modest, imaginative wines." "Excellent breakfasts." (*J Rudd, Patrick Jefferson; also Mrs Austin Gibbons, and others*) One couple was bothered by traffic noise from the road.

Open Mar–end Nov, weekends Nov, Dec. Restaurant closed for lunch.
Rooms 6 double. No TV. 3 on ground floor.
Facilities Sun lounge, parlour, bar, dining room; drying facilities. 4-acre grounds: garden, paddock, river, fishing. Golf, shooting, lake with fishing, sailing, nearby. Unsuitable for ♿.
Location 8 miles S of Dolgellau; at junction of A487 and B4405.
Restrictions Smoking in lounge bar only. No children under 5. Guide dogs only.
Credit cards Access, Visa.
Terms D,B&B £44.50–£65 (B&B terms by arrangement). Packed lunches available. Off-season breaks. *V*

THREE COCKS Powys Map 3

Three Cocks Hotel BUDGET
Three Cocks, nr Brecon LD3 0SL
Tel/Fax (01497) 847215

A welcoming restaurant-with-rooms in the Brecon Beacons National Park, close to the Wye. It is a 15th-century inn with a cobbled forecourt, ivy-clad walls, worn steps, great oak beams and a small flowery garden. Michael Winstone (the chef) and his Belgian wife, Marie-Jeanne, front-of-house, previously ran a restaurant in Belgium, and there's a Belgian accent to their repertoire of continental dishes, "consistently excellent, with first-class ingredients, beautifully cooked and served, ending with memorable desserts". Bread is freshly baked. The wine list is fairly priced. Service is "quiet and efficient". The spacious dining room has a rustic decor, with tapestries on the stone walls. Both lounges – one panelled, the other stone-walled and beamed – have an open fire. Recent endorsements: "The best hotel food I have had in years." "A wonderful place, charming hosts, excellent value for money. You would never think, driving by, that such a civilised place existed in such an otherwise austere hamlet. The restaurant and lounge are almost sumptuous in feeling. Bedrooms are cheerful and cosy, with sturdy old oak furniture and patchwork quilts." (*John E Borron, SG*) The hotel is on a busy road, but front rooms are double-glazed.

Open Mid-Feb–Nov. Closed Tues; restaurant closed for lunch Sun.
Rooms 7 double. No telephone, TV, etc.

Facilities 2 lounges, TV lounge, breakfast room, dining room. ½-acre grounds. Golf, canoeing, riding, fishing nearby. Unsuitable for ♿.
Location 5 miles SW of Hay-on-Wye on A438 Hereford–Brecon. Rear rooms quietest. Large carpark.
Restriction No dogs.
Credit cards Access, Visa.
Terms B&B: single £40–£62, double £62; D,B&B double (min. 2 nights) £95–£110. Set lunch/dinner £25.50; full alc £28. *V*

TINTERN Gwent — Map 3

Parva Farmhouse BUDGET — *Tel* (01291) 689411
Tintern, Chepstow NP6 6SQ — *Fax* (01291) 689557

"We loved it." "Welcome and hospitality most friendly, food outstanding." Recent endorsements for this unpretentious old creepered stone building, bedecked with flowers in hanging baskets and tubs. It is set beside a small church above an oxbow of the river Wye, a mile from the famous ruined abbey. The grounds are small, but there is excellent walking all around. The beamed lounge has a wood-burning stove, an honesty bar, and lots of board games. In the restaurant, where the walls are adorned with fishing gear and there is a huge inglenook fireplace, the four-course dinner, prepared by chef/proprietor Dereck Stubbs, includes traditional Welsh dishes. It is "remarkably good value". The wine list includes Parva wine, made from local grapes, and is "amazingly cheap: Châteauneuf du Pape for £12.50; nothing above £20". "Good traditional breakfast." Vickie Stubbs is "very much in evidence, helpful and friendly, but never pushy". The "simple but charming" bedrooms vary in size; some are good for a family. They have tea-making facilities, muted TV, and river or garden views. There is a busy road nearby, but this hasn't bothered our reporters. (*Ann and Fred Hammer, and others*)

Open All year.
Rooms 3 family, 6 double.
Facilities Lounge with honesty bar, restaurant. Small lawn alongside river. Fishing nearby. Unsuitable for ♿.
Location At N end of village, just off A466. M48 5 miles.
Restrictions No smoking in dining room. No dogs in public rooms.
Credit cards Access, Amex, Visa.
Terms B&B: single £42–£44, double £60–£64; D,B&B (min. 2 nights): single £59.50–£62, double £95–£99. Set dinner £17.50. Special breaks; 2 nights for price of 1 Oct–end Mar. Weekly rates. 1-night bookings occasionally refused. Children under 12 accommodated free in parents' room. *V*

WHITEBROOK Gwent — Map 3

The Crown at Whitebrook BUDGET — *Tel* (01600) 860254
Whitebrook, Monmouth NP5 4TX — *Fax* (01600) 860607

Sandra and Roger Bates's unpretentious restaurant-with-rooms, an extended and modernised 17th-century inn, has a peaceful setting in a steeply wooded valley near the river Wye (a designated area of outstanding natural beauty). There's excellent walking all around. Its decor may be unpretentious, but the cooking is of a high order of sophistication. In the beamed restaurant, popular with outside diners, French and British dishes, "using the best of Welsh ingredients", are cooked to order by Sandra Bates, who in 1994 won the Logis of Great Britain regional cooking competition. Our readers have found the food "excellent in every way, imaginative, beautifully cooked, and impeccably presented by a charming, efficient staff". The wine list is "excellent, with accurate descriptions". Some bedrooms are small; the best one has a four-poster and a whirlpool bath. They are well equipped, "with really comfortable beds and excellent bedside lighting". "Breakfast has everything one could have wished for, properly cooked; plenty of choice, lots of coffee and, above all, fresh hot toast. Very good value for money." "Exceptionally helpful hosts; friendly welcome." (*RAL Ogston, and others*) One couple this year thought the dining room decor was "spartan, with uncomfortably bright lighting".

Open All year, except Christmas, 2 weeks Jan. Restaurant closed to non-residents Sun evening/ midday Mon.
Rooms 12 double. 1 on ground floor.
Facilities Lounge, bar, restaurant; function room; terrace. 3-acre garden. Fishing in Wye 1 mile; golf nearby. Unsuitable for ♿.
Location 5 miles S of Monmouth on unclassified road from A466 and B4293 W of Bigsweir Bridge,
Restrictions No smoking in restaurant. No dogs in public rooms.
Credit cards All major cards accepted.
Terms B&B £26–£45; D,B&B £52–£70. Set lunch £16.95, dinner £26.95. Midweek, off-season, New Year breaks. *V*

Scotland

Kilcamb Lodge, Strontian

ABERFELDY Perthshire and Kinross **Map 5**

Farleyer House
Aberfeldy PH15 2JE

Tel (01887) 820332
Fax (01887) 829430

This impressive 16th-century former dower house of Castle Menzies stands in huge grounds with mature trees on a hillside overlooking the Tay Valley. There's been another change since last year: owner Janice Reid has a new manager, Andy Cole. However, the two restaurants, the smart set-menu, dinner-only *Menzies* and the cheaper *Scottish Bistro*, are still both supervised by chef Richard Lyth, with the help of Marc Guibert. "The young and enthusiastic staff were brilliant at their job – welcoming, attentive, but unobtrusive. The atmosphere is that of the perfect Scottish country house – very comfortable, big fires and an excellent table in the *Menzies* room. Each of the four courses was perfect. The library and drawing room were comfortably furnished and warm – incredible, as it was –20° and thick snow outside!" *(Scott Darby and Mark Tattersall)* There's a "challenging" six-hole golf course in the grounds; *Farleyer*'s residents may use a nearby country club with indoor swimming pool and other sporting and leisure facilities.

Open All year. House party only at Christmas.
Rooms 15 double. 4 (with shower) in Ghillie's Cottage. 1 adapted for ♿.
Facilities Drawing room, TV lounge, library, bar, 2 restaurants. 34-acre grounds: children's playground, garden, croquet, golf, woods. Shooting, riding arranged; salmon-, trout-fishing ½ m; country club with leisure facilities nearby.
Location From Aberfeldy, take B846 for 2 miles, towards Kinloch Rannoch.
Restrictions No smoking: *Menzies* restaurant. Dogs by arrangement; not in house (drying room available).
Credit cards All major cards accepted.
Terms B&B: single £55–£100, double £80–£150, suite £100–£170. D,B&B £65–£120 per person. Set dinner (*Menzies*) £32; full alc (*Scottish Bistro*) £22.50. Children under 14 accommodated free in parents' room.

ACHILTIBUIE Highland — Map 5

Summer Isles Hotel
Achiltibuie
by Ullapool IV26 2YG

Tel (01854) 622282
Fax (01854) 622251

César award in 1993

"Number one on the West Coast – a haven of hospitality, incredibly good in every sense. Part of the charm: the simply *beautiful* owners and the staff, and the excellent cuisine. Absolutely *nothing* to criticise – the perfect dream come true." "The food is, we think, magical, the bedrooms are comfortable, the lounges and dining room beautifully furnished, but it is the unique atmosphere that brings people back year after year. Mark and Geraldine Irvine maintain a consistently high standard; everything runs like clockwork, yet it is relaxed and informal; a combination of professionalism and personal involvement that is all too rare." More unbridled enthusiasm this year for this small hotel, with a red "Meals" in *Michelin*, in a remote and beautiful setting, up a 15-mile single-track road, with spectacular views of the sea and a great scattering of little islands. It's a splendid base for birdwatchers, walkers and fishermen. The gulf stream is nearby, though weather can change from Arctic to Aegean inside a week; guests are advised to bring wellingtons, binoculars, paint-boxes and midge cream. Bedrooms are pretty but not lavishly appointed; some are quite small. The Loghouse suite is recommended for families. (*Christian Bartoschek, Mrs MH Box*)

Open Easter–early Oct.
Rooms Suite (sleeps 2–5; can be self-catering Oct–May), 10 double, 1 single. 8 in annexe. Some on ground floor. No TV.
Facilities Sitting room, lounge with TV, 2 bars, dining room. Small garden. Sea, beaches, lakes nearby. Unsuitable for ♿.
Location NW of Ullapool; after 10 miles turn off A835 on to single-track road skirting lochs Lurgain, Badagyle and Oscaig. Hotel is just past village post office.
Restrictions No smoking in dining room, bedrooms. No dogs in public rooms.
Credit cards None accepted.
Terms B&B: single £47.50, double £80–£100, suite £130; D,B&B: single £81.50, double £168–£198. Set dinner £34. 10% discount for 6 or more nights. Children under 5 accommodated free in parents' room; under 13 half-price.

ARDUAINE Argyll and Bute **Map 5**

Loch Melfort Hotel *Tel* (01852) 200233
Arduaine, by Oban PA34 4XG *Fax* (01852) 200214

César award in 1996

Philip and Rosalind Lewis's white-walled Edwardian hotel lies on the coast road between Oban and Crinan, in a nonpareil position looking towards Jura and Scarba. The best rooms, brightly decorated, are in the main house; the custom-built ones in the Cedar Wing (suitable for families) are also comfortable and have their own terrace or balcony (but see below). Philip Lewis's cooking has been much praised, especially his excellent use of local shellfish and seafood. Salmon trout and prawn fishcakes with a tomato coulis or steamed fillets of Dover sole with Armoricaine sauce might be followed by Queen of Puddings or raspberry and blueberry almond tart. "The Sunday evening buffet is outstanding, with so many fresh and beautifully prepared dishes." "Such langoustines, such shrimps!" Breakfasts are substantial, with "wonderful kippers". The hotel lawn runs down to the water's edge, and its grounds adjoin a fine National Trust garden. Passing yachtsmen use the hotel's moorings, drying facilities and hot showers. Children are welcomed. (*W and AR; also Good Pub Guide*) The difference between the rooms in the Cedar wing and those in the main building must be emphasised: there have been continued complaints about the sound insulation in the Cedar Wing (Mrs Lewis tells us that they have improved it, and plan to do more this year), and its decor has also been criticised.

Open 23 Feb–5 Jan.
Rooms 26 double, 1 single. 20 in Cedar Wing. Some on ground floor.
Facilities Ramps. 2 lounges, 2 bars, dining room. 20-acre grounds; National Trust garden adjoins; small beach, fishing, windsurfing.
Location 19 miles S of Oban, on A816. Large carpark.
Restrictions No smoking in dining room. No dogs in main house.
Credit cards Access, Amex, Visa
Terms B&B £35–£60; D,B&B £45–£77.50. Bar meals. Set dinner from £26.50. Off-season, Christmas, New Year breaks. *V*

ARDVOURLIE Western Isles **Map 5**

Ardvourlie Castle *Tel* (01859) 502307
Aird a Mhulaidh *Fax* (01859) 502348
Isle of Harris HS3 3AB

A romantic Victorian shooting lodge on the shores of Loch Seaforth, in the far reaches of the Western Isles, described by its nominator as "a wonderful place to relax in a peaceful and scenic setting": "The lawns run down to the shore where you sometimes see otters playing. Our spacious, comfortable room had superb views over the loch, and a large Victorian bath in the adjoining bathroom. The lounge and library, with open fires, are ideal places to take your ease after a hard day's walking on the hills. There are gas lights in the dining room, giving a lovely mellow glow. The food, cooked by the owner, Derek Martin, who uses much local produce, is superb. Breakfasts include fresh home-baked bread, and real porridge cooked slowly overnight. The service is informal but helpful and attentive." Some rooms have gas and oil lamps and "splendid Victorian beds", and there are mahogany-panelled baths with brass fittings. More reports, please.

Open Apr–Oct.
Rooms 4 double. 1 on ground floor.
Facilities Lounge, library, dining room. 13-acre grounds. Sandy beaches, loch and river fishing nearby.
Location Off A859 8 miles NE of Tarbet, 24 miles S of Stornoway.
Restriction Smoking banned in restaurant, by arrangement in lounges, discouraged in bedrooms. Dogs by arrangement only.
Credit cards None accepted.
Terms B&B £45–£50; D,B&B £70–£75. Set dinner £25. Packed lunches available.

ARISAIG Highland — Map 5

Arisaig House — *Tel* (01687) 450622
Beasdale, by Arisaig PH39 4NR — *Fax* (01687) 450626

"Expensive, but well worth the cost if you want pampering," writes an American visitor on a return visit to this grand 19th-century mansion (Relais & Châteaux). "It is beautiful and well maintained, and we consider the walk through the garden, woodland and meadows down to the shore of the sea loch to be one of the most beautiful in Scotland." Other praise: "A notable hotel. I was treated with great courtesy, and felt more like a friend than a guest." "Everywhere beautifully furnished and immaculately kept." Owned by Ruth and John Smither and their son Andrew, who takes care of the magnificent grounds, the house is both luxurious and welcoming, with wellingtons in the porch, an entrance hall with high windows, oriental rugs and a carved oak staircase, a drawing room with vaulted ceiling and log fire, and a billiard room decorated with college oars. In summer, light lunches and teas are served on a terrace. Bedrooms, priced according to size and view (most are spacious), are traditional, with "highest quality furniture, sheets and towels, flowery fabrics, soft colours, books and fresh flowers"; best ones overlook the sea. Award-winning chef Gary Robinson, a graduate of *Gidleigh Park, Inverlochy Castle* and *Ston Easton Park* (*qqv*), among others, recently took over the kitchen from the Smithers' son-in-law David Wilkinson who, with his wife Alison, has moved to front of house. We'd like reports on the food, please. (*Martha Prince, RCC Sandys, and others*) One visitor found the reception cool.

Open Mar–Nov inclusive.
Rooms 2 suites, 12 double.
Facilities 3 lounges, lounge bar, billiard room, dining room; meeting room. 20-acre grounds: croquet, sea loch 10 mins' walk. Unsuitable for ♿.
Location On A830 Fort William–Mallaig. 1 mile past Beasdale railway station; 3 miles before Arisaig village.
Restrictions No smoking in restaurant. No children under 10. No dogs.
Credit cards Access, Amex, Visa.
Terms [1996] B&B £80–£120. Set dinner £38. Reductions for 3 or more nights; off-season breaks.

> If you have had recent experience of a good hotel that ought to be in the *Guide*, please write to us at once. Report forms are to be found at the back of the book. Procrastination is the thief of the next edition.

AUCHENCAIRN Dumfries and Galloway Map 5

Balcary Bay Hotel
Auchencairn
nr Castle Douglas DG7 1QZ

Tel (01556) 640217
Fax (01556) 640272

The "friendly and lively" Clare Lamb, her husband Graeme and their red setter provide a warm welcome in their ever-popular, large white country house, idyllically set on the edge of the bay. From the front bedrooms – "much sought after and more expensive" – you can hear the water lapping at night, and see birds on the foreshore in the morning. Rooms vary – the best are large, well appointed and generously supplied with fresh fruit, shortcakes, and do-it-yourself drinks, including Bovril and Horlicks. The food, based on delicacies such as Galloway beef and local lobster and salmon, is "even better than last year", and "universally splendid", according to recent visitors. Breakfast is "super with lots of choice: haggis, kippers, etc; excellent brown toast". There is good walking nearby and the hotel will provide packed lunches. (*Alan Thwaite, Eric Dodson, and others*) A complaint this year about rigid allocation of tables, and one guest thought the food "no-nonsense nothing-special".

Open Mar–early Nov.
Rooms 14 double, 3 single.
Facilities Lounge, residents' lounge, cocktail bar / conservatory, snooker room, restaurant. 3½-acre grounds on bay: sand / rock beach. Safe bathing, fishing, sailing, golf, riding, shooting nearby. Unsuitable for ♿.
Location Off A711 Dumfries–Kircudbright, 2 miles S of Auchencairn on shore road.
Restrictions Smoking discouraged in restaurant, banned in residents' lounge, conservatory. No dogs in public rooms.
Credit cards Access, Visa.
Terms [1996] B&B £46–£52; D,B&B (min. 3 nights) £57–£62. Set lunch (Sun) £8.50, dinner £20.50; full alc £23. Low-season rates; reductions for 3–7-night stays. Children under 12 in parents' room half-price. *V*

Collin House
Auchencairn
nr Castle Douglas DG7 1QN

Tel (01556) 640292
Fax (01556) 640276

Much praise again this year for Pam Hall and John Wood's charming pink 18th-century house by Auchencairn Bay. It has wonderful views across the Solway Firth to the Cumbrian hills beyond, and a splendid location, with good walking and interesting towns to visit. "A lovely house. It is furnished with comfortable traditional and antique furniture, and has the ambience of a much-loved home into which guests are welcomed. Very relaxing." "Large, pretty bedrooms and good bathrooms. The meals were excellent. Our six-year-old son was given marvellous suppers in the kitchen every evening. The breakfasts were astounding." "The owners are very professional, and friendly without being obsequious. We were introduced to fellow diners but not expected to mingle uncomfortably and (horror!) dine at the same table." John Wood ("a first-class chef") produces a short menu of inventive, fairly modern dishes, which changes daily, and features fresh local produce, with fish and game in season. The wine list, also short, is carefully chosen, and there is an interesting, mainly Scottish, cheeseboard. Breakfast includes plump kippers and freshly squeezed orange juice. Fresh flowers everywhere. (*Ann Fletcher, Caroline Thomson, B Spratt, JC, and many others*)

Open Mar–Jan. Closed Jan/Feb.
Rooms 6 double.
Facilities Drawing room, sitting room, dining room. 20-acre grounds: 2-acre garden. Beach, fishing nearby. Unsuitable for ♿.
Location Turn right off A711 ¼ mile E of Auchencairn. Small signs.
Restrictions No smoking: dining room, 1 bedroom. No children under 11 at dinner. Dogs by arrangement; not in public rooms.
Credit cards Access, Amex, Visa.
Terms [1996] B&B £40–£57; D,B&B £68.50–£85.50. Set lunch (residents only) £12, dinner £28.50. Off-season rates; 3-day packages. Christmas, New Year breaks. Young children accommodated free in parents' room.

AUCHTERARDER Perthshire and Kinross — Map 5

Auchterarder House — *Tel* (01764) 663646
Auchterarder PH3 1DZ — *Fax* (01764) 662939

This fine baronial mansion, set in large grounds, with rhododendrons, firs, oaks and beeches, amid Perthshire hills and glens, was built for a Victorian industrialist, and is now owned and run by the hospitable Ian and Audrey Brown. The ambience is one of relaxed, old world luxury – the ideal place to unwind, in total comfort. Rooms are large and elegantly furnished, with complimentary decanters of sherry and fruit bowls. The entrance has a grand *porte cochère*; inside one comes upon a sunken marble conservatory which is used for summer dining, parties and in-house weddings. A recent visitor, lunching alone on a February Monday, was surprised and touched by the trouble taken: "A fire had been lit in the library, a charming small room in which drinks, and then the meal, were served. I was treated like royalty. The chef had gone to the trouble to make a game soup. The quality of food was exceptional, the service charming." "A vast bath sat in the middle of our sumptuous bathroom, which was very large, warm, and panelled, with large mirrors," writes another sybarite. "One might never have moved from it, and just called for room service." Fires burn in the handsome fireplaces everywhere. The dining room is romantic at night, with masses of flowers, and candlelight. Breakfasts are splendid and room service "outstanding". "Even when using the *Guide* voucher, I was upgraded to a large suite." (*RCC Sandys, MW, JS, and others*)

Open All year.
Rooms 3 suites (2 in courtyard), 12 double.
Facilities Drawing room, library, billiard room, dining room, conservatory; conference/function facilities. 17-acre grounds: croquet, putting, pitching hole. Fishing, shooting, golf nearby. Not really suitable for ♿, "but we help".
Location 1½ miles NW of town on B8062 (signposted Crieff).
Restrictions No smoking in dining room. Children under 10 by arrangement.
Credit cards All major cards accepted.
Terms B&B: single £80–£125, double £130–£225, suite £135–£160. Set lunch £18.50, dinner £37.50. D,B&B breaks. Reductions for 2 or more nights. *V*

Give the *Guide* positive support. Don't leave feedback to others.

AUCHTERHOUSE Angus — Map 5

The Old Mansion House *Tel* (01382) 320366
Auchterhouse *Fax* (01382) 320400
by Dundee DD3 0QN

Nigel and Eva Bell's mansion dates back to the 16th century and stands on a knoll, surrounded by fine gardens, beautifully kept, with a small stream, good-sized swimming pool, and croquet and tennis lawns. It has a vaulted entrance hall and fine plasterwork in the drawing room and in the restaurant, which has a Jacobean fireplace, now a wine store. The Bells are professional hosts in the best sense and, with their friendly staff, provide a high standard of service – shoes are cleaned, morning tea brought to bedrooms. The restaurant is popular locally (among business people on weekdays) for traditional French/Scottish cooking, on a menu with plenty of choice; vegetarians are catered for. Bar lunches and suppers are also available. Bedrooms at the top of the house (some are enormous attics under the eaves) are traditional in decor, with antiques and some four-posters; there's good family accommodation. More reports, please.

Open 4 Jan–24 Dec.
Rooms 6 double.
Facilities Lounge bar, cocktail bar, restaurant; private dining room. 11-acre grounds: squash, tennis, croquet, swimming pool, woodland walks. Beaches 10 miles. Unsuitable for ♿.
Location 6 miles NW of Dundee. From A923 fork right at Muirhead on to B956. Hotel 3 miles on left.
Restrictions No smoking in restaurant. No dogs in public rooms.
Credit cards All major cards accepted.
Terms B&B £62.50–£75. Set lunch £15.50; full alc £30. Bar meals. Off-season rates.

BALLATER Aberdeenshire — Map 5

Balgonie Country House *Tel/Fax* (013397) 55482
Braemar Place
Ballater AB35 5RQ

John and Priscilla Finnie's Edwardian country house, in the heart of the "Whisky Trail", just outside Ballater, is peacefully set in lovely grounds with mature trees and lawns: it overlooks the golf course, with the hills of Glen Muick beyond. "The comfort of our room, the friendliness of the staff and the welcome we received from Mr and Mrs Finnie were wonderful," wrote one of last year's guests. "The chef, David Hindmarch, who once cooked for the Queen, uses local fish, game and beef to great effect in his elegant four-course menus: fillet of salmon on a bed of leeks is topped with a horseradish crust, breast of duck comes with a beetroot and apple gateau and a caramel orange jus – everything is beautifully presented." (*AN*) Salmon fishing can be arranged, with notice.

Open All year, except mid-Jan–Mid-Feb.
Rooms 8 double, 1 single.
Facilities Sitting room, bar, restaurant. 3-acre grounds: croquet. Fishing on river Dee, golf, hill-walking nearby. Unsuitable for ♿.
Location On outskirts of Ballater, off A93 Aberdeen–Perth.

Restrictions No smoking in restaurant. Children under 8 must have supper at 6 pm. No dogs in public rooms, unattended in bedrooms.
Credit cards Access, Amex, Visa.
Terms [1996] B&B £35–£57.50; D,B&B £55–£86. Set lunch £17.50, dinner £29.00. Off-season rate: D,B&B £50. 1-night bookings occasionally refused. *V*

Darroch Learg
Braemar Road
Ballater AB35 5UX

Tel (013397) 55443
Fax (013397) 55252

This hotel is composed of two pink-and-grey granite listed country houses, one a former hunting lodge, the other baronial and turreted. It is set amid lovely scenery on the side of a wooded mountain, ten minutes' walk up from Ballater. Overlooking the Dee Valley and the Grampians, it makes a good base for a golfing or fishing holiday. "First class food, good bedrooms and a very warm welcome," write visitors this year, endorsing earlier praise of the "friendly and unintrusive" proprietor, Nigel Franks, the "exceptionally pleasant staff", and the welcome accorded to children (though there are no specific facilities for them). Chef David Mutter's modern Scottish cooking is admired too: three choices for each course, which might include home-smoked wild rabbit with black pudding, and duck breast with foie gras and Hunza apricots with risotto and jus of morels. "Excellent wine list. Good value." Breakfasts are generous and substantial. (*RT and K Johnson, and others*) Bedrooms vary: those on the upper floors can be slightly cramped; most have lovely views.

Open Feb–Dec.
Rooms 17 double, 1 single, in 2 buildings. 1 on ground floor.
Facilities 2 lounges, drawing room, dining room, conservatory; drying room. 4-acre grounds. River Dee ¼ mile, fishing. Birdwatching, shooting, golf, hang-gliding, riding, etc nearby.
Location On A93, ½ mile W of Ballater.
Restrictions No smoking: dining room, drawing room, 4 bedrooms. No dogs in public rooms.
Credit cards All major cards accepted.
Terms B&B: single £35–£45, double £60–£110; D,B&B: single £54–£68, double £98–£156. Set lunch £13.75, dinner £24.75. Spring, summer, autumn breaks; New Year package. Children under 12 accommodated free in parents' room. *V* (Oct–Mar)

Tullich Lodge NEW
Ballater AB35 5SB

Tel (013397) 55406
Fax (013397) 55397

Tullich Lodge returns to our pages after a long absence, with this encomium from an old friend of the *Guide*: "Set on a hillside on the outskirts of Ballater, overlooking Strathdee and distant Lochnagar, this fortified mansion with its arrow-slit windows and fashionable Victorian crenellation has been cherished by its co-owners, Hector Macdonald and Neil Bannister, since 1968. Filled with period furniture and appropriate bygones, it never appears to change. There are huge, brass-tapped baths, throne-like loos, even bells to attract the services of long-dead valets and housemaids. If it pours with rain, the fine first-floor drawing room with its Broadwood piano, or the smaller chintzy sitting room are perfect places in which to sit quietly and read. But it is in the mahogany-panelled dining room that *Tullich* comes into its own. Neil Bannister's food is locally sourced and seasonal. There's no choice on the set dinner menu but it is so carefully orchestrated that choice is made redundant. Salmon, venison, grouse, lobster, halibut, chanterelles; excellent bread, classic soups, roasts and stews are treats to look forward to at the end of the day. Cheeses are usually Scottish and chosen with care; puddings might be nectarine frangipane or cranberry clafoutis. This is the kind of food which never palls. While others diminish themselves with over-elaboration, Neil practises reticence. Naturally the porridge at breakfast is made from oats from a local mill, the kippers are undyed, the marmalade home-made. As tranquil as any Relais du Silence, *Tullich* is a legend among those who come to the Highlands in search of peace and comfort." (*Derek Cooper*)

Open 1 Apr–31 Oct
Rooms 7 double, 3 single. TV on request.
Facilities Drawing room, sitting room, bar, dining room. 8 acre woodland garden. Unsuitable for ♿.
Location 1½ miles E of Ballater on A93 Braemar–Aberdeen.
Restrictions No smoking in dining room. No dogs in public rooms.
Credit cards All major cards accepted.
Terms [1996] B&B £80; D,B&B £100. Light lunch £7, set dinner £25. Reductions for 2 nights or more. 1-night bookings sometimes refused.

BALQUHIDDER Stirling — Map 5

Monachyle Mhor NEW/BUDGET — *Tel* (01877) 384622
Lochearnhead FK19 8PQ — *Fax* (01877) 384305

On the narrow road that winds along Loch Voil, this pink-washed converted farmhouse lies surrounded by fields, with stunning views on all sides. The "genial and caring" hosts, Rob, Jean and Tom Lewis, offer a warm welcome and excellent value to those prepared to make the detour from the Stirling to Crianlarich road. The compact dining room is in a covered veranda running along the front of the house. It serves French-influenced cooking on two fixed-price menus. "The food was delicious," say our nominators, "every item prepared with real care and thoroughness; excellent local fish and game. We did not expect scrambled eggs and smoked salmon for breakfast at such a moderately priced hotel." Good bar meals too. Bedrooms in the courtyard are more modern than those in the main house. (*Margaret and Alan Clarke*) Rob Roy McGregor is buried in the church in Balquhidder village, four miles away.

Open All year.
Rooms 3 suites, 7 double. 5 in courtyard. Self-catering cottages.
Facilities Lounge with TV, lounge bar, dining room. 2,000-acre estate: walking, salmon/trout-fishing, stalking.
Location 11 miles NW of Callander. Turn off A84 at Kingshouse; 6 miles along glen.
Restrictions No smoking: dining room, bedrooms. No children under 12. No dogs.
Credit cards Access, Visa.
Terms [1996] B&B £27.50–£35. Set dinner £18, £21.

> Most hotels have reduced rates out of season and for children, and offer "mini-break" rates throughout the year. It is always worth asking about special terms.

BANAVIE Highland **Map 5**

Torbeag House NEW/BUDGET *Tel/Fax* 01397 772412
Muirshearlich
Banavie, by Fort William PH33 7PB

A welcome addition to our budget category, recently opened, and nominated by a regular *Guide* reporter. "Run by Ken and Gladys Whyte with a bouncy labrador, it is a modern country house, in a large woodsy azalea garden up a steep drive off a quiet back road. It overlooks the Great Glen, and has spectacular views of the north face of Ben Nevis. Everything is newly decorated in Sanderson-style fabrics and wallpaper. It is immaculately clean, with all the 'extras' you find in larger places – flowers and fruit in room, interesting toiletries, good bedside lamps, and glossy magazines. Dinner [at 7.30; four courses, no choice; preferences discussed in advance] is freshly prepared to a high dinner-party standard, and served at separate tables in a dining room with dark Georgian-type furniture, beautiful silver and china, and old oil paintings of prize cattle. Vegetables and fruit come from the garden; bread, jams, oatcakes, yogurt, fudge, etc are home-made. No nightlife nearby; it's a place for people who want peace and quiet, an early night – and value for money." (*Kate Kelly*) Ken Whyte is a self-taught cook; dinner might include smoked salmon and langoustine rolls, followed by venison and red cabbage and bread and butter pudding. Unlicensed; bring your own drink (no corkage charge). Breakfast is a "real Scottish" affair. No smoking.

Open All year. Guests should not arrive before 4 pm except by prior arrangement. Dinner for residents only.
Rooms 3 double.
Facilities Drawing room, dining room. Garden: tennis. Walking, climbing, fishing, sailing, skiing nearby. Unsuitable for ♿.
Location 5 miles N of Fort William. A830 towards Mallaig 1 mile, then B8004 Banavie–Gairlochy 2½ miles. Entrance on left.
Restrictions No smoking. No children under 12. No dogs in public rooms.
Credit cards Access, Visa.
Terms [1996] B&B: £22–£33; D,B&B: £38–£48. Set dinner £16. Packed lunch £5.

BANCHORY Aberdeenshire **Map 5**

Banchory Lodge *Tel* (01330) 822625
Banchory AB31 3HS *Fax* (01330) 825019

In a "marvellous position by the river Dee", this white-painted Georgian house, once a coaching inn, is filled with Victorian and Edwardian furniture and bric-à-brac collected over 30 years by resident owners, Mr and Mrs Jaffray. The hotel has many loyal regulars, and is popular with fishing folk and golfers (there are three courses close by). Floral chintzes abound in bedrooms, "lovely flower arrangements and log fires in public rooms". The food is unashamedly traditional fare: haggis, beef, salmon. Traditional afternoon teas are also served. (*JS*) The Jaffrays offer several specialist breaks, including one devoted to the artist Joseph Farquharson, RA, who lived nearby and whose work they collect.

Open All year, except New Year.
Rooms 1 suite, 21 double.

Facilities 2 lounges, cocktail bar, pool room with TV, 2 restaurants. 10-acre grounds: river with salmon-, trout-fishing (book well in advance). Golf nearby. Unsuitable for ♿.
Location 5 mins' walk from centre. Private carpark.
Credit cards All major cards accepted.
Terms B&B £65–£85; D,B&B £85–£95. Packed lunches available. 3-night specialist breaks: gardens, fishing, golf. *V*

BLAIRGOWRIE Perthshire and Kinross — Map 5

Kinloch House — *Tel* (01250) 884237
by Blairgowrie PH10 6SG — *Fax* (01250) 884333

César award in 1991

This grand 19th-century Scottish mansion, "where cosy opulence and a relaxed atmosphere are the keynote", is peacefully set in a large estate with woods, parklands and highland cattle. Inside are oak panelling, family portraits, *objets d'art*, fresh flowers and books everywhere, and a conservatory. David and Sarah Shentall and their son, Charles, are accommodating hosts, providing a country house ambience alongside impressive attention to detail. "My bedroom had a four-poster bed; its bathroom, larger than the bedroom, had a marvellous full-sized Victorian bath with plumbing to match. The food was excellent, with a large selection for breakfast ranging from smoked salmon kedgeree to sirloin steak, all included in the price." Dinners feature much Scottish fare – haggis, cullen skink, smokies and the like – served in an elegant dining room, with a kilted Mr Shentall to elucidate the menu. There is a good and reasonably priced wine list, and a huge selection of malt whiskies. Breakfasts include a decorative fruit platter. Service is friendly without being effusive. The hotel is popular with shooting parties, having a game larder, drying facilities and kennels for gun-dogs, and with fishermen (plenty of lochs and rivers nearby) and golfers (40 golf courses within an hour's drive). (*John Stirling*) A recent dissenter found it pretentious and over-priced, and the food "indifferent".

Open All year, except 18–30 Dec.
Rooms 2 suites, 16 double, 5 single. 4 on ground floor.
Facilities Lounge, lounge bar, conservatory, restaurant; private dining room. 25-acre grounds. River/loch fishing, shooting, stalking, golf nearby.
Location 3 miles W of Blairgowrie on A923 to Dunkeld.
Restrictions No smoking in restaurant. No children under 7 in restaurant. No dogs in public rooms.
Credit cards All major cards accepted.
Terms D,B&B: single £83, double £173, suite £205. Bar lunches. Set lunch £14.95, dinner £28.90. Reductions for 3 or more nights. 1-night bookings occasionally refused.

> "Set meals" refers to fixed-price meals, which may have ample, limited or no choice on the menu. "Full alc" is the hotel's own estimated price per person of a three-course meal taken *à la carte*, with a half-bottle of house wine. "Alc" is the price of a *carte* meal excluding the cost of wine.

BRIDGE OF MARNOCH Aberdeenshire — Map 5

The Old Manse of Marnoch — *Tel/Fax* (01466) 780873
Bridge of Marnoch
by Huntly AB54 7RS

Patrick and Keren Carter's immaculate early 19th-century house stands amid large grounds with mature gardens and a herb parterre, in a tranquil setting on the banks of the river Deveron. It is popular with the fishing fraternity. Its decor reflects the many years the Carters spent in the Middle East. Bold colours predominate in the public rooms; in the dark red dining room, with original nautical paintings, meals are served with Victorian silver, Edinburgh crystal and fine china. Tea, with two sorts of cake and biscuits, is served without charge (in the beautiful garden in fine weather). Dinner, "eclectic Scottish, traditional/modern" cooking, with choices, includes such dishes as roasted aubergine and red pepper soup, and fillet of beef with rowan sauce. The large breakfast menu is also eclectic, ranging from Turkish figs and Afghan apricots to venison sausages and kedgeree, via "rough meal porridge, served in a wooden bowl with horn spoon"; there is a vast selection of teas. Not everyone appreciates the owners' enthusiastic dogs. More reports, please.

Open All year, except 1 week Oct/Nov, odd days in winter, Christmas, New Year.
Rooms 5 double. No telephone.
Facilities Lounge, study, dining room. 4-acre grounds: garden, herb parterre; river: fishing; stalking, shooting arranged. Unsuitable for ♿.
Location On B9117 less than 1 mile W of A97 Huntly–Banff.
Restrictions No smoking in dining room. No children under 12. No dogs in public rooms.
Credit cards Access, Visa.
Terms B&B: single £54–£60, double £81–£90; D,B&B: single £79–£85, double £131–£140. Set lunch £15, dinner £25. 2-day/weekly rates.

BUSTA Shetland — Map 5

Busta House — *Tel* (01806) 522506
Busta, Brae ZE2 9QN — *Fax* (01806) 522588

This white-painted 16th-century laird's home is said to be the oldest continuously inhabited building in Shetland. It lies in a remote and sometimes windswept position overlooking the sea, and has its own small harbour, and fine views over Busta Voe. "Very friendly, informal, competent and warm-hearted. An island on the island!" "A delightful hotel; the long lounge is both beautiful and comfortable, and, like the library, well stocked with books. Charming staff – one young lady guided me through the malts, remembering what I had taken on each previous night." The library and large sitting room, with flowery fabrics, polished wooden floor, oriental rugs and fresh flowers, are inviting places to spend a wet or lazy day. Meals in the bar and restaurant are popular locally. Lots of traditional Scottish fare. Wholemeal rolls are baked daily; soups and puddings, including ice-creams, are home-made. (*Christian Bartoschek, Michael and Duora Lewis*) One recent visitor, although endorsing most of our entry, would have liked a more regular supply of hot water, and fewer strange sauces (eg, skate with honey).

Open 3 Jan–22 Dec.
Rooms 1 suite, 17 double, 2 single.
Facilities Lounge, library, bar, restaurant. 4-acre grounds on loch: small harbour, loch/sea fishing. Sailing, diving, pony-trekking, indoor swimming pool nearby. Unsuitable for ♿.
Location Clearly signposted from A970 Voe–Hillswick, 1 mile N of Brae.
Restrictions No smoking: restaurant, library. No dogs in public rooms.
Credit cards All major cards accepted.
Terms B&B: single £63, double £86.50, suite £110. Set dinner £22.50. 3-day packages; off-season breaks: painting, archaeology, etc.

CALLANDER Stirling — Map 5

Brook Linn BUDGET — *Tel* (01877) 330103
Leny Feus, Callander FK17 8AU

Fiona and Derek House are the sociable though non-interfering proprietors of this small, elegant but unpretentious Victorian house, built 150 years ago. It is on a hill, ten minutes' walk from the town centre, in a large garden with stream and waterfall (*linn* in Gaelic) and fine views over the Trossachs. A recent visitor praises "the service, and the happy atmosphere provided by Mr and Mrs House – first class in every respect". "Beautiful, quiet setting; hotel spacious, warm and comfortable. We couldn't have asked for a more pleasant stay." The atmosphere is informal; children are welcome. Cooking is slightly adventurous traditional (vegetarians are catered for); excellent home baking. (*JC Dixon, SG, and others*) Mealtimes are fixed: breakfast at 8.15–8.45 am; dinner at 7 pm.

Open Easter–end Oct.
Rooms 6 double, 1 single. 1 on ground floor. No telephone.
Facilities Residents' lounge, dining room. 2-acre garden. Unsuitable for ♿.
Location Through town on A84 from Stirling; right at *Pinewood* nursing home into Leny Feus; right, up hill, at hotel's sign. Private parking.
Restrictions No smoking. No dogs in public rooms.
Credit cards None accepted.
Terms B&B £18–£25; D,B&B £30–£37. Set dinner £12. Weekly rates. Children under 2 £5; under 13 half price.

The Roman Camp — *Tel* (01877) 330003
off Main Street — *Fax* (01877) 331533
Callander FK17 8BG

This 17th-century hunting lodge is owned, like *Auchterarder House* (*qv*), by the Brown family, and run by Eric and Marion Brown. It stands in romantic grounds in a secluded setting on the banks of the river Teith, but is just off Callander's main street. The public rooms retain many original features. There is an oak-beamed bar. The dining room, with modern light wood stencilled beams, is hung with 1930s tapestries of British cathedrals. The older bedrooms on the first floor are "in traditional style, very stylish, some quite grand". Spacious modern ones are on the ground floor in a new wing. Simon Burns' contemporary Scottish cooking, thought "delicious, and very elegant" by some, may be too *nouvelle* for others. Copious breakfast includes porridge, haggis and black pudding, as well as more usual cooked and uncooked items. One couple this year enjoyed their stay, but found their bathroom "grotty".

Open All year.
Rooms 3 suites, 11 double. 7 on ground floor (1 adapted for ♿).
Facilities Drawing room, library, bar, conservatory, restaurant; conference/function facilities. 17-acre grounds: river, ¾-mile fishing.
Location E end of Main Street (small driveway between 2 pink cottages).
Restrictions No smoking in restaurant. No children under 5 in restaurant after 7 pm. No dogs in public rooms.
Credit cards All major cards accepted.
Terms B&B: single £69–£109, double £89–£139, suite £129–£159; D,B&B: single £103–£143, double £157–£207, suite £197–£227. Set lunch £18, dinner £34. Full alc £45. 2-day breaks off season. *V*

CANONBIE Dumfries and Galloway — Map 5

Riverside Inn NEW — *Tel* (013873) 71512 and 71295
Canonbie DG14 0UX

Returning to the *Guide*, now that Robert and Susan Phillips have decided not to sell, this small inn on the banks of the Esk is popular with fishing folk. It continues to provide high class dinners and bar meals for travellers on their way north or south, and is a useful base for exploring Hadrian's Wall and the Solway coast. Reports this year are enthusiastic: "Delightful couple, restrained and rather shy, but kind and very helpful. Good rooms, good beds, good food, attractive surroundings. The service is efficient, unobtrusive and quietly friendly. We had bar meals each evening – *very* good value, well-cooked food, quality ingredients. Plenty of good cheer in the cosy bar with its open fire, real ale, and huge variety of malts. Excellent breakfasts." "Sue Phillips makes all her own preserves, jams, marmalades, sauces, stuffings." Bedrooms have chintz curtains and covers and lots of welcoming touches – flowers, bowls of fruit, etc. (*Stephanie Sowerby, Good Pub Guide, and others*) One visitor reported a decidedly cool welcome.

Open All year, except 2 weeks Nov, Christmas, 2 weeks Feb.
Rooms 7 double. 2 in cottage in garden. 1 on ground floor.
Facilities 2 lounges, lounge bar, restaurant. Small garden. River Esk 50 yds: fishing available.
Location M6 exit 44. 10 miles N on A7; turn into Canonbie. Bottom of hill by Esk bridge. Private carpark.
Restrictions No smoking in restaurant. Dogs by arrangement.
Credit cards Access, Visa.
Terms [1996] B&B: single £55, double £75. Bar meals £5–£15. Set dinner £18.50–£22.50; full alc £20–£25. 2-day winter breaks.

CARDROSS Argyll and Bute — Map 5

Kirkton House BUDGET — *Tel* (01389) 841951
Darleith Road — *Fax* (01389) 841868
Cardross G82 5EZ

This 160-year-old converted farmhouse built round a courtyard, and with superb views of the Clyde, is described by its owners, Stewart and Gillian Macdonald, as "country guest accommodation". It is unpretentious and informal; the bedrooms are comfortable, with charming, simple furniture. The "high quality" plain country food is prepared by Gillian Macdonald, and there's a simple and well-chosen wine list. "Excellent Scottish breakfast." Despite its tranquil setting, the house is only 18 miles from Glasgow; the airport is about 25 minutes away by car. Some of the rooms are suitable for families; cots, high chairs, laundry facilities and baby-sitting are available. A 1996 report: "Pleasant in every way, and very good value." (*Lisa and Peter Simon*)

Open All year, except Christmas, New Year. Lunch not served.
Rooms 6 double. 2 on ground floor.
Facilities Lounge, dining room (no-smoking). 2-acre grounds: children's play area, paddock, stabling for visiting horses. River Clyde 1 mile; fishing, walking, birdwatching, golf nearby.
Location 18 miles NW of Glasgow. Turn N off A814 at W end of Cardross, up Darleith Rd. Drive on right after ½ mile, past 3 cottages.
Credit cards Access, Amex, Visa.
Terms B&B: £26–£37.50; D,B&B £40–£55. Set dinner £18. Off-season breaks.

COLONSAY Argyll and Bute — Map 5

Isle of Colonsay Hotel NEW — *Tel* (01951) 200316
Isle of Colonsay PA61 7YP — *Fax* (01951) 200353

Kevin and Christa Byrne's long-popular hotel overlooking Scalasaig harbour. On one of Argyll's remotest islands, reached by ferry 3 times a week; guests can be marooned by storms. Golden beaches, rocky cliffs, plenty of wildlife, sea and loch fishing. Free loan of bicycles to adults. Informal atmosphere. Good cooking, with emphasis on seafood. Bedrooms vary in size; most have en suite *shower. Garden bungalow for families. Open 1 Mar–5 Nov. Not really suitable for* ♿ *"but help available". No dogs in public rooms. All major credit cards accepted. B&B £45–£80. Set dinner £21. Was for sale, but the Byrnes have decided to stay; fresh reports badly needed.* *V*

CONTIN Highland — Map 5

Coul House NEW — *Tel* (01997) 421487
Contin, by Strathpeffer IV14 9EY — *Fax* (01997) 421945

Martyn and Ann Hill's mansion, built in 1821, stands in a splendid position at the end of a winding drive, with views towards the mountains and forests of Strathconon. "The hallway is immediately welcoming," writes its nominator, "log fire, comfortable seats, sleeping dogs." The fine octagonal drawing room is more formal, and the dining room has a huge window overlooking the garden. Chef Chris Bentley's cooking – "good and interesting" – includes ambitious "Taste of Scotland" dishes, as well as vegetarian options and "one very plain dish for the smattering of guests who have reached an age where a good night's sleep is preferable to rich food in fancy sauces". Bedrooms vary in size, but are well equipped. (*Prof. Peter and Mrs Andrina Robson*) A bagpiper plays in the garden on Friday evening in the summer.

Open All year.
Rooms 1 suite, 16 double, 3 single. 4 on ground floor.
Facilities Ramp. Entrance lounge, drawing room, 2 bars, restaurant. 8-acre grounds: 9-hole pitch and putt course. Salmon- and trout-fishing, golf nearby.

Location In village, ½ mile up drive, to right off A835 to Ullapool.
Restrictions No smoking in restaurant. No dogs in restaurant, bar.
Credit cards All major cards accepted.
Terms B&B £35.00–£68.50; D,B&B £49.50–£83.50. 6-course set dinner £26.50. Full alc £30. 3/7-day breaks. Christmas, New Year, fishing, golf, pony-trekking packages. *V*

CRIANLARICH Stirling — Map 5

Allt-Chaorain House BUDGET
Crianlarich FK20 8RU
Tel (01838) 300283
Fax (01838) 300238

Conflicting reports this year for this home-like hotel, set amongst wooded hills in a remote part of Perthshire. Roger McDonald is described as "an excellent host with a quiet manner and a quirky sense of humour, who looks after your every need". Other compliments: "a warm welcome and very good food"; "comfortable beds"; "good value for money". (*Jean Ekins-Daukes, John Campbell, Geraldine Terry*) On the downside, there have been complaints about the decor; bedrooms can be small, with fairly basic bathrooms; and some visitors complain of slapdash "take it or leave it" service. Traditional Scottish three-course dinners are served in a panelled dining room. The house party atmosphere includes communal dining (residents only), six guests to a table, at 7 pm, traditional home-cooked dishes in generous portions with plenty of fresh vegetables. For breakfast there are "healthy" and "heart-attack" choices. There's excellent walking nearby, with "a great concentration of Munroes [mountains over 3,000 feet] for the intrepid". More reports, please.

Open 20 Mar–27 Oct. Dining room closed for lunch.
Rooms 8 double. 4 on ground floor.
Facilities Lounge with honesty bar, sun lounge, dining room. 10-acre grounds: gardens, croquet. Lochs all around; fishing, walking.
Location 1 mile N of Crianlarich, 500 yds on left off A82 towards Tyndrum.
Restrictions Smoking in sun lounge only. No children under 7. No dogs in dining room.
Credit cards Access, Amex, Visa.
Terms B&B £33–£52; D,B&B £48–£67. Set dinner £15–£18. Reductions for long stays. Children 7–12 accommodated at half price in parents' room.

CRINAN Argyll and Bute — Map 5

Crinan Hotel
Crinan PA31 8SR
Tel (01546) 830261
Fax (01546) 830292

This incomparably positioned hotel stands at the seaward end of the eight-mile Crinan Canal, which connects Loch Fyne to the Atlantic. Nicolas and Frances Ryan have been here for 25 years. No beauty outside, it has lovely views from all its rooms across to the mountains of Mull and the Isle of Jura. Simple bedrooms have pastel colours and pine furniture; nine have a private balcony. The rooftop bar, recently refurbished, has a light oak central bar, a "colonial" decor and paintings by Mrs Ryan (the artist Frances Macdonald). There are two restaurants. Nick Ryan is chef in the top-floor decidedly pricey gourmet *Lock 16* (the last lock on the canal is number 15), where picture windows make the most of the view. Seating only 20, it specialises in seafood straight off the boats, perfectly cooked. Angela Burns is chef in the cheaper ground-floor restaurant, the *Westward*, which features Angus beef, local salmon and seafood and other Scottish delicacies. The public bar also serves fish and seafood, and home-made soups. "Staff are outstanding – the receptionist insisted on carrying our bags," wrote correspondents last year. Poor sound insulation can be a problem in some rooms. More reports, please.

Open All year, except 1 week Christmas. Restaurants closed midday; *Lock 16* also closed Oct–May, Sun/Mon.
Rooms 1 suite, 19 double, 2 single.
Facilities Lift. 2 lounges, 3 bars, 2 restaurants. ½-acre garden. Safe, sandy beaches nearby; fishing.
Location At centre of Lochgilphead follow A83 over small roundabout; right at next roundabout on to A816 to Oban; left after 2 miles on to B841 to Crinan.
Restrictions No smoking in restaurants. No dogs in restaurants.
Credit cards Access, Amex, Visa.
Terms D,B&B: single £75, double £130. Bar lunches. Set dinner: *Westward* £30; *Lock 16* £40. Winter rates.

DERVAIG Argyll and Bute — Map 5

Druimard Country House BUDGET
Dervaig, Tobermory
Isle of Mull PA75 6QW
Tel (01688) 400291
Fax (01688) 400345

"A haven for wildlife and a must for theatre-goers, with a friendly atmosphere, total peace, and the sound of curlews late in the evening." Haydn and Wendy Hubbard's Victorian house stands "amid superb scenery" on a hillside just outside a pretty village at the head of Loch Cuin, on the north-west side of the island. It has stunning views across the glen and the river Bellart. A converted cow byre in its grounds houses the world's smallest professional theatre, the 43-seat Mull Little Theatre, which "plays to packed houses" from April to October. There's a pretty conservatory, and a cosy lounge. Bedrooms are of reasonable size, and simply furnished, with flowery fabrics, fresh flowers and small but well-equipped shower or bathroom. Mrs Hubbard's excellent cooking puts the emphasis on local produce – Mull scallops, langoustines, local cheeses. Breakfasts "are well cooked, with plenty of choice". Calgary beach, a wide expanse of white sand, is close by. (*PF*)

Open 1 Apr–end Oct.
Rooms 1 suite, 5 double, 1 single.
Facilities Lounge, conservatory, restaurant. 1 acre grounds: theatre. Beaches, fishing nearby (ghillie available).
Location From Craignure ferry, A849 W through Salen. Left to Dervaig after 1½ miles. Hotel on right before village.
Restrictions No smoking in restaurant. No dogs in public rooms.
Credit cards Access, Visa.
Terms [1996] B&B £34–49.50; D,B&B £50.50–£66. Set dinner £18.50. *V*

> The *V* sign at the end of an entry indicates hotels in the UK and Ireland that have agreed to take part in our Voucher scheme and to give *Guide* readers a 25% discount on their room rates, subject to the conditions explained in *How to read the entries* and listed on the backs of the vouchers.

DULNAIN BRIDGE Highland — Map 5

Auchendean Lodge BUDGET — *Tel* (01479) 851347
Dulnain Bridge
Grantown-on-Spey PH26 3LU

Ian Kirk and Eric Hart's Edwardian hunting lodge, run on house party lines, is gloriously set in the Cairngorms, overlooking the Spey valley. Its gardens back on to a pine-covered hill with plenty of wildlife, fine views and good walking. Much of the original Art Nouveau decor has been maintained. Furnishing of bedrooms and drawing room (which has a log fire) is traditional, with antiques and period furniture, fresh flowers, miscellaneous knick-knacks, collections of china, pictures, and books and games; it may be a bit kitsch for some tastes. "The owners are professionals," writes a fan. "They anticipate one's needs, they stop and talk, and they provide many extra services that most hoteliers don't consider." Others have praised the "very good" cooking, "French/Scottish with an emphasis on game", with limited choice on the menu. "Home grown vegetables and honey, home-made jams all excellent." In the autumn, Eric Hart takes guests on "wild fungal forays", and menus often include ceps and chanterelles from the local woods. There is an extensive wine list, particularly strong in bottles from New Zealand, Eric Hart's home country. (*J Moody, Mr EM Arnold, and others*) One single room is "very small".

Open All year, except 4 weeks in winter. Lunch not served.
Rooms 6 double, 2 single.
Facilities Ramps. Lounge, drawing room, dining room. 1½-acre grounds: 9-hole pitch and putt, access to 200-acre woods. Fishing, golf, tennis, skiing nearby. Only dining room suitable for ♿.
Location 1 mile S of Dulnain Bridge, on A95 to Aviemore.
Restrictions No smoking: dining room, drawing room. No dogs in public rooms, except lounge.
Credit cards All major cards accepted (*3.5% commission added*).
Terms B&B £17–£47; D,B&B £40–£70. Set dinner £23.50.

DUNKELD Perthshire and Kinross — Map 5

Kinnaird — *Tel* (01796) 482440
Kinnaird Estate — *Fax* (01796) 482289
by Dunkeld PH8 0LB

This luxurious yet unstuffy 18th-century dower house, Grade B listed (Relais & Châteaux), is set in a vast estate, with magnificent views over the Tay valley and "soothing Scottish scenery as far as the eye can see". There's a wide variety of sporting facilities (see below), and excellent walking and birdwatching. It is run by its American proprietor Mrs Constance Ward, with manager Douglas Jack. Public rooms are much as they would have been 80 years ago, with family portraits, photographs, memorabilia, antiques and flowers. The main lounge is cedar-panelled; there is a fine snooker room. Bedrooms are sumptuously decorated; each has a gas log fire. In the impressive restaurant with chandeliers and italianate frescoed landscapes, chef John Webber (Mosimann-trained) serves such dishes as tortellini of squat lobster with a risotto of lemon zest and herbs, confit of quail, and hot raspberry soufflé. The wine list is comprehensive, with many half bottles.

Breakfasts are "well above average". "Probably the best hotel we have visited in the United Kingdom; a smoothly unobtrusive and efficient operation," wrote one visitor last year; another was so moved by the romance of the location that he successfully proposed marriage by the log fire in the drawing room. But a recent dissenter thought the atmosphere somewhat cool, and the food not up to its previous standard. More reports, please.

Open All year. Thurs–Sun only 6 Jan–16 Mar.
Rooms 1 suite, 8 double. 1 on ground floor. 4 holiday cottages.
Facilities Lift. Drawing room, morning room, study, billiard room, 2 dining rooms; function facilities. 9,000-acre estate: gardens, tennis, croquet, shooting, clay pigeon-shooting, 3 trout lochs, riding. Salmon- and trout-fishing on river Tay ½ mile.
Location NE of Dunkeld. From A9 Perth–Pitlochry left on to B898 to Dalguise/Balnaguard. *Kinnaird* 4½ miles on right.
Restrictions No smoking in dining rooms. No children under 12. No dogs in house (kennels available).
Credit cards Access, Amex, Visa.
Terms D,B&B single £195–£269.50, double £225–£319, suite £225–£354. Set lunch (2–3 courses) £19.50–£24, dinner (4 courses) £39.50. Winter rate (not Christmas, New Year): D,B&B double £225.

DUNOON Argyll and Bute — Map 5

Enmore Hotel — *Tel* (01369) 702230
Marine Parade, Kirn — *Fax* (01369) 702148
Dunoon PA23 8HH

David and Angela Wilson's Victorian villa on the edge of Dunoon was originally the retreat of a rich Glasgow businessman. The decor is a happy combination of modern comforts with antique furniture and a country atmosphere. Visitors enjoy the log fires, the good food, and evening walks along the boardwalk. Rooms are large and well appointed, with plenty of cupboard space. Some have a four-poster bed, and there are plenty of extras: tins of sweets, a good selection of books, towelling dressing-gowns; also a jacuzzi and – an innovation – a *digital* trouser-press. The Wilsons make good use of home-grown vegetables ("excellent soup"), and local ingredients – sea trout, prawns and Argyll smoked venison. "*Amuse-gueule* served in the lounge were the most generous and original encountered anywhere." Breakfast includes fresh orange juice, local kippers, and French or cinnamon toast. The hotel also has two "international standard" squash courts. Children are welcome. "All in all a *delightful* hotel." (*J Ford, J Eunson, Derek Smith, and others*)

Open All year, except Christmas week.
Rooms 1 suite, 7 double, 2 single. 2 on ground floor.
Facilities 2 lounges, bar, dining room; conference room; shop; 2 squash courts. 1-acre grounds. Private shingle beach across road: safe but cold bathing, boating. Golf, swimming pool, tennis, pony-trekking nearby. Unsuitable for ♿.
Location On Marine Parade between 2 ferries, 1 mile W of town centre. Private parking.
Restrictions No smoking in dining room. No dogs in dining room.
Credit cards Access, Amex, Visa.
Terms B&B £25–£80; D,B&B £45–£95. Set lunch £15, dinner £20; full alc £30. Romantic, New Year, winter, spring, etc, breaks. V

DUNVEGAN Highland Map 5

Harlosh House *Tel/Fax* (01470) 521367
by Dunvegan
Isle of Skye IV55 8ZG

"A beautiful situation on the edge of a sea-loch, with the Cuillins behind, seals and herons in the water, and lambs at the door. Exceptionally good dinners and breakfasts, quality showing in all the details; fresh flowers on the tables. Comfortable rooms and excellent, friendly staff. If you want remote peace, beauty, comfort and good food, this is it!" "Peter is a magnificent cook – unusual juxtapositions of flavours all worked extremely well: monkfish with lemon grass, and a sensational turbot with caramelised shallots on leeks. Lovely puddings, too." More praise this year for Peter and Lindsey Elford's small croft-style house in a remote and peaceful setting on a peninsula jutting into Loch Bracadale. Breakfasts are excellent, and seafood is a speciality at dinner; bread, pasta, ice-cream, and sorbets are home-made. Wide range of malt whiskies. No grounds to speak of – "but who cares when you can stroll straight down to the loch?" Excellent walking nearby, and lots of wildlife. (*Ben Whitaker, Mary Milne-Day, and others*) The food has now earned a red "Meals" in *Michelin*.

Open Easter–mid-Oct.
Rooms 6 double.
Facilities Lounge with bar, sun lounge, dining room. Loch 50 yds: fishing, sailing; pony-trekking, shooting nearby. Unsuitable for ♿.
Location 4 miles S of Dunvegan by A863. Between Roag and Caroy take minor road, signposted to Harlosh, for 2 miles.
Restrictions No smoking: restaurant, bedrooms. No dogs.
Credit cards Access, Visa.
Terms B&B £34–£65. Set dinner £24.50.

EDINBURGH Map 5

Drummond House *Tel/Fax* (0131) 557 9189
17 Drummond Place, EH3 6PL

Alan and Josephine Dougall's fine Georgian house, with its spacious rooms, high ceilings and tall windows remains popular with our readers. "As nice as ever." "*Fine*. Full of good taste; grand host." From a pillared hallway with flagstones and oriental rugs, a spiral staircase leads up to a cupola. It is in the city's 18th-century New Town, like most of our Edinburgh entries, in a handsome square opposite a garden, only minutes from Princes Street. (*William Bentsen, and others*) Breakfast is very good, with lots of different home-made jams, although one guest found it "too communal". The house can be cool, but rooms are provided with electric blankets, which are switched on early. No smoking.

Open All year, except Christmas.
Rooms 3 double. No telephone/TV.
Facilities Lounge with TV, breakfast room. Unsuitable for ♿.
Location Just N of St Andrew Sq and Waverley Stn, at E end of Gt King St.
Restrictions No smoking. No children under 12. No dogs.
Credit cards Access, Visa.
Terms B&B: single £60–£85, double £90.

Malmaison
1 Tower Place
Leith EH6 7DB
Tel (0131) 555 6868
Fax (0131) 555 6999

Joint César award in 1996

The idea behind the two *Malmaisons* – there's a sister hotel in Glasgow (*qv*) – is simple: no extras, and concomitantly low prices. *Malmaison* has halved the cost of a first-class room in Edinburgh by reducing staff to a minimum and omitting some of the "frills". What you get is crisply designed rooms with good beds and "cleverly assembled" fabrics, TV and CD player. This innovative "short on luxury, high on comfort" formula, invented by Ken McCulloch, owner of the much grander *One Devonshire Gardens* in Glasgow (*qv*), is clearly working, as this year's reports confirm: "The location in the port of Leith, two miles from the city centre, is both trendy and attractive, and I liked the second-empire decor of this turreted former seaman's mission, with an open-air café on the plaza in front. My bedroom was large, light, and stylish; blue-and-white striped bedcover, deep blue blinds; bathroom with traditional fittings, wooden loo seat etc." "The hotel was informal, and everybody very helpful; delicious breakfasts." The brasserie serves well-executed traditional French dishes – steak-frites, coq au vin, etc. (*CR, Antony Hill, and others*) One recent visitor found the background music in the café, "even at breakfast", obtrusive.

Open All year, 25 Dec.
Rooms 6 suites, 17 double.
Facilities Lift. Café bar, brasserie.
Location Leith dockside, 10 mins' drive from city centre.
Restrictions No smoking in bedrooms. No dogs in public rooms.
Credit cards All major cards accepted.
Terms Rooms £80, suite £110. Breakfast: continental £6, Scottish £10. Full alc £28.

---

17 Abercromby Place BUDGET
17 Abercromby Place, EH3 6LB
Tel (0131) 557 8036
Fax (0131) 558 3453

Mrs Eirlys Lloyd (she has reverted to her maiden name) recently renovated this large and handsome house, built in 1815 and originally the home of Edinburgh's famous architect, William Playfair. Now a Wolsey Lodge, it overlooks private gardens, has private parking, and is only five minutes' walk (uphill) from Princes Street. "Lovely, convenient location; overwhelming impression of staying in a friend's house. Excellent breakfast – proper food, and not a packet in sight." "As nice as ever," writes another *aficionado*. "We very much like the mews room at the back, which suits us with our baby." Breakfasts are taken communally; there's "one huge table for all the guests to eat at or hide behind *The Scotsman*". An evening meal is now available; guests should bring their own wine. (*Jon Hughes, William Keegan, and others*) One prospective visitor found his attempts to book thwarted by the "private house" element: telephone calls not answered, even by a machine; no billboard, etc.

Open All year.
Rooms 7 double, 2 single. Unsuitable for ♿.
Facilities Sitting room, breakfast room.
Location 5 mins' walk from city centre, in road parallel to Princes St. Private parking.
Restrictions No smoking. No dogs.

Credit cards Access, Visa.
Terms B&B £35–£45. Set dinner £25.

Sibbet House *Tel* (0131) 556 1078
26 Northumberland Street *Fax* (0131) 557 9445
EH3 6LS

Jim and Aurore Sibbet offer an exceptionally warm welcome and "very good value" in their beautifully proportioned Georgian house in a grey stone terrace in New Town, a couple of blocks from Princes Street. It has a fine staircase, lit by a huge domed rooflight, and a large drawing room on the first floor. The Sibbets (he something of a character, she very French) were formerly interior decorators, and the hotel is stuffed with antiques and knick-knacks in public rooms and bedrooms alike. The bedrooms, described by one recent guest as "amazingly luxurious", mostly have *en suite* facilities; the smallest has a private bathroom across a landing. All have comfortable chairs and "lights you can actually read by". Visitors are given a key to come and go as they please. They are introduced to one another, but there is no pressure to socialise. Lavish breakfasts are laid out on an antique sideboard with real silver cutlery. Departures are on occasion serenaded by bagpipes. A simple evening meal is available, with "menus at the instruction of guests", and there are plenty of restaurants nearby. (*KK, and others*) One warning: the basement self-contained apartment (not in the same building) is "dreary".

Open All year, except Christmas/New Year.
Rooms 4 double. 2 self-contained apartments 2 blocks away.
Facilities Drawing room, dining room. Unsuitable for ♿.
Location 5 mins' walk from centre. Private garage (£3 a night); parking in private lane.
Restrictions No smoking. No dogs.
Credit cards Access, Visa.
Terms B&B £35–£40. Set dinner £25. 1-night bookings sometimes refused.

ERISKA Argyll and Bute Map 5

Isle of Eriska NEW *Tel* (01631) 720371
Ledaig, by Oban PA37 1SD *Fax* (01631 720531

Back in our pages after a long absence, the Buchanan-Smiths' splendid Victorian mansion on a tiny private island off the west coast (linked by a bridge to the mainland) has been transformed by their energetic son Beppo. "He is," write recent visitors, former super-hoteliers themselves, "breathing fresh life into the Scottish Baronial pile, which remains more country home than hotel. The large, light bedrooms have been refurbished with flair and attention to detail. Bathrooms are smart and tiled. The housekeeping fairy still tucks a pair of hot water bottles into double beds each night. The new chef, Euan Clark, with an all-but-Mohican haircut, is solemn and clever. He produced three truly excellent dinners, making good use of local scallops, shellfish and seafood, excellent Aberdeen Angus beef. Nice traditional touches like crisp fried whitebait appear, too, and a savoury as an alternative to cheese. Tame badgers come to the library door for their 'supper' of bread and milk every night; wildlife abounds on the island – otters, seals, herons and deer. Best of all, a smart 17-metre indoor swimming pool, a small gymnasium, and a six-hole golf course now augment the tennis court, boats and clay pigeon-shooting. Robin Buchanan-Smith, Church of Scotland minister, raconteur and character, has created an ambience of warmth and bonhomie, but those seeking tranquillity and seclusion will find all they want in this peaceful house." (*Eve and Ron Jones*)

Open All year, except Jan/Feb.
Rooms 15 double, 2 single. 2 on ground floor, with access for ♿.
Facilities 3 drawing rooms, bar/library, dining room; indoor swimming pool, gymnasium. 300-acre island: tennis, golf, boating, clay pigeon-shooting.
Location 12 miles N of Oban. 4 miles W of A828.
Restrictions No children under 10 in dining room at night. No dogs in public rooms.
Credit cards Access, Amex, Visa.
Terms B&B: single £148, double £185–£215. Set dinner £35.

EVIE Orkney — Map 5

Woodwick House BUDGET
Evie KW17 2PQ
Tel (01856) 751330
Fax (01856) 751383

"At ten o'clock one evening, eight Norwegians whose boat had broken down turned up unannounced, bringing a giant lobster and a large number of crabs. Ann cheerfully prepared them dinner, unaided, and they left satisfied at 1.30 am." A recent episode at Ann Herdman's "excellent small hotel", set in some of the island's only woods, with bluebells, rookery, and a small stream running down to the lapping waters of Woodwick Bay. The bedrooms are simple but well equipped. The food is healthy and varied; breakfasts, with home-made marmalade, are excellent. "Ann Herdman, a superb and imaginative cook, is friendly and interesting, and helpful in every respect." Food can be simply or more elaborately prepared according to guests' requirements, and will include all the local specialities – lobster, oysters, crab, beef and lamb. Special diets are catered for, too. (*Michael and Duora Lewis, Commander JC Dixon*) Concerts, poetry readings and musical recitals are held, and sometimes a spontaneous *ceilidh* in the evening.

Open All year.
Rooms 4 suites, 7 double, 1 single. 4 with *en suite* facilities. 2 on ground floor. No telephone/radio/TV.
Facilities Lounge, TV lounge, dining room; room with piano for entertainments. 12-acre grounds on bay: fishing, birdwatching; guided tours.
Location From A965 turn off to Evie. After *c.*15 mins, right at sign to *Woodwick House*, then left; house in trees at end of road.
Restriction Smoking in restaurant and bedrooms discouraged.
Credit cards None accepted.
Terms B&B £20–£36; D,B&B £30–£49. Set lunch from £2.00, dinner from £14.50. Terms negotiable. Christmas, New Year packages. *V*

> Our italicised entries indicate hotels which are worth considering but which, for various reasons – inadequate information, lack of feedback, ambivalent reports – do not at the moment warrant a full entry. We particularly welcome comments on these hotels.

FORT WILLIAM Highland — Map 5

Crolinnhe BUDGET — *Tel* (01397) 702709
Grange Road
Fort William PH33 6JF

"We wholeheartedly endorse your entry. The Mackenzies made us very welcome," write recent visitors to this unassuming no-smoking B&B, in a quiet residential area a short walk from the town centre. Its Gaelic name ("Above the Linnhe") describes its position on a hillside, with a fine view over the loch to the North Western Highlands. It is a carefully renovated Victorian villa, with a pretty, homey decor. Bedrooms, some with bathroom *en suite*, are spacious, with floral bedspreads and wallpaper, and TV. Most overlook the loch, as does the breakfast room. What makes it special is the warmth and friendliness of Flora and Kenneth Mackenzie. "Breakfast was the best of our trip, and included award-winning haggis; if you're trying haggis for the first time, this is the place." Rates are "amazingly reasonable". (*Jill and Steve Flinn, and others*)

Open Mar–Nov.
Rooms 5 double. 1 with bath, 2 with shower. No telephone.
Facilities Lounge, dining room. 1-acre grounds. Loch 200 yds. Unsuitable for ♿.
Location 10 mins' walk from centre. From High St take Lundavra Rd; fork right into Grange Rd. Private parking.
Restrictions No smoking. No dogs.
Credit cards None accepted.
Terms B&B double £56–£70.

The Factor's House — *Tel* (01397) 705767
Torlundy, Fort William PH33 6SN — *Fax* (01397) 701421

This early 20th-century house was once the home of the factor (estate manager) of *Inverlochy Castle* (see next page). They now run it as a much less pricey B&B for those who flinch at the castle's tariff, but may want to dine there. "The house is decorated with colourful fabrics, gentle wall colours and good lighting; furniture is a mix of antique and good repro. Bedrooms overlook Ben Nevis or the surrounding hills. They are modern, cosy and well equipped; with small but efficient bathrooms. Some are spacious. Efficient double-glazing mitigates the noise of traffic on the nearby main road. Generous breakfasts are served in a pretty room with a jolly, chatty atmosphere." (*PF*) More reports, please.

Open Mar–Dec. Closed Christmas, New Year.
Rooms 4 double, 1 single.
Facilities Lounge, breakfast room. 1-acre garden; access to castle grounds. Unsuitable for ♿.
Location On A82 3 miles NE of Fort William, after turning to *Inverlochy Castle*.
Restriction No dogs in public rooms.
Credit cards Access, Amex, Visa.
Terms B&B £50–£60.

> Inevitably some hotels change hands or close after we have gone to press. It may be prudent to check the ownership when booking, particularly in the case of small establishments.

Inverlochy Castle *Tel* (01397) 702177
Torlundy, Fort William PH33 6SN *Fax* (01397) 702953

César award in 1984

"The service was brilliant: we were treated both like royalty *and* like friends. Our every need seemed to be anticipated by telepathy. Food as good as ever." "The staff are as affable as any I have come across." "We had a truly sumptuous bedroom; its bathroom was sumptuous too, and the size of most hotel bedrooms." Praise this year and last for one of Britain's most luxurious country house hotels (Relais & Châteaux). Owned by Grete Hobbs, it has been a hotel for 28 years; the exemplary manager, Michael Leonard, is now in his second decade. It is a 19th-century Scottish baronial house, set in huge grounds amid magnificent Highland scenery. Its chief architectural glory is the Great Hall with crystal chandeliers and a frescoed ceiling with cherubs among clouds. There's a splendid billiard room with a high ceiling and a marbled fireplace. The drawing room has open fires and comfortable sofas and armchairs. Flowers everywhere. In the *Michelin*-starred restaurant, Simon Haigh, who trained with Raymond Blanc, serves fine classic cookery, with a strong emphasis on local fish and game; he will also turn out a good haggis. Servings are generous. And there is an outstanding wine list. (*S Beresford, and others*)

Open Mar–Nov.
Rooms 1 suite, 15 double, 1 single.
Facilities Great Hall, drawing room, 2 dining rooms, billiard room; facilities for small conferences out of season. 50-acre grounds in 500-acre estate: gardens, tennis, loch, fishing. Golf, skiing nearby. Chauffeur-driven limousines for hire. Unsuitable for ♿.
Location On A82 3 miles NE of Fort William, just past golf club. Follow signs to hotel; ignore signs to Inverlochy village/Inverlochy Castle (ruins).
Restrictions Smoking banned in restaurant, discouraged in bedrooms. Children under 12 must share parents' room. No dogs in hotel (kennels available).
Credit cards Access, Amex, Visa.
Terms B&B: single £150–£175, double £220–£280, suite £295–£350. Set dinner £42.50.

GLAMIS Angus Map 5

Castleton House NEW *Tel* (01307) 840340
by Glamis, Forfar DD8 1SJ *Fax* (01307) 840506

In a rather flat and uninspiring stretch of Scotland – "raspberry and potato country" – William and Maureen Little's "respectable grey stone Victorian pile" is approached by a long drive between tall flowering trees and bushes. "It is efficient, clean and well run, with a helpful staff and a luxurious feel," is an inspector's verdict. The bedrooms are newly decorated, with striped wallpaper, chintzy bedspreads and Queen Anne/Louis XV style furniture; exotic bathrooms have gold taps. Dinner is served in the conservatory dining room, which can be uncosy on a winter night: our inspector thought the old dining room, now the breakfast room, would have been more suitable. Ryan Young's traditional/modern cooking is popular with locals; puddings are a strong point. Good breakfast, with plenty of choice.

Open All year.
Rooms 6 double.

Facilities Lounge, bar, conservatory restaurant, breakfast room. 9-acre grounds. Fishing, shooting, pony-trekking nearby. Unsuitable for ♿.
Location 3 miles W of Glamis, on A94 midway between Forfar and Coupar Angus.
Restrictions No smoking in dining room. No dogs in house (kennels provided).
Credit cards Access, Amex, Visa.
Terms B&B: single £70, double £100; D,B&B: single £85, double £130. Set lunch £12.75, dinner £19.50; full alc £30. Reductions for 2 or more nights.

GLASGOW — Map 5

Babbity Bowster BUDGET — *Tel* (0141) 552 5055
16–18 Blackfriars Street, G1 1PE — *Fax* (0141) 552 7774

César award in 1995

A highly convivial café/bar/restaurant/hotel (named for an 18th-century dance), owned by bearded Fraser Laurie, "a great character who really seems to enjoy what he does". The ground floor is a down-to-earth pub; there's a restaurant above and bedrooms on the second floor. No reception (you apply to the bar), but the welcome is warm and informal; staff carry bags up and down. Rooms are small and very simple, but clean, with good wardrobe space; no "goodies", no TV. The listed Robert Adam house is in a pedestrian street in Merchant City, not far from the centre. You might expect it to be quiet but the noise of the pub, the sounds of cheerful street voices, and city activity bounce off the stone walls of the surrounding buildings: earplugs are recommended. Breakfast in the bar can be haphazard. The popular restaurant, *Schottische*, has cartoons of the owner/chef and staff on white walls, caricature sculptures, potted greenery and café-style furniture; Scottish fare, including haggis, neeps and tatties, is served along with more conventional items. Snacks are available all day, and there's a floodlit *boules* court. (*Good Pub Guide; also AD Budgen*)

Open All year, except Christmas Day, New Year's Day. Restaurant closed Sun.
Rooms 4 double, 2 single. All with shower. No TV. Apartment in opposite building.
Facilities Café/bar, pub, restaurant; patio. Unsuitable for ♿.
Location Pedestrian precinct in centre, between Glasgow Cross and cathedral. Small carpark.
Restriction No dogs.
Credit cards Access, Amex, Visa.
Terms B&B: single £45, double £65. Full alc £23–£25.

Malmaison — *Tel* (0141) 221 6400
278 West George Street — *Fax* (0141) 221 6411
G2 4LL

Joint César award in 1996

Smart, stylish, no frills, low cost – the *Malmaison* concept is the brainchild of Ken McCulloch, owner of the far grander and more expensive *One Devonshire Gardens* (*qv*). It's a new type of city hotel, with an equally youthful Edinburgh sibling (*qv*), which opened in summer 1994. *Malmaison* occupies a former Episcopalian church built at the turn of the century, in the Georgian area close to the city centre. It is smartly designed around a magnificent Art Nouveau central staircase with blue-and-gold ironwork. Furnishings in small but well-arranged bedrooms continue the theme. The young staff are "outstandingly friendly and relaxed". There's a deliberate policy of not providing services on tap in order to keep prices reasonable: guests carry their own bags up the steep stairs. The basement brasserie with a vaulted ceiling, stone pillars and a mahogany bar "has buzz, vitality, and a relaxed atmosphere", helped along by taped jazz. There's white linen on the tables, and a classic French brasserie menu. More reports, please.

Open All year.
Rooms 4 suites, 17 double. Some on ground floor.
Facilities Café bar, brasserie.
Location Corner of W George and Pitt Sts, opposite police station. Private parking.
Restriction No dogs in bar, brasserie.
Credit cards All major cards accepted.
Terms Rooms £80, suite £110. Breakfast £7.50. Full alc £25. Weekend rates.

One Devonshire Gardens *Tel* (0141) 339 2001
1–3 Devonshire Gardens, G12 0UX *Fax* (0141) 337 1663

"One of my two favourite hotels in the world," writes a regular *Guide* correspondent of Ken McCulloch's opulent establishment in the fashionable West End, a short distance from the city centre. It is composed of three town houses which are not interconnected; reception and restaurant are in Number One. The hotel aims at a private house atmosphere; guests must ring the bell to enter. Bedrooms, many huge, with four-poster, are richly endowed with heavy fabrics and drapes in deep colours, lights with dimmer switches, fruit, magazines, CD player, and marble bathroom with luxurious bath robes. In 1996, Andrew Fairlie was named Scottish Hotel Chef of the Year, and earned a *Michelin* star for his modern French-influenced cooking, using mainly Scottish ingredients. (*Mark Tattersall*) Some find the decor magnificent, but others think it oppressive. One recent visitor, while praising the service and food, had some criticisms of housekeeping, "and to have to pay extra for the Sunday paper at these prices was ridiculous." Room service breakfasts are also criticised. The hotel stands at a busy intersection of two roads, but windows are double-glazed.

Open All year.
Rooms 2 suites, 25 double. 1 on ground floor.
Facilities 2 drawing rooms, bar/club room, restaurant; 3 private dining rooms. Walled garden, patio. Unsuitable for ♿.
Location 2 miles from centre at intersection of Great Western and Hyndland roads. Back rooms quietest. Off-street parking in front.
Restrictions No smoking in restaurant. No dogs in public rooms.
Credit cards All major cards accepted.
Terms Rooms: single £135–£145, double £160–£170, suite £180–£200. Breakfast: continental £8.50, Scottish £13.50. Set lunch £25, dinner £40. Weekend breaks.

The Town House BUDGET *Tel* (0141) 357 0862
4 Hughenden Terrace, G12 9XR *Fax* (0141) 339 9605

"Spot on," is one reporter's verdict on Bill and Charlotte Thow's "upmarket B&B", a listed Victorian house with an impressive staircase, in the heart of Glasgow's West End, a quiet conservation area. It scores on other points too: "Very clean, well heated, spacious bedrooms"; "the bathroom had only a shower, but it was a hot, efficient one."

Breakfast was judged by one visitor to be "the best we'd eaten anywhere in Scotland". It's only 15 minutes' walk to Byres Road's restaurants and shops, and 15 minutes by taxi to the city centre. (*John P Wylie, Val Ferguson, Diana and Jack Taylor*)

Open All year, except Christmas/New Year.
Rooms 10 double.
Facilities Lounge, dining room. Small garden. Unsuitable for ♿.
Location 1½ miles W of centre. Leave A82 at Hyndland Rd, 1st right into Hughenden Rd, then right at mini-roundabout. Street parking.
Restrictions No smoking in dining room. No dogs.
Credit cards Access, Visa accepted.
Terms B&B £52–£62. Full alc £26.

GLENELG Highland — Map 5

Glenelg Inn BUDGET — *Tel/Fax* (01599) 522273
Glenelg
by Kyle of Lochalsh IV40 8JR

A venerable inn, immortalised by Boswell when he and Dr Johnson stayed here in 1773. "Our room," Boswell reported, "was damp and dirty, with bare walls and a variety of bad smells. Dr Johnson was calm. I said he was so from vanity. *Johnson*: "No, sir, it is from philosophy." The ghosts of these writers would not recognise today's inn, just a touch eccentric, in a wonderful setting on Glenelg Bay, with a view to Skye. "A delightful place in a delightful location; our large bedroom looked across to Skye. Dinner was glorious – the most delicious salmon with hollandaise we have ever tasted. *Strongly* recommended." The large, rather dark panelled bar with roaring fire is the village pub; occasional *ceilidhs* are held. The residents' dining room is separate, and quiet, with candlelight and roses. Christopher Main, "an attractive host", claims to be "the only young Scottish/local innkeeper on the West Coast of Scotland". There's plenty of wildlife and lots to do out of doors. (*Dr NB Finter*) Room maintenance may not be the inn's strong point. Reception and service may be offhand at times.

Open Easter–end Oct. New Year. Bar open all year.
Rooms 6 double. 1 on ground floor. No telephone.
Facilities Morning room, bar, dining room. 2-acre grounds: garden down to sea. Sailing, fishing, birdwatching, hill walking, golf nearby.
Location Seafront.
Restrictions No smoking in dining room. No dogs in bedrooms.
Credit cards None accepted.
Terms [1996] D,B&B £47–£80. Bar lunch from £3. Set dinner £22. Off season 4-day rates: D,B&B £50. *V*

GLENLIVET Moray — Map 5

Minmore House — *Tel* (01807) 590378
Glenlivet AB37 9DB — *Fax* (01807) 590472

A Victorian house in the beautiful Glenlivet valley, this popular hotel is run with enthusiasm by Belinda Luxmoore, much praised for her cooking. The bedrooms are large and airy; the decor is "ungimmicky" and the bath towels are huge. Breakfast includes freshly squeezed orange juice, eggs from the hens in the paddock, splendid coffee. Many have written in the past of the excellent service, congenial surroundings, and good value for money. Their comments have mostly been endorsed this year: "Excellent in every way. Food of the type one seldom finds – local, really fresh produce, deftly cooked. Our dinner, of fresh pea and mint soup, local langoustine, melt-in-the-mouth Châteaubriand and raspberries could not be faulted." "It is everything you have cracked it up to be. A very good place to return to." Daily rates include afternoon tea in the drawing room. Generous packed lunches can be provided. The no-choice menu features local salmon, beef, venison and organically grown vegetables. There are lovely views from the secluded garden above the river Livet on which *Minmore* has fishing rights; nearby are wonderful walks, castles and gardens to visit, and almost a score of golf courses. (*Mrs S Slocock, and others*) A reader this year found the top floor rooms obviously inferior to the others, but with no price difference; another objected to the proximity of the distillery, and was critical of the housekeeping.

Open May–mid-Oct. Dining room closed for lunch.
Rooms 8 double, 2 single.
Facilities Hall, drawing room, bar (occasional *ceilidhs*), dining room. 4-acre grounds: terraced garden, croquet, tennis, swimming pool (unheated). Fishing, golf nearby. Unsuitable for ♿.
Location Take A95 Grantown-on-Spey–Ballindalloch. Right on to B9008 at *Delnashaugh Inn*. Follow signs to Glenlivet Distillery.
Restrictions No smoking: dining room, drawing room, some bedrooms. No dogs in public rooms.
Credit cards Access, Visa.
Terms B&B £39; D,B&B £60. Set dinner £25. 3/7-day rates. 1-night bookings occasionally refused. *V*

GLENROTHES Fife **Map 5**

See Markinch

INNERLEITHEN Scottish Borders **Map 5**

The Ley NEW *Tel/Fax* (01896) 830240
Innerleithen EH44 6NL

"On my first visit to the area," writes a regular correspondent, "I didn't know a good place to stay. Now I do. It has large, beautifully furnished rooms, excellent bathrooms, and fine views over extensive and beautifully kept gardens. Dinner [four courses; no choice] was a splendid affair, served by Mrs McVicar." Doreen and Willie McVicar's handsome mid-Victorian house, a member of the Wolsey Lodge consortium, is set in large grounds, with garden and woodland, in lovely Border country, close to Walter Scott's Abbotsford. There's a nine-hole golf course at the bottom of the drive. Many Border abbeys and castles are close by. Edinburgh is 40 minutes' drive. (*Chris Kay*)

Open Mid Feb–mid Oct.
Rooms 3 double.
Facilities Drawing room, sitting room, dining room. Unsuitable for ♿.
Location 2 miles N of Innerleithen on B709 towards Heriot. Pass through golf course, then left over white bridge.

Restrictions No smoking: dining room, bedrooms. No children under 12. No dogs.
Credit cards None accepted.
Terms B&B £35.50–£38.50; D,B&B £57–£60; single occupancy supplement £10. Set dinner £21.50

INVERNESS Highland — Map 5

Culloden House NEW — *Tel* (01463) 790461
Inverness IV1 2NZ — *Fax* (01463) 792181

Ian and Marjory McKenzie's splendid 1772 Palladian mansion stands on the site of an earlier house, in a large park close to the tragic battlefield. A regular contributor brings it to our pages this year: "It was the home of Duncan Forbes, a very significant figure in the '45 uprising. The kilted proprietor is a local man who knows the area, which is awash with history. The hotel is reasonably formal, in keeping with the magnificent dining room, and the service is excellent. The food was superb – the best venison I have ever had; the wine list is comprehensive and fairly priced." The rooms vary in size and quality, ranging from ordinary comfort to four-postered *grand luxe*. The Garden Mansion in the grounds has four luxurious no-smoking suites. Chef Michael Simpson's largish menu offers such delicacies as medallions of ostrich with a tartlet of mushrooms coated with redcurrant jus, and also his own cured salmon, and a terrine of local game, venison and pigeon. There's a full-size billiard table, a sauna and sunbed near the old prisoner's dungeon, and a piper on the lawn most summer evenings. (*J Eunson; also Prof. P and Mrs A Robson*) Inverness Airport is not far.

Open All year.
Rooms 4 suites in Garden Mansion, 17 double, 2 single.
Facilities Lounge, morning room, billiard room, dining room; sauna, sunbed. 40-acre grounds: tennis. Golf nearby. Unsuitable for ♿.
Location NE of Inverness. Take A96 for 1 mile, right at sign to Culloden; Culloden House Ave 1 mile further on left.
Restrictions No smoking: dining room, suites. No children under 10. No dogs in public rooms, unattended in bedrooms.
Credit cards All major cards accepted.
Terms B&B: single £69–£125, double £220. Set lunch £16.50, dinner £35.

Dunain Park — *Tel* (01463) 230512
Inverness IV3 6JN — *Fax* (01463) 224532

"The food is excellent, the rooms are big, and the indoor swimming pool is a great idea on cold winter days," writes one recent visitor to this italianate early 19th-century house in large gardens and woodland, overlooking the river Ness and the Caledonian Canal. Another felt any criticisms last year were "totally unfounded" – he thought the service excellent and the food "irresistible" and "of the highest quality". Mr Nicoll is a genial host, devoted to his calling and constantly improving the rooms. The decor is homely and traditional with a fire in cold weather. The rooms, especially the six suites in the new wing (each has a small sitting room), are attractive, spacious and comfortable. The hotel's main strength, however, is Ann Nicoll's cooking: dishes like saddle of rabbit with mustard sauce, or mousseline of smoked haddock with sorrel sauce are accompanied by vegetables from the hotel's garden. Edward Nicoll now offers a choice of over 200 different malt whiskies. (*Christian Bartoschek, HJ Hamilton, Susanna Peck*).

Open All year, except 3 weeks Jan/Feb.
Rooms 8 suites (2 in cottages, 1 with access for ♿), 5 double, 1 single.
Facilities 2 lounges, restaurant; indoor swimming pool, sauna. 6-acre grounds: badminton, croquet. Fishing, shooting, golf, tennis, winter sports nearby.
Location 1 mile S of Inverness. Turn left off A82 after Craig Dunain hospital (on right).
Restrictions No smoking in dining room. No dogs in public rooms.
Credit cards All major cards accepted.
Terms B&B £35–£79; D,B&B £55–£99. Full alc £32. Low season rates; Christmas/New Year breaks.

ISLE ORNSAY Highland — Map 5

Eilean Iarmain Hotel NEW
Isle Ornsay, Sleat
Isle of Skye IV43 8QR
Tel (01471) 833332
Fax (01471) 833275

A small Victorian inn (also known as the *Isle Ornsay Hotel*), owned by Skye Bridge chairman Sir Iain Noble. Overlooking the Sound of Sleat and the Knoydart hills, "it is part of a wee group of white buildings at the end of a flower-lined lane with a grass-covered promontory, rocks, trees, and a small fishing dock," writes the enthusiastic nominator. "Six bedrooms are in the original building; six are across the drive in the Garden House. We ordered dinner in the attractive lounge and proceeded to the cosy panelled dining room. Yes, white linen, flowers and candles, at this faraway little place. The oysters were right from the bay, superbly fresh. We also had a mushroom, thyme and lemon tart, duck breast in plum sauce, and apple pie brûlée with ginger custard sauce. Service was pleasant and efficient. Breakfast included a good selection of fruits, stewed and fresh, and good bacon and black pudding." Another visitor liked the "professionally modulated Gaelic madness" and the "professional and agreeable local staff". Chef Patricia Gidgeon always includes local ingredients in her sophisticated menus – scallops and roe deer are much in evidence. (*Martha Prince, and others; also Good Pub Guide*)

Open All year.
Rooms 12 double. 6 in garden house.
Facilities Lounge, bar (live music weekly), restaurant. Loch fishing nearby. Unsuitable for ♿.
Location Above Isle Ornsay Bay; 15 mins' drive from Skye bridge and from Mallaig-Armadale ferry. Take A852, then A851.
Restriction No smoking: restaurant, some bedrooms.
Credit cards Access, Amex, Visa.
Terms B&B £39.50–£65. Set lunch £16.50, dinner £26. Winter breaks.

****

German grouse Standards of cooking in Britain have risen, but it is disappointing to see tons of shellfish and fresh fish arrive in harbour when all you get in the restaurants is fish fried in breadcrumbs. It's easier to get fresh Scottish salmon, venison and grouse here in Germany than in Scotland.

****

KENTALLEN Highland Map 5

Ardsheal House NEW
Kentallen, by Appin PA38 4BX
Tel (01631) 740227
Fax (01631) 740342

In a stunning position overlooking Loch Linnhe and the Morvern hills, this is the historic home of the Stewarts of Appin, and featured in Robert Louis Stevenson's *Kidnapped*. The Sutherland family, who were forced to sell the house in 1968 to pay death duties, have now regained ownership, and the resident managers, George Kelso, the chef, and his wife Michelle, front of house, are still here. They run it on family home lines. "We arrived to perhaps the warmest welcome we had ever had at a hotel," write recent visitors. "That set the standard of our stay. We had an excellent room. Breakfasts and dinners were superb, especially the local fish." Bedrooms vary in size; some have spectacular views of Loch Linnhe. The house is two miles from the main road, with nothing but the wind and the birds to disturb the tranquillity. (*Brian and Christine Kingston*)

Open All year.
Rooms 12 double, 1 single.
Facilities Sitting room, study, bar, billiard room, dining room. 900-acre estate: 20-acre garden, tennis. Rocky beach; fishing, boating. Unsuitable for ♿.
Location 17 miles SW of Fort William. On A828, 5 miles S of Ballachulish Bridge.
Restriction No smoking in dining room.
Credit cards Access, Amex, Visa.
Terms [1996] D,B&B £65–£100. Set lunch £18, dinner £32.50. Reductions for 2 or more nights. Christmas, New Year packages; winter rates. *V*

KILCHRENAN Argyll and Bute Map 5

Ardanaiseig
Kilchrenan, by Taynuilt PA35 1HE
Tel (01866) 833333
Fax (01866) 833222

This handsome Scottish baronial mansion stands by Ben Cruachan in showpiece gardens on the shore of Loch Awe, "probably one of the most beautiful situations in Scotland". It was recently given a fresh lease of life, with a new owner and chef, Bennie Gray and Dale Thornber respectively; Nigel Liston remains as manager. Recent visitors, arriving wet and bedraggled, "were greeted most kindly, as if there was nothing unusual about guests in socks asking for sustenance. We were ushered into a huge warm drawing room with a dramatic decor and fantastic views across the lake, and served beautifully made sandwiches and good warming soup; drinks were generous, and the service was charming." The splendid public rooms have recently been redecorated; bedrooms, although large, and furnished with antiques, are "a little threadbare"; bathrooms, "rather 1950s", have large towels and luxurious bath oils. We'd be grateful for more reports, especially on the cooking, described as "modern Scottish, with a classic French influence". (*P Flynn, and others*)

Open All year, but may close for refurbishment in Feb 1997.
Rooms 1 suite, 13 double.
Facilities Drawing room, library/bar, billiard room, dining room. 100-acre grounds: large gardens (open to public); on loch; boating, fishing. Not really suitable for ♿.
Location Take B845 off A85 1 mile E of Taynuilt; follow signs to hotel.

Restrictions No smoking: dining room, drawing room, 1 bedroom. No children under 8. No dogs in public rooms.
Credit cards All major cards accepted.
Terms B&B single £78–£110, double £84–£160. Set lunch £15, dinner £33.50; full alc £30. *V*

Taychreggan *Tel* (01866) 833211
Kilchrenan, by Taynuilt PA35 1HQ *Fax* (01866) 833244

"The setting is close to unbeatable. Our reception was kindly. Our room overlooked the loch; its decor was carefully coordinated, and the bed was still in its prime. Overall an atmosphere of pleasant calm. Meals to remember in the beautiful dining room (again the loch view), with excellent service, under the watchful eye of a French *maîtresse d'*. The chefs put the emphasis on local ingredients, and rightly so. Fillets of Highland beef melted on the tongue. Breakfast included porridge in true Scottish style and Loch Fyne kippers." "Annie Paul is a charming and vivacious hostess." "A delicious place. Everything was polished, professional and in excellent taste." This much-smartened and extended old stone drovers' inn, reached by a winding road, is set on the banks of Loch Awe. Its buildings are arranged around a cobbled courtyard, "filled to overflowing with flowers"; one houses several new bedrooms and a billiard room. The decor "successfully combines traditional furniture and contemporary art". (*Nick and Myriam Whalley, Martha Prince; also Keith Flinter, and others*) The odd caveat: soundproofing in the new annexe could be improved; "irritating taped music at dinner"; the service at dinner found a little too elaborate and slow for some.

Open All year.
Rooms 20 double.
Facilities 2 lounges, bar, dining room; function room. 25-acre grounds on loch: boats, fishing (ghillie available). Riding, deer-stalking, climbing, golf nearby.
Location 19 miles SE of Oban. Off B845, at end of 7-mile single track.
Restrictions No smoking in dining room. No children under 14. No dogs in public rooms.
Credit cards All major cards accepted.
Terms B&B £47–£62; D,B&B £75–£90. Set lunch £14, dinner £30. Autumn, winter, spring, themed breaks.

KILDRUMMY Aberdeenshire Map 5

Kildrummy Castle Hotel *Tel* (01975 5) 71288
Kildrummy, by Alford AB33 8RA *Fax* (01975 5) 71345

Tom Hanna, with a long-serving and loyal staff, has been running his turn-of-the-century Scottish baronial house in the heart of Donside for 17 years. It adjoins the grounds of a ruined 13th-century castle (guests may walk in the formal gardens), and has a private stretch of the river Don, two miles away, for trout- and salmon-fishing. The public rooms are large and comfortable, with masses of books and magazines. A fine carved wooden staircase leads up from the panelled hall to the bedrooms, which vary greatly in shape, size and outlook. There's plenty of choice on chef Kenneth Whyte's four-course dinner menu – "good plain cooking, much local produce and plentiful helpings; sweet trolley irresistible." (*LL*) More reports, please.

Open 7 Feb–2 Jan.
Rooms 1 suite, 14 double, 1 single.
Facilities Drawing room, lounge bar, library, restaurant. Adjacent to 15-acre castle gardens. 3½ miles private fishing on river Don. Unsuitable for ♿.
Location NE of Ballater on A97 Ballater–Huntly.
Restrictions No smoking in restaurant. No dogs in public rooms.
Credit cards Access, Amex, Visa.
Terms B&B: single £70, double £115–£145, suite £125–£145. Set lunch £14.50, dinner £28; full alc £34. Short breaks; Christmas, New Year packages. Reduced rates for children.

KILLIECRANKIE Perthshire and Kinross — Map 5

Killiecrankie Hotel — *Tel* (01796) 473220
Pass of Killiecrankie — *Fax* (01796) 472451
by Pitlochry PH16 5LG

"Another delightful visit. The situation, among hills and woods, is delightful. There are few walks pleasanter than the one along the river, approached by a gate just opposite the hotel. The food is excellent, with particularly good fish and traditional puddings. The full Scottish breakfast would set you up for the whole day. Good bread." "A very friendly hotel. Colin and Carole Anderson are most attentive. Excellent staff." "Good value." More praise this year for this small hotel in a beautiful wooded setting at the entrance to the Pass of Killiecrankie, overlooking the river Garry. Bedrooms, "attractive and well kept", are of varying sizes, with a simple decor, locally crafted pine furniture, and modern bathroom. The wine list includes a good selection of half bottles. Pre-theatre suppers are served to guests visiting the nearby Pitlochry Festival Theatre. (*Mrs MH Box, Mr RI Gravett, and others; also Good Pub Guide*)

Open Mid-Feb–3 Jan.
Rooms 1 suite, 7 double, 2 single.
Facilities Lounge, bar, restaurant. 4-acre grounds: putting, croquet. Fishing on river Garry ¼ mile; bird sanctuary nearby. Unsuitable for ♿.
Location 3 miles N of Pitlochry, just off A9.
Restrictions No smoking: bedrooms, restaurant. No children under 5 in restaurant at night.
Credit cards Access, Visa.
Terms [1996] D,B&B £67–£76. 2-night off-season breaks, wine-tasting weekends, Christmas, New Year programmes. 1-night bookings occasionally refused. Children accommodated free in parents' room.

KILMORE Argyll and Bute — Map 5

Glenfeochan House — *Tel* (01631) 770273
Kilmore, by Oban PA34 4QR — *Fax* (01631) 770624

More praise this year for David and Patricia Baber's imposing Victorian house, with its ornate plasterwork, high ceilings, finely carved staircase and family antiques. It stands in one of the major gardens in the Western Highlands (open to the public), on a huge estate at the head of Loch Feochan. "I found warm, unstinting and sincere hospitality, beautiful, restful surroundings, marvellous views, outstanding food." The bathrooms are modern and well equipped with large, fluffy towels. Patricia Baber smokes her own salmon, makes her own marmalade and bread, and cooks for a dinner party of guests (there are only three rooms and guests eat together using the family silver). Local "Argyll snails" are now used in many dishes; grilse is caught by the Babers' son James, who grows all the vegetables for the house too. Breakfasts have been described as "delicious and extravagant". (*Kathy Mansfield, and others*) But a dissenter this year found dinner and breakfast only so-so, and "over-priced".

Open April–31 Oct.
Rooms 3 double.
Facilities Drawing room, dining room. 350-acre estate: 8-acre garden (open to public), croquet, free salmon- and sea trout-fishing, clay pigeon-shooting, hill walking, loch bathing. Unsuitable for ♿.
Location 5 miles S of Oban, ¾ mile off A816.
Restrictions No smoking: dining room, bedrooms. No children under 10. No dogs in house.
Credit cards Access, Amex, Visa.
Terms B&B double £134. Packed lunch £6. Set dinner £30. 4-day breaks all year; 10% discount Mar, Oct. 1-night bookings refused May and June.

KINBUCK Stirling — Map 5

Cromlix House — *Tel* (01786) 822125
Kinbuck, by Dunblane FK15 9JT — *Fax* (01786) 825450

More accolades this year for this "quite excellent" hotel: "Delightful as ever. Peaceful and beguiling. Sheer luxury. Antique furniture. Rooms are palatial, with the most comfortable beds we've ever slept in. Bathrooms have every conceivable extra, and the most powerful showers outside the USA." "Dining at *Cromlix* is a memorable experience." David and Ailsa Assenti's massive turn-of-the-century house, "which started life as a rather grand cottage, hence its diverse architectural style", is informally run. It stands in a huge wooded estate with three lochs with wild brown trout, ducks and swans; rabbits, sheep, deer and pheasants abound; many outdoor activities are available (see below). It has panelled reception rooms, original furnishings, fine paintings and porcelain, and a private chapel, where weddings and christenings take place. (*William Davidson, Val Ferguson, and others*) One reader was very critical of room service.

Open All year, except 2–31 Jan. Lunch possibly not served in low season.
Rooms 8 suites, 6 double.
Facilities Sitting room, library, 2 dining rooms, conservatory; small meeting facilities; chapel. 3,000-acre grounds: tennis, croquet, walking, fishing, riding, shooting (clay pigeon, rough, pheasant, grouse). Unsuitable for ♿.
Location From Dunblane take A9 2 miles; left on to B8033 to Braco/Crieff, through Kinbuck village, across narrow bridge; drive 200 yds on left.
Restrictions No smoking in restaurant. No dogs in public rooms.
Credit cards All major cards accepted.
Terms B&B: single £80–£150, double £130–£195, suite £160–£270. Set lunch £18, dinner £37.50. Winter breaks. Christmas, New Year packages. *V* Oct–Apr, except Christmas, New Year, Easter.

> If you are nominating a hotel, please err on the side of saying too much. Many suggestions have to be rejected only because they are too brief.

KINCLAVEN Perth and Kinross — Map 5

Ballathie House NEW — *Tel* (01250) 883268
Kinclaven, by Stanley PH1 4QN — *Fax* (01250) 883396

A turreted Victorian mansion, in huge grounds on the banks of the Tay, not far from Perth. It is warmly nominated: "A beautiful, remote setting, with excellent walks nearby. The staff were welcoming and charming. The rooms vary greatly in size: ours was small but adequate, with a good bathroom – lots of fluffy towels and 'extras'. Others, however, are palatial. The food is truly outstanding. Tasty soups, beautifully cooked fish and meat and yummy hot sticky puddings." (*Val Ferguson*) Chef Kevin Macgillivray's modern Scottish cooking makes inventive use of local produce – medallions of venison with carrot and ginger purée, breast of pheasant with juniper sauce. There is free salmon fishing for guests in February. The Sportsman's Lodge in the grounds offers simpler accommodation.

Open All year.
Rooms 1 suite, 21 double, 6 single. 2 on ground floor.
Facilities Drawing room, morning room, cocktail bar, restaurant. 1,500-acre estate: tennis, croquet, putting, salmon-fishing in Tay. Golf nearby.
Location 8 miles N of Perth. A9 for 2 miles; B9099 through Stanley; right at sign for Kinclaven and Ballathie.
Restrictions No smoking in restaurant. No dogs in public rooms.
Credit cards All major cards accepted.
Terms B&B £57.50–£100; D,B&B £75–£112. Set lunch £11.45–£14.95, dinner £25–£29. Special breaks Oct–Easter £69 per person per night half board. Free fishing in Feb.

KINCRAIG Highland — Map 5

Ossian Hotel BUDGET — *Tel* (01540) 651242
The Brae, Kincraig — *Fax* (01540) 651633
by Kingussie PH21 1QD

In the Spey valley beside lovely Loch Insh, Mr and Mrs Rainbow's small hotel is endorsed this year: "Very friendly hosts. All in all great value for money. Excellent breakfasts, served personally by Johnny. We found some main courses at dinner disappointing, so stuck to plain steaks, which were excellent; the pudding trolley was the best we have seen for some years. Our bedroom was spacious and very well furnished. Mrs Rainbow's mother, Mrs Ramage, is knowledgeable on local fishing and walks." Dinners are *à la carte*, using "fresh local produce as much as possible"; special diets are catered for. "The whole place is cheerful; the owners have been in charge for years, and it shows." (*Janice Carrera, Stephen Samuels*) The hotel's "wee pub" serves snacks and drinks from 11 am to 9.30 pm. The Cairngorms, close by, provide a multitude of outdoor activities.

Open All year, except Jan, Nov.
Rooms 7 double, 2 single.
Facilities Lounge, cocktail lounge, restaurant; café/bar. Fishing, sailing, canoeing, riding, winter sports nearby.
Location Off B9152, equidistant (6 miles) from Kingussie and Aviemore.
Restriction No smoking in restaurant.
Credit cards Access, Visa.
Terms [1996] B&B £19.50–£29.50; D,B&B £35–£55. Full alc £23. *V*

KINGUSSIE Highland

The Cross
Tweed Mill Brae
Kingussie PH21 1TC

Tony and Ruth Hadley's well-c... tweed mill stands by the Gynack burn, ... ing and through its grounds. There are nat... and plenty of wildlife. The restaurant is a magn... area, and earns a red "Meals" in *Michelin*. Ruth... "Scottish eclectic" cooking makes inventive use of loc... boudin of seafood, mousseline of pike, venison with redcu... port; puddings might include hot chocolate fondant and rasp... shortbread. There's an impressive wine list, too. The bedrooms a... simple but stylish and comfortable, "but with not much view as the hotel is in a hollow". More reports, please.

Open 1 Mar– 1 Dec, 27 Dec–5 Jan.
Rooms 9 double. TV on request.
Facilities Ramp. 2 lounges (1 with TV), restaurant. 4-acre grounds, river. Only restaurant suitable for ♿.
Location 350 yds up Ardbroilach Rd from traffic lights at town centre. Left at sign down private road.
Restrictions No smoking: restaurant, bedrooms. No children under 12. No dogs.
Credit cards Access, Visa.
Terms D,B&B £85–£170. Set dinner £35. Guests staying 1 night only are expected to dine in. Wine weekends. *V*

KYLESKU Highland — Map 5

Kylesku Hotel NEW/BUDGET — *Tel* (01971) 502231
By Lairg, Sutherland IV27 4HW — *Fax* (01971) 502313

Marcel and Janice Klein's small white hotel at the ferry dock, now bypassed by the new Kylesku bridge, makes an ideal base for a tour of the wild and dramatic scenery of the far north-west of Scotland. "A very long drive, but worth it," writes the nominator. "Superb location – the views from the dining room conservatory are breathtaking. Marcel Klein is a congenial host, and the staff are friendly and helpful. Fabulous food. Local fishermen land fresh fish daily, which Marcel cooks in the evening: turbot, skate, salmon in super sauces. Very good bar food in the pub, where friendly locals congregate. Boat trips leave twice a day to see waterfalls, seals and flowers. The hotel has been recently refurbished and is very warm, with plenty of hot water; our room had a sofa and a large comfortable bed with good linen; our dogs were made welcome, too." (*Janice Carrera*) Marcel Klein is something of a wine buff, and has assembled an impressive cellar.

Open 1 Mar–31 Oct.
Rooms 7 double. No telephone.
Facilities Sitting room, lounge (both with TV), restaurant; drying room. Fishing (tuition arranged), walking, climbing, bird-watching nearby.
Location 35 miles N of Ullapool, on A894.
Restrictions No smoking in restaurant. No dogs in public rooms.
Credit cards Access, Visa.
Terms [1996] B&B £27.50–£35. Set lunch £12.50, dinner £18. *V*

A North Ayrshire Map 5

ge NEW/BUDGET *Tel/Fax* (01770) 830229
za
Arran KA27 8HJ

nally the village manse, John and Jeannie Boyd's small hotel ds in a small well-kept garden amid spectacular deer and eagle ntry in the north of the island, a mile from the Kintyre ferry. The edrooms are "luxuriously appointed", with original paintings and embroideries on the walls. "Excellent" dinners at 7 for 7.15 are served by candlelight, with crystal and fresh flowers. Jeannie Boyd's no-choice menus include locally smoked salmon, as well as "boozy bread-and-butter pudding with mango"; she will take guests' preferences into account. No licence; bring your own bottles. There is excellent hill-walking on the doorstep, and a golf-course too. (*Mr and Mrs JT Mills*)

Open All year, except Christmas.
Rooms 1 self-contained suite, 3 double.
Facilities Lounge, dining room. ¼-acre garden. Walking, golf, fishing, sailing nearby.
Location On A841, opposite golf-course.
Restrictions No smoking: dining room, bedrooms. No children under 12 May–Sept.
Credit cards None accepted.
Terms [1996] B&B £25–£30; D,B&B £38.50–£43.50. Packed lunch from £3.50. Set dinner £14.50. Weekend and midweek off-season breaks. 1-night bookings refused in advance for high season.

MARKINCH Fife Map 5

Balbirnie House *Tel* (01592) 610066
Balbirnie Park *Fax* (01592) 610529
Markinch, by Glenrothes KY7 6NE

"Stupendous luxury." This Grade A Georgian mansion, with an 18-hole golf course "just a chip shot away", stands in a Capability Brown-style landscaped park, with mature trees and an important collection of rhododendrons. It has been lovingly restored by the Russell family, Alan, Elizabeth, Nicholas and Imogen. It has a long gallery with *trompe-l'oeil* paintings, a library bar, well stocked with malt whiskies, and a comfortable drawing room; antiques everywhere. "*Not* in the budget class, but well worth the price for such pampering," writes a recent visitor. "Most bedrooms are spacious, with sofa, armchairs, lots of extras. Staff are without exception pleasant and friendly. First-class food." David Kinnes, a runner-up in the Northern Chef of the Year competition, is now head chef. His cooking – "classical with a Scottish approach" – won the AA's top award (four red stars) in 1996; only one other Scottish hotel was thus honoured. Lunch is served in the *Gamekeeper's Inn*, a country-style bistro. All manner of country pursuits are available (see below). (*Mrs EH Prodgers*)

Open All year.
Rooms 2 suites, 26 double, 2 single. 1 on ground floor.
Facilities Ramp. Gallery, drawing room, library, snooker room, 2 restaurants; function facilities. 420-acre estate: golf, fishing, riding, shooting, falconry, jogging, etc.

Location NW of Markinch, off B9130. Halfway between Edinburgh and St Andrews.
Restriction No smoking in restaurant. Dogs by arrangement.
Credit cards All major cards accepted.
Terms [1996] B&B £72.50–£112.50. Set Sun lunch £14.75, dinner £27.50; full alc £35. Weekend, golfing breaks.

MARYCULTER Aberdeenshire — Map 5

Maryculter House — *Tel* (01224) 732124
South Deeside Road — *Fax* (01224) 733510
Maryculter, Aberdeen AB1 0BB

Former Templar priory in 5-acre wooded grounds on river Dee, 8 miles south of Aberdeen. Ample public rooms. Efficient management. Somewhat functional decor and business/function-oriented clientele (riverside setting popular for weddings). 23 comfortable bedrooms (some on river) with pine furniture, flowery fabrics; 16 no-smoking; some on ground floor; ramps. Good bar meals; traditional French dinners in restaurant (closed Sun). Golf, fishing, shooting nearby. All major credit cards accepted. No dogs in eating areas. Rooms: single £55–£105, double £70–£120, suite £180; D,B&B single £75, double £99–£130. Set dinner £29. Recently endorsed: "Obliging staff, outstanding food." But we'd like more reports, please. *V*

MUIR OF ORD Highland — Map 5

The Dower House — *Tel/Fax* (01463) 870090
Highfield, Muir of Ord IV6 7XN

"A very good find" – an endorsement this year by a regular *Guide* contributor. Close to some of Scotland's most spectacular scenery, this 19th-century house, now a welcoming small country hotel in mature grounds, is owned by Robyn (the chef) and Mena Aitchison. "The gardens are a great pleasure and a lovely backdrop to this mildly eccentric building." The *cottage orné* decor combines Victorian pine and loose-covered chairs and sofas, in a riot of vibrant colours and patterns. The small lounge has a bar and lots of books; the dining room is warm and welcoming, with chairs upholstered in green, and green napkins tied with green tartan ribbons. The "modern British" cooking uses fresh local produce; there's limited choice on the menu. Breakfasts are generous. Some bedrooms are small, but cosily decorated; the bathrooms have Victorian fittings. (*JC*)

Open All year, except Christmas, 1 week Mar/Oct.
Rooms 1 suite, 4 double. All on ground floor.
Facilities Lounge, dining room. 4-acre grounds: small formal garden, swings, tree house. Fishing nearby.
Location 15 miles NW of Inverness. 1 mile N of Muir of Ord, on A862 to Dingwall: left at double bend sign; through maroon gates.
Restrictions No smoking: dining room, bedrooms. No dogs in public rooms.
Credit cards Access, Visa.
Terms B&B: single £35–£75, double £70–£110; D,B&B: single £65–£105, double £120–£170. Set lunch £17.50, dinner £30. Winter rates. *V*

For details of the Voucher scheme see page xxx.

NAIRN Highland — Map 5

Clifton House
Viewfield Street
Nairn IV12 4HW

Tel (01667) 453119
Fax (01667) 452836

César award in 1987

"Mr Macintyre's welcome, style and personal concern for his guests are unsurpassable." "Our eighth visit to what must be one of the most distinctive hotels in Scotland. From the simple stone exterior, festooned with roses, to the drawing rooms and bedrooms there are flowers everywhere – even our bathroom had foxgloves and roses. Everywhere, waiting to be read, are wonderful books. There are *objets d'art* on walls, stair landings and table tops. A fluffy orange cat, Oberon, provided much entertainment." "An old favourite, as much fun as ever. The encyclopaedic wine list was as wonderful as we remembered." Recent accolades for this Victorian seaside villa, which looks across the Moray Firth towards Ross-shire and the Sutherland hills. Owner, manager and chef Gordon Macintyre is as theatrical and exuberant as his extravagant Victorian interiors. The restaurant serves local fresh fish and wild salmon, meats and game, and the wine list reflects Mr Macintyre's passionate interest in the subject. There's plenty of choice; cooking is French, with well-executed traditional dishes, followed by British puddings and Scottish cheeses. Breakfast includes home-made bread, oatcakes, muesli and preserves. Snack lunches and picnics are available. Stylish bedrooms (some quite small) have antique furniture; duvets on beds can be changed to conventional bedding on request. The hotel has a theatrical licence; in winter plays, concerts and recitals are staged. (*E Lurphey, Martha Prince, and others*)

Open Mid-Jan–mid-Dec.
Rooms 8 double, 4 single. No telephone/TV.
Facilities Sitting room, drawing room, TV room/library, Green Room, 2 dining rooms; plays, concerts, recitals Oct–Mar (with price reductions). Beach, golf, tennis, public swimming pool, fishing, shooting, riding nearby. Unsuitable for ♿.
Location Turn E at roundabout on A96 in town centre. Private parking.
Restrictions No smoking in 1 dining room. No dogs in dining rooms.
Credit cards All major cards accepted.
Terms [1996] B&B: single £50–£54, double £85–£95. Full alc £25–£30 (including house wine).

NEWTON STEWART Dumfries and Galloway — Map 5

Creebridge House BUDGET
Minnigaff
Newton Stewart DG8 6NP

Tel (01671) 402121
Fax (01671) 403258

This peaceful grey stone former shooting lodge stands amid flowery gardens on the edge of a fairly unremarkable town close to the Galloway hills, convenient for the Stranraer ferry. A visitor this year found "a friendly and welcoming greeting, attentive staff, good value for money". The public rooms are large and comfortable, with fresh flowers and pot-pourri everywhere. "Dinner was very good indeed, with a varied menu, and several delicious puddings. Breakfast was excellent, with generous but not daunting portions, and plenty of coffee." Bedrooms vary in size and standard; the best have views over the garden. The hospitable owners, Chris and Sue Walker, are originally from Yorkshire. He does the cooking, and the four-course dinners offer a limited choice, but always include fish or game. The hotel makes a good base for a fishing holiday, and offers many country pursuits and sports. Children are welcome. (*Margaret and Alan Clarke, WD Richmond, SP*)

Open All year, except Christmas.
Rooms 18 double, 2 single. 1 on ground floor.
Facilities 2 lounges, bar, restaurant. 3-acre grounds: croquet, putting. Fishing, golf, pony-trekking, birdwatching, sailing, beach nearby.
Location Left over bridge in town, towards Minnigaff. Hotel 200 yds on left, after petrol station.
Restriction No smoking in restaurant.
Credit cards All major cards accepted.
Terms [1996] B&B: single £30–£40, double £60–£75; D,B&B: single £45–£55, double £90–£105. Set dinner £17.50. Golf packages. Children under 12 accommodated free in parents' room. *V*

OBAN Argyll and Bute — Map 5

Dungallan House NEW — *Tel* (01631) 563799
Gallanach Road — *Fax* (01631) 566711
Oban PA34 4PD

"Bliss," writes our sorely tried inspector. "At last somewhere I can unreservedly recommend. Welcoming, accommodating owners, delightful smiley young staff. Delicious dinners. Excellent value." George and Janice Stewart (she is chef) will be known to regular *Guide* readers from their time at the *Arisaig Hotel*, Arisaig. They recently took over this Victorian stone house on the outskirts of Oban. It is set on tree-lined cliffs, with panoramic views over Oban bay, the islands of Mull and Lismore, and the hills of Morvern. Bedrooms vary in size: all are chintzy and floral, with a good simple bathroom (plenty of hot water). The best are at the front – you can lie in bed watching the ferries go by in the distance. The large, handsome dining room, warmed by a fire, overlooks the bay (fine sunsets). The food has a distinct Scottish accent, with the emphasis on fresh local seafood, and traditional puddings to finish. Ferry services to many of the islands leave from Oban.

Open All year (possibly closed for renovation Nov, Feb).
Rooms 11 double, 2 single. 1 on ground floor.
Facilities Lounge, bar, dining room. 5-acre grounds. Sea 50 yds (cliff); sandy beaches, sea / loch fishing, golf nearby.
Location ½ mile from town centre. Follow signs to Gallanach, left 500 yds past ferry terminal.
Restrictions No smoking in dining room. Dogs by arrangement; not unattended in bedrooms.
Credit cards Access, Visa.
Terms B&B £40. Set dinner £23.50; full alc £31.75. *V*

There are many expensive hotels in the *Guide*. We are keen to increase our coverage at the other end of the scale. If you know of a simple place giving simple satisfaction, please write and tell us.

PEEBLES Scottish Borders Map 5

Cringletie House
Peebles EH45 8PL
Tel (01721) 730233
Fax (01721) 730244

This pink stone baronial mansion, with turrets, gables and dormer windows, was built by the renowned Scottish architect David Bryce in 1861 for the Wolfe Murray family of Quebec fame. It is set on a large estate on the edge of town, amid gardens and woodland, with extensive views over the surrounding hills and the Tweed valley. Despite the rural setting it is only half an hour's drive from Edinburgh. The Maguire family owners have been here for 24 years, attracting a loyal clientele. One of them writes this year: "Much new decoration and general smartening up since our last visit. Stanley and Alison Maguire were away on holiday, but their son and daughter-in-law were firmly in control. Excellent dinner; service lacked polish but was very willing." There is an extensive, reasonably priced wine list. The kitchen, under Sheila McKellar, produces "consistently good" meals on an eclectic menu, ending with luscious traditional puddings. Fruit and vegetables are supplied by the large walled kitchen garden. There is a panelled lounge with a fine painted ceiling, marble fireplace and antique furniture. A new conservatory has lovely views. Bedrooms, with flowery wallpaper and bedspreads and a mixture of antique and modern furniture, vary in size and quality; some require a climb up to the third floor, but are priced accordingly. (*Dr NB Finter, and others*)

Open 8 Mar–1 Jan.
Rooms 12 double, 1 single.
Facilities Lift. 2 lounges, conservatory, bar, 2 dining rooms. 28-acre grounds: walled kitchen garden, tennis, putting, croquet, children's play area. Golf, fishing nearby. Unsuitable for ♿.
Location 2 miles N of Peebles on A703.
Restrictions No smoking: dining rooms, 1 lounge. No dogs in public rooms, unaccompanied in bedrooms.
Credit cards Access, Amex, Visa.
Terms B&B £50–£55. Set Sun lunch £16, dinner £25.50. Spring, autumn breaks.

Park Hotel
Innerleithen Road
Peebles EH45 8BA
Tel (01721) 720451
Fax (01721) 723510

A dignified, traditional hotel in an excellent centre for sightseeing. A recent visitor, who spent four nights here, found it "truly excellent": "It fully deserves its place in the *Guide*. The staff were welcoming, caring and friendly. Our delightful bedroom had a splendid view of the Peebleshire hills; a thrush outside sang lustily all day. In the oak-panelled dining room, the menu was interesting, the Anglo/French food well cooked and attractively presented. Fresh flowers everywhere." Breakfasts are lavish. The facilities – swimming pool, sauna, tennis etc – of the *Peebles Hotel Hydro* (which owns the *Park*) are available to guests at no extra charge. (*MH*)

Open All year.
Rooms 20 double, 4 single.
Facilities Bar, lounge, restaurant; function room. ½-acre garden. Access to health facilities at *Peebles Hotel Hydro* 700 yds; fishing, golf nearby. Unsuitable for ♿.

Location Centre of town. Private parking.
Restriction No dogs in public rooms at mealtimes.
Credit cards All major cards accepted.
Terms B&B £40–£70; D,B&B £50–£80. Set dinner £18.80. 3/7-day rates. Christmas, New Year breaks; golfing holidays. *V*

PENNYGHAEL Argyll and Bute — Map 5

Pennyghael Hotel NEW/BUDGET — *Tel* (01681) 704288
Isle of Mull PA70 6HB — *Fax* (01681) 704205

"A stunningly beautiful place. Mrs Bowman, who runs it, is a first-class cook and provided huge breakfasts and substantial and imaginative dinners. Unbelievably reasonable." "A more beautiful location could not be imagined; Jess Bowman and her staff were genuinely friendly and welcoming." "We felt like one of the family; superb food – we had smoked goose breast as a starter one evening." Much praise for this low white house on the shores of Loch Scridain, with its herons and sea otters. The limited-choice menu makes imaginative use of local produce: wild salmon, scallops, Mull cheese and venison. (*Catherine and Anthony Storr, C and R Frieze, Mrs DF Hutchins*)

Open Easter–New Year.
Rooms 6 double. Some on ground floor. Also self-catering cottages.
Facilities Ramps. Lounge, dining room.
Location On A849, beside Loch Scridain.
Restriction No dogs in public rooms.
Credit cards Access, Visa.
Terms B&B £35; D,B&B £50. Set dinner £21. Reductions for 3 or more nights. Weekly rates out of season. Christmas, New Year packages.

PLOCKTON Highland — Map 5

The Haven NEW/BUDGET — *Tel* (01599) 544223
Plockton IV52 8TW — *Fax* (01599) 544467

This unassuming hotel is a converted merchant's house in a delightful West Highland village ("a crescent of white cottages opposite steep blue hills") on the shore of an inlet of Loch Carron. It returns to our pages with new owners, Annan and Jill Dryburgh. The decor is traditional. Bedrooms vary in size and position; the best are spacious and light. The large dining room, with a gold-toned pipe organ, is popular with non-residents; cooking is traditional Scottish, with plenty of choice on the menu, including local salmon, prawns and venison. All our readers have thought it delicious, though one couple would have liked more vegetables; service is friendly. "Very good value." (*Eve Gompertz, PJC Mead, Stephen Samuels, and others*)

Open 1 Feb–20 Dec.
Rooms 2 suites, 12 double. 1 single.
Facilities 2 lounges, conservatory, bar, restaurant. Beach 30 yds.
Location In village 7 miles N of Kyle of Lochalsh. Small carpark.
Restrictions No smoking: restaurant, 1 lounge, conservatory. No children under 7. No dogs in public rooms.
Credit cards Access, Visa.
Terms B&B £34–£41; D,B&B £50–£60. Set dinner £22.50 (non-residents). 3-day breaks.

PORT APPIN Argyll and Bute — Map 5

The Airds Hotel — *Tel* (01631) 730236
Port Appin, Appin PA38 4DF — *Fax* (01631) 730535

César award in 1994

"Fantastic. Worth every penny." "We have stayed regularly over 25 years. Eric Allen is a natural host. Courteous staff, headed by manager Kenneth Penman, who is never idle, tending fires, whisking off ashtrays, plumping up cushions." "Faultless service; neither too much nor too little, too formal nor too relaxed. Public rooms the best we have seen." More praise this year for the Allen family's small but sybaritic hotel (Relais & Châteaux), once a ferry inn. The bedrooms and bathrooms, though not large, are pretty and pleasant. The Scottish element is emphasised with touches of tartan, and thistles on the dining room carpet; Eric Allen is always kilted, the waitresses wear smart tartan skirts, short by day, long by night. The dining room decor is unfussy, with nothing to distract from the *Michelin*-starred food, the wines ("the list deserves a Booker prize"), and the view through the long window of the constantly shifting light on the loch. Graeme Allen has taken the kitchen over from Betty, his mother. "Food is unvaryingly of the best: deliciously smooth soups often of humble ingredients like leek and swede, venison, Loch Linnhe prawns, fillet of Angus beef, a long list of irresistible puddings." Afternoon tea comes with elegant china and damask napkins; there's home-made bread and marmalade for breakfast. "Gorgeos smoke sammon sandwiches for our picnic," wrote an eight-year-old visitor. (*Diana and Jack Taylor, Jean Dundas, Mr and Mrs DH Thomas, Emma Thomas; also Sybella Zisman*)

Open All year.
Rooms 1 suite, 10 double, 1 single. 2 on ground floor.
Facilities 2 lounges, bar, restaurant, conservatory. 1-acre garden. Near loch: shingle beach, bathing, fishing, boating; pony-trekking, forest walks.
Location 2 miles off A828, 25 miles from Fort William (N) and Oban (S). Parking.
Restrictions No smoking in restaurant. Dogs by prior arrangement.
Credit cards Access, Amex, Visa.
Terms [1996] D,B&B £85–£135. Set dinner (4-course with ½ bottle of wine) £45. Off-season reductions; Christmas, New Year breaks. Extra bed for child in parents' room £30.

PORT OF MENTEITH Stirling — Map 5

The Lake Hotel — *Tel* (01877) 385258
Port of Menteith FK8 3RA — *Fax* (01877) 385671

In a beautiful, peaceful setting on the shore of the only lake in Scotland, looking across to the Trossachs, this hotel was completely refurbished in 1989, but retains its stylish Art Deco atmosphere. A large, much-added-to manse, beside a small church, it has once again been warmly endorsed this year: "Excellent situation, warm welcome and first-class food. I recommend it without hesitation." "The staff could not have been more charming and helpful. The view over the lake from the conservatory restaurant was mesmerising. The food was delicious: wonderful fresh fish, vegetables cooked to perfection; agonising choice of puddings." "After dinner we lingered over coffee and home-made petits fours, watching the fishermen making their nightly sortie." "Absolutely quiet. Absolutely relaxing." The rooms are pleasant, with soft colours and large bathrooms. (*Valerie and Antony Gimons, Val Ferguson, Pamela and Glen Pomerantz, Prof. Peter and Mrs Andrina Robson; also Mary Milne-Day*)

Open All year.
Rooms 16 double.
Facilities Lounge, lounge bar, restaurant, conservatory. 1-acre grounds on lake: fishing. Golf, hill walking, mountain biking nearby.
Location Take A85 to Port of Menteith, B8034 to Arnprior. Hotel on right after 250 yds.
Restrictions No smoking in restaurant. No children under 12. No dogs in public rooms.
Credit cards Access, Amex, Visa.
Terms [1996] B&B £34–£75; D,B&B £58–£92. Set lunch £12, dinner £21.90; full alc £25. Off-season breaks. Christmas, New Year packages. *V*

PORTPATRICK Dumfries and Galloway Map 5

Knockinaam Lodge *Tel* (01776) 810471
Portpatrick DG9 9AD *Fax* (01776) 810435

Knockinaam stands at the end of a three-mile track, in a spectacular setting, with cliffs on three sides and the sea on the fourth. More plaudits this year for the relatively new, refreshingly informal, Canadian owners, Michael Bricker and Pauline Ashworth – "charming hosts, friendly, but entirely without false bonhomie" – and for the "incomparable" manager Lorna McMiken, a survivor of the previous regime. "The place is immaculate and perfect for a romantic weekend, with every kind of country house comfort: electric blankets and fluffy towels in the bedrooms and bathrooms, log fires and deep sofas in the lounges, and flowers everywhere. Tony Pierce has taken over as head chef, retaining the *Michelin* star earned by his predecessor. "The food is truly stunning. I couldn't fault a single dish; the chef's surprise one night, a piece of cod steamed on a bed of couscous dressed with balsamic vinegar, was magical." Breakfast is traditional Scottish, and there is a choice of 101 malt whiskies in the bar. (*Caroline Burton, Susan Chait*) One visitor would have preferred a less French bias to the wine list, and a wider selection of inexpensive bottles.

Open All year.
Rooms 9 double, 1 single.
Facilities 2 lounges, bar, dining room. 30-acre grounds: garden, croquet; private beach 100 yds. Sea fishing, golf nearby.
Location 7½ miles SW of Stranraer. Turn off A77 2 miles W of Lochans.
Restrictions No smoking in restaurant. No children under 12 in dining room at night (high tea 6 pm). No dogs in public rooms.
Credit cards All major cards accepted.
Terms [1996] B&B £58–£80; D,B&B £65–£115. Set lunch £27, dinner £35. Off-season 3-day breaks. *V*

****

Traveller's tale There were mice in the bedroom at one hotel I stayed at. *Three*. When I called to have something done, someone came up to help. But they were quite patronising. "Oh, you're afraid of a baby mouse?"

****

PORTREE Highland Map 5

Viewfield House BUDGET *Tel* (01478) 612217
Portree, Isle of Skye IV51 9EU *Fax* (01478) 613517

César award in 1993

Loyal visitors have sprung to the defence of this house of "unique charm", after the mild criticisms voiced in the *Guide* last year. "As you say, somewhat eccentric but very enjoyable. Our enormous bedroom had an utterly delightful Victorian bathroom – but modern plumbing and piping-hot water." "We were received courteously and elegantly by Hugh Macdonald, whose attention to his guests is as meticulous and considerate as ever. His young staff is friendly and effective. Breakfast and dinner were well-prepared, enticing and substantial." "Rather ramshackle in an elegant, faded sort of way. Hugh, complete with kilt, is a warm host. Enforced chat with other diners wouldn't suit everyone, but there are three small tables for those who don't want to join in." The family home of Macdonalds since the 18th century, and, apart from the plumbing, largely unchanged since before the first world war, the house is a repository of imperial mementos – Persian carpets, Indian tapestries, Burmese gongs, stuffed animals, Benares brass, and the bric-à-brac of the Raj. Meals generally take place around a central table, with gleaming family silver and crystal. Hugh's Californian wife Linda produces five-course traditional Scottish dinners – "good food, and lots of it, though peat-smoked salmon proved rather bizarre." (*Dr NB Finter, John and Moira Cole, C and R Frieze*)

Open Mid-Apr–mid-Oct.
Rooms 9 double, 2 single. No telephone/TV.
Facilities Drawing room, TV room, dining room. 20-acre grounds: croquet, swings, woodland walks. Sea 200 yds. Unsuitable for ♿.
Location S side of Portree, 10 mins' walk from centre. Driving towards Broadford turn right just after BP station on left.
Restrictions No smoking in dining room. No dogs in public rooms.
Credit cards Access, Visa
Terms [1996] B&B £30–£40; D,B&B £45–£55. Set dinner £15. 3/5-day rates. 1-night bookings sometimes refused.

QUOTHQUAN South Lanarkshire Map 5

Shieldhill Hotel *Tel* (01899) 220035
Quothquan, by Biggar ML12 6NA *Fax* (01899) 221092

Neil and Jean Mackintosh's dignified castle-type house dates in part from the 13th century. It is set amid the rolling hills of Lanarkshire, overlooking the river Clyde "with scarcely another dwelling in sight". Some accolades this year and last: "Excellent value for money – we fully endorse your entry." "Friendly and enthusiastic staff. Comfortable lounges, spacious dining room; food served with perfect timing. Wide-ranging, reasonably priced wine list. Gargantuan breakfast with freshly squeezed juice, porridge with honey and cream, a 'full house fry', kippers and smoked salmon and scrambled egg; butter and jams of the non-packaged variety." Bedrooms vary – most are large and floral, with huge beds and good Edwardian furniture. Some have a jacuzzi. (*Mr and Mrs R A Roxburgh, Esler Crawford, and others*) Drew Heron has replaced Paul Whitecross in the kitchen: more reports, please.

Open All year.
Rooms 1 suite, 10 double.
Facilities 2 lounges, bar, dining room; conference room. 6-acre grounds. Fishing nearby. Unsuitable for ♿.
Location 2 miles N of Biggar, left off B7016.
Restrictions No smoking in restaurant, bedrooms. No children under 10. Dogs in car only.
Credit cards All major cards accepted.
Terms B&B £47–£76; D,B&B £67–£96. Set lunch £15, dinner £27. 2-night breaks. Christmas, New Year packages. *V*

ST BOSWELLS Scottish Borders **Map 5**

Dryburgh Abbey Hotel *Tel* (01835) 822261
St Boswells TD6 0RQ *Fax* (01835) 823945

More plaudits this year for this luxuriously restored baronial mansion in a lovely setting, adjacent to the romantic ruins of Dryburgh Abbey on the banks of the Tweed: "Spacious, elegant, well run and peaceful." "An excellent place – when you have found it! The accommodation was marvellous; beautifully quiet." "We cannot fault this hotel. Staff were cheerful and helpful but not intrusive, and the food was of high quality." The beautiful dining room overlooking the Tweed, and the pillared Roman-style pool are also praised. (*Stephanie Sowerby, JC, Jane Bailey*) Most guests appreciate Patrick Ruse's imaginative cooking; his menus include a vegetarian dish and several "Taste of Scotland" options, eg, Pork Auld Alliance – medallions of pork on whisky, apple and prune cream. There are 14 golf courses within half an hour's drive, and the hotel will organise fishing or shooting parties.
Open All year.
Rooms 2 suites, 17 double, 6 single. Some in gate lodge 100 yds. Some on ground floor, suitable for ♿.
Facilities Lift, ramp. 2 lounges, bar, dining room; indoor swimming pool. 9-acre grounds: putting. Fishing, shooting, clay pigeon-shooting, golf nearby.
Location From St Boswells, 2 miles on B6404, signposted to Dryburgh Abbey, then B6356 for just over 1½ miles.
Restrictions No smoking: 1 lounge, dining room. No dogs in public rooms.
Credit cards Access, Amex, Visa.
Terms B&B £40–£55; D,B&B £52.50–£72.50. Set dinner £22.50. 2/5-night breaks. *V*

SHAPINSAY Orkney **Map 5**

Balfour Castle *Tel* (01856) 711282
Shapinsay KW17 2DY *Fax* (01856) 711283

"Great fun. Vast comfortable bedroom with views over to Kirkwall, dominated by St Magnus cathedral, with lowing herds passing backwards and forwards outside the window. The Zawadskis run a very amiable and slightly eccentric hotel/country house party in splendid surroundings." A warm endorsement this year for "the most northerly castle hotel in the world", which looms out of the mist on a small, fertile island given mainly to cattle- and sheep-rearing. Inside the same romantic atmosphere prevails: huge bedrooms, carpeted corridors, oak-panelled library, drawing room with plaster-gilded ceilings, log fires. Most of the fixtures and fittings are original, dating back to the castle's Victorian heyday. It is set in wooded grounds, with beautiful gardens and good walks. The Zawadski family eat breakfast and lunch with their guests in the kitchen, and in the evening serve a simple three-course dinner round one large table. Most of the produce comes from their own home farm and from Orkney waters. Dress is informal. "Other guests included a father and son heavily into shooting duck and rabbit, and an American lady vegetarian working for an animal welfare group." The family also own two uninhabited islands and will take guests by boat to see birdlife and seals. Most bedrooms have an *en suite* bathroom; one bedroom is suitable for families. (*Michael and Duora Lewis*)

Open All year.
Rooms 4 suites, 3 double, 1 single. No telephone/TV.
Facilities Drawing room, library with bar, TV room, billiard room, dining room. 2-acre garden on 70-acre estate. Boat trips, birdwatching, fishing. Unsuitable for ♿.
Location 20-minute ferry from Kirkwall. Travel information sent to guests.
Credit cards Access, Visa.
Terms D,B&B £68. Light lunch £4.50. 30% reduction for children. Weekly rates.

SHIELDAIG Highland — Map 5

Tigh an Eilean
Shieldaig
by Strathcarron IV54 8XN

Tel (01520) 755251
Fax (01520) 755321

"Charming. Informally run and not luxurious, it is wonderful for walking and relaxing. The staff are friendly. The food is tasty and filling, with lots of fresh fish and hot puddings, just what you need after being in the open all day. Plenty of hot water and fluffy towels to wrap yourself in." "Our favourite hotel. Guests return, as we do, year after year." "The village retains the atmosphere of a working fishing village, and the hotel is part of this. The proprietors are genuine, friendly and competent." Recent accolades for Callum and Elizabeth Stewart's small hotel, in a row of old buildings peacefully set by a sea loch amid the glorious Torridon hills of Wester Ross. It opens directly on to the village street, where hens and ducks wander. No garden, "but in fine weather most people want to be out in this magnificent area, and you can easily find sheltered places on the Shieldaig peninsula nearby to sit and admire the views." Local crab, lobster and game, and wild Atlantic salmon feature on the dinner menu. Breakfasts are "splendidly sustaining, with excellent porridge". The residents' lounge is small, but the dining room has a "light, open feeling". Bedrooms vary from "large, plainly but adequately furnished" to "small, without a view, quite a climb, but well planned". Simple bar meals available. (*Val Ferguson, Mr and Mrs JT Mills, and others; also Good Pub Guide*)

Open Apr–late Oct.
Rooms 8 double, 3 single. No telephone/TV.
Facilities Lounge, TV lounge, bar, dining room; drying room. Private fishing (salmon, sea trout) on river Balgy. Unsuitable for ♿.
Location Centre of village off A896 (but quiet). Parking opposite.
Restrictions No smoking: dining room, TV lounge. No dogs in public rooms.
Credit cards Access, Visa.
Terms B&B £45–£47.50. Set dinner £21. Reductions for 5 or more nights. Children under 8 accommodated free in parents' room.

SKIRLING Scottish Borders Map 5

Skirling House NEW/BUDGET *Tel* (01899) 860274
Skirling, Biggar ML12 6HD *Fax* (01899) 860255

Bob and Isobel Hunter's home, now an upmarket no-smoking B&B, is an Arts and Crafts period piece in the midst of splendid Border countryside. The drawing room has a 16th-century carved wood Florentine ceiling, and pieces of ironwork specially commissioned for the house, which was built in 1908. Our nominator could not fault anything: "Outstanding decor, taste, and level of comfort, and the warmest of welcomes. Excellent dinner: red pepper tart, chicken with watercress sauce, regional Scottish cheeses, chocolate fondant. For breakfast there are fresh orange juice, and home-made cherry, plum and walnut muffins; home-made bread and marmalade too. This new venture deserves to succeed." (*Mrs M Kershaw*)

Open Mar–Dec.
Rooms 3 double. 1 on ground floor. Also 2-bedroom self-catering cottage.
Facilities Drawing room, dining room, conservatory. 5½-acre garden: tennis, croquet. Fishing on River Tweed.
Location Centre of village, facing green.
Restrictions No smoking. Dogs by arrangement.
Credit cards None accepted.
Terms B&B £25–£35; D,B&B £42.50–£52.50. Set dinner £17.50. Weekly rates. *V*

SPEAN BRIDGE Highland Map 5

Corriegour Lodge BUDGET *Tel* (01397) 712685
Spean Bridge PH34 4EB *Fax* (01397) 712696

Rod and Lorna Bunney's Victorian hunting lodge on the shores of Loch Lochy is professionally run and unpretentious. It is praised again this year: "Excellent. The local staff are very helpful; cooking adventurous and plentiful; owners very friendly; there's a log fire in the lounge and the two golden retrievers (Sam and Jamie) are much in evidence." The house is freshly decorated, with plenty of "antiques and bits and pieces". At dinner, good local ingredients include Loch Lochy trout, haunch of venison and rack of Scottish lamb." Bedrooms vary in size; three large ones are suitable for families. (*W Ian Stewart, and others*) You can watch boats on their way through the Caledonian Canal from the conservatory dining room. The hotel has its own beach and jetty.

Open Mar–Oct.
Rooms 8 double, 1 single.
Facilities Lounge, bar, conservatory/dining room. 6-acre grounds, beach, jetty. Fishing, walking. Unsuitable for ♿.
Location On A82, 18 miles NE of Fort William, mid-way between Spean Bridge and Invergarry.
Restrictions No smoking in dining room. No dogs.
Credit cards Access, Amex, Visa.
Terms B&B £28–£35; D,B&B £46–£54. Special rates for 2 or more nights. *V*

We need detailed fresh reports to keep our entries up to date.

STRONTIAN Highland — Map 5

Kilcamb Lodge — *Tel* (01967) 402257
Strontian PH36 4HY — *Fax* (01967) 402041

César award: Scottish hotel of the year

One of our most popular Scottish hotels. Again this year there is a steady stream of praise, with not a dissenting note, for the generous and caring hospitality of the Blakeway family at their stone house on Loch Sunart. Some recent accolades: "Hotel of hotels. Food excellent; situation superb." "A totally enjoyable experience from start to finish." "Food as good as we remembered: beautifully cooked fish and yummy puddings – just the thing after a day's walking." "Rooms extremely comfortable." "Heaps of fresh towels and more than king-size bed." *Kilcamb*, Georgian with Victorian additions, stands in isolated splendour at the end of the Ardnamurchan peninsula in large grounds, which are ablaze in spring with rhododendrons, azaleas and rare wild flowers. Plenty of wildlife too: red deer, squirrels, hawks, otters, seals and golden eagles. Gordon and Ann Blakeway have now retired. The young Blakeways have taken the helm, with Peter in charge of the food, and his new wife Anne front of house. Stakker, an ebullient labrador welcomes one and all. There are fine views across lawns to the loch, and breathtaking sunsets. The lounges, with fires, fresh flowers, decorative plates and up-to-date magazines, have the feel of a well-loved home. The Gordon Girls – free-range chickens – provide fresh eggs every day. (*David Lipsey, Val Ferguson, Mary Milne-Day, Geraldine Terry, and many others*)

Open Mar–Nov, mid-Dec–mid-Jan.
Rooms 5 suites, 6 double. 2 self-catering cottages in grounds.
Facilities Drawing room, lounge/bar, dining room. 28-acre grounds: private beach, fishing, boating; mountain bikes available. Pony-trekking nearby. Unsuitable for ♿.
Location From A82 S of Fort William take Corran ferry, then A861 to Strontian.
Restrictions No smoking: drawing room, dining room, bedrooms. No dogs in public rooms.
Credit cards Access, Visa.
Terms [1996] D,B&B £69–£75. Set dinner £26.50. Discounts for 3/6 nights.

SWINTON Scottish Borders — Map 5

The Wheatsheaf BUDGET — *Tel/Fax* (01890) 860257
Main Street
Swinton TD11 3JJ

Alan and Julie Reid's popular and welcoming inn is in a village four miles from the river Tweed. The four bedrooms are simple but comfortable; three have *en suite* facilities. Alan Reid produces excellent unpretentious meals – the finest ingredients, skilfully cooked – on a large *carte*, as well as two set menus, both with several choices. "Food very good for a pub, and breakfast was outstanding," writes a recent visitor. "Fresh orange juice, eggs, bacon, excellent poached haddock all personally served by Mr Reid." Bar meals are also said to be "outstanding". (*Good Pub Guide*) Rooms on the road side can be noisy, and one visitor complained of a permeating smell of cigarette smoke.

Open All year, except Christmas, last 2 weeks Feb, last week Oct.
Rooms 4 double, 3 with *en suite* facilities.

Facilities Residents' lounge, lounge bar, 2 dining rooms. ½-acre garden: children's play area. Fishing on river Tweed by arrangement.
Location Centre of village. Parking beside hotel.
Restrictions No smoking: 1 dining room, sun lounge, bedrooms. No dogs in public rooms.
Credit cards Access, Visa.
Terms B&B £27.50–£45. Full alc £20. 3-night rates. *V*

TARBERT Western Isles — Map 5

Leachin House NEW/BUDGET

Tarbert, Isle of Harris HS3 3AH — *Tel* (01859) 502157

A Wolsey Lodge in the Outer Hebrides, enticingly recommended by a regular reader, an American enthusiast for Scotland: "A charming white house, immaculate and ship-shape, in a beautiful setting overlooking West Loch Tarbert and the mountains across the water. Diarmuid and Linda Wood, the friendly and very helpful hosts, have filled it with personal treasures, models and prints of sailing ships, seamen's knots mounted on plaques, and other things nautical. It has sparkling white walls and Harris tweed curtains [Norman MacLeod, the father of the Harris tweed industry once lived here]. The three bedrooms and bathrooms have lovely views, and all the amenities of a larger hotel – TV, fluffy towels on heated racks, bath gels, good soaps, etc. One of the bathrooms is *en suite*; the others are across a landing. Linda is the cook, and a very good one. The polished dining table is communally set with pretty linen and china. Dinner included delicious starters, eg, scallops in a Vermouth sauce and cream of capsicum soup; then coq au vin – fragrant and lovely. My husband, a chocolate person, adored the chocolate truffle torte. Tea (no extra charge), with flapjacks and carrot cake, is served by the drawing room fire. Breakfast is whatever you want; the complete Scottish affair or just porridge; excellent croissants too." (*Martha Prince*) Mr Wood organises specialist guides to take visitors to see eagles and sea otters; fishing can be arranged. In June and July the hills are carpeted with wild flowers.

Open Jan–Dec; closed Christmas and New Year.
Rooms 3 double. No telephone.
Facilities Drawing room, dining room. ½-acre garden. Sea 60 yds: safe bathing; fishing, walking nearby. Unsuitable for ♿.
Location 1 mile N of Tarbert on A859. Signposted on loch side.
Restrictions No smoking: dining room, bedrooms. Preferably children over 10. Dogs by arrangement.
Credit cards Access, Visa.
Terms B&B £35; D,B&B £55. Set dinner (with carafe of house wine) £20. 5-day breaks. *V* (as alternative to house discounts; Nov–Feb)

TIMSGARRY Western Isles — Map 5

Baile-na-Cille BUDGET

Timsgarry, Uig — *Tel* (01851) 672242
Isle of Lewis HS2 9JD — *Fax* (01851) 672241

César award in 1990

"This place is unique." Richard and Joanna Gollin's 18th-century manse lies by a huge white sand beach on the wild west coast of Lewis.

Others have written of "the *wonderful* food (I stayed a week and every meal was delicious)" and the "quirky, slightly eccentric charm of the Gollins, who manage to remain hospitable despite the non-stop demands of running an ever more successful operation on the edge of nowhere." "Breakfast the best in my travels; excellent porridge and home-made bread." Children are welcomed, and treated as equals. Simple bedrooms, varying in size, have double-glazing, electric blanket, etc; most have a sea view. Three, in the converted cowshed, are fairly basic and priced accordingly. Dinner is communally served; no choice, but preferences are discussed in advance. Richard Gollin drives frequently to Stornoway (about an hour away) and will drop guests at various points for walking and climbing. Mrs Gollin is a keen amateur flyer, and will take visitors for joy rides "if we have a machine staying". "It is true the pace of change out here makes evolution look like Nigel Mansell," writes Richard Gollin. "But we have a new grass tennis court; the first in Western Timsgarry." (*Christian Bartoschek, Brian Knox, and others*). One dissenter appreciated the dinners but thought breakfast a let-down, and the house shabbier than our entry suggested.

Open 15 Mar–15 Oct.
Rooms 2 family suites, 8 double, 2 single. 8 with bath. 3 in cottage annexe. Some on ground floor. No telephone/TV.
Facilities 3 lounges (1 with TV), dining room, conservatory; drying room. 3-acre grounds: walled garden, tennis, children's play area, cricket pitch, beach (dinghy, windsurfer, fishing rods available). Near 7 sandy beaches: safe bathing, fishing, sailing. Not really suitable for ♿.
Location 34 miles W of Stornoway. A858 from Stornoway or Tarbert to Garynahine, B8011 towards Uig; at Timsgarry shop turn right to shore. (Most road signs in Gaelic only.)
Restriction No smoking: dining room, 2 lounges, some bedrooms.
Credit card Access, Visa.
Terms B&B £22–£35; D,B&B £44–£57. Set lunch/dinner £21.15. Child in bunk room £12 including food. Packed lunches. Weekly rates.

ULLAPOOL Highland — Map 5

Altnaharrie — *Tel* (01854) 633230

Ullapool IV26 2SS

César award in 1987

"Uncompromising all-round excellence of food, decor, staff and location." "Fred Brown's quiet approach to the task of making each guest's stay perfect has rubbed off on his young staff. As you say, he maintains a degree of comfort astonishing for such a remote location. From the welcome as we stepped from the little boat on to the hotel jetty, to the feeling of leaving true friends as we waved goodbye this was a special experience. I cannot remember any hotel with fewer notices." Unstinted praise again for this old drover's house in an idyllic, remote setting on the southern shores of Loch Broom, opposite the fishing village of Ullapool. Cars are left there and visitors make the crossing in a comfortable launch, drawn by the tranquillity, the unassuming elegance and the "truly exquisite food". *Michelin* awards two stars – *Altnaharrie* is the only Scottish establishment to be thus recognised – for Norwegian-born Gunn Eriksen's cooking. Much of the food is grown or caught locally; there is no choice on the menu until dessert;

preferences are discussed at the time of booking. Some bedrooms are in the main house, smaller ones are in a cottage annexe; one is by a stream, with lovely views. They are attractively decorated in simple Scandinavian style, with king-size beds, and bathrooms both lavish and functional. No radio or TV, but lots of books. There's no mains electricity supply: the private generator is turned off after bedtime; a torch by the bed helps out in the middle of the night. There is limited walking from the hotel up a steep track. Guests are advised to bring stout footwear. (*Prof. NC Craig Sharp, Anthony Rota; also Sybella Zisman*)

Open Easter–mid-Nov.
Rooms 8 double. 2 in cottage near house, 1 in grounds 100 yds. No telephone/TV.
Facilities 2 lounges, dining room. 1½-acre grounds on loch: garden, pebble beach, safe (cold) bathing; trout/salmon-fishing by arrangement. Unsuitable for ♿.
Location On S shore of Loch Broom, reached by regular ferry (telephone from Ullapool). Free private parking in Ullapool.
Restrictions No smoking. No children under 8. Dogs by arrangement, not in public rooms.
Credit cards Access, Amex, Visa.
Terms D,B&B £145–£180. Set dinner £65–£70. 1-night bookings occasionally refused.

The Ceilidh Place BUDGET
14 West Argyle Street
Ullapool IV26 2TY
Tel (01854) 612103
Fax (01854) 612886

Exuberant, idiosyncratic establishment, originally just a coffee shop, now bar, hotel, bunk-house, gallery, performance room, book shop, wholefood shop and bakery. Plays, poetry readings, ceilidhs, *art exhibitions held regularly. 13 comfortable, if not lavish, bedrooms in main house; 11 basic ones (some shared), with bunk beds, in Clubhouse annexe. Traditional cooking, with emphasis on local seafood and vegetarian dishes. Robust breakfasts. Run by Jean Urquhart, widow of co-founder Robert Urquhart. No smoking: restaurant, some bedrooms. No dogs in public rooms. All major credit cards accepted. B&B: £35–£55. Full alc £27.50. More reports badly needed.*

WHITEBRIDGE Highland — Map 5

Knockie Lodge
Whitebridge IV1 2UP
Tel (01456) 486276
Fax (01456) 486389

"It has that certain something which sets it above other places," writes a regular visitor to Ian and Brenda Milward's 200-year-old hotel, formerly a hunting lodge for the Chief of Clan Fraser. Another recent accolade: "It must have one of the most peerless remote locations in the book. I appreciated more this time the quality of the house and its furnishings – fine panelling and carvings, impressive pictures, lots of interesting books, excellent silver and napery. A bonus is the extension to the sitting room, with a picture window overlooking one of the lochs; there's also a billiard room, and another sitting area. The bath towels are the best and largest I have come across *anywhere*." Cooking is sophisticated but not over-elaborate; there is a wide-ranging wine list. Bedrooms, varying in size, are unfussy and snug, with good hanging space, fresh flowers, and immaculate modern bathrooms. There is excellent fishing and deer-stalking. (*JC, and others*) Mr Milward has strong views about television: it is not an option for guests.

Open 4 May–26 Oct.
Rooms 8 double, 2 single. No TV.
Facilities Drawing room with bar, sitting room, billiard room, dining room. 10-acre grounds. Loch 5 mins' walk: private fishing rights. Deer-stalking, pony-trekking, golf nearby. Unsuitable for ♿.
Location 2 miles down single-track private road W off B862, 8 miles N of Fort Augustus.
Restrictions No smoking in dining room. No children under 10. No dogs in public rooms, unattended in bedrooms.
Credit cards All major cards accepted.
Terms [1996] B&B: single £50, double £90–£150. Set dinner £26.

WHITING BAY North Ayrshire — Map 5

Grange House BUDGET — *Tel/Fax* (01770) 700263
Whiting Bay
Isle of Arran KA27 8QH

Peaceful, unpretentious Victorian house with "friendly, almost domestic atmosphere, genuinely nice owners, Janet and Clive Hughes, lots of local literature". ¼ mile from village centre in 1-acre garden: putting lawn. Foreshore across small road, lovely views; good bird-watching, walking. 9 bedrooms (2 for families; 1 adapted for ♿), 7 with facilities en suite. *Sauna. Good traditional dinner at 7 pm on 3-course menu, "but rushed service". Open mid-Mar–mid-Nov, Christmas, New Year. No smoking. No dogs. Lunch not served. Access, Visa accepted. B&B £30–£35; D,B&B £45–£50 [1996]. More reports, please.*

Channel Islands

St Brelade's Bay Hotel, St Brelade

ROZEL BAY Jersey **Map 1**

Château La Chaire *Tel* (01534) 863354
Rozel Bay, St Martin JE3 6AJ *Fax* (01534) 865137

"A truly lovely hotel. All the staff, from the manager, Alan Winch, to the chambermaids, were charming; service at all times efficient, polite and welcoming." "Elegant and comfortable. Location idyllic and quiet." "We enjoyed leisurely breakfasts, afternoon tea on a sunny terrace, and excellent canapés before dinner. Bedrooms very well set up; the suite had two luxury bathrooms, and everything you could think of: fresh fruit, towelling robes, even a Scrabble board." Recent praise for this small luxurious hotel on the slopes overlooking the Rozel valley at the north-eastern tip of Jersey. It is set in terraced gardens above a picturesque fishing harbour: good cliff walks, safe beaches, "heavenly views". Inside are panelled public rooms, chandeliers, fine mouldings with cherubs and intricate scrollwork in the spacious Rococo lounge. In the restaurant, with oak panelling and an attractive conservatory, chef Simon Walker (new since January 1996) serves modern British cooking, specialising in seafood; we'd be grateful for reports on his work. (*Vicki George, and others*)

Open All year. Restaurant closed Christmas evening.
Rooms 1 suite (on ground floor), 13 double.
Facilities Lounge, bar, restaurant with conservatory. 6-acre garden. Sandy beach, safe bathing nearby. Unsuitable for ♿.
Location 5 miles NE of St Helier. Follow signs for St Martin's church, then Rozel. 1st left in village; hotel carpark 200 yds on left.
Restrictions No smoking in conservatory. No children under 7. No dogs.
Credit cards All major cards accepted.
Terms [1996] B&B: single £59–£105, double £80–£135, suite £155–£180; D,B&B: single £75–£121, double £112–£167, suite £187–£212. Set lunch £14.75, dinner £22.50; full alc £32.50. Winter breaks. 1-night bookings sometimes refused in season.

ST BRELADE Jersey — Map 1

Atlantic Hotel — *Tel* (01534) 44101
St Brelade JE3 8HE — *Fax* (01534) 44102

"One of the nicest hotels we have ever stayed in. Spotless throughout. Staff exceptional. Food excellent and imaginative." "I visited with my elderly mother. We were made to feel especially welcome, and upgraded to lovely large rooms with a magnificent sea view. The decor is quite exceptional; the designer's talents combine cleverly with the beauty of the situation. Pinks and greens give a relaxing feeling, large windows enable the beauty of the gardens to be thoroughly enjoyed. Service second to none." Two endorsements for this "truly luxurious" hotel which made its *Guide* debut last year. It was opened 26 years ago, by the father of the present owner, Patrick Burke; its manager, Simon Dufty is a member of the hotel-keeping family of *Longueville Manor*, St Saviour (*qv*). Its grounds adjoin La Moye championship golf course, and it overlooks the wonderful five-mile beach of St Ouen's Bay. Behind its plain exterior are a wrought iron staircase, rich carpeting, urns, fountains, antiques and specially designed modern furniture. Light lunches are served, by the pool in fine weather. The airport is ten minutes' drive away. (*Lynda Gillinson, Sarah Barrington*) Only caveats: "Some bedrooms and bathrooms a bit on the small side; shower pressure inadequate."

Open Mar–Dec.
Rooms 2 suites, 48 double.
Facilities Lounges, cocktail bar, restaurant; fitness centre: swimming pool, sauna. 3-acre grounds: tennis, swimming pool. Golf club, beach nearby. Unsuitable for ♿.
Location 5 miles W of St Helier.
Restriction No dogs.
Credit cards All major cards accepted.
Terms [1996] B&B: double £110–£200, suite £185–£325. Set lunch £15, dinner £22.50; full alc £40.

St Brelade's Bay Hotel — *Tel* (01534) 46141
St Brelade's Bay JE3 8EF — *Fax* (01534) 47278

A large hotel, which has been owned by one family for five generations. It is set in beautiful, large, landscaped gardens, in a fine position overlooking the vast expanse of the bay, though separated from the beach by a road. Behind the modern exterior is an old-fashioned, elegant decor, with moulded ceilings, chandeliers, and lots of fresh flowers. Traditional food is served in the panelled restaurant. There are plenty of outdoor facilities (see below), and evening entertainment. Sea-facing bedrooms have a balcony; others overlook the garden. There's good family accommodation. "We honeymooned here forty years ago," writes a recent visitor. "And had a very happy return visit. Our comfortable bedroom had a balcony overlooking the sea. The *maître d'* really added to the relaxed atmosphere. The owners were very much in evidence, particularly at mealtimes." "Lovely suite, with comfortable chairs for reading, and current magazines. The food was enjoyable, and we were impressed by the staff's attitude. They seemed genuinely to want to please the guests, and the quality of service permeated the hotel." (*Pauline Turner, Mrs C Wright*)

Open 25 Apr–6 Oct.
Rooms 4 suites, 76 double, 4 single.
Facilities Lift. Lounge, TV room, bar, restaurant; entertainments, disco twice weekly; games room, snooker room; sun veranda. 7-acre grounds: swimming pool with bar, barbecue, sauna, solarium, exercise room; children's swimming pool, lifeguard; tennis, croquet, putting, table tennis, *boules*, children's play area. Beach across road. Golf nearby.
Location 5 miles W of St Helier.
Restrictions No smoking in restaurant. No dogs.
Credit cards Access, Visa.
Terms B&B: single £52–£90, double £76–£180, suite £124–£220; D,B&B: single £57–£95, double £86–£190, suite £134–£230. Set lunch £12, dinner £18; full alc £30.

ST PETER PORT Guernsey — Map 1

La Frégate — *Tel* (01481) 724624
Les Côtils — *Fax* (01481) 720443
St Peter Port GY1 1UT

An old manor, much converted, set in terraced gardens on a hill above the harbour, which most bedrooms overlook. They are spacious, and have excellent, large bathrooms, "with baths designed for late-20th century bodies, and man-sized towels"; some have a balcony. "We enjoyed sitting at our window eating the room-service breakfast (this is encouraged); the view was so good that my wife got out her water colours. The staff are courteous without pushiness." The restaurant (popular with locals for its mainly French cooking) is "worth making the trip for – exquisite fish, and delicious desserts"; "good materials, enhanced, not spoilt, by cooking". The *table d'hôte* is "excellent value"; so are the weekend rates. (*Paul Palmer, Julian Currie*)

Open All year.
Rooms 13.
Facilities Lounge, bar, restaurant. Terraced garden.
Location Near Candie Gardens, 3 mins' walk from centre. Hard to find; hotel will send directions. Carpark.
Restrictions No children under 14. No dogs.
Credit cards All major cards accepted.
Terms B&B: single £55, double £70–£95. Set lunch £13, dinner £19; full alc £25–£35. Christmas package. *V*

ST SAVIOUR Jersey **Map 1**

Longueville Manor
Longueville Road
St Saviour JE2 7WF
Tel (01534) 25501
Fax (01534) 31613
E-mail Longman@itl.net

César award in 1986

This luxurious hotel (Relais & Châteaux) has been run by the Lewis and Dufty families for over 40 years. It is set in large grounds at the foot of a wooded valley, just inland from Jersey's capital, St Helier. "Everything of high quality: impressive rooms, exceptional housekeeping, very good food," writes a recent visitor, endorsing earlier praise: "The team of owners and front-of-house is charming. The staff (many Portuguese) are exceptionally hard-working, willing to please, and polite. Decor very smart without being brash or contrived – swagged curtains, colourful oriental rugs, original paintings, antiques, good repro furniture. Marvellous spacious bedrooms and suites, with comfortable settee, fresh flowers, masses of magazines. First-class swimming pool, heated to a constant 80°F, with a charming ambience and an excellent poolside lunch." In the *Michelin*-starred restaurant, the "modern English cooking with a French classical influence" by Andrew Baird, is "interesting and varied", with an emphasis on fresh meat, fish and home-grown vegetables: "The daily-changing three-course set menu was so seductive we were rarely tempted to eat off the *carte*, which is quite expensive." "Wonderful vegetarian dishes." The Royal Jersey Golf Club is close by. The winter package, which includes car hire, is "very good value". (*AG, and others*)

Open All year.
Rooms 2 suites, 30 double. 8 on ground floor.
Facilities Lift. 2 lounges, bar lounge, restaurant; conference facilities. 16-acre grounds: gardens, woodland, croquet, tennis, swimming pool. Golf, bowls, squash, nearby. Sandy beaches ¾ mile.
Location 1 mile E of St Helier by A3; hotel on left.
Restrictions No smoking in restaurant. No dogs in public rooms.
Credit cards All major cards accepted.
Terms B&B: single £125–£185, double £155–£240, suite £280–£330; D,B&B £30 per person added. Set lunch £19, dinner £32; full alc £40. Winter weekend breaks; Christmas package.

SARK **Map 1**

Hotel Petit Champ NEW/BUDGET
Sark, via Guernsey GY9 0SF
Tel (01481) 832046
Fax (01481) 832469

Late 19th-century granite hotel, popular with Guide *readers under previous management, now renominated under new owners, Mr and Mrs Robins. In secluded area on headlands of west coast, well away from day trippers – magnificent views, spectacular sunsets. "Location and tranquillity unparalleled on this most beautiful of islands." Rooms comfortable, but not luxurious (no telephone,* TV*, etc). Sun lounges, library, bar. 1-acre grounds: putting, solar-heated pool; steep walk down to sandy beach. Good food: fresh lobster, fresh fish, etc, "served with style and panache". Open Easter–early Oct. 16 bedrooms. Unsuitable for* ♿*. No smoking: dining rooms, library. "Children must be old enough to sit with parents at dinner." No dogs: bedrooms,* *restaurant. All major credit cards accepted. B&B £32.50–£39; D,B&B £42.25–£49. More reports, please.* *V*

La Sablonnerie BUDGET
Little Sark
Sark, via Guernsey GY9 0SD

Tel (01481) 832061
Fax (01481) 832408

Sark, only three-and-a-half miles long, but with nearly 40 miles of coastline, is the smallest of the four main Channel Islands. No cars, but all parts of the coast are easily reached on foot, by barouche, or on a bicycle. In Little Sark, the southernmost part of the island, this "charming and idiosyncratic" 16th-century farmhouse has been owned by the Perrée family for over 40 years; it is currently run by Elizabeth Perrée. "I have visited regularly since 1966," writes a devotee, "and have witnessed the improvement in the facilities and food. The menu is varied, with extensive choice, always including fish, excellent meat, and delicious vegetables, grown on the hotel's own farm. Desserts are exceptional, and there's a groaning cheeseboard. Breakfasts – 'whatever you want'. The relationship between kitchen and waiting staff is excellent; every meal progresses in a delightful manner." "Everything is done for guests' comfort: bedrooms are tidied during breakfast; on a dull day the barman lit a fire and offered us a game of chess. Not the lap of luxury; no TVs or telephones in bedrooms; ours, in a wing, was small and unheated. But the gorgeous situation, the beautiful gardens, the lure of the food and, most of all, the friendly, concerned staff will bring us back." (*DWB, and others*) More reports, please.

Open Easter–Oct.
Rooms 1 suite, 15 double, 6 single. Guests sometimes accommodated in nearby cottages.
Facilities 3 lounges, 2 bars, restaurant. 1-acre garden: tea garden, croquet. Bays, beaches, rock pools nearby. Sark unsuitable for ♿.
Location Southern part of island.
Restrictions No smoking in some bedrooms. No dogs in public rooms.
Credit cards Access, Amex, Visa.
Terms (*Excluding 10% service charge*) B&B £38–£60; D,B&B: £49.50–£78. Set lunch £18.50, dinner £21.50; full alc £29.50.

Stocks BUDGET
Sark, via Guernsey GY9 0SD

Tel (01481) 832001
Fax (01481) 832130

Armorgie family's old-established hotel, an 18th-century granite farmhouse, centrally situated in south-facing wooded valley, 20 minutes' walk from harbour. Welcoming lounge; 24 simple bedrooms – good family accommodation. Informal courtyard bistro serves moderately priced lunches and cream teas. Cider Press *restaurant specialises in local fish, meat and shellfish on quite ambitious menu. "Large young staff; service cheerful and efficient." Open Apr–Oct. 1-acre garden: unheated swimming pool. Bicycle hire. Sandy beach nearby. Unsuitable for ♿. Smoking discouraged throughout. All major credit cards accepted. B&B £29–£38; D,B&B £41–£50. Set lunch £12, dinner £18.50; full alc £19.50–£29.50. Good packages, inclusive of travel. More reports, please.* *V*

There is no VAT in the Channel Islands.

Northern Ireland

Beech Hill House, Derry

BELFAST **Map 6**

Ash-Rowan *Tel* (01232) 661758
12 Windsor Avenue *Fax* (01232) 663227
Belfast BT9 6EE

Evelyn and Sam Hazlett's B&B, a solid Victorian house in residential South Belfast, has been endorsed again this year. A business traveller, driven out of the big hotels by the Clinton contingent last year, was delighted with the place. "Cosy rooms with lovely linen, perhaps a touch frilly; genuinely kind and warm welcome. We had to make a 6 am start, so excellent bread and jam and a flask of coffee were left out for us." The house is full of old furniture, lace and curios. Mr and Mrs Hazlett are charming hosts – she cooks and they both bake. Breakfast includes two types of home-baked bread, home-made conserves, fresh fruit salad, and a large choice of cooked dishes, including the Ulster Fry, "not for the faint-hearted". Bedrooms are remarkably well fitted out, and all have a shower. There's a lounge for residents, with daily papers. (*AT Farrell-Ayub*) A dissenter this year thought it "over-rated and over-priced".

Open All year, except 23 Dec–mid Jan.
Rooms 2 double, 2 single.
Facilities Lounge, breakfast room. ½-acre garden.
Location Just off Lisburn Rd, 2 miles SW of centre. Carpark.
Restrictions No smoking: breakfast room, 2 bedrooms. No children under 12. No dogs.
Credit cards Access, Visa.
Terms B&B: single £46–£52, double £68–£72.

COOKSTOWN Co. Tyrone — Map 6

Tullylagan Country House NEW
40b Tullylagan Road
Cookstown BT80 8UP

Tel (016487) 65100
Fax (016487) 61715

Handsome 18th-century house, 4 miles from Dungannon, in splendid grounds beside the Tullylagan river. "A very warm and comfortable hotel with flowers everywhere, and excellent service." "All the rooms we saw were decorated to a high standard and the grounds round the hotel were lovely." Fishing on the estate. Closed Christmas Day. 1 suite, 16 double. No dogs. Access, Visa. B&B: single £40, double £60. Set lunch £8.95, dinner £15.95. More reports, please.

DERRY Co. Londonderry — Map 6

Beech Hill House
32 Ardmore Road
Derry BT47 3QP

Tel (01504) 49279
Fax (01504) 45366

Two miles outside Derry, in its own broad parkland, stands this handsome white country house. Once the home of a judge, now a hotel owned by local people, the Donnellys, it is one of the most highly reputed in the North. "The garden is lovely, beds and bedrooms comfortable; the food is excellent – they have a wonderful chef," writes an old friend of the *Guide*. Another says: "My room was bright and spacious, with a lovely view. Staff were friendly and flexible and the food superb – best fresh salmon and soup, best cooked breakfast I can remember." Seamus Donnelly is very much in evidence, carrying cases, and sometimes waiting at table, as is his cheerful sister Patsy. Bedrooms are mostly quite large, and well equipped. Noel McMeel's cooking is above average for these parts, with good-quality fish and meat, and excellent puddings. Local people use the big lounge as a kind of pub: "Everyone who is anyone in Northern Ireland seems to turn up there." One visitor had mild objections to the decor and the piped music in the hall, but felt "the kindness and willingness of the proprietors overcame everything". (*MA, and others*)

Open All year, except 24/25 Dec.
Rooms 2 suites, 15 double.
Facilities Ramps. Lounge, morning room, bar, restaurant; conference facilities. 32-acre grounds: tennis, ponds, waterfall.
Location 2 miles SE of Derry, off Belfast road (signposted to right). Carpark.
Restrictions No smoking in restaurant. No dogs.
Credit cards Access, Amex, Visa.

Terms B&B: single £62.50, double £75, suite £100. Set lunch £13.95, dinner £20.95; full alc from £33. Weekend, midweek breaks.

ENNISKILLEN Co. Fermanagh **Map 6**

Killyhevlin Hotel NEW

Tel (01365) 323481
Fax (01365) 324726

Rambling two-storey white building in "splendid position" in 5-acre grounds on shores of Lough Erne (boating, coarse fishing). Extended and refurbished in style "both luxurious and delightful". 45 straightforward bedrooms; huge bathrooms. Bar meals in boathouse-style bar, and lounge. Nightly music by resident pianist. Restaurant food a touch complicated (no recognisably Irish dishes); immense helpings. Excellent choice and value on wine list. Good breakfasts, freshly cooked (but weak coffee). 14 self-catering chalets on lake shore; conference complex. No smoking in restaurant. No dogs. All major credit cards accepted. B&B: single £50–£58.50, double £90–£110, suite £150–£200. Set dinner £19.50; full alc £22.50. *V* *Late news: as we went to press, the hotel reported that it expected to be in business again very soon, following bomb damage in July 1996.*

Republic of Ireland

Hunter's Hotel, Rathnew

The big international hotel chains are hardly represented in Ireland. There are one or two small Irish chains, notably Fitzpatrick's and Jurys, but they do not feature in this section. Almost all Irish hotels are privately owned and run, and indeed this country is a paradise of the kind of smallish, very personal hotel of character that the *Guide* seeks out and encourages.

Many of them are stately homes still lived in by their ancestral owners, the Anglo-Irish gentry, who have turned them into private hotels or guest houses to defray the costs of keeping up a big estate. Or newer owners have acquired them and run them in the same very personal way. Guests may be surrounded by old family portraits and heirlooms, fine old family antiques and furniture. It is all very civilised, though this kind of inspired amateurism in hotel-keeping can have its drawbacks. Often the wife of the house does the cooking, in "country house" style, ie, simple, rather bland, using local ingredients. In many such hotels, the owners try to give their paying clients the illusion that they are personal friends on a visit. They may try to create a "house party" atmosphere. Often the guests dine communally round one big table, at one sitting, and conversation is general, as at a private dinner party. This can work well, or it can be embarrassing, depending on the mix of guests and the hosts' personality. The hosts will sometimes preside: often they are great fun, full of local anecdotes and information, but at worst, you may feel that you are paying your host to amuse *him* at dinner. Most of the best of these stately home hotels are in this guide. In town and country alike, there are also guest houses of all kinds, private homes offering B&B, and – an Irish speciality – farmhouses providing simple bedrooms, big breakfasts, sometimes an evening meal too. You can stay in converted farm buildings or outhouses, get to know the country people, even share briefly in the life of the farm. The Irish Tourist Board, Bord Fáilte, grades all kinds of accommodation: the places it approves generally display at the gate its green shamrock sign.

All Irish accommodation provides a cooked breakfast, with bacon, sausages, eggs, etc – ample, but somewhat monotonous, and coffee is usually poor. Food in Irish hotels has been improving considerably, as witness some of the entries in this chapter. But standards remain erratic, and attempts at sophistication do not always succeed. Just a few places win a *Michelin* star or red "Meals" for quality, and we identify these. As in Britain, VAT is included in bills, but not service, and you are expected to add about 10 per cent for this. Service, usually by local people, may sometimes lack polish: but it makes up for this by an almost universal Irish cheerfulness and obligingness.

ADARE Co. Limerick — Map 6

Dunraven Arms — *Tel* (061) 396633
Main Street — *Fax* (061) 396541

Adare, near Limerick, is a pretty village on the banks of the river Maigue, with black and white timbered houses, an ancient church, and many ruins. There are plenty of sporting activities in the area, and this handsome old traditional inn, long, low and yellow, with a pretty garden, is popular with the local horse-riding fraternity. Its manager, Louis Murphy, is a keen huntsman, and will make arrangements for guests to hunt with famous local packs. The hotel has virtually doubled in size in the last two years, but a recent visitor enjoyed his stay nonetheless: "I was given an excellent, quiet large room, facing the garden. The food was good – not gourmet, but well presented and well cooked. The service was a bit amateur, but full of charm. The half board rate was good value. It might be a bit noisy in the fox-hunting season." The decor is traditional. Chef Mark Phelan has won awards for his cooking. A new leisure centre has just been built, with a large swimming pool, computerised gym studio, and steam room. More reports, please.

Open All year.
Rooms 8 suites, 53 double, 5 single.
Facilities Library, reading room, TV room, residents' bar (pianist, harpist at weekends), public bar, restaurant, conservatory; conference/function facilities; leisure centre: swimming pool, gym etc. 3-acre garden; river, fishing. Golf, riding, fox-hunting available.
Location In village 10 miles SW of Limerick. Private parking.
Restriction No dogs in house.
Credit cards All major cards accepted.

Terms [1996] Rooms: single IR£57–£72, double IR£84–£104, suite IR£130–£150. Breakfast: continental IR£6.80, Irish IR£9.95. Set lunch IR£8.95–IR£12.95, dinner IR£22.95; full alc IR£26.

AGLISH Co. Tipperary — Map 6

Ballycormac House BUDGET — *Tel* (067) 21129
Aglish, nr Borrisokane — *Fax* (067) 21200

Herbert and Christine Quigley's ancient farmhouse near Lough Derg offers American comfort and a high standard of cooking. Recent accolades: "We had such a successful hunting weekend with them that we returned with all the family for two and a half weeks in August – It was undoubtedly the best holiday of our life." "The location is not spectacular, but the house and small gardens are particularly charming. Our suite (we were upgraded without extra charge) had a four-poster, and was delightfully decorated. The food was very good, plentiful and reasonably priced." The Quigleys offer a "modern eclectic" cuisine, "with diverse ethnic menus using the best produce Ireland has to offer"; vegetarians are catered for. Families and people on their own are welcomed, and programmes of outdoor activities (riding, fox-hunting, shooting etc) can be arranged; so can packed or light lunches; "old-fashioned teas" are served by the fire. (*Carolyn Bullus, GD*)

Open All year.
Rooms 1 suite (with TV), 3 double, 1 single. No telephone.
Facilities Sitting room, dining room; drying room. 2-acre gardens. Lough Derg 5 miles; fishing, sailing, riding, golf nearby.
Location From Nenagh N on N52 to Borrisokane, then N65. Right at signs to hotel.
Restrictions No smoking: dining room, bedrooms. No young children. Dogs by arrangement; not in house.
Credit cards Access, Visa.
Terms B&B: single IR£30, double IR£60, suite IR£70; D,B&B: single IR£50–£54, double IR£100–£108, suite IR£110–£118. Set lunch IR£6–£10, dinner IR£20–£24. Off-season breaks; activity programmes; Christmas, New Year packages. 1-night bookings refused bank holidays. *V*

BALLINDERRY Co. Tipperary — Map 6

Kylenoe BUDGET — *Tel/Fax* (067) 22015
Ballinderry, Nenagh

An 18th-century house on a hilltop near Lough Derg. It is set in huge grounds with meadows, woods, a small stud farm, apple orchards and plenty of wildlife. Sadly, Ken Moeran died last year; his wife Virginia is now running it as a B&B. *Guide* reporters have found it as good as ever: "We arrived much later than expected, but were made very welcome with tea and biscuits. Our rooms were spacious and comfortable – it was like staying with friends." "An uncomplicated, friendly place. Our children were made particularly welcome." Others have found the house warm throughout, and written of the "immaculate housekeeping", and the "gleaming bathrooms, with plentiful hot water". "All in all, good value for money." (*D Kaars Sypesteyn, PC, and others*)

Open All year. Advance booking required.
Rooms 3 double, 1 single.

Facilities Drawing room, dining room. 150-acre grounds. Lake 1 mile: fishing. Unsuitable for ♿.
Location Between Ballinderry and Terryglass (signposted). 7 miles NW of Borrisokane.
Credit card Access, Visa.
Terms B&B IR£25. Set dinner IR£18.50–£20. Children under 12 accommodated at half price.

BALLYLICKEY Co. Cork Map 6

Ballylickey Manor *Tel* (027) 50071
Ballylickey, Bantry Bay *Fax* (027) 50124

The 300-year-old former shooting lodge of Lord Kenmare, for four generations the home of the Franco–Irish Graves family, is now a luxurious hotel (Relais & Chateaux). Its reception rooms are splendid, with log fires, antiques, paintings and handsome draperies; breakfast and light meals for residents only are served in the handsome green dining room. The poolside Mediterranean-style restaurant, *Le Rendezvous*, has a French chef, Gilles Eynaud, and a distinctly French atmosphere. It is open to the public. Some elegant guest bedrooms, "heavily draped and curtained, with exceptionally comfortable beds with French cotton embroidered sheets and frilly pillow cases", are in the main house. More rustic ones are in cottages in the garden. "Everything about the place was appealing," runs a recent report. "The gardens, the view, the comfort of the rooms and the faultless dinner and breakfast. Staff were agreeable, helpful and efficient. Expensive, but worth every penny." But one couple this year, while endorsing much of the above, had severe reservations about the restaurant, which they felt was run for the benefit of the public rather than residents, with a long pre-dinner wait and haphazard service. Cottage rooms have been criticised for furnishings, heating and insulation, and are "uncomfortably close" to the pool and restaurant.

Open Mid-Mar–mid-Nov.
Rooms 7 suites, 5 double. 7 in garden cottages 150 yds.
Facilities 3 drawing rooms, 2 bars, 2 restaurants. 10-acre grounds: swimming pool; private salmon/trout-fishing.
Location On N71 Bantry–Kenmare.
Restrictions No smoking in restaurants. Dogs "at discretion of owners and their dogs"; not in house.
Credit cards Access, Amex, Visa.
Terms B&B: double IR£90, suite IR£165–£180. Set lunch IR£10–£15, dinner IR£25–£30; full alc IR£45.

Sea View House BUDGET *Tel* (027) 50073 and 50462
Ballylickey, Bantry Bay *Fax* (027) 51555

More praise this year for Kathleen O'Sullivan's fine Victorian house overlooking Bantry Bay and the distant mountains. "Fully support the *Guide* entry. Mrs O'Sullivan runs a really delightful establishment, supported by a charming and helpful staff." There are good bedrooms with plenty of cupboard space, and personal touches everywhere; gleaming bathrooms with lots of extras. "The food was excellent," writes another enthusiast. "Lovely fish – Bantry Bay oysters and mussels, scallops, crab and Dover sole. Breakfasts also good with fresh

Irish potato cakes and potato pancakes and good bacon. Extraordinarily good value." Guests are greeted on arrival with tea and home-made biscuits, and are treated from then on with "extreme kindness". The warm welcome and hospitality centres on the personality of Miss O'Sullivan, "floating about in one of her lovely dresses, making sure that everyone is happy". Packed lunches are available. (*Hazel Astley, RM Sparkes*)

Open Mid-Mar–mid-Nov.
Rooms 17 double. 1 on ground floor, suitable for ♿.
Facilities Lounge/bar, TV room, 2 dining rooms. 5-acre grounds. Fishing, boating, beaches, riding, golf nearby.
Location 3 miles N of Bantry towards Glengarriff, 70 yds off main road.
Restrictions: No smoking in dining room. No dogs in public rooms.
Credit cards All major cards accepted.
Terms B&B: IR£30–£55; D,B&B (min. 3 days) IR£50–£95. Set dinner IR£25. Special breaks all year. *V* (low season only)

BALLYMOTE Co. Sligo **Map 6**

Temple House BUDGET *Tel* (071) 83329
Fax (071) 83808

"Continues to live up to its reputation; outstanding value for money." An endorsement this year for this Georgian mansion in 1,000 acres of farmland and woods, beside a lake and the ruins of a castle built by the Knights Templar in AD 1200. The Percevals, whose family has lived here for three centuries, are friendly and informal, but the main hall and stairway are decidedly imposing. Some of the five bedrooms are huge too: one is nicknamed "the half-acre". All are comfortably kitted out; beds have an electric blanket. At dinner, guests sit round one table, and Deb Perceval's cooking ("Irish with French connections") is much admired. The Percevals do not eat with their guests, but are ready to chat at all times. Mr Perceval, something of a Green, is proud to show visitors the farm on his huge estate, stocked with sheep and Kerry cattle (it is a classified lichen conservation area). Fishing is available on the lake and shooting parties are held in winter. Children are welcomed. One small caveat – guests are asked to observe a "no scent" rule as Mr Perceval is allergic to scented products. (*A O'D*)

Open 1 Apr–30 Nov.
Rooms 4 double, 1 single. No telephone/TV.
Facilities Sitting room, snooker room, dining room. Terraced garden: croquet. 1,000-acre farm and woodlands; lake: coarse fishing, boating. Unsuitable for ♿.
Location 14 miles S of Sligo on N17. Signposted beyond Esso garage in Ballymote.
Restrictions No smoking in dining room. No dogs in house.
Credit cards Access, Amex, Visa.
Terms B&B IR£40; D,B&B IR£58. Set dinner IR£18; full alc IR£22. Weekend breaks. Reductions for long stays. 1-night bookings refused public holidays.

****

Traveller's tale At dinner at one hotel, I ordered a bottle of white wine which arrived unchilled. I was informed the hotel was "right out of ice" – this on New Year's Eve! I then ordered champagne. The bottle arrived in an ice-bucket full of water, which only served to make the champagne warmer.

****

BANTRY Co. Cork — Map 6

Bantry House — *Tel* (027) 50047
Fax (027) 50795

César award in 1991

A grand classical country house, superbly situated in huge wooded grounds above Bantry Bay, with views of the Caha mountains. It is open to the public, and offers B&B in two of its wings. The owner, Egerton Shelswell-White, a direct descendant of the Earl of Bantry, is a keen trombone-player. The breakfasts, served in a "delightful and cosy room", are much admired, and recent visitors were enthusiastic about the bedrooms. "Ours, No. 25, was huge, decorated in fresh-looking blue and white, with breathtaking views of the bay. Furnishings are modern, but chosen with taste to harmonise with the old building." Guests have the use of a separate sitting room, billiard room, and small television room, and free access to the main rooms of the house, including the library with its fine period furniture, tapestries and family portraits. Simple three- or four-course dinners for residents are served at 7.30 pm on weekdays, and by arrangement at weekends. More reports, please.

Open New Year–end Oct. Dinner May–Oct only.
Rooms 1 suite, 8 double.
Facilities Sitting room, library (occasional concerts), TV room, billiard room, bar, tea room, dining room; craft shop. 100-acre estate: 20-acre garden. Sea, sandy beach ½ mile. Unsuitable for ♿.
Location ½ mile from centre, towards Cork; signposted on Inner Harbour wall.
Restrictions No smoking: restaurant, bedrooms. Dogs in grounds only.
Credit cards Access, Visa.
Terms B&B IR£50–£70. Set dinner IR£20–£25. Wine licence only. Reductions for 5 days or more; group bookings.

BEAUFORT Co. Kerry — Map 6

Beaufort House NEW — *Tel/Fax* (064) 44764

A handsome Georgian family home, complete with two children and a dog, in a small village near Killarney. The river Laune (with fishing for salmon and trout) runs through its large grounds. It is "unreservedly recommended" by a seasoned Irish traveller: "The setting by the river is idyllic; from the upper rooms there is a good view of the mountains – Magillicuddy's Reeks. The owners, Rachel and Donald Cameron, are a charming, extremely attentive couple, with an eye for interior design. They have spent lavishly on beautifully coordinated curtains and carpets; walls are painted to match. Our large front bedroom was superb, with a view of the river and mountains, a double bed wide enough for four, a very adequate bathroom, with good quality towels. Dinner is communal and the Camerons join their guests over dessert and coffee; the no-choice set menu was excellent on both evenings, with a carefully chosen wine list. Breakfast is generous Irish." (*Esler Crawford*)

Open 1 Apr–31 Oct.
Rooms 4 double. No telephone; TV on request.
Facilities Drawing room, library, dining room. 42-acre grounds: river, trout/salmon-fishing. Golf nearby.

Location 6 miles W of Killarney on R562. Left over bridge opposite petrol station. House immediately on left.
Restrictions No smoking, except in library. No dogs in house.
Credit cards Access, Visa.
Terms B&B IR£50–£55. Set dinner IR£25.

BIRR Co. Offaly — Map 6

Tullanisk

Tel (0509) 20572
Fax (0509) 21783

George and Susan Gossip's 18th-century dower house, set in the wooded grounds of the Earl of Rosse's vast Birr Castle estate, is run "with taste and care". Its elegant rooms are filled with the owners' own antique furniture, china and pictures, giving it a personal atmosphere. George Gossip "is a colourful character and a great sportsman". "He continues to preside with tremendous style," writes a regular visitor, "and goes to great lengths to talk to everyone." Dinner is taken communally and served by candlelight. No menu or choice, but preferences are discussed. Food is "quite adventurous" and cooked "with enthusiasm"; game is a speciality. Breakfasts are also admired. "Marvellous atmosphere."(*Esler Crawford, CF, and others*) Only complaint: "Poor bath towels."

Open All year, except Christmas. Advance booking required Nov–mid-Mar. Lunch not served.
Rooms 7 double. 5 with facilities *en suite*. 1 on ground floor.
Facilities Drawing room, sitting room, playroom, dining room. 2-acre grounds in 2,000-acre estate. Shooting, fishing, riding, golf available. Unsuitable for ♿.
Location 1½ miles NW of centre of Birr.
Restrictions No smoking: dining room, bedrooms. "Well-behaved children and dogs preferred."
Credit cards Access, Amex, Visa.
Terms B&B: single IR£38–£52, double IR£72–£90. Set dinner IR£22.50. Negotiable rates for longer stays. *V*

BLESSINGTON LAKE Co. Wicklow — Map 6

Tulfarris House NEW

Tel (045) 864574
Fax (045) 864423

"A venerable Georgian country house converted into a hotel, with sensitive extensions that blend new and old. It feels as remote and secluded as a hunting lodge, although Dublin is only a few miles away. Russborough House, the splendid mansion housing the Beit Collection, is a bracing four-mile walk away. The bar is friendly and efficient; the restaurant offers an imaginative menu; the bedrooms are airy, light and pretty. The atmosphere is relaxed and informal, and the staff are easy-going – when we woke one morning to find a young man sleeping off a heavy night's drinking on a couch in the corridor, the cleaners were unperturbed: they giggled behind their hands, tidied away his shoes, and tiptoed away so as not to disturb his sleep." The hotel is set on the shores of the Poulaphouca Lake, with the Wicklow Mountains behind. In its large landscaped grounds are a nine-hole golf course and two floodlit tennis courts. There is a large indoor swimming pool. (*Tony Thomas*)

Open All year, except Christmas.
Rooms 20 double, 1 single. Some on ground floor.
Facilities Ramps. 2 lounges, 2 bars, TV room, restaurant; swimming pool. Large grounds: gardens, tennis, golf, lake frontage, fishing, sailing, windsurfing. Riding, gliding, pony-trekking nearby.
Location 6 miles S of Blessington off N81.
Restriction No dogs.
Credit cards All major cards accepted.
Terms B&B IR£44–£79. Set lunch IR£13, dinner IR£23; full alc IR£30.

BUNCLODY Co. Wexford — Map 6

Clohamon House — *Tel* (054) 77253
Fax (054) 77956

Sir Richard and Lady Levinge's 18th-century house 1½ miles E of Bunclody. 180-acre grounds sloping down to river Slaney (salmon- and trout-fishing in season). 4-acre gardens, farm, well-known stud. Grand, if worn interior: fine furniture and paintings; charming bedrooms, but housekeeping not a strong point. "Friendly and amusing hosts. Excellent, straightforward dinners, communally served, using home-grown vegetables and home-laid eggs; good vegetarian dishes. Open 1 Apr–mid-Nov; dining room closed midday, Sun evening. 4 bedrooms (no smoking). Self-catering cottage with ♿ access. Dogs by arrangement. Access, Visa accepted. B&B IR£48. Set dinner IR£25.

CARAGH LAKE Co. Kerry — Map 6

Caragh Lodge — *Tel* (066) 69115
Fax (066) 69316

"Truly in a class of its own. A genuine country house feel. Superb decor, warm ambience, and wonderful, simply wonderful food." "A perfect place to unwind; quiet and secluded. Mrs Gaunt was welcoming and enthusiastic, giving personal attention to all her guests. The staff were courteous. We enjoyed high teas on the veranda overlooking the garden, and cycled round the lake on locally rented bicycles." Recent praise for Mary Gaunt's Victorian fishing lodge, a low white building "with a colonial feel". It stands in magnificent large gardens full of rare trees and shrubs, on the shore of Caragh Lake, with views of Ireland's highest mountains, the McGillycuddy Reeks. The Ring of Kerry is a mile away. The spacious bedrooms in the main building have splendid views, unlike the simpler rooms in the annexe. The cooking is modern in style: very good fish, chicken and Irish cheeses; bread is home-baked, wines are reasonably priced. Good breakfasts: freshly squeezed orange juice, scrambled eggs with smoked salmon. (*Julie Smith, Clare Harris*) There is unpolluted swimming in the lake. Sandy beaches are a short drive away; eight golf courses nearby.

Open 28 Mar–17 Oct.
Rooms 8 double, 2 single. 7 in annexe. Some on ground floor.
Facilities 2 lounges, dining room. 7-acre grounds: garden, tennis, sauna; on lake: swimming, fishing, boating. Sea 5 miles. Unsuitable for ♿.
Location 22 miles W of Killarney. N70 from Killorglin along Ring of Kerry, 2nd road signposted Caragh Lake; left at lake.
Restriction No smoking in restaurant. No children under 7. No dogs.
Credit cards Access, Amex, Visa.

Terms (*Excluding 10% service charge*) B&B: single IR£60, double IR£80–£100. Set dinner IR£25.

CARRIGBYRNE Co. Wexford — Map 6

Cedar Lodge — *Tel* (051) 428386 and 428436
Carrigbyrne, Newbawn — *Fax* (051) 428222

A modern family-run hotel west of Wexford, convenient for the Rosslare ferry. "It is consistently good," writes a regular visitor. "The bedrooms are prettily decorated, with impressive bathrooms. High standard of housekeeping. The omnipresent owner, Tom Martin, keeps things running smoothly. The food is good too: the home-made bread is the best we have had anywhere in Ireland." Others concur: "Smart and comfortable, with tasteful furnishings and a warm and friendly atmosphere. The restaurant is very attractive, with a big log fire in the middle of the room; we had beautifully cooked fish." Dinners include local mussels, oysters and crab. Carrigbyrne is within easy reach of the Wexford coast. (*Ruth West, Tricia Nash*)

Open 1 Feb–20 Dec.
Rooms 28 double. Some on ground floor.
Facilities Lounge, lounge bar, breakfast room, restaurant; Irish music twice weekly. ½-acre garden. Sandy beaches 12 miles.
Location On N25, 14 miles W of Wexford.
Restrictions No smoking in restaurant. Dogs by arrangement; not in public rooms.
Credit cards Access, Visa.
Terms [1996] B&B IR£35–£70; D,B&B IR£55. Set lunch IR£15, dinner IR£25. 3-day rates. *V*

CASHEL BAY Co. Galway — Map 6

Cashel House — *Tel* (095) 31001
Fax (095) 31077

Kay and Dermot McEvilly's civilised manor house (Relais & Châteaux) stands in the lovely wilds of Connemara, at the head of Cashel Bay. "Its excellence," runs a recent report, "derives not solely from the visible presence of the proprietors; the cheerful and helpful staff are superbly trained to provide the facilities of a really first-rate hotel." Public rooms include a comfortable lounge with antiques and fresh flowers, a library and a spacious modern bar. Breakfasts, in the large conservatory dining room, and snack lunches in the bar, are "excellent", though some have found the dinner menus over-ambitious. Some of the rooms have a sea view; the suites in the modern section are "superb and good value". (*WA, S and JL*) The hotel has its own tennis court, riding stable and tiny beach, and golf and fishing are close by.

Open All year, except 10 Jan–10 Feb.
Rooms 13 garden suites, 17 double, 2 single. Some on ground floor.
Facilities Drawing room, lounge, lounge bar, library, dining room/conservatory. 50-acre grounds: 15-acre gardens, tennis, riding; private beach, fishing.
Location 42 miles NW of Galway. 1 mile S of N59 at Recess.
Restrictions No children under 5. No dogs in public rooms.
Credit cards All major cards accepted.
Terms (*Excluding 12½% service charge*) B&B: IR£51–£90. Set dinner IR£29. Spring, autumn breaks.

Zetland House

Tel (095) 31111
Fax (095) 31117

John and Mona Prendergast's handsome white 1850s hunting lodge stands in large grounds with shrubs and trees, on the edge of Cashel Bay in the midst of the wild Connemara landscape. It has been warmly endorsed this year: "A delightful place to stay. The views are quite breathtaking." "Genuine Irish hospitality. We were greeted with great warmth; dinner was superb." "Spacious, comfortable bedroom." The lounges are large, with peat fires, antiques, soft colour schemes, fresh flowers, books, porcelain and a wide-ranging collection of paintings. Chef Paul Meehan's cooking is described as "progressive Irish with an emphasis on fresh seafood". (*HC Medcalf, Mrs SM Frith, Mrs L Byers, and others*) Sadly the Zetland fishery is not what it was: sea trout runs have been practically wiped out, and salmon are becoming scarce on the Gowla river too. John Prendergast is part of the "Save Our Seatrout" organisation which is trying to find the cause – sea lice from salmon farms are suspected. But happily there are signs of recovery for sea trout on the Gowla.

Open 15 Apr–31 Oct.
Rooms 17 double, 3 single. 1 on ground floor.
Facilities Drawing room, lounge, cocktail bar, restaurant. 6-acre grounds: tennis; rocky shore 200 yds. Lake/river fishing 3 miles. Sandy beach 10 miles.
Location 40 miles N of Galway, on N95.
Restriction No dogs in public rooms.
Credit cards All major cards accepted.
Terms B&B IR£51–£90. Set lunch IR£15, dinner IR£30. Full alc IR£37. Off-season rates. *V*

CASTLEBALDWIN Co. Sligo — Map 6

Cromleach Lodge
Ballindoon
Castlebaldwin, via Boyle

Tel (071) 65155
Fax (071) 65455

The panoramic setting is on a hillside above Lough Arrow, with hardly a house in sight. Here a local couple, Christy and Moira Tighe, have enlarged their own home into a sophisticated guest house. "A most perfect place," says a recent visitor. "The only sound is from occasional tractors, the view from the bedroom window is out of this world. Bedrooms are spacious, with fresh fruit, a welcoming drink, fully stocked bathroom, etc. The food is wonderful; excellent breakfasts set one up for a day's walk." Others have also admired Mrs Tighe's "serious and professional" cooking, well above average for an Irish guest house (*Michelin* red "Meals"), and the friendly and efficient service. All bedrooms have south-facing views over Lough Arrow. (*SP, and others*) A few caveats: some find the decor in the bar/lounge and bedrooms over-ornate. Others would prefer fewer exhortatory notices. Wines tend to be pricey, and the piped mealtime music can irritate, even though it is subdued and classical.

Open All year, except 1 Nov–15 Dec.
Rooms 10 double.
Facilities 2 lounges, 3 dining rooms, conservatory. 30-acre grounds. Private access to Lough Arrow: fishing, boating, surfing; walking, hill climbing. Unsuitable for &.

Location 9 miles W of Boyle, off N4 Dublin–Sligo. Turn E at Castlebaldwin.
Restrictions No smoking: 1 lounge, dining rooms, 5 bedrooms. No children under 7 in dining room. No dogs in house (kennels provided).
Credit cards All major cards accepted.
Terms B&B IR£50–£90; D,B&B IR£80–£120. Set lunch IR£20, dinner IR£35. Midweek, weekend rates. Cookery courses out of season. *V*

CASTLETOWNSHEND Co. Cork — Map 6

Bow Hall BUDGET — *Tel* (028) 36114

A guest house, "offering excellent value", with American owners, Dick and Barbara Vickery. It overlooks the harbour of a seaside village in the romantic far south of Cork. It is a handsome late 17th-century building, filled with family heirlooms and portraits, and set in a walled garden. "The charming owners run a relaxed operation, and delight in sharing with others their very American home," wrote one visitor. "Meals to dream about" are communally served. Barbara Vickery's American-inspired cooking is based on fresh local produce, and vegetables from the garden. Breakfasts are "outstanding", with fresh orange juice, hot apple bran muffins and buckwheat pancakes. (*SG*) More reports, please.

Open Jan–mid-Nov. Occasionally at other times in low season.
Rooms 1 suite, 2 double.
Facilities Library, dining room. ¾-acre garden. Harbour 3 mins' walk.
Location In village, 5 miles SE of Skibbereen. Parking.
Restrictions No smoking. No dogs.
Credit cards None accepted.
Terms B&B IR£30–£35. Set dinner IR£20.

CLARECASTLE Co. Clare — Map 6

Carnelly House — *Tel* (065) 28442 / *Fax* (065) 29222

Dermot and Rosemarie Gleeson's creeper-covered Georgian house stands on a large estate, with a farm, woodlands and plenty of wildlife, between Ennis and Shannon Airport. The interior is elegant, with tall windows, and a wide staircase. It has a beautiful drawing room, with a fine plaster ceiling and Corinthian pillars. Bedrooms are spacious, "with splendid bathrooms". The welcoming hosts, country house party atmosphere, and generous breakfasts all come in for praise. Dinner, good simple home cooking, is a four-course, no-choice affair, and requires prior notice. More reports, please.

Open All year, except Christmas, New Year.
Rooms 5 double. Self-catering accommodation in gate lodge (sleeps 4/5).
Facilities Lounge, drawing room, dining room. 100-acre grounds. Golf, fishing, hunting nearby.
Location 10 miles N of Shannon on N18; 3 miles SW of Ennis. Parking.
Restrictions No children under 10. No dogs in house.
Credit cards Access, Amex, Visa.
Terms [1996] B&B: single IR£95, double IR£125–£156. Set dinner (by arrangement) IR£28.

CLIFDEN Co. Galway — Map 6

The Ardagh NEW — *Tel* (095) 21384
Ballyconneely Road — *Fax* (095) 21314

"A modern, comfortable hotel in a delightful location looking out over Ardbear Bay. The owners, Stephane and Monique Bauvet, are friendly, charming and very helpful. Monique is the chef – her Belgian extraction shows in her excellent cooking. Our large sea-facing room was well equipped and had a good-sized bathroom. This makes a fine base to explore the western end of the Connemara peninsula. At the end of the day you return to be greeted by the smiling staff and the really delicious food." The emphasis is on fish – eg, "*Ardagh*'s famous seafood chowder" or halibut with sun-dried tomato, caper and basil vinaigrette. (*RM Sparkes*)

Open End Mar–end Oct.
Rooms 3 suites, 14 double, 4 single.
Facilities 2 lounges, bar, restaurant. Small garden. Beach, lake (fishing), golf nearby.
Location 1½ miles S of Clifden on R341 towards Ballyconneely.
Restrictions No smoking in restaurant. Dogs by arrangement.
Credit cards All major cards accepted.
Terms B&B IR£39.50–£62.50. Set dinner IR£25. Full alc IR£28. 2-day, weekend rates. *V*

The Quay House BUDGET — *Tel* (095) 21369
Clifden, Connemara — *Fax* (095) 21605

This Georgian house, Clifden's oldest building, in a "quiet and charming" position by the water, has been, in the last hundred years, harbourmaster's house, convent, and Franciscan monastery. It is now a restaurant-with-rooms, run by the "delightful" Paddy and Julia Foyle. The decor is eccentric – "a blend of antiques and Art Deco, creating an *avant-garde* style," write the Foyles. There's a corridor lined with deer heads; plenty of bold colours. Bedrooms, with garden or bay views, are comfortable and spacious, especially the downstairs ones. Peter McMahon, who has worked at the *Quay* for the past three years, has now taken over in the restaurant from Dermot Gannon, whose cooking received rave reviews last year – "the best meal we had in Ireland"; "the best we've *ever* had". We'd love to know if this dizzying standard has been maintained. (*Tricia Nash, JS*)

Open 15 Mar–30 Nov. Dining room closed Sun evening.
Rooms 10 double. 4 in courtyard.
Facilities 2 sitting rooms, dining room, conservatory. ½-acre garden. Fishing, golf, riding nearby.
Location Harbour; 7 mins' walk from centre. Courtyard parking.
Restrictions No smoking: restaurant, bedrooms. No dogs in house.
Credit cards Access, Visa.
Terms B&B IR£30–£35. Set lunch IR£10, dinner IR£22; full alc IR£35. *V*

> Please don't be shy of writing again about old favourites. Too many people feel that if they have written once, years ago, there is no need to report on a revisit.

CLONDALKIN Co. Dublin Map 6

See Dublin

CLONES Co. Monaghan Map 6

Hilton Park *Tel* (047) 56007
Scothouse, Clones *Fax* (047) 56033

César award in 1994

"'Great windows opening to the south', Yeats wrote of another Irish country house, but it could have been this one. All the rooms have floor-to-ceiling windows commanding views of the landscaped park." So writes a recent visitor to what has been the family home of the Maddens for some 250 years, a stately mansion standing amid rolling parkland, with a golf course and three lakes. "The style is relaxed and informal, but everything runs like clockwork." "The food continues to be a delight," adds another enthusiast. Lucy Madden makes use of "the best raw materials locally available, and organically grown vegetables often only picked at 5 pm". Evening meals, in the baronial dining room, are served communally or at separate tables, according to preference. Breakfast, by contrast, is in a "cosy, cheerful annexe to the kitchen". The "warmly hospitable" Maddens run the place on house party lines; they are always around to advise or to chat, but do not impose themselves on their guests. Public rooms are elegantly furnished, with memorabilia from past times. Bedrooms are huge, "and gracious without being luxurious". (*A O'Dowd, Brian Scott-McCarthy*)

Open 1 Apr–30 Sept. Dining room closed for lunch and to non-residents.
Rooms 1 suite, 6 double. No telephone/TV.
Facilities Drawing room, sitting room, games room, dining room, breakfast room. 500 acres parkland: golf, 3 lakes (swimming, boating, fishing). Unsuitable for ♿.
Location 4 miles S of Clones, on L46 to Ballyhaise.
Restrictions No smoking in bedrooms. Children under 7 by arrangement. No dogs.
Credit cards Access, Visa.
Terms [1996] B&B IR£45–£65.50. Set dinner IR£25. 3-night reductions. Winter shooting parties. 1-night bookings refused if too far in advance.

CORK Map 6

Lotamore House BUDGET *Tel* (021) 822344
Tivoli *Fax* (021) 822219

On a hillside above the river Lee, a fine old Georgian manor, now a 21-bedroom Grade A guest house, recently refurbished and efficiently run by the "charming and efficient Mr and Mrs Harty". Rooms are nicely furnished with comfortable, attractive older pieces of furniture. Breakfasts are excellent and the service is "friendly and personal". The front rooms have views, but the rear ones are quieter. (*JA*) More reports, please.

Open All year, except Christmas.
Rooms 20 double, 1 single.
Facilities Lounge. 4-acre garden.

Location 3 miles E of city centre, off N25.
Restriction No smoking in bedrooms.
Credit cards Access, Amex, Visa.
Terms B&B IR£20–£27. *V*

CROSSMOLINA Co. Mayo — Map 6

Enniscoe House — *Tel* (096) 31112
Castlehill — *Fax* (096) 31773

This handsome Georgian country house, whose plain façade belies the 18th-century plasterwork and sweeping staircase inside, stands in its own large and attractive grounds by the shores of Lough Conn. "Just as good as we remembered it," write returning visitors. "We were greeted warmly by Mrs Kellett, whose family home it has been for generations, and escorted to a *massive* room overlooking the lough. Plenty of hot water and a most comfortable four-poster bed. Good dinner and 'full house' Irish breakfast." Another couple "thoroughly enjoyed" this experience of country house living. "Mrs Kellett was tireless in her efforts to keep things running smoothly." The two big sitting rooms have the original furniture, paintings and bookcases, family memorabilia everywhere, and polished wood floors with rugs. The bedrooms are large and comfortable, with modern bathroom. Dinner, with limited choice, is Irish country house style with French touches – "good beef, turbot, salmon; delicious desserts, a praline meringue was memorable" – served on a charming eclectic mixture of china. There's a working farm on the estate; Mrs Kellett also runs a heritage centre there, helping returning emigrants to trace their Irish roots. (*Esler Crawford, Jean Dundas*) One niggle: "I wish Mrs Kellett would look for a new wine merchant."

Open 1 Apr–14 Oct, 31 Dec–1 Feb. Lunch not served.
Rooms 6 double. Self-catering units in yard behind house.
Facilities 2 sitting rooms, dining room. 150-acre parkland: lake frontage, fishing (tuition, ghillie). Golf, riding, cycling, shooting nearby. Unsuitable for ♿.
Location 2 miles S of Crossmolina on R315 to Castlebar.
Restrictions No smoking: restaurant, 2 bedrooms. Dogs by arrangement.
Credit cards Access, Amex, Visa.
Terms B&B: single IR£50–£60, double IR£80–£104; D,B&B IR£60–£80 per person. Set dinner (book by 4 pm) IR£20 (IR£23 for non-residents). 10% reduction for 3 or more nights. Children under 2 accommodated free in parents' room. *V* (except July/Aug)

DINGLE Co. Kerry — Map 6

Doyle's Townhouse — *Tel* (066) 51174
John Street — *Fax* (066) 51816

One of our most popular Irish entries, endorsed again this year. John and Stella Doyle's modest empire includes a much-admired restaurant, *Doyle's Seafood Bar* (red "Meals" in *Michelin*), a small hotel in the house next door, and four annexes, with sitting rooms, "furnished to a very high standard", 200 yards down the street. "As near perfect as any dinner, bed and breakfast could be," was one recent tribute. Other visitors have found the food "of world class quality and range, with prices the moderate end of normal expectation", and the Irish breakfasts substantial enough to last the day. The menu is rich in local fish and shellfish: oysters, hot poached lobster, salmon in puff pastry with sorrel sauce, and grilled mussels with garlic stuffing. The sitting room is furnished nostalgically in the style of a traditional Irish small-town hotel, and the bedrooms have brass bedsteads, antique furniture and good fabrics, as well as "white starched sheets and gigantic towels". Some marble bathrooms. (*Clare Harris, and others*)

Open Mid-Mar–mid-Nov. Restaurant closed Sun.
Rooms 8 double. 2 on ground floor.
Facilities Residents' lounge, cocktail bar, 2 dining rooms. Sea angling, golf, riding, windsurfing nearby.
Location Central.
Restrictions No smoking in 1 dining room. Not really suitable for young children. No dogs.
Credit cards Access, Diners, Visa.
Terms (*10% service charge added to meals*) B&B: single IR£42, double IR£66. Full alc IR£25.

Milltown House NEW/BUDGET *Tel* (066) 51372
Fax (066) 51095

John and Angela Gill's unpretentious B&B in beautiful situation, 1 mile outside Dingle, overlooking bay. Bright, pristine, large bedrooms, with pleasant decor, high quality bathroom fittings. Welcoming owners and staff. Good breakfasts (emphasis on home-baking). Plenty of restaurants within walking distance. 1-acre grounds; riding stable on premises (pony-trekking holidays); golf courses nearby. 10 bedrooms, some with private patio, 1 suitable for ♿. Open 15 Mar–15 Nov. No smoking in conservatory lounge. No dogs in public rooms. Access, Visa accepted. B&B IR£18–£40 [1996].

DUBLIN — Map 6

Ariel House NEW *Tel* (01) 6685512
52 Lansdowne Road *Fax* (01) 6685845
Dublin 4

1850s house in residential area, with modern bedroom extension at rear. Hospitable proprietor Michael O'Brien. Generous Irish breakfasts in Victorian room with conservatory extension overlooking garden. Wine bar, but food not served. Ramps. 3 suites, 25 bedrooms; some on ground floor. Open 13 Jan–24 Dec. No smoking: breakfast room, bedrooms. No children under 9. No dogs. Access, Visa accepted. Double room IR£50–£90, suite IR£90–£150. Breakfast IR£7.50. More reports, please.

Belcamp Hutchinson *Tel* (01) 8460843
Carrs Lane, Malahide Road *Fax* (01) 8485703
Balgriffin, Dublin 17

An unlikely find in N suburbs of Dublin, 15 mins' drive from airport and 10 mins' from beaches: smart Georgian country house, with ornate features and ambience of private home. Co-owned and run by Doreen Gleeson, "a good cook and pleasant hostess". 6 large bedrooms, stylishly furnished. "Excellent breakfast." 4-acre grounds. Closed 24–28 Dec. Unsuitable for ♿. Access accepted. B&B IR£38. Dinner IR£23. Endorsed this year, but fuller reports would be welcome.

The Grey Door
22–23 Upper Pembroke Street
Dublin 2

Tel (01) 6763286
Fax (01) 6763287

"A warm, comfortable and locally famous small hotel-cum-restaurant, in a historic area of the city. It combines friendliness with efficiency. All your telephone messages will be delivered promptly, and they will also remember whether you like your eggs sunny-side-up or easy-over. Food is of a high standard both at breakfast and in the evening." A 1996 endorsement for Barry Wyse's restored Georgian town house, "run in relaxed style, with a helpful, attentive and humorous staff". It has plenty of antiques in the public areas, and pretty bedrooms "with excellent bathrooms". The *Grey Door* restaurant, with a modern decor, serves contemporary Irish cooking; the informal, cheaper *Pier 32*, traditional in style, serves Irish seafood specialities, accompanied on most nights by Irish folk music. (*Tony Thomas, and others; also Lance Christopher*) Rooms at the front can get traffic noise.

Open All year, except 24–30 Dec. Restaurants closed Sun, bank holidays.
Rooms 1 suite, 6 double.
Facilities Lounge, bar, 2 restaurants; 2 private dining rooms. Unsuitable for ♿.
Location Near St Stephen's Green, a short ride or stiff walk from business centre. Street parking.
Restriction Guide dogs only.
Credit cards All major cards accepted.
Terms (*12.5% service charge added to meals*) Rooms: single IR£70, double IR£90, suite IR£100. Breakfast: continental IR£5, Irish IR£6.95. Set lunch IR£12.50, dinner IR£22.50; full alc IR£30. Weekend breaks. Children under 12 accommodated free in parents' room.

The Hibernian
Eastmoreland Place
Ballsbridge, Dublin 4

Tel (01) 668 7666
Fax (01) 660 2655

Once a nurses' home, this red and amber brick high Victorian building in a quiet street in residential Ballsbridge is now a stylish and expensive town house hotel. It is decorated with rich fabrics, deep upholstery and bright colours. The bedrooms are smallish but comfortable, with pocket-sprung mattresses, and superior toiletries. "Under the supervision of manager David Butt, the young staff give the impression that they genuinely want you to enjoy your stay," wrote the nominator. Public rooms are decorated in country house style. Chef David Foley, who comes from Tralee, produces sophisticated food ("modern Irish with French influences") in the Patrick Kavanagh room. The downtown shopping area of Grafton Street is ten minutes' walk away.

Open All year, except 23–27 Dec.
Rooms 10 suites, 31 double. 2 adapted for ♿.
Facilities Drawing room, library, restaurant. Guitarist Sat evening.
Location From Mespil Rd take Baggot St Upper, left into Eastmoreland Pl. Hotel at end on left. Private parking.
Restrictions No smoking in 13 bedrooms. No dogs.
Credit cards All major cards accepted.
Terms [1996] (*Excluding 12½% service charge on food*) B&B: IR£60–£150. Set lunch IR£13.95, dinner IR£23.50; full alc IR£32. *V*

Kingswood Country House *Tel/Fax* (01) 4592428
Naas Road
Clondalkin, Dublin 22

More accolades this year for this handsome Georgian country house seven miles west of central Dublin, once the home of the great Irish tenor Joseph Locke. Surrounded by a secluded walled garden, it has been converted into an elegant restaurant with seven bedrooms, well run by a young couple, Tom and Sheila O'Byrne. "So much thought and care goes into this place. My room was charming and cleverly decorated to suit the mood of the building – lace curtains and shutters, bare polished boards in the bathroom (but all washing facilities new). Home-made marmalade and quince jam for breakfast." "We arrived late. Mrs O'Byrne produced an excellent light meal which we ate in the pleasant conservatory. Friendly and helpful staff." "Dinner was excellent and breakfast a delight: coming down on a misty morning to a blazing fire, real orange juice and stupendous porridge made an excellent start to our Irish holiday." (*MA, Margaret Crick, AS*)

Open All year, except 3 days Christmas, Good Friday.
Rooms 7 double.
Facilities Lounge, bar, restaurant, function facilities. 1-acre garden. Riding, shooting, golf nearby. Only restaurant suitable for ♿.
Location On left side of N7 towards Naas, 7 miles W of Dublin centre, 1½ miles after Newlands Cross.
Restrictions Unsuitable for children, except Sun lunch. Guide dogs only.
Credit cards All major cards accepted.
Terms (*Excluding 12.5% service charge*) B&B: single IR£40–£50, double IR£55-£70. Set lunch IR£13.95, dinner IR£21.95. Weekend breaks.

DUNLAVIN Co. Wicklow Map 6

Grangebeg House *Tel* (045) 401367

"A beautiful Georgian house, standing grandly in huge grounds, and approached by a long winding driveway. Horses graze in the fields in the rolling countryside. *Grangebeg* has a sense of unpretentious homeliness. You can be sure of a warm Irish welcome from the friendly, caring owner, Mrs Aine McGrane. Delicious breakfasts (no time limit) are taken round an antique table in the elegant dining room. Evening meals are available on request. Bedrooms and public rooms are spacious, and tastefully furnished in a mixture of antique and traditional furniture. This corner of Ireland is famous for its racehorses, and Mrs McGrane's daughter runs a stables behind the house; there is a cross-country course for enthusiasts." But this is not just a horsey place, rather a haven of peace for exploring the quiet south-east of Ireland. And by the end of 1996, Mrs McGrane tells us, the lake will have been cleaned out and there will be coarse fishing for *Grangebeg* guests. (*MO*)

Open All year, except 20–28 Dec.
Rooms 5 double, 1 single. No telephone.
Facilities Drawing room, TV room, dining room. 86-acre grounds: parkland, gardens, tennis, lake, stables. Walking, shooting, fishing, water sports, golf, racing nearby.
Location 1 mile E of Dunlavin off R412.
Restriction No dogs in house.
Credit cards Access, Visa.

Terms B&B: single IR£30–£35, double IR£64–£84. Set dinner (by arrangement) IR£19.95. *V* (first night only)

GALWAY Map 6

Norman Villa BUDGET *Tel/Fax* (091) 521131
86 Lower Salthill

"The best breakfast I've had in any B&B or hotel," writes a recent visitor to Mark and Dee Keogh's carefully restored Victorian coach house on the edge of town. It has a pretty decor, with old pine furniture, plenty of paintings and sculpture, and good linen on antique brass beds. "Good value for money." (*John Fraher*) More reports, please.

Open All year.
Rooms 5 double. No telephone/TV.
Facilities Drawing room, breakfast room. ¼-acre garden. Sea, sandy beach, river, fishing nearby.
Location 1 mile W of centre, at Salthill. Courtyard parking.
Restrictions No smoking in bedrooms. Unsuitable for babies. No dogs.
Credit cards Access, Visa.
Terms B&B IR£23–£32. Christmas breaks.

GOREY Co. Wexford Map 6

Marlfield House *Tel* (055) 21124
Courtown Road *Fax* (055) 21572
César award in 1996

"Quite simply, the best. The lounges and bedrooms are a joy. It is a real talent that can present luxury without a hint of vulgarity. The gardens, from bird sanctuary, through 'rain forest' to manicured lawns and burgeoning herb garden are pleasant and interesting. The service is faultless and friendly, and Mrs Bowe, entertaining and welcoming to the manner born, clearly enjoys meeting her guests in the dining room." "The only hotel I have ever been motivated to photograph inside and out. The peacock at the entrance was the finest 'doorman' you could imagine. Mrs Bowe's taste, and her gentle guiding hand over her staff were evident at every turn." Tributes this year to Mary and Ray Bowe's sophisticated country house hotel (Relais & Châteaux), once the dower house of the Courtown estate. The Regency building is set in award-winning grounds with a lake and a wildfowl reserve. The entrance hall is "dazzling", with smart antique furniture, spectacular flower displays, and goldfish ponds by the front door. Bedrooms have dramatic wallpapers and curtains, hand-embroidered sheets, real lace pillows, and "splendid bathroom". The Bowes' daughter Margaret is the efficient general manager. The food has been called "some of the best we have ever eaten". Craig Jones, who trained at *Inverlochy Castle, Gravetye Manor*, and *Longueville Manor* (*qqv*), took over the kitchens in February 1996, and we'd like to know if he maintains this high standard – his cooking is described as "a modern approach to classical dishes, using the best of local produce". (*Richard and Sheila Owen, PJ and BA D'Arcy, and others*)

Open All year, except mid-Dec–31 Jan.
Rooms 6 suites, 11 double, 2 single. Some on ground floor.

Facilities Reception hall, drawing room, library/bar, conservatory/restaurant. 36-acre grounds: tennis, croquet, wildfowl reserve, lake. Sea 1 mile: sandy beaches, safe bathing.
Location 1 mile from Gorey on Courtown road.
Restrictions No smoking: dining room, bedrooms. No dogs in public rooms.
Credit cards Access, Amex, Visa.
Terms (*Excluding 10% service charge*) B&B: single IR£70–£85, double IR£132–£146, suite IR£160–£400. Set lunch IR£18, dinner IR£32. Off-season reductions. *V*

KANTURK Co. Cork **Map 6**

Assolas Country House *Tel* (029) 50015
Fax (029) 50795

César award in 1995

"A wonderful stay, as near to perfection as possible. Superb ambience, great friendliness and personal attention from Joe and Hazel Bourke and their lovely assistant Karen." "Run with style and great good humour – any guest should feel at home." Praise again this year for this elegant 17th-century manor house, set in beautifully kept grounds, with a little river, complete with swans, weir and mini-island. It has been the home of the Bourke family for over 70 years, and a hotel for more than a quarter of a century. Other visitors have written: "The charm is made up of innumerable small things. As soon as you enter, a log fire is lit for you. You are offered umbrellas and wellingtons as well as recipes. Afternoon tea, with lemon or chocolate cake, is served in the garden or by the fire." Service is "polished and unobtrusive". Bedrooms are tastefully furnished, with luxurious bathrooms. There is sparkling glass in the dining room, and damask napkins. Mrs Bourke's Irish country house cooking is "a highlight of every visit"; the accent is on fish and shellfish; many of the herbs and vegetables come from the hotel's walled kitchen garden; the soups, sauces and pastry are much admired, as are the brown scones and soda bread that are served at breakfast. (*Michael O'Flaherty, EC; also Major JA Comyn, and others*)

Open 1 Apr–1 Nov.
Rooms 9 double. 3 in courtyard building.
Facilities Hall, drawing room, 2 dining rooms. 15-acre grounds: gardens, tennis, croquet, river, boating, trout-fishing. Salmon-fishing, golf nearby. Unsuitable for ♿.
Location 3½ miles NE of Kanturk; turn off N72 Mallow–Killarney, towards Buttevant.
Restriction No dogs in house.
Credit cards All major cards accepted.
Terms B&B: single IR£53–£72, double IR£86–£160. Set dinner IR£30. *V*

KENMARE Co. Kerry **Map 6**

Park Hotel Kenmare *Tel* (064) 41200
Fax (064) 41402

Country house grandeur (five red *Michelin* gables) combines with sybaritic comfort and high gastronomy (*Michelin* star) in this characteristic Relais & Châteaux establishment. It has plenty going for it: an "idyllic" parkland setting, with beautiful views of the Kenmare estuary and the west Cork mountains; elegant public rooms with open fires and flowers; "gorgeous" bedrooms with smart antiques and fine china; large modern bathrooms with luxurious towels; and a friendly and efficient staff. "We could not fault the food," write recent visitors of Bruno Schmidt's cooking, which he describes as "progressive Irish, with a Pacific rim". Breakfast foodies will be glad to learn that the hotel was last year's winner of the Galtee Irish Breakfast Award. (*HC Medcalf*)

Open Mid-Apr–Nov; also 23 Dec–2 Jan.
Rooms 9 suites, 37 double, 4 single. 1 equipped for ♿.
Facilities Lift, ramps. Lounge, TV room, bar lounge (piano each evening), restaurant. 11-acre grounds: tennis, golf, croquet. Rock beach, safe bathing, fishing 5 mins' walk.
Location 60 miles W of Cork, adjacent to village. Signposted.
Restriction No dogs.
Credit cards All major cards accepted.
Terms B&B: single IR£116–£137, double IR£196–£280, suite IR£330–£398. Set dinner IR£39; full alc IR£80. Christmas, New Year programmes.

Sheen Falls Lodge *Tel* (064) 41600
Fax (064) 41386

In a stunning location, surrounded by hills, mountains and moors, this luxurious resort hotel (Relais & Châteaux) has a Danish owner, Bent Hoyer. A Cromwellian manor house, much extended, it stands in huge wooded grounds a mile outside this attractive town, beside the Sheen Falls, and has lovely views of Kenmare Bay. "The most perfect place in which to unwind," writes a regular *Guide* correspondent. "The warmth and friendliness of the staff is high even by Irish standards, the food and service are superb, and the bedrooms are huge, with crisp linen sheets and duvets, and large marble bathroom." "Kindness and food outstanding," adds another admirer. The *Michelin*-starred restaurant serves sophisticated modern Irish cooking by chef Fergus Moore. All manner of leisure activity is available (see below). There is a discreet conference centre. (*JH, and others*)

Open 9 Feb–3 Dec.
Rooms 9 suites, 31 double.
Facilities Lift, ramps. 2 lounges, bar, restaurant; health and fitness centre: jacuzzi, sauna, gym, beauty treatments. 360-acre grounds: fishing, riding, croquet, tennis, clay pigeon-shooting. Golf nearby. Sea 6 miles.
Location 1½ miles SE of Kenmare, just off N71 to Glengariff.
Restriction No dogs.
Credit cards All major cards accepted.
Terms Rooms: single IR£135–£185, double IR£160–£240, suite IR£255–£360. Breakfast IR£13. Set lunch IR£17.50, dinner IR£37.50.

KILLEAGH Co. Cork Map 6

Ballymakeigh House BUDGET *Tel* (024) 95184
Fax (024) 95370

"Margaret Browne has a gift for making her guests feel at home." "Food was outstanding." "Attractive and spotless rooms, beautiful, peaceful country setting." "Excellent value." Accolades continue to pour in for this modernised old farmhouse in the heart of the "emerald green countryside" of prosperous east Cork, now a well-decorated guest house. Most bedrooms are large and comfortable, although one guest found it hard to manoeuvre in a room with two double beds. The geranium-filled conservatory on the south side is a delightful place to sit and survey the Brownes' large dairy herd. Guests can ride, play tennis on the splendid new court, or watch the daily routines on the home farm, such as milking. There are fine beaches nearby, too. The breakfast recently won a national award. (*Ellin Osmond, Linda Peters, Mr and Mrs FT Easterbrook, HC Medcalf, and others*)

Open 1 Feb–1 Dec. Dining room open to non-residents by arrangement only.
Rooms 5 double.
Facilities Lounge, conservatory, dining room. 200-acre farm: 1-acre garden, tennis, children's play area. Unsuitable for ♿.
Location 6 miles W of Youghal, just NE of Killeagh. Signposted.
Restrictions No smoking in dining room. No dogs in house.
Credit card Visa.
Terms B&B IR£20–£30. Set dinner IR£20.

KILMALLOCK Co. Limerick — Map 6

Flemingstown House BUDGET — *Tel* (063) 98093
Fax (063) 98546

A large 18th-century farmhouse, set in open country just outside the interesting medieval town of Kilmallock, with its fine Dominican friary. "Imelda Sheedy-King and her daughter gave us a most warm and friendly welcome," wrote its nominator. "The salmon at dinner was beautifully cooked; so were the very fresh vegetables. Altogether a comfortable and friendly place to stay in away-from-tourists countryside; good value for money." Others, too, have enjoyed the food, particularly the home-made Sachertorte, "unusual in rural Ireland". Visitors can look around the working dairy farm. (*J and PG*) Bedrooms and bathrooms (showers only) have been enlarged this year. More reports, please.

Open 1 Mar–1 Nov.
Rooms 3 suites, 2 double.
Facilities Lounge, dining room. 1-acre garden. Golf, riding, fishing nearby. Unsuitable for ♿.
Location 2 miles SE of Kilmallock on R512 to Fermoy.
Restrictions No smoking. No dogs in public rooms.
Credit card Visa.
Terms B&B IR£20–£25. Set dinner IR£16.

KINSALE Co. Cork — Map 6

The Old Presbytery NEW/BUDGET — *Tel/Fax* (021) 772027
Cork Street

Returning to our pages after a change of ownership, this tall narrow house offers good value for money at the heart of a charming and now very fashionable old fishing port. "Mr and Mrs McEvoy are a chatty and friendly couple," writes the nominator. "Our bedroom had a magnificent brass bed and pine furniture. The march of time has definitely stopped in the sitting room which is Victorian in every detail, right down to the music on the upright piano." Breakfast is served in the old kitchen; all manner of dishes are on offer, including fruit-filled crêpes, chicken liver, bacon and sausages, and "full Irish breakfast with black and white pudding"; orange juice is freshly squeezed. Dinner is not served, but there are plenty of excellent restaurants nearby – *Man Friday*, overlooking Kinsale harbour, is particularly recommended. (*Esler Crawford, Cilla Langdon-Down*)

Open All year, except Christmas.
Rooms 6 double. Some on ground floor.
Facilities Lounge with TV, conservatory, breakfast room. Sea, river, fishing close by. Unsuitable for ♿.
Location 2 mins' walk from centre, near parish church. Private carpark.
Restrictions Unsuitable for children. No dogs.
Credit cards None accepted.
Terms B&B IR£20–£40.

LEENANE Co. Galway — Map 6

Delphi Lodge — *Tel* (095) 42211
Leenane, Connemara — *Fax* (095) 42296

The former sporting lodge of the Marquis of Sligo stands alone by a lake amid glorious unspoilt mountain country on the northern edge of Connemara. Peter and Jane Mantle run it as a private lodge for fly-fishing enthusiasts, and also welcome those who want just peace and rest, and walks amid this wild scenery. Recent praise: "A delightful setting – the most stunning view I have ever seen from a hotel bedroom." "It manages that tricky blend of friendliness and professionalism. Afternoon tea and chocolate cake served on arrival; big well-furnished bedroom; huge fluffy towels and piping hot water. Excellent home-cooked dinner, taken at a huge oak table, presided over by Peter Mantle, who is very good company. The wine list is a treat, and finely priced." "Friendly and relaxed atmosphere; dinner was lively, and fishing was hardly discussed, although one could understand the allure, seeing a curragh next morning on the calm peaty lough, with fishermen and a ghillie quietly sculling." Some rooms have a four-poster. There is a large but cosy library, and a billiard room. Several empty sandy beaches lie within easy reach, and the wildlife is exceptional: otters, badgers, peregrines, etc. Not for those in search of bell-hops and room service. (*JH, RC, and others*)

Open All year, except Christmas, New Year.
Rooms 11 double. 2 on ground floor. 4 self-catering cottages.
Facilities Drawing room, library, billiard room, dining room. 15-acre grounds in 600-acre estate: lake, fishing, bathing.
Location 9 miles N of Leenane on Louisburgh road. 20 miles SW of Westport.
Restrictions Children under 12 not encouraged. No dogs.
Credit cards Access, Visa.
Terms B&B: single IR£45–£70, double IR£60–£110. Set lunch IR£7, dinner IR£25. 7-night fishing breaks. Fly-fishing tuition weekends. *V*

The 1998 *Guide* will appear in the autumn of 1997. Reports are particularly useful in the spring, and they need to reach us by 1 June 1997 if they are to help the 1998 edition.

LETTERFRACK Co. Galway — Map 6

Rosleague Manor *Tel* (095) 41101
Letterfrack, Connemara *Fax* (095) 41168

"A wonderful hotel. Dramatic setting; first-class comfort and style; superb service; food of a high order." Praise for this handsomely rambling Regency house standing in large grounds above a sheltered bay, amid the Connemara mountains and forests. It is owned by a sister and brother, Anne and Patrick Foyle; brother-in-law, Nigel Rush, is chef. Anne, "friendly and amusing", is the manager. "She is very much in evidence – I cannot recall seeing such a hard-working owner." There are large bedrooms, two attractive drawing rooms, and a fine dining room with creaking floorboards and ancestral portraits. The menu specialises in Connemara lamb and fresh seafood. Breakfasts, including a seafood platter, have been much admired, as have the "charming staff" and the peaceful atmosphere, "not a clock in sight, no one is reminded of the passing of time". Beautiful beaches and numerous lakes with excellent fishing are nearby. (*Mr and Mrs JH Astle-Fletcher, and others*)

Open Easter–1 Nov.
Rooms 4 mini-suites, 15 double, 1 single. 2 on ground floor.
Facilities 2 drawing rooms, conservatory/bar, billiard room, dining room; sauna. 25-acre grounds: tennis, path to water's edge (no beach). Lakes, fishing nearby.
Location Off N59, 7 miles NE of Clifden. Parking.
Restrictions No smoking in dining room. No dogs in public rooms.
Credit cards Access, Amex, Visa.
Terms B&B IR£40–£80. Set dinner IR£25. Off-season weekend breaks. *V* (except July, Aug, bank holidays)

LETTERKENNY Co. Donegal — Map 6

Castle Grove House BUDGET *Tel* (074) 51118
Fax (074) 51384

Raymond and Mary Sweeney's fine late 17th-century house is splendidly placed at the end of a long drive, overlooking Lough Swilly. It makes an excellent base from which to explore the remote beaches and hills of south Donegal. "Letterkenny itself is unprepossessing," wrote the nominator, "but the hotel has a beautiful, peaceful setting on the shore of the lough, with woods all around. The public rooms are large and handsome, after the fashion of Irish country houses. Bedrooms are comfortable, with huge warm bathrooms. The food is conventional but good, breakfasts especially, and the staff are pleasant and attentive. The dining room is much patronised by the local professional classes." Much of the food is home grown. Deep sea fishing, shooting and riding can be arranged. (*AL*) More reports, please.

Open All year, except 23–26 Dec. Restaurant closed Sun, Mon in low season.
Rooms 8 double. 7 more (1 with ♿ access) planned for 1997.
Facilities Drawing room, library with TV, dining room. 4-acre grounds. Beaches, fishing, shooting, riding nearby.
Location Off Ramelton road, 3 miles NE of Letterkenny by N13, R245.

Restrictions No smoking: restaurant, library, bedrooms. Unsuitable for very small children. No dogs.
Credit cards All major cards accepted.
Terms B&B: single IR35–£45, double IR£70–£80; D,B&B: single IR£55–£70, double IR£120–£130. Set dinner IR£25. Golf, fishing parties. *V*

LOUGH ESKE Co. Donegal — Map 6

Ardnamona House BUDGET — *Tel* (073) 22650, *Fax* (073) 22819

Early-Victorian shooting lodge in 100-acre grounds: lake frontage (boating, swimming, fishing); ancient oak forest; National Heritage garden with internationally famous collection of rhododendrons. Run with enthusiasm and charm by Kieran and Amabel Clarke; house party atmosphere. "Romantic setting, complemented by vases of heavenly scented lilies in public rooms – an unforgettable impression." Dinners "excellent", but not always available. 6 no-smoking bedrooms, south-facing and brightly decorated. Open 1 Feb–1 Dec. No dogs in house. Access, Visa accepted. B&B IR£35–£45. Set dinner IR£17. More reports, please.

MALLOW Co. Cork — Map 6

Longueville Manor NEW — *Tel* (022) 47156, *Fax* (022) 47459

A splendid Georgian mansion (Relais & Châteaux) run by the O'Callaghans, Michael and Aisling, with son William (the chef). It stands in a large estate, with the river Blackwater running through, and overlooks the ruins of Dromineen Castle, owned by O'Callaghan ancestors and destroyed by Cromwell. The hotel was dropped from the *Guide* owing to lack of reports, but returns now, much renovated, and warmly nominated: "It is tastefully furnished without being ornate, and a sense of history pervades. There are portraits of all the Irish presidents in the main dining room. Our room, more like a suite, was immense, with a well-equipped bathroom, almost as large. The hostess was charming, the waiting staff were unfailingly cheerful and humorous, and the dinners were memorable. The parkland setting offers gentle, pleasant walks, but the garden is in need of attention. Not cheap, but good value; nice atmosphere." The cooking is French-style, "with the best of Irish ingredients". In warm weather, guests may dine in the new Victorian-style conservatory. (*PJ and BA D'Arcy*)

Open 1 Mar–20 Dec.
Rooms 5 suites, 13 double, 2 single.
Facilities Drawing room, bar, 2 dining rooms, conservatory, library/private dining room; function facilities. 500-acre farm; gardens, river, salmon- and trout-fishing, walking.
Location 3 miles W of Mallow on N72 to Killarney.
Restrictions No smoking: 1 dining room, 5 bedrooms. No dogs.
Credit cards All major cards accepted.
Terms [1996] B&B IR£53–£80; D,B&B IR£70–£97.50. Set lunch IR£17, dinner IR£30.

All our inspections are carried out anonymously.

MIDLETON Co. Cork **Map 6**

Bailick Cottage BUDGET *Tel* (021) 631244

A 19th-century cottage, now Ava Glasson's civilised guest house, creeper-clad, in a big village amid pleasant country two miles east of Cork city. It has an informal garden; inside are antiques and flowers. "Excellent breakfasts, with freshly squeezed orange juice, cereals, jams and breads all home-made." The comfortable rooms are prettily furnished in coordinating fabrics; windows overlook the garden and river estuary where herons and whimbrels can be seen. The staff are "friendly and helpful". More reports, please.

Open All year.
Rooms 6 double. No telephone/TV.
Facilities Lounge, dining room. 2-acre garden opposite river. Sea 2 miles. Unsuitable for ♿.
Location Off R630 on edge of Midleton, 10 miles E of Cork. Private parking.
Restriction No dogs in house.
Credit cards None accepted.
Terms B&B IR£21.50–£30.

MONKSTOWN Co. Dublin **Map 6**

Chestnut Lodge BUDGET *Tel* (01) 280 7860
2 Vesey Place *Fax* (01) 280 1466

"A Regency terrace house, overlooking a wooded park, in a cul-de-sac with no traffic noise. It is furnished with good taste. Breakfast is a delight, as was tea with freshly baked scones and Mrs Malone's home-made jam. Everything is beautifully presented: starched table napery, butter curls, proper tea." "Hospitality and breakfasts above average." Nancy Malone's B&B, in a quiet eastern suburb of Dublin, offers comfort and tranquillity within easy reach of the centre. It is also convenient for the ferry at Dun Laoghaire. (*Catherine Fraher, Linda Peters*) Plenty of restaurants nearby.

Open All year.
Rooms 4 double.
Facilities Lounge, breakfast room. Golf, riding, sailing nearby.
Location 6 miles from centre of Dublin. Off Monkstown Rd (R119 Dublin–Dun Laoghaire).
Restriction No dogs.
Credit cards Access, Visa.
Terms B&B IR£25–£40. Children under 10 sharing parents' room half price.

MOUNTRATH Co. Laois **Map 6**

Roundwood House *Tel* (0502) 32120
Fax (0502) 32711

César award in 1992

Frank and Rosemary Kennan's Palladian mansion, "a gem of mid-18th-century architecture", is set in large grounds at the foot of the Slieve Bloom mountains, in the almost empty Irish "Midlands". "Staying there is *fun*," writes one enthusiast. The Kennans' friendliness and welcome, in their beautiful old house full of pictures, books and furniture, make it easy to ignore a few creaking floorboards and cracked walls. *Roundwood* has been refurbished – the top floor and roof at any rate, but *aficionados* of its slightly shabby Irish charm need not worry. The Kennans say: "Our intention is to keep *Roundwood* as near as possible to what it should be – an aged beauty, dressed in her own slightly frayed clothes, not tarted up in modern fashion." Bathrooms are quaint, but the water is hot. Dinners, which are communally eaten, are substantial and well cooked, "with lively and intelligent conversation led by Mr Kennan, resumed in the morning over a very enjoyable breakfast". There's an unusually good wine list. (*JS; also Margaret Crick, and others*)

Open All year, except Christmas.
Rooms 10 double.
Facilities Drawing room, study, library, dining room. 18½-acre grounds: croquet, swings, stables. Golf, river fishing nearby. Unsuitable for ♿.
Location N7 Dublin–Limerick. Right at T-junction in Mountrath, then left to Kinnitty. Hotel 3 miles exactly.
Restrictions No smoking in bedrooms. No dogs.
Credit cards All major cards accepted.
Terms B&B IR£35–£41. Set Sun lunch IR£12, dinner IR£22. *V*

MUCKROSS Co. Kerry — Map 6

Muckross Park NEW — *Tel* (064) 31938, *Fax* (064) 31965

In the heart of Killarney's National Park, and conveniently placed for the lakes, Raymond Kelliker's modernised version of Killarney's oldest hotel, in business since 1795, offers an excellent base for riding and exploring lakeside and forest walks. "We didn't see the famed red deer, but we spotted a dappled Japanese deer within a couple of hundred yards of the hotel," wrote its nominator. "The staff could not have been more cheerful and helpful, and the food in *Molly Darcys* (the thatched 'traditional Irish pub and restaurant' next to, and owned by, the hotel) was ample, wholesome and tasty. The bedrooms are prettily furnished – Laura Ashley with an Irish brogue – and the public rooms have a hearty charm." In the gourmet *Blue Pool* restaurant, Matthias Elbel's extensive menu uses plenty of fresh local produce: crab fritters with dill mayonnaise, seafood chowder, Cromane oysters and so on. Kerry is a golfer's paradise; there are several championship courses within easy reach. (*Tony Thomas*)

Open Mar–Nov.
Rooms 2 suites, 25 double.
Facilities Drawing room, bar, restaurant; function facilities. Pub/restaurant next door. 5-acre grounds. Lakes, fishing, walking, riding, pony-trekking, golf nearby. Unsuitable for ♿.
Location 2½ miles S of Killarney, on N71 towards Kenmare.
Restrictions No smoking in restaurant. No dogs.
Credit cards All major cards accepted.
Terms B&B: single IR£60–£80, double IR£80–£120, suite IR£180–£250. Pub meals. Set dinner IR£18.50; full alc IR£28. Off-season breaks.

> If you are nominating a hotel, we'd be grateful if you could send us the brochure.

MULRANY Co. Mayo Map 6

Rosturk Woods BUDGET *Tel/Fax* (098) 36264

This "delectable, upper-crust guest house", with "exemplary hosts", Louisa and Alan Stoney, stands on the sandy seashore of a village on beautiful Clew Bay in the west of Mayo, real *Playboy of the Western World* country. Though recently built, the house has an old feel and a cottage atmosphere; interesting books and pictures abound. Bedrooms have stripped pine doors, soft shades of blue, cotton prints, good lighting, and views across the bay. Alan Stoney grew up in the castle next door; Louisa, "friendly, intelligent and down to earth", runs the house and cooks simple dinners – good soups, freshly grilled salmon, etc. Breakfast includes smoked salmon and scrambled egg. There are also self-catering cottages, whose guests may dine in the main house. More reports, please.

Open Apr–end Oct.
Rooms 1 suite, 3 double. 1 suitable for ♿. Also self-catering accommodation (available all year).
Facilities Sitting room with TV, dining room. Garden. Riding, golf nearby. On seashore: good bathing.
Location 7½ miles W of Newport, between main road and sea.
Restrictions No smoking: dining room, bedrooms. No dogs in public rooms.
Credit cards None accepted.
Terms B&B IR£20–£28. Set dinner IR£20.

NEWPORT Co. Mayo Map 6

Newport House NEW *Tel* (098) 41222
Fax (098) 41613

Between Achill Island and the mountains of Mayo, close to the wild splendours of Erris and Connemara lies "one of the finest hotels in Ireland", according to its nominator, a regular visitor over many years. "It's an old manor house close to the sea; great hospitality and a warm greeting from Thelma and Kieran Thompson and their staff; wonderful food." A member of the Relais & Châteaux consortium, the pedigree Georgian house boasts fine plasterwork and a splendid staircase surmounted by a lantern and dome. Chef John Gavin's cooking includes sophisticated dishes such as oysters Rockefeller, and quail stuffed with mousseline of venison and wild mushroom sauce, followed, perhaps, by an iced Benedictine soufflé. The hotel has its own fishery on the Newport river. (*Conrad Voss Bark*)

Open 19 Mar–Oct.
Rooms 16 double, 2 single. 5 in courtyard. 2 on ground floor.
Facilities Drawing room, sitting room, bar, billiard room, dining room. 20-acre grounds: walled vegetable garden. Private fishing; golf, riding, walking, shooting, hang-gliding nearby.
Location In village. 15 mins' drive N of Westport.
Restrictions No smoking in dining room. No dogs in public rooms.
Credit cards All major cards accepted.
Terms [1996] B&B IR£50–£76; D,B&B IR£78–£106. Set dinner (6 courses) IR£30. Children under 2 accommodated free in parents' room. *V*

OUGHTERARD Co. Galway — Map 6

Currarevagh House — *Tel* (091) 552312
Oughterard, Connemara — *Fax* (091) 552731
César award in 1992

This mid-Victorian country house, set in huge grounds by the shore of Lough Corrib (some of the best fishing in Ireland), has been owned by the Hodgson family for five generations. Harry and June Hodgson have been resident hosts since 1970. "It is warm, comfortable and welcoming, with a hotchpotch of carpets and furniture," runs a recent endorsement. "Nightly hot-water bottles in beds, effective radiators in bathrooms. Excellent set dinners, good breakfasts too. We caught two salmon and three trout in three days." The house is not at all smart; in fact it is openly old-fashioned and slightly run-down; but that is its appeal to many readers, who enjoy the huge beds and Edwardian furniture and write: "Because it lacks formal elegance, it is comfortable and relaxing; the overall effect is home-like and friendly, like visiting an old relative." The no-choice, four-course country house-style menu might include poached salmon, confit of duck with cassis sauce, bilberry brûlée, or a good roast; service is by local women, and guests are expected to be punctual. Breakfast is an Edwardian-style buffet, with a range of hot dishes on the sideboard. (*CM Horne, and others*)

Open Apr–Oct. Parties of 8 or more at other times (except Christmas, New Year). Lunch by arrangement (residents only).
Rooms 13 double, 2 single. 3 on ground floor in mews.
Facilities Drawing room, sitting room, library, bar, dining room. 150-acre grounds: lake fishing (ghillies available), boating, swimming, tennis, croquet. Golf, riding nearby. Not ideal for ♿.
Location 4 miles NW of Oughterard on Glann lakeshore road.
Restrictions No smoking in dining room. Children under 12 by arrangement. Dogs by arrangement; only on lead in public rooms.
Credit cards None accepted.
Terms (*Excluding 10% service charge*) B&B: single IR£45–£64, double IR£90–£98. Set dinner IR£20. 3/7-day rates. 1-night bookings sometimes refused far in advance in season.

RATHMULLAN Co. Donegal — Map 6

Rathmullan House — *Tel* (074) 58188
Rathmullan, Letterkenny — *Fax* (074) 58200

This early 19th-century mansion stands pleasantly in its own wide gardens, beside attractive Lough Swilly – not a lake but an inlet from the sea, with a broad sandy beach. It is run by the owners Bob and Robin Wheeler, with son Mark as manager, and a friendly staff. "Continues to offer comfortable hospitality and excellent food," writes a regular visitor. "The breakfast must be the best in Ireland." Endorsed in 1996: "Though professionally run, it has the feel of a private house. Staff efficient and helpful. My heavy suitcase was raced up the stairs." Public rooms have chandeliers, antiques, marble fireplaces and oil paintings. In the striking conservatory-style dining room, a lavish buffet lunch is served on Sundays. Chef Kevin Murphy recently returned after an interval of two years, and we'd be grateful for reports on his "new Irish" cooking. There are pleasant walks along the beach, up the lovely Fanad peninsula, and into Rathmullan, "a village full of unspoilt Donegal melancholy". A pretty indoor salt water swimming pool, and a sauna and steam room add to the pleasures. (*EC, D Kaars Sypesteyn*)

Open Early Mar–Nov.
Rooms 8 mini-suites, 11 double, 1 single.
Facilities Drawing room, Rajah room, library, TV room, smoking room, cellar bar, dining room; indoor salt water swimming pool, sauna, steam room. 10-acre grounds: tennis, croquet; direct access to sandy beach, safe bathing. Unsuitable for ♿.
Location ½ mile N of village, 14 miles NE of Letterkenny.
Restrictions No smoking in dining room. No dogs.
Credit cards All major cards accepted.
Terms [1996] (*Excluding 10% service charge*) B&B IR£37.50–£60; D,B&B IR£60–£92.50. Sun buffet lunch IR£13.50; set dinner IR£24. Weekend rates; 2-day breaks.

RATHNEW Co. Wicklow — Map 6

Hunter's Hotel NEW

Tel (0404) 40106
Fax (0404) 40338

Now modernised, but with its character emphatically unchanged, this ancient coaching inn by a river, owned and run by the Gelletlie family since 1825, returns to our pages with affectionate endorsements from two trusted correspondents. "My memory was of old-fashioned comfort, perhaps a little time-worn, with large amounts of very adequate food. Recently, however, I found the whole place gleaming with fresh paint, new carpets and polished wood. My single bedroom was generous in size; with a bed big enough for two, and no fewer than three mirrors. The extensive dinner menu provided hearty if not *haute cuisine* fare, and breakfast was 'full house Irish' with freshly squeezed juice, linen napkins and not a sign of pre-packed butter or preserves." "I have loved this place for 30 years. Mrs Gelletlie is my ideal Irish hotel-keeper, and the hotel itself, with all its quirks and its disdain for 'improvement', strikes me as the best possible indoctrination into Irishness." Whiskey and tea are served throughout the day, often simultaneously. Nobody bothers with keys. (*Esler Crawford, Jan Morris*)

Open All year, except 3 days over Christmas.
Rooms 13 double, 3 single. 1 on ground floor.
Facilities Residents' lounge, TV room, bar lounge, dining room. 2-acre garden: river, fishing. Golf, tennis, riding, sea, sandy beach, fishing nearby.
Location 28 miles S of Dublin. Turn off N11; ½ mile outside village. Carpark.
Restrictions No smoking in dining room. No dogs.
Credit cards All major cards accepted.
Terms [1996] B&B IR£45; D,B&B IR£65. Set lunch IR£14.50, dinner IR£22.

Tinakilly House

Tel (0404) 69274
Fax (0404) 67806

This grey stone mansion was built in the 1870s by the great navigator Captain Robert Halpin, one-time commander of Brunel's *Great Eastern*, as his retirement home. It stands close to the sea in large wooded grounds, and is efficiently run as a smart country hotel by the present owners, William and Bee Power. The furnishings include golden chandeliers and sconces, polished dark wood, Rococo fireplaces, softly upholstered formal sofas and chairs, red carpets, potted plants, and a magpie miscellany of glittering bric-à-brac. The rooms, including the bedrooms, some of which have a four-poster bed of imperial dimensions, are large and high-ceilinged with tall windows. The "high-quality" food might include such local ingredients as scallops or roast Wicklow venison. The staff are "cheerful and willing". A pianist plays on Friday and Saturday nights. Close by are the Wicklow Mountains, where the film *Braveheart* was shot. (*J and JR*)

Open All year.
Rooms 3 suites, 26 double. 5 on ground floor, 1 equipped for ♿.
Facilities Hall, residents' lounge, bar, 3 dining rooms; conference facilities. 7-acre grounds: tennis, putting green. Golf, bird sanctuary nearby.
Location Off N11 Dublin–Wicklow. Take R750 through Rathnew. Entrance on left after ¼ mile.
Restriction No dogs.
Credit cards All major cards accepted.
Terms B&B: IR£58–£100. Bar lunches. Set Sun lunch IR£18.50, dinner IR£30. Short breaks, Dickensian Christmas, New Year programme.

RECESS Co. Galway — Map 6

Ballynahinch Castle NEW

Tel (095) 31006
Fax (095) 31085

This splendid crenellated house stands on the banks of a river (excellent salmon fishing) in a large wooded private estate in the wild heart of Connemara. It is warmly nominated by a regular visitor: "We love its tranquil atmosphere, stunning location, relaxed style, and atmosphere of a private home. Fires burn in the entrance hall in winter, and guests are encouraged to sit around drying off walking gear and having tea or drinks. The restaurant and the bedrooms in the new annexe have wonderful views of the river, from huge windows. Food is very good, with plenty of local fish and game." This is the ancestral home of the Martin family ("Humanity Dick" Martin was the founder of the RSPCA); the English county cricketer and sportsman, Maharajah Ranjitsingh, also lived here. (*Lidia Ferritto*)

Open All year, except Christmas, Feb.
Rooms 13 double, 5 single.
Facilities Hall, drawing room, dining room. 350-acre grounds: river, fishing, tennis, shooting. Unsuitable for ♿.
Location 36 miles from Galway. Turn towards Roundstone off N59 Galway–Clifden. Entrance 2 miles.
Restriction No dogs.
Credit cards All major cards accepted.
Terms (*Excluding 10% service charge*) B&B: single IR£55–£69, double IR£80–£120. Set lunch IR£15, dinner IR£23.

RIVERSTOWN Co. Sligo — Map 6

Coopershill

Tel (071) 65108
Fax (071) 65466

César award in 1987

"A wonderful hotel. Brian and Lindy O'Hara are excellent hosts, efficient and attentive, but also relaxed." "We cannot praise it too much.

We enjoy the country house party style, the (agreeable to us) certain formality tempered by the good humour of the hosts, the walks through the woods, the dogs, the peacocks, and the gathering of guests in the drawing room before and after dinner. The house is filled with antiques; everything is impeccably cared for. The food was even better than last time, and so generous: large servings if you want to eat a lot, butter arranged in serried curls, wonderful fudge and chocolate with coffee, afternoon tea with cut-and-come-again cakes. Tumblers of fresh orange juice at breakfast. Good value." "A delightful, secluded place in idyllic countryside. The interior is something of a time warp, with spears, hunting trophies, and ancestors decorating the walls." More plaudits this year for this grey stone mansion, built by the O'Hara family in 1774, in a large estate south of Sligo town. Nearby are the knobbly hills beloved by Yeats. Bedrooms are lofty and well appointed, with old-fashioned furniture: most have a four-poster or a canopied bed. Dinner (no choice), a leisurely meal by candlelight, is at 8.30 pm. (*ML Povey, Jean and George Dundas, Richard and Sheila Owen; also A O'Dowd*)

Open Mid-Mar–end Oct. Out-of-season house parties by arrangement.
Rooms 7 double. No TV.
Facilities 2 halls, drawing room, TV room, dining room; table-tennis. 500-acre grounds: garden, tennis, woods, farmland, river with coarse fishing. Trout-fishing, sandy beach, championship golf course 18 miles. Unsuitable for ♿.
Location From N4 turn towards Riverstown at Drumfin crossroads, 11 miles SE of Sligo; follow *Coopershill* signs.
Restrictions No smoking: dining room, bedrooms. No dogs in house.
Credit cards All major cards accepted.
Terms B&B: IR£45–£60; D,B&B IR£68–£83. Light or picnic lunch IR£6; set dinner IR£23. Discounts for 3 or more nights. Christmas, New Year house parties. V

SHANAGARRY Co. Cork — Map 6

Ballymaloe House

Tel (021) 652531
Fax (021) 652021
E-mail bmaloe@iol.ie

César award in 1984

Myrtle and Ivan Allen's gracious and rambling hotel, more or less Georgian, with a Norman keep, is set in the middle of a large farm. Almost everything you eat in the renowned restaurant, apart from the fish, is home-grown or raised. Many outdoor activities are available (see below). The place remains hugely popular, despite occasional grumbles, for the special hospitality generated by the extended Allen family. "The food and service were excellent, and our two young children were treated extremely well," is one recent encomium. Lounges are comfortable, with log fires in winter; walls are hung with Ivan Allen's collection of modern Irish paintings. Bedrooms vary in size; those in the main house tend to be larger than annexe ones: "The six-pillowed Rose room was very comfortable, with pleasant views across the back lawns to the duck pond." The restaurant has steadily grown in size, and now has five rooms and a conservatory. Head chef is Rory O'Connell, brother of daughter-in-law Darina Allen, who runs the Ballymaloe Cookery School. The cooking remains careful and traditional, "unspoilt by *nouvelle* pretensions"; there's a splendid, if pricey, wine list. (*Mrs S Kinder, Richard and Sheila Owen, and others*) "After eager anticipation", one recent visitor was disappointed: "Disorganised reception; dinner not up to expectation." Another felt that *Ballymaloe* had become a victim of its own success, and detected a "conveyor-belt atmosphere". The swimming pool is said to be on the cool side.

Open All year, except 24–26 Dec.
Rooms 30 double, 3 single. 11 in courtyard. 3 on ground floor.
Facilities Drawing room, 2 sitting rooms, TV room, conservatory, 5 dining rooms. 400-acre farm: gardens, tennis, swimming pool, 6-hole golf course, croquet, children's play area; craft shop. Cookery school nearby. Sea 5 miles: sand and rock beaches; fishing, riding by arrangement.
Location 20 miles E of Cork; 2 miles E of Cloyne on L35 Ballycotton road.
Restrictions No smoking in some dining rooms. No dogs in house.
Credit cards All major cards accepted.
Terms B&B: IR£70–£90; D,B&B £81.50–£121.50. Set lunch IR£16 (Sun buffet IR£17), dinner IR£31.50. Winter, conference rates.

WICKLOW Co. Wicklow — Map 6

The Old Rectory — *Tel* (0404) 67048, *Fax* (0404) 69181

A pretty early Victorian house in the old harbour town. It stands in pleasant gardens, and is owned and run, with relaxed informality, by Linda and Paul Saunders. Their friendly welcome has been praised, as has Linda Saunders' cooking, "a joyful experience – waits between courses well rewarded by that aroma of freshness only achieved when the cooking is done while you dine". Linda is a pioneer of "floral cuisine", and the "gourmet floral menu" includes stuffed courgette flowers, breast of lamb and lavender sausages and "croquembouche with frosted rose petals and spun sugar". Many ingredients are home-grown. Breakfasts, "Irish, Scottish or Swiss", are also praised. Rooms, which vary in size, are individually designed, Victorian in style "and very comfortable". Lots of fresh flowers, as you might expect. This year there is a new wing, giving an extended lounge area, and with a fitness suite. More reports, please.

Open Mar–Dec. Restaurant closed Good Friday.
Rooms 7 double.
Facilities Drawing room, aperitifs lounge, dining room; fitness suite. 1-acre garden. Beach ½ mile, bathing, fishing.
Location Edge of town; on left off N11 Dublin–Wicklow.
Restriction No smoking: restaurant, aperitifs lounge. No dogs.
Credit cards All major cards accepted.
Terms B&B IR£48–£72. Set dinner IR£28.50; full alc IR£40. 2-day rates; special breaks. Children under 2 accommodated free in parents' room; under 12 half price. *V* (Oct–Apr)

YOUGHAL Co. Cork — Map 6

Aherne's — *Tel* (024) 92424
163 North Main Street — *Fax* (024) 93633

César award: best restaurant-with-rooms – Irish style

"A perfect stay. The warmest of welcomes, the most helpful of staff; friendliness and hospitality of the highest order." "I cannot recommend it too highly. The best of everything: service, food and rooms. A delight in every way." Once more, visitors pull out all the stops to express their joy at the Fitzgibbon family's popular restaurant-with-rooms in a historic walled port at the mouth of the Blackwater river, on the lovely Irish south coast. Long noted for its "particular flair with freshly caught seafood", it offers "a warm and Irish welcome". The bedrooms, in a modern wing, are huge and well furnished. "Ours had a lavishly fitted bathroom, and an extension, with a sitting room with a peat fire and a breakfast area; the overall effect was that of the best sort of French hotel." "The food was marvellous: amazing, perfectly cooked seafood at dinner, and a mammoth breakfast with freshly squeezed orange juice, scrambled egg and smoked salmon and fresh fish, if required." "Not cheap, but we had value for money and a night of comfort and pampering." (*Michael O'Flaherty, Rachel Burridge, Dr John Rowlands, and others*) Bar meals too.

Open All year, except Christmas.
Rooms 10 double. 3 on ground floor, 1 with facilities for ♿.
Facilities Drawing room, 2 bars, restaurant. Beach, bathing, sea/river fishing, riding, golf nearby.
Location On N25, ½ mile from centre. Courtyard parking.
Restriction No dogs.
Credit cards All major cards accepted.
Terms [1996] B&B IR£40–£60. Bar meals. Set lunch IR£15.50, dinner IR£26; full alc IR£30.

Part two

Austria
Belgium
The Czech Republic
Denmark
France
Germany
Greece
Hungary
Italy
Luxembourg
Malta
The Netherlands
Norway
Portugal
including Madeira
Slovenia
Spain
including The Balearics
and The Canaries
Sweden
Switzerland
including Liechtenstein

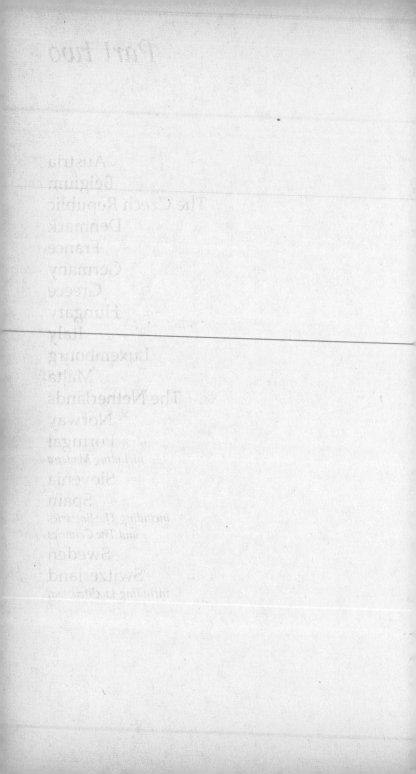

Austria

Sporthotel Singer, Berwang

Hotels follow much the same pattern in Austria as they do in Germany. The big chains, such as Hilton and Holiday Inn, are represented; but most hotels are smaller and individually run, of the kind we prefer. Some are well-converted castles, or members of the Romantik Hotel association, or chalet-style ski-hotels. Many simple country inns have the official *Gasthof* label. In the cities, some of the best smaller hotels are *pensions*, personal in character but not offering full hotel facilities (eg, the reception desk may not always be manned).

As in Germany, duvets, rather than sheets and blankets, are the norm; chocolates are often left on the bed as a goodnight gesture; and, except in the smallest places, breakfast is a buffet, generally included in the room price. Service, too, is included in the bill, but it is usual to leave a tiny extra tip if it has pleased you. Food is generally lavish in quantity, with an Austrian touch: *nouvelle cuisine* has not made many inroads. But neither has *Michelin*, which has no Austrian edition, so we spare our readers the constant references made to it in most other chapters.

BAD ZELL 4283 Oberösterreich — Map 16

Gasthof Gschwandtner NEW/BUDGET *Tel* (07263) 72 66-0
Marktplatz 24

Partly converted from an old farm, this modest and friendly inn stands in the market square of a small spa town east of Linz, amid pleasant country. Well run by Franz and Elfriede Gschwandtner, it fell from last year's *Guide* through lack of reports, but is now renominated: "Outwardly plain, but delightful, it provides a good buffet breakfast and interesting *pension* dinners (we were offered delicious *boletus edulis* mushrooms). Rooms and bathrooms are spacious, well furnished and appointed. We noted that a parent with a handicapped child was, quite discreetly, very well looked after." There's a pleasant garden with loungers, and sun-terrace for drinks. (*BW Ribbons*)

Open All year, except last week Nov / 1st week Dec. Restaurant closed Mon.
Rooms 1 suite, 5 double, 3 single.
Facilities Lounge, bar, restaurant; function room; terrace. Garden: sauna.
Location In town, 40 km NE of Linz. Garage, parking.
Credit cards None accepted.
Terms [1996] B&B 330 Sch; D,B&B 430 Sch. Set meals 100 Sch; full alc 200 Sch.

BERNSTEIN 7434 Burgenland — Map 16

Hotel Burg Bernstein *Tel* (03354) 63 82
Fax (03354) 65 20

This intriguingly eccentric hotel is a massive Gothic fortress, renovated in Renaissance and Baroque styles, and standing splendidly alone amid wooded hills near the Hungarian border. It is owned and run by the Bergers, whose family home it has been since 1892. "We loved it all," says a recent visitor, endorsing earlier accounts: "The husband wandered about, looking remarkable: very tall, in *Lederhosen*, with three gold rings in his left ear. Dinner, in a huge banqueting hall with a fine stucco ceiling, was informally delivered but tasty. Andrea Berger is the chef. There was an air of decay about the place, but everything worked and was very clean, and the staff were very good-natured. Most rooms are high-ceilinged suites with a haphazard collection of antiques." "Our huge rooms sported armour, helmets and swords, and the view was stunning." "Our rooms, with new elegant marble bathroom, were occupied years ago by an Arab diplomat, and still contained his library on world religions, his desk (complete with skull), fez and ceremonial sword. Dinner, by candlelight, was simple and rustic. Breakfast was served in the large inner courtyard. An atmospheric, friendly place, splendid for children." (*GSS, and others*) A further oddity: the telephone is always on an answering machine; to contact the hotel you must dictate a message or send a letter or fax, all of which get answered promptly. And there is no phone or TV in the rooms. "No technics!" write the Bergers, who add: "Living in a castle is more than exciting." Newer reports welcome.

Open 1 May–16 Oct.
Rooms 5 suites, 4 double.
Facilities Hall, lounge, bar; sauna. Park: garden, swimming pool; fishing. Tennis, golf, riding nearby; hunting arranged.
Location Just outside Bernstein village, 13 km N of Oberwart.

Credit cards All major cards accepted.
Terms B&B 710–990 Sch; D,B&B (min. 2 nights) 1,020–1,300 Sch. Set dinner 310 Sch.

BERWANG 6622 Tirol — Map 16

Sporthotel Singer

Tel (05674) 81 81
Fax (05674) 81 81-83

The Singer family's ever-admired hotel, made up of two big adjacent chalets, stands on a pine-studded slope, on the edge of this busy summer and ski resort, west of the towering Zugspitze – there's a modern ski-lift nearby. A Relais & Châteaux member, it is smart and cosmopolitan, spacious and quite large; it also has Tyrolean decor and a "family atmosphere", and it lays on various jollities such as yodelling and zither evenings. American visitors this year were pleased: "Our junior suite had charming decor, every comfort, and a huge window along one side. Johann, the *maître d'hôtel*, lent charm and liveliness to the festive dining room, where the food was good, notably the soups. Excellent staff." The personal touch of the "very hospitable" owners invites loyalty, and some devotees have visited more than 20 times in 17 years. "Marvellous views from the bedroom balconies." Facilities include jacuzzi, sauna and massage. (*Susan Hanley, SB*) Some discreet coach parties, mainly from France. The nearby walks have been called "uninteresting"; and the hotel is hard to reach by public transport. One plaint: "If only the restaurant were no-smoking!"

Open 19 Dec–2 Apr, 16 May–5 Oct.
Rooms 25 suites, 25 double, 10 single.
Facilities Lift. Lounge, 2 bars, *Stube*, 2 dining rooms; children's playroom; dancing, Tyrolean evenings; fitness centre (no-smoking): jacuzzi, sauna, massage, solarium. Small garden: terraces.
Location 80 km NW of Innsbruck, off Stuttgart road. Garages, open parking.
Credit cards Amex, Diners, Visa.
Terms B&B: single 780–1,200 Sch, double 1,380–2,700 Sch, suite 1,660–3,890 Sch. Set lunch from 200 Sch, dinner from 300 Sch; full alc from 300 Sch. Reductions for children.

BEZAU 6870 Vorarlberg — Map 16

Gasthof Gams

Tel (05514) 22 20
Fax (05514) 22 20-24

"The service and food were as good as ever," says a visitor this year to this converted 17th-century coaching inn, which faces green fields and wooded hills on the edge of a pleasant little town near the Bregenz forest. Public rooms are fitted out in traditional style, and bedrooms are modernised – some are two-room suites, suitable for families. The warm personal touch of the Nenning family owners has been praised by readers, who also enjoy the heated outdoor swimming pool and sauna. "A charming hotel, with friendly staff and outstanding food", which is freshly cooked and attractively prepared, with sensible use of local products. The terraces are pleasant for meals in hot weather, and the views to the mountains are inviting. "A real welcome for children." (*Anne E Sharp, and others*) Bedrooms vary in size: those above the public rooms can be noisy when one of the hotel's many lively events is going on. The hotel recently joined a new group, Europa Wanderhotels, offering special arrangements for hikers.

Open All year, except 15 Nov–20 Dec.
Rooms 7 suites, 25 double, 4 single.
Facilities Lounge, bar, TV room, 6 dining rooms; conference/functions rooms; games room, table-tennis; sauna, Turkish bath, solarium, hot whirlpool; terraces. Large garden: swimming pool (heated May–Oct), 3 tennis courts. Unsuitable for ♿.
Location Central. Bezau is 30 km SE of Bregenz, 37 km NW of Lech. Private parking.
Credit cards None accepted.
Terms B&B: single 680–1,030 Sch, double 1,060–1,360 Sch, suite 1,660 Sch; D,B&B 695–1,145 Sch per person. Set meals 250–300 Sch; full alc 350 Sch. Reduced rates for children.

ELIXHAUSEN 5161 Salzburg — **Map 16**

Romantik Hotel Gmachl — *Tel* (0662) 48 02 12
Dorfstrasse 14 — *Fax* (0662) 48 02 12-72

On edge of village 8 km N of Salzburg, with views over plain: a sturdy yellow-fronted hostelry, fairly smart, dating from 1334, owned by Gmachl family since 1583. Their butcher's shop next door helps ensure high quality of food (Austrian, plus some nouvelle *dishes) in their attractive* Gasthaus. *Good breakfast buffet, with meats. 52 well-modernised bedrooms, some in new annexe. Leisure centre: swimming pool, sauna, solarium. Garden: swimming pool, tennis, riding. Closed 24–26 Dec. All major credit cards accepted. B&B double 1,540–2,150 Sch; D,B&B double 2,060–2,750 Sch. Set meals 300–480 Sch. No recent reports; more welcome.*

EMMERSDORF 3644 Oberösterreich — **Map 16**

Landgasthof Pritz NEW — *Tel* (02752) 712 49
Fax (02752) 712 49 44

In ancient village on Danube opposite Melk, 84 km W of Vienna, handsome old inn stylishly modernised, well run by "charming" Pritz family owners. Spacious foyer, good modern bedrooms, fine cooking, "splendid" breakfasts. Outdoor heated pool, sauna, sun terrace. Good walking nearby. Closed 8 Jan–5 Mar. Diners card accepted. 45 rooms (some self-catering). B&B 460–750 Sch. Set meals 110–130 Sch.

FREISTADT 4240 Oberösterreich — **Map 16**

Gasthof Deim BUDGET — *Tel* (07942) 22 58-0
zum Goldenen Hirschen — *Fax* (07942) 22 58-40
Böhmergasse 8

In handsome old ramparted town 40 km NE of Linz, a characterful old inn full of tradition and period pieces, but modernised. 32 spacious, pleasant bedrooms, some with canopied bed. Lounge, atmospheric restaurant with terrace; generous cooking, cheerful service. Garden: swimming pool. Closed 7–21 Jan. Only Diners card accepted. B&B double 900 Sch; D,B&B double 1,130 Sch. Set meals 140–200 Sch. No recent reports; new ones, please.

GARGELLEN 6787 Vorarlberg — Map 16

Hotel Madrisa — *Tel* (05557) 63 31
Montafon — *Fax* (05557) 63 31-82

"The most *gemütlich* hotel we have ever stayed in," say regulars returning this year to this old *Guide* favourite. It is a ski-hotel next to nursery slopes in the beautiful Montafon valley, and would suit a family holiday, summer or winter. Not smart but informal, traditional in style yet well modernised, it has been in the hands of the Rhomberg family for three generations, and the present Rhomberg owners are "an exceptional couple": "One day they held a party for the guests with food and music." A view last year: "Our wood-panelled rooms had beautiful views. The sumptuous breakfast buffet included home-made muesli and four kinds of berries. Dinner was always delicious, with good use of local game; one evening, the 'Farmer's Buffet' was a table loaded with a vast array of hot meats, etc, charmingly served. We loved the leisure facilities – a large indoor pool, sauna, mountain bikes to be borrowed free. The Rhombergs were always in evidence, chatting with guests." "The balcony of our lovely room had a view of the village church and mountains" (rooms in the older part have no balcony, but are also pleasant). Children enjoy the table-tennis, the large-screen videos, the mountainside picnic breakfasts. (*Anne and Ian Steel, GP, and others*) One reader this year liked the "professional" staff and "excellent" swimming pool, but criticised her room's decor, the food, and the sometimes slow and clumsy service.

Open 16 Dec–17 Apr, 25 June–24 Sept. Restaurant closed Tues.
Rooms 5 suites, 45 double, 12 single.
Facilities Lounges, TV room, bar, restaurant; disco; children's playroom; indoor swimming pool, sauna, fitness room; terrace. Garden.
Location Central. Gargellen is 28 km S of Bludenz. Parking.
Credit card Access (for extras only).
Terms [1996] D,B&B: winter 1,090–1,710 Sch; summer 760–960 Sch. Set lunch 80 Sch, dinner 380 Sch; full alc 500 Sch. 1-night bookings sometimes refused in winter.

GMUNDEN AM TRAUNSEE 4810 Oberösterreich — Map 16

Parkhotel am See NEW — *Tel* (07612) 42 30
Schiffslaende 17 — *Fax* (07612) 42 30-66

Here's a happy story. Just outside this lively resort east of Salzburg, and by the lake, is this classic, fairly smart hotel. "One of the most civilised that we know," say visitors in 1996, who now restore it to the *Guide* after a period with no reports. "We spent our honeymoon here in 1954, and have just returned for the first time. It is still run by the same Holzinger family, and is as wonderful now as it was all those years ago. Set in park-like gardens by the lake, amid spectacular scenery, it's a substantial building dating from the 16th century, and once housed a brewery. It is now in the loving care of three Holzinger sisters, Gabriele, Barbara and Claudia: they and their staff are relaxed and welcoming. Perfectly run in every way, the hotel has a warm family atmosphere, and is beautifully furnished with fine antiques and heirlooms. Lounges are comfortable, the bar is cosy. Most bedrooms face the lake: ours, furnished in good modern Austrian style, had a balcony. The gardens have the right furniture for sun-bathing or lounging; snacks and refreshments are brought out on request. There's no pool, but the hotel has its own bathing-jetties on the lake. No formal meals are served, but there's a large, slightly rustic 'bistro' in a building in the garden: here sumptuous buffet breakfasts are served, and then light meals and snacks up to 9.30 pm. For a fuller meal, we liked the nearby *Schwan* hotel." In summer you can dine under the chestnut trees. (*Arlette and Brian Singleton*)

Open 23 May–21 Sept.
Rooms 2 suites, 39 double, 6 single.
Facilities 2 lounges, bar/bistro; conference room; sauna, solarium. Large garden: tennis, children's playground, lake swimming. Golf nearby. Unsuitable for ♿.
Location On Vienna side of town centre, by lake. 60 km SW of Vienna. Parking.
Credit cards Access, Visa.
Terms B&B 600–980 Sch. Light lunch 180 Sch, dinner 200 Sch.

GRAZ 8010 Styria — Map 16

Schlossberg Hotel — *Tel* (0316) 80 70-0
Kaiser-Franz-Josef-Kai 30 — *Fax* (0316) 80 70-160

This 400-year-old inn, in a quiet but central side-street of Austria's second city, was renovated recently: it has beamed ceilings and rambling corridors, but a modern lift. Guests have found it attractively furnished, with country-style antiques and interesting paintings. It has a large, comfortable lounge and bar, and a courtyard for drinks. "Our spacious suite had rustic furniture. Efficient service: good buffet breakfast." (*A and BW*) We should welcome reports on the new restaurant.

Open All year, except Christmas. Restaurant closed Sun.
Rooms 5 suites, 35 double, 15 single.
Facilities Lift. Lounge, TV room, bar, breakfast room; conference facilities. Roof garden: swimming pool; solarium, fitness room. Unsuitable for ♿.
Location Central. Garage.
Credit cards All major cards accepted.
Terms [1996] B&B: single 1,500–1,700 Sch, double 2,200–2,600 Sch. Set lunch 90 Sch; full alc dinner 250 Sch.

GSCHNITZ 6150 Tirol — Map 16

Berggasthof Gschnitzerhof NEW/BUDGET — *Tel* (0576) 213
Im Gschnitztal — *Fax* (0576) 321

Outside village in lovely, secluded Alpine valley, off motorway to Brenner pass 30 km SW of Innsbruck: "wonderful" family-run Gasthof, *amazing value. Helpful staff, good Austrian food. Large, charming rooms (hand-painted pine furniture), modern bathrooms. Outdoor swimming pool. Skiing. Open 15 May–early Oct, 20 Dec–Easter. No credit cards accepted. 19 rooms. D,B&B: summer 400–450 Sch, winter 435–485 Sch [1996].*

Report forms (Freepost in UK) will be found at the end of the *Guide*. If you need more, or larger ones, please ask. But it is not essential that you use them for reports.

HEILIGENBLUT 9844 Kärnten **Map 16**

Haus Senger NEW/BUDGET *Tel* (04824) 22 15
Fax (04824) 22 15-9

Hans and Rosina Senger's "charming mountain chalet" stands just outside a village below the Grossglockner, in wild upland country, good for walking or skiing. It has a cheerful decor, with lots of wood panelling. Dropped from recent editions of the *Guide* for lack of feedback, it was admired again this year: "The setting is beautiful, with wonderful views. Bedrooms are large, with sitting area and balcony. The dining room has a warm, wonderful atmosphere, and we enjoyed our dinners. The Senger family were charming." There's a garden, with a swing. (*Lee and Jim Stevens*)

Open End June–early Oct.
Rooms 8 suites, 6 double, 3 single.
Facilities Lift. Lounges with fireplace, TV room, restaurant; sauna, steam bath. Garden.
Location Edge of village, 40 km N of Lienz. Parking.
Credit cards All major cards accepted.
Terms B&B 450–960 Sch; D,B&B 700–1,200 Sch. Set meals 250–350 Sch; full alc 390 Sch. Reduced rates for children sharing parents' room.

INNSBRUCK 6020 Tirol **Map 16**

Gasthof Weisses Kreuz NEW *Tel* (0512) 594 79
Herzog-Friedrichstrasse 31 *Fax* (0512) 594 79-90

In traffic-free city centre, pleasant little family-run B&B hotel dating from 1465. Mozart stayed as a boy; well modernised since his day. 30 nicely furnished rooms (2 no-smoking), modern bathrooms. Good breakfasts. Private parking 3 mins' walk. Access, Amex, Visa accepted. B&B: single 670–870 Sch, double 1,020–1,400 Sch. Restaurant, separately owned, in same building. Renominated this year, but fuller reports welcome.

KITZBÜHEL 6370 Tirol **Map 16**

Romantik Hotel Tennerhof NEW *Tel* (05356) 31 81
Griesenauweg 26 *Fax* (0536) 36 36 70

In a smart resort, this smart yet cosy chalet-hotel lives up to its "Romantik" name, says its euphoric nominator: "Rooms are the epitome of what a Tyrolean hotel should be – hand-painted armoires, wood floors, pastel-coloured duvet covers, little chairs in flowered fabrics. The dining rooms are most atmospheric, with dark green and bright pink in one room, yellow in another, baby blue across the hall. In the candlelight, they just glow. Service is by young men and women in Tyrolean dress: a bit casual, but elegant. Cooking is *nouvelle* Austrian, and superb: the best rare saddle of lamb I had anywhere, and a Christmas Eve set dinner that included lobster in champagne jelly, peach-elderflower sorbet, soufflé of ginger bread and fig sabayon. All quite classy. One day I saw a whole pig being delivered, and sure enough next day we had fresh sausage patties on the breakfast table. The manager, Herr Oberhammer, is delightful. Four more suites are being added. They spend a lot of money in this region. My only criticism: the lobby chairs and upholstery need a facelift." The garden has a swimming pool amid trees. (*Karen Pasold and Sheila Bielich*)

Open May–Oct, Dec–Mar.
Rooms 44.
Facilities Lounges, bar, restaurant; conference facilities; indoor swimming pool, sauna, solarium, massage; terrace. Garden: swimming pool.
Location In resort. Parking.
Credit cards All major cards accepted.
Terms [1996] B&B double 1,250–2,260 Sch (winter), 920–1,810 Sch (summer); D,B&B 1,520–2,530 Sch (winter), 1,190–2,080 Sch (summer).

LIENZ 9900 Tirol — Map 16

Parkhotel Tristachersee — *Tel* (04852) 67 6 66, *Fax* (04852) 67 6 99

Lienz, capital of east Tyrol, is a pleasant town below the Dolomites, not far from Italy. To its east, set right beside a small lake, amid woods, is this modern chalet-style hotel: the dining terrace and many of the flowery bedroom balconies face over the water. Visitors now returning have confirmed their report last year: "Outstandingly good, and quiet, in a beautiful setting. An enthusiastic welcome, and up-to-date bedrooms. Excellent food: fresh fish from the lake, served with good Austrian wines, in a bright, airy dining room. Ample breakfast buffet. The owner, Herr Kreuzer, has made a conservation area in the lake – nesting ducks, birds, flowers." "Delightful and well run: the Kreuzers were most friendly. A pretty garden with loungers, and a fine new indoor pool." (*Maureen and Pat Campbell, REE*)

Open All year, except mid-Oct–mid-Dec.
Rooms 3 suites, 40 double, 4 single.
Facilities Bar, 2 dining rooms; indoor swimming pool; terrace. Large grounds on lake.
Location 5 km E of Lienz.
Credit cards None accepted.
Terms [1996] B&B 580–1,200 Sch; D,B&B 680–1,330 Sch. Set meals 200–640 Sch; full alc 500 Sch.

MILLSTATT AM SEE 9872 Kärnten — Map 16

Hotel Nikolasch BUDGET — *Tel* (04766) 20 41
Kaiser-Frank-Josefstrasse 74 — *Fax* (04766) 20 41-13

In resort on pretty Carinthian lake, modern hotel near water's edge, family-run and friendly. 30 rooms, most with balcony and lake views, all with shower. Terrace, private grassy bathing lido, surfing, kayaks, etc. Good local dishes; dancing, parties in season. Open 1 May–20 Oct, 20 Dec–10 Feb. Credit cards not accepted. B&B double 640–1,260 Sch; D,B&B 420–730 Sch per person. Set meals 95–275 Sch [1996].

****

Traveller's tale Charm is no substitute for standards, and there was nothing charming about being told at one hotel that there was no cold milk for my tea "at the moment", so I would have to have warm milk.

****

OBERALM BEI HALLEIN 5411 Salzburg — Map 16

Schloss Haunsperg NEW — *Tel* (06245) 80 662
Hammerstrasse 32 — *Fax* (06245) 85 680

Here is another example of a stately home transformed into a small hotel by its ancestral owners. It is a fine creeper-covered 14th-century manor in its own park, south of Salzburg. "Most comfortable and lovely, full of family antiques," say nominators. "The von Gerneths, husband and wife, live in the house and make your stay special. They sit and offer wine or something, and talk with every guest. Rooms and suites are large." There are elegant period furnishings, a baroque chapel, and a large music room with a grand piano and quite a history (Herr von Gerneth's great-grandfather wrote the words for *The Blue Danube*). No restaurant: several nearby. (*Karen Pasold and Sheila Bielich*) Fuller reports welcome.

Open All year.
Rooms 5 suites, 3 double, 1 single.
Facilities Lounges, breakfast room. Garden: tennis.
Location 15 km S of Salzburg, 3 km N of Hallein. Take *Autobahn* A8 exit 16 (Hallein). Parking.
Credit cards All major cards accepted.
Terms B&B: single 850–1,050 Sch, double 1,530–2,100 Sch, suite 1,890–2,500 Sch.

ST-WOLFGANG 5360 Oberösterreich — Map 16

Hotel Peter — *Tel* (06138) 2304
Fax (06138) 23044

In the same picturesque resort east of Salzburg as the much-sung *White Horse Inn* (now large and touristy) is this other hotel, smaller and simpler, rebuilt after a fire in 1993. A handsome chalet set above the lake, it has a folksy interior and is well run by the Elser family. "The rooms are beautifully furnished in wood, with balconies facing the Wolfgangsee and the mountains. The good and varied choice of food is served either on the terrace or in the lovely restaurant, both of which face the lake. The bar has evening entertainment. In the morning Frau Elser sits in the elegant lounge in Austrian costume. All the staff were very friendly." (*REE*)

Open Apr–Oct, Dec–Feb.
Rooms 6 suites, 14 double. Some no-smoking.
Facilities Lift. Lounge, bar, breakfast room, restaurant; coffee shop; disco; terrace. Lake nearby: beach, swimming.
Location At entrance to town, which is 50 km E of Salzburg. Parking.
Credit cards All major cards accepted.
Terms [1996] B&B 580–840 Sch; D,B&B 740–1,000 Sch. Set meals 60–250 Sch; full alc 300 Sch.

> The "Budget" label by a hotel's name indicates an establishment where dinner, bed and breakfast is offered at around £50 (or its foreign currency equivalent) per person, or B&B for about £30 and an evening meal for about £20. These are only rough guides and do not always apply to single accommodation; nor do they necessarily apply in high season.

SALZBURG Map 16

Hotel Altstadt Radisson Tel (0662) 84 85 71-0
Rudolfskai 28/Judengasse 15 Fax (0662) 84 85 71-6/8
5020 Salzburg

In the traffic-free heart of the old city, a pink-fronted 14th-century coaching inn, newly converted; rooms have views of the river, or of the cathedral and castle. Recent impressions: "It has genuine period charm and cosy elegance. In the rather pricey *Symphonie* restaurant, facing the river, service was attentive. We were warmly welcomed, and our top-floor room was quiet, spacious and sweet-smelling." "Expensive, but of high quality. It is part of a transatlantic chain, but has not lost its Austrian style. Large well-equipped bedrooms, friendly service, wide choice at buffet breakfast, good cuisine." Some rooms have old exposed beams, but the atrium is glass-roofed in modern style. (*JW*) The one-way traffic system can be "a nightmare".

Open All year.
Rooms 19 suites, 41 double. Some no-smoking.
Facilities Lift. Bar, restaurant.
Location Central. Car access for unloading; parking service.
Credit cards All major cards accepted.
Terms B&B: single 1,800–3,900 Sch, double 2,600–6,400 Sch, suite 4,900–9,600 Sch. Set lunch 420 Sch, dinner 570 Sch; full alc 570 Sch.

Hotel Elefant Tel (0662) 84 33 97
Sigmund-Haffnergasse 4 Fax (0662) 84 01 09-28
5020 Salzburg

A typical Salzburg town house on a quiet street in the city's historic heart. An inn for 400 years, and recently renovated, it has again been admired in 1995–96: "A fantastic location. Our rooms were quite small, but adequately furnished. The dining rooms were understaffed, but the food was delicious; breakfasts, served in a pretty room, were plentiful." "Everyone was cheerful and friendly." Some others have been less enthusiastic about the food, and have found the breakfast room gloomy, while bedroom upkeep may have small lapses. The staircase is "a bit of an art gallery, with pictures, prints, statuary"; "lots of newspapers in the beautifully decorated lounges". The area is a pedestrian zone, but you can drive up to load or unload. (*Kathy Gaston, C and S McFie, HG*)

Open All year. Restaurant closed Tues.
Rooms 1 suite, 23 double, 12 single. Some on ground floor.
Facilities Lift. Lounge, TV room, bar, 3 dining rooms; conference facilities.
Location Central. Municipal parking 5 mins' walk.
Credit cards All major cards accepted.
Terms [1996] B&B: single 800–950 Sch, double 1,250–1,850 Sch, suite 1,800–1,900 Sch. Full alc 300 Sch.

Hotel Kasererbräu Tel (0662) 84 24 45
Kaigasse 33 Fax (0662) 84 24 45-51
5020 Salzburg

This 14th-century building near the cathedral is now quite a smart hotel, with a flower-filled inner courtyard and heavily ornate furnishings, either in Biedermeier style or more modern. "A light and airy hotel, with good breakfasts in a nice room," says a visitor this year. Another, who had "a room with pine twin beds and matching wardrobe", adds: "We were asked to light the candles on the Christmas tree in the lobby." The bathrooms are up-to-date and the health centre is efficient. Staff are fairly friendly, "but not exactly effusive". (*Mr and Mrs M Strong, and others*) No restaurant, but readers have eaten well in the *trattoria* downstairs.

Open All year, except 3 Feb–7 Mar.
Rooms 5 suites, 32 double, 6 single.
Facilities Lift. Lounges, TV room, bar; sauna, steam bath, solarium. Unsuitable for ♿.
Location Central, in pedestrian zone. Garage.
Credit cards All major cards accepted.
Terms B&B: single 800–1,210 Sch, double 1,200–2,400 Sch, suite 1,850–2,900 Sch.

SCHRUNS 6780 Vorarlberg — Map 16

Hotel Krone BUDGET

Tel (05556) 72 255
Fax (05556) 74 879

"An excellent small hotel, with personal friendly service and a comfortable room reached by stairs, which helped digest the generous helpings of our half-board dinner." So runs this year's new praise for the Mayer family's very *gemütlich* hostelry, all wood panelling and chintzy curtains. It is near the centre of a pleasant market town in the Montafon valley. An earlier view: "It has character. Herr Mayer supervises the kitchen and the food is good. We took half board, and were not even charged extra when we ate *à la carte* some evenings. There are tables for eating outdoors, but no garden." Rooms are smallish but comfortable. (*Col. TE Huggan*)

Open All year, except mid-Oct–23 Dec, 30 Mar–18 May. Restaurant closed Thurs.
Rooms 8 double, 1 single.
Facilities Lounge, 2 dining rooms; terrace. Unsuitable for ♿.
Location 12 km SE of Bludenz. Central, near Kronen bridge. Parking.
Credit card Diners.
Terms [1996] B&B 350–460 Sch; D,B&B 520–630 Sch. Set meals 160–250 Sch; full alc 280 Sch.

SEEHAM 5164 Salzburg — Map 16

Hotel Walkner BUDGET

Tel (06217) 55 50 and 52 50
Fax (06217) 55 50-22

The Walkner-Haberl family's ever-popular hotel has a quiet pastoral setting on a hill above a lake, amid splendid scenery north of Salzburg. It is modern, but with "delightfully restored antique furnishings" in the public rooms. "A quiet rural gem," said a reader this year. "Our large room had a balcony with a pretty view of the lake. The *en pension* meals were interesting and good. Immaculate grounds." Others have praised the "enthusiastic staff and bright new decor". "We had meals on the sunny terrace facing the lake – well-presented Austrian fare." "The owners are charming." Bedrooms and bathrooms are modern; all have a balcony. The pleasant garden has a swimming pool, a sandpit, and games for children: "They are all within view of the dining patio, so the kids could play while the grown-ups lingered over their meal." (*Melissa McDaniel, AML, and others*)

Open All year, except 23–26 Dec.
Rooms 17 double, 5 single.
Facilities Lounge, bar, billiard room, restaurant/café; conference room; sauna, solarium, fitness room; terrace. Garden: swimming pool, children's playground. Unsuitable for ♿.
Location 20 km N of Salzburg, on Mattighofen road.
Credit cards Access, Amex, Visa.
Terms B&B: single 330–665 Sch, double 660–1,330 Sch; D,B&B 470–805 Sch per person. Set meals 150 Sch; full alc 310 Sch.

SEMMERING 2680 Niederösterreich — Map 16

Panoramahotel Wagner — *Tel* (02664) 25 12-0
Hochstrasse 267 — *Fax* (02664) 25 12-61

Set on a panoramic peak, on the edge of a once-fashionable mountain resort 90 km SW of Vienna, a charming traditional inn very well run by "charming" Wagner family. 26 pretty rooms, good bathrooms; some have large balcony with views. Excellent varied food; library, sauna, café-terrace, garden; guests can swim at larger hotel nearby. Open 20 Dec–1 Apr, 5 May–26 Oct. Restaurant closed Wed/Thurs. No credit cards. D,B&B double 1,670–1,870 Sch. Endorsed this year, but fuller reports welcome.

STEYR 4400 Oberösterreich — Map 16

Hotel Mader BUDGET — *Tel* (07252) 533 58-0
Stadtplatz 36 — *Fax* (07252) 533 50-6
E-mail hotel.mader@magnet.at

This old industrial town south of Linz has a beautiful market square. Here stands the Mader family's graceful hotel, made up of three 17th-century houses, one of them an inn since 1694. "An attractive town, and the best small hotel I've used in ten years," runs a recent report. "Rooms are large, tastefully done, and quiet; staff are courteous; breakfast buffet was above average." (*CB*) Dining is in a 400-year-old vaulted wine-cellar, or in the courtyard in summer; we'd be glad of reports on the food.

Open All year, except 24–26 Dec. Restaurant closed Sun, public holidays.
Rooms 2 suites, 38 double, 19 single. 10 no-smoking.
Facilities Lounge, TV room, bar, restaurant; wine cellar; courtyard. Garden. Unsuitable for ♿.
Location Follow "Zentrum" signs, then hotel signs. Garage (80 Sch).
Credit cards All major cards accepted.
Terms Rooms: single 675 Sch, double 830 Sch, suite 1,070 Sch. Breakfast 95 Sch. D,B&B 735–980 Sch per person. Alc meals 250–300 Sch. Reduced rates for children.

Romantik Hotel Minichmayr — *Tel* (07252) 53 410
Haratzmüllerstrasse 1–3 — *Fax* (07252) 48 20 255

In industrial town with fine medieval quarter, 25 km SE of Linz, a stylish traditional hostelry at point where rivers Steyr and Ems meet. Pleasant views of city from dining and breakfast rooms and some bedrooms. Good nouvelle-*ish cooking, rustic panelled* Stube. *Sauna, fitness room. All major credit cards accepted. 50 rooms. B&B 490–1,260 Sch, half board 645–1,415 Sch [1996]. Admired recently ("a beautiful room and view, terrific food"), but fuller reports welcome.*

VIENNA — Map 16

Hotel Amadeus — *Tel* (01) 533 87 38
Wildpretmarkt 5, 1010 Wien — *Fax* (01) 533 87 38-38

Opera people enjoy this small modern B&B hotel in a pleasant side street near St Stephan's. It is outwardly no beauty but full of other virtues, such as "a charming, correct staff" and reasonable prices for so central a location. Recent reports: "Excellent breakfast, with real orange juice." "Very friendly." "Flowers everywhere, fine prints on the walls; crystal chandeliers, rich red rugs and a red-and-white decor." Rooms vary in size. Noise levels seem to vary too, from "quiet at night" to "sounds of street traffic". Public rooms have been refurbished, but some readers have judged the red-and-white decor "pseudo-elegant". One nice touch: a stand full of umbrellas for rainy weather. Newer reports much needed.

Open All year, except Christmas.
Rooms 22 double, 8 single.
Facilities Breakfast room. Unsuitable for ♿.
Location Central, down small turning off Tuchlauben. Public garage 5 mins' walk.
Credit cards All major cards accepted.
Terms B&B: single 960–1,500 Sch, double 1,660–1,950 Sch.

Hotel Kaiserin Elisabeth — *Tel* (01) 51 52 60
Weihburggasse 3 — *Fax* (01) 51 52 67
1010 Wien

"A delightful stay"; "we were most impressed" – praise for this discreetly stylish old hotel where Liszt and Wagner stayed. It is in a historic building down a side street near St Stephan's cathedral. Its smart hall and lounge are lit by chandeliers. "There are wonderful staircases, salon-sized bedrooms, and huge bathrooms. The public rooms are effortlessly patrician – perfect for Vienna, whose charm depends on imaginative recreation of more elegant times." "Our rooms were large and well lit, with polished wood floors and rugs. Buffet breakfast was as good as ever." No restaurant, but light snacks are offered all day. (*A and BW, LT and JF*) Rooms on the third and fourth floors now have air-conditioning. Some single rooms are small and a bit drab. And some front rooms can suffer from noise from pedestrians and early deliveries.

Open All year.
Rooms 3 suites, 44 double, 16 single. Air-conditioning.
Facilities Lift. Lobby with bar, lounge. Garage parking service.
Location Central, in pedestrian zone near cathedral. Parking in nearby garage (cash only).
Credit cards All major cards accepted.
Terms B&B: single 1,450–1,550 Sch, double 2,100–2,500 Sch, suite 2,800 Sch. 3 nights for price of 2 31 Oct–24 Mar.

Hotel König von Ungarn
Schulerstrasse 10
1010 Wien

Tel (01) 515 84-0
Fax (01) 515 84-8

"Difficult to fault – a haven of tranquillity and charm": so runs praise again this year for this friendly *King of Hungary*, liked by most visitors but not all. It inhabits a 16th-century building near St Stephan's cathedral, in the heart of old Vienna. Finely restored, it is now "a very romantic Art Nouveau-decorated hotel", with "the feeling of an exclusive club". Its glass-domed courtyard serves as a "charming" bar-cum-lounge. The bedrooms, with walls painted deep rich reds, terracottas and pinks, lie off galleried halls around the courtyard. "Our large room was opulently rustic – antique pine furniture, a huge crystal chandelier." "A quite good breakfast served in an elegant room." The fashionable restaurant, under separate ownership, is good but expensive. (*Jon Hughes, Mrs H Langenburg, Karen Pasold and Sheila Bielich*) Some visitors have found the front desk arrogant; others, however, think them "formal, polite, crisply efficient", and the Hungarian bartender is said to be "truly charming". One visitor thought her room poky, and criticised both food and service. More reports, please.

Open All year. Restaurant closed Sat.
Rooms 8 suites, 21 double, 4 single.
Facilities Lift, ramps. Lounge, bar, restaurant (under separate ownership); conference room; courtyard.
Location Central; near St Stephan's cathedral, in maze of 1-way streets.
Credit cards All major cards accepted.
Terms B&B: single 1,550 Sch, double 1,850–2,200 Sch, suite from 2,600 Sch. Set lunch 350 Sch, dinner 500 Sch; full alc 600 Sch.

Hotel Nestroy NEW
Rotensterngasse 12
1020 Wien

Tel (01) 21 14 00
Fax (01) 21 14 07

In quiet street, B&B in affluent private mansion, well modernised. Handy for airport and motorways; 15 mins' walk from centre. Spectacular indoor garden: tall trees, balustrades, statues. Terrace with city views. Spacious, immaculate bedrooms; splendid bathrooms. Excellent buffet breakfast – huge choice. Charming staff. Garage. Business facilities. 62 rooms. B&B: single 1,350–1,750 Sch, double 1,700–2,400 Sch [1996].

Pension Nossek
Graben 17
1010 Wien

Tel (01) 533 70 41-0
Fax (01) 535 36 46

The fashionable Graben is a traffic-free street, very central. Here, this much-liked *pension* inhabits the three high-ceilinged top floors of an office building. Old in style but newly renovated, it is run by two sisters and their father, Dr Renato Cremona, whose family have owned it since 1914. "If anything better than before," writes one devoted regular. Other views: "The family supply enormous bunches of fresh flowers from their garden. Our big elegant room had a tiny balcony. The good breakfast sometimes included delicious black plum jam." Though most rooms are large, some back ones are small and a bit airless, and one has been described as "spartan but very adequate". (*ULP and others)* Bedside lighting is criticised. Double-glazing cuts out most street noise.

Open All year.
Rooms 3 suites, 18 double, 5 single.
Facilities Lift. TV room, breakfast room. Unsuitable for ♿.
Location Central, but quiet; on corner of Habsburgergasse. Underground carpark 1 min's walk.
Credit cards None accepted.
Terms B&B: single 500–800 Sch, double 1,100 Sch, suite 1,500 Sch.

Pension Pertschy *Tel* (01) 53 449-0
Habsburgergasse 5 *Fax* (01) 53 449-49
1010 Wien

Central, near Graben, this soigné *pension* inhabits the three upper floors of an old palace, built round a courtyard. Two more plaudits in 1995–96: "We had a spacious room with sofa, good bedlights, decent-sized bathroom. Generous breakfast, friendly and obliging service." "Excellent. Good breakfast buffet." Last year's view: "Our family room was big as a ballroom. Rooms are furnished in opulent style: huge armchairs, chandeliers. Coffee at any time." (*HR, R Townend, AML*) Rooms facing the street or pedestrian alley may suffer some noise; quietest rooms face the courtyard, but have no sunlight. No restaurant: lots nearby.

Open All year.
Rooms 41 double, 6 single. Some on ground floor.
Facilities Lift. Lounge, breakfast room; courtyard.
Location Central.
Credit cards Access, Diners, Visa.
Terms Rooms: single 680–740 Sch, double 980–1,280 Sch, suite 1,160–1,280 Sch. Breakfast 85 Sch. Children under 3 free.

Hotel Römischer Kaiser *Tel* (01) 512 77 51
Annagasse 16 *Fax* (01) 512 77 51-13
1010 Wien

Near opera house and cathedral, small, personal and fairly luxurious B&B hotel, built in 1684 as palace of imperial chancellor. Period furnishings. Helpful staff, good buffet breakfasts, coffee shop, pavement café. 24 rooms, back ones quietest; air-conditioning. Parking nearby. All major credit cards accepted. B&B: single 1,590–2,200 Sch, double 2,000–3,050 Sch. Endorsed this year, but fuller reports welcome.

ZELL AM SEE 5700 Salzburg — Map 16

Landhotel Erlhof *Tel* (06542) 566 37
Erlhofweg 11 *Fax* (06542) 566 37 63

Standing alone on the Zellersee, in a lyrically beautiful position facing the ring of mountains and the blue water, and backed by lovely trees, is this chalet hotel, handsome and much restored. "It is on the quieter south side of the lake, well away from the noise and dirt of Zell. Bedrooms are well furnished. Some face the lake or have a balcony, others have views of meadows and woods. The restaurant, using local produce, is popular with locals; we enjoyed eating on its terrace, and at breakfast we liked the gadget for boiling your egg. The owner, Dr Michael Piech, trained in England. The hotel has a garden and tennis courts, and its own lake frontage for bathing and boats." (*REE*)

Open All year, except 18 Mar–2 Apr, end Oct–early Dec. Restaurant closed Wed.
Rooms 8 suites, 8 double, 1 single.
Facilities Lift. Lounges, bar, restaurant; conference room; sauna, solarium, fitness room. Garden: tennis, children's playground. Swimming, sailing, surfing in lake (private beach).
Location 2 km S of Zell am See. Parking.
Credit cards All major cards accepted.
Terms B&B: single 550–650 Sch, double 960–1100 Sch, suite 1740–1860 Sch; D,B&B 730–1180 Sch per person. Set lunch 280 Sch, dinner 480 Sch; full alc 420 Sch.

Belgium

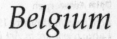

Château d'Hassonville, Marche-en-Famenne

AARTSELAAR 2630 Antwerpen — Map 9

Hotel Kasteel Solhof — *Tel* (03) 877 30 00
Baron Van Ertbornstraat 116 — *Fax* (03) 877 31 31

This "excellent" hotel is in a 14th-century castle just outside Antwerp, set in a lovely mature park surrounded by canal. "We had a lovely room, good breakfasts, and staff were helpful," says one visitor this year, although another thought the place functional, without warmth. "Idyllic, almost rural, setting, serene view, courteous staff," was an earlier verdict. Decor is luxurious but unfussy. (*Lisa and Peter Simon*) No meals: several restaurants about a kilometre away.

Open All year, except Christmas/New Year.
Rooms 24 double.
Facilities Lift. Lounge, breakfast room; conference room. Garden.
Location 10 km S of Antwerp, off A12. Parking.
Credit cards All major cards accepted.
Terms [1996] B&B: single 5,250–8,450 Bfrs, double 6,200–8,900 Bfrs.

ANTWERP Map 9

Firean Hotel
Karel Oomsstraat 6
2018 Antwerpen

Tel (03) 237 02 60
Fax (03) 238 11 68

B&B hotel in attractive 1920s building 2 km S of city centre, near S ringway. Public rooms are in Art Deco style; bedrooms have antique and repro furniture, fresh flowers, and are well equipped (trouser-press, etc). Generous breakfasts, on patio in fine weather. Garage. Closed 28 July–18 Aug, 24 Dec–early Jan. All major credit cards accepted. 15 rooms (some in annexe). B&B: single 4,000–4,600 Bfrs, double 4,950–5,900 Bfrs.

Hotel De Rosier
Rosier 23
2000 Antwerpen

Tel (03) 225 01 40
Fax (03) 231 41 11

"A beautiful hotel! Down a side street ten minutes' walk from the historic centre, it is a 17th-century mansion full of antiques, sumptuous yet not overpowering. They have even managed to incorporate a swimming pool into the historic structure. Our enormous high-ceilinged room overlooked a private garden, and we had a delicious breakfast on the terrace. Service was as impeccable as you'd expect at those prices." No main meals, but "cosy five-o'clocks".

Open All year, except Christmas/New Year.
Rooms 4 suites, 9 double.
Facilities Lift. Lounges, breakfast room; indoor swimming pool; terrace. Garden.
Location 800 m S of centre. Street parking.
Credit cards All major cards accepted.
Terms B&B: single 7,500 Bfrs, double 10,000 Bfrs, suite 12,000–25,000 Bfrs. High tea 750 Bfrs.

BRUGES West-Vlaanderen Map 9

Hotel Adornes
St Annarei 26
8000 Brugge

Tel (050) 34 13 36
Fax (050) 34 20 85

"Delightful," say visitors this year to the Standaert family's B&B beside a canal bridge. It consists of three adjacent picturesque 17th-century houses, well modernised without loss of character (polished wood floors and exposed beams). "Our lovely room had three windows facing the canals, and a beautiful white-tiled bathroom. The owners and staff were alert and charming, and gave us free coffee and biscuits. The buffet breakfast was copious: muesli, stewed fruits, lashings of good coffee, etc." Others have admired the cheerful if sometimes rather small rooms, elegant furnishings, and "lovely" breakfasts served in "a bright beamed room with candles, flowers and a fire in the hearth". "The top-floor rooms have oak roof-trusses, interestingly lit; ours had comfortable furniture in simple modern style." (*David and Margot Holbrook, Carole Hooper, Melissa McDaniel, and others*) Bicycles are available free, and in low season visitors staying two or more nights get a free ticket for the city's museums.

Open All year, except 1 Jan–14 Feb.
Rooms 20 double. 1 on ground floor.
Facilities Lift, ramps. 2 lounges, breakfast room (no-smoking). Bicycles available.
Location Fairly central. From ring road enter town via Dampoort; follow canal towards centre; hotel signposted. Private parking.
Credit cards Access, Amex, Visa.
Terms [1996] B&B: single 2,600–3,400 Bfrs, double 2,800–3,600 Bfrs.

Hotel Anselmus *Tel* (050) 34 13 74
Ridderstraat 15 *Fax* (050) 34 19 16
8000 Brugge

Liked again this year, this "excellent" B&B is owned and run by the friendly Dutoit-Schoore family. Set in a quiet street in the old town, it is in a handsome old gabled house with a massive wooden door, and has been skilfully and elegantly converted. It is named after an eminent humanist of Bruges who lived here and who may have been a contemporary of Erasmus. One recent guest had a "delightful" room with smart modern decor, and enjoyed the "huge breakfast and lovely copper coffee pots". The owners are "helpful and gracious", rooms may be "small, but are warmly furnished", and the breakfast room facing the garden is charming. (*D Bewley, Antony TR Fletcher, FD*) As in many such houses, the main stairs are steep and narrow.

Open All year, except Jan.
Rooms 1 suite, 8 double, 1 single. 2 on ground floor.
Facilities Hall, lounges, breakfast room.
Location 5 mins' walk from Markt. Garage; safe street parking.
Credit cards Access, Amex, Visa.
Terms B&B: single 2,500–2,800 Bfrs, double 2,900–3,500 Bfrs, suite 4,500–4,900 Bfrs.

Hotel Aragon *Tel* (050) 33 35 33
Naaldenstraat 24 *Fax* (050) 34 28 05
8000 Brugge

A small and neat B&B in a quiet street near the Markt, with a little garden. Owned and run by Luc and Hedwig Van Laere-Wulleman, "an interesting and charming couple", it has been liked again this year: "Peaceful and hospitable"; "how nice to find a well-lit hotel room"; "elegant taste". Rooms are smallish but comfortable, and breakfasts are admired. Tea, coffee and biscuits are provided free from noon to 6 pm. (*David Crowe, AJE Brennan, David Sebag-Montefiore, and others*) Credit cards are accepted: but a reader this year found a notice at reception discouraging them. The nearby, reasonably priced *St Joris* restaurant is admired – "excellent waterzooi".

Open All year, except Jan–mid-Feb.
Rooms 3 suites (1, with kitchenette, in adjacent annexe), 12 double, 3 single. 3 no-smoking.
Facilities Lounge, breakfast room, TV room. Small garden. Unsuitable for ♿.
Location Central (windows triple-glazed). Leave ring road via Ezelpoort; follow signs to Biekorf underground carpark. Hotel next door.
Restriction No smoking: breakfast room, 2 bedrooms.
Credit cards All major cards accepted.
Terms B&B: single 2,250–2,750 Bfrs, double 3,250–4,250 Bfrs, suite 4,200–5,500 Bfrs. 1-night bookings refused Sat in season.

Hotel Botaniek BUDGET *Tel* (050) 34 14 24
Waalsestraat 23 *Fax* (050) 34 59 39
8000 Brugge

Inexpensive for Bruges, yet central, a well-converted 18th-century mansion in quiet street. Pleasant young owners; 9 good bedrooms with modern furniture; buffet breakfast. No smoking in breakfast room. All major credit cards accepted. B&B: single 1,900–2,500 Bfrs, double 2,300–2,600 Bfrs. No restaurant. Special breaks. At Freren Fonteinstraat close by is Hotel Jan Brito, *which opened recently under the same management. We'd be glad of reports on that too* – tel *(050) 33 06 01.*

Hotel Bryghia *Tel* (050) 33 80 59
Oosterlingenplein 4 *Fax* (050) 34 14 30
8000 Brugge

Bruges, so accessible from Calais, has more hotels in the *Guide* than almost any other town on the Continent, bar Paris. One of the most typical is the Cools family's 15th-century merchant's house in a quiet location, still admired: "Delightful: helpful, friendly service, and quite a copious breakfast buffet." Some rooms overlook a square, others a canal. The decor is "beautiful", and the breakfast is served in a pleasant beamed room. "Our bedroom was small but pretty. Marvellous warm light from special bulbs." (*FD, MRF*)

Open All year, except 2 Jan–16 Feb.
Rooms 18 double.
Facilities Lift. Lounge/bar, breakfast room (no-smoking).
Location Central. Garage (250 Bfrs); open parking (200 Bfrs).
Credit cards All major cards accepted.
Terms B&B double 3,950–4,800 Bfrs. Children under 2 accommodated free in parents' room.

Oud-huis Amsterdam *Tel* (050) 34 18 10
Spiegelrei 3 *Fax* (050) 33 88 91
8000 Brugge

The Traen family's "old house" is a well-restored 17th-century mansion, centrally located, by a canal. It has a "club-like ambience", and recent visitors have been delighted: "Lovely decor and period furniture, a management and staff who run the job beautifully." "Expensive, but worth it. Our large attic room was beamed, with circular windows facing the canal. The sitting room is also lovely, with expensive fabrics and an air of elegant comfort. The garden with its shrubs and creepers is a lovely setting for a drink." No recent reports; more welcome.

Open All year.
Rooms 2 suites, 23 double. 2 on ground floor.
Facilities Lift. Lounge, bar, breakfast room; meeting room; terrace.
Location Central. Garage (300 Bfrs).
Credit cards All major cards accepted.
Terms B&B: single 3,900–5,500 Bfrs, double 4,750–6,250 Bfrs, suite 7,000–7,500 Bfrs. Children under 12 accommodated free in parents' room.

De Snippe *Tel* (050) 33 70 70
Nieuwe Gentweg 53 *Fax* (050) 33 76 62
8000 Brugge

"Sophisticated and stylish" (Relais & Châteaux), Luc and Francine Huysentruyt's restaurant-with-rooms is in an 18th-century house down a quiet side-street. It has been elegantly converted, using modern furniture but without spoiling the old interior. And it wins a *Michelin* star and two *Gault Millau toques* for such dishes as courgettes stuffed with frogs' legs. Again in 1995–96, readers have been delighted. "We enjoyed virtually everything. The beautiful bar and restaurant have original paintings, our large room was tastefully decorated. The staff could not have been nicer, and our meals were exceptional, but not cheap. Breakfast included Belgian waffles, wonderful rolls." "A superb menu. The glass-sided dining room extension made for wonderful summer dining." "Lovely linen and glasses." Behind is a pretty garden under big trees, and a small outdoor terrace for drinks; the lounge/conservatory is full of plants and rattan furniture. The 18th-century murals and wall-coverings of embossed gold leather are admired. (*Robert Freidus, N and M Whalley, and others*)

Open All year, except mid-Feb–mid-Mar, 1 week Nov, Sun Nov–Apr. Restaurant closed Sun/midday Mon.
Rooms 4 suites, 5 double.
Facilities Lift. Lounge, bar, restaurant; terrace. Small garden.
Location Central. Private parking.
Credit cards All major cards accepted.
Terms B&B: single 4,500 Bfrs, double 5,000 Bfrs, suite 6,000–7,000 Bfrs. Set lunch 1,500 Bfrs, dinner 2,500 Bfrs; full alc 3,000 Bfrs.

Die Swaene *Tel* (050) 34 27 98
Steenhouwersdijk 1 *Fax* (050) 33 66 74
8000 Brugge

The Hessels family's 15th-century house on a quiet canal remains admired by nearly all visitors. "Friendly service, excellent breakfasts, dinner superb," was one recent comment. It is an expensive, very *soigné* hotel, described as "full of gilt, red velvet, dark colours and copies of great masters, all somehow combining to create an impression of Flemish elegance" – its "splendid" lounge, with open fire and painted ceiling, was once the meeting room of the Guild of Tailors. Some rooms have a garden patio or an antique canopy bed. "Very friendly reception staff. Our pretty room overlooked a small garden. We dined in the 'winter garden', which was light and pretty; the main restaurant was a bit dark, but had atmosphere. Food was good, notably fish." "Splendidly elegant, with attentive service." Buffet breakfast. (*B and EH, and others*)

Open All year.
Rooms 3 suites, 17 double, 2 single. 4 on ground floor.
Facilities 2 lifts, ramps. Lobby, lounge, bar, breakfast room (no-smoking), restaurant; indoor swimming pool, sauna; terrace. Garden.
Location Central (but quiet); signposted from market square. Garage.
Credit cards All major cards accepted.
Terms B&B: single 4,500 Bfrs, double 5,500–6,800 Bfrs, suite 8,950–10,950 Bfrs. Set lunch 1,050 Bfrs, dinner 1,850–2,550 Bfrs; full alc from 2,500 Bfrs.

Hotel Ter Duinen
Langerei 52
8000 Brugge

Tel (050) 33 04 37
Fax (050) 34 42 16
E-mail terduinen@unicall.be

"A delightful spot." "Our fourth visit. We didn't think things could get better, but they have." "They have refurbished, and the new sound-proofing works wonders. The buffet breakfasts are substantial and delicious." "From our room with a balcony we enjoyed the moonlight over the canal." This trim white house, an old *Guide* favourite, is run by the "charming" Bossu-Van den Heuvels, and is not too expensive. Most rooms are a decent size, furnished with subtle fabrics and period pieces, with "flowers everywhere". (*Oliver and Delia Millar, B James, GE Samson, and others*)

Open All year, except Jan.
Rooms 20 double. 10 with air-conditioning.
Facilities Lift. Lounge/bar with TV, breakfast room (no-smoking). Unsuitable for ♿.
Location On canal 10–15 mins' walk from centre (double-glazing). Street parking; garage available (250 Bfrs).
Credit cards All major cards accepted.
Terms B&B: single 2,400–3,750 Bfrs, double 2,800–3,950 Bfrs.

BRUSSELS

Map 9

Hôtel L'Agenda BUDGET
6 rue de Florence
1050 Bruxelles

Tel (02) 539 00 31
Fax (02) 539 00 63

This small modern B&B hotel, quietly situated off the Avenue Louise, is remarkable value for expensive Brussels. A new owner, Amir Siwji, took over in July 1995: visitors since then have found it still good, and the staff friendly and efficient. All rooms have a kitchenette – "an amazing bonus" – and are decent-sized (even the singles), if simple. There are fresh rolls for breakfast "and real jam in bowls". (*Hillary de Ste Croix, and others*) Restaurant *Le Chou de Bruxelles* nearby is recommended.

Open All year.
Rooms 3 suites, 28 double, 7 single. 1 on ground floor.
Facilities Lounge, breakfast room. Small garden.
Location 700 m S of Place Louise. Garage.
Credit cards All major cards accepted.
Terms Rooms: single 2,500–3,300 Bfrs, double 2,800–3,600 Bfrs, suite 3,100–4,100 Bfrs. Breakfast 300 Bfrs. Reductions for children under 12. Christmas, Easter, summer breaks.

Hotel Rembrandt BUDGET
42 rue de la Concorde
1050 Bruxelles

Tel (02) 512 71 39
Fax (02) 511 71 36

Well placed for visiting the sites, and remarkable value for Brussels, Madame Grasset's small *pension* is a 19th-century building down a quiet, nondescript street off the Avenue Louise. It is full of Belgian character, decorated in period style and hung with reproductions of old-master paintings; many of them are framed jigsaw puzzles. Latest visitors were pleased with their large, quiet bedroom, "with ancient cabinet record player, sofa, and fine fireplace". "The attractive sitting room/reception is separated from the breakfast area by a splendid dresser. Breakfast is routine continental." "Friendly, if uneffusive welcome." (*CR, and others*) Some rooms now have TV.

Open All year, except 3 weeks Aug, Christmas/New Year.
Rooms 1 suite, 11 double, 1 single.
Facilities Lift. Sitting room, breakfast room (no-smoking).
Location Fairly central, off Ave Louise, near Pl Stéphanie.
Credit cards All major cards accepted.
Terms [1996] B&B: single 1,400 Bfrs, double 2,000 Bfrs, suite 2,300 Bfrs.

Hotel Welcome BUDGET *Tel* (02) 219 95 46
23 quai au Bois à Brûler *Fax* (02) 217 18 87
1000 Bruxelles

Quite central, on a canal near the fish market, this tiny, modest hotel has two recent admirers. "How rare to find an intimate hotel in the midst of a big city. Its six rooms are at once well equipped and reassuringly old-fashioned. Ours had a writing desk, comfortable armchairs. Breakfast came with fresh orange juice and sliced meats, in a bright tiled room that serves also as a neighbourhood café." "It's a quiet hotel, family run. We were served by the charming old father, whose welcome justifies the hotel's name." The family also own the *Truite d'Argent*, a reputed but more expensive restaurant in the same building. (*MH, MR*) Refurbishment is due in 1997, with the creation of four more rooms, say the owners.

Open All year.
Rooms 6 (10 in 1997).
Facilities Café/breakfast room.
Location Close to fish market. Free private parking.
Credit cards All major cards accepted.
Terms [1996] Rooms 2,200–3,000 Bfrs. Breakfast 250–350 Bfrs.

DURBUY 6940 Luxembourg Belge Map 9

Le Sanglier des Ardennes *Tel* (086) 21 32 62 and 21 10 88
Rue Comte Théodule d'Ursel 99 *Fax* (086) 21 24 65

Set amid pretty woodlands in the Ourthe valley, Durbuy is "a delightful grey stone village dating from the 1300s". Here four small hotels, the *Sanglier, Cardinal, Alexandre* and *Vieux Durbuy,* are run jointly, under the same ownership (Maurice Caerdinael). The *Sanglier* serves as restaurant for all four: two *Gault Millau toques* for sophisticated cooking, eg, rouget with wild mushrooms. "A super room at the *Cardinal*, and a good dinner once a busy *maître d'* had gracelessly moved us away from the *very worst* table." That report this year follows earlier accounts: "A delightful stay, with a friendly multinational staff. Some rooms can be a little poky, but mine, in a villa down the road, had a lounge, dining area and kitchen. Throughout, furniture is antique." Some rooms have views of the river and medieval castle. The cellar wine museum has 30,000 bottles, some over 100 years old. (*Mr and Mrs DA Lewis*) There are meeting and banqueting rooms geared to the conference trade.

Open All year. Restaurant closed Thurs, Jan.
Rooms 11 suites, 34 double. Some on ground floor.

Facilities Salon, 2 bars, 4 dining rooms (1 no-smoking); conference facilities; riverside terrace.
Location Central. 45 km SW of Liège. Parking.
Credit cards All major cards accepted.
Terms Rooms 2,800–4,700 Bfrs, suite 5,000–7,500 Bfrs. Breakfast 450 Bfrs. D,B&B 3,150–3,550 Bfrs per person. Set meals 1,200–2,350 Bfrs; full alc 3,000 Bfrs.

HASSELT-STEVOORT 3512 Limburg — Map 9

Scholteshof — *Tel* (011) 25 02 02
Kermtstraat 130 — *Fax* (011) 25 43 28

Michelin awards two stars, and *Gault Millau* four *toques,* to Roger Souvereyns, the distinguished owner/chef of this luxurious restaurant-with-rooms. Set amid fields outside Hasselt, it is an 18th-century manor house with inner courtyard and landscaped garden. These accounts hold good: "A lovely place to stay. A beautiful building, superbly converted and full of fine pictures, books, antiques and modern designs. The six- or seven-course menu can be tailored to your requirements if you want only fish or vegetables. There is a selection of wines for each course – generously served – and all for an inclusive price which is not too frightening." "Delicious, with the added attraction of the kitchen opening on to the dining room, so guests can view the amazing spectacle of a gourmet meal in the making. Most bedrooms are a bit small and charmless, though comfortable. The high-ceilinged suites have views over the garden."

Open All year, except 2–24 Jan. Restaurant closed Wed.
Rooms 7 suites (for 3–4 people, in 2 separate houses), 11 double.
Facilities Lounge, library, restaurant; conference facilities. Garden: tennis.
Location Edge of Stevoort village, 7 km W of Hasselt. Parking.
Credit cards All major cards accepted.
Terms Rooms 4,500 Bfrs, suite 8,500 Bfrs. Breakfast 600 Bfrs. Set lunch 2,650 Bfrs, dinner 4,750 Bfrs; full alc 4,800 Bfrs.

HERBEUMONT 6820 Luxembourg Belge — Map 9

Hostellerie du Prieuré de Conques — *Tel* (061) 41 14 17
Route de Florenville 176 — *Fax* (061) 41 27 03

This stylishly converted 18th-century priory, long, low and white, stands in neat gardens and long lawns set with apple trees, by the banks of the curving Semois in the vast Ardennes forest. The owner is "fatherly and friendly", his wife "pleasant and chatty". A 1996 visitor enjoyed traditional food such as pheasant cooked in cream, and liked the welcome and service. Furniture is either genuine rustic or good repro; public rooms are smartly furnished with antiques and old paintings; bedrooms vary in size and style; some are "lovely and large, with private terrace and view of the river". (*CM Burton, WAG*)

Open 15 Mar–Nov. Restaurant closed Tues–Thurs.
Rooms 15 double, 3 single. Some in annexe. Some on ground floor.
Facilities Salon, bar, 2 dining rooms; terrace. Garden.
Location 3 km SE of Herbeumont on N884. 23 km E of Bouillon. Private parking.
Restriction No smoking: 1 dining room, some bedrooms.
Credit cards Access, Amex, Visa.
Terms B&B: single 3,500–4,700 Bfrs, double 4,200–5,500 Bfrs; D,B&B double 6,500–7,500 Bfrs. Set meals 950–1,650 Bfrs; full alc 1,250 Bfrs.

HERSELT 2230 Antwerpen — Map 9

Hostellerie Agter de Weyreldt
Aarschotsebaan 2

Tel (016) 69 98 51
Fax (016) 69 98 53

In quiet country 43 km SE of Antwerp, 4 km SW of Herselt, low white-walled farmhouse attractively converted into stylish restaurant with some rooms, simple and quite small, but comfortable. Terrace; lovely gardens. Good food such as turbot in champagne sauce. Restaurant closed Sat midday, Sun evening/Mon. All major credit cards accepted. 6 rooms: 1,200–2,000 Bfrs. Breakfast 450 Bfrs. D,B&B 3,000–3,500 Bfrs per person [1996]. Newer reports needed, please.

KORTRIJK 8500 West-Vlaanderen — Map 9

Village Gastronomique Eddy Vandekerckhove
Sint-Anna 5

Tel (056) 22 47 56
Fax (056) 22 71 70

Kortrijk is a handsome old Flemish town by the French border – its French name is Courtrai. Here Eddy Vandekerckhove's modern gabled house has seven luxurious bedrooms. This may not quite add up to a "village", but certainly it is gastronomic (*Michelin* star, two *Gault Millau toques*). "Superb breakfasts, cooking as good as ever," say devotees who returned recently, endorsing their earlier view: "A happy ambience, service smooth and friendly. Eddy is an extrovert young chef of fairly ample girth; his charming wife Katherine runs the restaurant, and the whole place has that lovely atmosphere of operating like clockwork. Dinner was great fun. The new extension has an amazing water garden under a high glazed roof, with ponds, fountains, tropical plants and fish, and tables and chairs for coffee or drinks. The rooms are superb, all named after Belgian painters, with examples of their work on the walls. Our huge bathroom was all in marble." (*P and JT*)

Open All year, except two weeks Sept. Restaurant closed Sun evening/Mon.
Rooms 7 double. All on ground floor.
Facilities Lounge, bar, restaurant; conference facilities. Small garden.
Location 3 km S of town centre. 28 km NE of Lille. Private parking.
Credit cards All major cards accepted.
Terms B&B: single 4,500 Bfrs, double 4,750 Bfrs. Set meals 2,550–2,650 Bfrs; full alc 3,500 Bfrs.

LISOGNE 5501 Namur — Map 9

Moulin de Lisogne
Rue de la Lisonnette

Tel (082) 22 63 80
Fax (082) 22 21 47

A gracefully converted water mill, set pastorally beside a plashing stream in a village outside Dinant. A Relais du Silence, it is now a smart restaurant-with-rooms run by a young couple, the Blondiaux. They put the accent less on bedrooms than on *cadre* (lovely rugs and antiques, and *Michelin* red print) and cooking (*Gault Millau toque*): "Our large attic room was stylishly decorated but had only one tiny window, so was rather gloomy. However, the meal was excellent – fish soup, sole in chablis, etc." "If you can get a seat out on the terrace, you might see your trout caught by the *sous-chef*." Mussels in cream sauce come with the drinks before dinner, which might include quail mousse or young wild boar with mushrooms. This year, readers again enjoyed the dinners, but thought breakfast sparse, and friendly welcome even sparser. There is no TV or radio in the rooms. The owners have this year rebuilt the old mill tower. Further reports welcome.

Open 2 Feb–15 Dec.
Rooms 10 double. 2 in converted outbuilding. 1 on ground floor.
Facilities 2 salons, bar, 2 dining rooms; conference room; terrace. Garden: tennis, river, fishing.
Location In village, 4 km NE of Dinant, off N936 to Liège. A4/E411 exit 20. 3 garages; private carpark.
Credit cards All major cards accepted.
Terms B&B 2,800–3,500 Bfrs; D,B&B 3,400–3,700 Bfrs. Set meals 1,250–1,950 Bfrs; full alc 2,000 Bfrs.

MAARKEDAL 9681 Oost-Vlaanderen — Map 9

Hostellerie Shamrock
Ommegangstraat 148
Muziekbos
Tel (055) 21 55 29
Fax (055) 21 56 83

Some of the best sophisticated cooking in Belgium (*Michelin* star, three *Gault millau toques*) is on offer at this smart restaurant-with-rooms (Relais & Châteaux) in rolling wooded country near Ronse, a textile town west of Brussels. You go up a long drive in a well-kept garden, to what looks like a private house in half-timbered mock-Tudor style (where the Irish name comes from is not clear). Latest news: "A spacious room with enormous bathroom, tasteful decor. The garden is illuminated after dark. Staff were most friendly. Dinner was good, perhaps not quite as good as *Gault Millau* promised: food too ambitious." The main stairway with carved wood balcony descends directly into the elegant dining room.

Open All year, except 15–31 July, Tues/Wed.
Rooms 1 suite, 5 double.
Facilities Lounge, 2 dining rooms. Garden.
Location 5 km NE of Ronse, off N62, at Muziekbos.
Restriction No children under 8.
Credit cards All major cards accepted.
Terms B&B: single 6,200 Bfrs, double 6,800 Bfrs, suite 8,800 Bfrs; D,B&B double 10,800 Bfrs. Set meals 1,950–3,750 Bfrs; full alc 3,500 Bfrs.

MALMÉDY 4960 Liège — Map 9

Hostellerie Trôs Marets
2 route des Trôs Marets
Tel (080) 33 79 17
Fax (080) 33 79 10

This small modern Relais & Châteaux hostelry stands in a neat garden amid thick trees, in fine rolling countryside near the German border. Public rooms and bedrooms are furnished in heavy Belgian country style, but comfortable. "Probably our all-time European favourite," says an *habitué*. "We had a large room, the quiet and the trees were magnificent, the host attentive, and the food still *nouvelle*-ish but generous" (*Gault Millau toque*). The dining room has been called "delightful", as have the breakfasts, which include Ardennes ham. (*WAG*) Some visitors have felt rather oppressed by the tall trees round the main building: the hillside annexe has better views and a greater feeling of space.

Open All year, except mid-Nov–Christmas.
Rooms 4 suites (in nearby annexe), 7 double.
Facilities Lounge, restaurant; conference room; indoor swimming pool; terrace. Park: garden. Unsuitable for ♿.
Location At Mont, 5 km NE of Malmédy, on N68 to Eupen. Parking.
Credit cards All major cards accepted.
Terms B&B: single 3,500–4,000 Bfrs, double 4,900–8,500 Bfrs, suite 9,000–18,000 Bfrs. Set meals 1,750–2,750 Bfrs; full alc 2,750 Bfrs.

MARCHE-EN-FAMENNE 6900 Luxembourg Belge — Map 9

Château d'Hassonville — *Tel* (084) 31 10 25
Aye — *Fax* (084) 31 60 27

This grey 17th-century pepper-potted *château* on the outskirts of the Ardennes, owned and run by the Rodrigues family, stands in its own 120-acre grounds, with a garden designed by Le Nôtre. "We were very pleased," say its nominators. "Our spacious room, facing the scenery, had classic Louis XV painted furniture and original paintings. Housekeeping was first class. There's a cosy bar where a log fire crackles. Of the two dining rooms, one has magnificent period wall paintings. The cuisine is classical, using fresh produce (two *Gault Millau toques*), and the wine list is superb. They have 'the best *sommelier* of Belgium', the elegantly moustachioed Pierre Vicini. Breakfast, an amazing buffet, is served in the old *orangerie*, now a tropical conservatory: the friendly parrot got out of his cage and fancied my hair." (*F and IW*)

Open All year, except 1 week Jan. Closed Mon evening/Tues.
Rooms 1 suite, 20 double. 7 in annexe.
Facilities Lounge, bar, TV/snooker room, 2 dining rooms; function facilities. Park: garden, putting green, bicycling; river, fishing, golf nearby.
Location At Aye, 4 km W of Marche, which is 56 km S of Liège.
Credit cards All major cards accepted.
Terms B&B: single 3,500–4,500 Bfrs, double 4,800–6,800 Bfrs, suite 10,800 Bfrs. Set lunch 1,150 Bfrs, dinner 1,650–2,850 Bfrs; full alc 2,500 Bfrs [1996]. Gastronomic weekends.

NOIREFONTAINE 6831 Luxembourg Belge — Map 9

Auberge du Moulin Hideux — *Tel* (061) 46 70 15
Route de Dohan 1 — *Fax* (061) 46 72 81

Secluded in a wooded Ardennes valley near the French border, this stylishly converted mill house is now a small luxury hotel (Relais & Châteaux), quite idyllic. It is owned and run by Charles and Martine Lahire, who "know how to make their guests feel like friends", and the cooking of Christian Ulweling wins a *Michelin* star and three *Gault Millau toques*. "A storybook *auberge*," says a recent visitor, "with delicious dinners served in a somewhat sterile room. Good, if slow, breakfasts in a more cheerful room. We enjoyed cosying up to the fireplace, and can hardly wait to return, even at those prices." "Staff pleasant, food excellent." Bedrooms are admired; one bathroom was "a dream in beige marble". There's an ornamental pond with ducks, and tables and chairs for drinks on a well-kept lawn. (*G and SM, and others*) An indoor swimming pool is new this year. Some readers doubt value for money: prices of wines and some extras can be *very* high.

Open Mid-Mar–end Nov. Restaurant closed Wed/midday Thurs Mar–July.
Rooms 3 suites, 10 double.
Facilities Lounge, bar, breakfast room, restaurant; indoor swimming pool. Garden: tennis. Trout-fishing 2 km.
Location By N865, 2.5 km SE of Noirefontaine, which is 4 km N of Bouillon.
Credit cards All major cards accepted.
Terms B&B: double 7,600 Bfrs, suite 8,600 Bfrs. Set meals 2,000–2,500 Bfrs.

STAVELOT 4970 Liège — Map 9

Hostellerie Le Val d'Amblève NEW
7 route de Malmédy
Tel (080) 86 23 53
Fax (080) 86 41 21

On the edge of an attractive old town south of Liège, amid lovely hilly Ardennes countryside, stands this sturdy family house, now a Romantik Hotel, owned and run by Ruud and Marion Roxs. It fell from the 1996 *Guide* for lack of reports, but two new ones now bring it back. "A perfect welcome, a quiet and comfortable room. Every dish on the *demi-pension* menu was a creation, though for some it may have been a bit rich; service rather slow." "Elegant furnishings. A memorable dinner, prepared and served by M. Roxs." The spacious dining room has picture-windows opening on to a large terrace with umbrellas, backed by sloping lawns and noble trees. Bedrooms in the new annexe have been called light and airy. (*Julia de Waal, Eric Dodson*) Much renovation this year. But some beds have been found to lack bedside lights.

Open All year, except 1st 3 weeks Jan. Restaurant closed to non-residents Mon evening.
Rooms 13 double. 4 in nearby annexe.
Facilities 2 lounges, 2 dining rooms; terrace. Garden: tennis. Unsuitable for ♿.
Location Outskirts of Stavelot, 9 km SW of Malmédy. Garages, carpark.
Credit cards All major cards accepted.
Terms B&B: single 2,250 Bfrs, double 2,900 Bfrs; D,B&B double 5,500 Bfrs. Set meals 1,350–1,875 Bfrs; full alc 1,850 Bfrs.

TORGNY 6767 Luxembourg Belge — Map 9

Auberge de la Grappe d'Or NEW
Rue de l'Ermitage 18
Tel (063) 57 70 56
Fax (063) 57 03 44

Sympathetically furnished in period style, the Boulangers' Relais du Silence is a 19th-century house in a quiet village right by the French border, south of Virton. "Absolutely wonderful," say its nominators. "All rooms are nicely decorated. From ours we could hear church bells, and relax in spacious comfort. The restaurant is excellent (*Michelin* star, for, eg, nettle soup with frogs) and reasonably priced. Jacques Boulanger cooks, his wife Liliane is front of house – pleasant people, and so are their staff." (*Leonard Hill and Cathy Stevulak*)

Open All year, except one week early Feb (carnival), last week Aug/1st week Sept. Restaurant closed Sun evening/Mon.

Rooms 6 double.
Facilities Salon, 3 dining rooms (1 no-smoking). Garden. Unsuitable for ♿.
Location In village, 10 km SW of Virton. Left off N82 Arlon–Montmédy. Secure parking.
Credit cards All major cards accepted.
Terms B&B: single 2,550 Bfrs, double 3,300 Bfrs; D,B&B 2,950 Bfrs. Set lunch 1,100 Bfrs, dinner 1,995 Bfrs; full alc 2,000 Bfrs.

VIEUXVILLE 4190 Liège — Map 9

Château de Palogne — *Tel* (086) 21 38 74
Route de Palogne 3 — *Fax* (086) 21 38 76

On edge of small town in wooded Ardennes foothills 42 km S of Liège, grey mansion finely restored, with beautiful period decor. Pleasant owners, 11 stylish bedrooms, good substantial breakfast in room overlooking large garden. Some noise from nearby railway. No restaurant: Au Vieux Logis *in town recommended. Open all year on reservation. Access, Diners, Visa accepted. Rooms 2,500–3,600 Bfrs. Breakfast 350 Bfrs.*

WATERLOO 1410 Brabant — Map 9

Le Côté Vert — *Tel* (02) 354 01 05
Chaussée de Bruxelles 200g — *Fax* (02) 354 08 60

"I had spent the previous night in the Brussels *Hilton*, and the contrast could not have been greater – to the credit of *Le Côté Vert*," says a visitor this year to this small family-run hotel. A low white modern building, it is in the centre of a historically famous little town south of Brussels, yet stands amid greenery. "An excellent place, with courteous staff, good restaurant," is another new verdict. "The grounds are beautiful (even cows and sheep in the yard), the food is superb, service is quick and impeccable. Rooms are modern and functional; suites have a fully equipped kitchen." (*Michael Freeman, Dr Anthony Winterbourne*) The restaurant, *La Cuisine au Vert*, is now across the garden.

Open All year. Restaurant closed Sun, Christmas.
Rooms 8 suites (in separate building), 29 double. 7 on ground floor. Some no-smoking.
Facilities Lift. Bar, lounge, restaurant; conference room. Garden.
Location Central. Waterloo is 17 km S of Brussels. Parking.
Credit cards All major cards accepted.
Terms B&B: single 4,020 Bfrs, double 4,690 Bfrs, suite 9,320 Bfrs. Full alc 1,000 frs. Children under 6 accommodated free in parents' room.

****

Traveller's tale Why do hotel proprietors feel the need to perform the ritual circuit of diners' tables each evening? Few possess the necessary panache to carry it off, and in most cases everyone involved feels distinctly ill at ease. On occasion, I have sensed a rising tension in the dining room as the appointed time draws near. Conversations are interrupted, food grows cool, and the intimate moment is lost. If they *must* do it, why not in the bar, beforehand? Then we could spot them coming and make our escape.

****

Rooms 8 double.
Facilities Salon, 2 dining-rooms. Terrace. Large garden. Unsuitable for &.
Location In village, 20 km SW of Liège. Exit 6 of N62. [illegible]. Secure parking.

On edge of small town in wooded Ardennes foothills 45 km S of Liège, 19th-century mansion, finely restored, with fine period decor. Pleasant, discreet, English-speaking hostess; good substantial breakfast in cosy, cheerful-looking large cellar. Some rooms [illegible]. No restaurant: Au Vieux Logis in town recommended. Open all year except Christmas. Access, Diners, Visa accepted. Rooms 2,500–3,600 Bfrs. Breakfast 350 Bfrs.

The Czech Republic

Hotel Hoffmeister, Prague

For the first time, we have a full separate chapter for the Czech Republic. Most of the entries are for Prague, where, exploiting the city's huge new tourist popularity, many hotels have raised their room prices steeply. But their restaurants, frequented by local people too, tend to remain modestly priced and good value.

Many of Prague's grand hotels have now been restored; other new ones have been built. Nevertheless, for a city of this importance, the number of really good hotels is few, and many have standards of service or upkeep below western levels. In holiday periods, hotels are still very full and it is wise to book in advance; at other times, it is now much easier than it was three or four years ago to find a room at the last moment. If you bring a car to the centre of Prague, beware of a system of one-way streets and new ringways that, owing to the renovation, is utterly baffling. You need a detailed *new* street-map.

We have been told of very few good hotels in the other main cities, or in the countryside or the famous spas. Plenty of readers were last year in Prague, but who was last year in Marienbad (Mariánské Lázně) or Karlovy Vary? Where are the pleasant country inns, or farm guest houses, today common in Slovenia and appearing fast in eastern Germany? We should be glad of nominations.

BRNO Moravia — Map 14

Pegas Hotel BUDGET — *Tel/Fax* (05) 422 10 104
Jakubská 4
602 00 Brno

In centre of second city of Czech Republic, down quiet side street: small hotel, spotless, with friendly staff, good sizeable rooms. Hotel is attached to brewery and above lively bierkeller, *but not noisy. Lounge, restaurant. All major credit cards accepted. 14 rooms. B&B: single 700–1,050 Kč, double 1,200–1,700 Kč [1996]. Reports on food welcome.*

ČESKÝ KRUMLOV Bohemia — Map 14

Pension-Restaurant Belarie — *Tel/Fax* (0337) 55 90
Dlouhá 96
381 01 Český Krumlov

In charming medieval town 160 km S of Prague, near Austrian border, restored 15th-century house by river: "A real find, with magnificent rooms, best food of our trip." Beamed ceilings, bedrooms in period style. Outdoor summer dining, with view of castle. Open May-Oct. All major credit cards accepted. 5 rooms. B&B: single 1,940 Kč, double 2,640 Kč. Set meal 600 Kč.

PLZEŇ Bohemia — Map 14

Hotel Continental — *Tel* (019) 723 52 92
Zbrojnická — *Fax* (019) 722 17 46
305 34 Plzeň

Famous for its beer, this old industrial town has ancient cobbled streets and a huge main square. Just off this is the "personal favourite hotel in town" of its nominator, who has "seen them all". Like Plzeň as a whole, it is under intense renovation: "The son of the original owner is back, working hard to overcome the years of Communist mismanagement and neglect. The staff is of high quality, the crystal chandeliers are brilliantly polished. Our large, bright room had huge windows and was comfortably furnished. Breakfast was superb, with unlimited cups of strong coffee. Food in the large restaurant was excellent. There's even a night-club and casino." (*Jaye Lambert*)

Open All year.
Rooms 50.
Facilities Restaurant, café, lounge, night-club, casino.
Location Central, off main square. Guarded parking.
Credit Cards All major cards accepted.
Terms [1996] B&B: single 1,490 Kč, double 2,150 Kč.

> When a continental hotel has failed to return its questionnaire, we have quoted 1996 prices, with a note to that effect.

Hotel Škoda BUDGET *Tel* (019) 27 52 52
Námesti Českych Bratré 10
305 34 Plzeň

Bohemia's second city produces cars as well as beer, and Volkswagen today owns its huge car factory, which bears the same name as this "hideous grey Soviet era hotel", liked by its nominator even so: "It has some remaining problems, like windows difficult to open, but rooms were well equipped and comfortable, and staff friendly, efficient and English-speaking. Our room had a fine view of the lit-up spires of the cathedral, and the smog. The really good feature was the restaurant: good Czech food, lots of beer, all delicious and not internationalised. Breakfast, a lavish spread, included poppy-seed custard tarts and other Czech cakes." (*Anne-Marie Sutcliffe*)

Open All year.
Rooms 5 suites, 18 double, 44 single.
Facilities Lounge, restaurant, bar / *Weinstube*.
Location 10 mins' walk from main square. Secure parking.
Credit cards All major cards accepted.
Terms B&B: single 1,300 Kč, double 2,000 Kč.

PRAGUE Map 14

Hotel Adria *Tel* (02) 24 23 13 69
Václavské náměsti 26 *Fax* (02) 24 21 10 25
110 00 Praha 1

A much-liked medium-sized hotel, well modernised, on Wenceslas Square. Two recent reports: "Our room was small but quiet and comfortable, looking over the garden. Breakfast was a first-class buffet, in a pleasant room." "Recently renovated, with friendly, efficient reception. The cavern restaurant, fancifully decorated with stalactites etc, had good food (apricot stuffed dumplings), hurried service." Front rooms have views of the famous square (really a boulevard). (*DG Randall, and others*)

Open All year.
Rooms 66 double.
Facilities Lobby, restaurant; terrace.
Location Central. Private parking.
Credit Cards All major cards accepted.
Terms B&B: single 4,030 Kč, double 4,930 Kč.

Hotel Harmony *Tel* (02) 232 00 16
Na Poříčí 31 *Fax* (02) 231 00 09
110 00 Praha 1

Central, 1 km E of Old Town Square, on edge of old town, newly renovated hotel, lacking in atmosphere but "clean, warm and efficient, well furnished, with friendly young staff. Good buffet breakfast, restaurant "fair". Visa, Diners accepted. 60 rooms, 5 equipped for disabled. B&B: single 3,335 Kč, double 3,340 Kč. Alc 300 Kč [1996].

If you find details of a hotel's location inadequate, let us know.

Hotel Hoffmeister
Pod Bruskou 9
118 00 Praha 1

Tel (02) 561 81 55
Fax (02) 530 959

Set just below the Castle on the river side, this ambitious and expensive Relais & Châteaux member, newly renovated, has a pleasant inner courtyard with tables and chairs under white parasols. Two 1996 reports bring it to the *Guide*: "Everything is light and bright, lots of brass, elaborate chandeliers, a feeling of space. Our room was very comfortable, with excellent well-equipped bathrooms, hair-dryer, etc. All the staff spoke good English and were efficient. We had two excellent dinners, and a generous buffet breakfast, including a table of sliced fresh fruits." "It has character, a wealth of paintings and prints on the walls, and better food than that at most Prague hotels" – its chef, Václav Košnař, cooked for Queen Elizabeth II on her visit to Prague: one of his special dishes is stuffed quail with apples. (*John Rowlands, JW Makinson*) The owner, Martin Hoffmeister, has dedicated his hotel to his father, Adolf Hoffmeister, "elegant globe-trotter, lover of art, food and wine, caricaturist, writer and diplomat" (as the brochure describes him), whose Beardsley-like cartoons and paintings adorn its walls. Another plus: the Fort Knox-like garage.

Open All year.
Rooms 4 suites, 38 double. 1 especially equipped for ♿. Some no-smoking.
Facilities Bar, café, restaurant, wine cellar; terrace.
Location Central, between Castle and river. Garage.
Credit cards All major cards accepted.
Terms Rooms: single 4,200–6,600 Kč, double 4,800–7,400 Kč, suite 7,250–14,000 Kč. Breakfast 300 Kč. Set meals 500–600 Kč; full alc 980 Kč.

Hotel Maximilian
Haštalska 14
110 00 Praha 1

Tel (02) 21 80 61 11
Fax (02) 21 80 61 10

Just N of Old Town Square, newly renovated medium-sized hotel, "a delight", with quiet, comfortable, well-equipped rooms, small bar; "delicious" buffet breakfasts with fresh scrambled eggs. All major credit cards accepted. 72 rooms. B&B: single 4,780 Kč, double 5,700 Kč [1996]. No restaurant.

Hotel Obora
Libocká 1
162 00 Praha 6

Tel (02) 36 77 79
Fax (02) 316 71 25

8 km W of city centre, 8 km from airport, comfortable newly opened hotel, with 20 rooms. Recent praise: "Charming, with mainly good service. Room adequate if spartan; dinner not too good, but breakfast above average." Secure parking. All major credit cards accepted. B&B: single 1,900 Kč, double 2,600 Kč. Alc meals 170–270 Kč [1996].

> We ask hotels to estimate their 1997 tariffs, but many prefer not to think so far ahead and give their 1996 tariffs. Some hotels on the Continent do not return our questionnaire. Prices should always be checked on booking.

Hotel Paříž
U Obecního Domu 1
110 00 Praha 1

Tel (02) 24 22 21 51
Fax (02) 24 22 54 75

Quite near Old Town Square, this distinguished mansion was built in 1907 "in neo-Gothic style", according to its brochure, with "Art Nouveau elements". Back now in the hands of its original Brandejs family owners, it is a four-star hotel affiliated to France's Concorde group. "It's delightful, with comfortable rooms, splendid Art Nouveau detail," runs a recent report. "Buffet breakfasts were the best we've ever had: excellent bacon, sausages and scrambled egg, decent coffee, good ambience in the restaurant. The concept of service seemed to have got through totally." Endorsed this year: "An impressive building, with well-conserved decor. Good service and noise insulation." (*JW, G Avery*) More reports welcome on the restaurant, which, the brochure says, serves *nouvelle cuisine*. The hotel's *Café de Paris* is "just right for a drink or a light lunch".

Open All year.
Rooms 2 suites, 88 double, 10 single.
Facilities Bar, coffee shop, restaurant. Unsuitable for ♿.
Location Central, 400 m E of Staroměstské náměsti. Private parking.
Credit cards All major cards accepted.
Terms B&B: single 4,720–5,900 Kč, double 4,960–6,200 Kč, suite 7,680–9,600 Kč; D,B&B 600 Kč added per person. Set meals 500–1,100 Kč; full alc 600 Kč.

Pod Věží
Mostecká 2
110 00 Praha 1

Tel (02) 53 37 10
Fax (02) 53 18 59

Next to Three Ostriches *(see next page), a "pretty town* palais *of noble origin", now a newly redecorated hotel, fairly expensive. "Our room was large, well-furnished and quiet, with large bath." Breakfast excellent, service adequate. Guarded garage. All major credit cards accepted. 12 rooms. B&B: single 3,320–3,900 Kč, double 4,500–6,200 Kč. Alc meals 300-350 Kč [1996]. Reports on food welcome.*

Pension U Raka
Černínská 10/93
118 00 Praha 1

Tel (02) 205 111 00
Fax (02) 205 105 11

In a small street just west of the Castle, this newly opened six-room guest house (its name means "At the Sign of the Crayfish") is a stylish and quite ambitious venture, as its nominators relate: "The two new buildings are accurate reconstructions of 18th-century barns on this site, and the owner, photographer Alexandr Paul, clearly takes pride in his achievement. The furnishings are of modern unfinished wood; beds were comfortable, and the bathroom spacious and well equipped. Impeccable service, and the best breakfast ever, served on beautiful Bohemian porcelain. No real restaurant, but meals can be arranged ahead of time. Oil paintings by local artists cover the walls of the public rooms, and are for sale – the area is now an artists' haven, with many studios and galleries in old houses." The decor is tasteful and original, with tiled floors, much use of open brickwork; outside is a neat cobbled patio. (*Greg and Julie Brinks*)

Open All year.
Rooms 1 suite, 5 double.
Facilities Lounge, snack bar; terrace. Garden.
Location Off Loreto Square, 500 m W of Castle. Private parking.
Credit cards All major cards accepted.
Terms B&B: double 4,200 Kč, suite 6,900 Kč. Set meals US$50.

U Tří Pštrosů
Dražického náměsti 12
118 00 Praha 1

Tel (02) 24 51 07 79
Fax (02) 24 51 07 83

Close to the western end of Charles Bridge, this famous and picturesque 17th-century inn, "The Three Ostriches", is now privatised, back in the hands of its Dundr family owners. Recent visitors have admired it more for its looks and atmosphere than for the cuisine. "Excellent by Czech standards, if expensive. Friendly service. Lovely rooms with the famous painted ceilings; quite modern bathrooms." "Very Czech. Service mostly attentive, staff good fun." "All very romantic. Tiny entrance hall with beautiful modern glass chandelier." (*Jon Hughes, Mrs Beth Hughes Hall, WR Charlesworth, and others*) A reader this year thought the food poor. Food is not the hotel's strong point, but there are lots of other restaurants close by.

Open All year.
Rooms 3 suites, 10 double, 5 single.
Facilities Lounge, bar, restaurant. Unsuitable for ♿.
Location Central, west side of Karlův Most (Charles Bridge). Private parking.
Credit cards Access, Amex, Visa.
Terms B&B: single 3,900 Kč, double 3,900–5,300 Kč, suite 4,900–7,500 Kč. Set lunch 400 Kč, dinner 600 Kč; full alc 600 Kč.

Denmark

Falsled Kro, Millinge

COPENHAGEN **Map 7**

Hotel d'Angleterre *Tel* 33 12 00 95
Kongens Nytorv 34 *Fax* 33 12 11 18
1050 København K

The *Angleterre* is one of Copenhagen's monuments, an old-fashioned grand hotel, with all modern luxuries, including a pool and, new this year, a spa and fitness club. "Our big, handsome room had a balcony and a view over the square; because it was on the fourth floor, traffic noise was not a problem. It had a classy green and peach 19th-century decor, a big leather-topped desk, and a comfortable bed with high-quality cotton sheets and duvets, all carefully maintained. Walking through the wide corridors, lit by sconces, and with pots of orchids, was a pleasurable reminder of another era. The pretty wood-panelled bar has pictures of the hotel's past. Service from the well-trained young staff was gracious and never unctuous. Breakfasts were delicious, but they are expensive if you are not on the inclusive weekend rate." (*CM*) There are two restaurants, one an expensive gourmet set-up.

Open All year.
Rooms 18 suites, 90 double, 22 single.
Facilities Lift. Lounge, 2 restaurants; conference facilities; spa: fitness club, swimming pool.
Location Central.
Credit cards All major cards accepted.
Terms [1996] Rooms: single 1,850 Dkr, double 2,050–2,900 Dkr, suite 3,400–9,900 Dkr. Breakfast 120 Dkr. Set meals 395–440 Dkr. Weekend rates.

Ascot Hotel — *Tel* 33 12 60 00
Studiestræde 61 — *Fax* 33 14 60 40
1554 København V

A B&B town hotel on a pleasant street close to Tivoli and Strøget, a famous pedestrian area. Behind the elaborately moulded turn-of-the-century façade of ionic pilasters and balustrades lie a grand vaulted reception hall with columns of black granite, a large "ballroom-like" room where the buffet breakfast is served, and an old-fashioned winding stairway. The architectural complexities of the building (a conversion of three) necessitate some juggling with stairs and lifts. Quietest bedrooms overlook the "not particularly attractive" inner courtyard. Some rooms may be cramped, but the penthouse suite is "magnificent, with terraces facing both sides of the city". One report this year of poor housekeeping, and an impersonal atmosphere. More reports, please.

Open All year.
Rooms 26 suites (with kitchenette), 67 double, 50 single. Some with balcony.
Facilities Lift. Lounge, bar, breakfast room; conference facilities. Unsuitable for ♿.
Location Central, near town hall. Private parking.
Credit cards All major cards accepted.
Terms [1996] B&B: single 890–990 Dkr, double 1,090–1,390 Dkr; suite (excluding breakfast) 1,390–1,990 Dkr.

---

71 Nyhavn Hotel — *Tel* 33 11 85 85
Nyhavn 71 — *Fax* 33 93 15 85
1051 København K

Converted 19th-century warehouse (82 rooms) on Nyhavn (New Harbour) in old city. Admired for architectural charm and magnificent quayside location. Good buffet breakfast. Helpful staff; children welcomed (under-12s accommodated free in parents' room). Free parking. Unsuitable for ♿. All major credit cards accepted. B&B: single 995–1,310 Dkr, double 1,350–1,560 Dkr, suite 1,850–2,600 Dkr. Set dinner 130 Dkr. More reports, please.

FREDENSBORG 3480 Seeland — Map 7

Pension Bondehuset NEW — *Tel* 42 28 01 12
Sørupvej 14 — *Fax* 42 28 03 01
Sørup

This lakeside inn near the Queen's summer palace, not far from Copenhagen, fell from the *Guide* two years ago for lack of reports; it now returns with accolades from visitors beguiled by its idyllic setting amid carefully tended flowery gardens. "The thatched cottages are charming; our room was adorable, and immaculate; the hostess was gracious, and the garden and lake were quiet and restful after noisy Copenhagen. We felt very much at home." Breakfast is admired – jams are home-made, breads and pastries are baked every morning: "Those who only know what passes for a Danish pastry in England would do well to visit *Bondehuset* for educational purposes." A returning visitor thought the dinners "as good as ever, if not better": "The menu is limited to dishes of the day, but is excellent value and far cheaper than restaurants in the town centre." Others have liked the public rooms "filled with antiques, knick-knacks and family memorabilia, giving it a warm old-fashioned feel". Energetic visitors may borrow the hotel's rowing boat, or walk in the "most attractive" royal park which runs down to the lake. Fredensborg is convenient for Hamlet's castle at Elsinore and the "splendid" Louisiana art gallery. (*Pat Malone, Roger and Jytte Hardisty, Pauline O'Driscoll*)

Open All year.
Rooms 9 double, 6 single. Some on ground floor.
Facilities Lounge, TV room, restaurant; patio. Garden: private harbour: rowing, bathing, fishing. Golf nearby.
Location Fredensborg is 30 km NW of Copenhagen. Private parking.
Credit cards Access, Visa.
Terms [1996] Full board 555–720 Dkr.

Hotel Store Kro *Tel* 42 28 00 47
Slotsgade 1–6 *Fax* 42 28 45 61

This grand old country hotel dates from 1723, when Frederick IV decided to build an inn next to his splendid castle. "Efficient and friendly reception, a pretty single room under the roof, overlooking a big garden; good food on a short and well-considered menu; very attractive sitting room; admirable service; and breakfast with the best Danish rye bread I have ever eaten." Nearby are the Fredensborg Golf Club, the Karen Blixen Museum and the Louisiana Museum of Art, as well as castles and beaches galore. (*BK*)

Open All year, except Christmas, New Year.
Rooms 38 double, 11 single.
Facilities Restaurant, lounge; conference facilities; sauna. Golf, beaches nearby.
Location Central.
Credit cards All major cards accepted.
Terms B&B: single 850 Dkr, double 1,150–1,350 Dkr. Set lunch 295 Dkr, dinner 315 Dkr.

HORSENS 8700 Jylland — Map 7

Jørgensens Hotel *Tel* 75 62 16 00
Søndergade 17–19 *Fax* 75 62 85 85

The birthplace of the explorer Bering, who discovered the Bering Strait, is in the lake district of central Jutland. It has some elegant 18th-century buildings, and also "the widest main street in Denmark". Here, this splendid town house, built in the baroque style in 1744 and once the Lichtenbergske Mansion, has returned to private hands and has been beautifully refurbished in exquisite taste. The staff are pleasant and helpful. (*JH*) A new chef this year; we'd like more reports, please.

Open All year, except Christmas, New Year.
Rooms 2 suites, 21 double, 19 single.
Facilities Lounge, restaurant; conference facilities. Beach 6 km.
Location Central. Parking.
Credit cards All major cards accepted.
Terms B&B: single 675 Dkr, double 810 Dkr, suite 1,350 Dkr. Set lunch 98 Dkr, dinner 215–305 Dkr; full alc 310 Dkr. 20% reduction weekends.

MARSTAL 5960 Aerø — Map 7

Hotel Marstal BUDGET

Dronningestræde 1A — *Tel* 62 53 13 52

Marstal is a little port on the island of Aerø, with cobbled streets, ancient churches hung with intricate ship models, a maritime museum, sophisticated shops and a lively night life. It makes a perfect base for exploring the surrounding countryside and beaches, by bicycle or car, or on foot. "In a country famed for its hospitality, this hotel is a jewel," wrote its nominator. "It is in the centre of town, close to the harbour, and has six simply furnished, bright, clean rooms with gauzy curtains that blow in the sea breezes. Hosts Gurli and Flemming Houg provide flowers, baskets of fruit, and tourist information for the guests. Breakfast is included in the inexpensive price of the room. Lunch and dinner, freshly cooked, and served in generous portions, always include a selection of seasonal specialities – Danish gravlax, and eel prepared in many different ways. Locals gather in the cosy restaurant and bar. Service is unfailingly cheerful." (*MH*). One report this year criticised room maintenance and wished for more bathrooms.

Open All year.
Rooms 4 double, 2 single. No *en suite* facilities.
Facilities Lounge, bar, restaurant. Beaches nearby.
Location Central, near harbour. Marstal is in SE of Aerø.
Credit cards All major cards accepted.
Terms [1996] B&B 250–350 Dkr, D,B&B from 305 Dkr.

MILLINGE 5642 Funen — Map 7

Falsled Kro

Assensvej 513 — *Tel* 62 68 11 11
Fax 62 68 11 62

"One of Denmark's havens." An unusual luxury hotel (Relais & Châteaux) on the central island of Funen, once a 15th-century smugglers' inn, now a cluster of old thatched buildings around a cobbled courtyard. The decor in the bedrooms is more Spanish than Scandinavian, but all have working fireplaces. It is famous for the cuisine of French co-owner Jean-Louis Lieffroy, who smokes his own salmon in the garden kiln. Everything else too, including "the best asparagus and strawberries in the world", is grown, caught or cured locally. One reader gave it his ultimate hotel accolade, a 10. Another found his room small and the climb to the loft sleeping area steep, but thought "the charm oozing through made up for the astronomical prices". Other recent praise: "Idyllic setting and atmosphere, delicious food, and the Fyn countryside and seashore to walk along. Though French-run, a very Danish treat." (*JH, BK, and others*)

Open All year, except Christmas. Restaurant closed midday Mon.
Rooms 3 suites (across road, 100 m), 14 double, 2 single. Some on ground floor.
Facilities Lounges, bar, restaurant, coffee shop; conference facilities; terrace, courtyard. Garden: small golf course, tennis, helipad. Sea: sailing, surfing, fishing, 2 km.
Location 10 km NW of Faaborg.
Credit cards All major cards accepted.
Terms Rooms: single 700 Dkr, double 1,600 Dkr, suite 1,975 Dkr. Breakfast 130 Dkr. Set lunch 290 Dkr, dinner 390–690 Dkr.

NYBORG 5800 Funen — Map 7

Hesselet NEW — *Tel* 65 31 30 29
Christianslundsvej 119 — *Fax* 65 31 29 58

A luxurious modern building in a beautiful situation outside the town of Nyborg, it has lawns leading down to the sea, and spectacular views of the new bridge which, by 1998, will link Funen to Zeeland across the Store Bælt. Many of the large, stylishly furnished bedrooms look out to sea; all have granite bathrooms, with every possible extra. "Highly recommended. The staff are delightful and the owners very friendly," writes a regular visitor. There's a splendid indoor swimming pool, and outdoor activities are well catered for too: two new tennis courts, and seven golf courses are within easy reach. The hotel will even provide bicycles. (*C Buckmaster*)

Open All year, except Christmas, New Year.
Rooms 4 suites, 42 double. Some no-smoking. Some on ground floor.
Facilities Garden room, library, billiard room, restaurant; indoor swimming pool; terrace. Garden: beach, jetty, fishing. Golf, tennis nearby.
Location 2 km N of Nyborg. E20 exit 45.
Credit cards All major cards accepted.
Terms B&B 980 Dkr, double 1,420 Dkr, suite from 1,800 Dkr. Set lunch 180 Dkr, dinner 365 Dkr; full alc 490 Dkr.

RIBE 6760 Jutland — Map 7

Hotel Dagmar NEW — *Tel* 75 42 00 33
Torvet 1 — *Fax* 75 42 36 52

Absent from the *Guide* last year for lack of feedback, the *Dagmar* returns to our pages with an enthusiastic endorsement: "Staying there was the highlight of my trip – I felt I was in another world." Ribe, lying amongst the marshes and dunes of the west coast of Jutland, claims to be the oldest town in Denmark, with an 800-year-old cathedral, cobbled streets and nesting storks. The hotel, built in 1581, looks across the square to the cathedral. Bedrooms have low ceilings, sloping floors, thick walls and windows with deep sills, and are soberly decorated with paintings and antiques. There's an elegant, fairly expensive candlelit restaurant and a less formal one in the cellar, where there's good solid food at a reasonable price, and music and dancing on winter weekends; also an excellent and copious breakfast buffet. (*Sherrill Brown*)

Open All year, except 24/25/31 Dec, 1 Jan.
Rooms 47 double, 1 single.
Facilities Lounge, bar, 2 restaurants; conference facilities. Unsuitable for ♿.

Location Central, opposite cathedral. Open parking.
Credit cards All major cards accepted.
Terms [1996] B&B: single 645–945 Dkr, double 845–1,145 Dkr.

SØNDERHO 6720 Fanø — Map 7

Sønderho Kro — *Tel* 75 16 40 09
Kropladsen 11 — *Fax* 75 16 43 85

One of Denmark's oldest hotels, built in 1722, stands in a picturesque fishing village at the tip of the long sandy island of Fanø. The Sørensens, "shy, but charming on acquaintance", are the fifth generation to run it. "This must be the smallest and most remote member of Relais & Châteaux, a real must for the *Guide.*" It is only 17 kilometres from Esbjerg and the Harwich ferry. Spacious bedrooms, in a separate wing, are named after Fanø sailing ships. Excellent food in dining room, roaring fire in hall, antiques and modern paintings, good breakfasts with home-made jams. And miles of empty dunes and beaches. (*JH*)

Open 1 Mar–10 Nov, 26 Dec–1 Jan, Weekends only Nov/Dec/Jan.
Rooms 8 double. 5 on ground floor.
Facilities Lounge, restaurant. Garden. By sea: sandy beach, safe bathing. Golf, tennis nearby.
Location 20 mins by ferry from Esbjerg, then 20 mins' drive. In SE Sønderho, by dyke.
Credit cards All major cards accepted.
Terms Rooms: single 585–890 Dkr, double 710–1,090 Dkr. Breakfast 90 Dkr. Set lunch 200 Dkr, dinner 300 Dkr; full alc 375 Dkr.

SORØ 4180 Seeland — Map 7

Hotel Postgaarden — *Tel* 53 63 22 22
Storgade 27 — *Fax* 53 63 22 91

This "charming old town" is set between two lakes (it was originally an island). It has a 12th-century abbey church and many lovely old buildings. One of these is the *Postgaarden*, a long yellow house in the main street, which has been an inn since 1682 and was recently modernised. "The furnishings in the lounges and breakfast room are rather conventional and lacking in 'olde-worlde' atmosphere," wrote its nominator, "but we had an excellent bedroom with a bathroom which appeared to be all marble and mirrors. The restaurant is in a half-timbered barn, across a cobbled yard, with tables outdoors for summer meals. Our set dinner included the best gravlax ever, followed by beef fillet served on a red-hot iron hotplate – you cook it to your own liking. Breakfast was a traditional and generous buffet. Very friendly service. Good English spoken." (*AL*) More reports, please.

Open All year, except Christmas, New Year.
Rooms 19 double, 4 single.
Facilities Lounge, restaurant; conference facilities; sauna.
Location Central. Rear carpark.
Credit cards All major cards accepted.
Terms [1996] B&B: single 450 Dkr, double 650 Dkr. Lunch from 75 Dkr, dinner from 160 Dkr.

France

Château de la Treyne, Lacave

Despite the high level of the franc against the pound and the dollar, France can still provide visitors with value for money. Petrol may be expensive, but hotel bedrooms generally cost much less than in Britain, especially for two people sharing; and everywhere you can still find good *prix fixe* menus at reasonable prices.

Our readers are still eagerly touring France in large numbers, and once again this year it wins far more entries than any other country on the Continent. Readers continue to recommend the glossy high-priced conversions of old *châteaux*, abbeys and mill houses by streams; also the expensive super-gastronomic places, where some great chefs have been adding a few luxurious bedrooms to their smart restaurants, thus qualifying for this guide.

Happily, readers have also provided plenty of new entries for the simpler rural *auberges* and small-town inns that have long been the glory and originality of our French selection. We trust that readers will continue to seek these out. We also include a few *chambres d'hôtes*: many are farmhouses offering simple accommodation, maybe an evening meal too, plus a glimpse of real French rural life; others may be manors and *châteaux* where the same is done on a grander scale, but just as personally.

A note on the different kinds of hotel to be found in France, and on their classification in the main French guides, may come in useful. The generally efficient but impersonal hotels of the big chains (Concorde, Méridien, Pullman and Sofitel at the upper end of the market; Mercure and Novotel in the middle range; Campanile, Ibis and Fimotel in the cheaper bracket) do not feature in this book. The smaller hotels of character that we prefer are almost all individually owned and run; but many of them group together for the purposes of joint marketing and promotion. Of these associations, the most superior and expensive is Relais & Châteaux, many of whose members are converted *châteaux* or luxury inns; some are excellent, though our readers sometimes find them pretentious or overpriced. A rival grouping is that of the Châteaux et Demeures de Tradition, mostly middle-priced and often very attractive. The Logis de France is a huge fraternity of some 3,800 family-owned small-town hotels or rural *auberges*, identifiable by their bright green and yellow signboards. For the most part, they are quite simple but well-run places, offering value for money. Châteaux Accueil is a newer association of *châteaux* with just a few bedrooms, converted into guest houses offering bed and breakfast and sometimes an evening meal. Most are run by their family owners. The Relais du Silence are unusually quiet hotels, often in isolated settings – the kind of place to which *Michelin* may give a red rocking chair for being "very quiet and secluded". *Michelin* also bestows a red-print classification on a hotel whose looks or ambience it finds particularly pleasing.

As for food, so important in France, we make a point in these pages of stating whenever a hotel has won an award for its cuisine from *Michelin* or from its rival, the *Gault Millau* guide. Even one star in *Michelin* indicates cooking of a high standard; its top rating is three stars, given to only 20 establishments in France in 1996. *Gault Millau* awards *toques* (chef's hats), its top grade being four of them; it also differentiates between black-print *toques* for traditional cooking and red-print ones for the *cuisine créative* that it often prefers. We do not necessarily share the controversial *Gault Millau*'s tastes; nor will many of our readers, who may consider that this red-*toque*'d *nouvelle cuisine*, with its generally high prices and small portions, is less delectable than more classic French fare. For them a useful indicator could be the red "Repas" that *Michelin* awards for "good food at moderate prices" (also quoted in our text).

The often tricky subject of service is simple in France: by law 15% is added to hotel and restaurant bills. You need leave nothing extra.

ACCOLAY 89460 Yonne **Map 9**

Hostellerie de la Fontaine BUDGET *Tel* 03.86.81.54.02
Fax 03.86.81.52.78

In pretty village just off A6, 21 km SE of Auxerre, M. Guidon's small hotel, built of local golden stone and set around courtyard, wins accolade for his warm personal attention, plus good food in spacious airy dining room. "Inspiring" wine list. 11 comfortable rooms, some facing pretty garden. Closed Sun dinner 1 Nov–15 Mar. Amex, Visa accepted. Rooms from 250 frs. Breakfast 32 frs. D,B&B 250 frs per person. Set meals 95-230 frs [1996].

AGDE 34300 Hérault Map 10

La Tamarissière *Tel* 04.67.94.20.87
21 quai Théophile-Cornu *Fax* 04.67.21.38.40

The old fishing-port of Agde, with its fortified ex-cathedral made from the tufa-ash of a nearby extinct volcano, lies next to the new resort of Cap d'Agde, a pastiche of a Provençal fishing-village; close by is Europe's largest nudist holiday town. *La Tamarissière*, at the mouth of the Hérault, competes with these exotica by being a fishermen's *buvette* turned into a smart and sophisticated waterside inn, with a pretty garden and good swimming pool. You can dine outdoors beneath tamarisk trees. Owner/chef Nicolas Albano's cooking, defiantly *nouvelle*, earns two *Gault Millau toques*, but was too *nouvelle* for some *Guide* readers. Others have written: "The Albanos and staff were welcoming. We ate well." "A good-sized bedroom with balcony, excellent food." "Pleasant and comfortable, with excellent breakfasts, friendly *patronne*." More reports, please.

Open All year, except 2 Jan–15 Mar. Restaurant closed Sun evening/Mon 15 Mar–15 June, 15 Sept–2 Jan, midday Mon 15 June–15 Sept.
Rooms 27 double.
Facilities 3 lounges, TV room, restaurant. Garden: swimming pool (unheated). Unsuitable for ♿.
Location 4 km SW of Agde by D32.
Credit cards All major cards accepted.
Terms Rooms: single 310–350 frs, double 450–650 frs. Breakfast 65 frs; D,B&B 65 frs per person added. Set meals 149–350 frs; full alc 350–400 frs.

AIGUEBELETTE-LE-LAC 73610 Savoie Map 12

Hôtel de la Combe: Chez Michelon BUDGET *Tel* 04.79.36.05.02
Fax 04.79.44.11.93

Run for five generations by the Dufour family, this simple restaurant-with-rooms stands above a quiet, little-known lake west of Chambéry. Craggy mountains rise behind; there are fine views from most bedrooms, and from the dining room with its picture windows. The cooking has a local Savoyard touch, with fish from the lake. Recent praise: "A beautiful spot and a friendly welcome." "A good meal, a pleasant room with a view. The young staff were helpful and charming." An earlier report spelt it out: "The large terrace, shaded by a sweet chestnut, faces the lake and is a restful place to sit and watch the fishermen and listen to the nightingales. The modern building is light and airy, with plain, attractive bedrooms. The Alpha Plus communal lavatory has spectacular pink-and-gold flowered wallpaper *all* over. I would gladly return – for the comfort, peace, beauty and good food, in a room where the locals are packed in." (*O and DM, and others*)

Open All year, except Nov. Closed Mon evening/Tues.
Rooms 9 double. All with bath or shower, 5 with WC. 2 on ground floor.
Facilities Lounge, TV room, restaurant; terrace. Garden, beach.
Location S of *autoroute* A43 to Lyon, 24 km W of Chambéry.
Credit cards Access, Visa.
Terms Rooms 120–302 frs. Breakfast 36 frs. D,B&B 256–328 frs per person. Set meals 120–230 frs; full alc 200–300 frs.

AIGUES-MORTES 30220 Gard — Map 11

Hôtel des Arcades NEW
23 boulevard Gambetta

Tel 04.66.53.81.13
Fax 04.66.53.75.46

A restaurant-with-rooms in a famous medieval walled city by the Rhône delta. Dropped from the 1996 *Guide* for lack of feedback, it is restored this year: "We had a large pleasant room, an excellent dinner, with friendly staff." This endorses an earlier, wry account: "Aigues-Mortes is everything that Carcassonne isn't. No over-restoration, no hundreds of ghastly grockle shops, but a living, active town with enough bloodthirsty history to keep the children interested. My seven-year-old liked the places for tipping boiling oil down on to attackers. The hotel, like all the buildings, is ancient (16th-century), very attractive and nicely converted. Our rooms had views of the lovely garden at the back. Rooms slightly dark and furnished with what guide books used to call antiques. Still, very comfortable." (*David H Clark, and others*)

Open All year, except 11–27 Feb, 12–28 Nov. Restaurant closed Mon/midday Tues, except July/Aug, public holidays.
Rooms 6 double.
Facilities Restaurant. Garden.
Location Central. Aigues-Mortes is 42 km S of Nîmes.
Credit cards All major cards accepted.
Terms [1996] B&B 480–550 frs. Set meals 120–250 frs.

AIX-EN-PROVENCE 13100 Bouches-du-Rhône — Map 11

Hôtel des Quatre Dauphins BUDGET
54 rue Roux-Alphéran

Tel 04.42.38.16.39
Fax 04.42.38.60.19

Central, near Cours Mirabeau, small and friendly B&B hotel with 13 attractive bedrooms, renovated in Provençal style; pleasant breakfast room. Access, Visa accepted. B&B: single 322 frs, double 404–464 frs. Endorsed in 1996, but fuller reports welcome.

AIX-LES-BAINS 73100 Savoie — Map 12

Le Manoir
37 rue Georges Ier

Tel 04.79.61.44.00
Fax 04.79.35.67.67

The large and lovely Lac du Bourget is *Le Lac* where Lamartine mourned his lost love: there's a memorial to him on a hillside in this once-fashionable spa – still quite chic but "somewhat sad", as such places often are. *Le Manoir*, a Relais du Silence, is one of its best hotels, a big white gabled villa set quietly on a hill in the outskirts. It has been called "well run and welcoming", and has a large attractive garden with smart tables and chairs, plus two lounges with period furniture, and three dining rooms (one a conservatory). "We liked it a lot," is a recent view. "Our quite large, well-furnished room had a good bathroom and a balcony overlooking the *parc*. The service was good, so were the four-course *demi-pension* meals" (good local lake fish). Many guests are *curistes* at the thermal baths. The hotel has a stunning indoor swimming pool of its own. (*EHW*)

Open All year.
Rooms 60 double, 13 single. 11 air-conditioned.
Facilities Lift. 2 salons, bar, 4 dining rooms; conference/function facilities; indoor swimming pool, jacuzzi, sauna, Turkish bath. Garden. Opposite large park; lake: beaches, sailing 3 km.
Location 500 m from centre, SE of Thermes Nationaux. Private carpark.
Credit cards All major cards accepted.
Terms Rooms: single from 295 frs, double from 345 frs. Breakfast 55 frs. D,B&B 315–480 frs per person. Set meals 138–245 frs; full alc 250 frs.

AJACCIO 20000 Corse-du-Sud — **Map 17**

Hôtel Dolce Vita — *Tel* 04.95.52.42.42
Route des Sanguinaires — *Fax* 04.95.52.07.15

The Route des Sanguinaires runs west along the coast from Ajaccio, Corsica's torrid capital and birthplace of Napoleon. Five miles out is the *Dolce Vita*, where the sweet life centres round a lovely swimming pool and canopied dining terrace by the sea, with an "unbeatable view". "Very smart, in a beautiful position", is a recent plaudit. Many bedrooms have a balcony facing lawns and sea, and some are spacious. The *Michelin* star and two *Gault Millau toques* are "well deserved – langoustine ravioli, fresh fish, with many dishes incorporating the very good local sheep's cheese, brocchiù". There are some fine deserted beaches nearby. The small sandy beach is covered at high tide, but there is an iron ladder from the rocks into the sea, for swimming. (*C and AP*)

Open 1 Apr–31 Oct.
Rooms 32 double. Some on ground floor.
Facilities Lounge, bar, 2 dining rooms; conference facilities; night club. Air-conditioning. Garden: terraces, swimming pool, bathing from rocks; slipway for boats. Unsuitable for ♿.
Location 8 km W of Ajaccio, on coast. Parking.
Credit cards All major cards accepted.
Terms [1996] Rooms: single 435–565 frs, double 700–970 frs. Breakfast 60 frs. D,B&B double 1,330–1,755 frs. Set meals 250 frs; full alc 280–440 frs. 1-night bookings refused in season.

ALBI 81000 Tarn — **Map 10**

Hostellerie Saint-Antoine NEW — *Tel* 05.63.54.04.04
17 rue St-Antoine — *Fax* 05.63.47.1047

In the town centre, quite near the superb Toulouse-Lautrec museum and the wonderful pink cathedral, is this venerable old hotel. The Rieux family have owned and run it as an inn since 1734, and have now rebuilt it in modern style but with period furniture. After a time with no reports, it is restored to our pages: "It is run most efficiently, with real warmth and care. Dinner was good and breakfast exceptional, served in an attractive room." Or you can take breakfast, or drinks, on the terrace. Quietest bedrooms face the garden at the back. Guests have free use of the pool and tennis court at the *Saint-Antoine*'s luxurious sister hotel, *La Réserve* (*Gault Millau toque*), two miles away. (*Antonia Paul*)

Open All year.
Rooms 6 suites, 32 double, 6 single.

Facilities Lift. 3 lounges, bar, restaurant. Garden. Swimming pool, tennis at *La Réserve* 3 km.
Location Central. Parking.
Credit cards All major cards accepted.
Terms B&B: single 370–530 frs, double 520–850 frs, suite 900–1,000 frs. Set meals 140–200 frs; full alc 250 frs.

LES ANDELYS 27700 Eure — Map 8

Hostellerie de la Chaîne d'Or — *Tel* 02.32.54.00.31
27 rue Grande — *Fax* 02.32.54.05.68

In 1995–96, three more plaudits came for this 18th-century *auberge*, splendidly situated between the Seine and the main square of an old Norman town near Rouen. With its flowery courtyard and beamed dining room, it is very attractive, and most bedrooms have "Monet-style" views of a great loop in the river (Monet's garden at Giverny is not far away). "Lovely room facing the Seine." "We loved this hotel. The manager and his wife were hard-working and charming, service was impeccable and the food delicious." This year, *Michelin* bestows a star for the first time, and *Gault Millau* still gives two *toques*, for Norman cooking in a modern style, eg, oysters in champagne sauce. In the "charming dining room with cosy pink curtains", readers have enjoyed the "warm seafood salad in lemony herby cream sauce, fish in lobster sauce with spinach". "Our room was beautifully decorated, quite elegant, with a sitting area where we took breakfast looking at the river." "Our older room had antique furniture and a very creaky floor." (*Dr NB Finter, Dr and Mrs J Granger, Mr and Mrs A Andersen, and others*) "When our car was broken into in the night, the robbers were chased away by the owner's gun."

Open All year, except 1 Jan–2 Feb, Sun evening/Mon.
Rooms 10 double.
Facilities Restaurant, breakfast room; function room; courtyard. Unsuitable for ♿.
Location In Petit Andelys, on river. 39 km SE of Rouen. Parking.
Credit cards Access, Amex, Visa.
Terms [1996] Rooms 395–740 frs. Breakfast 65 frs. Set meals 140–298 frs; full alc 260–440 frs.

ANDLAU 67140 Bas-Rhin — Map 9

Hôtel Kastelberg BUDGET — *Tel* 03.88.08.97.83
10 rue du Général Koenig — *Fax* 03.88.08.48.34

In Alsatian wine village close to Route du Vin, 39 km SW of Strasbourg, gabled modern hotel in local style, run by friendly Wach family. Good Alsatian food and wines; 29 spacious, pleasant rooms, most with balcony; sun terrace. Restaurant closed Jan–Mar. Access, Visa accepted. B&B double 380–430 frs; D,B&B double 600–660 frs. Set meals 98–280 frs.

> If you have kept brochures and tariffs for continental hotels, do please enclose them with your reports. They are particularly useful if you are nominating a hotel.

ANIANE 34150 Hérault Map 10

Hostellerie St Benoit BUDGET *Tel* 04.67.57.71.63
Route de St-Guilhem *Fax* 04.67.57.47.10

On edge of village 30 km NW of Montpellier, near Hérault gorges, Clamouse caves and fascinating St-Guilhem village: modern Logis de France, family-run, with young, eager staff. 30 rooms, many with balcony facing piscine. *Clean and tidy, with somewhat kitsch decor. Good breakfast. Closed 4 Jan–14 Feb. Access, Visa accepted. Rooms 270–310 frs. Breakfast 37 frs. D,B&B 265–275 frs per person. Set meals 99–145 frs [1996]. Reports on food welcome.*

ANNOT 04240 Alpes-de-Haute-Provence Map 11

Hôtel de l'Avenue BUDGET *Tel* 04.92.83.22.07
Avenue de la Gare *Fax* 04.92.83.34.07

Set amid mountains with bizarre rock formations, Annot is a delightful tiny town of upper Provence – ancient archways, tall Renaissance houses, neatly paved alleyways with streams. "It's mostly ungentrified, and looks like a deserted set from an early French movie," says the nominator of the modest *Avenue*, which wins a *Michelin* red "Repas" and *Gault Millau toque* for owner/chef Jean-Louis Genovesi's regional cooking. "Food and presentation were excellent. The front-of-house ladies were charming and full of smiles. The dining room and bedrooms have been modernised in that peculiar French style. But the floors still creaked, and the old doors kept their original lovely locks. Our room was small but had nice views. You can eat on the terrace in fine weather." (*RH*)

Open 1 April–4 Nov.
Rooms 12 double, 2 single. 2 in annexe.
Facilities Salon with TV, restaurant. Unsuitable for ♿.
Location Central. Annot is 32 km NE of Castellane. Street parking.
Credit cards Access, Visa.
Terms Rooms 200–250 frs. Breakfast 30 frs. D,B&B 240–280 frs per person. Set meals 85–110 frs; full alc 180 frs.

ARBOIS 39600 Jura Map 12

Jean-Paul Jeunet *Tel* 03.84.66.05.67
9 rue de l'Hôtel de Ville *Fax* 03.84.66.24.20

Michelin this year awarded a second star to Jean-Paul Jeunet – who also wins three *Gault Millau toques*, above all for his clever use of local herbs – at his restaurant in the centre of a small, pretty town in the wine-growing Jura hills. "An excellent meal and a lovely room," said a reader this year, while the "enchanting atmosphere" has been extolled by devotees: "A clever interior designer has used natural textures and colours in the 17th-century public rooms (beamed ceilings and an old fireplace). Our delightful bedroom was, in contrast, bright and modern. Service was friendly and gracious. Fantastic, creative cooking: each dish lovingly prepared with fine ingredients. M. Jeunet and his wife were charming." (*JA Dyson, N and DA*) One recent visitor agreed about the food, and the "professional efficiency and niceness of the staff", but found the corridors sombre, and his room quite small and noisy. Two rooms have use of a small enclosed garden.

Open 1 Feb–30 Nov. Restaurant closed Tues/midday Wed (except school holidays, Sept).
Rooms 1 suite, 17 double. 6 in annexe.
Facilities Lift. Salon, restaurant; meeting room.
Location Central. Limited private parking.
Credit cards All major cards accepted.
Terms Rooms: single 350 frs, double 450 frs, suite 550 frs. Breakfast 68 frs. Set meals 190–500 frs; full alc 500 frs.

ARLES 13200 Bouches-du-Rhône **Map 11**

Hôtel d'Arlatan *Tel* 04.90.93.56.66
26 rue du Sauvage *Fax* 04.90.49.68.45

Down quiet side-street in heart of old Arles, distinguished 15th-century mansion, former home of counts of Arlatan. Courtyard with palms and fountain, lovely enclosed garden. 41 rooms with antiques, Provençal fabrics; but some are very small. All major credit cards accepted. Rooms 450–695 frs. Breakfast 58 frs. No restaurant: try Le Médiéval *or* Le Vaccarès. *No recent reports; more welcome.*

Hôtel Calendal NEW/BUDGET *Tel* 04.90.96.11.89
22 place du Docteur Pomme *Fax* 04.90.96.05.84

Central but quiet, near Roman arena, friendly hotel in three buildings, newly refurbished, with shady walled garden for drinks and breakfast. Bedrooms simple, with modern decor; some are large. All major credit cards accepted. 27 rooms: 250–460 frs. Breakfast 36 frs. Light meals available (soups, omelettes, salads). Renominated after recent change of owners. Fuller reports welcome.

ARPAILLARGUES 30700 Gard **Map 11**

Hôtel Marie d'Agoult *Tel* 04.66.22.14.48
Château d'Arpaillargues *Fax* 04.66.22.56.10

This 18th-century *château* is the former home of the d'Agoult family – the writer Marie d'Agoult was Franz Liszt's mistress, and their daughter Cosima married Richard Wagner. Situated on the edge of this village near fascinating Uzès, it is now a stylish country hotel, with a library, a park and views over the rolling hills. "Wonderful," runs our latest report. "We loved the swimming pool in the beautiful garden, and playing *boules* in the twilight. Dinner was magical – the food excellent with a different menu each night, and we watched the swifts and humming birds while we ate. Our room was large, and the staff friendly." Others have written: "Our light and spacious room had a private terrace with views." "The food was excellent, and we were warmly received." Opinions differ as to whether the rooms in the *château* itself, which are dearer, are preferable to those in the annexe (an old silkworm nursery); some in both houses are small, and the *château*, with many stairs and no lift, is not suitable for the disabled. (*PJAD, JER*) A new chef in 1996; reports, please.

Open Apr–Nov.
Rooms 2 suites, 26 double. 18 in annexe. 1 on ground floor. 22 with air-conditioning.
Facilities Lounge/bar, TV room, 3 dining rooms (1 no-smoking). Garden: swimming pool (unheated), tennis. Unsuitable for ♿.
Location 4 km W of Uzès.
Credit cards All major cards accepted.
Terms Rooms 400–800 frs, suite 800–1,150 frs. Breakfast 55 frs. D,B&B: single 640–1,040 frs, double 880–1,280 frs, suite 1,280–1,630 frs. Set lunch 125 frs, dinner 210 frs.

ARZON 56640 Morbihan — Map 8

Le Crouesty — *Tel* 02.97.53.87.91
Port du Crouesty — *Fax* 02.97.53.66.76

Castrated and banished from Paris for his affair with Héloise, Pierre Abelard spent the years 1128–34 as abbot of St-Gilda, here on the south side of the Gulf of Morbihan. As he wrote, he found "the country wild, the monks beyond control, the natives brutal and barbarous". They have changed. Madame Gloaguen, say the hotel's nominators, brings "a genuine friendly concern for her visitors" to the running of this spruce purpose-built B&B, near the marina of Le Crouesty and the wide clean beach of Navalo. "Its modern decor creates a light, airy ambience. Breakfast is noted for its fresh bakery. Front rooms can be a bit noisy in high season, but we rejoice in this hotel. No dinners, but *Auberge Kerstephanie* about ten kilometres away is favoured by locals for its good value." (*JBC and CL*)

Open All year, except 5 Jan–5 Feb.
Rooms 26 double.
Facilities Lounge, breakfast room; terrace. Garden.
Location At Port du Crouesty, 2 km SW of Arzon, 32 km SW of Vannes. Parking.
Credit cards Access, Amex, Visa.
Terms [1996] Rooms 350–450 frs. Breakfast 39 frs.

AUDINGHEN 62179 Pas-de-Calais — Map 9

La Maison de la Houve NEW/BUDGET — *Tel* 03.21.32.97.06
Fax 03.21.83.29.95

Useful for tunnel or ferry goers, this old farmhouse **has** a quiet rural setting north of Boulogne. It has been well modernised, with plenty of pink in the decor, by its owner from Paris, Mme Danel. She has a botanic and rose garden in the grounds, and has filled the house with good furniture. The hotel fell from the 1996 *Guide* after criticisms, but an American family were pleased this year: "Simple and charming, with a friendly atmosphere – '*pas de clefs*,' said Madame. Her breakfast-brunch came with fruit, eggs, local cheeses. The roses were in full bloom. Vista of cows in the pasture." (*G Scott Briggs*) No restaurant: several nearby. Further reports welcome.

Open All year.
Rooms 6 double, 1 single. 2 on ground floor.
Facilities Salon, breakfast room. Garden.
Location 12 km N of Boulogne, off D940: 1.5 km SE of Audinghen, by D191 to Marquise.
Credit cards None accepted.

Terms B&B: single 105–150 frs, double 125–170 frs. Children under 15 accommodated free in parents' room.

AUTUN 71400 Saône-et-Loire **Map 12**

Hôtel des Ursulines NEW *Tel* 03.85.86.58.58
14 rue Rivault *Fax* 03.85.86.23.07

Close to Autun's superb 12th-century cathedral is this graciously elegant hotel, a former convent built into the ramparts at the top of the town, and finely converted. "Splendidly equipped rooms and a beautiful outlook towards the Morvan hills," says its nominator. "Food excellent, staff attentive. Breakfast in a former chapel" (with fine stained-glass). You can dine on the terrace facing the hills (*Gault Millau toque*), or take drinks in the formal garden. (*Michael and Betty Hill*)

Open All year.
Rooms 6 suites, 32 double.
Facilities Lift. Salons, bar, restaurant; conference facilities. Garden.
Location On S edge of inner town, by ramparts. Garage.
Credit cards All major cards accepted.
Terms [1996] Rooms 350–465 frs, suite 515–820 frs. Breakfast 60 frs. D,B&B 480–675 frs per person. Set meals 90–375 frs; full alc 385 frs.

Vieux Moulin *Tel* 03.85.52.10.90
Porte d'Arroux *Fax* 03.85.86.32.15

Just outside a Roman gateway of this superb historic Burgundy town (fine cathedral, museum): elegant restaurant with 16 quiet, spacious bedrooms, comfortable lounge, shady garden. Excellent food. Closed 2 Dec–28 Feb, Sun evening/Mon in low season. Access, Amex, Visa accepted. Rooms 230–370 frs. Breakfast 45 frs. Set lunch 90 frs, dinner 150–250 frs [1996].

AUXERRE 89000 Yonne **Map 9**

Le Parc des Maréchaux *Tel* 03.86.51.43.77
6 avenue Foch *Fax* 03.86.51.31.72

In a quiet part of an old cathedral city, this converted 1850s mansion is now a stylish B&B hotel, run in a personal way by its *patronne*, Espérance Hervé, a doctor's wife. It remains popular with readers of all ages. "It's a great place for us children." "Madame is charming and very efficient." "Warm, enthusiastic welcome; airy, well-equipped rooms." Breakfast is "excellent" and "generous", and you can take it under the limes in the big garden. The comfortable bedrooms, newly renovated, are named after French marshals such as Lyautey, and there are "interesting Napoleonic memorabilia". The plushy American bar, "with its welcoming fire", is called *L'Araucaria*, after the 100-year-old Chilean monkey-puzzle tree in the garden. Quiet classical muzak plays – too repetitively, say some – in the comfortable Napoleon III sitting room where breakfast is served. (*SL, and others*)

Open All year.
Rooms 25 double. 2 on ground floor.
Facilities Lift. Lounge, bar, breakfast room; conference room. Large grounds: children's play area, table-tennis.

Location 500 m W of town centre. Private parking.
Credit cards All major cards accepted.
Terms Rooms: single 275–295 frs, double 310–390 frs. Breakfast 47 frs. Children accommodated free in parents' room.

AVALLON 89200 Yonne — Map 9

Château de Vault-de-Lugny

Tel 03.86.34.07.86
Fax 03.86.34.16.36

"Elegant, beautiful and romantic" is a recent verdict on the Audan family's stately 16th-century *château*, set in spacious grounds west of Avallon. Sumptuously renovated, full of antiques, it has also been called "splendidly idiosyncratic", and this earlier report holds good: "You announce your arrival at the ornate iron gates which then quietly swing open – and you are met by a cacophony of geese, hens, peacocks and barking dogs. At the entrance steps, maids are waiting and a vast old hall serves as reception. Shades of *Brideshead*, until Mlle Audan greets you in American English. The rooms are beautifully furnished (at least one has a four-poster). Everything creaks, smells of polish, and has a worn, well-used feel." (*JR*) We'd be glad of fuller reports, especially on the food.

Open End Mar–mid-Nov.
Rooms 7 suites, 5 double. 1 on ground floor.
Facilities Lounge, restaurant (no-smoking). Garden.
Location 6 km W of Avallon. Turn right off D957 at Pontaubert, then right on to D142 after church.
Credit cards Access, Amex, Visa.
Terms B&B: double 700–1,200 frs, suite 1,500–2,200 frs. Set dinner 280 frs. Discount for longer stay.

AVIGNON 84000 Vaucluse — Map 11

Hôtel d'Europe

12 place Crillon

Tel 04.90.14.76.76
Fax 04.90.85.43.66

"Civilised, quiet and gastronomically excellent," writes a veteran this year, anatomising this famous hotel, a 16th-century aristocrat's house in a small square near the Papal Palace. It was already an inn in 1799 when Napoleon stayed here, and today is an elegant and stylish hotel, rather formal – "a cool and expensive haven in noisy hot Avignon". Public rooms are filled with flowers and antiques; the dining room is a little dull, but when it's warm you can eat under the plane trees beside a fountain in the charming small courtyard. This expensive *Vieille Fontaine* restaurant has lost its *Michelin* star but keeps the *Gault Millau toque*: most readers admire its food. Bedrooms are superior: one couple had "a suite with an elegant marble bath, and a large private sun terrace with parasol and a terrific view of Avignon". Reports on service and welcome are mixed: again this year, a visitor thought the staff impersonal, "but not unfriendly". Breakfast, says one reader, is good but "overpriced". There is a pleasant bar, and gentle piped classical music. Rooms vary in size, and some at the back can suffer from traffic noise. (*Sally and Anthony Sampson, P Yarnold, and others*)

Open All year. Restaurant closed Sun/midday Mon.
Rooms 3 suites, 44 double. Some on ground floor. Air-conditioning.

Facilities Lift. Lounge, TV room, bar, restaurant; conference facilities; terrace, courtyard. 5 mins' walk from Papal Palace.
Location By Porte de l'Oulle on W side of city. Private garage (50 frs).
Credit cards All major cards accepted.
Terms Rooms: 620–800 frs., suite 2,100 frs. Breakfast 90 frs. Set lunch 160 frs, dinner 280–380 frs.

La Ferme BUDGET
Chemin des Bois
La Barthelasse

Tel 04.90.82.57.53
Fax 04.90.27.15.47

Just north of the city, this Logis de France, a converted farmhouse with beamed ceilings, stands quietly amid trees on an island in the Rhône. It has been liked recently for its "excellent food, nice swimming pool", and a pretty patio where you can eat outdoors. Others have written: "Pleasant owners, comfortable rooms, cosy dining room." On the menu, such dishes as raviolis d'escargots, escalope de sandre. Cheerful decor, a log fire in winter. But beds can be small: "You may have to sleep diagonally." (*IB and TR*)

Open Mar–Nov, 26 Dec–2 Jan. Closed for lunch Sat.
Rooms 18 double, 2 single. 2 no-smoking. 10 air-conditioned.
Facilities Salon, bar, restaurant. Garden: swimming pool (unheated).
Location 5 km N of walled city. Cross Édouard Daladier bridge towards Villeneuve; right on island along D228. Private parking.
Credit cards Access, Amex, Visa.
Restriction No children under 8.
Terms B&B: single 325–368 frs, double 380–526 frs; D,B&B 305–400 frs per person. Set meals 105–210 frs.

BAGNOLES-DE-L'ORNE 61140 Orne — Map 8

Le Manoir du Lys
Route de Juvigny

Tel 02.33.37.80.69
Fax 02.33.30.05.80

Paul and Marie-France Quinton's gabled and half-timbered manor house, typically Norman without, neatly modernised within, stands in a lush forest outside a well-known spa town. "It just keeps getting better," wrote returning fans this year. "Excellent baths, beautiful gardens, warm welcome, food amazingly good – *bon Dieu* what foie gras, what cheeses, what wonderful fresh fish" (*Gault Millau toque*). A 1996 visitor thought it "very well run, fully professional while remaining friendly", while another reader had "a lovely light and spacious room with its own balcony, facing the beautiful gardens and peaceful countryside". (*Ruth and Derek Tilsley, JT, and others*) It's a Relais du Silence, but stags may roar at night in the forest.

Open All year, except 5 Jan–14 Feb, Christmas, Sun evening/Mon 1 Nov–Easter.
Rooms 23 double. 1 especially equipped for ♿.
Facilities Lift. Lounge, bar, billiard room, 2 dining rooms; conference facilities; terrace. Garden: swimming pool, tennis, golf practice.
Location 3 km NW of Bagnoles, near golf course.
Credit cards All major cards accepted.
Terms Rooms 300–580 frs, suite 680–780 frs. Breakfast 57 frs. Set meals 135–265 frs; full alc 280–380 frs.

BARFLEUR 50760 Manche **Map 8**

Hôtel le Conquérant BUDGET *Tel* 02.33.54.00.82
16–18 rue St-Thomas-Becket *Fax* 02.33.54.65.25

"Delightful" 18th-century stone manor house in attractive small fishing port 27 km E of Cherbourg. Nicely converted, with big beautiful garden; welcoming owners, the Delomenèdes. 16 spacious rooms. Closed 16 Nov–14 Feb. Access, Visa accepted. B&B double 372–422 frs. Simple set meals (crêpes, fish soup, etc), for residents only. Or try restaurant Moderne (Michelin *red "Repas") in village.*

BARJAC 30430 Gard **Map 11**

Le Mas du Terme NEW *Tel* 05.66.24.56.31
Fax 05.66.24.58.54

In open hilly country 4 km SE of Barjac off D901, and just SW of superb Gorges de l'Ardèche: converted 18th-century mas *with rustic furnishings, stone vaulted ceilings, lounge, courtyard, swimming pool with loungers. 19 comfortable rooms. Food good, but menu restricted; buffet breakfast a bit slapdash. Open Apr–Dec. Access, Visa accepted. Rooms 390–450 frs. Breakfast 45 frs. D,B&B 385–565 frs per person. Set meals 160–240 frs [1996].*

LE BARROUX 84330 Vaucluse **Map 11**

Hôtel Les Géraniums BUDGET *Tel* 04.90.62.41.08
Place de la Croix *Fax* 04.90.62.56.48

This modest family-run *auberge* ("outstanding value") is an old stone building in an out-of-the-way Provençal hill village, complete with medieval castle, amid glorious country up near Mont Ventoux. "Our room was small but nicely decorated, with an unforgettable view. Madame was wonderful to us, and the food was good too" (eg, navarin d'agneau à la provençale). Rooms in the newer annexe are "small but nicely furnished" and many have views over the Rhône valley and the hills. You can eat on the terrace with a view, or in a beamed *salle*. "The food was tasty, served by an enthusiastic young woman." The owners, Jacques and Agnès Roux, have been called "charming", "busy but helpful". (*S and LC*) Some tour groups.

Open All year, except 4 Jan–1 Mar, Wed 15 Nov–15 Mar.
Rooms 22 double. 9 in nearby annexe.
Facilities Salon with TV, bar, restaurant; function room; 2 terraces. Garden: solarium, table-tennis. Unsuitable for ♿.
Location 10 km N of Carpentras. Garage.
Credit cards All major cards accepted.
Terms [1996] Rooms 210–250 frs. Breakfast 35 frs. D,B&B 230–370 frs per person. Set meals 80–250 frs; full alc 200 frs.

A number of continental hotels have quoted their rates exclusive of tourist tax or value added tax. Please check when booking.

LA BAUME DE TRANSIT 26790 Drôme — Map 11

Domaine de St-Luc BUDGET

Tel 04.75.98.11.51
Fax 04.75.98.19.22

"Transit" does little to convey the rustic appeal of this converted 18th-century farmhouse, in remote upper Provence, north-east of Bollène. It has "friendly and attentive young owners", Ludovic and Éliane Cornillon, and is classified as *chambres d'hôte*, rather than as a hotel (rooms are quite simple). There is a large handsome lounge, an old hearth and some antiques. This year, one visitor thought the food disappointing, but earlier reports praised the "high standard of meals" and the quiet calm. "A beautiful complex of old stone buildings, tastefully restored. Our comfortable room opened on to a private terrace." All the guests (the hotel is particularly popular with Americans) sit round one table for the no-choice four-course dinner, which comes with wine from the owner's vineyards. (*JD, DR*)

Open All year.
Rooms 1 triple, 4 double. 1 on ground floor.
Facilities Lounge, restaurant. Garden.
Location 1.5 km S of La Baume de Transit. 12 km NE of Bollène.
Credit cards None accepted.
Terms B&B double 330 frs. Set dinner 135 frs.

LES BAUX-DE-PROVENCE 13520 Bouches-du-Rhône — Map 11

Le Mas d'Aigret

Tel 04.90.54.33.54
Fax 04.90.54.41.37

Bestowing two *toques* on the cuisine, *Gault Millau* praises *"l'humour* so British *de Pip Phillips et sa grande affabilité"* as other key assets of this converted 17th-century stone *mas*. Owned and run by this jovial Englishman and his French wife Chantal, it lies in the valley below the famous ruined hill village-cum-castle of Les Baux, a magnet once for troubadours, now for mass tourists. Pip tells us that rumours of his own departure have been much exaggerated, and that if he was closed for a few months in the summer of 1996, it was simply because the municipal council was repairing the rocky cliff behind his hotel, but this is now done. "Service, accommodation and food were first class," is our latest report. Meals in summer are served on a large shady terrace with a view over the valley and castle, floodlit at night. Readers enjoy the "personal welcome", "elegant clientele" and "delicious" food, which uses local Provençal recipes and produce: "Not a place for weight-watchers." The owner "blazes with enthusiasm, talking to all his guests at dinner". "The public rooms are full of antiques, personal objects; on the terrace the tables are candlelit." "Service is by local girls who chatter to you delightfully." Bedrooms are "small but pretty". (*MM, and others*)

Open All year, except 3–22 Feb. Restaurant closed Wed midday.
Rooms 16 double.
Facilities Salon, bar, restaurant; terrace. Garden: swimming pool. Unsuitable for ♿.
Location 400 m E of village on D27A. 19 km NE of Arles. Private parking.
Credit cards All major cards accepted.
Terms [1996] Rooms 600–950 frs. Breakfast 70 frs. D,B&B 620–845 frs per person. Set meals 190–350 frs.

Auberge de la Benvengudo *Tel* 04.90.54.32.54
Vallon de l'Arcoule *Fax* 04.90.54.42.58

In valley 2 km SW of Les Baux, off D78, creeper-covered farmhouse, quite glamorous, with floodlit patio, large swimming-pool in big garden; tennis. Good Provençal cooking by owner/manager Daniel Beaupied. Attractive rooms, some with antiques. Open 1 Feb–31 Oct. Restaurant closed Sun evening. Access, Amex, Visa accepted. 20 rooms: 450–680 frs. Breakfast 60 frs. Full alc 285 frs. No recent reports; new ones welcome.

BAYEUX 14400 Calvados **Map 8**

Château de Bellefontaine *Tel* 02.31.22.00.10
49 rue Bellefontaine *Fax* 02.31.22.19.09

Rural, yet only 1.5 km SE of centre, off ring road to Caen, 18th-century château *in 5-acre park with fountain, stream and tennis. "Peaceful and delightful." Good beds, pleasant decor, helpful staff, breakfast any time. No restaurant. Closed 15 Jan–15 Feb. All major credit cards accepted. 15 rooms: 380–650 frs. Breakfast 50 frs.*

Le Lion d'Or *Tel* 02.31.92.06.90
71 rue St-Jean *Fax* 02.31.22.15.64

"An elegant hotel full of character, with friendly staff"; "our bedroom was excellent, so was the food" – more praise, this year and last, for a dignified old coaching inn, "old-fashioned in a nice nostalgic way". It is in the town centre, but quiet (a Relais du Silence). Rooms are set back from the street around a paved courtyard with flowers and trees; many are spacious, and one was "attractively decorated with Chinese wall fabrics". In the "rather formal" dining room, the food wins a *Gault Millau toque*, and has again been praised by our readers this year, notably the trout in orange butter sauce and fondue of camembert. Yet *Michelin* has now withdrawn its star. (*Jill Douglas, Martin and Karen Oldridge, and others*). Large groups can be an irritation.

Open 21 Jan–20 Dec.
Rooms 2 suites, 24 double.
Facilities Salon, reading room, bar, 2 dining rooms; courtyard. Unsuitable for ♿.
Location Central, near Halle aux Grains, but quiet. Courtyard parking.
Credit cards All major cards accepted.
Terms [1996] Rooms 300–470 frs, suite 600–900 frs. Breakfast 60 frs. D,B&B 380–655 frs per person. Set meals 100–320 frs; full alc 280 frs. Children accommodated free in parents' room in low season.

BEAULIEU-SUR-MER 06310 Alpes-Maritimes **Map 11**

Hôtel Métropole NEW *Tel* 04.93.01.00.08
15 boulevard Maréchal Leclerc *Fax* 04.93.01.18.51

Beaulieu with its casino and floodlit palms remains sedately elegant, if less fashionable than in pre-war days. A survivor from that epoch is the *Métropole,* right by the sea. Not large but grand and stylish (Relais & Châteaux, five red *Michelin* gables), it is still one of the great hotels of the Côte d'Azur, and was restored to the *Guide* by a devotee writing in 1996: "It all seems very formal and elegant, yet the staff are friendly, making you feel welcome. Bedrooms are classical French in style: from ours it was a delight to enjoy the view of the well-tended garden and the sea. Breakfast was delicious by French standards, with lots of fresh pastries. Cooking is creative, making the *Michelin* star [and two *Gault Millau toques*] well deserved. The *table d'hôte* is five-course. You can eat on the terrace when it's fine, while the dining room also faces the sea." The heated salt-water pool is "a dream". Some cheaper rooms are small, face inland, and may be a bit noisy. (*Mrs H Langenberg*) Jean Rauline, the first new manager for 23 years, arrived in 1995.

Open All year, except 20 Oct–20 Dec.
Rooms 3 suites, 40 double, 10 single. Air-conditioning.
Facilities 2 lounges, bar, restaurant; terrace bar. Garden: swimming pool.
Location Central, by sea, 10 km NE of Nice. Parking.
Credit cards Access, Amex, Visa.
Terms D,B&B: single 1,240–2,200 frs, double 1,940–3,930 frs, suite 3,360–6,330 frs. Set meals 400–490 frs; full alc 500 frs.

LE BEC-HELLOUIN 27800 Eure — Map 8

Auberge de l'Abbaye — *Tel* 02.32.44.86.02
Pl. Guillaume le Conquérant — *Fax* 02.32.46.32.23

One of Europe's great Benedictine monasteries once stood in this picturesque village south-west of Rouen, and in medieval times it produced three archbishops of Canterbury. It has now been restored from ruin, and again houses a religious community – the Gregorian chant in the abbey church is worth hearing. On the village green is the Sergent family's 18th-century half-timbered *auberge*, full, apart maybe from its neon sign, of tasteful character: "Low beams, sloping floors, creaking boards and tiny windows all make for atmosphere." Rooms, though comfortable, are old-fashioned for some tastes, but recent visitors wrote: "Delightful. Caring owners, and an excellent dinner (duck salad, lovely Norman puddings)." Previous praise: "Our baby was greeted with enthusiasm." "Comfortable beds in a large, pretty room which had lost nothing of its 18th-century character. Bright cheerful dining room, with fresh flowers, attractive glassware. Breakfast good, too." (*David Griffith, and others*) One couple were accorded a chilly reception, and "half the dishes on the menu were not available".

Open All year.
Rooms 1 suite, 9 double. Some on ground floor.
Facilities Salon, TV room, 2 dining rooms; function room; terrace.
Location 5 km N of Brionne, which is 41 km SW of Rouen. Private parking.
Credit cards Access, Amex, Visa.
Terms Rooms 390–580 frs. Breakfast 40 frs. D,B&B 400 frs per person. Set meals 130–250 frs; full alc 250 frs.

BELCASTEL 12390 Aveyron — Map 10

Le Vieux Pont — *Tel* 05.65.64.52.29
Fax 05.65.64.44.32

"Here is a kind of dream French hotel," writes a recent visitor. "It is in a tiny remote hamlet of medieval houses, rising on the sides of a steep cliff, topped by a feudal castle. At the foot of the cliff, a 500-year-old cobbled bridge crosses the swift-flowing Aveyron. On one side is the family home of two sisters, Nicole and Michèle Fagegaltier, whose parents and grandparents ran a restaurant here. Now Nicole (early thirties and self-taught), helped by her husband Bruno, wins a *Michelin* star, as well as a red 'Repas', and two *Gault Millau toques* for inventive regional cooking: her way with turnips and lentils, cèpes and girolles, helped us towards a memorable meal. Michèle does front-of-house. They have now converted a ruined building across the bridge into a tiny hotel, simple, almost austere, but elegant too: modern lighting, a fine view of the river. No boutiques, no tourist tat." "The staff were charming in a direct, open way. The restaurant has picture windows facing the river, and a relaxed up-market chic, typically French. Delicious breakfast." To these earlier views was added this fresh encomium in 1996: "This is the hotel for me. The setting is magic. Dinner was exactly what we wanted – each a different fish dish, preceded by an amuse-bouche of magret in orange sauce and succeeded by stunning puddings. All dishes were nicely balanced and intelligently timed." (*Elizabeth and Bernard Biggs, HR, JCB*)

Open All year, except Jan/Feb. Closed Sun evening/Mon except July/Aug.
Rooms 7 double. 1 on ground floor.
Facilities Restaurant. River: fishing.
Location 23 km W of Rodez, off D994 to Villefranche. Parking.
Credit cards Access, Visa.
Terms Rooms: single 400 frs, double 480 frs. Breakfast 50 frs. D,B&B 415–450 frs per person. Set meals 135–330 frs; full alc 320 frs.

BELLE-ILE-EN-MER 56360 Morbihan — Map 8

Castel Clara NEW — *Tel* 02.97.31.84.21
Port Goulphar — *Fax* 02.97.31.51.69

Belle-Ile, the largest of Brittany's offshore islands, has rocky headlands, sandy beaches and creeks. On a hill above one creek, in a lovely setting on the south coast, is this smart white modern Relais & Châteaux hotel. Dropped from the 1995 *Guide* for lack of feedback, it is restored eagerly this year: "Beautiful and sophisticated. Our room and the view were top rate. A relaxed ambience; restaurant run by female staff. Clients mainly French BCBG" (ie, posh). Others have written: "Our large room had a terrace facing the sea. There's a huge heated salt-water pool, and wonderful food" – *Gault Millau toque*. (*Martin and Karen Oldridge*)

Open Mid-Feb–mid-Nov.
Rooms 11 suites, 32 double.
Facilities Lift. Lounge, bar, breakfast room, 2 dining rooms; games room; conference facilities; terrace. Garden: sea-water swimming pool, tennis.
Location 7 km W of Le Palais, at Port Goulphar (cove). 45-min car/passenger ferry service several times daily from mainland. Private parking.
Credit cards Access, Amex, Visa.
Terms Rooms: double 1,095–1,390 frs, suite 1,490–1,950 frs. Breakfast 120 frs. D,B&B 1,350–1,880 frs. Set meals 175–370 frs.

> The "New" label is used for hotels which are appearing in the *Guide* for the first time or have been readmitted after an absence.

BÉNODET 29950 Finistère Map 8

Hôtel Menez-Frost *Tel* 02.98.57.03.09
4 rue Charcot *Fax* 02.98.57.14.73

This popular resort in south Brittany stands at the mouth of the calm river Odet, which is studded with pleasure boats. The *Menez-Frost*, made up of several buildings in a well-kept garden, is fairly central, near to the port and good beaches, but quiet. It has tennis, ping-pong and an outdoor swimming pool, and has been called "ideal for children's holidays, with a young and cheerful staff". "A very enjoyable week in a large self-catering apartment, with views over the excellent large pool and pretty garden. The owner/managers were charming" – they are a "true Breton" family, very active. Bedroom decor is rather dull, but many rooms have a balcony, and the lounge has deep, comfy chairs. No restaurant, which some families might find a handicap; but there are good eating places nearby, eg, the *Café du Port* at Ste-Marine across the river. (*NMM and others*) Two more self-catering apartments have been added this year.

Open Hotel: 1 May–30 Sept; 12 self-catering apartments: 1 Mar–30 Nov.
Rooms 4 suites, 28 double, 12 single. 5 on ground floor. 10 self-catering apartments.
Facilities Salon, TV room, reading room, bar; conference facilities. Garden: swimming pool, solarium, sauna, tennis, table-tennis.
Location Central, near post office, port and ferry. Private carpark.
Credit cards Access, Visa.
Terms Rooms: single 320–395 frs, double 350–550 frs, suite 600–840 frs. Breakfast 45 frs.

BÉNOUVILLE 14970 Calvados Map 8

La Glycine BUDGET *Tel* 02.31.44.61.94
11 Place du Commando n°4 *Fax* 02.31.43.67.30

In village, cheaper alternative to Manoir *(below). A family-run Logis de France, "The Wisteria" has 25 simple adequate rooms, patio, "excellent" food and good service. Closed 15 Feb–15 Mar; restaurant closed Sun evening out of season. Access, Visa accepted. B&B: single 263–313 frs, double 346 frs; D,B&B 280–395 frs per person. Set meals 95–225 frs.*

Restaurant Le Manoir d'Hastings et Hôtel La Pommeraie *Tel* 02.31.44.62.43
Avenue de la Côte de Nacre 18 *Fax* 02.31.44.76.18

Brittany Ferries' port at Ouistreham is a five-minute drive from this converted 17th-century priory, now a stylish restaurant-with-rooms, in the first village to be liberated by Anglo-Canadian airborne forces on D-Day. Creeper-covered, with a pretty courtyard for drinks, it is set amid gardens and indeed a *pommeraie*, and is nicely run by its owners, José and Carole Aparicio. Readers this year enjoyed "fantastic" warm terrine de foie gras in the dining room, which is in the old priory building, and, like the hall, has an open log fire. Previous praise: "We thoroughly enjoyed it. Our suite was superbly equipped, with luxurious bathrobes, lots of freebies, fresh fruit. The sea bass was superb." "Our room was spacious, with casement windows opening on to an old orchard." (*Sir John and Lady Burgh, J and DT, RH*)

Open All year, except 12 Nov–5 Dec.
Rooms 15 double (4 in *Manoir*, 11 in *Pommeraie*). Some on ground floor.
Facilities Salons, bar, 3 dining rooms. Garden. Sea 3 km.
Location 7 km NE of Caen, off D515 to Ouistreham. Carpark.
Credit cards All major cards accepted.
Terms [1996] Rooms: single 400–600 frs, double 500–800 frs. Breakfast 50 frs. D,B&B 450–850 frs per person. Set meals 120–360 frs; full alc 300 frs.

BEUZEVILLE 27210 Eure — Map 8

Le Petit Castel BUDGET
et Auberge du Cochon d'Or

Place du Général de Gaulle

Tel 02.32.57.70.46
Fax 02.32.42.25.70

In a small town near Honfleur, *Le Castel* is a neat Logis de France, with some rooms opening on to a walled garden. Next door is its ever-popular restaurant, *Le Cochon d'Or*, an old Norman *auberge* (*Michelin* red "Repas" for good value). It is an old family concern, and the Folleau parents have just retired and handed over to their children. Readers this year were again content: "A true gem. We've been coming here for ten years, and if anything it gets better. Welcome always warm, food excellent, and the whole place spotless and well kept." Others wrote earlier: "A charming restaurant with pink decor, splendid food. All staff were most friendly: the receptionist carried our heavy suitcase up the winding staircase with enthusiasm" (that's almost unique). "An atticky room (adequate) with good bathroom, a superb meal." "Norman cooking at its best", and copious. Some rooms are very small; those at the front by the main road have double-glazing. (*PB Roots, Greg Brinks, Bill and Marcia Griffith, P and SR, and many others*)

Open 15 Jan–15 Dec. Restaurant closed Sun evening (Oct–end Mar)/Mon.
Rooms 20 double. 16 at *Petit Castel*, 4 at *Auberge*.
Facilities 2 lounges (1 at *Auberge*), restaurant; 2 function rooms. Garden.
Location Centre of town. 15 km SE of Honfleur, just N of Paris–Caen *autoroute*. Parking.
Credit cards Access, Visa.
Terms B&B: single 240 frs, double 330–395 frs. Set meals 81–240 frs; full alc 260 frs.

BLÉRÉ 37150 Indre-et-Loire — Map 9

Le Cheval Blanc BUDGET

Place de l'Église

Tel 02.47.30.30.14
Fax 02.47.23.52.80

Michel and Micheline Blériot own and run this "charming little hotel", in a town on the Cher near Chenonceaux and its lovely *château*. In summer, you can sit or eat in a picturesque patio/garden, but there are no public rooms other than the "two elegant dining rooms". *Michelin* awards a star, and *Gault Millau* a *toque* for cooking again admired this year: "Food superb: the 198 frs menu [1996] was imaginative, with large portions. A good welcome, polite staff, comfortable room in modern extension – but the beams are plastic." "Very enjoyable." Earlier views: "We had breakfast in the courtyard amid flowers ablaze with colour. The bedroom and bathroom were fine, with tiles in pretty pastel shades." M. Blériot is "a lovely sincere fellow". (*WD Richmond, Dr NB Finter, AN*) Some rooms and bathrooms are very small.

Open All year, except 2 Jan–10 Feb. Restaurant closed Sun evening/Mon, except July/Aug.
Rooms 12 double.
Facilities Hall, 2 dining rooms; courtyard. Small garden: swimming pool. Unsuitable for ♿.
Location Central pedestrian precinct. Bléré is 27 km E of Tours. Garage.
Credit cards All major cards accepted.
Terms Rooms 290–310 frs. Breakfast 38 frs. D,B&B 345–490 frs per person. Set meals 99–270 frs; full alc 320 frs.

BOISSET 15600 Cantal — Map 10

Auberge de Concasty NEW — *Tel* 04.71.62.21.16
Fax 04.71.62.22.22

In the remote and hilly Pays de la Châtaigneraie (chestnut grove country) of southern Auvergne, readers have unearthed this idyll: "We think this is quite the prettiest countryside in France. At this family farmhouse hotel, Martine Causse and her staff offer a genuine and warm welcome. There were lots of young children: the large rooms had plenty of extra beds. In the grounds were three families of donkeys each with a ten-day-old foal, and a nice splash pool; pleasant views, and plenty of shade under the apple trees. The road carries one tractor an hour and the occasional car. There are easy walks all round. The *demi-pension* meals were never repeated: delicious, plentiful, straightforward food. Service was charming and competent. The breakfast buffet varied too, offering chestnut purée [of course], fromage frais, etc. Our two beefs: horrible foam pillows and a dreadful wardrobe. But we were made to feel so welcome that one feels churlish to mention it." (*Richard and Sheila Owen*)

Open All year, except 20–30 Nov, 18–26 Dec. Restaurant closed Wed.
Rooms 16. Some on ground floor.
Facilities Restaurant. Garden: swimming pool.
Location 3 km NE of Boisset by D64. 29 km SW of Aurillac.
Credit cards All major cards accepted.
Terms [1996] Rooms 305–490 frs. Breakfast 45 frs. D,B&B 370–440 frs per person. Set meals 150–200 frs.

BORDEAUX — Map 10

Saint-James NEW — *Tel* 05.57.97.06.00
Place Camille Hostein — *Fax* 05.56.20.92.58
Bouliac, 33270 Bordeaux

Formerly called *Les Jardins de Hauterive*, this bizarrely unusual hotel-plus-brilliant-restaurant stands by a church on a hillside in the south-eastern suburb of Bouliac, facing across the broad Garonne to the city. The high-tech modern bedrooms are in a structure of oxidised metal, not what you'd expect of a Relais & Châteaux member; the stylish restaurant (*Michelin* star, three *Gault Millau toques*) is walled in glass, with sophisticated decor. All is the brainchild of owner/chef Jean-Marie Amat, a very innovative and fashionable cook. Yet so untrendy are our own readers that they did not report for a while, and the hotel fell from the 1996 *Guide*. Now back it comes: "It combines a classic dining experience with daringly futuristic bedrooms. We were greeted by an urbane and voluble porter. Bedrooms are all different styles: in ours, the lighting was mainly a theatrical spotlight thrown casually on the floor; the bathroom was like an operating theatre, with weird taps; the huge bed, arranged in the middle of the room on a high plinth, was ultra-comfortable once you managed to climb into it. Surrounded by windows, we felt on a stage. We dined in the older part of the hotel, on a large terrace with stunning views over Bordeaux. The food was almost beyond reproach. An expensive experience, but unforgettable." Also a cheaper restaurant, *Le Bistroy*. (*Martin and Karen Oldridge*)

Open All year. *Le Bistroy* closed Sun.
Rooms 17 double.
Facilities Lift. 2 restaurants; conference room; terrace. Garden: swimming pool.
Location In Bouliac, 5 km SE of city centre, off avenue G. Cabannes. Parking.
Credit cards All major cards accepted.
Terms [1996] Rooms: 600–1,300 frs. Breakfast 75 frs. D,B&B 770–1,020 frs per person. *Saint-James*: set meals 185–360 frs; alc 280–420 frs. *Le Bistroy*: alc 150 frs.

BOURBON-L'ARCHAMBAULT 03160 Allier — Map 10

Hôtel des Thermes BUDGET — *Tel* 04.70.67.00.15
Avenue Charles-Louis-Philippe — *Fax* 04.70.67.09.43

Talleyrand once took a cure for rheumatism at this spa town in the northern Auvergne, where the Barichard brothers own and run this spruce and confident little hotel. "We commend their charm and professionalism," say devotees returning this year. "It's an immaculate hotel, with a timeless atmosphere and delectable food." This is cooked by Guy Barichard, who wins a *Michelin* star and *Gault Millau toque* for, eg, pavé de boeuf en croûte. Last year's verdict: "The best small hotel we have found in 14 years of touring France. M. Barichard's welcome, the maid who carried our bags, the comfort of our large room overlooking the park, all showed a rare standard of hospitality." Everything is traditional in the best sense: staff in formal dress, bedrooms with matching wallpapers on floor and ceiling, a neat garden terrace facing the thermal centre. Breakfasts are "beautifully served". (*Dr CH Maycock, JDS*) Front rooms may be a bit noisy; rooms in the main house are said to be better than annexe ones.

Open 15 Mar–31 Oct.
Rooms 1 suite, 15 double, 5 single.
Facilities Salon, restaurant; terrace. Garden.
Location 200 m from centre. Bourbon is 23 km W of Moulins. Parking.
Credit cards Access, Visa.
Terms Rooms: single 320 frs, double 360 frs, suite 420–450 frs. Breakfast 45 frs. D,B&B 360–420 frs per person. Set meals 140–225 frs.

BOUZIGUES 34140 Hérault — Map 10

Côte Bleue BUDGET — *Tel* 04.67.78.31.42
Fax 04.67.78.35.49

Bouzigues village lies on the big lagoon of Thau, opposite the enchanting seaport of Sète with its canals and the famous clifftop cemetery that inspired Paul Valéry (he lies buried there). The *Côte Bleue* is recommended as "quite unusual" – a very good seafood restaurant (*Gault Millau toque*) with a modern hotel next door: "This building circles a large garden with a huge swimming pool. There are loungers, sofa hammocks, and masses of terracotta bowls full of geraniums. Our decent room had a large terrace, and a view over the lagoon. The restaurant, very smart, with more geranium bowls, has a terrace extending to the lagoon and its oyster *parc*, and a view of the old port of Bouzigues. The waiters were young and dashing. Good coquillages and salmon on the 148 frs menu. The corpulent figure selling oysters at the bar is in *The Guinness Book of Records*, we were told, for eating 100 oysters in record time at a competition in Paris." (*N and KV*)

Open All year. Restaurant closed Jan, Tues evening/Wed except July/Aug.
Rooms 32.
Facilities Restaurant; function room; terrace. Garden: swimming pool.
Location Outside Bouzigues, 4 km NE of Mèze by N113. Parking.
Credit cards Access, Amex, Visa.
Terms [1996] Rooms 280–350 frs. Breakfast 36 frs. Set meals 148–380 frs.

BRANCION 71700 Saône-et-Loire — Map 12

La Montagne de Brancion — *Tel* 03.85.51.12.40
Col de Brancion — *Fax* 03.85.51.18.64

Owned and run by the Million family, this newish hotel, long, low and white, stands secluded amid vineyards in the rolling Mâconnais hills west of Tournus. Recent praise: "Brancion, now mostly deserted, is enchanting, with an old Romanesque church and ruined castle. On a hillside nearby, with a glorious view, is this quite smart hotel. In the delightful dining room, with recorded classical music, we enjoyed exquisite modern food in decent portions, charmingly served. They gave me verveine tisane made with leaves from their garden." Endorsed this year: "Charming owners, beautiful flowers – Monsieur is obviously a keen gardener." (*Harriet and Tony Jones, Prof. P and Mrs A Robson*) Cold lunches, and drinks, are served in the garden, by the heated pool. Breakfast includes a boiled egg, yogurt and freshly squeezed orange juice. All bedrooms, quite simple but attractive, overlook the view.

Open 15 Mar–early Nov.
Rooms 20 double. 7 on ground floor.
Facilities Bar/salon, restaurant (no smoking); terrace. Garden: swimming pool.
Location 14 km W of Tournus by D14, 2 mins' drive from Brancion.
Credit cards Access, Diners, Visa.
Terms Rooms 460–750 frs. Breakfast 70 frs. D,B&B 580–730 frs per person. Set meals 200–390 frs; full alc 400 frs.

BRANTÔME 24310 Dordogne — Map 10

Le Moulin de l'Abbaye — *Tel* 05.53.05.80.22
1 route de Bourdeilles — *Fax* 05.53.05.75.27

"A quite wonderful setting": this handsome old creeper-covered mill, set on the banks of the river Dronne, is now a luxurious small hotel (Relais & Châteaux), owned and run by Régis and Cathy Bulot. The dining room, with its lovely yellow decor, extends to a terrace over the river for summer eating, and Guy Guénégo's cooking lives up to this idyll (*Michelin* star, three *Gault Millau toques*). Readers again this year are full of praise ("Cathy Bulot is a delightful hostess"), save that opinions on the service vary hugely. "Lunch was maybe *the* best we had in France, wildly inventive, with marvellous service." "Our comfortable room, decorated in pretty rustic style, looked over the river. Dinner on the terrace was pleasant, but the professional service lacked warmth. And one feels like a bird in a gilded cage, as the public looks on from the park opposite, even photographing the terrace." This gilded cage has "a clever balance of antique and modern decor". "We had a superb room overlooking the weir, with beautiful fabric decoration and four-poster bed." "The furniture looked antique in our triangular bedroom, and we could lie in bed with superb views." Food has been called "excellent, if a bit too *nouvelle*" – a starter of "squid stuffed with snails amid a mound of fried frogs' legs". The old water wheel is still working, and "the rushing water is almost hypnotic". Rooms in an annexe, *La Maison du Meunier*, are said to be quieter than those in the mill. Another annexe, *La Maison de l'Abbé*, is further away. (*Neil French, Mrs Lydia Heah, and others*)

Open 26 Apr–2 Nov. Restaurant closed Mon midday.
Rooms 3 suites, 17 double, in three buildings. 1 on ground floor.
Facilities Salon, restaurant; terrace. Garden.
Location On edge of town. 27 km N of Périgueux. Garage.
Credit cards All major cards accepted.
Terms [1996] Rooms 550–900 frs, suite 950–1,350 frs. Breakfast 70 frs. D,B&B 750–960 frs per person. Set meals 220–450 frs; alc 280–450 frs.

BRINON-SUR-SAULDRE 18410 Cher — Map 9

La Solognote

Tel 02.48.58.50.29
Fax 02.48.58.56.00

On the edge of the strange forests and marshlands of the Sologne, a rustic *auberge* in a village by a river. It is noted for the cuisine of its congenial owner/chef Dominique Girard (*Michelin* star, *Gault Millau toque*). "A good dinner, with copious girolles from the forests," said a visitor this year, who found his small bungalow room "a useful overnight stop". Service is friendly and "highly professional". Bedrooms are simple, varying in size. The best ones face a patio garden where drinks and breakfasts are served in fine weather; others get slight traffic noise. "Excellent breakfast, beautifully served." (*Felix Singer, William and Ann Reid*)

Open All year, except 4 Feb–12 Mar, 20–28 May, 16–25 Sept.
Rooms 2 suites for 3–4 people, 13 double.
Facilities Salon, restaurant; terrace. Garden. Unsuitable for ♿.
Location In village, 57 km SE of Orléans, on D923. Private open parking.
Credit cards Access, Visa.
Terms Rooms 320–410 frs, suite 510 frs. Breakfast 57 frs. Set meals 165–330 frs; full alc 320 frs.

BRIOUDE 43100 Haute-Loire — Map 10

Hôtel de la Poste et Champanne — BUDGET

Tel 04.71.50.14.62
Fax 04.71.50.10.55

1 boulevard Docteur Devins

In the busy main street of this old Auvergne market town, close to one of the Auvergne's finest Romanesque churches, as well as to a salmon museum and a lace-making museum, stands this finely traditional hostelry, owned and run by the lively Chazal-Barge family, and ever popular with readers: "What lovely people, and what food!" "It lived up to its reputation for warmth of welcome, value for money and prodigal generosity. Everyone seemed to be taking the 105 frs [1996] set menu, which is all of seven courses, with the soup tureen left on the table, and an amazing choice of desserts. All good honest regional fare, served with brio: excellent trout with a sorrel sauce. Breakfast included eggs, cheese, ham. Our room was simple but had the important things, including a small balcony with recliner, and a view towards the hills." Only snags: bad insulation, noisy plumbing; some street noise. The public rooms and bedrooms have been renovated. (*BWR, and others*)

Open All year, except Jan. Restaurant closed Sun evening Oct–May.
Rooms 2 for 4 people, 18 double. 14 in nearby annexe.
Facilities Reading room, TV room, bar with terrace, 4 dining rooms (1 no-smoking); conference facilities. Small garden in annexe. Unsuitable for ♿.
Location Central; annexe has parking and garage.
Credit cards Access, Visa.
Terms Rooms 160–250 frs. Breakfast 32 frs. D,B&B 220 frs per person. Set meals 70–180 frs; full alc 140 frs.

BUXY 71390 Saône-et-Loire — Map 12

Château de Sassangy — NEW

Tel 04.85.96.12.40
Fax 04.85.96.11.44

In pleasant wine-growing country 6 km W of Buxy, 23 km W of Chalon-sur-Saône, a stately château *well restored as* chambres d'hôte *guest house. Elegant furnishings, spacious rooms with antiques; library, lounge, summer terrace; working vineyard on huge estate. Quiet and peaceful. "Gracious host", André Marceau, sells his own Burgundy. Good breakfasts; "excellent" dinner, by arrangement. Open mid-Mar–mid-Nov. Children preferably over 10. Access, Visa accepted. 8 rooms. B&B double 550–700 frs.*

BUZANÇAIS 36500 Indre — Map 10

L'Hermitage — BUDGET

Route d'Argy

Tel 02.54.84.03.90
Fax 02.54.02.13.19

This "haven of old-fashioned charm" has become one of the most widely praised of all our French entries. It is an idyllic white creeper-covered mansion, a Logis de France, set in "beautiful shady grounds" by the quiet river Indre on the edge of a small town. Though inexpensive ("superb value for money"), it is full of discreet elegance: its decor shows a happy sense of colour rare in French hotels of this kind. What's more, the food of *patron*/chef Claude Sureau earns a red "Repas" from *Michelin* for careful good value. "The food is fabulous, service excellent in a pleasant dining room," runs one report this year. Breakfast, with "best ever" croissants, is served under coloured awnings in the garden, when it's fine. Madame is "charming if reserved" and "totally dedicated". "The hotel dog is quite a character." (*J Rudd, Elizabeth Robey, Neil French, and countless others*) One dissenter thought the grounds in need of attention.

Open All year, except 1–15 Jan, 14–23 Sept. Closed Sun evening/Mon (except hotel July/Aug).

Rooms 12 double, 2 single. 4 in annexe. 2 no-smoking.
Facilities Salons, 2 dining rooms (1 no-smoking); terrace. Large grounds by river: fishing. Unsuitable for ♿.
Location Edge of town. 26 km W of Châteauroux. Garage.
Credit cards Access, Visa.
Terms Rooms: single 230 frs, double 285 frs. Breakfast 29 frs. D,B&B 245–335 frs per person. Set meals 88–155 frs; full alc 260 frs.

CABOURG 14390 Calvados — Map 8

Pullman Grand Hôtel — *Tel* 02.31.91.01.79
Promenade Marcel Proust — *Fax* 02.31.24.03.20

"We loved it all, it caught the aura of a bygone age", "fantastic faded charm", are latest commendations for the great white 1900s wedding-cake which Proust stayed at so often and wrote about so poetically, and where our readers, who have admired the "marvellous seaside position" in this Normandy resort, as well as the "vast rooms with balcony, the wonderful atmosphere" and the same shifting colours of the sunlight on the sea that Proust described in his novel, which transmuted Cabourg into "Balbec", have gazed out through the picture windows of the huge dining room that Proust called "the aquarium", to the sandy beach where his hero first glimpsed Albertine with her brilliant, laughing eyes and black polo-cap, beside a hotel that Pullman have restored quite well, with the same marble pillars and chandeliers in the vast foyer (even if it now mainly hosts business seminars, for Cabourg no longer has the social cachet it had in the Duchesse de Guermantes's day), and where you may ask if you wish for the "*chambre* Marcel Proust", which has *belle époque* furnishings such as brass bedstead (but a modern white telephone), and can enjoy a "very good breakfast buffet" (though the madeleines served to all guests now come in plastic wrappers) or eat in the winter restaurant called, of course, *Le Balbec*, where a reader has called the food "below average", thus inspiring us to solicit further insights from correspondents, please, provided they write in the master's style with nothing more obtrusive than a comma. (*Dr and Mrs J Granger, and others, with a big nod to MP*)

Open All year.
Rooms 68 double.
Facilities Lift. Salons, bar, piano bar in season, restaurant; conference facilities. Garden.
Location Central, by beach. Large carpark.
Credit cards All major cards accepted.
Terms [1996] Rooms 770–1,020 frs. Breakfast 75 frs. D,B&B 650–800 frs. Set meals 150–195 frs.

LA CADIÈRE-D'AZUR 83740 Var — Map 11

Hostellerie Bérard — *Tel* 04.94.90.11.43
Rue Gabriel Péri — *Fax* 04.94.90.01.94

In main street of hill-village 9 km inland from Bandol, attractive 19th-century auberge, *newly renovated, with beamed ceilings, tiled floors, spacious yet cosy lounge/bar, and bright dining room with panoramic views of hills and valley. Owned and run by the Bérards, she an exuberant front-of-house, he an excellent cook* (Gault Millau toque)*: Provençal plus* nouvelle *dishes. Good breakfast buffet. Pool and sun terrace charming, but can get crowded. Closed 11 Jan–19 Feb. Access, Amex, Visa accepted. 40 rooms, in 4 buildings. B&B: single 435–600 frs, double 610–770 frs. Set meals 95–415 frs [1996]. No recent reports; more welcome.*

CAHORS 46000 Lot **Map 10**

Hôtel Terminus NEW *Tel* 05.65.35.24.50
5 avenue Charles-de-Freycinet *Fax* 05.65.22.06.40

Central, opposite station, classic family-run hotel newly and expensively modernised. Stylish period furniture. "Superb food" in hotel's restaurant, Le Balandre *(two* Gault Millau toques*). Bar, terrace. Restaurant closed Sun evening/Mon, except July/Aug. Access, Amex, Visa accepted. 22 rooms: 280–480 frs. Breakfast 50 frs. D,B&B double 950–1,080 frs. Set meals 250–320 frs [1996]. Renominated this year, but fuller reports welcome.*

CALVI 20260 Haute-Corse **Map 17**

La Signoria *Tel* 04.95.65.23.73
Route de la Forêt de Bonifato *Fax* 04.95.65.38.77

Just outside Calvi, this 17th-century residence in a park of palms, olives and pines has been stylishly converted into a glamorous restaurant-with-rooms. It is near the airport, but recent visitors "were not conscious of any noise". "The swimming pool sits in a delightful garden with views of the mountains. We had a comfortable suite, also with views. The cooking is ambitious, and on the whole successful [*Gault Millau toque*]: we had two excellent meals outdoors. A restful yet sophisticated place." Riding, tennis, etc. (*H and CP*)

Open 1 Apr–15 Oct. Restaurant closed midday July / Aug.
Rooms 2 suites, 8 double. 6 in annexe. Some on ground floor.
Facilities Bar / lounge, restaurant; terrace. Garden: swimming pool, hamman, tennis.
Location 5 km S of Calvi, near airport.
Credit cards Access, Amex, Visa.
Terms [1996] Rooms 450–1,100 frs, suite 1,200–2,000 frs. Breakfast 70 frs. Set meals 360 frs; full alc 340 frs.

CALVINET 15340 Cantal **Map 10**

Le Beauséjour BUDGET *Tel* 04.71.49.91.68
Route de Maurs *Fax* 04.71.49.98.63

Set amid glorious upland scenery, Calvinet is a typically dour Auvergne village of grey stone houses. One of them, in the main street, has been converted into this neat well-modernised restaurant-with-rooms, where owner / chef Louis-Bernard Puech wins a *Michelin* star *and* red "Repas", plus a *Gault Millau toque* for his intelligent adaptation of local cuisine. "The entrées and pastry were superb," says a reader this year. "The staff are courteous, the service is generous, the decor elegant and restrained." Last year's view: "M. Puech was welcoming. Our top-floor room was vast, with a good view, decent hand-made wood furniture. Poor breakfast coffee, but our dinner was good. The waiter couldn't help with our stumbling questions, so I cannot say what it was we ate" – maybe *Michelin*'s suggestions of stuffed pigs' trotters, or oxtail with duck's livers? (*Penny and Mark Marshall, DH*) Some have found the modern rooms lacking in character.

Open All year, except 15 Jan–10 Mar. Closed Sun evening/Mon, except public holidays.
Rooms 12 double.
Facilities Lounge, dining room. Unsuitable for ♿.
Location Central. 36 km SW of Aurillac.
Credit cards Access, Visa.
Terms [1996] Rooms 240–300 frs. Breakfast 35 frs. D,B&B 250 frs. Set meals 130–260 frs.

CAMBRAI 59400 Nord — Map 9

Hotel Beatus — *Tel* 03.27.81.45.70
718 avenue de Paris — *Fax* 03.27.78.00.83

Rubens's painting *Mise en Tombeau* hangs in the church of St Géry, in this interesting town. The *Beatus*, a low building set back from the road, has a dullish suburban setting but a nice garden, and, says a visitor this year, "is the perfect overnight stop". He and others have liked the bedrooms, and the welcome from the Gorczynski family owners. Breakfast is described as "excellent" or "adequate". New this year is a restaurant (for residents): "exceptional cooking", "food first class, with superb desserts", are readers' comments. "A spacious, beautifully decorated bedroom, superb bathroom." "Comfortable quiet rooms": many are furnished in Louis XV/XVI style. Elegant bar. (*BW Ribbons, JC Dixon, Dr ACM Codd, Greg Brinks, Oliver and Delia Millar, and others*)

Open All year.
Rooms 1 suite, 31 double. 12 on ground floor.
Facilities 2 lounges, bar, restaurant; conference room (no-smoking). Garden.
Location 1 km SW of town centre on N44 to St-Quentin. Protected parking.
Credit cards All major cards accepted.
Terms Rooms 320–440 frs, suite 580–600 frs. Breakfast 50 frs. Full alc 190 frs.

CANCALE 35260 Ille-et-Vilaine — Map 8

Les Rimains et Maison de Bricourt — *Tel* 02.99.89.64.76 — *Fax* 02.99.89.88.47
1 rue Duguesclin

Owner/chef Olivier Roellinger provides distinguished modern cuisine (two *Michelin* stars, four red *Gault Millau toques*), at his very chic restaurant *Maison de Bricourt* in this popular Breton fishing-port. A recent admirer writes: "It's formal, yes, but not pompous. The young attractive staff did seem to care about doing everything perfectly, and the food was sublime. A charming and enjoyable place." Accommodation, just six bedrooms, is in a handsome villa, *Les Rimains*, 500 metres away; here our reporter had too small a room, with almost no closet space. "Clever decorating could not make up for this, but the great view of the bay could. And the hospitable *concierge* gave us a delicious breakfast bright and early, including tuna pâté and prune custard cake." Every room has a marble bathroom. A small garden with chairs reaches to the clifftop where the view extends across the bay to Mont-St-Michel. (*B and BK*) Newer reports needed, please. The Roellingers also own the *Hôtel de Bricourt-Richeux*, which has 13 luxurious rooms and views over the bay. It is about four kilometres from *Les Rimains* and the *Maison de Bricourt*, and has its own restaurant, *Le Coquillage*. On these, too, we should welcome reports.

Open All year. Restaurant closed mid-Dec–mid-Mar, Tues/Wed (open Wed evening in season).
Rooms 6 double.
Facilities Salon, restaurant. Garden.
Location Central. 14 km E of St-Malo. Parking.
Credit cards All major cards accepted.
Terms [1996] Rooms 850 frs. Breakfast 85 frs. Set lunch 250 frs, dinner 660 frs.

CARSAC-AILLAC 24200 Dordogne — Map 10

Le Relais du Touron — BUDGET

Tel 05.53.28.16.70
Fax 05.53.28.52.51

Secluded amid woodland scenery near a small village east of Sarlat is this 19th-century *gentilhommière*, owned by the "charming" Claudine Carlier. This year and last, its summery qualities have again been enjoyed: "Delightful. Food excellent, rooms spacious, garden and pool kept to a high standard. The ever-present Mme Carlier kept a close eye on running the hotel." "A beautiful hotel in a lovely setting. All staff were friendly. Our room overlooked the large, well-situated swimming pool. We dined on the terrace, or in a very pretty room. Food was simple but delicious" (it can include regional dishes, but the set menus offer little choice). "Breakfast wonderful." "Our large room was tastefully decorated. Plenty of loungers round the pool." The dining room has white walls, green plants and pink table-linen, "creating an impression of serenity". The hotel is not designed for wet weather: "the only lounge is dominated by a TV." (*Ross Taggart; also Renée Robson, GA McKenzie, and others*) Some rooms are quite small. One reader felt overheated in bed because of a plastic mattress cover.

Open 1 Apr–14 Nov. Restaurant closed midday in low season; Tues midday, Fri in high season.
Rooms 12 double. 2 on ground floor.
Facilities Salon with TV, restaurant; terrace. Garden: swimming pool (unheated). River 1 km: canoeing, fishing.
Location 2 km N of Carsac, off D704 to Sarlat. Carpark.
Credit cards Access, Visa.
Terms Rooms: single 245–300 frs, double 265–375 frs. Breakfast 36 frs. D,B&B 288–389 frs per person. Set meals 92–270 frs; full alc 158 frs.

CARTERET 50270 Manche — Map 8

La Marine

11 rue de Paris — *Tel* 02.33.53.83.31
Barneville-Carteret — *Fax* 02.33.53.39.60

A solid old holiday hotel by an estuary, in a small fishing port-cum-summer resort, with splendid beaches. Liked again this year, it is quite smart and sophisticated, "with the Cesne family owners much in evidence". Readers much admire young Laurent Cesne's cuisine

(*Michelin* star, two *Gault Millau toques*) and the "efficient and pleasant" service. A recent view: "We had a fish dish with a delightfully aromatic sauce, and an amazingly light andouille. Mme Cesne and her staff are welcoming. Our room overlooking the estuary was spacious, warm, well equipped, and in tip-top decorative order." Rooms vary: the newer annexe ones have good facilities but lack estuary views. There's a pleasant terrace for drinks by the river. (*Peter Wade, PEC*)

Open Mid-Feb–Nov. Restaurant closed Mon Feb/Mar/Oct.
Rooms 2 family suites, 27 double, 2 single. 3 in annexe.
Facilities Salon, bar, 2 dining rooms; terrace. Beach 400 m. Unsuitable for ♿.
Location In village (part of Barneville-Carteret). 37 km SW of Cherbourg.
Credit cards All major cards accepted.
Terms Rooms: single 290 frs, double 395 frs, suite 620 frs. Breakfast 49 frs. D,B&B 405–495 frs per person. Set meals 140–400 frs.

CASSIS 13260 Bouches-du-Rhône — Map 11

Hôtel de la Plage de Bestouan NEW — *Tel* 04.42.01.05.70
Plage de Bestouan — *Fax* 04.42.01.34.82

Matisse, Dufy and Dali all once painted at this famous Provençal fishing port-cum-resort, still picturesque but now sadly over-built and over-visited (its big casino is besieged by the nearby Marseillais). Among the pines at the western end of the shingly beach is this breezy modern hotel, family-owned, with a sea-facing sun terrace. Lack of reports pushed it from the 1996 *Guide*: but a reader this year was "made most welcome", and reports: "Dining on the terrace was delightful, the food excellent, the staff polite." Rooms vary: some have balcony and sea view but are small, with thin walls; others are larger, but have no view. (*PK Nissaire*)

Open 1 Apr–31 Oct.
Rooms 27 double, 2 single.
Facilities Lounge, bar, restaurant; terrace. Access to beach.
Location By beach, 1 km W of centre. Public parking nearby.
Credit cards All major cards accepted.
Terms Rooms: single 300–420 frs, double 420–650 frs. Breakfast 50 frs. D,B&B 390–600 frs per person. Set meals 130–160 frs; full alc 190–240 frs.

CELONY 13090 Bouches-du-Rhône — Map 11

Le Mas d'Entremont — *Tel* 04.42.23.45.32
Montée d'Avignon — *Fax* 04.42.21.15.83
Celony, Aix-en-Provence

Just north-west of Aix, near the busy N7 *autoroute* but quiet, stands this elegantly converted old *mas*, spacious and quite glamorous. It has beamed ceilings, and a big garden with a lily pond – you can dine here on the terrace, while the open-air swimming pool has smart, comfortable loungers. Plenty of recent admiration: "Beautifully decorated rooms, cooking of a high standard." "Very good cuisine, service both charming and professional. During some spectacular storms and power failures, the staff coped admirably, as did the German shepherd dogs. The views are spectacular." There are "excellent" bungalows: "Ours was furnished with walls of dark blue fabric, antique desk and marble bathroom, and had a *cuisinette*." (*C and LS, and others*)

Open 15 Mar–end Oct. Restaurant closed Sun evening/midday Mon.
Rooms 2 suites, 15 double, 1 single. 12 in garden annexe. Some on ground floor.
Facilities Lift. 2 salons, restaurant. Garden: tennis, swimming pool (unheated).
Location 3 km NW of Aix, just off N7. Private parking.
Credit cards Access, Visa.
Terms Rooms 560–840 frs, suite (for 3) 940–960 frs. Breakfast 70 frs. D,B&B double 1,190–1,400 frs. Set meals 200–240 frs; full alc 340 frs.

CÉRET 66400 Pyrénées-Orientales — Map 10

La Terrasse au Soleil

Route de Fontfrède — *Tel* 04.68.87.01.94 — *Fax* 04.68.87.39.24

Up in the Pyrenean foothills south of Perpignan, this stylish modern Relais du Silence, in local Catalan style, has views of the mountains and distant sea. There's an outdoor dining terrace, and a swimming pool with loungers and parasols. Bedrooms, mostly in two annexes, are decorated in different colours (some can be startling). "We had a warm welcome from Madame Leveillé, and charming attention from all her staff – the best service ever," write recent guests. "Our room, in pretty pale pink and green, with Catalan furniture, had a huge window with private balcony, and a knock-out view of the Pyrenees. The blue-and-yellow dining room and green-and-yellow breakfast room are attractive. The *en pension* dinner was interesting, and beautifully presented; breakfast was copious, with cereals, omelettes and delicious breads. The heated outdoor pool is in a sun-trap sheltered by hedges. The garden has several seating places, in sun or shade." (*AM Appleby, Richard and Sheila Owen, and others*) Some have said of the food: "Never too much; in no way fattening." But another guest wrote: "Portions on the half board menu were tiny, and all the more annoying for the long gastronomic descriptions to which one was subjected. But staff were charming, and we enjoyed the plethora of well-behaved pedigree dogs."

Open 1 Mar–31 Oct.
Rooms 1 suite, 26 double. 14 in 2 annexes. Some on ground floor. Air-conditioning.
Facilities Ramps. 2 lounges, bar lounge, 2 dining rooms (1 no-smoking); conference room; terrace (meal service). Garden: swimming pool, tennis, golf practice.
Location 1.5 km W of Céret. 31 km SW of Perpignan. Limited parking.
Credit cards Access, Amex, Visa.
Terms Rooms 595–795 frs, suite 1,100 frs. Breakfast 80 frs. D,B&B double 995–1,355 frs. Set meals 160–240 frs.

CHABLIS 89800 Yonne — Map 9

Hostellerie des Clos

Rue Jules Rathier — *Tel* 03.86.42.10.63 — *Fax* 03.86.42.17.11

The list of Chablis wines is "telephone directory size" at this converted almshouse, now an elegant modern hostelry, where *patron*/chef Michel Vignaud wins a *Michelin* star and two *Gault Millau toques*, for cuisine once *nouvelle*, but now "moving towards classicism". Devotees this year extolled the food, found the rooms "not luxurious, but perfectly adequate for a night's stay", and marvelled: "We hadn't been for four years, but Madame remembered us." "The buffet breakfast is outstanding, and room 10 is the best 'disabled' room I know in France." Guests are expected to dine in the restaurant. Service can be slow. (*Harriet and Tony Jones, Dennis O'Mulloy, and others*)

Open All year, except 20 Dec–10 Jan. Closed Wed 1 Oct–30 Apr (restaurant also closed midday Thurs).
Rooms 26 double. 1 suitable for ♿.
Facilities Lift. Salon, bar, restaurant; terrace. Garden.
Location Central. Chablis is 19 km E of Auxerre. Limited private parking.
Credit cards Access, Amex, Visa.
Terms D,B&B 480–770 frs. Set meals 178–420 frs; alc 300–400 frs.

CHAGNY 71150 Saône-et-Loire — Map 12

Hôtel Lameloise — *Tel* 03.85.87.08.85
Place d'Armes — *Fax* 03.85.87.03.57

"A wonderful meal, so professional: a night to remember" – more praise in 1996 for this renowned venue, an elegantly converted 15th-century mansion (Relais & Châteaux) in the main street of a dullish Burgundy town. Owner/chef Jacques Lameloise's cooking still wins three *Michelin* stars, and three *Gault Millau toques*, and our readers concur: "Outstanding food." Recently praised dishes include the aiguillettes de boeuf, tête de veau and ravioli of snails in garlic. The welcome is friendly, the service efficient. The air-conditioned dining room, with its "quietly luxurious atmosphere", is a series of beamed and vaulted rooms, some quite small. "Madame and her staff were nice and helpful as ever." "Lovely bedroom and bathroom." Rooms in the new wing are very quiet and comfortable; the older ones are more elegant, with antiques, beamed ceilings and fireplaces, but road traffic is audible from some. (*Mrs Pat Brown, and others*)

Open All year, except 18 Dec–23 Jan. Closed Wed (except dinner 1 July–30 Sept)/midday Thurs.
Rooms 17 double.
Facilities Lift. Salon, bar, restaurant.
Location Central. Garage.
Credit cards Access, Amex, Visa.
Terms [1996] Rooms 650–1,500 frs. Breakfast 90 frs. Set meals 370–600 frs; alc 390–560 frs.

CHALLANS 85300 Vendée — Map 10

Château de la Vérie NEW — *Tel* 02.51.35.33.44
Route de Saint-Gilles-Croix-de-Vie — *Fax* 02.51.35.14.84

The Vendée wars of the 1790s still echo in local hearts, in this curious haunting region close to the Atlantic. Here this "slightly crumbling 16th-century *château* in the middle of nowhere" (a *monument historique classé*, with a 17-hectare park) makes a fascinating debut: "It has been exquisitely renovated inside by its charming owners, the Martins, who have been there five years. They have put a lot of thought into the decorations: the dining areas are done in soft golden yellow and the lounge in red. M. Martin asked us anxiously what we thought of them. Our room, also done in good taste, had a matching set of old prints; corridors were full of plants and cut flowers. We arrived amid a reception for guests in dinner suits, but despite our dusty appearance on bikes, our welcome was impeccable. Dinner was beautiful – the chef, Jean-François Delanné, is a *maître cuisinier de France*. Breakfast on the terrace was informal: it was a pleasure to sit among the young children of the family playing with their toys; and to drink in the history. One gripe: plastic sheet on bed." (*Martin and Karen Oldridge*)

Open All year.
Rooms 1 suite for 4 people, 11 triple, 9 double. 2 in nearby annexe. 2 on ground floor.
Facilities Salon, 2 dining rooms; conference/function room; terrace. Garden: swimming pool (unheated), tennis, children's playground.
Location 2.5 km SW of Challans, which is 56 km SW of Nantes.
Credit cards All major cards accepted.
Terms Rooms 300–880 frs. Breakfast 60 frs. D,B&B 365–1,070 frs per person. Set meals 100–300 frs; full alc 350 frs.

CHÂLONS-EN-CHAMPAGNE 51000 Marne — Map 9

Hôtel d'Angleterre — *Tel* 03.26.68.21.51
19 place Monseigneur Tissier — *Fax* 03.26.70.51.67

"A model example of a smart city hotel, combining high professionalism with sympathetic warm welcome" – a 1996 judgment on this old *Guide* favourite in the town centre, a small hotel, sophisticated but with "a good, solid old-fashioned feel". "Breakfast was a superior buffet, and dinner included wonderful chocolate soufflé": owner Jacky Michel's "creative" cooking (*Michelin* star, *Gault Millau toque*) makes much use of the local drink (eg, crabs in champagne, kidneys in red champagne). Other plaudits this year: "A superb meal, with friendly service." "Relaxed atmosphere in formal surroundings. Large comfortable room with efficient air-conditioning." Earlier visitors admired "the sophisticated dining room bedecked in blue and yellow." One bedroom "seemed twice its size by having mirrors on two sides, while a glass ceiling doubled the light value". Jacky Michel has now opened two cheaper eateries, *La Cuisine d'à Côté* and *Le Pré St-Alpin*, in an "enchanting Art Deco-ish house": the second was enjoyed this year. (*HR, Anne and Ian Steel, Garry Wiseman, and many others*)

Open All year, except Sun, 12 July–3 Aug, Christmas school holidays. Restaurant also closed midday Sat.
Rooms 18 double. Most air-conditioned.
Facilities 2 salons, bar, restaurant; conference room; small terrace (meal service). Unsuitable for ♿.
Location Central (rooms double-glazed), near Notre-Dame-en-Vaux. Limited private parking.
Credit cards All major cards accepted.
Terms Rooms 390–490 frs. Breakfast 65 frs. Set meals 150–450 frs; full alc 450 frs.

CHAMALIÈRES 63400 Puy-de-Dôme — Map 10

Hôtel Radio — *Tel* 04.73.30.87.83
43 avenue Pierre-Curie — *Fax* 04.73.36.42.44

A sedate white hotel, aloof on a hillside in a residential suburb of Clermont-Ferrand (the baths and casino of Royat spa are quite close). The public rooms and stylish bedrooms are in Art Deco style, and the garden is "lovingly tended". The owners are Michel and Yvette

Mioche: she, very chic, "keeps the front of house with flair and style". A recent visitor thought breakfast dull, but liked the bedrooms and the "superb" dinners. However, there is now a new chef, Frédérick Coursol, and we should be glad to hear whether he is keeping the *Radio*'s cuisine as finely tuned as ever (*Michelin* star and *Gault Millau toque* in 1996).

Open All year, except Jan. Restaurant closed Sun / midday Mon in low season.
Rooms 1 suite, 26 double. 6 with air-conditioning. Some no-smoking.
Facilities Lift. 2 salons, restaurant. Garden.
Location 2 km W of centre of Clermont-Ferrand.
Credit cards All major cards accepted.
Terms Rooms: single 250 frs, double 350 frs, suite 750 frs. Breakfast 60 frs. D,B&B double 770 frs. Set meals 160–420 frs; alc 350 frs.

CHAMPAGNAC-DE-BELAIR 24530 Dordogne — Map 10

Hôtel Moulin du Roc — *Tel* 05.53.02.86.00
Fax 05.53.54.21.31

For years, a moneyed international clientèle has flocked to the Gardillou family's sophisticated and very gastronomic operation (*Michelin* star) – a gracefully converted 17th-century walnut mill, idyllically located by a stream in a village near Brantôme. It is full of flowers and antiques, and has pretty bedrooms, some quite small. Returning devotees found it "still going well" this year: "M. Gardillou looks prosperous, the soul of slightly patrician courtesy. A capable young woman now runs front-of-house – we were impressed by her kind personal attention to a badly disabled guest in a wheelchair. The supporting staff did well on the whole, but betrayed signs of pressure. The grounds are delightful." Others wrote recently: "Delightful in all respects. We climbed a spiral staircase to our lovely spacious suite – antique desk, walls covered in pale pink silk. The salon and two restaurants were cosy, though the decor of one *is* too opulent, maybe tasteless." "The breakfast tray was a feast for the eyes." "The hotel is crammed with *objets*, some verging on kitsch. But I'm a sucker for exposed beams, a four-poster bed, a heated pool (bliss in early summer)." (*James and Anthea Larken, GA McKenzie, K and N Varley*) Only one dissenting voice this year, a visitor who criticised upkeep and service. The swimming pool, now covered, is in a separate building in the grounds, quite a walk from the hotel. Most important, Solange Gardillou, regarded by many as the best woman chef in France (*Michelin* star, etc) has this year retired from the kitchen. This is now in the hands of her son Alain, who is also manager in place of his father. Reports on his work are much needed.

Open All year, except 2 Jan–10 Mar. Restaurant closed Tues / midday Wed.
Rooms 4 suites, 10 double. 2 on ground floor.
Facilities Lounge, bar, restaurant. Park: garden, covered swimming pool, tennis, river fishing.
Location 6 km NE of Brantôme by D78 and D83. Parking.
Credit cards All major cards accepted.
Terms Rooms: single 400 frs, double 400–630 frs, suite 690 frs. Breakfast 60 frs. Set meals 150–285 frs; full alc 350 frs.

Report forms (Freepost in UK) are at the end of the *Guide*.

CHAMPILLON 51160 Marne **Map 9**

Hôtel Royal Champagne

Tel 03.26.52.87.11
Fax 03.26.52.89.69

On a hillside near Épernay, with wide views over the champagne vineyards and the Marne valley, stands this 18th-century coaching inn. It has been smartly modernised, and is a Relais & Châteaux member. Its grand restaurant bears a *Michelin* star, two *Gault Millau toques*, for classic cooking. Bedrooms are in superior chalets in the grounds; most have their own terrace and view. Latest admiration: "In the handsome dining room, the atmosphere of enjoyment is not unconnected with the wonderful champagnes. Most of the food is very good, and service runs smoothly. The bedrooms are quiet, individually furnished, and bathrooms are splendid. We took breakfast on our private terrace with its lovely view." Or you can go for a buffet in the main breakfast room. (*JMM, MLNF, and others*) The decor has been called "mock-baronial".

Open All year.
Rooms 3 suites, 27 double. All in bungalows.
Facilities Salons, bar, restaurant; terrace. Large grounds: golf practice, club house, tennis.
Location 7 km N of Épernay on N2051 to Reims. Garage, private parking.
Credit cards All major cards accepted.
Terms Rooms 870 frs, suite 1,500 frs. Breakfast 85 frs. D,B&B double 1,560–1,730 frs. Set meals 275–350 frs.

CHÂTEAU-ARNOUX 04160 Alpes-de-Haute-Provence **Map 11**

La Bonne Étape NEW

Chemin du Lac

Tel 04.92.64.00.09
Fax 04.92.64.37.36

In an ordinary little town in the broad Durance valley, just off the Grenoble-Marseille highway, stands this 17th-century coaching inn, elegantly converted and quite expensive. In the hands of the Gleize family, it offers superb creative variations on Provençal cuisine (*Michelin* star, three *Gault Millau toques*), and after a time with no reports it is now restored to the *Guide*: "Food was indeed splendid, if very rich. Delicious breakfast, with yummy home-made jams. The restaurant is a glistening affair in warm yellows and golds. Family run, service unstuffy. Our room had antique furniture, and looked over the small garden: lots of herby plants giving off lovely smells at night. Swimming pool only just heated in late October, but we braved the water and enjoyed a quick dip." Others have extolled the breast of wild chicken, the chocolate-filled croissants for breakfast, and the service, "warm to children and animals alike". Some rooms and bathrooms are small; quietest ones face the back. (*Fiona Dick*) Three conference rooms are new this year.

Open All year, except 3 Jan–14 Feb, Christmas Eve, Sun evening/Mon 1 Nov–31 Mar.
Rooms 7 suites, 11 double. Some on ground floor.
Facilities Bar, 2 dining rooms, 4 conference rooms. Garden: swimming pool.
Location Central. 14 km S of Sisteron. Garage, parking.
Credit cards All major cards accepted.
Terms Rooms 500–1,100 frs, suite 900–1,500 frs. Breakfast 85 frs. Set meals 225–530 frs; full alc 370 frs.

CHÂTEAU-GONTIER 53200 Mayenne — Map 8

Le Jardin des Arts — *Tel* 02.43.70.12.12
5 rue Abel Cahour — *Fax* 02.43.70.12.07

This happily named hotel is a newly converted old mansion by the river Mayenne, in a small town north of Angers. It has an enterprising owner/manager, Raphaël Triquet, and succeeds in being both sophisticated and homelike, with reasonable prices. Recent praise: "Madame was warm, with a nice sense of humour. Dinner on the terrace was delicious: service a bit chaotic, but somehow that added to the charm." "Dining room very charismatic. Even the piped jazz was good." Some rooms are spacious, "with a good mix of antique and modern furnishings" – these face the river and garden, where breakfast can be served; some are more basic. You can take breakfast in the garden. (*JT, and others*) A few readers have found the food disappointing. The hotel's setting is not entirely pastoral: it also faces an industrial area and a bridge with heavy traffic.

Open All year, except Christmas/New Year, Feb holidays. Restaurant closed midday Mon/midday Sat/evening Sun in low season.
Rooms 20 double. 2 on ground floor.
Facilities Salon, 2 dining rooms; conference facilities. Garden: golf practice, table-tennis; bicycles, canoes.
Location Central. 43 km NW of Angers. Parking.
Credit cards Access, Visa.
Terms Rooms 320–530 frs. Breakfast 47 frs. Set meals 75–200 frs; full alc 200 frs.

CHÊNEHUTTE-LES-TUFFEAUX 49350 Maine-et-Loire — Map 8

Le Prieuré NEW — *Tel* 02.41.67.90.14
Fax 02.41.67.92.24

Converted from a medieval priory, this Relais & Châteaux member, smart and luxurious, stands imposingly on a bluff above the Loire, in a large private wooded park, and has beautiful gardens. After a time with no feedback, it is renominated by readers who admired the courteous service and "excellent" restaurant (two *Gault Millau toques* for inspired use of regional produce). "Airy and exhilarating, with a wonderful view down the river," was an earlier comment. The elegant rooms in the main building may suffer slight train noise; the bungalows amid the trees are quieter, each with its own garden, but they are smaller and less bright. (*Martin and Karen Oldridge*). Visit the nearby caves in the tufa cliffs: some are used for mushroom-growing, some have ancient sculptures, some are still lived in by troglodytes.

Open All year, except end Jan–early Mar.
Rooms 2 suites, 33 double. 15 in bungalows in park. Some on ground floor.
Facilities Lounge, bar, restaurant; function room. Park: garden, mini-golf, tennis, swimming pool.
Location 7 km NW of Saumur, off D751.
Credit cards All major cards accepted.
Terms Rooms 450–1,100 frs, suite 1,350 frs. Breakfast 85 frs. D,B&B 280 frs added per person. Set meals 160–400 frs; full alc 350 frs.

We are particularly keen to have reports on italicised entries.

CHENONCEAUX 37150 Indre-et-Loire — Map 8

Hôtel du Bon Laboureur et du Château — NEW

Tel 02.47.23.90.02
Fax 02.47.23.82.01

6 rue du Dr Bretonneau

This good ploughman is just by the gates of one of the loveliest of the Loire *châteaux*. After a brief appearance in the 1989 *Guide*, it is now renominated: "Run by the fourth generation of the original owners, it has the sense of quiet assurance and competence of a long-time family hotel. Bedrooms are good-sized and well furnished: ours had a view of the pretty kitchen garden with fruit trees. Lounges are large, though the modern decor seemed a bit out of kilter with the hotel's old-fashioned charm. Service was excellent. We ate dinner on a large terrace under a beautiful plane tree; then the next night, as it was cooler, in the pretty beamed dining room. Food is traditional, good; wines include some produced on the Chenonceaux estate." (*Carolyn Mathiasen*) Rooms on the main road can be a bit noisy.

Open All year, except 2 Jan–15 Feb, 15 Nov–15 Dec.
Rooms 4 suites, 28 double.
Facilities Lounges, restaurant; terrace. Garden: swimming pool.
Location By *château*. 33 km E of Tours. Parking.
Credit cards All major cards accepted.
Terms [1996] Rooms 320–700 frs. Breakfast 45 frs. D,B&B 350–550 frs. Set meals 150–300 frs.

Hostellerie de la Renaudière — BUDGET

Tel 02.47.23.90.04
Fax 02.47.23.90.51

Close to the *château* is this "rather austere old house, recently refurbished", with a big garden where tables, chairs and parasols stand invitingly on the lawn. "A good welcome; our room was comfortable, nay elegant." "Dinner served in the garden was a joy. Lovely house." Those reports this year and last echo an earlier eulogy: "We were welcomed effusively by the owner, Joël Camus, who really seems to enjoy his role. The dining room, an anachronism of functional glass walls, was packed with French families enjoying the excellent food at reasonable prices. Our superb feuilleté of quail came up garnished with its own poor little head. In the pleasant gardens was an aviary where a sole guinea-fowl paced anxiously, fearful perhaps of losing his." "While eating we could see the garden which, with its stone tables and colourful parasols, looked like a set for a film such as *Last Year in Marienbad*. We expected an enigmatic heroine in flowing veil to walk wraith-like across the lawn." (*John Willmington, L and AC*)

Open All year (weekends/school holidays only 15 Nov–15 Mar). Restaurant closed Wed, except July/Aug.
Rooms 13 double, 2 single. 5 in annexe. 5 on ground floor.
Facilities Salon with bar, 2 dining rooms (1 no-smoking); function room; fitness room, sauna. Garden.
Location On edge of village, 33 km E of Tours. Closed parking.
Credit cards Access, Amex, Visa.
Terms B&B: single 250 frs, double 290–310 frs; D,B&B double 480–510 frs. Set meals 98–230 frs; full alc 250 frs.

CHINON 37500 Indre-et-Loire Map 8

Hôtel Diderot BUDGET *Tel* 02.47.93.18.87
4 rue Buffon *Fax* 02.47.93.37.10

An unassuming B&B, in a handsome old creeper-covered building, built of pale stone, with a wrought iron balcony reached by a spiral staircase. It continues to be much liked, especially for its "jovial and delightful" Cypriot owner, Theodore Kazamias. "He is a great and generous hotelier, and his welcome is genuine. The decor and furnishing is rustic, and comfortable." Rooms vary in size and quality: "The annexe on the courtyard has been refurbished in charming style, using the old timbers." "Our room was a dream – high beams, large beds, banana tree thriving outside. And aperitifs twice the normal size." Breakfast is admired, particularly for "Madame's famous home-made jams" (eg, peach-and-ginger), and is taken communally, which some readers like more than others. (*Jeremy and Anthea Larken, and many others*) It was in the now half-ruined hilltop castle of this historic wine town that St Joan met the Dauphin.

Open 10 Jan–20 Dec.
Rooms 28 double. 4 in nearby annexe. Some on ground floor. 4 no-smoking.
Facilities Bar with TV, breakfast room; courtyard.
Location Near Pl Jeanne d'Arc; well signposted. Courtyard parking.
Credit cards All major cards accepted.
Terms B&B: single 265–360 frs, double 330–480 frs.

CHONAS L'AMBALLAN 38121 Isère Map 12

Domaine de Clairefontaine BUDGET *Tel* 04.74.58.81.52
Fax 04.74.58.80.93

Owned and run by the friendly Girardon family, this pleasant country hotel puts its accent firmly on food, not bedrooms. A converted 18th-century mansion, once the home of the bishops of nearby Vienne, it stands at the edge of a Rhône valley village, and has "a big garden, a lovely lawn, a pond, birdsong, an idyllic farm-like feeling". Bedrooms are inexpensive, and some are quite basic, though clean, as readers reported this year. Philippe Girardon's cooking, which wins a *Michelin* star and a *Gault Millau toque* for such dishes as pigeonneau en cocotte cooked with cherry wine, is served "very professionally" by bow-tied waiters in a lovely formal restaurant: "It has been beautifully refurbished in yellow, with grey marble floors and a peacock theme." "A superb dinner, friendly service, adequate breakfast," was one comment this year, backing much earlier praise. In the main building, most rooms are "spacious and well decorated", but some at the top can be dingy; those in a converted outhouse are small and simple, sometimes a bit shabby, but quiet. (*Mr and Mrs RL Marks, Harriet and Tony Jones, and many others*)

Open All year, except 1 Dec–1 Feb. Restaurant closed Sun evening/Mon (open Mon evening July/Aug), Sat midday July/Aug.
Rooms 2 suites, 14 double. 6 in annexe. 1 on ground floor.
Facilities Salon, 2 dining rooms; terrace. Garden: tennis.
Location *Autoroute* A7 exit Condrieu. Village W of N7, 9 km S of Vienne (signposted). Parking.
Credit cards All major cards accepted.

Terms [1996] Rooms 180–370 frs. Breakfast 45 frs. D,B&B 280–380 frs per person. Set meals 150–380 frs; alc 240–330 frs.

CLÉCY 14570 Calvados — Map 8

Hostellerie du Moulin du Vey NEW

Tel 02.31.69.71.08
Fax 02.31.69.14.14

The Suisse Normande is not as mountainous as its name might imply, but pleasantly hilly and rural. Here stands this old creeper-covered corn mill, with snug period decor and a beamed dining room – the wide windows of which open on to a terrace beside the gently flowing Orne, where you can eat out in summer. Lack of reports took it out of the *Guide* last year, but a reader this year found it "charming". Earlier views: "The pretty restaurant has a jolly ambience and serves good food (particularly the puds) with friendly efficiency." "Very good five-course *demi-pension* meals: sole with cucumber, marvellous cheeseboard, etc." Breakfast has been judged "ordinary". Rooms are in the mill and in two annexes: one, the *Relais de Surosne*, two miles away, has large and comfortable rooms. Some other rooms vary in quality. (*Peter Wade*)

Open All year, except Dec/Jan (open New Year).
Rooms 2 suites, 23 double. 6 in nearby annexe. 7 in annexe 3 km away.
Facilities Lounges, bar, TV room, restaurant; conference facilities; terrace (meals served). Garden: children's playground. Unsuitable for ♿.
Location On D133a, 2 km E of Clécy, 37 km S of Caen. Private parking.
Credit cards All major cards accepted.
Terms [1996] Rooms 390–520 frs. Breakfast 50 frs. D,B&B 450–620 frs per person. Set meals 138–360 frs; full alc 300 frs.

CLOYES-SUR-LE-LOIR 28220 Eure-et-Loir — Map 8

Hostellerie St-Jacques

Place du Marché aux Oeufs

Tel 02.37.98.40.08
Fax 02.37.98.32.63

Cloyes is a small town on the old pilgrim route to Santiago, now the Chartres–Tours main road. Here Émile Zola lived while researching *La Terre*, his savage novel of peasant life, set in this part of the Beauce wheat plain. This *relais*, built round a courtyard, with a terrace, is in the town centre: but, says its nominator, it has "a lovely garden going down to the river Loir". "The atmosphere was right, the service friendly, the bedroom and bathroom attractive and roomy. Dinner was very good – brioche with hot sausage, navarin d'agneau, crème brûlée, etc, and a good red Saumur. The dining room is enchanting" (with Renaissance-style decor). (*CM*) Meals are also served in a cheaper bistro.

Open 15 Mar–2 Nov. Bistro closed 15 Dec–21 Jan, Mon Nov–Mar.
Rooms 21.
Facilities Lift. Restaurant, bistro; terrace, courtyard. Garden.
Location Central, parking. Cloyes is 55 km SW of Chartres.
Credit cards Access, Visa.
Terms [1996] Rooms 360–450 frs. Breakfast 53 frs. D,B&B 435–470 frs per person. Set meals: bistro 98 frs, restaurant 175 frs.

CLUNY 71250 Saône-et-Loire — Map 12

Hôtel de Bourgogne — *Tel* 03.85.59.00.58
Place de l'Abbaye — *Fax* 03.85.59.03.73

"A warm welcome, cooking of a high standard," writes one guest this year, after her 12th visit to the ever-popular *Bourgogne*. It has been an inn since the 18th century: Lamartine often stayed here and guests can still sleep in his bed. Rambling but dignified, it stands in the main square of this picturesque medieval town, amid the ruins of the mighty Romanesque abbey, which, in the Middle Ages, was one of Europe's leading religious, artistic and intellectual centres. Most bedrooms look out on to its towers or on to green hills. Recent comments: "Food was the best we had anywhere in Austria, Italy or France – tender snails, wonderful chicken with truffles. Wines were superb, but the mark-ups were horrendous." "Good friendly service, personal attention from the Gosse family owners." "A country house atmosphere, like sharing a family home." "It strikes the right balance of gracious living and informality. Superb cheeses and desserts. Breakfast, with hot croissants, stood out too." Rooms vary in size and quality. (*Mrs EH Prodgers, SRP, and others)* There's a cheaper brasserie for lunch.

Open All year, except Christmas/New Year. Restaurant closed 15 Nov–5 Mar.
Rooms 3 suites, 12 double. 2 no-smoking.
Facilities Ramps. Lounge, bar, restaurant, brasserie. Small courtyard (breakfast, drinks served in fine weather). Films, concerts.
Location Central. In abbey ruins (back rooms quietest). Garage.
Credit cards All major cards accepted.
Terms Rooms 410–520 frs, suite 990 frs. Breakfast 55–75 frs. D,B&B double 1,050–1,500 frs. Restaurant: set meals 160–350 frs; full alc 350 frs. Brasserie: set meal 85 frs.

COCURÈS 48400 Lozère — Map 11

La Lozerette BUDGET — *Tel* 04.66.45.06.04
Fax 04.66.45.12.93

Pierrette Agulhon has won an EU and national prize, "Madame Commerce en milieu rural", for modernising her family's trim villa in a Cévenol village near Florac. It stands amid gorgeous scenery, by the road where Robert Louis Stevenson and Modestine plodded in 1878 (he described Cocurès as "a cluster of black roofs . . . sitting among vineyards and meadows and orchards thick with red apples"). Latest visitors have found Pierrette "warm and charming", "effervescent yet controlled", and have liked the "beautifully appointed" bedrooms. Most people appreciate the regional cooking too ("imaginative and well prepared"), though some are less sure. The dining room is "light and pleasant"; the garden doubles as a *boules* alley. "Comfortable, warm (a log fire in October) and good value. The new rooms, with their handsome wood furnishings, have been done with an eye on Cévenol atmosphere, and Cévenol produce is used in the menu planning." "Our room had a splendid view down the valley. At breakfast, vast pots of home-made jam and local honey." (*DH, and many others*) The hotel is on a main road, quiet at night – but a reader notes that cars are noisier than RLS's donkey-traffic.

Open Easter–1 Nov. Restaurant closed to non-residents Tues.
Rooms 20 double, 1 single. 3 on ground floor, 1 adapted for ♿.
Facilities Lounge, bar, restaurant. Garden: *boules*.
Location 5 km NE of Florac, just off CD998. Parking.
Credit cards Access, Amex, Visa.
Terms Rooms 240–380 frs. Breakfast 38 frs. D,B&B 260–370 frs per person. Set meals 80–100 frs; full alc from 160 frs.

COGNAC 16100 Charente — Map 10

Domaine du Breuil — *Tel* 05.45.35.32.06
104 avenue Robert Daugas — *Fax* 05.45.35.48.06

The "delightful dining room with superb food" could well be full of wine merchants come to buy cognac, at this converted 18th-century manor, quietly set in a park on the edge of town. "It has been elegantly refurbished," says its nominator, "and has terraces front and back. Staff were charming. The bedroom was good, apart from the pillows filled with foam bits." (*NJY*)

Open All year.
Rooms 2 suites, 12 double, 10 single. Some no-smoking.
Facilities Lift. Salon, bar, restaurant; conference room. Large grounds.
Location 3 km E of town centre. Parking.
Credit cards All major cards accepted.
Terms [1996] Rooms 280–310 frs. Breakfast 40 frs. D,B&B 280–350 frs per person. Set meals 100–280 frs.

COLMAR 68000 Haut-Rhin — Map 12

Hostellerie Le Maréchal — *Tel* 03.89.41.60.32
4 place des Six Montagnes Noires — *Fax* 03.89.24.59.40

Three 16th-century half-timbered houses form this stylish little hotel in the picturesque Petite Venise quarter. The dining room and some bedrooms (all named for musicians, Bach, Wagner, etc) face the river. There are four-poster beds and old-world decor, but modern bathrooms, some with jacuzzi. "Our room was rather small but beautifully appointed, food was superb," says a recent visitor. The cooking is imaginative (eg, fillet of duck with sauté of langoustines) and is served in the garden when it's fine; good breakfasts. (*GAW*) More reports, please.

Open All year.
Rooms 30. Some no-smoking.
Facilities Lift. Breakfast room, restaurant. Garden.
Location Central. Garage.
Credit cards Access, Amex, Visa.
Terms [1996] Rooms 450–900 frs. Breakfast 65 frs. D,B&B 700–800 frs per person. Set lunch (with wine) 155, dinner 195–365 frs.

COLY 24120 Dordogne — Map 10

Manoir d'Hautegente — *Tel* 05.53.51.68.03
Fax 05.53.50.38.52

Euphorically admired again in 1995–96, this picturesque creeper-covered mansion stands by a hillside in deep country north of Sarlat.

For 300 years it has been the home of the Hamelin family, who now run it in personal style as a small delectable hotel: it is certainly the *Guide*'s finest example of this genre, in France. "A very special place", "delightful" – praise this year, echoing last year's: "Our first reaction was 'WOW!' – and so it remained. It really is too beautiful for words. Our room was charming, with yellow fabric-covered walls, lovely old bits of furniture. We dined by the millpond – delicious food, best scallops I've had for years, hot apple tart a must. The Hamelins are charming: son Patrick has real lighthearted warmth." "We were enthusiastic. The old watermill with associated river, pools and weirs has been skilfully adapted, making a wonderful garden. In summer you dine on the terrace, in such elegance, as the sun sets on the hills. Food is imaginative, and the staff all courteous, charming and ready to chat. Our room was very pretty." "Our room had a rustic balcony by the millstream. The whole effect is in keeping with the old buildings, and fun." In the salon, a log fire blazes when the evenings get cool. The owners' home-made foie gras is "outstanding". (*Ruth and Derek Tilsley, Ian McClaren, Richard and Sheila Owen, and many others*)

Open Early Apr–early Nov. Restaurant closed midday Mon/Tues/Wed.
Rooms 2 suites, 8 double. Some in separate building 50 m. 1 on ground floor.
Facilities Lounge, library, 3 dining rooms (1 no-smoking). Garden: swimming pool; river, private fishing.
Location 19 km N of Sarlat. From N89, take D704 and D62. Parking.
Credit cards Access, Amex, Visa.
Terms B&B: single 500 frs, double 700–950 frs; D,B&B: single 620 frs, double 820–1,070 frs. Set lunch 150 frs, dinner 170–250 frs.

COMPIÈGNE 60200 Oise — Map 9

Hostellerie du Royal-Lieu — *Tel* 03.44.20.10.24
9 rue de Senlis — *Fax* 03.44.86.82.27

A sturdy, comfortable half-timbered hostelry, on the outskirts of this historic town with its huge royal palace. It is on a dull main road, but rooms look on to a quiet garden at the back. Recent reports: "Friendly staff, lovely rooms, and excellent if rather rich food. With orchids on the table, hovering white-jacketed waiters, some of us felt that dinner was over-the-top. We were laughing; other diners looked so solemn." "An elegant hotel, and a splendid copious meal." "Owner/chef Angelo Bonechi gave us a warm welcome. The baby wild boar was delicious. Our room was well furnished, but a bit dark." There's a beamed lounge. (*KGA, and others*)

Open All year.
Rooms 3 suites, 15 double. 1 on ground floor.
Facilities Salon, bar, restaurant; function room. Garden.
Location 3 km SW of town, on Senlis road. Private parking.
Credit cards All major cards accepted.
Terms Rooms 475 frs, suite 625 frs. Breakfast 45 frs. D,B&B 445–685 frs per person. Set meals 170–360 frs; full alc 400 frs.

The length of an entry need not reflect the merit of a hotel. The more interesting the report or the more unusual or controversial the hotel, the longer the entry.

CONDRIEU 69420 Rhône — Map 12

Hôtellerie Beau Rivage *Tel* 04.74.59.52.24
2 rue du Beau Rivage *Fax* 04.74.59.59.36

"We loved the place: the new owners are friendly and helpful," say visitors this year to this old *Guide* favourite, a creeper-covered hotel, smart and stylish, beside the *beau rivage* of the Rhône in Côtes-du-Rhône vineyard country. In summer you can take drinks under parasols on the pretty terrace by the river, or dine on the stone-flagged patio. *Michelin* bestows a star, and *Gault Millau* a *toque*, on Reynald Donet's cooking. "Don't miss the famous but rare Condrieu wines." A 1996 report, since the change of owners: "The meal was expensive but superb, with enormous richness of taste. The bedroom was delightful, but it was a strange sensation to sit on a lavatory that rocks from side to side." Others have written: "We enjoyed dining in the garden and breakfast on the terrace. Our attractive bedroom had a terrace facing the view. Staff were friendly, highly organised." Some rooms have fabric-covered walls. (*Elizabeth Robey, and others*) The petro-chemical works down the river are not intrusive, but there is some noise from the main-line trains.

Open All year.
Rooms 4 suites, 20 double. 16 in annexe. 1 on ground floor. 15 air-conditioned.
Facilities Salon, bar, restaurant (no-smoking); terrace overlooking Rhône. Garden: fishing. Unsuitable for ♿.
Location On N86, 40 km S of Lyon. A7 exit Condrieu (from N), or exit Chanas (from S). Garages, closed parking.
Credit cards All major cards accepted.
Terms [1996] Rooms: double 520–750 frs, suite 820 frs. Breakfast 65 frs. Set meals 170–610 frs; full alc 310–420 frs.

CONQUES 12320 Aveyron — Map 10

Hôtel Sainte-Foy *Tel* 05.65.69.84.03
Fax 05.65.72.81.04

A fine 17th-century mansion, gracefully furnished, facing the massive abbey church in a famous old village on a wooded hillside above a gorge, between Figeac and Rodez. The church is known for the Romanesque stone carving on its west doorway, and for its rich gold and silver treasure. The hotel, which is named after the martyred girl whose weird gold relic is still to be seen in the abbey museum, is modern, inside an old building. You can dine in a leafy, gently floodlit courtyard. One visitor thought his bedroom "rather plain and not over-burdened with comfort", but he liked the comfort of the public rooms and found the food well cooked and presented: "Silver domes, of course, but something good under them: confit de canard with (cheers) green vegetables, and a chocolate pudding with glazed carrots – unusual combination but utter heaven." Some rooms face the courtyard, while others overlook the abbey. (*Endorsed this year by David Wyatt and Wendy Baron*) There's a new chef this year. Cars can reach the hotel to unload baggage, but they must then be parked below the village.

Open Easter–Nov.
Rooms 3 suites, 14 double. Some air-conditioned.

Facilities Lift. Lounges (1 no-smoking), TV room, bar, 3 dining rooms; conference room; terraces, courtyard.
Location Central, opposite abbey church. Parking.
Credit cards Access, Amex, Visa.
Terms B&B: single 450–810 frs, double 510–1,100 frs; suite 1,320 frs; D,B&B 415–970 frs per person. Set meals 100–320 frs; full alc 300 frs.

CONTRES 41700 Loir-et-Cher — Map 9

Château de la Gondelaine

Tel 02.54.79.09.14
Fax 02.54.79.64.92

A 1996 visitor admired the 17th-century wood panelling in the salon, at Odile and Philippe Mellerio's handsome pink hunting lodge in the heart of the Sologne forests, south of Blois. Others have written: "Beautiful, romantic and restful: we could hear nothing but birds. Our beamed floral room was perfect, service was attentive, and food was almost too perfect to eat, with delicious local wines." "Our smallish attractive room had a fine marble fireplace; everything was spanking new. The meal, served by an eager young waiter, was of high quality." (*Martin and Karen Oldridge, and others*) One reader strongly criticised room maintenance and restaurant service.

Open All year, except 15 Jan–1 Mar, Christmas. Restaurant closed Mon midday/Wed in low season.
Rooms 13 double, 2 single. 2 on ground floor.
Facilities 2 salons, 3 dining rooms. 200-acre park: garden, tennis, fishing, hunting, falconry, mountain-biking. Riding, golf nearby.
Location 6 km NE of Contres, 21 km S of Blois, by D122, D99. Up private drive.
Credit cards All major cards accepted.
Terms Rooms: single 450 frs, double 490–830 frs. Breakfast 45 frs. D,B&B 490–600 frs per person. Set meals 155–280 frs.

CORDES 81170 Tarn — Map 10

Le Grand Écuyer

Rue Voltaire

Tel 05.63.56.01.03
Fax 05.63.56.18.83

Built in the 13th century as a defence against Simon de Montfort and his cruel crusaders, this famous old ramparted hilltop village is today packed with chic boutiques and craft shops. Here stands this former hunting lodge of the counts of Toulouse, very swish, with fine antiques and baronial furnishings. Owner/chef Yves Thuriès, famous for his pastries, wins a *Michelin* star and two *Gault Millau toques* for cuisine that "like his hotel, oscillates between the discreet and the flamboyant". "Superb", "the best meal ever", say some readers. But one this year thought the menu "pretentious", with no local daily specials. "We also found it a little much when the silver domes were removed and the contents of our plates were solemnly announced in detail: it was hard not to giggle at the hapless waitress. But it's a beautiful place to stay: the bar is charming and the staff pleasant." Others have written: "Our room had two four-posters, antiques, marbled bathroom, and a superb view. Expensive, but worth it." "The *sommelier* remained friendly, even when we ordered one of the cheapest bottles. Light sauces and beautifully decorated dishes: the langoustine ravioli was divine." (*GD, and others*)

Open Easter–15 Oct. Closed Mon/midday Tues.
Rooms 1 suite, 12 double. Air-conditioning.
Facilities Lounge, TV room, bar, 3 dining rooms; terrace.
Location In village centre, 25 km NW of Albi. Public parking down hill, crowded in season.
Credit cards All major cards accepted.
Terms Rooms 450–850 frs, suite 1,200 frs. Breakfast 70 frs. D,B&B 650 frs per person. Set meals 170–420 frs; alc 250 frs.

CORDON 74700 Haute-Savoie — Map 12

Le Cordonant BUDGET

Tel 04.50.58.34.56
Fax 04.50.47.95.57

A small family-run chalet-style hotel, "done out in the usual Alpine rustic style", in a village-cum-ski resort west of Chamonix. Half of the rooms face Mont-Blanc, the others look on to ski slopes; many have a balcony. "Excellent", "very good" are epithets in 1995–96, endorsing earlier praise for "the enthusiasm and dedication" of the "charming" owners, Gisèle and Alain Pugnat (and their daughter Cendrine). "The *table d'hôte* meals were excellent [*Michelin* red 'Repas'], making extensive use of local dairy products, pork and pastas." When it's fine, meals are served on the garden terrace (lovely views). Madame is the "kindly, smiling front-of-house", Monsieur is ebullient and rotund: "Hearing that it was my birthday, he produced a delectable home-made birthday cake as a gift. Many more meals like this and I shall begin to resemble him!" (*BW Ribbons, AG Don, and others*)

Open 15 May–20 Sept, 20 Dec–15 Apr.
Rooms 14 double, 2 single.
Facilities 2 salons, reading room, restaurant; small meeting room; sauna, jacuzzi, fitness room; terrace. Garden.
Location On edge of village, 4 km SW of Sallanches, 30 km W of Chamonix. Parking.
Credit cards Access, Visa.
Terms B&B 290–320 frs; D,B&B 269–365 frs per person. Set meals 120 frs; full alc 160 frs.

Les Roches Fleuries

Tel 04.50.58.06.71
Fax 04.50.47.82.30

Also facing across the valley to Mont-Blanc, this flower-decked chalet-hotel, spacious and informal, has "attentive" family owners, the Picots, and was much liked in 1995–96. "All front bedrooms and the dining room offer one of the best views in Europe, notably at sunset. Rooms in the new building are small but pleasant, furnished in Alpine style, with some antiques. There is a cosy, beautifully decorated salon/library/bar. A buffet breakfast is served on the terrace with a fine view. Cooking was good, but *pension* dinner selections were rather average. Very nice outdoor swimming pool. And Jimmy the labrador is the most entertaining member of the family." Others have thought the cuisine "excellent": Savoyard dishes, such as pela des aravis, are served in the *Boîte aux Fromages* restaurant. All rooms have a balcony. (*Andrew and Anna Niedzwiecki, JAP*)

Open Mid-Dec–mid-Apr, early May–end Sept.
Rooms 2 suites, 25 double, 1 single. 2 in annexe.

Facilities Salon, library, 2 bars, 2 restaurants; conference room; gym. Garden: swimming pool, table-tennis. Unsuitable for ♿.
Location 4 km SW of Sallanches on D113. Parking.
Credit cards All major cards accepted.
Terms Rooms: single 380 frs, double 580–650 frs, suite 750–900 frs. Breakfast 60 frs. D,B&B 440–570 frs per person. Set meals 145–295 frs; full alc 340 frs.

COTIGNAC 83570 Var — Map 11

Hostellerie Lou Calen — *Tel* 04.94.04.60.40
Cours Gambetta — *Fax* 04.94.04.76.64

This village in the Var hills is curiously located at the foot of a brown cliff holed with caves, some of them once inhabited. Here the *Lou Calen* (Provençal for "the place of the oil lamp") is a vine-covered *auberge*, friendly and unassuming, owned and run by Claudine Mendes. Rooms are simple, furnished in local rustic style, but have modern plumbing (some front ones suffer traffic noise). You can dine out on a terrace with wide views (dishes such as grilled shark, skewered goat). The descent to the swimming pool is steep. This year, one couple thought the hotel "lovely". Another wrote: "Charming. Lovely big bedroom. Tasty meal in large dining room, fire crackling. Pleasant service; enjoyable breakfast with good fig jam." And another: "They were very kind to our baby daughter." (*Fiona Dick, C and AP, and others*) But one veteran traveller thought the place badly run-down, with a "cheerful but rather *ad hoc* young staff". More reports, please.

Open All year, except 2 weeks Feb. Restaurant closed Wed, except July–Sept.
Rooms 16 double. 2 in garden annexe. Some on ground floor.
Facilities Salon, TV room, restaurant; conference room. Garden: swimming pool (unheated).
Location In village, 20 km NE of Brignoles. Parking.
Credit cards All major cards accepted.
Terms Rooms 300–550 frs. Breakfast 40 frs. D,B&B double 660–810 frs. Set meals 90–185 frs; full alc 230 frs.

COULANDON 03000 Allier — Map 10

Le Chalet BUDGET — *Tel* 04.70.44.50.08
Fax 04.70.44.07.09

A holiday *chez* the Hulots, Henry and Nicole, has again been recommended: "An excellent dinner and comfortable rooms." Their Relais du Silence/Logis de France is a former hunting lodge, set in its own big park with a small lake full of fish, halfway between Moulins and the village of Souvigny (fine priory church). Readers have liked the "lush pastoral setting with nightingales", and the pretty bedrooms, some with exposed beams. (*JMC*) More reports, please.

Open All year, except 16 Dec–31 Jan.
Rooms 28 double. 19 in annexe. 9 on ground floor.
Facilities Lounge, library, breakfast room, 2 dining rooms; 2 terraces. Large garden: swimming pool, pond, river, fishing.
Location 6 km W of Moulins, off D945 towards Souvigny.
Credit cards All major cards accepted.
Terms Rooms: single 290 frs, double 340–360 frs. Breakfast 45 frs. D,B&B 350–440 frs per person. Set meals 110–230 frs; full alc 300 frs.

COURCELLES-SUR-VESLE 02220 Aisne — Map 9

Château de Courcelles *Tel* 03.23.74.13.53
Fax 03.23.74.06.41

Set amid parkland between Reims and Soissons, this handsome white-fronted 1694 *demeure*, with a neat *jardin français*, typifies the French style of formal *château*-hotel. It offers tennis, riding, rowing on the lake, wooded walks, and "a pleasant swimming pool beside an attractive terrace". "Very high quality, matched by high prices," says an admirer this year, endorsing earlier praise: "Immaculately kept, peaceful and elegant. Super spacious room. Dinner had reasonable choice of classic French dishes with a modern touch." "To walk in the grounds by moonlight was most romantic; and in the heavily beamed, candelit dining room our meal was mostly excellent [*Gault Millau toque*] – rissoles de foie gras chaud, etc. Breakfast was lavish, with excellent coffee. The bar was cosy, the manager friendly." (*JE Robbs, Ann and Denis Tate, and others*) A few caveats about room upkeep. A new bypass to the village is being built round the hotel's park: this may or may not reduce the noise from juggernauts.

Open All year, except 15 Jan–15 Feb, 24 Dec.
Rooms 3 suites (2 in annexe), 11 double.
Facilities Salon/bar, 2 dining rooms (1 no-smoking). Garden: swimming pool (heated May–Sept), tennis.
Location 20 km E of Soissons, on N31 to Reims. Parking.
Credit cards Access, Amex, Visa.
Terms [1996] Rooms 600 frs, suite 1,400 frs. Breakfast 75 frs. D,B&B 550–975 frs per person. Set meals 230–360 frs.

COURSÉGOULES 06140 Alpes-Maritimes — Map 11

Auberge de l'Escaou NEW/BUDGET *Tel* 04.93.59.11.28
Fax 04.93.59.13.70

In remote hill-village 16 km NW of Vence, amid grandiose scenery, pleasant modern auberge *run by cheerful young couple. Good food (menus for* "toute la famille"*), gorgeous view from dining terrace. 10 clean, modern rooms. Lift. Closed Monday out of season. Access, Visa accepted. B&B double 320 frs; D,B&B 260 frs per person. Set meals 98–165 frs. Renominated this year. More reports welcome.*

CRÈCHES-SUR-SAÔNE 71680 Saône-et-Loire — Map 12

Hostellerie du Château de la Barge *Tel* 03.85.37.12.04
Fax 03.85.37.17.18

Again much admired in 1995–96, for its food far more than its rooms, this handsome creeper-covered 17th-century manor stands on the edge of a village near Mâcon, with large grounds and a pretty flowery garden. It is not a smart hotel, but informal, cheerfully run by its owner Claude Nebout. Reports this year: "An excellent place. Rooms wall-papered (floor and ceiling), basic, but very French – and who cares about the room, given the quality of the Burgundian food and wine? The outstanding 210 frs menu included home-cured salmon, and good cheese trolley (much goat) and puds. Local red wine better than the white, and my digestif was the most enormous I've ever been served in a restaurant." "Warm and welcoming owner, rooms fairly basic but clean." Others have agreed: not much pretence at decor, but "public rooms are endearingly old-fashioned, with high beamed ceilings and motley pictures". Breakfast was "generous", although "everything was in wrappings". You can take lunch on the terrace in summer. (*Garry Wiseman, Alyssa Armstrong, PM Pullie, AS Carr, and many others*) "Nightingales sing at night", but so does the nearby TGV.

Open All year, except 24 Oct–19 Nov, 19 Dec–4 Jan, Sat/Sun Nov–Easter.
Rooms 2 suites, 22 double. 2 on ground floor.
Facilities Lift. Salon, TV room, restaurant; terrace. Garden: children's playground.
Location A6 exit Mâcon Sud; follow signs for Gare TGV. Courtyard parking.
Credit cards All major cards accepted.
Terms B&B: single 290 frs, double 310 frs; D,B&B (min. 3 days) 310 frs per person. Set meals 100–210 frs; full alc 160 frs.

CRÉPON 14480 Calvados — Map 8

Ferme de la Rançonnière NEW/BUDGET *Tel* 02.31.22.21.73
Fax 02.31.22.98.39

"A real find", yet close to Bayeux and the Normandy beaches – and quite a curiosity. It is a fortified crenellated farmhouse dating from the 13th to the 15th century, and according to its discoverer has "fantastic atmosphere and character". "The buildings stand round a huge courtyard. Our room, in a newly renovated building, had stone walls, a ceiling with huge oak beams, stone/tiled floors, pieces of antique furniture but very comfortable beds, a good bathroom. The dining room too was oak-beamed and stone-walled – and iron-chandeliered! A wood fire roared in a big open fireplace. The food was good, the service smooth and efficient, even though two groups of business men were dining." Large garden. (*Jill Douglas*)

Open All year. Restaurant closed 13–23 Jan.
Rooms 34 double/family. 7 more in annexe *Ferme de Mathan* 500 m.
Facilities Ramps. Lounge, breakfast room, 2 dining rooms (1 no-smoking). Garden: courtyard.
Location 12 km E of Bayeux, 7 km SE of Arromanches. Parking.
Credit cards All major cards accepted.
Terms [1996] Rooms 295–400 frs; in annexe 380–480 frs. Breakfast 45 frs. D,B&B 270–310 frs per person. Set meals 88–255 frs.

CRILLON-LE-BRAVE 84410 Vaucluse — Map 11

Hostellerie de Crillon le Brave *Tel* 04.90.65.61.61
Place de l'Église *Fax* 04.90.65.62.86

This very stylishly converted Provençal mansion, in a hill-village below Mont Ventoux, is the brain-child of Peter Chittick, a Canadian ex-lawyer, who owns it with Craig Miller: they have new managers this year, a Canadian/French couple, Hector and Pamela de Galard. Old oak beams, local antiques and colourful Souleidado fabrics go to make up the decor, while the regional cooking wins a *Gault Millau toque*. Praise came again this year: "The style is of elegant simplicity, and the old buildings of honey-coloured stone have been superbly renovated. The vaulted stone dining room leads on to a terrace with cypresses, where breakfast is on a par with the view. The exceptional cuisine includes game from the local hills, and some wines are from vineyards by the hotel." Nearly all readers agree on the views, superb service, good food, though some have found the cooking over-elaborate, with a lack of fresh vegetables and salads – "but breakfast was delicious". The rooms are pretty, and the terrace is "a magical place to eat in the warm evenings". "Provençal smellies in the bathroom and a complimentary bowl of pistachio nuts, replenished daily." (*Michael and Valerie Miller, and others*)

Open All year, except 2 Jan–14 Mar. Restaurant closed Tues Nov–Mar, midday except Sat/Sun.
Rooms 5 suites, 19 double. In 4 buildings.
Facilities 4 lounges, breakfast room, dining room. Garden: swimming pool, terraces; bicycles. Unsuitable for ♿.
Location 14 km NE of Carpentras, off D974 to Bédoin. Garages.
Credit cards Access, Amex, Visa.
Terms [1996] Rooms 750–1,250 frs, suite 1,450–2,300 frs. Breakfast 80 frs. D,B&B 280 frs per person added. Set meals 240–290 frs; full alc 360 frs.

LA CROIX-VALMER 83420 Var — Map 11

Les Moulins de Paillas et Résidence Gigaro

Plage de Gigaro

Tel 04.94.79.71.11
Fax 04.94.54.37.05
E-mail 101564.1050@compuserve.com

Although St-Tropez and other busy resorts are quite near, this gorgeous bit of coast is "wholly unspoilt". This pleasant modern hotel, named after three ruined windmills on the hills behind, and quiet save for the sound of surf, is beside a beach that is "rarely overcrowded", with good walks all round. It is fairly large, a long low building with cheerful decor, and was enjoyed again recently: "The coast here has been bought by local councils and conservation groups as a nature reserve. All the rooms have a little garden or balcony, and are comfortable if not lavish. But there are lounges, or you can sit round the good big pool. Most guests are Swiss. Staff are alert and friendly. Breakfasts pleasant, with a variety of breads. And we like the hotel's *La Brigantine* restaurant, with super fish [*Gault Millau toque*]." (*RBR*)

Open Mid-May–30 Sept.
Rooms 68 double in 2 buildings. Some on ground floor.
Facilities Lounges, TV room, bar, café, 3 restaurants; terrace. Garden: swimming pool, tennis. Private beach.
Location At Gigaro, 5 km E of La Croix-Valmer.
Credit cards Access, Amex, Visa.
Terms [1996] B&B: single 620–1,140 frs, double 690–1,210 frs; D,B&B 560–1,200 frs per person. Alc meals 290 frs.

CUQ-LE-CHÂTEAU 81470 Tarn — Map 10

Cuq en Terrasses

Tel 05.63.82.54.00
Fax 05.63.82.54.11

"A truly blissful place", "a lovely stay", say visitors this year. London designer Tim Whitmore (he worked for Biba, and for Paul McCartney) and his wife Zara have restored an old presbytery and opened it as a small and special hotel. It is in a hamlet on a hilltop east of Toulouse, looking over a "breathtaking" landscape. The decor is "traditionally *midi*", with hand-plastered walls, old terracotta tiled floors and beamed ceilings. "The owners are congenial and the house is ravishing – from the rear, a four-storey *maison de maître*, with beautiful flower-decked terraces leading down to the pool. Every object of furniture and decor has been chosen with care and taste. There's a fine staircase, and unusual exposed beams." "The decor is inspired, with bright colours, the food is delicious", is one report this year. Another: "Our room was a delight. Drinks on a beautiful terrace looking over the garden to a magnificent pool. You're made so welcome. We even enjoyed the soft music over dinner." "Warm, friendly hosts. Sympathetic home cooking." (*HR, Linda Brook, Virginia Pearce, and others*) Meals are served by prior arrangement, with 24 hours' notice.

Open All year, except 4 Jan–5 Feb.
Rooms 1 apartment (in separate tower by swimming pool), 2 suites, 5 double.
Facilities Ramp. Library/lounge with TV, bar/dining room; meeting facilities. Garden: swimming pool, croquet, badminton. Lake 12 km: water sports, fishing. Unsuitable for ♿.
Location Off N126 Toulouse–Castres. At Cadix-Cuq-Toulza take D45 to Revel for 2 km. Hotel on left.
Credit cards Access, Diners, Visa.
Terms Double room 400–500 frs, suite 700 frs, apartment 900 frs. Breakfast 55 frs. Set lunch 130 frs, dinner 150 frs (24 hrs notice required).

LES DEUX-ALPES 38860 Isère — Map 12

La Bérangère NEW — *Tel* 04.76.79.24.11, *Fax* 04.76.79.55.08

This smart modern hotel (Relais & Châteaux) stands close to a ski-run, in a large, popular resort south-east of Grenoble. Its broad sun-terrace faces the mountains; and it has unusually good food for a holiday hotel of this kind (*Michelin* star, *Gault Millau toque*). Dropped from the 1996 *Guide* for lack of reports, it now returns *cum laude*: "Improved by its new manager, it is better than ever. The mountain views from the pool are marvellous. Lunch on the terrace in the sun, if you can manage it after the wonderful buffet breakfast (fruit flans, etc). We had some memorable meals even on the no-choice half-board menu; good-value wine list, considerate staff. Relaxed and informal." "Slightly formal, but relaxed. A wonderfully chatty manager, but not intrusive. The games room is good for children. Rooms vary in price: cheaper ones have poor views, while the best overlook the terrace, pool and Alps." (*G and E Watt, Erick Davidson*) The drive up by car is very steep.

Open 1 Dec–29 Apr, 15 June–1 Sept.
Rooms 59 double. 1 on ground floor.
Facilities Lift. Salon, bar, games room, restaurant; conference room; indoor swimming pool, sauna, jacuzzi; terrace (lunch served in fine weather): swimming pool.
Location At entrance to resort, 74 km S of Grenoble. Garage.
Credit cards Access, Amex, Visa.
Terms [1996] Rooms 600–800 frs. Breakfast 65 frs. D,B&B 580–800 frs per person. Set meals 200–400 frs; full alc 270–450 frs.

La Farandole *Tel* 04.76.80.50.45
18 rue du Cairou *Fax* 04.76.79.56.12

This big modern chalet, fairly smart, stands near the centre of a large popular ski resort. Many rooms have a balcony with spectacular views of Alps and glaciers. "Our mixed bag of a party found it just right for skiers. Rooms are light and spacious. Kind and concerned staff and Martin family owners. Breakfast buffet for carnivores and fruit compotes to die for. Dinner five courses of unwavering high quality – fish and meat prepared deliciously, fruit tarts, creamy concoctions. Excellent leisure facilities: big panoramic pool, hammam, fitness room, solarium, etc. Minibus to the slopes." (*SM*)

Open 20 June–10 Sept, 1 Dec–1 May.
Rooms 14 suites, 42 double, 4 single.
Facilities Lift. Lounge, restaurant; conference facilities; indoor swimming pool, fitness room. Garden.
Location In resort, 74 km SE of Grenoble. Garage.
Credit cards All major cards accepted.
Terms B&B: single 400–500 frs, double 600–700 frs, suite 800–1,000 frs; D,B&B 550–750 frs per person. Set meals 200–250 frs.

DEUX-CHAISES 03240 Allier **Map 10**

Château de Longueville *Tel* 04.70.47.32.91

Two km W of Deux-Chaises, 10 km NE of Montmarault on N145 to Moulins: 19th-century château *with garden and pond, newly redecorated in clever period style by "charming and inventive" American-born owner Michael Jumonville. Antiques, rugs,* faux marbre *loos. Relaxed ambience. Candlelit dinners with owner (eg, pintade sauce champagne); nightly piano music and dancing. 2-acre grounds. Credit cards not accepted. 4 rooms. B&B double 400 frs; D,B&B 400–490 frs per person. Set meals 200 frs. Reports on meals and that night-life welcome.*

DIJON 21000 Côte-d'Or **Map 9**

Hôtel Wilson *Tel* 03.80.66.82.50
10 place Wilson *Fax* 03.80.36.41.54

This 17th-century post house on one of the city's main squares has been nicely converted, keeping some of the old exposed beams and an exterior gallery in the courtyard. "Excellent, friendly staff, good breakfast," is a recent plaudit. But bedrooms are simple: "Ours was somewhat spartan, but comfortable," writes one visitor. Another liked the "charming decor" and added: "Our room seemed to have been just redone, while retaining old 'post house' features." Bathrooms vary in quality. (*LB, and others*) No restaurant, but readers like the adjacent *Thibert* (*Michelin* star, three *Gault Millau toques*), which is distinguished without being *too* pricey.

Open All year, except New Year.
Rooms 27 double. 1 on ground floor.
Facilities Lift. Salon, bar, breakfast room (no-smoking).
Location Central (rooms double-glazed, courtyard ones quietest). Parking in courtyard.
Credit cards Access, Visa.
Terms Rooms 340–480 frs. Breakfast 55 frs.

DINAN 22100 Côtes d'Armor — Map 8

Hôtel Arvor BUDGET — *Tel* 02.96.39.21.22
5 rue Auguste Pavie — *Fax* 02.96.39.83.09

In centre of historic and delightful old Breton town, former convent, recently imaginatively converted. 23 bedrooms of character, excellent service, relaxed ambience. Access, Amex, Visa accepted. Rooms 260–360 frs. Breakfast 35 frs. No restaurant. Good value: more reports welcome.

DOLUS D'OLÉRON 17550 Charente-Maritime — Map 10

Le Grand Large NEW — *Tel* 05.46.75.37.89
Baie de la Rémigeasse — *Fax* 05.46.75.49.15

On W coast of holiday island of Oléron, 2 km SW of Dolus, "excellent up-market seaside hotel", modern, ivy-covered, smart and pricey (Relais & Châteaux). View of rolling dunes, direct access to sandy beach. Very good food, notably local seafood (two Gault Millau toques*); friendly owners and staff. Fine bedrooms facing sea or large gardens; indoor swimming pool, tennis. Open April–end Sept. Access, Amex, Visa accepted. 5 suites, 21 double: 780–1,680 frs. Breakfast 90 frs. D,B&B 780–1,230 frs per person. Set lunch 160 frs, dinner 260–370 frs. Fuller reports welcome.*

DOMME 24250 Dordogne — Map 10

Hôtel de l'Esplanade — *Tel* 05.53.28.31.41
Fax 05.53.28.49.92

"A model of the French small regional hotel," writes a recent guest at this medium-priced Logis de France, run with style by *patron*/chef René Gillard and his amiable wife. Its position is superb, on a cliff above the Dordogne, in a showpiece village, full of daytime trippers but quiet at night. The cuisine (*Michelin* star, *Gault Millau toque*) has been found "faultlessly good", in quality and quantity: "On the 150 frs [1996] menu, a huge plate of asparagus with millefeuille, a creamy mussel soup, magret of duck, a royal chariot of desserts, and a very good Cahors at 110 frs. Our room, with a picture window over the river, was good apart from poor bedside lighting." "What a view! It's worth waking at dawn to see the mist over the river, the sun catching the cliffs" – but not all rooms have that view, nor all tables on the panoramic dining terrace. Madame is said to direct operations "with great aplomb". "The hotel has charm, from the old wood panelling in the foyer to the chic decor of the bedrooms. Mine was small but exquisitely furnished, with a marble bathroom." (*Bill and Marcia Griffith, HR, and others*) Rooms at the top can be hot in summer. Some are in old houses in the village, but are nicely furnished. The dining room has been redecorated this year.

Open 14 Feb–3 Nov. Restaurant closed Mon in low season.
Rooms 1 suite, 24 double. 10 in 3 houses in village.
Facilities Salon, bar, restaurant; terraces. Unsuitable for ♿.
Location 12 km S of Sarlat.
Credit cards Access, Amex, Visa.
Terms Rooms 300–590 frs, suite 800 frs. Breakfast 50 frs. D,B&B 350–640 frs per person. Set meals 160–350 frs; full alc 400 frs.

DURAS 47120 Lot-et-Garonne Map 10

Hostellerie des Ducs *Tel* 05.53.83.74.58
Boulevard Jean Brisseau *Fax* 05.53.83.75.03

The author of *L'Amant*, whose real name was Donnadieu, chose the nom-de-plume of Marguerite Duras because her father once owned a house in this wine-growing townlet south of the river Dordogne. Here this converted convent has been totally renovated this year, with air-conditioning, new furniture, and a new terrace overlooking the 14th-century fortress. Visitors before the change enjoyed the "family atmosphere, small but comfortable rooms, superb food (*Gault Millau toque*), beautiful garden and small swimming pool". Others concurred, adding "excellent breakfasts". (*J and DM*) Reports on the new developments would be most welcome.

Open All year. Restaurant closed Sun evening/Mon in low season.
Rooms 14 double, 2 single.
Facilities Salon, TV room, billiard room, restaurant (no-smoking). Garden: swimming pool (unheated). Unsuitable for ♿.
Location On D708, 23 km N of Marmande. Parking.
Credit cards Access, Visa.
Terms Rooms: single 200 frs, double 250–450 frs. Breakfast 40 frs. D,B&B 280–340 frs per person. Set meals 80–210 frs; full alc 350 frs. Off-season reductions.

ENCAUSSE-LES-THERMES 31160 Haute-Garonne Map 10

Aux Maronniers BUDGET *Tel* 05.61.89.17.12

In village 11 km SE of St-Gaudens in Pyrenean foothills, small family-run Logis de France beside a stream, with terrace for summer dining, and garden shaded by – yes! – chestnut trees. Friendly owners, good inexpensive "peasant cooking". 10 rooms, small, simple, but clean, all with bidet; showers and WCs on landing. Open Apr–end Oct, except Sun evening/Mon out of season. Restaurant open all year, except Jan, Sun evening/Mon out of season. Access, Visa accepted. B&B double 214 frs; D,B&B 175 frs per person. Set meals 70–140 frs. Recently renominated.

L'ÉPINE 51460 Marne Map 9

Aux Armes de Champagne *Tel* 03.26.69.30.30
31 avenue du Luxembourg *Fax* 03.26.66.92.31

This well-modernised old coaching inn stands in the square of a village east of Châlons-en-Champagne. Most bedrooms face the huge floodlit basilica of Notre Dame. And so does the dining room, where *Michelin* awards a star, and *Gault Millau* two *toques,* to Patrick Michelon's cooking. More praise in 1995–96: "Dining was a delight, and the service most efficient. The wine waiter is a real character. A comfortable room, but breakfast not so well organised." Earlier views: "Food the best of our holiday. The flower garden was wonderful." "A quiet, pretty room in the annexe. All staff are very thoughtful. Unforgettable food, eg, marmite of lobster and scallops, a superb chocolate marquise" (but another reader thought the wines overpriced). The waiters have a habit of describing each dish in high theatrical style as they present it. The owner, Jean-Paul Pérardel, is full of friendly welcome, and room service is much admired. (*Dr Arthur and Mrs Naylor, Ian and Dorothy Young, and others*) Lorries passing outside the dining room can be a nuisance. Annexe rooms are quietest; others are within earshot of the basilica's hourly chimes.

Open All year, except Christmas, New Year, 5 Jan–12 Feb, Sun evening/Mon Nov–Mar.
Rooms 2 suites, 35 double. 16 in annexe (200 m). Some on ground floor.
Facilities TV room, bar, 2 dining rooms; function facilities; concerts in summer. Garden: mini-golf. Tennis, golf nearby. Unsuitable for ♿.
Location Central. L'Épine is 8.5 km E of Châlons, on N3. Private parking.
Credit cards All major cards accepted.
Terms Rooms: single 320 frs, double 690 frs, suite 1,250 frs. Breakfast 55 frs. Set meals 200–475 frs; full alc 400–450 frs.

ESPEZEL 11340 Aude — Map 10

Hôtel Grau BUDGET

Tel 04.68.20.30.14
Fax 04.68.20.33.62

This is remote and hilly Cathar country, where you can visit the tiny hill-village of Montaillou, setting of Emmanuel Le Roy Ladurie's masterly case-study of medieval life. Along the same scenic road is Espezel, another old village on a plateau, where Michel Grau, a local man, and his Geordie wife Orwina own and run this modest Logis de France, with the help of their "jolly" daughter, and "engender an air of enjoyment". Two recent plaudits: "Madame is quite a card. And Michel Grau gave us a very fine dinner – sea bass with a delicious sauce, complemented by the local white Corbières." "Michel, a rugby player, serves superb local produce in generous portions. For breakfast, he provides his own jams, such as fig with walnuts and raisins. Orwina is as down-to-earth and friendly as you'd expect a Tynesider to be. They offer good value." (*Elizabeth and Bernard Biggs, J and AL*) Some bathrooms are large, but shower rooms may be poky.

Open All year.
Rooms 7 double, 1 single.
Facilities Salon with TV, bar, restaurant.
Location 21 km SW of Quillan. Private parking.
Restriction Smoking discouraged in dining room.
Credit cards Access, Visa.
Terms Rooms: single 150 frs, double 200–280 frs. Breakfast 35 frs. D,B&B 190–245 frs per person. Set meals 75–190 frs; full alc 220 frs.

ESTRABLIN 38780 Isère — Map 12

La Gabetière NEW/BUDGET

Tel 04.74.58.01.31
Fax 04.74.58.08.98

This old creeper-covered manor near the Rhône valley has a haunting history. It belonged to a *seigneur*, Jacques Gabet, whose family turned Protestant at the Reformation; he himself was shot by the Catholics in 1573. Today it is owned and run as a guest house by René Lentillon and her daughter, and we hope it is free of ghosts: "It is full of nooks and crannies, odd staircases and crooked hallways – quite fun," says its nominator. "Our room was adequate, service pleasant, breakfast nice. There's a lounge/bar, an attractive garden, and a playground for kids. No restaurant, but the one they recommended nearby, in a bright pink shopping centre, turned out to be very good." Outdoor pool. (*Kaye Sykes and Ed Ackert*)

Open All year.
Rooms 1 suite, 9 double, 2 single. 2 in annexe.
Facilities Salon, bar; conference room. Garden: swimming pool, children's playground. Unsuitable for ♿.
Location Outside Estrablin, on D502, 9 km E of Vienne. Locked parking.
Credit cards Access, Diners, Visa.
Terms Rooms: single 230 frs, double 300–350 frs, suite 470 frs. Breakfast 34 frs.

EUGÉNIE-LES-BAINS 40320 Landes — Map 10

Les Prés d'Eugénie et Le Couvent des Herbes
Tel 05.58.05.06.07
Fax 05.58.51.10.10

Famous as the birthplace of his *cuisine minceur*, Michel Guérard's "grand and special institution" inhabits an imposing Second Empire mansion north of Pau, on a site where hot springs bubble. In the French guides he earns the topmost food ratings, and our inspector thought this deserved: "He still delivers the gourmet goods, at a high but fair price: we felt we were not just paying through the nose for flunkies and glitter. We are still talking about the density of taste of the chicken soup, the sea bass cooked in goose fat, the brilliant chocolate desserts. The long wine list includes some local items at reasonable price. Our only complaint: the over-attentive waiters rushing to top up even your water glass as you take a sip. The Guérards were much in evidence and seemed a cordial couple. However, our bedroom had a dated feel, very plain, lacking in character, despite the French windows leading on to a pleasant terrace." "The groaning cheeseboard needed two people to lift it." The hotel caters for *curistes* who wear dressing gowns much of the day, drink the waters and eat *cuisine minceur*: more robust guests can choose from Guérard's *menu gourmand*. Rooms vary, and not all are plain: the suites in the 18th-century nunnery in the garden have been called "rustic chic". The huge outdoor pool is warm and well kept, and "breakfast on the terrace was a delight, as were drinks at night on the patio with its illuminated fountains and statues". (*Endorsed this year by Lawrence Brass*)

Open All year, except 2 Dec–27 Feb. Restaurant closed Wed/midday Thurs in low season, except public holidays.
Rooms 10 suites, 33 double. 8 in *Couvent*.
Facilities Lift. Salon, TV room, gallery, bar, billiard room, restaurants; beauty salon, thermal baths, sauna. Garden: tennis, swimming pool.
Location Off D944 near St-Sever-Aubagnan, 53 km N of Pau.
Credit cards All major cards accepted.
Terms [1996] Rooms 1,300–1,700 frs. Breakfast 110 frs. *Menu minceur* (residents only) 320 frs; set meals 390–690 frs.

> Deadlines: nominations for the 1998 edition should reach us not later than 25 May 1997. Latest date for comments on existing entries: 1 June 1997.

EYGALIÈRES 13810 Bouches-du-Rhône — Map 11

Hostellerie Mas du Pastre NEW/BUDGET — *Tel* 04.90.95.92.61
Quartier St-Sixte — *Fax* 04.90.90.61.75

In Alpilles foothills, 1 km E of Eygalières village, 11 km SE of St-Rémy, old farmhouse converted by owners, Roumanille family, into small hotel, superbly decorated in Provençal style with colourful modern additions. Friendly welcome. Large pool, boules *in idyllic garden (loungers under parasols). Access, Visa accepted. 10 rooms, varying in size and price. B&B double 350–600 frs. No restaurant; lots nearby. Fuller reports welcome.*

LES EYZIES-DE-TAYAC 24620 Dordogne — Map 10

Les Glycines — *Tel* 05.53.06.97.07
Fax 05.53.06.92.19

This "cradle of prehistory" (as Les Eyzies calls itself) gets deluged with visitors. However, set quietly on the edge of the village, in a lovely garden by a river, is Henri and Christiane Mercat's creeper-covered hostelry, admired as ever this year: "A lovely oasis, with caring and friendly staff, mostly in their twenties, and Madame always gracious and elegant. Our ground-floor room opened directly on to the wonderful garden, where we took breakfast. On the dining terrace, we enjoyed good food (some dishes outstanding), but presentation was over-fussy and sauces very rich." Others, writing in similar vein, have praised the gardens and pool, the views from the terrace. "Our children were given child-sized meals as delicious as our five-course dinners." "Mme Mercat is a fantastic hostess, with a good sense of humour." But some rooms, both in the annexe and in the main building, are quite small, and one reader disliked the "gaudy orange wallpaper, even on the doors" and the plumbing noises. Service at dinner can be slow. (*Mrs Lydia Heah, and others*) "The delightful half-dog/half-cat, Fanny, likes to sit on the reception counter."

Open Mid-Apr–mid-Oct. Restaurant closed midday Sat, except July–Sept.
Rooms *Pavillon* for 4 people in grounds, 24 double. 4 on ground floor.
Facilities Salon, bar, reading room (no-smoking), restaurant; terrace (meals served). Large garden: swimming pool (unheated). Canoeing, fishing nearby.
Location On D47 Périgueux–Sarlat, by river. Parking.
Credit cards Access, Amex, Visa.
Terms Rooms: single 312–395 frs, double 350–409 frs. Breakfast 50 frs. D,B&B 398–520 frs per person. Set meals 140–180 frs; full alc 330 frs.

ÈZE-VILLAGE 06360 Alpes-Maritimes — Map 11

Château de la Chèvre d'Or NEW — *Tel* 04.92.10.66.66
Rue du Barri — *Fax* 04.93.41.06.72

The best-known and most touristy of Côte d'Azur hill-villages stands in a dramatic site beside the Middle Corniche, on a rocky outcrop almost sheer above the sea. It has been carefully restored, and the many souvenir shops are not *too* vulgar; at night, when the trippers have departed, it can be hauntingly quiet. There is no motor traffic, but a short walk along its main alley leads to this small but celebrated luxury hotel (Relais & Châteaux), *very* expensive, and renominated this year: "It was built in 1920 in medieval style to blend into the side of Èze village – a spectacular setting. The rooms and terraces are spread cunningly over five levels and set out in great style. The two small swimming pools are beautifully sited, with sumptuous loungers and views. Even the smaller, cheaper rooms are of a high standard and have a balcony: to sit there with an excellent breakfast and view of the coast is both relaxing and exciting. The restaurant with large windows and the same stunning outlook has varied, enjoyable food (*Michelin* star, two *Gault Millau toques*). Staff are solicitous, friendly and efficient. A delight." (*Felix Singer*) Meals can be taken alfresco in summer.

Open 1 Mar–30 Nov. Restaurant closed Wed Mar/Nov.
Rooms 6 suites, 23 double.
Facilities Bar/salon, 4 restaurants; terrace. Garden: 2 swimming pools. 10 mins' drive to sea; tennis, golf nearby.
Location 10 km NE of Nice, by Moyenne Corniche road. Public parking at entrance to village.
Credit cards All major cards accepted.
Terms [1996] Rooms 1,600–2,600 frs. Breakfast 105 frs. *Chèvre d'Or*: set lunch 250 frs, dinner 560 frs; alc 420–540 frs. *Café du Jardin*: set meals 100–160 frs.

FLAGY 77940 Seine-et-Marne — Map 9

Hostellerie du Moulin — *Tel* 01.60.96.67.89
2 rue du Moulin — *Fax* 01.60.96.69.51

"We loved it," says a 1996 visitor, heaping yet more praise on this idyllic *Guide* favourite: a 13th-century mill house, "beautifully converted" into a rustic-style restaurant-with-rooms, in a pretty village south of Fontainebleau. "A warm welcome from the owner, Claude Scheidecker, and his staff. Excellent service, and memorable food with slightly offbeat flavours. An old atmospheric rustic building, spotlessly maintained, with some antiques. Our rooms were over the water, whose sound created the most profound sleep." Others this year also praised the "welcoming" owners and the food, "good value". There's a pleasant lounge with some of the old mill wheels and pulleys, a "romantic dining room", and in summer you can eat out under weeping willows beside a stream, with the murmur of rushing water. Rooms are inevitably small, but comfortable. (*Mike Shepherd, DB McLean, and others*)

Open All year, except 15–27 Sept, 22 Dec–24 Jan, Sun evening/Mon (except public holidays, when closed Mon evening/Tues).
Rooms 10 double.
Facilities Lounges, bar with TV, restaurant; small conference room; terrace. Riverside gardens: fishing. Unsuitable for ♿.
Location 9 km S of Montereau, 23 km SE of Fontainebleau. From N6 turn right on to D403, immediately left on to D120.
Credit cards All major cards accepted.
Terms Rooms: single 260–320 frs, double 320–500 frs. Breakfast 50 frs. D,B&B (min. 3 days) 366–502 frs per person. Set meals 180–240 frs; full alc 280–350 frs.

> Don't trust out-of-date editions of the *Guide*. Hotels change hands, deteriorate or go out of business. Many hotels are dropped and new ones added every year.

FLORENT-EN-ARGONNE 51800 Marne — Map 9

Le Jabloire BUDGET — *Tel* 03.26.60.82.03
Fax 03.26.60.85.45

In village deep in Forest of Argonne, 7 km NE of Ste-Menehould, former staging-post now a pleasant small B&B hotel run by local mayor and his wife, both charming. 12 clean, modernised rooms. Excellent breakfasts. Closed Feb, Sun evening Nov–Mar. Access, Amex, Visa accepted. Rooms 250–380 frs. Breakfast 35 frs. Endorsed recently, but fuller reports welcome. Restaurant La Ményère *(closed Sun evening/Mon) recommended.*

FLORIMONT-GAUMIERS 24250 Dordogne — Map 10

La Daille — *Tel* 05.53.28.40.71

Derek and Barbara Brown, typical Dordogne expats, own and run this small restaurant/guest house in personal style. It is in the hills south of Domme, an old stone farmhouse with an outside staircase and pigeon tower. Inside it has been sensitively modernised; bedrooms, in a purpose-built annexe and a converted barn, enjoy fine views across the valley. "Peaceful, friendly, super food"; "welcoming hosts, dinner a delight in the stone dining room", are two recent plaudits. Mrs Brown was treasurer of the British Epicure Society, and her cooking, a mix of English and French, uses home-grown vegetables. "Breakfast, beside our room on the terrace, was delicious, with superb brioche. Dinner was really nice, but too abundant for hot weather, and the wine offered was rather poor." "How pleasant to sit under the walnut tree. Then there is the evening gathering in the courtyard to meet one's fellow guests." But there's no lounge. (*A and D Toft, Giovanna Davitti, and others*) No lunches, but you can buy your own snacks and enjoy them in the garden.

Open 1 May–30 Sept. Restaurant closed for lunch.
Rooms 3 double, 1 single. 1 in converted barn.
Facilities Restaurant; terrace. Large grounds. Unsuitable for ♿.
Location Signposted from Gaumiers village, just W of D46. 13 km S of Domme, 5 km NW of Salviac.
Restrictions No smoking in restaurant. No children under 7.
Credit cards None accepted.
Terms D,B&B (min. 3 days) 390–455 frs. Set dinner 150 frs.

FONTAINEBLEAU 77300 Seine-et-Marne — Map 9

Hôtel de l'Aigle Noir NEW — *Tel* 01.60.74.60.00
27 place Napoléon Bonaparte — *Fax* 01.60.74.60.01

Bedrooms vary from Victorian plush to modern plain at this, the town's grandest hotel, which has Louis XVI and Empire decor and faces the gardens of Napoleon's favourite palace. It is family owned and run, and has excellent service; also a piano bar and small heated swimming pool. Dropped from the *Guide* for lack of reports, it is renominated by two readers this year: "Very good and reliable, with excellent restaurant" (this is *Le Beauharnais*, which wins a *Michelin* star and two *Gault Millau toques*). "My room was excellent, staff were most helpful, but food was ordinary." Some bedrooms have a balcony overlooking the town, some a marble bathroom, but those on the third floor are "small and attic like". The lock-up garage is a boon. (*Mr and Mrs DA Lewis, Mrs EH Prodgers*)

Open All year. Restaurant closed 5–25 Aug.
Rooms 6 suites, 55 double, 6 single. 2 equipped for ♿. Air-conditioning.
Facilities Lift, ramps. Salons, bar, restaurant; conference facilities; indoor swimming pool, sauna; 2 patios
Location Central (double-glazing). Garage.
Credit cards All major cards accepted.
Terms [1996] Rooms 800–1,050 frs, suite 1,500–2,000 frs. Breakfast 95 frs. D,B&B 930–1,205 frs per person. Set meals 180–450 frs; full alc 290–450 frs.

FONTVIEILLE 13990 Bouches-du-Rhône — Map 11

Auberge La Régalido NEW — *Tel* 04.90.54.60.22
Rue Frédéric Mistral — *Fax* 04.90.54.64.29

Tourists flock to Daudet's windmill (or rather, *one* of his windmills), which stands on a hill outside this tiny town in the foothills of the Alpilles, near Arles. Down a side-street is this former oil-mill, now a delightful flowery *auberge,* luxurious yet unpretentious. After some time with no reports, it is brought back to the *Guide* with enthusiasm, by a devotee: "Each year it gets marginally better. The boss / chef, Jean-Pierre Michel, is always around; he even mans reception. His cooking is Provençal at its best (*Michelin* star, *Gault Millau toque*): bouillabaisse, Alpilles lamb. Rooms are scattered all over this old house, higgledy-piggledy: all delightful, and decorated in a charming, somewhat chintzy manner. Breakfast, maybe in the wonderful flower-filled garden, is as good, varied and well presented as any we've had in France." You can eat out on fine days. Rooms have flowery light fabrics, smart new tiled bathrooms, and in some cases beamed ceilings and their own roof-terrace. (*Neil French*)

Open All year, except 3–31 Jan. Restaurant closed Mon, except July–Sept when closed midday Mon / midday Tues.
Rooms 2 suites, 11 double, 2 single. 1 on ground floor.
Facilities 3 lounges, bar, restaurant. Garden: patio.
Location In village, 10 km NE of Arles. Parking.
Credit cards All major cards accepted.
Terms Rooms: single 430–450 frs, double 650–1,160 frs, suite 1,490–1,510 frs. Breakfast 97 frs. D,B&B double 1,440–1,945 frs. Set meals 160–390 frs; full alc 400 frs.

FORCALQUIER 04300 Alpes-de-Haute-Provence — Map 11

Le Colombier NEW — *Tel* 04.92.75.03.71
Fax 04.92.75.14.30

Four km S of town, on D16, cleverly converted stone farmhouse with pleasant views from shady terrace, swimming pool. "Delightful" owners. Attractive dining room, with roaring fire; goodish food and breakfast. 15 bedrooms, all different. Open 1 Mar–17 Nov; restaurant open 1 Jan–15 Nov, closed lunch except Sun/Mon. Access, Amex, Visa accepted. Rooms 310–460 frs. Breakfast 42 frs. D,B&B 345–470 frs per person. Set meals 128–190 frs [1996]. Fuller reports welcome.

FORGES-LES-EAUX 76440 Seine-Maritime **Map 9**

Auberge du Beau Lieu *Tel* 02.35.90.50.36
Le Fossé *Fax* 02.35.90.35.98

Two km SE of small spa town 42 km NE of Rouen, which may have been original for Flaubert's Yonville in Madame Bovary, *excellent restaurant with Norman-based cooking* (Gault Millau toque)*; just 3 formal bedrooms, each with own patio. Pleasant service. Closed Tues, except July/Aug. All major credit cards accepted. Rooms 335 frs. Breakfast 38 frs. Set menus 105–325 frs [1996]. Endorsed this year for good food and welcome and "small cottage in garden, clean and bright", but fuller reports welcome.*

FOUESNANT 29170 Finistère **Map 8**

Hôtel de la Pointe de Mousterlin *Tel* 02.98.56.04.12
Pointe de Mousterlin *Fax* 02.98.56.61.02

On S Brittany coast, 6 km S of Fouesnant, and right by sandy beach, a white, very modern Logis de France, with pleasant staff and family owners. Wide lawns, tennis, gym, sauna. Good food (local fish), and breakfast choice. Open 1 May–30 Sept. Access, Visa accepted. 52 rooms: 235–435 frs. Buffet breakfast 38 frs. D,B&B 265–430 frs per person. Set meals: lunch 80–160 frs, dinner 210 frs [1996]. Special summer rates for families.

FRÉHEL 22240 Côtes-d'Armor **Map 8**

Relais du Fréhel NEW/BUDGET *Tel* 02.96.41.43.02
Route du Cap

On lovely stretch of North Brittany coast, 2.5 km S of Cap Fréhel headland, converted creeper-covered 19th-century farmhouse, "a real gem, with rustic charm, and wonderful garden". Rooms small but with good views. Meals served in wood-walled room with log fire. Friendly service. Tennis, table-tennis. Open 1 Apr–3 Nov. Access, Visa accepted. 13 rooms: 187–267 frs. Breakfast 33 frs. D,B&B 257–287 frs per person. Set meals 68–172 frs [1996].

FROENINGEN 68720 Haut-Rhin **Map 12**

Auberge de Froeningen NEW *Tel* 03.89.25.48.48
2 route d'Illfurth *Fax* 03.89.25.57.33

The "very welcoming" Renner family own and run this sophisticated restaurant-with-rooms, a Logis de France, in a village south-west of Mulhouse. It is in a spruce modern house built in local style with flower-decked balconies, and it returns to the *Guide* with three plaudits in 1995–96. "A warm atmosphere. Food of a high standard (save for disappointing fish courses) in a restaurant run with calm efficiency. Our bedroom comfortable but rather small." "A pretty bedroom, excellent food, friendly staff." The restaurant has been called "elegant, in a warm way, with red walls and curtains, wooden beams and oriental rugs". Or you can eat on a pretty terrace. (*Dr Arthur and Mrs Irene Naylor, J Osborne, C Leeming*) Bedrooms were renovated this year. Some face the rear courtyard.

Open All year, except 6–27 Jan, 11–25 Aug. Closed Christmas.
Rooms 7 double.
Facilities 2 dining rooms (1 no-smoking); terrace. Garden.
Location 7 km SW of Mulhouse. From A36 exit Dornach, approach Froeningen on D18 via Didenheim, Hochstatt. Private parking.
Credit cards Access, Visa.
Terms Rooms 325–400 frs. Breakfast 42 frs. Set meals 80–350 frs; full alc 300–350 frs.

FUTEAU 55120 Meuse — Map 9

À l'Orée du Bois

Tel 03.29.88.28.41
Fax 03.29.88.24.52

The Aguesse family's restaurant-with-rooms stands on a wooded hillside in the pretty Argonne countryside where Lorraine meets Champagne. It is both a Logis de France and a Relais du Silence, while Paul Aguesse's "imaginative" cooking wins a *Gault Millau toque.* Returning devotees were again pleased this year: "We enjoyed the sophistication of the comfortable rustic restaurant, and the warm foie gras with grapes, pigeon with coriander, lamb with honey and lemon. Good cheeseboard, and excellent breakfast, with pain au chocolat, wonderful home-made jams. Lots of locals were dining. Bedrooms are simple, with limited wardrobe space, but very clean, with good lighting. We find the Aguesses very friendly, with a keen sense of humour." Others too have liked Madame's "extrovert charm". This year, a visitor loved the "super views from the glass extension to the dining room", whose tables have fresh flowers and candles. "The five-course *menu touristique* one of the best meals ever." Bedrooms, light and spacious, are in a new wing. (*Padi and John Howard, A and I Naylor, and many others*) There was one gripe this year about "motel-like" room furnishings.

Open All year, except 3 weeks Jan, Nov public holidays.
Rooms 7 double. Some on ground floor.
Facilities Lounge, TV room, bar, 2 dining rooms; 2 meeting rooms. Small garden.
Location 1 km S of Futeau. 13 km E of Ste-Menehould. Turn S off N3 at Les Islettes.
Credit cards Access, Visa.
Terms Rooms: single 315 frs, double 355 frs. Breakfast 50 frs. D,B&B 420–500 frs per person (min. 3 nights). Set meals 115–350 frs; full alc 300–320 frs.

GASSIN 83580 Var — Map 11

Hôtel du Treizain

Domaine du Treizain

Tel 04.94.97.70.08
Fax 04.94.97.67.25

This ever-popular little hotel, informal but quite sophisticated, stands just outside busy St-Tropez and is relatively quiet. Though modern, it is built in local rustic style, with tiled floors, patio, stucco walls and pretty interiors (beamed ceilings). It centres on a beautiful swimming pool and has terraces with flowering trees; most bedrooms have lovely views of the sea or hills. Its exceptional Dutch owners, Hans and Helen Jans, were again warmly praised this year: "They were amazingly hospitable, even let us borrow their car a few times! Breakfast by the pool was a treat." "He brought us English papers every day." Previous reports: "There's a real warmth about the place. Service excellent." "Lovely room, good pool, tasty snacks, a home-like atmosphere." "The owners were at the poolside for most of the day but in a friendly, helpful way, not obtrusively. "Fresh orange juice for breakfast, mosquito blinds in all rooms, a large selection of videos, and a night porter." No restaurant, but "decent" snacks are available both at lunch and at dinner time. (*Meg Pearce, PK Nissaire, JR Osborne, and others*)

Open Apr–15 Oct.
Rooms 5 suites, 11 double. 6 air-conditioned.
Facilities Bar/TV room; terraces. Garden: swimming pool (unheated), snack bar, sauna, table-tennis. Unsuitable for ♿.
Location 3 km SW of St-Tropez, off D98A coast road.
Credit cards All major cards accepted.
Terms Rooms 750–1,000 frs. Breakfast 50 frs. Snacks 100 frs.

GAVARNIE 65120 Hautes-Pyrénées — Map 10

Hôtel Club Vignemale NEW

Tel 05.62.92.40.00
Fax 05.62.92.40.08

The famous Cirque de Gavarnie, a vast amphitheatre of glacial mountains with thundering waterfalls, towers above this village in the high Pyrenees. Here, by a river, this odd-looking stone building is owned by Sandra Marchand and run by "sa maman Danielle". "Gavarnie gets thronged with day-trippers in season," say its nominators, "but this small, friendly hotel is set quietly apart, across the stream from the busy main street. It is well managed by Danielle and her husband, who keeps a herd of Merens horses (a rare Pyrenean species) which can be hired for trekking. There are well-appointed bedrooms, as well as an airy lounge, a games room, and a fitness room with jacuzzi. Views over the Cirque are superb, and mountain walking is excellent. We planned to stay three days but ended up staying a week." Cheerful modern decor. (*Dr and Mrs KR Whittington*) Reports on the food welcome.

Open Hotel: 1 Apr–15 Oct. Restaurant: 1 June–15 Sept.
Rooms 6 suites for 3–4 people, 19 double. Some no-smoking.
Facilities Lift. 2 salons, TV room, billiard room, 2 dining rooms (1 no-smoking); banqueting room; fitness room, jacuzzi; terrace. 2-hectare grounds: river; riding, walking.
Location In village, which is 50 km SE of Lourdes.
Credit cards Access, Amex, Visa.
Terms Rooms: single 390–520 frs, double 490–620 frs. Breakfast 58 frs. D,B&B 398–690 frs per person. Set meals 130–250 frs.

GÉMENOS 13420 Bouches-du-Rhône — Map 11

Relais de la Magdeleine

Rond-Point de la Fontaine

Tel 04.42.32.20.16
Fax 04.42.32.02.26

Michelin gives lots of red print for charm and quality to the Marignane family's much-loved country hotel, outside a small town not far from the coast at Cassis and the wild massif of La Ste-Baume. Peaceful, happy and cultured, yet smart and elegant, it is a 17th-century *bastide* in a large walled garden with a lovely bathing pool. "Very good dinner and breakfast, a large comfortable bedroom," say visitors this year, following earlier praise. "Wonderful food, good service, relaxed hosts." "The strains of Schubert and Mozart predominate in the evening. The contrasts of flavours were a real pleasure. The tables, spread under towering plane trees, were prettily laid. Our bedroom had Provençal antiques, a good firm bed and superb reading lights." "M. Marignane achieved the right balance of warmth without being effusive." Drinks are served on the terrace before dinner – five courses on a menu that changes daily. (*Betty and Percy Brower, and others*)

Open 15 Mar–1 Dec. Restaurant closed Sun evening/midday Mon.
Rooms 1 suite, 24 double.
Facilities Lift, ramps. 2 lounges, 2 dining rooms (1 no-smoking); function room. Garden: swimming pool (unheated).
Location Outskirts of Gémenos. 23 km E of Marseille. *Autoroute* A52 exit Pont de l'Étoile. Private parking.
Credit cards Access, Visa.
Terms Rooms: single 395–480 frs, double 530–750 frs, suite 890–1,100 frs. Breakfast 68 frs. D,B&B 570–850 frs per person. Set meals 255 frs; full alc 350 frs.

GÉRARDMER 88400 Vosges — Map 9

Hostellerie des Bas Rupts et Chalet Fleuri
Bas Rupts
Tel 03.29.63.09.25
Fax 03.29.63.00.40

The Philippe family's stylish and rather glamorous modern hostelry stands just outside this lake resort, amid hilly meadows and pinewoods. In modern chalet style, with Virginia creeper and Alsatian flowery decor, it has been keenly admired again recently, notably for its food (*Michelin* star, two *Gault Millau toques*): "Our room in the chalet, facing the pool, had magnificent adorned beams, a flower-decked balcony, smart modern bathroom. Cheerful and efficient staff, sophisticated ambience despite lots of small children. Germanic ornaments everywhere. Food is excellent, eg, strong rich terrine de volaille and foie gras, tripes au riesling à l'ancienne, civet de joues de porcelet en chevreuil, warm fruit salad with sabayon. German-style buffet breakfast." Rooms in the main building are pretty, though not as large as those in the annexe. Leather armchairs, parasols in the garden, and terraces with wide views add to the delights. (*I and FW, and others*)

Open All year.
Rooms 1 suite, 25 double, 4 single (13 in *Chalet*, 17 in *Hostellerie*). Some on ground floor.
Facilities Ramp. Lounge, bar, restaurant. Garden: swimming pool, tennis.
Location 3 km S of Gérardmer. Parking.
Credit cards Access, Amex, Visa.
Terms [1996] Rooms 360–740 frs. Breakfast 80 frs. D,B&B 500–700 frs per person.

GIEN 45500 Loiret — Map 9

Hôtel du Rivage
1 quai de Nice
Tel 02.38.37.79.00
Fax 02.38.38.10.21

Christian Gaillard's neat little modern hotel overlooks the broad Loire, in a fine old town with a castle floodlit at night. Long a *Guide* favourite, alike for its service, setting and cuisine (*Michelin* star, *Gault Millau toque*), it has again won praise this year: "Our meal was outstanding, so was our room. Very good breakfast." "It never fails to please. The owners always seem ready to improve their facilities, and the views over the water at dusk and dawn are memorable. Our huge top-floor room was the height of luxury, if a little impersonal. Food was splendid, with Madame very much in charge, but discreetly so. Breakfast marred by packet orange juice and butter." "Beautifully run. A warm welcome, fine linen, impeccable waiting." "Our room had modern four-poster, splendidly crafted." "Dishes were works of art, served on the richly coloured Gien porcelain." "Pigeon and calf's liver perfect." The dining room faces the Loire, as do many bedrooms (all are double glazed). Bathrooms are much admired. (*Peter and Susan Ranft, Betty and Terry Brower, and others*)

Open All year, except Christmas Eve. Restaurant closed early Feb–early Mar, Sun evening in winter.
Rooms 3 suites, 16 double. Some air-conditioned.
Facilities Salon, piano bar, restaurant; small conference facilities. River terrace. Unsuitable for ♿.
Location By banks of Loire, 200 m from centre, on N7 to Nevers (double-glazed throughout). Private parking.
Credit cards All major cards accepted.
Terms Rooms: single 305 frs, double 370 frs, suite 705 frs. Breakfast 48 frs. Set meals 145–385 frs; full alc 250–380 frs.

GIGONDAS 84190 Vaucluse — Map 11

Les Florets — *Tel* 04.90.65.85.01
Route des Dentelles — *Fax* 04.90.65.83.80

The Bernards' country hotel lies outside Gigondas, below the toothy limestone crags of the Dentelles de Montmirail ("superb views") and near to some of the best Côtes du Rhône vineyards. "A wonderful idyllic spot" and "exceptional value" were among the new plaudits this year. An inspector was more reserved, finding his bedroom lacking in character and breakfasts undistinguished. However: "The two Bernard families, *père et fils*, were everywhere dispensing cordiality. The place has a settled professional air of knowing what it is doing and doing it well at a reasonable price." And others have written: "Eating out on the shady terrace was delightful, and the gardens were well looked after. Food of high quality, service effective." "You always hear the sound of a burbling stream." "We had a simple, clean room in a bungalow with a patio in front." (*J Osborne, Dr Arthur and Mrs Irene Naylor, and others*) You can buy wines from the Bernards' award-winning vineyard nearby.

Open Mar–end Dec. Closed Tues evening/Wed Nov/Dec/Mar (restaurant also closed Wed Apr–Oct).
Rooms 13 double. 4 with terrace in annexe. Some on ground floor.
Facilities Salon, bar, restaurant; terrace. Garden. Unsuitable for ♿.
Location 1.5 km E of Gigondas, by route des Dentelles de Montmirail. Parking.
Credit cards All major cards accepted.
Terms [1996] Rooms 410 frs. Breakfast 50 frs. D,B&B double 780 frs. Set meals 95–210 frs; full alc 280 frs.

We need detailed fresh reports to keep our entries up to date.

Hôtel Montmirail *Tel* 04.90.65.84.01
par Vacqueyras *Fax* 04.90.65.81.50

This is wine country. South of Gigondas, and near to Beaumes de Venise with its famous sweet muscat, is the Nicolet family's *château*, set amid vines. More enthusiasm this year: "The ambience was delightful, the staff willing and friendly, the food fresh and good. We dined at pretty tables on the large terrace, with all nationalities intermingled: most guests were French." Others have admired the "beautiful swimming pool". "Charming owner, lovely food, breakfast on terrace, with home-made jams, a sheer delight." "Service was marvellous, by an army of well-trained young people. Bedrooms are a bit small, but comfortable." The set menus, changing daily, might include Provençal dishes such as tapenade and fillet of rascasse with wild mushrooms. (*MJ Levitt*) Some renovation this year.

Open Mid-Mar–early Nov.
Rooms 41 double, 4 single. Some on ground floor. 1 adapted for ♿.
Facilities 2 lounges, bar, 2 dining rooms; function facilities. Garden: swimming pool.
Location 6 km S of Gigondas, just E of Vacqueyras, off road to Montmirail. Guarded parking.
Credit cards Access, Visa.
Terms [1996] Rooms: single 265–286 frs, double 390–405 frs. Breakfast 50 frs. D,B&B double 810–825 frs. Set meals 99–160 frs; full alc 280 frs.

GINCLA 11140 Aude **Map 10**

Hostellerie du Grand Duc BUDGET *Tel* 04.68.20.55.02
Route de Boucheville 2 *Fax* 04.68.20.61.22

In a remote village in the hilly, forested heart of the Cathar country stands this old manor, gracefully converted, now a three-star Logis de France run by three generations of the "very pleasant" Bruchet family. Rooms are well furnished, but on the third floor. No lift, so not recommended for the infirm. Recent guests have liked it a lot: "A real treasure of a place, and such a bargain. The location is a delight. Bedrooms have dried flower arrangements; but in the dining room we had two dozen real rosebuds on our table. Food was good and plentiful, with plenty of local wine bargains. Madame, skimming in and out, picked up pace as the evening went on." "Our room was spacious and warm, and smelt of polish. Ample breakfasts." (*ND, and others*) One couple loved the place, but found the cooking disappointing.

Open 1 Apr–15 Nov. Restaurant closed midday Wed, except school holidays.
Rooms 10 double.
Facilities Salon, bar/breakfast room, restaurant; conference rooms. Garden. Unsuitable for ♿.
Location 23 km SE of Quillan. At Lapradelle take D22 off D117 to Perpignan. Private parking.
Credit cards Access, Visa.
Terms Rooms 255–290 frs. Breakfast 38 frs. D,B&B 285–365 frs per person. Set meals 130–250 frs.

Sterling and dollar equivalents of foreign currencies at the date of going to press will be found at the back of the *Guide*.

GIVRY 71640 Saône-et-Loire — Map 12

Hôtel de la Halle BUDGET — *Tel* 03.85.44.32.45
Place de la Halle — *Fax* 03.85.44.49.45

This warmly traditional Logis de France is a venerable building in the centre of a highly picturesque small town west of Chalon. It has a pretty dining room popular with locals, and is a fine place for an overnight stay if you care more about Burgundian food and jollity than bedrooms: "M. and Mme Perrot are the type of hosts one reads about in old novels, he boisterous, she extrovert. They involved their French guests in the gossip of the day; little cognacs kept appearing. In that wonderfully old-fashioned room, panelled, lots of dark red furnishings, we had one of the nicest meals, for 90 frs [1996] – rustic jambon du Morvan, lapin aux deux moutardes and a superb gratin dauphinoise, perfect with the bunny. Lovely traditional large balloons in which to swirl the Givry 1990, purple colour, lovely nose. Friendly service. Bedrooms are small but adequate." (*PW, K and SM-S*) Front rooms can have traffic noise.

Open All year, except Nov/Feb school holidays, Sun evening/Mon (open July/Aug).
Rooms 1 for 4 people, 1 triple, 8 double.
Facilities Bar, restaurant. Garden. Unsuitable for ♿.
Location Central. Givry is on D69, 9 km W of Chalon-sur-Saône. Parking.
Credit cards Access, Visa.
Terms [1996] Rooms 230 frs. Breakfast 30 frs. Set meals 90–180 frs; alc 300 frs.

GLUGES 46600 Lot — Map 10

Les Falaises BUDGET — *Tel* 05.65.37.33.59
Fax 05.65.37.34.19

Beside the Dordogne river on the edge of a small village, this modest creeper-covered Logis de France, well decorated, stands below high dramatic cliffs opposite a vineyard. It has a vine-covered terrace, and a garden with plane and walnut trees. And it has been much admired again recently, notably for its food. "We found this delicious. We liked the friendly calm efficiency of the staff, and the feeling of space in the dining room and on the terrace." "Excellent local wine and good regional food." "On arriving, you almost enter the family living room and hotel kitchen. Mme Dassiou at once makes you feel at home. The *demi-pension* dinners were first class. Our room was not large but nicely got up." Some bathrooms are very small. (*D and MM, and others*) One snag for high summer: an oppressive camp-site nearby.

Open 1 Mar–30 Nov.
Rooms 17 double.
Facilities Lounge, TV room, restaurant; terrace. Garden.
Location 5 km S of Martel, 20 km E of Souillac.
Credit cards Access, Visa.
Terms [1996] Rooms 220–320 frs. Breakfast 38 frs. D,B&B 220–270 frs per person. Set meals (with wine) 100–300 frs.

> Before making a long detour to a small hotel, do check that it is open. Some are known to close on impulse.

GORDES 84220 Vaucluse — Map 11

Hôtel Les Bories — *Tel* 04.90.72.00.51
Route de Vénasque — *Fax* 04.90.72.01.22

Just north of this so-chic hill-village, on the road to the splendid Cistercian abbey of Sénanque, is this dazzling modern hotel created from ancient buildings. Some rooms are in a small *mas*, others in authentic *bories*, the strange beehive-shaped stone huts found in this area (comforts are modern). Recent views: "Delightful, with an efficient and caring staff. Our room's balcony had wonderful views of the Lubéron and of hilltop Gordes. The indoor and outdoor pools are both a delight. The chef makes imaginative use of local products." "Spectacular, but expensive. Candlelit dinner was pleasant." (*AM, I and CG*)

Open Mid-Feb–end Nov. Restaurant closed Mon (open in season, public holidays).
Rooms 1 suite, 17 double. 7 in annexe. 1 suitable for ♿.
Facilities Lifts. 4 salons, restaurant; indoor swimming pool. Garden: swimming pool, tennis.
Location 2 km N of Gordes. Parking.
Credit cards All major cards accepted.
Terms [1996] Rooms 950–1,800 frs. Breakfast 85 frs. D,B&B 810–1,160 frs per person. Set lunch 160 frs, dinner 205–380 frs.

Les Romarins — *Tel* 04.90.72.12.13
Route de Sénanque — *Fax* 04.90.72.13.13

Across a ravine from this famous and very fashionable hill village 35 km E of Avignon, 18th-century bastide *nicely converted. Period furniture, 10 pretty rooms, large bathrooms; pleasant terrace, superb views, swimming pool. Closed 15 Jan–15 Feb. Access, Amex, Visa accepted. Rooms 430–700 frs. Breakfast 54 frs.*

GOSNAY 62199 Pas-de-Calais — Map 9

La Chartreuse du Val-St-Esprit — *Tel* 03.21.62.80.00
1 rue de Fouquières — *Fax* 03.21.62.42.50

The setting amid now defunct coalfields is unpromising. But this ambitious hotel has other virtues: it is near the *autoroute* to Calais and began life as a monastery, later rebuilt in classic *château* style. As a hotel, it has now again been rebuilt, and enlarged, and latest visitors have been mostly impressed. "It is elegant, and everyone fell backwards to please us," says one this year. Earlier views: "The spacious new salon, very comfortable, has sofas upholstered in gold damask; the colour scheme is dark blue and gold, rather opulent. There's a new brasserie, and two restaurants, both large and rather lacking in character." But: "Food as good as previous years [*Gault Millau toque*], and service too." "Excellent breakfasts. But the hotel has changed its character: it now has banquets, and Rotary meets there – not a good recommendation for food, and I speak as a Rotarian." (*Mrs EH Prodgers, Ann and Denis Tate, and others*)

Open All year.
Rooms 3 suites, 49 double, 4 single. Some on ground floor.

Facilities Lift. Lounge, bar, breakfast room, 3 dining rooms; conference/function rooms. Garden: tennis.
Location 5 km SW of Béthune. *Autoroute* A26 exit 6, then follow signs to Les Chartreuses
Credit cards All major cards accepted.
Terms Rooms: single 300–700 frs, double 450–850 frs, suite 1,000 frs. Breakfast 50 frs. Set meals 210–365 frs; full alc 450 frs.

LA GOUESNIÈRE 35350 Ille-et-Vilaine — Map 8

Hôtel Tirel-Guérin — *Tel* 02.99.89.10.46
Gare de la Gouesnière — *Fax* 02.99.89.12.62
St-Méloir-des-Ondes

The setting – just inland from Cancale and St-Malo, beside fields and a railway station – is nothing special. But this modern white holiday hotel, family-run, has many assets. It is not far from good Breton beaches; it wins a *Michelin* star and *Gault Millau toque* for food much reputed locally (eg, braised duck's liver with apples). And though not expensive it was said recently to offer "superb luxury – pleasant service, a beautiful elegant meal". It also has a huge and "beautiful" indoor pool and jacuzzi, and "lovely large bedrooms". A report this year: "A delightful stay: our large room, with excellent bathroom, overlooked the small garden, very peaceful. Staff were friendly, breakfast was served in the lovely dining room." And last year: "Excellent meals, notably lamb in ginger." (*Greg Brinks, P and AJ*) Some readers find the set menus lacking in variety. Back rooms are quietest, but passing trains are not disturbing on this small line (front rooms are double-glazed). More rooms were air-conditioned this year.

Open Mid-Jan–mid-Dec. Restaurant closed Sun evening in low season.
Rooms 8 suites, 52 double. Some on ground floor. Some air-conditioned.
Facilities Ramps. 2 salons, TV room, bar, 3 dining rooms; 3 conference rooms; indoor swimming pool, sauna, fitness room, jacuzzi. Garden: tennis.
Location At La Gouesnière station, on D76 between La Gouesnière and Cancale. 12 km E of St-Malo. Garage (30 frs), parking.
Credit cards All major cards accepted.
Terms Rooms: single 270 frs, double 400 frs, suite 600 frs. Breakfast 40 frs. D,B&B double 700–900 frs. Set meals 120–380 frs; full alc 280–350 frs.

GOUMOIS 25470 Doubs — Map 12

Hôtel Taillard — *Tel* 03.81.44.20.75
Fax 03.81.44.26.15

For over a century the Taillard family have owned and run this handsome chalet-style Logis de France/Relais du Silence, which occupies a secluded position on the slopes of a wooded valley near the Swiss border. "Food and comfort are excellent, and the views are splendid, but there's not much sense of welcome," says a recent visitor. Others have broadly agreed about a hotel sometimes erratic in its standards (although it offers many local Jura dishes, it has lost both its *Michelin* star and its *Gault Millau toque* since 1995). But the site is splendid: "The large terrace has lovely views, the small open-air pool is pleasant, and the loudest noise was the tinkling of cowbells." Many bedrooms have a balcony with a view and all have been newly renovated; some at the back are small. (*CM*) A new seven-room *Résidence*, with sauna and gym, has just opened.

Open Mar–mid-Nov. Closed Wed Oct/Nov/Mar.
Rooms 6 suites, 18 double. 7 in annexe. Some on ground floor.
Facilities Bar, reading room, 2 dining rooms; conference room; sauna, gym. Garden: swimming pool (unheated), table-tennis. Unsuitable for ♿.
Location 50 km SE of Montbéliard. *Autoroute* A36 exit Montbéliard Sud. D437 to Maiche, then E 18 km to Goumois. Hotel near church. Private parking.
Credit cards All major cards accepted.
Terms [1996] Rooms 275–440 frs. Breakfast 52 frs. D,B&B 350–440 frs per person. Set meals 135–380 frs; full alc 300–380 frs.

LA GRAVE 05320 Hautes-Alpes — Map 12

Hôtel La Meijette BUDGET — *Tel* 04.76.79.90.34
Fax 04.76.79.94.76

Friendly family hotel amid glorious mountain scenery, on main road in small skiing and climbing resort 78 km SE of Grenoble. Well heated, well run. Spectacular views from modern restaurant (good homely food) and from many bedrooms. Most are chalet-style; some are small; those on road may suffer traffic noise. Open 1 Mar–30 Apr, weekends May, 1 June–30 Sept. Closed Tues except July/Aug. Access, Visa accepted. 18 rooms: 300–500 frs. Breakfast 37 frs. D,B&B 300–500 frs per person. Set meals 120–180 frs. Fuller reports welcome.

GRAY 70100 Haute-Saône — Map 12

Château de Rigny NEW — *Tel* 03.84.65.25.01
Rigny — *Fax* 03.84.65.44.45

Outside Rigny village, 5 km NE of Gray, 17th/18th-century château *set in large, lovely grounds, nicely converted into country house hotel. Baronial salon, period furnishings, 23 stylish bedrooms. New conservatory for lunch, breakfasts; terrace for drinks; outdoor swimming pool. All major credit cards accepted. Rooms 370–800 frs. Breakfast 60 frs. Set meals 200–330 frs. Renominated this year: "Food of highest calibre." Fuller reports welcome.*

GRÉSY-SUR-ISÈRE 73460 Savoie — Map 12

La Tour de Pacoret BUDGET — *Tel* 04.79.37.91.59
Montailleur — *Fax* 04.79.37.93.84

This village perches above the Isère valley, downstream from Olympic Albertville. Here at the foot of a handsome 14th-century watchtower is this unassuming Relais du Silence, praised again this year: "Charming, friendly, with excellent cooking, most agreeable rooms." Last year's view "The gardens are unkempt, but have chairs and tables for sunbathing, etc. The hotel and its terrace, where we drank and watched the sunset, are *not* unkempt. Food superb. Staff couldn't have been nicer." "Superb views, a cheerful atmosphere where guests chat to each other." (*Elizabeth Robey, SC*) The steep circular staircase might not suit the infirm.

Open Apr–1 Nov.
Rooms 7 double, 2 single.
Facilities Salon, restaurant; terrace. Garden. Unsuitable for ♿.
Location 1.5 km NE of Grésy, which is 19 km SW of Albertville. Private parking.
Credit cards Access, Visa.
Terms [1996] Rooms: single 280 frs, double 450 frs. Breakfast 50 frs. Set lunch 90–205 frs, dinner 120–205 frs; full alc 250 frs.

GUÉTHARY 64210 Pyrénées-Atlantiques — Map 10

Hôtel Pereria BUDGET — *Tel* 05.59.26.51.68
Rue de l'Église

In attractive seaside resort 9 km SW of Biarritz, old Basque house in big garden with sea views, now unassuming holiday hotel with friendly owners. 30 large rooms, best ones in annexe. Good food, served out on terrace when it's fine; some Basque dishes, but no choice on half board menu. Open end Mar–1 Nov. Parking. Access, Visa accepted. B&B double 168–280 frs. D,B&B 180–270 frs per person. Set meals 78–190 frs.

HALLINES 62570 Pas-de-Calais — Map 9

Hostellerie St-Hubert — *Tel* 03.21.39.77.77
1 rue du Moulin — *Fax* 03.21.93.00.86

In a village inland from Calais, this elegant *belle époque* stately home is now a family-run hotel, hugely admired again this year: "We had a really first-class stay. The *château* is in a beautiful park, with natural gardens and a delightful 'Monet-type' bridge. The plush interior has a grand entry hall, with orchids and other flowers in reception area, and a lovely stained-glass window on the stairs. The hotel has a family-run feel. A warm welcome from Madame, whose son is chef: in the palatial dining room, the food was good and good value, though it did not look as if the menu changes much. Service very formal, very good. Breakfast well presented. Our room was excellent, with chandelier, marble fireplaces, coordinated pink and green colours, view of the gardens." (*Jennifer Keeble*)

Open All year. Closed Sun evening/Mon.
Rooms 9 double.
Facilities Hall, restaurant. Garden.
Location In village 6 km SW of St-Omer, 52 km SE of Calais, off N28 to Abbeville. Parking.
Credit cards Access, Diners, Visa.
Terms [1996] Rooms 350–800 frs. Breakfast 50 frs. Set meals 120–340 frs; full alc 260–380 frs.

HAUT-DE-CAGNES 06800 Alpes-Maritimes — Map 11

Le Cagnard — *Tel* 04.93.20.73.21
Rue Pontis-Long — *Fax* 04.93.22.06.39

The Barel family's very smart and mostly much-admired hotel (Relais & Châteaux) stands in a fashionable hill-village just inland from a hideously overbuilt stretch of the Côte d'Azur. It is artfully converted out of 13th-century houses by the ramparts, virtually clinging to the side of a cliff. Devotees returning this year enthused: "Our favourite hotel in France, with a superb rustic charm. Our lovely room was spacious, combining luxury and artistry. The meal was magnificent: book early to get a table on the terrace." *Michelin* gives a star, and *Gault Millau* two *toques*, for adaptations of local dishes. "Lovely owners" (the Barels' daughter is manageress). "Our huge room had a small balcony with views to the sea and mountains. The old stone floor had large wool rugs in nice modern designs; the bathroom was marble-tiled." But not all rooms have the sea view. The "beautiful hand-painted ceiling" of the ever-busy dining room "slides away on command to reveal the sky"; you can also eat in a graceful candlelit former guardroom where sometimes there is guitar music. "I loved the higgledy-piggledy corridors, daftly decorated but comfortable rooms, unforgettable views. Breakfast was a gourmet feast." (*Carey and Nigel Newton, and others*) Rooms, however, vary in size and comfort, and some can be hot in summer. One critic complained of a small room, poorly furnished. Parking is tricky: best use the carpark just below the village, or leave it to the hotel. The fascinating museum in the village, and Auguste Renoir's old house down in Cagnes-Ville, are not to be missed.

Open All year. Restaurant closed Nov–mid-Dec, midday Thurs.
Rooms 10 suites, 14 double, 4 single. 18 in annexe.
Facilities Lift. 2 lounges, breakfast room, 2 dining rooms; terrace. Unsuitable for ♿.
Location On ramparts, 2 mins from *château*. Valet parking, garage.
Credit cards All major cards accepted.
Terms Rooms: single 400 frs, double 650–900 frs, suite 1,050–1,500 frs. Breakfast 80 frs. Set lunch 275 frs, dinner 300 frs; full alc 500 frs.

HESDIN-L'ABBÉ 62360 Pas-de-Calais — Map 9

Hôtel Cléry — *Tel* 03.21.83.19.83, *Fax* 03.21.87.52.59

This elegantly converted 18th-century *château* stands just south of Boulogne (useful for tunnel- or ferry-users). Set in "very pretty gardens" plus 12 acres of parkland, it is approached by a tree-lined avenue. It has a splendid façade and handsome entrance hall, with a lovely curving Louis XV wrought-iron staircase. New young owners, Didier and Catherine Legros, arrived in 1995, and three readers since then have approved their efforts: "A delightful, quiet hotel in beautiful order." "Friendly ambience. The 120 frs menu [1996] was good value: food of excellent quality. Breakfast with fresh orange juice, cereals, etc. Our comfortable room, facing the park, had delicious white linen sheets." "Comfortable lounges, lovely grounds." Some rooms are in the nearby converted stables, and although pretty can be small. (*J Rudd, Barbara Hill, Lisa and Peter Simon*) A new chef arrived in 1996. Meals are not served at weekends.

Open All year, except 15 Dec–31 Jan. Restaurant closed weekends, midday.
Rooms 1 suite, 20 double. Some in cottage annexe.
Facilities Lounge, bar, 2 dining rooms; conference facilities. Park: garden, tennis, walks. Sandy beach nearby. Unsuitable for ♿.
Location 9 km SE of Boulogne, off N1.
Credit cards All major cards accepted.
Terms Rooms 290–590 frs, suite 990–1,100 frs. Breakfast 50 frs. Set dinner 120–150 frs; full alc 150–250 frs.

HUISMES 37420 Indre-et-Loire Map 8

Château de la Poitevinière *Tel* 02.47.95.58.40
Fax 02.47.95.43.43

This handsome 18th-century *château* in large well-landscaped grounds, just north of Chinon, has been described by readers as a "marvellous haven". Owned by Californians Dianne and Mark Barnes, and run by them and Charles and Nancy Loewenburg, it has been much praised again this year, for its "generous breakfasts, warm and personal attention", by an American reader who adds: "Your needs are actually thought about and acted on. Alas, there's none of that wonderful French 'ambience'– but you can't have everything! Dianne Barnes served breakfast for us at 6 am one morning, for our early departure, and found local olives for us" – to go with the local wines and cheeses served at cocktail time. Earlier plaudits: "Like staying in a beautiful, cosy home." "Bedrooms are large, with big modern bathrooms. Nancy and Charles helped entertain our children – though their dog Max did most of the work. We were offered after-dinner drinks in their living room. Breakfast buffet included muffins, home-made juices." Volleyball, badminton, bicycles and assorted animals are for guests to enjoy. There are good restaurants in the area – though, if a whole group rents the *château*, dinners will be laid on. There is no smoking in the *château*. (*Adam Platt, Mike and Rindie Powers, DS*) *Note*: the hotel can be contacted through its San Francisco office: *tel* (415) 922 4795; *fax* (415) 928 2863.

Open 1 Apr–10 Nov.
Rooms 5 double.
Facilities 2 salons, library, dining room. Park: croquet, *pétanque*, golf, jogging paths, volleyball, bicycles. Unsuitable for ♿.
Location 3 km S of Huismes, 6 km N of Chinon, at junction of D16 and D118.
Restriction No smoking.
Credit cards None accepted.
Terms B&B double 980 frs.

HUSSEREN-LES-CHÂTEAUX 68420 Haut-Rhin Map 9

Hôtel Husseren les Châteaux NEW *Tel* 03.89.49.22.93
Rue du Schlossberg *Fax* 03.89.49.24.84

Owned and run by a Dutch couple, Karin and Lucas de Jong, this striking modern Logis de France, white-walled and red-roofed, is terraced along a wooded hillside above the vineyards near Colmar, with views over the Rhine plain. It has been designed in modern style by a Danish architect, with light and airy public rooms; each bedroom has a lounge and south-facing terrace. Dropped from the 1996 *Guide* for lack of feedback, it now wins "a resounding yes" from a new admirer: "Food was excellent and fairly priced: outstanding choucroute à la confiture de canard, while the local pinot noir served chilled was refreshing on a warm evening. The ability to eat outside on the terrace was appreciated. Breakfast was of high standard, too. Our only reservation concerned the architect: the view from the rooms is spoilt by careless siting of the dining area, and the duplex split-level bedrooms may look very trendy in a magazine but they are at best inconvenient, and downright dangerous for the young or old." (*Peter Jowitt*)

Open All year.
Rooms 2 suites, 36 double. Some on ground floor.
Facilities Lift. Lounge, TV room, bar, restaurant; conference facilities; indoor swimming pool, sauna, fitness room. Grounds: tennis; children's playground.
Location On edge of village, 8 km SW of Colmar. Turn off N83 at Eguisheim; follow road 2.5 km. Parking.
Credit cards All major cards accepted.
Terms Rooms 310–520 frs, suite 1,100 frs. Breakfast 55 frs. D,B&B 530–740 frs per person. Set meals 105–335 frs; full alc 157 frs. Children under 12 accommodated free in parents' room.

IGÉ 71960 Saône-et-Loire — Map 12

Château d'Igé

Tel 03.85.33.33.99
Fax 03.85.33.41.41

This former hunting lodge of the dukes of Mâcon stands by a stream on the edge of the Mâcon hills and is now a luxury hotel (Relais & Châteaux). "A real treat, with gorgeous gardens, helpful staff, heavenly food" (*Gault Millau toque*), says a reader this year. It is "a beautiful little medieval castle", with rounded turrets, ivy-covered walls, stone-flagged floors and stairways, and a light conservatory facing the garden. Some rooms have antiques, or are multi-level turret suites. One reader wrote of "an excellent dinner", but others have found the food variable (overdone frogs' legs); and the set menu changes little. "Our turret room had charming views across the village. The gardens are delightful, with posh loungers, and ducks to feed." Others have enjoyed the piped classical music. (*Mrs J James, and others*) Steps up to some rooms are steep.

Open 1 Mar–30 Nov.
Rooms 6 suites, 7 double.
Facilities Salon, restaurant, conservatory; conference facilities; terrace. Garden. Unsuitable for ♿.
Location 6.5 km N of N79, 14 km NW of Mâcon, 11 km SE of Cluny.
Credit cards All major cards accepted.
Terms [1996] Rooms 555–720 frs. Breakfast 65 frs. D,B&B 490–598 frs per person. Set meals 190–360 frs.

ILLHAEUSERN 68970 Haut-Rhin — Map 12

Hôtel des Berges

Tel 03.89.71.87.87
Fax 03.89.71.87.88

The Haeberlin family's *Auberge de l'Ill* has a pastoral setting in a village by the river Ill north of Colmar. For a long time the most distinguished restaurant in Alsace (French guides' top ratings), it now has bedrooms, by the river bank at the end of the lovely gardens. They are very expensive, exquisite, and original, and are run "with charm and enthusiasm" by the Baumanns, daughter and son-in-law of one Haerberlin. "The hotel block is built in the style of the old tobacco-drying barns of the area – the architect was Yves Boucharlat, responsible for *L'Aubergade* at Puymirol (*qv*). The Baumanns have created a spacious country atmosphere, with antiques, modern cane chairs, rough stone tile floors, modern lighting. At night the illuminated riverside complex looks fantastic. Weeping willows line the banks, where old punts swing gracefully for guests' use. Dinner at the *Auberge* was as excellent as expected. The local storks (revered in Alsace) know a winner when they see one: one family has built its nest on the hotel's roof, and goes to the *Auberge*'s kitchen to be fed." (*A and PH, and others*)

Open All year, except Feb. Closed Christmas, Mon (restaurant open midday Apr–Oct)/Tues.
Rooms 4 suites (1 in riverside cottage), 7 double. Air-conditioning.
Facilities Lounge, TV room, bar, restaurant; terrace. Garden.
Location By river, in village. 16 km N of Colmar. Garage, parking.
Credit cards All major cards accepted.
Terms Rooms 1,300–1,500 frs, suite 1,750–2,500 frs. Breakfast 130 frs. Set lunch 500 frs, dinner 710 frs; full alc 500–660 frs [1996].

La Clairière *Tel* 03.89.71.80.80
50 route d'Illhaeusern *Fax* 03.89.71.86.22

Set peacefully amid fields beside road to Guémar, 16 km NE of Colmar, an up-market B&B, smartly furnished, in newish gabled Alsatian building. 25 bedrooms, varying in size, nicely decorated; some antiques, attractive lounge; good breakfasts. Lift. Garden: tennis, swimming pool. Useful for diners at Haeberlins' celebrated Auberge, *close by (see above). Open 1 Mar–31 Dec. Access, Visa accepted. Rooms 430–980 frs. Breakfast 70 frs [1996]. New reports welcome.*

LA JAILLE-YVON 49220 Maine-et-Loire Map 8

Château du Plessis *Tel* 02.41.95.12.75
Fax 02.41.95.14.41

This small 18th-century *château*, set amid woods north of Angers, has been likened to "a large and mellow English vicarage", and is run in personal style by its owners, Paul and Simone Benoist. "They were charming, and treated us like their private guests," say recent guests. "The food was better than good, and we enjoyed walking in the grounds." Others wrote earlier: "We had a friendly, fun evening, all so relaxed, with good, generous regional cooking." Antiques and family portraits abound in the stylishly furnished public rooms. A circular staircase leads to the bright, comfortable bedrooms. Mme Benoist is "an unusually good cook for a stately home *patronne*", and guests if they wish can dine with their hosts, round an elegantly appointed candlelit table. (*RT, and others*)

Open 1 Mar–1 Nov. Dinner by arrangement (not Sun).
Rooms 8 double.
Facilities Hall with self-service bar, 2 lounges (1 no-smoking), dining room. Large park: *boules*. Unsuitable for ♿.
Location Just S of La Jaille-Yvon. 35 km N of Angers.
Credit cards All major cards accepted.
Terms B&B: single 520–580 frs, double 650–750 frs; D,B&B 630–860 frs per person. Set dinner (incl. aperitif and 3 Loire wines) 270 frs.

JOIGNY 89300 Yonne Map 9

La Côte Saint-Jacques *Tel* 03.86.62.09.70
14 Faubourg de Paris *Fax* 03.86.91.49.70

"Wonderful food and restaurant"; "very expensive but not a rip-off": readers this year and last have extolled the Lorain family's renowned cuisine at their superior old coaching inn beside the river Yonne (three-star, three-*toque* ratings in the French guides). An earlier view: "Very glamorous, with luxurious bedrooms, opulent dining room and good service. Mirrors, clever lighting and huge flower arrangements are all used to dazzling effect." While one reader this year criticised the "glossy, kitschy effect, such a mish-mash, spoiling the old coaching inn", others enjoy it, and endorse this account: "Slightly outrageous. The dining rooms have candlelight and very sensuous food. But it all works, because it is totally professional – and fun. Our bedroom had dark beams, Berber carpets over plank floors, a huge marble bathroom." Ten rooms are in the main building; others, across a main road, are reached by a tunnel decorated with local Roman remains. Here "substantial and interesting" breakfasts are served in an airy and bright lounge by the river, where there is also a small garden, which is "a visual delight". (*MLNF, and others*)

Open All year.
Rooms 4 suites, 25 double. Some on ground floor. 15 air-conditioned.
Facilities Lift. 2 salons, bar, 3 dining rooms; conference facilities; indoor swimming pool, sauna. Garden: lake, tennis, helipad.
Location 27 km NW of Auxerre. N6 exit Sens.
Credit cards All major cards accepted.
Terms Rooms: single 600 frs, double 1,780 frs, suite 1,950 frs. Breakfast 110 frs. Set meals 380–720 frs; full alc 700–800 frs.

JOSSELIN 56120 Morbihan — Map 8

La Carrière BUDGET — *Tel* 02.97.22.22.62
8 rue de la Carrière

In central Brittany 73 km W of Rennes, in small town with a splendid castle, imposing private house run as chambres d'hôte *by "charming" Alain and Jacqueline Bignon. 6 spacious bedrooms, antiques in public rooms; quiet. No meals, but restaurants nearby. Access, Visa accepted. B&B double 300–350 frs. Endorsed in 1996: "Breakfast in sun on the terrace, with large garden. A house of quality."*

JOUÉ-LÈS-TOURS 37300 Indre-et-Loire — Map 8

Château de Beaulieu — *Tel* 02.47.53.20.26
67 rue de Beaulieu (D207) — *Fax* 02.47.53.84.20

A modernised 17th-century manor on the south-west outskirts of Tours, run with style by owner/chef Jean-Pierre Lozay (his wife is Scottish). It looks over a well-kept parterre with topiary and *putti* cavorting in the pool. Reporters in 1996 were "over the moon": "What incredible value for money! Dinner, served outside on the terrace with a view towards Tours, was far more than 'congenial' [last year's description], with home-baked baguettes intensely yummy. The welcome was beyond reproach. Our room had a state-of-the-art air-conditioning unit." An earlier view: "Inside, the place seemed at first a bit pretentious, with medieval armoury and chinoiserie up a pair of curving stairways. But our small room was comfortable and well furnished. Dinner, served in a lovely light room, was delicious, notably the coquilles St-Jacques." "The surroundings are quiet, once the municipal swimming pool at the bottom of the gardens is closed." (*Martin and Karen Oldridge*) Rooms vary in size and price. Half board is required in summer.

Open All year.
Rooms 19 double. 3 with jacuzzi. 10 in pavilion annexe.
Facilities Salon, TV room, bar, 2 dining rooms (1 no-smoking); conference facilities. Large garden. Free swimming (public pool) July/Aug, tennis nearby. Unsuitable for ♿.
Location 4 km SW of Tours, by D86, D207.
Credit cards Access, Amex, Visa.
Terms Double room 380–750 frs. Breakfast 50 frs. D,B&B 390–590 frs per person. Set meals 195–440 frs; full alc 350 frs. Half board obligatory June–Sept; special rates Nov–Easter.

KAYSERSBERG 68240 Haut-Rhin — Map 12

Hotel Constantin BUDGET — *Tel* 03.89.47.19.90
10 rue Père Kohlmann — *Fax* 03.89.47.37.82

In pretty Alsatian village where Albert Schweitzer was born (his home is a museum), beautiful, nicely converted house in quiet side street. 20 simple but attractive rooms, with local painted wardrobes. Comfortable lounge, delightful conservatory for breakfast. No restaurant, but same family's Au Château *has good food. Access, Visa accepted. B&B double 398–448 frs.*

LACAVE 46200 Lot — Map 10

Le Pont de l'Ouysse — *Tel* 05.65.37.87.04
Fax 05.65.32.77.41

Not far from Rocamadour, this very smart restaurant-with-rooms has an idyllic setting by a river, with a *château* looming above and a tree-shaded dining terrace for fine weather. *Patron*/chef Daniel Chambon offers inventive variations on local cuisine (*Michelin* star, two *Gault Millau toques*). "In fact it's hard to find main dishes without foie gras and truffles." The food and the "wonderful" setting have won three more plaudits this year: "We had a comfortable suite with our own little garden. Dinner and breakfast were on the delightful shady terrace. Friendly proprietors." "Excellent food, helpful *sommelier*, splendid large airy room." "Cheerful rooms, relaxed welcome. Breakfast, with scrambled egg and truffles, home-made yogurt, was one of the best." Others have relished the cassoulet, fillets of rouget, and "sublime" puddings, with generous portions. Some rooms overlook the terrace, and have a "garden look". The heated pool is enjoyed. (*Felix Singer, Elizabeth Biggs, J Rudd*)

Open Early Mar–11 Nov. Closed Christmas, Mon in low season.
Rooms 1 suite, 10 double, 3 single. 5 rooms in 2 annexes.
Facilities Lounge, TV room, 2 dining rooms; terrace. Garden: swimming pool. Unsuitable for ♿.
Location 10 km NW of Rocamadour. Private parking.
Credit cards All major cards accepted.
Terms Rooms: single 350 frs, double 550–600 frs, suite 750–800 frs. Breakfast 60 frs. D,B&B 650 frs per person. Set meals 160–350 frs; full alc 350–400 frs.

Château de la Treyne *Tel* 05.65.27.60.60
Fax 05.65.27.60.70

This 14th–17th century castle, now a luxurious Relais & Châteaux hotel, stands on a low cliff beside the Dordogne. It has wide grounds and a superb formal garden. Good food (two *Gault Millau toques*) is served on a terrace with fine river views; breakfast is taken on the lawn under massive old trees; there's a Louis XIII salon, and a lounge with an open fire. Readers this year were again enthusiastic: "Very expensive but worth every penny. A fairy tale dream, with stone stairs and creaking doors. Our beautiful room overlooked the river. The staff greeted us like old friends, and the food was outstanding: we fell in love with the passion fruit soufflé." Earlier views: "Our suite was vast, with a large four-poster, real antiques and a triangular bathroom. Young attentive staff." "Wonderful setting. Cheerful, light rooms. Difficult to find dishes without foie gras, but breakfast with scrambled eggs (truffé) was one of the best." Or try a non-foie gras dish such as pigeon stuffed with nuts and endives. (*Mike and Rindie Powers, FS*)

Open Easter–mid-Nov. Restaurant closed for lunch Tues, Wed.
Rooms 2 suites, 12 double. Air-conditioning.
Facilities 2 lounges, bar, breakfast room, restaurant; terrace. Park: garden, tennis, swimming pool. Unsuitable for ♿.
Location 3 km W of Lacave. 10 km NW of Rocamadour.
Credit cards All major cards accepted.
Terms Rooms 700–1,800 frs. Breakfast 80 frs. Set meals 180–280 frs; full alc 350 frs.

LAGUIOLE 12210 Aveyron **Map 10**

Michel Bras *Tel* 05.65.44.32.24
Route de l'Aubrac *Fax* 05.65.48.47.02

High in the Aubrac uplands, outside this small Massif Central town, the talented chef Michel Bras runs a brilliant operation: food of high quality (two *Michelin* stars, four *Gault Millau toques*) in a small hotel of striking modern design – "our bedroom was like a spacecraft" and "he's a genius" are recent comments. These earlier accounts hold good: "Outstanding cuisine, boldly imaginative design, enthusiastic and high-spirited service and, as added value, thrilling views of the mountains. We chose the 'Évasion et Terre' set menu – six courses plus bonuses for 410 frs [1996] – and were suitably awed by nearly all the master's offering" (it might include gargouillou de jeunes légumes, pois crispy avec lapin à l'huile d'olive). "Bras is passionate about this region and its produce, and strives to bring out the essence of each ingredient. The same purity is evident in the design and decor – glass, granite and basalt, with the furniture in light blond wood. Bright, bright spotlights in bedrooms and public rooms. Not a cosy place, and some people might hate the stark simplicity. But we were exhilarated by the shock of this new minimalism, especially as the coolness of the decor was mitigated by the warmth of the staff." (*B and EB*) Newer reports welcome.

Open Early Apr–end Oct. Closed Mon. Restaurant also closed midday Tues, except July / Aug.
Rooms 15 double. Some on ground floor.

Facilities Lift. Lounge, restaurant (no-smoking); conference room. Large garden.
Location 6 km E of Laguiole, towards Aubrac. Private parking.
Credit cards Access, Amex, Visa.
Terms [1996] Rooms 980–1,600 frs. Breakfast 90 frs. Set meals 200–620 frs; full alc 600 frs.

LAMASTRE 07270 Ardèche — Map 12

Hôtel du Midi et Restaurant Barattéro

Place Seignobos — *Tel* 04.75.06.41.50 — *Fax* 04.75.06.49.75

"A lovely hotel, with excellent food, very friendly Mme Perrier and head waiter. And a large, nicely furnished room in the annexe." Thus one recent visitor sums up a sure *Guide* favourite, in the market square of a small town west of Valence. It's a traditional hostelry, where locals gather in the dining room of owner / chef Bernard Perrier (*Michelin* star for solid regional cooking). On the *menu traditionnel*, poularde en vessie and pain d'écrevisses have been liked, while breakfast, taken outdoors, may include a bowl of local cherries and peaches. The Perriers are "a charming young couple, making a success of the place". The wine list is best on local Rhône wines, but the accent is on quality, with few cheap bottles. Most bedrooms are across the road in an annexe, "beautiful inside, with large, quiet rooms and excellent bathrooms". Rooms in the main building are less special, but OK. There's a pleasant quiet garden. (*JME, and others*) *Gault Millau* has dropped its entry this year – why, we wonder?

Open Early Mar–end Dec. Closed Sun evening / Mon (open Mon evening July / Aug).
Rooms 12 double. 1 on ground floor. Some in annexe.
Facilities Ramps. 2 salons, 2 dining rooms. Garden.
Location Central (front rooms double-glazed). Parking.
Credit cards All major cards accepted.
Terms Rooms: single 300 frs, double 395–475 frs. Breakfast 65 frs. D,B&B 400–450 frs per person. Set meals 175–425 frs.

Château d'Urbilhac

Route de Vernoux — *Tel* 04.75.06.42.11 — *Fax* 04.75.06.52.75

"A wonderful setting, really romantic." High on a wooded hillside in its own 150-acre park stands this imposing building, admired again in 1996: "It is a 19th-century mansion designed to look like a 16th-century *château*, but has the intimate atmosphere of a private country home. Bedrooms are furnished with real 19th-century antiques, all different, some a little faded. The spectacular terrace and swimming pool overlook distant hills, and are shaded by a huge pine tree. Breakfast, on splendid china, is taken on the terrace; dinner has a more formal setting, and was uneven: some dishes delicious (eg, very good foie gras, guinea fowl), some less so." Others have written: "Incredible pool and patio area." "Mme Xompero tries to preserve a tranquil atmosphere. The elegant glasses, linen napkins, help to create *la vie du château*." The attractive rooms have fine views. There are cats, a green parrot, and "the largest dog we have seen, timid as a sheep". (*Andrew and Anna Niedzwiecki, and others*)

Open 1 May–1 Oct. Restaurant closed midday, except weekends.
Rooms 10 double, 2 single. 1, in *pavillon*, on ground floor.
Facilities Salon, bar, 2 dining rooms (1 no-smoking); terrace. Large park: garden, swimming pool, tennis.
Location 2 km S of Lamastre, on D2 to Vernoux.
Credit cards All major cards accepted.
Terms Rooms: single 500 frs, double 700 frs. Breakfast 65 frs. D,B&B 500–650 frs per person. Set meals 230 frs; full alc 250 frs.

LANGRES 52200 Haute-Marne — Map 12

Le Cheval Blanc — BUDGET

4 rue de l'Estres — *Tel* 03.25.87.07.00 — *Fax* 03.25.87.23.13

This family-run Logis de France is in the centre of a fine hilltop town north of Dijon, with a 13th-century cathedral and ancient ramparts. The hotel, once a church, has been an inn since 1793. Its restaurant (named after Diderot, who was born in Langres) was found "most enjoyable" again this year. "Wonderful food"; "food beautifully presented"; "a warm welcome," others have written. There's a pleasant terrace for drinks and breakfast. Some rooms are large, with stone-vaulted ceiling; but some can be "a bit poky", while those in the annexe are said to be spacious but charmless. (*G Child, Mrs J James, Michael and Betty Hill, and others*) Front rooms suffer from traffic noise.

Open All year, except 15 Dec–15 Jan, Tues evening/Wed.
Rooms 17 double. 6 in annexe.
Facilities Salon, bar, restaurant; 2 meeting rooms; terrace.
Location Central. Langres is 25 km SE of Chaumont. Garage.
Credit cards Access, Visa.
Terms [1996] Rooms 275–370 frs. Breakfast 40 frs. D,B&B 280–330 frs per person. Set meals 105–250 frs.

Grand Hôtel de l'Europe — BUDGET

23–25 rue Diderot — *Tel* 03.25.87.10.88 — *Fax* 03.25.87.60.65

An inexpensive old stone-fronted hostelry, not as "grand" as its name suggests, and very good value. Several reports brought more praise this year. "An excellent overnight stop, in a delightful town. Restaurant charming and food delicious." "Everything that's best about Logis de France." "Staff friendly and welcoming. Breakfast and dinner in a very pretty panelled room." "Our bedroom was pretty, with floral prints and antique cupboards. Very tender scallops in cream." The ever busy restaurant is said to be "more like a *relais routier* than an elegant place", yet service is *very* good. Rooms, some a little basic, vary in size and amenities; rear ones are quietest. (*Kate Trelford, Mike Knight, Amanda and Gillian Rogers, WR, and others*) One report of noisy plumbing.

Open All year.
Rooms 2 suites, 25 double, 1 single. 9 in annexe behind hotel.
Facilities Lounge, bar, 3 dining rooms. Unsuitable for ♿.
Location Central (quietest rooms overlook garden). 35 km SE of Chaumont, 66 km N of Dijon. Private parking.
Credit cards All major cards accepted.
Terms Rooms: single 150–215 frs, double 170–290 frs, suite 350 frs. Breakfast 33 frs. Set meals 73–205 frs.

LAPOUTROIE 68650 Haut-Rhin **Map 12**

Les Alisiers BUDGET *Tel* 03.89.47.52.82
Fax 03.89.47.22.38

Ella and Jacques Degouy's farmhouse, with beamed ceilings, stands high in a secluded valley in the Vosges, but only 19 km from Colmar. More than ever this year it has pleased readers: "Brilliant. Friendly owners, magnificent views from restaurant and terrace. Food wonderful. Excellent value." "Ella Degouy was very nice. Our room, under the eaves, was quite large, with simple decor. Excellent set dinner, good buffet breakfast." "Remarkable value, perhaps because the rooms are somewhat shabby, but comfortable." Others wrote: "Owners and guests all seem to get on like one large family." "The food is simple but good and free of attempts at *nouvelle cuisine*." (*R Barratt, Dr NB Finter, TW Miller Jones, PM Pullie*)

Open All year, except Christmas, 4 Jan–1 Feb.
Rooms 12 double, 1 single.
Facilities Salon, bar, 2 dining rooms (1 no-smoking); terrace. Garden. Unsuitable for ♿.
Location 3 km from centre, off N415 to St-Dié; from church follow signs for Alisiers.
Credit cards Access, Visa.
Terms Rooms: single 180 frs, double 310 frs. Breakfast 45 frs. Set meals 80–190 frs; full alc 215 frs.

Hôtel du Faudé BUDGET *Tel* 03.89.47.50.35
28 rue du Général Dufieux *Fax* 03.89.47.24.82

This pretty Alsatian village has three hotel/restaurants with the coveted *Michelin* red "Repas" for good food at modest prices. This one, a Logis de France in the main street, is run with "enthusiasm and competent care" by the go-ahead Baldinger family. "They take obvious pride in their Alsatian heritage. Superb courteous service. We enjoyed the informal gardens with streams, and the evening's musical entertainment during which the *patron* went from keyboard to chopping-board. Rooms were spacious and well equipped." Others have written: "Informal, lively and very good value. We ate outside on a covered terrace, with a lovely hilly backdrop with trees. The local cooking was plentiful, delicious." "The public rooms lack ambience but we had a good bedroom, newly decorated in vaguely rustic style. Lighting was a bit dim." (*AML, endorsed this year by Dr ACM Codd*)

Open All year, except 15 days Mar, early Nov–early Dec, 25 Dec, 1 Jan.
Rooms 1 suite, 25 double. 12 in annexe behind restaurant.
Facilities Lift. Salon, bar, billiard room, 2 dining rooms (1 no-smoking); indoor swimming pool; terrace. Garden. Unsuitable for ♿.
Location In village, 21 km NW of Colmar. Garage, private parking.
Credit cards All major cards accepted.
Terms Rooms 310–475 frs. Breakfast 45 frs. D,B&B 300–495 frs per person. Set meals 75–375 frs; full alc 265 frs.

> We asked hotels to quote 1997 prices. Not all were able to predict them in the late spring of 1996. Some of our terms will be inaccurate. Do check latest tariffs at the time of booking.

LESTELLE-BÉTHARRAM 64800 Pyrénées-Atlantiques Map 10

Le Vieux Logis BUDGET *Tel* 05.59.71.94.87
Route des Grottes *Fax* 05.59.71.96.75

Despite recent modern expansion, this old *auberge* west of Lourdes "still keeps its French ambience", according to one returning devotee: "It is still our favourite hotel." It has long been liked for its quiet rural charm and for the Gaye family's personal hospitality: "They never lose their warmth and charm." It has a park where you can sit under trees listening to the cowbells, and a sunny terrace for drinks, where peacocks strut. But it also has a new extension with conference facilities: here the bedrooms are simply but tastefully furnished, and some have a balcony facing lovely scenery. Some visitors since the change have judged "the welcome as warm and charming as ever" and the food just as good (*Gault Millau toque*). But one reader disliked the piped music and thought the ambience "more motel than French". (*M and JB*) A few rooms are in garden chalets or converted barns.

Open 15 Mar–15 Jan. Closed Christmas, Sun evening/Mon in low season.
Rooms 40 double. 5 in chalets in garden, 2 equipped for ♿.
Facilities Lift, ramps. Bar lounge, 3 dining rooms; 2 conference rooms. Garden: swimming pool.
Location 3 km E of Lestelle-Bétharram, on N937. 12 km W of Lourdes.
Credit cards Access, Amex, Visa.
Terms Rooms 220–270 frs. Breakfast 35 frs. D,B&B double 505–555 frs. Set meals 75–210 frs; full alc 220–260 frs.

LEVERNOIS 21200 Côte-d'Or Map 12

Hostellerie de Levernois *Tel* 03.80.24.73.58
Route de Verdun-sur-le-Doubs *Fax* 03.80.22.78.00

Near Beaune, a luxurious country house in a huge and lovely park, with illuminated gardens and fountains. It's an ideal setting for the high-class cooking of Jean Crotet and his son, Christophe (two *Michelin* stars, two *Gault Millau toques*), which is served to the accompaniment of live music. "Superb food, presented in an inspired way. When it's fine you can dine outside, and take aperitifs on the lawn under modern canopies. The main house is the restaurant: bedrooms, cool and spacious, are in a pavilion nearby. Superb breakfast." Others have spoken of "hedonism, sensuality". Most bedrooms are furnished in French rustic style and have a private patio, beside a wooded park with a stream and lake. One reader struck a quizzical note this year: "The bedroom/bathroom reminded me of a luxurious *parador*: lots of stone, wood and marble, hardly *château*-style. The restaurant is stylish, but the art on its walls (bright blue and green Medusa-like figures) is a bit off-putting. Food good, but what prices! The wine 'list' is a 78-page book, worth studying properly for an hour or two before dinner. Staff, mainly young, were charming. The toilets have a captivating *cordon sanitaire* device, a plastic sleeve operated by pressing a red button." (*MI Walker, DES*)

Open All year, except 15 days Feb, 24–28 Dec. Restaurant closed midday Tues/midday Wed 1 Dec–31 Mar.
Rooms 2 suites, 14 double. 12 in garden annexe. Some on ground floor.
Facilities Bar, 2 dining rooms. Park: garden, tennis.

Location Edge of village, 5 km SE of Beaune. Private parking.
Credit cards All major cards accepted.
Terms Rooms 950–1,100 frs, suite 1,500–1,700 frs. Breakfast 95 frs. D,B&B 1,150–1,500 frs per person. Set meals 220–550 frs; full alc 500 frs.

LIMOUX 11300 Aude — Map 10

Grand Hôtel Moderne et Pigeon — *Tel* 04.68.31.00.25
1 place du Général Leclerc — *Fax* 04.68.31.12.43

This market town near Carcassonne produces a well-known sparkling wine, the *blanquette* – one of many drinks and other goodies on offer at this graceful little Logis de France, former home of the parents of the Countess du Barry. "A friendly welcome," say recent visitors, "and a rather grand staircase with dark murals. Our room above the courtyard had a big *armoire*, and a superb marble bathroom. Dinner in the courtyard or in the big grand dining room was accompanied by Wagner. The owners were full of smiles and courtesy. On the *demi-pension* menu, splendidly traditional cooking" (eg, magret of eponymous pigeon). (*B and DD*) Early Friday, market day, could be noisy.

Open Feb–end Nov. Restaurant closed Mon, midday Sat.
Rooms 19 double.
Facilities Lounge with TV, bar, 3 dining rooms; terrace. Unsuitable for ♿.
Location Central. 25 km S of Carcassonne. Parking.
Credit cards All major cards accepted.
Terms [1996] Rooms 310–510 frs. Breakfast 52 frs. D,B&B 320–405 frs per person. Set meals 145–215 frs.

LOCHES 37600 Indre-et-Loire — Map 8

Hôtel de France BUDGET — *Tel* 02.47.59.00.32
6 rue Picois — *Fax* 02.47.59.28.66

In centre of Loire valley town with superb old château, *43 km SE of Tours, a classic hostelry with pretty, flowery courtyard: quietest rooms face this. Warm welcome. Open 15 Feb–9 Jan. Closed Sun evening/Mon, except July/Aug. Access, Diners, Visa accepted. 19 rooms: 215 frs. Breakfast 33 frs. Set meals 85–255 frs. Reports on restaurant welcome.*

LODS 25930 Doubs — Map 12

La Truite d'Or BUDGET — *Tel* 03.81.60.95.48
Rue du Moulin Neuf — *Fax* 03.81.60.95.73

At this "delightful" white-walled Logis de France, the well-named Joël Vigneron serves excellent local wines, as well as local trout cooked in various ways. It stands in a lovely Jura valley, upstream from picturesque Ornans where Gustave Courbet was born and where he painted. It is an old mill converted into a rustic but comfortable hotel, beside the sparkling river Loue, with good walking country all around. The pretty rooms are quiet, the characterful dining room is well patronised locally. "A lovely, friendly place, with delicious food and Arbois wines." "Fillet of sandre cooked in local vin jaune was especially good. Excellent cheeses. A beautiful area, especially in autumn, when the hills are on fire with colour." (*L and AC, and others*)

Open 1 Feb–mid-Dec. Closed Sun evening/Mon in low season.
Rooms 12 double.
Facilities Salon, bar, 2 dining rooms (1 no-smoking); terrace. Garden. Unsuitable for ♿.
Location Edge of village, on D67. 36 km SE of Besançon. Garage.
Credit cards Access, Visa.
Terms Rooms 250 frs. Breakfast 32 frs. D,B&B 280 frs per person. Set meals 100–185 frs; full alc 250 frs.

LOURMARIN 84160 Vaucluse — Map 11

Moulin de Lourmarin — *Tel* 04.90.68.06.69
Rue du Temple — *Fax* 04.90.68.31.76

Albert Camus lived for a while in this lovely village, on the southern slopes of the Lubéron hills, and he lies buried in its cemetery. Opposite its Renaissance *château* is this "stunningly attractive" little hotel, an 18th-century mill luxuriously converted. You can dine outdoors under trees, or in the old mill house with its light, bright decor. Owner/chef Édouard Loubet's cuisine has this year won its first *Michelin* star; he also earns two *Gault Millau toques*, for his "inordinate passion for local produce". A visitor in 1996 was impressed: "There's a really good atmosphere among the bright, intelligent staff, anxious to please. They are serious about their food, and dinner is something of a theatre, with all acting out their parts. The ambitious cooking was mostly excellent. Édouard uses a lot of local herbs, sprinkling whole branches of them on many dishes. Portions are small, but you get extra things like *amuse-bouche* and *avant-dessert*. Breakfast, with yogurt, home-made jams, was really good. Double-glazing (with air-conditioning) cuts out village noises." Decor is bright and modern, in bold Provençal colours. "Our attractive room had wonderful views. The swimming pool is two kilometres away in a large garden: towels, fridge, etc provided." (*Martin and Karen Oldridge, and others*)

Open All year, except mid-Jan–mid-Feb. Restaurant closed Tues/midday Wed in low season.
Rooms 2 suites, 20 double.
Facilities Lift. Sitting room, bar, restaurant; terraces. Garden. Swimming pool (unheated) 2 km.
Location In village, 33 km N of Aix-en-Provence. Secure parking (50 frs).
Credit cards All major cards accepted.
Terms Rooms: single 500–600 frs, double 700–1,200 frs, suite 1,600–1,900 frs. Breakfast 80 frs. D,B&B 700–950 frs per person. Set meals 180–380 frs; full alc 500 frs. Children under 7 accommodated free in parents' room.

LUNÉVILLE 54300 Meurthe-et-Moselle — Map 9

Château d'Adoménil — *Tel* 03.83.74.04.81
Rehainviller — *Fax* 03.83.74.21.78

Set in its own park outside a workaday Lorraine town, this much-turreted *château* (Relais & Châteaux) is a grand house but has a "nice homely atmosphere". It was admired again this year for the "excellent food" prepared by owner/chef Michel Million: his classic Alsatian dishes with a modern touch win him a *Michelin* star and two *Gault*

Millau toques. In summer you can eat on the small terrace overlooking the park, with swans and ducks in the moat. These earlier reports hold good: "The bedrooms are all beautiful and original. Ours, in the converted stables, had marble floors, an arched mullioned window, a huge double bed. Food was first class (foie gras, langoustines, pigeonneau, lamb noisettes). Madame, smiling and attentive, was much in evidence, and Monsieur chatted amicably with us about his imaginative sauces." "The great dane and two playful Siamese cats give the place the feel of a home. We had one of the older, slightly cheaper rooms in the main house. It had a charming faded elegance, with antique furniture, lovely views across the park. The restaurant is three smallish pretty rooms with lovely chandeliers, nice paintings – some of them of Dartmoor." "The entrance hall with its marble floors is stunning." (*JE Robbs, J and PH, and others*) Some slight noise from a railway. Four suites and a swimming pool are new this year.

Open All year. Restaurant closed Mon (except evenings 16 Apr–31 Oct)/midday Tues/evening Sun.
Rooms 5 suites, 7 double. 4 in annexe.
Facilities Lounge, bar, restaurant; conference room. Large grounds: swimming pool; pond; walks. Unsuitable for ♿.
Location 5 km S of Lunéville, off D914 to Épinal.
Credit cards All major cards accepted.
Terms Rooms 630 frs, suite 1,050 frs. Breakfast 70 frs. Set meals 245–460 frs; full alc 625 frs.

LYON Rhône — Map 12

Hôtel des Artistes — *Tel* 04.78.42.04.88
8 rue Gaspard-André — *Fax* 04.78.42.93.76
69002 Lyon

Very central, near Place Bellecour, a neat, fairly priced B&B hotel. 45 well-decorated bedrooms, modern, light and airy, and double-glazed. Good buffet breakfast, promptly served, in pleasant room. Lift. Public parking nearby. All major credit cards accepted. Rooms 330–450 frs. Breakfast 48 frs [1996]. 10% reduction weekends.

La Tour Rose — *Tel* 04.78.37.25.90
22 rue du Boeuf — *Fax* 04.78.42.26.02
69005 Lyon

A stunner. In the narrow streets of Le Vieux Lyon are various fine Gothic or Renaissance houses, once the homes of silk merchants. One of them is this *Tour Rose*, a luxury restaurant-with-rooms that unites the city's great traditions of silk, architecture and gastronomy (owner/chef Philippe Chavent has a *Michelin* star and two *Gault Millau toques*). "It's a captivating place. Part gives the impression of being in a large glass box in a courtyard. Here we had dinner with the magnificent Tour Rose all floodlit; a cascade of blue water hid the kitchen area. M. Chavent comes from a silk family, and silks cover the walls of the bedrooms, each of which is named after a silk house. Bedrooms and bathrooms are luxurious; ours was on two levels with a stained glass partition. We enjoyed oeufs pochés aux feuilles de capucine, mousseline d'huîtres et pétoncles, jus aux citrons confits et à la coriandre, etc. The *sommelier* with a handsome moustache was helpful. A good breakfast arrived on a large tray. The welcome, service, general tone were all one would want." (*A and SC*)

Open All year. Restaurant closed Sun.
Rooms 1 suite, 11 double. 3 on ground floor.
Facilities Salon, bar, restaurant; 2 conference rooms.
Location Central, in Vieux Lyon. Pay parking.
Credit cards All major cards accepted.
Terms Rooms 950–2,800 frs, suite 1,650–2,800 frs. Breakfast 95 frs. Set meals 295–595 frs; full alc 500–600 frs.

Villa Florentine NEW *Tel* 04.72.56.56.56
25 montée St-Barthélémy *Fax* 04.72.40.90.56
69005 Lyon

*On hillside in Vieux Lyon, former convent now a luxurious and very expensive hotel (Relais & Châteaux), well run by attentive manager and staff. Many rooms overlook city. Good food (*Michelin *star), by a chef new this year. Garden, swimming pool. All major credit cards accepted. 16 rooms: 1,200–1,900 frs. Breakfast 80 frs. Set meals 160–380 frs [1996]. Fuller reports welcome.*

MADIÈRES 34190 Gard — Map 10

Château de Madières *Tel* 04.67.73.84.03
Fax 04.67.73.55.71

Michelin gives plenty of red print to this "magical place" – a 14th-century fortress, with a garden, set above the gorge of the river Vis in the southern Cévennes (Relais du Silence). The Parisian owners, Bernard and Françoise Brucy, restored it themselves, and readers are thrilled: "We spent a blissful three days at this splendid hotel. Everything pleases: a superb and unusual room with vast bathroom, the utter peace, the fine view, the delicious food, the library, the fine swimming pool, the helpful staff. We found the Brucys charming." "I would recommend it for everything, except the 80 frs *petit déjeuner*." "Beautiful rooms with a view of the gorge. Very friendly service. Lots of cats. A special place, good for the soul and the kids; good walks nearby (but steep!)." (*ATRF, AM*) *Gault Millau* awards a *toque* to the new chef, Guy Bonafous. More bedrooms were restored this year.

Open 28 Mar–2 Nov.
Rooms 3 suites, 7 double.
Facilities 2 lounges, TV room, library, 2 dining rooms (1 no-smoking); fitness room. Park: garden, swimming pool, children's pool / playground, table-tennis. River nearby: safe swimming.
Location 18 km SW of Ganges, by D25 to Lodève. Parking.
Credit cards All major cards accepted.
Terms Rooms: 585–1,150 frs, suite 1,330 frs. Breakfast 80 frs. D,B&B double 1,200–1,795 frs. Set meals 195–380 frs; full alc 350 frs.

MARQUAY 24620 Dordogne — Map 10

Hôtel Restaurant des Bories BUDGET *Tel* 05.53.29.67.02
Fax 05.53.29.64.15

Most readers continue to be pleased by this unassuming Logis de France, in a tiny hilltop village between Les Eyzies and Sarlat (lovely views). It has beamed ceilings and a big pool with panoramic vistas. "I love this place, for its food and quiet location, even if the annexe rooms are small and dull," says a visitor this year, endorsing last year's plaudits: "The Dalbavies are charming, bedrooms simple but spotless." "The two Dalbavie daughters handled the restaurant with charm and efficiency. Excellent food." In the restaurant, which is down the road, the dearer menus offer real Périgord cuisine. (*Bill and Marcia Griffith, and others*) The hotel gets full of overnight coach parties in high season, and service may suffer. Bedrooms have been called "basic but acceptable".

Open 23 Mar–2 Nov. Restaurant closed midday Mon (except public holidays).
Rooms 3 suites, 27 double. 19 in 2 annexes. Some on ground floor.
Facilities Ramp. 2 salons, TV room, bar, restaurant; conference room; terrace. Garden: 2 swimming pools (unheated). Lake 4 km: water sports.
Location 12 km NW of Sarlat. Take D47 towards Les Eyzies, then D6. Large carpark.
Credit cards Access, Visa.
Terms Rooms 210–285 frs, suite 410–450 frs. Breakfast 32 frs. D,B&B 270–415 frs per person. Set meals 85–180 frs; full alc 135 frs.

MAUROUX 46700 Lot — Map 10

Hostellerie Le Vert BUDGET — *Tel* 05.65.36.51.36
Fax 05.65.36.56.84

This nicely restored old farmhouse, now a Logis de France, is set amid Cahors vineyards in a hamlet south of the lovely Lot valley. Its Belgian owner, Bernard Philippe, cooks, while his German wife, Eva, runs the place. "Excellent in every way: delightful owners, superb food, lovely surroundings." That praise this year endorses last year's: "Our room in a converted barn had beams, armchairs, a large fireplace and a grand piano. Our *menu pension* included a generous plate of smoked salmon and canard aux pêches. Ample breakfast." "Excellent service, and beautifully quiet." There's a big patio and garden, an outdoor *piscine*, and a children's playground. (*Mr and Mrs WM Lee, and others*) All rooms were renovated this year.

Open 14 Feb–12 Nov. Restaurant closed Thurs/midday Fri.
Rooms 6 double, 1 single. 2 in annexe.
Facilities Lounge, restaurant; terrace. Garden: swimming pool. Bicycles for hire. Unsuitable for ♿.
Location 12 km SW of Puy-l'Évêque. Private parking.
Credit cards Access, Amex, Visa.
Terms Rooms 230–380 frs. Breakfast 38 frs. D,B&B double 620–720 frs. Set meals 100–160 frs; full alc 200–250 frs. Reductions for longer stays.

MELLECEY 71640 Saône-et-Loire — Map 12

Le Clos Saint-Martin NEW/BUDGET — *Tel/Fax* 03.85.45.25.93
Le Bourg

This attractive B&B, in a Burgundy wine-growing village, has just been opened by a civilised young English couple, Kate and Stephan Murray-Sykes – for him, it is quite a change from being an international banker in Frankfurt. Their house, "comfortable, rather rambling", is mostly 19th-century but part is 13th-century, with the remains of a chapel dating apparently from the 8th century. "All the bedrooms are large, well furnished," say nominators. "Breakfast, including cereals, fruit, etc, is served on the attractive terrace, facing a spacious walled garden and swimming pool." Among the attractions of the garden are a Gothic folly and a grotto. The Murray-Sykes export local wines, and can take their guests to vine-growers in the village for wine-tastings; they also run cookery courses. (*David and Patricia Hawkins*)

Open All year, except 1 week late Feb, 1 week late Oct, Christmas.
Rooms 6 double (no-smoking).
Facilities Lounge, TV room, dining room, kitchen; terrace. Garden: swimming pool, children's play area.
Location 10 km W of Chalon-sur-Saône. Take D48 off D978 to Autun. Safe parking.
Credit cards Most major credit cards accepted.
Terms B&B: single 300–360 frs, double 430 frs. Advance booking recommended.

MERCUREY 71640 Saône-et-Loire — Map 12

Hôtellerie du Val d'Or — *Tel* 03.85.45.13.70
Grande Rue — *Fax* 03.85.45.18.45

On the busy main street of a leading Burgundy wine village stands this "very pretty" old hostelry, neat and cosy, where Monique and Jean-Claude Cogny earn a *Michelin* star and *Gault Millau toque* for cooking that combines Burgundian tradition with *nouvelle*-ish touches. Our readers this year have again been pleased: "A very hospitable family." "Our meal was superb, and breakfast outstanding too, with gorgeous breads, home-made jams. The smiling owners have a splendid young team and show great pride in the cooking." "The best meal of our holiday, making up for the smallness of bedroom and bathroom." The small bedrooms are charmingly decorated, and meals are served on Limoges china in a "lovely" room. The cheaper set menus have been found good value but limited (the same sauces keep reappearing): the dearer *carte* is more interesting ("wonderful snail soup"). The food has been called "more robust than average in flavour and portion", so not *too nouvelle*. Light and colour in the garden, armchairs in the salon, and a blazing fire in winter – but rooms by the road can be noisy. (*P and S Ranft, Ms MI Walker, J Osborne, and others*)

Open All year, except 15 Dec–17 Jan, 26–30 May, 1–4 Sept, Mon/midday Tues.
Rooms 12 double, 1 single.
Facilities Salon, bar, 2 dining rooms (no-smoking). Garden. Unsuitable for ♿.
Location Central. Private parking.
Credit cards Access, Visa.
Terms Rooms: single 180 frs, double 430 frs. Breakfast 52 frs. Set meals 120–345 frs; full alc 350 frs.

MEURSAULT 21190 Côte-d'Or — Map 12

Les Magnolias — *Tel* 03.80.21.23.23
8 rue Pierre-Joigneaux — *Fax* 03.80.21.29.10

Several readers have recently enjoyed this charming 18th-century residence, really a cluster of old houses round a flowery courtyard, and now a small and select hotel. It is down a quiet street in this famous wine village. "A lovely informal atmosphere. The owner and his staff were helpful. Our beautifully furnished room had huge bed, two small balconies, luxurious bathroom." "A warm welcome, and our room was palatial." Others have liked the home-made jams for breakfast. The owner, Antonio Delarue, is half-English despite his name. *Gault Millau* says his bedrooms are *"au confort très* british", but one *Guide* reader thought them "so lovely and French". Some are only medium-sized. (*JT, and others*) Front rooms can have early traffic noise. No restaurant; several in the village.

Open 15 Mar–30 Nov.
Rooms 1 suite, 11 double. 4 on ground floor.
Facilities Lounge; terrace, courtyard. Garden.
Location Central. Courtyard parking.
Restriction Smoking discouraged in bedrooms.
Credit cards Access, Amex, Visa.
Terms Rooms 380–600 frs, suite 700–750 frs. Breakfast 45 frs.

MEYRONNE 46200 Lot — Map 10

La Terrasse BUDGET

Tel 05.65.32.21.60
Fax 05.65.32.26.93

This converted monastery, former residence of the bishops of Tulle, stands imposingly above the Dordogne. Yet it's not at all grand, more "a fun type of place, not sophisticated, good value for money", as a reader puts it this year, adding: "Amazing castle-style hotel. Lots of creaky floorboards and spiral staircases! Simple cleanish rooms. Shower was a bit dodgy. Food was more into quantity than quality but good wholesome stuff. Wonderful terrace facing the river where you eat in summer. Freezing pool, very refreshing. Friendly hard-working Madame." Others have written warmly of the cooking of her husband, Gilles Liébus: "We had delicious salmon in sorrel sauce, lambs' sweet-breads, garlicky potatoes. Service was by a charming girl, and the attractive dining room gave a fantastic view of the valley." "Excellent buffet breakfast." "We had a large room with beamed ceiling. Staff were polite, but the beef was tough." Garden areas have little shade. Some bedrooms are in an adjacent castle said to date from the 9th century: they vary in size but all have mod cons. (*Carey and David Newton, J Rudd, and others*)

Open 28 Feb–15 Nov.
Rooms 17 double.
Facilities 2 salons, TV room, bar, 3 dining rooms; terrace. Garden: swimming pool. Unsuitable for ♿.
Location On the Dordogne, 13 km E of Souillac, 12 km NW of Rocamadour.
Credit cards Access, Visa.
Terms Rooms 260–400 frs. Breakfast 50 frs. Set meals 100–270 frs; full alc 290 frs.

MEYRUEIS 48150 Lozère — Map 10

Château d'Ayres

Tel 04.66.45.60.10
Fax 04.66.45.62.26

A 12th-century monastery, rebuilt as a *château*, set alone in open country on the edge of the limestone *causses* and the Cévennes National Park, close to the Jonte and Tarn gorges. Large bedrooms overlook a park of sequoias, chestnuts and cedars. This year and last, readers have been pleased: "A three-star, historic house, full of antiques both decorative and human!! Impeccable service, discreet to a fault (we spotted at least two 'notables' with companions clearly not Mme Notable). Not cheap, but worth it. Food not outstanding but adequate." "Lovely setting, excellent food, friendly staff." An earlier view: "The owners, the Comte and Comtesse de Montjou, make you feel like family friends. The staff too are all courtesy. Beautiful breakfasts, and an air of peace and elegance – especially in the evening, when small candlelit tables and chairs are set under the trees in the park, and subtle floodlighting tints the *château*'s façade and the trees, creating perfect reflections in the pool." (*Mrs Blethyn Elliott, RP*) One bathroom was found poky.

Open 1 Apr–15 Nov.
Rooms 6 suites, 20 double, 1 single.
Facilities 2 lounges, games room, restaurant; terrace. Garden: swimming pool (heated June–end Sept), tennis, riding.
Location 1.5 km SE of Meyrueis, 41 km NE of Millau.
Credit cards All major cards accepted.
Terms Rooms: single 350–400 frs, double 420–770 frs, suite 850–950 frs. Breakfast 64 frs. D,B&B 435–650 frs per person. Set meals from 155 frs; full alc 280 frs. Reduced rates for children.

MIMIZAN 40200 Landes — Map 10

Au Bon Coin du Lac — *Tel* 05.58.09.01.55
34 avenue du Lac — *Fax* 05.58.09.40.84

Popular resorts, with splendid sandy beaches, line the long flat Atlantic coast south-west of Bordeaux. Just inland are freshwater lakes amid the Landes forest, also with resort facilities. Here, this elegant restaurant-with-rooms has an "idyllic setting" beside flowery lakeside gardens, and has long been admired: "Our room was excellent," says a reader this year. The food carries a *Michelin* star and two *Gault Millau toques* for, eg, lasagne de foie gras de canard, pigeon rôti au chou. "We loved eating out in the tree-shaded courtyard. Madame seemed a little formidable at first, but did thaw. We stayed in one of the potentially self-catering villas near the hotel: comfortable, though the bathroom was a bit basic." Bedrooms can be a bit dark because of the trees – "a good fault on very hot days". (*Elizabeth Biggs, and others*) Service can be erratic, and as it's not really a hotel staff tend to disappear outside mealtimes.

Open All year, except Feb, Sun evening/Mon Sept–June.
Rooms 4 suites, 4 double. Some on ground floor.
Facilities Lounges, bar, dining room; function rooms; terrace. Garden: lake, fishing, rowing boats. Sea 4 km.
Location 1 km N of Mimizan. 98 km SW of Bordeaux.
Credit cards Access, Amex, Visa.
Terms [1996] Rooms 510–650 frs, suite 580–700 frs. Breakfast 65 frs. D,B&B 650 frs per person. Set meals 160–350 frs; alc 350–450 frs.

Please make a habit of sending in a report as soon as possible after a visit when details are still fresh in your mind. The more you can tell us of your impressions the better.

MIONNAY 01390 Ain Map 12

Alain Chapel

Tel 04.78.91.82.02
Fax 04.78.91.82.37

"Very civilised and enjoyable," say expert travellers this year, revisiting this grand and elegant restaurant-with-rooms north of Lyon, which has been much extended from an old rural *auberge*. It has stone-flagged halls and patios and a floodlit garden. Here the great Alain Chapel held sway till his death in 1990; today his widow is in charge, with his *protégé* Philippe Jousse as head chef. And, like *Michelin* (two stars) and *Gault Millau* (three *toques*), our own reporters regard the food as still "superlative" – one of this year's epithets. Recent letters have also praised the *accueil*, the comfort, and the quiet, although a main road runs past (most rooms face the garden). "We arrived at 10 pm, but were encouraged to have a relaxed, leisurely meal." "The staff were both friendly and professional, and breakfast was very good too." "A very warm welcome from Mme Chapel. Our room had bright curtains and fabrics. The restaurant was flower-filled, busy and bustling." You eat in a series of small discreet rooms, where tables are well spaced and the ambience is quiet and dignified. Jacket and tie expected. (*Pat and Jeremy Temple, and others*)

Open All year, except Jan, midday Mon–Tues 4 pm.
Rooms 11 double, 2 single.
Facilities 3 lounges, bar, restaurant; terrace (meal service in summer). Unsuitable for ♿.
Location 17 km N of Lyon, on N83. From A46 NE of Lyon take exit Les Echets on to N83, direction Bourg-en-Bresse. Garage parking.
Credit cards All major cards accepted.
Terms [1996] Rooms: single 600 frs, double 750–800 frs. Breakfast 87 frs. Set meals 330 (midweek lunch)–795 frs; full alc 800 frs. Children under 6 accommodated free in parents' room.

MIREPOIX 09500 Ariège Map 10

Hôtel Le Commerce BUDGET

20 cours du Docteur Chabaud

Tel 05.61.68.10.29
Fax 05.61.68.20.99

This small town in Cathar country was sacked by Simon de Montfort, then rebuilt with a cathedral. Just below the latter is this archetypal small provincial hotel, a half-timbered building above an arcade: "We went back after many years, and found it entirely unchanged. We had the same room, with large solid furniture, wallpaper with huge orange flowers. A pleasant welcome, and a splendid meal in the courtyard under big trees – soup left on the table, beautifully cooked quail with haricots verts. Friendliness, a modest bill – and no muzak!" (*B and DD*)

Open 1 Feb–30 Sept, 15 Oct–31 Dec. Restaurant closed Sat, except July/Aug.
Rooms 29 double, 1 single. 10 in annexe.
Facilities TV lounge, restaurant (1 no-smoking room); terrace. Garden.
Location Central. Mirepoix is 36 km NE of Foix, on D119 to Carcassonne. Parking.
Credit cards All major cards accepted.
Terms Rooms 180–300 frs. Breakfast 30 frs. D,B&B 180–270 frs per person. Set meals 67–160 frs; full alc 150 frs.

MOLINES-EN-QUEYRAS 05350 Hautes-Alpes Map 12

L'Équipe BUDGET
Route de St-Véran

Tel 04.92.45.83.20
Fax 04.92.45.81.85

Amid wooded hills and ski-slopes in broad Alpine valley outside Molines village on St-Véran road, 46 km SE of Briançon: neat chalet-style Logis de France, owned and run by friendly Catalin family. Informal ambience; generous country cooking on demi-pension; *good breakfasts; 22 "spacious" bedrooms, many with balcony and view. Terrace, garden by river; ski-lifts close by. In skiing season: folk concerts, firework displays, some fondue parties. Open 15 Dec–31 Mar, 17 May–30 Oct. All major credit cards accepted. B&B double 371–392 frs; D,B&B double 568–612 frs. Set meals 74–158 frs. No recent reports: more most welcome.*

MOLITG-LES-BAINS 66500 Pyrénées-Orientales Map 10

Château de Riell

Tel 04.68.05.04.40
Fax 04.68.05.04.37

Specialising in skin and lung diseases, Molitg is a spa beside a small lake in the Pyrenean foothills, close to Prades with its annual Pablo Casals festival (he spent his exile there). On a hill above is this "very special place" – a neo-Gothic crenellated castle, now a smart but oddly decorated luxury hotel owned and run by Biche Barthélemy, sister-in-law of Michel Guérard (see Eugénie-les-Bains). "The rooftop garden with swimming pool has mountain views. The staff were attentive – flowers with every tray delivered. Good regional food" (*Michelin* star, *Gault Millau toque* for dishes such as lasagne aux langoustines, all copiously served in *non-minceur* style, and Catalan-influenced). There's a pretty tiled courtyard for drinks, and loungers by a second *piscine* under the trees. More praise recently: "The tiger-skin bar almost scared us off, but in fact it added to the charm. Food excellent, service welcoming." Less expensive rooms are in an annexe near the pool. (*G and SM, and others*)

Open 30 Mar–1 Nov.
Rooms 3 suites, 18 double. 7 in garden annexe.
Facilities Lifts. 2 lounges, bar, restaurant; conference centre; fitness and beauty centre: sauna; rooftop terrace: swimming pool. Park: 2 swimming pools, tennis; lake, beach, fishing.
Location On edge of spa, which is 7 km NW of Prades. Garage, parking.
Credit cards All major cards accepted.
Terms Rooms 1,000–1,300 frs. Breakfast 90 frs. Set meals 190–430 frs.

MONTE CARLO 98000 Monaco Map 11

Maison d'Or
21 rue du Portier

Tel 04.93.50.66.66
Fax 04.93.30.76.00

Near Casino, facing the sea and Japanese garden, a tiny, very elegant hotel with lush Empire furnishings on "precious stones" themes. Piano bar, outdoor terrace, friendly staff; sandy beach 200 m. Public parking. All major credit cards accepted. 10 rooms. B&B double 820–1,170 frs [1996]. No restaurant.

MONTFAVET 84140 Vaucluse Map 11

Les Frênes *Tel* 04.90.31.17.93
645 avenue des Vertes-Rives *Fax* 04.90.23.95.03

"Away from the crime and grime of Avignon", in a wooded park on its eastern outskirts, is the Biancone family's small luxury hotel – an old mansion well renovated, with a series of cottages/suites, set in two acres of formal gardens with fountains and a pretty swimming pool. It was loved again lately: "Wonderful, with smiling, helpful staff, and Madame very efficient. Our pool room was luxurious. The seven-course meal, served with precision on the terrace, was hugely expensive but worth every penny." *Gault Millau* bestows two *toques* on the Italo-Provençal cooking of the young chef, Antoine Biancone. The hotel has superb bathrooms equipped for *la balnéothérapie*", as our balneophile reporter has explained: "Our large modern room's bathroom was among the nicest I have ever seen in a hotel: the shower had eight different heads, each with three settings, the jacuzzi was large, the bath fixtures were by Rolex (new to me). The power skylight over the bed, with a power shade, was a lovely touch." Dinner is served on the front patio when it's fine. "The wonderful food served amidst the quiet beauty of the night in the gardens provided a romantic and memorable evening." (*LA, and others*) One reader thought the staff snooty. Newer reports needed, please.

Open Mid-Mar–Nov.
Rooms 3 suites, 17 double. Some in separate buildings.
Facilities Lift. Lounge, bar, restaurant (no-smoking); patio. Garden: swimming pool.
Location 7 km E of Avignon by avenue Avignon. Parking.
Credit cards All major cards accepted.
Terms [1996] Rooms: single 595 frs, double 990 frs, suite 1,880 frs. Breakfast 90 frs. Set meals 195–495 frs.

LES MONTHAIRONS 55320 Meuse Map 9

Château des Monthairons *Tel* 03.29.87.78.55
Dieue-sur-Meuse *Fax* 03.29.87.73.49

South of Verdun, the Meuse runs through the large, walled park of this stately 19th-century *château*, converted into a country hotel. It has a slightly sombre decor, but is well run by its owners, the Thouvenin family (the son is chef, and wins a *Gault Millau toque* for his carpaccio of wild boar and red-currant soufflé). Two recent plaudits: "Very peaceful. Our two-bedroom suite had a sunken tub you could almost swim in. Delicious meal: coffee and drinks were served in the book-lined parlour. The staff were young, helpful, and very hard-working." "Excellent rooms, good service, food good but not outstanding." (*FF, DWT*)

Open All year, except 31 Dec, 2 Jan–12 Feb. Closed Mon, Sun evening/Tues midday 2 Nov–15 Mar.
Rooms 2 suites, 9 double. Some on ground floor.
Facilities Library, breakfast room, 4 dining rooms; conference room. Garden: river, swimming.
Location 13 km S of Verdun, W of Meuse, on D34.
Credit cards All major cards accepted.

Terms [1996] Rooms 450–790 frs. Breakfast 60 frs. D,B&B 450–700 frs per person. Set lunch 120 frs, dinner 165–395 frs.

MONTIGNAC 24290 Dordogne — Map 10

Relais du Soleil d'Or BUDGET — *Tel* 05.53.51.80.22
16 rue du 4 septembre — *Fax* 05.53.50.27.54

Close to Lascaux II caves and 25 km N of Sarlat, in a main street of this small town yet with large beautiful grounds behind (tall trees, lawns, fishpond, unheated swimming pool and patio): characterful old hotel with period decor, good regional food; café for snacks. Staff friendly. Closed Feb. Restaurant closed Sun evening/Mon Oct–Mar. Access, Amex, Visa accepted. 32 rooms: 250–405 frs. Breakfast 50–55 frs. D,B&B 240–515 frs per person. Fuller comments welcome.

MONTPELLIER 34000 Hérault — Map 11

Hôtel Le Guilhem — *Tel* 04.67.52.90.90
18 rue Jean-Jacques Rousseau — *Fax* 04.67.60.67.67

Despite Montpellier's metamorphosis from sleepy wine capital to industrial boom town, its *vieille ville*, superbly restored, is as charming as that of Arles or Aix. Here, down a narrow street, is this sympathetic B&B hotel, well converted by its Parisian owners, the Charpentiers. This year and last, readers have again found it "cosy and welcoming", and have enjoyed the copious breakfasts, which come with flowers, newspaper, etc, and in fine weather can be taken on the lovely terrace amid greenery. Many rooms have a view of the cathedral. They are all well equipped (hair-dryer, good reading lights), although some are small. Those in the annexe, "very clean and fresh", may be quietest – the garden overlooked by some rooms in the main building belongs to a restaurant which can be noisy at night in summer. (*P Yarnold, and others*) Rooms not air-conditioned (see below) can be stiflingly hot in warm weather. No restaurant, but *Chez Marceau* and *Isadora* are recommended; so is the more expensive *Cercle des Anges*.

Open All year.
Rooms 4 suites, 25 double, 4 single. 9 in annexe. 9 air-conditioned.
Facilities Lift. Salon, breakfast room (no-smoking); terrace. Unsuitable for ♿.
Location Central, in pedestrian zone. Hard to find. Best approached from W, from Promenade du Peyrou. Public parking 100 m.
Credit cards All major cards accepted.
Terms Rooms: single 330 frs, double 380–650 frs. Breakfast 49 frs.

MONTREUIL 62170 Pas-de-Calais — Map 9

Château de Montreuil — *Tel* 03.21.81.53.04
4 chaussée des Capucins — *Fax* 03.21.81.36.43

Montreuil is the medieval hilltop town of which Jean Valjean became mayor in Victor Hugo's now famously musicalised epic, *Les Misérables*. Close to its ruined citadel, within a lovely walled garden, stands this large old house, now a luxurious Relais & Châteaux hotel. Its owner/chefs are Christian Germain and his English wife Lindsay, who this year are far from *misérables* as they have just regained a *Michelin* star (they also have two *Gault Millau toques*), for their *nouvelle*-ish cooking – eg, duck dishes, and langoustines on a bouillabaisse of mussels. Most of our own readers enjoy it, too. And breakfast has been called "a dream, including an indescribably rich jam, a whole round loaf of warm brown bread". Bedrooms were liked again this year: some are "large and full of comforts", with big beds and "lovely" bathroom; others are more modest. Children are welcomed. French locals patronise the restaurant, but the hotel itself is heavily Briton-besieged.

Open Early Feb–mid-Dec. Closed Mon Oct–May. Restaurant closed Thurs midday.
Rooms 1 suite, 10 double, 3 single. 3 on ground floor.
Facilities Lounge, bar, restaurant. Garden. Sea 18 km.
Location Opposite Roman citadel. 38 km S of Boulogne, off N1. Garage.
Credit cards All major cards accepted.
Terms [1996] Rooms: single 730 frs, double 880 frs, suite 980 frs. Breakfast 60 frs. D,B&B double 1,600–1,700 frs. Set lunch 200–270 frs, dinner 300–400 frs; full alc 380 frs. Special breaks.

Auberge de la Grenouillère *Tel* 03.21.06.07.22
La Madelaine-sous-Montreuil *Fax* 03.21.86.36.36

Day-trippers to Boulogne may think of the French as "frogs". If they went just a few miles south, their fears might be confirmed. Big 1930s frescoes of frogs at dinner adorn the *salle* of this intriguing Froggery Inn, where cuisses de grenouilles à l'ail are on the menu – but there is much else too, winning owner/chef Roland Gauthier his *Michelin* star and two *Gault Millau toques*. "It's a small farmhouse converted into a delightful restaurant-with-four-rooms, beside the river Canche. The rooms, full of charm and character, are set around a courtyard where you can dine or drink when it's fine. In the restaurant, with its huge fireplaces and rustic beams, M. Gauthier offers a celebration of imaginative food – traditional, with contemporary ideas, and young fresh vegetables and salads from the farm. The game and the varied fish dishes are served with his own outstanding sauces. He and his staff are friendly, courteous. It's like being in a small house party." "A convivial atmosphere of local French," adds a reader this year. (*Felix Singer, MJ Gooding, and others*)

Open New Year, 1 Feb–15 Dec. Closed Tues/Wed, except July/Aug.
Rooms 1 suite, 3 double. Some on ground floor.
Facilities Bar, 2 dining rooms. Garden.
Location 1.5 km W of Montreuil, by D917 and D139.
Credit cards All major cards accepted.
Terms Rooms 400–600 frs. Breakfast 50 frs. Set meals 150–380 frs; full alc 450 frs.

Les Hauts de Montreuil NEW *Tel* 03.21.81.95.92
21–23 rue Pierre Ledent *Fax* 03.21.86.28.83

An enticing discovery this year, only a short drive from the Channel ports and Tunnel. This picturesque 16th-century half-timbered house in the centre of the old town offers, say its nominators, "a charming welcome, delicious food, jolly young waitresses, buffet breakfast of gargantuan proportions, large comfortable room in an annexe (very quiet)." Parking in the hotel yard was "brilliantly organised as 15 GB cars arrived". What's more, there's a charming courtyard with a fountain and tables with blue parasols; attractive open brickwork in the public rooms; a 16th-century cellar with a range of old and rare wines; and regional dishes such as carbonade de boeuf flamande. (*Oliver and Delia Miller*) More reports eagerly awaited.

Open All year, except evening 24–31 Dec.
Rooms 27 double. Some on ground floor.
Facilities Bar, billiard room, 2 dining rooms (1 no-smoking); conference facilities; terrace.
Location Central, parking.
Credit cards All major cards accepted.
Terms [1996] Rooms: single 365 frs, double 435 frs. Breakfast 55 frs. D,B&B 460–580 frs per person. Set meals 95–235 frs; full alc 280 frs.

MOUDEYRES 43150 Haute-Loire — Map 10

Le Pré Bossu

Tel 04.71.05.10.70
Fax 04.71.05.10.21

Moudeyres is a hamlet south of Le Puy in the Massif Central, not far from Le Monastier where Robert Louis Stevenson began his hike with a donkey over the Cévennes. This old thatched farmhouse already existed in those days; today it is a fairly smart restaurant whose Flemish owner/chef, Carlos Grootaert, wins a star and a *toque* for innovative twists to local recipes. "We were enchanted by this wild beautiful place, the best kind of sophisticated rusticity," writes an inspector in 1996. "Madame is a bit shy, Monsieur more extrovert. Rooms lacked nothing in comfort, and were furnished in a style fitting to the place: lots of buttons and bows. Our meal was full of unusual delights, an interesting mix of French and Flemish dishes: asparagus with quails' eggs, lentils with morilles, kid mousse, waterzooi of salmon. The slight formality of the decor is modified by the jolly pix by the Grootaerts' young children." "Our room overlooked the pretty gardens. Dinner, rather *nouvelle*, was one of the best meals I've ever tasted: every dish, its sauces and spices, was explained in detail, a bit OTT maybe." Wine mark-ups are high. Fly-screens have now been fitted to the windows.

Open 1 Apr–11 Nov. Restaurant closed for lunch weekdays in low season.
Rooms 10 double.
Facilities Salon, TV room, bar, restaurant (no-smoking); terrace. Garden.
Location In hamlet, 25 km SE of Le Puy, 5 km beyond Laussonne.
Restriction No smoking: salon, restaurant.
Credit cards Access, Amex, Visa.
Terms Rooms 365–490 frs. Breakfast 55 frs. D,B&B 440–590 frs per person. Set meals 168–295 frs; full alc 300–350 frs. 25% reduction on half board prices on presentation of *Guide*.

MOUGINS 06250 Alpes-Maritimes — Map 11

Hôtel de Mougins NEW

205 avenue du Golf

Tel 04.92.92.17.07
Fax 04.92.92.17.08

Just inland from Cannes, the area round the smart hill-village of Mougins has a remarkable concentration of luxury hotels and restaurants. One of them is this clever conversion of four farmhouses, part of the very individual Concorde hotel group. "Staff are charming and rooms comfortable," writes our 1996 nominator. "The restaurant is good and its muzak not too intrusive in the evening, though it can spoil the excellent buffet breakfast. Some dining tables are out on the terrace by the garden, near the pleasant pool and poolside bar." Balconies overlook rosemary and mimosa, lavender, fig and vine. Golf course nearby. (*P Yarnold*)

Open All year. Restaurant closed Sun evening 1 Nov–28 Feb.
Rooms 1 suite, 50 double. Rooms in 4 farmhouses (1 no-smoking). Some on ground floor suitable for ♿.
Facilities Lounge, 2 bars, 2 restaurants (no-smoking). Garden: swimming pool. Golf nearby.
Location 2 km E of Mougins on Antibes road, 7 km N of Cannes.
Credit cards All major cards accepted.
Terms Rooms 780–980 frs, suite 1,600 frs. Breakfast 80 frs. D,B&B double 1,170–1,270 frs. Set meals 180 frs; full alc 250 frs. Children under 12 accommodated free in parents' room. Golf packages.

MOURÈZE 34800 Hérault — Map 10

Hôtel Navas BUDGET — *Tel* 04.67.96.04.84
"Les Hauts de Mourèze" — *Fax* 04.67.96.25.85

In hilly *garrigue* country west of Montpellier, this half-ruined village has a fantastic setting of strangely shaped rocks; the nearby man-made lake of Salagou is good for bathing and boating. Against this wild background, the Navas family's simple and friendly little hotel, set amid trees, has again been liked this year: "Madame is an outgoing, friendly soul. Bedrooms are large, with adequate bathrooms: each has a patio giving on to the rugged scenery. Breakfasts are basic. The pool is pleasant." Lovely outdoor terrace. (*Elizabeth Biggs*) The son of the house serves good regional dishes, quite cheaply, in the restaurant – which is 200 metres from the main house "pour respecter le calme". Or try the more expensive *Mimosa* in nearby St-Guiraud.

Open 26 Mar–1 Nov.
Rooms 14 double, 2 single. Some on ground floor.
Facilities Breakfast room; terrace: swimming pool.
Location 8 km W of Clermont-l'Hérault.
Credit card Visa.
Terms Rooms 250–300 frs. Breakfast 30 frs. D,B&B 95 frs added per person.

MUR-DE-BRETAGNE 22530 Côte-d'Armor — Map 8

Auberge Grand'Maison — *Tel* 02.96.28.51.10
1 rue Léon le Cerf — *Fax* 02.96.28.52.30

Owner/chef Jacques Guillo's much-admired restaurant-with-rooms (*Michelin* star, two *Gault Millau toques*) inhabits a sturdy old granite house, in a big village in the wild heart of Brittany, near a large and pleasant lake. It is quite smart and stylish, yet very good value, as visitors found again this year: "Very good food, friendly staff, rooms beautifully furnished, and the bathrooms gleamed." An earlier view: "An excellent place, with really serious and innovative cuisine. We especially enjoyed the homard aux cinq accords – five dishes of lobster served with five different sauces. Guillo advised us to eat them anticlockwise round the plate – lighter to heavier sauces. Breakfast included home-made fruit compôte, and the best croissants ever, also home-made." (*Nick Hayward, and others*) There is a new bar and a new lounge this year.

Open All year, except Oct. Closed Sun evening/Mon.
Rooms 8 double, 4 single. 6 with TV.
Facilities Lounge, bar with TV, restaurant; private dining room. Unsuitable for ♿.
Location Central (rooms sound-proofed). Mur is 16 km NW of Pontivy. Public parking.
Credit cards All major cards accepted.
Terms Rooms: single 300 frs, double 300–650 frs. Breakfast 60 frs and 100 frs. D,B&B: single 610 frs, double 790 frs. Set meals 170–400 frs; full alc 380–420 frs.

MUZILLAC 56190 Morbihan — Map 8

Domaine de Rochevilaine NEW — *Tel* 02.97.41.61.61
Pointe de Pen Lan, Billiers — *Fax* 02.97.41.44.85

On a rocky headland of the south Brittany coast, this old manor has been converted into a stylish and unusual hotel, whose cuisine wins a *Michelin* star and two *Gault Millau toques*. Some bedrooms are in ancient buildings, others in palatial modern pavilions with sitting rooms, suitable for families. All are scattered in well-tended gardens dotted with ancient Breton sculptures and crosses. The furniture is all antique Breton, eg, huge carved wardrobes in some rooms. There's an outdoor swimming pool above the rocks; sandy beaches are nearby. After a time with no reports, three new plaudits came in 1995–96: "A top class hotel, if a little impersonal. Our magnificent room had a marble bathroom, and a view over the sea which lapped the rocks below our windows. The restaurant was superb, with faultless service: crépinette de lotte was fantastic. Breakfast was in the sun in the courtyard." Here you can also take lunch. "The setting above the rocks was spectacular." (*Martin and Karen Oldridge, Curzon Tussaud; also Richard Graham*)

Open All year.
Rooms 2 suites, 38 double. In several buildings.
Facilities Lounge, bar, restaurant; health centre: swimming pool, sauna, massage, beauty treatment. Garden: swimming pool. Beaches, safe bathing nearby. Unsuitable for ♿.
Location At Pointe de Pen, 5 km S of Muzillac. 33 km SE of Vannes. Parking.
Credit cards All major cards accepted.
Terms Rooms: single 495–795 frs, double 580–1,195 frs, suite 1,200–2,000 frs. Breakfast 60 frs. Set meals 195–250 frs; full alc 400 frs.

NAJAC 12270 Aveyron — Map 10

L'Oustal del Barry BUDGET — *Tel* 05.65.29.74.32
Place du Bourg — *Fax* 05.65.29.75.32

In this remote but scenic part of the Massif Central, Najac is a beautiful medieval village above the Aveyron gorges, with an old castle high on a hill above the river. This hotel is on the village square, yet it also has a "delightful" large garden with a children's playground. Some rooms have a balcony, with lovely views. The owner/chef Jean-Marie Miquel died in a tractor accident in 1994, but his widow, Catherine, carries on, "graciously and efficiently", says a 1996 visitor, who adds: "We had five splendid meals, with fresh produce, good portions, tasty and imaginative [*Michelin* red "Repas", *Gault Millau toque*]. Excellent breakfasts. Service throughout was charming, from the young receptionists to the elderly chambermaids. Our two rooms had wonderful views." (*Caroline McIntosh, and others*) Rooms vary in size and quality (some are a bit basic).

Open 1 Apr–1 Nov. Restaurant closed Mon midday Apr–June/Oct.
Rooms 19 double, 2 single. Some on ground floor.
Facilities Lift. 2 lounges, TV room, 2 dining rooms (no-smoking); terraces. Garden: children's playground. Guests staying a few days have free entry to Najac's public swimming pool.
Location Central. 19 km SW of Villefranche-de-Rouergue, off D122. Parking.
Credit cards Access, Amex, Visa.
Terms [1996] Rooms: single 260 frs, double 300 frs. Breakfast 48 frs. D,B&B 300–350 frs per person. Set meals 130–320 frs.

NANCY 54000 Meurthe-et-Moselle — Map 9

Grand Hôtel de la Reine — *Tel* 03.83.35.03.01
2 place Stanislas — *Fax* 03.83.32.86.04

The queen is Marie-Antoinette, who stayed in this 18th-century palace on the exquisite Place Stanislas on her way to meet her husband-to-be, Louis XVI. It is now a member of the Concorde hotel group: "A great building in a lovely square. A wonderful experience," was a 1996 compliment. Another recent view: "It is unusual and fabulous. All rooms are done up in Louis XVI style: ours, very quiet, overlooked the inner courtyard, and had every luxury. Superb service, and we had an excellent dinner from a menu featuring regional dishes" (*Michelin* star, *Gault Millau toque*). (*Prof. Wolfgang Stroebe, and others*)

Open All year.
Rooms 3 suites, 42 double.
Facilities Salons, bar, restaurant; conference rooms; courtyard.
Location Central. Public parking nearby.
Credit cards All major cards accepted.
Terms [1996] Rooms 600–1,350 frs. Breakfast 80 frs. Set meals 240–290 frs; full alc 200–350 frs.

NICE Alpes-Maritimes — Map 11

La Pérouse — *Tel* 04.93.62.34.63
11 quai Rauba-Capeu — *Fax* 04.93.62.59.41
06300 Nice

It is the location that makes *La Pérouse* so special among Nice's 350 hotels: halfway up the castle rock at the east end of the promenade, it offers "breathtaking" views of the bay from many rooms. It also has a small swimming pool below high rocks, and a calm roof terrace with lemon trees where breakfasts are served, and light lunches too in summer. After much renovation in 1995, it is quizzically re-approved by a regular: "I'm a sucker for this place. The front desk is now much smarter, with charming, well-drilled receptionists. Many rooms are smallish, but our beautiful one, on the top floor, was of Sheraton USA proportions, with its own terrace sun-beds. It had modern 1970s decor, mainly green: the French still hanker to be back on the land, so most rooms are like one of Emma Bovary's orgasmic dreams. In the huge bathroom, toffee-coloured marble rules, OK. Breakfast is so-so and overpriced." The director, Bruno Mercadal, is "a smasher, with an English wife". "A good average breakfast was served charmingly by an elderly maid." But there have been some reports of younger, less helpful staff. Rooms vary: not all have that view. But by Nice standards they are fairly quiet, being so high above the city's Latin clamour. (*Paul Palmer, Ann and Sydney Carpenter*) At this bend on a main road, stopping to unload luggage is not easy.

Open All year. Restaurant closed mid-Sept–mid-May.
Rooms 3 suites, 58 double, 3 single. Air-conditioning.
Facilities Lifts. Lounge, bar; conference room; terrace. Garden: swimming pool (unheated), sauna, solarium. Beach across road. Unsuitable for ♿.
Location E end of Promenade des Anglais, by castle. Some private parking.
Credit cards All major cards accepted.
Terms Rooms 670–1,325 frs, suite 1,640–2,200 frs. Breakfast 85 frs. Set meals 200 frs; full alc 220 frs. 1 child under 12 accommodated free in parents' room.

Le Petit Palais NEW — *Tel* 04.93.62.19.11
10 avenue Émile-Bieckert — *Fax* 04.93.62.53.60
Cimiez, 06000 Nice

This stately white *belle époque* mansion stands quietly on a hill above Nice (it's a Relais du Silence), in the elegant residential quarter of Cimiez. Its nominator writes: "The actor / playwright Sacha Guitry had style and taste, and this was his home. The rooms at the back, preferably on the first floor, have unparalleled views over the roofs of the Vieille Ville and the sea. Rooms are medium-sized, newly decorated and comfortable. The breakfast room is somewhat gloomy, but there's a flowery terrace, also for breakfast." (*Felix Singer*). There's not really a restaurant, but light meals are served.

Open All year.
Rooms 1 suite, 25 double.
Facilities Lift. Bar, breakfast room, restaurant; function room; terrace.
Location 1.5 km N of seafront on S edge of Cimiez. Private parking.
Credit cards All major cards accepted.
Terms Rooms 390–780 frs, suite 1,160–1,290 frs. Breakfast 30–75 frs. Light meals 80 frs. Children under 12 accommodated free in parents' room.

NIEUIL 16270 Charente — Map 10

Château de Nieuil — *Tel* 05.45.71.36.38
Fax 05.45.71.46.45

This moated Renaissance *château*, once a hunting lodge of François I, stands in its own big wooded park north-east of Angoulême. It is luxurious (Relais & Châteaux), with lovely gardens, fine antiques, imposing marble staircase. The friendly owner, Jean-Michel Bodinaud, is always liked, and his wife Luce's cooking earns a *Michelin* star and *Gault Millau toque*. Three recent visitors have written warmly: "Upkeep and food excellent, service swift. In our large room, we had a lavish breakfast in bed with many lovely different breads." "Impeccable service, a huge bathroom, and a cosy atmosphere in the wood-panelled restaurant, posh but *décontracté*." "A beautiful room, bed the most comfortable ever, and bathroom *le dernier cri*. Food, eg, simmered oysters, was fine." M. Bodinaud writes this year: "Good news for your readers: I no longer put the national flags of guests on their tables." (*Martin and Karen Oldridge, and others*) There's a winter restaurant, *La Grange aux Oies*, in the converted stables.

Open End Apr–early Nov.
Rooms 3 suites, 11 double. 2 on ground floor.
Facilities Ramps. Hall, lounge, bar, restaurant, winter restaurant (mid-Dec–mid-Apr). Park: garden, swimming pool (unheated), tennis, lake, fishing.
Location Off D739, between Nieuil and Fontafie, 40 km NE of Angoulême.
Credit cards All major cards accepted.
Terms [1996] Rooms: single 675–1,080 frs, double 750–1,300 frs, suite 1,300–2,000 frs. Breakfast 80 frs. D,B&B double 1,545–2,760 frs. Set meals 190–330 frs; full alc 360 frs.

NOIZAY 37210 Indre-et-Loire — Map 8

Château de Noizay NEW — *Tel* 02.47.52.11.01
Route de Chançay — *Fax* 02.47.52.04.64

"We could imagine Louis XIV and his entourage enjoying happy days here," say readers renominating this sturdy 16th-century *château* (Relais & Châteaux) in the Loire valley. The eulogy goès on: "It was like a fairy tale, in a superb setting with magnificent old trees. Lots of antique furniture, large imposing wooden staircase, wonderful large rooms with enormous four-poster bed. Superb lamb at dinner [*Gault Millau toque*]. Lazing by the lovely pool with attentive waiters was delightful." Set in a small village amid the Vouvray vineyards, the hotel has neat gardens *à la française*, a swimming pool, and a tennis court. (*Carey and Nigel Newton*)

Open Mid-Mar–mid-Jan.
Rooms 14 double.
Facilities Salon/bar, library; meeting room with TV. Large grounds: gardens, swimming pool (unheated), tennis. Unsuitable for ♿.
Location 8 km E of Vouvray, via N152, D78.
Credit cards Access, Amex, Visa.
Terms Rooms: single 650–995 frs, double 950–1,300 frs. Breakfast 80 frs. D,B&B double 1,880–2,160 frs. Set meals 150–360 frs; full alc 320 frs.

NONTRON 24300 Dordogne — Map 10

Grand Hôtel Pélisson BUDGET — *Tel* 05.53.56.11.22
3 place Alfred Agard — *Fax* 05.53.56.59.94

This busy old walled hilltop town lies between Périgueux and Angoulême, in the "Périgord Vert". In its main square is this former coaching inn, warmly enjoyed again recently: "A lively hotel, with a feeling of great cheerfulness. An excellent four-course dinner from the 115 frs [1996] menu – far too much good food. Service was polite and, after a time, friendly. Bedrooms were modest and unpretentious, but quiet and comfortable, if a little gloomy. The main wooden staircase is wonderfully decrepit, curving, creaking and subsiding to crazy angles – worth the journey." There are deckchairs and lawns around the swimming pool, beside a terrace for drinks and summer eating. "Mme Pélisson is an elegant and gracious host." (*RH, and others*)

Open All year.
Rooms 22 double, 4 single.
Facilities Lift. 3 salons, bar, 3 dining rooms; 2 conference rooms. Garden: swimming pool (unheated).
Location Central. Nontron is 45 km SE of Angoulême. Enclosed parking.
Credit cards Access, Visa.
Terms Rooms 140–180 frs. Breakfast 34 frs. Set meals 80–250 frs; full alc 165 frs.

ORNAISONS 11200 Aude — Map 10

Relais du Val d'Orbieu — *Tel* 04.68.27.10.27
Fax 04.68.27.52.44

Out on the vine-growing plain west of Narbonne, not far from the lovely Cistercian abbey of Fontfroide, is this gracefully converted old mill house, white-walled and wood-beamed. It has a flowery garden and big pool, and "delightful" owners, Jean-Pierre and Agnès Gonzalvez, plus the golden labrador, Daphne, who is expert at *accueil*. "Charming," say recent guests. "We took a room with a terrace and enjoyed Monsieur's cooking. He seemed to take real pleasure in discussing it and the wines with us." "Our smallish room with four-poster overlooked vineyards, and was very peaceful. Excellent breakfast in our room, and pleasant service." (*ND, B and DD*)

Open All year, except Sun evening Nov–Feb. Restaurant closed for lunch Nov–Feb.
Rooms 6 suites, 12 double, 2 single. 1 on ground floor, equipped for ♿.
Facilities Lounge, bar, TV room, restaurant. Garden: swimming pool.
Location On D24, S of N113 14 km W of Narbonne.
Credit cards All major cards accepted.
Terms B&B: single 490–520 frs, double 630–890 frs, suite 830–1,190 frs; D,B&B double 1,220–1,780 frs. Set meals 145–375 frs; full alc 300–350 frs.

OTTROTT 67530 Bas-Rhin — Map 9

Clos des Délices — *Tel* 03.88.95.81.00
17 route de Klingenthal — *Fax* 03.88.95.97.71

At the foot of the Vosges, along the Alsace Wine Road, is this sympathetic new hotel in local style, set in its own pretty park. "We liked it very much," say readers this year. "The public rooms are in one building, the bedrooms in another, reached by a glass-walled corridor. A covered walkway leads through the garden to the pool, which is also glass-walled but feels very open. When children arrived and discovered the whirlpool button a brilliant time was had by all. We used the loungers on the lawn, then dined outside at elegant black metal tables. All the menus were interesting, and the staff were efficient and friendly: the young *maître d'* had personality." (*Prof. P and Mrs A Robson*)

Open All year. Restaurant closed Sun evening, Wed.
Rooms 23 double. Some on ground floor.
Facilities Lift. Salon, restaurant; conference room; indoor swimming pool, whirlpool, sauna, solarium; terrace. Large grounds: garden, walks.
Location 4 km W of Obernai, 35 km SW of Strasbourg. Parking.
Credit cards All major cards accepted.
Terms [1996] Rooms 480–680 frs. Breakfast 70 frs. D,B&B 480–520 frs per person. Set meals 120–380 frs.

PAILHEROLS 15800 Cantal — Map 10

Auberge des Montagnes BUDGET

Tel 04.71.47.57.01
Fax 04.71.49.63.83

Typical of *la vieille France profonde* that we all love (plus an outdoor swimming pool, beside fields, and a brand-new indoor one), this snug and simple Logis de France, an old farmhouse, stands on the edge of a village in the remote Cantal uplands. "I heartily recommend it," says its nominator. "This is what they all used to be like in fond memories! This is tough-towel-and-no-soap two-star country – small rooms, and in some the plumbing is simple. BUT the beds are comfy, and Madame is a joy. We arrived at 4 pm as the lunchtime session of the old and bold was leaving, so Madame bid them a fond farewell and gave us a cup of tea. The air was like wine, the water like silk, and dinner was simple, copious, tasty, and served by a jolly smiling local girl with untidy hair. The soup was left for us to serve ourselves, then came local ham, chicken in flaky pastry, cheese, dessert – all for 70 frs. We could have worked out in the gym. It's a long winding road up from Vic-sur-Cère, but *il vaut le détour*" – the French guides agree, awarding a red "Repas" and red print for good value. (*E and BB*) There's an outdoor terrace for drinks.

Open All year, except 13 Oct–21 Dec.
Rooms 24 double, 1 single. 7 in nearby annexe, 2 suitable for ♿.
Facilities 3 salons, bar, 2 dining rooms (1 no-smoking); gym. Garden: swimming pool, children's playground. Tennis, fishing nearby.
Restriction No children under 18 months.
Location 14 km E of Vic-sur-Cère, 34 km E of Aurillac.
Credit cards Access, Visa.
Terms Rooms 198–268 frs. Breakfast 28 frs. D,B&B 230–270 frs per person. Set meals 70 frs.

PARIS — Map 9

Hôtel de l'Abbaye
10 rue Cassette 75006

Tel 01.45.44.38.11
Fax 01.45.48.07.86

A former monastery, restored with simple elegance, on a small street near St-Sulpice. Windows open on to a flagged courtyard with greenery, where breakfast or drinks can be taken. Much recent praise: "We had the cheapest room, but it was warm and comfortable, the water hot. Tea was nicely served." "Our room's decor was not luxurious (eg, exposed painted pipes) but it was tasteful. The two luxurious sitting rooms have fresh flowers. Breakfast was abundant, for Paris." Others have spoken of "charming staff", and "very good bathrooms – but they have not got the lighting right". Alexander Solzhenitsyn stayed recently for three weeks. (*L and PS, and others*) The four duplex suites have a balcony with views. Some rooms are small.

Open All year.
Rooms 4 suites, 42 double. All air-conditioned.
Facilities 3 salons, TV room, bar, breakfast room. Small garden.
Location Central, near St-Sulpice church. (Métro: St-Sulpice.)
Credit cards Access, Amex, Visa.
Terms B&B double 900–1,500 frs, suite 1,800–1,900 frs.

Hôtel d'Angleterre *Tel* 01.42.60.34.72
44 rue Jacob, 75006 *Fax* 01.42.60.16.93

This handsome old house, built round a courtyard "in a most convenient location", was long ago the British Embassy (hence its name). Now it is a hotel of character, enjoyed again this year, with a slightly faded elegance and some beamed ceilings. The stairway and some bedrooms have just been renovated, and "there's no more shabbiness", claim the owners – though the "unique blend of shabbiness and calm efficiency" was rather enjoyed by one earlier reader. Service has been judged "pleasant and efficient" and breakfast "excellent"; and one visitor liked the "wonderfully old-fashioned feel, slight formality, bedroom with country-style decor, painted ceramic tiles, and the sitting area with newspapers on wood frames" – less Angleterre than Autriche. Rooms do vary. Some have been found darkish and unkempt. Quietest ones face the courtyard. (*Sir Alan Cook, Leonard Hill and Cathy Stevulak, and others*)

Open All year.
Rooms 3 suites, 23 double, 1 single. Some on ground floor.
Facilities Lift. Lounge/bar, breakfast room; courtyard. Unsuitable for ♿.
Location Close to St-Germain-des-Prés. (Métro: St-Germain-des-Prés.)
Credit cards All major cards accepted.
Terms Rooms: single 500 frs, double 600–1,100 frs, suite 1,400 frs. Breakfast 50 frs.

Hôtel Bradford *Tel* 01.45.63.20.20
10 rue St-Philippe-du-Roule *Fax* 01.45.63.20.07
75008

Liked again this year for its "very pleasant" staff, this hotel off the Champs-Elysées has solid traditional virtues. Recent views: "Bathroom fittings were old-fashioned and manageable, a nice change from the space-age trappings fashionable in France these days. Staff were friendly. But the place is expensive for what it is. The small lounge would have been nice to sit in but had muzak." "My personal, slightly eccentric favourite in Paris. A wonderful wrought iron lift, a huge bathroom tiled in soft sea green, and a view of the Eiffel Tower from my attic room." (*Andrew Palmer, CMcF*) Air-conditioning is new. And double glazing has reduced traffic noise, say the owners.

Open All year.
Rooms 41 double, 7 single.
Facilities Salon, breakfast room (no-smoking). Unsuitable for ♿.
Location Central (windows double-glazed). (Métro: St-Philippe-du-Roule.)
Credit cards All major cards accepted.
Terms Rooms: single 610–790 frs, double 750–990 frs. Breakfast 55 frs. No restaurant; room service meals available. Children under 12 accommodated free in parents' room.

We ask hotels to estimate their 1997 tariffs, but many prefer not to think so far ahead and give their 1996 tariffs. Some hotels on the Continent do not return our questionnaire. Prices should always be checked on booking.

Hôtel Caron de Beaumarchais *Tel* 01.42.72.34.12
12 rue Vieille du Temple, 75004 *Fax* 01.42.72.34.63

Recorded strains of *Le Mariage de Figaro* suitably fill the foyer of this very *soigné* little hotel, named after the author of the play, who lived up the street. It is in the fashionable Marais just off the rue de Rivoli, and is owned and run by a father and son, the Bigeards. Three more plaudits came this year. "Lovely: a pretty bedroom, and no noise." "The father is a delightful character. Service, decor and ambience were very good. Our room had wooden beams, a small but bright modern bathroom." The hotel is cosily furnished, with painted bathroom tiles. Rooms are small – far *too* small for comfort, said one reader this year. But all agree on the good quality of the breakfasts, served in a pretty basement room. Framed mementoes of the playwright are in all the rooms." And *no* prizes for guessing which Paris morning paper is provided free to guests. (*Anthea Morton, L Abeles, K and B McCann*)

Open All year.
Rooms 19 double.
Facilities Breakfast room; air-conditioning. Small garden.
Location Central. (Métro: Hôtel de Ville.)
Credit cards All major cards accepted.
Terms [1996] Rooms 620–690 frs. Breakfast 48 frs. Children under 6 accommodated free in parents' room.

Châtillon Hôtel BUDGET *Tel* 01.45.42.31.17
11 square de Châtillon, 75014 *Fax* 01.45.42.72.09

One of our two budget entries for Paris: a no-frills hotel with a touch of eccentricity, in a quiet cul-de-sac near the Porte d'Orléans. Latest reports are enthusiastic: "Charming, helpful proprietors." "Mme Le Coq has an irrepressible good nature. Her husband, less outgoing, is constantly redecorating. Bedrooms are large, spotless if sparse, with comfortable beds and generous bathrooms. Birds cough and wheeze in the trees outside." Breakfasts, "promptly served", are generally liked – "splendid bread and croissants" – though some have found them spartan, and opinions vary on the coffee. But everyone agrees: "Amazing value." (*D and MH, and others*) Visitors showing a copy of the *Guide* get a free breakfast. No restaurant: the nearby *Bistro Romain* ("cheap and cheerful") and *Le Layer* are recommended. Also *La Régalade*, "a good little bistro".

Open All year.
Rooms 6 suites, 25 double. 1 on ground floor.
Facilities Lift. Lounge, bar/TV room, breakfast room.
Location Entrance to square is by 33 ave Jean Moulin. Garage parking nearby. (Métro: Alésia.)
Restriction No smoking: breakfast room, bedrooms.
Credit cards Access, Visa.
Terms Rooms: single 290 frs, double 330 frs. Breakfast 32 frs.

> Most hotels have reduced rates out of season and for children, and offer "mini-break" rates throughout the year. It is always worth asking about special terms.

Relais Christine *Tel* 01.43.26.71.80
3 rue Christine, 75006 *Fax* 01.43.26.89.38

Sixteenth-century abbey converted into small, luxury hotel, in ancient narrow street by Seine, near St-Germain-des-Prés. Some bedrooms small, but all finely furnished, with colourful fabrics; quietest are round the pretty courtyard. Attractive lounge, log fire, good breakfasts served in cellar with antiques. Friendly staff; no restaurant, but light meal room service. Garage. All major credit cards accepted. 51 rooms: single 1,630 frs, double 1,690–1,780 frs. Breakfast 95 frs [1996]. Warmly endorsed in 1996 – "gloriously peaceful, not cheap, but good value" – but we'd be glad of fuller reports.

Le Clos Médicis *Tel* 01.43.29.10.80
56 rue Monsieur-le-Prince *Fax* 01.43.54.26.90
75006

Near Jardins de Luxembourg, 18th-century hôtel particulier *now a* soigné *small hotel, well decorated. Lounge, small garden, good buffet breakfast, courteous staff. All major credit cards accepted. 38 rooms: 606–1,212 frs. Buffet breakfast 60 frs.*

Hôtel Eber *Tel* 01 46.22.60.70
18 rue Léon Jost, 75017 *Fax* 01 47.63.01.01

A neatly renovated Relais du Silence with a helpful owner, Jean-Marc Eber, and a "personable staff". It stands in a quiet side street near the Parc Monceau, and is a short walk from the Étoile. Rooms are cheerful, with a simple decor. They vary in size – some are large and high-ceilinged; many overlook the inner patio. Again *Guide* readers have been pleased: "Nicely furnished bedroom, with good modern shower room." "Staff immensely accommodating." "Delightfully French. The lift, mirrored all round, was the slowest ever. Comfortable bed (with pillows, not bolsters). Very good breakfast served in the small bar or on the patio: delicious croissants, good jams (a different one each day)." (*Meg Pearce, Mr and Mrs SC Glover, A and CR*) No restaurant: but meals, brought in from nearby, will be served in the bedrooms. Only gripe: background music in the public area all day.

Open All year.
Rooms 5 suites, 13 double.
Facilities Reception (no smoking), salon/bar; patio. Unsuitable for ♿.
Location Central. Paid parking 150 m. (Métro: Courcelles.)
Credit cards All major cards accepted.
Terms [1996] Rooms 610–660 frs, suite 1,050–1,360 frs. Breakfast 50 frs. Long-stay, weekend, Aug, winter reductions. Children accommodated free in parents' room.

> Hotels often book you into their most expensive rooms or suites unless you specify otherwise. Even if all room prices are the same, hotels may give you a less good room in the hope of selling their better rooms to late customers. It always pays to discuss accommodation in detail when making a reservation and to ask for a free upgrade on arrival if the hotel isn't full.

Hôtel des Grands Hommes *Tel* 01.46.34.19.60
17 place du Panthéon, 75005 *Fax* 01.43.26.67.32

The "great men" are those entombed in the Panthéon across the street, as well as Surrealist painters and writers like André Breton who stayed at this congenial little hotel, run by the "warm and helpful" Brethous family. Its claim to be the place where Surrealism was created has been formally recognised by the city with a marble plaque. Modified praise again this year: "A quiet location, pleasant and helpful staff, delicious breakfasts, modern bathrooms. Bedrooms were acceptable, nothing special (beds and pillows had seen better days)." There has been redecoration, however, since that report. Rooms vary in size (some are "pretty but tiny"), but all are furnished in period style. Some have exposed beams, or "stylish canopy beds". Front ones may have "the floodlit Panthéon to gaze at". Breakfast is taken in a charming vaulted cellar. (*Val Ferguson, EF, and others*)

Open All year.
Rooms 2 suites, 30 double.
Facilities Lounge with bar, breakfast room (no-smoking); conference rooms; air conditioning. Small garden. Unsuitable for ♿.
Location Opposite Panthéon. Underground carpark 100 m. (Métro: Luxembourg.)
Credit cards All major cards accepted.
Terms Rooms: single 520–670 frs, double 720–770 frs, suite 810–1,200 frs. Breakfast 45 frs.

Hôtel Jeu de Paume NEW *Tel* 01.43.26.14.18
54 rue St-Louis-en-l'Ile, 75004 *Fax* 01.40.46.02.76

Down quiet side-street on Ile St-Louis, 17th-century royal tennis (jeu de paume) *court, cleverly converted into elegant, unusual hotel combining antique grace with modern high-tech. Half-timbered atrium lobby, glass lift; patio garden. 32 rooms, newly renovated; some are small. All major credit cards accepted. Rooms 820–1,395 frs. Breakfast 80 frs. No restaurant. Renominated this year. Fuller reports, please.*

Le Relais du Louvre *Tel* 01.40.41.96.42
19 rue des Prêtres- *Fax* 01.40.41.96.44
St-Germain-l'Auxerrois, 75001

Puccini set *La Bohème* in this 18th-century building down a quiet street near the Pont Neuf. Now it is an elegant little hotel, newly renovated, with modern bathrooms. More plaudits, this year and last: "We loved it." "Nice friendly staff." "It is smartly decorated, with attractive coordinated fabrics. Our room was small but adequate, and breakfast (served only in the bedroom) very satisfactory. No traffic noise, but you can hear conversations as party walls are thin." (*Lisbeth W Ruderman, and others*) One complaint this year of "haphazard housekeeping", including tepid bathwater – not what you need if your tiny hand is frozen.

Open All year.
Rooms 3 suites, 13 double, 5 single. 2 on ground floor. Some no-smoking.
Facilities Lift. Reception, bar. Courtyard garden.
Location By Seine at Pont Neuf. (Métro: Pont Neuf.)
Credit cards All major cards accepted.

Terms Rooms: single 606–756 frs, double 832–962 frs, suite 1,292–1,962 frs. Breakfast 50 frs. 15% discount July/Aug, Christmas.

Hôtel des Marronniers *Tel* 01.43.25.30.60
21 rue Jacob, 75006 *Fax* 01.40.46.83.56

A B&B hotel close to St-Germain-des-Prés, set back from the street. It is lent a somewhat rustic air by the eponymous chestnut trees in its flowery courtyard, where tables and chairs stand beneath parasols: here in summer you can take drinks or breakfast. "Friendly staff, lovely breakfast," says a 1996 visitor. "Delightful," said another last year. The recently renovated rooms are "charming, with beautiful fabrics". An earlier view: "A pretty lobby. Our comfortable top-floor room looked over rooftops. I imagine it could get hot in summer." Some period furniture, but some rooms and bathrooms are small. The lift is "*very* slow, very Parisian". (*Clive and Sue Burton, WJR, and others*) No traffic noise, but some guest and plumbing noises: the party walls are very thin.

Open All year.
Rooms 2 suites, 34 double, 3 single.
Facilities Lift. Lobby, small bar, breakfast room; courtyard. Unsuitable for ♿.
Location Central. (Métro: St-Germain-des-Prés.)
Credit cards None accepted.
Terms [1996] Rooms 715–870 frs. Breakfast 46 frs.

Hôtel Montalembert *Tel* (01) 45.49.68.68
3 rue de Montalembert, 75007 *Fax* (01) 45.49.69.49

Between the Boulevard St-Germain and the river, a classic building has been turned into a luxury hotel with a striking design and decor, a mix of old and new. 1996 visitors found it "enchanting. The staff could not have been more charming and efficient". Earlier guests have admired the "handsome bright rooms, brilliant marble and stainless steel bathrooms; the three miniature suites on the top (8th) floor must be the most luxurious 'garrets' in Paris, with spectacular city views." Each bedroom has a mobile phone – "no need to hang about waiting for that important call". As last year, however, the restaurant has come in for some criticism.

Open All year.
Rooms 5 suites, 51 double.
Facilities Lounge, bar, restaurant; meeting room. Unsuitable for ♿.
Location Central. Public parking nearby. (Métro: Rue du Bac.)
Credit cards All major cards accepted.
Terms [1996] Rooms: double 1,625 frs, suite 2,750–3,600 frs. Breakfast 100 frs. Set meals 170 frs; full alc 250–300 frs.

> The "Budget" label by a hotel's name indicates an establishment where dinner, bed and breakfast is offered at around £50 (or its foreign currency equivalent) per person, or B&B for about £30 and an evening meal for about £20. These are only rough guides and do not always apply to single accommodation; nor do they necessarily apply in high season.

Hôtel Notre-Dame BUDGET *Tel* 01.47.00.78.76
51 rue de Malte, 75011 *Fax* 01.43.55.32.31

On side street near Place de la République, Mme Ades's friendly little hotel with 48 simple, clean if unexciting rooms, newly renovated. Breakfast room. Guarded parking adjacent. Access, Visa accepted. Rooms 195–450 frs. Breakfast 35 frs. "Wonderful restaurants nearby." Newer reports, please.

Hôtel du Panthéon *Tel* 01.43.54.32.95
19 place du Panthéon *Fax* 01.43.26.64.65

"It is wonderful to wake up to that noble view of the Panthéon," says an inspector in 1996, after taking a front room in this 18th-century building. Next door to the *Grands Hommes (qv)*, it is also owned and run by the Brethous family and is fairly similar in price and kind, with Louis XVI style furnishings. "The rooms, though small, have been well modernised, while retaining the house's old beams. Excellent lighting, but a tiny loo, where you have to manoeuvre yourself in." Some rooms are "reasonably spacious". Breakfast is in a pleasant *sous-sol;* service and reception are helpful. Triple-glazing removes nearly all noise – and in any case the *place* has little night traffic.

Open All year.
Rooms 34 double.
Facilities Lounge/bar, breakfast room (no-smoking). Air conditioning. Tiny garden. Unsuitable for ♿.
Location Opposite Panthéon. Underground carpark 100 m. (Métro: Luxembourg.)
Credit cards All major cards accepted.
Terms Rooms: single 520–670 frs, double 720–770 frs. Breakfast 45 frs.

Pavillon de la Reine *Tel* 01.42.77.96.40
28 place des Vosges, 75003 *Fax* 01.42.77.63.06

This luxury hotel just off a beautiful square in the Marais has recently been described as "delightful", and praised for its "great style and comfort" and "excellent personal service". Skilfully converted from a handsome old building, it has an attractive lobby with antiques and large open fireplace. Rooms, individually furnished, vary in size and price: some are small, but all are free from traffic noise, especially those that face the flower-filled patio. No restaurant, but there are plenty nearby. Endorsed this year, but fuller reports welcome.

Open All year.
Rooms 25 suites, 30 double. Some on ground floor. Air-conditioning.
Facilities Lounge with fireplace, breakfast room; courtyard. Garden.
Location Central. Garage. (Métro: St-Paul.)
Credit cards All major cards accepted.
Terms Rooms: single 1,300–1,500 frs, double 1,500–1,700 frs, suite 1,900–2,700 frs. Breakfast 95–140 frs.

Hôtel de Saint-Germain NEW *Tel* 01.45.48.91.64
50 rue du Four, 75006 *Fax* 01.45.48.46.22

Near St-Germain-des-Prés, small, neat hotel with charming staff, good breakfasts, rooms furnished with rustic pine, described by owners as "un style anglais raffiné". *Room upkeep not always perfect. All major credit cards accepted. 30 rooms. B&B: single 460–740 frs, double 610–785 frs. No restaurant. Métro: St-Sulpice.*

PASSENANS 39230 Jura — Map 12

Auberge du Rostaing BUDGET — *Tel* 03.84.85.23.70 *Fax* 03.84.44.66.87

A Franco-Swiss couple, Félix and Colette Eckert (she cooks, he hosts), are the much-admired owners of this "charming", "unusual" and modest *auberge*, situated amid unspoilt countryside on the edge of a quiet village between the Jura hills and the rich Bresse farmlands. "Excellent", "housekeeping of a high standard", are among this year's endorsements, backing earlier praise: "We were treated royally and at once felt at home. The Eckerts were most congenial." "Better value than ever. Delicious *en pension* meals." There's a pleasant courtyard where meals can be taken in summer. The white 18th-century main building contains a spacious dining room with open fireplace, large peasant cupboards and modern art, and a "parlour" upstairs with a piano, records, games and books (many of these reflect M. Eckert's previous career as a teacher in Africa). There is *no* television in the house. Bedrooms are "small but prettily decorated"; some are in an attractive vine-balustraded building with an outside staircase. (*DB McLean, BW Ribbons, and others*)

Open 1 Feb–30 Nov. Closed Mon evening in low season.
Rooms 2 suites, 5 double, 2 single. 7 with shower, 5 with WC.
Facilities Lounge, restaurant (no-smoking); courtyard. Garden. Bicycle hire. Unsuitable for ♿.
Location Off N83, 11 km SW of Poligny. 70 km S of Besançon.
Credit cards Access, Visa.
Terms Rooms 132–248 frs, suite 328–388 frs. Breakfast 25 frs. D,B&B 140–303 frs per person. Set meals 62–176 frs.

PAU 64000 Pyrénées-Atlantiques — Map 10

Grand Hôtel du Commerce NEW/BUDGET — *Tel* 05.59.27.24.40
9 rue Maréchal Joffre — *Fax* 05.59.83.81.74

Central, near castle and river, a friendly, comfortable, traditional hotel. Breakfast buffet in Louis XIII lounge, with wood fire. Large, pleasant restaurant; courtyard for outdoor meals. Pavillon *annexe rooms may be best. All major credit cards accepted. 51 rooms: 235–320 frs. Breakfast 36 frs. D,B&B double 515–535 frs. Set meals 92–155 frs. Children under 10 accommodated free in parents' room.*

PÉGOMAS 06580 Alpes-Maritimes — Map 11

Le Bosquet BUDGET — *Tel* 04.92.60.21.20
74 chemin des Périssols — *Fax* 04.92.60.21.49

On the edge of a village in mimosa country, just inland from Cannes and quietly secluded from the madding coast, is this simple family-run holiday hotel. The Cattet family owners have been found "competent" and "extremely friendly" by recent visitors who add: "Overall, superb value for money in this area. We took one of the studios, small and functional, with kitchen area. The swimming pool had good pool furniture." No restaurant, but *L'Écluse* in the village is recommended. (*Shirley Tennant, I and WS, ER*) But one reader complained of the absence of heating in a cold October, and mean bedside lighting. More reports welcome.

Open All year, except 15 Feb–2 Mar.
Rooms 7 studios, 15 double, 2 single.
Facilities Salon, TV room. Garden: swimming pool (unheated), tennis, children's playground. Unsuitable for ♿.
Location In outskirts of village, 11 km NW of Cannes on road to Mouans-Sartoux. Covered parking.
Credit cards None accepted.
Terms Rooms: single 200 frs, double 250–340 frs, studio 340–430 frs. Breakfast 30 frs.

PEILLON 06440 Alpes-Maritimes — Map 11

Auberge de la Madone

Tel 04.93.79.91.17
Fax 04.93.79.99.36

Only 19 kilometres from Nice, yet remote in the high hills, the Millo family's characterful Logis de France stands on the edge of one of the most striking *villages perchés* of the area. Rooms have tiled floors and country furniture, and many of the best also have a balcony facing the valley and mountains. This view is shared by the broad terrace used for drinks and meals (true *cuisine Niçoise*, and dishes such as loup au fenouil, winning a *Gault Millau toque*). "Out of season, the hotel was almost empty and a bit gloomy. But we had a good dinner and breakfast; nice waiter." That report this year backs earlier praise: "We loved our room, the friendly service and family atmosphere." "Excellent food, rooms with good lighting and storage space." "A cheerful fire was lit each evening, though it was not cold. The porter, a great character, doubles as waiter" – prompting the comment: "Slightly eccentric staff, just right for so eccentric a location. A wonderful contrast after the horrors of Nice." (*Betty and Percy Brower, and others*)

Open All year, except 7–24 Jan, 20 Oct–20 Dec. Closed Wed.
Rooms 2 suites, 18 double. 4 no-smoking. 7 in annexe 50 m.
Facilities Salon, TV room, bar, 2 dining rooms (1 no-smoking). Large garden: tennis, *boules*. Unsuitable for ♿.
Location 19km NW of Nice.
Credit cards Access, Visa.
Terms Rooms 420–780 frs. Breakfast 58 frs. D,B&B 440–700 frs per person. Set meals 140–300 frs.

PERNES-LES-FONTAINES 84210 Vaucluse — Map 11

Saint Barthélémy BUDGET

Tel 04.90.66.47.79
Chemin de la Roque

This historic little town near Carpentras is noted for its medieval walls, Renaissance gates, and 36 eponymous fountains, mostly 18th-century. Nearby is this *trouvaille*: "We came by chance upon this 18th-century stone house, lovingly restored, set off the main road in lovely grounds – well-tended garden with sun chairs, table-tennis, swing, games facilities, outdoor table for breakfast. It's a *chambres d'hôtes* run by a charming couple, the Mangeards (he's almost too chatty, but nice). Rooms are delightfully done in Provençal style, with good lights. Tilleul from the garden was delicious." (*ULP*) No restaurant, but Madame will sometimes provide a light evening snack, *"pour rendre service"*. In Carpentras, the *Michelin*-rosetted *Vert Galant* is pricey but excellent.

Open All year.
Rooms 1 triple, 4 double.
Facilities Lounges, TV room, restaurant; terrace. Garden: minigolf, table-tennis, badminton; bikes.
Location 2 km E of Pernes, 8 km S of Carpentras.
Credit cards None accepted.
Terms B&B: single 200 frs, double 260–340 frs.

PÉROUGES 01800 Ain — Map 12

Ostellerie du Vieux Pérouges

Tel 04.74.61.00.88
Fax 04.74.34.77.90

With its ramparts and half-timbered houses, this medieval hilltop village north-east of Lyon is so well preserved that historical feature films are often shot here. The hotel, converted from 13th-century buildings on the village square, is part of this decor. Its studied folksiness might irritate some readers, but it delights others, as it did recently: "A charming place, with very good food (rabbit stew and smoked carp). You are served by mature waitresses in 'costume', and the wine list is on a vellum scroll. Our quiet room in the annexe had a little garden where we took breakfast and had a picnic." Some rooms are in the tower, with glorious views, marble bathrooms, "mock Gothic splendour, and a wainscot shaped as a dragon – highly entertaining". In the dining room, where a fire roars, you can enjoy poulet de Bresse aux morilles and "wonderful" galettes. (*O and DM*)

Open All year.
Rooms 2 suites, 26 double (in 4 different buildings). 2 on ground floor.
Facilities Salon, bar, restaurant; terrace. Garden.
Location Village square. 39 km NE of Lyon. Parking.
Credit cards Access, Visa.
Terms Rooms: single 390–700 frs, double 480–980 frs. Breakfast 60 frs. Alc meals 290 frs.

LA PETITE-PIERRE 67290 Bas-Rhin — Map 9

Aux Trois Roses BUDGET

Tel 03.88.89.89.00
Fax 03.88.70.41.28

Set amid rolling forests in northern Alsace, this old hilltop village is today much visited by German trippers from across the border. In its pretty main street is this flower-decked 18th-century *auberge*. The dining room has a fine view of the castle, floodlit on summer evenings; dinners are also served on a terrace facing the valley. Run busily by the Geyer family and a bevy of other Alsatians, it's an informal and lively place, somewhat Central European, with comfy salons and a big *Stüberl* where snacks and cakes are served all day. Some bedrooms in the old building are a bit cramped (back ones are quietest): those in the modern wing are better ("ours was a joy, very peaceful") and some have a balcony. Food comes in hefty helpings (eg, help-yourself hors-d'oeuvre), but quality is unremarkable. The buffet breakfast is liked, and the indoor pool. (*MJG*) You may find coach parties.

Open All year.
Rooms 16 suites, 20 double, 7 single.
Facilities 2 lifts. 3 lounges, bar, 4 dining rooms; conference facilities; indoor swimming pool; terrace. Garden: tennis, children's play area.
Location Central. Parking.
Restriction No smoking: 1 lounge, 1 dining room.
Credit cards Access, Visa.
Terms Rooms 275–590 frs. Breakfast 53–66 frs. D,B&B 340–530 frs per person. Set meals 98–265 frs; full alc 260 frs.

PEYREHORADE 40300 Landes — Map 10

Hôtel Central NEW/BUDGET — *Tel* 05.58.73.03.22
Place Aristide-Briand — *Fax* 05.58.73.17.15

*In main square of little town on N117, 41 km E of Bayonne, small, friendly family-run hotel "with personal touch" yet very professional. 16 comfortable rooms; excellent food popular with locals (*Michelin *star and red "Repas",* Gault Millau toque*). Closed 4–12 Mar, 16–30 Dec, Sun evening/Mon (except July/Aug). All major credit cards accepted. Rooms 280–350 frs. Breakfast 40 frs. D,B&B 345–370 frs per person. Set meals 110–220 frs [1996].*

LE POËT-LAVAL 26160 Drôme — Map 12

Les Hospitaliers — *Tel* 04.75.46.22.32
Le Vieux Village — *Fax* 04.75.46.49.99

The "charming" Morin family's hotel stands on a hilltop in a medieval village, where wooded Alpine foothills descend to the Rhône valley. It is an old building tastefully restored, with a ruined 12th-century chapel above, and a beamed and vaulted lounge. The huddle of buildings of golden stone creates an idyllic setting, and many bedrooms enjoy the superb views. Long a *Guide* favourite, it was enjoyed again this year for its "delightful rooms, excellent food" (*Gault Millau toque*), "very good breakfasts". And: "We dined and breakfasted on the roof terrace, enjoying the breathtaking views. Sweets were delicious." To which one reporter adds, wryly: "All very comfortable, a superb setting: I look forward to going back. Meals are swiftly served, very enjoyable. There's a wonderful wine waiter, a general factotum with a sense of humour. Pleasant visitors; high-bourgeois ambience, correct but a bit frumpy. But in bad weather the place can be gloomy: one notices that the furniture is shabby, beds sag, doors bang." Others have praised the "large and airy" rooms, some with view of the floodlit castle. "M. Morin, a delight, entertained us and himself by playing jazz on the piano. Breakfast by the pool is most pleasant – even though the bees agree. We enjoyed smoked haddock soup, salmon in raspberry sauce." (*ABX Fenwick, Betty and Percy Brower, John Derry, Felix Singer, and others*) The sun goes off the pool early. Rooms near it can suffer from noisy children.

Open 15 Mar–15 Nov, weekends 15 Nov–1 Feb, New Year.
Rooms 2 suites, 21 double, 1 single. 15 in annexe. 5 on ground floor.
Facilities Salon, TV room, bar, 2 dining rooms (1 no-smoking); conference facilities. Garden: terraces, swimming pool (unheated).
Location At top of old village. On D540, 25 km E of Montélimar. Private parking adjacent.
Credit cards All major cards accepted.
Terms Rooms: single 250–310 frs, double 300–1,100 frs, suite 900–1,100 frs. Breakfast 50 frs. D,B&B 210 frs per person added. Set meals 160–320 frs; full alc 220 frs.

POLIGNY 39800 Jura — Map 12

Hostellerie des Monts de Vaux

Tel 03.84.37.12.50
Fax 03.84.37.09.07
E-mail mtsvaux@hostellerie.com

Beside N5 to Geneva, 4 km SE of Poligny, Carrion family's smart but mildly eccentric old coaching inn, in garden with tennis, and wonderful views. Friendly owners. Elegant country antiques; good Jura specialities served in pretty dining rooms (1 for non-smokers). Rooms vary in size and quality. Open end Dec–end Oct. Closed Tuesday/midday Wed, except July/Aug. All major credit cards accepted. 10 rooms: single 500–750 frs, double 600–900 frs. Breakfast 70 frs. D,B&B double 1,500–1,600 frs. Set meals 170–400 frs. Fuller reports, please.

PONT-DE-L'ISÈRE 26600 Drôme — Map 12

Michel Chabran
Avenue du 45e-Parallèle

Tel 04.75.84.60.09
Fax 04.75.84.59.65

"An excellent dinner, with good Rhône wines from a nearby vineyard" – our latest report on Michel Chabran's renowned and stylish restaurant (Relais & Châteaux; two *Michelin* stars, two *Gault Millau toques*, for such dishes as raw scallops with truffles, quail with foie gras of duck). The setting is dull, on the busy main road of a suburb of Valence. But you eat in a warmly attractive dining room, or in a small garden beside it: "Madame runs the show in style." Service is friendly, rooms are comfortable and quiet, with double-glazing. An earlier account: "Public rooms are an odd assortment, reflecting the architecture of M. Chabran's great-grandad's café / restaurant, now much enlarged. The little-used lounge is in 1960s style. The food is delicious and helpings generous." (*T and RR, and others*)

Open All year.
Rooms 11 double, 1 single. Air-conditioning.
Facilities 2 salons, bar, restaurant (1 no-smoking room); terrace. Unsuitable for ♿.
Location On N7, 9 km N of Valence.
Credit cards All major cards accepted.
Terms [1996] Rooms: single 330–600 frs, double 390–690 frs. Breakfast 80 frs. Set meals 215–655 frs; full alc 480–610 frs. Children accommodated free in parents' room.

All our inspections are carried out anonymously.

PONT-AUDEMER 27500 Eure — Map 8

Belle-Isle sur Risle — *Tel* 02.32.56.96.22
112 route de Rouen — *Fax* 02.32.42.88.96

Just outside this small Norman town is this sturdy *deuxième empire* mansion, rather expensive but prettily located: it is on a small island that forms its five-acre garden, where there are easy chairs and parasols on the lawn. "The hotel has an air of Edwardian elegance. Our bedroom had a charming breakfast alcove. Dinner was imaginative (eg, fricassée of oysters) and well served: there was a family party, and a pianist entertained us till midnight." Rooms are furnished in period style; upper ones have the best views. The owner, Marcelle Yazbeck, has given them exotic names like Shéhérazade, Bohème. (*C and JRD*)

Open All year.
Rooms 4 suites, 16 double.
Facilities 3 lounges, bar, 2 dining rooms; indoor swimming pool, sauna, gym; terrace. Garden: swimming pool, tennis, table-tennis, boating. Unsuitable for ♿.
Location 1.5 km E of town centre. Parking.
Restriction No smoking: 2 lounges, 1 dining room.
Credit cards All major cards accepted.
Terms Rooms: single 600 frs, double 1,250 frs, suite 1,300 frs. Breakfast 75 frs. D,B&B double 1,440–2,150 frs. Set lunch 189–230 frs, dinner 390 frs; full alc 400 frs.

Auberge du Vieux Puits — *Tel* 02.32.41.01.48
6 rue Notre-Dame-du-Pré — *Fax* 02.32.42.37.28

Three bouquets and a few brickbats have come this year for a firm *Guide* favourite – a very picturesque old inn, made up of three 17th-century timbered houses round a courtyard. The Foltz family owners are welcoming and offer good Norman cooking, eg, duck with cherries and truite Bovary au champagne. "Delightful staff, comfortable room, delicious dinner and breakfast." "Our room in the old part was 'awash' with oak beams and antique furniture. In the charming dining room with its roaring log fire, the owner guided everyone through choosing the menu." "The lavatory was spectacularly small, but this somehow added to the amusement of this very special hotel. Food was extremely good but very expensive" – indeed, another reader this year called it "a rip-off", and felt that staff put pressure on guests to over-order. A cool reception was another complaint. But others recently have written: "One of our favourite hotels; it doesn't change, and Madame is as warm and cosy as ever." "A charming girl carried our bags to delightful attic rooms with lovely views of rooftops." "In our room were fresh flowers and antique chests. Excellent orange soufflé, good breakfast" (this, and drinks too, you can take in the garden). The older bedrooms by the courtyard are sweet but small; the newer ones have more comfort but less character. (*AS Carr, Jill Douglas, and others*) Stairways can be twisting. Guests are expected to dine in.

Open 25 Jan–15 Dec. Closed Mon evening/Tues, except in summer.
Rooms 12 double. In 2 separate buildings. 2 equipped for ♿.
Facilities 2 small salons, 2 dining rooms (no-smoking). Small inner garden.
Location 300 m from town centre (signposted), but quiet. Private parking.
Credit cards Access, Visa.

Terms Rooms 270–430 frs. Breakfast 45 frs. Set meals 200 (lunch only)–320 frs; full alc 260–350 frs.

PONTEMPEYRAT 43500 Haute-Loire **Map 10**

Mistou BUDGET *Tel* 04.77.50.62.46
Craponne-sur-Arzon *Fax* 04.77.50.66.70

This idyllic Relais du Silence, remote in the eastern Massif Central, is an old converted mill in a pine-clad valley. Terraces open on to lawns with garden furniture; interiors are freshly decorated, cool and attractive. Bedrooms, some in an annexe, are simple but tasteful, with furniture ranging from antique rustic to sophisticated modern. The young owners, Jacqueline and Bernard Roux, have again been found "delightful and friendly", and the rooms "comfortable, well lit". M. Roux's cooking exploits the produce of the region – smoked breast of duck, rabbit in mustard, local cheeses and wines. Readers approve the *demi-pension* menus, but one found the dishes on the *carte* a bit pretentious. Everyone likes the peaceful setting (ducklings in a pond, etc), and the breakfasts with home-made jams. Some insects from the mill stream, but each room has a killer device. (*RBR, and others*) Much renovation is planned for winter 1996–97.

Open Easter–1 Nov.
Rooms 19 double, 4 single. 10 in nearby annexe.
Facilities Lounge, 2 dining rooms. Garden. Unsuitable for ♿.
Location On D498 7 km NE of Craponne. 36 km N of Le Puy.
Credit cards Access, Amex, Visa.
Terms Rooms: single 280 frs, double 440–540 frs. Breakfast 50 frs. D,B&B double 410–500 frs. Set meals 125–305 frs; full alc 450 frs. .

PORNICHET 44380 Loire-Atlantique **Map 8**

Hôtel Sud-Bretagne NEW *Tel* 02.40.11.65.00
42 boulevard de la République *Fax* 02.40.61.73.70

A fairly smart holiday hotel, blue-and-white fronted, 200 metres from the sea, in a resort at the less fashionable end of La Baule's long sandy beach, with a modern marina nearby. Dropped from last year's *Guide* for lack of reports, it was admired again in 1996: "Well run, and idiosyncratic. The rooms are full of character: the theme in ours was ducks – duck hooks, duck loo roll holder, duck painting. The wallpaper echoed the artificial Greek temple visible from our window. A large stuffed fish lay under a glass panel near reception. Our innovative dinner was good value [*Gault Millau toque*], notably the fondue au chocolat – wickedly scrummy. Breakfast, beside the indoor pool, included fresh orange juice." According to an earlier report, the owner, Michel Bardouil, "clearly loves being in charge and service is impeccable". (*Martin and Karen Oldridge*) The hotel has a private beach club, and two boats of its own.

Open All year.
Rooms 4 suites, 26 double.
Facilities Lift. lounge, bar, billiard room; restaurant; conference facilities; indoor swimming pool. Garden: swimming pool, tennis. Unsuitable for ♿.
Location 250 m from beach. 7 km E of La Baule. Parking.
Credit cards All major cards accepted.

Terms Rooms: single 350–450 frs, double 450–800 frs, suite 1,00[illegible] Breakfast 60 frs. D,B&B 550–850 frs per person. Set meals 130–[illegible] alc 300 frs.

PORQUEROLLES 83400 Var — Map 11

Mas du Langoustier — *Tel* 04.94.58.30.09
Fax 04.94.58.36.02

This most seductive luxury hotel is a long pink-walled building, secluded in its own 75-acre pine-wooded park, at the almost deserted eastern end of a very lovely island off the Côte d'Azur, just south of Hyères. Most of the island is a national park, with sandy beaches and wooded cliffs (but no cars, and no smoking outside the village). A recent eulogy: "Lovely. We had a huge bedroom, large bathroom and balcony, fantastic views. There's free use of mountain bikes: we took an exceptional picnic, provided by the hotel, to one of the many sandy coves. The restaurant left me speechless. We had about 12 courses, all exquisite, red mullet, lobster, duck, etc, fully deserving the two *Gault Millau toques* and *Michelin* star." Meals are served on a large terrace. (*HN*)

Open End Apr–mid-Oct.
Rooms 3 suites, 47 double. 5 without wc.
Facilities Lounge/bar, outside bar, 2 dining rooms (1 for residents only); terrace. Park: garden, tennis; beach 200 m.
Location 3.5 km E of port of Porquerolles (15 mins by boat from La Tour Fondue – frequent services). Free bus service from port. No cars on island.
Credit cards All major cards accepted.
Terms [1996] D,B&B 945–1,693 frs.

PORTO-VECCHIO 20137 Corse-du-Sud — Map 17

Grand Hôtel Cala Rossa — *Tel* 04.95.71.61.51
Cala Rossa — *Fax* 04.95.71.60.11

This stylish modern hotel stands alone in its own big park, in a landscape of pines, rocks and distant hills; its beach with parasols, crowded in summer, is in a pretty cove with mountain views. And, rare for a seaside beach hotel, it serves remarkable *nouvelle*-ish cuisine (*Michelin* star and two red *Gault Millau toques* for wonders like pigeon roasted in myrtle wine, and Corsican dishes such as wild boar with chestnuts). "Exceptionally pleasant and well run, with superb food, and relaxed atmosphere," ran a recent report. Others wrote: "Impeccable service from a pleasant staff. Superb dinners, and a nice room facing the garden. Our only complaints: no balcony, and nowhere to hang wet swimming costumes." There are marble floors and a spacious open-plan dining room. Few rooms have a sea view, because of the trees: front ones face the lush garden; back ones are smaller and face the road. A big buffet lunch is served by the beach, where there's a bar for drinks. A drive through cork forests leads to Porto-Vecchio. (*MWA*)

Open 6 Apr–2 Nov.
Rooms 60. Air-conditioning.
Facilities Salon, TV room, bar, dining room; conference facilities. Large garden: tennis; direct access to sandy beach with bar. Golf 20 mins. Unsuitable for ♿.

Location On peninsula 10 km NE of Porto-Vecchio, by N198, D568, D468.
Credit cards All major cards accepted.
Terms [1996] D,B&B (obligatory) 1,450–1,900 frs. Set meals 350–400 frs; alc 270–420 frs.

POUDENAS 47170 Lot-et-Garonne — Map 10

La Belle Gasconne — *Tel* 05.53.65.71.58
Fax 05.53.65.87.39

A 14th-century mill house in a remote Gascony hamlet, now a stylish but not expensive restaurant-with-rooms. Marie-Claude Gracia, whose husband died in 1995, now adds the role of owner to that of chef, and her "impressive" regional cuisine wins two *Gault Millau toques*. "The quality of the food has not changed, and she is now assisted by her daughter and son-in-law," says a reader this year, backing last year's praise: "The mill is truly gorgeous, with cool stone floors, and beamed bedrooms soothingly decorated; the meals are imaginative: second helpings of some starters and all desserts are generously offered. A genuinely hospitable atmosphere." The mill stream has been cleverly integrated with the dining room; and glass doors lead into a flagstoned hall, where logs burn cosily in winter. Bedroom windows have views over mill pond and river, where guests can take a canoe ride. A short walk through a pine grove takes you to a small and "idyllic" swimming pool in the garden, on an island formed by the mill stream. (*Laurence Brass, PJC Wadsley, and others*)

Open All year, except early Jan–mid-Feb.
Rooms 1 suite, 6 double.
Facilities Salon with TV, bar, restaurant. Garden: swimming pool. Unsuitable for ♿.
Location In village. 17 km SW of Nérac on D656. Private parking.
Credit cards All major cards accepted.
Terms Rooms: single 380 frs, double 520–570 frs, suite 650 frs. Breakfast 55 frs. D,B&B 590–710 frs per person. Set meals 180–285 frs; alc 290 frs.

PULIGNY-MONTRACHET 21190 Côte-d'Or — Map 12

Le Montrachet — *Tel* 03.80.21.30.06
10 place des Marronniers — *Fax* 03.80.21.39.06

Thierry Gazagnes's handsome old stone-walled hostelry stands in the main square of a classic Burgundy wine village. It has been discreetly modernised to retain a rustic air: one or two bedrooms have fake beamed ceilings. But there's nothing fake about the Burgundian cuisine (*Michelin* star, *Gault Millau toque*, notably for the apple tart). Our reporter, who had a "marvellous" salad of quail, wrote previously: "The head waiter scored highly for talking to us only in French. The list of white Montrachets is naturally of telephone directory size, and the one we chose was excellent. When I asked for a *marc* with coffee, the bottle was left on the table to tempt me further, with no charge other than the initial 50 frs. Breakfast seemed ordinary though maybe I was suffering from that *marc*." There's a terrace on the square for drinks. (*DO'M, CC*) Some bedrooms are "huge and luxurious", but some bathrooms are tiny. One recent report of very slow service at dinner. There is no lounge, and the village "goes to bed early".

Open All year, except 1 Dec–9 Jan. Restaurant closed Wed midday.
Rooms 2 suites, 30 double. 1 on ground floor suitable for ♿. 10 in annexe.
Facilities Bar with TV, restaurant; terrace.
Location Central. Enclosed parking.
Credit cards All major cards accepted.
Terms Rooms 450–515 frs, suite 750–995 frs. Breakfast 55 frs. D,B&B 565–795 frs per person. Set meals 195–425 frs; full alc 450 frs.

PUYMIROL 47270 Lot-et-Garonne — Map 10

Les Loges de l'Aubergade — *Tel* 05.53.95.31.46
52 rue Royale — *Fax* 05.53.95.33.80

Owner/chef Michel Trama continues to win two *Michelin* stars and four red *Gault Millau toques* at this 13th-century house, brilliantly converted, in a hill-village near the Garonne valley. It is a luxurious venture (Relais & Châteaux), where bold cuisine marches with ambitious design: striking modern furniture, mostly Italian, has been blended into an interesting old building with wit and style. Rooms are "a superb mixture of modern and ancient". The creamy white stone is set off by clever modern lighting, the dining room chairs are high-tech leather. Again this year, readers tended to admire the design more than the high gastronomy – unusual for France. "Thrilling, exhilarating. The details astonish: sleek blue switches, the most comfortable white sofa ever, a huge bed with a flamboyant cover matched by ethereal curtains. Two stylish patios. But breakfast was ordinary." "Excellent breakfast. Dinner a bit pretentious. Staff not very friendly. Marvellous room. But the plastic grass round the pool cheapens the place." "Witty design, professional service, but food not so memorable." Yet who could forget this one? "Our eight-course meal was wonderful, served with impeccable ritual – a lasagne of lobster with truffles (ambrosial), salmon with asparagus, tarragon lamb. A powerful goat's cheese startled the palate; desserts were equally sensational." The set menus vary *selon le marché*. M. Trama and his wife Maryse are "charming". (*Felix Singer, Neil French, Lydia Heah, and others*) Reception is not always staffed, so you may get locked out unless you ask for a key.

Open All year, except Feb school holidays, Mon out of season.
Rooms 10 double. 2 on ground floor. Air-conditioning.
Facilities Lounge, bar lounge, smoking room, restaurant; conference facilities. Garden: jacuzzi.
Location 17 km E of Agen (leave N113 at Lafox). Garage.
Credit cards All major cards accepted.
Terms Rooms 750–1,410 frs. Breakfast 90 frs. D,B&B double 2,100 frs. Set meals 180–680 frs; alc 400 frs.

QUESTEMBERT 56230 Morbihan — Map 8

Hôtel de Bretagne — *Tel* 02.97.26.11.12
13 rue St-Michel — *Fax* 02.97.26.12.37

In small town 27 km E of Vannes, very distinguished and exotic restaurant-with-rooms (Relais & Châteaux), serving probably the best food in Brittany (two Michelin *stars, three* Gault Millau *toques), cooked by owner/chef Georges Paineau and son-in-law Claude Corlouer. Exciting mix of aromas; panache and daring originality, alike in cuisine, smart decor of bedrooms and dining rooms (one a lovely conservatory), and flamboyant charm of owners. Lovely spacious garden full of oriental cats. Access, Amex, Visa accepted. 12 rooms: double 780–980 frs; D,B&B double 850–950 frs. Set lunch 180 frs, dinner 295 frs. Why, why no recent reports? Please send some.*

RABASTENS 81800 Tarn **Map 10**

Le Pré-Vert BUDGET *Tel* 05.63.33.70.51
54 promenade des Lices *Fax* 05.63.33.82.58

"A wonderful old-fashioned two-star Logis de France," writes a recent visitor to this creeper-covered 18th-century hotel in the centre of a pleasant, untouristy little town between Toulouse and Albi. "It is full of charm and character. We had a warm welcome from the *patronne* and her friendly son, and a thrilling view of the Saturday morning *marché* beneath our window." The hotel has a big shady garden. Meals are served in summer on a terrace under the trees, and in winter in a wood-panelled dining room. Portions are generous; the *carte* may be a better bet than the set menus. The decor has been called "a ramshackle mix of nice old furniture, tapestries, gilt mirrors and, for us, a hideous bathroom with a clashing mix of primary colours". (*GS*) Most readers find the food adequate, if not inspired.

Open All year, except 2–31 Jan. Restaurant closed Sun evening/midday Mon.
Rooms 14 double, 1 single.
Facilities Bar, 2 dining rooms (1 no-smoking); terrace (meal service). Garden. Unsuitable for ♿.
Location Central. 37 km NE of Toulouse. Parking.
Credit cards Access, Amex, Visa.
Terms [1996] Rooms 160–350 frs. Breakfast 30 frs. D,B&B 280–350 frs per person.

RASTEAU 84110 Vaucluse **Map 11**

Hôtel Bellerive *Tel* 04.90.46.10.20
Route Violès *Fax* 04.90.46.14.96

A cheerful modern Relais du Silence, enjoyed again this year. It looks outwardly dull but has a lovely setting, amid gardens and Côtes du Rhône vineyards, with fine views to Mont Ventoux and the Dentelles de Montmirail. Two recent accounts: "As welcoming as ever. Mme Pétrier runs it efficiently, her husband's cooking is *soigné*, for example the casserole of snails, chicken with rice timbale and crayfish; good local wines." "It has antiques in the corridors, and an obliging staff. Our family room, with attractive fabrics, had its own terrace and private garden. Ceiling fans kept the rooms cool. The restaurant, with fine views, served local dishes on the excellent *demi-pension* menu." (*John Derry, W and AR*) The smallish sheltered swimming pool, with loungers, gets crowded in high summer. The Roman ruins at Vaison, though damaged in the 1992 floods, are worth a visit. So are the sung vespers at Le Barroux monastery.

Open 30 Mar–mid-Nov.
Rooms 20 double. Some on ground floor.
Facilities Salon with TV, restaurant. Large garden: swimming pool.
Location 9 km W of Vaison-la-Romaine, off D975 to Orange.
Credit cards Access, Visa.
Terms [1996] Rooms 485–495 frs. Breakfast 50 frs. D,B&B 435–445 frs per person. Set meals 145–185 frs.

REIMS 51100 Marne — Map 9

Boyer Les Crayères — *Tel* 03.26.82.80.80
64 boulevard Henri-Vasnier — *Fax* 03.26.82.65.52

Owner/chef Gérard Boyer's awesomely superior Relais & Châteaux hotel is an elegant cream-coloured mansion in a stately park, in the southeast suburbs of Reims. It is used by magnates of some of the big champagne houses for entertaining important clients. Its renowned cuisine still wins three *Michelin* stars, but *Gault Millau*, detecting a decline in quality, dropped its rating this year from 19.5 to 17 (three *toques*). Our own readers' views, too, can be mixed. "Wonderful food," was one comment this year, while others have written: "Beautiful bedrooms overlooking a large garden, outstanding food beautifully served." "Such grand *château* luxury, such French flair and style." But: "The food was not as good as at some other *Michelin* *** places, and the *maître d'* was almost rude." "The food was superb and copious, and the service efficient, though only the Boyers themselves displayed real charm. The dining rooms were beautiful. We got the smallest room: its *belle époque* proportions had been spoilt by the carving out of it of a very small bathroom. The room was newly and expensively decorated in deep green." There is no salon, just a small bar which can get crowded. The new winter garden is "Proustian, very elegant and spacious". (*T and RR, and others*) More reports welcome.

Open All year, except 23 Dec–13 Jan. Restaurant closed Mon/midday Tues.
Rooms 3 suites (in cottage), 16 double. Air-conditioning.
Facilities Lift. Hall, bar, restaurant; private dining room; terrace, winter garden. Park: gardens, tennis, helipad.
Location 3 km from town centre. *Autoroute* A4 exit St-Rémi; follow direction Luxembourg for 0.5 km; hotel at roundabout with N44 to Châlons-sur-Marne. Parking, garage.
Credit cards All major cards accepted.
Terms [1996] Rooms 990–1,940 frs. Breakfast 102 frs. Alc 520–740 frs.

RENNES 35000 Ile-et-Vilaine — Map 8

Lecoq-Gadby — *Tel* 02.99.38.05.55
156 rue d'Antrain — *Fax* 02.99.38.53.40

In NE suburbs of Brittany's capital, on road to Caen, small elegant hotel with rooms in different period styles, beautifully furnished, newly appointed. Some have balcony facing garden, as does restaurant. Excellent main meals and breakfast. Helpful staff. All major credit cards accepted. 11 rooms. B&B 355–610 frs. Set meals 100–300 frs [1996]. Fuller reports welcome.

REPLONGES 01750 Ain — Map 12

La Huchette — *Tel* 03.85.31.03.55
Fax 03.85.31.10.24

This smart old *auberge*, which stands at the edge of a village east of Mâcon, has broad lawns, a big swimming pool with loungers, and some surprising decor; and it is well run by its owners, the Gualdieri. The new chef, Vincent Rivon, wins a *toque* from *Gault Millau*, and approval from a *Guide* reader too, this year: "Dinner was first-class, including foie gras de canard, méran, delicious desserts. Our room facing the garden and swimming pool was very comfortable. The spacious lounge is nicely furnished." Last year's praise: "A warm welcome, a large well-furnished room with big bathroom. The tranquil restaurant, also facing the garden, has big murals of lofty castles and idyllic country scenes." "Despite its fierce crimson and purple wallpaper, we liked our room, also the family." (*Joan Powell, and others*) The hotel is on a main road, but back rooms are very quiet.

Open All year.
Rooms 1 suite, 11 double. Some on ground floor.
Facilities Salon, bar, restaurant; function room. Garden: swimming pool.
Location Edge of village, 4 km E of Mâcon, off N79. Parking.
Credit cards All major cards accepted.
Terms Rooms: single 450–550 frs, double 500–600 frs, suite 900–1,200 frs. Breakfast 60 frs. D,B&B double 940–1,040 frs. Set meals 160–230 frs; full alc 300 frs.

RIBEAUVILLÉ 68150 Haut-Rhin — Map 12

Le Clos Saint Vincent — *Tel* 03.89.73.67.65
Route de Bergheim — *Fax* 03.89.73.32.20

The Chapotin family's elegant restaurant-with-rooms, in a neat white Alsatian villa, stands alone amid Riesling vineyards, with three ruined castles on the hills behind. Interiors are smart and spacious; many bedrooms have a balcony, where you can take breakfast, facing the garden and vines. Again this year and last, praise has been lavish: "Everything about it is charming. Staff are cheerful, prices are good value, the food is chosen to complement the wine." "A lovely stay in a beautiful hotel." Owner/chef Bertrand Chapotin's cooking is "excellent", eg, veal chop with cèpes. There is "a lovely terrace above the valley", and a "superb" new indoor swimming pool, the side of which is glass with sliding doors. (*Robin Riley, and others*)

Open 15 Mar–15 Nov. Restaurant closed Tues/Wed.
Rooms 3 suites, 12 double. Some on ground floor.
Facilities Lift. 2 lounges, bar, restaurant; indoor swimming pool. Garden.
Location NE outskirts on Bergheim road. 15 km N of Colmar. Private parking.
Credit cards Access, Visa.
Terms B&B: single 630–700 frs, double 730–810 frs, suite 1,030–1,140 frs; D,B&B double 1,310–1,678 frs. Set meals 150–250 frs; full alc 350 frs.

RIMBACH 68500 Haut-Rhin — Map 12

L'Aigle d'Or NEW/BUDGET — *Tel* 03.89.76.89.80
Fax 03.89.74.32.41

In a tiny village up a remote valley of the southern Vosges foothills is this unpretentious Logis de France, owned and run by the Marcks. "It is an oldish building but well kept and equipped. The atmosphere was warm and peaceful. Madame runs the restaurant, often packed with local families; Monsieur is the excellent chef, providing many good local dishes (but desserts were unimaginative). We had two connecting double rooms for our family. There is a terrace café, a garden, and games equipment. We thoroughly enjoyed our stay." (*Michael and Judi Smith*)

Open All year, except 19 Feb–14 Mar, Mon in low season.
Rooms 21 double.
Facilities Restaurant; terrace cafe. Garden.
Location 11 km W of Guebiller by D51, 33 km NW of Mulhouse. Parking.
Credit cards All major cards accepted.
Terms [1996] Rooms 100–210 frs. Breakfast 22 frs. D,B&B 175–210 frs per person. Set meals 70–165 frs.

ROANNE 42300 Loire — Map 10

Troisgros — *Tel* 04.77.71.66.97
Place de la Gare — *Fax* 04.77.70.39.77

As you might expect in France, one of the world's greatest restaurants stands facing the railway station of a humdrum little town. Here Pierre Troisgros, a leading pioneer of so-called *nouvelle cuisine*, and his son Michel won the French guides' top ratings yet again in 1996, and our readers have again concurred: "Dinner was superb, with wonderful desserts"; "excellent food, superb breakfast, helpful staff". Scrambled eggs with caviar, and foie gras in raspberry wine have been especially enjoyed. Pierre Troisgros "calls at table in an unaffected manner". The bedrooms are also remarkable – a "surrealist paradise" with abundant use of glass (including the doors between bedrooms and bathrooms) and Mirós on some walls. This account holds good: "The warmth is tangible, the staff are charming and unpretentious, the rooms luxurious. The older ones are charming too: one is Japanese in inspiration. The delightful inner courtyard has a Japanese water-garden lit up at night, from which you have a panoramic view of the superbly organised kitchen, like a ballet. The wine list is sumptuous. Breakfast included smoked ham and fruit." (*T and RR, and others*)

Open All year, except Feb school holidays, 1st half Aug, Tues evening/Wed.
Rooms 5 suites, 14 double. Air-conditioning.
Facilities Lift. Salon, bar, restaurant. Garden.
Location Central (rooms double-glazed). Private underground carpark.
Credit cards All major cards accepted.
Terms Rooms 700–1,600 frs. Breakfast 120 frs. Set meals 300 (lunch Mon–Fri only)–730 frs; full alc 750 frs.

LA ROCHE-L'ABEILLE 87800 Haute-Vienne — Map 10

Le Moulin de la Gorce — *Tel* 05.55.00.70.66
St-Yrieix-la-Perche — *Fax* 05.55.00.76.57

The setting is a hamlet in pleasant hilly country, between the two porcelain centres of Limoges (large and ugly) and St-Yrieix (small and lovely). Also small and lovely is this converted mill house, now an elegant restaurant-with-rooms, owned and run by Jean and Annie Bertranet: *Michelin* gives two stars, and *Gault Millau* two *toques*, for the cuisine of Yves Brémont. There are pretty grounds, and a large pond. After some recent criticisms of room upkeep, this year brought only praise: "We again loved it. Dinner was delicious: foie gras, marinade of salmon, coquilles St-Jacques *beautifully* undercooked, ris de veau aux cèpes whose earthiness went well with a Volnay." "Worth a visit for the silence, and the excellent food served in cathedral-like seriousness: all very admirable. The room decor, much of it pale blue, or pink, is not really cottagey, more suited to a *château* than a mill." "One breakfast is enough for two people." Some bedrooms have antiques, old beams. You can take lunch or breakfast by the pond, dinner in dining rooms either "rustic" or "Louis XVI". (*Mrs Curzon Tussaud, Felix Singer, Elizabeth Ring*) "The only noise is from the ducks/geese on the millpond at dawn."

Open All year, except Jan. Closed Sun evening/Mon 20 Sept–15 Apr.
Rooms 1 suite, 9 double. 6 in mill, 3 in main building, suite in small separate mill.
Facilities Salon, 2 dining rooms (1 no-smoking). Garden. Unsuitable for ♿.
Location 12 km NE of St-Yrieix, off D704; 2 km S of La Roche off D17. Parking.
Credit cards All major cards accepted.
Terms Rooms: single 350 frs, double 750 frs, suite 1,300 frs. Breakfast 75 frs. D,B&B double 1,500–1,600 frs. Set meals 180–480 frs; full alc 350 frs.

LA ROCHELLE 17000 Charente-Maritime — Map 10

Hôtel Les Brises
17 Chemin Digue de Richelieu — *Tel* 05.46.43.89.37 — *Fax* 05.46.43.27.97

This old fortified seaport is one of France's loveliest towns. About a mile west of the centre is the point where, in 1627, Cardinal Richelieu built a dyke to keep out the English fleet, which was then allied with the town's Huguenot defenders. Here, in a quiet position by the sea, is this "good-quality" B&B hotel. It offers views of the islands and harbour from many bedrooms, and from the sun terrace with loungers and parasols – "an enthralling non-stop theatre". "The rectangular 1950s building is unattractive," say 1996 visitors, "but the view is splendid, and housekeeping was top-notch. Breakfast on the terrace was OK." General agreement that bedrooms are good and well kept, even "excellent". A foghorn and revolving foglight might sometimes disturb sleep. (*Martin and Karen Oldridge, and others*) For meals, try *L'Entracte* (much liked this year), or the lively *Bar André* by the harbour.

Open All year.
Rooms 2 suites, 45 double, 3 single.
Facilities Lift. TV lounge, bar; terrace. Direct access to sea, rocky beach; sandy beach, safe bathing 1.5 km.
Location Seafront, 1.5 km W of town centre. Garage, carpark.
Credit cards All major cards accepted.
Terms Rooms: single 250–310 frs, double 300–630 frs, suite (for 4 people) 650–950 frs. Breakfast 49 frs.

Hôtel de la Monnaie NEW
3 rue de la Monnaie — *Tel* 05.46.50.65.65 — *Fax* 05.46.50.63.19

Much more central than *Les Brises* (above), this stately 17th-century mansion has, says its nominator, a "splendid location" in this marvellous old city, close to the ramparts and the harbour entrance. "The building's age is visible in the lovely tiled lobby and inner courtyard. The bedrooms are quite modern, rather out of character, with built-in furniture and fabrics in geometric designs. But they are very well equipped, with good lighting. The welcome is warm, the hotel is well run, and a generous breakfast includes good coffee." (*Carolyn Mathiasen*) No restaurant: lots, such as *La Marmite* (expensive) and the *Toque Blanche* (medium price), nearby.

Open All year.
Rooms 4 suites, 32 double. Air-conditioning.
Facilities Lift. Lobby, breakfast room; conference facilities. Courtyard.
Location Central, 300 m W of Vieux Port. Private garage.
Credit cards All major cards accepted.
Terms [1996] Rooms 450–580 frs. Breakfast 52 frs.

LES ROCHES-DE-CONDRIEU 38370 Isère — Map 12

Le Bellevue NEW/BUDGET — *Tel* 04.74.56.41.42
Quai du Rhône — *Fax* 04.74.56.47.56

This modern creeper-covered hotel stands beside the broad majestically curving Rhône south of Lyon, in a busy stretch of the valley: vine-clad hills rise on the far bank. Dropped from last year's *Guide* for lack of reports, it won a new admirer this year: "A very attractive bargain staging-post: outstandingly friendly service from the owner, M. Bouron, and excellent food and wine, in a pleasant restaurant with river views." Rooms are comfortable and quiet, but some are quite simple: best are the few with a balcony facing the river.

Open All year, except 10 Feb–12 Mar, 22–28 Oct. Restaurant closed Mon, Sun evening Oct–Jan.
Rooms 16.
Facilities 2 salons, restaurant.
Location In village, 12 km SW of Vienne. Parking.
Credit cards All major cards accepted.
Terms [1996] Rooms 200–310 frs. Breakfast 35 frs. D,B&B 200–450 frs per person. Set meals 110–300 frs.

ROMANÈCHE-THORINS 71570 Saône-et-Loire — Map 12

Les Maritonnes — *Tel* 03.85.35.51.70
Fax 03.85.35.58.14

Set at the foot of the vine-clad Beaujolais slopes, Guy Fauvin's quite sophisticated little hotel wins a *Michelin* star and a *Gault Millau toque* for classic local dishes such as frogs' legs sauté'd with herbs, and coq au vin. Three more plaudits this year: "We enjoyed our eight-night stay – excellent food, very good bedroom, obliging staff. A well-run hotel, with atmosphere too. A good swimming pool with loungers, within a beautiful garden." "Delightful. Notable sweet trolley. Lovely breakfast room with elegant antiques." "Hospitable staff, excellent breakfast. Food good, but the cheaper menu is too limited, and there's a surfeit of bonnes bouches and petits fours, which one would rather not have to pay for." Much furnishing is in rustic style. Some rooms are small, but nearly all are pretty. (*Mr and Mrs R Bishop, Andrew Hillier, Joan Powell, MJG*) An outdoor terrace is new this year. Slight noise from trains.

Open End Jan–mid-Dec. Closed Sun evening/Mon, midday Tues in low season.
Rooms 20 double.
Facilities Lounge, bar, restaurant. Garden: swimming pool. Unsuitable for ♿.
Location Near station (double glazing). Private parking.
Credit cards All major cards accepted.
Terms Rooms 370–560 frs. Breakfast 60 frs. Set meals 160–420 frs; full alc 420 frs.

ROMORANTIN-LANTHENAY 41200 Loir-et-Cher — Map 9

Grand Hôtel du Lion d'Or — *Tel* 02.54.94.15.15
69 rue Georges-Clémenceau — *Fax* 02.54.88.24.87

Expensive, smart and stylish (Relais & Châteaux, four red *Michelin* gables), this handsome old post house stands in the main street of a market town south of Orléans. Even more superior is Didier Clément's cooking (two *Michelin* stars, three *Gault Millau toques*), and it was again admired by our own readers this year: "Lovely risotto of crayfish, and a roasted partridge elegantly dismembered, set on a slice of hot foie gras. Breakfast in our room was spectacular." Most bedrooms are set round a splendid flower-decked courtyard. "The reception rooms are stunning," runs a recent account, "with floor-to-ceiling mirrors, enchanting flower arrangements, and a lit candelabra on the grand piano. The dining room has 18th-century panelling, sparkling silverware, a giant low-slung lit chandelier. And the food is exquisite. The Barrat family owners and their daughter, who is married to the brilliant young chef, make a fine team, and their staff are very stylish. We loved the place and found nothing to fault." (*Mrs Curzon Tussaud, Francine and Ian Walsh, and others*) Upkeep of cheaper rooms has been criticised. Rooms facing the street can be a bit noisy, despite double glazing.

Open All year, except mid-Feb–mid-Mar.
Rooms 3 suites, 13 double. 6 air-conditioned.
Facilities Lift, ramps. 2 salons, restaurant. Garden (meal service).
Location Central. Town is 67 km SW of Orléans. Parking.
Credit cards All major cards accepted.
Terms Rooms: single 600 frs, double 750–1,500 frs, suite 1,200–2,100 frs. Breakfast 100 frs. Set meals 410–600 frs; full alc 620 frs.

ROSCOFF 29681 Finistère — Map 8

Hôtel Brittany NEW — *Tel* 02.98.69.70.78
Boulevard Sainte-Barbe — *Fax* 02.98.61.13.29

Convenient for the ferries to or from Plymouth, this old manor house stands by the sea, at the edge of the port. "We have often used it as an overnight stop, and have always been welcomed with great charm," says its renominator this year. "It is peaceful. We have liked the rooms both in the older and in the newer parts, especially those with a veranda by the covered swimming pool. Service is courteous and meals are excellent – alike in the beautiful restaurant and on the terrace facing the sea. An extensive breakfast is served by the pool." *Gault Millau toque*, notably for local fish, eg, lotte rôtie au basilic. (*Mrs BE Dunford*)

Open Mar–Nov. Restaurant closed midday Mon.
Rooms 2 suites, 23 double.
Facilities Bar, restaurant. Garden: swimming pool, sauna, solarium.
Location At E end of harbour, 1 km from town centre. Parking.
Credit cards Access, Amex, Visa.
Terms Rooms 350–610 frs, suite 650–940 frs. Breakfast 55 frs. D,B&B 480–840 frs per person.

RUGY 57640 Moselle **Map 9**

La Bergerie BUDGET *Tel* 03.87.77.82.27
15 rue des Vignes *Fax* 03.87.77.87.07

This Relais du Silence is in a hamlet just off the motorway north of Metz (but traffic noise is slight). It's an attractive old stone building, with a creeper-covered terrace, tables and chairs on the lawn, and modern bedrooms in a new block facing fields. A 1996 report: "We had a good-sized room, simply furnished but with a decent bathroom, and very peaceful at the back. The restaurant is gourmet class; we had a splendid old-fashioned meal – *cuisine grande-mère* – beautifully prepared and served. breakfast, buffet style, was unusually varied and copious for France." (*Arlette and Brian Singleton*)

Open All year, except 23 Dec–2 Jan.
Rooms 48 double. 20 in annexe. Some on ground floor.
Facilities Ramps. Restaurant; conference/function facilities; terrace. Garden.
Location 15 km NE of Metz. *Autoroute* A4 exit Argancy; take D1 to Ennery, then right to Rugy. Parking.
Credit cards Access, Visa.
Terms Rooms 310–390 frs. Breakfast 45 frs. D,B&B 325–470 frs per person. Alc meals 200 frs.

ST-AIGNAN-SUR-CHER 41110 Loir-et-Cher **Map 8**

Clos du Cher *Tel* 02.54.75.00.03
Route de St-Aignan *Fax* 02.54.75.03.79

Sixty km SE of Tours, on edge of small town by river Cher (remarkable 12th-century murals in church crypt), old mansion in wooded park, newly converted into elegant small hotel, family-run. 10 individually decorated rooms, modern bathrooms. Stylish restaurant in converted stables: excellent food. Closed early Jan–mid-Feb, 18–25 Nov, Wed out of season. All major credit cards accepted. Rooms 390–550 frs. Breakfast 60 frs. D,B&B 395–460 frs per person. Set meals 135–340 frs [1996].

ST-BONNET-LE-FROID 43290 Haute-Loire **Map 12**

Auberge des Cimes *Tel* 04.71.59.93.72
Fax 04.71.59.93.40

Amid glorious hilly Massif Central scenery 26 km W of Annonay, village auberge *stylishly renovated, with 18 bright bedrooms in new annexe. Owner/chef Régis Marcon's "outstanding" and mostly expensive cuisine wins* Michelin *star, three* Gault Millau *toques. Friendly service. Open 15 Mar–15 Nov, except Sun evening/Mon out of season. Access, Visa accepted. Rooms 550–700 frs. Breakfast 60–80 frs. D,B&B 600–750 frs per person. Set meals 140–550 frs [1996].*

A number of continental hotels have quoted their rates exclusive of tourist tax or value added tax. Please check when booking.

ST-CLÉMENT-DES-BALEINES 17590 Charente-Maritime Map 10

Le Chat Botté *Tel* 05.46.29.21.93
Place de l'Église *Fax* 05.46.29.29.97
Ile de Ré

At far W end of this long flat holiday island near La Rochelle, village of St-Clement-of-the-whales contains this modest Puss-in-Boots hotel, newly renovated with pale wood and yellow paint. Breakfast room by garden, health and fitness centre; good beaches close by. Same family own separate restaurant of same name (Gault Millau toque) *across road. No babies. Closed 1–15 Dec, 6 Jan–6 Feb. Access, Visa accepted. 19 rooms (1 on ground floor). B&B: single 343–353 frs, double 466–586 frs. 1-night bookings refused July/Aug.*

ST-CLOUD 92210 Hauts-de-Seine Map 9

Villa Henri IV *Tel* 01.46.02.59.30
43 boulevard de la République *Fax* 01.49.11.11.02

In well-known bourgeois Paris suburb 11 km W of Eiffel Tower, near park: quiet and spacious hotel set back from road. 36 rooms, lounge, pleasant staff, and good breakfasts. Parking. Hotel's own restaurant, Le Bourbon *(closed 20 July–20 Aug), only so-so, but good ones nearby. All major credit cards accepted. Rooms: single 460–500 frs, double 510-550 frs. Breakfast 48 frs. Set meals 115–178 frs [1996]. Newer reports needed, please.*

ST-CYPRIEN 66751 Pyrénées-Orientales Map 10

Hôtel Belvédère NEW/BUDGET *Tel* 04.68.21.05.93
Fax 04.68.37.19.38

In the old village of St-Cyprien, just inland from its big modern beach-resort (see next page), is this white modern block: it is not beautiful, but has palm-trees in its garden, balconies for all bedrooms, and other assets, says its irrepressible nominator: "This little gem, great value, perches above the village, in a residential area for retired people, mercifully removed from St-Cyprien-sur-Hullabaloo. M. Bellais, the owner, is pleasant and anglophile. Our room was large and pure French flop-house, with funereal-looking yet comfy beds. The view of sea and neighbours was stunning: blissful were the evenings watching the sunsets from our spacious balcony. In the small but adequate bathroom, everything worked. In the vast dining room, popular with locals for Sunday lunch, we really ate well. No TV in the bedrooms: we anyway found it more fun to watch the communal telly and listen to the litany of abuse our fellow guests heaped on their politicians." (*Paul Palmer*)

Open Apr-Oct.
Rooms 30. Many with balcony.
Facilities Lounge, restaurant, bar; terrace. Garden. Unsuitable for ♿.
Location On hill in village, 3 km E of St-Cyprien beaches. 14 km SE of Perpignan. Parking.
Credit cards Access, Diners, Visa.
Terms Rooms 210–280 frs. Breakfast 35 frs. Set meals from 80 frs.

ST-CYPRIEN-SUD 66750 Pyrénées-Orientales Map 10

L'Ile de la Lagune *Tel* 04.68.21.01.02
Boulevard de l'Almandin *Fax* 04.68.21.06.28

St-Cyprien, near Perpignan, is one of the seven modernistic resorts built on this coast since the 1970s. The style may not please everyone, but it has its own glamour. Here this holiday complex, a modern hotel in local Catalan style, with some bungalows, is on a tiny island in a lagoon. Its nominator was delighted: "A dozen or so rooms have a balcony, where over breakfast you can enjoy the Pyrenees, the sea, and a wide sandy beach. The manager/chef Jean-Paul Hartmann and his charming wife Catherine make guests feel at home. His food in the hotel's *Almandin* restaurant (*Michelin* star, two *Gault Millau toques*) is varied, imaginative, and excellent value – the sardines, gambas and other seafood were succulent. We dined out on the beautiful terrace by the lagoon – a bit windy. The gorgeous pool is lit up at night." (*CN-R and HB-B*)

Open All year, except Jan/Feb. Restaurant closed Sun evening/Mon in low season.
Rooms 4 suites, 18 double. Some on ground floor with access for ♿.
Facilities Lift. Lounge, TV room, bar, restaurant; 2 function rooms; terrace. Garden: swimming pool (unheated), private beach.
Location 3 km E of St-Cyprien, 19 km SE of Perpignan. Parking.
Credit cards Access, Amex, Visa.
Terms [1996] Rooms 490–900 frs, suite 800–1,250 frs. Breakfast 65 frs. D,B&B 520–960 frs per person. Set meals 160–380 frs; full alc 360 frs.

ST-DIDIER 35220 Ille-et-Vilaine Map 8

Hôtel Pen'Roc BUDGET *Tel* 02.99.00.33.02
La Peinière *Fax* 02.99.62.30.89

"Marvellous hospitality," say visitors to Mireille and Joseph Froc's Logis de France, set quietly amid meadows beside an historic Romanesque pilgrimage church, east of Rennes. It is a modern hostelry, not picturesque but bright and cheerful, and has long been liked for the cheerful warmth of the staff and owners, and for their cooking (*Michelin* red "Repas", *Gault Millau toque*), which includes dishes with herbs and vegetables from their garden. More praise came in 1996: "Fresh, well-cooked food beautifully presented, and a genuine interest in you as a guest, from Madame and all her staff." Rooms are "airy and attractive", though one reader found them too modern and "mass produced". There is a heated outdoor pool, and a pleasant lounge, busy at midday, quiet in the evening. (*John and Helen Wright, and others*)

Open All year, except 25 Feb–23 Mar, 28 Oct–3 Nov. Restaurant closed Sun evening Sept–Apr.
Rooms 30 double, 3 single. 2 on ground floor, suitable for ♿.
Facilities Lift, ramp. Lounge/bar, 3 dining rooms (1 no-smoking); conference facilities. Park: garden, swimming pool, sauna, fitness room, children's play area.
Location 4 km E of Châteaubourg. Turn off D857 towards St-Didier at St-Jean-sur-Vilaine, then left to La Peinière.
Credit cards All major cards accepted.
Terms [1996] Rooms: single 330–380 frs, double 400–520 frs. Breakfast 48 frs. D,B&B 350–390 frs per person. Set meals 105–260 frs.

ST-EMILION 33330 Gironde — Map 10

Auberge de la Commanderie BUDGET — *Tel* 05.57.24.70.19
Rue des Cordeliers — *Fax* 05.57.74.44.53

In the heart of this famous wine-village, a former Templar house newly renovated, now a graceful small hotel. "Very pleasant and friendly, with an excellent breakfast spread," is one plaudit this year. Another: "We had a quiet, pretty room at the back, overlooking the vines. Breakfast included hot toast." No restaurant; *Francis Goullée* opposite recommended. (*GA McKenzie, H and M Strong*) "In the shops of St-Emilion we found it impossible to buy any liquid other than that derived from the grape. No mineral water anywhere." What do you expect?

Open All year except 15 Jan–15 Feb.
Rooms 1 suite, 16 double. 7 in annexe.
Facilities Lift. Salon, bar, breakfast room.
Location Central. Parking. St-Emilion is 41 km E of Bordeaux.
Credit card Access.
Terms Rooms 220–450 frs, suite 500–700 frs. Breakfast 38–48 frs.

Hostellerie de Plaisance — *Tel* 05.57.24.72.32
Place du Clocher — *Fax* 05.57.74.41.11

Well worthy of St-Emilion and its famous wines is this "stylish up-market hostelry", in a former monastery built of local stone. The site is curious, atop a sandstone cave-filled cliff that contains a troglodyte church dating from the 9th century. The hotel's terrace offers a fine view of the town and vineyards. Some readers recently found staff aloof and inefficient, but a visitor this year fared better: "Service was impeccable, and we struck up an excellent relationship with the previously criticised *sommelier*. Superb menu gastronomique [*Michelin* star, *Gault Millau toque*]. From our table we looked out at a vista of vineyards, castle and amorous pigeons, one of which I ate the next day. The restaurant is charming, if formal, the public rooms are a bit lacking in ambience. Pity there's no bar. Breakfast on the terrace. A rather small but well-appointed bedroom; luxurious bathroom. Ensure that you park carefully, or your car can get locked in by a curious rising bollard in the road." (*Jon Hughes*)

Open All year, except Jan.
Rooms 2 suites, 9 double, 1 single. 3 on ground floor. Some air-conditioned.
Facilities Salon, TV room, restaurant; function room; terrace. Garden.
Location Central, near Syndicat d'Initiative. Open parking.
Credit cards All major cards accepted.
Terms [1996] Rooms 500–790 frs. Breakfast 56 frs. Set meals 140–270 frs.

Le Logis des Remparts — *Tel* 05.57.24.70.43
18 rue Guadet — *Fax* 05.57.74.47.44

On the edge of the village, this old stone building has a broad terrace with tables and chairs under parasols, facing some of the famous vineyards. More praise this year: "A warm welcome and excellent service. It was a pleasure to breakfast on the terrace, and our room was tastefully decorated." Rooms are spacious and newly renovated: modern furniture, with the occasional antique. Back rooms are quietest.

No restaurant, but *Le Tertre* and *Francis Goullée* are recommended. (*Mrs Lydia Heah, EF, and others*) There will probably be a swimming pool in 1997.

Open All year, except 16 Dec–14 Jan.
Rooms 17 double. Some on ground floor.
Facilities Salon, bar, breakfast room (no-smoking); terrace. Garden.
Location Central, in main street. Protected parking.
Credit cards Access, Visa.
Terms Rooms 320–620 frs. Breakfast 48 frs. 10–30% reductions in winter. Children under 3 accommodated free in parents' room.

ST-FÉLIX-LAURAGAIS 31540 Haute-Garonne — Map 10

Auberge du Poids Public BUDGET — *Tel* 05.61.83.00.20 *Fax* 05.61.83.86.21

You can dine on the terrace, "with the sun going down over the mountains", at this excellent *auberge* in a pretty hilltop village amid rolling country south-east of Toulouse. The views extend to the snowy Pyrenees and the Montagne Noire to the east. The *Poids Public* is a low building, extended from the original village inn where produce was weighed (hence its name) before the proceeds were split between landlord and tenant. Today *patron*/chef Claude Taffarello wins a *Michelin* star *and* a red "Repas", plus two *toques* from *Gault Millau*, and praise again this year and last from our readers: "A delicious meal, beautifully served on a shady terrace facing a great sunny panorama." "Strong, rich fish soup with rouille, gigot roasted pink with garlic cloves." "A dish of tender mixed vegetables out of this world." "Excellent service: they go in for simultaneous raising of domes, but do it nicely." The "wonderful, old-fashioned bedrooms with mahogany bedheads" are admired, though some have found walls too thin. One couple had twin beds at right-angles. Front rooms are biggest, but suffer from traffic noise. (*Elizabeth Biggs, David Wyatt and Wendy Baron, and many others*)

Open All year, except Jan. Closed Sun evening Oct–Apr.
Rooms 4 triple, 9 double.
Facilities Salon, bar, restaurant; 2 function rooms. Small garden. Unsuitable for ♿.
Location On D622, 43 km SE of Toulouse. Back rooms quietest.
Credit cards Access, Amex, Visa.
Terms [1996] Rooms 250–295 frs. Breakfast 42 frs. D,B&B 265–300 frs per person. Set meals 135–305 frs; full alc 250–380 frs.

ST-FLORENT 20217 Haute-Corse — Map 17

Hôtel Bellevue — *Tel* 04.95.37.00.06 *Fax* 04.95.37.14.83

Set by the sea in a pretty pleasure-port west of Bastia, this much-liked holiday hotel has lovely gardens, a good swimming pool, and a noted restaurant, *La Table du Roy* (*Gault Millau toque* for its Mediterranean dishes). Returning devotees have written: "We were again delighted. François Prudent's food gets more delicious (fillets of rouget in thyme and herbs, etc); the daily half board is always tempting. Simple white walls, very friendly staff, and a view that justifies the name." Earlier comments: "It is chic, sophisticated and meticulously run, under the scrutiny of the charming Mme Loubet. The decor is fresh, with jolly prints and touches of bold colour." Light lunches are served by the pool, with views of sea and mountains, and dinner is taken in an open-air restaurant, also with sea views. There is a large, well-kept garden, and a shingly bathing beach is 700 metres away. (*H and CP, and others*) Some tour groups.

Open End Apr–early Oct.
Rooms 2 suites, 21 double. 3 on ground floor. Air-conditioning.
Facilities Salon / bar, restaurant; conference room. Garden: swimming pool, tennis, children's playground. Beach nearby.
Location 300 m from harbour. 23 km W of Bastia. Protected parking.
Credit cards All major cards accepted.
Terms Rooms 350–850 frs. Breakfast 50 frs. D,B&B double 700–1,700 frs. Set meals 150–180 frs.

ST-FLORENTIN 89600 Yonne — Map 9

La Grande Chaumière — *Tel* 03.86.35.15.12
3 rue des Capucins — *Fax* 03.86.35.33.14

This quietly elegant restaurant-with-rooms, an up-market Logis de France, is a long cream-coloured building off the main square of a pleasant little town near Auxerre. Owner / chef Jean-Pierre Bonvalot's efforts (*Michelin* star, *Gault Millau toque*) have again been admired this year: "An enjoyable meal in a very grand restaurant. Excellent breakfast, and a pleasant welcome. We had a suite full of mirrors." Others have written: "Staff charming. Lovely quiet room facing the garden." "Very trim and well kept. A delightful formal garden and terrace full of roses and Grecian statuary. We enjoyed foie gras, soufflé de brochet, with local chablis not overpriced." You can eat on a pretty patio. (*Joan Powell, J and JD*)

Open All year, except 21 Dec–17 Jan, end Aug–6 Sept. Closed Wed / midday Thurs except July / Aug.
Rooms 4 suites, 6 double. 1 in garden annexe.
Facilities Hall, bar, 2 dining rooms (no-smoking); terrace. Garden. River, fishing 1 km. Unsuitable for ♿.
Location Central. 31 km NE of Auxerre, on N77 to Troyes. Private parking.
Credit cards Access, Amex, Visa.
Terms Rooms: single 300–490 frs, double 350–550 frs, suite 650–750 frs. Breakfast 56 frs. Set meals 200–275 frs; full alc 470 frs.

ST-GALMIER 42330 Loire — Map 12

La Charpinière NEW/BUDGET — *Tel* 04.77.54.10.20
Fax 04.77.54.18.79

Just outside this small town north of St-Étienne is the large production plant of the Badoit mineral spring, and close by is this Relais du Silence, whose nominator preferred "a fine and expensive bottle of Condrieu" to go with his "quite excellent" meal of sautéed goats' cheese, poached monkfish and baby lamb cutlets in red wine sauce. It is a low, fairly modern building with a curious creeper-covered tower, next to a big lawn set with chairs and tables, and a swimming-pool. "The *patronne*, Annick Mazenod, was courteous. Breakfast was copious, and our room was spacious, with comfortable chairs, pleasant view of the grounds." (*Malcolm Seymour*)

Open All year.
Rooms 1 suite, 34 double. 17 on ground floor.
Facilities Lounge, TV room, bar, billiard room, 4 dining rooms (some no-smoking); fitness centre (65 frs): indoor swimming pool, sauna, hammam, exercise room. Garden: tennis, swimming pool (unheated), golf practice. Unsuitable for ♿.
Location 22 km N of St-Étienne, 2 km SW of St-Galmier by D12. Parking.
Credit cards Access, Diners, Visa.
Terms Rooms: 330–430 frs, suite 550–750 frs. Breakfast 50 frs. Set meals 95–240 frs; full alc 190 frs.

ST-GERMAIN-EN-LAYE 78100 Yvelines — Map 9

Cazaudehore-La Forestière — *Tel* 01.34.51.93.80
1 ave Kennedy — *Fax* 01.39.73.73.88

Just west of Paris, secluded in the heart of the forest of St-Germain, the Cazaudehore family run a fashionable restaurant bearing their name, and next door a stylish small hotel in a wooded garden. A recent plaudit: "We had excellent meals [*Gault Millau toque*], with good service, in a sophisticated ambience. Exciting salads: one was of warm quail. Exciting breads for breakfast, too. Our bedroom was beautifully furnished." The modern rooms and suites have prints and antiques; the dining room, with its fresh flowers and gleaming silverware, is packed at weekends with *le beau monde parisien* – a place to dress for dinner. Or you can dine in the garden. "In the flower-filled courtyard, we heard only the birdsong. The people were charming, service was swift but personal." (*EB, and others*)

Open All year. Restaurant closed Mon, except holidays.
Rooms 5 suites, 25 double.
Facilities 2 salons, 2 dining rooms; function rooms; courtyard. Garden. Unsuitable for ♿.
Location 1.5 km NW of St-Germain, by N284 and route des Mares.
Credit cards Access, Amex, Visa.
Terms Rooms: single 770 frs, double 980 frs, suite 1,350 frs. Breakfast 75 frs. Set meals 290–360 frs; full alc 440 frs. Children under 8 accommodated free in parents' room.

ST-GIRONS 09200 Ariège — Map 10

Château de Seignan — *Tel* 05.61.96.08.80
Montjoie — *Fax* 05.61.96.08.20

Just outside this little town near the Pyrenees, a trim white *château* in a park with ancient chestnut trees, by a river with a sandy beach. "Young M. de Bardies's family have lived here for 300 years," says its nominator. "He has now converted it into a lovely nine-room hotel. We spent a week, in a room furnished in genuine period style, overlooking the river and a terrace, where meals can be served when it's fine. The welcome was delightful, and the food delicious" (eg, fillet of sea-bass with oysters). Elegant period furnishing throughout. (*JBT*)

Open Apr–Oct.
Rooms 1 suite, 8 double.

Facilities Lounge, TV room, bar, restaurant; terrace. Park: garden, swimming pool, tennis. Unsuitable for ♿.
Location 2 km E of town, off D117.
Credit cards All major cards accepted.
Terms Rooms 360–890 frs, suite 600–1,200 frs. Breakfast 42 frs. D,B&B 372–650 frs per person. Set meals 98–380 frs; full alc 250 frs.

ST-HIPPOLYTE 68950 Haut-Rhin — Map 12

Le Parc NEW — *Tel* 03.89.73.00.06
6 rue du Parc — *Fax* 03.89.73.04.30

At centre of pretty village on Alsace Wine Road, 20 km N of Colmar, modern pink-and-red-façaded hotel energetically run by owner/chef Joseph Kientzel and his wife, with friendly, well-trained staff. Cheerful rooms in new wing, some with views. Good food, including Alsatian dishes, in main restaurant and Weinstube *(tavern, a local meeting place). Indoor swimming pool, sauna, hammam, gym, solarium. Garden. Closed 26 Feb–11 Mar, 18 Nov–2 Dec; restaurant closed Mon, 1–6 July. All major credit cards accepted. 42 rooms: 250–360 frs. Breakfast 50 frs. D,B&B 320–450 frs per person. Set meals 85–300 frs [1996].*

La Vignette BUDGET — *Tel* 04.89.73.00.17
Route du Vin — *Fax* 04.89.73.05.69

Attractive old half-timbered auberge *with cheerful service, very good food. Good modern rooms in new wing; simpler older ones. Lift, ramp. Lounge; friendly bar with pub atmosphere. Open 14 Feb–20 Dec; restaurant closed Wed. Access, Visa accepted. 25 rooms. B&B double 365–425 frs; D,B&B double 565–625 frs. Set meals 90–250 frs.*

ST-JEAN-DE-LUZ 64500 Pyrénées-Atlantiques — Map 10

Hôtel Parc Victoria — *Tel* 05.59.26.78.78
5 rue Cépé — *Fax* 05.59.26.78.08

A charming Basque resort-cum-fishing port, where Louis XIV married the Infanta Maria Teresa of Spain. Two blocks back from its broad sandy beach, in a big garden with handsome old trees, is this stylish new hotel in a stately white turn-of-the-century mansion (Relais & Châteaux). It is furnished in a mix of Art Deco and Art Nouveau styles, but with ultra-modern bathrooms. "A delightful friendly welcome, cool, quiet bedroom, very good food, beautiful gardens," runs a report this year, following previous enthusiasm: "A charming place. In the new restaurant by the magnificent swimming pool, the food was good and the service outstanding." "Breakfast on the terrace was as pastoral as ever." "The pool was filled with environment-friendly water; even sun-hats provided." (*PJC Wadsley, and others*)

Open 15 Mar–15 Nov.
Rooms 2 suites, 10 double. 1 on ground floor.
Facilities Salon, 2 dining rooms; terrace. Garden: swimming pool. Beach 200 m.
Location Central, but quiet (well-signposted). Private parking.
Credit cards All major cards accepted.
Terms Rooms: single 820–960 frs, double 1,050–1,280 frs, suite 1,250–1,500 frs. Breakfast 75 frs. Set lunch 180 frs, dinner 210 frs.

ST-JEAN-DU-BRUEL 12230 Aveyron Map 10

Hôtel du Midi-Papillon BUDGET *Tel* 05.65.62.26.04
Fax 05.65.62.12.97

For four generations the "delightful" Papillon family have owned and run this former *relais de poste*, now an unassuming Logis de France, in an old village on the river Doubie, in the western Cévennes. Though *very* popular with the Germans and British (including *Guide* readers), it manages to retain a true French rural ambience; and, as one reader puts it this year, it "still offers wonderful value for money, even with the pound at its present rate". All visitors warm to the Papillons, especially to Mme Butterfly herself, "so charming and efficient, with the gift of making everyone feel special". Service is "swift and personal", and the food wins a *Michelin* red "Repas" and *Gault Millau toque*. All agree that the standard of meals is "fantastic": the no-choice but varied menu for residents (main courses may include quail, civet de chevreuil, cassoulet, confit de canard aux lentilles) is far better than the usual *en pension* fare in France. Madame writes to us beguilingly of the local produce – of pigs *"élevés par un paysan du coin,* of mushrooms gathered by shepherds as they watch their flocks on the Causse du Larzac – and points out that *"la quasi-totalité"* of all fruit and vegetables used comes from the hotel's garden. (*JP Berryman, PE Carter, and others*) Improvements go ahead – a new lounge and heated swimming pool, much room and bar renovation.

Open 25 Mar–11 Nov.
Rooms 1 suite, 17 double, 1 single. 2 pairs communicating rooms in annexe.
Facilities Ramps. Salon, TV room, bar, 3 dining rooms (2 no-smoking); terrace. Garden: swimming pool, whirlpool; on river, fishing. Unsuitable for ♿.
Location 40 km SE of Millau on D991; 20 km E of N9. Public parking.
Credit cards Access, Visa.
Terms Rooms: single 81 frs, double 128–200 frs, suite 326 frs. Breakfast 24 frs. D,B&B double 360–452 frs. Set meals 74–204 frs; full alc 160 frs.

ST-LÉONARD-DE-NOBLAT 87400 Haute-Vienne Map 10

Le Grand Saint-Léonard NEW/BUDGET *Tel* 05.55.56.18.18
23 avenue Champs-de-Mars *Fax* 05.55.56.98.32

In porcelain-making town 19 km E of Limoges, small and spruce hostelry, family-run and well modernised, with period furnishings. Good varied food (Gault Millau toque)*; smallish but well-kept rooms, double-glazed. Closed 15 Dec–15 Jan, Mon (except in high summer). All major credit cards accepted. 14 rooms: 270–300 frs. Breakfast 45 frs. D,B&B 290–310 frs per person. Set meals 115–290 frs [1996]. Fuller reports welcome.*

ST-MALO 35400 Ille-et-Vilaine Map 8

Le Valmarin *Tel* 02.99.81.94.76
7 rue Jean XXIII *Fax* 02.99.81.30.03

In suburb of St-Servan, graceful creeper-clad 18th-century house in large grounds near beach and port, newly renovated as civilised B&B: "Absolutely beautiful, tremendous breakfasts." Sumptuous furnishings, 12 airy rooms, large bathrooms, all now renovated; quietest rooms face gardens at rear.

Closed 16 Nov–24 Dec, 8 Jan–14 Feb. Access, Amex, Visa accepted. Rooms 500–700 frs. Breakfast 55 frs.

ST-MARTIAL-VIVEYROLS 24320 Dordogne — Map 10

Les Aiguillons BUDGET — *Tel* 05.53.91.07.55
Beuil — *Fax* 05.53.90.40.97

In remote Périgord countryside, 5 km NW of Verteillac, 47 km S of Angoulême, charming modern hostelry, good value: warm welcome; 8 attractive rooms, some on ground floor; spruce restaurant offering Gault Millau-*betoque'd cooking of owner Christophe Beeuwsaert. Garden: swimming pool (unheated), views of valley. Open Mar–Dec. Restaurant closed Sun evening/Mon in low season. Ramps. Access, Visa accepted. B&B double 420 frs; D,B&B 350 frs per person. Set meals 120–225 frs.*

ST-MARTIN-EN-BRESSE 71620 Saône-et-Loire — Map 12

Au Puits Enchanté BUDGET — *Tel* 03.85.47.71.96
Route de Verdun — *Fax* 03.85.47.74.58

Jacky Château's hotel is not itself a *château*, nor an enchanted well, but a modest white-walled Logis de France in a Burgundy village east of Chalon-sur-Saône. Friendly and family-run, it has pleased recent visitors: "Quiet, and an excellent dinner." "Poulet de Bresse full of flavours." "Recommended by us all. A delightfully tasty navarin of lamb. Helpful owners. Willing service, much of it by the grandparents." Pretty bedrooms and dining room. (*PT, and others*)

Open All year, except 8–24 Jan, 23 Feb–3 Mar, Tues.
Rooms 13 double. Some on ground floor.
Facilities Lounges, TV room, bar, restaurant. Garden.
Location In village, 17 km E of Chalon-sur-Saône. Parking.
Credit cards Access, Visa.
Terms Rooms 170–280 frs. Breakfast 37 frs. D,B&B double 205–370 frs per person. Set meals 95–220 frs; full alc 180 frs.

ST-MARTIN-VALMEROUX 15140 Cantal — Map 10

Hostellerie de la Maronne — *Tel* 04.71.69.20.33
Le Theil — *Fax* 04.71.69.28.22

In the lush valley of the Maronne, near the superb Renaissance hill-village of Salers, stands this 19th-century Auvergnat house, now a Relais de Silence, in its own informal garden. It is owned and run by Alain de Cock and his Malagasy wife (she does the cooking), with a friendly staff. Another eulogy came this year: "Quietly ironic host who has an efficiently run hotel in a near-idyllic landscape. Good service and food: a luscious langoustine ravioli and a superb Hermitage are fond memories. We could have stayed weeks." An earlier view: "The only sounds are the bells on the mahogany-red Salers cattle and the sheep grazing nearby. Some rooms have a south-facing balcony and comfortable armchairs. There's a good secluded small swimming pool and one tennis court. The bar is cosy but over-endowed with Scotch malt whiskies to the detriment of French drinks. Excellent local cheeses, crème brûlée well up to the standard of Trinity, Cambridge." "The *demi-pension* meals were exceptional value; good breakfast, too." M. de Cock has been called "laid back" by readers. But he is hands-on enough to have done lots of refurbishing this year, he tells us. (*PJC Wadsley*)

Open 1 Apr–5 Nov.
Rooms 1 suite, 20 double. Some on ground floor.
Facilities Lift, ramps. Salon, bar, breakfast room, restaurant; sauna; terrace. Garden: swimming pool, tennis.
Location Outside hamlet of Le Theil, 3 km E of St-Martin-Valmeroux on D37. Parking.
Credit cards Access, Amex, Visa.
Terms Rooms 460–580 frs, suite 650–700 frs. Breakfast 60 frs. D,B&B 440–500 frs per person. Set meals 150–250 frs.

ST-PALAIS-SUR-MER 17420 Charente-Maritime — Map 10

Hôtel Primavera NEW

12 rue du Brick

Tel 05.46.23.20.35
Fax 05.46.23.28.78

This pleasant white *belle époque* "folly", built as a wealthy private house, stands in its own large gardens close to the sea, in a small town near the big resort of Royan. There's a rocky beach at 300 metres, and good bathing at 800 metres. Now a Relais du Silence, the hotel makes its *Guide* debut: "It is a family holiday hotel, and is run like one, with Madame very much in charge. In our room, in a nearby annexe, all was correct; and it had period furniture. An excellent holiday hotel dinner, in a spacious airy room with super sea views." Some rooms have a balcony, also with that view. The heated covered pool is large. (*Martin and Karen Oldridge*)

Open All year, except 12–26 Feb, 1–25 Dec. Restaurant closed Tues evening/Wed Oct–Mar.
Rooms 45 double. Some with balcony. 22 in 2 nearby annexes.
Facilities Lift. 2 salons, breakfast room, restaurant; conference room; indoor swimming pool. Garden: tennis. Unsuitable for ♿.
Location By sea, 1.5 km W of town centre, 7 km NW of Royan. Parking.
Credit cards All major cards accepted.
Terms [1996] Rooms 260–360 frs, suite 440–620 frs. Breakfast 50 frs. D,B&B 310–507 frs per person. Set meals 115–225 frs; alc 250 frs.

Hôtel Téthys BUDGET

Plage de Nauzan

Tel 05.46.23.33.61

On bluff above sandy beach 1.5 km SE of St-Palais, towards big resort of Royan, at mouth of Gironde, pleasant unassuming seaside hotel, family run ("Mme Fouché is a dear"). Good simple food and bedrooms. Open May–Sept. Access, Visa accepted. 23 rooms: 270–330 frs. Breakfast 35 frs. D,B&B 300–350 frs per person. Set meals 95–200 frs [1996].

> "Budget" labels indicate hotels offering accommodation for up to about £50 (or its foreign currency equivalent) for dinner, bed and breakfast, or £30 for B&B and £20 for an evening meal. But we would emphasise that this is a rough guide only, and does not always apply to single rooms or in high season.

ST PATRICE 37130 Indre-et-Loire — Map 8

Château de Rochecotte — *Tel* 02.47.96.16.16
Fax 02.47.96.90.59

Set just across the Loire from the large romantic Château d'Ussé, this handsome white 18th-century pile is also quite romantic (Talleyrand gave it to the Duchesse de Dino). *Gault Millau*, bestowing two *toques* for cuisine, calls it *"le plus séduisant château-hôtel de la région"*, and our readers too were much impressed this year: "It is set amid 17 acres of old forest, rich with birds and wildlife. A formal 18th-century garden leads to the swimming pool. The landscaped Italian terrace, spectacularly lit at night, has a lily-pond teeming with goldfish at one end, a wonderful unrestored private chapel at the other. An elegant and charming young woman greeted us. All the public rooms, including the library, are exquisitely decorated: the warm pastel colours and avant-garde lighting indicated the touch of an interior designer. But though grand the *château* has an un-museum-like lived-in quality: the sound of children's laughter, toys, the alsatian dog sleeping in the sun, kittens at play, all were reminders that this is also the home of the Pasquier family owners. Our bedroom was spacious, elegantly but comfortably furnished; housekeeping was faultless. Dinner was formal, presented with the flair of a well-choreographed ballet, and food was excellent. When I was feeling unwell, a plate of best-ever scrambled eggs, plus fruit, was sent to our room: the cost of my half-board dinner was deducted, and we were charged only 30 frs. Other guests? The elegant, elderly patrician French couple playing bezique on the terrace. The good-looking jeans-clad twosome who swept up in a Rolls-Royce, maybe minor royalty off-duty. The silk-scarved Gauloises-smoking roué, a master of the expansive Gallic gesture, eager to impress his doe-eyed gymslip-clad young mistress. Rochecotte has a timeless elegance." And so has that report of *Jennifer and David Williams*.

Open All year, except Feb, Christmas.
Rooms 3 suites, 29 double. 4 in nearby annexe.
Facilities 2 lounges, breakfast room, library, 3 dining rooms (1 no-smoking); terrace. Garden: swimming pool. Unsuitable for ♿.
Location 30 km W of Tours. 10 km W of Langeais, off D 35 to Bourgueil. Parking.
Credit cards All major cards accepted.
Terms Rooms 580–930 frs, suite 1,250 frs. Breakfast 55 frs. D,B&B double 1,010–1,630 frs. Set meals 195 frs, 285 frs; full alc 350 frs.

ST-PAUL-DE-VENCE 06570 Alpes-Maritimes — Map 11

Hôtel Le Hameau — *Tel* 04.93.32.80.24
528 route de la Colle — *Fax* 04.93.32.55.75

"Charming"; "we spent six days of unqualified pleasure" – again this year, enthusiasm has rolled in for this nicely converted 18th-century farmhouse. It stands on a hillside outside touristy St-Paul, well away from the crowds and chaos of the coast. "The setting, views and swimming pool were delightful. Service was diligent. Breakfast average, but with home-made marmalade." Earlier accounts: "Comfortable rooms with easy chairs, substantial breakfasts, cheerful and helpful staff." "A beautiful view from our bedroom of the walled hill-village of St-Paul." "Bedroom slightly shabby, but owner's friendly welcome more than made up." The low white buildings are on several levels. You can breakfast amid flowerbeds, trellised arbours and citrus trees. There's a spacious lounge with a big stone fireplace, tables for playing games, and lots of books in English and French. The white-walled bedrooms are attractively furnished in country style, with many antiques. Rooms vary in size and shape, some being a bit low-ceilinged and dark. Some have a kitchenette. No restaurant. (*David Lodge, Nicholas Roberts, and others*) Peaceful, save that "ferocious dogs bark from nearby houses".

Open 15 Feb–15 Nov, 22 Dec–6 Jan.
Rooms 3 suites, 13 double, 1 single. In 4 different buildings. Air-conditioning.
Facilities Lounge with TV, library, breakfast room (no-smoking); terraces. Garden: swimming pool. Unsuitable for ♿.
Location 1 km SW of St-Paul on D7 to La Colle. Garages, closed parking.
Credit cards Access, Visa.
Terms Rooms 400–620 frs, suite 700–720 frs. Breakfast 55 frs.

ST-QUENTIN-SUR-LE-HOMME 50220 Manche — Map 8

Le Gué du Holme NEW — *Tel* 02.33.60.63.76
Fax 02.33.60.06.77

In village 5 km SE of Avranches, by D78, spruce and soigné *little restaurant-with-rooms (Logis de France), run by owner/chef Michel Leroux and "very welcoming" wife Annie. Very good food in small, chic dining room. Comfort, good period furniture. Closed 23 Dec–18 Jan, Sat lunch/dinner Sun Oct–Easter. All major credit cards accepted. 10 rooms: 400–500 frs. Breakfast 50 frs. D,B&B 480–500 frs per person. Set meals 140–365 frs.*

ST-RÉMY-DE-PROVENCE 13533 Bouches-du-Rhône — Map 11

Les Antiques — *Tel* 04.90.92.03.02
15 avenue Pasteur — *Fax* 04.90.92.50.40

On the southern edge of St-Rémy, near the mental hospital where Van Gogh spent a year, are the remarkable Roman remains of Les Antiques (Glanum). Hence the name of this hotel, a finely converted 19th-century mansion near the town centre. It has a grand entrance with marble floors and tapestries, and comfortable and airy bedrooms. You can stay in the main building, or in a *pavillon*, which most readers prefer. Reports this year were again enthusiastic. "Delightful. Grand, old and a little worn, but a most pleasant sort of seediness. Friendly staff, excellent breakfast in a wonderful sun room facing the large garden." "Our spacious pavilion room had its own terrace with table, chairs and parasol. Lovely gardens, good pool, elegant public rooms. But breakfast service was disorganised." "Such friendliness." (*Monte Dale Witte, JR Osborne, and others*) Some plumbing noises, and some bathrooms are tiny. Bedrooms vary in size, and those by the road are within earshot of the morning traffic.

Open 26 Mar–20 Oct.
Rooms 26 double, 1 single. 10 on ground floor.
Facilities 3 salons, TV room, breakfast veranda (no-smoking). Large grounds: swimming pool (unheated). Unsuitable for ♿.
Location Central. Closed parking.

Credit cards All major cards accepted.
Terms Rooms 380–600 frs. Breakfast 62 frs.

ST-SATURNIN-DE-LENNE 12560 Aveyron — Map 10

Château St-Saturnin

Tel 05.65.70.36.00
Fax 05.65.70.36.19

An 18th-century *château*, elegantly converted, in a small village south of the Lot valley. It is now run as a personal hotel by its Anglo-American owners, Cliff and Victoria Lenton. The spacious bedrooms are furnished in period style; the lovely public rooms include a library and a music room. There's a large garden, a terrace, and an outdoor pool. Mrs Lenton's cooking (she has just done training with Prue Leith in London) has been called French-Californian, using local ingredients. Recent American guests were delighted: "A warm greeting, and caring attention throughout our stay. Victoria prepared us a superb dinner. Bedrooms are high-ceilinged, luxurious." An English visitor, liking the rooms and setting, found the family-style informality a bit disconcerting: but the Lentons now write to us that this has "been replaced by a more professional approach to service". (*BBF and RLF*) Unusually for France, there is no smoking in the bedrooms or in most public rooms.

Open All year, except 8 Jan–30 March. Restaurant closed midday, Sun evening.
Rooms 3 suites (for 3 or 4), 9 double. 1 on ground floor, suitable for ♿.
Facilities Lounge, library/TV/games room, bar, dining room; terrace. Garden: swimming pool, croquet.
Location In village, 42 km E of Rodez, 8 km SE of St-Geniez. *Autoroute* A75 exit 41.
Restriction No smoking, except TV room/bar.
Credit cards Access, Amex, Visa.
Terms [1996] Rooms 600–900 frs. Breakfast 50 frs. D,B&B (3 nights min) 475–1,000 frs per person. Picnic lunch 90 frs. Set dinner 120–200 frs. "Adventures for food lovers", painting courses, Christmas break.

ST-SERNIN-SUR-RANCE 12380 Aveyron — Map 10

Hôtel Carayon BUDGET

Place du Fort

Tel 05.65.98.19.19
Fax 05.65.99.69.26

In a village on the Albi–Millau road, just south of the lovely Tarn valley, is this rural Logis de France. Now much enlarged and modernised by its "cheerful and helpful" *patron*/chef, Pierre Carayon (he spent a year at the *Savoy* in London), it remains essentially a family affair, with elegant Claudette Carayon playing front-of-house. There are two panoramic dining rooms above the valley, and *Michelin* grants a red "Repas", notably for the inexpensive regional *menu rouergat*. Many rooms share the view across the valley; the "spacious and modern" ones in the new wing on the hillside are better than the more basic ones in the old building. The garden offers diversions for children, and a second swimming pool has just been built. M. Carayon is "quite an ambitious empire-builder", and again this year one reader felt that service and quality were suffering from the expansion and the "holiday camp style". But another wrote: "If this is trying too much it succeeds, and should serve as an example to other hoteliers of how to provide excellent rooms, service and meals at acceptable cost. The 119 frs [1996] seven-course menu was tremendous value. On a visit in September, we found all rooms full, but M. Carayon offered us a charming room in his mother's house!"

Open All year, except Nov, Sun evening/Mon in low season.
Rooms 60. Most with bath/shower. Some in buildings in grounds. Some on ground floor. 3 adapted for ♿.
Facilities Lifts. 2 salons, 2 TV rooms, 2 bars, restaurant; terrace. Park: 2 swimming pools (unheated), sauna, tennis, children's playground, table-tennis, mini-golf; river: fishing.
Location Central. 50 km E of Albi on D999. Parking.
Credit cards All major cards accepted.
Terms Rooms 199–700 frs. Breakfast 35 frs. Set meals 75–300 frs; full alc 200–300 frs.

ST-VAAST-LA-HOUGUE 50550 Manche — Map 8

Hôtel de France BUDGET — *Tel* 02.33.54.42.26
Restaurant des Fuchsias — *Fax* 02.33.43.46.79

Before the battle of Crécy, Edward III landed his troops at this oyster-breeding port east of Cherbourg. Today troupes of Britons still land at the Brix family's appealing Logis de France in the village centre. It is very pretty, festooned indeed with red fuchsias, and has a cobbled courtyard and thatched canopy. *Michelin* gives a red "Repas" and *Gault Millau* a *toque* for the food. Lots more praise in 1995–96: "Staff delightful, food excellent, room comfortable if a bit shabby." "On New Year's Eve, we had an outstanding five-course dinner, with the gardens candlelit." "You can dine in the lovely walled garden, complete with banana tree, or in an elegant new conservatory with smart green awnings and big murals. Polished service by courteous young men in white jackets. It's quite a smart place now, but menus are very good value, with the accent on fresh local fish, including oysters. Good soupe de poissons, fish cassoulet, crème brûlée." No main lounge, but plenty of sitting space. (*Mr and Mrs WM Lee, Ian Dewey, and others*)

Open All year, except 5 Jan–22 Feb. Closed Mon mid-Sept–mid-May, Tues midday mid-Nov–Mar.
Rooms 1 suite, 29 double, 3 single. 14 across garden. 1 on ground floor.
Facilities Ramps. 2 salons, bar, 2 dining rooms; conference room; free chamber music concerts last 10 days Aug. Garden: bicycle hire. Sandy beach, tennis nearby.
Location In village, 29 km E of Cherbourg. Public parking.
Credit cards All major cards accepted.
Terms Rooms: single 150 frs, double 300–425 frs, suite 495 frs. Breakfast 43 frs. D,B&B 295–385 frs per person. Set meals 78–265 frs; full alc 230 frs.

Hôtel La Granitière NEW — *Tel* 02.33.54.58.99
74 rue du Maréchal Foch — *Fax* 02.33.20.34.91

Like Brittany, this part of western Normandy is made of granite. Hence the name of this neat "granite-mason's house", now a tiny, very *soigné* hotel, set back from the sea in its own grounds. "Our room was very pretty, neatly furnished, with a good bathroom," says its nominator. "The small dining room had lots of atmosphere, with stone walls, antiques; dinner was enjoyable and breakfast good. An open wood fire blazed. Service was efficient and charming." (*Jill Douglas*)

Open All year, except 15 Feb–20 Mar, Tues in low season.
Rooms 1 suite, 8 double, 1 single. Some with air-conditioning.
Facilities Salon/bar, restaurant. Garden. Sandy beach 300 m. Unsuitable for ♿.
Location On edge of village, which is 29 km E of Cherbourg. Safe parking.
Credit cards All major cards accepted.
Terms Rooms 285–458 frs, suite 550–750 frs. Breakfast 40 frs. D,B&B double 594–746 frs. Set meals 85–190 frs; full alc 230 frs.

STE-ANNE-LA-PALUD 29550 Finistère — Map 8

Hôtel de la Plage

Tel 02.98.92.50.12
Fax 02.98.92.56.54

With its long sandy beach, and food unusually good for a seasonal seaside hotel (*Michelin* star, *Gault Millau toque*), the Le Coz family's stylish and quite expensive *Plage* continues mainly to please readers. "Our room was smallish, but with an amazing sea view. The food is outstanding: a whole lobster each, or a dozen langoustines, on the *demi-pension* menu, which changes daily. Breakfast came with high-quality fruit salads and a glorious selection of tiny brioches and croissants." Earlier views: "A lovely place oozing atmosphere, with its waitresses in Breton costume and its bar in a thatched cottage." "The restaurant tries to keep its French flavour in the face of a lot of foreigners, by insisting upon guests using French." You eat char-grilled lobster "with a special pinny draped tenderly round you by a maternal waitress". But another reader felt that the hotel "favoured minimum contact with guests". (*P and SR, and others*) Some front rooms can be noisy; others may have thin party walls. Surprisingly, the hotel has few facilities for small children.

Open Apr–mid-Nov.
Rooms 5 suites, 24 double, 1 single. 2 on ground floor.
Facilities 2 lifts, ramps. Salons, TV room, bar, restaurant; conference facilities; sauna. Garden: tennis, swimming pool; safe, sandy beach.
Location On coast, W of Plonevez-Porzay by D61. Carpark.
Credit cards All major cards accepted.
Terms [1996] Rooms 650–1,000 frs, suite 1,100–1,300 frs. Breakfast 75 frs. D,B&B 700–950 frs per person. Set meals 220 frs.

STE-PREUVE 02350 Aisne — Map 9

Château de Barive

Tel 03.23.22.15.15
Fax 03.23.22.08.39

This big 18th-century hunting lodge, with a spacious courtyard, stands alone on the Picardy plain east of Laon (fine hilltop cathedral). Now a hotel, it has a German owner, Senator Helmut Aurenz, and a Dutch manageress, whose husband, Jos Bergman, is chef. He wins two *Gault Millau toques* for such dishes as warm oysters with caviar – but there's also "*petit déjeuner anglais sur demande*". More praise in 1996: "We were delighted. An enormous room, with two sofas and a basket of sweets – to my small son's delight. Dinner was delicious, staff friendly." "Dinner and breakfast excellent." There's a spacious terrace. Rooms are luxurious, with period furnishings. (*I and E Kemahli, Prof. P and Mrs A Robson, LM*)

Open All year, except mid-Dec–mid-Jan.
Rooms 3 suites, 10 double, 1 single.
Facilities Lounge, restaurant, conservatory; conference facilities; indoor swimming pool, sauna; terrace. Garden: tennis. Unsuitable for ♿.
Location 23 km NE of Laon. Left off road between Sissonne and Ste-Preuve.
Credit cards All major cards accepted.
Terms Rooms: single 380 frs, double 480 frs, suite 880 frs. Breakfast 55 frs. D,B&B 460–660 frs per person. Set meals 130–330 frs; full alc 380 frs.

SAINTES 17100 Charente-Maritime — Map 10

Relais du Bois St-Georges — *Tel* 05.46.93.50.99
Rue de Royan, Cours Genêt — *Fax* 05.46.93.34.93

This stylish and most original hotel stands on the outskirts of a fascinating town, known for its Roman amphitheatre, lovely Romanesque churches and July music festival. An inspector's recent report: "The hotel is the love-child of Jérôme Emery, its super-dedicated owner, who has converted it from an old farm. Two buildings are 12th-century, now high-tech conference rooms decked out in medieval style. The spacious open-plan foyer / salon / restaurant has an amazing decor of beams, old candlesticks, tapestries, etc, all a bit contrived, but glamorous. And right *in* the salon, at one end, is the small heated swimming pool bedecked with Roman statuary: no, we didn't find that kitschy either. Through picture windows it faces the glorious landscaped garden, with a floodlit lake and peacocks. Here we dined on the terrace: the young chef Philippe Gault wins two *toques* from his namesake (no kin), but we were a bit disappointed, except for the lovely dessert of soupe froide de fruits rouges and the super Bordeaux wines. Service was impeccable. The bedrooms in the older wing are large, and well equipped. In the newer block are the smaller, famously gimmicky rooms: one looks like a submarine; another is an igloo; a third, Monte Cristo's prison, with the loo hidden in a treasure-chest. But don't be put off. It really is a lovely hotel."

Open All year.
Rooms 3 suites, 27 double. Some no-smoking. 6 on ground floor, with access for ♿.
Facilities Lounge, TV room, 2 bars, restaurant; conference facilities; indoor swimming pool; terrace (meal service in summer). 14-acre grounds: gardens, croquet, *boules*, table-tennis, lake, jogging track. Tennis, golf, riding nearby.
Location W outskirts. 2 km from *autoroute* A10 exit 35. Garage.
Credit cards Access, Visa.
Terms Rooms: single 380–750 frs, double 550–900 frs, suite 1,150–1,800 frs. Breakfast 74 frs. Set meals 190–480 frs; full alc 240–290 frs.

LES STES-MARIES-DE-LA-MER 13460 Bouches-du-Rhône — Map 11

L'Étrier Camarguais — *Tel* 04.90.97.81.14
Chemin bas des Launes — *Fax* 04.90.97.88.11

On the edge of the Camargue just north of Les Stes-Maries, the *Étrier* (stirrup) is one of several ranch-like hotels that cater mainly for riders: it has its own herd of white Camarguais horses for hire to guests by the hour (not cheap). "Excellent all round," says a recent visitor. "Friendly staff, good food and service. Our beautiful room had a loft for the children's beds, and a glass door looking on to a canal with horses, ducks etc. The big swimming pool was delightful. The stables provide a chance to see the Camargue wildlife close up." It's a spacious, breezy and youthfully informal place, with log-cabin decor; bedrooms, in chalets in the garden, have their own patio. Dinner may include a fish buffet. The nearby disco is just out of earshot. Les Stes-Maries's gipsy festival, held every 23–27 May, is worth seeing. (*C and LS*)

Open 1 Apr–15 Oct.
Rooms 27 double.
Facilities Bar, breakfast room, restaurant; disco; conference facilities; terrace. Garden: swimming pool (unheated), tennis, riding. Sea 2 km.
Location 3 km N of town, just off N570 to Arles.
Credit cards All major cards accepted.
Terms Rooms 400–540 frs. Breakfast 50 frs. D,B&B: single 520–660 frs, double 840–980 frs. Set meals 170 frs; full alc 250 frs.

SARS-POTERIES 59216 Nord — Map 9

Hôtel Fleuri BUDGET — *Tel* 03.27.61.62.72
65 rue du Général de Gaulle

"Intriguing is the word – we recommend it," runs renewed praise this year for this small, unusual B&B hotel in a village near the Belgian border. Next to it is a more ambitious restaurant, *L'Auberge Fleurie*, very pretty and separately owned and managed. A reader arrived "in none too good a mood after visiting towns straight out of *Germinal*", but then found all just as described in this earlier report: "The hotel, mildly eccentric, is run by identical twins, Claudine and Thérèse, and they both love pink. Just about everything is pink, from the flowers and curtains to the handles on the breakfast knives and spoons. Our bedroom was basic but clean, with a view of the courtyard; huge antique furniture, marble bedside lockers, tiled floor with sheepskin rugs, but the bed-springs did twang. Small, simple bathroom. Breakfast, simple but good, is served communally at a large table in the hall, and it was hilarious. The *Auberge*, a handsome white roadside inn, surrounded by neat lawns and flower-beds, is simply but elegantly decorated. We loved its atmosphere and the service was charming. Owner/chef Alain Lequy's cooking was excellent [*Michelin* star, *Gault Millau toque*]: salade de pigeonneau aux girolles, sandre au giniève de Houlle." There's a pretty patio where you can dine out in summer. (*JM Eunson*) Some traffic noise.

Open All year, except Feb. *Auberge* closed Mon, 16 Jan–8 Feb, 16–31 Aug.
Rooms 3 double, 8 single.
Facilities Salon. Garden: tennis. Unsuitable for ♿.
Location In village, on D962 10 km NE of Avesnes. Courtyard parking.
Credit cards Hotel: Visa. Restaurant: all major cards accepted.
Terms Rooms 235–285 frs. Breakfast 40 frs. Set meals (*Auberge*) 150–320 frs; alc 210–330 frs.

****

Traveller's tale The service at one hotel we stayed at displayed a staggering over-confidence. The waiter volunteered to my wife as she sat down at table that he liked her dress, but it reminded him of Tarzan and Jane. This would have been unacceptable in a corner café, let alone a *Michelin*-starred restaurant.

****

SAUMUR 49400 Maine-et-Loire Map 8

Hôtel Anne d'Anjou *Tel* 02.41.67.30.30
32 quai Mayaud *Fax* 02.41.67.51.00

This enticing hotel has a fine setting, beside the broad Loire and below the great hilltop castle of Louis X. Owned and run by Yves and Anne-Marie Touzé, it is "a beautifully restored" 18th-century building with a garden. "Bedrooms are simple and modern; views are of the river or castle. Buffet breakfast is adequate. The hotel's *Menestrels* restaurant is first class, in an old converted barn with glass roof: very clever cooking, and thank God we have moved away from the pretentious minute portions of a few years ago." There's a noble stairway; some bedrooms are in Empire style, with decorated panelled walls. (*MAF, endorsed this year by Anthea Morton*)

Open All year, except 23 Dec–4 Jan.
Rooms 2 suites, 43 double, 5 single. Some on ground floor.
Facilities Lift. 2 salons, restaurant. Garden.
Location Central (double glazing). Parking.
Credit cards All major cards accepted.
Terms Rooms: single 280 frs, double 430–560 frs. Breakfast 50 frs. Set meals 160–340 frs; full alc 320 frs.

SAUVETERRE-DE-COMMINGES 31510 Haute-Garonne Map 10

Hostellerie des 7 Molles *Tel* 05.61.88.30.87
Fax 05.61.88.36.42

This modern white-fronted hotel, quite smart yet informal, lies in a wooded valley of the Pyrenean foothills. Well run by a pleasant couple, the Ferrans, it is admired for its service, comfort and food (*Gault Millau toque*), but less for its decor: "It may lack the usual stylishness of many other Relais & Châteaux hotels – eg, the Holiday Inn-type decor in the refurbished corridors. But it has the feel of a large family home, with service always professional yet also very warm. Our large, comfortable room has an old-fashioned feel, and its balcony overlooks the lush green valley. Meals have been excellent: a wonderful gigot of milk-fed lamb, and good breakfasts with thick local yogurt." Others have written: "Our large bedroom was beautifully appointed in soft colours; breakfast was served on our balcony facing the mountains." Gilles Ferran's cooking has been called "a balanced mixture of *nouvelle cuisine* and Pyrenean traditional": "he knows the secret hiding-places of the coveted boletus mushroom," says his brochure. Swimming pool and tennis court in the lawned garden; table-tennis in the gazebo. "Sounds of cowbells" – but also some of traffic in front rooms.

Open All year, except 2 Jan–31 Mar, Nov, Tues in low season.
Rooms 2 suites, 15 double, 2 single. Some with balcony.
Facilities Lift. Salon, bar, 2 dining rooms. Garden: swimming pool, tennis.
Location At Gesset, 2 km SE of Sauveterre, 13 km SW of St-Gaudens. Parking.
Credit cards All major cards accepted.
Terms Rooms: single 350–690 frs, double 420–780 frs, suite 845–920 frs. Breakfast 75 frs. Set meals 190–295 frs; full alc 300 frs.

SÉES 61500 Orne — Map 8

L'Ile de Sées BUDGET — *Tel* 02.33.27.98.65
Macé — *Fax* 02.33.28.41.22

A picturesque ivy-covered manor, amid lush pastoral country in southern Normandy. It is a modestly priced Logis de France, yet, says a reader this year, "with tennis courts, and manicured garden areas for relaxation amid umbrella'd groups and sunbathing loungers, it has the paraphernalia of a classy French establishment". It is owned and run by the Orcier family, with a cheerful staff, and again this year most – though not quite all – reports are favourable. "Excellent: Madame a great character, lovely garden, good food especially those delicious Normandy cheeses." "Madame runs the place with a refreshing and brisk directness. A good dinner." Earlier views: "Madame bustles and sings, running the place well. We liked the pretty garden terrace." "Breakfast with big bowls of fromage frais and fruit salad." (*J and A Larken, Anthea Morton, SN, and others*) However, the rooms are modest ("clean, but utilitarian"), and there have again been some reports of imperfect upkeep, even of poor food.

Open All year, except Christmas. Closed Sun evening/Mon.
Rooms 16 double. Some on ground floor.
Facilities Bar, restaurant; conference/function facilities; terrace. Garden: tennis. Unsuitable for ♿.
Location At Macé, 5 km N of Sées, via D303 off N158 Sées–Argentan. Private parking.
Credit cards Access, Visa.
Terms Rooms 290–310 frs. Breakfast 35 frs. Set meals 78–170 frs. Children under 3 accommodated free.

SÉGOS 32400 Gers — Map 10

Domaine de Bassibé — *Tel* 05.62.09.46.71
Fax 05.62.08.40.15

In quiet rolling countryside north of Pau, a handsome creeper-covered 18th-century farmhouse converted into a luxurious small hotel (Relais & Châteaux), where Sylvie and Olivier Lacroix are "charming and urbane hosts". There's an attractive pool, with a terrace for drinks. "We stayed a week and found it marvellous, in friendliness, service, bedrooms and food." That recent report backs previous praise: "All is enchantment, in the best French country house style. The salons are cool and inviting, with interesting books. Our ground-floor room, in the sophisticatedly rustic annexe, opened on to a meadow full of wild flowers. Service is by smiling waitresses and the food is excellent and inventive [*Gault Millau toque*] but with too little choice on the cheaper menus." (*MLNF*) "The house hound did invade our room one morning, but with the friendliest of demeanours." Insects, less friendly, sometimes do so too.

Open All year, except 2 Jan–20 Mar. Restaurant closed Tues/midday Wed in low season.
Rooms 7 suites, 11 double. 10 in annexe. Some on ground floor.
Facilities 2 lounges, bar, restaurant; terrace. Park: swimming pool.
Location 8 km S of Aire-sur-l'Adour, just E of N134 to Pau.
Credit cards All major cards accepted.

Terms [1996] Rooms 650–825 frs. Breakfast 75 frs. D,B&B 650–910 frs per person. Set meals 180–250 frs.

SÉGURET 84110 Vaucluse Map 11

La Table du Comtat *Tel* 04.90.46.91.49
Fax 04.90.46.94.27

The *Table* is noted for its *table (Michelin* star, *Gault Millau toque)*, provided by owner/chef Franck Gomez. It has a superb setting, too, above the Rhône vineyards, with wide views of the plain. It is a chic restaurant-with-rooms in a fine 15th-century house, just above the ancient hill-village of Séguret (a key centre of Provençal culture, with its Christmas church pageant and craftsmen who make *santons*; Vaison and Orange are nearby). Recent visitors have enjoyed such dishes as cold fish soup with langoustines, guinea fowl with summer fruits. "The local wine was tangy and characterful. M. Gomez is friendly and endearing, and the view from our room will live in the memory." Many diners are "smart and international". It is best to eat by daylight, by a window seat; the place is a bit dull and formal after dark. The small *piscine*, floodlit at night below its high rock, is "a stunner". (*GW, JAP, and others*) One returning devotee this year found the food less good than usual.

Open 6 Mar–23 Nov, 11 Dec–30 Jan. Closed Tues evening/Wed except 1 July–23 Sept.
Rooms 8 double.
Facilities Salon, 2 dining rooms; terrace. Small garden: swimming pool (unheated). Unsuitable for ♿.
Location Off D23, 8 km S of Vaison-la-Romaine, at entrance to Séguret. Parking.
Credit cards All major cards accepted.
Terms [1996] Rooms: single 400–480 frs, double 480–600 frs. Breakfast 70 frs. D,B&B 600–850 frs per person. Set meals 150–450 frs; alc 400 frs.

SÉLESTAT 67600 Bas-Rhin Map 9

Abbaye de la Pommeraie *Tel* 04.88.92.07.84
8 avenue Maréchal Foch *Fax* 04.88.92.08.71

On a quiet road near the centre of this handsome old Alsatian town, a 17th-century abbey is now a stylish and expensive hotel, owned and run by the François family. "We love it," say devotees who visited twice recently. "We had an enormous suite with a huge bed on a dais in an alcove, antiques, and rugs on the parquet floor. All very light and bright, and a marble bathroom. Another time, our room had old pine and beams. The charming manageress Nicole managed our good dinner well, and breakfast was superb. There's a new cheaper restaurant too, Alsatian in style." The main dining room has flower displays, and there's a small garden. *Gault Millau toque* for such dishes as pigeon in pastry with cabbage and coriander. (*P and JT*)

Open All year. Restaurant closed 15 July–5 Aug, Sun evening/Mon.
Rooms 3 suites, 11 double. Air-conditioning.
Facilities Lift. Lounge, salon, 3 dining rooms. Small garden.
Location Central. 47 km SW of Strasbourg. Garage.
Credit cards All major cards accepted.
Terms [1996] Rooms 850–1,500 frs. Breakfast 90 frs. D,B&B 675–1,150 frs per person. Set meals 150–290 frs; alc 200 frs.

SEMUR-EN-AUXOIS 21140 Côte-d'Or — Map 12

Hostellerie d'Aussois — *Tel* 03.80.97.28.28
Route de Saulieu — *Fax* 03.80.97.34.56

Semur is one of the finest little medieval towns in Burgundy, and just outside is this complete contrast – a very modern new hotel, long and low, with a touch of stylish glamour, yet not expensive (a Logis de France). Its owner/manageress, Mme Jobic, is "charming". A 1996 report: "The terrace, restaurant and front rooms have a spectacular view of the ramparted town, floodlit at night. Our welcome was warm. The hotel's stylish restaurant, *La Mermoz*, is popular with locals; the young staff were friendly. The buffet breakfast was excellent, save for the synthetic orange juice. We enjoyed the heated outdoor pool. Of our two rooms, the standard one was fine, but housekeeping was poor in the more spacious one." Other recent views: "Rather impersonal, but good ample Burgundy cooking." "Our quiet room at the back had a view of fields with cows grazing." (*David and Jennifer Williams, PJC Wadsley, Prof. and Mrs Robson, and others*) A new chef this year: reports on his work welcome.

Open All year. Restaurant closed 3 weeks in winter.
Rooms 1 suite (for 4 people), 42 double. Some on ground floor.
Facilities Bar, TV room, restaurant; 5 meeting rooms; sauna, fitness room; terrace. Garden: swimming pool; bicycle hire.
Location 1 km E of town. Parking.
Credit cards Access, Amex, Visa.
Terms [1996] Rooms 280–360 frs, suite 500–600 frs. Breakfast 35 frs. D,B&B 265–480 frs per person. Set meals 90–195 frs; full alc 150 frs.

SEURRE 21250 Côte d'Or — Map 12

Le Castel BUDGET — *Tel* 03.80.20.45.07
20 avenue de la Gare — *Fax* 03.80.20.33.93

Cheerful modern Logis de France in small town 26 km E of Beaune, on Dole road. Friendly owners. Good and copious local cooking, plus some Martinique dishes, served in big, bright dining room. No lounge, but flowery terrace. Mainly quiet, but some train noises. Closed 2 Jan–6 Feb, Mon out of season. Access, Visa accepted. 22 rooms: 240–265 frs. Breakfast 35 frs. Set meals 95–180 frs [1996].

SÉVRIER 74320 Haute-Savoie — Map 12

Auberge de Létraz NEW — *Tel* 04.50.52.40.36
Létraz — *Fax* 04.50.52.63.36

Four km S of Annecy town, stylish modern hotel in fine setting with garden stretching right down to beautiful Lake Annecy: many rooms have lake-facing balcony. Delicious cooking (Michelin *star). Restaurant closed Sun evening/Mon out of season. All major credit cards accepted. 25 rooms: 525–780 frs. Breakfast 56 frs. D,B&B 509–639 frs per person. Set meals 195–395 frs [1996]. Fuller reports welcome.*

SOMMIÈRES 30250 Gard **Map 11**

Auberge du Pont Romain *Tel* 04.66.80.00.58
2 rue Émile Jamais *Fax* 04.66.80.31.52

Lawrence Durrell lived and died in this big Languedoc village on the edge of the *garrigue*. Its Roman bridge provides the name for this hotel, which itself is something quite else, a converted 19th-century carpet factory, by a river. "The factory chimney is rather off-putting, but then all changes: massive quiet rooms, looking over the lovely swimming pool; good bathroom, though its decor was eccentric. Lovely dining room with log fire, an excellent meal and young, enthusiastic service." "Rugs, antique furniture, tapestry chairs are impressive features, along with the warm welcome." "Immaculate housekeeping. A delightful garden with large old trees, medium-sized pool well placed for sun or shade. An excellent breakfast on the terrace." Food portions are "large and rich", eg, the "excellent" filet de sole Lawrence Durrell, the writer's favourite. (*LB, and others*)

Open 15 Mar–30 Oct, 1 Dec–15 Jan. Restaurant closed Wed, except July / Aug.
Rooms 2 suites, 17 double. Some on ground floor.
Facilities Lift. Salon, bar, restaurant; conference / function rooms; terrace. Garden: swimming pool.
Location On edge of village, 28 km SW of Nîmes.
Credit cards All major cards accepted.
Terms Rooms 240–450 frs. Breakfast 45 frs. D,B&B 320–545 frs per person. Set meals 125–245 frs; full alc 250 frs.

STRASBOURG 67000 Bas-Rhin **Map 9**

Romantik Hotel Beaucour *Tel* 03.88.76.72.00
5 rue des Bouchers *Fax* 03.88.76.72.60

Central, across river Ill from cathedral, new Romantik hotel formed from three handsome half-timbered 18th-century mansions, finely modernised, with old interior courtyard but bright new decor. Amiable staff, good comfort, huge breakfasts. Public parking next door. All major credit cards accepted. 49 rooms, with some high-tech facilities (eg, jacuzzi); 2 adapted for ♿. Rooms: single 380–680 frs, double 780–950 frs. Breakfast 65 frs. No restaurant. Weekend reductions. Again liked this year, but fuller reports welcome.

Hôtel de la Cathédrale *Tel* 03.88.22.12.12
12 place de la Cathédrale *Fax* 03.88.23.28.00

"Oh, to go back to this romantic hotel without the children!" says a reader this year, adding, "The decoration was warm and updated, the bathroom excellent, and breakfast very good. Our room at the back overlooked a wonderful restaurant that smelled great. Even the cathedral bells were not overpowering, thanks to double glazing." The hotel, facing the cathedral, is neat and modern with sophisticated decor in its bar and foyer. "The helpful staff really seem to enjoy their work." Rooms vary in size (some are small), and the stairs are steep. (*Greg Brinks, Leonard Hill and Cathy Stevulak*) The hotel is to be enlarged early in 1997. It now has a part-time porter / driver to help with luggage. A new wine tavern, *Zum Sternstebele*, is recommended this year.

Open All year.
Rooms 5 apartments (in annexe 100 m), 35 double. 2 no-smoking.
Facilities Lift. 2 lounges, TV room, bar, breakfast room (no-smoking); conference facilities.
Location Central. Underground carpark nearby.
Credit cards All major cards accepted.
Terms Rooms 340–800 frs. Breakfast: continental 48 frs, buffet 60 frs. Children under 12 accommodated free in parents' room. Weekend rates.

Hôtel du Dragon — *Tel* 03.88.35.79.80
2 rue de l'Écarlate — *Fax* 03.88.25.78.95

Just south of the river Ill, down a quiet street of the old town, a 17th-century house has been strikingly converted into a modern B&B hotel, with cool modern decor and a pleasant patio for drinks. Some upper rooms have views of the cathedral. "Recommended without reservation," is one recent plaudit. "A helpful young man showed us to a delightful white-and-grey room under the eaves, ultra-modern. A pleasant breakfast in a nice room." Everyone finds the young owner "charming", and enjoys his Gallic humour. (*C and MC, KMR, and others*) Non-touristy restaurants recommended nearby: *Le Pont Corbeau, Le Strussel.*

Open All year.
Rooms 2 suites, 26 double, 4 single. Some no-smoking.
Facilities Lift. Salon, TV room, bar; patio.
Location Central, off Quai St-Nicolas, near Pl d'Austerlitz. Public parking only.
Credit cards All major cards accepted.
Terms Rooms: single 430–495 frs, double 475–640 frs. Breakfast 58 frs.

Hôtel Gutenberg NEW — *Tel* 03.88.32.17.15
31 rue des Serruriers — *Fax* 03.88.75.76.67

Central, near cathedral, characterful old building with a variety of rooms, some elegant and modern, others quaint and cosy; some air-conditioned, some on ground floor. Period furniture, good comfort, friendly service, nice breakfast. Lift. Closed 1–12 Jan. Access, Visa accepted. 45 rooms: 245–450 frs. Breakfast 42 frs. No restaurant. "Everyone's favourite in Strasbourg, so it's often full."

Hôtel des Rohan — *Tel* 03.88.32.85.11
17–19 rue du Maroquin — *Fax* 03.88.75.65.37

Central, by cathedral, "charming" small family-run hotel in traditional style with modern comforts. Caring management and staff, superior breakfast in elegant salon. 36 bedrooms, some quite small; 24 air-conditioned; some no-smoking. Quiet at night (double-glazing). All major credit cards accepted. Public parking. Rooms: single 360–410 frs, double 495–695 frs. Breakfast 50 frs. Children accommodated free in parents' room. Endorsed this year, but fuller reports welcome.

> The length of an entry need not reflect the merit of a hotel. The more interesting the report or the more unusual or controversial the hotel, the longer the entry.

TALLOIRES 74290 Haute-Savoie Map 12

Hôtel de l'Abbaye NEW

Tel 04.50.60.77.33
Fax 04.50.60.78.81

In a select village-resort on lovely Lake Annecy, this gracefully converted old abbey is one of several small, luxurious hotels by the lake. Built by Benedictines in 1694, it has been a hotel since 1844, now family run. Dropped from the 1990 *Guide* after some criticisms, it is now warmly renominated: "There is a grandeur to this delightful atmospheric building, so well blended into its fine setting. Two vast galleries with monks' cells turned into bedrooms of varying size, entered through the original stone-framed wooden doors. Nothing spoilt: polished wood floors, original furniture, sculpted stone figures. There's an indoor patio; chamber music plays discreetly. Knarled ancient trees on the front terrace lead to a private jetty. All rooms have idyllic views; some have a balcony above the slightly neglected garden. Old roses from the garden are put in the rooms (bathrooms are renovated). The traditional local food is of good quality; the wine list is famous for its range and modest price. It shames *Michelin*'s taste to have taken away the hotel's red symbol, which it gives constantly to vulgar interiors." (*Felix Singer*)

Open Apr–end Oct.
Rooms 2 suites, 28 double, 2 single. 1 on ground floor.
Facilities Salon, TV room, library, bar, restaurant; conference facilities; concerts/exhibitions in cloisters; medical centre with hydrotherapy, whirlpool, massage; terrace. Garden: private lakeside beach, windsurfing. Unsuitable for ♿.
Location On E shore of lake, 12 km SE of Annecy. Parking.
Credit cards All major cards accepted.
Terms [1996] Rooms 1,195–1,395 frs. Breakfast 70 frs. D,B&B 700–1,020 frs per person. Set meals 180–360 frs.

Hôtel Beau Site NEW

Tel 04.50.60.71.04
Fax 04.50.60.79.22

The Conan family's hotel is a handsome white late-19th-century villa in the centre of this resort village. "It is in the middle of Talloires, but full of peace and quiet," write its renominators. "It has a large garden with lawns reaching to the lake. Here are lounge chairs, with plenty of room to sunbathe. You can take breakfast in the garden, and lunch under the trees; food is quite good, and the amiable M. Conan is ready to offer an alternative on the set menu. The villa has been renovated and furnished in a modern style that spoils its otherwise charming character. However, bedrooms are large, pleasant, with well-designed bathrooms. And the old atmosphere has been kept in the one room escaping 'modernisation', a salon with antiques, painted a warm red. Front rooms have balconies with breathtaking lake views." (*Andrew and Anna Niedzwiecki*)

Open 6 May–7 Oct.
Rooms 28 double, 1 single. 11 in a nearby annexe.
Facilities 2 lounges, restaurant; terrace. Garden: tennis; private beach at lake.
Location Centre of village. 12 km S of Annecy. Parking.
Credit cards All major cards accepted.
Terms B&B: single 375–395 frs, double 535–860 frs, suite 1,010–1,080 frs; D,B&B 430–710 frs per person. Set meals 170–240 frs; full alc 290–320 frs.

Les Prés du Lac *Tel* 04.50.60.76.11
Clos Beau-Site *Fax* 04.50.60.73.42

"A sybaritic paradise, we cannot praise it too highly," is this year's plaudit for an enchanting modern villa. Select and expensive, it stands serenely by the lake, with neat lawns stretching to its private beach. The cheerful rooms have views of the lake and hills, patios are large and private, the ambience is "informal and relaxed", and the manager and co-owner Marie-Paule Conan is "a delight". Many rooms have a balcony; some others are in well-converted older buildings. "We enjoyed the wonderful breakfast on our private terrace." The salon has a bar. No restaurant, but you can eat well at the adjacent *Beau Site*, also owned by the Conan family; and the hotel will prepare light snacks. (*Dr NB Finter, and others*)

Open 1 Mar–31 Oct.
Rooms 2 suites, 16 double. Some in 2 garden houses. 2 on ground floor. 5 air-conditioned.
Facilities Salons, library / card room, bar; solarium. Lakeside garden: tennis.
Location On lake, 12 km S of Annecy. Garages; private parking.
Credit cards All major cards accepted.
Terms Rooms: double 700–1,125 frs, suite 1,540–1,895 frs. Breakfast 80 frs.

TAMNIÈS 24620 Dordogne Map 10

Hôtel Laborderie BUDGET *Tel* 05.53.29.68.59
Fax 05.53.29.65.31

A modern hotel built of mellow local stone, secluded on a hilltop between Sarlat and Les Eyzies, with beautiful quiet views in all directions. Inside are beamed ceilings, and a log fire for winter. There's a "lovely swimming pool", an attractive terrace, and a new dining room extension with light, bright decor. An inspector visited in 1996: "Our annexe room was of fair size, with decent decor, but the bed had seen younger days. Dinner impressed by its generosity: a large slice of foie gras, hors d'oeuvre with a help-yourself bowl of rillettes. Breakfast included ham, cheese and yogurt, all for 35 fr. Lots of children, and plenty of children's facilities." Others have called the Laborderie family owners "marvellous". The Périgourdin country cooking is always admired (*Michelin* red "Repas", *Gault Millau toque*). On the four-course *demi-pension* menu, local duck and goose are much in evidence. Some rooms have a small terrace: those at the back, above the kitchens, are noisy. Quite close, and worth a visit, is Lascaux II, a meticulous copy of the prehistoric Lascaux caves that are closed to the public.

Open 30 Mar–3 Nov.
Rooms 36 double. Some in garden annexe. Some on ground floor.
Facilities 2 salons, TV room, 2 dining rooms; function rooms; terrace. Garden: swimming pool. Lake nearby: swimming, fishing, windsurfing, sandy beach.
Location Central. 14 km NE of Les Eyzies. Parking.
Credit cards Access, Visa.
Terms [1996] Rooms 230–470 frs. Breakfast 35 frs. D,B&B 285–380 frs per person. Set meals 95–240 frs.

TARGET 03140 Allier **Map 10**

Château de Boussac *Tel* 04.70.40.63.20
Target, Chantelle *Fax* 04.70.40.60.03

When a stately home is turned into a private hotel run by its owners, who treat their paying guests like friends, it can be a risk for both sides – in France, as in Britain or Ireland. But it works well *chez* the Marquis and Marquise de Longueil, at their 17th-century fortified *château* in rolling country north-west of Vichy. It has four round towers, a moat, a lake and pleasant gardens. Part of the estate has been sold off for hunting, part they still run as a working farm. An inspector stayed recently: "The house is slightly untidy in a pleasant way, with personal bric-à-brac, books, a Gainsborough, other family heirlooms and portraits. Our suite had a grand piano, antiques, a hair-dryer and mediocre pictures. We were four couples for dinner round an elegant table, where our affable, talkative (and bilingual) host led the conversation. He and his wife had cooked the meal themselves – good if conventional, with local farm duck, Auvergne cheeses and wines. Good breakfast, also communal, with home-made jams. In winter, many guests come for the high-priced hunting. All very pleasant, but no special house-party atmosphere."

Open 1 Apr–30 Nov; Christmas/New Year by arrangement.
Rooms 1 suite, 4 double.
Facilities 2 salons, dining room. Garden. Unsuitable for ♿.
Location 10 km SE of Montmarault, S of D46 Montluçon–St-Pourçain.
Credit cards Access, Amex, Visa.
Terms Rooms 600–800 frs, suite 950–1,100 frs. Breakfast 55 frs. Set meals 220–320 frs (including wine).

THANNENKIRCH 68590 Haut-Rhin **Map 12**

Auberge la Meunière NEW/BUDGET *Tel* 03.89.73.10.47
Fax 03.89.73.12.31

On edge of village in lovely wooded Vosges foothills, 24 km N of Colmar, a charming old inn with wooden façade, authentic rustic decor, cheerful furnishings old and new. Glorious views from outdoor dining terrace and some bedrooms. Good Alsatian cooking by owner/chef Jean-Luc Dumoulin; nice welcome by his Italian wife. Open Easter–30 Nov. Access, Amex, Visa accepted. 15 rooms. B&B double 330–420 frs; D,B&B 235–330 frs per person. Set meals 95–195 frs. Fuller reports welcome.

****

Perennial plaint We were dismayed to find refurbishment under way at our chosen hotel, and no fewer than two private dinner parties on the second evening of our stay, so that the resources of the staff were pretty much at full stretch. I had failed to make all the necessary enquiries when booking – about building works, conferences, large parties or anything else that might interfere with a quiet, civilised stay. Hardly any hotels volunteer this information when initial enquiries are made.

****

THIONVILLE 57100 Moselle — Map 9

L'Horizon — *Tel* 03.82.88.53.65
50 route du Crève-Coeur — *Fax* 03.82.34.55.84

The Speck family's much-admired vine-clad hostelry, strikingly decorated, stands on a quiet hillside above a workaday Lorraine steel town. The flower-filled foyer, light and spacious, has "a ceiling like something from the *Arabian Nights*, very pretty when lit up". The dining room has velvet drapes and panoramic views, rural and industrial; there's a well-kept flower-filled garden, and an elegant terrace for tea and drinks. "A lovely hotel," say visitors this year. "We dined on the terrace as the sun went down. All was most professional, save that service was a bit slow. Breakfast was delightful." This backs other recent praise: "Superb and sumptuous. Fantastic decorations." "I have never enjoyed any hotel more. Mme Speck and all her staff were charming, our room with a balcony was prettily furnished and the food excellent – foie gras, stuffed pigeon, apple and calvados sorbet" (*Gault Millau toque*) "The restaurant was bustling with family parties – lots of children and laughter, everyone friendly." (*Maureen and Pat Campbell, C and MC, and other*)

Open All year, except Jan/Feb. Restaurant closed Sat midday.
Rooms 10 double.
Facilities Ramp. 4 salons, TV room, bar, restaurant; conference facilities; terrace. Large grounds: garden. Unsuitable for ♿.
Location 2 km NW of Thionville: follow signs to Bel-Air hospital, then Crève-Coeur.
Credit cards All major cards accepted.
Terms Rooms 480 frs. Breakfast 60 frs. Set meals 225–295 frs; full alc 325 frs.

THOISSEY 01140 Ain — Map 12

Au Chapon Fin et Restaurant Paul Blanc — *Tel* 04.74.04.04.74
Fax 04.74.04.94.51

"Elegant and well run; meals of high quality, served with delicacy," runs a 1996 report on this fairly smart, well-modernised hotel, set quietly in a village near the Saône south of Mâcon. The Maringue family's welcome is "courteous" and "heart-warming". And young Bruno Maringue wins a *Michelin* star and two *Gault Millau toques* for his Bressan and Burgundian cooking ("delicious", says a reader). The hotel was created by Bruno's grandfather, and is owned and run by his mother. This year's view: "Bedrooms spacious. We had breakfast on our terrace looking on to the gardens. Dining room most attractive and well organised, with many waiters hovering. But some specialities were a little disappointing." "Bathrooms verge on the luxurious." Lovely terrace under the trees for summer dining. (*Dr Arthur and Mrs Irene Naylor, JAP*) Guests are expected to dine in.

Open All year, except fortnight end Nov–early Dec. Closed Tues/midday Wed.
Rooms 16 double, 4 single. Some in annexe.
Facilities Lift. Bar, restaurant; function room. Garden.
Location Centre of village. 16 km S of Mâcon. Private carpark.
Credit cards All major cards accepted.
Terms [1996] Rooms: single 250 frs, double 460–680 frs. Breakfast 55 frs. Set meals 250–520 frs; full alc 450 frs.

THOMERY 77810 Seine-et-Marne Map 9

Le Vieux Logis NEW *Tel* 01.60.96.44.77
5 rue Sadi Carnot *Fax* 01.60.70.01.42

In a small town by the Seine near Fontainebleau, this trim white 18th-century mansion, noted for its food (two *Gault Millau toques*), makes an appealing *Guide* debut: "A most attractive conservatory-dining room, shady courtyard dining area, and pleasant pool with comfortable loungers. Food very good: sleek businessmen lunching, smart cars in park. Rooms well fitted, shades of beige, and named after flowers. We were moved after first night (they got us a bit mixed up with our flowers). Mme Plouvier (owner) much in evidence at dinner, not at breakfast where service was not so good. Noisy bin lorries churned up street at unearthly hour." (*Prof. P and Mrs A Robson*) On Saturdays, candlelit dinner and piano bar.

Open All year.
Rooms 14 double
Facilities Salon, bar, 2 dining rooms; function room; terrace. Garden: swimming pool, tennis.
Location In town, 9 km E of Fontainebleau. Parking.
Credit cards Amex, Visa.
Terms Rooms 300–400 frs. Breakfast 50 frs. Set menus 140/240 frs; full alc 300–350 frs.

TOULOUSE 31000 Haute-Garonne Map 10

Hotel Mermoz NEW *Tel* 05.61.63.04.04
50 rue Matabiau *Fax* 05.61.63.15.64

Quite central, on main street near station, but set back from road, so quiet: spruce B&B hotel in Art Deco style, named after famous Toulouse pioneer aviator. Buffet breakfast in conservatory or leafy patio. Bar. Helpful staff. 52 smallish, pleasant rooms; poor lighting. All major credit cards accepted. Locked parking. B&B: single 400–515 frs, double 450–565 frs [1996].

****

Traveller's tale In one hotel we stayed at, our room was quite dirty, but it was getting late and we were tired and hungry, so we agreed to take it. When we prepared for bed, we noticed large spiders crawling in the dust that covered every corner of the room. I tried to take a shower; the pipe kept popping from the wall, with a rattling sound. My husband went to ask the owner for assistance. What happened next was beyond comprehension. I could not at first understand why my husband looked so upset. He told me we had to leave. The owner was yelling that we Americans were nothing but trouble, that we were making a noise (obviously due to the shower pipe); she accused me of damaging the plumbing. My husband and I are soft-spoken and easy-going. I dressed and packed and we left. By now it was nearly 10 pm. Fortunately the small inn nearby had a vacancy.

****

TOURTOUR 83690 Var — Map 11

La Bastide de Tourtour NEW

Tel 04.94.70.57.30
Fax 04.94.70.54.90

The medieval hill-village of Tourtour is today a fashionable residential centre and a showpiece: its lovely façades of golden-brown stone have been scoured clean. There are wide vistas on all sides and the Gorges du Verdon are quite close. *La Bastide*, smart and expensive (Relais & Châteaux), was custom-built in the 1960s in mock-castle style, and stands in its own wooded garden. It fell from the *Guide* in 1992 after criticisms of service and decor, but was liked this year: "It is excellently run, with very good food, friendly owners and staff. The outdoor terrace and pool areas are nice. The 'fake' round tower is the main staircase, furnished with various pieces of ancient machinery, some of them looking like instruments of torture." An earlier visitor had "a large and cheery room with cloth-covered walls and matching bedcovers", and found the dining room "intimate and romantic". (*Michael Forrest*) The chef is new this year. And we wonder whether the owners, Étienne and Francine Laurent, still have their rare collection of 200 peasant bonnets and hats.

Open 10 Mar–31 Oct. Restaurant closed midday Tues, Mon in low season.
Rooms 23 double, 2 single.
Facilities Lift, ramps. Salon, restaurant, conference room; terrace. Garden: swimming pool, tennis court.
Location On SE edge of Tourtour. *Autoroute* A8 exit Le Muy: follow signs to Draguignan, then Salernes, then Tourtour. Parking.
Credit cards All major cards accepted.
Terms Rooms: single 380–530 frs, double 520–1,400 frs. Breakfast 75 frs. D,B&B double 610–1,050 frs. Set lunch 160 frs, dinner 290–350 frs; full alc 400 frs.

TRÉBEURDEN 22560 Côtes-d'Armor — Map 8

Ti al Lannec
Allée de Mézo-Guen

Tel 02.96.23.57.26
Fax 02.96.23.62.14

Rocks in strange shapes alternate with sandy coves along this attractive stretch of the north Brittany coast, where Trébeurden is a busy bathing resort. Set apart in its quiet garden, high above the sea, is this handsome grey-and-white mansion, a fine hotel run with skill by the "warm and friendly" Jouanny family. It is "well organised for small children", and has a new health and massage centre, and private steps down to the beach. Food is well above average for a seaside hotel (*Gault Millau toque*). Recent praise: "Fantastic bathroom, gardens beautiful." "Dinner and buffet breakfast were excellent." Many of the finely furnished rooms have a big balcony with the view across the bay; some have a four-poster. A lounge with period decor; tables and chairs under parasols and trees on the lawn. A bulletin appears on one's breakfast table, giving times of the tides, details of local markets and events. (*P and AJ, and others*) Service is mostly affable, though one young couple found it aloof. Normal peace can be disturbed at times by a disco on the beach.

Open 16 Mar–11 Nov.
Rooms 7 suites, 20 double, 2 single.
Facilities Lift, ramps. 2 salons (1 no-smoking), billiard room, bar, restaurant;

conference facilities; fitness centre. Garden: outdoor chess, table-tennis, *boules*; path to sandy beach, safe bathing, fishing.
Location Central. Signposted from Lannion (10 km).
Credit cards All major cards accepted.
Terms [1996] Rooms 450–1,050 frs. Breakfast: continental 65 frs, buffet 90 frs. D,B&B 575–775 frs per person. Set meals 105–390 frs.

TRÉGUIER 22220 Côtes-d'Armor — Map 8

Kastell Dinec'h — *Tel* 02.96.92.49.39
Fax 02.96.92.34.03

This old grey Breton town (fine cathedral) is quite near to the beaches of Trébeurden and Perros-Guirec. Just outside it, down a country lane, is this 17th-century stone farmhouse in a pretty garden (with small swimming pool), daubed in red print by the French guides. "A very pretty building hidden in a little copse. Helpful staff, pleasant bedroom, and a pretty restaurant like an old banqueting hall. Here the food was delicious, served on good china." Some rooms are in a converted stable block. (*NH*)

Open All year, except 1 Jan–19 Mar, 11–27 Oct, Tues evening / Wed in low season. Restaurant closed for lunch.
Rooms 12 double, 3 single.
Facilities Lounge, restaurant. Garden: swimming pool.
Location 2 km SW of Tréguier, off Lannion road.
Credit cards Access, Visa.
Terms [1996] Rooms 420–460 frs. Breakfast 55 frs. D,B&B 440–460 frs per person. Set dinner 130–310 frs.

TRELLY 50660 Manche — Map 8

La Verte Campagne BUDGET — *Tel* 02.33.47.65.33
Le Hameau Chevalier — *Fax* 02.33.47.38.03

"Very peaceful, tea in garden, lovely meals," says a recent guest at this 18th-century farmhouse, set in deep Normandy countryside, and cosily converted into a highly rated restaurant with seven inexpensive rooms (*Michelin* star, *Gault Millau toque*). Covered with creepers and roses, it has a garden, and a large, comfortable lounge with beamed ceiling. Visitors have warmed to its owners: "Caroline Bernou is charming, like her hotel. The food, served by an obliging and ubiquitous young man, was of good quality, presented without pomposity. A pretty house, and peaceful." "Excellent value. Our bedroom was adequate, with ivy round the windows and a view of the little garden. The staff were friendly and the food was wonderful: a 220 frs [1996] menu of eight or nine courses included tomato sorbet, pâté de foie gras of duck with fig purée, good cheeseboard, apple-based desserts." (*L and AC*) More reports, please.

Open All year, except 1st week Dec, Christmas Eve.
Rooms 6 double, 1 single.
Facilities Salon, bar, 2 dining rooms. Garden. Unsuitable for ♿.
Location 2 km SE of Trelly, which is 12 km S of Coutances, between D171 and D7. Private parking.
Credit cards Access, Visa.
Terms Rooms: single 220 frs, double 380 frs. Breakfast 35 frs. D,B&B 280–350 frs per person. Set meals 140–350 frs; full alc 350 frs.

TROYES 10000 Aube — Map 9

Le Champ des Oiseaux NEW — *Tel* 03.25.80.58.50
20 rue Linard Gonthier — *Fax* 03.25.80.98.34

"What a find!" The name sounds so rural, but this appealing *Guide* newcomer is actually in the medieval heart of a biggish town, near the cathedral. The name comes from storks who used to nest nearby. "It's an extraordinary 15th-century building, restored, sympathetically on the whole, by its owner, Monique Boisseau (a former teacher), and opened as a hotel in 1995. Our spacious, well-appointed room had a good-sized bed." "Our charming host and hostess have fulfilled their long-established dream of converting the old building next to their own house. Sumptuous fluffy towels, sumptuous bathroom. Breakfast, with home-made lemon curd, freshly squeezed juice, etc, in a pretty room overlooking the small walled garden and delightful courtyard." (*P Yarnold, Jan and Alan Codd*) No restaurant: try the moderate-priced *Horloge*.

Open All year.
Rooms 3 suites, 9 double. Some on ground floor.
Facilities Ramps. Salon, bar, breakfast room; courtyard. Garden.
Location Central, near cathedral. Garage, private parking.
Credit cards All major cards accepted.
Terms Rooms 430–450 frs. Breakfast 55 frs.

Le Relais Saint-Jean — *Tel* 03.25.73.89.90
Rue Paillot de Montabert 51 — *Fax* 03.25.73.88.60

In pedestrianised medieval heart of old Troyes, lovely beamed building modernised inside, with elegance plus comfort. Quiet, with good service. Lift; easy access to underground carpark. All major credit cards accepted. 23 rooms: single 430–550 frs, double 470–650 frs. Breakfast 55 frs. Bar but no restaurant (lots nearby). Endorsed in 1996, but fuller reports needed.

TURENNE 19500 Corrèze — Map 10

La Maison des Chanoines NEW/BUDGET — *Tel* 05.55.85.93.43
Route de l'Église

Tucked below the huge, imposing castle of a small, lovely village in Dordogne, 16 km S of Brive, a 16th-century mansion now a pleasant restaurant-with-rooms, owned and run by local Cheyroux family. Traditional food served in old stone-vaulted room. 3 nicely decorated rooms (no-smoking), pretty shaded terrace. Open 1 Apr–15 Nov, New Year. Closed Tues evening/Wed, except in season. Access, Visa accepted. B&B double 370–440 frs. Set meals 100–195 frs. Criticised last year regarding welcome, but now renominated for "excellent food, delightful ambience". Fuller reports, please.

If you have had recent experience of a good hotel that ought to be in the *Guide*, please write to us at once. Report forms are to be found at the back of the book. Procrastination is the thief of the next edition.

URIAGE-LES-BAINS 38410 Isère **Map 12**

Hôtel Les Mésanges BUDGET *Tel* 04.76.89.70.69
Le Vacher *Fax* 04.76.89.56.97

This small spa town near Grenoble has a lovely forested sub-Alpine setting. On its edge is this small and quiet hotel, efficiently run by the Prince family. A *mésange* is a tit, and readers have found "lots of them dancing about and singing" as they dined on the terrace. "There's a nice swimming pool, and our spacious room had beautiful views." Another recent view: "Splendid location, excellent restaurant, genuine hospitality." The buffet breakfast is liked too, and the garden with parasols. (*S and LC, BH*)

Open 1 May–20 Oct, Feb school holidays, weekends 1 Feb–Easter. Restaurant closed Tues to non-residents.
Rooms 38 double, 1 single. 25 with TV.
Facilities Ramps. TV room, bridge room, restaurant (no-smoking). Garden: swimming pool, table-tennis, children's playground.
Location 11 km SE of Grenoble, just outside Uriage, towards St-Martin d'Uriage. Parking.
Credit cards Access, Amex, Visa.
Terms Double room 290 frs. Breakfast 38 frs. D,B&B 250 frs per person. Set meals 80–230 frs; full alc 180 frs.

UZÈS 30700 Gard **Map 11**

Hôtel d'Entraigues BUDGET *Tel* 04.66.22.32.68
8 rue de la Calade *Fax* 04.66.22.57.01

Set in the rolling *garrigue* country north of Nîmes, Uzès is a fascinating old town of narrow streets and tall towers; the highest is that of the massive turreted ducal castle. There's a pig fair in February, a garlic fair in June. Down one alley below the castle is this 16th-century mansion, once the home of a general. It has been tastefully converted into a select hotel, with soft-hued stone and dimly lit low-vaulted ceilings. "It has a Gothic feel. Staff were friendly, and dinner, taken on the rooftop terrace on a summer evening, was excellent. But the swimming pool is tiny." Rooms too are mostly small, even cramped, but many have a modern bathroom. The chef, new this year, offers such dishes as ragoût of sweetbreads, calf's head and tongue with morilles. Our latest report warmly approves his efforts. The pool, we're told, may be small, but "it's very pretty, and you can go into a room beneath to watch legs flap around". (*JB and JN, Linda Brook*)

Open All year.
Rooms 5 suites, 29 double, 2 single. 17 in annexe opposite. Some air-conditioned.
Facilities Lift. Salon, TV room, restaurant with bar; terrace: swimming pool (unheated).
Location Central, opposite cathedral, but quiet. Garage, protected parking.
Credit cards All major cards accepted.
Terms Rooms: single 185–195 frs, double 285–325 frs, suite 500–600 frs. Breakfast 45 frs. Set meals 110–270 frs; full alc 300 frs.

If you find details of a hotel's location inadequate, let us know.

VALBONNE 06560 Alpes-Maritimes — Map 11

Hôtel Les Armoiries
Place des Arcades
Tel 04.93.12.90.90
Fax 04.93.12.90.91

Just inland from Cannes, in the arcaded main square of a small, very pretty town, is this ochre-coloured 17th-century building, classed as a historic monument and restored as a stylish small hotel. Its helpful owners live on the top floor. "Service excellent, warm atmosphere," is one of several recent plaudits. "Our comfortable corner room looked over the square, affording a continuing panorama of village life. The third-floor breakfast room is interestingly designed." "Beautiful furnishings and Provençal fabrics, plus modern *luxe* comforts. Our room was even scented with perfumes from Grasse." No restaurant; several in town. (*TW, and others*)

Open All year.
Rooms 16 double. Air-conditioning.
Facilities Lift, ramps. Lounge, TV room, bar, breakfast room.
Location Central. 12 km N of Cannes. Public carparks nearby.
Credit cards All major cards accepted.
Terms [1996] Rooms 450–900 frs. Breakfast 50 frs.

LE VAL D'AJOL 88340 Vosges — Map 12

La Résidence BUDGET
5 rue des Mousses
Tel 03.29.30.68.52
Fax 03.29.66.53.00

Amid wooded hilly country in the south-west part of the Vosges, in an area of spas and small textile firms, is Mme Bongeot's Logis de France, a handsome old house with modern additions. "It is on the edge of the village in its own extensive grounds, with hard tennis court, swings and other games, old farm instruments and a handsome tethered goat. We had a warm welcome, and the pool was quickly uncovered for our sole use. In the dining room, light and unfussy, we sat beside a large tank of tropical fish. Our only complaint about the food: there was too much of it. The lounge looked cosy." Bedrooms are in modern or Louis XV/XVI style. (*R and JH*)

Open All year, except mid Nov–early Dec.
Rooms 53 double, 2 single in 3 buildings. Some on ground floor.
Facilities Ramp. 2 lounges (1 with TV), bar, restaurant. Garden: swimming pool, tennis. Only restaurant suitable for ♿.
Location 17 km SW of Remiremont, on D23.
Credit cards All major cards accepted.
Terms Rooms: single 230–320 frs, double 300–400 frs. Breakfast 42 frs. D,B&B 290–450 frs per person. Set meals 65–265 frs. Children under 12 accommodated free in parents' room.

VALENCE 26000 Drôme — Map 12

Restaurant Pic
285 avenue Victor-Hugo
Tel 04.75.44.15.32
Fax 04.75.40.96.03

When Jacques Pic, one of the giants of French cuisine, died in 1993, his son Alain took over his celebrated restaurant-with-rooms. This Relais & Châteaux house, which stands in a shady garden in a tree-lined street on the edge of a dusty Rhône valley town, remains a true family operation, for which Alain Pic now wins two *Michelin* stars, four black *Gault Millau toques*. It has always been one of the warmest and least snooty of the great French gastronomic temples, and our readers find it still that way: "Alain Pic deserves all the accolades that his forebears gathered. A kindly welcome, and a beautifully decorated bedroom with a fine marble bathroom. My husband took the 650 frs [1996] Menu Rabelais, well-named indeed, and I had asparagus, caviar and turbot. We couldn't stop paying compliments. The wines were superb, too, though the *sommelier* was like a cabaret. The kitchen was visible behind a glass door. The warm, kind and generous atmosphere was to me unique, and M. Pic is charming. His menus are less innovative than some, but he makes one feel one is staying with a friend." "Pure delight." Breakfast, which comes with a bottle of *marc*, is also lauded. (*E and BB, O and DM*) Ten more bedrooms, and an outdoor unheated swimming pool, are planned for spring 1997.

Open All year. Closed Sun evening.
Rooms 2 suites, 3 double.
Facilities Lift. Salon, dining room; terrace. Garden.
Location 1 km S of centre. *Autoroute* A7 exit Valence Sud; follow sign for Ave Victor-Hugo. Parking.
Credit cards All major cards accepted.
Terms Rooms 750–1,000 frs. Breakfast 100 frs. Set meals 290–920 frs; alc 620–820 frs.

VAL-SUZON 21121 Côte-d'Or — Map 12

Hostellerie du Val-Suzon

Tel 03.80.35.60.15
Fax 03.80.35.61.36

In a hamlet north-west of Dijon, this restaurant-with-rooms has a rustic setting but is itself quite smart, and popular with local diners-out and executives. Some rooms are in the main building; others, larger and quieter, with views of the hills, are in an annexe, the *Chalet de la Fontaine aux Géais*, just up the hill. Some readers have found the hotel pretentious, but this year it was called "charming, with quiet rooms, friendly staff, reasonable prices, excellent dinner" (*Gault Millau toque*). Last year's views: "Our rooms were spacious and pleasant, and breakfast a feast of brioches and petits pains." "Our room in the main building was a little poky but with a huge bath. We had a good dinner in the garden, preceded by the strongest kirs we've ever had in France." In the garden is an aviary (*geai* is a jay), with peacocks, etc. Also bantam cocks which start crowing before dawn. (*ABX Fenwick, and others*)

Open All year, except Wed / midday Thurs in low season.
Rooms 1 suite, 15 double, 1 single. 9 in *Chalet*.
Facilities Lounge, TV room, bar, restaurant; function room. Garden. Unsuitable for ♿.
Location 16 km NW of Dijon, just off N71 to Châtillon. Parking.
Credit cards All major cards accepted.
Terms [1996] Rooms 420–520 frs. Breakfast 58 frs. D,B&B 453–550 frs per person. Set meals 200–420 frs.

> We are particularly keen to get more reports on our italicised entries.

VELLERON 84740 Vaucluse Map 11

Hostellerie La Grangette *Tel* 04.90.20.00.77
Chemin de Cambuisson *Fax* 04.90.20.07.06

Beautifully converted grey stone manor, alone in open country just east of D938, 11 km S of Carpentras. Semi-wild grounds with swimming pool, tennis. 16 soigné bedrooms with oak beams, antiques, draped curtains, views of Provençal hills. Friendly owners and staff, good Provençal food in pretty dining room. Access, Amex, Visa accepted. B&B double 690–1,090 frs; D,B&B double 900–1,300 frs.

VENCE 06140 Alpes-Maritimes Map 11

La Roseraie *Tel* 04.93.58.02.20
Avenue Henri Giraud *Fax* 04.93.58.99.31

Modest but appealing: a converted villa in a garden, with a small kidney-shaped swimming pool, on the edge of a crowded but historic Provençal town. "We were delighted both with the hotel and with its owners, Maurice and Monica Ganier. Our wonderful room, decorated in local style, opened on to the lovely terrace overlooking the pool, where large and good breakfasts were served in a friendly atmosphere." "We spent five very happy days here. Rooms are small but pretty, some with views of the old town. Breakfast was far better than French average, and the Ganiers are very pleasant." (*JC and DC, GC*) No restaurant: try *La Farigoule*, not expensive.

Open All year.
Rooms 10 double.
Facilities Lounge; terrace. Garden: swimming pool, children's play area. Unsuitable for ♿.
Location 500 m from centre. Parking.
Credit cards Access, Amex, Visa.
Terms [1996] Rooms 430–550 frs. Breakfast 50 frs.

VERDUN 55100 Meuse Map 9

Hostellerie du Coq Hardi *Tel* 03.29.86.36.36
8 avenue de la Victoire *Fax* 03.29.86.09.21

As strategically located for today's tourists as it was for the generals of 1914–18, Verdun lies just off the Paris–Frankfurt *autoroute*. The main battlefields, in the hills just to the north-east, are worth visiting for the museum of agonising war scenes, next to happy photos of post-1945 Franco-German youth exchanges. The *Coq Hardi*, in the town, is a venerable half-timbered building, "in antique/rustic style, with a log fire in the hall". Family-run, it is noted for its food (*Michelin* star, *Gault Millau toque*). Again this year, readers have been pleased: "Madame made us very welcome. We had a comfortable room with smart bathroom, and an excellent meal." "Service was gracious." (*Anne and Ian Steel, Virginia Spargur*) Front rooms have good river views, but rear ones are quietest.

Open All year.
Rooms 3 suites, 33 double.

Facilities Lift. Hall, restaurant; conference facilities.
Location Central, near river. Lock-up garage.
Credit cards Access, Amex, Visa.
Terms [1996] Rooms 310–750 frs. Breakfast 68 frs. D,B&B 500 frs per person. Set meals 200–465 frs; alc 385–480 frs.

VERGÈZE 30310 Gard — Map 11

La Passiflore BUDGET — *Tel* 04.66.35.00.00
11 rue Neuve — *Fax* 04.66.35.09.21

Down the road from this village near Nîmes is the underground Perrier spring that today produces 800 million bottles a year. It was first commercialised by an Englishman, St-John Harmsworth of the newspaper family; he bought it in 1903, modelling the tapering green bottle on Indian clubs he used for exercise. Today others from Britain, Anthony and Linda Booth, own and run this creeper-covered Logis de France, loved by recent guests: "The Booths are priceless, he an artist manqué, she a poppet – the French queue up at her door." "You would not know they were not French, unless you asked. She cooks, *à la française*: terrine of venison, quiche with roquefort sauce, magret de canard, mouthwatering desserts. A pretty courtyard leads to this haven of tranquillity, which is quiet despite main roads nearby. The bedrooms are spacious, with modern tiled bath/shower rooms." (*Paul Palmer, RCT*)

Open All year. Restaurant closed 15 Nov–26 Dec, Mon Apr–Oct, Sun/Mon Nov–Mar, midday.
Rooms 11 double. Some on ground floor.
Facilities Lounge, breakfast room, restaurant. Garden.
Location In village, 10 km SW of Nîmes. Secure parking.
Credit cards Access, Amex, Visa.
Terms Rooms 200–325 frs. Breakfast 38 frs. D,B&B double (min. 4 days) 490–600 frs. Set dinner 135 frs; full alc 185 frs. Children under 6 accommodated free in parents' room.

VERTEILLAC 24320 Dordogne — Map 10

La Guide NEW/BUDGET — *Tel* 05.53.91.53.54

Each year, we hear of more British families starting up small rural hotels or guest houses in the Dordogne: there's been nothing like it since the Hundred Years' War. Pat and Geoffrey Burnstone have taken over a converted stone farmhouse, with barns and *pigeonnier*, in a hamlet amid the rolling Périgord landscape. *La Guide* (rein) has inspired three nominations to *Le Guide* in 1995–96: "You can stay in the main house, or in a large converted barn. There's a large garden and nice swimming pool." "Patricia's dishes might include duck with ginger sauce, iced fruit pudding. Home-made jams. Great informality." "A tranquil, homely atmosphere." There are lounges, with beams and stone walls, and a large garden with fine trees, and seats and tables suitable for picnicking. (*Sir Angus Stirling, Mr and Mrs MP Baker, Alan Baker*) More reports please.

Open 3 May–18 Oct.
Rooms 6 double, 1 single. In 3 buildings.
Facilities Lounges, TV room, restaurant (no-smoking). Garden: swimming pool.
Location 4 km N of Verteillac, 15 km N of Ribérac.

Credit cards None accepted.
Terms B&B £28–£56. Dinner 150 frs (residents only, Mon/Wed/Fri/Sat).

VERVINS 02140 Aisne — Map 9

La Tour du Roy — *Tel* 03.23.98.00.11
45 rue du Général Leclerc — *Fax* 03.23.98.00.72

This turreted manor house stands on the ramparts of a small town near the Belgian border, in an area of orchards and streams. It has character: some bedrooms are in the three round towers, and all are individually designed, with fine fabrics, and good-quality ceramics in the bathrooms; some are hung with original tapestries. There's a pretty garden, a courtyard terrace and a first-floor balcony where drinks and breakfast are served. Service is "efficient and friendly", and the lively owner/chef Annie Desvignes wins a *toque* for what *Gault Millau* has called "*une cuisine féminine sage et maîtrisée*". "Food was delicious, breakfast especially good, and our large room was attractive," says a *Guide* reader this year. Others have written: "The welcome was warm, and our bedroom decor was exquisite, with a view over the ramparts and a colourful bathroom." "New stained-glass windows on the main staircase depicting local scenes, delightful Art Deco objects, antiques." (*Barbara Hill; also Kaye Sykes and Ed Ackert, and many others*) A few readers have been less impressed by the food.

Open All year.
Rooms 5 suites, 13 double. 3 in annexe. 2 adapted for ♿.
Facilities Salon, 3 dining rooms; courtyard. Garden.
Location Central. 71 km N of Reims, off N2. Guarded parking.
Credit cards All major cards accepted.
Terms Rooms: single 350 frs, double 450 frs, suite 600 frs. Breakfast 70 frs. D,B&B 600–700 frs per person. Set meals 180–280 frs; full alc 400 frs.

VÉZELAY 89450 Yonne — Map 9

Hôtel Crispol BUDGET — *Tel* 03.86.33.26.25
Fontette — *Fax* 03.86.33.33.10

"What an amazing place!" A recent verdict on this strikingly modern hotel, in a hamlet east of the famous north Burgundy hilltop village – its bright dining room has picture windows facing the stunning Romanesque basilica. It is owned and run by Christian and Marie-Paule Schori, "charming and good looking"; the fact that Mme Schori is a design expert helps to explain the bold contemporary decor, "a bit over-the-top, like a chic Parisian flat, but not chi-chi". Bedrooms are in a separate building. "It's a bit like a *very* up-market motel," said a recent visitor, "with a superb restaurant (but choice is limited): we served ourselves from enormous casseroles, and our son was given an entire bowl of chocolate mousse. Breakfast, also lavish, was the best of our holiday. But although not unfriendly, the place is very impersonal." For so much chic, prices are reasonable. And the gardens are "very unsmart".

Open All year, except Jan/Feb, Mon (hotel open in season).
Rooms 2 suites, 10 double.
Facilities Ramp. Salon, 2 dining rooms (1 no-smoking); terrace. Garden.
Location 3 km E of Vézelay, on D957 to Avallon. Parking, garage.

Credit cards Access, Visa.
Terms Rooms 350–420 frs, suite 420 frs. Breakfast 40 frs. D,B&B 360 frs per person. Set meals 110–280 frs; full alc 220 frs.

L'Espérance *Tel* 03.86.33.39.10
St-Père *Fax* 03.86.33.26.15

In a valley to the east of the village is Marc Meneau's very sophisticated restaurant: it is made up of three glass pavilions full of plants, and looks on to a garden with a rose arbour and a stream, lit up at night. Its cuisine still wins three *Michelin* stars and three *Gault Millau toques,* and most readers have again concurred: "Food amazingly good, fantastic combinations of flavours and colours." "Our main course was a whole turbotin for three, cooked in red wine: it was worth the 50-minute wait." Another report spells out the ambience: "It's not dinner, it's grand opera! Everyone eyeing everyone else, and wondering what they do to be able to afford the stratospheric prices. But the food was delicious, and the staff most pleasant." "The Meneaus remain so caring and unassuming." Rooms in a nearby converted mill have been found either "gloomy" or "tastefully luxurious". Those in the new annexe on the main road are more spacious but can suffer traffic noise. This *Pré des Marguerites* also has a swimming pool, and a cheaper restaurant with simpler regional dishes. (*R and SO, and others*) Some dislike seeing "the name 'Marc Meneau' stamped on everything". And one dissenter complained of "a real mish-mash of expansion without a unifying style".

Open All year, except end Jan–early Mar. *Espérance* closed Tues/midday Wed; *Pré* closed Mon, in low season.
Rooms 6 suites, 29 double, in 3 buildings. Some on ground floor. 14 air-conditioned.
Facilities Lounge, bar, 2 restaurants. Garden: swimming pool.
Location 3 km E of Vézelay on D957. Closed parking.
Credit cards Amex, Diners, Visa.
Terms Rooms 600–1,400 frs, suite 1,600–2,900 frs. Breakfast 140 frs. *Espérance*: set lunch 390 frs, dinner 680–890 frs; full alc 900 frs.

VICHY 03200 Allier Map 10

Arverna Hôtel NEW/BUDGET *Tel* 04.70.31.31.19
12 rue Desbrest *Fax* 04.70.97.86.43

Central, in tree-lined side-street 400 m from fashionable thermal centre, friendly family-run B&B hotel, simple but modernised. 26 rooms, back ones very quiet; small garden, for breakfast in summer. Good help-yourself breakfasts. Garage nearby. Closed 20–25 Oct, 21 Dec–5 Jan, Sun 1 Dec–1 Mar. All major credit cards accepted. Rooms 200–280 frs. Breakfast 32 frs [1996] 10% discount for those carrying Guide. *Renominated this year.*

> "Set meals" refers to fixed-price meals, which may have ample, limited or no choice on the menu. "Full alc" is the hotel's own estimated price per person of a three-course meal taken *à la carte,* with a half-bottle of house wine. "Alc" is the price of a *carte* meal excluding the cost of wine.

LE VIGEANT 86150 Vienne **Map 10**

Hôtel Val de Vienne NEW *Tel* 05.49.48.27.27
Port de Salles *Fax* 05.49.48.47.47

Beside river Vienne, at Port de Salles, 7 km SW of L'Isle-Jourdain and SE of Poitiers, modern functional bungalow-style B&B hotel managed efficiently by Susan Brooker-Carey. 20 sizeable rooms, each with private terrace (1 adapted for disabled); "exquisitely powerful and consistent showers". Large garden, swimming pool. 5-acre grounds: gardens, river, fishing; Val de Vienne racing circuit nearby. Access, Visa accepted. Rooms 420–520 frs. Buffet breakfast 45 frs. Good restaurants nearby, but hotel hopes to open its own restaurant, La Grimolée, *in adjacent building in 1997.*

LA VILLE-AUX-CLERCS 41160 Loir-et-Cher **Map 8**

Le Manoir de la Fôret NEW *Tel* 02.54.80.62.83
Fort-Girard *Fax* 02.54.80.66.03

The name, and the setting, could evoke *Le Grand Meaulnes*: from a village way west of Orléans, you drive down a side-road past a lake, through a tunnel of trees, and there it is, a handsome ivy-covered mansion in woods and well-kept gardens. The building itself is less well kept, and criticisms pushed it from the 1995 *Guide*. But two reports this year urge its return: "We spend a night here each year, and cannot fault it for good value. Excellent food with a large choice, friendly service, a most elegant dining room. Charlotte the dog took us on a 35-minute walk round the lake." And, on a slightly less certain note: "Hard to find but worth the effort, this old hunting-lodge has an air of genteel decay about its fabric: but the food was first-class. Some new furniture is needed for the terrace, which is the hotel's best feature, with a view of garden and forest. Our bedroom was dark and old-fashioned, just like French hotels used to be." But others have had a light and airy room, with antiques and "some bizarre pictures". "Family-run, friendly, and quiet." (*Mrs Blethyn Elliott, Ross Taggart*)

Open All year, except Sun evening/midday Mon.
Rooms 1 suite, 18 double.
Facilities Lounge, bar, restaurant; conference room; terrace. Garden. Unsuitable for ♿.
Location 1.5 km E of La Ville-aux-Clercs (turn to Fort-Girard by police station).
Credit cards Access, Amex, Visa.
Terms [1996] Rooms 290–450 frs. Breakfast 45 frs. D,B&B 580 frs per person. Set meals 150–265 frs.

VILLEFRANCHE-DE-ROUERGUE 12200 Aveyron **Map 10**

Le Relais de Farrou BUDGET *Tel* 05.65.45.18.11
Le Farrou *Fax* 05.65.45.32.59

The Bouillard family owners "create a happy relaxed atmosphere" at this modestly priced Logis de France . It is a holiday hotel, with modern buildings grouped around a "delightful" garden and an L-shaped swimming pool (lots of loungers). A 1996 report: "A very pleasant stay. Attractive restaurant; service friendly. Breakfast unexceptional." You can also dine on an outdoor patio. Bedroom decor can be garish:

"strong brown and mauvey-pink". (*Caroline McIntosh, GA McKenzie*) Rooms on the main road can be noisy: but most face the gardens and are quiet. A new chef this year. We'd like reports on the food, please.

Open All year, except Christmas. Restaurant closed Sun evening/Mon in low season.
Rooms 1 suite, 25 double. Some on ground floor. Air-conditioning.
Facilities Lounges, bars, TV room, dining rooms; fitness room, hammam, jacuzzi; terrace. Grounds: garden, river, tennis, swimming pool, mini-golf, children's play area; helipad.
Location On D922 to Figeac, 4 km N of Villefranche. Garage, carparks.
Restriction No smoking: 1 dining room, 8 bedrooms.
Credit cards Access, Visa.
Terms Rooms 270–450 frs, suite 520–580 frs. Breakfast 44 frs. D,B&B 315–487 frs per person. Set meals 80–310 frs; alc 300 frs.

VILLEFRANCHE-SUR-MER 06230 Alpes-Maritimes — Map 11

Hotel La Flore — *Tel* 04.93.76.30.30
Av. Princesse Grace de Monaco — *Fax* 04.93.76.99.99

Villefranche, so close to Nice, has a fine natural harbour on a deep bay and is often visited by NATO warships; the tiny 14th-century fishermen's chapel has frescoes by Jean Cocteau. Above the harbour is this classic hotel newly rebuilt in modern style, liked again in 1996: "It is remarkably quiet, and my double room was excellent. I had a good dinner in the bright, cheerful restaurant." This endorses last year's view: "We stayed a week, but it takes a day before you meet all the staff and the warmth of the place gets to you. A very friendly atmosphere. All rooms are furnished in traditional Provençal taste, delightfully cool. Many have a balcony giving a superb view of the bay. Our larger room had a spacious bathroom with jacuzzi. Breakfast on the veranda by the swimming pool is a memorable occasion, very cheerful, full of goodies." (*P Yarnold, GJ*)

Open All year.
Rooms 4 suites, 27 double. 8 in annexe. Some on ground floor.
Facilities Lift. Bar, restaurant; meeting room; terrace with restaurant. Garden: swimming pool. Sandy beaches 1 km.
Location Central. 3 km E of Nice. Parking.
Credit cards All major cards accepted.
Terms B&B: single 360–760 frs, double 420–820 frs. D,B&B 350–870 frs per person. Set meals 130–240 frs.

VILLENEUVE-LÈS-AVIGNON 30400 Gard — Map 11

Le Prieuré — *Tel* 04.90.25.18.20
7 place du Chapître — *Fax* 04.90.25.45.39

Across the Rhône from Avignon, this historic old town has a mighty Charterhouse and other noble buildings. One is this 14th-century priory, well converted into an elegant and luxurious hotel (Relais & Châteaux), owned by Marie-France Mille and managed by her son. Her chef, Serge Chenet, wins a *Michelin* star and two *Gault Millau toques* for variations on Provençal dishes, such as roast scallops with truffles and purée of peas. Latest reports have praised the "friendly staff", the lavish buffet breakfast, the "beautiful gardens with big swimming pool". Others have liked the poolside lunch, the big shady terrace, and dining by candlelight under the plane trees. "Superb in every way." "Our big room in the new annexe had a balcony facing the pool." "Characterful" bedrooms are in the old building, and larger, more expensive ones in the two smart new annexes. Some cheaper rooms may need redecoration. (*KZ, RL and HJM*) Some noise from night trains.

Open Early Mar–early Nov. Restaurant closed 1 May.
Rooms 10 suites, 19 double, 7 single. 1 on ground floor. Some in annexes: *Atrium* and *Chapître.*
Facilities Lifts, ramps. 2 salons, bridge room, library/TV room, breakfast room, dining room; function facilities; air-conditioning; dining patio. Large garden: tennis, swimming pool.
Location 3 km N of Avignon. Central, behind church. Enclosed parking.
Credit cards All major cards accepted.
Terms Rooms 550 frs, suite 1,450–1,800 frs. Breakfast 80 frs. Set meals 200–460 frs; full alc 450–550 frs.

VILLENEUVE-SUR-YONNE 89500 Yonne — Map 9

La Lucarne aux Chouettes

Quai Bretoche — *Tel* 03.86.87.18.26 — *Fax* 03.86.87.22.63

The actress Leslie Caron has returned to what she calls *"mes vieilles pierres bourguignonnes"*. In the little town where she now lives she has restored four derelict 17th-century houses by the river Yonne, to create this "delectable" restaurant-with-rooms. She runs it herself. "The conversion has been beautifully done, keeping all the old character of ancient stones and beams, flagged floors and old tiles. The four bedrooms are all different. Ours, under the eaves, was huge, with rugs and antiques; the bathroom was on a raised tiled area, its privacy secured by a 'stage curtain'. A small window overlooked the rapid river and its swans, ducks and long barges. There's a terrace for summer dining. In the restaurant, under a huge vaulted ceiling and by a blazing fire, we enjoyed the *prix fixe* menu of mainly Burgundian specialities. The wine list, mainly local, was keenly priced, and service was excellent. Breakfast was traditional, served by the charming manageress." (*P and JT*) A new chef this year, Noelle Samson. More reports, please.

Open All year.
Rooms 4 double.
Facilities Bar, restaurant; riverside terrace. Access to river: bathing, fishing, boating; bicycles available. Unsuitable for ♿.
Location Central, by bridge. 13 km S of Sens.
Credit cards Access, Amex, Visa.
Terms Rooms 490 frs. Breakfast 50 frs. Set lunch 98 frs, dinner 170 frs; full alc 220 frs.

VILLERAY 61110 Orne — Map 8

Le Moulin de Villeray

Villeray, Condeau-au-Perche — *Tel* 02.33.73.30.22 — *Fax* 02.33.73.38.28

Nothing could be more studiously romantic than this beautifully converted old mill house, set quietly beside a small river in the pretty Perche district of southern Normandy. Now a smart restaurant-with-rooms, with enthusiastic owners, the Eelsens, it has won more praise this year: "Delightful, with beautiful gardens and swimming pool." Others have written: "Very atmospheric, with splendid beams and old glass in the dining room. A warm welcome and a well-trained staff. Rooms are well furnished in provincial style. It is out-of-doors on a warm summer evening that the place comes into its own – a lovely garden by the river, and a courtyard where meals are served." "We were greeted warmly, given a beautiful room above the mill cottage." François Lagrue's cooking has been called "marvellous", eg, tête de veau avec foie gras de canard. (*J Rudd, and others*) A few small signs of neglect: "They need to replace the railings of the millrace before they lose a guest."

Open All year, except Feb.
Rooms 2 suites, 16 double. 8 in garden annexe. Some on ground floor.
Facilities Salon, bar, restaurant. 3-hectare grounds: garden, swimming pool, river: fishing.
Location 8 km N of Nogent-le-Rotrou, by D918, D10.
Credit cards All major cards accepted.
Terms Rooms: single 390–590 frs, double 450–950 frs, suite 750–1,150 frs. Breakfast 68 frs. D,B&B double 982–1,746 frs. Set meals 145–330 frs; full alc 250–350 frs. Cookery, pottery courses.

VILLERS-COTTERETS 02600 Aisne — Map 9

Hôtel Le Régent NEW/BUDGET — *Tel* 03.23.96.01.46
26 rue du Général Mangin — *Fax* 03.23.96.37.57

This historic town in the forest of Retz, north-east of Paris, has a small museum devoted to Alexandre Dumas *père*, who was born here. There are several fine old buildings with inner courtyards, which used to be coaching inns on the Paris–Brussels route. One of them is the *Régent*, 16th- to 18th-century, tastefully converted into a hotel where real character counts for more than smart upkeep. Dropped from the *Guide* for lack of reports, it is now renominated: "Wonderful! The lobby was charming, as was the manager. Our room was large, comfortable, clean, with big windows facing the lovely courtyard/garden (where we had a good breakfast). The room had clearly been very elegant, but was a bit run down (cracked antiques and panelling, worn carpet), as was the hallway. However, some other parts of the hotel have apparently just been carefully renovated." The reception room has country antiques, including a real sedan chair that you are welcome to sit in. Many rooms have their large original beams. (*Martin V Ferer*) No restaurant: the nearby *Commerce* is recommended.

Open All year.
Rooms 1 suite, 15 double, 2 single. 4 on ground floor.
Facilities Lobby, breakfast room; terrace.
Location Central. Villers is 78 km NE of Paris on N2. Garage, interior parking.
Credit cards Access, Diners, Visa.
Terms Rooms: single 155–215 frs, double 330–370 frs, suite 370–650 frs. Breakfast 30.50–44.50 frs.

If you have kept brochures and tariffs for continental hotels, do please enclose them with your reports. They are particularly useful if you are nominating a hotel.

VINCELOTTES 89290 Yonne — Map 9

Auberge des Tilleuls NEW/BUDGET — *Tel* 03.86.42.22.13 *Fax* 03.86.42.23.51

*On banks of river Yonne, 16 km SE of Auxerre, off N6, attractive rural inn with welcoming owner/chef, simple but adequate rooms, excellent meals (*Michelin *red "Repas") and breakfasts served on terrace under lime trees in summer. Closed 18 Dec–end Feb, Wed evening/Thurs out of season. Access, Visa accepted. 5 rooms: 275–400 frs. Breakfast 38 frs. D,B&B 350–400 frs per person. Set meals 120–275 frs [1996].*

VONNAS 01540 Ain — Map 12

Georges Blanc — *Tel* 04.74.50.90.90 *Fax* 04.74.50.08.80

Half-timbered and pink-bricked, Georges Blanc's famous and sophisticated restaurant (Relais & Châteaux) has a pretty setting beside a river on the edge of a *village fleuri* south-east of Mâcon. It still wins the French guides' topmost ratings for cuisine, and has other qualities, too: "The dining rooms are really beautiful," runs a report this year, "with their beams, grand fireplaces and tapestried chairs. Our huge bathroom in marmalade-coloured marble was also lovely." The maestro now has a cheaper eating-place, too, *L'Ancienne Auberge,* across the road in his grandparents' former café. "For 150 frs [1996], the meal was a bargain," say devotees. "We stayed in a huge split-level suite by the river. Super food, excellent family and staff." This year, another reader also found it delightful, and adds: "We had breakfast in the main hotel to see how the rich live, and they were mostly Japanese." In the main restaurant, where M. Blanc is usually much in evidence, one reader thought the dishes "individually sensational", but together "a stunningly rich Edwardian combination unsuitable for most 1990s stomachs", and she found the staff flustered and snooty. The hotel has some medium-priced rooms in a newly renovated building; but most admired are the large bedrooms in the new "winter garden" area, many of them facing the river. Here the lounge has a log fire in winter and becomes a riverside terrace in summer. (*ABX Fenwick, P and JT*)

Open All year, except 2 Jan–8 Feb, Christmas. Restaurant closed Mon/Tues (open Tues evening 19 June–15 Sept).
Rooms 10 suites, 38 double. 21 in 2 annexes. Air-conditioning.
Facilities Lift. 2 lounges, bar, breakfast room, dining room; conference room; winter garden/river terrace. Garden: tennis, putting, swimming pool, helipad.
Location 20 km SE of Mâcon. *Autoroute* A6 from N: exit Mâcon Nord, from S: exit Villefranche. Follow signs to Châtillon-sur-Chalaronne, then Neuville-les-Dames, then Vonnas.
Credit cards All major cards accepted.
Terms Rooms 550–1,750 frs, suite 1,850–3,000 frs. Breakfast 105 frs. Set meals 470–850 frs.

Report forms (Freepost in UK) will be found at the end of the *Guide*. If you need more, or larger ones, please ask. But it is not essential that you use them for reports.

VOUVANT 85120 Vendée Map 10

Auberge du Maître Pannetier BUDGET *Tel* 02.51.00.80.12
Place du Corps de Garde *Fax* 02.51.87.89.37

The ruined castle in this ancient ramparted townlet in pastoral south-east Vendée was allegedly built by the fairy Mélusine in one night in 1242. The owners of this Logis de France claim that it, too, has a "rather magic ambience", but our reporter found it more practical: "A charming village by a river, with narrow winding streets. The restaurant is popular locally, and we could see why. The local wines are good, too. There's a 1930s-style cocktail bar, where charming girls served an excellent breakfast. Madame was helpful. Our room was well fitted out with new 'antique pine' furniture. Top floor rooms have substantial roof beams: tall people should watch out." (*JA; endorsed this year by Elizabeth Biggs, who specially appreciated the hotel's welcome to families with young children*)

Open All year, except Feb school holidays.
Rooms 7 double.
Facilities Salon, bar, 3 dining rooms; terrace. Unsuitable for ♿.
Location In village, 15 km N of Fontenay-le-Comte. Public parking.
Credit cards Access, Visa.
Terms Rooms 210–280 frs. Breakfast 35 frs. D,B&B 245–260 frs per person. Set meals 70–350 frs; full alc 280–300 frs.

LA WANTZENAU 67610 Bas-Rhin Map 9

Le Moulin de la Wantzenau *Tel* 03.88.59.22.22
Impasse du Moulin 3 *Fax* 03.88.59.22.00

Outside a village north of Strasbourg is this charmingly converted old mill house, quite idyllic, with its garden and broad terraces by the river Ill. It is owned and run by two grand-daughters of the last "working" mill-owner, while their brother Philippe Clauss runs *Au Moulin*, the good restaurant opposite. More recent praise: "A favourite of ours, with its bird-filled garden and good welcome. The rooms are pleasantly decorated: we had a split-level top-floor suite." (*AS*)

Open All year, except 24 Dec–2 Jan. Restaurant closed 1–15 Jan, 5–25 July.
Rooms 1 suite, 19 double.
Facilities Lift. Salon, library, bar, breakfast room (no-smoking); terrace. Unsuitable for ♿.
Location By river, 1.5 km E of Le Wantzenau, which is 12 km NE of Strasbourg by D468. Private parking.
Credit cards Access, Amex, Visa.
Terms Rooms 340 frs, suite 550 frs. Breakfast 55 frs.

WIERRE-EFFROY 62720 Pas-de-Calais Map 9

Ferme du Vert BUDGET *Tel* 03.21.87.67.00
Route du Paon *Fax* 03.21.83.22.62

More than ever this year, the tributes have poured in: "What a lovely place", "wonderful", "quite marvellous", etc. But does this simple farmhouse between Calais and Boulogne receive such ecstatic praise simply because it's the first bit of rural France you come to, arriving via ferry or tunnel? No: it has its own amazing qualities, too. The "kind and gentle" Bernard family have converted part of their working farm into a Logis de France, now doing a roaring tourist trade but still genuinely pastoral. Its unique atmosphere owes a lot to its farmyard, with free-ranging ducks and geese, an enormous rooster, a turkey, doves and kittens, an energetic labrador. "M. Bernard was so lovely it wasn't true. We loved all the animals, and the silence. We had a good meal with excellent soup and lots of it, in the cosy restaurant with log fire and friendly waiter." "The scene at breakfast was enchanting – children playing with animals in the yard, merriment all round. We felt we were taking part in *Jean de Florette*." "A courteous staff served a delightful meal, with a huge and wonderful apple tart." "An enchanting rural haven: just what a small family hotel should be." "There's a lovely half-wild garden, where we drank wine on an old stone patio under a tree." And so on . . . The pine-clad bedrooms, "warm and cosy", but a little basic for some tastes, are fashioned from barns; many readers love sleeping in a converted hayloft. "Our lovely room had a four-poster bed: the loo was in a cupboard." One son runs a *fromagerie* on the farm where they make their own cheeses – "excellent". (*Linda Brook, Gillian Gadsby, BC Kay, Carey and Nigel Newton, and countless others*) The restaurant, separately managed, has a new chef this year. First reports are contradictory: one highly critical, one "getting better".

Open All year, except 15 Dec–15 Jan. Restaurant closed midday, Sun.
Rooms 16 double, in 4 buildings. 4 on ground floor.
Facilities Salon, bar, breakfast room, restaurant; meeting room. Garden: tennis, putting; bicycle hire.
Location *Autoroute* A16 exit Marquise–Rinxent. Go to Marquise. Follow signs for *Ferme du Vert*.
Credit cards Access, Amex, Visa.
Terms Rooms: single 300 frs, double 350–400 frs. Breakfast 50 frs. D,B&B double 680–800 frs. Set dinner 150 frs.

YVOIRE 74104 Haute-Savoie — Map 12

Hôtel-Restaurant du Port

Tel 04.50.72.80.17
Fax 04.50.72.90.71

Yvoire is "a tiny flower-decked medieval village", inevitably full of tourists and souvenir shops (but also with a curious museum of live reptiles), near Geneva on the south side of Lac Léman. Here this restaurant-with-four-rooms has been called "as picturesque as can be, Swiss chalet style". Recent praise: "The best room, facing the lake, has a jacuzzi. Our quieter room had balcony, charming view. M. Kung gave us a warm welcome. Service was friendly. The large foyer, which doubles as bar and breakfast area, has excellent design. The main restaurant has views over the lake, with a terrace. The cooking seems to be famous locally. We enjoyed the salade savoyarde, foie de veau with garlic in a good sauce, boeuf stroganoff, a light red Jura wine." More reports, please.

Open 15 Mar–30 Oct. Closed Wed Apr/Oct.
Rooms 4 double. Air-conditioning.
Facilities Salon, bar, 3 dining rooms; conference room; 2 terraces on lake.
Location In village, 30 km NE of Geneva. Cars allowed for access only (hotel arranges parking).
Credit cards Access, Amex, Visa.
Terms B&B 550–800 frs. Set meals 105–190 frs; full alc 220 frs.

Germany

Wald- und Schlosshotel, Friedrichsruhe

This year, we have eight new entries for former East Germany, which brings up to 15 our selection for that region. This, together with our new separate chapters for the Czech Republic and Slovenia, indicates that more readers are now visiting those ex-Communist lands, and that more smallish privately run hotels, of the kind that the *Guide* prefers, are now appearing there. In eastern Germany, hotels of the old regime have now been privatised, and often renovated. And many new ones have been purpose built. Some belong to chains, but others are family owned: in some cases, as with our entries for Magdeburg and Quedlinburg, former owners from the pre-GDR days have got their old property back. Most hotels in the east are now coming close to western standards of service, food and comfort.

In Germany as a whole, chain hotels are far less numerous than they are in the UK or the USA. At the upper end of the market, the principal German chains are Maritim and Steigenberger; some foreign chains, such as Crest, Holiday Inn and Mercure, are also represented. Hotels of this kind are generally efficient, but impersonal and very large. None of them features in the *Guide*.

In fact, nearly all German hotels are individually owned and run. Some of these, as in France, group together for joint promotion and marketing. Perhaps the best association is Romantik Hotels: its members are in the medium to upper price bracket, and nearly all are in old buildings with some character and atmosphere. Many are most attractive, and they are seldom formal or pretentious. Gast im Schloss, another good association, consists of well-converted castles, some still run by their family owners; several feature in this book. The large Ring Hotel association is diverse: it includes some dullish city hotels for businessfolk, as well as some very attractive ones. The Silencehotels, part of the French Relais du Silence group, are quiet hotels, mostly in secluded settings.

Standards of service and cleanliness tend to be high in Germany, even in the cheapest hotels. There are some peculiarities, however, that may puzzle a first-time visitor. As in most of central Europe, duvets (*Federbetten* or down comforters) are universally used in place of top sheets and blankets. German beds tend to be rather hard, with small, thin pillows, for this is considered healthy. Most double rooms have twin beds, often placed close together to form one bed – "it makes snuggling a challenge," said one reader this year. In many hotels, a chocolate or sweet will be left on the bed as a tiny goodnight gift. Soap and shampoo are not usually provided in guest houses. Breakfast is generally a buffet, included in the room price. Service is always included in the bill; you need leave nothing extra for room service, though in a restaurant it is customary to give a tip of about 3 to 5 per cent directly to the waiter or waitress when paying the bill.

As in France, we make a point of indicating when a hotel has won an award from *Michelin* for its cuisine. The top rating of three stars is given to only three restaurants in all Germany (compared with 20 in France), but even one star indicates food of high quality. We also indicate when *Michelin* bestows a red "Menu", the equivalent of the coveted red "Repas" in France, for "good food at moderate prices".

ASCHAU IM CHIEMGAU 83229 Bayern — Map 14

Residenz Heinz Winkler — *Tel* (08052) 17 99-0
Kirchplatz 1 — *Fax* (08052) 17 99 66

Heinz Winkler is owner/chef of this distinguished 15th-century coaching inn, much modernised, in the pretty village of Aschau, at the foot of the Chiemgau Alps. This year, *Michelin* withdrew one of its three stars. But the cooking remains imaginative, among the best in Bavaria. The dining room is huge (many visitors drive over from Munich for a meal), but it affords privacy as the tables are well spaced. "Our large room facing the mountains was beautifully furnished in Biedermeier style, with cheerful fabrics. The breakfast buffet had exceptional delicacies, and the staff made us welcome." There is no lounge, only a "large, rather ostentatious lobby", and a bar; also a garden with loungers, and a patio for drinks in summer. An indoor swimming pool is planned for autumn 1996. Newer reports are much needed.

Open All year.
Rooms 12 suites, 20 double. Some on ground floor.
Facilities Lift. Lobby, bar, TV room, restaurant. Garden.

Location In village, 82 km SE of Munich. Parking.
Credit cards All major cards accepted.
Terms B&B: single 180 DM, double 220–450 DM, suite 450–580 DM. Set meals 145–195 DM; alc 150 DM.

AUGSBURG 86152 Bayern — Map 14

Romantik Hotel Augsburger Hof — *Tel* (0821) 31 40 83
Auf Dem Kreuz 2 — *Fax* (0821) 3 83 22

Bertolt Brecht scorned the noble city of his birth as being much too bourgeois. But today it has a Brecht museum among its many remarkable attractions. Others include the Golden Hall of the Renaissance *Rathaus*, the 16th-century Fuggerei almshouse estate, plus the MAN factory where Rudolf Diesel invented his fuel engine. Between this and the cathedral is this classic hotel, newly renovated. Recent praise: "Nice and homey, with pine furniture, enough chintz to make it comfortable but not cutesy. Nice staff." "The restaurant serves good Swabian fare" – as befits the capital of the Swabian part of Bavaria. More reports, please.

Open All year. Restaurant closed 24 Dec, 1 Jan.
Rooms 29 double, 7 single.
Facilities Lift. Restaurant, bar; sauna; terrace.
Location 1 km N of centre. Parking.
Credit cards All major cards accepted.
Terms B&B: single 115–165 DM, double 145–230 DM; D,B&B double 195–270 DM. Set meals 40–82 DM; full alc 65 DM.

AYING 85653 Bayern — Map 14

Brauereigasthof Aying NEW — *Tel* (08095) 705
Zornedingerstrasse 2 — *Fax* (08095) 2053

The Inselkammer family's huge creeper-covered beer-pub "embodies everything you expect a Bavarian hotel to be", says a 1996 visitor, restoring it to the *Guide* after a while with no reports. It stands next to a famous brewery in a picturesque flower-decked village near Munich, where dairy farmers and commuters rub shoulders. The airy bedrooms have Biedermeier furniture; and you can eat out in the courtyard when it's fine (some delicate dishes, such as carbonnade of lamb in garlic sauce, plus the usual hefty local pork-based ones). "The food in the beautiful restaurant was grand. Staff were gracious, and our sunny room had lovely pine furniture. Beer is everywhere." In fact, there's no point in *not* being here for the beer: they serve it with their "walloping" breakfasts, if you wish, they even leave free bottles of it on your pillow at night. "Go in to dine armed with a guide to German beer. Imaginative food: our first encounter with dried wild-boar ham." Rooms have painted furniture. (*Kathy Gaston*)

Open All year, except 23/24 Dec.
Rooms 1 suite, 21 double, 5 single.
Facilities 3 lounges, breakfast room, restaurant; function room. Garden: children's playground. Bicycles for hire. Unsuitable for ♿.
Location Central. 26 km SE of Munich. Parking.
Credit cards All major cards accepted.
Terms B&B: single 160 DM, double 220 DM, suite 350 DM. Alc meals 60 DM.

BAD LAASPHE-GLASHÜTTE 57334 Nordrhein-Westfalen Map 14

Jagdhof Glashütte NEW
Glashütterstrasse 20

Tel (02754) 39 90
Fax (02754) 39 92 22

In a little-known part of central Germany, remote amid hilly forested country on the southern edge of the Sauerland, is this very stylish mock hunting-lodge, all half-timbering, gabled turrets and pretty lights. "The brochure's glossy photos, of young sophisticates enjoying the high life, should not put one off," says its nominator. "The public and private rooms are all exposed beams and country cottons. Although it has only 29 rooms, the hotel offers the services of a much larger place, including massages, sauna, theme weekends. Yet the atmosphere is intimate. A cosy fire in reception, thick bathrobes, a sumptuous buffet breakfast. We look forward to returning." There's also a piano bar, a barbecue in the garden, a heated pool. More reports, notably on the food, would be welcome.

Open All year.
Rooms 10 suites, 16 double, 3 single.
Facilities 2 lifts. Lobby with fire place, piano bar, 3 dining rooms; function rooms; indoor swimming pool, sauna, solarium, massage, hairdressing. Garden. Unsuitable for ♿.
Location Outside Volkholz village, 14 km W of Bad Laasphe, on road from Siegen. Parking.
Credit cards All major cards accepted.
Terms B&B: single 188–208 DM, double 350–390 DM, suite 410–580 DM; D,B&B 50 DM per person added. Set lunch 58 DM, dinner 89 DM; full alc 80 DM. Reduced rates for children.

BADEN-BADEN 76530 Baden-Württemberg Map 14

Hotel Am Markt BUDGET
Marktplatz 18

Tel (07221) 2 27 47
Fax (07221) 39 18 87

This small, modest family-run hotel is not what you might expect to find in the heart of fashionable Baden-Baden. "It is in the oldest part of town, on the top of the hill by the cathedral. There are no frills here, but our quiet room overlooking the city was basically comfortable. The narrow reception area adjoins the *Stüble*. Here we had freshly cooked, plentiful, truly German dishes from the limited menu, served till 8 pm. You can also eat on a pleasant terrace in the square. Adequate breakfast." (*J and MS*)

Open All year. Restaurant (residents only) closed midday.
Rooms 10 double, 17 single. 12 with bath or shower, 2 with WC.
Facilities 2 lounges with TV, restaurant (residents only); small terrace. Unsuitable for ♿.
Location Central. In pedestrian zone (car access for unloading). Parking.
Credit cards All major cards accepted.
Terms B&B: single 55–90 DM, double 100–150 DM. Set dinner 10–20 DM; full alc 35 DM.

> Inevitably some hotels change hands or close after we have gone to press. It may be prudent to check the ownership when booking, particularly in the case of small establishments.

BAMBERG 96047 Bayern Map 14

Romantik Hotel Weinhaus Messerschmitt *Tel* (0951) 2 78 66
Langestrasse 41 *Fax* (0951) 2 61 41

A handsome old winehouse-with-rooms, where Professor Willy Messerschmitt, the aircraft engineer, built the model of his first plane. It has been in the family's hands since 1832 (old portraits adorn the hallways) and is now owned by a descendant, Otto Pschorn. "Good food and comfort, an old-fashioned feel," say readers this year. Others have admired the decor of dark wood beams, carved stair-rails and oriental rugs, the large bedrooms with matching fabrics, and the "splendid" service. "A nice breakfast buffet was served in a proper Bavarian room, with a lovely old porcelain stove." Notable wines. (*W Cottingham, and others*). The hotel is on the junction of two busy roads. Earplugs are provided free by the management.

Open All year, except 24 Dec, 13–18 Jan.
Rooms 2 suites, 14 double, 1 single. 4 no-smoking.
Facilities Restaurant, *Stube*, wine cellar; conference room. Garden. Unsuitable for ♿.
Location Central. 4 private parking spaces; underground carpark nearby.
Credit cards All major cards accepted.
Terms B&B: single 125 DM, double 195 DM, suite 225 DM. Set meals 25–59.50 DM; full alc 75 DM. Children under 6 accommodated free in parents' room.

BAYREUTH-SEULBITZ 95448 Bayern Map 14

Waldhotel Stein *Tel* (0921) 90 01
Fax (0921) 9 47 25

"A relaxing atmosphere, mildly eccentric in the nicest way. A warm welcome, friendly service, unpretentious cooking with generous helpings: the 'after-opera buffet' has a huge and diverse range of dishes. We had a spacious, well-equipped room." An endorsement this year for Irmgard Stein's peaceful modern hotel in this pleasant village near Bayreuth (you can see the floodlit *Festspielhaus* from your window). The rooms are in five bungalows in the big garden, close to the main house, which holds the restaurant, lounge and pool. "We enjoyed our stay," wrote British hoteliers last year; "you can relax in the garden, enjoy the pool and the views across rolling farmland to orchards. The mother and daughter Stein arrange affairs confidently, and their staff are charming. Breakfasts were copious." Many ingredients are organically produced locally. (*Michael MacKenzie and Frederic Symonds, J and MS*) Some rooms are large and luxurious, some are bedsitters with balcony. One couple were not impressed by room or food.

Open All year, except Christmas/New Year.
Rooms 20 suites, 20 double, 10 single. Some on ground floor. Some no-smoking.
Facilities 2 lounges, restaurant; conference room; indoor swimming pool, sauna, solarium, massage. Large grounds.
Location 6 km E of Bayreuth, near Seulbitz village; follow signs for *Eremitage*. Garage, carpark.
Credit cards All major cards accepted.
Terms B&B: single 98–250 DM, double 146–360 DM, suite 500–600 DM. Set meals 30 DM; full alc 48 DM. (Prices increase hugely during opera festival.)

BEILSTEIN 56814 Rheinland-Pfalz Map 14

Haus Lipmann *Tel* (02673) 15 73
Marktplatz 3

Metternich was the last overlord of this picturesque village on the Mosel, and his ruined castle stands on the hill above. Tucked between the river and the tiny main square is this half-timbered old *Gasthof*, modest but full of character, and long admired. Readers have enjoyed eating on its flower-decked terrace facing the river, or in the fine old panelled dining room: dishes might include smoked Mosel eel with scrambled eggs. An inspector was there in 1996: "It's very simple, but delightfully traditional and personal, well run by the Lipmann/Thülen family. Rooms are old-fashioned, but comfortable: ours had a poky shower room but superb antique porelain wash-basin, and a balcony facing the river (slight traffic noise). In the hall is a 1920s phonograph with old 33 and 78 rpm records, lovingly kept. In the family's wine-cellar opposite (1577), vaulted and candlelit, we spent a convivial evening drinking and singing, arms locked, swaying gently. A Lipmann brother owns the nearby *Altes Zollhaus* hotel – *tel*: (02673) 18 50) – and its modern *Am Klosterberg* annexe, up a hill: these have less charm than the Haus Lipmann, but they are inexpensive, and bedrooms are more modern. (*JA and KA, and others*)

Open 15 Mar–15 Nov.
Rooms 5 double. 20 more in annexes (see text).
Facilities Restaurant; conference/function facilities; wine cellar (wine tastings); terrace on Mosel. Unsuitable for ♿.
Location Central, near marketplace. Parking.
Credit cards None accepted.
Terms B&B: single 110 DM, double 120–150 DM; D,B&B 20 DM per person added; full board 30 DM added. Full alc 55 DM.

BERCHTESGADEN 83471 Bayern Map 14

Hotel Krone BUDGET *Tel* (08652) 6 20 51
Am Rad 5 *Fax* (08652) 6 65 79

This famous little town has a glorious setting of mountains and Alpine lakes. Little remains to be seen of Hitler's upland eyrie; but a visit to the local salt-mines is a "must". On a quiet hill in the outskirts is the modest but ever popular *Krone*, white-walled, blue-shuttered and furnished in Bavarian rustic style: many rooms open on to balconies facing the valley and hills. The snug, wood-panelled rooms have Bavarian hand-painted furniture. "Delightful," say visitors this year. "Frau Grafe and her son were very pleasant, the food was first class." Others have written: "We had a lovely room, and the breakfast and the home cooking were good." Frau Grafe, dressed in Bavarian costume, "offers a warm welcome". (*Ian N Harris*)

Open 21 Dec–28 Oct. Closed Mon.
Rooms 2 suites, 13 double, 6 single.
Facilities Lounge, 2 dining rooms (1 no-smoking); terrace. Garden.
Location 1 km N of centre, off Salzburg road. Private parking.
Credit card Access.
Terms B&B: 50–78 DM; D,B&B 68–96 DM. Full alc 30 DM.

BERLIN Map 14

Hotel Belvedere *Tel* 82 60 01 0
Seebergsteig 4 *Fax* 82 60 01 63
Grunewald, 14193 Berlin

Three miles west of the city centre, down a quiet, leafy side street in the wealthy and well-named suburb of Grunewald, is this big gabled turn-of-the-century villa – quite a contrast to the Ku'Damm hotels. "High-grade *pension*, with a *Gemütlichkeit* not common in Berlin; remarkable value for this city. Public rooms have the air of a bourgeois private home. Most bedrooms are furnished in period style and are large and bright – there's even a grand piano in one – but some basement ones may be gloomy. The owner, Erwin Opel, is pleasant, and the garden lovely." The nearby forest extends to the big Havel lake with its beaches. A bus goes to city centre. No restaurant (lots nearby).

Open All year.
Rooms 12 double, 7 single.
Facilities Salon with TV, breakfast room. Garden: solarium. Unsuitable for ♿.
Location In Grunewald, 4 km SW of city centre. (S-Bahn: Grunewald.)
Credit cards Access, Diners, Visa.
Terms Rooms: single 65–140 DM, double 120–180 DM. Breakfast 10 DM.

Hotel Brandenburger Hof *Tel* (030) 21 40 50
Eislebenerstrasse 14 *Fax* (030) 21 40 51 00
Wilmersdorf, 10789 Berlin

Near to the Zoo and Ku'damm, this large turn-of-the-century mansion (Relais & Châteaux) has been stylishly modernised, and has Bauhaus decor. Rooms are around a glassed-in courtyard, with a Japanese garden, where meals are served from 7 am until midnight in the *Wintergarten* restaurant, and exhibitions are held. There is also a gourmet restaurant, the *Quadriga*. "Both the hotel and restaurant were excellent," says a visitor this year, echoing last year's praise: "The sumptuous breakfast buffet includes gravlax. Bedrooms are cool and airy, with modern design. Restful meditation poems are on your pillow. Good food, knowledgeable reception staff." "Known in Berlin as one of the very best city-centre hotels." (*Michael LN Forrest, and others*)

Open All year. *Quadriga* closed Sat/Sun, 1–12 Jan, 19 July–17 Aug.
Rooms 83 double, 4 single.
Facilities Piano bar, winter-garden, 2 restaurants; 3 conference rooms.
Location Central. Garage (18 DM). (U-Bahn: Augsburgerstrasse.)
Credit cards All major cards accepted.
Terms B&B: single 250–395 DM, double 290–445 DM. Set lunch 48 DM, dinner: *Wintergarten* 65 DM, *Quadriga* 85–160 DM; full alc: *Wintergarten* 85 DM, *Quadriga* 120 DM. Children under 6 accommodated free in parents' room.

Hotel-Pension Dittberner *Tel* (030) 881 64 85
Wielandstrasse 26 and 884 69 50
10707 Berlin *Fax* (030) 885 40 46

"Very good value, and warmly welcoming" – latest praise for Frau Lange's mildly idiosyncratic *pension*, just off the Ku'Damm. It is on the third floor of the same building as another modestly priced *pension*, the *Modena* (also recommended; *tel* 885 70 10), and it uses the same creaky old lift. Rooms vary in size. The best have tall French windows leading on to balconies. "It is plain except for the sitting/breakfast room, which is very atmospheric, in late 19th-century style. Frau Lange runs the hotel with the help of her daughter. Her husband runs a classy art gallery on the ground floor, and the rooms are full of interesting wooden pictures. You go for the wayward charm, not for the upkeep or housekeeping, both sometimes criticised. Recommended restaurant close by, *Marjellchen*, inexpensive and *gemütlich*, specialising in East Prussian cuisine.

Open All year.
Rooms 12 double, 9 single. 11 with *en suite* facilities.
Facilities Lift. TV lounge, breakfast room. Unsuitable for ♿.
Location Central, off Kurfürstendamm, 800 m W of Memorial Church. Carparks nearby. (U-Bahn: Adenauerplatz.)
Credit cards None accepted.
Terms [1996] B&B: single 90–130 DM, double 140–200 DM.

Hecker's Hotel — *Tel* (030) 88 90-0
Grolmanstrasse 35 — *Fax* (030) 88 90-260
10623 Berlin

Central, just off top of Ku'Damm (U-Bahn: Uhlandstrasse): B&B hotel with roof terrace, ultra-modern decor, 72 large, bright cheerful bedrooms (back ones quietest), most with marble bathroom, some with kitchenette; 1 equipped for ♿. Good breakfasts. All major credit cards accepted. B&B: single 00–310 DM, double 250–390 DM [1996]. Endorsed this year: "We would not hesitate to stay here again." More reports, please.

Hotel Residenz — *Tel* (030) 88 44 30
Meinekestrasse 9 — *Fax* (030) 882 47 26
10719 Berlin

Two big houses with *Jugendstil* façade have been knocked together to form this "most elegant" hotel, just off the Kurfürstendamm. It remains popular: "The front rooms are like private apartments: high, light ceilings with Art-Deco designs, substantial quality furniture and well-equipped bathrooms. Our room had a king-size bed, and a large writing desk. The buffet breakfast was superb; we had an ordinary, well-served dinner in the hotel's *Grand Cru* restaurant." Breakfast "embraces the hot, the German and the healthy". Back rooms are quietest, but smaller, and with less character. (*J and MS, and others*)

Open All year.
Rooms 10 suites, 70 double, 4 single.
Facilities Lift. Salon, bar, restaurant; conference facilities.
Location Central, off Ku'damm. Street parking difficult. (U-Bahn: Uhlandstrasse.)
Credit cards All major cards accepted.
Terms B&B: single 210–220 DM, double 266–310 DM, suite 390–450 DM. Set meals 25–35 DM; full alc 45 DM.

Hotel Seehof — *Tel* (030) 3 20 02-0
Lietzensee-Ufer 11 — *Fax* (030) 3 20 02-251
14057 Berlin

Central but quiet, a fairly smart and formal hotel in Charlottenburg, well run, with amiable staff. Best feature is small lake in garden, overlooked by airy dining room and most bedrooms, some with balcony. Attractive terraced gardens, cosy bar, good conventional food. Swimming pool for summer. Underground garage. (U-Bahn: Sophie-Charlotten-Platz.) Access, Amex, Visa accepted. 77 rooms. B&B: single 223–357 DM, double 277–444 DM. Set meals 42–69 DM. More reports welcome.

BURG 03096 Brandenburg **Map 14**

Waldhotel Eiche NEW *Tel* (035603) 643
Eicheweg 1 *Fax* (035603) 60184
Burg-Kauper

One of our eight new entries this year for former East Germany. It is an ambitious holiday hotel in the Spreewald, a flat watery region where the Spree divides into various streams, amid woods, meadows and orchards; many of the locals are Sorbs, a Slav minority with their own culture, and their own language, similar to Polish. The *Eiche*, an inn since 1765, was visited by Theodore Fontane, who described it in one of his books. Owned for five generations by the Roschke family, it survived GDR blight and has now been enlarged and rebuilt as a big red mansion by owner/chef Wilhelm Roschke. Our nominator relates: "The bedrooms, comfortable if not very exciting, all have peaceful river or pasture views. The food is hearty and very good; ample breakfast buffet." Delights include terrace and beer-garden, outdoor dining, boat trips, dancing, "speciality evenings".

Open All year.
Rooms 7 suites, 53 double, 2 single. Some on ground floor.
Facilities Lift. Lounges, bar, 4 restaurants; 4 conference rooms; sauna, steam bath, fitness room; terrace. Garden: beergarden; children's playground; on river: fishing.
Location At Burg-Kauper, 9 km N of Burg, 27 km NW of Cottbus.
Credit cards Access, Amex, Visa.
Terms B&B: single 120–140 DM, double 160–200 DM, suite 220–260 DM; D,B&B 30 DM added per person. Full alc 50 DM.

COLOGNE Nordrhein-Westfalen **Map 14**

Hotel Buchholz BUDGET *Tel* (0221) 12 18 24
Kunibertsgasse 5 *Fax* (0221) 13 16 65
50668 Köln

Just north of the cathedral and main station, central but quiet, this small and friendly B&B hotel, newly renovated, has a British owner, Carole Ann Buchholz. Bedrooms are "comfortable, pleasantly old-fashioned". "When I checked in exhausted at 11.30 pm," says a recent visitor, "the welcoming night porter willingly produced some bread and soup. My room was tiny but perfectly equipped. Pleasant breakfast room." (*BA*)

Open All year, except Christmas/New Year.
Rooms 10 double, 7 single.
Facilities Lounge, TV room, bar, breakfast room.
Location Central, 300 m N of station. Public parking.
Credit cards All major cards accepted.
Terms B&B: single 55–150 DM, double 95–280 DM. Special rates off season. 1-night bookings sometimes refused in season.

Hotel im Wasserturm *Tel* (0221) 2 00 80
Kaygasse 2 *Fax* (0221) 2 00 88 88
50676 Köln

This most unusual luxury hotel is a 19th-century water tower, a great brick cylinder, hardly beautiful, but now converted in bold ultra-modern style: it is "full of excellent modern art", as befits a city that is a German modern art capital. But readers' views vary sharply, about the service as well as about the hotel's quirky design. Its most ardent devotees, returning this year, again liked the food, the "very pleasant" staff, the "excellent" beds and duvets, thus endorsing their earlier accounts: "Its design is inspired and exciting, done with style, panache and lots of money. The staff are relaxed but professional, the panoramic top-floor restaurant is spectacular, with very good food." Bedrooms are split-level, with striking modern furniture and spiral staircases. The lounge and bar serve good snacks, and often a pianist or singer is there. Chairs, tables and parasols are set in the garden in summer. (*Pat and Jeremy Temple*) Others have disliked the split-level design, the room lighting has been found too dim, and: "Our bathroom was minute, and so ultra-modern that it was impossible not to flood the place when having a shower." One visitor found staff most unhelpful about making restaurant bookings. More reports, please.

Open All year.
Rooms 42 suites, 38 double, 10 single. Some no-smoking.
Facilities Lounge, bar, piano bar, restaurant; conference/function rooms; sauna, solarium; terrace. Garden. Unsuitable for ♿.
Location Central, 1.5 km SW of cathedral. Free underground garage.
Credit cards All major cards accepted.
Terms Rooms: single 390–490 DM, double 490–590 DM, suite 590–2,400 DM. Breakfast 29 DM. Set lunch from 55 DM, dinner from 85 DM; full alc from 105 DM. Special breaks. Children under 7 accommodated free in parents' room.

DAUN 54550 Rheinland-Pfalz Map 14

Schlosshotel Kurfürstliches Amtshaus *Tel* (06592) 30 31
Auf dem Burgberg *Fax* (06592) 49 42

In a small resort amid the lovely Eifel hills, north of the Mosel. Inside the town, but quietly secluded on a hilltop, is this handsome yellow-walled 18th-century *Schloss*, converted into a very stylish family-run hotel. Inspectors were there in 1996: "We were delighted. The owner, Gunter Probst, is a kindly man of creative taste, who has filled his hotel with a remarkable collection of unusual antiques, tapestries, old portraits. Some might find the effect a bit too baronial, but for us it worked; and though smart, it's an intimate, warm, family place: daughter is at reception. In the elegant restaurant, food was fairly *nouvelle* but unstinted – the stuffed smoked quail with oriental juice was daringly undercooked, and served with a good Mosel white. The wonderful buffet breakfast included the best muesli ever, fresh strawberries, all kinds of fruit. The tiled heated swimming pool, carved from the volcanic rock, is very stylish. Bedrooms, all different, mostly medium-size, are well furnished, some in period style, some more modern. Many have fine views of the hills. We had a suite with a huge green triangular bath, and a famous orange-canopied bed acquired by

Herr Probst from a government hotel near Bonn, where it had been used by Brezhnev, the Shah of Iran, etc. Even so, we slept well."

Open All year, except 2–3 weeks Jan.
Rooms 1 suite, 24 double, 17 single.
Facilities Lift. Lounge, bar, restaurant; function rooms; indoor swimming pool, sauna, steam bath; terrace. Garden.
Location Hilltop. From centre (Forum), follow signs. Carpark.
Credit cards All major cards accepted.
Terms B&B: single 115–155 DM, double 220–260 DM, suite 360 DM. Set lunch 57 DM, dinner 85–125 DM; full alc 100 DM.

DETMOLD Nordrhein-Westfalen — Map 14

Detmolder Hof — *Tel* (05231) 2 82 44
Langestrasse 19 — *Fax* (05231) 3 95 27
32756 Detmold

In main street of characterful town, former capital of Lippe principality, a much-gabled hotel combining old-world charm with efficiency. Sizeable rooms, some with antique furnishings. Lavish breakfast buffet; varied main meals, "successfully attempting nouvelle cuisine*". All major credit cards accepted. 39 rooms (18 in annexe). B&B: single 128 DM, double 220 DM. Alc 47–75 DM [1996]. Endorsed again this year, but fuller reports welcome.*

DINKELSBÜHL 91550 Bayern — Map 14

Goldener Anker — *Tel* (09851) 57 80-0
Untere Schmiedgasse 22 — *Fax* (09851) 57 80-80

In picturesque town on Romantische Strasse, *43 km S of Rothenburg, attractive old flower-decked inn in local style. Friendly family owners, cheerful ambience. 15 well-equipped, well-lit rooms; good Franconian dishes and wines; lavish buffet breakfast. All major credit cards accepted. B&B: single 80 DM, double 150 DM. Alc 27–62 DM [1996].*

DREIS 54518 Rheinland-Pfalz — Map 14

Waldhotel Sonnora NEW — *Tel* (06578) 4 06
Auf dem Eichelfeld — *Fax* (06578) 14 02

On edge of Eifel massif amid wooded hills and meadows, 8 km SW of Wittlich, 30 km NE of Trier, pleasant, inexpensive chalet-style hotel with outstanding, expensive restaurant, very elegant (2 Michelin *stars); excellent friendly service; good wines at fair prices. Bedrooms with shared balconies, overlooking oddly ornamented garden. Closed 6 Jan–6 Feb; restaurant closed Mon/Tues. Access, Amex, Visa accepted. 20 rooms: B&B: single 80 DM, double 140 DM. Set meals 135–165 DM [1996]. Renominated this year, but fuller reports welcome.*

> Important reminder: terms printed must be regarded as no more than a rough guide to the size of the bill to be expected at the end of your stay. For latest tariffs, it is vital that you check when booking.

DRESDEN 01097 Sachsen **Map 14**

Hotel Bülow Residenz *Tel* (0351) 8 00 30
Rähnitzgasse 19 *Fax* (0351) 8 00 31 00

Central but quiet, just north of the Elbe, a handsome 18th-century baroque mansion newly renovated as small luxury hotel. "Very friendly staff, and a well-equipped room with elegant modern furniture. Good buffet breakfast, and well-presented food in an elegant restaurant." That report last year is now endorsed: "Select and charming. The meal was excellent. We liked the spirit of management and staff" – but another reader found service slow and cool. The Swabian chef prepares good Swabian dishes, and others. There is a vaulted cellar bar, and you can dine in the courtyard in summer. (*Walter Cottingham, PPR*) Many breakfast items are charged extra.

Open All year, except 2 weeks Jan.
Rooms 7 suites, 23 double, 1 single.
Facilities Lift. Lounges, bar, restaurant; courtyard.
Location 600 m N of historic centre. Parking.
Credit cards All major cards accepted.
Terms [1996] Rooms: single 290 DM, double 340 DM, suite 420–550 DM. Breakfast 25 DM. Set lunch 60 DM, dinner 80 DM; full alc 98 DM. Children under 7 accommodated free in parents' room.

Hotel Martha Hospiz *Tel* (0351) 5 67 60
Nieritzstrasse 11 *Fax* (0351) 804 32 18

The splendid old Baroque buildings in Saxony's capital can never recover fully from the allied bombing of 1945, but the city as a whole is now fast recovering from the years of communist neglect. Symptomatic of this, the post-war GDR palace hotels have mostly been bought up by western chains – one is now a Hilton, another a Maritim. Far smaller and cheaper than either is this *Hospiz*, a late 19th-century building in a suburb north of the Elbe, ten minutes' walk from the historic centre. It was founded by the Lutheran churches as a hostel, and is still church-owned today. But it has been carefully renovated into a discreet medium-price hotel of sober elegance. The aura is slightly monastic, but the sizeable rooms are comfortable, the buffet breakfast is good, and service is pleasant. One snag: no bar in daytime. But after 6 pm you can eat and / or drink in the locally popular *Kartoffelrestaurant* in the basement, where potato-based and other dishes are served at low prices (pity about the assertive piped German folk music)." "Excellent value, and friendly staff." (*CKB*) "We love children," says the hotel.

Open All year, except 21–27 Dec.
Rooms 24 double, 12 single. Some adapted for ♿.
Facilities Lift. Lounge, breakfast room (no-smoking), restaurant.
Location 1 km N of historic centre. Garage, private parking.
Credit cards Access, Amex, Visa.
Terms B&B: single 95–150 DM, double 190–230 DM. Children under 6 accommodated free in parents' room, reductions for older children.

If you think we have over-praised a hotel or done it an injustice, please let us know.

EISENACH 99817 Thüringen Map 14

Sophien Hotel NEW *Tel* (03691) 25 10
Sophienstrasse 41 *Fax* (03691) 2 51 11

This historic city, where Bach was born and Luther lived, is best known for the hilltop Wartburg castle, where Luther translated the Bible. "It is also one of the boom cities of the east," write inspectors this year, "with new Opel and BMW car factories, masses of new shops and restaurants. In a town centre now in the grip of urban renovation, we found this brand-new hotel owned by the Göbel family from Hessen – a typical example of *Wessi* hotel investment. It's a big white modern block, with smart modern interior design: a spiral stairway leads up to a wide open-plan bar/reception/restaurant area. Here we had a superb buffet breakfast, nicely served. The salad buffet at dinner looked good, too, but we had to dine elsewhere. Reception was efficient, but impersonal. Sizeable, well-equipped bedrooms (hair-dryer, etc): a monthly magazine gave details of what's on in this actively cultural city. All in all, a hotel typical of the new-style eastern Germany." Reports on the main meals welcome.

Rooms 3 suites, 51 double, 2 single. Some no-smoking.
Facilities Lift. Bar, restaurant; 2 meeting rooms; sauna, solarium.
Location Central. Parking.
Credit cards All major cards accepted.
Terms B&B 75–115 DM; D,B&B 25 DM added. Alc meals 30 DM. Children under 12 half price.

FRANKFURT AM MAIN 60325 Hessen Map 14

Hotel Westend *Tel* (069) 74 67 02 and 74 50 02
Westendstrasse 15 *Fax* (069) 74 53 96

Near to the big skyscrapers, but in a quiet, mainly residential district, the Mayer family's small personal hotel is unusual for downtown Frankfurt with its big brash modern ones. It is furnished with antiques and old pictures, and offers old-world service by discreet men in black suits who address lady guests as "*Gnädige Frau*" (esteemed Madam). "Eccentric but decent staff, and good breakfasts." "Exquisite bed-linen, terrific coffee, five kinds of freshly baked bread for breakfast." "The little terrace was enjoyable." These are recent comments. Prices are moderate for central Frankfurt: but some rooms do not have a bathroom, and there is no lift. There is a pleasant garden, but no restaurant (lots nearby). More reports, please.

Open All year, except Christmas, New Year, Easter.
Rooms 9 double, 11 single. Not all with facilities *en suite*.
Facilities 3 lounges (1 with TV); terrace (drinks served). Garden. Unsuitable for ♿.
Location Central. 5 mins' walk from station, off Mainzer Landstrasse. Private parking.
Credit cards All major cards accepted.
Terms Rooms: single 120–280 DM, double 160–350 DM, triple 330–560 DM. Breakfast 18 DM.

We are particularly keen to have reports on italicised entries.

FRIEDRICHSRUHE 74639 Baden-Württemberg Map 14

Wald- und Schlosshotel Friedrichsruhe NEW

Tel (07941) 60 87-0
Fax (07941) 6 14 68

This large white-walled red-roofed mansion, in the hilly and wooded Hohenlohe country, was built in 1712 by the *Fürsten* of that ilk and is owned today by the Fürst Kraft zu Hohenlohe-Öhringen. It has been converted into a *very* superior hotel (Relais & Châteaux), partly renovated this year, and run in lordly style by manager/chef Lothar Eiermann, who provides some of the most ambitious cooking in Germany (two *Michelin* stars). Rooms are in the old mansion or, along with the restaurant, in a modern and stylish extension. After some criticisms in the late 1980s, a renomination has come this year: "Perhaps there is no better hotel in Germany at present. I have been visiting for the past 20 years. The food is ambrosial, served with flair. The parkland setting, the swimming pools, delightful golf course, add to the pleasures. The absence of suitable lounges, and the high wine mark-ups, are blemishes." (*Gordon Campbell*)

Open All year.
Rooms 16 suites, 23 double, 6 single. In 3 buildings.
Facilities Lifts. Salons, bar, 2 restaurants; function room; indoor swimming pool, sauna, beauty farm. Large grounds: swimming pool, tennis, 18-hole golf course. Unsuitable for ♿.
Location 6 km N of Öhringen. *Autobahn* A6 exit Öhringen, direction Friedrichsruhe. Parking.
Credit cards All major cards accepted.
Terms B&B: single 195–340 DM, double 295–420 DM, suite 490–700 DM. Set meals 145–195 DM. 1-night bookings refused New Year.

GOHRISCH 01824 Sachsen Map 14

Annas Hof BUDGET
Neue Hauptstrasse 118

Tel (035021) 6 82 91
Fax (035021) 6 70 98

The beautiful region south-east of Dresden, with its odd-shaped rocky hills and old castles, is known as the "Saxon Switzerland". Here, in a little resort near the curving Elbe, is this neat pink villa, now run as a small private hotel by a young local couple, Sabine and Rainer Roske. British hoteliers who visited recently were enthusiastic: "The Roskes are visibly busy, and accessible, and offer excellent value for money. Our room was most comfortable, with pleasing decor, a view, a large bathroom with shower (no baths). We dined twice, and much appreciated the varied use of pork in all forms, smoked, boiled, roasted, in the Saxon tradition. The Elbe wine is eminently quaffable." Furnishings are quite modest, but not unattractive. (*J and MS*) The hotel sometimes lays on dances, and organises hiking and sightseeing excursions.

Open All year, except Nov. Restaurant closed Wed/Thurs Dec–Mar.
Rooms 11 double, 2 single. 3 in annexe.
Facilities Bar, restaurant; terrace. Garden. Unsuitable for ♿.
Location 25 km SE of Dresden. Just S of Elbe, near Königstein. Limited private parking.
Credit cards Access, Amex, Visa.
Terms B&B: single 55–65 DM, double 85–130 DM; D,B&B 20 DM per person added. Full alc 30 DM.

GOTHA 99867 Thüringen Map 14

Pannonia Hotel am Schlosspark NEW *Tel* (03621) 44 20
Lindenauallee 20 *Fax* (03621) 44 24 52

Gotha, one of those charming eastern towns now being rediscovered by tourists, has a well-restored *Altstadt* and a Renaissance *Rathaus*. A foyer of the German Socialist Workers' movement in the 1870s, it was also the home of a firm which used to publish the *Almanach de Gotha*, a guide to the nobility, like *Debrett*. Between these two social extremes is this very new and sleek hotel, part of the Pannonia chain. "It is set quietly on the edge of the park that surrounds the baroque *Schloss*. Large comfortable rooms, courteous staff, and a sumptuous buffet breakfast. Dinner was international *nouvelle cuisine* with a Hungarian flavour" (the chef is Hungarian). The restaurant and lounge are very light, with sloping glass roof. (*Julia de Waal*)

Open All year.
Rooms 16 suites, 80 double. 12 no-smoking. 2 suitable for ♿.
Facilities Lift, ramps. Lounge, bar, restaurant, *Stüberl*; conference/function facilities; fitness room, sauna, solarium, whirlpool; terrace. Garden.
Location Central, near *Schloss*, market square. Garage. Shuttle service to Erfurt airport (25 km).
Credit cards All major cards accepted.
Terms B&B: single 125–170 DM, double 180–235 DM, suite 300–350 DM. Set meals 18–26 DM; full alc 55 DM. Children under 12 accommodated free in parents' room.

GREVENBROICH 41515 Nordrhein-Westfalen Map 14

Zur Traube *Tel* (02181) 6 87 67
Bahnstrasse 47 *Fax* (02181) 6 11 22

In a dull little town between Cologne and Düsseldorf is this distinguished Relais & Châteaux restaurant-with-rooms: its owner/chef, Dieter Kaufmann, wins two stars from *Michelin* and in 1994 was named Germany's Chef of the Year by *Gault Millau* (pigeon is a speciality). "Delightful, sophisticated, calm and comfortable," say seasoned travellers. "It was packed, and our superb meal went on till well after midnight, with the staff seemingly enjoying it as much as the guests. Breakfast is amazing, course after course. The 1890s building is rather austere at the front, but has a rear garden and terrace. The rooms are very German in the high quality of their furniture, fabrics, lighting, easy chairs, marble-tiled bathroom. Frau Kaufmann advises on the fantastic wine list with quiet charm. Tables are well spaced, the friendly service is mainly by girls, drilled to perfection but not in a robot manner."

Open All year, except week before Easter, 15–31 July, 23 Dec–23 Jan. Restaurant closed Sun/Mon.
Rooms 2 suites, 4 double.
Facilities Lounge. Restaurant. Garden.
Location Central. 31 km NW of Cologne. Parking.
Credit cards Access, Diners, Visa.
Terms B&B: single 190–290 DM, double 290–490 DM. Set meals 155–185 DM; full alc 98–132 DM.

HAMBURG

Map 14

Hotel Abtei
Abteistrasse 14
20149 Hamburg

Tel (040) 44 29 05
Fax (040) 44 98 20

In Harvestehude, the rich merchants' quarter north-west of the Alster lake, is this handsome Jugendstil mansion. Converted now into a small, elegant hotel (Relais & Châteaux), it is owned and run by Fritz and Petra Lay. "It feels like a private home and is full of good furniture, fine mirrors, family paintings. There's a charming garden at the back. Only a view of the Alster is missing. Mr Lay is fanatical about his hotel and his personal touch is apparent. He is a bathroom designer, too, and our bathroom was a joy, full of brilliant *trompe-l'oeil*. Thus the shower / loo was a garden bower, with real creepers leading out of the trompish ones. Superb breakfast, with perfect muesli." That admirer later returned: "We had a splendid garden suite: neo-baroque ceiling mouldings, state-of-the-art hi-fi." In the small, very *soigné* restaurant – open in the evenings only, for residents and their guests – young Ulrich Heimann's cooking is much admired (*Michelin* star). More reports, please.

Open All year, except 2 weeks early Jan. Restaurant closed midday, Sun / Mon, to non-residents.
Rooms 3 suites, 8 double. Some on ground floor.
Facilities Lounge, bar, restaurant; terrace. Small garden. Unsuitable for ♿.
Location Just NW of Alster, 3 km from city centre. Private parking (20 DM). (U-Bahn: Klosterstern.)
Credit cards All major cards accepted.
Terms [1996] B&B: single 250–300 DM, double 350–410 DM, suite 450 DM. Set menu 86–155 DM.

Hotel Hanseatic
Sierichstrasse 150
22299 Hamburg

Tel (040) 48 57 72
Fax (040) 48 57 73

"It goes from strength to strength" – the latest comment on this very personal little luxury hotel, a white patrician villa in a quiet residential area north of the Alster lake. Opera, film and theatre people often choose to stay here. Its special ambience is created by its delightful owner / manager Wolfgang Schüler, whom our own readers have admired for many years. "Breakfast was imaginative, and the flowers were changed daily in our enormous garden-level room." "Everything is carefully thought out, and breakfasts are healthy and delicious. We had the wonderful suite, which looks out on to a huge green space at the back." "Our bedroom was elegantly furnished with antiques, the bathroom was huge, and tea came in an antique silver pot."

Open All year.
Rooms 12 double. 5 no-smoking.
Facilities Lounge / bar, breakfast room (no-smoking); fitness room, sauna. Small garden. Alster lake, city park 800 m. Unsuitable for ♿.
Location In Winterhude, 4 km N of centre. Street parking (difficult); garage 5 mins' walk. (U-Bahn: Sierichstrasse.)
Credit card Amex.
Terms [1996] Rooms: single 200–230 DM, double 250–320 DM. Breakfast 27.50 DM.

HANNOVER Niedersachsen — Map 14

Landhaus Ammann — *Tel* (0511) 83 08 18
Hildesheimerstrasse 185 — *Fax* (0511) 843 77 49
30173 Hannover

By main road 3 km S of city centre, but quiet, with nice garden, luxurious restaurant. Good staff. "Dinner merited its Michelin *star." All major credit cards accepted. 16 spacious, tastefully furnished rooms. B&B: single 245 DM, double 330–398 DM. Set meals 60–170 DM.*

HEIDELBERG 69117 Baden-Württemberg — Map 14

Hotel Backmulde NEW — *Tel* (062211) 53 66 0
Schiffgasse 11 — *Fax* (062211) 53 66 60

In old town centre, just off main Hauptstrasse with its jolly students pubs, a tiny, spruce, well-modernised hotel. 13 large bedrooms, good breakfasts. Restaurant (closed Sun/midday Mon); no lounge or bar. All major credit cards accepted. Parking. B&B: single 98–125 DM, double 158 DM [1996]. Fuller reports welcome.

HELLENTHAL 53940 Nordrhein-Westfalen — Map 14

Haus Lichtenhardt BUDGET — *Tel* (02482) 6 14
An der Lichtenhardt 26 — *Fax* (02482) 18 68

The picturesque old town of Monschau, set in a narrow gorge, and the interesting outdoor museum of rural life at Kommern, are both quite close to this unassuming modern hotel in the northern part of the Eifel Massif – a lovely area that, like its fruity red Ahr wines, deserves to be better known abroad. Painted white, the hotel stands quietly amid hills, next to a nature reserve with deer and falcons. There's a patio, with white tables and chairs under parasols. Bedrooms are large and comfortable, but simple. A reader this year found the staff pleasant and the food "wonderful". Earlier views: "Breakfasts in the best German tradition." "Good food, very professional owners." "Friendly and peaceful." (*Virginia Spargur, and others*)

Open All year, except Christmas.
Rooms 1 suite, 11 double, 4 single. 10 in nearby annexe.
Facilities Lounge, restaurant; meeting room; terrace. Garden. Unsuitable for ♿.
Location Edge of village, 56 km SE of Aachen. Parking.
Restriction No children under 10.
Credit cards All major cards accepted.
Terms B&B: single 45 DM, double 90 DM; D,B&B double 120 DM. Set meals 18 DM; full alc 50 DM.

HINTERZARTEN 79856 Baden-Württemberg — Map 14

Hotel Sassenhof — *Tel* (07652) 15 15
Adlerweg 17 — *Fax* (07652) 4 84

On village green of fashionable Black Forest resort 26 km SE of Freiburg, with view of hills, a select B&B, gabled and flower-decked. Charming owners, elegant public rooms, large indoor swimming pool, sauna, solarium, copious breakfasts. Closed 15 Nov–15 Dec. Credit cards not accepted. 24 rooms, including four new holiday apartments. B&B double 148–178 DM. No restaurant, lots nearby.

HOFGEISMAR 34369 Hessen — Map 14

Dornröschenschloss Sababurg — *Tel* (05671) 80 80
Sababurg — *Fax* (05671) 80 82 00

The brothers Grimm used to come for hunting parties to this former country home of the Princes of Hessen, which is said to have inspired *The Sleeping Beauty*, hence its name. It is a 14th-century *Schloss*, alone on a rolling wooded plateau above the Weser valley – a bit "self-consciously romantic", but seductive, as a recent visitor agrees: "Touristy on summer weekends, but in winter it was wonderful. We had two beautiful rooms, one small in the turret, one quite large with views of fields and hills. Dinner was a delight." Pheasant and venison in season are recommended. The hotel is popular for local weddings. And concerts and fairy-tale plays are put on in its private theatre, an old wine cellar. Newer reports welcome.

Open All year.
Rooms 17 double.
Facilities Salon, restaurant; conference/function facilities; theatre, museum; courtyard. Garden. Zoo adjacent. Unsuitable for ♿.
Location 14 km NE of Hofgeismar. 30 km N of Kassel.
Credit cards All major cards accepted.
Terms [1996] B&B: single 170 DM, double 350 DM. Alc 55–81 DM.

HOLZAPPEL 56379 Rheinland-Pfalz — Map 14

Altes Herrenhaus zum Bären — *Tel* (06439) 70 14
Marktplatz 15 — *Fax* (06439) 70 12

This village west of Limburg lies amid pleasant wooded country. In its main square is this half-timbered 17th-century building, now an elegantly decorated restaurant-with-rooms, with a garden terrace, and friendly owners. A recent view: "Our welcome was warm. The house is beautifully kept, the rooms are lovely, and in the cosy restaurant the food is excellent, with lavish portions and ample choice." Breakfasts are lavish too, and include fish and meat. "Even attic rooms are good, and our meal was four-star." More reports, please.

Open All year, except Jan, 24 Dec. Restaurant closed Mon.
Rooms 2 suites, 7 double.
Facilities Lift, ramps. Hall, restaurant; banqueting room, conference facilities; terrace.
Location In village 16 km SW of Limburg, on Bad Ems road. Parking.
Credit cards All major cards accepted.
Terms B&B: single 98.50–135 DM, double 198.50–250 DM, suite 275 DM; D,B&B double 330 DM. Set meals 49–95 DM; full alc 70–80 DM.

> Hotels are dropped if we lack positive feedback. If you can endorse an entry, we urge you to do so.

HORBRUCH IM HUNSRÜCK 55483 Rheinland-Pfalz Map 14

Historische Schlossmühle *Tel* (06543) 40 41
Fax (06543) 31 78

Edgar Reitz, who was born nearby, set and filmed his masterly *Heimat* on the Hunsrück plateau, where the Liller family's 17th-century mill house, now a smart hotel, stands by a stream. Its studied folksiness (knick-knacks everywhere) irritates some visitors, but delights others, as again this year: "Our comfortable room, quite small, was crowded with furniture and ornaments. Dinner was enjoyable, with tables set out on different levels and corners. The unusual dishes (halibut with mango, etc) were more ambitious than successful. The Lillers are welcoming hosts." Earlier views: "Idyllic restfulness and bucolic beauty." "Exquisite. There was a lot of clutter – dolls and the like – on the way to our room, but this was tastefully furnished, and opened on to a small patio with tables and chairs. Our seven-course dinner was superb, and the breakfast buffet an *embarras de richesses*, with brown eggs from the Lillers' own hens, eight types of tea, and the teapot filled from a magnificent samovar." The huge old mill wheel turns by the dining room, where tables are oddly strewn with marbles. (*Alex and Beryl Williams, and others*) A dissenter this year thought the welcome cold, the cooking ordinary, the decoration pretentious – "but yes, the breakfast *was* excellent".

Open All year, except Christmas. Restaurant closed Mon.
Rooms 1 suite, 9 double.
Facilities Lounge, reading room, breakfast room (no-smoking), restaurant, *Stube*; function room; terrace. Garden: children's playground. Unsuitable for ♿.
Location Horbruch is 12 km E of Bernkastel. Private parking.
Credit cards Access, Visa.
Terms B&B: single 120–160 DM, double 180–265 DM, suite 265–295 DM. Set lunch 50 DM, dinner 85 DM; full alc 60–70 DM. 1-night bookings sometimes refused.

JOHANNESBERG 63867 Bayern Map 14

Hotel Sonne – Meier's Restaurant NEW *Tel* (06021) 47 00 77
Hauptstrasse 2 *Fax* (06021) 41 39 64

In village in hills, 8 km N of Aschaffenburg, "delightful" restaurant-with-rooms, owned and run by Meier family: welcoming, relaxed ambience, friendly and skilled service; excellent but expensive food (Michelin star), *served on garden terrace in fine weather. Good breakfasts, pleasant rooms with tiled bathrooms. Restaurant closed Mon, first 2 weeks Sept. All major credit cards accepted. 8 rooms: with breakfast 68–118 DM. Alc 73–106 DM.*

KAMPEN 25999 Schleswig-Holstein Map 14

Golf- und Landhaus Kampen NEW *Tel* (04561) 46 910
Braderuper Weg 12 *Fax* (04561) 46 91 11
Kampen, Sylt

This is our first-ever entry for the North Sea island of Sylt, part nature reserve, and also northern Germany's leading holiday playground. Its windy yet invigorating climate has long made it fashionable: Thomas

Mann and Marlene Dietrich used to stay, then in the 1960s it was dubbed "The St-Tropez of the North". That ritzy era has now ended, but many of the rich and famous still come. Almost all guests are German, and only now has a *Guide* reader reported on this tiny but very select and expensive B&B hotel, set by the sand dunes in Kampen village, chief focus of the showy smart set. "Built in local Friesian style, it has blue-carpeted bedrooms in keeping with the sea. Generous buffet breakfast." No restaurant: *Lysieffer*, *Rotes Kliff* and the pricier *Kupferkanne* are the places to eat, amid the glossy, amusing throng. Excellent sea bathing.

Open All year.
Rooms 3 suites, 6 double. Some on ground floor.
Facilities Lounge with fire place, bar, breakfast room; indoor swimming pool, sauna. Garden. Sea 3 mins' walk. Unsuitable for ♿.
Location In village, 3 mins' walk from centre. Sylt is reached via causeway from Niebüll: train, or frequent rail shuttle for cars.
Credit cards Access, Amex, Visa.
Terms B&B: single 250–370 DM, double 300–420 DM, suite 410–670 DM. Children under 7 accommodated free in parents' room.

KÖNIGSTEIN IM TAUNUS 61462 Hessen — Map 14

Hotel Sonnenhof — *Tel* (06174) 29 08 0
Falkensteinerstrasse 9 — *Fax* (06174) 29 08 75

This small resort in the Taunus foothills is crowned by a ruined feudal fortress. But standing a little lower in its own large park with giant trees is this big gabled hunting lodge, formerly owned by Baron Rothschild. As Frankfurt is only 20 minutes' drive away (more at rush hour), business people with a car might find it a useful alternative to the routine downtown hotels. A recent account: "Superb food, ultra-friendly service, lovely grounds. We had a bright room with a rather small bathroom, in the old part of the hotel." Most rooms are in a modern extension: repro antiques, balconies facing the gardens. You can dine on a large terrace. Good breakfast buffet, nice pool. (*EW*)

Open All year.
Rooms 25 double, 17 single. 23 in modern extension. Some on ground floor.
Facilities Hall, salon, bar, 2 restaurants; function room; indoor swimming pool, sauna, solarium; sun terrace. Large garden: tennis.
Location Edge of town, 23 km NW of Frankfurt. Parking.
Credit cards All major cards accepted.
Terms B&B: single 150–190 DM, double 230–330 DM; D,B&B 40 DM per person added. Set lunch 35 DM, dinner 69–98 DM; full alc 60–80 DM.

KONSTANZ 78464 Baden-Württemberg — Map 14

Seehotel Siber — *Tel* (07531) 6 30 44
Seestrasse 25 — *Fax* (07531) 6 48 13

A handsome Jugendstil villa beside the Bodensee (Lake Constance) is the home of the Siber family's distinguished and elegant restaurant-with-rooms (Relais & Châteaux). It has been admired again for its food (*Michelin* star) and "beautifully furnished rooms", endorsing earlier praise: "Staff were nice, if a bit slow, and the food was good. There's an outdoor terrace by the lake for meals in fine weather; breakfast there was elegant. Our bedroom, decorated in pale green and yellow, had a view of the lake; large bathroom but no shower, only a tub. The disco in the basement did not keep us awake, as we had feared." Excellent local fish: Bodensee bouillabaisse a speciality. (*CM*)

Open All year, except 2 weeks Feb.
Rooms 1 suite, 11 double. 2 air-conditioned.
Facilities Lounge, 3 dining rooms; dance-bar; terrace.
Location By lake, 2 km NE of town centre. Private parking.
Credit cards Access, Diners, Visa.
Terms Rooms 150–390 DM, suite 490–590 DM. Breakfast 35–50 DM. Set lunch 55–68 DM, dinner 115–185 DM.

LÜBECK 23560 Schleswig-Holstein — Map 14

Hotel Kaiserhof — *Tel* (0451) 70 33 01
Kronsforder Allee 11–13 — *Fax* (0451) 79 50 83

"It was lovely, and the staff were grand" – praise for this smart conversion of two adjacent patrician houses, owned and run in personal style as a hotel by Ruth Klemm and her daughter. It is said to combine sophisticated elegance with cosiness, and it stands just across the Elbe-Lübeck canal from the historic centre of this glorious old Hanseatic city, birthplace of Thomas Mann and the setting for his masterpiece *Buddenbrooks*. Other recent views: "Attractive and comfortable, with friendly staff, excellent breakfast." "Charming decor. Breakfast, in a pleasant room with a nice garden terrace, was a good German display." Rooms are double-glazed, and most face away from the main road. The "beautifully designed" swimming pool and the health club are open till 10 pm. (*SR and ELH*) No restaurant, but the hotel owns one nearby; we'd be glad of reports on it.

Open All year.
Rooms 6 suites, 46 double, 12 single. 15 in nearby annexe.
Facilities Lift. 2 lounges, bar (open 6 pm–1 am; closed Sat/Sun); 3 conference rooms; indoor swimming pool, sauna, solarium, fitness centre; terrace. Garden. Unsuitable for ♿.
Location 1.5 km S of city centre. Garages (12 DM), carpark.
Credit cards All major cards accepted.
Terms B&B: single 145–195 DM, double 195–250 DM, suite 280–430 DM. Children under 6 accommodated free in parents' room.

MAGDEBURG 39112 Sachsen-Anhalt — Map 14

Residenz Joop — *Tel* (0391) 62 62-0
Jean-Burgerstrasse 16 — *Fax* (0391) 62 62 100

This large industrial town was heavily bombed, then gracelessly rebuilt under the GDR – save for the baroque *Rathaus*, the ancient Gothic cathedral, and a few other monuments, all well restored. Quite near the centre, amid trees in a garden, is this sturdy white gabled villa, which the grandfather of the present owners, the Joops, built in 1903 and used as the Swedish Consulate (he was himself the consul). Later the family fled the Communists, but they, like so many others, have now regained their old home, and have turned it into an elegant B&B hotel, of a kind still uncommon in the former GDR – a "*Privathotel mit* flair", to use the Joops' own description. It is gracefully furnished in modern style. "Bernd and Ursula Joop are friendly, and have preserved the ambience of their grand old villa, while adding modern convenience," says a recent visitor. "It compares very favourably with *any* small hotel or inn I have stayed in *anywhere*." (*WS*)

Open All year, except end Dec–early Jan.
Rooms 1 suite, 15 double, 9 single. 20 no-smoking.
Facilities Breakfast room (no-smoking); terrace. Garden.
Location 1.5 km SW of centre, off Leipziger Chaussee. Garages, carpark.
Credit cards Access, Amex, Visa.
Terms [1996] B&B: single 165 DM, double 270 DM.

MARKTHEIDENFELD 97828 Bayern — Map 14

Hotel Anker — *Tel* (09391) 60 04-0
Obertorstrasse 6–8 — *Fax* (09391) 60 04-77

In a small wine-growing town on the Main, west of Würzburg, the Deppisch family own and run a smart white modern hotel, furnished in good taste. Opposite, in their elegant restaurant, *Weinhaus Anker* (*Michelin* star), they serve such dishes as pigeon in wine sauce, venison with rowanberry sauce. They also own some local vineyards, and you can buy their good Franconian wines. "A lovely hotel," is a recent view. "Rooms large and efficient, food excellent, service friendly." Many rooms have a balcony over the lovely courtyard. The "lavish" bathrooms and the "family house atmosphere" have been praised. (*Endorsed this year by David and Patricia Hawkins*) There's now a second and cheaper restaurant, with simpler cooking, and a new wine cellar. Children are warmly welcomed.

Open All year. Restaurant closed Mon/midday Tues.
Rooms 4 suites, 22 double, 13 single. Some on ground floor.
Facilities Lifts, ramp. Lounge, TV room, breakfast room, 2 restaurants, cellar (wine tastings); conference facilities; courtyard (drinks service). Garden: playground.
Location Central, next to church. Best approached from *Autobahn* A3 exit Marktheidenfeld. Garage.
Restriction Smoking discouraged in restaurant, banned in some bedrooms.
Credit cards All major cards accepted (Diners in restaurant only).
Terms B&B: single 108–148 DM, double 175–220 DM, suite 320–450 DM. Set lunch 40 DM, dinner 55 DM. Children under 6 accommodated free in parents' room.

MEERSBURG 88709 Baden-Württemberg — Map 14

Hotel Löwen — *Tel* (07532) 4 30 40
Marktplatz 2 — *Fax* (07532) 43 04 10

In 1848, Germany's greatest woman poet, Annette von Droste-Hülshoff, died of consumption and a broken heart, gazing out across Lake Constance from her room (now open to visitors) in the awesome old fortress at Meersburg, the prettiest town on the lake. Here in the tiny market square is this picturesque vine-clad 15th-century building, with red geraniums in its window-boxes. A recent visitor was "most impressed", especially by the food served in its cosy three-room restaurant (this could include fresh Bodensee trout, ragout of lamb in red wine sauce). The interior is filled with a mix of antiques, heirlooms and potted plants. Breakfast is a lavish buffet. Bedrooms have a sofa and easy chairs. (*RE*)

Open All year. Restaurant closed Wed in winter.
Rooms 17 double, 4 single. 4 no-smoking.
Facilities Restaurant, *Weinstube*; function room. Unsuitable for ♿.
Location Central. Public parking.
Credit cards All major cards accepted.
Terms B&B: single 70–120 DM, double 130–190 DM; D,B&B 30 DM added per person. Set meals 42 DM; full alc 59 DM. Children under 6 accommodated free in parents' room.

MUNICH Bayern **Map 14**

Gästehaus Englischer Garten *Tel* (089) 39 20 34
Liebergesellstrasse 8 *Fax* (089) 39 12 33
80802 München

This creeper-covered 18th-century mill house, now a select guest house, stands by a stream on the edge of the Englischer Garten, down a quiet lane. How rural and idyllic! – yet the city centre is only two miles away, and studenty Schwabing with its animated night-life is much closer. In summer you can take drinks and breakfast in the secluded garden by the stream. "So appealing and home-like," runs a recent report. "Irene Schlüter-Hübscher is the family owner, and her staff have the personal touch. Thick carpets, some antiques, pictures of old Munich – what could be *hübscher*? There are several large yet cosy bedrooms: ours, almost a suite, had a comfortable sitting area, big bathroom, garden views. But some rooms, notably in the annexe, are smaller and duller. The breakfast room is pretty but cramped." Endorsed this year: "All the staff were charming, helpful. For our last night, we were asked to move from our ground-floor room to a higher one, as a guest was arriving 'with a very old dog who cannot manage the stairs'. It was put with such charm that we didn't mind moving." (*Richard and Anne Hobson, and others*) Twelve rooms are in the mill house itself, six with bathroom *en suite*. Fifteen are one-room self-catering apartments in an annexe across the street.

Open All year.
Rooms 25 double, 2 single. 15 in nearby annexe. Some on ground floor.
Facilities Lift. Breakfast room. Small garden.
Location On E edge of Schwabing, 5 mins' walk from U-Bahn station. By car, approach from Leopoldstrasse, not Mittlerer Ring. Garage. (U-Bahn: Münchner Freiheit.)
Credit cards None accepted.
Terms Rooms: single 110–175 DM, double 130–195 DM. Breakfast 6 DM.

Hotel Neumayr *Tel* (089) 71 60 54
Heiglhofstrasse 18 *Fax* (089) 719 33 76
81377 München

In the south-west suburb of Grosshadern, close to a forest and the city's leading hospital, is this new hotel in local style, owned and run by the Neumayrs. It has neat and pleasant rooms, some with a balcony facing the garden. "Joseph Neumayr was kind and witty, and his buffet breakfast was good, in a busy, rather cramped room." This room now also serves main meals, with a small, conventional menu. You may well eat better at the 16th-century inn across the road, now separately owned, with a new name, *Erdinger Weissbräu*: visitors this year thought it "really excellent, with real Bavarian dishes at modest prices, lots of ambience". It also has a beer-garden. (*KA and JA*) Reports on the *Neumayr*'s food welcome.

Open All year.
Rooms 37 double, 18 single. Some on ground floor.
Facilities Lift. 2 lounges, breakfast room, restaurant. Garden: beer garden.
Location 7 km SW of centre. From *Altstadt,* take Lindwurmstrasse, Würmtalstrasse. Parking. (U-Bahn: Grosshadern.)
Credit cards All major cards accepted.
Terms B&B: single 115–145 DM, double 180–200 DM. Alc meals 33–45 DM.

Hotel An der Oper *Tel* (089) 29 00 27-0
Falkenturmstrasse 10 *Fax* (089) 29 00 27 29
80331 München

Much used by visitors to the nearby Opera, this friendly B&B hotel lies down a side street off the smart Maximilianstrasse. "Small and cosy, with high-quality breakfast," is a recent comment. Staff are very helpful, especially in finding tickets for the opera when it's full. The white-walled, white-furnished bedrooms have chandeliers, and modern bathroom; some rooms are quite small. There's a comfortable lobby, where newspapers on wooden handles are available in the best *Mitteleuropa* tradition. Double-glazing cuts out most street noise. (*S and F-PG*) Newer reports welcome.

Open All year.
Rooms 55.
Facilities Lift. Lounge, TV room, breakfast room; conference room. Unsuitable for ♿.
Location Central, near Opera House. Multi-storey carpark nearby. (U-Bahn: Marienplatz.)
Credit cards All major cards accepted.
Terms [1996] B&B: single 150 DM, double 250 DM.

Hotel Schrenkhof *Tel* (089) 61 00 91-0
Leonhardsweg 6 (restaurant 611 62 36)
Unterhaching, 82008 München *Fax* (089) 61 00 91-50

A modern building, but very traditional. From outside it looks like a big chalet; inside, it is smart and stylish, full of beautiful wood panelling and Bavarian carved furniture. Not easy to find, it has a quiet semi-rural setting in a south-eastern outer suburb of Munich. "A lovely place, full of warmth and charm," says a reader this year. Breakfast was lavish. The owners did not seem present, but all the people at front desk were helpful and pleasant." "Outstandingly good". (*Virginia Spargur, and others*)

Open All year, except Christmas, New Year, Easter.
Rooms 1 suite, 18 double, 5 single. Some on ground floor.
Facilities Lift. Lobby, breakfast room (no-smoking); conference facilities; fitness room, sauna, solarium.
Location 10 km SE of city, via Tegernseer Landstrasse and B13. Parking.
Credit cards All major cards accepted.
Terms B&B: single 140–210 DM, double 180–300 DM, suite 380 DM.

Hotel Uhland NEW *Tel* (089) 54 33 50
Uhlandstrasse 1 *Fax* (089) 54 33 52 50
80336 München

Between main station and Theresien Wiese (where Oktoberfest is held), a converted 1890s mansion with 25 "large though not always stylish" rooms, good bathrooms. Family owners, personal service; lounge/TV room with coffee/tea-making facilities; lavish breakfast buffet. All major credit cards accepted. Parking. B&B: single 115–190 DM, double 150–270 DM.

MÜNSTERTAL 79244 Baden-Württemberg Map 14

Romantik Hotel Spielweg *Tel* (07636) 70 90
Spielweg 61 *Fax* (07636) 7 09 66
Obermünstertal

Set amid hilly meadows south of Freiburg, this quietly elegant old hostelry has been owned and run by the Fuchs family for five generations. It exudes Black Forest tradition, but there's not *too* much folksiness in its cosy comforts. Rooms are in three adjacent buildings: those in the oldest, the *Stammhaus*, are cheapest but tastefully decorated, while the *Haus am Bach* and *Haus-Sonnhalde* have larger, newer rooms and suites, all with balcony. Recent eulogies: "Most excellent: a warm atmosphere, friendly staff and owners – and oh, the breakfasts!" "A jewel of a place, very relaxed and peaceful. Mr Fuchs is a charming, quiet man. Breakfast is a scrumptious buffet, and the main meals were delicious – wild boar, duck, etc." The serious *nouvelle*-ish cooking, with traditional dishes too, earns a *Michelin* star. Once a week Mr Fuchs takes guests on a long walk with a picnic, which is much enjoyed – as are the indoor and outdoor pools. (*RJ and SHM, LM*) A dissenter this year liked the rooms, but was critical of the restaurant (both food and service).

Open All year. Restaurant closed Mon/Tues.
Rooms 5 suites, 30 double, 9 single.
Facilities Lift, ramps. Lounge, 2 dining rooms; indoor swimming pool, sauna. Garden: swimming pool, tennis, children's playground.
Location Above Münstertal, 27 km S of Freiburg. Garages, parking.
Credit cards All major cards accepted.
Terms B&B: single 150–200 DM, double 190–440 DM, suite 440–600 DM. Set meals 75 DM.

NECKARGEMÜND 69151 Baden-Württemberg Map 14

Hotel zum Schwanen *Tel* (06223) 70 70
Uferstrasse 16, Kleingemünd *Fax* (06223) 24 13

Newly redecorated, this neat and appealing little hotel stands quietly across the Neckar from a village east of Heidelberg. "The river view was marvellous, the food delicious and the owners and staff very gracious," runs our latest report, backing earlier plaudits: "At Christmas, we were served Glühwein in the enclosed garden terrace. The service, setting and food (eg, pork medallions in a calvados cream sauce) were extraordinary and even a *kleine* portion was generous."

There's a glassed-in dining room with views. Or you can dine under the trees by the river. (*RB, and others*)

Open All year.
Rooms 1 suite, 12 double, 6 single.
Facilities Winter garden, restaurant; conference facilities; terrace. Garden.
Location On river, across from Neckargemünd. 9 km E of Heidelberg. Open parking.
Credit cards All major cards accepted.
Terms B&B: single 140–180 DM, double 195–240 DM, suite 270 DM. Set lunch/dinner 45–80 DM. Children under 6 accommodated free in parents' room.

NEUWEIER 76534 Baden-Württemberg — Map 14

Hotel Heiligenstein — *Tel* (07223) 5 20 25
Heiligensteinstrasse 19a — *Fax* (07223) 5 89 33

"Excellent, with a good restaurant," says a visitor this year to this modern hotel in traditional chalet style, set below vineyards in a typical wine-village on the *Badische Weinstrasse.* It has a charming young staff and owner, Barbara Beck, and it offers good, copious local cooking (eg, ragout of venison with Spätzle) in a cosy restaurant full of locals. Plenty of wry praise: "Our room was large, with a balcony, and beautifully equipped, with heavenly beds (but the birds make a lot of noise at Dawn Chorus time). The room had a massive door, with massive wood fitments, carved to death. At dinner, we enjoyed ample, simple dishes, such as grilled trout, with delicious local wine. Breakfast was ample, too. The hotel was full of costly and elaborate kitsch, which they sold. We were given a little painted duck when we paid the bill." Others have written less wittily of the friendly staff, tiled baths, home-cured ham, splendid views. (*Lisa and Peter Simon, D and MH*)

Open All year, except 23–25 Dec. Restaurant closed Tues.
Rooms 2 suites, 24 double, 3 single. Some no-smoking. Some on ground floor.
Facilities Lift, ramps. Lounge, TV room, billiard room, restaurant; 2 conference rooms; sauna, jacuzzi, solarium; terrace. Garden.
Location On edge of village, 10 km SW of Baden-Baden, 7 km NE of Bühl. Private parking.
Credit card Access.
Terms B&B: single 98–108 DM, double 155–165 DM, suite 290 DM; D,B&B double 235–245 DM. Set dinner 40 DM, full alc 62 DM.

NUREMBERG-BOXDORF 90427 Bayern — Map 14

Landhotel Schindlerhof — *Tel* (0911) 93 02 0
Steinacherstrasse 6–8 — *Fax* (0911) 93 02 620

In Boxdorf village on the city's north-west outskirts is this unusual and "delightful" hostelry. A large 17th-century farmhouse, all red-roofed and white-walled, has been converted into a rustic yet sophisticated hotel, with timber beams, pine furniture, and rooms in four separate buildings. "We dined in the courtyard under umbrella awnings, with very good draught Franconian wine. The *Frühstück* buffet was the best we've ever had." "Our room was large and rustic in an eco-friendly way, with a pine four-poster and a cane sofa; yet we also had a CD player and choice of CDs, plus video, plants and magazines. The breakfast buffet in a converted barn was superb – best Bircher muesli ever.

And our dinner was spectacular, amid Christmas decorations of golden suns, moons and blue globes: superb food included papillon of lobster and stuffed sole, presented as a colourful butterfly which tasted as delicious as it looked. Service was friendly and helpful. Fresh fruit is available *ad lib* in the hallway. Despite the business conferences at its Kreativecentrum, the hotel has not forfeited its sophisticated 'country hotel' atmosphere." "The attractive cobbled courtyard is a super place for Glühwein parties in winter." Or you eat in a great barn, below bare beams. (*DQ, and others*)

Open All year.
Rooms 57 double, 14 single. In 4 buildings. Some no-smoking.
Facilities Lounges, restaurant; conference facilities; sauna; courtyard (meals served in summer). Unsuitable for ♿.
Location In Boxdorf village, 9 km NW of Nuremberg (Nürnberg), off A73 to Erlangen.
Credit cards All major cards accepted.
Terms B&B: single 210 DM, double 270 DM. Set meals 38–75 DM; full alc 95 DM.

OBERAMMERGAU 82487 Bayern — Map 14

Gasthof Zur Rose BUDGET — *Tel* (08822) 47 06
Dedlerstrasse 9 — *Fax* (08822) 67 53

In a famous Bavarian village N of Garmisch (its next Passion Play is in 2000), this "friendly Alpine inn, the quintessence of gemütlichkeit", *is warmly run by the Frank family. It has simple, well-heated bedrooms, a garden, public rooms full of fine furniture and family heirlooms; good copious food; excellent breakfasts. Closed Nov, 24 Dec; restaurant closed Mon. All major credit cards accepted. 22 rooms. B&B: single 65 DM, double 110 DM; D,B&B 25 DM added per person. No recent reports; more welcome.*

OBERWESEL 55430 Rheinland-Pfalz — Map 14

Burghotel Auf Schönburg — *Tel* (06744) 93 93 0
Fax (06744) 16 13

This converted medieval castle, once the fief of the dukes of Schönburg, perches high above the Rhine's west bank, with a fantastic view. It is one of the *Guide*'s favourite German hotels, classy and romantic, and was extolled again this year: "The food is superb, service is flawless, and the rooms are lovely." While the outward aspect is severe, inside all is intimate and cosy – small beamed courtyards and dining rooms, a handsome library, slightly twee bedrooms, inevitably a bit small, with four-posters (best are those with balcony in the old tower). Inspectors were there in 1996: "It is stylish and up-market, and managed with taste and grace by its owners, the Hüttls – he a stately bearded figure with an incongruous pony-tail. Food was elaborate, a bit *nouvelle*, very *soigné*, and expensive. We had a good local Bacharach red (44 DM!) – and for breakfast smoked salmon with Sekt." The Hüttls have painted one of the outer walls bright red, because that's how it was in the 16th century, when painted walls were a sign of wealth. Recent praise: "A delightful room, with red velvet canopy above the bed." "Antiques in the bedroom, and a free decanter of sherry. The food, such as lamb in mustard sauce, was beautifully served." You can dine in the courtyard. Luggage is brought up by tractor from the carpark. Slight train noise from far below in river-facing rooms. (*Virginia Spargur, S and F-PG, and others*). Some tour groups.

Open Apr–Dec. Restaurant closed Mon.
Rooms 2 suites, 17 double, 3 single.
Facilities Lift. Sitting room, small library, 3 dining rooms; conference room; courtyard (meals in fine weather), riverside terrace. Unsuitable for ♿.
Location 2 km S of town. 42 km S of Koblenz. Carpark below castle (luggage brought up by tractor).
Credit cards All major cards accepted.
Terms B&B: single 125 DM, double 230–320 DM, suite 340–360 DM; D,B&B 60 DM added per person. Set meals 60–85 DM; full alc 80 DM.

PEGNITZ 91257 Bayern — Map 14

Pflaums Posthotel Pegnitz — *Tel* (09241) 72 50
Nürnbergerstrasse 12–16 — *Fax* (09241) 8 04 04

The Pflaum family's "eccentric and expensive" old post house (Relais & Châteaux), in a small Franconian town. Irradiated by the warmth of the owners ("Frau Pflaum is an enthusiastic hostess"), it has an international and musical flavour – patrons include famous musicians visiting nearby Bayreuth, and the Pflaums offer Wagner from Bayreuth on a large screen. Part of the hotel is still traditional, part strikingly modernised: it has four new "Laura Ashley" rooms, each with its own garden, while the boldly designed ultra-modern suites have won a US award for "the most exciting world-wide", with brilliant lighting. "Food is excellent, the staff young and friendly. Rooms vary from the luxurious to the plain and adequate. Unusual full-size papier-mâché figures in the dining room." "The indoor pool, sauna, etc, are superb, but the large erotic murals round the pool may force parents with children to do some unexpected explaining. The hotel's newer part is surreal, like being in a dream." But there's also a rustic *Stube*, plus a gourmet restaurant. Also a museum of modern art, and a new Internet Bar. Some rooms have traffic noise. Newer reports welcome.

Open All year.
Rooms 25 suites, 25 double. 1 on ground floor. 80% no-smoking. Air-conditioning.
Facilities Lift. Lounges, TV room, bar, restaurant (no-smoking); conference facilities; health club: swimming pool, sauna, indoor golf; dining terrace. Garden.
Location 1 km SW of Pegnitz. 33 km NE of Nürnberg.
Credit cards All major cards accepted..
Terms B&B: single 150–268 DM, double 195–590 DM, suite 395–1,500 DM. Set meals 59–165 DM. Reduced rates for children.

PESTERWITZ 01705 Sachsen — Map 14

Hotel Pesterwitzer Siegel NEW — *Tel* (0351) 460 20 68
Dresdnerstrasse 23 — *Fax* (0351) 460 20 72

Smallish, personal family-run hotels are finally appearing in former East Germany. This one, a new white building in a village overlooking Dresden, makes a welcome *Guide* debut: "It is owned and run by the friendly and helpful Siegel family, and has modern, well-serviced rooms. The excellent restaurant, with outside patio, is popular locally." The modern furnishings and decor are somewhat functional. There's a large beer-garden with white chairs and tables and a dance-floor. (*JR Williamson*)

Open All year, except Christmas.
Rooms 26 double. Some on ground floor.
Facilities Lift. Bar, breakfast room, restaurant; conference facilities; sauna, whirlpool. Garden: beer garden, children's playground.
Location In village, 5 km W of city. Parking.
Credit cards All major cards accepted.
Terms B&B: single 115–160 DM, double 150–180 DM; D,B&B 95–135 DM per person. Alc meals 35–40 DM.

PFRONTEN 87459 Bayern — Map 14

Berghotel Schlossanger Alp — *Tel* (08363) 60 86
Am Schlossanger 1 — *Fax* (08363) 66 67

"A friendly holiday hotel with surprisingly good food" – recent praise for the Schlachter-Ebert family's modern chalet, full of wood beams and Bavarian folk ornaments, but fully renovated in 1995. It stands amid open fields, on the edge of a straggling ski and summer resort in the Allgäu Alps, below the high Falkenstein mountain with its gaunt ruined castle. "A cordial welcome from the owners, a comfortable room, an excellent breakfast, and a good dinner, including perch and venison, served by a pleasant waitress in traditional costume." "Before us was the incredible panorama of peaks, and cowbells tinkled in the meadows at our feet." Geraniums festoon the balconies, and "jolly beer-drinkers" are said to mix with "quiet wine-drinkers". There are lounges, and an outdoor terrace-café for walkers. Children are welcomed. (*WR, and others*)

Open All year, except mid-Jan–mid-Feb. Restaurant closed Tues early Nov–early May.
Rooms 30 suites.
Facilities Lounge, TV room, breakfast room (no-smoking), restaurant; children's playroom; indoor swimming pool, sauna, solarium, whirlpool, fitness room; terrace. Garden: children's playground. Unsuitable for ♿.
Location At Pfronten-Obermeilingen, 4 km from centre of Pfronten.
Credit cards All major cards accepted.
Terms B&B double 77–202 DM, suite 220–300 DM; D,B&B 30 DM added per person. Set lunch 25–35 DM, dinner 35–65 DM; full alc 52 DM.

POTSDAM 14469 Brandenburg — Map 14

Schloss Cecilienhof — *Tel* (0331) 3 70 50
Neuer Garten — *Fax* (0331) 29 24 98

This, the most famous hotel of the former GDR, stands in a pleasant park, close to the Havel lake that here forms the border with Berlin. It was built in 1913 in English mock-Tudor style, as the residence of Kaiser Wilhelm II's daughter-in-law Cecilie (Sans Souci is nearby). Then, in 1945, the four-power Potsdam Treaty was negotiated and signed in a part of the house that is now a museum – you can see the chairs in which Churchill sat puffing while Stalin sat plotting. The rest of the house was turned by the GDR into a small, select state hotel, today privatised, and this year "completely restored with original

English furniture", say the owners. Before that, readers reported: "Comfortable rooms, excellent buffet breakfast, food unexceptional." "Service was polite and efficient, if a bit formal for a country hotel. Dinner in the panelled restaurant was good." There's a garden, and a terrace for summer dining. This year, a reader found the service "full of charm and concern", but noted faults in upkeep (broken TV, eccentric bath taps) and added: "It represents an enthusiastic attempt to bring the former East into the 1990s, but they are still on the learning curve." (*PJC Wadsley*)

Open All year.
Rooms 5 suites, 28 double, 10 single. 5 on ground floor.
Facilities Salons, bar, restaurant; conference facilities; sauna; terrace. Park: garden; lake 100 m.
Location In Neuer Garten, 2 km N of centre (signposted). Parking.
Credit cards All major cards accepted.
Terms B&B: single 195–255 DM, double 290–470 DM, suite 550–1,500 DM. Full alc 75 DM. Children under 12 accommodated free in parents' room.

QUEDLINBURG 06484 Sachsen-Anhalt — Map 14

Hotel am Brühl NEW — *Tel* (03946) 96 18-0
Billungstrasse 11 — *Fax* (03946) 39 52

This ultra-picturesque medieval town near the Harz mountains, with its old castle, Gothic town hall and half-timbered houses, is now being tactfully restored after its years of GDR neglect, and is a UNESCO World Heritage site. The *Brühl*, a stately white town house built in 1922, was bought in 1948 by the Schmidt family, who used it as a liquor factory; the state then took it over. Now, as happens in the former East, the Schmidts have got their property back, and have renovated it as a small family-run hotel. "The interior," says its nominator, "is high-ceilinged, bright and welcoming. The bedrooms offer sage-green carpeting, painted country furniture and yellow curtains. Bathrooms are spacious and modern. A copious buffet breakfast is served in a cheerful room." We should be glad of reports on the restaurant.

Open All year. Restaurant closed Sun (except Easter).
Rooms 2 suites, 19 double, 5 single. 2 no-smoking.
Facilities Lift. Restaurant; 2 conference rooms; sauna, solarium. Garden. Occasional concerts. Unsuitable for ♿.
Location Close to historic centre. 71 km SW of Magdeburg. Private parking.
Credit cards None accepted.
Terms B&B: single 120–140 DM, double 170–190 DM, suite 240–290 DM. Alc meals from 50 DM.

RAVENSBURG 88212 Baden-Württemberg — Map 14

Romantik Hotel Waldhorn — *Tel* (0751) 36 12-0
Marienplatz 15 — *Fax* (0751) 36 12-100

This impressive old Swabian town of towers and painted gateways was once a Guelph stronghold. The *Waldhorn* is worthy of it – an old building of character that has been run as a hotel by the same family since 1860. Its panelled rooms are full of flowers and interesting pictures; and the cooking wins a *Michelin* star (for, eg, mixed seafood hors d'oeuvre). A recent visitor confirms earlier praise: "The excellent restaurant has a fairly short menu of modern dishes, and breakfast is a big buffet." There is also a *Weinstube* for cheaper meals. The large rooms in the annexe have attractive fabrics and "a sophisticated feel". Rooms vary in size and price. (*SRH*)

Open All year. Restaurant closed Sun/Mon, Christmas; *Weinstube* closed midday.
Rooms 3 suites, 18 double, 12 single.
Facilities Lift. Lounge, restaurant, *Weinstube*; conference facilities; terrace.
Location Central. 35 km NE of Konstanz. Parking.
Credit cards All major cards accepted.
Terms [1996] B&B: single 115 DM, double 272 DM. Set meals: restaurant 87–114 DM, *Weinstube* 45–62 DM.

REGENSBURG Bayern — Map 14

Bischofshof am Dom — *Tel* (0941) 5 90 86
Krauterermarkt 3 — *Fax* (0941) 5 35 08
93047 Regensburg

Beside the majestic cathedral, a former bishop's residence, neatly converted. Owner Herbert Schmalhofer was private chef of Germany's richest man, the late Fürst von Thurn und Taxis: but prices are reasonable. Courteous staff; bedrooms with all comfort; copious breakfasts; good classic dishes served in a lovely room, or out in the patio/beer-garden with its curious comic goose-cum-fox fountain. Closed 22–25 Dec. All major cards accepted. Garage. 54 rooms: single 110 DM, double 195 DM; D,B&B 35 DM added per person. More reports, please.

Hotel Münchner Hof — *Tel* (0941) 58 44-0
Tändlergasse 9 — *Fax* (0941) 56 17 09
93047 Regensburg

In traffic-free heart of old town (but cars may enter to load or unload), "a gem" – neat and friendly family hotel in old building, well modernised. Good Bavarian cooking and buffet breakfasts. Credit cards not accepted. 52 rooms, some no-smoking. B&B: single 95–125 DM, double 140–170 DM. Set meals 19–22 DM. New reports welcome.

ROTHENBURG OB DER TAUBER 91541 Bayern — Map 14

Hotel Eisenhut NEW — *Tel* (09861) 7050
Herrngasse 3–5 — *Fax* (09861) 70545

Enclosed within its 14th-century ramparts above the Tauber, this famous old town of cobbled streets, fountains and tall gabled houses is as picturesque as any in Germany: but of course it gets crowded. In a main street, and very much in character, is the famous old *Eisenhut*. Made up of four medieval houses, it is a luxury hotel (Relais & Châteaux), furnished with antiques and original paintings. It fell from the *Guide* in 1989, after lack of feedback and some criticisms. Now it is renominated, oddities and all: "Probably our favourite hotel in Germany, and breakfasts the second best of our trip. Staff were very courteous, and one of our rooms was spacious and well equipped. The other was rather strange, being entirely red – red walls, curtains, bedspread, lampshades, flocked furniture. The bed was encased in an iron cage-type affair, and the entire room looked like a New Orleans bordello. After a day or so we got used to it." But many rooms are less odd, quite white. The name *Eisenhut* means "iron hat" or "wolfsbane", a poisonous plant. (*Kathy Gaston*) More reports please, especially on the food.

Open All year.
Rooms 2 suites, 64 double, 13 single. 2 no-smoking. 24 in annexe.
Facilities Lobby, bar, restaurant; function room, conference facilities; terrace. Garden: beer-garden. Unsuitable for ♿.
Location Central (front rooms could be noisy). Garage.
Credit cards All major cards accepted.
Terms [1996] Rooms: single 155–225 DM, double 195–380 DM, suite 520–640 DM. Breakfast 20 DM. Set lunch 40 DM, dinner 95 DM. Children under 10 accommodated free in parents' room.

Hotel Garni Hornburg NEW/BUDGET *Tel* (09861) 84 80
Hornburgweg 28 *Fax* (09861) 55 70

Peacefully apart from the tourist throng, yet an easy walk to the busy town centre, this tall, gabled half-timbered villa stands just outside the city walls. It is a guest house, restored to the *Guide* this year by two readers, after a change of owners: "Martin and Gabriele Wetzel were most welcoming, offering fine service and a bountiful breakfast. Our ground floor room was large and quiet." "A hearty breakfast in a pleasant Victorian-style room. Gracious hosts, tastefully decorated bedroom." The large garden can be used for barbecues. (*Virginia Spargur, Kari B Schilling*) As in all Germany, the juxtaposed twin beds "can make snuggling a challenge". No restaurant, but the *Altfränk Weinstube* was liked this year.

Open All year, except Christmas, 2 weeks Nov.
Rooms 1 suite, 9 double.
Facilities Lounge, breakfast room. Garden.
Location E of city walls, near Galgentor. Parking.
Credit cards All major cards accepted.
Terms B&B: single 85–125 DM, double 125–155 DM, suite 180 DM. Children under 12 accommodated free in parents' room.

ROTTACH-EGERN 83700 Bayern Map 14

Hotel Franzen NEW *Tel* (08022) 60 87
Karl-Theodorstrasse 2a *Fax* (08022) 56 19

On the lovely Tegernsee, Rottach-Egern is quite a smart lake resort (but cows stroll down its main street: this is Bavaria). Here the Franzen family's "delightful small hotel", a sturdy flower-girt chalet, is eagerly nominated: "Our room had beautiful antiques, large easy chairs, elegant bedspreads, flowers, fresh fruit, and two balconies with superb mountain views. The Franzens' welcome was personal, service was cheerful. The lounge had plenty of reading lamps. In the intimate *Pfeffermühle* dining room, the food was generous: good home-made soups. Once a week, guests can cook their own indoor barbecue meals, from an array of meats and vegetables." There are terraces for outdoor meals, and lawns and trees. (*Ann Chedlow*)

Open All year. Restaurant closed 2 weeks Apr, 2 weeks Nov.
Rooms 3 suites, 11 double, 1 single.
Facilities Ramps. Hall, lounge, TV room, restaurant; terrace. Garden.
Location On edge of town, 50 km S of Munich. Parking.
Credit card Access.
Terms B&B: single 85–125 DM, double 150–220 DM, suite 230–260 DM. Set lunch 20 DM, dinner 25 DM; full alc 40–60 DM.

ST GOAR 56329 Rheinland-Pfalz — Map 14

Schlosshotel und Villa Rheinfels — *Tel* (06741) 80 20
Schlossberg 47 — *Fax* (06741) 76 52

High above W bank of Rhine, 35 km SE of Koblenz, quite smart and well-modernised hotel built into walls of huge, mainly ruined old Rheinfels castle, once "a cross between Neuschwanstein and Carcassonne". Superb views down over Rhine from terrace and cheerful dining room. 58 elegantly decorated rooms, some inside castle, some in annexe, with equally inspiring views. Good food and service; indoor swimming pool, sauna. All major credit cards accepted. Rooms (with breakfast) 135–240 DM. Alc 42–72 DM [1996].

SCHALKENMEHREN 54552 Rheinland-Pfalz — Map 14

Landgasthof Michels BUDGET — *Tel* (06592) 9 28-0
St-Martinstrasse 9 — *Fax* (06592) 9 28-160

In the lovely Eifel hills, near Daun, is a region of small round volcanic lakes with clear blue water. Close to one of these, in a quiet village, is this neat family-run holiday hotel, with "cosy charm and a dash of elegance", as its nominators put it: "Our room in the new wing was large, light and airy, with tasteful decor, and a geranium-decked balcony with chairs. There's a comfortable lounge, and three dining rooms, one wood-panelled, one with lovely stained-glass windows depicting rustic scenes. The home-cooking was good and plentiful, and service was natural and charming, with a touch of humour. Breakfast was a hearty buffet, with the accent on wholefoods. The tiled indoor pool is attractive. All in all, good value for money." In the garden is a giant chess set, and a barbecue stand. (*D and JW*)

Open All year.
Rooms 2 suites, 30 double, 6 single.
Facilities Lift, ramps. Lounge, 3 dining rooms; conference facilities; indoor swimming pool, sauna, steam bath, massage, fitness room. Garden: chess.
Location 6 km SE of Daun. Parking.
Credit cards All major cards accepted.
Terms B&B: single 84–92 DM, double 134–188 DM, suite 150–260 DM; D,B&B 94–120 DM per person. Set meals 28 DM; full alc 48 DM.

SCHÖNWALD 78141 Baden-Württemberg — Map 14

Hotel Dorer — *Tel* (07722) 95050
Franz-Schubertstrasse 20 — *Fax* (07722) 950530

On quiet street of Black Forest resort 56 km NE of Freiburg, a smart and stylish little hotel with wood panelling, elegant furnishings, owned and run by "very welcoming" Scherer family. Good cooking. Indoor swimming pool, beauty salon; garden, tennis. All major credit cards accepted. 19 rooms: B&B double 140–154 DM; D,B&B double 200–226 DM. Set meals 45 DM. Fuller reports welcome.

Hotel Zum Ochsen NEW *Tel* (07722) 10 45
Ludwig-Uhlandstrasse 18 *Fax* (07722) 30 18

Near the centre of this resort village is the Martin family's typical Black Forest hotel, built in a manner at once smart and folksy, with lots of light wood and some antiques. The ambience likewise is informal yet sophisticated. Dropped from the 1996 *Guide*, it is now renominated: "We were greeted warmly, and our room had a balcony bordered by a flowery lawn. Breakfast was a feast, and the staff genuinely seemed to enjoy looking after my children." Good Baden cooking (snail soup, etc) is served by waitresses in local costume, on the patio in summer, by a log fire in winter. Musical evenings are organised. There is a pleasant indoor pool. (*Melissa McDaniel*)

Open All year. Restaurant closed 5 Nov–12 Dec, Tues/Wed.
Rooms 3 suites, 45 double. Some no-smoking.
Facilities Lounge, 4 dining rooms; conference room; indoor swimming pool, sauna, solarium; terrace. Large grounds: tennis, lake with fishing; bicycles. Unsuitable for ♿.
Location On edge of village, on road to St-Georgen, 8 km S of Triberg. Garages, parking.
Credit cards All major cards accepted.
Terms [1996] B&B: single 102 DM, double 320 DM; D,B&B 145–203 DM per person. Alc 48–85 DM.

SCHWANGAU 87645 Bayern **Map 14**

Hotel Müller *Tel* (08362) 8 19 90
Alpseestrasse 16 *Fax* (08362) 81 99 13
Hohenschwangau

The two great royal castles of Neuschwanstein and Hohenschwangau are in full view of the Müller family's handsome and stylish hotel, wood-panelled, and much enjoyed for its spacious rooms, good food, noteworthy wine-list and pleasant staff. "Breakfast was outstanding, our room comfortable but plainly furnished." "Our room opened on to an upper terrace with a view of one floodlit castle. Excellent dinner in a beautiful room." You can dine in a winter garden with those castle views. "The place is a circus during the day, with all the tour groups trouping from one *Schloss* to another in front of and sometimes through the hotel. But things quieten down at night." (*S and F-P Gingras, and others*)

Open All year, except 1 Nov–20 Dec.
Rooms 3 suites, 34 double, 8 single. 2 in nearby annexe.
Facilities Lift. Lounge, bar, restaurant, winter garden; conference facilities; terrace.
Location 6 km SE of Füssen. Parking.
Credit cards All major cards accepted.
Terms [1996] B&B: single 140 DM, double 260 DM; D,B&B 115–165 DM per person. Alc 36–78 DM.

SCHWARZENBERG 08340 Sachsen — Map 14

Am Hohen Hahn NEW
Gemeindestrasse 92
Bermsgrün

Tel (03774) 2 53 07
Fax (03774) 2 30 33

High on wooded hill at Bermsgrün, 4 km S of old town near Erzgebirge (mountains) and Czech border, holiday hotel with sweeping views. Nice staff; pleasant modern bedrooms with light wood furniture. Bar; good local cuisine, bountiful breakfast buffet; meals served on terrace. Fitness room, sauna, games room; minigolf, tennis, riding. Access, Amex, Visa accepted. 45 rooms. B&B: single 95–135 DM, double 160–210 DM. Set meals 32–53 DM [1996].

SCHWERIN 19063 Mecklenburg-Vorpommern — Map 14

Strand-Hotel NEW/BUDGET
Am Strand 13
Zippendorf

Tel (0385) 21 30 53
Fax (0385) 32 11 74

Beside Schwerin's big lake, in Zippendorf suburb, 6 km SE of town centre, classic 1920s holiday hotel on sandy beach. Privatised and renovated, with large rooms rather dully furnished. Pleasant service, decent food. Lakeside terrace for drinks, meals; bar/dance-hall. Access, Amex, Visa accepted. 26 rooms. B&B: single 100 DM, double 110–130 DM. Set meals 19–30 DM [1996]. Renominated this year, but fuller reports welcome.

TRIER Rheinland-Pfalz — Map 14

Hotel Deutschherrenhof NEW
Deutschherrenstrasse 32
54290 Trier

Tel (0651) 97 54 20
Fax (0651) 4 23 95

Central, quite near Porta Nigra, cheerful little modern hotel run with eager efficiency by owner Hans Jürgen Schmitz. 15 large rooms; generous breakfast served in elegant room (no-smoking). Garages. Access, Amex, Visa accepted. B&B: single 80–95 DM, double 120–160 DM. Renominated this year, but fuller reports welcome.

Hotel Eurener Hof
Eurenerstrasse 171
54294 Trier

Tel (0651) 8 80 77
Fax (0651) 80 09 00

Trier, centre of the Mosel wine trade and birthplace of Karl Marx (his home is now a museum), was a major Roman capital under the emperors Diocletian and Constantine. This past grandeur is today evoked by the Porta Nigra, finest Roman relic in Germany, and other imperial buildings. Across the Mosel, in the suburb of Euren, is this spruce white-fronted hotel, owned by the Haag family since 1906 and modernised in local style. Liked again this year, notably for its good food, it has an air of quality and comfort. An earlier view: "Our bedroom was large, and our meal was delicious, with vast helpings; the buffet breakfast was excellent, too." Two restaurants: an informal one is open all day." (*CF*)

Open All year, except Christmas.
Rooms 6 suites, 39 double, 18 single.
Facilities Lift. 2 lounges, bar, 2 dining rooms; indoor swimming pool, sauna, solarium. Unsuitable for ♿.
Location In Euren, across Mosel 3 km W of centre. Parking.
Credit cards Access, Amex, Visa.
Terms B&B: single 123–140 DM, double 185–215 DM, suite 235–255 DM; D,B&B 32–40 DM added per person. Set meals 17.50–35 DM; full alc 40–50 DM.

Hotel Petrisberg *Tel* (0651) 4 64-0
Sickingenstrasse 11–13 *Fax* (0651) 4 64-50
54296 Trier

You get a fine view down over Roman Trier from any of the rooms with balcony at this modern B&B hotel, ever popular with readers, and liked again this year. It sits splendidly amid garden, woods and vineyards, high on a hill above the city, and has finely landscaped grounds. It is admired also for its friendly staff, and for the warm personal service of its owner, Herr Pantenburg: "He was charming. Our room was excellent, with a balcony overlooking Trier, and the copious breakfast buffet was outstanding." "Our light, spacious room was enjoyable, with that spectacular view." There are all kinds of plants, statues, pictures, antiques – "massive kitsch throughout, with a gnome presiding over the splendid breakfast spread", which may include home-made liver dumpling soup. Herr Pantenburg sometimes offers wine from his own vineyards, leased to the Bishop of Trier. (*Franz Opitz, PD, and others*) Some rooms are in an annexe: they can be more ordinary, and not all have a view.

Open All year.
Rooms 5 triple, 25 double, 2 single. 2 on ground floor. 16 in annexe, 100 m.
Facilities Salon, TV room, breakfast room, wine bar. Garden, terraces.
Location Near Roman amphitheatre, 20–30 mins' walk from centre. Parking, garages.
Restriction No smoking: TV room, breakfast room, bedrooms.
Credit cards None accepted.
Terms B&B: single 100 DM, double 160–170 DM, triple 250–264 DM.

Hotel Villa Hügel NEW *Tel* (0651) 3 30 66
Bernhardstrasse 14 *Fax* (0651) 3 79 58
54295 Trier

This white chalet-like Jugendstil villa rises up amid trees in the southern suburbs, with good views over city and countryside. Owned and run by the Schütt family, it returns to the *Guide* after a time with no reports: "An excellent place, in a fairly quiet street within walking distance of the centre. Courteous welcome, lovely rooms with big windows. A friendly atmosphere, outstanding buffet breakfasts, excellent indoor pool and a patio. Bedrooms good for the price. The slight noise from the railway didn't disturb us." (*Dr Anthony Winterbourne*) No restaurant.

Open All year, except 22 Dec–8 Jan. Restaurant closed Fri/Sat/Sun.
Rooms 30 double, 4 single. Some on ground floor.
Facilities 4 lounges, bar; indoor swimming pool, sauna; terrace. Garden.
Location In S suburbs, 10 mins' walk from centre. Garage, parking.
Restriction No smoking: 2 lounges, 6 bedrooms, swimming pool.

Credit cards All major cards accepted.
Terms B&B single 100–150 DM, double 160–225 DM.

TÜBINGEN 72074 Baden-Württemberg — Map 14

Landhotel Hirsch
Schönbuchstrasse 28
Bebenhausen

Tel (07071) 6 80 27
Fax (07071) 60 08 03

In Schönbuch forest, in the northern suburbs of the old university city of Tübingen, is the beautiful Cistercian abbey of Bebenhausen, which dates from the 12th century. Here, say recent visitors, the old village inn is now "a charming hotel, owned and sympathetically managed by a young couple", Ernst and Brigitte Fischer. "Our spacious top-floor attic was enchanting, furnished with rustic elegance, with clever use of the exposed beams to give a feel of intimacy. Lovely small marble bathroom, and nice view of the forest. Good food in the elegant restaurant, candlelit in the evening. A cheerful atmosphere, with all the staff enthusiastic." Outdoor terrace for drinks and summer dining. (*GB and CH*) More reports, please.

Open All year. Restaurant closed Tues.
Rooms 8 double, 4 single.
Facilities Lounge, restaurant, *Stüble;* terrace.
Location 4 km N of centre. Parking.
Credit cards All major cards accepted.
Terms B&B single 135 DM, double 240 DM. Set meals 29.50–45 DM.

WALTERSDORF 02799 Sachsen — Map 14

Gastätte Grenzbaude BUDGET
Hauptstrasse 161

Tel (035841) 33 90
Fax (035841) 33 99-9

In ski-resort close to Czech border, 16 km SW of Zittau, lively and inexpensive rustic-style restaurant with 22 well-modernised (but poorly lit) bedrooms. Newly privatised, friendly owners, good food. "In the Stübl, *wonderful happy atmosphere" (it's good to hear that from former East Germany). Beer garden, swimming pool, sauna. Amex, Access accepted. B&B 70 DM; D,B&B 180 DM. Set meals 10–30 DM.*

WEIMAR 99423 Thüringen — Map 14

Christliches Hotel Amalienhof
Amalienstrasse 2

Tel (03643) 54 90
Fax (03643) 54 91 10

Near town centre and Goethehaus, 1826 mansion with garden, now run by Lutheran church association (see Martha Hospiz, *Dresden) as simple, friendly hotel ("religion not pushed").* Weinstube *but no restaurant; good breakfast. Parking. Beds can be hard, in German manner. Access, Amex, Visa accepted. 22 rooms. B&B: single 125–150 DM, double 186–196 DM. Some apartments are new this year.*

> Please write and confirm an entry when it is deserved. If you think that a hotel is not as good as we say, write and tell us.

Hotel Elephant NEW
Markt 19

Tel (3643) 802–0
Fax (3643) 65310

In 1999, Goethe's Weimar will be the first smaller town to be named European City of Culture (following upon Athens, Dublin, etc). Many more famous guests will then follow the likes of Wagner and Tolstoy, who stayed at this renowned 300-year-old inn in the past. Another guest was Hitler, who, in the days when Weimar was a staunch Nazi fief, greeted the cheering crowds from its balcony on the market-place. Dreary in the GDR days, the *Elephant* is now privatised (Flamberg Hotels), and has been totally refurbished in the Art Deco style of the Bauhaus (which was born in Weimar in 1919). The nominator liked her room (with small bathroom) facing the market square, and the elaborate breakfast: "To escape the main restaurant's *nouvelle cuisine*, we dined in the *Keller*, which provided excellent German food: duck with red cabbage, etc." Modern art on the walls; smart tables and chairs on the garden terrace. (*Julia de Waal*) A dissenter found the hotel rather formal and cheerless, with dull food. More reports, please.

Open All year. Restaurant closed Jan.
Rooms 20 suites, 63 double, 19 single. Some no-smoking.
Facilities Lift. Lounge, bar, bistro, restaurant; conference facilities; terrace. Garden.
Location Central. Private parking.
Credit cards All major cards accepted.
Terms [1996] Rooms: single 200–260 DM, double 260–380 DM, suite 480 DM. Breakfast 25 DM. D,B&B 55 DM per person added. Set lunch 40 DM, dinner 75 DM; full alc 85 DM.

WIESBADEN 65185 Hessen — Map 14

Hotel Admiral
Geisbergstrasse 8

Tel (0611) 5 2 86 60
Fax (0611) 52 10 53

Near centre of large spa town, Hessen's capital, a 19th-century hotel newly renovated, with good repro furniture; double glazing. Friendly staff, "super" buffet breakfast. All major credit cards accepted. B&B: single 125–145 DM, double 175–195 DM. No restaurant.

Alexander Hotel NEW
Rheinstrasse 72

Tel (0611) 99 28 5-0
Fax (0611) 99 28 55-5

Very central, small and soigné *B&B hotel opened in 1996 by multilingual young couple, he Portuguese, she German/American, both attentive. 23 spruce rooms with repro furniture, some no-smoking. Lounge, bar. Lift, ramps. Public garages nearby. All major credit cards accepted. B&B: single 115–135 DM, double 155–175 DM. Weekend rates.*

***

Traveller's tale We enjoyed everything at our hotel except the breakfast tea, which was rotten. I mentioned this to the owner, while settling the bill – not rudely, just querying why, when everything else was so spot on, this item, crucial to the pleasures of a tea-drinker's breakfast, should be so dire. "Oh, is it?" she said. "I wouldn't know. I drink Lapsang myself."

***

Greece

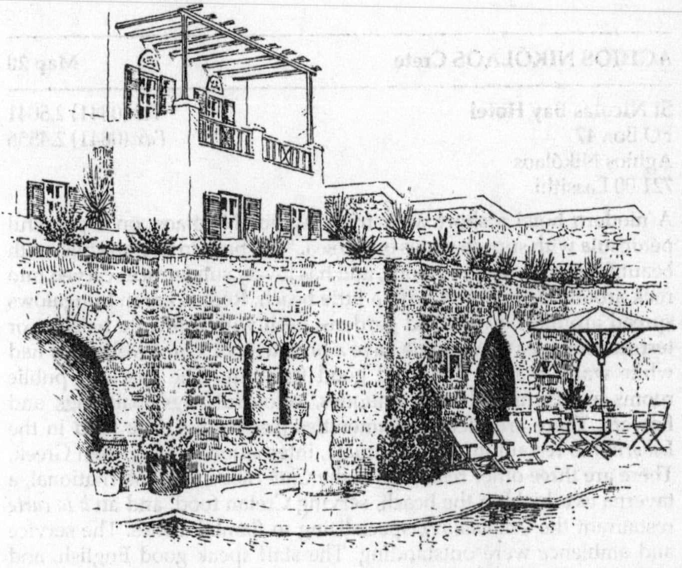

Kivotos Clubhotel, Mykonos

Greek hotels are officially graded, L (luxury), A, B, C, D and E (in the latter two categories they are simple, sometimes with shared bathrooms). Standards can vary greatly within each grade. In the cities, there are just a few international chain hotels of the Hilton or Holiday Inn type. The principal Greek chain is Xenia, with state-run medium-priced hotels developed in the 1960s to stimulate tourism in rural areas and resorts. In the larger coastal resorts there are some modern concrete eyesores, but the trend now is towards pleasanter bungalow developments, neatly sited in gardens. There are some expensive and sybaritic hotels, often on islands, but simple B and C class hotels in the countryside are often preferred by our readers.

In recent years, rather than encourage the building of more large hotels, the Greek National Tourist Organisation (EOT) has introduced a programme of remodelling old buildings in rural settings. The aim is to maintain their authentic feel while offering simple accommodation, generally with self-catering facilities. Towers in the Mani, wooden houses on Mount Pelion, and entire small villages on Santorini have been converted.

Another option is to stay in a private house (many of these, too, are officially graded), where the price is sometimes open to negotiation. On islands, the local police station will help in cases of need. Breakfast is not included.

Small hotels generally do not accept credit cards, preferring eurocheques or travellers' cheques. Service is included in the bill, and you need leave only a token extra tip. Breakfast is often not included in the room rate, and there is no obligation to take it in the hotel. L- and A-class hotels outside Athens may sometimes insist on half board, and expect bookings of at least a week in high season. Except in some luxury establishments, hotel food is seldom of high quality; a local taverna is probably more fun.

AGHIOS NIKÓLAOS Crete — Map 20

St Nicolas Bay Hotel
PO Box 47
Aghios Nikólaos
721 00 Lassithi

Tel (0841) 2.5041
Fax (0841) 2.4556

A modern hotel a short walk from Aghios Nikólaos, on a peaceful peninsula with superb views out to sea. "It is built in Cretan style, with beautiful use of slate and stone, and has lovely sun terraces carved into rock around a small bay with a little beach. Rooms are in bungalows spread around flower-filled gardens, each with a private balcony or terrace and a sea view; some have a private pool. Our lovely suite had white walls, marble floor and good furniture. The spacious public rooms are furnished with antiques, colourful rugs, paintings and flowers. There are plenty of amenities [see below]. The food in the *Labyrinthos* restaurant was adequate, international rather than Greek. There are three other restaurants: the *Club House*, also international, a taverna overlooking the beach, serving Cretan food, and an *à la carte* restaurant the (*Minotaure*), specialising in flambé dishes. The service and ambience were outstanding. The staff speak good English, and make a point of getting to know you. Only drawback: muzak in the public rooms." (*MF*)

Open Apr–end Oct.
Rooms 125 bungalows: 22 suites, 92 double, 11 single. 16 with private pool.
Facilities 2 lounges, cocktail lounge, TV lounge, 2 bars, 3 restaurants (1 no-smoking); games room; health club: indoor swimming pool, jacuzzi, gym, massage. Garden: terraces, 2 swimming pools, 2 children's pools, children's play area, tennis, beach with restaurant, water sports, sea excursions. Unsuitable for ♿.
Location 2 km N of Aghios Nikólaos.
Credit cards All major cards accepted.
Terms [1996] B&B: single 23,000–52,000 drs, double 30,000–110,000 drs, suite 42,000–135,000 drs; D,B&B: single 29,000–58,000 drs, double 42,000–122,000 drs, suite 54,000–147,000 drs. Set lunch 6,500 drs, dinner 9,500 drs; full alc 8,500–22,500 drs. Special rates for long stays, families, etc.

Don't trust out-of-date editions of the *Guide*. Hotels change hands, deteriorate or go out of business. Many hotels are dropped and new ones added every year.

ATHENS Central Greece **Map 20**

Hotel Hera BUDGET *Tel* (01) 923.6682
9 Falirou *Fax* (01) 924.7334
Makrigianni, 117 42 Athens

"For convenience, a pleasant downtown location (with a tiny tree-lined triangular 'square' in front) and extremely good value for money, try the *Hera*. It is modern and very clean, with basic, comfortable rooms. Each has private bath, air-conditioning and telephone; some have TV. Ask for a front one on the fourth or fifth flour with a balcony (no extra charge). The top (sixth) floor is a roof garden, more roof than garden, with a spectacular view of the floodlit Acropolis at night. You can take a drink up here to enjoy the lovely Athenian night. The young manager, Katia Depaoli, was most cordial. Two of the city's main tram lines are just across the 'square', but one can easily walk to Syntagma Square and the fascinating restaurants of the Plaka, on the other side of the Acropolis." (*C and JD*)

Open All year.
Rooms 43 double/triple, 6 single. Some with balcony.
Facilities Lounge, bar with TV; coffee shop; roof garden.
Location 5 km from centre, near Acropolis and Syntagma Sq. Garage.
Credit cards Amex, Visa.
Terms [1996] B&B: single 9,060–13,600 drs, double 12,250–19,300 drs, triple 14,650–23,100 drs. Children under 2 accommodated free in parents' room.

Herodion Hotel *Tel* (01) 923.6832
Rovertou Galli 4 *Fax* (01) 923.5851
117 42 Athens

Cool, clean modern hotel near the Acropolis. Pleasing, well-insulated bedrooms. Large, comfortable public rooms. Rooftop terrace; patio garden (drinks served beneath trees). Plentiful self-service breakfast. Readers generally eschew restaurant, preferring nearby taverna, Socrates' Prison. *Staff considered friendly by some; others complain of impersonal atmosphere. Some noise from day-care centre at back. 90 rooms. All major credit cards accepted. B&B: single 20,250–29,000 drs, double 26,500–38,000 drs, suite 32,500–47,000 drs. Set meals 5,000 drs; full alc 9,000 drs. More reports, please.*

CHANIA Crete **Map 20**

Hotel Amphitriti BUDGET *Tel* (0821) 5.6470
31–33 Lithinon *Fax* (0821) 5.2980
731 32 Chania

A welcoming family-run B&B, in Crete's sympathetic former capital. "The rooms are small but clean and neat. Two open on to a huge flower-lined balcony (in June the jasmine aroma is wonderful). Continental breakfast includes jam made by the mother of the family. On the morning when we had to leave at 6.15, she gave us an early breakfast, and squeezed excellent oranges into juice rather than give us them whole as usual, because it would be quicker and easier to consume. They recommended a good restaurant for dinner nearby. The attention of the staff was outstanding." The hotel is located above the old mosque, and has wonderful views of an old lighthouse, and of the Venetian waterfront, which can be a bit noisy at night, but double-glazing and air-conditioning were recently installed. (*KB and CS*) There are good bus services, so a car is not essential. Bar snacks are available.

Open All year, except Jan/Feb.
Rooms 2 triple, 14 double, 4 single.
Facilities Lounge, TV room, breakfast room (no-smoking), snack bar. Safe sandy beaches nearby; bicycle, motor-cycle hire. Unsuitable for ♿.
Location Off old harbour. Last right turn off Kanevaro before chains. Street parking.
Credit cards None accepted.
Terms Rooms: single 13,000 drs, double 17,000 drs. Breakfast 2,500 drs. Children under 5 accommodated free in parents' room.

Amphora Hotel BUDGET
2 Parados Theotokopoulou 20
731 31 Chania
Tel (0821) 9.3224
Fax (0821) 9.3226

In the Venetian quarter of Chania, with its narrow streets and little shops, is this "lovely hotel", a converted 13th-century building. Its restaurant ("highly recommended") is right on the harbour, which some of the balconies also overlook; and there are two charming roof terraces. "It is elegantly furnished, with high ceilings, whitewash and stone walls, striped fabrics, nicely painted woodwork, lovely wooden floors. The bedrooms have good lighting and smart bathrooms; some have a kitchenette. There is a grand suite with a huge fireplace." "Everything in first-class order. Helpful staff. Breakfast included fresh orange juice and home-made preserves." (*Ben Rubinstein and Sarah Chrisp, and others*) Some rooms are quiet, but those near reception can get noise from arrivals and departures, and those on the waterfront might be disturbed by the nightlife.

Open All year. Restaurant closed 15 Nov–31 Mar.
Rooms 1 suite, 18 double, 1 single.
Facilities Bar, breakfast room, restaurant; roof garden. Unsuitable for ♿.
Location At old Venetian harbour (2 rooms could be noisy). Public parking adjacent.
Credit cards Access, Visa.
Terms [1996] Rooms: single 11,000–12,000 drs, double 14,000–16,000 drs, suite 21,000–25,000 drs. Breakfast 2,000 drs. Full alc 3,500–4,000 drs. Children under 12 accommodated in parents' room half price.

Villa Andromeda
El. Venizelou 150
731 33 Chania
Tel (0821) 2.8300
Fax (0821) 2.8303

In the eastern suburbs of Crete's former capital, in a fine position above the sea, is a residential district of faded elegance where foreign powers built consulates during the brief period of Cretan autonomy (1898–1913). Here, the former German consulate, a neo-classical villa "with a posh interior" (ornate ceilings), has been converted into an exclusive bed-and-breakfast hotel. It consists entirely of suites on two levels with a modern decor, not particularly Cretan in style, but "comfortable and elegant, with lots of marble". Most have modest cooking facilities. "The manager, Athina Naxaki, and her assistant, Barbara, were wonderfully helpful, and generous with advice," writes an American visitor. "A high-grade continental breakfast is delivered to the suite on guests' schedule. The rear pool/bar area is attractive, though it could be better separated from the adjoining properties." "Nice views at the front over the sea, sunny rooms at the south-facing rear." No restaurant, but snacks are served. (*Adam Platt, and others*)

Open All year, except 20 Nov–20 Dec.
Rooms 8 suites. Air-conditioning.
Facilities Garden: terraces, swimming pool, children's pool (from mid-April), snack bar. Unsuitable for ♿.
Location 1.5 km from town centre. Private parking.
Credit cards Access, Amex, Visa.
Terms [1996] B&B double 22,000–34,000 drs.

ELOUNDA Crete **Map 20**

Elounda Mare *Tel* (0841) 4.1102
PO Box 31 *Fax* (0841) 4.1307
Elounda 721 00 Lassithi

On a peninsula on Crete's north coast, this glamorous modern Greek-owned *de luxe* hotel is set amid lush grounds ("quite an achievement in Crete"), with green lawns, shady trees and flowery shrubs, and a church. They slope gently to a sandy beach and rocky cove, where guests may indulge in all manner of water sports. Bedrooms are in the main building, with balconies facing the sea, and in white bungalows linked by paths in the form of a Cretan village; many of the latter, which are the best, have a private pool, and a large sitting room with a marble floor. There are "splendid" lounges, a little chapel, a games room, and three restaurants. *The Deck*, on a terrace, serves a five-course *table d'hôte* dinner; *The Yacht Club*, above the mini-harbour, serves international and Greek specialities; *The Old Mill* is expensive and formal. Lunch may be brought to the room. Breakfast is a copious buffet. "Cloistral calm; unostentatious, courteous and friendly service, by an English-speaking staff; food of five-star standard," *Guide* reporters have written. Predictably (this is the only Relais et Châteaux hotel in Greece), the atmosphere is international, and extras are expensive. But there are cheerful tavernas in Elounda village, a short taxi ride away, and "if you go out of peak season, and stay in the main building, it's almost affordable." More reports, please.

Open Apr–Oct.
Rooms 2 suites, 47 double (in main building). 44 bungalows (33 with private swimming pool). Air-conditioning.
Facilities 2 lounges, TV room, 2 bars, 3 restaurants; boutique, coiffeur. Garden: swimming pool, tennis; beach, water sports. Leisure facilities (including golf) at sister hotel *Porto Elounda Mare*, next door. Unsuitable for ♿.
Location 3 km from Elounda. 10 km N of Aghios Nikólaos.
Credit cards Access, Amex, Visa.
Terms [1996] B&B: single 26,000–49,000 drs, double 33,000–69,000 drs, suite 48,000–96,000 drs, bungalow 58,000–330,000 drs. Set dinner 9,000 drs; full alc 15,000 drs.

Sterling and dollar equivalents of foreign currencies at the date of going to press will be found at the back of the *Guide*.

GAVRION Aegean Islands — Map 20

Hotel Perrakis NEW/BUDGET
Kipri, Gavrion 845 01 Andros
Tel (0282) 71456
Fax (0282) 71459

"Andros, the most northern of the Cyclades, is a pleasant, unspoilt island, with plenty of wildlife and wonderful spring flowers. This white modern hotel is well positioned at the western end of a sheltered bay, just across the road from a clean sandy beach with clear warm water. Dennis Perrakis spent 25 years in San Francisco, before returning to build the hotel 12 years ago. His sister-in-law, Marie, runs the restaurant. The bedrooms, most with balcony, are simply furnished and comfortable, with a shower and modern plumbing. All overlook the sea, as do the bar, the lounge and the pleasant dining room, where good home-cooked Greek dishes are served. The buffet breakfast includes cereals, yogurt and nutty brown bread. The staff are friendly and the resident owners extremely helpful. Dennis will run guests into the nearby ferry port of Gavrion, or to the next village/port, Batsi, where there are other restaurants and tavernas, in his comfortable air-conditioned mini-bus." (*Denis Jukes*)

Open Apr–Oct.
Rooms 44 double.
Facilities Lounge, bar, games room, restaurant; terraces. By beach. Unsuitable for ♿.
Location Kipri. Near Gavrion, on W side of Andros island.
Credit cards Probably some accepted.
Terms [1996] Rooms: single 8,500–12,000 drs, double 9,750–13,000 drs. Breakfast 1,500 drs. Set meals 3,000 drs.

HYDRA Central Greece — Map 20

Hotel Orloff BUDGET
Rafalia 9
180 40 Hydra
Tel (0298) 5.2564 and 5.2495
Fax (0298) 5.3532
Athens office: *Tel* (01) 822.6210
Fax (01) 825.1778

The island of Hydra, south of Athens, "quiet and traffic-free but rather arid", has a fashionable capital with a beautiful harbour. Here, this small, pretty *pension* with friendly hosts is favoured by artists, diplomats and politicians, and is thought "delightful" and "marvellously relaxing" by *Guide* readers. It's an 18th-century family house, lovingly restored, with large high-ceilinged rooms, cool white walls, beams, blue doors and window frames, period furniture, and unobtrusive but effective air-conditioning. A copious breakfast is served in a day room or the "lovely flowery courtyard". Lots of tavernas nearby. There is a rocky beach five minutes' walk away; sandy beaches are ten minutes away by boat. (*JS, and others*) A new manager this year; we'd like more reports, please.

Open End Mar–end Oct.
Rooms 3 suites, 7 double.
Facilities Lounge, bar. Courtyard garden. Air-conditioning. Beach 5 mins' walk.
Location Central, 100 m from harbour. Regular ferry services from Piraeus, Ermioni.
Credit cards Access, Diners, Visa.
Terms [1996] B&B double 18,000–32,000 drs.

IMEROVIGLI Aegean Islands **Map 20**

Chromata NEW *Tel* (0286) 24850
PO Box 14 *Fax* (0286) 23278
Imerovigli 847 00 Thira (Santorini)

Attractive new small B&B hotel on rim of volcanic Caldera, overlooking sea. Colourful italianate design; stunning public areas. Sizeable pool "meandering from cliff's edge into lobby". 17 bedrooms, suites and apartments: spacious, adequately furnished, some with kitchenette, some reached up many steps; but "uncomfortable if innovative cave-like bathrooms". Terrace. Very helpful staff. Generous buffet breakfast. Bar. Open Apr–Nov. All major credit cards accepted. B&B: single 26,000–29,000 drs, double 37,000–46,000 drs [1996]. More reports, please.

KARDAMYLI Peloponnese **Map 20**

Kalamitsi Hotel BUDGET *Tel* (0721) 7.3131
Kardamyli 240 22 Messinias *Fax* (0721) 7.3135

In this small town ("a charming balance of civilisation and quiet") in the lush Messinian part of the Mani, where Patrick Leigh Fermor has made his home, is this "lovely" hotel. "Beautifully situated in an olive grove leading down to a small pebble beach, it is well designed, and built in an attractive pinky local stone, a change from the ubiquitous white and blue. Accommodation is a mixture of traditional hotel rooms and bungalows; the latter have simple catering facilities. Ours was well furnished, with comfy beds, fridge, and super *en suite* shower and bath. The food was so good that, though we had booked on a B&B basis, we ate in every evening. Portions were generous, and the set menu more traditionally Greek than in many tourist tavernas. Pleasant English-speaking owners. The surrounding area is pretty spectacular." (*"Wholeheartedly endorsed" in 1996 by Dr and Mrs Rampton*)

Open Apr–Oct. Lunch not served.
Rooms 26 (including bungalows, with kitchenette).
Facilities Lounge, restaurant. Garden; beach.
Location W coast of Mani peninsula. 1 mile from Kardamyli, SE of Kalamáta.
Credit cards Access, Visa.
Terms [1996] Rooms: single 13,500–14,500, double 16,000–17,000 drs, bungalow 17,500–25,000 drs. Breakfast 1,500 drs. Set dinner 3,000 drs.

KASTRON Peloponnese **Map 20**

Hotel Chryssi Avgi BUDGET *Tel* (0623) 9.5224
Loutropoleos 9 and 9.5380
Kastron 270 50 Ilias

Kastron is an attractive village in the north-western Peloponnese, crowned by a well-preserved old Frankish castle, with stunning views. This friendly, informal hotel, in its main street, is run by the Franco-Greek Lepidas family. The Parisian hostess, Catherine Lepidas, is much admired: "she is charming, witty and truly gracious". Accommodation is "simple but adequate", and breakfast, served on the terrace in fine weather, is "outstanding". There's a beautiful, safe, sandy beach three kilometres away. The family also run a bar/pizzeria, but we don't have up-to-date reports on the food; we'd be glad to hear from recent visitors.

Open Early May–mid Oct, "or later, depending on weather and guests".
Rooms 10 double. 1 with bath, 9 with shower.
Facilities Lounge, bar, dining room; terrace. Unsuitable for ♿.
Location Centre of village 60 km SW of Patras. Rear rooms quietest. Parking.
Credit cards None accepted.
Terms [1996] B&B: single 8,000 drs, double 11,000 drs. Full alc at pizzeria 4,500 drs.

MYKONOS Aegean Islands — Map 20

Hotel Adonis BUDGET
PO Box 68
846 00 Mykonos
Tel (0289) 2.3433
Fax (0289) 2.3449

Set above the main road a short walk from the centre of town, stands this cool white-walled hotel. A sandy beach is five minutes' walk away, and buses to the superb beaches on the south side of the island pass the door. "An all-time favourite," writes an American visitor, "with a relaxed atmosphere. The staff went out of their way to please each guest; someone was always on hand to recommend local restaurants or to serve a drink from the bar. Generous breakfast. Our simple bedroom was comfortable and clean, with some interesting pieces of furniture. Our fellow guests, many of them regular visitors to the hotel, were knowledgeable about the island." Some bedrooms are small; most have a sea-facing balcony. (*M Kulanda*)

Open Apr–Oct.
Rooms 3 suites, 27 double, 2 single. Air-conditioning.
Facilities Ramps. Lounge, TV room, 2 bars.
Location From centre take road towards Ornos Bay; hotel on left.
Credit cards Access, Amex, Visa.
Terms B&B: single 9,350–18,000 drs, double 12,250–22,250 drs, suite 23,000–45,000 drs. 1-night bookings refused during Greek Easter.

Kivotos Clubhotel
Ornos Bay
846 00 Mykonos
Tel (0289) 2.5795
Fax (0298) 2.2844
Athens office: *Tel* (01) 724.6766
Fax (01) 724.9203

A luxurious hotel overlooking Ornos Bay. Built in 1993, white-walled and set on terraces with sculptures, mosaics and frescoes, it was nominated by an awestruck British hotelier: "For those who, like me, remember Mykonos of the late sixties and early seventies, this hotel will come as something of a shock. Exceptional service, home-made pastries to go with the full range of Greek, American and English breakfast options. Air-conditioning and a magnificent pool overlooking Ornos Bay. But the real treat is the understated success of the design, and the way in which all the luxury somehow remains in harmony with the island. This little slice of heaven does not come cheap, however, and extras are pricey." Indoors and out are works by local craftsmen. Bedrooms have satellite TV, video, safe and mini-bar. A poolside barbecue is held once a week. (*JW*) More reports, please.

Open May–Oct.
Rooms 4 suites, 24 double. Air-conditioning.
Facilities Lounge, bar, restaurant; fitness centre, sauna, games room, squash court; terraces: bar, swimming pool with bar. Private beach
Location 3.5 km from Mykonos town.
Credit cards All major cards accepted.
Terms [1996] B&B: single 34,000–57,000 drs, double 39,000–66,000 drs, suite 68,000–125,000 drs. Set lunch 9,500 drs, dinner 10,500 drs; full alc 15,000 drs.

MYRINA Aegean Islands — Map 20

Akti Myrina Hotel — *Tel* (0254) 2.2681
Myrina 814 00 Lemnos — *Fax* (0254) 2.2352
Athens office: — *Tel* (01) 413.8001
Vas. Pavlou 107 — *Fax* (01) 413.7639
185 33 Piraeus, Athens

Lemnos is a flat, sometimes windy, but beautiful island. This luxurious hotel is just outside the "charming, unspoilt" little capital. Its stone cottages are spread over a hillside in a flowery terraced garden leading down to a private beach. Each has its own little garden or patio, where breakfast can be served. Most have a view to the sea, which is shallow for a long way out and very clean. As ever, *Guide* reporters are enthusiastic: "Delightful, friendly atmosphere. Attentive staff, present when needed, discreetly absent when privacy is preferred. Expensive, but good value for money." "Perfect for a family holiday. Long, safe, clean beach, plenty of space, children's playground. Charming local staff. Room servicing perfect." Others happily remembered "restful days amid peace and beauty", "watching wild birds from our bungalow garden", and sitting in the courtyard under a full moon, enjoying the music of the resident pianist. Guests are ferried by the hotel's two caiques to otherwise inaccessible beaches, and they may go for sea trips on the hotel yacht, skippered by Captain Yannis (he sometimes teaches visitors to dance). Plenty of choice for meals, from the formal gourmet one, to the little taverna by the shore, which serves salads and hot dishes, including local fish and meat dishes. The bars serve snacks and drinks. (*B Milner, AC, and others*)

Open May–1 Oct.
Rooms 15 suites, 110 double. All in cottages with veranda, small garden, air-conditioning.
Facilities Lounge, TV lounge, 3 bars, café, 4 restaurants; hairdresser; disco. 25-acre grounds: tennis, swimming pool, children's pool, mini-golf, volley-ball, table-tennis, private sandy beach with restaurant; fishing, bathing, water sports. Unsuitable for ♿.
Location 1 km from Myrina town. Direct flight from Athens, or boat from Piraeus.
Restriction No smoking in main restaurant.
Credit cards All major cards accepted.
Terms D,B&B: single 44,000–56,000 drs, double 63,000–120,000 drs, suite (for 4) 135,000–175,000 drs. Children under 6 accommodated free in parents' room. 15% discount for returning guests who book direct with the hotel.

> Deadlines: nominations for the 1998 edition should reach us not later than 25 May 1997. Latest date for comments on existing entries: 1 June 1997.

NAFPLION Peloponnese — Map 20

Byron Hotel NEW/BUDGET — *Tel* (0752) 2.2351
Platonos 2, Platia Agiou Spiridona — *Fax* (0742) 26338
Nafplion 211 00 Argolis

In the centre of the old town, the first capital of modern Greece ("now quite elegant, clean and pedestrianised"), is this "lovely" old pink and blue house, set below the Catholic church. It has been carefully restored by the friendly owner, Aristidis Papaioannoy, who speaks excellent English. "It is efficiently run," write the nominators. "Our top-floor room was spotless, with a double bed, *en suite* bathroom (decent size towels), marble floors, and amazing views over the old town and harbour. Breakfast is served on the very pretty terrace in summer, and includes real coffee." (*Dr and Mrs Rampton*) No restaurant but there are plenty nearby. There is safe parking in a small square 30 metres away.

Open All year, except 1 Nov–15 Dec.
Rooms 18 double. Air-conditioning.
Facilities Breakfast room, terrace. Rocky beach nearby.
Credit cards Access, Amex, Visa.
Location Central, near Catholic church. Parking nearby.
Terms B&B: single 12,500 drs, double 17,000–21,000 drs. Breakfast 1,200 drs.

SKALA Aegean Islands — Map 20

Skala Hotel BUDGET — *Tel* (0247) 3.1343
Skala 855 00 Patmos — *Fax* (0247) 3.1344

Skala is the hub of Patmos's commercial life, and has some lively tavernas and discos, and a number of recently built hotels. Right by the harbour is this one, "personal and welcoming, offering excellent value", and evocatively nominated: "We arrived at night by boat. The hotel, well lit, was just two minutes' walk away – just what the weary traveller needed. The receptionist was enormously friendly and helpful, and the bedroom, with its *en suite* bathroom, 100 per cent comfortable. Only next morning did we discover the hotel's most wonderful feature. When you enter from the street, your breath is taken away by the glorious pinks and purples of the bougainvillea filling the courtyard; you breakfast on a porch under a bougainvillea canopy. There's a salt-water swimming pool, with a bar where you can sit on stools submerged in the water. If you want atmosphere, peace, yet immediate access to everything Patmos has to offer, this is the place." No restaurant, but light meals by arrangement. (*FP*) More reports, please.

Open Apr–Oct.
Rooms 78 double.
Facilities Lounge with TV, bar, breakfast room. Large garden: swimming pool.
Location Near harbour.
Credit cards All major cards accepted.
Terms [1996] B&B: single 9,000–12,500 drs; double 12,500–18,000 drs. Set meals 3,000–3,500 drs.

> In your own interest, always check latest tariffs with a hotel when you make your booking.

Hungary

Hotel Senator-Ház, Eger

BUDAPEST **Map 19**

Alba Hotel NEW *Tel* (1) 175-9244
Apor Péter út. 3 *Fax* (1) 175-9899
1011 Budapest

Down quiet side-street in Buda, between river and castle, sizeable modern B&B hotel owned by Swiss chain. "Clean, efficient, no frills, good value." 95 rooms: functional, varying in size. Helpful staff; generous buffet breakfast. Parking (22 DM). All major credit cards accepted. B&B double 120–200 DM.

Beatrix Panzió BUDGET *Tel* (1) 275-0550
Széher út. 3 *Fax* (1) 176-3730
1021 Budapest

This spruce white-walled villa, now a "delightful" up-market *pension*, stands, surrounded by a garden, in a residential area on the western edge of town. Its owner/managers, the Martinecz family, have won the "Guest House of the Year" award, and new praise came in 1996: "It was friendly, delightfully warm, also quiet and clean. We had an enjoyable stay. Small bar downstairs (but who needs a big one?), with good selection of local liqueurs and brandies. Facilities basic (built-in shower), and some noise from other rooms, but all have satellite TV. Well placed for a tram-ride into town." Goodish breakfasts are served in a new well-decorated room. There's a gazebo, a pond with goldfish, and a garden where barbecues are sometimes held, but no restaurant. (*Tony Balacs*)

Open All year.
Rooms 4 suites, 12 double. Some on ground floor.
Facilities Ramps. Bar, breakfast room (no-smoking); terrace. Garden.
Location 8 km W of city centre; tram service. Secure parking.
Credit cards None accepted.
Terms B&B: single 70–90 DM, double 90–100 DM, suite 120–150 DM.

Hotel Erzsébet
Károlyi Mihály út. 11–15
1053 Budapest
Tel (1) 138-2111
Fax (1) 118-9237

In fairly quiet street in Pest inner city, classic 1900s hotel completely refurbished, now "efficient and comfortable". Good buffet breakfast and restaurant with Hungarian dishes; popular beer hall. Lift. Parking. All major credit cards accepted. 123 rooms: single 155 DM, double from 195 DM. Set meals 20 DM [1996]. "Still reasonably priced, compared with hotels belonging to western chains." More reports, please.

Hotel Gellért
Szent Gellért tér 1
1111 Budapest
Tel (1) 185-2200
Fax (1) 166-6631

The palatial old *Gellért*, a great white turn-of-the-century wedding cake, stands in all its Baroque glory at the foot of the Gellért hill, above the Danube. Once the city's premier hotel, it is now overtaken by the *Hilton* and others, but there's still plenty to impress visitors – lavish Art Nouveau decor, marbled halls, wrought ironwork and majestic stairway, huge high-ceilinged bedrooms, and the giant thermal baths in the basement, fed by nearby hot springs. The baths are separately managed and often crowded, but hotel guests get special comfy robes to visit them: they are said to be "stupendous" but "in need of some tarting up". There are also spa water baths, and an outdoor swimming pool adorned with arbours and statues (closed in winter), where the world's first artificial wave machine (1916) still operates for ten minutes each hour. Latest visitors have judged the hotel slightly run down, and service muddled – "but the swimming pool made up for it all". Others have admired "the army of polyglot receptionists, the huge buffet breakfast, though it comes with muzak", and the "virtually instant laundry service". The inevitable gipsy orchestra is said to be inferior to others in town. Bedrooms vary. Some are small and "spartanly furnished"; river-facing front ones are best, but their double-glazing does not quite blot out the noise of clanging trams. (*WG, and others*)

Open All year.
Rooms 14 suites, 102 double, 123 single.

Facilities Hall, lounges, bar, brasserie, coffee shop, 2 dining rooms; banqueting hall, conference rooms; nightclub; thermal baths. Garden: terraces, swimming pool.
Location 3 km from centre, at foot of Gellért hill. Guarded parking opposite.
Credit cards All major cards accepted.
Terms [1996] B&B: single 200 DM, double 348 DM, suite 450 DM; D,B&B 40 DM added per person. Children under 12 accommodated free in parents' room.

Budapest Hilton *Tel* (1) 214-3000
Hess András tér 1–3 *Fax* (1) 156-0285
1014 Budapest

Built soon before the fall of Communism, this exceptional *Hilton* has a fine position on Castle Hill in the historic heart of Buda: it is next to the 13th-century Matthias Church, and has been cleverly designed to incorporate the remains of the 13th-century monastery that once flourished here. Communism may come and go, but on this sacred site modern American capitalism now reaches back to the roots of medieval Christianity. "The front has been rebuilt to copy the destroyed building it replaces, but the back is modern and sympathetically done, with a lot of smoked glass." While the public rooms are colourful, the bedrooms are plainer and more impersonal, but nice. "Bathrooms are showing their age but still function well. Staff are genuinely pleasant and helpful. The coffee shop serves a lavish buffet breakfast. The *Kalocsa* Hungarian restaurant is pretty. Here and in the *Dominican* restaurant we found the food variable: superb soups, and good fish from Lake Balaton, but vegetables pre-*nouvelle cuisine*. It's hearty peasant grub in posh surroundings." The gipsy violinist has been called "one of Hungary's best". "Wonderful views, two excellent restaurants, impeccable service." (*LT and JF, and others*) A fitness centre is new this year. No recent reports; more welcome.

Open All year.
Rooms 27 suites, 295 double. 3 suitable for ♿. 1 floor no-smoking. Air-conditioning.
Facilities Lounge, 2 bars, 2 cafés, 2 restaurants; conference/function facilities; fitness centre.
Location In Buda, on Castle Hill. Indoor/outdoor parking.
Credit cards All major cards accepted.
Terms (*Excluding 15% tax*) Rooms: single 280–425 DM, double 365–535 DM, suite 530–1,500 DM. Breakfast 29 DM. Set lunch 60 DM, dinner 70 DM; alc 50 DM. Children accommodated free in parents' room.

EGER 3300 Map 19

Hotel Korona BUDGET *Tel* (36) 313-670
Tündérpart 5 *Fax* (36) 310-261

Eger, north-east of Budapest, is a lovely historic old town in a valley. It has an ancient castle, even a 17th-century Turkish minaret, and it produces some of Hungary's best wine, the Egri Bikavér (bull's blood). The *Korona*, a modern white building in a quiet street, calls itself "the first family-run hotel of Eger". "It was charming, its management nice and helpful, speaking good English and German. The rooms were simple and spacious, and in the quaint outdoor dining patio the food was excellent, the Eger wine exceptional (a visit to the cellars is a must)." (*BL*)

Open All year.
Rooms 1 suite, 39 double. 20 in annexe 5 m. Some on ground floor. 4 no-smoking.
Facilities Lounges, bar, wine cellar, restaurant; conference room; patio.
Location Central. 130 km NE of Budapest. Parking.
Credit cards All major cards accepted.
Terms B&B: single 55–65 DM, double 60–90 DM, suite 100–130 DM; D,B&B 12 DM added per person. Children under 10 accommodated free in parents' room.

Hotel Senator-Ház BUDGET *Tel/Fax* (36) 320-466
Dobó tér 11

"This wholly professional hotel/brasserie deserves the highest praise," writes its nominator. "It is on the edge of the pedestrianised area, just below the castle walls. Some athleticism is needed for climbing the 18th-century staircase to the bedrooms. They are small but adequate and very comfortable. The staff have little English, but are friendly and well motivated. Breakfast was very well prepared." (*DS*) No proper lounge, but pleasant outdoor cafés nearby.

Open All year.
Rooms 9 double, 2 single.
Facilities Reception/lounge, bar, breakfast room, grill room; terrace. Unsuitable for ♿.
Location Central, below castle. Unsupervised parking.
Credit cards Access, Amex, Visa.
Terms B&B: single 3,500–5,000 fts, double 4,800–8,800 fts.

FERTÖD 9431 Map 19

Kastélyszálló BUDGET *Tel* (99) 370,971
Bartok Béla út. 2

In a town dominated since the 18th century by the Esterházy dynasty, the best-value accommodation in the *Guide* this year, despite the grand setting. "Not a hotel, rather a palace with rooms – the very fine Esterházy summer palace where Haydn wrote and directed the 'Farewell' Symphony. Accommodation is on the second floor (steep stairs!) of the east wing. We had a quiet, very large corner bedroom with separate sitting area and a balcony giving on to the garden. *En suite* basin and mirror, with serious communal facilities just down the corridor. Just £6.77 for two, payable in advance. There is a chance that an over-excited Hungarian school party will live it up in the corridors until 3 am. However, the walls are thick, there is a lot of space and the guardian takes care to lodge the young as far away as possible from us retired musicians. You eat and drink well for almost nothing at the new café across the road, open until 10.30 pm, but not for breakfast." (*DS*) The palace is one of the top tourist sights in Hungary.

Open Probably all year. No meals.
Rooms 19.
Facilities Large lounge. Access to palace garden.
Location East wing of palace. 2 mins' walk from centre.
Credit cards None accepted.
Terms [1996] Rooms: single 1,300 fts, double 1,500 fts.

Italy

Luna Convento, Amalfi

Italian hotels are officially classified and range from five-star *de luxe* down to small one-star inns and guest houses. The big international chains, such as Hilton, Holiday Inn and Novotel, are represented, but sparsely. The main Italian-owned luxury chain is CIGA; Jolly Hotels are more numerous, more down-market. The great majority of Italian hotels are individually owned, although some are grouped into associations, as in other countries – Relais & Châteaux, Romantik Hotels, etc. There is now a branch of the excellent Logis de France association, Logis d'Italia, with over 100 members.

It has become harder to find a good, modestly priced hotel in Italy, especially in the cities, which are now very expensive. Many hotels have upgraded themselves, installing smart bathrooms, hair-dryers, mini-bars, etc, and put up their prices. At the upper end of the market, Italy has quite a number of strikingly beautiful hotels, furnished and decorated with true Italian flair, in modern or traditional style; they are among the best of their kind in Europe, and this chapter has a good selection. Then, especially in Tuscany, there are many villas and manors that have been converted and are now run as personal hotels, sometimes by their ancestral owners. Finally there is the *locanda*, which is a country inn similar to a French *auberge*. *Agroturismo* is a recent movement that encourages the conversion of farmhouses and rural dwellings into small hotels.

We include a selection of these country hotels, which can be delightful. However, we have found few good individual hotels in big cities. Our total number of entries for Rome has risen this year from seven to nine: but we still have only three for Milan, one for Genoa, and none at all for Turin or Naples.

As is usual on the Continent, prices include a service charge, and you need leave only a token tip, if service has been especially good. A double room usually costs 30 to 50 per cent more than a single one. Some hotels include breakfast in the room rate; but generally you pay extra for it, and are therefore free to take it or not, as you wish. As Italian hotel breakfasts are often poor, it can be more fun, and cheaper, to go to a café for a good espresso or cappuccino.

In many Italian hotels. the food, often regional, tends to be better than the bedrooms. We quote the *Michelin* star ratings – there are lots of these in northern Italy, extremely few in the south, and only three establishments in the entire country with three stars, compared with 19 in France.

ALPE FAGGETO 52033 Arezzo — Map 17

Fonte della Galletta BUDGET *Tel/Fax* (0575) 793925 and 793652
Alpe Faggeto
Caprese Michelangelo

For lovers of mushrooms and Michelangelo: near the artist's birthplace and the great monastery of Verna, alone in the wild forested Apennines, is this 5,000 feet-up, down-to-earth chalet-like restaurant-with-rooms. Owned and run by the Berlicchi-Boncompagni family, it has just been refurbished. But it is still perhaps more of a "typical Italian experience" than an ordinary hotel, and has a "vivacious local ambience". Recent visitors have enjoyed its very special gastronomy: "The son prepared an entire dinner of the local wild mushrooms – sliced raw mushrooms, then ravioli with a mushroom sauce, deep-fried mushrooms in batter, grilled porcini and uovi mushrooms. We had no room for dessert, even if it had been made from mushrooms." Others enjoyed the flambé'd chestnuts, ravioli with truffles, and added: "Very friendly service, delicious air. Delicious water from the local spring is pressed on guests. Modern bathrooms, simple but comfortable wooden furniture." Rooms too are simple, but adequate. The grounds are surrounded by "a marvellous beech wood". (*DFP, JW*)

Open All year (weekends only Jan–Mar).
Rooms 16 double, 3 single. 6 in bungalows 30 m. 1 suitable for ♿.
Facilities Ramps. 2 lounges, TV room, bar, billiard room, restaurant. Large grounds.
Location 6 km SW of Caprese Michelangelo; 50 km NE of Arezzo.
Credit cards All major cards accepted.
Terms [1996] Rooms: single 65,000–70,000 L, double 75,000–80,000 L. Breakfast 12,000 L. D,B&B 63,000–68,000 L per person. Set meals 45,000 L; full alc 35,000 L.

AMALFI 84011 Salerno — Map 18

Luna Convento *Tel* (089) 871002
Via Pantaleone Comite 33 *Fax* (089) 871333

Perched above Amalfi's gorgeous coast is this cool, white-walled convent. It was founded originally by St Francis of Assisi, and men of genius have since stayed there, including Wagner and Ibsen, who wrote *A Doll's House* in room 5. Bedrooms have good views and are fair-sized, with antique furniture (but some fittings are worn). "Notably civilised", "a delightful stay", are two plaudits this year. "Our room was recently and tastefully decorated, food was pleasing, breakfasts well above average, notably the pastries." "Our large and bright room had magnificent sea views. Service was friendly; food was fresh, simple and well presented" – "spectacular" lasagne, grilled local prawns, good local wine. There is traffic noise by day, but it quietens at night; the "wonderful" inner cloister is very quiet, and looks gorgeous in winter with its fruit-laden lemon trees. The hotel has been owned by the Barbaro family for generations, and has its own rococo chapel, which can be hired for a wedding. The unheated sea-water swimming pool is liked, but it's a climb down from street level. You can also sunbathe on huge rocks, then jump into the sea. (*PW Gamble, SC Glover*)

Open All year.
Rooms 2 suites, 44 double.
Facilities Lift. Lounge with TV, restaurant; function facilities; cloister. Swimming pool in rocks below; night club (July/Aug) opposite.
Location On coast road, 200 m E of centre. Garage nearby (20,000 L).
Credit cards All major cards accepted.
Terms B&B: 105,000–160,000 L per person. D,B&B 150,000–230,000 L. Set meals 65,000 L; full alc 70,000–80,000 L.

ARGEGNO 22010 Como — Map 17

Hotel Belvedere *Tel* (031) 821116
Via Milano 8 *Fax* (031) 821571

This solid ochre-painted 18th-century villa is owned and run by Giorgio Cappelletti and his Scottish wife Jane, who are both "very much in evidence". It stands right by the lake in a village north of Como, and you can take breakfast or main meals on its broad terrace by the water. Comfortable rather than smart, it has won lots more praise this year and last: "A very pleasing ambience, with warm, forthcoming staff and very good food. A wonderful bed redeemed the lino floor of our room." "Stunning view over lake from spacious bedroom. An atmospheric dining room, with a lengthy oral menu ('well, what would you like?'), ample helpings." There are Scottish-baronial touches to the furniture, and tartan covers on the sofas, but mostly the tone is simple. "On the terrace, dishes were brought in copper saucepans – gnocchi, grilled lake fish, gorgeous dessert of red berries." For chilly days, "a log fire in the lovely sitting room". (*Mike Shepherd, and others*) Not all bedrooms face the lake, and those by the road can be noisy. The ladder down to the lake for bathers is "steep and rickety".

Open Mar–Nov.
Rooms 17 double.

Facilities Sitting room, bar/TV room, restaurant; terrace. Garden. Unsuitable for ♿.
Location On lake. 20 km N of Como. Private parking.
Credit cards Access, Visa.
Terms D,B&B 130,000 L per person; full board 160,000 L. Set meals 45,000 L; full alc 60,000 L.

ASOLO 31011 Treviso — Map 17

Villa Cipriani — *Tel* (0423) 952166
Via Canova 298 — *Fax* (0423) 952095

An old town of arcaded streets, Venetian palaces and villas: one of them is this lovely luxury hotel (part of the big CIGA chain), where Robert Browning once lived, and wrote "God's in his heaven, all's right with the world!" Who could say that today? But a 1996 reader found that all *was* right with the *Cipriani*: "Our room was lovely, dinner was expensive but nice." Other praise, this year and last: "Marvellous for a peaceful holiday. Food delectable, notably the risottos." "It is visually idyllic, lovely gardens." There are views of valley and mountains. Rooms are ornate: those in the main building, not the annexe, are best. One visitor had "a beautiful sitting area with oriental rug, burgundy velvet love-seat and marble-topped credenza". Vegetables are from the garden; and breakfast on the terrace might include wild strawberries and black figs. You can dine in the garden. Service was this year called "amazingly helpful", though some visitors in the past have found waiters slow and aloof. (*Karen Pasold and Sheila Bielich, and others*) A few gripes: in summer, the small garden may fill up with functions; one reader was given a seriously sub-standard room.

Open All year.
Rooms 29 double, 2 single. Some on ground floor. Air-conditioning.
Facilities Lift. Lounge, bar, 2 dining rooms; function facilities; terrace. Garden.
Location 300 m from centre. 35 km NW of Treviso. Garages.
Credit cards All major cards accepted.
Terms [1996] Rooms 385,000–484,000 L. Breakfast 27,000 L. D,B&B 344,000–382,000 L per person. Alc 82,000–138,000 L.

ASSISI 06081 Perugia — Map 17

Hotel Country House BUDGET — *Tel/Fax* (075) 816363
San Pietro Campagna 178

An old house just outside the city walls, now a quiet and inexpensive B&B *pensione*. In its garden is a fountain, and the views from its terrace extend to the hills beyond the river. Rooms vary in size. Some are "small but comfortable, with individuality"; but a visitor this year had a "glorious large room", and found breakfasting on the terrace "pure joy, as regards ambience", with good coffee and juices but poor food. Others have written: "A friendly, hospitable atmosphere, and Silvana Ciammarughi is a real hostess, with a nice sense of humour." There are loungers in the well-kept garden. The hotel doubles as an antique shop, so if you take a fancy to any of the excellent antique furniture in your bedroom, you can make an offer for it. (*Dr ACM Codd, and others*) Bathrooms can be cramped, and upkeep may not be perfect.

Open All year.
Rooms 10 double, 2 single. 4 in garden annexe. Some on ground floor.
Facilities Lounge/bar, TV room. Garden: terraces.
Location 1.5 km from Assisi, off S147 to Perugia. Ample free parking.
Credit card Visa.
Terms B&B: single 85,000 L, double 110,000 L.

Residenza di Campagna Santa Maria degli Ancillotti NEW *Tel/Fax* (075) 8039764
Sterpeto 42

A farmhouse converted into comfortable small hotel, outside Assisi: "We recommend it highly," say its nominators. "It is very peaceful, off the beaten track, and as this is Umbria, the views are good. The host, Paolo Villa, is very helpful and friendly. His wife does the cooking, good but not sophisticated (typical Umbrian dishes); the ever-smiling son acts as waiter and handyman, daughter does the book-keeping. The grounds are well tended; the swimming pool is kept very clean by an unusual small plastic gizmo that works through the night. Each apartment consists of two rooms and bathroom; furniture is of good quality. Powerful but small shower (no baths)." (*C and J Eastaugh*)

Open All year.
Rooms 8 suites. 2 in annexe 30 m.
Facilities Bar, restaurant. Garden: swimming pool (unheated), table-tennis, *boccia*, archery, mountain bikes; horses for hire. Unsuitable for ♿.
Location 6 km NW of Assisi, off road to Sterpeto. Parking.
Credit cards None accepted.
Terms B&B 120,000 L; D,B&B 175,000 L. Set meals 55,000 L.

Albergo Umbra *Tel* (075) 812240
Via degli Archi 6 *Fax* (075) 813653

Down a quiet alley off the main square is the Laudenzi family's "charming" hotel, medium-priced and long popular with readers. This year, devotees on their third long visit waxed euphoric: "It warrants our warmest praise. Each time, we have marvelled at the friendliness of the staff, the magic of the setting, the deliciousness of the food. Breakfasts have got better and better. Sitting on one's balcony overlooking the Umbrian plain and the dome of Santa Maria degli Angeli, with the swallows diving, one feels near to heaven. And lunch on the terrace, under a vine-laden pergola, is a pretty good imitation of the Earthly Paradise." Earlier visitors more modestly praised the risotto and funghi salad, also the "cosy ambience". Public rooms have some elegance. Some bedrooms are spacious, some much smaller; some overlook an orchard. (*DKW, and others*)

Open All year, except 15 Jan–15 Mar. Restaurant closed Tues.
Rooms 21 double, 4 single. 15 with air-conditioning.
Facilities 2 lounges, bar, restaurant; terrace (meals served in fine weather). Garden.
Location Town centre, near main square.
Credit cards All major cards accepted.
Terms [1996] Rooms: single 95,000–100,000 L, double 130,000–160,000 L. Breakfast 15,000 L. Full alc 45,000–50,000 L.

BELLAGIO 22021 Como — Map 17

Hotel du Lac NEW — *Tel* (031) 950320
Piazza Mazzini 32 — *Fax* (031) 951624

This classic and stylish holiday hotel, well run by pleasant owners, stands right by Lake Como, in a well-known resort. It is renominated this year: "We had a spacious, well-equipped room. Staff were friendly. Dinner was delicious, and a bargain to boot." Others have praised the buffet breakfast and lunches, the roof garden, the "lovingly polished traditional furniture". You can eat with a view of the lake. (*Kaye Sykes and Ed Ackert*)

Open 21 Mar–end Oct.
Rooms 38 double, 9 single.
Facilities Lounge, TV room, 2 bars; roof-garden. Unsuitable for ♿.
Location Central, opposite landing stages. Garages.
Credit cards Access, Visa.
Terms B&B 115,000–199,000 L; D,B&B 135,000–140,000 L; set lunch 42,000 L; dinner 46,000 L.

BERGEGGI 17042 Savona — Map 17

Hotel Ristorante Claudio — *Tel/Fax* (019) 859750
Via XXV Aprile 37

Claudio Pasquarelli's smart modern restaurant-with-rooms has a fine cliffside location above the Riviera, and an outdoor swimming pool. The decor is bright and cheerful, and on the dining terrace facing the sea the fish-based cuisine of Giorgio Baracco wins a *Michelin* star. "High quality fish, a friendly family, delightful bedroom with dramatic view of the sea." That report this year backs earlier praise, plus caveats: "Spacious white bedrooms with tiled floor and balcony, and above all the fish, wonderfully fresh and superbly cooked. Presided over by a charmingly laid-back and slightly vague Claudio. He needs to take a grip, if the place is not to get tattier." "Gadgets such as jacuzzi put up the room prices, but service was friendly, and the good breakfast included home-baked bread." The set fish meal can include pasta with scampi and truffles, grilled sea bass." (*MJ Gooding, CJ Daintree, and others*)

Open All year, except Jan. Restaurant closed Mon / midday Tues.
Rooms 16 double.
Facilities Lift. Lounges, bar, dining room; conference facilities; terrace. Garden: swimming pool. Unsuitable for ♿.
Location 7 km W of Savona. Garage.
Credit cards Access, Amex, Visa.
Terms B&B: single 110,000–120,000 L, double 200,000–230,000 L; D,B&B 170,000–200,000 L per person. Set meals 90,000–120,000 L.

BETTOLLE 53040 Siena — Map 17

La Bandita BUDGET — *Tel/Fax* (0577) 624649
Via Bandita 72

In the Tuscan countryside east of Sinalunga, an old restored farmhouse with antique furnishings. "It is quietly secluded up a side road, surrounded by a garden, orchards, vineyard and olive trees," says a recent guest. "A nice young couple, the Fiorini, own and run it. Her cooking is truly *casalinga*, and her home-made peach and apricot jams are the best. They also press their own olive oil, which is for sale. Rooms are tastefully furnished and bathrooms are modern. We stayed in an annexe, where it was pleasant to sit on the patio and watch the sunset." Many vegetables are home-grown. (*DFP*) A garden gazebo for meals was due to open in summer 1996.

Open All year. Restaurant closed Tues.
Rooms 8 double. 2 in adjacent building. 2 on ground floor.
Facilities Sitting room, library, restaurant; terrace. Garden.
Location 1.5 km NW of Bettolle village, 6.5 km E of Sinalunga. *Autostrada* A1 exit Val di Chiana 1 km.
Credit cards Access, Visa.
Terms Rooms 100,000 L. Breakfast 15,000 L. Set meals 40,000 L. Reduced rates for children.

BOLOGNA — Map 17

Hotel Corona d'Oro 1890

Via Oberdan 12
40126 Bologna

Tel (051) 236456
Fax (051) 262679

In the heart of old Bologna, in a narrow street close to its glorious *centro storico*, is this characterful old building, a hotel from 1890, but in parts far older – in its inner courtyard is a 14th-century portico, and some bedrooms have panelled ceilings with paintings from the 15th and 16th centuries. It is also friendly, says a recent visitor: "Charming lobby with sofas, under a glass roof which opens in summer, and a bar, where breakfast is served. Rooms are comfortable." No restaurant, but in the world capital of pasta, you have a hundred good choices.

Open All year, except 20 July–20 Aug.
Rooms 26 double, 9 single. Air-conditioning.
Facilities Lift. Lounges, bar; conference facilities.
Location Central. Public garage nearby.
Credit cards All major cards accepted.
Terms [1996] B&B: single 185,000–290,000 L, double 275,000–420,000 L.

Hotel Roma

Via Massimo d'Azeglio 9
40123 Bologna

Tel (051) 226322
Fax (051) 239909

Also in the heart of the city, and right by its stunning Piazza Maggiore (finer than anything in Florence), is this sizeable hotel mainly for business people (nothing wrong with that: Bologna's medieval splendour grew from its business prowess). "Our charming room was decorated in the style of an Italian William Morris," says a recent visitor, "with a big balcony facing a skyline of *campanili*." Others have commended the staff and "better than average" breakfasts. The food has been found "enjoyable", and the decoration "nicer than it need be for a businessman's hotel". (*H and RT, R and JH*)

Open All year.
Rooms 4 suites, 80 double. Air-conditioning.
Facilities Lift. Restaurant.
Location Central. Car access at rear. Garage.

Credit cards All major cards accepted.
Terms [1996] Rooms: single 130,000 L, double 180,000 L. Breakfast 20,000 L. D,B&B 150,000 L per person. Alc meals 40,000–50,000 L.

BORDIGHERA 18012 Imperia — Map 17

Villa Elisa
Via Romana 70
Tel (0184) 261313
Fax (0184) 261942

An "Edwardian atmosphere" and "an air of calm and luxury" pervade this handsome white villa, 800 metres from the seafront of a busy Riviera resort. Owned and run by the Oggero family for over a century, it has public rooms furnished with antiques, and a playground for *bambini* in the lovely garden. Many rooms have a big south-facing balcony, but only top-floor ones get a sea view. A devotee returning this year found it "almost as delightful as before, save that they have put a roof over the terrace restaurant". She, and others, wrote earlier: "The building and grounds are pretty, and the swimming pool is exceptional – sunny, but with shade around it too. Meals are very good, and breakfast elaborate." "Our quiet room at the back faced a small orange and lemon grove. We took breakfast on the terrace, by the enchanting garden. The friendly staff had a personal touch." (*Jane Gibbs, and others*) There is some traffic noise. An unheated outdoor swimming pool is new this year.

Open All year, except early Nov–22 Dec.
Rooms 1 suite, 31 double, 3 single.
Facilities 2 salons, TV room, bar, restaurant, *tavernetta* (no-smoking); terrace. Garden: swimming pool (unheated), children's playground.
Location Central, 800 m from seafront. 12 km W of San Remo. Garage, free open parking.
Credit cards All major cards accepted.
Terms B&B: single 110,000–140,000 L, double 150,000–200,000 L; D,B&B 103,000–173,000 L per person. Set lunch/dinner 60,000 L; full alc 70,000 L. 10–50% reductions for children. In Aug half or full board only.

BORGO PACE 61040 Pesaro e Urbino — Map 17

La Diligenza – Da Rodolfo BUDGET
Tel (0722) 89124

An expert on Italy commends the "authentic Italian domesticity and rusticity" at this restaurant-with-a-few-simple-rooms in a stone village on a river, in the Apennine foothills west of Urbino. "The hub is the grocery shop, bar and dining room, noted amongst Italians far and wide, especially for Sunday lunch in the mushroom and truffle season (down the valley at S. Angelo in Vado is one of Italy's great truffle markets, with a truffle museum to boot). We were regaled with wave upon wave of sometimes mysterious dishes, with no written menu, so you have to *know* what's going on. It was traditional Italian regional food, variable in quality but served with enthusiasm and relish. The Rodolfi are lovely, welcoming people: he is thoughtful and joking. The few rooms are old-fashioned, with huge bedsteads and not much space; the dark landing is all family pictures on the walls, and silver and porcelain treasures in a vast old cabinet. A staging-post to be chosen for human, even anthropological reasons, not sybaritic ones." (*ALL*)

Open All year.
Rooms 8 double.
Facilities Ramps. Bar with TV, dining room.
Location In village, 38 km W of Urbino.
Credit cards Access, Amex, Visa.
Terms Rooms 60,000 L. Breakfast 10,000 L. Set meals 25,000–35,000 L; full alc 35,000 L.

BRESSANONE 39042 Bolzano — Map 17

Hotel Elefante — *Tel* (0472) 832750
Via Rio Bianco 4 — *Fax* (0472) 836579

This 16th-century building near the town centre is now a stylish hotel, called "delightful" and "charming" by recent visitors. Lavishly furnished with antiques, tapestries and old paintings, it is traditional in the best sense ("it is nice to have your luggage carried by porters in green baize aprons"). "Excellent food, in rather too large portions. Pleasant if slightly run-down garden, with a small pool." "Good service, food of a high standard, menus changing daily. Some fine paintings, mostly religious." But: "Not a place for the squeamish, for it is covered in 17th- and 18th-century daubs of saints dying in disgusting ways. But it's comfortable, with pleasant service. Food is hotel international with some local touches. The bar is funereal. Excellent buffet breakfast." (*CMB, DJ*) Ask for a quiet room: those facing the garden can be noisy.

Open All year, except 7 Jan–Mar, 10 Nov–Christmas. Restaurant closed Mon, except 30 July–10 Nov.
Rooms 44. Air-conditioning.
Facilities Lounge, bar, 3 dining rooms; conference facilities. Garden: swimming pool, tennis.
Location Central. Garage.
Credit cards All major cards accepted.
Terms B&B 130,000 L.

BRISIGHELLA 48013 Ravenna — Map 17

Relais Torre Pratesi — *Tel* (0546) 84545
Via Cavina 11 — *Fax* (0546) 84558

Occupying a *"posizione molto panoramica"* in the Apennine foothills near Faenza is this curiosity – a sturdy 16th-century tower of mellow brick, linked to a farmhouse. "It is one of those very special places you come across by accident. The tower is massive with tiny windows and narrow slits, but the rooms inside are modern, served by a lift and winding metal staircase. In fact the rooms are a bit high-tech. The owners, Nerio and Letizia Raccagni, have restored the tower, and they treated us like personal guests. Their staff, too, were kindness itself. Breakfast, carefully served, was taken at a long oak table. It included home-made yogurt, cake, meats, a whole cheese, breaded mushroom balls, home-made jams. There's a library, and a music room with a 19th-century piano." (*M and KO*) Reports on the main meals welcome.

Open All year. Restaurant closed Tues.
Rooms 3 suites, 4 double.
Facilities Salon, lounge, reading room, restaurant. Garden. Unsuitable for ♿.

Location At Cavina, 8 km E of Brisighella, which is 13 km SW of Faenza.
Credit cards All major cards accepted.
Terms B&B: double 200,000 L, suite 250,000 L; D,B&B 150,000–190,000 L per person. Set meals 50,000 L.

BUONCONVENTO 53022 Siena — Map 17

Fattoria Pieve a Salti BUDGET — *Tel/Fax* (0577) 807244

Converted farmhouse and outbuildings on lonely hilltop, 3 km NE of Buonconvento. Ambitious project, part of Tuscan Agrituristica scheme, to restore buildings and revitalise land on 700-hectare estate 26 km SE of Siena. New this year: 17 additional bedrooms in two separate buildings; beauty farm with sauna. Good country cooking in spacious beamed room. "Super-quiet. Extraordinary value for money." Lounge, bar; conference facilities. Big swimming pool with superb views; tennis, fishing, riding. Closed Christmas, Jan. Access, Diners, Visa accepted. 29 rooms. B&B 60,000–72,000 L; D,B&B 90,000–100,000 L [1996].

CANNERO RIVIERA 28051 Verbania — Map 17

Hotel Cannero — *Tel* (0323) 788046 (788113 in winter)
Lungo Lago 2 — *Fax* (0323) 788048

By the landing-stage of a small Lake Maggiore resort stands this ever-popular family hotel, "professionally yet personally run". It has just been extensively refurbished, and was again much admired this year – "excellent", "we love it", "superb value for money", "the Gallinotto family owners were as charming and helpful as ever" are typical reactions. "They have true Italian warmth," says another. "I had one of the new rooms, very comfortable, with a terrace and lake view" (most rooms are spacious and modern). "Sig.a Gallinotto is gracious, caring and ever-present, and treats her staff well." Food is "quite good, not exceptional", and the full board menu has limited choice: but it changes daily, and "the *carte* is superb". "Good buffet breakfast", served on the terrace by the lake. Upper rooms have a balcony over the lake, and get sun much of the day as the hotel faces south-east. The pool is liked, too. (*Prof. P and Mrs A Robson, Mrs C Leeming, Dr ACM Codd, R Gilbert, and many others*) Some night noise from landing-stage. Guests tend to dress formally for dinner. Attractions for children include "Wichy, our little friendly dog".

Open 8 Mar–4 Nov.
Rooms 36 double, 4 single. 2 suitable for ♿. 15 air-conditioned.
Facilities Lift. 2 lounges, TV room, bar/café, restaurant. Garden: tennis, swimming pool, lakeside terrace, water sports.
Location Central, on Lake Maggiore. Garage, parking.
Credit cards All major cards accepted.
Terms B&B: single 100,000–120,000 L, double 170,000–200,000 L; D,B&B 110,000–140,000 L per person. Set meals 40,000–50,000 L.

> If you are nominating a hotel, please tell us enough to convey its character and quality. We can't make good bricks without plenty of straw. We find brochures very helpful.

CAPRESE MICHELANGELO 52033 Arezzo — Map 17

Buca di Michelangelo BUDGET

Tel (0575) 793921
Fax (0575) 793941

"An enchanting place", "an excellent restaurant amid beautiful scenery", up in the wild Apennines. Some readers find the rooms *too* basic, at this modest village pub, and there is no proper lounge. But most guests echo this evocative account: "It's a homely family concern, with a feeling of old-fashioned decency. The good, honest cooking is well patronised by locals. After the dark rusticity of the entrance-cum-bar, one passes into a large, light, handsome room with a wooden ceiling. One wall is covered with a mural depicting Michelangelo's early life in these mountains (he was born nearby); another, entirely glass, looks out over the spectacular wooded view; a narrow balcony is beyond, and in hot weather the glass is folded back to make an open-air eyrie for the diners. From the hotel it's a short walk to Michelangelo's house, on a hilltop in picturesque scenery. Endorsed recently: "When a party led by several priests arrived and a special dinner was served, we were given the same food – a gargantuan feast." (*BWR, JR*) But even admirers have complained of poor heating, scruffy rooms.

Open All year, except 10–25 Feb. Restaurant closed Wed.
Rooms 19. Some in annexe.
Facilities Lounge/bar with TV, restaurant. Garden.
Location 45 km NE of Arezzo.
Credit cards Access, Amex, Visa.
Terms [1996] Rooms: single 45,000 L, double 70,000 L. Breakfast 6,000 L. D,B&B 55,000–65,000 L per person. Alc 24,000–38,000 L.

CASTELLINA IN CHIANTI 53011 Siena — Map 17

Tenuta di Ricavo

Tel (0577) 740221
Fax (0577) 741014

This elegant manor in the Tuscan hills, near Siena, is a member of the Romantik Hotels association and is independently owned and run by a Swiss-Italian family, the Lobrano-Scotoni. Long admired by readers, it has attractive rooms in rustic period style: some have a balcony and views, and many are in outbuildings. More praise came this year: "Glorious quiet, comfortable rooms and splendid views. The grounds were well kept, the two small pools were clean and attractive. The restaurant was superb." "It remains one of my favourite hotels. Their restaurant has greatly improved; they now have an excellent chef" – earlier reports had described the food as "more international than regional". (*Antonia Paul, Denise and Warren Levy*) Meals (booking essential, even for hotel guests) are served in the piazza or garden when it's fine.

Open Easter–end Oct. Restaurant closed Mon/midday Tues, midday in low season.
Rooms 9 suites, 13 double, 1 single. Some on ground floor.
Facilities 3 salons, reading room, TV room, restaurant. Garden: 2 swimming pools, table tennis, *boccia*.
Location 22 km NW of Siena, 34 km S of Florence. Leave *superstrada* at San Donato exit.

Credit cards Access, Visa.
Terms [1996] B&B: single 120,000–240,000 L, double 210,000–365,000 L, suite 300,000–420,000 L. Alc meals 48,000–77,000 L. Bookings 21 days before arrival.

CASTEL RIGONE 06060 Perugia — Map 17

Relais La Fattoria NEW — *Tel* (075) 845322
Via Rigone 1 — *Fax* (075) 845197

"A delightful small hotel in a tiny hill village above Lake Trasimeno," says the nominator of this old farmhouse with beamed ceilings, well modernised but full of character. "The staff are welcoming, the public rooms have comfortable sofas, and there's a small bar. Our bedroom, with lovely bathroom, was a bit noisy but from locals chattering, not traffic. The terrace and swimming pool overlook the Umbrian countryside. The restaurant (service can be long-winded) offers a wonderful buffet of starters. On Friday night there's an 'American-style buffet', for which the whole neighbourhood comes in, complete with children and grannies." (*Sara A Price*)

Open All year. Restaurant closed 10 Jan–early Feb.
Rooms 3 suites, 23 double, 3 single.
Facilities Lounge, TV room, bar, restaurant. Garden: swimming pool. Unsuitable for ♿.
Location In village, 26 km NW of Perugia. Parking nearby.
Credit cards All major cards accepted.
Terms B&B 50,000–175,000 L; D,B&B 30,000–40,000 L per person added. Set meals 30,000 L; full alc 60,000 L.

CETONA 53040 Siena — Map 17

Convento di San Francesco NEW — *Tel/Fax* (0578) 238015

"Magical and intriguing", and not really a hotel at all. It is "a supremely beautiful monastery high in the Chianti hills, converted with flair and good taste into a very plush hotel/restaurant". Founded by St Francis in 1212, it was recently taken over by Fr Eligio, "a somewhat controversial priest" involved in the social rehabilitation of delinquents. Here he set up a community of these youngsters, who rebuilt the place and live and work in it. Part of his complex is a luxurious high-priced restaurant-with-rooms, previously known as *La Frateria di Padre Eligio*, which was dropped from the 1995 *Guide* for lack of reports, but has now been revisited by earlier visitors: "We were welcomed by the restaurant manager, a pleasant member of the community. Our large suite contained a mixture of antiques, beams, modern rustic furniture and modern Italian lighting. *En suite* was a massive sunken bath. The set menu is long and the food good, but not outstanding. Breakfast was wonderful, but ask for what you want." Earlier reports admired the frescoes in the beautiful chapel, the gardens beside the old cloisters, the huge polished tables carved from tree-trunks. "The restoration has been done with total integrity, loving care, and plenty of money." Five bedrooms are smallish; the suites have "dramatic views, and huge paintings, mainly religious, which should have been in a museum". (*David and Kate Wooff*)

Open All year, except Jan/Feb.
Rooms 2 suites, 5 double.

Facilities Lounge, restaurant. Large grounds.
Location 1 km from Cetona, which is 50 km SW of Perugia, 10 km SW of Chiusi. Parking.
Credit cards Access, Amex, Visa.
Terms B&B: single 220,000 L, double 280,000 L, suite 380,000 L. Set meals 120,000 L.

COGNE 11012 Aosta — Map 17

Hôtel Bellevue — *Tel* (0165) 74825
Rue Grand Paradis 22 — *Fax* (0165) 749192

"We enjoyed our stay. Excellent breakfasts and dinner, glorious views, a clean and pretty room, and pleasant staff." That recent letter endorses earlier praise for the Jeantet Roullet family's sturdily traditional hotel, on the edge of a hiking and skiing resort in a French-speaking mountain valley south of Aosta. "Our room was luxuriously equipped with old Alpine furniture, but also had an impressive new bathroom; a small balcony overlooked meadows of Alpine flowers and the Gran Paradiso massif. The cosy sitting room and the lovely dining room, with its large windows, enjoy the same view. Here we had a superb meal of real Italian food. The buffet breakfast was generous, and the proprietor kind and gracious." (*GD*)

Open 21 Dec–28 Sept.
Rooms 4 chalets, 9 suites, 24 double.
Facilities Lift. Lounge (no-smoking), 2 bars, video pub, 3 dining rooms; indoor swimming pool, Turkish bath, sauna, whirlpool. Garden.
Location 27 km S of Aosta. Parking.
Credit cards Access, Diners, Visa.
Terms B&B: single 162,000 L, double 250,000 L, suite 360,000 L; D,B&B (min. 3 days) 126,000–290,000 L per person. Set meals 40,000–60,000 L.

CORTONA 52044 Arezzo — Map 17

Hotel San Michele — *Tel* (0575) 604348
Via Guelfa 15 — *Fax* (0575) 630147

Near main square of fascinating Tuscan hilltop town, elegantly modernised Renaissance palazzo *with beamed ceilings, tiled floors; friendly family service. Rooms vary in size, and not all are quiet. 2 lounges (1 no-smoking). Parking 300 m away, down steep hill. Swimming pool close by. Closed 12 Jan–14 Mar. All major credit cards accepted. 37 rooms. B&B double 150,000–170,000 L. No restaurant;* Il Falconiere, *just outside town, recommended. Endorsed this year, with caveats.*

CORVARA 39003 Bolzano — Map 17

Romantik Hotel La Perla — *Tel* (0471) 836132
Alta Badia — *Fax* (0471) 836568

In big summer and skiing resort in Dolomites – "storybook village" 65 km NE of Bolzano: stylish, expensive chalet-style holiday hotel, lots of wood. Family run, "professional but informal"; excellent pension *meals; first-class rooms (some no-smoking) with balcony, splendid views. Large outdoor pool, children's games. Unsuitable for ♿. Open 6 Dec–6 Apr, 28 June–28 Sept;*

main restaurant closed Mon. Access, Amex, Visa accepted. 52 rooms. B&B double 240,000–560,000 L; D,B&B double 276,000–596,000 L. Set meals 52,000–72,000 L. Endorsed this year, but fuller reports welcome.

CUNEO 12100 **Map 17**

Hotel Principe NEW *Tel* (0171) 693355
Piazza Galimberti 5 *Fax* (0171) 67562

The main hotel of a biggish market town between Turin and Nice. It fell from the 1996 *Guide* for lack of reports, but was admired again this year for its individual charm: "Recently modernised, it has spacious rooms with good lighting, excellent bathrooms; very quiet. The manager/owner and his wife were charming." Others have called the breakfast "delicious", and the decor "an agreeable mix of Art Deco and contemporary Italian styling. (*G, E and L Watt, Betty and Percy Brower*) No restaurant, but the *Ligure*, fairly close, is warmly recommended.

Open All year.
Rooms 31 double, 11 single. 31 with air-conditioning.
Facilities Lift, ramps. Bar, TV room, breakfast room; meeting room.
Location Centre of town. 94 km S of Turin. Private garage.
Credit cards All major cards accepted.
Terms Rooms: single 150,000 L, double 190,000 L. Breakfast 15,000 L.

ERBUSCO 25030 Brescia **Map 17**

L'Albareta – Gualtiero Marchesi NEW *Tel* (030) 7760550
Bellavista *Fax* (030) 7760573

This former country estate, outside a village near lake Iseo, has been converted into one of the most stylish and superior hotel operations in Italy. It is owned by the Moretti family, and its restaurant, in the hands of master-chef Gualtiero Marchesi, is one of the three in Italy to win three *Michelin* stars. The *Guide*'s leading experts on Italian high living were there this year: "It warrants a detour on any hedonistic itinerary. The house, surrounded on three sides by vine-covered hills, has been lavishly refurbished. Our room in the old tower had a bucolic view. Ceilings were vaulted, the floor was parquet with rugs (and marble in the bathroom). The bed was a four-poster, windows had Burgundy curtains, a chest and desk were antiques. But there was a lot of technical gimmickry, too: lights and plug sockets were controlled by a confusing plethora of switches. The Marchesis, a charming, shy couple, run the place personally. And the food in the lofty beamed dining room was wonderful – potato ravioli filled with calamaretti, risotto with saffron." "The design of our room was simple but luxurious and tasteful. Public rooms are spacious. Our meal was excellent, but service was sometimes slow. The estate's own wines are well priced." "The cuisine is *minceur*, but by no means minimally so. An eight- or nine-course *dégustation* menu and you get up feeling well and wonderful." (*David and Kate Wooff, Pat and Jeremy Temple, Felix Singer*)

Open All year, except Jan. Restaurant closed Sun evening/Mon.
Rooms 3 suites, 41 double (2 no-smoking). 3 in nearby annexe. Air-conditioning.

Facilities Lift. 2 lounges, bar, billiard room, restaurant; 2 function rooms; indoor swimming pool, sauna, jacuzzi. Garden; tennis, riding, mountain bikes. Golf club nearby.
Location 1 km from Erbusco, 22 km NW of Brescia, near Corte Franca. Garages.
Credit cards All major cards accepted.
Terms [1996] Rooms: single 180,000–220,000 L, double 260,000–320,000 L, suite 370,000–420,000 L. Breakfast 20,000–45,000 L. Set meals 65,000–140,000 L; full alc 120,000–160,000 L. Reduced rates for children accommodated in parents' room

---

ERICE 91016 Trapani, Sicilia **Map 18**

Elimo Hotel NEW *Tel* (0923) 869377
Via Vittorio Emanuele 75 *Fax* (0923) 869252

In centre of lovely town (see below), old stone building finely converted in a series of styles, now a smart hotel, owned and run by friendly Tilotta family. 21 quiet, pleasant rooms, some with sea views. Restaurant excellent but expensive (cheaper ones nearby). Bar, terrace. All major credit cards accepted. B&B double 190,000–250,000 L; D,B&B 140,000–150,000 L per person. Set meals 40,000 L. Renominated this year. Fuller reports welcome.

Hotel Moderno NEW *Tel* (0923) 869300
Via Vittorio Emanuele 63 *Fax* (0923) 869139

This ancient and lovely (but tourist-filled) town stands at the top of a high rock, with views of the sea. The hotel, in a 19th-century building, is as modern inside as its name suggests, and its rooms look over Trapani, not the sea. It is run in a friendly manner by the Catalano family, and is furnished with style and originality. After a period with no reports, it returns to our pages: "Spacious, quiet rooms with attractive furniture, individual paintings; statues in the communal areas. Good restaurant." Lounges, and large terrace. (*S Wright*) Driving through the narrow one-way streets is hard: best park in the square just inside the town gate.

Open All year.
Rooms 34 double, 7 single. 17 in annexe. Air-conditioning.
Facilities Lift. 2 lounges, 2 bars, 2 TV rooms, dining room; meeting room; terrace.
Location Central. Parking.
Credit cards All major cards accepted.
Terms B&B: single 100,000–130,000 L, double 150,000–180,000 L; D,B&B 120,000–150,000 L per person. Alc meals 60,000 L.

FERRARA 44100 **Map 17**

Duchessa Isabella *Tel* (0532) 202121
Via Palestro 70 *Fax* (0532) 202638

This marvellous Po Valley city has a wealth of palaces, several of them connected with its former rulers, the renowned Este family. And Isabella d'Este, "a gentle lady who loved symposia and banquets", has given her name to Ferrara's premier hotel (Relais & Châteaux), in a 16th-century mansion. "Our beautiful suite overlooked a lovely garden," runs our latest report. "The owners work hard and provide delicious food, including their home-smoked meats. Some rooms are small." (*BB*) The restaurant, says the brochure, has painted wooden ceilings bordered in gold, 16th-century doors, and coloured frescoes of the Ferrara school. "We owe to the *duchessa* the beautiful table service in *graffito* ceramics, dating from 1490, and the staff wear costumes of that period. A landau, drawn by a white horse and bearing Isabella d'Este's image, is available for guests. Comforts include fax." We'd be glad to hear more about the banquets, if not the symposia.

Open All year, except 1–28 Aug. Restaurant closed Mon evening.
Rooms 6 suites, 21 double. Air-conditioning.
Facilities Lift. Salons, bar, restaurant; meeting rooms. Garden.
Location Central. Parking.
Credit cards Access, Visa.
Terms [1996] B&B: single 330,000 L, double 430,000 L; D,B&B 260,000–280,000 L per person. Alc meals 65,000–111,000 L.

FIÉ ALLO SCILIAR 39050 Bolzano — Map 17

Hotel Emmy — *Tel* (0471) 725006
Via Putzes 5 — *Fax* (0471) 725484

Set amid open fields below the craggy Dolomites, a smart modern chalet-style holiday hotel in a German-speaking area (the town's local name is Völs am Schlern). The owner, Frau Kasslatter, "is anxious to please, and her staff are excellent". Several visitors have given her their own Emmy awards: "Wonderful new bathroom." "We spent a cosy, quiet, friendly week over Christmas, and loved it. Our room had a balcony with a view across to the snowy mountains and the village with its floodlit church. The hotel's star feature was the six-course dinner, including a salad buffet. The swimming pool is a good size, so is the lounge. Skiing is at least an hour away by bus." Lots of wood panelling, panoramic terrace for drinks and breakfast. (*SB, and others*) New this year, a *Centro Beauty* and a *Centro Cure*. Newer reports welcome.

Open All year, except 4 Nov–20 Dec.
Rooms 29 suites, 20 double, 3 single. Some on ground floor.
Facilities Lift. Bar, breakfast room, restaurant; indoor swimming pool, sauna, solarium; terrace. Garden. Skiing 14 km (free bus).
Location On edge of resort, 16 km E of Bolzano. Large garage.
Credit cards Access, Visa.
Terms Rooms: single 90,000–150,000 L, double 160,000–280,000 L, suite 200,000–370,000 L. Breakfast 10,000 L. D,B&B double 220,000–340,000 L. Set meals 50,000–59,000 L; full alc 65,000 L.

FIESOLE 50014 Firenze — Map 17

Pensione Bencistà BUDGET — *Tel/Fax* (055) 59163
Via B da Maiano 4

Set in a park amid olive groves, this *pensione* in a "beautiful old villa" is remarkably inexpensive and has a superb view of Florence (you should ask for a room with a view). An admirer this year caught the flavour: "Huge and old-fashioned. All the books in the lounge are English and the furniture is EM Forster period. The Simoni family owners are helpful and congenial, the rooms are ugly and the view is stunning. The food is plonked down for you and is very good indeed.

Interesting wines. A fascinating place, and so cheap." Similar praise last year: "The large staff were all friendly, and, oh, how well trained. At 7.30 pm a bell sounded, and we all trouped down to a large room, where the no-choice dinner was excellent. You could then take coffee in one of the beautiful sitting-rooms." From the terrace you can enjoy the view. "Must be one of the best-value *pensioni* in Italy." (*David Holbrook, N and DA, and others*) Some rooms are small.

Open All year.
Rooms 36 double, 8 single, 32 with bath. 2 in annexe 10 m.
Facilities 3 lounges, restaurant. Large grounds. Unsuitable for ♿.
Location On hillside NE of Florence. 10 mins' drive from centre; regular buses. Parking.
Restriction No smoking: 2 lounges, restaurant.
Credit cards None accepted.
Terms D,B&B 110,000–130,000 L; full board 15,000 L added.

FLORENCE **Map 17**

Hotel Helvetia and Bristol *Tel* (055) 287814
Via dei Pescioni 2 *Fax* (055) 288353
50123 Firenze

In the late 19th century, when it was built, this became Florence's leading hotel (Pirandello and Stravinsky were among its *habitués*). Now newly renovated, it is still very grand, and has again been liked recently: "Bedrooms are luxuriously appointed with fabric wall coverings, antiques and fine works of art. Our marble bathroom had a large jacuzzi. Public areas are elegant, with fine paintings, flowers. There's a foyer lounge with library and open fire, and a much-admired winter garden bar doubling as a breakfast room. The smartly attired staff were friendly. In the small *Bristol* restaurant the food was reliable, with some Tuscan dishes. The superior breakfast was accompanied by stirring operatic muzak, which we personally found preferable to the live pianist in the evenings." Others have called the public areas "small and cosy rather than palatial", and have enjoyed the views across to the *duomo* from upper floors. The jacuzzi is popular with children. (*MM and FS*)

Open All year.
Rooms 17 suites, 26 double, 9 single. Air-conditioning. Some no-smoking.
Facilities Lifts. Lounge, TV room, winter garden/bar, restaurant. Unsuitable for ♿.
Location Central, near Strozzi Palace; in traffic-free zone (access for guests' cars). Garage.
Credit cards All major cards accepted.
Terms B&B: single 354,750–393,250 L, double 495,000–605,000 L, suite 753,500–1,490,500 L. Set meals 75,000–95,000 L; full alc 90,000–125,000 L.

Hotel Hermitage *Tel* (055) 287216
Vicolo Marzio 1 *Fax* (055) 212208
50122 Firenze

"What a delight," wrote the nominator of this small friendly hotel next to the Uffizi gallery and Ponte Vecchio. "The rooftop garden has inspiring views, so does the sunny all-window breakfast room. There's a cosy lounge with lemon-coloured over-stuffed chairs, antique tables, vases of fresh flowers. The continental breakfast was not special, but alternatives are available. The atmosphere is delightful. Our room, decorated with charm, had modern beds, an antique painted armoire, oriental carpets. The young desk staff were friendly. My only criticism: too many guests were fellow Americans. Our favourite nearby restaurant: across the Arno, the *Osteria del Cinghiale Bianco*, specialising in wild boar." (*RG*)

Open All year.
Rooms 26 double, 3 single. Air-conditioning. Unsuitable for ♿.
Facilities 2 lounges, TV room, bar; roof garden.
Location Central, by Ponte Vecchio. Public garage nearby.
Credit cards Access, Visa.
Terms B&B: single 190,000 L, double 290,000 L.

Romantik Hotel J and J NEW
Via di Mezzo 20
50121 Firenze
Tel (055) 2345005
Fax (055) 240282
E-mail jandj~@dada.it

We do not know who J and J are, or were: but their B&B hotel near the Duomo is quite *Romantik*, as its nominator relates: "The building began life as a convent in the 16th century. Traces of frescoes remain on the old walls. Period furnishings combine with modern pieces to create an ambience far more comfortable than that which the original residents enjoyed. Our suite, with three large windows overlooking the street, was enormous, and quiet." Fuller reports welcome.

Open All year.
Rooms 7 suites, 13 double. Some on ground floor. Air-conditioning.
Facilities Lounges, bar.
Location Central, 400 m E of Duomo. Private garage (40,000 L).
Credit cards All major cards accepted.
Terms [1996] B&B: double 330,000–375,000 L, suite 450,000–500,000 L.

Villa Liberty
Viale Michelangiolo 40
50125 Firenze
Tel (055) 683819 and 6810581
Fax (055) 6812595
E-mail hotel.villa.liberty@dada.it

In residential area c. 2 km S of Ponte Vecchio, small converted villa set in a shady garden, with Art Nouveau feel (curved decorated mirrors, painted ceilings). 17 large, pleasant rooms with marble floor: those at back are quietest. Friendly staff. Unsuitable for ♿. Private parking. All major credit cards accepted. B&B: single 180,000 L, double 230,000 L. No restaurant.

Loggiato dei Serviti
Piazza SS. Annunziata 3
50122 Firenze
Tel (055) 289592
Fax (055) 289595

This lovely ex-monastery was built in 1527 for the order of the Serviti, and stands in a beautiful piazza. It has been gracefully restored and furnished: one bedroom, for example, has a big 19th-century bed in open gilded ironwork, beside a 17th-century wardrobe. The place is popular with visiting art lecturers – and with our readers. Recent views: "It's austerely elegant, unchintzy, with charming staff. Delightful breakfast and vaulted bedrooms: ours had a magical view of an empty garden and a field of terracotta roofs." "Our room was not only cool but quiet – unheard of in Italy. Service extremely pleasant." Another reader however found reception erratic and traffic noise disturbing – "but we'd go back, to wake up to the view of the Ospedale degli Innocenti, and the sound of the fountain in the square." "Glossy oak floors, a beautiful carved wooden bedstead, and a modern marble bathroom." (*JW, and others*) Rooms vary in size and quality, but many have just been renovated.

Open All year.
Rooms 4 suites, 19 double, 6 single. Air-conditioning.
Facilities Lift. Lounge, TV room, bar, breakfast room. Unsuitable for ♿.
Location Central. In pedestrian zone, 200 m from *duomo*. Garage parking.
Credit cards All major cards accepted.
Terms B&B: single 200,000 L, double 280,000 L, suite 350,000–600,000 L.

Hotel Monna Lisa *Tel* (055) 2479751
Borgo Pinto 27 *Fax* (055) 2479755
50121 Firenze

A Renaissance palace, five minutes' walk from the *duomo*, its cool, spacious public rooms filled with antiques, oil paintings and sculpture. "For travellers not tourists," wrote its nominator, "with an atmosphere of patrician domesticity, rather like staying in a National Trust property, and being looked after by family retainers. They are friendly and natural, with always helpful receptionists. My first room, in the villa, was charming and pretty, but small, so I moved to a plainer, larger one in the newly converted *dipendenza*. It had splendid new mahogany fitted furniture, a gorgeous, well-equipped shower room, and a view of the lovingly tended flowery garden, a rare thing in Florence, where one day I sat in the sun with Bessie, the Old English sheepdog. Breakfast is a daily pleasure, served in a grand yet comfortable, authentically Florentine room, with beautifully laid tables, and a cold self-service buffet." (*ALL*) Most rooms overlook the garden or the courtyard. Those on the street side have double-glazing.

Open All year.
Rooms 29 double, 5 single. 10 in garden annexe. Air-conditioning.
Facilities Lounge, bar, TV room, breakfast room. Garden. Unsuitable for ♿.
Location E of *duomo*. Private parking (20,000 L) at Vicolo della Pergola 1a (off Via della Pergola, parallel to Borgo Pinto).
Credit cards All major cards accepted.
Terms B&B: single 180,000–250,000 L, double 280,000–400,000 L.

Hotel Morandi alla Crocetta *Tel* (055) 2344747
Via Laura 50 *Fax* (055) 2480954
50121 Firenze

An elderly Irish lady, Kathleen Doyle Antuono, and her two sons run this extraordinary B&B hotel, near the Academy of Fine Arts. "Atmospheric", "utterly charming", "civilised and elegant", are among the latest bouquets. The building has an amazing history: it was used as a brothel by Lorenzo de' Medici, then rebuilt as a convent in the 16th century by Sister Domenica of Paradise, a saintly Dominican who taught her nuns to weave gold and silver cloth. Today, it arouses delight tinged with alarm: "A bit like sleeping in a museum." "We were met with Gregorian chant and given a room with a bed surrounded by [17th-century] frescoes of the death of Blessed

Domenica – I'm not sure I'd stay here for my honeymoon. But I've seldom been in a lovelier room." "Baroque music, antique furniture, oriental carpets, old oil paintings on the walls." "Mrs Doyle enchants guests with her knowledge and insights – for instance, informing us about the oddities of Italian culture when we asked about laundry." Her staff too have been found erudite, and this year her sons were "very helpful". The modern bathrooms are praised. Some rooms have a balcony. (*AC Skinner, and others*) Rooms vary in size: some are small and subject to traffic noise, notably students' motor-bikes.

Open All year.
Rooms 8 double, 2 single. Air-conditioning.
Facilities Lounge, bar, breakfast room. Unsuitable for ♿.
Location Central, behind archaeological museum. Parking difficult: public garages some way away.
Credit cards All major cards accepted.
Terms Rooms: single 110,000 L, double 190,000 L. Breakfast 20,000 L.

Pitti Palace *Tel* (055) 2398711
Via Barbadori 2 *Fax* (055) 2398867
50125 Firenze

Near N end of Ponte Vecchio, Anna Colzi's well-modernised B&B hotel with decent bedrooms, spacious lounge, roof terraces with bar and superb views, where buffet breakfast is served. Unsuitable for ♿. All major credit cards accepted. 72 rooms; air-conditioning, double-glazing. B&B 200,000–300,000 L. Enthusiastically endorsed in 1996 for location, views, room and bathroom: "A lot of hotel for the money!"

FONTIGNANO 06070 Perugia — Map 17

Villa di Monte Solare *Tel* (075) 832376
Via Montale 7 *Fax* (075) 8355462

"A jewel, it borders on the idyllic" – one of several new plaudits this year for a 1780s patrician villa in a large estate near Perugia. It is reached by a narrow climbing road that peters out into a rough track before you park under the olive trees. The owners, Rosemarie and Filippo Jannarone, run it in civilised, personal style, and "let you feel you have the run of the house and its grounds". You can take a light lunch under the cedars of Lebanon in the formal garden; beyond is a private chapel, a tennis court, and a panoramic swimming pool with loungers and parasols. Breakfast is simple; dinner is no-choice, served at 7.30 pm, using vegetables and fruit from the estate. This also produces wines, olive oil and honey, which guests can purchase. The owners wait on the guests at table. "Our suite was perfect, with stone floors, breathtaking views." "Rosi is charming." "The pools, tennis court and grounds make it a wonderful place." "A warm welcome, and the nightingales sang us to sleep most nights." (*David and Moyna Ross, Sharon A Watt, JFG*) Once again, though, it is the cooking that is mildly controversial. "Umbrian cuisine of the highest quality", "a gem of a cook", are two recent comments, but another reader this year, who liked the home-made pasta, found the meat dishes poorly cooked – "a pity, because in most other respects it's a lovely place". Bedrooms in the villa have antiques. Some modern rooms and suites are in a converted farmhouse nearby, down a very steep road.

Open All year, except Christmas.
Rooms 7 suites (5 in annexe), 8 double. All with shower.
Facilities 2 lounges, TV room, bar, breakfast room, 2 dining rooms (1 no-smoking). In 120-acre estate: 4-acre garden, tennis, 2 swimming pools, riding. Unsuitable for ♿.
Location 25 km W of Perugia, near SE corner of Lake Trasimeno.
Credit cards Access, Diners, Visa.
Terms D,B&B (obligatory) 120,000 L.

GARGONZA 52048 Arezzo — Map 17

Residence Castello di Gargonza — *Tel* (0575) 847021
Monte San Savino — *Fax* (0575) 847054

This unusual and beguiling place, which is situated on a hilltop in the Tuscan woodlands, is not exactly a hotel. Rather, it is a partly self-catering hotel-cum-conference centre and rural community, in an intact 13th-century walled village which Count Roberto Guicciardini's family has owned for centuries. Below the *Castello*, with its tall, turreted tower, are old red-roofed cottages which can be hired for a week or more on a self-catering basis, or else as hotel rooms (three nights minimum). The conversions have been done with Italian flair – clean stone walls, beamed ceilings, pretty country decor, cobbled alleys. "All wonderful – always a treat to visit," says a returning devotee. "The restaurant, *La Torre di Gargonza* by the castle walls, has a stylish, sophisticated-rustic atmosphere. Our cottage had comfortable, tweedy, easy furniture; and the residents' garden was a riot of flowers, with new elegant Japanese sunshades, while nature all around yielded up delights – lizards, bats, fireflies, glow-worms, even black squirrels." "Breakfast in the old olive-press building was delicious." (*ALL, and others*) A new chef this year. Hotel service as such hardly exists; no food or drink is on sale in the village outside mealtimes; and cars can enter only for loading or unloading baggage.

Open All year, except 15–30 Nov, 10 Jan–28 Feb. Restaurant closed Tues.
Rooms 38 bedrooms, in self-catering cottages (sleeping 2–7). 7 double in guest houses. Some on ground floor.
Facilities Lounge, TV room, bar, restaurant; auditorium, meeting halls, conference rooms. Large grounds: gardens, children's play area, woods, farm. Unsuitable for ♿.
Location 8 km W of Monte San Savino on SS73 to Siena. *Autostrada* A1 exit 27. Follow blue sign to Gargonza and *Ristorante La Torre di Gargonza*.
Credit cards All major cards accepted.
Terms [1996] (Min. 3 nights) B&B 80,000–125,000 L per person; D,B&B 110,000–155,000 L; full board 140,000–185,000 L. Full alc 45,000–50,000 L.

GENOA 16126 — Map 17

Hotel Vittoria BUDGET — *Tel* (010) 261923
Via Balbi 33-45 — *Fax* (010) 262656

Upper rooms have a distant view of the port, at the Gerolla brothers' hotel up a side-alley, usefully near the station. Decor is nothing special, but recent visitors have praised the "helpful, gracious staff, modern and quiet rooms, great coffee". An earlier view: "Breakfast was good, and I enjoyed the simple, workmanlike evening meals, normal Italian with no frills for tourists: good fresh fish, pasta and delicious home-made pesto." (*CA, and others*) Many rooms are singles; quietest ones lack a view. Air-conditioning is new this year.

Open All year.
Rooms 36 double, 20 single. All air-conditioned.
Facilities Lift. TV room, bar, restaurant; conference room; terrace. Unsuitable for ♿.
Location Near station, 1.5 km W of city centre. Garage 150 m.
Credit cards All major cards accepted.
Terms Rooms: single 60,000–100,000 L, double 100,000–140,000 L. Breakfast 5,000 L. D,B&B 80,000–130,000 L per person. Set meals 25,000 L; full alc 32,000 L.

GHIFFA 28055 Novara — Map 17

Park Hotel Paradiso — BUDGET

Tel (0323) 59548
Fax (0323) 59878

"This idiosyncratic hotel is a gem," runs a report this year on the Anchisi family's villa, set amid sub-tropical vegetation on a hillside above Lago Maggiore, facing south. "The gardens and grounds were most attractive, and Sig. Anchisi was charming. Our room with balcony faced the glorious lake: we liked its tiled floor, but not the curious flocked wall-covering. The Art Deco furnishings in the public rooms might not suit all tastes, but we thought them splendid. The choice for dinner is limited, but they can usually prepare alternatives. Fish from the lake and steak from local beef were delicious. Breakfast on the terrace was memorable, with wonderful free-range eggs." Others wrote: "The Liberty-style stained glass and woodwork were amazing. There were lounging chairs in the garden; the heated pool was clean and pretty but rather sunless." Food is with a Spanish touch: Signora is from Madrid. Many rooms face the lake. Meals are served on the terraces when it is fine." (*NM Mackintosh*)

Open 20 Mar–20 Oct.
Rooms 15 double, 5 single. Some no-smoking.
Facilities Lounge, TV room, dining room; terrace. Garden: swimming pool, whirlpool, *boccia*, table-tennis.
Location Outside Ghiffa, which is 22 km N of Stresa. Parking.
Credit cards None accepted.
Terms B&B: single 117,000 L, double 176,000 L; D,B&B 117,000–120,000 L per person. Set meals 25,000–50,000 L. Full alc 55,000 L. Reductions for children.

GIARDINI-NAXOS 98035 Messina, Sicily — Map 18

Arathena Rocks — BUDGET

Via Calcide Eubea 55

Tel (0942) 51348 and 51337
Fax (0942) 51690

"Still delightful" (a comment this year), this cheerful white seaside hotel lies down a quiet private road, on the edge of a busy resort below Taormina. It has colourful decor, lots of flowers, and a pool hewn from the lava rocks (or you can swim in the clear sea). Recent enthusiasm: "The resort has no claim to beauty, but is set in a wide bay, with Etna and its plume of smoke at one end. The hotel is built on the rocky shore, with a pool and bathing terraces out on the rocks; there's also a beautiful shady garden with palm trees and statuary. The style of furnishings is individual, with vibrant Sicilian colours, interesting antiques, paintings, ceramics. All bedrooms good size, with excellent beds. The large elegant dining room leads to a wide shady terrace where breakfast and lunch are served; the foyer is beautiful, the salon spacious. Management and staff were beyond praise. A relaxed atmosphere – and quiet, save for some disco noise. The food is acceptable plain Italian, with very good fish and pasta." Lunches were thought better than dinners this year, alike for food and service. (*Eve Gompertz*) Many rooms have a sea-facing balcony. Some package tours.

Open 1 Apr–25 Oct.
Rooms 2 suites, 42 double, 10 single. 4 in adjacent building.
Facilities Lift. Lounge, 2 bars (1 with TV, 1 with piano 6 nights), restaurant (no-smoking). Garden: swimming pool (unheated), tennis.
Location In Naxos, 5 km S of Taormina. Hotel minibus takes guests to Taormina.
Credit cards Access, Amex, Visa.
Terms D,B&B 98,000–104,000 L; full board 120,000–125,000 L. Set meals 45,000 L. 30–50% reductions for children under 12.

GUBBIO 06024 Perugia — Map 17

Hotel Bosone Palace NEW — *Tel* (75) 9220688
Via XX Settembre 22 — *Fax* (75) 9220552

Dante once stayed at this sumptuous palace, 13th-century in origin, now beautifully restored. It is not, however, a grand luxury hotel, but two-star, reasonably priced. An inspector found it "very friendly", and writes: "It has a lofty prime position above this staggeringly beautiful hill town, close to the ducal palace. Most rooms have standard decor, but we had a supremely grand suite, full of 18th-century baroque splendour: putti galore, and a characteristic negligéed beauty in the high ceiling fresco. The big window gave a panoramic vista of the town and hills beyond. Breakfast, average Italian, was in another splendid room with its original painted walls and ceilings. For other meals, the hotel has an arrangement with the *Taverna del Lupo* close by. Parking not easy (see below).

Open All year.
Rooms 5 suites, 24 double, 1 single. 5 on ground floor.
Facilities Lift. TV room, breakfast room; meeting room.
Location Central. Car access (not easy) for loading and unloading. Private garage 300 m.
Credit cards All major cards accepted.
Terms Rooms 65,000–290,000 L, suite 240,000–290,000 L. Breakfast 10,000 L. D,B&B 130,000–140,000 L. Set meals 35,000 L; full alc 35,000 L.

LEVANTO 19015 La Spezia — Map 17

Hotel Nazionale BUDGET — *Tel* (0187) 808102
Via Jacopo 20 — *Fax* (0187) 800901

On the beautiful mountain coast west of La Spezia, Levanto is a little town below a castle, next to the curious Cinqueterre villages. Here, this family-run hotel, simple but pleasant, with a panoramic roof-terrace and a garden for outdoor dining, was liked again this year: "Very friendly service from polyglot Signora. *Pension* menu restricted, but good plain cooking. Bedrooms plain but adequate: rear ones are quietest." "Rooms and baths were lovely, food good." (*Eric Dodson*)

Open 23 Mar–3 Nov, 7 Dec–8 Jan.
Rooms 1 suite, 27 double, 4 single.
Facilities Lift. Lounge, bar, restaurant (no-smoking); roof terrace. Garden. Sandy beach 100 m.
Location Central. 36 km NW of La Spezia. Parking.
Credit cards All major cards accepted.
Terms [1996] Rooms: single 110,000 L, double 130,000 L, suite 190,000 L. Breakfast 15,000 L. D,B&B double 200,000–230,000 L. Set meals 35,000–50,000 L; full alc 40,000–60,000 L.

LORANZÈ 10010 Torino — Map 17

Hotel Panoramica BUDGET
Via San Rocco 7
Tel (0125) 669966
Fax (0125) 669969

You can dine and drink on a terrace, with a view of hills and valleys: hence the name of this "real gem", a small modern hotel north of Turin – though one admirer felt that *gastronomica* might be more appropriate (*Michelin* star). "The proprietor laid on an excellent lunch and took a lot of trouble with me personally," said a reader this year. Previous praise: "Smartly decorated, with some rather stark modern abstracts on the walls. We had a smart bedroom with small balcony facing the valley, and dined on the terrace, where the food was imaginative, well cooked and nicely presented. Breakfast buffet outstanding." "The rooms were sophisticated, with bold yet subtle decor; the sitting room was pretty, the dining room cool and beautiful; the owners were informal and friendly. And the cuisine was distinguished: a surprise starter of acacia flowers deep-fried in batter, then green-and-white tagliatelle, warm asparagus soufflé, radicchio-filled ravioli, pink duck with cherries. We drank the owners' wine from vines they grow nearby." Strong business lunch links (but not at weekends) with the Olivetti factory six miles away. (*ABX Fenwick, and others*)

Open All year, except 23 Dec–10 Jan.
Rooms 8 double, 8 single.
Facilities Sitting room, bar, dining room; function room. Garden: tennis. Unsuitable for ♿.
Location 10 km from Ivrea. 52 km NE of Turin. Private parking.
Credit cards All major cards accepted.
Terms B&B: single 98,000 L, double 125,000 L; D,B&B 97,000–133,000 L per person. Set meals 45,000 L; full alc 60,000–80,000 L.

LUCCA 55050 — Map 17

Villa La Principessa
Massa Pisana
Tel (0583) 370037
Fax (0583) 379136

Set at the foot of wooded hills just south of Lucca, this stately house in its beautiful park was, in the 14th century, the home and court of the Duke of Lucca. It is now a luxuriously elegant hotel. The vast hall has a ceiling the height of two floors, an immense fireplace, chandeliers and old pictures. It is all very well run, but rather impersonal, "with no visible host". But mostly it is enjoyed: "We arrived on bicycles," say recent guests, "and a uniformed maid came to carry our bags. Our room had a high painted ceiling, its modern bathroom was startlingly white, the lift was quaint and narrow. At dinner, atmosphere and service were faultless: a waitress from Cheshire has been there 25 years. I had traditional dishes (Tuscan bean soup, thick and tasty, rabbit stuffed with spinach), good but expensive." The new chef has been judged "excellent". The restaurant, called *Gazebo,* is in "a most attractive pavilion with poor acoustics" in the sister hotel, the *Principessa Elisa,* across the main road. "Our suite overlooked the lovely gardens; it had a wrought iron balcony, unsuitable for sitting out but romantic. Breakfast was the finest we had in Italy." (*M and KO, PJH*)

Open All year, except 6 Jan–6 Feb. Restaurant closed Sun.
Rooms 5 suites, 27 double, 5 single. Air-conditioning.
Facilities Lift. Salon, bar, snack bar, restaurant; conference facilities. Park: swimming pool. Unsuitable for ♿.
Location 3 km S of Lucca, along SS12bis towards Pisa.
Credit cards All major cards accepted.
Terms [1996] Rooms: single 270,000 L, double 355,000 L. Breakfast 22,000 L. D,B&B 269,000 L per person. Alc meals 58,000–82,000 L.

MASSA LUBRENSE 80061 Napoli — Map 18

Hotel Bellavista Francischiello *Tel* (081) 8789181
Via Partenope 26 *Fax* (081) 8089341

A hotel on the scenic corniche road south of Sorrento, three minutes' drive from the beach. "Rooms, all with balcony, overlook Sorrento bay and Capri: fantastic sunsets. Very quiet. Spacious white-walled entrance, Art Deco style. The outdoor swimming pool on the roof, built against a rock, has superb views, a well-stocked bar, wonderful flowers, and plenty of deckchairs with umbrellas. Dining room tastefully decorated, attended by owner Riccardo Gariulo and his friendly parents. But the food at his sister's nearby restaurant, *Antico Francischiello – Da Peppino* is more exciting." (*S and F-PG*)

Open All year. Restaurant closed Tues.
Rooms 2 suites, 30 double, 1 single. 10 in annexe. Air-conditioning.
Facilities Lift, ramps. 4 lounges, TV room, 2 bars, 3 dining rooms (no-smoking); 4 conference rooms. Rooftop swimming pool (unheated).
Location 4 km S of Sorrento. Parking.
Credit cards All major cards accepted.
Terms B&B: single 82,000–95,000 L, double 124,00–140,000 L, suite 184,000–200,000 L; D,B&B 95,000–135,000 L per person. Set meals 24,000 L; full alc 45,000 L.

MELE 16010 Genova — Map 17

Hotel Fado 78 BUDGET *Tel* (010) 6971060
Via Fado 82

On the road winding up inland from Voltri, west of Genoa, this hardy *Guide* annual is owned and run by the "very friendly" Canepa family (Christine Canepa is English). "The room was nice, the restaurant good, and children were given special attention and special meals," says a reader this year. Others have called the hotel "ideal for an overnight stop". "A marvellous welcome, and a long chat with Christine over an excellent breakfast. The lasagne was memorable." "Housekeeping is immaculate. Pleasant light furnishings, and good views across the valley. Nice secluded garden: they gave us unlimited plums to pick and take away, plus home-made plum jam. A good dinner, with veal in a succulent sauce." "After dinner we sat on a swing in the garden and watched the sun set over the valley." Bedrooms are in a modern extension, all with views. (*Melissa McDaniel, and others*) A motorway and railway nearby, but noise is only slight.

Open All year. Restaurant closed Mon/Tues.
Rooms 6 double, 2 single.
Facilities Lounge, bar, 2 dining rooms. Large garden. Unsuitable for ♿.
Location 7 km N of Voltri on SS456 to Ovada. *Autostrada* A26 exit Masone or Voltri.
Credit cards None accepted.
Terms Rooms: single 60,000 L, double 105,000 L. Breakfast 15,000 L. Full alc 42,000–48,000 L.

MENAGGIO 22017 Como — Map 17

Grand Hotel Victoria — *Tel* (0344) 32003
Lungolago Castelli 7/11 — *Fax* (0344) 32992

In this "charming quiet town", a fairly smart resort on the west shore of Lake Como, the *Grand Hotel Victoria*, redolent of our yesterdays, stands amid trees by the promenade. "It is a large *belle époque* building, but has the atmosphere of a small family-run hotel, thanks mainly to its very friendly staff [there's even an interpreter, Danilo]. During our stay all guests were invited to a cocktail party and a classical concert. No garden as such, but a well-appointed pool where drinks etc are available all day. Meals are served on the front lawn under a white-and-yellow striped canopy: excellent sumptuous antipasto and dessert buffet. Meat and fish courses lacked inspiration, but pastas were delicious. Public rooms have been restored in 19th-century style, and are comfortable. The bedrooms are more modern, with dark wood furniture which does not fit the decor. Bathrooms are pleasant and bright. Many rooms face the lake with magnificent views, and some have a balcony. Half of the building is now condominiums. (*A and AN*)

Open All year.
Rooms 4 suites, 38 double, 11 single. Some on ground floor.
Facilities Lift. Salon, bar, TV room, restaurant; conference facilities; terrace. Garden: swimming pool. Tennis, golf, lake nearby.
Location In town, 35 km N of Como. Parking.
Credit cards All major cards accepted.
Terms B&B: single 210,000 L, double 310,000 L, suite 430,000 L. D,B&B double 375,00–400,000 L. Set meals 55,000–65,000 L; alc 65,000–70,000 L. Special off-season rates.

MERANO 39012 Bolzano — Map 17

Hotel Fragsburg (Castel Verruca) — *Tel* (0473) 244071
Via Fragsburg-Labers 3 — *Fax* (0473) 244493

High on a hill above a big spa resort in the Alto Adige, this handsome white chalet-style Relais du Silence is surrounded by woods, meadows and mountains, and its own orchards. The main building, 300 years old, is perched on the mountainside. Again this year and last, praise has been warm: "A large bedroom with balcony and lovely view.

Good food, excellent breakfast, helpful owners." "We were welcomed by the omnipresent Ortner family, who have owned and run the hotel for generations and take their meals with their guests. Meals are served on attractive terraces hanging over the valley; there are rustic pine-panelled dining and reading rooms inside." "Very quiet, save for the nightingales." Every meal starts with a self-service salad bar. Breakfasts can include fresh fruit from the garden. The "delightful" large swimming pool faces the mountains. On Fridays the Ortners offer drinks on the house and a lavish hot buffet, which they serve themselves dressed in Tyrolean *Tracht*. "One day they invited us all to a garden party for their son's birthday." (*Mrs C Leeming, and others*) New this year: a sauna and gym, and lounge chairs by the pool. Not all rooms have the view. Tour parties may be given rooms overlooking the carpark.

Open Easter–5 Nov. Restaurant closed Mon.
Rooms 2 suites, 12 double, 2 single. Some no-smoking. Some on ground floor. 2 in chalet.
Facilities Lift, ramps. 3 lounges, TV room, bar, restaurant; sauna, gym; 2 dining terraces. Garden: swimming pool, children's play area, table-tennis, chess.
Location 5 km E of Merano. Right towards Schenna off S38 Bolzano (Bozen)–Merano, right after 2.5 km at Rametz. Hotel 5 km along this road.
Credit cards None accepted.
Terms B&B: single 110,000–155,000 L, double 195,000–300,000 L, suite 220,000–330,000 L; D,B&B double 250,000–380,000 L. Set lunch 40,000–60,000 L, dinner 45,000–70,000 L; full alc 45,000–70,000 L.

MILAN Map 17

Hotel Manzoni NEW — *Tel* (02) 76005700
Via Santo Spirito 20 — *Fax* (02) 784212
20121 Milano

Central, in side-street near Brera gallery (but not easy to reach by car), modern B&B hotel, well run and not too expensive by Milan standards. Recently redecorated in traditional contemporary style. Staff helpful, breakfast fair. No air-conditioning except in basement bar. Some noise from nearby houses: front rooms quietest. Rooms on lower floors are gloomy, facing a courtyard. Invaluable bonus: garage parking. Closed Christmas/New Year, 25 July–25 Aug. All major credit cards accepted. 52 rooms: single 170,000 L, double 220,000 L. Breakfast 19,000 L. Renominated this year.

Hotel Pierre Milano — *Tel* (02) 72000581
Via Edmondo de Amicis 32 — *Fax* (02) 8052157
20123 Milano

"A very *svelte* little luxury hotel" with a striking decor, a mix of new and ancient, not far from the cathedral. "Arriving by car involves a steep climb and a tight turn under the hotel's canopy," write recent visitors. "The hotel offers a very personal service: desk staff are formal, but welcoming. The reception area has a shiny marble floor with rugs, opulent leather seating and equestrian sculptures. Our suite was sublimely quiet, if a little dark (it had smoked glass windows looking on to a central wall), but lighting was excellent, the decor stylish, and the bathroom very well equipped. The buffet breakfast was excellent." "The staff greet us as old friends," write regulars.

Open All year, except 3 weeks Aug.
Rooms 6 suites, 25 double, 18 single.
Facilities Lift. Lounge, piano bar, breakfast room, restaurant.
Location 1 km SW of *duomo*. Garage: valet parking.
Credit cards All major cards accepted.
Terms B&B: single 230,000–330,000 L, double 320,000–500,000 L, suite 560,000–690,000 L. Set lunch 60,000–70,000 L, dinner 70,000–80,000 L. Weekend discounts.

Hotel Spadari al Duomo Tel (02) 72002371
Via Spadari 11 Fax (02) 861184
20123 Milano

In side street just W of duomo, *chic small hotel with contemporary art works and "modern-romantic ambience". Rooms small. Good breakfasts, obliging staff, bathrooms with whirlpool. Closed Christmas, New Year. All major credit cards accepted. 38 rooms. B&B double 330,000–420,000 L. Leading restaurant,* Peck, *just opposite. More reports, please.*

MONFORTE D'ALBA 12065 Cuneo — Map 17

Giardino – Da Felicin Tel/Fax (0173) 78225

In Piedmont townlet amid Barolo vineyards 50 km E of Cuneo, facing panorama of hill-towns and distant Alps, a family-run Michelin-starred *restaurant with 12 adequate rooms (some have terrace). Excellent Piedmont specialities, informal friendly ambience. Large garden with bar. Unsuitable for ♿. Closed Jan/Feb, 2 weeks July; restaurant closed Sun evening/Mon. Access, Visa accepted. Half board (obligatory) 130,000 L. Alc 40,000–65,000 L [1996].*

MONREALE 90046 Palermo, Sicily — Map 18

Carrubella Park Hotel NEW/BUDGET Tel (091) 6402187
Via Umberto I 233 Fax (091) 6402189

In superbly sited town with famous cathedral, 8 km W of Palermo, smallish modern hotel with good breakfasts, plain, pleasant rooms (some have balcony with sweeping coastal views). Air-conditioning. Safe parking. Open 1 Mar–30 Oct. All major credit cards accepted. 30 rooms. B&B 64,000–89,000 L; D,B&B 95,000–105,000 L per person. Set meals 38,000 L. Reports on food welcome.

MONTEFOLLONICO 53040 Siena — Map 17

La Chiusa NEW Tel (0577) 669668
Fax (0577) 669593

Set in the hills south-east of Siena, this carefully renovated old farmhouse in a small medieval hill town "is a perfect example of a *ristorante con camere*", writes its nominator, an expert in the field. "The restaurant is a stylish conversion of a Tuscan olive oil mill, with brick arches, fresh flowers, good linen and cutlery. The owner, Umberto Lucharini, and his staff are professional and congenial. His wife, Dania, cooks like a dream; soups are notable, main courses delicious, puddings outstanding. There is a heart motif on many dishes, particularly starters and desserts, and the bill comes on a heart cut out of coloured paper, with a single figure – none of the boring detail of computerised bills. The wine list is exceptional; it is worth asking Umberto's advice; he often comes up with rare bottles. The bedrooms are good to very good; the two newest use huge granite olive oil presses in the decor, and have a sybaritic bathroom. There is a quiet garden with *chaises longues* and wonderful views of Montepulciano and Pienza, both 15 minutes' drive away." (*Paul Henderson*)

Open All year, except 10–26 Dec, 8 Jan–25 Mar. Restaurant closed Tues.
Rooms 1 apartment, 2 suites, 9 double. 1 on ground floor.
Facilities Restaurant; courtyard. Garden. Unsuitable for ♿.
Location 60 km SE of Siena; just N of Montepulciano.
Credit cards All major cards accepted.
Terms B&B: single 240,000 L, double 280,000 L. Full alc 110,000 L.

MONTERIGGIONI 53035 Siena — Map 17

Albergo Ristorante Casalta BUDGET — *Tel/Fax* (0577) 301002
Strove

This "fine budget hotel, that tries so hard to please its guests" is in the tiny village of Strove, amid glorious scenery near Monteriggioni and quite near Siena. It has a flowery courtyard for outdoor drinks and dining. More praise, this year and last: "Rooms though smallish are carefully decorated, and service was elegant." "It is simple, but has atmosphere, and is charmingly run by Giorgio Cellerai." "A charmingly converted old house. Rooms were spacious. Dinner was excellent, with a variety of Tuscan specialities, including wild game." (*Sharon A Watt, and others*)

Open 1 Mar–1 Nov.
Rooms 10 double.
Facilities Lounge, restaurant; courtyard.
Location In Strove, 4 km W of Monteriggioni, off road to Colle Val d'Elsa. 16 km NW of Siena. Public parking.
Credit cards None accepted.
Terms [1996] Rooms 110,000 L. Breakfast 12,000 L. D,B&B 104,000 L per person. Alc meals 40,000–50,000 L.

MONTEROSSO AL MARE 19016 La Spezia — Map 17

Hotel Porto Roca — *Tel* (0187) 817502
Via Corone 1 — *Fax* (0187) 817692

Thirty-two km W of La Spezia, on edge of one of 5 Cinqueterre villages high on rugged Ligurian coast: "lovely" modern hotel on rocky headland, offering comfort, quiet, superb sea views. Nice staff. Best rooms have balcony or patio; back rooms dreary. Generous breakfasts; dinners "wholesome and enjoyable". Lounge, sunbathing terrace; small sandy beach – crowded in summer, but hotel has reserved area. Best approached by train: corkscrew roads difficult. Unsuitable for ♿. Open 23 Mar–3 Nov. Access, Amex, Visa accepted. 42 rooms. B&B double 210,000–295,000 L; D,B&B 160,000–250,000 L per person. Set meals 55,000–60,000 L. Renominated, but fuller reports welcome.

OLIENA 08025 Nuero, Sardegna — Map 18

Su Gologone *Tel* (0784) 287512
Fax (0784) 287668

The Palimodde family's hotel lies in the wooded foothills of rocky mountains, near a small town in the east of Sardinia. An intriguing recent account: "It is like a small village: with its white walls and blue doors, it recalls Tunisia, while the pink-tiled roofs remind one of Andalucia. The terraced rooms are set among cascades of flowering vegetation. Large paintings and sculptures adorn the arched lobby, woven baskets and other local handicrafts line the corridors – and carcasses of sheep or wild boar roast on spits by a log fire in the dining room. Not a place for strict vegetarians, but the vegetables and fruit are also delicious, and most of the local wines, especially the *rosés*. I reached my large bedroom, with its *en suite* bathroom, across a courtyard with cacti and a farm cart. There's a big swimming pool, tennis courts, etc. Service was good, apart from small lapses. An original hotel, that any able-bodied traveller with an umbrella would enjoy." Cryptic; less so is the warning that the elderly or disabled might not like the many steps. (*TB*)

Open Mar–Nov.
Rooms 8 suites, 57 double. Air-conditioning.
Facilities Bar, reading room, 4 dining rooms. Garden: swimming pool, tennis, mini-golf, bowls, riding. Unsuitable for ♿.
Location 8 km NE of Oliena, which is 193 km N of Cagliari.
Credit cards Access, Amex, Visa.
Terms B&B: single 100,000–105,000 L, double 140,000–165,000 L, suite 180,000–245,000 L; D,B&B 115,000–210,000 L per person. Alc meals 60,000 L.

ORTA SAN GIULIO 28016 Novara — Map 17

Villa Crespi NEW *Tel* (0322) 911902
Fax (0322) 911919

On the shore of lovely Lake Orta, set in a large park and backed by mountains, stands this amazing "no-expense-spared" folly. Benigno Crespi, a cotton industrialist who travelled widely in the Orient, built it in 1880 as his private villa, in ornate Moorish style: "Poets, princes and sovereigns were received there as guests," says the brochure. Turned into a luxurious hotel by a Milanese lawyer, it now makes its *Guide* debut: "The *Villa Crespi* is excellent for a bizarre night of pseudo-oriental splendour. The shape and structure are totally Islamic, right up to the minaret. Marble and terracotta, splendid wooden floor designs, elaborately painted tiles on walls and ceiling. The rooms are vast, furnished with genuine antiques which somehow blend together within the Islamic cocoon. Four-poster beds, immense curtains. All this could be hateful, vulgar, but somehow it is rather fun, including the green water fountain and the black glass lift. Reception is kind and subdued – save that the chef officiates in the elegant restaurant more than in his kitchen. We did not think that his *Michelin* star was quite justified, but breakfast was excellent. A swimming pool is coming this year." (*Felix Singer; also Prof. P and Mrs A Robson*) The regular conference business from Milan may not seem entirely in place.

Open All year, except 15 Nov–1 Dec, 15 Jan–1 Feb.
Rooms 8 suites, 6 double. Air-conditioning.
Facilities Lift, ramps. Hall, lounge, bar, summer bar, restaurant; sauna, fitness centre; terrace. Park.
Location 1 km E of Orta village. 84 km NW of Milan. Parking.
Credit cards All major cards accepted.
Terms B&B: single 180,000–230,000 L, double 320,000–380,000 L, suite 380,000–480,000 L; D,B&B 210,000–290,000 L per person. Set meals 85,000–100,000 L; full alc 90,000–100,000 L. Children under 3 accommodated free in parents' room.

Hotel San Rocco NEW *Tel* (0322) 911977
Via Gippini 11 *Fax* (0322) 911964

This former monastery, built in the 17th century, is now a fairly grand hotel, on the edge of an old village on Lake Orta. After a time with no reports, it is renominated by a 1996 visitor: "It is silently situated by the side of this charming lake, away from the tourist bustle. Solidly built, probably between the wars, with a modern extension, it is conventional and very comfortable. Rooms are smallish, but well designed with Italian care; good colour scheme. Some rooms have a balcony; all have romantic views, best at night with illuminated churches and island. Large reception rooms; better than average hotel food. The garden does not amount to much: but there's a medium-sized swimming pool, and a spacious terrace by the lake" – this is set with tables and chairs. (*Felix Singer*)

Open All year.
Rooms 14 suites, 54 double, 6 single. Air-conditioning.
Facilities Salon, billiard room, 2 bars, 3 dining rooms; conference facilities; sauna, whirlpool, massage. On lake: terrace, swimming pool, private beach, water sports. Unsuitable for ♿.
Location 500 m from village centre. 46 km N of Novara. Garage, carpark.
Credit cards All major cards accepted.
Terms [1996] B&B 120,000–190,000 L; D,B&B (min. 3 nights) 170,000–280,000 L. Set lunch 70,000 L, dinner 80,000 L.

OTTONE 57037 Isola d'Elba Map 17

Villa Ottone *Tel* (0565) 933042
Fax (0565) 933257

Secluded beside a small bay just east of Portoferraio, Elba's capital, stands this sturdy white 19th-century villa, in its own spacious wooded grounds. In the hands of the Di Mario family, it is now a very well-run beach hotel: "Service was exceptional, and food was above average for a tourist hotel, with excellent wines, too," says a visitor this year, endorsing earlier praise: "It has a private beach with glorious views, also a private pool, with bar. Each bedroom is assigned beach chairs, parasols, and large bathing towels laundered daily. The villa has a large sea-facing veranda, with chairs, a lounge, and a bar with resident pianist. The larger first-floor rooms have a balcony. Ours had a magnificent painted ceiling and a large tiled bathroom, and it overlooked the bay. Breakfast is served outdoors under shady trees. Dinner, in an adjacent building, is good and plentiful but not flamboyant. We enjoyed the local fish." (*Mike Hutton, and others*)

Open 10 May–30 Sept.
Rooms 80, some in *Villa*, remainder in bungalows. Some on ground floor. Air-conditioning.
Facilities Lift. Lounge, TV room, bar, piano bar, restaurant; terraces. Garden: swimming pool, tennis, children's playground; private beach: boating, sailing, water-skiing, wind-surfing, fishing. Access to golf club 3 km.
Location 11 km E of Portoferraio; ferries from mainland (Livorno, Piombino). Carpark.
Credit cards All major cards accepted.
Terms Rooms: single 85,000 L, double 160,000 L. Breakfast 10,000 L. D,B&B 105,000–230,000 L per person. Set meals 50,000 L, full alc 60,000 L.

PANZANO IN CHIANTI 50020 Firenze — Map 17

Villa Le Barone

Via San Leolino 19 — *Tel* (055) 852621 — *Fax* (055) 852277

This graceful villa, high on a hill between Florence and Siena, with wide views from its garden and swimming pool of vineyards, cypresses and olive groves in a rolling Tuscan landscape, is the former home of the della Robbia family. It is owned today by Franca Viviani della Robbia, who runs it as a sophisticated *pensione*. "Excellent, at reasonable prices," says a devotee returning this year, and endorsing his 1995 view: "Quiet, with good food and wine, and comfortable rooms, though our peculiar hip bath was not exactly relaxing." Dinners are served in the old winery: good pasta, local dishes, and home-made desserts. You can take breakfast or lunch in a tree-shaded courtyard. Most bedrooms are elegantly furnished with antiques and flowers. Some are more basic, as they would be in a private home. There is still the feeling of being a country house guest in "this most individual hotel, with its charming staff". (*Esler Crawford, SC, and others*)

Open 1 Apr–1 Nov.
Rooms 25 double, 1 single. 6 air-conditioned. 16 in 3 garden annexes.
Facilities 2 lounges, TV room, bar, restaurant. Garden: swimming pool (unheated), tennis. Unsuitable for ♿.
Location 1.5 km SE of Panzano, off SS222 to Siena. 31 km SE of Florence.
Credit cards Access, Amex, Visa.
Terms [1996] D,B&B 185,000–210,000 L per person. Set meals 60,000 L.

Villa Sangiovese

Piazza Bucciarelli 5 — *Tel* (055) 852461 — *Fax* (055) 852463

This "civilised" *Guide* favourite, south of Florence, is owned and well run by a friendly Swiss couple, Ueli and Anne Marie Bleuler, in the best Swiss manner. Very Tuscan is its soft golden stone, and it stands in a tiny, quiet village square; rooms at the back look over the rolling Tuscan hills, with vines, olive trees and cypresses nearby. A "stunning" swimming pool is carved into the hill. You can dine on the terrace, when it's fine. Inside, there's a "lovely" lounge with log fire, and a library. "The public rooms are decorated mainly in soft yellows and fawns to give a cool, cheerful atmosphere." More praise, plus some niggles, this year: "Breakfast, the finest we had in Italy, is served in a bright room with tall windows, facing the Tuscan hills, or outside in warm weather. Bedrooms are decorated in a somewhat spartan modern style, softened with a few antiques. Ours was quiet at night." "The cooking is good, but the menu might be changed more often, and though service is faultless, Herr Bleuler can keep his guests waiting when taking orders. Staying in the village, almost entirely unspoilt by tourism, is like being in a time-warp." (*Alan Blyth, Larissa and Michael Milne, Esler Crawford, and others*)

Open All year, except Christmas, Jan/Feb. Restaurant closed Wed.
Rooms 3 suites, 15 double, 1 single.
Facilities 2 lounges, library, bar, restaurant. Garden: terraces, swimming pool (unheated); mountain bicycles. Unsuitable for ♿.
Location Central, on square; back rooms quietest. Parking.
Credit cards Access, Visa.
Terms [1996] B&B: single 130,000 L, double 160,000–240,000 L, suite 240,000–280,000 L. Full alc 34,000–40,000 L.

PARMA 43100 Map 17

Hotel Torino *Tel* (0521) 281047
Borgo A. Mazza 7 *Fax* (0521) 230725

This pleasant B&B hotel, family run, is near the *duomo*, right in the *centro storico* of a fine old city. The pretty rooms, newly redecorated, vary in size, and bathrooms can be cramped. "A warm welcome from the owner, and breakfast above average, in the newly renovated foyer," runs a report this year. Others too have found the staff pleasant, but some find the breakfast only so-so. (*NF Scholes, Jane Gibbs, SC*)

Open All year. Closed 1–22 Aug.
Rooms 33. Air-conditioning.
Facilities Lounge, bar, TV room, breakfast room. Courtyard. Unsuitable for ♿.
Location Central. Private garage.
Credit cards All major cards accepted.
Terms Rooms: single 98,000 L, double 148,000 L. Breakfast 12,000 L.

PEDEMONTE 37020 Verona Map 17

Villa del Quar *Tel* (045) 6800681
Via Quar 12 *Fax* (045) 6800604

Set amid Valpolicella vineyards in a valley near Verona, this mellow patrician mansion is mostly 16th-century, with later additions and farm buildings. Many rooms have old beamed ceilings; 18th-century wooden choir stalls adorn the foyer. Our nominator found the hotel itself (Relais & Châteaux) worthy of this heritage: "All rooms are well equipped and the staff were helpful. The swimming pool was beautifully kept. The excellent buffet breakfast and main meals were served on a pleasant terrace, and although the food at dinner was not quite as good as the ambience, it was served with panache. The wine waiter, a tremendous enthusiast, completely changed my views about Valpolicella wines: we had some excellent ones." (*AF*)

Open All year, except 6 Jan–28 Feb. Restaurant closed Mon.
Rooms 4 suites, 18 double. 2 on ground floor. Air-conditioning.
Facilities Lift, ramps. Salon, bar, breakfast room, 2 dining rooms; meeting room; terrace. Large grounds: gardens, swimming pool, jogging track.
Location 7 km NW of Verona, on road to San Pietro in Cariano.
Credit cards All major cards accepted.
Terms B&B: double 330,000–430,000 L, suite 450,000–650,000 L. Full alc 75,000–90,000 L.

PERUGIA Map 17

Hotel La Rosetta NEW *Tel/Fax* (075) 5720841
Piazza Italia 19
06121 Perugia

Central, just off main corso, *sizeable but friendly hotel with excellent, stylish bedrooms, well-equipped bathrooms; pleasant food, served in shady courtyard when it's fine. Back rooms quietest. Salon, bar, games room, reading room. All major credit cards accepted. Restaurant closed Mon. 95 rooms. With breakfast 120,000–240,000 L; D,B&B 133,000–156,000 L per person [1996]. Renominated this year, but new reports on food needed.*

PETTENASCO 28028 Novara Map 17

Hotel Giardinetto BUDGET *Tel* (0323) 89482
Via Provinciale 1 *Fax* (0323) 89219

Many rooms have a balcony facing the lake, at this white modern hotel in a resort by lake Orta. Again this year, readers were happy there: "It is not luxurious or sophisticated, but very pleasing. It stands right on the lake: from your balcony, you can see the fish swimming. The Primatesta family owners generate a relaxed, friendly atmosphere, and the north Italian cuisine is of a high standard." "I have stayed five times, and am happy to call it my 'second home'." Readers enjoy the seafood buffet, the live music on Thursday nights, the dining terrace over the lake, and the diverse water-based activities. Service "has a real, not professional, charm". The swimming pool has been renovated: "The water fluctuates at the time," say the owners, "and it has a flowery terrace." Children are most welcome. (*Eira Lewis, L Pellett, and others*) But standards can slip in high summer, when package tours come: they eat in a separate dining room from the other guests. Rooms facing the busy main road can be noisy. And one visitor this year found his bathroom too small.

Open 1 Apr–end Oct.
Rooms 2 suites, 45 double, 7 single. Air-conditioning.
Facilities Lift, ramps. Lounge, TV room, 2 bars, restaurant, coffee shop; conference room; gala evening with dancing Thurs in summer; terrace. Garden: swimming pool, solarium, children's playground. Fishing, boating, water-skiing on lake.
Location 500 m from village centre. 4 km N of Orta San Giulio. Private parking.
Credit cards All major cards accepted.
Terms B&B 85,000–155,000 L; D,B&B 125,000–200,000 L. Set lunch 40,000–45,000 L, dinner 55,000 L.

PIENZA 53026 Siena Map 17

Il Chiostro di Pienza *Tel* (0578) 748400
Corso Rossellino 26 *Fax* (0578) 748440

In a Tuscan Renaissance hill town, a 15th-century monastery newly converted into a classy hotel. "Pienza is delightful, like a stage set (Zeffirelli filmed *Romeo and Juliet* here). The *Chiostro* has a stunning setting near the cathedral, with a wonderful view at the rear. The cloister has tables and chairs for drinks: a bit bare, but creepers have been planted. The decor is not that great – purpose-built furniture. But our room was large, well lit, with tiled floor, arched frescoed ceiling, and overlooking a garden with glorious view beyond. Breakfast was adequate. Nice reception lady. All was quiet, save for church bells, and birds at dawn." (*GA*) A reader this year agreed about the "functional" furnishings and "very jolly and elegant" receptionist, but found the food "only average" in the "hushed grand-hotel style" restaurant.

Open All year. Restaurant closed 10 Nov–20 Dec, 10 Jan–20 Mar.
Rooms 14 suites, 20 double, 3 single. 2 suitable for ♿.
Facilities 3 lounges, TV room, restaurant; terrace. Garden: swimming pool (unheated).
Location 52 km SE of Siena. Central (but quiet). Parking 5 mins' walk.
Credit cards All major cards accepted.
Terms [1996] B&B: single 110,000 L, double 170,000 L, suite 220,000 L; D,B&B 130,000–155,000 L per person. Alc meals 70,000 L.

La Saracina *Tel/Fax* (0578) 748022

On a large estate, with olive grove and vineyard, amid glorious Tuscan scenery, Donald and Jessie McCobb run a "luxurious bed-and-breakfast" in a restored farmhouse. Its nominator was beguiled: "The beautifully furnished rooms are in a converted barn and combine the best of old and new: beamed ceiling, tiled floor and antiques, with jacuzzi bath. Traffic noise is replaced by the tinkle of sheep bells and the sound of cuckoos. The buffet breakfast was excellent. No restaurant, but the McCobbs will advise on first-rate ones in nearby villages." (*ER*) Swimming, tennis, and panoramic views.

Open All year, except Christmas.
Rooms 3 suites, 3 double. All on ground floor.
Facilities Breakfast room. Garden: tennis, swimming pool (unheated).
Location On SS146, 7 km NE of Pienza.
Credit cards Access, Amex, Visa.
Terms [1996] B&B: single 190,000–280,000 L, double 230,000–300,000 L, suite 320,000 L.

PIEVE D'ALPAGO 32010 Belluno — Map 17

Ristorante Albergo Dolada *Tel* (0437) 479141
Via Dolada 21 *Fax* (0437) 478068
Plois

High in the Dolomite foothills, by a lake above the hamlet of Plois, is this attractive *Michelin*-starred restaurant-with-rooms. "It's a turn-of-the-century house with a small pretty garden, and a small terrace with hammock in front. Made up of several connecting rooms, the lovely restaurant has tiled floors and old beams, but modern chairs and lighting, huge vases of flowers. The enticing menu changes daily: it and the wines are very reasonably priced. Bedrooms, bright and modern, are all similar but each with a different colour: ours was Orange, even down to its coat-hangers and door knobs. The owners, Enzo and Rossana De Pra (he cooks), are very welcoming." (*P and JT*)

Open All year, except Feb. Restaurant closed Mon/midday Tues, except July/Aug.
Rooms 7 double.
Facilities Restaurant; terrace. Small garden.

Location At Plois, outside Pieve d'Alpago, 17 km NE of Belluno. Parking.
Credit cards All major cards accepted.
Terms Rooms 140,000–160,000 L. Breakfast 15,000–25,000 L. Alc meals 50,000–75,000 L.

POGGIO CATINO 02040 Rieti — Map 17

Borgo Paraelios — *Tel* (0765) 26267
Località Valle Colicchia — *Fax* (0765) 26268

This "*piccolo paradiso*" lies in hilly country north-east of Rome, and for the third year running has delighted our connoisseurs of Italian civilised luxury: "A wonderful hotel, food delicious, the best staff in Italy." It is a small country club-style hotel, built as a private residence, with a dozen chalet-style rooms now added in a garden setting, with orchards and terraces. "It combines sophistication with extreme rusticity. The range of leisure amenities includes tennis, two swimming pools, Turkish bath, billiard room, and chapel. The lounges are lavishly furnished. The dining room, in smart Italian rustic style, offers food that is excellent: inventive dishes such as cannelloni with nettle sauce, duck breast with honey caramel; the reasonably priced wines included some powerful reds. A buffet breakfast is served in a charming room. Bedrooms have cheerful floral fabrics, antiques, and summery decor; bathrooms are modern and well supplied with toiletries, etc. Each room has a small terrace – the views evoke arty Tuscan calendars, and farmyard noises drift across the valley." This year, a devotee wrote: "Food is unadventurous but sound, breakfast is impeccable, staff are dedicated." (*Kate and David Wooff, P and JT*) "The only sour note: in the hall, family photos including one taken in the company of Mussolini, and another of a group of officers in Fascist uniforms."

Open All year.
Rooms 2 suites, 13 double. Air-conditioning.
Facilities Lift. Lounge, TV room, billiard room, restaurant; games room; indoor swimming pool. Huge grounds: garden, swimming pool, tennis, golf. Unsuitable for ♿.
Location 4 km N of Poggio village, which is 59 km NE of Rome, off A1 to Florence. Parking.
Credit cards All major cards accepted.
Terms [1996] B&B: single 375,000 L, double 500,000 L, suite 650,000 L; D,B&B double 720,000 L. Set meals 110,000–130,000 L.

POMPONESCO 46030 Mantova — Map 17

Il Leone — *Tel* (0375) 86077
Piazza IV Martiri 2 — *Fax* (0375) 86770

"Spacious and enchanting" is recent praise for this *trattoria*-with-rooms in an old house beside the Po, in the wide main square of a quiet village between Mantua and Parma. Its authentic Emilian cooking varies with the season. "Our delectable dinner included slices of raw funghi, ravioli with aubergines, guinea fowl, house desserts. A copious breakfast was served with a smile." The house is full of antiques and bric-à-brac – its dining room even has a 16th-century blue-tinted frieze of classical scenes, just below the beamed ceiling. Bedrooms have been renovated, and some beds are huge (two metres square). Some rooms face the courtyard, where you can dine out in summer, beside a "well-kept" swimming pool. "Family-run with informal professionalism. Best Italian wine list I have ever come across." "A large selection of locally made grappa." (*BWR, and others*)

Open All year, except 27 Dec–25 Jan.
Rooms 4 double, 4 single.
Facilities Bar/TV room, restaurant; conference room. Garden: swimming pool (unheated).
Location In village, off S420 Mantova–Parma, 38 km from Mantova; signposted off Viadana–Guastella road. Safe public parking.
Credit cards All major cards accepted.
Terms [1996] B&B: single 100,000 L, double 145,000 L; D,B&B 130,000–140,000 L per person. Full alc 65,000 L.

PORTO CONTE 07041 Sassari, Sardegna — Map 18

El Faro NEW — *Tel* (079) 942010, *Fax* (079) 942030

Secluded on rocks by the sea on wild lovely Sardinian coast 13 km NW of Alghero, a fairly big and luxurious holiday hotel, very beautiful (Michelin red print). *Fine antique furnishings. Good food, friendly staff. Sun-bathing terraces, two swimming pools, beach; sauna, tennis. Open 12 May–15 Oct. 92 rooms. With breakfast 220,000–430,000 L; D,B&B 210,000—240,000 L per person. Set meal 75,000 L [1996]. Fuller reports needed.*

PORTO ERCOLE 58018 Grosseto — Map 17

Il Pellicano — *Tel* (0564) 833801
Cala dei Santi — *Fax* (0564) 833418

You can dine on a candlelit terrace at this well-known luxury hotel. It is built into the hillside, on a lovely rocky peninsula north-west of Rome: its wooded garden slopes down to a pretty swimming pool and then to the cliff edge. Sea bathing is from a rocky beach, with clean, clear water (but it's 90 steps down). Many of the spacious bedrooms have a sea-facing terrace. The hotel was for many years run by Ennio and Nadia Emili, much loved by readers. But latest reports suggest that the high quality of food and service is unchanged under the more formal management of the owner, Roberto Scio, who now runs it himself: "The nicest hotel we've ever stayed in, with terribly kind staff, delicious supper, a lovely bedroom terrace." "Friendly reception, a beautiful newly renovated room, and brilliant food at lunchtime barbecues." (*EC, and others*) "The hotel's perfection attracts the ritzier sort of international clientele." More reports, please.

Open 29 Mar–2 Nov.
Rooms 4 suites, 32 double. Some in cottages. Air-conditioning.
Facilities Lounge, TV room, 2 bars, 2 restaurants; conference facilities; gala buffet Fri July/Aug; terrace. Large grounds: tennis, sea-water swimming pool with bar/barbecue; rocky beach with safe bathing, water-skiing. Unsuitable for ♿.
Location 3.5 km S of Porto Ercole on Monte Argentario coast. Parking.
Credit cards All major cards accepted.
Terms [1996] B&B: double 774,000 L; D,B&B 472,000–562,000 L per person. Set meals 100,000 L.

PORTONOVO 60020 Ancona — Map 17

Hotel Emilia — *Tel* (071) 801145
Collina di Portonovo — *Fax* (071) 801330

This beautiful modern hotel stands on a cliff above the sea, south-east of Ancona, with Monte Cónero rising behind. "First class," runs a recent plaudit. "There's a full-size outdoor pool with diving board, and snack bar alongside. The double rooms are large and airy, with sea views; some rooms are smaller, but OK. Food and service are what one would expect, and the hotel is family-run, by the Fiorini, and warmly personal. It keeps a collection of modern art ["more and more beautiful", according to Sig. Fiorini] and awards an annual prize for it. Clientele are mainly Italian, up-market. This bit of the Adriatic coast has kept its rural character and is picturesque." You can dine on the clifftop terrace. And there's sea bathing down at Portonovo beach. (*SWB-S*)

Open All year.
Rooms 3 suites, 25 double, 2 single. 1 suitable for ♿.
Facilities Lift. Lounge with TV, bar, restaurant; conference facilities. Park: swimming pool, tennis. Sea 1.5 km.
Location 12 km SE of Ancona, above Portonovo. *Autostrada* A14 exit Ancona Sud.
Credit cards All major cards accepted.
Terms B&B: single 130,000–200,000 L, double 160,000–250,000 L, suite 200,000–400,000 L; D,B&B 150,000–180,000 L per person. Set lunch 50,000 L, dinner 70,000 L.

PRATO 50047 Firenze — Map 17

Villa Rucellai BUDGET — *Tel/Fax* (0574) 460392

Up in the lovely hills above Prato, amid vineyards and olive groves, this fine 16th-century mansion has been the home of the Rucellai family since 1759; now they let out some rooms to bed-and-breakfast guests. It is a very special place, described as "the closest most foreigners will get to staying in a well-off Italian home". "What a fabulous place!" "An experience," say readers this year, endorsing this earlier account: "The cosmopolitan Rucellai Piqué family give the impression of enjoying their guests' company. The great shady courtyard is stunning, and the heated spring-water pool. The public rooms with their high vaulted ceilings are gorgeous, full of beautiful old furniture and paintings; the dining room has dramatic frescoes, and there's a wisteria-festooned loggia with cane furniture." The pool and patio are wonderful, with sun-chairs and umbrellas. Breakfast is satisfactory." "Our high-ceilinged bedroom had a piano in it; the baroque garden is exquisite." "Redolent of a bygone era. Paolo Piqué and his charming wife were perfect hosts." (*Melissa McDaniel, Eve Gompertz, and others*) Two caveats: no air conditioning, and some noise from trains. And some readers have found that the "air of faded glory" of house and garden verged on shabbiness, and thought the service fitful. *Logli* and *La Fontana* are good restaurants nearby, but it's a winding drive on a narrow road.

Open All year.
Rooms 3 suites, 9 double.
Facilities Hall, 2 living rooms (one with TV), dining room. Large grounds:

garden, swimming pool, woods, farmland. Unsuitable for ♿.
Location 4 km NE of Prato, along narrow winding road.
Credit cards None accepted.
Terms Double room 100,000–130,000 L. Breakfast 10,000 L.

PUGNANO 56010 Pisa — Map 17

Casetta delle Selve BUDGET — *Tel* (050) 850359
San Giuliano Terme

"This highly individual B&B, in a converted farmhouse, was the discovery of our Tuscan trip," write inspectors. "Perched high on a hill south of Lucca, it is not for the timid driver: you wind your way up a steep track – best not done in the dark first time. Our abiding memories are of bright colours, a stunning view, and an eccentric but welcoming hostess, Nicla Menchi. She greeted us with a paintbrush stuck in her hair. Husky voiced, surrounded by her six cats, she sits painting at her easel some of the time. Bedrooms, which are not locked, are decorated in individual style, with different colour schemes: ours was very pink, with pretty beds, nice old furniture. It had a pink shower room/loo. The house is immaculate and colourful, full of our hostess's paintings – nudes and landscapes – plus some slightly dotty notices. She was kind, lit a fire of olive wood in the lounge for us. Beautifully quiet at night, and the best breakfast of our trip: boiled eggs, and *fresh* orange juice, rare in Italy, served after 9 am, when the sun arrives on the flowery terrace. There is a stunning view across the plain to Pisa."
Open All year.
Rooms 6 double.
Facilities Lounge with TV; terrace. Garden
Location Off SS12, 10 km SW of Lucca. From Pugnano take road to San Giuliano Terme, then winding track to right.
Restriction No children under 12.
Credit cards None accepted.
Terms Double room 100,000 L. Breakfast 13,000 L.

RADDA IN CHIANTI 53017 Siena — Map 17

Relais Fattoria Vignale — *Tel* (0577) 738300
Via Pianigiani 9 — *Fax* (0577) 738592

In the heart of the lush Chianti hills, on the edge of a big village north of Siena, stands this 18th-century wine-producing manor house, now converted with elegant taste into a stylish, well-kept and expensive B&B. Devotees returning this year found it "as good as ever", and extolled the "cheerful and helpful staff". Last year they spent two weeks: "It is the best-managed, most welcoming and comfortable hotel that we know in Tuscany or Umbria: meticulous housekeeping, excellent breakfasts, bright and attractive lounges, and a decent-sized swimming pool. The operation is supervised in detail by the delightful Silvia Kummer, who replies swiftly to letters." You can breakfast in an old vaulted room, or on a veranda facing the panorama, which the pool also shares. (*Mr and Mrs PJ Hall*) Readers like the *Michelin*-starred *Vignale* restaurant in Radda, separately owned.
Open 15 Mar–15 Nov.
Rooms 3 suites, 23 double, 3 single. 10 in annexe across road.

Facilities 2 lounges, lounge bar, TV room/library, breakfast room; conference room; chapel; terrace. Garden: swimming pool.
Location On edge of village, 33 km N of Siena. Parking.
Credit cards Access, Amex, Visa.
Terms B&B: single 200,000 L, double 350,000 L.

RANCO 21020 Varese Map 17

Albergo-Ristorante del Sole NEW *Tel* (0331) 976507
Piazza Venezia 5 *Fax* (0331) 976620

Charmingly set by the water in a village on the south-east coast of Lake Maggiore, this brilliant restaurant has been owned and run by the Brovelli family for over a century, and now carries two *Michelin* stars. Carlo Brovelli and his son do the cooking; his wife is front-of-house. Lack of reports thrust it from the *Guide* last year, but a 1996 letter urges its return: "It is a Relais & Châteaux member, but there's nothing glossy here. The bedrooms are warmly decorated in the best modern Italian style, and all but one have a balcony with distant view of lake and mountains. Some old family heirlooms mingle with the new. Cooking is minimal sophisticated (but there are enough courses), served with charm in elegant surroundings. An unminimal un-Italian breakfast. The setting is calm and unspoilt, with a vine-covered terrace, and lawns sloping to a lakeside promenade." Earlier visitors admired the welcome, the "light and innovative" cooking, the lake fish and "delicious" chilled desserts. Meals are served in an elegant white-walled dining room, or on the terrace. Bedrooms are all split-level: some are quite small. (*Felix Singer*) Some road noise.

Open All year, except Dec/Jan; closed Mon in low season. Restaurant closed Tues.
Rooms 4 suites, 4 double. Air-conditioning.
Facilities Lounge, bar, restaurant; function room; terrace (meal service). Garden. Unsuitable for ♿.
Location 67 km NW of Milan. *Autostrada* 8 exit Sesto Calende towards Angera. Parking.
Credit cards All major cards accepted.
Terms B&B: single 280,000–300,000 L, double 330,000–400,000 L. Set meals 70,000–120,000 L.

RAVELLO 84010 Salerno Map 18

Hotel Caruso Belvedere *Tel* (089) 857111
Via Toro 52 *Fax* (089) 857372

This converted Renaissance palace, set on a cliff above lemon groves that plunge down to the blue Gulf of Salerno, has been owned and run by the Caruso family for four generations. The dining terrace, the marble-pillared dining room and many bedrooms all have "wonderful" sea views. "An exquisite hotel, with excellent food," wrote a recent visitor, while another this year spelt it out: "It has an old-fashioned atmosphere, but I would recommend it. Our bedroom, rather small, had an open balcony with stunning views. Staff were friendly, the head waiter was excellent, and food was adequate but not exciting. Apart from the ghastly gold doilies on the table, all was well set up. Attractive gardens and beautiful terraces." Others have thought the cooking imaginative, with good salads from the garden. Half-board is obligatory in high season. "The hotel's own local wine is sound." The comfortable lounge has a wood fire, "but its painted ceiling is decrepit". (*David Craig, NK*) Views are divided on whether the hotel retains its past glory – but mostly the ayes have it.

Open All year. Restaurant closed Feb.
Rooms 2 suites, 22 double, 2 single.
Facilities Lounge, TV room, restaurant; terrace. Garden. Unsuitable for ♿.
Location 300 m from centre. Public parking.
Credit cards All major cards accepted.
Terms [1996] B&B: single 126,000–160,000 L, double 149,000–270,000 L, suite 244,000–320,000 L; D,B&B 115,000–195,000 L per person. Set meals 42,000 L.

Giordano e Villa Maria *Tel* (089) 857255
Via Santa Chiara 2 *Fax* (089) 857071

These two small hotels, close to each other, are both owned by the Palumbo family, and have a quiet setting up a winding lane from the village square, with views of the hills and sea far below. *Villa Maria* is a pink converted villa with large bedrooms and a pleasant terrace; the *Giordano*, more modern, has a big solar-heated swimming pool, and a shady garden for meals in summer. This year, a guest at the *Villa* liked his private veranda, and the "good reliable Italian *table d'hôte* food" served on the restaurant's tree-shaded terrace. An earlier visitor was similarly seduced: "If the view doesn't sell this charming place, the staff will: Vincenzo Palumbo and his waiter, Fidele, treated us like part of the family, and we spent hours playing cards with them after a candlelit dinner in a beautiful salon with parquet floor and indoor bougainvillea." Although some rooms are very small, all have "beautiful country antiques" and a tiled floor, and the luxurious upper rooms also have a jacuzzi. (*CJ Daintree*) In high season, half board may be obligatory. We need more reports on the *Giordano*.

Open All year, except Christmas.
Rooms 2 suites, 15 double.
Facilities Lounge, sitting room, bar, 2 dining rooms; terrace (meals served). Garden: swimming pool. Unsuitable for ♿.
Location 400 m from centre of old town. Carpark.
Credit cards All major cards accepted.
Terms [1996] B&B: single 130,000–150,000 L, double 200,000–225,000 L, suite 310,000–425,000 L; D,B&B 150,000–280,000 L per person. Set meals 60,000–70,000 L.

REGGELLO 50066 Firenze Map 17

Hotel Archimede *Tel* (055) 869055
Strada per Vallombrosa *Fax* (055) 868584

This rustic venue is up a mountain road outside a small town south-east of Florence, in the Pratomagno *massif*. It is in "a landscape of headily scented *maquis* and deciduous woods, rising to high windy pastures where 'wild' horses roam". The restaurant is characterful, and much reputed locally, and the small modern hotel has grown out of it. "The restaurant is a revelation," runs a recent account. "Approached through a tunnel, it is superglued on to the mountain-side, with a vertiginous ramp that makes you think. Lots of function rooms, all with rather a log-cabin *après-ski* feel. Very busy, and with very good food, reasonably priced. Bedrooms are basic but not poky, with tiled floors. The upper floor balconies may have sensational views: ours was impeded by trees." Others have agreed: "Dinner, with the fire blazing in the kitchen, was a most enjoyable feast: the colossal bistecca fiorentina was full of charcoal grill flavour." (*R and SO*) Some traffic noise.

Open All year, except 11–22 Nov. Restaurant closed Tues, except July–15 Sept.
Rooms 18.
Facilities Sitting room, restaurant; terrace. Garden.
Location 3.5 km N of Reggello on Vallombrosa road, 500 m beyond Pietrapiana.
Credit cards All major cards accepted.
Terms [1996] Rooms: single 95,000, double 130,000 L. Breakfast 10,000 L. D,B&B 100,000 L per person. Alc meals 35,000–50,000 L.

RIVA DI SOLTO 24060 Bergamo — Map 17

Miranda – Da Oreste BUDGET — *Tel/Fax* (035) 986021
Via Cornello 8
Zorzino

The friendly Polini family's pretty white villa, always popular with readers, stands high above little Lake Iseo, in Zorzino village, amid hills and olive groves. There is a large sun terrace, and a swimming pool; many bedrooms (upper ones are best) have a balcony with glorious views. Again this year, it has been found excellent value: "Enjoyed it. Superb view from the outdoor dining terrace; friendly staff, good pasta and fish. Our family room was simple, but nothing to complain about at the price; bathroom modern." "Nice, jolly atmosphere. Owner anxious to please. Food simple and plain but plentiful." Children, as is usual in Italy, are treated like normal guests. The hotel has been called "folksy and rather Alpine", but also "new and purpose-built". (*Prof. and Mrs Robson, BW Ribbons, and others*) Bedlights are poor.

Open All year.
Rooms 3 suites (in annexe), 20 double, 2 single.
Facilities TV room, restaurant. Garden: swimming pool, table-tennis, children's playground. Unsuitable for ♿.
Location In Zorzino village, 1.5 km above Riva di Solto. 40 km E of Bergamo. Parking.
Credit cards All major cards accepted.
Terms Rooms: single 57,000 L, double 73,000 L. Breakfast 7,000 L. D,B&B 61,000–65,000 L per person. Alc meals 31,000–45,000 L.

ROME — Map 17

Hotel Campo de' Fiori — *Tel* (06) 6874886
Via del Biscione 6 — *Fax* (06) 6876003
00186 Roma

A modestly priced little hotel near the Piazza Navona, on a sunny corner of the colourful outdoor fruit and vegetable market. The duplex roof-deck, which serves as a terrace, has a view over Rome's golden terracotta rooftops towards St Peter's. Rooms range from the top-floor "honeymoon suite" – "decor a little frayed, but we liked the ceiling painted blue with fluffy clouds, and the glittery drapery that can be drawn close round the beds" – to the small ones, "designed with style and whimsy", on the first floor: "The walls have large arched mirrors within ancient-looking Roman brickwork, the high original-beamed ceilings allow the bathrooms to have their own terracotta-tiled roofs – like a little cottage within the room. The Dutch desk manager was delightful." Many rooms have no bathroom. And there's no lift, for six floors. Breakfast is "merely adequate", but in summer it is served on the roof with its view; in winter, in a cosy basement, lined with mirrors. (*David and Margot Holbrook, RG*) The booking system is "a bit crazy", says one reader this year.

Open All year.
Rooms 1 suite, 26 double. 13 with bath and/or shower, 9 with WC.
Facilities TV room, breakfast room (no-smoking); roof garden. Air-conditioning. Unsuitable for ♿.
Location Central, near Piazza Campo dei Fiori.
Credit cards Access, Visa.
Terms B&B 100,000–190,000 L.

Albergo Cesàri *Tel* (06) 6792386 and 69940632
Via di Pietra 89a *Fax* (06) 6790882
00186 Roma

This former palace has been a hotel since the 18th century: Stendhal and Garibaldi were among its guests. Old-fashioned, simple, and reasonably priced for Rome, it is enjoyed for its "prompt and helpful staff", and its setting in the heart of old Rome, down a cul-de-sac off the busy Via del Corso. "It's far more comfortable than first appears, and we loved it – cool, clean and well run. A large bathroom, and we enjoyed using the most antique lift I have ever seen." The spacious rooms have high ceilings and antiques. Breakfasts are plain but adequate. (*MH, and others*) Most rooms suffer from some traffic noise, as so often happens in downtown Rome.

Open All year.
Rooms 40 double, 10 single. Some on ground floor. Air-conditioning.
Facilities Lift. Lounge, TV room, bar.
Location Central, off Via del Corso (windows double-glazed). Private garage nearby.
Credit cards All major cards accepted.
Terms [1996] B&B: single 150,000–188,000 L, double 170,000–256,000 L, suite 230,000–355,000 L.

Hotel Gregoriana *Tel* (06) 6794269
Via Gregoriana 18 *Fax* (06) 6784258
00187 Roma

Liked again this year and last, this converted convent is now a stylish little hotel with 1930s decor, and prices reasonable for Rome. It is conveniently located near the top of the Spanish Steps, close to a Metro station. It is on a side street, but front rooms can be noisy: back ones are quieter and larger, but dearer. Recent accounts: "Charming. Our room had a small balcony and attractive bathroom. Good coffee." "The 1930s style is carried through in detail throughout the hotel, and meticulously renovated: the original is supposed to be by Erté. The owner is civilised and courteous" – and staff too are friendly. Rooms are bright and pretty; some upper ones look out over roof-gardens and orange and lemon trees. One reader had "a big, sunny bathroom in blues and mauves". Pleasant bar and lounge. (*L Gillinson, KR, and others*)

Open All year.
Rooms 15 double, 4 single. 4 on ground floor. Air-conditioning.
Facilities Lift. Hall.
Location Central, above Spanish Steps. Parking.
Credit cards None accepted.
Terms B&B: single 180,000 L, double 300,000 L.

Albergo Internazionale *Tel* (06) 6793047
Via Sistina 79 *Fax* (06) 6784764
00187 Roma

Superbly located at the top of the Spanish Steps, this 16th-century building, first a monastery, then a home of artists, has been owned and run as a hotel by the Gnecco family since 1870. "Our room was large, with a good view, though somewhat sparsely furnished. A large tub, great for soaking away the aches caused by climbing those 137 steps! The staff are crisp and professional. The breakfast room is delightful and the breakfast tasty." (*FV*)

Open All year.
Rooms 2 suites, 32 double, 8 single. Air-conditioning.
Facilities Lounge, TV room, breakfast room.
Location Central, near Spanish Steps. Garages nearby.
Credit cards Access, Amex, Visa.
Terms [1996] B&B: single 210,000 L, double 295,000 L, suite 600,000 L.

Lord Byron NEW *Tel* (06) 3220404
Via Giuseppe de Notaris 5 *Fax* (06) 3220405
00197 Roma

"Expensive, but good value – an oasis of peace and good taste in the hurly burly of Rome." This highly sophisticated hotel (Relais & Châteaux) lies down a narrow street in a quiet neighbourhood of opulent villas near the Borghese gardens. You enter up a flight of white marble steps, leading from a small paved garden with orange and lemon trees. A returning visitor renominates it this year: "Being small, it offers more personal service than bigger places. After much refurbishment (new stair carpets), it looks newly decorated, and housekeeping is of a high standard. In the restaurant, service was impeccable, the food sophisticated (*Michelin* star) and the bill a pleasant surprise. The buffet breakfast has improved, save for the coffee. In the bar, the singer/pianist in the evenings is obtrusive, but the drinks are superb." Others have admired the decor: "Dazzling, very Italian. Our large and beautiful room had a sculpted arched ceiling, walls lined with mirrors or floral fabric, and a small terrace with shrubs." (*Kate and David Wooff*)

Open All year. Restaurant closed Sun.
Rooms 9 suites, 27 double, 1 single. 1 suite in separate building.
Facilities Two lounges, piano bar, restaurant; function room. Small garden. Unsuitable for ♿.
Location Just NW of Borghese gardens in Parioli district. Garage.
Credit cards All major cards accepted.
Terms B&B: single 295,000–370,000 L, double 360,000–550,000 L, suite 800,000–1,200,000 L. Alc meals from 100,000 L.

Hotel Margutta NEW
Via Laurina 34
00187 Roma

Tel (06) 3223674
Fax (06) 3200395

In cobbled street S of Piazza del Popolo, quiet and friendly hotel with 21 simple, newly renovated rooms, above-average breakfasts. Good value for Rome. Open all year. All major credit cards accepted. 21 rooms. B&B double 147,000 L.

Hotel Portoghesi
Via dei Portoghesi 1
00186 Roma

Tel (06) 6864231
Fax (06) 6876976

An old building near the Piazza Navona: it has been a hotel for 150 years, and is still family-run and friendly, with furnishings in period style. Rooms vary in size. One reader's was large, "with an odd assortment of antiques", and a good view; another, at the back, was tiny, but clean and quiet. It's "nice, friendly and central"; with a rooftop terrace for fine weather. (*BB, and others*)

Open All year.
Rooms 3 suites, 18 double, 7 single.
Facilities Lift. Breakfast room, TV room; rooftop terrace. Unsuitable for ♿.
Location Central, near Piazza Navona. Private parking.
Credit cards Access, Visa.
Terms B&B: single 160,000 L, double 240,000 L, suite 290,000–400,000 L.

La Residenza
Via Emilia 22–24
00187 Roma

Tel (06) 4880789
Fax (06) 485721

Down a quiet street off the Via Veneto is this small but very *soigné* hotel, ochre-façaded in Roman style. Most guests are American, and our own US readers liked it a lot again this year: "This inn was intimate and cosy, reception was very welcoming. Our good room had a patio balcony with comfortable seating for outdoor reading (we also hung out some laundry to dry, just like the Romans!). Decor is tasteful, with an artful blending of Victorian and modern. The library doubles as an evening bar." "The staff were wonderful, helpful, friendly, and the buffet breakfasts fabulous." Rooms vary in size: some are "a bit small and dark", but all are comfortable, and have TV, with in-house video films in English as well as Italian, plus CNN. Lots of foreign newspapers are available, free. No restaurant; but there are good ones nearby, such as the *Giovanni* in Via Marche. (*K and B Jinnett, Mary McGuire, NK*)

Open All year.
Rooms 5 suites, 18 double, 5 single.
Facilities Lift. 2 lounges, bar, breakfast room; terrace, patio. Air-conditioning. Unsuitable for ♿.
Location Central, near Via Veneto and American Embassy (back rooms quietest). Some parking.
Credit cards Access, Amex, Visa.
Terms [1996] B&B: single 130,000 L, double 270,000 L.

Villa del Parco NEW
Via Nomentana 110
00161 Roma

Tel (06) 44237773
Fax (06) 44237572

The Bernardini family's small hotel, once a private villa, makes its *Guide* debut: "It sits among trees down a long driveway, in Rome's embassy district, just east of the Borghese gardens. Rooms are decorated in a mix of standard 'period hotel' pieces plus a few antiques. Our room was quite large: there are also some tiny singles. The bathroom, rather dated, had porcelain fixtures from the 1940s, but all worked just fine. The public areas downstairs have comfortable sofas. Breakfast, served on the terrace in fine weather, is fairly simple. No restaurant: but the very courteous staff will prepare salads and sandwiches." A small garden has tables and chairs. (*Larissa and Michael Milne*)

Open All year.
Rooms 19 double, 6 single.
Facilities Sitting rooms, bar, TV room, breakfast room; terrace. Garden.
Location Fairly central, 2 km E of Borghese gardens. Guarded parking.
Credit cards All major cards accepted.
Terms [1996] B&B single 165,000–175,000 L, double 215,000–230,000 L. Special weekend rates.

SAN GIMIGNANO 53037 Siena — Map 17

L'Antico Pozzo
Via San Matteo 87

Tel (0577) 942014
Fax (0577) 942117

Liked again this year, this discreetly elegant B&B in the old town inhabits a building with an old and startling history. Trials were held here by the Inquisition; then in the 18th century it was a "salon" for high society, and balls took place in what is now the breakfast room. Further back, Dante Alighieri is said to have stayed in the frescoed room that is now number 13; in those days, girls who refused to submit to the *droit de seigneur* were suspended in the well (the eponymous *antico pozzo*) for three days and nights. But no such fate befell our reporter: "It has been sympathetically restored: some rooms have their original ceiling frescoes, others look out over the city's towers. Rooms vary in size: ours was smallish but comfortable, and its modern locally designed furniture blended well with the beautiful simplicity of the hotel." Again this year, readers found the staff very courteous, and enjoyed an "appetising" buffet breakfast, which you can take out in the patio when it's fine. Back rooms are quietest. All have air-conditioning, but in winter they can be under-heated. Three recommended *trattorie* close by: *La Stella, La Mangiataoia* and *L'Antica Taverna*. (*Larissa and Michael Milne, and others*)

Open All year, except Feb.
Rooms 3 suites, 14 double, 1 single. Air-conditioning.
Facilities Lift, ramps. Lounge, TV room, bar, breakfast room (no-smoking); terrace. Garden.
Location Central. Parking nearby.
Credit cards All major cards accepted.
Terms B&B: single 130,000 L, double 180,000 L, suite 230,000 L.

Hotel Bel Soggiorno BUDGET *Tel/Fax* (0577) 943165
Via San Giovanni 91

Just inside the ramparts of this stunning medieval town is this lovely 13th-century building, its wide windows offering views of the Tuscan hills and olive groves. Run by the Gigli family since 1886, the hotel has again been liked recently: "An effusive welcome. Our room was small but well equipped, and had that view. So did the large but atmospheric restaurant, very panoramic. Dinner, with unusual home-made bread and excellent pasta, was above average." "Only average, save for my superb wild boar," chimes in another diner. Many rooms have a terrace. Those facing away from the street are quietest, *and* have the best views. (*M and KO, NK*)

Open All year. Restaurant closed 7 Jan–25 Feb.
Rooms 4 suites, 18 double. Air-conditioning.
Facilities Salon, bar, restaurant; terrace. Access to swimming pool at sister hotel, *Pescille*.
Location Central. Cars allowed in for unloading. Carpark nearby.
Credit cards All major cards accepted.
Terms B&B: single 110,000–130,000 L, double 140,000–160,000 L, suite 180,000–200,000 L; D,B&B 110,000–170,000 L per person. Full alc 48,000–65,000 L.

SAN GREGORIO 06081 Assisi — Map 17

Castel San Gregorio BUDGET *Tel* (075) 8038009
Fax (075) 8038904

"Friendly cows greet you in the parking lot" – a good start to a stay at this offbeat and convivial hotel, a creeper-covered neo-Gothic castle set amid vines and meadows between Assisi and Perugia. Some rooms have antique beds, others a four-poster with linen drapes; the bathrooms in the towers are circular. Beamed ceilings, spiral stairways, fancy lighting add to the atmosphere. Dining tends to be communal, round one big table, at a single sitting. "Definitely charming," is the latest praise. "The comfortable living room is elegantly furnished, and we enjoyed our aperitif in the arbour above the valley. Food not exciting but plentiful. Waitresses are hurried, but the single table gives ambience to the meal, as guests from diverse countries share experiences." Good local cheap wine. (*MF*) Rooms above kitchen can be noisy. The plumbing can be "doubtful". Newer reports, please.

Open All year, except 15–30 Jan. Restaurant closed to non-residents.
Rooms 12.
Facilities Reading room, dining room. Small garden. Unsuitable for ♿.
Location 13 km NW of Assisi.
Credit cards All major cards accepted.
Terms [1996] Rooms: single 85,000 L, double 130,000 L. Breakfast 13,000 L. D,B&B 110,000 L per person. Set meals (residents only) 42,000 L.

The "Budget" label by a hotel's name indicates an establishment where dinner, bed and breakfast is offered at around £50 (or its foreign currency equivalent) per person, or B&B for about £30 and an evening meal for about £20. These are only rough guides and do not always apply to single accommodation; nor do they necessarily apply in high season.

SAN MAMETE 22010 Como **Map 17**

Hotel Stella d'Italia BUDGET
Piazza Roma 1
San Mamete, Valsolda
(postal address: PO Box 46,
6976 Castagnola, Switzerland)
Tel (0344) 68139
Fax (0344) 68729

For many years, the "kind and gracious" Ortelli family have owned and run this old *Guide* favourite, an unpretentious hotel beside Lake Lugano at the Swiss border. The bedrooms, "simply furnished in bright colours", and each with its own balcony on which you can breakfast, have views across the lake to distant mountains. The dining terrace has a canopy of climbing roses; an "enchanting" garden leads down to a lido for swimming or sunbathing. A devotee returned this year: "Its charm is to be right on the lake: you can step off the terrace into the water, with superb views of the mountains. It is very much a family hotel of the old kind, with unfinished bottles of wine being put away for the next meal. The company might have been from a Terence Rattigan play: English guests talking to English ones; a table of noisy Germans; young American couples. There are now new kitchens, and a larger *carte*: the grilled fish from the lake was especially good." Others have spoken of smiling service, welcoming owners, a library of English books, and "fun taking the hotel's boat out on the lake". (*Lord Rodgers; also Elizabeth Robey, and others*)

Open Apr–Oct.
Rooms 31 double, 4 single.
Facilities 2 lounges, bar, restaurant (no-smoking). Garden: restaurant; lake: beach, bathing, fishing, surfing, boating. Unsuitable for ♿.
Location 10 km NE of Lugano, on lake between Gandria and Menaggio; road signposted Menaggio. Garage.
Credit cards Access, Amex, Visa.
Terms B&B: single 85,000 L, double 150,000–170,000 L; D,B&B 110,000–120,000 L. Set meals 35,000 L; full alc 55,000–65,000 L. 20–30% reduction for children.

SAN MARINO 47031 San Marino **Map 17**

Hotel Titano BUDGET
Contrada del Collegio 21
Tel (0549) 991006
Fax (0549) 991375

In central street of this tiny, fascinating, tourist-besieged republic: friendly hotel with 46 smallish but freshly decorated rooms; fine views, good breakfasts and main meals. Unsuitable for ♿. Open 15 Mar–15 Dec. All major credit cards accepted. B&B double 120,000–140,000 L; D,B&B 90,000-115,000 L per person [1996].

SAN PAOLO APPIANO 39050 Bolzano **Map 17**

Schloss Korb
Missiano
Tel (0471) 636000
Fax (0471) 636033

This medieval castle, family-owned and run, has a fine open setting amid terraced vineyards and rocky hills, west of Bolzano. And it has been lavishly converted, with beamed ceilings, rough stone walls, antiques, bizarre statuary. "We enjoyed the Bram Stoker touches," say recent guests. "Indeed, we loved everything about it – gourmet food, superb wines, excellent breakfast." Earlier comments: "A superb view from our wide battlemented balcony. The set dinner menu was excellent, delicately cooked. The buffet breakfast included everything from scrambled egg to chocolate cake. All staff were pleasant." "From our room we enjoyed the sunset over the Dolomites." Some rooms are small. The hotel now has a health and beauty centre. (*NK*)

Open 23 Mar–5 Nov.
Rooms 3 suites, 63 double, 2 single. 33 in annexe.
Facilities Lift. Lounge, TV room, bar, 3 dining rooms; conference facilities; health centre: swimming pool, sauna; terrace. Garden: tennis, swimming pool. Lake, fishing nearby.
Location 10 km W of Bolzano. Parking.
Credit cards None accepted.
Terms [1996] B&B 100,000–190,000 L; D,B&B 130,000–220,000 L. Set meals 60,000 L; full alc 70,000 L.

ST WALBURG IN ULTEN 39016 Bolzano — Map 17

Gasthof Eggwirt BUDGET

Tel (0473) 795319
Fax (0473) 795471

This white holiday hotel, simple but attractive, has Alpine furnishings and is well run by the Schwienbacher family owners. It lies in the remote and beautiful Ulten (Ultimo) valley of the German-speaking South Tyrol, near Merano. "As good as ever, very good value: it is warmly heated, has a friendly welcome, excellent food and wines," wrote a regular this year, endorsing her own praise last year: "Our room was spacious and comfortable. The family also own the bakery/teashop in the square, selling scrumptious Tyrolean cakes and strudels. On Tuesdays, when the hotel is closed, the owner took us for a nine-hour trek, supplying all the food and drink. We also went fly-fishing and wild mushroom-picking, and sun-bathed on the terrace." (*Janice Carrera*) The *Eggwirt* does not supply soap: "But this is compensated for by the hospitality and good food."

Open All year, except 3 Nov–25 Dec, Tues.
Rooms 17 double, 3 single.
Facilities Bar, TV room, 4 dining rooms; terrace. Garden. Unsuitable for ♿.
Location In Ulten valley, *c.* 22 km SW of Merano.
Credit cards None accepted.
Terms [1996] B&B 42,000–50,000 L; D,B&B 62,000–68,000 L. Set meals 24,000 L; full alc 30,000–32,000 Sfrs.

SANTA MARIA DI CASTELLABATE 84072 Salerno — Map 18

Hotel Sonia BUDGET

Tel/Fax (0974) 961172
Via G. Landi 25

On beach in old fishing port 70 km S of Salerno, unpretentious family-run seaside hotel: kindly staff, "happy atmosphere", excellent for children. Good plain cooking, but dull breakfast. 35 rooms (15 new this year), simple but nice, some with balcony facing beach. Unsuitable for ♿. Amex, Visa accepted. Rooms 50,000–85,000 L. Breakfast 8,000 L. D,B&B 75,000 L per person Set meals 25,000–30,000 L. Recently endorsed, but fuller reports welcome.

SESTO 39030 Bolzano — Map 14

Hotel St Veit NEW/BUDGET
Europaweg 16

Tel (0474) 710390
Fax (0474) 710072

In a German-speaking skiing and summer resort in the Dolomites (Sexten in German), a young couple, the Happacher-Karadar, own and run this extremely *gemütlich* chalet-hotel, warmly furnished in local style. "Friendly welcome, superb views from the restaurant," says its nominator. "Attentive head waiter and excellent food: wonderful buffet breakfast, buffet antipasto and salad bar at night, good regional wines. Superb bedrooms, many with a balcony. In the summer, they hold a weekly barbecue in the gardens. One gripe: they failed to put on the heating, in a chilly September." Indoor pool with panoramic views, shared also by many bedroom balconies. (*Janice Carrera*)

Open Christmas–Easter, June–15 Oct.
Rooms 26.
Facilities Hall, *Stube*, restaurant; indoor swimming pool, sauna, whirlpool, solarium. Garden.
Location In resort, near Austrian border. 116 km NE of Bolzano, off road to Lienz. Parking.
Credit cards None accepted.
Terms [1996] D,B&B 95,000–120,000 L. Set meals 23,000–40,000 L.

SIENA 53100 — Map 17

Certosa di Maggiano
Via Certosa 82

Tel (0577) 288180
Fax (0577) 288189

Of the oldest Carthusian monastery in Tuscany (1314) only the cloister and tower remain, now forming part of this elegantly luxurious (and *very* expensive) little hotel (Relais & Châteaux), a kilometre outside the city walls. All is idyllic: the big swimming pool is in a garden of peach and apricot trees, overlooking vineyards. "Probably the best hotel we have stayed in. Although luxurious, it felt friendly and relaxed. The gardens were beautiful, the meals delicious, and the swimming pool was a delight. A magical experience." That rave this year follows others: "Wonderful. You enter through huge wooden doors into the cloister. In the library/games room you can sit amid books and play chess, already laid out on a lovely carved table. Service is quietly attentive. Our room was large and well equipped. The food was first-class Italian of a *nouvelle* type." Some rooms have antiques. You can dine or breakfast in the courtyard, or in a "ravishingly pretty" room. "All in all, the manners and civilised charm of an earlier epoch, bolstered by 20th-century plumbing." (*Caroline Thomson, M and KO*) But: "Some might find the intimacy, relentless good taste and attention to detail a little precious."

Open All year.
Rooms 11 double, 6 single. 3 in nearby annexe. Some on ground floor. 3 no-smoking. Air-conditioning.
Facilities 2 bars, 2 dining rooms, TV room, games room, reading room. Large grounds: garden, swimming pool, tennis, helipad.
Location 1 km SE of Siena, outside Porta Romana. Parking.
Credit cards All major cards accepted.
Terms B&B: single 400,000–500,000 L, double 500,000–700,000 L, suite

750,000–950,000 L; D,B&B double 740,000–1,190,000 L. Set lunch 80,000 L, dinner 130,000 L; full alc 140,000 L. 1-night bookings refused New Year, Easter, during the *Palio*.

Hotel Santa Caterina *Tel* (0577) 221105
Via Piccolomini 7 *Fax* (0577) 271087

Just outside Porta Romana, 2 km SE of centre, converted 18th-century villa. Attractive public rooms; 19 "large, charming bedrooms", many facing flowery terrace; "generous breakfast". No restaurant. Closed 8 Jan–7 Mar. All major credit cards accepted. B&B: single 150,000 L, double 190,000 L [1996].

Villa Scacciapensieri *Tel* (0577) 41441
Via Scacciapensieri 10 *Fax* (0577) 270854

On a hillside just outside Siena, amid olives and vines, is this handsome 19th-century villa. It stands in a park with large and delightful gardens, so views of the town are obscured by trees, but you can see the *campanile* and *duomo* and hear the bells ringing. The Nardi family owners and their staff are amiable. More praise in 1996: "A cool and welcoming haven. The gardens and pristine swimming pool were a delight, meals were copious and well served, though dinner was too expensive." Others have written: "Our split-level room in the modern annexe was large and airy, with views over the gardens. The food was good Italian bourgeois. Lots of loungers round the pool." Others have spoken of the quiet atmosphere and prettily furnished rooms. (*Hillary de Ste Croix*)

Open 14 Mar–mid-Dec.
Rooms 5 suites (1 adapted for ♿), 22 double, 5 single. 3 buildings. Air-conditioning.
Facilities Lift. Lounge/bar, TV room, restaurant (no-smoking); conference room; terraces (meals served in summer). Park: gardens, swimming pool (unheated), tennis.
Location 2.5 km N of Siena. Regular bus service. Parking.
Credit cards All major cards accepted.
Terms [1996] B&B: single 100,000–200,000 L, double 190,000–330,000 L, suite 250,000–400,000 L. Set lunch 54,000 L, dinner 65,000 L; full alc 85,000 L.

SIUSI ALLO SCIALAR 39040 Bolzano **Map 17**

Hotel Bad Ratzes *Tel* (0471) 706131
Razzes

Seis am Schlern is the German name of this skiing and summer resort north-east of Bolzano, at the foot of the Dolomites. Just outside it is this sympathetic if dour-looking hotel, which commands fine views, and is well run by two sisters of the Schmerlin family. A 1996 visitor was delighted: "A wonderful hotel: charm and efficiency abound. The widowed father joins his daughters in inviting guests to drink in the lounge by the fire. Comfortably furnished bedrooms and lounges with exquisite pieces. The food was delicious and copious." This follows earlier plaudits: "There's an excellent buffet breakfast, and superb food at main meals (despite limited choice), with huge salad and vegetable buffet. The owners seem to love children." "The rooms were large, with balcony. One feels part of the family: we were all invited to drinks on the terrace one evening." "The cakes at tea were a disaster for the waistline." There's lots for children to do. (*BW Ribbons, JR*)

Open 17 Dec–23 Apr, 20 May–1 Oct. Restaurant closed Mon.
Rooms 51. Air-conditioning.
Facilities Lift. Lounge, restaurant; indoor pool, sauna; terrace.
Location 3 km SE of Siusi which is 23 km NE of Bolzano. Garage.
Credit cards None accepted.
Terms [1996] B&B: single 92,000 L, double 184,000 L; D,B&B 106,000–141,000 L per person. Set meals 43,000–59,000 L.

SOVICILLE 53018 Siena — Map 17

Albergo Borgo Pretale — *Tel* (0577) 345401
Località Pretale — *Fax* (0577) 345625

Set on a wooded hill near Siena, this severe-looking stone tower (*c.* 1100) and its adjacent buildings have been converted into a stylish hotel in wide grounds. The large swimming pool amid trees, the "delicious dinners and good buffet breakfast" are all admired. An inspector wrote recently: "It is very remote, utterly quiet at night. We sat on the lawn, enjoying the glorious view. The food is genuinely Italian, changing daily on the four-course menu, with generous helpings. Service was delightful and friendly." There is a pretty dining room, but when the weather is fine meals are served on a terrace with views – for lunch in summer, there's an excellent poolside buffet, with tables amid trees. Some bedrooms are in cottages, furnished in excellent taste; some can be small and a bit dark. The main suite in the tower has panoramic views. (*D and KM*) Warning: large groups can arrive, spoiling the calm. And, last year, staff reductions appeared to be affecting the quality of service.

Open All year, except 3 Jan–14 Mar. Restaurant closed midday.
Rooms 11 suites, 24 double. 8 in main tower, 27 in cottages.
Facilities Bar, TV room, restaurant; conference facilities; terrace. Large park: garden, swimming pool (unheated), tennis, bowls, putting, archery, hunting, fishing. Unsuitable for ♿.
Location 7 km W of Sovicille, which is 15 km SW of Siena. Private parking.
Credit cards All major cards accepted.
Terms B&B: single 210,000 L, double 320,000 L; D,B&B 220,000–270,000 L per person. Set dinner 60,000 L.

SPELLO 06038 Perugia — Map 17

La Bastiglia BUDGET — *Tel* (0742) 651277
Piazza Valle Gloria 7 — *Fax* (0742) 301159

Set on the edge of a medieval town near Assisi, this "super little hotel", "very new and most comfortable", wins lots more praise this year. It is a well-modernised old mill house, with cool white walls and stone arches: there are wide views of wooded hills and valleys from some bedrooms, and from the broad sun-terrace where meals are served in summer. "Food is excellent and staff pleasant," runs one report this year. "Our room had a nice terrace garden. It was wonderful to look out over the Umbrian hills, sipping wine in the evening light." "At night, only a nightingale broke the quiet. The restaurant serves good typical Italian dishes, such as tender veal with truffles. The Faucelli family owners were generously helpful." "Staff were helpful, lending us umbrellas." (*Eve Gompertz, Dr M Holbrook, Mrs J James, Paul Palmer*) Breakfasts are mostly praised, but are "the usual rag-bag buffet" according to one report. The rooms vary in size, and not all of them have views.

Open All year. Restaurant closed 7 Jan–7 Feb.
Rooms 22 double.
Facilities Lounge/bar, TV room, restaurant; meeting room; terrace. Air-conditioning. Unsuitable for ♿.
Location On edge of town, 12 km SE of Assisi. Public parking.
Credit cards All major cards accepted.
Terms [1996] B&B: single 110,000 L, double 130,000 L, suite 160,000 L; D,B&B 100,000–145,000 L per person. Set meals 30,000 L; full alc 35,000 L.

SPOLETO 06049 Perugia — Map 17

Hotel Gattapone NEW — *Tel* (0743) 223447
Via del Ponte 6 — *Fax* (0743) 223448

This "discreetly elegant" small hotel, just inside the old city walls of very cultured town, is much patronised by leading musicians during the Spoleto festival. After a period with no reports, it is now renominated: "Pricey, but you pay for the privileged position away from the centre, overlooking the 13th-century Ponte delle Torri, the viaduct built over a Roman aqueduct straddling a wide wooded gorge. Rooms vary in size. Breakfast was better-than-average." There's a patio with views, and modern decor. (*HR*)

Open All year.
Rooms 9 suites, 7 double.
Facilities 2 lounges, bar; patio. Unsuitable for ♿.
Location On E edge of town, 300 m from *duomo*. Parking.
Credit cards All major cards accepted.
Terms [1996] Rooms: single 140,000–220,000 L, double 170,000–300,000 L. Breakfast 15,000 L.

TAORMINA 98039 Messina, Sicily — Map 18

Villa Belvedere — *Tel* (0942) 23791
Via Bagnoli Croce 79 — *Fax* (0942) 625830

"A blissful place", "a delightful hotel", "magical" – more admiration in 1995–96 for this B&B hotel owned and run by a cultivated Franco-Italian family, the Pécauts, and superbly sited high above the sea. Its lush semi-tropical garden is full of palm trees, one of which stands in the middle of the swimming pool: here "excellent" lunches are served. "What pleasure to have orange blossom growing through your balcony railings." Bedrooms are simply furnished but comfortable, and most have lovely views. The public lounges "are attractively furnished with antiques, and books". "The Pécauts were much in evidence and helpful, and the maids were friendly." The hotel is quite close to Taormina's busy centre, yet far enough away to be quiet and private. The gardens are "delightful", the view from the pool is "stunning". (*J Mainwaring, Alice Sennett, and others*) Top-floor rooms have a balcony; those facing the street can be noisy, but double-glazing has just been installed, and some quiet ones face the garden.

Open 16 Mar–10 Nov, 20 Dec–11 Jan.
Rooms 1 suite, 42 double, 5 single. Some on ground floor. Some air-conditioned.
Facilities Lift. 2 lounges, TV room, library, bar, breakfast room; terraces. Garden: swimming pool, snack bar. Sea 4 km: safe bathing.
Location Central, near public gardens/tennis court. Guarded parking (7,000 L).
Credit cards Access, Visa.
Terms [1996] B&B: single 70,000–146,000 L, double 130,000–228,000 L, suite 250,000 L.

San Domenico Palace Hotel *Tel* (0942) 23701
Piazza San Domenico 5 *Fax* (0942) 625506

This renowned palace hotel, on its high promontory, began life in 1430 as a monastery. In 1943, first Kesselring, then Montgomery, used it as headquarters and much of the original 15th-century building, apart from the cloister, was destroyed by bombing. In our own time, *Michael Frayn* has called it "the most delightful hotel we've ever stayed at anywhere", and *Frederic Raphael* has added: "It retains a certain tranquil gravity but is neither pompous nor intimidating, apart from its immodest prices. The rooms are lofty and quiet, although nothing can exclude the rasping buzz of the Vespas passing below the terrace, from which you have a vertiginous view of the despoiled coastline and the unspoiled sea. The bedrooms and bathrooms are sumptuous. The gardens, with swimming pool, are colourful; you can gaze at Etna from among the lemon trees." The newer Edwardian block is less attractive, but its bedrooms have the best balconies. Newer reports welcome.

Open All year.
Rooms 22 suites, 65 double, 24 single. In 2 buildings. Air-conditioning.
Facilities Lift. Hall, 4 lounges, bar, TV room, games room, piano bar, dining room; conference rooms (no-smoking); courtyard terrace. Garden: swimming pool, snack bar. Private beach (car service).
Location Central; on promontory on W side of town.
Credit cards All major cards accepted.
Terms B&B: single 275,000–400,000 L, double 440,000–685,000 L, suite from 500,000 L; D,B&B 320,000–495,000 L per person. Set meals 95,000 L; full alc 95,000–150,000 L.

Villa Sirina *Tel* (0942) 51776
Contrada Sirina *Fax* (0942) 51671

On steep hill leading down to coast, 2 km W of town centre, stylishly converted private villa amid shrubs and fruit trees, with swimming pool (unheated). Excellent food and service, interesting pictures and design. Closed 11 Jan–14 Mar. All major credit cards accepted. 15 rooms, all with sea or mountain view. Unsuitable for ♿. B&B double 160,000–190,000 L; D,B&B double 210,000–250,000 L [1996]. More reports, please.

TELLARO DI LERICI 19030 La Spezia **Map 17**

Il Nido di Fiascherino BUDGET *Tel* (0187) 967286
Via Fiascherino 75 *Fax* (0187) 964225

Just outside Lerici, above the lovely gulf of La Spezia where Shelley drowned, stands this bright and airy modern hotel, again much admired this year and last: "A real gem. It has a marvellous position on the clifftop – on the cliffside are little slots with tables and chairs, from which to enjoy a post-dinner glass. Delicious varied antipasto changing daily, good simply grilled fish, best pasta ever. Staff all friendly." The pretty white restaurant has splendid sea views; so do many bedroom balconies, but not those in the annexe. The main snag: it is 140 steps down to the small private beach, which is crowded in summer. (*GW*)

Open All year.
Rooms 32 double, 4 single. 20 in annexe 15 m.
Facilities TV room, bar, 2 dining rooms. Garden. Unsuitable for ♿.
Location 2 km SE of Lerici, 800 m from Tellaro. Parking.
Credit cards All major cards accepted.
Terms B&B: single 90,000–120,000 L, double 120,000–186,000 L; D,B&B 80,000–130,000 L per person. Set meals 43,000 L; full alc 60,000 L.

TORGIANO 06089 Perugia — Map 17

Le Tre Vaselle — *Tel* (075) 9880447
Via Giuseppe Garibaldi 48 — *Fax* (075) 9880214

"Always a favourite," say visitors this year returning to this elegant hotel on a hillside, in a charming Umbrian village south of Perugia. A former village hostelry, it has been expensively renovated by its owners, the Lungarotti wine firm, which also has a wine museum in Torgiano and runs wine courses. The hotel is very ambitious, full of ideas for special events, and its new manager, Giovanni Margheritini, comes from the *Hilton* in Rome. "We had an excellent dinner and buffet breakfast, staff were welcoming," say regulars, who last year took one of the new luxury apartments: "Rugs on polished tiled floors and plenty of space, but lighting could have been brighter." Older rooms are simpler. Public rooms are huge, with beamed ceilings, thick white walls, archways, terracotta tiles, comfortable sofas. Cooking is regional, using first-rate local ingredients. Breakfast is served in an attractive cellar. (*Pat and Jeremy Temple*) The hotel has been "moving up-market" and "the chef often appears in the restaurant". But one reader found that service was slow and poor when large outside groups were being catered for: "A waiter knocked a lighted candle into my lap, and they ran out of cash at the desk so we couldn't leave tips."

Open All year.
Rooms 13 suites, 46 double, 2 single. Some no-smoking. 5 in annexe, *La Bondanzina*, 100 m. Air-conditioning.
Facilities Lift. Reading room, TV room, games room, 2 bars, breakfast room, restaurant; conference facilities; terrace (meal service). Unsuitable for ♿.
Location 15 km SE of Perugia, just E of *autostrada*. Carpark.
Credit cards All major cards accepted.
Terms [1996] B&B: single 190,000 L, double 290,000 L, suite 400,000 L; D,B&B 60,000 L added per person. Full alc 65,000–70,000 L.

> There are many expensive hotels in the *Guide*. We are keen to increase our coverage at the other end of the scale. If you know of a simple place giving simple satisfaction, please write and tell us.

TORRI DEL BENACO 37010 Verona — Map 17

Hotel Europa BUDGET — *Tel* (045) 7225086
Via d'Annunzio 13–15 — *Fax* (045) 6296632

Quietly secluded from this busy Lake Garda resort, this converted Venetian villa stands a steep four-minute walk up the hill behind. It has a woodland setting, backed by its own large olive grove, with views over the lake and mountains; you can eat out in the garden in fine weather. The owners, Enrica and Franco Casarotti, are "charming people", all agree, and most recent guests, though not all, have been delighted. "We liked the well-tended gardens." "It is quiet and cool, with a good pool. To get such marvellous food in a budget hotel was stunning. Buffet breakfasts outdoors were lavish and a visual delight. One night there was a special show for dinner: a guinea fowl and salmon trout from the lake, both in a salt crust, were brought out with floral decorations." Others have written: "The hard-working Signora is amazing, as she passes from Italian to English, to German, to French, with total fluency." Many rooms have a balcony and lake view, and most are nicely furnished and of adequate size; a few are cramped and spartan. (*D and MH, and others*) Not everyone likes dining sharp at 7 pm, nor having to choose from the dinner menu at breakfast time. And a few readers are not impressed by the food.

Open Easter–mid-Oct. Restaurant closed Apr.
Rooms 17 double, 1 single.
Facilities Reading room, TV room, bar, restaurant (no-smoking). Park: garden, swimming pool (unheated); bicycle hire. Unsuitable for ♿.
Location 10 mins' walk from village. 45 km NW of Verona. Private parking.
Credit cards None accepted.
Terms B&B double 155,000–200,00 L; D,B&B (min. 3 days) 89,000–115,000 L per person.

TRISSINO 36070 Vicenza — Map 17

Relais Ca' Masieri — *Tel* (0445) 490122
Via Masieri 16 — *Fax* (0445) 490455

"Birdsong filled the air, and the distant views of the farm were magical. The food (*Michelin*-starred) was exciting." That lyrical description is for an old farmhouse that has been converted into a small, elegant restaurant-with-rooms, amid pleasant hilly country north-west of Vicenza. It is run by the grandson of one of the former farming families, and has eight guest bedrooms of varying sizes, renovated with style. "Ours was huge, with smart lacquered cabinets, large marble dining table, good modern lighting and a picture window with views. The shower room (no baths) was also huge. The basement made a charming room for the breakfast buffet. The small attractive restaurant had candlelight, old beams, restored frescoes on the walls, interesting old photos of how the farm used to be. An excellent dinner with local specialities. There's a large terrace for summer dining." (*Warmly endorsed by Felix Singer*)

Open All year, except end Jan–mid Feb. Restaurant closed Sun/midday Mon.
Rooms 1 suite, 4 double, 3 single.
Facilities 2 lounges, TV room, bar, restaurant; terrace. Garden: swimming pool (unheated). Unsuitable for ♿.

Location 2 km NW of Trissino. 21 km NW of Vicenza. Guarded parking.
Credit cards Access, Amex, Visa.
Terms Rooms: single 100,000 L, double 140,000 L, suite 180,000 L. Breakfast 12,000 L. Set lunch 60,000 L, dinner 80,000 L; full alc 60,000 L.

URBINO 61029 Pesaro e Urbino — Map 17

Albergo Italia NEW/BUDGET — *Tel* (0722) 2701
Corso Garibaldi 52

Near ducal palace, in main street of superb walled hill-town poorly served by hotels, small, unassuming B&B hotel with lovely views of hills. Charming padrona. *Rooms very clean, water very hot, but lighting poor. Pleasant terrace for breakfast; garden. Closed Sept. No credit cards accepted. 45 rooms: single 53,000 L, double 80,000 L. Breakfast 8,000 L.*

VARENNA 22050 Como — Map 17

Hotel du Lac — *Tel* (0341) 830238
Via del Prestino 4 — *Fax* (0341) 831081

By the water's edge, in an old unspoilt fishing village on the east side of Lake Como, stands this traditional little hotel. It has fairly modern decor, and a recent devotee: "A wonderful position in a lovely village, with no traffic noise. It's family-run, with excellent service and enjoyable *demi-pension* meals." Many rooms have a balcony with views of lake or mountains. Part of the restaurant is open-air, "perfect for a balmy night, watching the sun set". (*HJMT*) Some rooms are small.

Open 1 Mar–31 Dec. Restaurant closed 1 Nov–28 Feb.
Rooms 1 suite, 12 double, 5 single. 1 on ground floor.
Facilities Lift. 2 lounges, TV room, bar, restaurant; terrace. On lake: safe bathing.
Location In village, 22 km N of Lecco. Private parking.
Credit cards All major cards accepted.
Terms [1996] Rooms: single 135,000 L, double 225,000 L. Breakfast 19,000 L; D,B&B 170,000–190,000 L per person. Set meals 52,000 L. Reduced rates for children sharing parents' room.

VENICE — Map 17

Pensione Accademia — *Tel* (041) 5210188
Dorsoduro 1058 — *Fax* (041) 5239152
30123 Venezia

This popular B&B *pensione* is in a charming 17th-century villa beside a side canal, close to the Grand Canal at the Accademia bridge – a super location. The public rooms are attractive, but bedrooms vary in size and quality: those not facing the canal are quietest. You can take breakfast and drinks on the front terrace, or in the patio garden at the back. But a recent visitor, who found the staff courteous, and room upkeep much improved, added: "Guests are no longer allowed to bring snacks and picnics to eat in the garden or on the terrace, as the *Guide* used to state. Apparently it all got out of hand. Probably too many people reading their *Rubinstein*." (*A and AK*) First floor rooms were renovated this year, says the hotel.

Open All year.
Rooms 1 suite, 21 double, 5 single. Air-conditioning. 2 on ground floor.
Facilities Lounge, bar, TV room, breakfast room. Garden. Unsuitable for ♿.
Location Central, near Grand Canal.
Credit cards All major cards accepted.
Terms [1996] B&B: single 110,000–150,000 L, double 165,000–280,000 L, suite 225,000–280,000 L.

Hotel Ala
Campo Santa Maria del Giglio 2494
30124 Venezia

Tel (041) 5208333
Fax (041) 5206390

This neat, efficient if somewhat impersonal hotel stands on a small canal just off the Grand Canal, near St Mark's. It has its own jetty for gondolas, also a roof-terrace with easy chairs and a view. Recent guarded approval: "Our well-appointed room overlooked a busy square, visible through prolific geraniums. There was some noise, but not seriously disturbing, and acceptable as part of the ambience of Venice. Room staff were pleasant, desk staff helpful but a bit condescending, very Venetian." Other views: "We had a great little terrace. Room furniture was modern." "Our newly redecorated room had painted furniture and pieces of Venetian glass. Excellent breakfast (lots of pastries)." (*J and AL, and others*) Some have found rooms very quiet. They vary in size; some are said to be cramped. No restaurant: hotel guests get a 10 per cent discount at *Da Raffaele* nearby, where "the food is fine, and you can eat by a canal where serenading gondoliers pass by". A new suite with views this year.

Open All year.
Rooms 1 suite, 68 double, 18 single. Air-conditioning.
Facilities 3 lounges, TV room, breakfast room (no-smoking); roof-terrace. Unsuitable for ♿.
Location Just off Grand Canal, near public boat stop 13 (lines 1 and 2).
Credit cards All major cards accepted.
Terms B&B: single 130,000–190,000 L, double 190,000–270,000 L, suite 300,000–400,000 L.

Hotel Flora
San Marco 2283/A
30124 Venezia

Tel (041) 5205844
Fax (041) 5228217

Down an alleyway near St Mark's is this B&B hotel with a quiet walled garden where drinks and good breakfasts are served. The period furnishings are very *soigné*. "Our stay in Venice was turned into magic by the spectacular staff," say Americans this year. "The waiters were charming to our children: they made my eldest daughter feel like an adult." Others praised the comfort and warmth. Rooms, some newly redecorated, vary hugely: some are "large and wonderful", some "small but satisfactory", some "extremely poky".

Open All year.
Rooms 38 double, 6 single. 2 on ground floor.
Facilities Lift. Reading/TV room, breakfast room; small courtyard.
Location 300 m W of Piazza San Marco.
Credit cards All major credit cards accepted.
Terms [1996] B&B: single 170,000–205,000 L, double 230,000–280,000 L.

Londra Palace NEW
Riva degli Schiavoni 4171
30122 Venezia

Tel (041) 5200533
Fax (041) 5225032

Splendidly located facing broad canal, just E of St Mark's: smallish luxury hotel with beautifully decorated rooms, some overlooking canal, all quiet owing to effective glazing. Good, copious food, unremarkable breakfasts. All major credit cards accepted. 53 rooms: B&B: single 230,000–400,000 L, double 280,000–610,000 L. Alc meals 84,000–136,000 L [1996]. Fuller reports welcome.

Hotel Monaco e Grand Canal
Calle Vallaresso 1325
30124 Venezia

Tel (041) 5200211
Fax (041) 5200501

"We were very taken by this lovely hotel" – another plaudit recently for the *Monaco,* on the Grand Canal near St Mark's. It has a leafy courtyard, impeccably kept public rooms and "a thrilling restaurant on the waterfront, full of activity". Earlier views: "We had a peaceful room facing the courtyard, and enjoyed breakfast on the terrace. The food was delicious and the staff were friendly." "The reception room had the aura of Coutts & Co. Dinner on the terrace was enlivened by a rising tide which squirted water through the duckboards on to the guests. We learned to lift our feet every time a wave hit us, and the waiters served on tiptoe, affecting surprise as Venice continued sinking." (*KP, and others*) Some single rooms may be small and ill-lit.

Open All year.
Rooms 5 suites, 54 double, 11 single. Air-conditioning.
Facilities Lift. Salon, TV room, bar, piano bar, restaurant; conference room.
Location Central, near Piazza San Marco.
Credit cards All major cards accepted.
Terms B&B: single 350,000–380,000 L, double 470,000–590,000 L, suite 700,000–900,000 L; D,B&B double 550,000–750,000 L. Alc meals 150,000 L.

Hotel Saturnia e International
Via 22 Marzo 2398
30124 Venezia

Tel (041) 5208377
Fax (041) 5207131

Liked again this year, this "cool haven" is a smartly converted 14th-century *palazzo,* near St Mark's – "a lovely hotel, quite large, but not impersonal". Decor is stylish: the reception area is a Gothic patio with elaborate inlaid ceiling. Some bedrooms too have a carved and gilded ceiling. Reports this year: "Our room was large, pleasantly furnished, and quiet. The reception staff were welcoming, the bar was friendly, the breakfast buffet one of the best." "Excellent bathroom." The hotel's busy *Caravella* restaurant offers outdoor dining in summer, with good seafood dishes. (*Mr and Mrs John Hunt, and others*)

Open All year.
Rooms 80 double, 15 single. 1 suitable for ♿. Air-conditioning.
Facilities Lift. Lounge with TV, restaurant; courtyard, roof terrace/solarium.
Location Just W of Piazza San Marco. 40% discount at Tronchetto carpark.
Credit cards All major cards accepted.
Terms B&B: single 210,000–336,000 L, double 280,000–494,000 L; D,B&B 74,000 L per person added. Full alc 100,000 L. Children under 12 accommodated free in parents' room.

VERONA 37121 **Map 17**

Hotel Gabbia d'Oro NEW *Tel* (045) 8003060
Corso Porta Borsari 4a *Fax* (045) 590293

Admired in 1996 as "small, comfortable and friendly", this expensive B&B hotel lies in the traffic-free heart of the old town, near the Piazza delle Erbe. "The charming owner and her daughter were always behind the reception desk, giving help. There was a small panelled bar, a quiet beamed reading room with plenty of books, a peaceful inner courtyard with tables and chairs for drinks or snacks; the buffet breakfasts were enormous, excellent. The silk flower arrangements struck the only peculiar note. A tiny lift took us to our fourth-floor room, heavily beamed, but with good lighting, a small sitting area, excellent housekeeping, and a view of part of the *piazza*. For meals, we can recommend *Il Desco* (*Michelin* star), in a lovely old palace, and *Le Arche* (for fish)." Both are expensive. (*Pat and Jeremy Temple*)

Rooms 20 suites, 7 double. Air-conditioning.
Facilities Lift. Lounge, bar, reading room, breakfast room; courtyard. Unsuitable for ♿.
Location Central, in pedestrian street: car access for unloading, staff arrange secure parking.
Credit cards All major cards accepted.
Terms Rooms: single 250,000–450,000 L, double 310,000–450,000 L, suite 410,000–1,200,000 L, Breakfast 45,000 L.

Hotel Torcolo BUDGET *Tel* (045) 8007512 and 8003871
Vicolo Listone 3 *Fax* (045) 8004058

This "excellent" but inexpensive little B&B lies down a side-street near the Arena, and was popular again this year: "The two owners, Silvia Pomari and Diana Castellani, are distinguished and charming. Our spacious room had some antiques." Rooms do vary in size and facilities; all are double-glazed, but traffic noise can penetrate. "The owners and a charming daughter were always ready to help." There is a small breakfast room with attractive prints of Verona; in summer, breakfast is served on a terrace. (*NM Mackintosh, Sir Alan Cook, DA O'Bryen, and others*) "Taking a car into Verona is nightmarish", but the hotel has a street parking concession. The *Olivo* in the Piazza Brà is recommended for superb pasta and pizzas.

Open All year, except 10–30 Jan.
Rooms 15 double, 4 single. 4 on ground floor in annexe (5 mins' walk). Air-conditioning.
Facilities Small breakfast room; terrace (for summer breakfast). Unsuitable for ♿.
Location Central, off Piazza Brà, near Arena. Street parking.
Credit cards Access, Amex, Visa.
Terms B&B: single 90,000–112,000 L, double 125,000–155,000 L.

We quote either prices per room, or else the range of prices per person – the lowest is likely to be for one person sharing a double room out of season, the highest for a single room in the high season.

Hotel Victoria NEW *Tel* (045) 590566
Via Adua 6 *Fax* (045) 590155

Central, near Arena, newly enlarged and renovated, quite expensive. Pleasant, efficient staff; well-furnished rooms (but adjacent plumbing can be audible); elegant new reception area, "sumptuous" buffet breakfast in spacious room. No restaurant, but "seductive" snacks, including flambé'd dishes, served in piano bar. Sauna. All major credit cards accepted. 79 rooms. B&B: single 195,000 L, double 284,000–350,000 L [1996].

VICCHIO 50039 Firenze Map 17

Villa Campestri *Tel* (055) 8490107
Via di Campestri 19/22 *Fax* (055) 8490108

"Staying here was like being the private guests of nobility in their ancient country seat," say readers who arrived by bicycle and found Signor Pasquali "immediately warm and interested in our trip". This Relais du Silence is a handsome white villa with 13th-century origins, in its own huge park in the Apennine foothills north-east of Florence. "It is high up in a valley with panoramic views, from the house itself and from the swimming pool. We were led up a cool stone staircase into a 15th-century Great Hall, then to our room which had double doors three inches thick, with their original ironmongery beautifully restored. The room could have been a stage set for *Romeo and Juliet* – billowing white drapes, a large carved bed and antique wardrobe, a beautiful bathroom straight out of *Homes and Gardens*. Dinner on the terrace was an intimate affair, presided over by *Il Padrone* in relaxed aristocratic style, with a little notebook. No menu, but he carefully described the freshly prepared regional dishes. He chatted to the guests, or went inside to give us a minute or two of enthusiastic jazz on his early American piano, slightly out of tune (better for jazz, he said). After all this, breakfast was almost ordinary. But what a special hotel!" (*M and KO*)

Open 15 Mar–31 Dec.
Rooms 6 suites, 10 double, 1 single. 8 in nearby annexe. 2 suitable for ♿.
Facilities Hall, lounge, 3 dining rooms; terrace. Garden: swimming pool.
Location 5 km S of Vicchio. 35 km NE of Florence.
Credit card Access.
Terms B&B: single 160,000 L, double 220,000 L, suite 350,000 L; Set meals 50,000 L. Special winter rates.

VOLTERRA 56048 Pisa Map 17

Villa Nencini BUDGET *Tel* (0588) 86386
Borgo Santo Stefano 55 *Fax* (0588) 80601

Just outside city walls of this lovely medieval Tuscan town, a handsome 17th-century stone villa, very quiet, with amiable wine-selling owner. Large garden with lovely pool, fine views of countryside. Bedrooms adequate, if basic, with poor lighting; some have balcony. Bar. Restaurant planned for 1998. Parking easy. Access, Visa accepted. 35 rooms, mostly in new annexe. B&B: single 70,000–90,000 L, double 105,000–125,000 L. Reports on annexe rooms much needed.

Luxembourg

Hôtel Bel-Air, Echternach

BOURSCHEID-PLAGE 9164 **Map 9**

Hôtel Theis BUDGET *Tel* 9 00 20
Fax 9 07 34

Beside winding river Sure, 14 km NW of Diekirch, quiet and simple hotel in pretty wooded country. "Pleasant, chatty owner", good food and bedrooms. Outdoor dining possible. Tennis, children's games, bathing, fishing. Open 15 Mar–15 Nov. Access, Diners, Visa accepted. 19 rooms, plus 12 holiday bungalows. B&B double 2,400–2,900 Lfrs; D,B&B 1,820–2,770 Lfrs per person.

ECHTERNACH 6409 **Map 9**

Hôtel Bel-Air NEW *Tel* 72 93 83
1 route de Berdorf *Fax* 72 86 94

On the edge of this pleasant resort, in the wooded hills of the Luxembourg Suisse, stands this fairly palatial country house hotel

(Relais & Châteaux). It has large grounds, with pools, a huge fountain and Doric columns: pity that the façade by the gardens is such an ugly mix of styles. In fact, some readers have found the hotel too formal, and lacking in style in other ways, and it fell from the 1996 *Guide*. But it has its own qualities, such as good cuisine (*Michelin* star), and a reader this year was mainly happy: "Service is formal, but friendly. The gentleman at reception was very solicitous, and all the staff pampered us. Dinner was carefully prepared and service prompt; a decent buffet breakfast. The lounges are by far the nicest parts of the hotel: in the huge dining room, the glaring light from the chandeliers does not make for intimacy, and the furnishing of our room was functional rather than elegant, but it was spotlessly clean, with a well-equipped bathroom." (*Mrs H Langenberg*)

Open All year.
Rooms 9 suites, 21 double, 2 single. 6 no-smoking.
Facilities Lift. Salon, TV room, bar, 2 dining rooms; conference facilities; 2 terraces. Garden: tennis, children's playground.
Location W of town: turn off Diekirch road to Berdorf. Garage, carpark.
Credit cards All major cards accepted.
Terms B&B: single 2,800–4,300 Lfrs, double 3,500–5,900 Lfrs, suite 5,000–6,000 Lfrs; D,B&B 3,350–5,650 Lfrs per person. Set meals 1,650–2,700 Lfrs; full alc 2,500 Lfrs. 1-night bookings sometimes refused.

LUXEMBOURG — Map 9

Grand Hôtel Cravat — *Tel* 22 19 75
29 boulevard Roosevelt — *Fax* 22 67 11
2450 Luxembourg

Central, near cathedral, but quiet: efficient traditional hotel with very attractive rooms, newly renovated, many with good views. "Marvellous antique elevator." Restaurant and brasserie. Buffet breakfast. Underground carpark 50 m. All major credit cards accepted. 58 rooms. B&B: single 5,400–5,900 Lfrs, double 6,200–7,200 Lfrs. Set meals 950–1,050 Lfrs. Fuller reports, please.

Hostellerie du Grunewald — *Tel* 43 18 82 and 43 60 62
Route d'Echternach 10 — *Fax* 42 06 46
Dommeldange, 1453 Luxembourg

"A typical plush old-style hostelry, very Luxembourgeoise," says a recent visitor to this white hotel, set indeed beside a *Grunewald*, in the northern outskirts. "It's a smart place, heavy in feel, but with far more character than the modern hotels high-rising over the city. We had a very quiet but somewhat small and dark room. Breakfast was an *embarras de richesses*, served promptly by Turkish maids in a pretty conservatory. The restaurant, separately owned, has very fine food, such as rouget in herbs, or leg of quail, and is fronted by a charming young woman. But wine mark-ups are very high." "It's a rare treat to find a hotel where management is so genuinely concerned to be helpful, especially in a town like Luxembourg, which has been swamped by the Euro-bland and the Euro-brash. Rooms comfortable if slightly over-prettily done out (eg, pink chinoiserie). They are quiet, for the main road no longer passes this way." (*F and IW; endorsed by Lisa and Peter Simon*)

Open All year. Restaurant closed 1–24 Jan, Sat midday / Sun, public holidays.
Rooms 5 suites, 12 double, 8 single. Some no-smoking.
Facilities Lift. 2 lounges, bar, 3 dining rooms, 2 breakfast rooms (1 no-smoking); conference facilities.
Location At Dommeldange, 3 km N of centre, just off new Echternach road. Parking.
Credit cards All major cards accepted.
Terms [1996] B&B: single 3,900–4,200 Lfrs, double 4,700–4,900 Lfrs, suite 5,500–5,900 Lfrs. Set meals 1,590–2,700 Lfrs; full alc 2,700 Lfrs. Children under 7 accommodated free in parents' room.

Malta

Hotel Ta' Cenc, Sannat

ST PAUL'S BAY **Map 17**

Gillieru Harbour Hotel BUDGET *Tel* (356) 572720
Church Square *Fax* (356) 572745
St Paul's Bay SPB 01

New, comfortable, white-painted hotel, attractively sited on water's edge in old fishing harbour, now a populous seaside resort. Lovely views, large swimming pool. 2 lifts. Exceptionally helpful staff. Neat, clean bedrooms with balcony. Restaurant (no-smoking), pizzeria; new chef in 1996. Roof terrace; unheated outdoor swimming pool. Rock beach 50 m. All major credit cards accepted. 50 rooms. B&B LM12.50–LM26; half board LM4.50 added [1996]. More reports, please.

Please make a habit of sending a report if you stay at a *Guide* hotel, even if it's only to endorse the existing entry.

SANNAT Gozo **Map 17**

Hotel Ta' Cenc
Sannat VCT 112

Tel (356) 556819
Fax (356) 558199

This large luxury hotel, set back from cliffs on a small island off Malta, led to the genesis of the *Guide* in 1978 when the Editor, after a particularly happy visit, wished to share his pleasure with others. "One of the most captivating hotels in Europe," a reader wrote in 1981. Since then it has almost doubled in size, and its facilities have also expanded. It has a magnificent site by dramatic cliffs and is set in large grounds with olive and orange trees, cacti and geraniums, dolmens and temple ruins. Accommodation is in cottages, *trulli* and suites, built with the local honey-coloured stone, each with a private veranda. "Superb views, precious privacy and tranquillity," enthused a visitor last year. "Beautiful rooms: plain white decor, locally manufactured rugs on stone floors; furnishing of a high standard; well-equipped bathroom." Others found their *trullo* "cool, comfortable and attractive", and added: "They were accommodating about the needs of our two-and-a-half-year-old daughter. Service was good-humoured, if sometimes erratic." There are two huge swimming pools and a small one for children; they are unheated, and therefore cold early and late in the season. There is a tiny rock "beach" below the cliffs, "a bone-shaking" ride down by mini-bus. Plenty of other outdoor activities (see below) but not much indoor entertainment for children, which can be a problem in spring if the weather is stormy. The food (Italian with Gozitan dishes) has not always been liked, but a recent reporter wrote: "It matched the quality of the rest." At times the tranquillity is shattered by the popping guns of hunters of migrant birds on the cliffs. More reports, please.

Open All year, except end Dec/early Jan–mid-Mar.
Rooms 9 suites, 8 *trulli*, 7 family, 59 double.
Facilities Lounge, TV room, bar, wine bar/night club, snack bar, restaurant; conference facilities; shops. Large grounds: 2 swimming pools, children's pool, jacuzzi, tennis (coach available), bowls. Private rock beach with grill (free transport); scuba diving; boat trips; speedboat for hire.
Location S part of island, near Ta' Cenc cliffs. Gozo reached by helicopter or ferry from Malta.
Credit cards All major cards accepted.
Terms [1996] D,B&B LM35.20–LM60.50; full board LM41.80–LM68.20. Children under 2 accommodated free in parents' room; under 12 35% discount.

The Netherlands

Hotel Ambassade, Amsterdam

ADUARD Groningen **Map 9**

Herberg Onder de Linden
Burg. van Barneveldweg 3
9831 RD Aduard

Tel (050) 403 14 06
Fax (050) 403 18 14

The pretty village of Aduard, with its ruined 12th-century Cistercian abbey, lies just west of Groningen. Here, Geerhard and Petra Slenema own and run this low red-brick 17th-century inn, finely restored, full of red print in *Michelin*, and liked again recently: "A very enjoyable stay. The bedroom was simply but stylishly furnished. Food excellent, and a good breakfast is brought to you in the bar by a roaring fire. Plenty of flowers." The "delicious" food wins a *Michelin* star, and breakfast can include scrambled eggs, strawberries and six kinds of bread. There are five spacious bedrooms, under the exposed beams of the roof; also a terrace where you can breakfast or take drinks. "The owners do everything to make their guests welcome," was an earlier comment. (*JS*)

Open All year, except 1–10 Jan, last week July/1st week Aug, Sun/Mon.
Rooms 5 double.
Facilities Salon, restaurant; terrace. Garden. Unsuitable for ♿.
Location 6 km NW of Groningen. Private parking.
Credit cards All major cards accepted.
Terms B&B: single 110 glds, double 120–155 glds. Set meals 65–95 glds; full alc 120 glds. Residents are expected to dine in.

ALMEN Gelderland **Map 9**

De Hoofdige Boer BUDGET
Dorpsstraat 38
7218 AH Almen

Tel (0575) 43 17 44
Fax (0575) 43 15 67

This quiet village is near the charming old town of Zutphen, and not too far from Arnhem and the Kröller-Müller museum (splendid Van Goghs). This year, readers have again praised the Holtslag family's traditional country hotel, whose name means "the stubborn farmer". It offers a cordial welcome, copious and excellent main meals, plus a pleasant lounge with unusual beamed decor, and a tea garden giving on to open fields. "The rural locale is charming (cows in the field behind), and the busy staff were friendly." "There's an ambience of tranquil village life." The bedrooms are quite modern in decor, spacious, and well lit and equipped. Children are well catered for. (*Melissa McDaniel*)

Open All year, except 1–14 Jan.
Rooms 3 suites, 18 double, 2 single. 3 on ground floor.
Facilities Lounge, TV room, bar, restaurant; function room; table-tennis; tea garden, dinner terrace. Garden. Outdoor swimming pool, free to hotel guests, 5 mins.
Location Central, near church. Parking.
Credit cards All major cards accepted.
Terms B&B: single 97.50 glds, double 147.50–185 glds, suite 185 glds; D,B&B 110–127.50 glds per person. Set dinner 57.50 glds; full alc 65 glds.

AMSTERDAM Noord-Holland **Map 9**

Hotel Ambassade
Herengracht 341
1016 AZ Amsterdam

Tel (020) 626 23 33
Fax (020) 624 53 21

"The paragon of virtue, the hotel by which we judge all others" – one of several more eulogies in 1995–96 for this "delightful" B&B hotel, with its "lovely atmosphere". Always the most admired of our Dutch entries, it comprises nine adjoining 17th-century patrician houses on the city's grandest canal. Its "extremely courteous" co-owner, Mr Van der Velden, has now handed over day-to-day management to WJ Schopman, but his own influence is still felt. Praise this year: "The hotel is full of light streaming in from the long graceful windows, and from the crystal chandeliers. Gleaming pieces of antique furniture are everywhere." "We had a pretty, cosy room up under the eaves, with a view across the canal." Rooms, varying in size according to their altitude in these tall buildings, are furnished in period or modern Dutch style: "Ours, high-ceilinged, had a beautiful antique desk, two large velvet easy chairs, and a balcony facing the canal." The public rooms have many items from the owner's personal collection of antiques – old china, clocks, paintings. "Charming service, breakfast in a large bright room." This is "a vast selection, not for slimmers (cooked dishes cost extra). The coffee is plentiful, hot, delicious." The steps to upper floors are steep (normal in these old Amsterdam houses), but eight of the buildings are now accessible by lift. (*Paul Palmer, Ruth West, Lady Milford, and many others*) No restaurant, but light refreshments are served, and there is 24-hour room service. Ground-floor rooms can be noisy.

Open All year.
Rooms 6 suites, 44 double, 2 single. 6 on ground floor. 5 in annexe.
Facilities Lifts. 2 lounges, breakfast room (no-smoking).
Location Central. Meter parking; public garage 5 mins' walk.
Credit cards All major cards accepted.
Terms B&B: single 240 glds, double 295 glds, suite 395 glds.

Het Canal House *Tel* (020) 622 51 82
Keizersgracht 148 *Fax* (020) 624 13 17
1015 CX Amsterdam

The "entertainingly eccentric" Len Irwin, from Detroit, and his wife Jane own and run this handsome 17th-century merchant's house, set on a canal close to the Anne Frank House. It has a pretty walled garden, illuminated at night, and has long been a *Guide* favourite. "Friendly and characterful," said a visitor this year, while others wrote earlier: "Full of antiques, the house has a charm all its own. Our room at the top was smallish but well decorated, with a large bathroom and a charming view over the canal. Breakfast was help-yourself in a large, airy room full of flowers, overlooking the garden" (it has huge mirrors and a grand piano). Rooms vary in size: some are small, some big ones overlook the canal; the new modern ones at the back face the garden. "Our top-floor room had the original wheel hoist." Service is by friendly Irish or English girls in period costume. Breakfast is "plentiful". (*Christina Baron, and others*) Stairs are steep, as in most canal houses of this type, but there is a lift. No restaurant.

Open All year.
Rooms 22 double, 4 single. 3 on ground floor.
Facilities Lift. Lounge, bar, breakfast room. Garden.
Location Central, near Westerkirk. Street parking; garage nearby.
Restriction No children under 12.
Credit cards All major cards accepted.
Terms B&B: single 210 glds, double 225–265 glds.

Hotel de L'Europe *Tel* (020) 623 48 36
Nieuwe Doelenstraat 2–8 *Fax* (020) 624 29 62
1012 CP Amsterdam

"This was my first visit for 40 years, and I thought it even better than I remembered it – just the right mix, for my tastes, of the grand and the easygoing, something that the Dutch are especially good at." A veteran travel writer's view, this year, of an imposing "grand hotel" that gleams out beside the broad Amstel, in the heart of old Amsterdam. Built in 1896, and redecorated to mark its centenary, it has long been liked by readers. One recent account: "Our large top-floor room had a balcony overlooking the canal, and a marble bathroom. The public rooms were lovely, the service at reception superb. We enjoyed the food in the hotel's cheaper restaurant, *Le Relais*. The swimming pool has a wave machine." And another view: "Truly luxurious but not overbearing." Various kinds of breakfast are offered, from French to American, at varying prices. Bedrooms facing the river are quietest. (*Jan Morris, and others*)

Open All year.
Rooms 20 suites, 64 double, 17 single.
Facilities Lift, ramp. Lounge, bar, 2 restaurants; banqueting/conference facilities; indoor swimming pool, sauna, solarium; terrace overlooking Amstel (meals in summer).
Location Central, opposite Mint Tower and Flower Market (rooms double-glazed; quietest at back). Garage.
Credit cards All major cards accepted.
Terms [1996] Rooms: single 415–515 glds, double 515–650 glds, suite 715–1,475 glds. Breakfast 27.50–37.50 glds. Set lunch from 65 glds, dinner from 80 glds; full alc 110 glds. Children under 6 accommodated free in parents' room.

Jan Luyken Hotel — *Tel* (020) 573 07 30
Jan Luykenstraat 58 — *Fax* (020) 676 38 41
1071 CS Amsterdam

Near Rijksmuseum and Concertgebouw, in smart residential area, tall late 19th-century town house, now a private hotel with "personal atmosphere" and "an air of considerable elegance". 63 smallish, adequate bedrooms (some no-smoking); "splendid" breakfast in charming basement room; small patio. All major credit cards accepted. B&B: single 290–330 glds, double 330–435 glds. No restaurant, lots nearby.

Toro Hotel — *Tel* (020) 673 72 23
Koningslaan 64 — *Fax* (020) 675 00 31
1075 AG Amsterdam

This handsome mansion, newly renovated and painted yellow, has a fine setting beside the quiet Vondelpark, fairly near the Rijksmuseum. Its garden and terrace, "full of flowers and birdsong", face a long lake. The owners, Jaap and Mies Plooy, are "full of sincerity and devotion", "very friendly", likewise their cats. This year and last, readers have again been pleased. "A large, well-furnished bedroom, excellent breakfast in an attractive room. Beautiful gardens." "It is lovely, full of antiques in the public rooms, and good new repro furniture in the bedrooms. The Art Nouveau glass ceiling in the dining room is spectacular." "My room had huge windows that made it very light." (*Amos F Hutchins, and others*) No restaurant, but *Delikt* is commended among the several good ones nearby.

Open All year.
Rooms 20 double, 2 single. Some on ground floor.
Facilities Lift. Lounge, breakfast room (no-smoking). Garden. Not really suitable for ♿.
Location 1 km W of Rijksmuseum. Parking.
Credit cards All major cards accepted.
Terms B&B: single 140–170 glds, double 190–200 glds.

Report forms (Freepost in UK) are at the end of the *Guide*.

Amsterdam Wiechmann Hotel *Tel* (020) 626 33 21
Prinsengracht 328–332 *Fax* (020) 626 89 62
1016 HX Amsterdam

Fairly central, but quiet: converted canal house, now an elegant family-run B&B hotel with antiques in hall, cosy lounge, pleasant no-smoking room with canal view where good buffet breakfasts are served. Lots of stairs, no lift. 38 sizeable bedrooms (some for families), some facing quiet courtyard. No credit cards accepted. B&B: single 135–150 glds, double 225–250 glds. Endorsed again this year: "Lovely traditional ambience, splendid rooftop view."

BLOKZIJL Overijssel Map 9

Kaatje bij de Sluis *Tel* (0527) 29 18 33
Brouwerstraat 20 *Fax* (0527) 29 18 36
8356 DV Blokzijl

"Katie by the lock" is one of only six restaurants in the Netherlands to win two *Michelin* stars in 1996 (none has three), and suitably it is named after a 17th-century local heroine who became an expert cook. Owned and run by the "very enthusiastic" van Groeningens, it is "a delightful place, with very good food, friendly service and welcome", says a 1996 visitor. An earlier report described the curious setting: "Blokzijl is a tiny and beautiful Hanseatic town, clustered round a horseshoe-shaped harbour in a region of lakes, canals and marshes. The horseshoe is broken by a lock, which is itself crossed by a swing bridge – regularly in action as yachts (and ducklings) navigate the lock. This is overlooked by *Kaatje,* whose comfortable, well-equipped bedrooms are in a large white building across the bridge. The food is original, with superb breakfasts." "Our room was in stylish design. Dinners were wonderful." André Mol's cooking is French-influenced (eg, goose liver with choucroute) and beautifully presented. Breakfast is served on the terrace or in a room with views of the garden and the boating manoeuvres. (*Michael MacKenzie and Frederic Symonds*)

Open All year, except Feb. Closed Christmas/New Year, Mon/Tues.
Rooms 8 double. Air-conditioning.
Facilities Conservatory/breakfast room, 2 dining rooms; 2 terraces. Garden. Unsuitable for ♿.
Location Central (rooms double-glazed). Blokzijl is 33 km NW of Zwolle. Hotel across canal at Zuiderstraat 1. Parking.
Credit cards All major cards accepted.
Terms B&B: single 235 glds, double 325 glds. Set meals (3–7 courses) 80–145 glds; full alc 150 glds.

DELFT Zuid-Holland Map 9

Hotel Leeuwenbrug *Tel* (015) 214 77 41
Koornmarkt 16 *Fax* (015) 215 97 59
2611 EE Delft

Some rooms have a flowery balcony, at this spruce hotel on a picturesque canal, near the centre of historic Delft. A devotee returning in 1996 liked it as much as ever, alike for its rooms, its staff, and the breakfasts, which include salami, currant bread and eggs. An earlier view:

"We were given a warm welcome, and a large airy ground-floor room at the back of the annexe, with picture windows facing a small garden. It had a sitting area, and a large modern bathroom." "The olde worlde atmosphere was attractive." (*Andrew Palmer, Prof. Sir Alan Cook*) Rooms vary greatly in size (some are small). No restaurant: the *Klikspaan* down the road is liked – intimate, with French cuisine.

Open All year, except 24 Dec–1 Jan.
Rooms 1 suite, 27 double, 9 single. 6 on ground floor.
Facilities Lift. Lounge/bar (no-smoking during breakfast), TV room; conference facilities.
Location A16 Rotterdam–Amsterdam exit Delft-Zuid or Delft-Pijnacker; follow signs to Centrum, then Centrum West. Hotel marked "C" on white hotel signs. Pay parking adjacent.
Credit cards Access, Amex, Visa.
Terms B&B: single 95–131 glds, double 119–158 glds, suite 165–195 glds.

THE HAGUE Zuid-Holland — Map 9

Hotel Corona NEW
Buitenhof 39–42
2513 AH Den Haag

Tel (070) 363 79 30
Fax (070 361 57 85

Very central, on attractive square near Mauritshuis museum, old hotel now taken over by Golden Tulip *chain. Comfortable good-sized rooms, excellent service. Good breakfasts. Pretty restaurant; outdoor dining terrace; new chef in 1996. All major credit cards accepted. 26 rooms: 240–285 glds. Breakfast 25 glds. Set meals 45–50 glds [1996]. More reports, please.*

HEEZE Noord-Brabant — Map 9

Hostellerie van Gaalen
Kapelstraat 48
5591 HE Heeze

Tel (040) 226 35 15
Fax (040) 226 38 76

Heeze, near Eindhoven, is a pleasant town with a castle amid pretty scenery ("like a Cuyp"). Here, this elegant and expensive restaurant-with-rooms has a yellow façade, dark green shutters, lots of tables for outdoor eating and drinking. Owned and run by Jules and Josephine van Gaalen, it has been found "very enjoyable" again recently: "Rooms are comfortable, bright and well equipped. The restaurant has been redesigned in 'Mediterranean style', with bare floors, rustic chairs, a very relaxed ambience. Cooking was good, with Italian and Provençal influences (herbs and olive oil). There's a pleasant garden terrace." Others have spoken of the "helpful staff", "tremendous breakfasts". (*P and JT*) Some stairs to the bedrooms are steep.

Open All year, except carnival week, last week July/1st week Aug, 27 Dec–5 Jan. Restaurant closed Sun.
Rooms 1 suite, 13 double.
Facilities Lounge, bar, 2 dining rooms; conference facilities; terrace. Garden. Unsuitable for &.
Location 10 km SE of Eindhoven, between E34 and E25. Garage, carpark.
Credit cards All major cards accepted.
Terms [1996] Rooms 125–150 glds. Breakfast 18 glds. D,B&B 138–175 glds per person. Set meals 53–90 glds.

HILVERSUM Noord-Holland — Map 9

Lapershoek — *Tel* (035) 23 13 41
Utrechtseweg 16 — *Fax* (035) 28 43 60
1213 TV Hilversum

On S edge of city, 34 km SE of Amsterdam, fairly new modern hotel with 63 excellent smart bedrooms, mostly large, some with water bed. Attentive staff, "lovely breakfast with wonderful breads". Good nouvelle*-ish food with generous portions, not cheap. All major credit cards accepted. B&B 226–245 glds. Alc meals 46–69 glds [1996].*

LEUSDEN Utrecht — Map 9

Huize den Treek — *Tel* (033) 286 14 25
Treekerweg 23 — *Fax* (033) 286 30 07
3832 RS Leusden

Just south of Amersfoort (convenient for the wonderful Kröller-Müller museum), this handsome white 17th-century mansion has a quiet woodland setting beside a lake with wild ducks and swans. It has been called "an elegant and romantic hideaway" and "full of antiques, but needing renovation". A 1996 visitor was more explicit: "The rooms are spacious, but furnished in a 1950s seaside B&B style. It could be dreary on a foggy day in November. But in a hot summer, when you can make full use of the terrace, dine by the lake and walk in the woods, it is wonderful. The staff are friendly and relaxed. We enjoyed our August stay enormously." The cooking has been called "good and French". (*MV Jones*)

Open All year, except 20 Dec–3 Jan.
Rooms 1 suite, 10 double, 7 single.
Facilities Lift. Lounge with TV, restaurant; conference facilities. Garden.
Location 2 km S of Leusden, 6 km S of Amersfoort. Parking.
Credit cards All major cards accepted.
Terms [1996] B&B 89–163 glds; D,B&B 117 glds. Alc meals 75 glds.

ROOSTEREN Limburg — Map 9

De Roosterhoeve NEW/BUDGET — *Tel* (046) 44 93 131
Hoekstraat 29 — *Fax* (046) 44 94 400
6116 AW Roosteren

Owned and run by the Féron family, a sturdy low red brick house in a village near the river Maas (Meuse) and the Belgian border, just off the Maastricht-Amsterdam motorway. "Large, comfortable bedrooms in modern style with Dutch traditional features. Friendly, helpful reception. Excellent restaurant serving French and Dutch dishes. We arrived after the kitchen was officially closed, but they managed a good meal for us. Excellent buffet breakfast." A light dining room faces the garden and the outdoor swimming pool. Tables outdoors in the patio. Cosy bar. (*John Hurst*)

Open All year. Restaurant closed 1 Jan.
Rooms 30 double, 5 single. 10 in nearby annexe.
Facilities Lift, ramp. 2 bars, 2 TV rooms, restaurant; 3 conference rooms; indoor swimming pool; sauna, steambath, solarium. Garden: swimming pool; skittles.

Location 31 km N of Maastricht: turn W off motorway, towards Maasiek (Belgium). Parking.
Credit cards All major cards accepted.
Terms B&B: single 105–120 glds, double 145–165 glds; D,B&B 98–112 glds per person. Set lunch 30 glds, dinner 60 glds; full alc 75 glds.

VASSE Overijssel — Map 9

Hotel Tante Sien BUDGET — *Tel* (0541) 68 02 08
Denekamperweg 210 — *Fax* (0541) 68 01 22
7661 RM Vasse

"Full of rural charm", a modern red-roofed building with pretty, traditional furnishings, in a small village near the German border. It is named after "Auntie Sien", a forebear of the present owners, the Masselinks. "A wonderful little place," runs a recent account. "It was quiet and comfy. A roaring fire in the lounge, and fresh roses even in the bathrooms. Breakfast was excellent and copious. The owners greeted us warmly." (*RAL*) There's a large, pleasant garden and patio. We'd like more reports on the cooking.

Open All year, except 2–15 Jan.
Rooms 15 double, 1 single.
Facilities 2 lounges, TV room, bar, restaurant; conference rooms; terrace. Garden. Unsuitable for ♿.
Location In village, 15 km NE of Almelo. Parking.
Credit cards None accepted.
Terms B&B: single 82.50 glds, double 140 glds; D,B&B 95–99 glds per person. Set lunch 37.50 glds, dinner 42.50 glds; full alc 47.50 glds. Reduced rates for children.

WITTEM Limburg — Map 9

Kasteel Wittem — *Tel* (043) 450 12 08
Wittemer Allee 3 — *Fax* (043) 450 12 60
6286 AA Wittem

A royal-red carpet leads to the bedrooms, at this grey-walled 15th-century castle east of Maastricht. It has been revamped in neo-Gothic style and is now an elegant restaurant-with-rooms. The turret suite has windows facing the moat, and the grounds are "gorgeous" – a flower garden, ancient trees and a pond with black swans. Our latest report commended the breakfast, which is "well served by a waiter in formal attire" and has been called "outstanding" (there are several kinds of fruit bread, and maybe cherries or strawberries in season). "Excellent food, prompt service, a relaxed atmosphere." "Our second-floor turret room was large, with terrific views." "The personal attention of the Ritzen family gives warmth and cosiness." Main meals could include ravioli filled with scallops, grilled goat's cheese with quince sauce. Some lorry noise from the nearby bypass.

Open All year.
Rooms 12 double.
Facilities Lounge, bar, 2 dining rooms. Large grounds. Unsuitable for ♿.
Location On N278 between Maastricht (17 km) and Vaals. Parking.
Credit cards All major cards accepted.
Terms Rooms: single 160 glds, double 210 glds. Breakfast 25 glds. D,B&B 210–260 glds per person. Set lunch 65 glds, dinner 95 glds; full alc 175 glds.

Norway

Fossheim, Lom

BALESTRAND 5850 **Map 7**

Kvikne's Hotel *Tel* 57 69 11 01
Balholm

American visitors this year were delighted with this large chalet-style fjordside hotel, owned by the Kvikne family since 1877. Much visited by VIPs now and in the past (Kaiser Wilhelm II was a frequent guest), it's popular too with coach tours which, according to our correspondent, do not intrude, but only add to the gaiety and bustle of the place. For the splendid evening buffet, residents sit separately at quiet tables with lake views. Rooms vary in size: some in the old building are smaller and less sunny than in the modern annexe. One lounge is entirely decorated with handcarved ornaments and furniture in the local "dragon" style. There are "dragon houses" in the village too. (*Mr and Mrs A Andersen*)

Open 1 May–30 Sept.
Rooms 11 suites, 156 double, 43 single. 4 suitable for ♿.

Facilities 4 lounges, TV room, 2 bars, restaurant; disco, live music 6 nights weekly; meeting room. Garden: sundeck; beach. Walking, climbing, fishing nearby.
Location Centre of village.
Restriction No smoking: restaurant, some lounges, some bedrooms.
Credit cards All major cards accepted.
Terms B&B: 570–1070 Nkr; D,B&B: 770–1270 Nkr. Set lunch 135 Nkr; full alc 500 Nkr.

BERGEN — Map 7

Augustin Hotel
C. Sundtsgt. 22–24
5004 Bergen
Tel 55 30 40 00
Fax 55 30 40 10

"Charming, convenient, comfortable. Very much a city hotel." A warm endorsement this year for what its owners, Egil and Kjetil Smørrås describe as "the most traditional hotel in Bergen". Like many of the best Norwegian hotels, it has been in the same family for more than 75 years, and is popular for its convenient location opposite the ferry terminal and near the main shops. Rooms at the back are quieter than those overlooking the harbour. High quality modern decor blends well with the more traditional parts of the building. Breakfasts are said to be "Viking-sized". (*Mr and Mrs A Andersen*)

Open All year, except Christmas/New Year.
Rooms 2 suites, 74 double, 10 single. 2 suitable for ♿.
Facilities Lift. Lounge, TV room, bar, 2 restaurants, coffee shop; conference facilities.
Location Central, near harbour. Street parking.
Credit cards All major cards accepted.
Terms B&B: single 595–795 Nkr, double 990–1,190 Nkr, suite 1,500–1,800 Nkr; D,B&B: single 780–980 Nkr, double 1,360–1,560 Nkr. Set meals 145 –185 Nkr; full alc 325 Nkr. Weekend rates.

FJÆRLAND 5855 — Map 7

Mundal Hotel
Tel 57 69 31 01
Fax 57 69 31 79
E-mail fjaerland@bre.museum.no

"We have fond memories of sitting round the fire on a cold day in the cosy reception area, reading, and listening to Grieg CDs," writes a visitor this year to one of Norway's oldest and most traditional hotels. It is serenely set beside the country's longest and deepest fjord, in the shadow of its largest glacier, the Jostedalsbreen. A trim white clapboard building, it has been run by the Mauritzen family since it was built in 1891. *Guide* readers have long appreciated its lovely position and friendly atmosphere. It is furnished with antiques and objects of genuine family interest, such as a hand-woven stair-carpet; the bedrooms are "basic – cottage-type – but comfortable". Dinners tend to be adequate, "graciously served" but not very interesting, breakfasts, on the other hand, were "uniformly good". The hotel now has a "book-café", a combined book and coffee shop. (*Mr and Mrs A Andersen*). There's excellent walking all around.

Open 1 May–1 Oct.
Rooms 1 suite, 26 double, 8 single. Some no-smoking.

Facilities Lounge, music room, library/billiard room, bookshop/café. Garden: by fjord (boat, bike hire). Unsuitable for ♿.
Location Central. 180 km NE of Bergen. Boat and bus services. Carpark.
Credit card Visa.
Terms B&B 385–685 Nkr; D,B&B 795–935 Nkr. Set 4-course dinner (including wine) 370 Nkr.

GEILO 3580 — Map 7

Dr Holms Hotel — *Tel* 32 09 06 22
PO Box 38 — *Fax* 32 09 16 20

A large white building with a huge veranda, set amid the mountains of central Norway. It makes a good base for cross-country and Alpine skiing; there's fishing (through a hole in the ice in winter) and good walking in summer. "We spent an enjoyable week at this comfortable, well-run hotel," writes a recent visitor. "The plentiful breakfast buffet set you up for the day, and the three-course dinners were excellent. One evening we had a traditional Norwegian buffet, with delicious seafood. We enjoyed dog sledding and horse-drawn sleigh rides, and there are three indoor swimming pools." (*JB*)

Open All year.
Rooms 17 suites, 91 double (44 no-smoking), 15 single.
Facilities Lounge, conservatory, 2 bars, 2 restaurants; fitness centre, 3 swimming pools, games room; terrace. Skiing, fishing, walking nearby.
Location Central, near station. Large garage.
Credit cards All major cards accepted.
Terms [1996] B&B: 390–540 Nkr; D,B&B 660–1,230 Nkr. Set lunch 195 Nkr, dinner 295 Nkr.

HOLTER 2034 — Map 7

Trugstad Gård — *Tel* 63 99 58 90
Fax 63 99 50 87

A genuine working farm, timber-built in the 15th century, with sympathetic later additions, set amid pastureland and forest about half-an-hour's drive from Oslo; "a sophisticated yet homely experience". Everything is in the best of taste, and spick and span. The bar/pool room has the original pine walls, ceiling and wall cabinets, and small, typically Scandinavian windows. In the dining room and lounge, with white-painted wooden floors, the walls are hung with pictures and traditional artefacts. Bedrooms, furnished in traditional style, are in wooden houses dotted around the grounds. Martin Haga is a personable, friendly host, his wife Tove an excellent cook: her specialities include local smoked salmon, grilled reindeer steak, and aromatic wild strawberries spiked with green peppercorns; there's a wide-ranging wine list as well.

Open Hotel: May–Oct; restaurant: all year.
Rooms 1 suite, 4 double. All in houses in garden.
Facilities Lounge, bar, dining room, *caramboule* room. Large grounds: garden.
Location 42 kms N of Oslo. Take route 120 off E6, through 2 roundabouts (Skedsmokorset, Eltonåsen) to Trugstadvegen. Turn left to hotel 800 m.
Credit cards All major cards accepted.
Terms Rooms: single 350–430 Nkr, double 700 Nkr, suite 1,100 Nkr. Breakfast 55–95 Nkr. Set lunch 150–180 Nkr, dinner 220–280 Nkr; full alc 450 Nkr.

LILLEHAMMER 2600 Map 7

Mølla Hotell Tel 61 26 92 94
Elvegt. 12 Fax 61 26 92 95

Unusual hotel in converted mill in centre of town which hosted 1994 Winter Olympics. 58 small, cosy bedrooms with traditional decor: pine furniture, rag rugs, rocking chairs; mod cons include cable TV, shower room with heated floor; 3 suitable for ♿ and "allergy sufferers". Attractive, helpful staff. Good traditional breakfast, Rooftop bar with panoramic views, intimate restaurant; sauna, gym. All major credit cards accepted. B&B: single 595–850 Nkr, double 790–995 Nkr. Alc from 150 Nkr [1996].

LOEN 6878 Map 7

Hotel Alexandra Tel 57 87 76 60
Box 40, Nordfjord Fax 57 87 77 70

A large, modern hotel in extensive grounds amid spectacular fjord and mountain scenery. Warmly recommended for its well-equipped bedrooms, good facilities, excellent food and welcoming atmosphere. The staff are helpful and friendly, and the buffet meals "superb", with a huge choice of dishes: "I never imagined that I'd see salmon presented in so many different ways. The sweet buffet was equally breathtaking." A recent endorsement from a seasoned Norwegian traveller: "I quickly got over the battery hen feeling, and had an immensely enjoyable two-day stay." In the resort are splendid opportunities for summer skiing, mountain climbing, fishing, cycling and walking. (*LL, ES*)

Open All year, except Jan, 14–27 Dec.
Rooms 9 suites, 153 double, 36 single. 2 floors no-smoking.
Facilities Lift, ramps. Lounge, cocktail lounge, piano bar, restaurant, café; conference facilities; playroom; indoor swimming pool, sauna, solarium, fitness room; live orchestra, dancing Mon–Sat. Park: tennis, mini-golf, *boccia*, pedalos, rowing boats. Beach nearby: bathing, fishing, water sports. Cross-country and summer skiing.
Location 10 km SE of Stryn, on Nordfjord. Garage, free carpark.
Credit cards All major cards accepted.
Terms B&B: single 800 Nkr, double 1,130 Nkr, suite 1,970 Nkr; D,B&B 775–1,145 Nkr per person. 1-night bookings refused New Year, Easter.

LOM 2686 Map 7

Fossheim NEW Tel 61 21 12 05
Fax 61 21 15 10

The Garmo family have owned and run this old coaching inn since 1897. A stylish hotel nowadays, arranged around a courtyard which includes one of Norway's best-preserved 17th-century houses, it prides itself on its Norwegian cuisine; Arne Brimi is the energetic and inventive young chef. "A delightful, very Norwegian hotel, quiet although central, full of antiques. Our room was adorable, the staff extremely helpful; good breakfast buffet." (*Pat Malone*)

Open 1 Feb–23 Dec.
Rooms 1 suite, 39 double, 10 single. 3 cabins. 20 no-smoking. 1 suitable for ♿. Some in annexe.

Facilities Lounge, TV room, bar, restaurant; weekend disco. Fishing 100 m.
Location 100 m from centre.
Credit cards All major cards accepted.
Terms B&B 590–990 Nkr. Dinner 195–495 Nkr.

OSLO Map 7

Hotel Continental *Tel* 22 82 40 00
Stortingsgt. 24–26 *Fax* 22 42 96 89
0161 Oslo 1

A grand hotel in a prime setting, this venerable establishment, dating from 1900, has been in the same family for four generations. The hotel epitomises Oslo in its well-heeled comfort, without fuss or ostentation. Edvard Munch liked it so much that he gave it nine drawings, which hang in the bar. Our readers, too, have been pleased: "One of the best hotels we have stayed in; though large, it has a family atmosphere. We were upgraded to a lovely suite, with a large, well-equipped bathroom. The staff are charming and attentive, and the house-keeping is of a high standard. The buffet breakfast is average, but the Danish pastries are to die for, being home-made, as are all the bread and cakes – the bakers start work at 5 am. Excellent light lunches are served in the bar. We greatly enjoyed dinner in the famous *Theatercafeen*, which was fully booked every evening – and for a year ahead at weekends." Most bedrooms are huge, with a sitting area, and triple-glazed against street noise. Willy Wyssenbach, said to be Norway's most famous chef, runs the three restaurants. (*Alex and Beryl Williams*)

Open All year, except Christmas, New Year.
Rooms 18 suites, 102 double, 43 single. Some no-smoking. Air-conditioning.
Facilities Lifts. Lounge, bar, pub, breakfast room, 3 restaurants, café; conference/banqueting facilities; terrace. Unsuitable for ♿.
Location Central, between Royal Palace and National Theatre. Underground garage.
Credit cards All major cards accepted.
Terms [1996] B&B: single 1,085–1,585 Nkr, double 1,950 Nkr, suite 2,500–5,500 Nkr. Set lunch 150 Nkr, dinner 350 Nkr.

RINGEBU 2632

Venabu Fjellhotell NEW/BUDGET *Tel* 61 28 40 55
2632 Venabygd *Fax* 61 28 41 21

A find in 1996: "Way north of Lillehammer, on a splendid broad isolated plateau ringed by snowy peaks, is this excellent holiday hotel, popular for *Langlauf* in winter, hiking in summer. Austere-looking outside, it is cosy and friendly inside, yet spacious, with plenty of Norwegian character. Built in the late 1940s, and much modernised since, it has always belonged to the Tvete family and is now run by affable Lars Tvete and his shyer sister Line. We hugely enjoyed our stay. Our compact twin-bedded room was well equipped, with heated shower room floor. And, in the dining room, which has big panoramic windows, the Norwegian food was much more interesting than we'd expected – smoked reindeer ham, delicious marinaded trout and salmon, moose stews, fruit desserts with yellow cloudberries, etc. We even liked the strange Norwegian porridges, taken at all meals. The breakfast buffet had various kinds of pickled herring. Good coffee. In a big lounge with a log fire, there was dancing to the tunes of the hotel musician, Ralf, a joky character. Skilful skiing instruction; and intriguing *après-ski*, such as sleigh-rides with Alaskan huskies, and horse-rides with flaming torches to a Lapp wigwam in the woods. Neither rowdy nor glossy, it's a discreet hotel for families, with a warm, informal ambience. We did have two gripes. First, the odd meal times (lunch at 2 pm, dinner at 6.30 while you're still full), which are due to skiing routines and local custom. Second, the horrific Norwegian taxes on alcohol (a small beer in the hotel is £3.70). Oh, and the hotel cat, Mamapuss, slept on our bed (not a gripe)." (*KA and JA*)

Open 20 Dec–1 May, 1 June–10 Oct.
Rooms 3 suites, 43 double, 10 single. 6 suitable for ♿. 30% no-smoking.
Facilities Sitting room (no-smoking), lounge with bar/dance-floor, TV room, restaurant (no-smoking); games room, sauna, solarium; crafts shop; ski-room, resident ski instructor. Lake 100 m: fishing.
Location 18 km NE of Ringebu, 80 km N of Lillehammer. Parking.
Credit cards Access, Diners, Visa.
Terms [1996] D,B&B 390–1,620 Nkr. Set lunch 60 Nkr. Reductions for children.

UTNE 5797 — Map 7

Utne Hotel

Tel 53 66 69 83
Fax 53 66 69 50

This white clapboard building is one of Norway's oldest hotels. First opened in 1722, it was run until very recently by successive generations of the Blokhus family which founded it. That tradition came to an end in 1996, when it was handed over to the Utne Trust, but Fru Aga Blokhus, the last of the dynasty, who has now retired, still "pops in every so often", as she puts it, "to talk to old and new guests". Splendidly placed at the foot of a steep promontory where the Hardangerfjord branches into two small fjords – "high blue mountains across the water, sheer cliffs above it, a waterfall plunging down the cliff face and rushing through the village, apple orchards on each side". The decor is charmingly rustic, with painted Norwegian furniture. A visitor this year writes: "Our room had a large comfortable bathroom and a balcony overlooking the fjord. Dinner seating, by arrangement of the hostess, was a little like being on a cruise." "Good food in a convivial dining room. There are interesting drives, to the ice-fields for example, and fine walks along the fjord in both directions." Some rooms are in a small annexe up the hill. (*Mrs A Andersen, JM, ES*)

Open All year, except Christmas/New Year.
Rooms 1 family, 21 double, 3 single. 19 with facilities *en suite*. 8 in annexe.
Facilities 2 lounges, bar, games room; restaurant; terrace. Garden. Walking, water sports nearby. Unsuitable for ♿.
Location Central. Opposite boat landing.
Restriction No smoking: restaurant, 1 lounge.
Credit cards All major cards accepted.
Terms [1996] B&B 460–580 Nkr per person. Set lunch 125–140 Nkr, dinner 210 Nkr.

> Few of our readers visit Norway. If you have been recently and can recommend a hotel or comment on any of our entries, please let us hear from you.

Portugal

Hotel da Lapa, Lisbon

Nearly half of our Portuguese entries are government-sponsored *pousadas (pousar* means to set down, to rest). Like the *paradores,* their Spanish counterparts, many *pousadas* are converted castles, monasteries or other historic buildings, often found atmospheric or even romantic by our readers. Some other *pousadas* are purpose-built, usually in a rural style, to help tourists in areas where hotels are lacking. Except in the case of the luxury *pousadas,* their amenities are often fairly simple. It is advisable to book well ahead if possible: *pousadas* are not very big, and they tend to be used by coach tours, or, in towns, by business people. The central booking office in Lisbon is: Enatur, Avenida Santa Joana a Princesa 10, 1700 Lisbon; *tel* (01) 848 12 21, *fax* (01) 848 43 49.

Simpler accommodation can be found at *estalagemes.* These are country inns that usually do not offer a full range of hotel services. Some are featureless and modern, but those in older buildings may have a charm that compensates for their simplicity. *Estalagemes* and *pousadas* are signposted at the entrance to towns and villages. In larger towns and resorts, some international chains are represented – Holiday Inn,

Novotel, for example – but they lack the individuality that could earn them a place in these pages.

There are also private country house or manor hotels that offer B&B, and sometimes other meals too by arrangement. Some are called *quintas*. They are registered with the tourism department and display a metal plaque with the symbol TER. There are three categories. *Turismo de Habitação* (TH), the most upmarket, comprises manors or residences of recognised architectural value; you might be hospitably received in an elegant *palacete* or *solar*. Simpler accommodation is offered by *Turismo Rural* (TR), in rustic houses with rural or village settings. Simplest of all is the *Agroturismo* (AT) accommodation in farmhouses or farm buildings: here visitors can even take part in farm work, normally unpaid! Advance booking is advised for all these categories, either directly with the owners, or through specialist operators whose names are listed in tourist offices. For *Turismo de Habitação*, you should contact: Privetur, Rua Castilho, 209-1 Ft, 1000 Lisbon; *tel* (01) 65 49 53.

Portugal is a well-organised tourist country. Even in quite remote hotels, you will often find staff speaking good English, or maybe French.

AMARANTE 4600 Porto — Map 13

Pousada de São Gonçalo BUDGET — *Tel* (055) 46 11 23
Serra do Marão — *Fax* (055) 46 13 53

Up a steep winding road, between the picturesque little towns of Amarante and Vila Real, is this mountain-top *pousada*. The views and sunsets are superb, the interior is warm and cosy, and there's a "country house atmosphere". "A pleasant place, with charming staff, good food, nicely served breakfast," runs a recent report. "The bedroom furniture had brightly painted carvings. The wind howled off the mountains, but windows are being double-glazed." Bedrooms are "a bit old-fashioned, but adequate". Some local dishes. (*JW*)

Open All year.
Rooms 15 double. Some on ground floor.
Facilities Lounge, TV room, bar, restaurant. Small garden.
Location 9 km E of Amarante on N15 to Vila Real.
Credit cards All major cards accepted.
Terms B&B: single 8,500–12,500 esc, double 10,000–14,500 esc. Set meals 3,500 esc.

BUÇACO 3050 Aveiro — Map 13

Palace Hotel NEW — *Tel* (031) 93 01 01
Floresta do Buçaco, Mealhada — *Fax* (031) 93 05 09

North of Coimbra, this unusual, indeed "bizarre", luxury hotel lies in the midst of a famous walled forest of oak and cypress, high on the ridge of Buçaco. It dropped from the 1995 *Guide* after reports of "tatty" bedrooms. Whether or not they have now been improved, the hotel and its setting entranced an American reader in 1996: "As you enter the gates of this magical forest, there's a sense of having strayed into a fairy-tale realm. It's an astonishing building, this *fin de siècle* hunting-lodge grafted on to a medieval monastery, beautifully tended and graciously welcoming. The interior is filled with antiques – fabulous *azulejos*, stained glass, and armour, yet there's no 'preserved in amber' air. The atmosphere is of unruffled calm and warmth, and the staff are impressive. In the grand dining room, the food matches the setting: the wine from the hotel's own vineyards is superb, and reasonably priced. I loved eating on the large terrace overlooking the gardens. My high-ceilinged, spacious bedroom looked over the woods, which are incredible. Mossy paths wind past medieval Benedictine hermitages, sacred well-springs, an abundance of exotic trees brought from all over the world by Portuguese explorers in the 16th/17th centuries." (*Lynn S Hay*) "Very Byronic"; "food the best we had in Portugal", were earlier comments. The "pleasant, smart staff", and the bathrooms are also admired.

Rooms 6 suites, 59 double. Air-conditioning.
Facilities Lift. Lounge, bar, restaurant. Large garden: tennis. Unsuitable for ♿.
Location 22 km N of Coimbra on N234. Garage, carpark.
Credit cards All major cards accepted.
Terms [1996] B&B 25,000–33,000 esc; D,B&B 11,000 esc. Set meals 6,500 esc.

CANIÇADA 4850 Braga — Map 13

Pousada de São Bento — *Tel* (053) 64 71 90
Vieira do Minho — *Fax* (053) 64 78 67

On N103 E of Braga, in Peneda-Gerês National Park, small former hunting lodge in lovely valley with mountain views. Dull-looking outside, but charming inside with welcoming, intimate ambience. 29 spacious air-conditioned rooms, with leather bedheads and rustic furniture. Food unremarkable, but service obliging. Swimming pool; river and lake nearby. All major credit cards accepted. B&B double 14,500–22,000 esc. Alc 4,200 esc [1996]. More reports needed.

CASCAIS 2750 Lisboa — Map 13

Hotel Albatroz — *Tel* (01) 483 28 21
Rua Frederico Arouca 100 — *Fax* (01) 484 48 27

Built in 1873 as a royal residence, this opulent villa stands on a rocky headland in a well-known fishing port west of Lisbon. Most bedrooms are in a modern wing, but the best are in the older part. Readers are rapturous: "From the moment we arrived it was a love affair. Charming and efficient staff, ancient tiled frescoes, beautiful flowers, rugs and antiques, lovely bar hanging out over the ocean. All was wonderful, *not* grand. Our smallish room over the bay was light and bright, bathroom luxurious. Dining room handsome, food and service excellent." "Pool small but ideal for sunbathing. Good breakfast, lovely view from restaurant." Endorsed this year: "Superb, very quiet, with superb food." (*Diana Nairn, and others*) A new manager this year, José Tomáz de Mello Breyner.

Open All year.
Rooms 3 suites, 35 double, 2 single. 2 on ground floor. Air-conditioning.
Facilities Lifts. Lounge, bar with terrace, restaurant; conference facilities; terrace: swimming pool.
Location Central, near beach. Garage, parking.
Credit cards All major cards accepted.

Terms B&B: single 21,500–37,000 esc, double 25,000–44,000 esc, suite 35,000–65,000 esc. Full alc 5,000 esc.

CONDEIXA-A-NOVA 3150 Coimbra **Map 13**

Pousada de Santa Cristina *Tel* (039) 94 40 25
Fax (039) 94 30 97

In small town 15 km SW of Coimbra, near superb Roman ruins of Conimbriga, new modern white pousada *built in local style. 45 comfortable rooms, good bathrooms; "delightful young staff", if sometimes slow. Varied breakfast. Swimming pool, tennis. All major credit cards accepted. B&B: single 17,000 esc, double 19,000 esc. Set meals 3,000 esc [1996]. Reports on meals welcome.*

ÉVORA 7000 **Map 13**

Pousada dos Lóios *Tel* (066) 240 51
Largo Conde de Vila Flor *Fax* (066) 272 48

Évora, a showpiece of Portugal, is a fascinating walled town with a Roman temple, Moorish architecture, and a superb cathedral. This *pousada* is also a showpiece – a converted 16th-century monastery, its spacious public rooms furnished with antiques. "The public rooms are exquisite, the swimming pool glorious. Our room was small but very fine." That 1996 report echoes other recent praise: "We enjoyed the patio, where after dinner a pianist played discreetly – oh, so romantic. Dinner competent, breakfast a bountiful buffet, service a bit slow but friendly." "Our room had two single beds carved with ferocious-looking eagles, and contained a mass of orange blossom – the scent was wonderful." But rooms vary: some are spacious, facing a courtyard, others are more like "austere and cramped" monks' cells; and one reader felt the public rooms were "dead and museum-like". Food has been called "adequate". (*Claire Wrathall, R and DT, and others*) One reader found staff "rude and unhelpful" when she reported that money had been stolen from her locked room.

Open All year.
Rooms 1 suite, 31 double.
Facilities Salons, restaurant, refectory; cloisters. Swimming pool.
Location Central, opposite Temple of Diana. Limited parking.
Credit cards All major cards accepted.
Terms [1996] B&B: single 25,000 esc, double 28,000 esc. Alc 3,300–5,500 esc.

Quinta do Pintor NEW/BUDGET *Tel* (066) 269 15
Estrada dos Canaviais

"We had a lovely time in this wonderful spot," say 1996 visitors to this low white farmhouse outside Évora, newly converted, with just five bedrooms. "The charming rooms have tiled floors and hand-painted traditional furniture from the Alentejo; bathrooms are new, with large showers. The comfortable public rooms are similarly furnished. We had dinner with the family: the food was all home-made and delicious. The friendly owners don't really speak English, but their son acted as interpreter." (*Suzanne Gallee*)

Open All year.
Rooms 5 double.
Facilities Lounge, dining room; patio.
Location 3 km W of Evora, on Canaviais road. Parking.
Credit cards None accepted.
Terms D,B&B double 8,000 esc. Set meals 1,800 esc.

FUNCHAL 9000 Madeira — Map 13

Quinta da Penha de França BUDGET — *Tel* (091) 22 90 87
Rua da Penha de França — *Fax* (091) 22 92 61

"An absolute winner. We spent seven happy days in one of the garden rooms, sharing a private tropical garden with three others. The staff were so kind" – another plaudit this year for a hotel of character near the harbour, owned and run by Muriel Ribeiro, who is very much in evidence. Others have written: "Pool, poolside service, bar and restaurant all excellent"; "lying by the pool listening to the birds in the jacaranda trees was quite an experience"; "a pleasant atmosphere and superb staff". The original handsome villa has been tactfully extended over the years: the newest wing, overlooking the ocean, is down a steep path from the old hotel. This wing was enjoyed again this year, save that it can suffer from traffic noise. All its bedrooms have a terrace or balcony and a sea view. There are lovely gardens and sea-water swimming pools. There is no full restaurant, but light meals are served on the terrace, or in *Joe's Snack Bar* ("an absolute delight", "food quite good", are this year's verdicts) (*Mr and Mrs J Keeble, Andrew and Celia Payne, Antony Fletcher, and many others*) Guests are given a complimentary Madeira cake on their birthday.
Open All year.
Rooms 3 suites, 70 double. 29 in garden annexe. 33 in new annexe by sea.
Facilities Lounge, TV lounge, 2 bars, 2 snack bars (no-smoking); terrace. Large garden: 2 swimming pools (1 heated); sea, rock beach nearby. Unsuitable for ♿.
Location Central, near harbour, between *Savoy* and *Casino Park* hotels. Parking.
Credit cards All major cards accepted.
Terms B&B: single 10,000–15,500 esc, double 13,600–19,000 esc, suite 17,300–20,400 esc. Dish of the day in snack bar 1,500 esc.

Reid's Hotel — *Tel* (091) 700 71 71
Estrada Monumental 139 — *Fax* (091) 700 71 77

An orchestra plays in the bar at night, and old traditions are kept up, eg, afternoon tea on the terrace and formal dress for dinner in the main restaurant. Such is *Reid's*, survivor from an earlier era of travel, when it was quite a British institution. For more than a century it has played host to celebrities of all sorts (Churchill's name is in the visitors' book) – and nowadays to well-heeled package tourists. "It has genuine colonial charm, but can still feel stuffy," says one writer. The subtropical gardens, and the clifftop setting above Funchal bay, are superb. There are two swimming pools, where a buffet lunch is served; or you can walk down through the gardens to swim in the sea or a rock pool. All sea-facing bedrooms have a balcony. The public rooms, impressive and high-ceilinged, include "a superb, pre-war-style billiard room". Guests without glad rags can dine informally in the clifftop trattoria, or in the French restaurant. Recent reports suggest that meals, both in the dining room and at the poolside, are not as good as they used to be. As we went to press, we learned that Reid's had changed hands. The new owner, Orient-Express, has promised "to preserve the hotel's grand traditions", while adding further bedrooms. We'd be grateful for reports on this new development.

Open All year.
Rooms 22 suites, 131 double, 15 single. All air-conditioned. 73 in garden annexe. Some on ground floor.
Facilities Lifts. 3 lounges, TV room, 2 bars, card room, billiard room, 3 restaurants, breakfast room; bar terrace, tea terrace. 10-acre garden: 2 swimming pools, poolside buffet, tennis, children's play area; lift/stairs to swimming pool, sea: windsurfing, sailing, fishing. Unsuitable for ♿.
Location 1 km from town centre. Parking.
Credit cards All major cards accepted.
Terms B&B: single 27,000–64,000 esc, double 41,000–90,000 esc, suite 74,000–215,000 esc; D,B&B (obligatory in high season) 7,100 esc per person added. Full alc 6,000–10,000 esc. Min. stay 14 days Christmas/Easter.

GUIMARÃES 4800 Braga — Map 13

Pousada de Santa Marinha — *Tel* (053) 51 44 53
Estrada da Penha — *Fax* (053) 51 44 59

"The enormous public rooms are wonderful, as are the formal gardens and the woods behind." More recent acclaim for an above-average *pousada*, a finely converted 12th-century monastery overlooking the town, with views of the hills north-east of Porto. Earlier views: "Someone has managed to get the decor exactly right. The staff were lovely – young and friendly." "The huge reception rooms are filled with antiques, oil paintings, luxurious carpets, hand-painted wall-tiles." Food, served in the arcaded monks' hall, is thought "acceptable", with "delicious cakes" for breakfast. (*GEW, and others*) Readers consider the former cells, each with private bath, to be more attractive ("ours even had a prayer stool") than those in a modern wing, which are luxurious but more impersonal.

Open All year.
Rooms 2 suites, 48 double. Air-conditioning.
Facilities Lift. Salons, bar, 3 dining rooms; conference facilities; courtyard, terrace. Garden.
Location 2.5 km E of town, on road to Penha. Parking.
Credit cards All major cards accepted.
Terms [1996] B&B: single 25,000 esc, double 28,000 esc. Alc 3,500–5,200 esc.

LISBON — Map 13

Hotel da Lapa NEW — *Tel* (01) 395 00 05
Rua do Pau de Bandeira 4 — *Fax* (01) 395 06 65
1200 Lisboa

This 19th-century palace, built for the Count of Valanças, was converted six years ago into a luxury hotel by the owners of the *Albatroz*, in nearby Cascais (*qv*). It is set in a residential area above the city (stunning views), surrounded by a large garden with mature trees, cascades, and a huge swimming pool. Palatial bedrooms in the original building are decorated with Portuguese motifs, and original paintings and etchings by local artists; a magnificent suite has large terraces and a view of the Tagus; there are apartments in former stables for long-term visits. Lower down, a large new building houses modern bedrooms, each with a secluded flowery balcony and a luxurious modern bathroom with *azulejos* (glazed tiles). The grand public rooms are hung with tapestries and have patterned marble floors. There is a health club with a large indoor pool. "A fabulous hotel with a great staff," writes the nominator, "they aim to please, and they do. The restaurant serves Portuguese and international food. There are terraces for coffee, snacks, etc. Breakfast is a huge buffet." (*Alfred Knopf Jr*)

Open All year.
Rooms 8 suites, 78 double. 22 in main house. Many with balcony.
Facilities Lounge, bar, breakfast room, restaurant; conference/function facilities; health suite: swimming pool, gym, etc. Large garden: swimming pool.
Location Near Monsanto Park and zoo; 15 mins by car to centre. Underground carpark.
Credit cards All major cards accepted.
Terms [1996] Rooms 32,000–35,000 esc. Breakfast 2,750 esc. Alc meals 5,750–7,600 esc.

Albergaria Senhora do Monte *Tel* (01) 886 60 02
Calçada do Monte 39 *Fax* (01) 887 77 83
1100 Lisboa

"Certainly one of the most spectacular views of any hotel in any city": this B&B stands high on one of Lisbon's many hills, in a slightly rundown residential area of coloured tile-faced houses, quite close to the historic Alfama district. Bedrooms are simple but clean and bright, with modern bathrooms. More praise this year: "Our comfortable modern room had a little balcony and pretty tiled bath. Staff were a bit reserved but not unfriendly." Most rooms have the admired city view, which is best from the rooftop bar where breakfast is served. "Watching the lights in the city, on the river and on the castle was magic." Breakfast is considered adequate, nothing special; but most readers find the staff friendly. Several good, cheap fish restaurants nearby, such as *Via Graça*. And Lisbon's most impressive viewing park, "with panoramic views over the city", is 75 metres away. (*AD Canning-Jones, Carolyn Mathiasen, NFC*) A visitor this year warns that the bar, the lift and the plumbing can be noisy: "Best avoid floors 2 and 3, and any rooms near the lift."

Open All year.
Rooms 4 suites, 20 double, 4 single. Some on ground floor with terrace. Air-conditioning.
Facilities TV lounge, rooftop bar/breakfast room. Unsuitable for ♿.
Location In upper town above Castelo São Jorge. Tram to centre 500 m.
Credit cards All major cards accepted.
Terms B&B: single 12,000–13,500 esc, double 15,000–16,500 esc, suite 22,500–26,000 esc.

In Portugal, reservations for *pousadas* can be made direct or through Enatur, Avenida Santa Joana a Princesa 10, 1700 Lisbon; *tel* (01) 848 12 21, *fax* (01) 848 43 49. Keytel International is the officially appointed UK agency for *pousadas:* tel (0171) 402 8182, *fax* (0171) 724 9503.

Hotel Tivoli Jardim *Tel* (01) 353 99 71
Rua Julio Cesar Machado 7 *Fax* (01) 355 65 66
1200 Lisboa

This modern hotel has a central downtown position, and was liked again this year: "Convenient and efficient"; "rooms are pleasant, and quiet". Others have written: "Some of the best food I have had in Portugal: salt cod *the* best. Staff helpful." But some find the food "bland" and breakfasts "basic", with slapdash service. Next door is the 329-room *Tivoli Lisboa*, more expensive. The hotels share a swimming pool and exercise complex. The *Tivoli Lisboa*'s rooftop restaurant, *O Terraço*, commands a great view of the city. (*Jan Morris, Jacqui Buffton and Richard Ingham, and others*)

Open All year.
Rooms 74 double, 45 single. Air-conditioning.
Facilities Lift. Lounge/bar, restaurant; conference facilities. Gardens: swimming pool, tennis.
Location 10 mins from centre, off Avenida da Liberdade; NE of Botanical Gardens. Garage, carpark.
Credit cards All major cards accepted.
Terms [1996] B&B: single 23,500 esc, double 29,000 esc. Set meals 4,600 esc.

York House NEW *Tel* (01) 396 27 85
Rua das Janelas Verdes 32 *Fax* (01) 397 27 93
1200 Lisboa

This converted 17th-century convent, about two kilometres west of the city centre, is one of Lisbon's loveliest hotels. Dropped from recent editions of the *Guide* for lack of feedback, it was warmly renominated in 1995–96: "The most delightful and beautifully appointed hotel I've ever stayed in. Our beautiful, spacious room, simply furnished with fine old pieces, had a view extending over the bougainvillaea-covered courtyard as far as the city's big Jesus statue. The staff were charming, informal but correct. We dined in the elegant courtyard, dominated by a huge palm: food was excellent (and not just by dodgy Portuguese standards), especially the wild mushroom starters and the puddings." "Delightful. All antiques." Courtyard rooms are quietest: front ones may suffer tram noise. (*Claire Wrathall, Amos F Hutchins*)

Open All year.
Rooms 29 double, 5 single. 5 no-smoking.
Facilities Bar, TV room, restaurant. Unsuitable for ♿.
Location 2 km W of centre, near Museu Nacional de Arte Antiga. Public parking.
Credit cards All major cards accepted.
Terms [1996] B&B: single 18,200–25,200 esc, double 20,900–31,500 esc. Alc 4,500 esc.

MACEDO DE CAVALEIROS 5340 Bragança Map 13

Estalagem do Caçador *Tel* (078) 42 63 54
Largo Manuel Pinto de Azevedo *Fax* (078) 42 63 81

Macedo is a small town in wild and hilly country near Bragança. Here, the former town hall is now a five-star *estalagem*, beguiling recent visitors: "It is on the main road, but the sides and back of this elegant house are set quietly behind a high wall, and overlook a flowered garden and a small swimming pool with comfortable sunbeds. The hotel is furnished with genuine furniture of its period. The public rooms are opulent, with hunting trophies, relatively restrained, and glass cabinets stuffed with a fascinating collection of porcelain jugs, shoes, cups and pots. Everything gleams. The bedrooms are large, with high ceilings and beds high off the ground – one almost needs a ladder to get in. They have feather pillows and are covered with two layers of embroidered and crocheted bedcovers. The service is gracious, gentle and shy. The place is run like a private country house – nothing as vulgar as bathroom freebies and hotel notices. The cooking was excellent, the helpings large and the price low. Two girls kept running in and out, bringing more. Language had its problems; each time we smiled and said, 'Thank you, it's all too much,' more freshly prepared food arrived. A wonderfully pampered night: rich style in a poor countryside. Outside, alas, quite a lot of road noise and stray dogs." Newer reports, please.

Open All year.
Rooms 25.
Facilities Lift. Salon, restaurant. Garden: swimming pool.
Location Central. Garage.
Credit cards All major cards accepted.
Terms [1996] Rooms 11,500–15,200 esc. Breakfast 1,000 esc. Alc 3,500 esc.

MANTEIGAS 6260 Guarda — Map 13

Pousada de São Lourenço — *Tel* (075) 98 24 50
Estrada de Gouveia — *Fax* (075) 98 24 53

Attractive modern "ski-lodge" pousada, *amid Portugal's highest mountains, Serra da Estrela, 13 km N of Manteigas, 61 km SW of Guarda. Useful log fires; garden, terrace, splendid views; pleasant young staff. Local food generous but patchy. 20 spacious, warm bedrooms, nicely furnished. All major credit cards accepted. B&B: single 12,500 esc, double 14,500 esc. Alc 3,200 esc [1996]. Newer reports welcome.*

MONCHIQUE 8550 Faro — Map 13

Estalagem Abrigo da Montanha — *Tel* (082) 921 31
Corte Pereira/Estrada de Fóia — *Fax* (082) 936 60

Between the Algarve hill-town of Monchique and the peak of Fóia is this small, pretty, family-owned inn. The setting is peaceful, amid cork, chestnut and eucalyptus forests, with fine views over hills and coast, now much developed and "horrible". But a snack bar/restaurant across the road "absorbs most of the lunch-time coach-party trade". Visitors have enjoyed the warm welcome from the owner and manageress, José and Esmerelda. The flower-filled garden contains a swimming pool. The food is liked, especially at breakfast ("fresh orange juice and lovely honey"); also the fish dishes and desserts. Lounges with open fires are a welcome retreat in chilly weather. Newer reports welcome.

Open All year.
Rooms 5 suites (4, with terrace, in garden annexe), 5 double.

Facilities Bar, restaurant; terrace. Garden: swimming pool. Unsuitable for ♿.
Location 2 km from Monchique on Fóia road. 25 km inland from Portimão. Parking.
Credit cards All major cards accepted.
Terms [1996] B&B 13,000–17,000 esc. Set meals 3,000–5,000 esc.

NAZARÉ 2450 Leiria — Map 13

Albergaria Mar Bravo NEW — *Tel* (062) 55 11 80
Praça Sousa Oliveira 67-A — *Fax* (062) 55 39 79

A restaurant-with-rooms on a small square by the beach, in an attractive old fishing-port-cum-bathing-resort north of Lisbon. "It's a modest place, but terrifically nice," says its 1996 nominator. "The rooms are small but comfortable and prettily furnished in a neo-Deco style; front ones have a balcony facing the sand. They are not tranquil, though to be disturbed by the bright lights of the fishing-boats is charming in its way. The bathroom looked a treat, but the shower inclined to flood. This could have been irritating, save that the staff were so sweet and helpful that you forgave them everything. If they met you in town, they would greet you like their oldest friend. The restaurant, quite formal and expensive, specialises in seafood: though it's good, you can eat elsewhere in town for much less money." (*Claire Wrathall*)

Open All year.
Rooms 16 double. Air-conditioning.
Facilities Lift. Restaurant; terrace. Garden.
Location Central. Nazaré is 123 km N of Lisbon.
Credit cards All major cards accepted.
Terms [1996] Rooms 11,000–16,100 esc. Breakfast 700 esc. Set meals 2,900–4,500 esc.

ÓBIDOS 2510 Leiria — Map 13

Pousada do Castelo — *Tel* (062) 95 91 05
Paço Real — *Fax* (062) 95 91 48

Óbidos, near the coast north of Lisbon, is a medieval hilltop town of cobbled alleys and flower-girt squares, so picturesque that it's very touristy. Built into its walls is this handsome 15th-century castle, now a fairly expensive *pousada*. It "maintains the ambience of an old castle without too many of the discomforts", and has "charming places to sit, inside and out". Most double rooms overlook the flowery courtyard, and are "of necessity small, with tiny bathroom"; there are also three suites in the tower. A recent visitor liked the *pousada*, including its food ("delicious salt cod"), but felt that rooms by the restaurant may suffer disturbance. But: "Óbidos itself is lovely, especially early in the morning, before the coaches arrive." More reports welcome.

Open All year.
Rooms 3 suites, 6 double. Air-conditioning.
Facilities Lounge, TV room, bar, restaurant. Unsuitable for ♿.
Location Central. In city walls.
Credit cards All major cards accepted.
Terms B&B: single 21,000–26,250 esc, double 24,150–29,400 esc, suite 32,000–51,000 esc; D,B&B double 37,000 esc. Set meals 4,150–5,900 esc.

Estalagem do Convento BUDGET *Tel* (062) 95 92 16
Rua Dom João d'Ornelas *Fax* (062) 95 91 59

Just outside the city walls is this "friendly inn", small and white, part ancient, part modern. Reports on the food can vary, although latest visitors have found it "the best we had in a Portuguese hotel, with excellent wines and service". You can dine in the garden, or in a charming room with an open fire. "A hotel full of character, with stylish decor." "We had a lovely quiet room overlooking the garden." Some of the bedrooms are small. Those in the new wing are "beautifully designed to blend with the existing house": "Ours was very pretty, with a balcony overlooking the countryside and the city walls." (*H and JNP*)

Open All year. Restaurant closed Sun.
Rooms 4 suites, 27 double.
Facilities 2 lounges, TV room, 2 bars, dining room. Garden. Unsuitable for ♿.
Location Central. Street parking.
Credit cards Access, Amex, Visa.
Terms B&B: single 6,300–13,000 esc, double 9,500–15,200 esc, suite 13,100–20,450 esc. Set meals 3,000–4,000 esc; full alc 4,500 esc.

Casa de San Tiago do Castelo NEW *Tel* (062) 95 95 87
Largo de San Tiago

Near castle, a large old manor house (Turismo de Habitaçã), *beautifully decorated, with white walls, wood ceilings, pretty fabrics, hand-painted tiles. Lounge, library, bar, terrace with barbecue. Friendly owner, Carlos Lopes; very helpful service; free after-dinner drinks. All major credit cards accepted. 7 rooms. B&B: single 10,000–12,500 esc, double 12,500–15,000 esc [1996].*

PORTO Map 13

Infante de Sagres *Tel* (02) 200 81 01
Praça D. Filipa de Lencastre 62 *Fax* (02) 31 49 37
4050 Porto

In heart of old town, very grand traditional Anglo-Portuguese hotel with opulent furnishings: chandeliers, oriental rugs, stained-glass windows. 74 bedrooms with antiques (some four-posters). Courtyard, with loungers (meals served in summer). French and Portuguese cooking. Pleasant staff. All major credit cards accepted. B&B double 22,500–29,500 esc. Meals alc. "Wonderfully ostentatious. Large room, but hard beds. Staff pleasant – if slightly grand." More reports, please.

REGUENGOS DE MONSARAZ 7200 Évora Map 13

Horta da Moura *Tel* (066) 552 06
Apartado 64 *Fax* (066) 552 41

Set on a hillside amid quiet farmland, outside the old fortified townlet of Monsaraz, is this newly renovated luxurious complex in Alentejan style. "A delightful place, in a remote location," says a visitor in 1996. "Much money has been spent, creating a kind of comfy rustic ambience. My large suite opened on to a patio with views of the glorious

Alentejo countryside. Furnishings were of good quality, but bland. The lounge area was spacious and nicely decorated, but a little dark. Breakfasts were a bit skimpy, but at dinner the lusty regional specialities were wonderful. Mr Albuquerque, the manager, is much in evidence and speaks excellent English." There are firelit lounges, large grounds, and guided jeep tours organised to local places of interest. There is also a riding enclosure, and guides are available for trips on horseback. (*Lynn S Hay*) Work on an extension to the hotel was under way in 1996.

Open All year.
Rooms 7 suites, 8 double.
Facilities Lounges, bar, games room, restaurant. Garden: swimming pool (unheated), tennis, riding; bicycles, horse-drawn carriages. River fishing, canoeing nearby.
Location 2 km outside Monsaraz, 36 km SE of Évora. Parking.
Credit cards All major cards accepted.
Terms B&B: single 14,500 esc, double 16,500 esc, suite 20,000–22,000 esc. Set meal 3,500 esc. Children under 4 accommodated free in parents' room.

SINTRA 2710 Lisboa — Map 13

Quinta da Capela — *Tel* (01) 929 01 70
Estrada Velha de Colares — *Fax* (01) 929 34 25
Monserrate

Byron wrote in *Childe Harold* about this famous hill-town, strikingly situated. The *Quinta*, rebuilt after the 1755 earthquake, is today a peaceful country inn, tastefully restored. Some readers are spellbound: "Real flowers, joyous music, an ample cool bedroom. It's magically unhotel-like: there's no reception desk, yet everything is efficient and welcoming." "The gardens are Eden itself, with idyllic valley views to the distant sea. The lounges, music and decor deter you from getting on with the day's sightseeing." Others have written: "Its absence of formality makes one feel one is staying in a friendly Cotswold manor house." "Staff cheerful and obliging." "No one is around to break your fantasy of being the owner of the place." (*BW, and others*) A car is essential; most Sintra sites and restaurants are at least five kilometres away. More reports, please.

Open All year, except Christmas.
Rooms 2 suites, 7 double. Some on ground floor. Self-catering cottages.
Facilities 3 lounges, bar, breakfast room; gym, sauna. Garden: small swimming pool (unheated). Sandy beaches, safe bathing, fishing, riding, tennis nearby.
Location 4 km W of Sintra on Colares road (follow signs to *Palácio de Seteais*), just past Monserrate gardens.
Credit cards Access, Amex, Visa.
Terms B&B: single 15,000–21,000 esc, double 17,000–24,000 esc, suite 24,000–28,000 esc.

Casa Miradouro NEW/BUDGET — *Tel* (01) 923 59 00
Rua Sotto Mayor 55 — *Fax* (01) 924 18 36
Sintra-Vila

"By far the nicest place we stayed in, on our visit to Portugal", say the nominators of this appealing *Guide* newcomer. "It is a converted 1890s family villa, newly opened in 1994 by retired Swiss economist

Friedrich Kneubuhl, who likes to talk to his guests and is always much in evidence. The six large rooms are variously decorated in restrained modern style, but with choice pieces of old furniture. Rooms facing the sea have lovely panoramic views (bring binoculars!). Breakfasts are copious buffets. There's a well-furnished drawing room with bar, administered by the owner." (*Jacqui Buffton and Richard Ingham*) No restaurant; lots nearby.

Open All year, except 20 Jan–28 Feb.
Rooms 6 double.
Facilities Reception, lounge with TV/bar, breakfast room; terrace. Garden. Unsuitable for ♿.
Location Turn left off route 17 after National Palace, towards Hotel Tivoli; then 450 m down Rua Sotto Mayor. Street parking.
Credit cards Access, Visa.
Terms B&B: single 12,500–15,500 esc, double 14,500–18,500 esc.

Palácio de Seteais *Tel* (01) 923 32 00
Rua Barbosa do Bocage *Fax* (01) 923 42 77

A *de luxe* country house hotel in an 18th-century palace. It has an elegant formal garden on one side; wilder gardens, terraces and lemon groves spill down the hillside on the other. Recent visitors were delighted: "It is kept very well, with beautifully polished floors. Service is courteous and individual, also efficient." Public rooms are grand and splendid, with murals, tapestries and antiques. Bedrooms too are elegantly furnished, with luxurious bathrooms. Those in the new wing blend in well. The gardens, "a real delight", have been restored to provide private corners with fine old stone seats and secret paths. There's a good wine list, but views on the cooking vary. Newer reports welcome.

Open All year.
Rooms 1 suite, 29 double. Some air-conditioned.
Facilities Lift. Salons, TV room, bar, restaurant (piano/harp music); terrace. Large grounds: garden, swimming pool, tennis, riding. Beach 10 km. Unsuitable for ♿.
Location 1 km W of Sintra on Colares road. Parking.
Credit cards All major cards accepted.
Terms [1996] Rooms: single 40,000 esc, double 43,000 esc. Breakfast 1,600 esc. Alc 6,800 esc.

VILA NOVA DE CERVEIRA 4920 Viana do Castelo Map 13

Pousada de Dom Dinis *Tel* (051) 79 56 01
Praça da Liberdade *Fax* (051) 79 56 04

In a charming townlet below a mountain on the bank of the Rio Minho, which divides Portugal from Spain, this atmospheric *pousada* occupies almost the whole of the tiny walled inner city, and is reached up a cobbled path through a double-walled gate. Its attractive well-equipped rooms are carved out among the old castle walls; they are spacious (some are large suites) and most have a pleasant private courtyard. Readers have admired this "novel and interesting design", also the view from the dining room (but its high roof is ugly) and the glassed-in breakfast room. Service is friendly. "Our bedroom was pleasingly furnished in keeping with the period style of the buildings, and had a patio with sun umbrella below the old walls." (*SEW, and others*) Two church clocks strike at night.

Open All year.
Rooms 3 suites, 25 double. Air-conditioning.
Facilities 3 lounges, TV room, bar, dining room; games rooms; banqueting room; terraces, patios. Small garden. Unsuitable for ♿.
Location Central. Reception in small office facing square. Parking.
Credit cards All major cards accepted.
Terms [1996] B&B: single 17,000 esc, double 19,000 esc. Set meals 3,500 esc.

Slovenia

Vila Bled, Bled

Yugoslavia had its own chapter in the *Guide* until 1991, when the war began. Since then, we have received no reports on the Croatian coastal resorts (Dubrovnik, etc), where conditions may still be insecure. But Slovenia is a different matter, and now has a full chapter of its own for the first time.

John and Katinka Ardagh write: "We have just spent a working holiday here, and we loved it – a small nation, which, since 1991, when it fought and won a week-long war against the Serb-led Yugoslav Army, has fully escaped the violence and chaos to the south. Peaceful and democratic, it is happy in its new and well-deserved independence, and economically has long been the most advanced of all the former 'socialist' countries, including Hungary and the Czech Republic. For a holiday it has everything, from Alps to Adriatic beaches, plus old baroque towns; the people are multilingual, intensely cultured, bursting with poetry and music. There are plenty of hotels up to western standards, plus scores of charming farm guest houses, very modestly priced. The two luxury hotels in Bled have also been praised by other *Guide* readers."

AJDOVŠČINA 65270 Primorska — Map 17

Hotel Planika BUDGET — *Tel* (065) 6 36 65
Goriška 25č — *Fax* (065) 6 32 11

In centre of small town 27 km E of Nova Gorica, ideal for visiting Karst region (Postojna caves, Lipica horses, etc): simple hotel with large, comfortable rooms, nice restaurant. All major credit cards accepted. 34 rooms. B&B: single 3,600 SIT, double 6,850–9,415 SIT. Set meals 430–860 SIT.

BLED 64260 Gorenjska — Map 17

Pavovc BUDGET — *Tel/Fax* (064) 74 17 02
Selo pri Bledu

"Slovenia has many farm guest houses, and this delightful place is a model of what they can be. It is a real working farm with guest house attached, in a hamlet outside Bled, amid glorious country. Danica Lukanc, warm and exuberant, greeted us with her home-made fruit brandy, laughed a lot, and gave us a simple but pleasant room, with shower, TV and Alpine views. The farm's poultry, pigs and fruit form the basis of the bland but sound home cooking: a whole roast chicken was put on our table. Ask for the plum dumplings. We woke to the sound of cowbells, and enjoyed a breakfast that included more fruit brandy, pancakes, and walnuts. Prices are amazingly low. Lovely walking country. The Lukancs are building a larger hotel nearby: we hope this will not spoil the rural charm." (*JA and KA*)

Open All year.
Rooms 6 double.
Facilities Sitting room, restaurant.
Location In hamlet, 2 km SW of Bled. Parking.
Credit cards None accepted.
Terms D,B&B 40 DM per person.

Grand Hotel Toplice — *Tel* (064) 79 10
C. Svobode 12 — *Fax* (064) 74 18 41

The smartest and best-known of Slovenia's resorts has a glorious position on the small and lovely Lake of Bled, facing the Julian Alps. One of its two grandest hotels is the *Toplice*, right by the lake, on the edge of town. Built in 1920, and since much modernised, it has long been admired by readers. Here's a recent view: "It has a better setting than the *Vila Bled* (see next page), and more charm and elegance too, with somewhat lower prices. We liked the panoramic salon and dining room, the terrace under chestnut trees by the lake, the colonnaded heated pool." The best rooms face the lake and mountains; some have furniture upholstered in gold velvet, with curtains to match. Service has been praised, but opinions of the food vary. Some prefer eating elsewhere. The British group tours are "somewhat upper crust".

Open All year.
Rooms 10 suites, 74 double, 37 single.
Facilities Lift. Lounges, bar, TV room, bridge room, café, 2 restaurants, bistro; conference room; indoor thermal swimming pool, sauna, solarium, gym; terrace. Garden: swimming pool.
Location By lake, 500 m from town centre. Parking.

Credit cards All major cards accepted.
Terms B&B: single 102–122 DM, double 154–184 DM, suite 254–304 DM; D,B&B double 214-244 DM. Full alc 40 DM.

Vila Bled *Tel* (064) 79 15
C. Svobode 26 *Tel* (064) 74 13 20

This former royal palace, set outside town on a hill above the lake, in its own 13-acre park, was remodelled by Tito after 1945 and used as his summer residence – here, he entertained Brandt, Eden, Nehru and others. Since his death it has been Slovenia's most sumptuous hotel (Relais & Châteaux), although by western standards prices are not too high. A returning devotee wrote recently: "The flowers are abundant, the food is better than ever, the staff are enthusiastic, the glass, silver and marble all shine, and a red carpet welcomes you." An inspector has since liked the elegant gardens, but thought the furnishings heavy and styleless. "But," he added, "we enjoyed talking with the witty and jovial manager, Janez Fajfar. Tito's murals of Socialist revolution have been carefully covered, but you can visit his top-floor concert hall." Many of the bedrooms were built without a lake view, for security reasons. Just along the lake, and separately owned, is the amazing *Café Belvedere,* built in the 1930s by King Alexander and also much used by Tito. "Outwardly an austere blockhouse, it's hypnotic inside. A waitress in a mauve miniskirt served us caviar sandwiches in Tito's tearoom, while Wagner and *The Sound of Music* played gently. On the wall behind us, frescoes showed sturdy farm girls and factory workers building a Socialist Utopia."

Open All year.
Rooms 21 suites, 10 double.
Facilities Lounges, bar, music room, 2 breakfast rooms, restaurant; conference room; games room; terraces. Garden: tennis; access to private lido mid-June–mid-Sept: safe bathing, boating. Golf, riding, fishing nearby.
Location 2 km W of Bled, just above lake. Safe parking.
Credit cards All major cards accepted.
Terms B&B: single £68–£81, double £100–£112, suite £108–£248. Set meals £20; full alc £25.

KAMNA GORICA 64246 Gorenjska — Map 17

Pension Krona BUDGET *Tel* (064) 71 40 04
Fax (064) 71 51 60

Just off the Bled-Ljubljana road, a few miles south of Radovljica, is this "incredible find", as its nominator describes it. "The restaurant is excellent, and there's a small cosy bar. Almost every room has a balcony, with a view of the mountains. Lighting is very good. Bathrooms have bathtubs and hair-dryer. Service is unfailingly friendly. When I dropped my eyeglasses and the frame broke, the receptionist, with a cry of 'My Man!', took them from me, and within half an hour 'her man' returned them to me, repaired. In the valley nearby are a marvellous Bee Museum, an Iron Forging Museum, a castle housing a Museum of Lace and a large and fascinating museum of mercury mining. At Kostanjevica, a Cistercian monastery has been converted into one of the most elegant museums of modern art I have ever seen." (*Marie Harris*)

Open All year.
Rooms 42 beds. Most rooms with balcony.
Facilities Bar, restaurant; sauna.
Location 15 km SE of Bled, 5 km SE of Radovljica. Parking.
Credit cards All major credit cards accepted.
Terms [1996] B&B double 7,200–9,000 SIT. Set meals 1,400–2,200 SIT.

KOSTANJEVICA NA KRKI 68311 Dolenjska — Map 17

Pod Gorjanci BUDGET — *Tel* (0608) 8 70 46
Ljubljanska C. 5 — *Fax* (0608) 3 10 06

In fine medieval townlet with noted monastery, 20 km E of Nove Mesto, small hotel with well-equipped rooms, good food, ample breakfast. Very quiet. 7 rooms. B&B double 5,600 SIT. Set meals 1,000–2,000 SIT [1996].

LIPICA 66210 Primorska — Map 17

Hotel Maestoso BUDGET — *Tel* (067) 3 10 09
Lipica 5 — *Fax* (067) 3 14 09

Founded in 1580, the famous Lipica stud farm is the cradle of all the elegant white Lipizzaner horses in the world: some were used by the Spanish Riding School in Vienna. Neatly kept, the stud is on a lovely pastoral plateau of the Karst region east of Trieste, and attracts many visitors. Some of them stay at this fairly big modern hotel. "It lies next to the stables, amid fields and woodlands. The price of room and breakfast includes a tour of the stud farm and admission to daily dressage displays. For an extra charge, you can actually ride these magnificent beasts (recreational outings, lessons, carriage rides and fox hunts!). The place is really a kind of resort (swimming pool, sauna, tennis, etc) and for the price it's fantastic." (*Marie Harris*) Reports on the food welcome.

Open All year.
Rooms 134 beds.
Facilities Restaurant; indoor swimming pool, sauna, beauty treatment. Garden: tennis.
Location By Italian border, 5 km S of Sežana. Parking.
Cards All major cards accepted.
Terms [1996] B&B: single 5,600–7,700 SIT, double 8,800–11,600 SIT; D,B&B 700 SIT added per person.

LJUBLJANA 61000 — Map 17

Austrotel — *Tel* (061) 132 61 33
Miklošičeva 9 — *Fax* (061) 30 11 81

"Slovenia's capital," writes an inspector, "is a true central European city of cafés, music and baroque, lively and civilised, crowded with students and a bit shabby. It is crowned by an old castle and graced by Plečnik's 1920s architecture. Near the historic part of town, in a drab main street leading to the station, is this modern Austrian-managed hotel, super-efficient, mainly for business people. It has smallish well-equipped rooms, pleasant staff, an outdoor café, and a superb buffet breakfast that includes wine if you want it." Reports on main meals welcome.

Open All year.
Rooms 62 double.
Facilities Breakfast room, bar, restaurant; conference rooms; terrace.
Location Central. Secure garage.
Credit cards All major cards accepted.
Terms [1996] B&B: single 14,000–17,200 SIT, double 21,500–26,700 SIT; D,B&B 2,600 SIT per person added.

OTOČEC OB KRKI 68222 Dolenjska — Map 17

Grad Otočec — *Tel* (068) 32 18 30
Grajska C. 1 — *Fax* (068) 32 25 90

80 km SE of Ljubljana, just off highway to Zagreb, 7 km E of Novo Mesto, handsome medieval castle converted into fairly sophisticated restaurant-with-rooms, secluded on small wooded island, between two arms of Krka. Comfortable rooms, but furnishings rather heavily baronial. Good straightforward food, pleasantly served (in floodlit courtyard in fine weather). Big leisure complex nearby. All major credit cards accepted. 19 rooms. B&B: single 12,000–13,400 SIT, double 16,800–18,880 SIT [1996]. Fuller reports welcome.

PIRAN 66330 Primorska — Map 17

Hotel Tartini BUDGET — *Tel* (066) 74 62 22
Tartinijev Trg 15 — *Fax* (066) 74 63 24

"Piran is magical," write inspectors, "a tiny medieval Venetian seaport, set on a narrow cape extending like a finger into the Adriatic, backed by green hills. It is a popular summer haunt of the Ljubljana smart set, and has excellent seafront restaurants. The small piazzas with statues and food markets, the clothes hanging to dry in the alleys, all evoked Italy. Our hotel, named after the composer Giuseppe Tartini (born in Piran), stood in the small main square. Here the view from our balcony was like an operetta set: a tiny dinghy-filled harbour, a small round marble-floored *piazza* with old Venetian palaces. Newly renovated, the hotel has excellent personal service, good food (notably fish) served in a patio in summer, so-so buffet breakfasts. Bedrooms are pleasant, save for their fussy modernist design."

Open All year.
Rooms 87 beds.
Facilities Restaurant; terrace.
Location Central. Town is 25 km SW of Trieste. Hotel will arrange outdoor parking, hard in Piran.
Credit cards All major cards accepted.
Terms [1996] B&B: single 3,600–8,200 SIT, double 5,500–12,900 SIT.

Some of our Slovenian telephone numbers may not be accurate; changes were taking place in 1996.

STRANICE 63206 Staderska **Map 17**

Urška BUDGET *Tel* (063) 762 180
Križevec 11 A

On edge of village 3 km SW of spa resort of Zreče (mud baths), 40 km SW of Maribor, delightful small guest house in glorious sub-Alpine setting. Convivial Topolšek family owners also run working farm with vineyards and in 1993 won Slovenia's Best Farm Guest House of the Year award, well merited, for good food and hospitality. "Amazing value." Simple Alpine-type rooms with mountain views. Credit cards not accepted. 5 rooms. D,B&B 2,900 SIT [1996].

Spain

Parador de Chinchón

The chain of state-owned luxury hotels, the *paradores,* of which there are now about 85, was created under the Franco regime in order to raise tourist standards and give a lead to the rest of the hotel industry, much of it then backward. The idea succeeded. Privately owned hotels of all kinds have since blossomed in Spain, and while many are ugly, others are full of character, even the simpler ones. To find good food and comfort in Spain, you certainly need not pay *parador* prices.

The *paradores* have cornered the market in historical grandeur. Most of the best are housed in splendid old buildings – medieval castles, former monasteries, rural mansions – that have been finely renovated. There are also newer purpose-built *paradores,* mostly on good sites by the coast or near main roads. These are now earmarked for privatisation. But the state will keep the prestigious historical ones.

Some *paradores* are quite small, but most are spacious, with large comfortable bedrooms, huge public lounges, and air-conditioning. Decor tends to the baronial: lots of tapestries and suits of armour. Piped music is common; and service, though efficient, tends to be rather formal. Menus include some regional dishes, well prepared. But *parador* food is usually rather bland, even dull, compared with the bold flavours found in many other restaurants.

For advance reservations, often advisable, the appointed agency in London is Keytel International: *tel* (0171) 402 8182, *fax* (0171) 724 9503. Its US equivalent is Marketing Ahead Inc: *tel* (212) 686 9213, *fax* (212) 686 0271. Keytel will ask you for a deposit, charge for breakfast whether you want it or not, and impose a booking fee. It may be better to contact the Madrid office: Central de Reservas de los Paradores de España, Calle Requena 3, 28013 Madrid; *tel* (91) 435 97 00, 435 97 44 or 435 97 68.

Ordinary hotels are plentiful, and advance booking is seldom essential, except in some resorts in high summer. All hotels are officially graded, from the five-star places down to one-star *pensions*; and by law the official price must be shown inside each room. In tourist areas, prices vary by around 30 to 40 per cent between low and high season (high summer, Christmas, Holy Week, local *fiestas*). And a room for two costs only about 50 per cent more than a room for one. But twin beds, rather than double beds, are the rule.

At the cheaper end of the scale, two-star *hostales* in towns are usually fine: the entrance may be drab and off-putting and decor minimal, but comfort is generally adequate. In rural areas, a good budget bet could be a *mesón*, a restaurant which offers country dishes, and may have a few rooms with loo and shower *en suite*. Simpler still, and more atmospheric, are the *hospederias* attached to monasteries, usually in beautiful settings. Navarra in particular has been developing these. Built for pilgrims and people on retreat, they are very cheap and quite jolly. Most are open in summer only.

Recently, a number of rural buildings, such as manors or farmsteads, have been converted as holiday homes or hotels, especially in the northern coastal zones. You will find self-catering enterprises, *casas rurales* (rustic cottages) and *casas rusticas* (farmhouses); also, especially in Asturias, farmhouses of character, converted (with government funding) into attractive hotels. Two examples in the 1997 *Guide* are *La Rectoral* in Taramundi and *La Tahona* in Besnes-Alles.

Even the simpler hotels, with one gable or less in *Michelin*, offered decent comfort and efficiency. You generally get a bath *en suite*, at least a small one, rather than a shower. While in expensive hotels breakfast may be a lavish buffet, more often the Spanish hotel breakfast is somewhat sparse and basic (and extra to the room price), and many small hotels do not offer it at all; in any case, it can be more fun to take a good coffee and a croissant in a bar, the way the Spanish do.

The food in northern Spain, except in some touristy hotels, is often superb – strong-flavoured, varied, with large helpings. Fish and seafood are marvellous, while even the beef can be very tender. And, unlike in Britain, the more down-market you go the better the food can become. Even in rough-looking *tapas* bars on waterfronts, you may be regaled with piles of fresh fish and seafood in spicy sauces, at £2 a platter. The Spanish stick to their own cooking, remaining largely unaffected by *nouvelle cuisine* or, at the other extreme, American fast food. They also stick to their strange late mealtimes. If you go into a restaurant at 10 pm and find it empty, don't think that it is unpopular with the locals: by 11 pm it may well be buzzing.

Note that there is a 6 or 7 per cent tax on hotels with a one- to four-star rating, and a 15 per cent tax on five-star or luxury hotels.

ALCAÑIZ 44600 Teruel Map 13

Parador de la Concordia *Tel* (978) 83 04 00
Castillo de Calatravos *Fax* (978) 83 03 66

On a hilltop, in this little town set among orchards and olive groves, stands this 12th-century castle-convent. It has a cloister, 14th-century murals in the keep, and a Gothic chapel (now a concert hall), but has been "rather too ruthlessly converted". An 18th-century addition is now this tiny *parador*: "Service is personal and relaxed. Our room was pleasant, and the window, though small, gave superb views over the countryside. Two pleasant lounges. In the quite grand dining room, which shared the views, dinner was only average for a *parador*." Aragonese lamb and chicken dishes are on offer. (*RH*) "I thought it rather institutional," said a visitor this year.

Open All year, except 18 Dec–2 Feb.
Rooms 10 double, 2 single. Air-conditioning.
Facilities Lift. Lounge, bar, restaurant. Garden.
Location Central. 103 km SE of Zaragoza, 102 km NW of Tortosa. Parking.
Credit cards All major cards accepted.
Terms [1996] Rooms: single 11,600–13,200 pts, double 14,500–16,500 pts. Breakfast 1,200 pts. Set meals 3,500 pts.

ALHAURIN EL GRANDE 29100 Málaga Map 13

Finca La Mota NEW/BUDGET *Tel* (95) 249 09 01
Partido Urique *Fax* (95) 259 41 20

Set in its own wide grounds just inland from Málaga, this 17th-century farmhouse/inn is owned and run by an amiable British/American couple, Jean and Arun Narang. Its rustic interior has English and Spanish antiques. It is all *very* informal, and upkeep was so badly criticised last year that we dropped the entry. But the place does have its devotees, including a well-known Irish hotelier: "There's a dusty semi-tropical lazy-daisy untidiness about it. Nobody bothers, because they are all so happy. Bedrooms are spotless, the pool is well looked after. Jean is very nice and efficient, and they have a super waiter. Food is not great but good and natural, eg, Spanish lamb grilled with wild rosemary. Children have a great time here. It's not quiet, with a lot of coming and going." Others this year have also liked the informality, friendliness, "interesting" food, including some unusual Indian dishes. (*Myrtle Allen, AV Neal*) But one reader this year thought the restaurant "pretty basic", and described the public areas as "tatty". More reports clearly needed.

Open All year.
Rooms 3 suites, 9 double, 1 single. 4 in nearby annexe. Some on ground floor.
Facilities Lounge, bar, restaurant; dining terrace. Garden: swimming pool (unheated), tennis, mini-golf, children's playground. Horses for hire (1,500 pts per hour). Golf nearby.
Location 40 km W of Málaga, 2 km SW of Alhaurin on Nijas road. Parking.
Credit cards All major cards accepted.
Terms [1996] B&B: single 5,000 pts, double 7,000–9,000 pts, suite 10,000 pts; D,B&B double 14,000 pts. Alc meals 2,800 pts.

ARCOS DE LA FRONTERA 11630 Cádiz — Map 13

Parador Casa del Corregidor — *Tel* (956) 70 05 00
Plaza del Cabildo — *Fax* (956) 70 11 16

Arcos stands on a cliff above the Guadalete river, with stupendous views of the Andalusian countryside. The *parador*, "a lovely hotel", is a Renaissance-style building on the main *plaza*, backing on to the edge of the cliff. Its interior has been restored in Moorish style and the spacious public rooms are set round a central open patio. "We had a magnificent huge bedroom." "Service firm but polite. The dining room is a delight, on the cliff's edge, with dramatic views." Best rooms have a private patio, overlooking the cliff. Reports on the food vary, but the buffet breakfast is popular. The *parador* is reached through a convoluted maze of narrow streets: driving and parking can be difficult. Tipping the parking attendant in the main square is recommended. (*Endorsed in 1996 by D and P Hawkins*)

Open All year.
Rooms 20 double, 4 single. Air-conditioning.
Facilities Lift. Salons, TV room, bar, restaurant; meeting room; 2 terraces.
Location On main square.
Credit cards All major cards accepted.
Terms [1996] Rooms from 13,500 pts. Breakfast 1,100 pts. Set meals 3,200 pts.

El Convento BUDGET — *Tel/Fax* (956) 70 23 33
Marques de Torresoto 7

"A superb hotel, with attentive family hosts, great views and excellent food" – recent praise for this eight-room inn, housed in a 16th-century convent on a quiet street off the main square. It enjoys the same view over the plain of Arcos as the more expensive *parador* almost next door. Access and parking are similarly tricky (see above). *El Convento* is crammed with family memorabilia, and its helpful owners are much in evidence. Bedrooms are quite small, simply furnished in local style, with modern bathroom. The best have a private terrace overlooking crumbling yellow cliffs – "from ours we watched the kestrels quartering over the plains of Arcos". There is no lounge or bar. But breakfast is above average, with fresh orange juice. The restaurant, in a beautiful 16th-century mansion close by, serves Andalusian specialities. (*JT, and others*) Not all rooms have a view. And a reader this year was disappointed by the food, which others have thought "excellent".

Open All year.
Rooms 8 double. Most with terrace.
Facilities Breakfast room, restaurant (in separate building). Unsuitable for ♿.
Location Side street in town centre near main square (follow directions to *parador*, and park in square).
Credit cards All major cards accepted.
Terms Rooms: single 4,280–5,350 pts, double 6,420–7,490 pts. Breakfast 700 pts. Set meals 2,500 pts.

Please make a habit of sending in a report as soon as possible after a visit when details are still fresh in your mind. The more you can tell us of your impressions the better.

ARRECIFE 35500 Canary Islands — Map 13

Hotel Lancelot BUDGET *Tel* (928) 80 50 99
Avenida Mancomunidad 9 *Fax* (928) 80 50 39
Lanzarote

Lovely Lanzarote has lots to offer (volcanic mountains, crashing seas, magnificent grottoes, pretty whitewashed villages). In its capital, Arrecife, this large, modern purpose-built hotel was found "good value" by a visitor this year, who liked its seafront position, with views of the bay from its panoramic dining room and from many bedrooms. These are well equipped and have "beautiful bathrooms with tiled floors". A recent account: "The manager is charming and all staff are attentive. The delightful chef, Sr Ramón, cooks wonderfully: excellent fish, and we ate masses of the local dish, papas arrugadas, small potatoes served with a very hot garlicky sauce. The package tours can be noisy, but they eat in a separate room. This area, beautifully furnished, has a little dance floor where on Saturdays they have a singer and one of those electronic gadgets that sound like a band." A swimming pool has just been built on the roof. (*Moira Jarrett*)

Open All year.
Rooms 77 double, 33 single.
Facilities Lounge, piano bar, snack bar, restaurant; roof-top swimming pool (unheated).
Location Central, by beach.
Credit cards All major cards accepted.
Terms Rooms: single 5,800 pts, double 7,200 pts. Breakfast 600 pts. Set meals 1,600 pts; full alc 1,800 pts.

ÁVILA 05001 — Map 13

Hostería de Bracamonte NEW/BUDGET *Tel* (920) 25 12 80
Calle Bracamonte 6

This "old building of charm and character" stands in a narrow street near to Ávila's famed 12th-century walls, and to the mighty cathedral. "The style is olde-worlde Castilian but not overdone (only one suit of armour!). White walls and exposed beams are agreeably festooned with pictures and dried flowers, and the floors covered with stone, quarry tiles and rugs. Bedrooms are smart, bathrooms attractively tiled, and service is helpful and sprightly. The bar serves a typical Spanish breakfast (*carajillo*, strong black coffee laced with brandy, keeps out the cold, in Spain's highest city)." The restaurant wins a red *Comida* in *Michelin* for its Castilian dishes. (*Lindsay Fisher*)

Open All year.
Rooms 2 suites, 16 double, 2 single.
Facilities Salon, bar, 2 dining rooms; patio. Unsuitable for ♿.
Location Central. Parking can be tricky.
Credit cards Access, Visa.
Terms Rooms: single 5,000–6,000 pts, double 7,000–8,000 pts, suite 17,000–19,000 pts. Breakfast 400 pts. Set meals 2,000 pts.

> Don't let old favourites down. Entries are dropped when there is no endorsement.

BAGUR 17255 Gerona — Map 13

Hotel Aigua Blava *Tel* (972) 62 20 58
Playa de Fornells *Fax* (972) 62 21 12

Always popular, this quite luxurious family seaside hotel is superbly located on various levels amid trees and rocks, on a lovely stretch of coast, and is built in local style round a small harbour. It is family-owned and run, with Juan Gispert now in charge, after the death of the former owner, his uncle. "We had a lovely time," say readers this year, echoing earlier praise: "Our attractive suite had fine views out to sea." "At the breakfast buffet there's Spanish omelette which you can eat on the terrace in the sunshine. In the restaurant, with its view of sea and boats, there's a lot of style and atmosphere: no jackets and ties, but everyone looks smart, and the coloured chairs are lovely. The staff are always joking with the guests, and the food is very good – many Catalan dishes, wonderful local fish, and of course 'The Cake', made in the hotel. Wonderful service in the many bars." There's a large swimming pool, with a bar; or you can swim from tiny beaches or off the rocks. Children are warmly welcomed. (*James Kite; also Celia and Andrew Payne*) Many guests are older British people, returning annually across the decades: "We, in our late twenties, got 'vetted' by these regulars, and once they found we were not riff-raff they were very friendly! It amused us greatly."

Open 15 Feb–10 Nov.
Rooms 14 suites, 67 double, 8 single. In 5 different buildings. 66 air-conditioned.
Facilities 4 lounges, TV room, 3 bars, 4 dining rooms; conference/banqueting rooms; boutique, hairdresser. Gardens: tennis, volleyball, swimming pool (disco nightly in season), paddling pool, children's play area. Sand and rock beaches: safe bathing, water sports, marina. Concessions at local golf courses. Unsuitable for ♿.
Location 4 km SE of Bagur, 8 km E of Palafrugell. Garage, carpark.
Credit cards Access, Amex, Visa.
Terms [1996] Rooms: single 7,700–10,000 pts, double 10,000–16,500 pts, suite 16,300–21,500 pts. Breakfast 1,400 pts. D,B&B 7,950–12,000 pts per person. Set meals 3,400 pts.

BAÑALBUFAR 07191 Mallorca — Map 13

Hotel Mar i Vent BUDGET *Tel* (971) 61 80 00
Calle Major 47-49 *Fax* (971) 61 82 01

The "convivial atmosphere" of this unpretentious hotel continues to delight visitors. The setting, too, is splendid, above steeply terraced fields in a fishing village on Mallorca's rugged west coast. It has been in the same family for four generations and is now owned and run by a brother and sister, Tony and Juanita Vives, whose "warm and genuine" welcome is backed by the "laughing, friendly and laid-back service" of their staff. "Very relaxing. Good, simple family food – gazpacho, fried fish, tricolour vegetable paté. Breakfasts are on the terrace, facing the bay. Our room was comfortable, simply furnished: the donkey on the terrace sometimes acted as alarm clock." "It's like revisiting old friends." "A simple hotel with excellent swimming in the pool and uncrowded sea coves, in an area which has managed to avoid the ravages wrought by tourism elsewhere on the island." There are fine views of the sea, and the hills behind offer exhilarating walking. Bedrooms are furnished in local style; some are small, but all are bright, with "delightful balconies". (*DH, and others*) A few niggles about overcooked vegetables, faulty soundproofing. A car is essential for touring.

Open All year, except Dec/Jan. Restaurant closed midday.
Rooms 20 double, 3 single. 12 in annexe.
Facilities 3 salons (1 with TV, 1 no-smoking), bar, restaurant; terraces. Garden: swimming pool, tennis. Sea cove down cliff: bathing. Unsuitable for ♿.
Location At entrance to village. 24 km NW of Palma. Garage, parking.
Credit cards Access, Visa.
Terms B&B: single 7,300 pts, double 10,300 pts; D,B&B: single 9,500 pts, double 14,700 pts. Set meals 2,200 pts. 1-night bookings sometimes refused in season.

BARCELONA 08002 **Map 13**

Hotel Colón *Tel* (93) 301 14 04
Avenida de la Catedral 7 *Fax* (93) 317 29 15
Regencia Colón *Tel* (93) 318 98 58
Calle Sagristans 13–17 *Fax* (93) 317 28 22

Two hotels under the same management in the Barrio Gótico, within walking distance of the waterfront, Museo Picasso and newer shopping districts. The *Colón*, larger and more expensive, faces the cathedral and its pedestrianised square. "It still has the feel of aristocratic old Spain. The bar is calm and intimate," said a recent visitor, endorsing this warm appraisal: "It is grand in a restrained way, refurbished in traditional style, clean and fresh. The public rooms are spacious, but there is little of the bustle and vulgarity of chain hotels. In some ways too little: no sign that room service is available. Bedrooms are comfortable and quiet behind double doors, with flower prints, white-painted furniture, superb lighting and excellent bathroom. Front rooms face the floodlit cathedral; from them one can watch the Catalan dancing to a brass band at the weekend. Top-floor rooms have a terrace and cost 20% more." The *Regencia*, in a narrow side street behind – "a plain hotel, clean and pleasant, with good breakfast and helpful staff" – is considered "good value at modest price". Rooms are small; those on the fifth floor have a balcony and the best outlook. There is a good breakfast buffet, served in a turn-of-the-century bistro. No restaurant, but snacks (brought from the *Colón*) are available all day in the bar. (*MAF, and others*)

Open All year.
Rooms *Colón*: 9 suites, 138 double/single. *Regencia*: 40 double, 15 single. Air-conditioning.
Facilities *Colón*: Lift. Salons, piano bar, restaurant, grill room; conference/function facilities. *Regencia*: Lift. Foyer lounge, bar/breakfast room. Unsuitable for ♿.
Location Central, near cathedral.
Credit cards All major cards accepted.
Terms [1996] *Colón*. Rooms: single 13,750 pts, double 20,500 pts. Breakfast 1,500 pts. Alc meals 4,000 pts. *Regencia*. Rooms: single 7,900 pts, double 13,500 pts. Breakfast 1,000 pts.

BAYONA 36300 Pontevedra — Map 13

Parador Conde de Gondomar — *Tel* (986) 35 50 00
Carretera de Bayona — *Fax* (986) 35 50 76

The setting is superb, within the grounds of a 16th-century fortress on a headland, with "idyllic views across the bay". This large, well-known *parador* is itself a modern building, a white-walled mock-*pazo* (Galician manor). Again this year, reports have been a bit mixed. A returning visitor enjoyed the large blue swimming pool, "very well kept, with loungers on very green grass", but found some upkeep of the hotel less perfect: "The open courtyard for drinks needed weeding, which is very un-*parador*." An earlier view: "Acceptable meals in the restaurant, with a picture window looking across the bay. Excellent breakfast, good bedrooms and friendly service." The *parador* is often busy with groups and conferences, and not everyone likes the insistent background music and Tannoy announcements. The food in the formal dining room, and in the tavern, simpler and cheaper, is no better than *parador* average. Bedrooms have traditional furnishings, good lighting and well-equipped bathrooms. Best rooms have views of the sea. (*Prof. P and Mrs A Robson*)

Open All year.
Rooms 2 suites, 116 double.
Facilities 2 salons, TV room, bar, restaurant; conference facilities; sauna, fitness room. Park: swimming pool (unheated), tennis, children's play area. Beach, bathing, fishing nearby. Unsuitable for ♿.
Location On coast, 21 km SW of Vigo by C550. Garage, parking.
Credit cards All major cards accepted.
Terms [1996] Rooms: single 8,500–10,750 pts, double 12,500–16,500 pts, suite 23,500–30,000 pts. Breakfast 1,200 pts. Set meals 3,500 pts; full alc 4,815 pts.

BENAOJÁN 29370 Málaga — Map 13

Molino del Santo BUDGET — *Tel* (52) 167151
Bda Estación — *Fax* (52) 167327

A British couple, Andy Chapell and Pauline Elkin, own and run this much-loved small hotel near Ronda. "A Mecca for tired pilgrims"; "probably the best hotel I have ever stayed in" – two more plaudits this year. A converted water mill with white pantiled buildings in typical *andaluz* style, it shelters beneath a steep mountain ridge, in the national park of Grazalema. The approach is off-putting, along a railway line, past factories, but then you arrive in this "lush little oasis". Bedrooms are strewn around gardens containing exotic Mediterranean vegetation and weeping willows beside a roaring stream; all rooms have their own terrace, with trees. Many guests are British, but "the inn is part of the local cultural landscape, and a focus of local life". The location is quiet, ideal for walking, mountain biking, or just lounging. There's an above-average selection of books, and a buffet breakfast. Bedrooms are simply furnished; some have a sun-trap terrace. The hotel is "very child-friendly", and the dining room with its "lovely atmosphere" is popular with locals. (*Canon M Bourdeaux, Gillian Gadsby, Martine Packer and Andy Kinch, William and Ann Reid, and many others*) The hotel's altitude can make it chilly out of season.

Open 21 Feb–10 Dec.
Rooms 11 double/family, 1 single. Some on ground floor.
Facilities Ramp. Lounge, bar, library, restaurant; terrace (meals served). Garden: swimming pool. Unsuitable for ♿.
Location Below village, by station. Take C339 N from Ronda; follow signs to Benaoján. Hotel sign-posted. Parking.
Credit cards All major cards accepted.
Terms Rooms: single 5,500–8,400 pts, double 7,800–12,000 pts. Breakfast 925 pts. D,B&B 7,800–12,400 pts per person. Full alc 2,800 pts.

BESNES-ALLES 33578 Asturias — Map 13

La Tahona BUDGET — *Tel/Fax* (985) 41 57 49

"A great place to soak up the beauty of nature," says a visitor to this rustic hotel, set quietly down a rough track in beech woods, on the edge of the dramatic Picos de Europa mountains. It is a converted bakery; and though it calls itself a rural tourist centre, the bar is still a focus of genuine village life (little English is spoken). The small beer garden is a good place to sample cabrales, the ferocious local blue cheese, together with sour Asturian cider served in jugs. Everything is bare stone, logs, red tiles and whitewashed plaster. The furnishing is simple but well done, and the restaurant is "very pleasing". The neat, clean bedrooms and well-equipped modern bathrooms are poorly sound-proofed (those near the bar and restaurant are noisiest): but when the noises cease, all you will hear is a babbling stream and the sound of birds. "One day we were up in Alpine-style mountains in the morning and on a Cornish-style beach in the afternoon." You can rent bicycles or hire a horse for exploring the mountains from the hotel. The new management has just opened a library and laundry: but there's no news yet of the much-needed sound-proofing. More recent reports welcome.

Open All year.
Rooms 1 suite, 19 double. 7 in *Casa de Molino* 50 m. Some on ground floor.
Facilities Lounge/TV room, reading room, bar, restaurant; terrace. Garden: bicycles/horses for hire; guided walks, river fishing nearby. Unsuitable for ♿.
Location 2 km from Alles. 10.5 km W of Panes on Cangas de Onís road.
Credit cards All major cards accepted.
Terms Rooms: single 4,800–6,800 pts, double 6,200–8,400 pts, suite 8,400–10,300 pts. Breakfast 800 pts. Set meals 1,800 pts; full alc 3,400 pts. Off-season rates.

BIELSA 22350 Huesca — Map 13

Parador de Bielsa — *Tel* (974) 50 10 11
Valle de Pineta — *Fax* (974) 50 11 88

Below the high Pyrenees, and near a tunnel leading to France, this modern grey stone building stands in "an awesome setting", by a rushing river at the head of the Valle de Pineta. "It is surrounded by mountains, devastatingly beautiful, and is purpose-built, therefore very spacious, and mostly wood. A large lounge with an open fire, a good large dining room with views, and a terrace. Our bedroom was large and well glazed against the worst that winter might throw at it; all rooms appeared to share the view." We'd be glad of reports on the food, said to include Aragonese chicken and lamb dishes *"al chilindrón"*. (*Lindsay Fisher*)

Open All year.
Rooms 24 double.
Facilities Lift. Salon, TV room, reading/billiard room, restaurant; terrace. Garden: children's playground.
Location 14 km NW of Bielsa, at entrance to National Park.
Credit cards All major cards accepted.
Terms [1996] Rooms 10,500–13,500 pts. Breakfast 1,200 pts. Set meals 3,200 pts.

CALA RAJADA 07590 Mallorca **Map 13**

Hotel Ses Rotges *Tel* (971) 56 31 08
Calle Rafael Blanes 21 *Fax* (971) 56 43 45

A small and friendly hotel in an old stone mansion of character, a few blocks away from the busy main street of a small fishing resort on Mallorca's east coast: nearby are clean sandy beaches and the mighty Artá caves. Inside, colours, fabrics and pictures have been chosen with care. The owner/chef, Gérard Tétard, is French, and his *Michelin*-starred cooking has again been admired recently: "A lovingly cared-for old building, full of interesting furniture and pictures, and masses of flowers arranged by Mme Tétard, who is charming, and arranged special meals for our small grandson. M. Tétard's cooking is marvellous. Breakfast was of high quality. Our room was cool and well lit, with a fine bathroom." "Madame runs a fiercely efficient dining room, and food was beautifully presented, if a bit rich." There's a terrace for summer dining, and a garden. Bedrooms are well appointed, and the air-conditioning works well.

Open Mar–end Nov.
Rooms 4 suites, 17 double, 3 single. Air-conditioning.
Facilities Salon, TV room, bar, 2 dining rooms; solarium; terrace for summer meals. Garden. Beach 200 m. Unsuitable for ♿.
Location Near centre of town, 79 km E of Palma.
Restriction Not suitable for young children.
Credit cards All major cards accepted.
Terms [1996] Rooms 7,810–9,845 pts, suite 16,905 pts. Breakfast 1,285 pts. Set meals 4,550 pts; full alc 6,000–10,000 pts.

CAMARIÑAS 15123 La Coruña **Map 13**

La Marina BUDGET *Tel* (981) 73 60 30
Miguel Freijo 4

"There's a breezy sense of space about this wild, remote north-west corner of Galicia, so Celtic, recalling Brittany or Co. Mayo. Bold cliffs alternate with deep bays enclosing fishing villages, such as Camariñas, quite untouristy, a bit shabby. On the headland, by a high lighthouse, 20 tall white wind-machines swirl in graceful unison (there's no lack of wind). In the village, women sit in the streets making lace, or grilling fresh sardines. Here, by the harbour, we found *La Marina*, a trim but modest restaurant-with-rooms, owned and run by a charming young woman, Azucena Canosa. Her partner, Juan Carlos, cooks, regally: his parrillada de pescados y mariscos was stunning, a huge platter of fresh mixed fish, with delicate sauces, and one 1,600 pts portion enough for two. Good dry white Galician wines. Our room, fine for a night stop, was small and plain but modern, with a gleaming marble-floored bathroom. Can one ask for more?" (*JA and KA*) Sea-facing rooms are the ones without a bathroom.

Open All year, except early Jan–early Feb.
Rooms 11 double, 4 single.
Facilities Restaurant; outdoor eating in summer.
Location In village, 90 km SW of La Coruña. Street parking.
Credit cards Access, Visa.
Terms Rooms: single 2,100–2,700 pts, double 3,100–4,200 pts. Breakfast 325 pts. Set meals 1,500–3,000 pts; alc 2,500 pts.

CARMONA 41410 Sevilla — Map 13

Parador Alcázar del Rey Don Pedro — *Tel* (95) 414 10 10, *Fax* (95) 414 17 12

This ancient walled town east of Seville is worth visiting for its Roman and medieval ruins. An extra attraction is this *parador*, regarded as one of Spain's finest, and again much liked recently: "The views are lovely; the pool is gorgeous." It is built on a hilltop inside the massive walls of the ancient Moorish *alcázar* and has wide views over the green plain of the Guadalquivir valley, with mountains behind. Moorish influences prevail in its decor – pierced wooden shutters and doors in the public rooms, a patio with a fountain. The interior walls, white-washed or of honey-coloured brick, are complemented by black or brown wood and leather furniture. The gardens are wonderful. The food is international, with repetitive menus: but the varied breakfast buffet is admired. Top-floor rooms have a balcony. Sound insulation, as in many Spanish hotels, can be poor. (*J and TA, S and AK*)

Open All year.
Rooms 1 suite, 62 double. 6 on ground floor. Air-conditioning.
Facilities Lifts. Hall, sitting room with TV room, bar, dining room; function room; patio. Garden: swimming pool.
Location Central; signposted. Parking.
Credit cards All major cards accepted.
Terms [1996] Rooms 16,500–18,000 pts. Breakfast 1,200 pts. Set meals 3,500 pts.

Casa de Carmona NEW — *Tel* (95) 414 33 00
Plaza de Lasso 1 — *Fax* (95) 414 37 52

In the centre of this fine old town (see above) is this "splendid Renaissance town house", refurbished ten years ago by a wealthy local lady, Marta Medina, and now a luxury hotel. An English hotelier nominates it, with caveats: "The rooms are beautiful, with splendid linen, attractive furniture. Owners and staff are charming. Reception is friendly, but unprofessional, and housekeeping is unreliable. The restaurant serves decent international fare, cooked by an Indian chef. Breakfast service can be very slow. Rooms are cunningly designed to avoid the sun, which means that none of them has any view, light or air. And the hotel has no sitting space with an outlook, or where you can sit in the sun. Despite these frustrations, it is possible to have a very happy stay, as we did." However, you can sit in a covered courtyard, and there's an ornamental Arab garden, and a small outdoor pool amid palm trees. (*Tim Hart*) In addition to a lift and ground-floor rooms, the hotel offers "plenty of care and attention" for disabled guests. Reports on meals and breakfast are needed, please.

Open All year.
Rooms 16 suites, 14 double. Air-conditioning. Some on ground floor.
Facilities Lift. 3 lounges, bar, 4 court yards; sauna, fitness room, massage; terrace. Garden: small swimming pool.
Location Central. Parking.
Credit cards All major cards accepted.
Terms Rooms 17,000–34,000 pts, suite 24,000–39,000 pts. Breakfast 1,500 pts. Set meals 3,500 pts; full alc 4,000 pts.

CERVO 27891 Lugo — Map 13

Pousada O Almacén BUDGET — *Tel* (982) 55 78 36
Carretera de Sargadelos 2 — *Fax* (982) 55 78 94

If the *Guide* gave *César* awards for the Continent, here's a candidate for our "utterly enjoyable mild eccentricity" category. On the edge of a Galician village near the coast, it's a sturdy 18th-century stone building, once a warehouse, now neatly restored. "This restaurant-with-rooms has no name outside, no sign that it sells food, drink or accommodation. So you have to ask your way. You enter through a rough bar full of locals. Upstairs, off a loggia with quaint country furniture, are sizeable and comfortable bedrooms, with good modern bathrooms; ours had a balcony above a wayward stream. To reach the handsome restaurant, we were led unceremoniously backstage from the bar, down a cluttered corridor past rooms packed with messy junk – then to be regaled by a jolly waiter with a marvellous copious meal: succulent fish soup, Galician fish dishes, a large and tender entrecôte. The dry Galician white wines were at give-away prices. Rafael Blas Basante is the elderly owner. His son, Fernando, cook and factotum, is a well-known guitarist. He also promotes *turismo rural* and will take guests on horse-treks. Or you can use the hotel's joky stagecoach, 'Cervo City'." Endorsed this year: "A magnificent find. Our room had cool flagged floors, Spanish furniture. In a converted old mill across the road, the hotel owners have created a bizarre night-bar with comfortable seats, attracting people from a hundred miles away. As an eclectic mix of music got toes tapping, the mill filled with a strange mix of Lolitas and Lotharios from the village, weathered farmers, and carloads of wealthy young things from the big smoke. We caroused till 3 am and were probably the first to leave." (*Victoria Heywood and Chris Clark, JA and KA*)

Open All year.
Rooms 8 double.
Facilities Restaurant, bar.
Location On edge of village, on Sargadelos road. 19 km E of Vivero. Parking.
Credit cards All major cards accepted.
Terms [1996] Rooms: single 2,750–3,000 pts, double 4,500–5,500 pts. Breakfast 400 pts. Set meals 1,500 pts.

> Always let a hotel know if you have to cancel a booking, whether you have paid a deposit or not. Hotels sustain huge losses due to "no-shows".

CHINCHÓN 28370 Madrid Map 13

Parador de Chinchón *Tel* (91) 894 08 36
Avenida Generalísimo 1 *Fax* (91) 894 09 08

"The very amiable new manager is improving what was already good," says a visitor this year to an above-average *parador*, a converted 17th-century Augustinian convent in a village south-east of Madrid. "Nice waitresses, and the occasional waiter, serve you cheerfully." Last year's view: "Bedrooms have painted furniture, white walls. There are gardens, a glassed-in cloister for drinks or coffee, a stunning colonnaded swimming pool. And the buffet breakfast prevents one eating for the rest of the day. Chinchón is an interesting little town, with an amazing double-balconied *plaza mayor*." Some suites have a huge terrace. Most visitors approve the food. (*Peter Harryman, and others*)

Open All year.
Rooms 2 suites, 36 double. Some on ground floor. All air-conditioned.
Facilities Lounge, bar, restaurant; conference facilities. Garden: swimming pool.
Location Central. 46 km SE of Madrid. Garage, carpark.
Credit cards All major cards accepted.
Terms B&B: single 13,200–14,400 pts, double 16,200–17,700 pts, suite 19,200–21,200 pts. Set meals 3,500 pts; full alc 4,500 pts.

COFIÑO 33548 Asturias Map 13

Halcón Palace *Tel* (98) 584 13 12
Fax (98) 584 13 13

This renovated manor house has a peaceful setting in the scenic foothills of the Picos de Europa, 15 minutes' drive from the sea. It was liked again this year: "The views across to the Picos are breathtaking, and must remind Leo Benz, the owner, of his native Switzerland, cows and their bells included. His wife is Spanish, and his brother from St-Moritz is chef, providing ample and well-presented food: our memorable *à la carte* dinner included a large mixed hors d'oeuvre and tender fillet steak with local cabrales (ewes' milk cheese). Value for money was very good. We had lunch outdoors with many Spaniards: the hotel's food has a high local reputation. The swimming pool is nicely sited in the garden, with views, but was out of action during our visit." "Our room had full-length windows with small balconies facing the mountains, and a large, well-equipped bathroom." (*William and Anne Reid, and others*) Six new rooms are planned for 1997.

Open All year, except Christmas: possibly 1–2 months for building works.
Rooms 1 suite, 12 double, 1 single. 1 in tower annexe. Some on ground floor. 6 more planned for 1997.
Facilities 2 lounges, bar, restaurant. Function facilities. Garden: swimming pool. Beaches 15 mins; fishing, riding, canoeing nearby.
Location In old village 6 km NW of Arriondas, just off AS260 Colunga road. Parking.
Credit cards All major cards accepted.
Terms Rooms: single 7,000–9,500 pts, double 9,000–13,000 pts, suite 16,000 pts. Breakfast 650 pts. Set meals 1,600 pts.

CÓRDOBA 14003 **Map 13**

Hotel Albucasis BUDGET *Tel/Fax* (3457) 47 86 25
Calle Buen Pastor 11

Friendly, intimate B&B, a whitewashed, shuttered old house in Jewish quarter close to Mezquita. *Simple furnishings, with many personal touches. 15 rooms, all air-conditioned, and modern bathrooms. Breakfast served in plant-filled patio in fine weather.* TV *room, bar. No restaurant, but plenty nearby (try* El Churrasco*). Garage. Access, Visa accepted. B&B: single 6,250 pts, double 10,000 pts. Endorsed this year, but fuller reports welcome.*

Hotel Marisa NEW/BUDGET *Tel* (957) 47 31 42
Cardenal Herrero 6 *Fax* (957) 47 41 44

Central, in old Jewish quarter, picturesque B&B hotel with good views of Mezquita. *Renominated this year for simple but comfortable rooms (some are spacious), friendly staff. Garage. Rooms at back quietest: others may be noisy. All major credit cards accepted. Bar, salon; no restaurant. 28 rooms: double 7,500–8,200 pts. Breakfast (500 pts) not recommended: cafés nearby.*

COSGAYA 39539 Cantabria **Map 13**

Hotel del Oso Pardo BUDGET *Tel* (942) 73 30 18
Fax (942) 73 30 36

Cosgaya is in the Picos de Europa, on the spectacular tourist road leading up from Potes to the Fuente Dé cable car. Here on the edge of the village is this modern hotel in traditional style, with wood balconies and heavy stone walls, but described as "a superior road-house". Recent verdicts: "Rooms are ordinary and a little dark, but such views! The swimming pool, tennis court, café by a stream, are all excellent. Staff are welcoming. And we felt we were eating real local food, very good." "A very well-run hotel, with lots of flowers, beautiful scenery, friendly staff, vast helpings of good food. But the tall new annexe looks soulless, and though the road is quiet at night, there's unceasing traffic during the day." Bedrooms are small but prettily furnished. Dishes include hearty soups, bean and chorizo stew, served generously. There is riding, fishing and skiing in the area. Some British tour groups.

Open All year, except 7 Jan–15 Feb, 24/25 Dec.
Rooms 32 double, 2 single.
Facilities Lounges (1 with TV), bar, restaurant; meeting room. Garden: swimming pool (unheated), tennis. River fishing nearby. Unsuitable for ♿.
Location Edge of village. 14 km W of Potes on Fuente Dé road. Parking.
Credit cards Access, Diners, Visa.
Terms Rooms: single 5,400–6,400 pts, double 7,000–8,000 pts. Breakfast 550 pts. Full alc 3,850 pts

Our italicised entries indicate hotels which are worth considering but which, for various reasons – inadequate information, lack of feedback, ambivalent reports – do not at the moment warrant a full entry. We particularly welcome comments on these hotels.

DEYÁ 07179 Mallorca **Map 13**

Hotel Es Molí *Tel* (971) 63 90 00
Carretera de Valldemossa *Fax* (971) 63 93 33

This old *Guide* favourite, a civilised hotel for civilised people, has a spectacular mountain setting on Mallorca's rugged north-west coast. "Excellent, friendly and well run, with very good food", is how it has been described again this year. The fragrant gardens are filled with blossom and fruit. From the terraces (on which summer meals are served) there are lovely views towards the sea; a meandering walk through olive, orange and lemon groves leads down to a rocky cove. "Stunning views from our balcony. Breakfast and lunch by the pool delicious. The courteous staff were quietly efficient." "Wonderful for a swimming/walking/exploring holiday." Pepe, the "very *simpatico*" reception manager, takes guests on "walks through magnificent unspoilt terrain, followed by long, jovial lunches". The hotel also provides a minibus to its small private beach, for deep-water bathing from a rocky platform (there is no nearby sandy beach). The lighter, more modern rooms in the annexe have "the highest and therefore the best view of the sea" (but some people find the steps too much). (*Audrey Connall, and others*)

Open Mid-Apr–end Oct. Restaurant closed for lunch.
Rooms 3 suites, 59 double, 9 single. Most with terrace. 16-room annexe up steep steps 50 m. Air-conditioning.
Facilities Lift. 3 lounges, TV room, card/writing room, 2 bars, 2 restaurants; dining terrace (dancing weekly in summer). Large gardens: swimming pool, tennis. Free minibus to rocky beach with bar. Unsuitable for ♿.
Location 500 m from village centre. 29 km from Palma. Parking.
Credit cards All major cards accepted.
Terms [1996] B&B 11,700–23,500 pts per person; D,B&B 2,100 pts added. Advance booking essential; min. 2 nights.

La Residencia NEW *Tel* (971) 63 90 11
Fax (971) 63 93 70

Richard Branson owns this very stylish and exclusive Relais & Châteaux hotel, a converted 16th-century manor in a mountainous setting outside the village. It is elegantly decked with antiques and traditional Spanish furnishings; its lovely gardens have orange and lemon trees; there are two swimming pools, and floodlit tennis courts. After some criticisms (eg, lack of any personal touch), it fell from the *Guide*: but five reports in 1995–96 urge that it be restored. "It was wonderful. Our sitting room looked on to the mountains. In *El Olivo* restaurant, the food was delicious" (*Michelin* star). "Excellent bedrooms and service, with towels and robes changed twice daily. Breakfasts were taken on shaded terraces with mountain views. In the main restaurant, all the men were wearing jackets. I was surprised at the formality: I have never seen a picture of Branson in a jacket. The second restaurant, near the main pool, is informal, with a simpler menu." "Terribly expensive, but worth it, though I do wish they would dispense with the synchronised cloche-lifting." A beauty centre is new. Two miles away is the hotel's private cove, with beach, bar and terrace (glorious views of this idyllic coast). (*Mrs C Ainley, Dr John Lunn, Isobel A Kempton, Michael LN Forrest, Tony Balacs*) "One night, we could not eat in *El Olivo* because it was 'fully booked'. The reason: the King of Spain was giving dinner to the Emperor of Japan." Only criticism: poor room insulation.

Open All year.
Rooms 2 suites, 55 double, 8 single. Air-conditioning.
Facilities 5 lounges, 2 bars, reading room, TV room, snooker room, 2 dining rooms; beauty centre, massage; gym; terrace. Garden: 2 swimming pools. Unsuitable for ♿.
Location 200 m from village centre, on Sóller road. Car park.
Credit cards All major cards accepted.
Terms B&B: single 12,000–19,350 pts, double 19,500–32,250 pts, suite 33,000–51,750 pts. Set lunch 6,000 pts, dinner 8,000 pts; full alc 10,000–12,000 pts.

FIGUERAS DEL MAR 33794 Asturias **Map 13**

Palacete Peñalba *Tel* (985) 63 61 25
El Cotarelo *Fax* (985) 63 62 47

Figueras del Mar is a small fishing port on the estuary opposite Ribadeo. Here, this idiosyncratic building, "a delightful original place", stands amid fine old trees on a hill above the sea. "It is a beautiful country house built in 1912 by a disciple of Gaudí, but in a more classically restrained style. Now it's a family-owned hotel. The atrium is surrounded on the first floor by nine bedrooms, mostly small, each with a terrace. They are carefully furnished, so as not to damage the original design; bathrooms are well equipped and seamlessly added. Many details delight: the splashes of coloured glass in the windows; slatted blinds on the outside of the terrace doors and folding solid ones inside; everything newly painted; breakfast served with Art Deco-style crockery on white wicker furniture. The crowning moment comes when you stroll down to the sea and the restaurant, and have a glass of cider in the bar before enjoying the freshly caught fish." The restaurant is in a separate building, down by the harbour.

Open All year.
Rooms 3 suites, 11 double.
Facilities Salons, bar, restaurant; terrace. Large garden. On sea: safe bathing. Special arrangements for guests at golf club 5 km.
Location On hill above port, off Ribadeo road. Private parking.
Credit cards Access, Amex, Visa.
Terms [1996] Rooms 10,500 pts, suite 14,500 pts. Breakfast 700 pts. Full alc 4,500 pts.

FUENTERRABÍA 20280 Guipúzcoa **Map 13**

Hotel Pampinot *Tel* (943) 64 06 00
Calle Mayor 5 *Fax* (943) 64 51 28

On hill in old part of this town close to French border, aristocratic 16th-century mansion, tastefully converted, with 8 attractive bedrooms. Elegant, grand but personal furnishings, antiques, chandeliers. Welcoming owners. No restaurant; lots nearby. All major credit cards accepted. Unsuitable for ♿. Rooms: single 10,500 pts, double 14,000 pts. Breakfast 1,100 pts [1996]. Endorsed this year: "Marvellous, with friendly staff, superb breakfast."

Parador de Hondarribia NEW *Tel* (943) 64 55 00
Plaza de Armas 14 *Fax* (943) 64 21 53

In main square of old town (see previous page), grey stone fortress once palace of Charles V, now small quite luxurious parador, *just restored. Fine views across bay to France. "Excellent" larger rooms; others smaller but also pleasant. Adequate breakfasts. All major credit cards accepted. 36 rooms: single 10,000–13,200 pts, double 13,500–21,000 pts. Breakfast 1,200 pts [1996]. No restaurant: try nearby* Sebastián *(medium price) or* Ramón Roteta (Michelin *star, expensive). Renominated this year; fuller reports welcome.*

GOMERA 38800 Islas Canarias — Map 13

Parador Conde de la Gomera *Tel* (922) 87 11 00
Cerro de la Horca *Fax* (922) 87 11 16
San Sebastián de la Gomera

Tiny, lush, mountainous Gomera is only 35 minutes by hydrofoil from busy Tenerife. In its capital, San Sebastián, Christopher Columbus prepared his ships to sail for the New World. This clifftop *parador* above the town is a long stone-and-tile mansion surrounded by a garden of date palms. A reader this year found it "welcoming, comfortable, with a good dinner table", echoing earlier praise: "One of the nicest hotels we have ever stayed in. It looks old, but was built in 1972, in Canarian style – a series of two-storey buildings with white walls, dark brown shutters, terracotta tiles, and inside polished wood floors, blue-and-white fabrics. Service is friendly, reading lights are powerful. Charming large garden with tropical plants, excellent swimming pool – and above all, perfect peace and quiet, just birdsong." Furnishings are "typical *parador* mock-antique". "Varied food, with local as well as Spanish dishes." "Beautifully run, with a monastic feel." (*Dr NB Finter, Joe Bourke, and others*) Not all rooms have a balcony. One or two gripes about the food, including the absence of fresh juice at breakfast; and about "impersonal" service. Sixteen rooms were added this year.

Open All year.
Rooms 2 suites, 58 double.
Facilities 2 salons, TV room, bar, restaurant. Large grounds: garden, swimming pool, bar. Black sand beach 15 mins' steep walk: safe bathing. Unsuitable for ♿.
Location 600 m from centre, overlooking port. Parking.
Credit cards All major cards accepted.
Terms [1996] Rooms 15,000 pts. Breakfast 1,200 pts. Set meals 3,000 pts; full alc 4,000 pts.

GRANADA — Map 13

Hotel América *Tel* (958) 22 74 71
Calle Real de la Alhambra 53 *Fax* (958) 22 74 70
Granada 18009

Far less expensive than the nearby *parador* (see next page), this delightful small hotel on the Alhambra hill has an interesting collection of art and sculpture, and has delighted readers again this year: "Marvellous. Pretty rooms, a lovely large patio where meals are served when fine. The food is simple but good; owners most pleasant." "Some dishes were really delicious." "Incredibly friendly, in a wonderful situation," ran an earlier report. The hotel was started by the present owner's father in 1929, and Maribel and Rafael Garzón continue that tradition. Architecture and furnishings are typically Andalusian, with many plants around the windows and doors. Rooms are small, some very small. (*Gillian Gadsby, Maureen Hunt, and others*)

Open 1 Mar–9 Nov. Restaurant closed Sat.
Rooms 1 suite (on ground floor), 8 double, 4 single. 9 air-conditioned.
Facilities Salon, dining room (no-smoking); patio. Unsuitable for ♿.
Location Alhambra hill. No private parking facilities.
Credit cards All major cards accepted.
Terms Rooms: single 7,000 pts, double 10,500 pts, suite 13,500 pts. Breakfast 1,000 pts. Set meals 2,100 pts; full alc 3,000 pts.

Hotel Reina Christina BUDGET *Tel* (958) 25 32 11
Calle Tablas 4 *Fax* (958) 25 57 28
Granada 18002

Federico García Lorca spent his last days here, in 1936, before the Nationalists murdered him: a fountain in the patio pays homage. It's a small hotel near the cathedral, well appointed and renovated this year; and though in a busy downtown street it is described as "beautifully quiet and cool" by recent visitors, who add: "The combination of marble and plants made for a relaxing atmosphere. Staff were charming, every comfort was provided, breakfasts were good buffet affairs, and our evening meal was simple but wholesome." Others too have liked it, save that "air-conditioning turned off at night was a problem in hot July". (*R and AS, and others*) The car park is four blocks away, but: "We were able to park outside the hotel for three days."

Open All year.
Rooms 3 suites, 31 double, 9 single. Air-conditioning.
Facilities Lift. Salon, TV room, snack bar, restaurant.
Location Central, near cathedral. Parking.
Credit cards All major cards accepted.
Terms [1996] Rooms: single 6,200 pts, double 9,750 pts, suite 11,550 pts. Breakfast 700 pts. D,B&B double 14,350–18,450 pts. Set meals 1,600 pts; full alc 3,000 pts.

Parador de San Francisco *Tel* (958) 22 14 40
Alhambra *Fax* (958) 22 22 64
Granada 18009

This flagship *parador*, right next to the Alhambra, is at core a 15th-century Franciscan monastery with lovely courtyards. "It was excellent, with very good food," is a 1996 comment, endorsing previous plaudits: "You feel as if you're staying *at* the Alhambra, it's so beautifully decorated in Moorish style, and lush with gardens." "The restaurant may lack views, but there's an outdoor terrace for drinks and breakfast, and some rooms have delightful views across to the Generalife." "Our palatial room in the original building had a balcony looking over the superb gardens. The courtyard was a delight, with plants, trickling water, and comfortable armchairs and sofas." Rooms in the modern wings are spacious but lack character. Food is mostly described as "OK". The *parador* is often heavily booked, and many guests stay for one night only, so small wonder that we get some reports of poor reception and service. (*Avis Port, and others*)

Open All year.
Rooms 2 suites, 36 double. Air-conditioning.
Facilities Salon, bar, tea room, restaurant; conference room; terrace. Garden. Unsuitable for ♿.
Location By Alhambra. Parking.
Credit cards All major cards accepted.
Terms [1996] Rooms 28,500 pts. Breakfast 1,200 pts. Set meals 3,500 pts.

GUADALUPE 10140 Cáceres — Map 13

Hospederia del Real Monasterio BUDGET — *Tel* (927) 36 70 00
Plaza Juan Carlos 1 — *Fax* (927) 36 71 77

This small town in the mountains between Toledo and Cáceres was a pilgrimage centre in the Middle Ages, and the image of the Virgin in its church is still venerated. The *Hospederia* forms part of the famous and majestic 14th-century Franciscan monastery, and has again been much admired: "A real prize. Since this is a royal monastery, you can imagine what the guest quarters are like. Our room was 30 feet by 30 feet, with 14-foot ceiling, antique furniture and a gigantic bed with huge carved headboard. Modern fittings in the bathroom. The restaurant serves excellent food at reasonable prices, and staff were helpful. The large courtyard was filled with flowers." (*LS, AR*)

Open All year, except mid-Jan–mid-Feb.
Rooms 1 suite, 45 double, 1 single.
Facilities Lift. Salons, TV room, bar, restaurant; cloister.
Location Central. 129 km E of Cáceres. Parking.
Credit cards Access, Visa.
Terms [1996] Rooms: single 4,700 pts, double 6,900 pts, suite 15,750 pts. Breakfast 750 pts. Full board 9,490 pts. Set meals 2,300 pts; full alc 3,500 pts.

Parador de Guadalupe — *Tel* (927) 36 70 75
Marqués de la Romana 12 — *Fax* (927) 36 70 76

Next to monastery (see above), elegant parador *installed in two 15th-century buildings, one a former hospital for pilgrims, one a former college. Cobbled courtyard with orange trees; lovely gardens: swimming pool, tennis. 40 attractive bedrooms, 20 in modern annexe with views (roomier but less characterful than those in original building), all air-conditioned. Lavish breakfasts. All major credit cards accepted. Rooms 9,500–12,500 pts. Breakfast 1,200 pts. Set meals 3,200 pts [1996]. Fuller reports welcome.*

GUALCHOS 18614 Granada — Map 13

La Posada — *Tel/Fax* (958) 65 60 34
Plaza Constitución 3–4

William Job (Australian) and José González (Spanish) own and run this admired restaurant-with-rooms, made up of two restored 18th-century houses, in the main square of an untouristy village in the foothills of the Sierra de Lújar. Devotees have written glowingly: "A haven of beauty and tranquillity, furnished in exquisite taste." Sr González's cooking is admired: "Imaginative, with beautifully flavoured sauces." "Delicious dinner (stuffed artichokes, roast partridge with rosemary)." Half board is obligatory. The garden and hillsides are ablaze with flowers in spring, but the polythene covers of market gardeners can blemish the view. Hosts and staff are "charming". (*C and AP, and others*) This hill village can be chilly, and the steep access is difficult with a large car. No recent reports: more welcome.

Open 15 Mar–30 Nov. Restaurant closed Mon.
Rooms 7 double, 2 single.
Facilities Lounge, bar, restaurant; patio/terrace. Small garden: pergola, tiny swimming pool (unheated). Beach 9 km. Unsuitable for ♿.
Location In village centre, 9 km from coast. Leave car at edge and walk; hotel will collect and park it.
Restriction No children under 12.
Credit cards Access, Visa.
Terms B&B (Mon only) 6,500 pts; D,B&B (obligatory, except Mon) 12,000 pts.

GUERNICA 48300 Vizcaya — Map 13

Hotel Gernika BUDGET — *Tel* (94) 625 03 50
Carlos Gangoiti 17 — *Fax* (94) 625 5874

In Basques' spiritual capital, small town famous for its ancient symbolic oak tree, German 1937 air blitz and Picasso's painting of that (now in Madrid): spruce, simple modern B&B hotel in N outskirts, on Bermeo road. Friendly staff, 24 serviceable bedrooms, decent breakfast in drab room. Garden. Beaches nearby. Unsuitable for ♿. Closed 25–31 Dec. All major credit cards accepted. Rooms 5,785–8,872 pts. Breakfast 630 pts.

JAÉN 23001 — Map 13

Parador de Santa Catalina — *Tel* (953) 23 00 00
Carretera del Castillo — *Fax* (953) 23 09 30

Set high on a crag above the town, and visible from far away, this *parador* is "modern and breathtaking". A recent view: "The contrast between the beautifully landscaped modern swimming pool, and its approach from the high steps of a rebuilt medieval castle, leaves an indelible impression." Only south-facing rooms have a balcony, but all have remarkable views. The ante-room to the dining room has high vaulted arches worthy of a cathedral. The dining room itself is hung with banners and tapestries, and the food is admired: "Local *cuisine*, the most interesting *parador* dinner we had." "Delicious fish soup." "Breakfasts were a veritable feast." Staff are "helpful and courteous". (*DB and FB, and others*) Newer reports welcome.

Open All year.
Rooms 45. 11 on ground floor. Some with balcony. Air-conditioning.
Facilities Lift. 2 lounges, chess/card room, bar, 2 restaurants. Large garden: swimming pool.
Location 3 km SW of Jaén. Follow signs for castle.
Credit cards All major cards accepted.
Terms [1996] Rooms 15,000–16,500 pts. Breakfast 1,200 pts. Set meals 3,500 pts.

Many hotels put up their prices in the spring. Tariffs quoted in the text may therefore be more accurate before April/May 1997 than after.

JARANDILLA DE LA VERA 10450 Cáceres — Map 13

Parador de Jarandilla de la Vera NEW

Tel (927) 56 01 17
Fax (927) 56 00 88

In a small town off the beaten track, way north-east of Cáceres, is this converted late-14th-century fortress, where Charles V once spent a year. It has mighty round stone towers, and an imposing courtyard. What's more, it is "one of the friendliest of *paradores*", according to its nominator this year: "The air conditioning was just right. There's a fine clean swimming pool in a pleasant garden. The cheerful waitresses were dressed in smart local costume. Food was good, eg, hake en papillote, grilled fish, figs in chocolate, local cheese tart – and hot tortilla for breakfast. Such a change from the service at another *parador* we visited, where Bernarda Alba herself was presiding, slow, surly and inefficient." "The dining room is beautiful." (*William and Ann Reid, EP Fooks*)

Open All year.
Rooms 43 double, 10 single. Air-conditioning.
Facilities Bar, restaurant; 3 conference rooms. Garden: swimming-pool, tennis.
Location In town, 132 km NE of Cáceres, 53 km E of Plasencia. Parking.
Credit cards All major cards accepted.
Terms [1996] Rooms: 15,000 pts. Breakfast 1,200 pts. Set meals 3,500 pts.

LEÓN 24001 — Map 13

Parador de San Marcos
Plaza de San Marcos 7

Tel (987) 23 73 00
Fax (987) 23 34 58

This former monastery is now a flagship *parador*, almost as much a showpiece as León's great Gothic cathedral. Dating from the 16th century, it has a splendid Renaissance façade, a monumental cloister, and palatial public rooms, newly refurbished. "My dinner was enjoyable, and I liked the mix of good quality new and old pictures," is a recent comment. Others have admired the fine reproductions of Spanish furniture and tapestries, softening the cool stone walls. Most bedrooms, large and well appointed, are in a modern extension: the luxurious principal suite was much praised this year. The restaurant, modern in style, gives on to a summer terrace, with the river beyond. The buffet breakfasts are liked. (*Peter Harryman*) Tour groups and coaches are much in evidence. Service was again rebuked this year: "surly", "disappointingly corporate".

Open All year.
Rooms 15 suites, 185 double. Air conditioning.
Facilities Lift. Salons, bar, restaurant, breakfast room; conference facilities; beauty parlour. Garden.
Location On river. Parking.
Credit cards All major cards accepted.
Terms [1996] Rooms 18,500 pts. Breakfast 1,200 pts. Set meals 3,500 pts.

> Be warned: in luxury hotels in Spain a value added tax will increase your bill by 15%. In one- to four-star hotels the surcharge is 6%.

MADRID 28014 Map 13

Hotel Prado NEW
Prado 11
Tel (91) 369 02 34
Fax (91) 429 28 29

Central, 400 km W of Prado museum, smallish five-storey hotel, recently modernised; efficient staff, 47 small but comfortable rooms (top-floor ones have balcony with rooftop views); tiled bathrooms. Breakfast with fresh orange juice. All major credit cards accepted. Rooms 14,000–17,500 pts. Breakfast 650 pts. Set meals 1,600 pts [1996]. Renominated this year. Reports on food welcome.

Hotel Villa Real
Plaza de las Cortes 10
Tel (91) 420 37 67
Fax (91) 420 25 47

Near to the Prado and the popular Santa Ana district of bars and restaurants: a fairly large, stylish hotel that skilfully blends old and new in its 18th/19th-century building, and was enjoyed in 1996. Public areas are traditionally furnished with mahogany, and pastoral embroideries. Food is expensive and elaborate (eg, linguine with garlic and baby eels; seafood and saffron soup loaded with lobster and shrimp). "This place is about service and charm." Staff are "the best I've ever encountered in Spain – they even made checking out a pleasure". (*Mrs C Ann Sweeney*)

Open All year.
Rooms 19 suites, 96 double. All air-conditioned.
Facilities Lift, ramps. Lounge, bar, TV room, snack bar, restaurant; conference/banqueting facilities; sauna, hairdresser, massage. Unsuitable for ♿.
Location Central, near Parliament, next to *Palace Hotel*. Garage.
Credit cards All major cards accepted.
Terms B&B: single 26,500 pts, double 34,400 pts, suite 65,000 pts. Full alc 6,000 pts.

MARANGES 17539 Gerona Map 13

Can Borrell BUDGET
Calle Regresco 3
Tel (972) 88 00 33
Fax (972) 88 01 44

In the Pyrenean resort area of Cerdanya, near Andorra, is this rambling farmhouse, stone-walled and much-beamed, now a "charming" restaurant-with-rooms. "The setting at the head of a valley is superb. A track leads up the mountain near some lakes. The hotel is owned and run by Antonio Forn and his wife, with the help of their three daughters. Service is friendly and personal. The food is excellent, with a Catalan touch, eg, conill amb cargos (rabbits with snails), also fresh local fungi, wild raspberries." Endorsed this year: "Señora is charming and very efficient." (*Mr and Mrs WM Lee*)

Open Apr–Dec, weekends Jan–Mar. Restaurant closed Mon evening/Tues in winter.
Rooms 6 double, 2 single.
Facilities Lounge, TV room, bar, 2 dining rooms; 2 terraces, veranda. Lakes, golf, skiing nearby; good walking in summer.
Location 18 km W of Puigcerdá. Large carpark.
Credit cards Access, Visa.
Terms [1996] Rooms: single 6,000 pts, double 8,000 pts. Breakfast 800 pts. Alc meals 2,900–4,050 pts. Off-season reductions. Special interest weekend courses: cookery, birdwatching, etc.

MÉRIDA 06800 Badajoz — Map 13

Parador de Mérida NEW
Plaza de la Constitución
Tel (924) 31 38 00
Fax (924) 31 92 08

Central, near Roman ruins and superb new Roman museum: former convent, with cloister, quiet rooms, luxurious modern bathrooms; small garden. Domed chapel now lounge. Excellent food, good friendly staff. Lift; carpark. All major credit cards accepted. 80 rooms: 16,500 pts. Breakfast 1,200 pts. Set meals 3,500 pts [1996]. Warmly renominated this year.

MIJAS-COSTA 29648 Málaga — Map 13

Casa Aloha
Playa El Chaparral
Carratera de Cádiz 203
Tel/Fax (52) 49 45 40

On sandy beach 30 km W of Málaga, off N340, Andalusian villa run as personal guest house, a Wolsey Lodge, by English couple Trish and Ray Goddard, he a former professional footballer. Terrace, gardens, attractive swimming pool; lounge in Mozarabic style (no-smoking). Water sports of all kinds available. Evening meal by arrangement (4,000 pts); paella admired. Children over 12 preferred. Access, Diners, Visa accepted. 5 bedrooms (no-smoking). B&B 6,500–7,500 pts. More reports, please.

NERJA 29780 Málaga — Map 13

Parador de Nerja NEW
Playa de Burriano-Tablazo
Tel (95) 252 00 50
Fax (95) 252 19 97

Splendidly located on a cliff above the beach, on the edge of this resort near Málaga, a civilised modern *parador* with beautiful gardens and courtyard, fountains and flowers. It is renominated this year: "It's good value, with a sense of space and peace, plenty of loungers and room to be alone. Bedrooms are spacious, each with a balcony and a view of the delightful gardens and sea. In the large, attractive dining room, the food was very good, and the breakfast buffet excellent, with masses of fresh fruit. Reception staff were helpful." There's a large swimming pool, and a lift down to the beach. "Nerja is said by many to be the most pleasant resort on the Costa." (*Maureen Hunt*)

Open All year.
Rooms 73. Air-conditioning.
Facilities Lift. Salons, bar, restaurant; conference room. Garden: swimming pool with snack bar, tennis.
Location E edge of resort. 52 km E of Málaga. Parking.
Credit cards All major cards accepted.
Terms [1996] Rooms 16,500 pts. Breakfast 1,200 pts. Set meals 3,500 pts.

> We asked hotels to quote 1997 prices. Not all were able to predict them in the late spring of 1996. Some of our terms will be inaccurate. Do check latest tariffs at the time of booking.

OLITE 31390 Navarra Map 13

Parador del Príncipe de Viana *Tel* (948) 74 00 00
Plaza de Los Teobaldos 2 *Fax* (948) 74 02 01

In this small and pleasant town on the plain south of Pamplona stands one of Spain's great castles, which was restored in the 15th century as a residence for the kings of Navarre. Near this massive and much rebuilt edifice, with its jumble of towers, porticoes, huge halls and winding stone stairways, is a much smaller and even older royal castle, where Carlos III, *El Noble*, spent his final years. This is now a *parador*, rather enclosed ("too much frosted glass"), with no garden, but decked out with the usual tapestries, armour and heavy baronial furniture. "Lovely building, one of the best meals we've had in a *parador*, terrific breakfast," runs a report this year. An earlier view: "Our room in the old building was superb – twin four-posters, enormous stone fireplace, lots of space and, of course, all mod cons." (*Linda Brook*) There is a new manager this year.

Open All year.
Rooms 42 double, 1 single. Some on ground floor. Air-conditioning.
Facilities Lift. Lounge with TV, bar, breakfast room, restaurant; conference facilities.
Location Central; next to castle.
Credit cards All major cards accepted.
Terms Rooms 10,800–13,500 pts. Breakfast 1,200 pts. Set meals 3,200 pts; full alc 5,000 pts.

PALMA DE MALLORCA Map 13

Hotel Born *Tel* (971) 71 29 42
Calle San Jaime 3 *Fax* (971) 71 86 18
Palma de Mallorca 07012

Not itself too spoilt by tourism, Mallorca's capital remains a real old Spanish city with a nucleus of picturesque narrow streets and alleys. Down one of them is this surprise: "A grand 18th-century mansion, with a sweeping staircase, chandeliers, a splendid courtyard and a regal air. The brass is always polished. All rooms are simply but adequately furnished, with sparkling bathrooms. The best overlook the palm-tree'd courtyard where an average breakfast is taken. Staff seemed reserved at first, but became friendly." (*DC*) No restaurant.

Open All year.
Rooms 3 suites, 20 double, 7 single. Air-conditioning.
Facilities Lounge with TV, bar; patio. Unsuitable for ♿.
Location Central.
Credit cards Access, Amex, Visa.
Terms B&B: single 9,500 pts, double 11,000–15,000 pts, suite 19,000 pts.

PERAMOLA 25790 Lérida Map 13

Hotel Can Boix NEW *Tel/Fax* (973) 470266

Off the main road from Andorra to Lérida, this white modern hotel, fairly smart, has a splendid isolated setting at the foot of the craggy Roca del Corb, and it overlooks the green valley of the Rio Segre.

Most rooms, in a nearby annexe, are large and very well equipped; service is attentive. "A haven of comfort amid the wilds of Catalonia," says our nominator. "There's a fountain-centred patio with a view to the snowy Serra del Cadi. The owner/chef, Joan Pallarés, is delightful, much in evidence, and he produced some excellent dinners (eg, seafood ravioli, duck with sweet roasted onion, apple gratin with cava sauce). There's good walking from the hotel, to explore hidden valleys and tiny Romanesque churches." There are wide lawns, and a large pool with loungers. (*Mrs Romney Bathurst*)

Open All year, except Jan, 15 days Nov.
Rooms 20 suites, 11 double, 4 single. 20 in nearby annexe. 1 suitable for ♿.
Facilities Lounge, TV room, bar, restaurant; sauna, solarium. Garden: swimming pool (unheated), tennis, table-tennis, children's play area.
Location 2.5 km NE of Peramola, which is 47 km S of Seo de Urgel, just W of main road to Lérida. Parking.
Credit cards Access, Amex, Visa accepted.
Terms Rooms: single 3,710 pts, double 4,735 pts, suite 16,430 pts. Breakfast 850 pts. D,B&B 5,865–11,713 pts per person. Set meals 2,835 pts; full alc 3,370 pts.

PONTEVEDRA 36002 — Map 13

Parador Casa del Barón — *Tel* (986) 85 58 00
Calle Barón 19 — *Fax* (986) 85 21 95

A 16th-century manor house (*pazo*) in the elegant heart of this old Galician city. "Like the whole town it has a quiet charm," says a recent visitor, "even if the rooms do not have much character. The small garden with its terrace, fountain and lawn with a large tree is attractive. Interesting old objects, and a sympathetic ambience. Nearby is the *Michelin*-starred *Doña Antonia*, a welcome escape from the hotel's dining room, and at no greater cost." An earlier visitor thought the *parador*'s own menu "imaginative" (Galician seafood, etc), and the buffet breakfast ample and varied. Rooms vary; some have been found "superb". There's an impressive stone staircase, and antique-style furniture. Staff are pleasant. (*Endorsed this year by Prof. and Mrs Robson*)

Open All year.
Rooms 44 double, 3 single. Some on ground floor.
Facilities Ramps. Lounge, bar, breakfast room, restaurant; meeting room; terrace. Garden. Sea, beaches nearby.
Location Old town centre; signposted.
Credit cards All major cards accepted.
Terms [1996] Rooms: single 8,400–11,600 pts, double 10,500–14,500 pts. Breakfast 1,200 pts. Set meals 3,200 pts.

REBOREDO 36988 Pontevedra — Map 13

Bosque Mar BUDGET — *Tel* (986) 73 10 55
Fax (986) 73 05 12

On Galician coast 32 km NW of Pontevedra, near resort of El Grove, a modern family-run holiday hotel amid pinewoods, close to sandy beaches. Friendly owners, pleasant bedrooms (best are in new annexe), many with balcony and sea views. Pretty garden, small but lovely swimming pool with parasols and loungers; sitting and breakfast rooms a bit formal. Fairly good food (or try Beiramar *in El Grove). Open Apr–Oct. Access, Visa accepted. 64 rooms: 4,000–9,500 pts. Breakfast 900 pts. D,B&B 6,000 pts per person. Set meals 2,000 pts [1996].*

RIBADESELLA 33560 Asturias **Map 13**

La Playa BUDGET *Tel* (98) 586 01 00

This pleasant little seaside town is close to the giant Tito Bustillo cave (wall paintings of *c.* 20,000 BC) and not far from the Picos de Europa. It has cliff walks, and a broad sheltered sandy beach with holiday hotels. One of these is a modest B&B, *La Playa*, liked by inspectors: "It's old-fashioned, but in a nice way – a 1920s yellow italianate villa of faded elegance, with flowers and creepers at the front. The Quesada Garcia family have owned it for 40 years, their family photos line the hall, and they run it in laid-back style. Our big room had a wood-panelled ceiling, coloured tiles, solid beds. The telephone, light switches and plumbing all looked unchanged since the 1930s, yet they worked. A friendly girl served us a simple, decent breakfast, which you can take on the terrace in summer. Some rooms have a balcony with sea view. There's a comfortable lounge, a sort-of patio with loungers, and the beach at your feet. Plenty of good eating-places by the harbour, across the bridge: try the *Tixin* for seafood tapas, the *Xico* for main meals.

Open 1 Apr–30 Sept.
Rooms 11 double.
Facilities Lounge, bar with TV, breakfast room; terrace. Garden.
Location On beach, 1 km W of town centre. 67 km E of Gijón. Parking.
Credit cards Access, Visa.
Terms Double: B&B 6,300–8,800 pts; D,B&B 12,800 pts. Set meals 2,000 pts.

RONDA 29400 Málaga **Map 13**

Hotel Don Miguel NEW/BUDGET *Tel* (95) 287 77 22
Villanueva 8 *Fax* (95) 287 83 77

Small friendly hotel close to Parador *(see below), and likewise right beside bridge and gorge. Some bedrooms have "spectacular" balcony overlooking gorge; same view from dining terrace (mainly very good food), but not for those who suffer from vertigo. Closed 2 weeks Jan. All major credit cards accepted. 19 rooms: single 4,500–5,500 pts, double 7,500–9,000 pts. Breakfast 375 pts. Meals alc 2,500–4,500 pts [1996].*

Parador de Ronda NEW *Tel* (528) 77500
Plaza de España *Fax* (528) 78188

Splendidly situated beside the top of Ronda's mighty gorge, this modern *parador* is built on the site of the old town hall and was opened in 1994. It makes its *Guide* debut: "The restaurant, with views of the mountains from every window, is breathtaking. Food was far above *parador* average (very good braised partridge) and service was friendly. Bedrooms are spacious. They all overlook the gorge, which does sometimes give off a smell of sewage: you should then keep the windows shut and use the air-conditioning." (*EP Fooks*)

Open All year.
Rooms 8 suites, 70 double. Air-conditioning
Facilities Lift. Salons, restaurant; conference facilities. Garden: swimming pool.
Location Central. Private underground parking.
Credit cards All major cards accepted.
Terms Rooms: single 10,800–13,200 pts, double 13,500–16,500 pts, suite 18,000–21,000 pts. Breakfast 1,200 pts. Set meals 3,000 pts; full alc 4,280 pts.

SALAMANCA Map 13

Residencia Rector *Tel* (923) 21 84 82
Rector Esperabé 10 *Fax* (923) 21 40 08
Salamanca 37008

"Salamanca has many hotels but none hold a candle to this place. The rooms are splendidly opulent, and service was most obliging." That report this year endorses an earlier panegyric: "A dream of a place. From the outside it looks like one of the city's grand palaces, with a pink stone façade carved in Renaissance style. But it dates back only to 1945. It is near a traffic junction on the city's noisy circular road. You enter down a few steps, to silence and a visual wonder of proportion and luxury. Recently restored by the family owners and a gifted architect, the interior is a *tour de force* of elegance. The style, though eclectic, is totally harmonious. Every detail is perfect: bathroom lined in marble, with the best shower fitting ever, soundless air-conditioning, remote-control garage doors, leaf tea with strainer. . . . Most rooms are on the first floor, grouped around patios. You feel strangely cocooned in this inward-turned design, amid high tech and sparkling restrained beauty." (*Lindsay Fisher, FS*) No restaurant.

Open All year.
Rooms 1 suite, 11 double, 1 single. Some on ground floor. Air-conditioning.
Facilities Lift. Salons, bar, breakfast room.
Location On ring road, near Roman bridge at S end of historic quarter, 400 m from centre. Garage.
Credit cards All major cards accepted.
Terms Rooms: single 12,000 pts, double 16,000 pts, suite 20,000 pts. Breakfast 950 pts.

SANLÚCAR DE BARRAMEDA 11540 Cádiz Map 13

Posada de Palacio BUDGET *Tel* (956) 36 48 40
Calle Caballeros 11 *Fax* (956) 36 50 60

This small and quiet *pension*, a whitewashed house with a stone courtyard, is in the old quarter of this sherry town, "where the scent of the local salty manzanilla haunts the *bodegas*". It is a building of some distinction, as a recent visitor found: "We were bowled over by our suite: two gorgeous and palatial rooms, plus a sitting room with easy chairs, and a sumptuous bathroom. Steps led up to the guests' sun-terrace, which was dotted with mattresses and potted plants. All very good value – as was the breakfast, with fresh orange juice and home-made cherry jam. A wonderful place." Some bedrooms are much simpler. (*MB*) Reports on food and service welcome.

Open Mar–end Dec. Restaurant closed for lunch.
Rooms 3 suites, 10 double, 2 on ground floor.
Facilities TV room with honesty bar, bar, restaurant; patio, roof-terrace. Garden. Beaches 2 km.
Location In old quarter, near church of Nuestra Señora de la O.
Credit cards Access, Diners, Visa.
Terms Rooms: single 5,000 pts, double 6,000–8,000 pts, suite 10,000 pts. Breakfast 700 pts. Set dinner 1,700 pts; full alc 2,200 pts.

SANTA MARIA DE MAVE 34492 Palencia — Map 13

Hosteria El Convento NEW/BUDGET — *Tel* (979) 12 36 11 *Fax* (979) 12 54 92

In village 8 km S of Aguilar, just W of main Santander–Palencia road, modest hotel in cleverly converted convent, next to fine Romanesque church. Family-run and friendly; simple rooms with good modern bathrooms; views over farmlands and orchards. Lively café/bar, quiet lounges with traditional decor; good food in stylish restaurant. Access, Amex, Visa accepted. 19 rooms: 4,000–6,000 pts. Breakfast 500 pts. Set meals 1,500 pts [1996].

SANTANDER — Map 13

Hostal Carlos III BUDGET — *Tel/Fax* (942) 27 16 16
Av. de la Reina Victoria 135
El Sardinero, 39005 Santander

Santander is not only a lively port and university city: its suburb of El Sardinero, with a long elegant beach and large white 1920s casino, is northern Spain's most fashionable seaside resort after San Sebastián. A smaller white 1920s villa, facing the beach, houses this sympathetic B&B hotel. "It is run by a friendly family and has a bright and cosy lounge, and a patio with Grecian statuary, where an adequate breakfast is served. Bathrooms are modern; bedrooms have good lighting, solid period furniture, and ours had a sea view. An ideal night stop before the morning ferry to Plymouth. And Santander has superb restaurants: try the *Bodega del Riojano* or *Posada del Mar*, both medium price." "Charming, full of smiles." (*Albert and Patricia Grant, JA and KA*)

Open 16 Mar–3 Nov.
Rooms 16 double, 4 single.
Facilities Lounge/breakfast room with TV; patio. Opposite sandy beach: safe bathing. Unsuitable for ♿.
Location In El Sardinero, 3 km E of centre and port. Public parking.
Credit cards Access, Amex, Visa.
Terms Rooms: single 4,000–6,200 pts, double 5,800–8,200 pts. Breakfast 390 pts.

SANTILLANA DEL MAR 39330 Cantabria — Map 13

Hotel Altamira BUDGET — *Tel* (942) 81 80 25
Calle Cantón 1 — *Fax* (942) 84 01 36

Besieged by tourists all day, this little medieval town is quieter at night. Here, a finely converted 17th-century palace, with richly beamed interior, has long been liked for its helpful staff, reasonable rates and solid comfort: some bedrooms have a balcony over the cobbled street. "Adequate bedroom in pleasant hotel with good friendly service; dinner superb, breakfast rather poor." That report this year backs earlier views: "Charming and atmospheric." "Exquisite and imaginative meals, elegant service." There are two restaurants, one for regional dishes, the other for simpler *platos combinados*. For ambitious eaters, the *Michelin*-starred *Molino* at Puente Arce, to the east, is "a wonderful restaurant", but it may be too *nueva cocina* for some tastes. To visit the famous caves of Altamira, near Santillana, you should apply months in advance: numbers are restricted, to protect the prehistoric paintings from damage. (*Findlay family*)

Open All year, except New Year.
Rooms 2 suites, 25 double, 5 single.
Facilities 2 dining rooms, bar; terrace. Garden. Beach 15 km. Unsuitable for ♿.
Location Central, by *parador*. Street parking.
Credit cards All major cards accepted.
Terms [1996] Rooms 6,300–10,200 pts. Breakfast 550 pts. Set meals 1,600 pts.

SANTO DOMINGO DE LA CALZADA 26250 La Rioja — Map 13

Parador de Santo Domingo *Tel* (941) 34 03 00
Plaza del Santo 3 *Fax* (941) 34 03 25

It's a surprise to find a live white hen and a cock, crowing loud, in a cage in the cathedral: they relate to a complicated story about an 11th-century hermit, Santo Domingo, whose miraculous powers kept a German pilgrim alive on the gallows after he had been falsely accused of theft. The saint also built a causeway (*calzada*) to help pilgrims on their way to Santiago. Later, opposite the cathedral, a hostel was created for them, and this forms the kernel of today's *parador*, quite smart, and liked again recently: "A pleasant surprise. It seems to have been rebuilt and redecorated, and is light and modern. Reception was friendly, and our quite large room had a stunningly large bathroom, modern and sparkling. The split-level dining room had a pleasant atmosphere, but service there was a bit thoughtless." "Food undistinguished," says another report. But they serve good Rioja wines from the vineyards just to the north, round Haro. (*RH*)

Open All year.
Rooms 61. Air-conditioning.
Facilities Lift. Restaurant; courtyard.
Location In town on Burgos road, 47 km W of Logroño. Public parking.
Credit cards All major cards accepted.
Terms [1996] Rooms: 13,500–20,000 pts. Breakfast 1,200 pts. Set meals 3,500 pts.

SEGOVIA — Map 13

Hotel Infanta Isabel NEW *Tel* (921) 44 31 05
Plaza Mayor *Fax* (921) 43 32 40
Segovia 40001

In the main square, by the cathedral, is this stately 19th-century building, opened as a hotel in 1992. "I think it is better, and better value, than the *Parador*, Segovia's other *Guide* entry," says its nominator, an expert on Spain. "It is a skilful conversion of an old town house, elegantly decorated and furnished in a kind of *fin de siècle* style. Unusually tasteful, in greens and yellows, it has damask wall coverings, restrained gilt wall lighting and ornate Spanish stoves. The breakfast room is charming, with pretty china and very attractive chairs. Bedrooms are equally appealing and well equipped. Breakfast is good by Spanish standards." Some rooms have a balcony facing the square. (*Lindsay Fisher*) No other meals served: but try the local speciality, roast sucking pig, in the *Mesón de Cándido*.

Open All year.
Rooms 5 suites, 21 double, 3 single. Air-conditioning.
Facilities Breakfast room, meeting room.
Location Central. Garage.
Credit cards All major cards accepted.
Terms B&B: single 6,625–8,175 pts, double 10,250–13,150 pts.

Parador de Segovia *Tel* (921) 44 37 37
Carretera de Valladolid *Fax* (921) 43 73 62
Segovia 40003

Set on a hilltop outside Segovia, this efficient modern *parador* has a pretty garden, and all of its rooms have picture windows and a balcony facing the city. It was partly redecorated this year, and has been much liked recently: "Stunning modern building. Huge awe-inspiring slate-floored public areas. Some rooms may be small, but ours in the newer part was fine. Wonderful views over Segovia from the dining room and circular indoor swimming pool. Staff might seem distant, as happens in large hotels, but porters are willing to discuss football at length, and are very knowledgeable about Dundee United!" (*AR*) What more can you want? – save to know that the outdoor heated pool has been renovated. And please tell us about the food, which is said to be good.

Open All year.
Rooms 7 suites, 93 double, 13 single. Air-conditioning.
Facilities Lift. Lounges, bars, TV room, café, restaurant; conference facilities; indoor swimming pool, sauna, fitness room. Garden: swimming pool, tennis.
Location 3 km N of Segovia, on N601. Parking.
Credit cards All major cards accepted.
Terms Rooms: single 13,200 pts, double 16,500 pts, suite 25,000 pts. Breakfast 1,200 pts. D,B&B double 25,900–34,400 pts. Set meals 3,500 pts; full alc 4,700 pts.

SEVILLE Map 13

Hotel Abril BUDGET *Tel* (95) 422 90 46
Jerónimo Hernández 20 *Fax* (95) 456 39 38
Sevilla 41003

Again this year, several readers have approved this unassuming B&B hotel in Seville's historic quarter. It has been finely restored, with true Spanish decor. "Excellent. Our room was spacious; a good breakfast in a pretty dining room." "Rather impersonal, but the decor was light, and breakfast fine." Another visitor found staff cheerful. Rooms vary: some may be noisy. (*Anthea Morton, Martine Packer, J and M Garrad, Maureen Hunt*) Warning: the hotel is not easy to find, tucked down narrow one-way streets, and parking is hard.

Open All year.
Rooms 18 double, 2 single. Some on ground floor.
Facilities Lift. Bar, TV room, breakfast room.

Location Central. Directly N of Pl. de la Encarnación. Public parking nearby.
Credit cards All major cards accepted.
Terms Rooms: single 5,000–8,000 pts, double 6,500–14,500 pts. Breakfast 500 pts.

Hotel Doña María *Tel* (95) 422 49 90
Don Remondo 19 *Fax* (95) 421 95 46
Sevilla 41004

This "lovely hotel, with a very nice staff" (a verdict this year) is well located in a quiet side street near the cathedral. Smart and sophisticated, its star asset is a small rooftop terrace with swimming pool (open only in summer) which overlooks the nearby Giralda tower. "We had a lovely stay. Our room was cool, service was cordial, breakfast ample." "Very good value, efficient staff." Those two recent reports follow earlier praise. "Quiet and charming, with antique furniture." "Our room's interesting decor was almost old Parisian/Art Deco." "From our balcony we could *watch* the Giralda's bells ringing." The entrance lounge has a glass wall giving on to the small inner courtyard – rooms facing on to this are a little small or dark, but much quieter. Self-service breakfasts are in a bright, cheery first-floor room. The hotel is on the German coach circuit and "can become crowded". (*Daisy Berger, David Bewley, and others*) One report of faulty plumbing. Car access and parking in the old quarter are a problem, though the hotel has a small underground garage.

Open All year.
Rooms 2 suites, 47 double, 10 single. 3 on ground floor. Air-conditioning.
Facilities Lift. Lounge, bar, breakfast room; meeting room; rooftop terrace: bar, swimming pool.
Location Central. 3 mins' walk from Giralda. 7-space garage.
Credit cards All major cards accepted.
Terms Rooms: single 7,000–16,500 pts, double 12,000–26,000 pts, suite 15,000–21,000 pts. Breakfast 1,300 pts.

Las Casas de la Judería NEW *Tel* (95) 441 51 50
Callejón de Dos Hermanas 7 *Fax*(95) 442 21 70
Sevilla 41004

"A gem." "The real thing. It mirrors the city's culture." Warmly nominated by regular *Guide* correspondents, this characterful B&B hotel is on the fringe of the Barrio Santa Cruz (historic quarter), "a perfect position". Not easy to find: "It is reached through a maze of narrow one-way streets. Access is through a chink in the side of the *plaza*, and it is without identification as a hotel until you reach reception. It is a 17th-century house in traditional Seville style. Original tiles line many of the twisting corridors and the charming courtyards, which are shady on sunny days, with hanging flower baskets; the main one has a soothing fountain. Accommodation is mostly in suites; ours was spacious and well furnished, with a sitting room and small kitchen. Breakfast is an extensive cold buffet; drinks are available all day. Plenty of restaurants nearby." (*David and Patricia Hawkins, Ruth Luborsky*)

Open All year.
Rooms 31. Most are suites, some with kitchen.
Facilities Lounge, dining room; courtyards.
Location Central, in historic quarter. Underground carpark.

Credit cards All major cards accepted.
Terms [1996] Rooms 10,000–12,500 pts. Breakfast 950 pts.

SIGÜENZA 19250 Guadalajara — Map 13

Parador de Sigüenza *Tel* (949) 39 01 00
Plaza del Castillo *Fax* (949) 39 13 64

"There can be no more impressive setting and ambience for a hotel in Spain," claims a recent report on this converted medieval fortress. It majestically crowns a small historic hill-town with a fine cathedral, north-east of Madrid. "It has been beautifully restored, with impressive lounge and quadrangle for drinks. Bathrooms and bedrooms are large (ours came with four-poster bed), but windows are generally in the turrets, so light is limited. Dinner did not quite match the setting or the high-quality service." Furnishings have been called "usual *parador*", with suits of armour guarding the TV. Some bedrooms, but not all, have a balcony, and there are fine views from the ramparts. The breakfast buffet has been praised. But some have found the hotel too touristy (it takes groups). (*Ian C Dewey*)

Open All year.
Rooms 2 suites, 76 double, 2 single.
Facilities Lift. Lounge, bar, restaurant; conference facilities. Small garden. Unsuitable for ♿.
Location In town, 129 km NE of Madrid. Parking.
Credit cards All major cards accepted.
Terms Rooms: single 10,800 pts, double 12,500–13,500 pts, suite 18,500–19,500 pts. Breakfast 1,200 pts. D,B&B double 22,900 pts. Set meals 3,500 pts; full alc 4,600 pts.

SOBRADO DE LOS MONJES 15312 La Coruña — Map 13

Hotel San Marcus NEW/BUDGET *Tel* (981) 78 75 27

This remote Galician village west of Lugo is dominated by a massive, if somewhat neglected, Cistercian monastery. Facing the monastery is this intriguing little hotel, a modest white building with a façade of *miradores* (glassed-in balconies), typically Spanish. Its nominators write: "We liked it very much, also its owners, a Spanish couple who worked for eight years in Britain. Our room, overlooking the square and monastery, had a *mirador*, a brass four-poster, and even a mirrored ceiling. It was quiet at night, as the village itself was quiet. A water-bed, the first in the area, was being installed in one room, for the publicity value. There is a flowery garden, with a play area for children, and a pool with loungers. Breakfasts are taken on the veranda facing the square. The dining room and bar were full of local people." (*Prof. P and Mrs A Robson*) Reports on the food welcome.

Open All year, except Jan.
Rooms 3 suites, 5 double, 4 single.
Facilities Lounge, bar, restaurant; small disco; terrace. Garden: swimming pool; children's playground. Unsuitable for ♿.
Location In village, 46 km W of Lugo. Public parking in square.
Credit cards Access, Visa.
Terms Rooms: single 3,500–6,000 pts, double 6,000–7,000 pts. Breakfast 475 pts. D,B&B 4,500–5,900 pts per person. Set meals 1,800 pts; full alc 2,475 pts.

SOMO 39140 Cantabria Map 13

Posada Mies de Villa NEW/BUDGET *Tel* (942) 51 00 73
Barrio Jorganes 14

On the edge of a small secluded resort across the bay from Santander, Antonio and Dorothy Ucelay Sainz have converted an old oak-beamed farmhouse to form a "delightful" *posada* that makes a welcome entry to the *Guide*: "Bedrooms are spacious, comfortable and tasteful, with English-style pillows, and green-and-white colour coordination. Breakfast, of a high standard (home-made jams, good coffee), is taken communally by the guests on the terrace in fine weather, with sublime views to the Picos de Europa." The Ucelay Sainz worked in large hotels in Britain – but "our customers are mostly Spanish". Sandy beaches are 8 km away. (*Albert and Patricia Grant*) No restaurant: lots nearby. Also, say the owners, "no music, no coin machines, no TV room, no telephone in rooms, no dance, no parties, no noise".

Open All year.
Rooms 9 double.
Facilities Lounge, bar, terrace. Garden. Unsuitable for ♿.
Location On edge of resort, 21 km E of Santander by road. Parking.
Credit cards None accepted.
Terms Rooms: 4,800–7,500 pts. Breakfast 375 pts.

SOS DEL REY CATÓLICO 50680 Zaragoza Map 13

Parador Fernando de Aragón *Tel* (948) 88 80 11
Fax (948) 88 81 00

This tiny medieval Aragón hill-town, now being much renovated, is named after King Fernando, who united Christian Spain under one crown in 1479, and was born here. The *parador*, modern but in regional style, stands beside the ramparts, with good views. Reports this year: "Pleasant but not remarkable." "Bedrooms, plainly but tastefully decorated, look out on to a vast area of golden corn. The airy top-floor dining room, lounge and terrace have the same view. Food standard *parador* but regional and robust, eg, ragout of mushrooms and squid, oxtail Aragon style. Delightful girl at front desk." Quiet rooms in traditional Spanish style. (*Lindsay Fisher, Dr I Anderson, SSD*)

Open All year.
Rooms 59 double, 6 single.
Facilities Lift, ramps. TV room, restaurant, snack bar. Garden.
Location In town, 59 km SE of Pamplona. Outdoor parking.
Credit cards All major cards accepted.
Terms Rooms: single 8,400–10,000 pts, double 10,500–12,500 pts. Breakfast 1,200 pts. D,B&B double 19,300–21,300 pts. Set meals 3,200 pts; full alc 4,000 pts.

In Spain, reservations for state-run establishments can be made direct or through their central booking office: Central de Reservas de los Paradores de España, Calle Requena 3, 28013 Madrid; *tel* (91) 559 00 69, *fax* (91) 559 25 40. Keytel International is the officially appointed UK agency for *paradores*: *tel* (0171) 402 8182, *fax* (0171) 724 9503.

TAMARIU 17212 Gerona Map 13

Hotel Tamariu BUDGET *Tel* (972) 62 00 31
Passeig del Mar 3
Playa de Tamariu

"Very, very pleasant," says a visitor this year to this small and friendly family-run hotel, beside the beach in a pretty Costa Brava fishing village, near sandy coves. Rooms are simple but cheerful, some with a balcony full of geraniums, looking to the sea. "The restaurant, on the seafront, was lovely: fish was certainly fresh, from the boats in the bay. And the cove was a delight: sandy beaches, pink rocks, and pine trees. Tamariu is a lovely friendly spot, though it may get a bit noisy in season." (*Elizabeth Robey, LB*)

Open 15 May–30 Sept.
Rooms 20 double, 5 single. 20 in annexe.
Facilities Salon, TV room, bar, restaurant. Direct access to beach. Unsuitable for ♿.
Location On seafront, 10 km E of Palafrugell.
Credit cards Access, Visa.
Terms B&B: single 4,000–4,300 pts, double 7,800–8,500 pts; D,B&B 6,100–6,300 pts per person. Set meals 2,200 pts.

TARAMUNDI 33775 Asturias Map 13

La Rectoral *Tel* (98) 564 67 67
La Villa *Fax* (98) 564 67 77

Up inland from Ribadeo, in an unspoilt visual paradise, is this "quiet and tasteful hotel". "From Ponte Nove on the N640, a picturesque road brings you to this small village in the depths of rural Asturias. At the church, a small wooden sign directs you up a steep lane and through an old stone arch to the rickety entrance of a 17th-century farmhouse. Here you enter the small reception area of a four-star hotel, where a smiling (Spanish-only) welcome awaits you. Opposite is a sitting room with a high vaulted ceiling and the original blackened stone walls and slate floors. Yellow leather sofas and spotlights make this somewhat over-dramatic, but the dining room is simple, and has some tables on a balcony. A bar leads to an outdoor terrace. The rest is new: six large bedrooms on the ground floor with large terrace, six above, without, all built in the same weathered materials. Beyond is an amazing sweep of meadow, valley, woods and mountains to the horizon. The decor is spoilt only by a profusion of twirly gold attachments in the bathroom. Dinner is average, but cheap; breakfast is very good. The staff are young and friendly. The hotel is publicly funded but privately run. Horses and bicycles can be hired. Nearby are small paths, minor roads and walks; like the lower Alps, but less developed." Newer reports needed on this idyll.

Open All year.
Rooms 18 double. 6 with terrace.
Facilities Lounge, bar, dining room. Garden; bicycles. Riding nearby.
Location S of Ribadeo, E of N640 to Lugo.
Credit cards All major cards accepted.
Terms [1996] Rooms 11,000–15,000 pts. Breakfast 1,000 pts. Set meals 2,200 pts.

TARANES 33557 Asturias — Map 13

La Casona de Mestas BUDGET
Las Mestas

Tel (98) 584 30 55
Fax (98) 584 30 92

Amid "wonderful mountain scenery" on the west side of the high Picos de Europa, this severe-looking stone building was converted from a thermal centre in 1986 and is now a "wonderfully peaceful" rustic hotel: "Our comfortable bedroom had plain wood furniture and a balcony window above a river. This was the only sound and we slept like logs. The floors are of quarry tiles or polished stone. The *menu de la casa* was the best we've had in Spain, with hearty portions, good home-made bread and house wine. On the *carte*: wild river salmon, bean soups and stews all well cooked. There's a large comfortable bar, and a stone-floored bar frequented by national park rangers. Bicycles are for hire." (*C and DW*)

Open All year, except 21 Jan–2 Mar.
Rooms 14 double.
Facilities TV room, bar, restaurant. Unsuitable for ♿.
Location 23 km S of Cangas de Onis, via Priesca or Viego.
Credit cards Access, Visa.
Terms Rooms: single 4,200–5,390 pts, double 6,000–7,700 pts. Breakfast 600 pts. D,B&B double 10,200–11,900 pts. Set meals 1,500 pts; full alc 2,500 pts.

TOLEDO — Map 13

La Almazara BUDGET
Carretera de Cuerva
Toledo 45080

Tel (925) 22 38 66
Fax (925) 25 05 62

This most beguiling little B&B hotel is inexpensive, simple, even basic, but full of character. It stands on a hillside outside the town, amid country estates known as *cigarrales*, where olive, oak and fruit trees grow. The old house, built round a courtyard, was the home of a 16th-century cardinal; many bedrooms overlook the city. "It was quite delightful. Our room, simple but clean, was perfect; the view from our balcony was breathaking." That plaudit this year endorses a previous one: "French windows, and a rickety mesh door, led on to a sizeable tiled balcony. We brought out chairs and table from our room, and made our own dinner, so we could sit and drink as the sun went down, lighting up the towers and houses of the city in gold. We were observed before sunset by martins and swallows, and after the sun had gone down by bats. Reception staff are extremely friendly. Breakfast was a simple continental affair, efficiently served." (*Judy Rothenburg, RH*) Beds are "not the most comfortable", and sound-proofing is non-existent.

Open 1 Mar–10 Dec.
Rooms 19 double, 2 single. 12 in annexe.
Facilities Lounge, breakfast room. Garden. Unsuitable for ♿.
Location 3.5 km SW of city off Cuerva road. Gate leads to unmade drive up to hotel. Secure parking.
Credit cards All major cards accepted.
Terms Rooms: single 3,400 pts, double 5,100–6,000 pts. Breakfast 450 pts.

Hostal del Cardenal *Tel* (925) 22 49 00
Paseo de Recaredo 24 *Fax* (925) 22 29 91
Toledo 45004

Built up against the city walls, this 18th-century residence of the archbishops of Toledo, which is central but quiet, has been liked again this year. Nearly all previous reports were positive, too: "What a superb place; we loved the setting in that garden with fountains. Room comfortable, if a little old-fashioned. The two dinners we had were superb." "A lovely large balcony, a pleasant dinner." "Our room overlooking the garden had a spacious feel. The bathroom was well equipped." (*RS*) More reports welcome.

Open All year. Closed evening 24 Dec.
Rooms 2 suites, 22 double, 3 single. All air-conditioned.
Facilities TV room, bar, breakfast room, restaurant; patios, courtyards. Garden. Unsuitable for ♿.
Location Just outside the old walls at Puerta de Bisagra. Parking.
Credit cards All major cards accepted.
Terms [1996] B&B: single 7,450 pts, double 12,350 pts, suite 16,550 pts. Set meals 2,550 pts; full alc 4,000 pts.

TORDESILLAS 47080 Valladolid Map 13

Hotel El Montico NEW *Tel* (983) 79 50 00
Apartado 12 *Fax* (983) 79 50 08
Carretera Burgos–Salamanca

Set in pinewoods just off N620 Burgos–Salamanca, 5 km E of historic town of Tordesillas: comfortable and quiet modern hotel, no beauty, but with good restaurant and leisure facilities, friendly staff. Outdoor dining. Swimming pool, tennis, squash, golf practice. All major credit cards accepted. 55 rooms: single 6,000–7,500 pts, double 8,500–11,000 pts. Breakfast 900 pts. Set meal 2,750 pts [1996].

TORTOSA 43500 Tarragona Map 13

Parador Castillo de la Zuda *Tel* (977) 44 44 50
Fax (977) 44 44 58

This old Moorish palace stands high on a rocky prominence, overlooking the city and the Ebro valley. The view in all directions is dramatic. The public rooms are embellished with pictures, sculptures and huge stone vases full of flowers. A recent view: "Our favourite *parador*, with a swimming pool that's not empty (unlike some others). Staff are mostly friendly, by *parador* standards. Spanish-style bedrooms are comfortable, and some have a balcony." The dining room, in the original palace building, offers "an excellent and varied menu", with unusual Duero wines and good seafood, served rather earlier than is usual in Spanish hotels. (*JGSS*)

Open All year.
Rooms 3 suites, 70 double, 9 single. Air-conditioning.
Facilities Lounge, TV room, bar, restaurant; 2 conference rooms. Large grounds: swimming pool. Unsuitable for ♿.
Location 500 m from town centre, on hilltop. Parking.
Credit cards All major cards accepted.

Terms [1996] Rooms: single 9,200–10,800 pts, double 11,500–13,500 pts, suite 14,400–16,900 pts. Breakfast 1,200 pts. Set meals 3,200 pts; full alc 4,000–5,000 pts.

TRUJILLO 10200 Cáceres — Map 13

Parador de Trujillo — *Tel* (927) 32 13 50
Plaza Santa Beatriz de Silva — *Fax* (927) 32 13 66

"A stunningly beautiful medieval town, as yet unspoilt by tourism." It was the birthplace of Pizarro, *conquistador* of Peru, and his equestrian statue stands in the magnificent main square. The *parador*, one of Spain's most delightful, is on a hilltop in the ancient citadel, a short walk away, secluded in shady gardens. It is a former convent, a rambling old building with courtyards, plus a modern annexe. "We had a lovely spacious room with caryatid beds. The breakfast buffet was beautiful, and the staff friendly and helpful." Others have praised the tranquil atmosphere, and regional Estremaduran dishes like casserole of pigeon in beans. "All *paradores* claim to be air-conditioned, but here it really worked." Newer reports welcome.

Open All year.
Rooms 1 suite, 45 double. Some in annexe. Air-conditioning.
Facilities TV room, bar, dining room; conference facilities. Garden: swimming pool. Unsuitable for ♿.
Location Central. 47 km E of Cáceres. Garage.
Credit cards All major cards accepted.
Terms [1996] Rooms 13,500–15,000 pts. Breakfast 1,200 pts. Set meals 3,500 pts.

TURRE 04639 Almería — Map 13

Finca Listonero BUDGET — *Tel* (950) 47 90 94
Cortijo Grande — *Fax* (950) 46 80 04

In the mountains near Mojácar is this stylishly converted old farmhouse, owned and run by a half-Australian, half-Northern Irish team, David Rice and Graeme Gibson, former restaurateurs in Sydney and Marbella. Readers have raved about it more than ever this year: "A true joy, with excellent imaginative food, delightful pool area." "Fabulous peaceful setting amid dramatic rugged scenery. It was like a private house party: pre-dinner drinks are taken together, and the owners are highly entertaining – within half an hour everybody is 'darling'. We all ate at the same time (at separate tables) and food was delicious. The farmhouse is decorated in great style: each bedroom is in a different colour, and has a comfortable armchair. The sitting room is a glorious vivid green, the dining room a stunning bright yellow. Photos, antiques, mementos are everywhere." But the cooking is English/international and makes no concessions to Spain. Bedrooms open on to a central courtyard, full of greenery. There's an interesting library. Long sandy beaches are nearby. (*Martine Packer, Roger Heading, and others*)

Open All year.
Rooms 6 double.
Facilities Lounges, bar, restaurant; terraces. Large garden: swimming pool. Golf, tennis, riding, walking (rough) nearby. Beaches 20 mins' drive: sailing, snorkelling, windsurfing.

Location 10 km W of Mojácar. Take L150 towards Mojácar, Turre, Garrucha. Follow signs from Cortijo Grande (3 km off road).
Restriction No children under 15.
Credit cards Access, Visa.
Terms B&B: single 8,000–9,000 pts, double 10,000–12,000 pts. Set dinner 4,000 pts; full alc 4,500 pts.

TUY 36700 Pontevedra Map 13

Parador de Tuy *Tel* (986) 60 03 09
Fax (986) 60 21 63

This "delightful" modern *parador* stands on a hill, on the edge of a historic town at the Portuguese border. "It has a pastoral view down the valley to Tuy's cathedral (illuminated at night), the gently flowing Miño, and distant mountains. The building is a copy of a Galician manor house, with stone and beautiful woods. Bedrooms, smaller than the norm for *paradores,* are decorated in simple country style, with gleaming newly renovated bathrooms. There is a terrace for drinks, and an enormous garden. A lawn dotted with trees and shrubs drops steeply on either side of an elaborately decorated stone staircase, down to an unusually large swimming pool and a tennis court. The atmosphere is calm, delightfully different from most *paradores.* I can find no fault; they even change the sheets daily. The food was excellent, on a daily-changing menu, with a drinkable local wine for only 425 pesetas! A *parador* with a heart; such a change from being an object in a museum." More reports, please. And there's a new manager this year.

Open All year.
Rooms 2 suites, 23 double, 1 single. Some on ground floor.
Facilities Lift. Lounge, bar, restaurant. Garden: swimming pool, tennis.
Location On edge of town, 15 km S of Vigo.
Credit cards All major cards accepted.
Terms [1996] Rooms 7,600–12,500 pts, suite 13,300–17,500 pts. Breakfast 1,200 pts. Set meals 3,200 pts.

ÚBEDA 23400 Jaén Map 13

Parador Condestable Dávalos *Tel* (953) 75 03 45
Plaza de Vásquez Molina *Fax* (953) 75 12 59

Long a *Guide* favourite, this lovely 16th-century stone palace fronts the historic main square of a beautiful and superbly preserved Renaissance city with many fine buildings and churches. "One of the nicest of *paradores,* with polite service, good food," says a visitor this year, backing earlier plaudits: "The best food we've ever had in a *parador* – a delicious selection of *tapas,* then a choice of Andalusian specialities." "Splendid architecture, stylishly adapted to comfort; competent reception. Memorable suckling pig." The attractive internal patio is framed by tiled corridors leading to cool rooms, many of them spacious. The best look on to the square or small courtyards. Antiques add to a sense of nobility; but some rooms have bright modern furnishings. Bathrooms can be "cavernous". (*Daisy Berger*)

Open All year.
Rooms 1 suite, 30 double. Air-conditioning. Some on ground floor.
Facilities 3 salons, TV room, bar, restaurant; patio courtyard.

Location Central, near town hall and San Salvador. Unguarded parking.
Credit cards All major cards accepted.
Terms [1996] Rooms: single 12,000–13,200 pts, double 15,000–16,500 pts, suite 18,400–20,400 pts. Breakfast 1,200 pts. Set meals 2,500–3,500 pts; full alc 4,200 pts.

VEJER DE LA FRONTERA 11150 Cádiz — Map 13

Hospederia Convento de San Francisco
La Plazuela 6
Tel (956) 45 10 01
Fax (956) 45 10 04

Just inland from Cape Trafalgar lies this small medieval town (dubbed by Jan Morris the most beautiful *pueblo* in Spain). Here on an isolated hill is this 17th-century convent, Moorish in style. Many original features have been carefully preserved: Roman mosaics, bits of medieval pottery, the old choir-stalls in the lounge. All the solid wood furnishings (hand-made in Valencia), as well as the simple, stone-vaulted bedrooms, echo the original style: any monastic austerity is offset by decent modern bathrooms. The refectory is still used as a dining room. Endorsements this year and last: "An excellent hotel, with friendly staff. We loved the decor and quietness. But breakfast was poor." "The food was not over-ambitious but of high quality, splendidly presented. Service was first rate." Breakfast and informal snacks are served in the large Andalusian bar. (*AV Neal, JT*)

Open All year. Restaurant closed Tues.
Rooms 21 double, 4 single.
Facilities Lift. Salons, bar/café, restaurant; cloister; conference facilities. Beaches 14 km. Unsuitable for ♿.
Location Central.
Credit cards All major cards accepted.
Terms Rooms: single 5,985–6,883 pts, double 7,615–8,757 pts. Breakfast 525 pts. D,B&B double 11,985–13,127 pts. Set meals 2,205 pts; full alc 3,500 pts.

VILLALBA 27800 Lugo — Map 13

Parador Condes de Villalba
Calle Valeriano Valdesuso
Tel (982) 51 00 11
Fax (982) 51 00 90

This little six-bedroom *parador* is one of Spain's most charming – a medieval fortified bastion with a drawbridge, in a ramparted Galician town. There are wide views from the large top bedrooms in the high octagonal tower: "Ours had a narrow window carved out of the rounded, ten-foot-thick walls. Service is excellent and informal." The cellar dining room has a huge fireplace and the air of a baronial hall. "Quite unusual and atmospheric," adds a reader this year, who claimed to have been visited in the night by the resident ghost: "It was a man of about thirty. Next morning, the girl on the staff was scared at my story, but the two older staff seemed to have heard it all before and had knowing looks on their faces." (*Charles Belair, and others*)

Open 11 Feb–22 Dec.
Rooms 6 double.
Facilities Lift. Lounge with TV/bar, restaurant. Garden. Unsuitable for ♿.
Location Central. 36 km N of Lugo. Parking.
Credit cards All major cards accepted.

Terms Rooms: single 10,800 pts, double 13,500–15,000 pts. Breakfast 1,200 pts. Set meals 3,200 pts.

VITORIA-GASTEIZ **Map 13**

Parador de Argómaniz *Tel* (945) 29 32 00
Vitoria-Gasteiz 01192 *Fax* (945) 29 32 87

Vitoria, the Basque capital, is a delightful old city with a breezy, youthful atmosphere. It has Renaissance palaces, a remarkable museum of playing cards, and a curious festival in August when a life-size puppet descends into the main square with an umbrella and everyone in the crowd lights a cigar. The *parador*, on a hill to the east, is a Renaissance palace at core, and enjoys wide views; its restaurant is a barn-like room on the second floor with a cat's cradle of roof-timbers. Bedrooms are in the modern wings on either side; front ones are best, as others face into the hillside. A recent view: "Our room was impeccable, with a wide view. Service in the restaurant was pleasant and lively. Breakfast was good; excellent coffee." More reports, please.

Open All year.
Rooms 53 double.
Facilities Lift. Salons, TV room, bar, restaurant. Garden. Unsuitable for ♿.
Location 10 km E of Vitoria by N1 Madrid–Irún.
Credit cards All major cards accepted.
Terms Rooms 10,000–13,500 pts. Breakfast 1,200 pts. Set meals 3,200 pts; full alc 6,000 pts.

ZAFRA 06300 Badajóz **Map 13**

Parador Hernán Cortés *Tel* (924) 55 45 40
Plaza Corazón de María 7 *Fax* (924) 55 10 18

In a remote whitewashed Moorish cattle town, superbly preserved, stands this very good *parador*, named after Mexico's founder, a local hero. Newly renovated, it is set in a drum-towered fortress, and was admired again this year: "Fabulous. A central almost cloistered yard with a well. Here you can sit with a drink. Super breakfast, and a good set menu served by friendly staff. But beware of taking 'extras' which you didn't order but which nevertheless appear on the bill." (*Linda Brook*) Bedrooms are large, stylish and well equipped. The huge pool is set romantically in a lush garden bordered by castle walls.

Open All year.
Rooms 45 double. Some on ground floor. Air-conditioning.
Facilities Lift. Bar, 2 dining rooms. Garden: swimming pool.
Location Central. Zafra is 75 km SE of Badajóz. Public parking.
Credit cards All major cards accepted.
Terms Rooms 10,800–18,500 pts. Breakfast 1,200 pts. D,B&B double 22,900–27,900 pts. Set meals 3,500 pts. Special discounts.

****

Traveller's tale The *pousada* was hung with heavy religious paintings. We found them somewhat depressing, particularly one in the dining room, which featured John the Baptist's head being served on a platter.

****

Sweden

Åkerblads, Tällberg

BÅSTAD 269 35 Skåne **Map 7**

Buena Vista NEW *Tel* (0431) 760 00
Tarravägen 5 *Fax* (0431) 791 00

This fine old house is splendidly positioned overlooking the small town of Båstad in the far south of the country, with a magnificent view over the Baltic. Bedrooms have antique furniture and patchwork quilts. "Ours was so cosy we felt we were in a home, and the bathroom was a real treat," writes our nominator. "The hotel was quiet and the staff very friendly. The breakfast buffet was beautifully presented." There's a chapel within the hotel, used for weddings, and five golf courses nearby. (*Pat Malone*)

Open All year.
Rooms 4 suites, 26 double. 6 in annexe. Some no-smoking.
Facilities Lift. 2 lounges, 2 bars, restaurant; chapel. Garden. Park, tennis, golf courses nearby.
Location Centre of town. Signposted. Parking.

Credit cards Access, Amex, Visa.
Terms B&B: single 710 Skr, double 910 Skr, suite 1,195–1,395 Skr. Set lunch 75 Skr, dinner 150 Skr. Full alc 225–250 Skr. Christmas, Easter packages.

GRYTHYTTAN 712 81 Västmanland — Map 7

Grythyttans Gästgivaregård — *Tel* (0591) 147 00
Prästgatan 2 — *Fax* (0591) 141 24

This village is well off the beaten track, in a region of small lakes just north of huge lake Vanern, some 270 kilometres west of Stockholm. Here Carl-Jan Granqvist ("quite a celebrity") has restored a 17th-century house and the adjacent shops and cottages to make a sophisticated hotel (Relais & Châteaux), fashionable for Swedes as well as tourists. Some bedrooms are lavish, with chintzy four-poster beds, lots of cushions, period lamp-fittings, old pictures (often cartoons), pot plants, and stylish but practical bathroom; others are much simpler. The restaurant, a series of interconnecting rooms, is known for its expensive French-influenced cuisine and goes in for synchronised cloche-lifting which some find pretentious. "But the food is undoubtedly very good, and the 'flying waitresses' are charming." A 1996 endorsement: "Utterly romantic. How everyone thinks Sweden should look, with its red-painted wooden houses with white framed windows. Trolls might pop up among the trees at any moment." (*Suzanne Bagner, AL*)

Open All year.
Rooms 10 suites, 60 double, 15 single. In separate houses.
Facilities 8 lounges, 2 TV rooms, bar, restaurant. Gardens: tennis. 150 lakes in area: boating, sailing, fishing; golf nearby. Unsuitable for ♿.
Location Centre of village, 70 km NW of Örebro. Parking.
Credit cards All major cards accepted.
Terms [1996] B&B: single 715–960 Skr, double 960–1,430 Skr; D,B&B 905–1,150 Skr per person. Reductions for 2 or more nights. Weekend packages.

KNIVSTA 741 95 Uppland — Map 7

Åby Gård NEW/BUDGET — *Tel* (0183) 88 218 and 88 123

"A real Swedish experience," writes the nominator of Gittan and Ingemar Johansson's 17th-century farmhouse hotel with 600 sheep, cattle, pigs and sheep dogs. "This charming house was once the kitchen and laundry for the manor house and it retains all its charm. Our room, simple but immaculate, reminded me of visits to my grandmother's farm as a child. We arrived late, and to save us going out to a restaurant, the owner fixed us a fantastic dinner. In the morning we were invited into the kitchen where we found a real Swedish breakfast *feast*: porridge, cold meats (smoked on the farm), home-made rolls and loganberry jam. It was so relaxing and refreshing, out in the country with all the animals." (*Pat Malone*) No smoking.

Open May–Sept.
Rooms 5 double. 2 with facilities *en suite*.
Facilities Lounge with TV and open fireplace. 7 golf courses nearby
Location Between Stockholm and Uppsala, 20 km N of Arlanda airport at junction of routes 77 and 273.
Restriction No smoking in house.

Credit cards None accepted.
Terms [1996] B&B 200 Skrs.

ORSA 794 98 Dalarna **Map 7**

Fryksås Hotell NEW
Fryksås Fäbodvall
Orsa Grönklitt
Tel (0250) 460 20
Fax (0250) 460 90

"A wonderful place," writes an enthusiastic visitor to this family-run farmhouse hotel in a hamlet on a high plateau overlooking Lake Orsa. "Quiet, restful, relaxing, tastefully decorated and utterly charming. The owners and staff are very helpful. Dinners were first rate, and breakfast was one of the best buffets of our trip, beautifully presented with antique wooden bowls and spoons. The view is spectacular, and it was fun walking out at night. No tour buses – just warm and friendly Swedes." An earlier encomium: "Fryksås is a collection of wooden huts, where farmers brought their cows for summer pasture in the old days. The nature-loving owner ran a celebrated restaurant in town before escaping here. He specialises in Nordic game dishes, and also serves wonderful fish, and incomparable home-baked bread." (*Pat Malone, and others*) A famous ski resort is within walking distance.

Open All year.
Rooms 15 double.
Facilities Lounge, dining room; sauna. Walking, climbing, skiing.
Location In hamlet above Lake Orsa, 10 km from Orsa.
Credit cards All major cards accepted.
Terms [1996] B&B: single 525 Skr, double 750 Skr. Set dinner 275 Skr.

STOCKHOLM **Map 7**

Bentley's Hotel
Drottninggatan 77
111 60 Stockholm
Tel (08) 14 13 95
Fax (08) 21 24 92

Run by enthusiastic anglophiles, Aggi and Klas Källström, this unusual hotel in the centre of Stockholm is made up, rather confusingly, of several apartments joined together, each section with a security code which changes regularly. It has the atmosphere of a private house. The bedrooms are cosily and quirkily decorated "with a touch of the 19th century". Breakfasts are "splendid", with all manner of hot and cold dish on offer, both Swedish (pickled herrings, cheese, sliced meats) and traditional English. "We offer 12 different teas, five kinds of marmalade, and eggs, bacon and sausage," writes Mr Källström, "but *no* kippers, which I hate since my younger days at King's School, Rochester." *Bentley's* has a wine and champagne bar; a restaurant, under separate management, is in the same building. (*AW*)

Open All year.
Rooms 3 suites, 17 double, 13 single.
Facilities Bar, restaurant; sauna. Swimming pool 2 mins' walk.
Location Central, near station.
Restriction No smoking in bedrooms.
Credit cards All major cards accepted.
Terms [1996] B&B: single 795 Skr, double 995 Skr.

Värdshuset Clas på Hörnet
Surbrunnsgatan 20
113 48 Stockholm

Tel (08) 16 51 30
Fax (08) 612 53 15

A low-lying traditional wooden building, set amid high-rises on the north side of town, 15 minutes' walk from the centre. It first opened as an inn in 1731, then became successively a ballroom, a hospital, an apartment block and a garage, before reverting to its original vocation. It is now an elegant restaurant-with-rooms. "The food is of the highest standard," wrote the nominators. "The owners' care and kindness were quite staggering, and the staff were helpful throughout. A most enjoyable stay." Bedrooms, some small, are light and airy, "and charming, with antique furniture". (*EW*) More reports, please.

Open All year.
Rooms 10 double.
Facilities Bar, dining rooms; conference room.
Location 1 mile N of centre.
Credit cards All major cards accepted.
Terms B&B: single 840-940 Skr, double 940–1,160 Skr. Dinner from 250 Skr.

Lady Hamilton Hotel
Storkyrkobrinken 5
111 28 Stockholm

Tel (08) 23 46 80
Fax (08) 411 11 48

"The location in the beautiful Old Town, with gabled mansions, cobbled lanes and courtyards, is wonderful," writes an admirer of this stylish B&B hotel. "It is in one of the quieter streets, close to the Royal Palace and the cathedral (the chimes of the bells every quarter of an hour were a bonus); excellent restaurants and shops are a five- to ten-minute walk away. Someone had a wonderful time decorating the hotel; the whimsical mixture of folk art and tongue-in-cheek tribute to Emma Hamilton made me grin every time I entered the public rooms. Our room had almost no empty floor space, but it was so pretty that it didn't matter. Service couldn't have been friendlier or more accomplished." Unusual features include a basement plunge pool (a 15th-century well) and medieval vaults (used as meeting rooms). (*CM*) The *Victory*, close by, and similarly nautical in decor, is under the same ownership (see next page).

Open All year.
Rooms 3 triple, 18 double, 13 single. Some no-smoking.
Facilities Lounge, bar, breakfast room; conference rooms; sauna, plunge pool. Unsuitable for ♿.
Location Central. In Old Town by Royal Palace. Valet parking (210 Skr a night).
Credit cards All major cards accepted.
Terms B&B: single 790–1,670 Skr, double 1,180–2,040 Skr, triple 1,390–2,280 Skr. Weekend reductions. Children under 12 accommodated free in parents' room.

Victory Hotel
Lilla Nygatan 5
111 28 Stockholm

Tel (08) 14 30 90
Fax (08) 20 21 77

"Still our Stockholm favourite." "All that I hoped it would be." "Absolutely wonderful – quaint, charming and first class." Just a few of this year's accolades for one of our most popular Swedish entries. In the Gamla Stan (the old town), like its sister hotel, the *Lady Hamilton* (previous page), it has a nautical theme; unlike her, it has its own restaurant, *Leijontornet*, which is warmly recommended. The *Victory* is built on the ruins of a 14th-century fortified tower, and in 1937 Sweden's largest treasure hoard was unearthed from the floorboards – a substantial cache of silver, part of which is on display. The hotel is furnished with a mix of stylish contemporary fittings and antiques. Each bedroom (some are decidedly small) commemorates a different sea captain from the great age of sailing ships. There's an atmospheric but cramped medieval dining room, where the breakfast is "first class". Staff are "exceptionally pleasant". (*Brian and Lesley Knox, Sherill Brown, Pat Malone, Gerald and Mary Clark, and others*).

Open All year, except Christmas, New Year. Restaurant closed Sun, July.
Rooms 4 suites, 20 double, 24 single. 1 floor no-smoking.
Facilities Lift. Library, bar, restaurant; conference rooms; sauna, plunge pool; courtyard (summer meal service). Unsuitable for ♿.
Location Central, on Old Town island. Valet parking.
Credit cards All major cards accepted.
Terms B&B: single 890–1,880 Skr, double 1,330–2,180 Skr, suite 2,190–4,900 Skr. Set lunch 70–100 Skr, dinner 210–450 Skr; full alc 400–500 Skr. Weekend rates. Children under 12 accommodated free in parents' room.

Wallin Hotel *Tel* (08) 20 15 20
Wallingatan 15 *Fax* (08) 791 50 50
107 24 Stockholm

"A conveniently central, quiet, moderate-sized B&B hotel," wrote its nominator. "The decor is modern, new and fresh; everything is sound and workmanlike. My room was not large, but it was well organised and attractive, with a nice shower room. Breakfast in the airy dining room is a comprehensive buffet. Not much in the way of public rooms, but the hotel owns a flat down the street, with an ample and elegant meeting room, useful if you are on business. A good base for sightseeing if you enjoy walking the quarter or half mile on the city streets (many are pedestrianised) to the Old Town or to the spectacular Wasa Museum (housing Sweden's Mary Rose)." (*ALL*) Light meals are available.

Open All year.
Rooms 83 double, 14 single. 2 floors no-smoking.
Facilities Lift. Bar, breakfast room; conference facilities.
Location Central, near Drottninggatan.
Credit cards All major cards accepted.
Terms [1996] B&B: single 865–935 Skr, double 1,065 Skr.

TÄLLBERG 793 70 Dalarna **Map 7**

Åkerblads *Tel* (0247) 508 00
Fax (0247) 506 52

Åkerblads, set beside Lake Siljan, halfway between Leksand and Rättvik, is a 17th-century farmhouse with new extensions, all comfortable and spacious. The rooms are Swedish-rural with pale wood, four-posters and painted panelling, in the style of Carl Lårsen. The owners, Christina and Arne Åkerblad and their sons, are the 19th and 20th generations of the founding family – among the oldest hotel families in Europe. Visitors have mostly been delighted with the ambience, the food, and the child-friendly atmosphere. There is a splendid smörgåsbord at lunchtime. Recently, however, a correspondent wondered if the hotel, now a member of the Romantik group, is not becoming too much part of the international circuit, which might detract from its rural charm. He found it slickly run and touristy, with too much emphasis on Swedish handicrafts and rural furniture, although the staff were very friendly and helpful. More reports, please.

Open All year, except Christmas.
Rooms 18 suites, 34 double, 11 single. Some in annexes. 10 no-smoking. Some on ground floor.
Facilities Lift, ramps. 5 lounges, 2 dining rooms (no-smoking), conference centre, wine bar, pub; sauna, solarium, whirlpool; occasional live music and dancing. Large grounds: garden, tennis, badminton, table-tennis, skating, sleigh-rides, children's games. Lake 400 m: beach, bathing, fishing, boating.
Location Equidistant (12 km) from Leksand and Rättvik; signposted. Outdoor parking.
Credit cards All major cards accepted.
Terms [1996] B&B 395–495 Skr; D,B&B 635–735 Skr. Set meals 165–275 Skr; full alc 385 Skr. Reductions for longer stays. "Last-minute prices": B&B from 175 Skr.

VÄRMDÖ 139 60 Stockholm — Map 7

FågelbroHus NEW

Tel (08) 571 401 00
Fax (08) 571 401 71

A large modern hotel in the heart of the Stockholm archipelago, set in large grounds near the water. It has its own golf course, and many other activities are available for the sportingly inclined, (see below). "We felt at home immediately," writes its American nominator. "The beautifully decorated public rooms, with well-stuffed chairs and sofas, abound with good lighting, inviting you to sit and read. Our bedroom was immaculate, and we enjoyed sitting on our deck, watching the swallows. Breakfast on the patio included a splendid buffet: lots of fresh fruit, cheeses, meat, etc, and unusual toppings for the muesli; everything helpfully labelled. Excellent walking in the beautiful grounds. A great place to stay." Meals may be taken in the clubhouse as well as in the more formal restaurant. (*Pat Malone*)

Open All year.
Rooms 72 double.
Facilities Lounge, restaurant, billiard room; sauna, solarium; patio. Large grounds: clubhouse, golf, tennis, croquet, *boules*, squash, riding, jogging, fishing, boat tours.
Location 31 km E of Stockholm. Route 222 exit Gustavsberg; right at 2nd roundabout towards Stavnäs/Djurö; after 6 km cross Strömna Channel; after 1 km, right at sign "Fägelbro Säteri". Hotel is after sports centre.
Credit cards All major cards accepted.
Terms [1996] B&B: single 850 Skr, double 980–1,200 Skr; D,B&B: single 1,183 Skr, double 1,766 Skr. Set dinner 333 Skr.

> There is inevitably less feedback from Scandinavia than from other more touristy parts of Europe. If you have been to Scandinavia and stayed in a good hotel, whether it is in the current *Guide* or not, we'd be particularly grateful for reports.

Switzerland

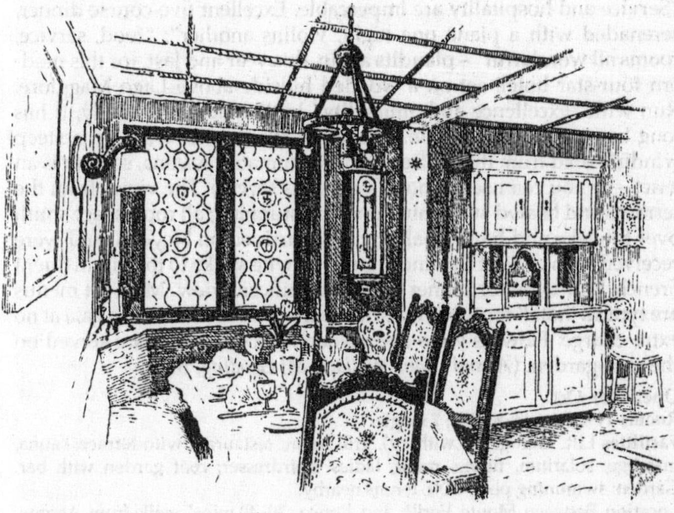

Hotel Bergsonne, Rigi-Kaltbad

Swiss hotel standards are among the world's highest, in terms of smooth professional service, cleanliness, comfort, well-equipped bedrooms and bathrooms, and food well prepared and presented. But prices are accordingly lofty. And that subtle ingredient, charm, is not always present. Many of the classic resort hotels, three- or four-star, cater for a staid clientele and are sedate by today's standards. If you want lively *Gemütlichkeit*, you could do better in a smaller family-run mountain inn or village *auberge*.

Some 80 per cent of hotels are part of the Swiss Hotel Association, which grades its members rigorously by fixed criteria: a five-star hotel must change bed-linen daily, a two-star hotel must at least have soap in the rooms, etc. But these rules take no account of decor, setting, ambience, warmth of welcome, interesting food – the qualities the *Guide* cares about. Most hotels are privately owned; very few (and none in this book) are part of the big international chains such as Hilton; some are members of the major associations, Relais & Châteaux, Romantik Hotels, etc.

Breakfast is generally a buffet, especially in German-speaking areas.

At main meals, the food is usually served copiously. Many hotels have a bland "international" menu, but quite a number serve local Swiss specialities, or are turning to the kind of *nouvelle cuisine* favoured by *Gault Millau* (we identify that guide's *toque* awards, and the stars of *Michelin*, which publishes a Swiss volume).

Service is included in all bills; only in expensive places are you expected to leave a few extra francs for special service.

ASCONA 6612 Ticino **Map 15**

Casa Berno *Tel* (091) 791 32 32
Fax (091) 792 11 14

"Service and hospitality are impeccable. Excellent five-course dinner, serenaded with a piano one night, violins another"; "food, service, rooms all wonderful" – plaudits again, this year and last, for this modern four-star hotel, set on a wooded hillside above Lago Maggiore. Run with "excellence and amiability" by the Goetschi family, it has long been a *Guide* favourite. It is some 40 minutes' walk up a steep winding road from the centre of smart, animated Ascona, so a car is an asset – or you can use the hotel's minibus service. The views from the terraces and heated swimming pool are stunning; all rooms face south over the lake and have a balcony. "We arrived on bicycles, and were received with a slight frostiness until my wife spoke to the girl in fluent French. Our table for dinner had a magnificent view. Most set menus are typical 'hotel' food; but on Fridays there's a seven-course gala at no extra charge. Flowers were everywhere." Good snacks are served on the roof-garden. (*Al and Diana Wallace, MJ Gooding, BB*)

Open Mar–Oct.
Rooms 11 suites, 43 double, 7 single.
Facilities Lift. Lounges (1 with TV), grill room, restaurant with terrace; sauna, massage, solarium, fitness room, ladies' hairdresser; roof garden with bar. Garden: swimming pool. Golf, tennis nearby.
Location Between Monte Verità and Ronco; 30–40 mins' walk from Ascona. Minibus service.
Credit cards Access, Amex, Visa.
Terms B&B 170–238 Sfrs; D,B&B 190–258 Sfrs.

BLITZINGEN 3981 Valais **Map 15**

Aparthotel Castle NEW *Tel* (028) 71 33 71
Fax (028) 71 33 41

NE of Brig, in superb setting high above Blitzingen, a modern hotel with large rooms, restrained contemporary decor, efficient-cum-friendly owners. Varied, imaginative cooking. Bar; indoor swimming pool, jacuzzi. Good facilities for ♿. Fine views down Goms valley. Open 1 June–30 Oct, 15 Dec–15 May. All major credit cards accepted. 40 rooms (some no-smoking). B&B double 160–185 Sfrs; D,B&B 95–185 Sfrs per person. Set meals 10–100 Sfrs. Fuller reports welcome.

When a continental hotel has failed to return its questionnaire, we have quoted 1996 prices, with a note to that effect.

CHAMPEX 1938 Valais **Map 15**

Relais du Belvédère BUDGET *Tel* (026) 83 11 14
Champex-Lac from 1.11.96: (027) 783 11 14
Fax (026) 83 25 76
from 1.11.96: (027) 783 25 76

In remote "cross-country skiing paradise" 17 km S of Martigny, small and simple chalet-hotel, family-run, by lake amid pinewoods, with access to many outdoor pursuits. 9 pleasant bedrooms in stripped pine, all with balcony. Mountain view from dining room; good Swiss dishes. Closed end Nov–23 Dec, 1 weekend after 15 May. Access, Visa accepted. 9 rooms. B&B double 130–150 Sfrs; D,B&B double 170–190 Sfrs.

DAVOS 7260 Graubünden **Map 15**

Hotel Flüela *Tel* (081) 410 17 17
Bahnhofstrasse 5 *Fax* (081) 410 17 18

Close to Davos's main ski-lift, the Parsenn Bahn, stands this large, imposing and rather grand ski-hotel, much modernised. Owned and run by the Gredig family for over a century, it continues to inspire strong loyalty. "A wonderful hotel," says a returning fan this year. "Superb food, friendly staff, brilliantly efficient head waiter, Hans. After Swissair managed to lose one of my suitcases, Herr Gredig lent me his own skiing trousers and ski glasses – in how many other hotels could this happen? When I went moonlight skiing, the hotel gave me a special late dinner." And a visitor coming back last year: "I had not stayed there for 55 years, since I went as a child with my family. Of its kind it is still superb: courteous staff, delicious food." This is described as "a mix of traditional and *nouvelle*". In the lounge, with its glowing log fire, a pianist plays. Bedrooms are "superb", table settings sumptuous, and there's a candlelit six-course dinner weekly. The staff's caring attitude towards children is admired: "the chambermaid on our floor was on duty all evening". (*Prof. TJ David*)

Open Nov–Apr.
Rooms 10 suites, 55 double, 20 single.
Facilities Bar/lounge (with pianist), sitting rooms, restaurants; conference/function rooms; games room; indoor swimming pool, sauna, solarium, massage, fitness room; ski boutique, barber, hairdresser; bank; terrace. Unsuitable for ♿.
Location Town centre. Roadside rooms may be noisy. Parking.
Credit cards All major cards accepted.
Terms [1996] D,B&B 165–480 Sfrs per person.

FTAN 7551 Graubünden **Map 15**

Haus Paradies *Tel* (081) 861 08 08
Fax (081) 861 08 09

This particular corner of paradise is the lovely Unter-Engadin valley, just west of Scuol, with views of the Lischana peaks and the hilltop castle of Tarasp. Here stands this smart and expensive modern hotel (Relais & Châteaux), built not in the usual Alpine chalet style but in a mode closer to Le Corbusier, and its bold design has Scandinavian touches. It has a new owner, Horst Rahe, but the manager/chef

Eduard Hitzberger remains, and his ambitious cuisine wins a *Michelin* star. "Paradise indeed" says a reader this year, backing earlier praise: "Idyllic. The food, service and atmosphere are all excellent." "An unusual and bewitching hotel with a *Thunderbirds* feel – concealed luxury and high-tech gadgetry. Our ultra-comfortable bedroom had a balcony with loungers, and a huge picture window: the view of craggy mountains was so spectacular it could have been fake. The staff are young, outgoing and friendly, and dinner is excellent in elegant *nouvelle* style – a fixed five-course menu. We were lucky to be there in mushroom season. There's an extensive library, a grand piano, and an on-site masseur/physiotherapist." (*Mrs Blake Foster, P and AH, and others*)

Open 30 Nov–27 Apr, 1 June–30 Oct.
Rooms 10 suites, 10 double, 6 single.
Facilities Lounge, library, reading room, restaurant; sauna, solarium, massage; terrace. Music evening once a fortnight. Unsuitable for ♿.
Location 3 km W of Scuol. Parking.
Credit cards Access, Amex, Visa.
Terms D,B&B: single 290 Sfrs, double 440–530 Sfrs, suite 630–890 Sfrs. Set lunch 68 Sfrs, dinner 165 Sfrs; full alc 90 Sfrs.

GENEVA — Map 15

Hôtel Les Armures
1 rue du Puits St-Pierre
1204 Genève
Tel (022) 310 91 72
Fax (022) 310 98 46

This intimate and elegant little hotel inhabits a 17th-century stone building in a small square of the old town, near the cathedral: it makes a pleasant contrast to the grand, impersonal palaces down by the lake, though it's almost as expensive. Again this year it has been popular: "What comfort! A quiet room overlooking the courtyard; discreet and charming furnishings. Staff were very helpful, especially over parking the car. The restaurant was atmospheric, with good, plentiful food, 'folksy' rather than gastronomic. Breakfast was less successful – eg, packet cheese, surely not necessary in Switzerland." Another reader thought breakfast "excellent" – and everyone likes the restaurant. Cosy lounge and *Stube*. Umbrellas in the rooms. (*P and S Ranft, Patrick Friesner, DMW*)

Open All year.
Rooms 4 suites, 20 double, 4 single. Air-conditioning.
Facilities Lift. Lounge, bar, breakfast room, restaurant. Unsuitable for ♿.
Location Central, near cathedral. Public carparks nearby.
Credit cards All major cards accepted.
Terms B&B: single 279–340 Sfrs, double 410 Sfrs, suite 520 Sfrs. Full alc 70–75 Sfrs.

> Hotels often book you into their most expensive rooms or suites unless you specify otherwise. Even if all room prices are the same, hotels may give you a less good room in the hope of selling their better rooms to late customers. It always pays to discuss accommodation in detail when making a reservation and to ask for a free upgrade on arrival if the hotel isn't full.

La Cigogne *Tel* (022) 311 42 42
17 place Longemalle *Fax* (022) 311 40 65
1204 Genève

Central but quiet, near Mont-Blanc bridge on left bank of Rhône. Not cheap, but with spacious, elegantly furnished rooms, good breakfasts. Lift; air-conditioning. All major credit cards accepted. 50 rooms. B&B: single 325 Sfrs, double 430 Sfrs. Set meals 36–52 Sfrs; alc 82–114 Sfrs [1996]. Reports on food welcome.

GLION-SUR-MONTREUX 1823 Vaud — Map 15

Hôtel Victoria *Tel* (021) 963 31 31
Fax (021) 963 13 51

This classic white hotel, smart and stylish (Relais & Châteaux), has a splendid position on a hillside above Montreux. "Very friendly, lovely views, flowers everywhere," is a recent comment, endorsing this earlier view: "Wonderful. The hotel perches so steeply above the town that you cannot see the latter from the rooms or garden; instead you look straight over Lake Geneva to the mountains beyond. In the new wing, we had a huge, light room, restfully decorated and superbly well equipped, with a balcony along its entire width. The big bathroom had a jacuzzi. All quiet at night. The gardens are spacious, so is the pool. We had a lovely welcome, and dined outdoors by the garden. Main dishes were ordinary, but breakfast was excellent." Another reader too found the food disappointing." (*T and RR, and others*)

Open All year.
Rooms 9 suites, 35 double, 10 single. Some on ground floor. Some in annexe.
Facilities Lift. Salons, TV room, restaurant; function facilities. Large grounds: garden, swimming pool, tennis, golf practice.
Location Outside Glion village, 5 km NE of Montreux. Private parking.
Credit cards All major cards accepted.
Terms [1996] B&B: single 130–240 Sfrs, double 220–340 Sfrs, suite 420–570 Sfrs; D,B&B 70 Sfrs added per person. Set lunch 60 Sfrs, dinner 70 Sfrs; full alc 85 Sfrs.

GRINDELWALD 3818 Bern — Map 15

Hotel Belvedere *Tel* (036) 54 54 34
Fax (036) 53 41 20

This classic hotel, fairly smart, stands on the edge of a leading Bernese Oberland resort, with mountains rising behind. Since it was built in 1907 it has been owned and run by the Hauser family, who have recently modernised and renovated it. "They run it with the precision of a Swiss watch," says one visitor. Another adds: "The view of the Eiger is magnificent. The six-course evening meals are superb, and the breakfast buffet is copious. Staff are friendly, and the owners accompany guests on activities, at a small charge." The health centre is well equipped. (*PG*)

Open All year, except 22 Oct–22 Dec.
Rooms 6 suites, 48 double, 2 single.
Facilities Lift. Lounge, salon (no-smoking), bar (pianist 6 days a week), restaurant; indoor pool, sauna, fitness room; children's playroom; terrace. Garden.
Location 200 m from centre. Parking.

Credit cards All major cards accepted.
Terms [1996] B&B: single 150–300 Sfrs, double 240–450 Sfrs, suite 450–950 Sfrs; D,B&B double 280–490 Sfrs. Set dinner 48–70 Sfrs; full alc 70 Sfrs.

Romantik Hotel Schweizerhof NEW *Tel* (036) 53 22 02
Fax (036) 53 20 04

On edge of resort, amid green pastures, sizeable and fairly smart chalet-hotel, owned and run for over 30 years by Hauser family. Traditional decor of stripped pine; lots of comforts. 50 large rooms, very good meals and breakfasts, cheerful staff, fine views. Games room; indoor swimming pool with views, sauna, solarium, etc, big garden with loungers. Open 21 Dec–31 Mar, 1 June–5 Oct. Access, Amex, Visa accepted. D,B&B single 172–227 Sfrs, double 314–408 Sfrs. Set lunch 17.50 Sfrs, dinner 38–90 Sfrs.

GSTAAD-SCHÖNRIED 3778 Bern Map 15

Hotel Alpenrose *Tel* (030) 4 67 67
Fax (030) 4 67 12

Set amid upland meadows and pinewoods, Schönried is a village resort with excellent skiing, 180 metres higher than Gstaad. Here this handsome family-run Alpine chalet was found "comfortable, with very friendly staff" by one visitor this year. Another last year spent "a wonderful week, with superb set menus": but a third was less happy, finding the food "only moderate". An earlier report: "There's a family atmosphere, and young Madame von Siebenthal has a real sense of caring for her guests. The cosy lounge felt more like an elegant home than a hotel. In the candlelit dining room we were served wonderful food. We had one of the new bedrooms, furnished in modern Alpine style, with a smart bathroom." Most rooms are large and have a balcony: some enjoy fine views, but others face woods and road and are not very bright. The hotel has a terrace, but no grounds. (*Mrs Blake Foster, CC*)

Open All year, except 20 Oct–15 Dec. Restaurant closed midday Mon/Tues, mid-Apr–mid-June.
Rooms 4 suites, 15 double. Many with balcony. Some on ground floor.
Facilities Lift, ramps. Lounge, bar, 2 restaurants; terrace.
Location 8 km NE of Gstaad. Garage, parking.
Credit cards All major cards accepted.
Terms [1996] Rooms 195–420 Sfrs (with breakfast); D,B&B 45 Sfrs per person added. Set meals 55–135 Sfrs; alc 43–118 Sfrs.

HOFSTETTEN BEI BRIENZ 3858 Bern Map 15

Landgasthof Alpenrose NEW *Tel* (033) 951 14 10
Fax (033) 951 44 81

Set amid fields in hamlet outside Brienz, near lake, small new hotel owned and run by charming young couple, Denise and Daniel Wälti. Stripped pine walls and furnishings, flowery balconies; good food. Lounge, small garden. Good facilities for disabled. Open Christmas–end Oct. All major credit cards accepted. Lounge, garden. 12 rooms (5 no-smoking). B&B double 100–180 Sfrs; D,B&B 35 Sfrs per person added. More reports, please.

ISELTWALD 3807 Bern — Map 15

Chalet du Lac NEW

Tel (036) 45 11 12
Fax (036) 45 11 44

"We loved it," says a visitor this year, restoring to the *Guide* this converted chalet in a prime site beside Lake Brienz. "Our room in the new part was furnished with care, and had a balcony overlooking the lake. Lovely evening meals." Another view: "Rooms were newly remodelled, with exposed cedar and white-washed wood. The mountain view was fine. The owner, Frau Abegglen, was friendly, and the food good: but service at dinner was slow." All rooms have a balcony, but some face the mountain. You can dine on a lakeside terrace when it's fine. The buffet breakfast is admired, though not always the breakfast service. (*Lisa and Peter Simon, Al and Diana Wallace*) Rooms above the rear carpark can be noisy.

Open 10 Mar–20 Dec. Restaurant closed Mon.
Rooms 21.
Facilities Restaurant; functions room; terrace.
Location S shore of Lake Brienz, 10 km E of Interlaken. Private parking.
Credit cards All major cards accepted.
Terms [1996] Rooms 125–230 Sfrs (with breakfast); D,B&B 30 Sfrs added. Alc meals 28–70 Sfrs.

KANDERSTEG 3718 Bern — Map 15

Royal Hotel Bellevue

Tel (033) 75 12 12
Fax (033) 75 13 33

"The best-run hotel I've ever stayed at," says a devotee who returned this year to this modern luxury hotel, owned and managed by Albert Rikli. It is quite small, in chalet style, but has grandiose public rooms with period decor. Set in gorgeous, well-kept gardens on the edge of this well-known Alpine resort, it has been liked again for its buffet meals and its young staff, "well trained, and with a nice sense of humour". An earlier view: "We enjoyed swimming in the heated outdoor pool, looking up at the mountains. The large lawn has lots of chairs, and taking tea on the terrace was a delight. The bar is cosy, with comfortable leather chairs. At dinner we were given a lovely window table; lots of help-yourself salads, main courses such as duck à l'orange, all very tasty, and varied desserts. Our pretty room had a superb view. The railway nearby does not disturb sleep." (*Susan B Hanley*)

Open 18 Dec–24 Mar, 2 June–29 Sept.
Rooms 7 suites, 35 double.
Facilities Lifts. Hall, 2 salons, bar, TV room, billiard room, 2 restaurants; swimming pool, whirlpool, sauna, solarium, massage. Garden: swimming pool, tennis, putting green, *boccia*, croquet, table-tennis. Riding, sailing, water-skiing nearby. Unsuitable for ♿.
Location On edge of resort. Private parking, garage.
Credit cards All major cards accepted.
Terms [1996] Rooms 350–610 Sfrs. Breakfast 25 Sfrs. Set dinner 100 Sfrs; alc 43–137 Sfrs.

We are particularly keen to have reports on italicised entries.

Landgasthof Ruedihaus *Tel* (033) 675 15 80
Fax (033) 675 18 28

Set amid meadows on the edge of the resort, this picturesque 18th-century chalet has rustic period furnishings (some four-posters); staff in country garb add to the local colour. "Our large room had heavy wooden furniture. There are two restaurants, one cheaper and less formal than the other. Food in both was excellent." Breakfasts are also admired. Some noise from trains at back. Guests have access to the owners' much more expensive *Doldenhorn* hotel, across the road, which readers have liked for its food but found a little impersonal.

Open All year. Restaurant closed Tues/midday Wed.
Rooms 1 suite, 7 double, 1 single.
Facilities Lounge, 2 restaurants; terrace. Garden. Unsuitable for ♿.
Location On edge of resort. Parking.
Credit cards All major cards accepted (residents only).
Terms B&B 85–115 Sfrs per person; D,B&B 30 Sfrs added. Set lunch 30 Sfrs, dinner 45 Sfrs; full alc 70 Sfrs. Children under 6 accommodated free in parents' room; under 12 50% reduction.

Hotel Victoria Ritter *Tel* (033) 675 80 00
Fax (033) 675 81 00

Set in a wide garden below a rocky mountain, this "marvellous family hotel" has been found ideal for a skiing holiday and is children-geared. "We were made to feel very welcome. The nursery was a godsend, staffed by a very caring and enthusiastic Swiss girl. Our children loved the entertainment and indoor swimming pool. Food was good, not exceptional." That 1996 report backs earlier similar praise: "The Platzer owners themselves have young ones. Nannies supervise the playroom with super toys and the high tea (delicious food). Adults' food was good too, in a restaurant with big windows facing the mountains. Sledges can be borrowed, and there's a bus service to the chairlift. Our suite had plenty of space, mountain views, big wooden cots for the children." There's a library. (*John and Julie Moseley, and others*)

Open 20 Dec–12 Oct. Restaurant closed Wed/Thurs in Apr/May.
Rooms 8 suites, 42 double, 28 single.
Facilities Lift, ramp. Lounge, library, 2 bars, restaurant; swimming pool; supervised children's playroom; terrace. Park: tennis, stream, fishing.
Location Central. Parking.
Credit cards All major cards accepted.
Terms B&B: single 92–125 Sfrs, double 174–240 Sfrs, suite 210–280 Sfrs; D,B&B double 224–290 Sfrs. Set lunch 35 Sfrs, dinner 40–50 Sfrs; full alc 50–60 Sfrs. Reductions for children. 1 night bookings refused Christmas/New Year.

MONTREUX 1820 Vaud **Map 15**

Golf Hotel René Capt *Tel* (021) 963 46 31
35 rue du Bon Port *Fax* (021) 963 03 52

In full view of Byron's romantic Château de Chillon, this sturdy white 1890s edifice, yellow-shuttered, stands in its lovely gardens by the lake. It's a classic Swiss hotel like they used to make them, but medium-price, not grand (only one *Michelin* gable). Recent approval: "Family-owned by the Capts, it has a very competent staff and is in impeccable repair, with spacious public rooms, parquet floors, some typical *belle époque* stained-glass panes, and a grand piano in the lounge. Meals are ample and well cooked. Rooms facing the lake are quietest: most if not all have double windows." (*KP*)

Open Easter–31 Oct.
Rooms 40 double, 20 single.
Facilities Lift. Lounges, restaurant; conference/function facilities; terrace. Garden. Indoor swimming pool next door; lake: swimming, fishing.
Location Central. Pay parking.
Credit cards All major cards accepted.
Terms [1996] B&B: single 119–130 Sfrs, double 186–204 Sfrs; D,B&B: single 139–150 Sfrs, double 226–244 Sfrs. Set meals 25–32 Sfrs.

LE NOIRMONT 2340 Jura — Map 15

Hôtel-Restaurant de la Gare

Tel (032) 953 11 10
Fax (032) 953 10 59

"This tiny gem of a sophisticated restaurant" (*Michelin* star, two *Gault Millau toques*) was again hugely enjoyed this year by its original discoverer. It is an unlikely place: a comic-looking steep-gabled little house, with three guest bedrooms, in a remote Jura townlet amid pinewoods near the French border. Here Georges Wenger, son of the local baker, and his German wife Andrea harness local farm produce to modern styles of cuisine, and a leading British hotelier has written: "I have never seen a small team better organised to please clients or more willing to do so." This year's view: "The *menu dégustation* is a magnificent procession of dishes with vibrant taste and subtle textures. Some dishes are influenced by Thai cooking. We enjoyed loup de mer en croûte de gingembre, agneau poché, plus a Falstaffian chuck of a wine list. The three bedrooms are furnished individually; a large plate of mixed fruit was in our room. The Wengers are charming, modest and caring. During breakfast, a very elderly farmer came in with a muslin pouch full of chanterelles, which appeared on the menu that evening. The rolling Jura hills around are wonderful." Earlier comments: "The building is spick-and-span. Our room was spacious and airy, decorated in pastel shades of apricot, lilac and blue. There's a garden with loungers, and a terrace for drinks." (*John and Padi Howard, once again, and others*)

Open All year, except Christmas. Restaurant closed Sun evening/Mon.
Rooms 2 suites, 1 double.
Facilities Hall/bar, dining room; terrace. Garden. Unsuitable for ♿.
Location In town, 19 km NE of La Chaux-de-Fonds. Street parking.
Credit cards Access, Amex, Visa.
Terms B&B: single 140–160 Sfrs, double 220–270 Sfrs; D,B&B 60 Sfrs added per person. Set lunch 52 Sfrs, dinner 60–140 Sfrs; full alc 92 Sfrs.

PONTRESINA 7504 Graubünden — Map 15

Hotel Chesa Mulin

Via Mulin

Tel (081) 838 82 00
Fax (081) 838 82 30

The ski-resort of Pontresina is quieter and prettier than its larger neighbour, St-Moritz. Here the *Chesa Mulin* was found "better than ever" by a devotee returning recently. On the edge of the resort, it is a modern family-run B&B hotel formed of two big chalets; its big garden, where you can take drinks, has fine mountain views; there are good summer walks across meadows and glaciers. Readers have enjoyed the "friendly atmosphere" created by the hard-working Schmid family. Rooms are pleasant, with lots of stripped pine, good reading lights. And the buffet breakfast, served in a bright Alpine-style room, is described as "excellent". (*RP*)

Open Dec–Apr, June–Oct.
Rooms 24 double, 6 single. 1 designed for ♿.
Facilities Lift. Lounge, snack bar, breakfast room (no-smoking); sauna, solarium; terrace. Garden.
Location Central. 7 km E of St-Moritz. Garage.
Credit cards All major cards accepted.
Terms B&B: single 95–130 Sfrs, double 170–240 Sfrs. 1-week min. (Sat–Sat) preferred in winter, obligatory over New Year. Special off season rates for senior citizens; ski packages.

RIGI-KALTBAD 6356 Luzern — Map 15

Hotel Bergsonne

Tel (041) 397 11 47
Fax (041) 397 12 07

"A dream of what Switzerland is like." Everyone enjoys the cowbells ("good for the soul", "a relaxing melody", "a most peaceful week here despite, or because of, the cowbells") at this up-in-the-sky hotel, three-quarters of the way up the Rigi mountain beside Lake Lucerne. Owned and run by the "charming" Willy and Dorly Camps-Stander, it is a sturdy modern building with a sun-terrace, reachable only by rack or cable railway. And it was hugely popular again this year and last: "A delight. Best food we tasted in Europe. The view from the dining room and its balcony was breathtaking." "The meals were delicious." "The owner was most gracious. We had good-size rooms, with a decor of Swiss pine, and an amazing view of sunrise above the clouds with the lake below. Breakfast was a bountiful buffet. And the music of the mountain was not only cowbells but groups of Alpine horns being blown in different areas." (*AD and JE Stokes, Al and Diana Wallace, Earl and Phyllis Jacobs, and others*)

Open Mid-Dec–Apr, June–Nov.
Rooms 4 suites, 13 double.
Facilities Lounge, restaurant, *Stube*; terrace. Garden. Unsuitable for ♿.
Location 3 km NE of Weggis. No access by car: take rack or cable railway from Vitznau or Weggis.
Credit cards Access, Amex, Visa.
Terms B&B 75–95 Sfrs; D,B&B 35 Sfrs added per person; full board 60 Sfrs added. Set lunch 25 Sfrs, dinner 40 Sfrs; full alc 50 Sfrs.

SCHAFFHAUSEN — Map 15

Rheinhotel Fischerzunft NEW

Rheinquai 8
8200 Schaffhausen

Tel (052) 625 32 81
Fax (052) 624 32 85

This picturesque medieval town is close to the powerful Rhine Falls. Here this former fishermen's guild house by the river is now a stylish and celebrated restaurant (Relais & Châteaux), with sumptuous bedrooms (most have river views). Owner/chef André Jaeger wins a *Michelin* star and four *Gault Millau toques* for cooking that has an oriental accent (he met his Chinese wife Doreen in Hong Kong). The food comes served on clear glass plates set on black lacquer trays decorated with flower petals. Some readers have found this over-fussy, and for this and other reasons the *Fischerzunft* fell from the *Guide*. But two readers in 1995–96 have pleaded for its return: "We have never stayed in a better inn. Lovely food and welcome, wonderful rooms." "A marvellous place. It is not pretentious, but filled with genuine warmth and charm: super friendly staff. Our bedroom was fresh looking and modern. We dined on the terrace by the fast-flowing Rhine, and had their medium-price menu, all fish and sensational, with fresh flowers adorning each course. The next night I had a special menu printed for my birthday (nine courses, such as squid filled with scampi): first-class cooking, and amazingly proficient service." The lavatory-flushing system is very high-tech; and beds are adjustable, "enabling 'his half' and 'her half' to be raised or lowered at different angles from each other". (*Ruth Luborsky, Francine and Ian Walsh*)

Open All year, except last week Jan–mid-Feb. Restaurant closed 1 Jan.
Rooms 4 suites, 6 double.
Facilities 2 lounges, restaurant; conference facilities; terrace. Unsuitable for ♿.
Location On banks of Rhine, 500 m E of centre. Limited parking.
Credit cards All major cards accepted.
Terms Rooms: single 195–310 Sfrs, double 280–430 Sfrs. Breakfast 25 Sfrs. Set meals 100–185 Sfrs; full alc 170 Sfrs.

SCHWANDEN 3657 Bern — Map 15

Gasthof Rothorn

Tel (033) 251 11 86
Fax (033) 251 33 86

"The setting is pure *Heidi*, with distant snowy mountains and unbelievably lush meadows. Mrs Amstutz-Rentsch was charming and the food wonderful (except perhaps for the puddings)" – another accolade for this *Guide* favourite, a sturdy brown chalet-hotel amid meadows backed by pine woods, in a village high above Gunten. Many rooms have views of the Bernese Alps. This report holds good: "We were delighted with the fine rural charm and quiet peace. Our room's furnishings were new; it even had a sofa and sitting area. We had simple but wonderful meals out on the terrace – pork in red wine sauce, duck with apricots. The bar, a local gathering spot, was full of yodellers and singers: we traded some sleep for good hospitality and authentic charm." Others have spoken of "local pensioners gossiping at the bar", of the modern bedrooms, of good service, and of the Amstutz-Rentsch family's "friendly and gracious hospitality". On some evenings they play Swiss folk music – "a most enjoyable free concert". (*Endorsed this year by R Barratt*) Bedrooms at the back look on to the hillside and are quiet; those at the front are larger and have a balcony, but can suffer from some noise.

Open All year, except 3 weeks Nov, 3 weeks Apr. Restaurant closed Mon.
Rooms 13 double. 3 in chalet annexe.
Facilities Lounge, TV room, dining room, restaurant; occasional folk music.
Location 20 mins' drive NW of Interlaken, 15 mins SE of Thun.
Credit cards Access, Amex, Visa.
Terms B&B: single 50–85 Sfrs, double 90–160 Sfrs; D,B&B double 146–216 Sfrs.

Set meals 13–32 Sfrs. Discount for children in parents' room: under 6 50%, 6–12 30%.

SOGLIO 7610 Graubünden — Map 15

La Soglina

Tel (081) 822 16 08
Fax (081) 822 15 94

High in the mountains south-west of St-Moritz, remote and unspoilt, Soglio has been described as the typical *Heidi* village, "rustic, traditional, romantic". *La Soglina* itself is a modern hotel, but modest: well run by the Nass-Schumacher family owners, it won another rave this year: "This is our favourite spot in the world. The views of the Alps from your private balcony are unparalleled. Our bedroom was large, waiters were friendly and thoughtful, the five-course dinners were excellent." "Our huge room was well furnished, and food was fresh, tasty and colourful." The old hotel has now been closed, and the former annexe on the hill (superb views) is now the main hotel, very modern, full of light stained oak. Rooms are "warm, cosy and very Swiss, with splendid hand-painted shutters on the windows". A new bedroom wing has just opened. (*Al and Diana Wallace, RAD and JD Booth*) Visitors may be charged extra for paying by credit card.

Open All year.
Rooms 33 double. Some on ground floor.
Facilities Lift. Lounge, TV room, restaurant; sauna, Turkish bath, whirlpool, solarium, fitness room; terrace (meals served). Garden.
Location On edge of village, just N of N3 Chiavenna–Maloja pass. Garden.
Credit card Visa.
Terms B&B double 130 Sfrs; D,B&B 30 Sfrs added per person. Set meals 35 Sfrs.

VADUZ 9490 Liechtenstein — Map 15

Hotel Real
Städtle 21

Tel (075) 232 22 22
Fax (075) 232 08 91

In busy main street of principality's tiny capital, restaurant-with-rooms renowned for superb expensive food, light and delicate (Michelin *star), served in smart, flower-filled room. Bedrooms at back spacious, quiet; those at front smaller, more modern. Cheerful service, OK breakfast. Closed 24–26 Dec. All major credit cards accepted. 13 rooms. B&B: single 170–250 Sfrs, double 185–225 Sfrs. Alc 85–135 Sfrs. Still owned and run by Real family, but the chef, Karl Armbrecht, is new. More reports, please.*

Park-Hotel Sonnenhof
Mareestrasse 29

Tel (075) 232 11 92
Fax (075) 232 00 53

Just outside the city, in mountain-backed parkland setting, luxurious elegant villa-hotel (Relais & Châteaux) owned and run by Real family (see above). Cordial staff. 29 large, well-fitted rooms, most with balcony and view; spacious lounges; indoor swimming pool. Garden. Excellent food. Open 15 Feb–22 Dec. All major credit cards accepted. B&B: single 210–270 Sfrs, double 280–380 Sfrs; D,B&B 68 Sfrs added per person. More reports, please.

VÉSENAZ 1222 Genève **Map 15**

La Tourelle NEW/BUDGET
26 route d'Hermance

Tel (022) 752 16 28
Fax (022) 752 54 93

In lakeside village 5 km NE of Geneva, down quiet street just inland, handsome white villa in garden with lawns, nominated as "absolute gem": "Friendly, superb service, excellent breakfast. Only drawback: thin walls." B&B only: nearby Vietnamese restaurant recommended. Closed 26 Dec–1 Feb. All major credit cards accepted. 23 rooms. B&B 100–195 Sfrs [1996].

VITZNAU 6354 Luzern **Map 15**

Terrasse am See

Tel (041) 397 10 33
Fax (041) 397 21 55

In a small and smart resort on Lake Lucerne, this relatively unsophisticated hotel was enjoyed warts-and-all by recent guests: "It is good value for Switzerland, and the friendliness of the owners more than makes up for its rather dowdy appearance. Also, it has a fine location right on the lake. The decor is strictly institutional and rooms are small, but clean. Some have a superb lake view, but those who, like us, draw the short straw have an intimate view of the rack railway station. This generates little night noise, but revellers in the open-air café forming part of the hotel can be heard clearly. In the dining room, superbly located, nearly all tables have a view of the lake and its beautiful sunsets." Others have written: "We were made very welcome by the Fassbind family and other staff. Ambience generally bucolic: no TV, but cowbells. Our bedroom most attractive in pink and white. Dining room built right out over the lake. No choice of dishes on the *pension* menu, but what we had was enjoyable." "Magical sunsets, tasty meals, and the staff made a great fuss of our baby," adds a reader this year. (*EC, Mrs J Kleeman, and others*)

Open Apr–Oct.
Rooms 19 double, 8 single.
Facilities Library, TV / games room, restaurant; sun-terrace. On lake: swimming, rowing boats / kayaks available.
Location Near mountain railway station and jetty. Parking.
Credit cards Access, Visa.
Terms [1996] B&B: single 80–110 Sfrs, double 120–200 Sfrs; D,B&B 30 Sfrs per person added. Set lunch 15 Sfrs, dinner 35 Sfrs; full alc 30–50 Sfrs. Children under 6 accommodated free in parents' room.

VULPERA 7552 Graubünden **Map 15**

Villa Maria

Tel (081) 864 11 38
Fax (081) 864 91 61

In remote Lower Engadin valley, near river Inn, 3 km SW of summer/winter resort of Scuol, attractive and peaceful holiday hotel with fine mountain views. Spacious rooms, excellent food, pleasant staff and family owners – he is a golf pro, and a course is close by. Outdoor dining, garden. Open 21 Dec–14 Apr, 21 May–31 Oct. No credit cards accepted. 15 rooms. B&B 124–296 Sfrs; D,B&B 30 Sfrs added per person. Set meals 68–108 Sfrs [1996]. Fuller reports welcome.

WEGGIS 6353 Luzern — Map 15

Hôtel Beau Rivage

Tel (041) 390 14 22
Fax (041) 390 19 81

The Geerings' bright and stylish family hotel stands on the lake near Lucerne, with a pretty garden where you can sit watching the steamers. It remains much loved by readers, one of whom writes this year: "A return here after ten years proved an absolute delight – it comes near to my ideal hotel. The Geerings have gone from strength to strength; their personal touch is everywhere. The five-course *demi-pension* dinner is cooked with infinite care: main dishes are rich but not unduly so, the salad and dessert buffets are varied. Public rooms are furnished in discreet good taste." "Enthusiastically endorsed." Others wrote: "The dear old *Beau Rivage*, utterly dependable, like a well-organised aunt, seemed better than ever this summer." "Most beautiful, with a magnificent setting." "Stunning tiles in the bathroom." Many rooms have a balcony facing the lake. The restaurant has an outdoor terrace, with matching yellow cushions and blinds. The pool is kept warm enough to swim in until the end of September. (*Alan Blyth, JA Dyson, Ronald McNeill, and many others*) Some night sounds from church bells – "but they are part of the ambience".

Open Early Apr–end Oct.
Rooms 4 suites, 28 double, 9 single. Some suitable for ♿.
Facilities Lift. Hall, lounges, bar, garden room, restaurant. Garden: swimming pool, lakeside terrace (band twice a week), beach, fishing.
Location On lake, near quay. Look for signs to Küssnacht. Garages, parking.
Credit cards All major cards accepted.
Terms B&B: single 120–160 Sfrs, double 200–300 Sfrs, suite 320–380 Sfrs; D,B&B 50 Sfrs per person added. Set meals 55–65 Sfrs; full alc 90 Sfrs. Reduced rates for children.

WENGEN 3823 Bern — Map 15

Hotel Alpenrose

Tel (036) 55 32 16
Fax (036) 55 15 18

There is no access by car, only by narrow-gauge railway, to this classic resort high in the Bernese Oberland. Here on the edge of the village, facing across to the Jungfrau, is an old but newly renovated hotel, owned and superbly run by the von Allmens (she is a Scot). Some balconies face the valley; you can lie in bed and gaze at the Jungfrau. An American visitor in 1996 was delighted by the warmth of welcome, the food and the bedrooms, echoing earlier praise: "Staggering views, the sound of sheepbells. Frau von Allmen is delightful, serving at reception and at dinner. This was fine – five huge courses, including help-yourself salad. Most guests, like me, were in their Feisty Fifties." But not all: "The staff treated our baby affectionately. An ambience of relaxed informal warmth. Our room was furnished in pine, with good lights. The lounges have lots of chairs, and food was excellent." Large garden. Most guests tend to be British. And Wengen: "It seems to attract old-fashioned people – single German ladies, doughty hikers, quiet English couples reading *The Daily Telegraph*." (*Carey and Lance Devin, PJG Ransom, Mrs Blake Foster, PE Carter, and others*)

Open May–Oct, Dec–Apr.
Rooms 36 double, 12 single. 5 in adjacent chalet.
Facilities 2 lounges, TV room, bar, restaurant; terrace. Garden.
Location Edge of resort. No cars in Wengen; park in Lauterbrunnen and take train.
Credit cards All major cards accepted.
Terms D,B&B 89–140 Sfrs. Set dinner 39 Sfrs.

Park Hotel Beausite *Tel* (033) 856 51 61
Fax (033) 855 30 10

Sizeable modern-style hotel looking over resort to Jungfrau. Most rooms have balcony. Commended for "warm and charming" staff and Strässle family owners, relaxed atmosphere, excellent food at buffet breakfast and dinner (some Swiss dishes). Indoor swimming pool, sauna; terrace with meal service. Closed 9–25 Apr, 20 Oct–17 Dec. Access, Visa accepted. 53 rooms. Rooms 210–370 Sfrs (with breakfast); D,B&B 35 Sfrs added per person. Set meals 38–85 Sfrs [1996].

Hotel Eiger *Tel* (033) 855 11 31
Fax (033) 855 10 30

Many balconies have views of the Eiger, Mönch and Jungfrau, at the Fuchs family's ski-hotel. Conveniently close to the station for the mountain railway, it has been rebuilt in traditional style (stripped pine, a new south-facing terrace), and has lots of ambience: "A cocktail party with the owners was interesting"; "the charming staff join in the fun of your being on holiday". Others have enjoyed the "beautifully designed" modern bedrooms, where the beds are pushed away each morning to create a sitting area. There are spacious family rooms with kitchen corner, and drying racks in the bathrooms, ideal for visits with children. "The hotel is run with polished efficiency, and has simple yet sophisticated good taste." The breakfast buffets are excellent and dinner, though not *haute cuisine*, is well presented (a new chef this year). The small bar is a focal point of Wengen *après-ski*. (*AVW*)

Open All year, except 13 Apr–7 Aug, 1–30 Nov. Restaurant closed Mon June–Oct.
Rooms 9 suites, 20 double, 4 single.
Facilities Lift, ramps. Lounge, TV room, 2 bars, 2 restaurants (no-smoking); terrace with restaurant. Outdoor swimming pool nearby.
Location Same as *Hotel Alpenrose* (see entry).
Credit cards All major cards accepted.
Terms B&B: single 85–128 Sfrs, double 190–280 Sfrs, suite 210–298 Sfrs; D,B&B: 106–170 Sfrs per person. Set meals 16–50 Sfrs; full alc 48–60 Sfrs. Children under 2 accommodated free.

ZERMATT 3920 Valais **Map 15**

Hotel Antares *Tel* (028) 67 36 64;
from 1.11.96 (027) 967 36 64
Fax (028) 67 52 36
from 1.11.96 (027) 967 52 36

"One of the highlights of our Swiss tour. Wonderful dinners, and a view of the Matterhorn from our balcony" – more enthusiasm this year for a quite smart modern chalet-style hotel, next to the cable-car for the Klein Matterhorn and the Schwarzsee, a summer skiing area. Recent reports have praised the Schnidrig-Holenstein family owners: "Gerhard's cooking is delicious, his wife Monika is a wonderful hostess. One can lie in bed and watch the sun rise over the Matterhorn." "Stylish and friendly, with a pleasant staff. We had a lovely spacious room with superior bathroom. Breakfasts above average. Convivial wood-panelled English-style bar." The sun-terrace has been heated, "so you can enjoy an *après-ski* drink and listen to the splendid pianist without freezing". (*Charles and Laura Waller, and others*) Some rooms are on the small side, and not all have a balcony.

Open All year.
Rooms 2 suites, 29 double, 5 single. 1 on ground floor.
Facilities Lift. TV lounge, 2 bars, restaurant; sauna, steam bath, solarium; terrace (meal service). Free use of swimming pool at nearby hotel.
Location 10 mins' walk from centre. No cars in Zermatt.
Credit cards Access, Visa.
Terms B&B 87–215 frs; D,B&B 112–240 frs. Set dinner 58 frs; full alc 80 frs.

Hotel Bristol *Tel* (028) 66 22 70
from 2.11.96 (027) 966 33 66
Fax (028) 66 22 74
from 2.11.96 (027) 966 33 65

"Central but not noisy, it was a delight. Mostly Swiss and French custom, no British. It has so established a reputation that it can eschew package tourism." So runs a recent report on the Perren family's 3-star hotel, set between two main ski-lifts, with a small garden for summer. "It's exceptionally well run by an enthusiastic family with an excellent chef – and here speak two foodies. Dinner with five smallish courses might include kangaroo meat, fondue. OK, the furnishing style wasn't *House and Garden*, but it was comfortable, nice and warm. An armchair lounge for *après-ski* tea, delightful duvets in our room, and a balcony with Matterhorn view. Sauna, and bar with live music (well soundproofed in basement)." (*BA and PS*)

Open All year, except end Apr–15 June, 15 Oct–end Nov. Dining room closed to non-residents.
Rooms 4 suites, 35 double, 11 single. All with balcony.
Facilities Lift. Lounge, bar with TV, dancing bar, restaurant; sauna, steam-bath, whirlpool, solarium; terrace.
Location Central. No cars in Zermatt.
Credit cards Access, Visa.
Terms B&B: single 115–140 Sfrs, double 210–270 Sfrs, suite 250–310 Sfrs; D,B&B 125–180 Sfrs per person. Full alc 45 Sfrs.

Hotel Metropol *Tel* (028) 67 32 31
from 1.11.96: (027) 966 35 66
Fax (028) 67 23 42
from 1.11.96: (027) 966 35 65

"A perfect hotel", "wonderful, intimate", "nowhere else do I feel so comfortable and relaxed" – the *Metropol* has featured in the *Guide* every year since 1981, and inspires strong loyalties. It has "stunning" views of the Matterhorn from bedrooms with a balcony on the south side, and is well run by the "charming and highly professional" Taugwalder family. After Zermatt's massive building boom, few of its 109 hotels today enjoy this view, but the *Metropol* is lucky; it is also next to a "soothing" river, yet only three minutes' walk from the lively main street. The muesli at the "famous breakfast table" is always enjoyed. The hotel is "modern and functional rather than characterful, yet in its very Swiss way a model of its kind". There is no restaurant as such, but "simple Swiss dishes" are available most evenings, and these have been found excellent and copious. (*RP, DG*) The *Alfa*, the Taugwalders' slightly cheaper sister hotel next door, is also warmly recommended.

Open 1 Dec–5 May, 10 June–25 Oct.
Rooms 20 double, 4 single. Some on ground floor.
Facilities Lift, ramps. Lounge, TV room, bar, dining room; terrace. Garden.
Location Central, near station. No cars in Zermatt; hotel will fetch you.
Credit cards All major cards accepted.
Terms B&B 70–150 Sfrs per person. Light meals available.

Hotel Riffelalp *Tel* (028) 66 46 46
Riffelalp from 1.11.96: (027) 966 46 46
Fax (028) 67 51 09
from 1.11.96: (027) 967 51 09

"This is heaven!" says a reader, and we take her point: in a sky-high position, it's a small hotel alone in a meadow on the mountainside above Zermatt, reached by cable railway. It might be ideal for skiing or serious mountain walking, but is perhaps too isolated for a general holiday. Run by a Swiss with Irish-sounding name, Thomas Moor, its endearing charms include views of the Matterhorn, an outdoor terrace for meals, good Swiss dishes at lunch, classic French cooking at dinner, and a good buffet breakfast. "Staff were excellent, our room was very nice, and the restaurant a pleasant surprise," runs a 1996 letter. (*Mrs Blake Foster, Bruce and Jane Watson*)

Open Mid-Dec–15 Apr, Mid-June–early Oct.
Rooms 24.
Facilities Lift. Restaurant; sauna; terrace. Garden: tennis.
Location On Riffelalp (2,222 m), 4 km S of Zermatt. Reached by Gornergrat cable railway.
Credit cards All major cards accepted.
Terms [1996] Rooms 178–320 Sfrs (with breakfast); D,B&B 45 Sfrs added per person. Set meals 20–34 Sfrs; alc 31–75 Sfrs.

Hotel Walliserhof *Tel* (028) 67 11 74
Bahnhofstrasse from 1.11.96: (027) 966 65 55
Fax (028) 67 55 31
from 1.11.96: (027) 966 65 50

In the main street near the station is this spruce and spacious hotel, once a farmhouse. It is furnished in local style, with lots of light wood. "Excellent, and well managed," runs a 1996 report. "The manager, Eugen Diethelm, has a wicked sense of humour, staff are very friendly. Our Matterhorn Club Room (worth paying the extra for size and view) was quiet, with superior cupboard space. Food was first rate: wonderful cheese fondue. Breakfasts adequate." This backs earlier praise: "Our large room was superbly serviced in the usual Swiss manner. The food was excellent, alike in the grill room and in the *Stube*, with its scrubbed pine tables and nice atmosphere." In season, guests on half board must expect to dine in a large, less attractive room at the back. (*NM Mackintosh, and others*)

Open All year.
Rooms 2 suites, 34 double, 4 single.
Facilities Lift. Lounge, bar, TV room, 2 dining rooms; sauna; terrace. Swimming pool at *Hotel Christiania* 5 mins' walk.
Location Central. No cars in Zermatt.
Credit cards All major cards accepted.
Terms B&B: single 90–175 Sfrs, double 160—330 Sfrs; D,B&B double 210–380 Sfrs. Full alc 55 Sfrs.

ZUOZ 7524 Graubünden — Map 15

Posthotel Engiadina — *Tel* (081) 854 10 21
Fax (081) 854 33 03

In the Inn valley near St Moritz, a picturesque Engadin village turned summer resort, with painted façades and built-in barns. Here the five-storey pink-façaded *Engiadina,* over 100 years old, looks outwardly sedate but is inwardly elegant, with "sumptuous" public rooms. The "warm and hospitable" owners, Giachem and Gisela Arquint, are always praised: once a week, at least in winter, they bring guests together for a fondue party. Food is "excellent" – four-course dinners, and buffet breakfasts. A regular visitor praised the "extreme politeness and professionalism of the staff", even though they seem to change every season. "The Arquints will sit with you in the evening for serious conversation" (he speaks six languages). Many rooms overlook mountains or the garden; those without views are still "perfectly nice", and cheaper. (*EC, and others*)

Open Dec–Apr, May–Oct.
Rooms 1 suite, 33 double, 10 single.
Facilities Lift. Salon with TV, 2 bars (one with piano), 2 dining rooms; banqueting room; terrace. Garden: tennis, swimming pool, sauna, solarium. Winter sports, lake nearby.
Location Centre of village, 10 km NE of St Moritz. Outdoor parking.
Credit cards All major cards accepted.
Terms B&B 88–158 Sfrs; D,B&B 122–182 Sfrs. Set lunch 38–42 Sfrs, dinner 40–49 Sfrs; full alc 60–72 Sfrs. Children under 6 accommodated free in parents' room.

ZÜRICH — Map 15

Hotel zum Storchen — *Tel* (01) 211 55 10
Am Weinplatz — *Fax* (01) 211 64 51
8001 Zürich

Paracelsus and Wagner are among the guests to have nestled down "*chez* the storks", in this pleasant if expensive riverside hotel. It dates back 600 years as an inn, though the present building is fairly new. About half of the bedrooms face the river and have the classic view of the cathedral and baroque town hall. That view is shared by the lovely canopied terrace by the river, where drinks and light meals are served. Here a reader this year had a "sumptuous" breakfast. Others have spoken of the "delightful ambience". The main restaurant is oak panelled, "with the atmosphere of one of Zürich's old guildhalls". Service is friendly and efficient. All the riverside bedrooms have just been refurbished. Some noise on both sides. (*Alan Blyth*) Some rooms are small. Reports on the food would be welcome.

Open All year.
Rooms 2 suites, 37 double, 39 single.
Facilities Lounge, bar, restaurant; terrace. Unsuitable for ♿.
Location Central. Valet parking.
Credit cards All major cards accepted.
Terms [1996] B&B 240–530 Sfrs. Set meals 44 Sfrs; full alc 64–95 Sfrs.

Hotel Tiefenau *Tel* (01) 251 24 09
Steinwiesstrasse 8–10 *Fax* (01) 251 24 76
8032 Zürich

This small family-run hotel, furnished in Louis XV style, with "bowls of fresh fruit everywhere", stands on a quiet side street near the Kunsthaus (wonderful Munchs, and Impressionist and post-Impressionist collections). It has been called "cosy without being Swiss-stuffy", and has a terrace where you can eat or drink under huge shady trees. One visitor was "delighted by the room, the breakfast, the general helpfulness", but thought that the "antiques" were not really so very old. Others have written: "Charming, spacious room, very quiet." "Hyper-Swiss, with a family feeling. In the bathroom a mini-bar offering gold-plated toothbrushes." The new restaurant, *Züri-Stube,* features local specialities and wines. (*RSMcN, and others*) "We thought it a bit threadbare, but staff were kind," is a report this year. More, please.

Open All year, except 22 Dec–7 Jan.
Rooms 7 suites, 20 double, 6 single. Some on ground floor. Air conditioning.
Facilities Lift. Salon, bar, restaurant, coffee shop; conference facilities; terrace. Garden.
Location Fairly central, by Schauspielhaus. Private parking.
Credit cards All major cards accepted.
Terms B&B: single 200–300 Sfrs, double 300–400 Sfrs, suite 400–450 Sfrs. Set meals 23–29 Sfrs; full alc 40–84 Sfrs.

with the atmosphere of one of Zürich's old guildhalls'. Service is friendly and efficient. All the elegant bedrooms have just been redecorated, [illegible] on both sides [illegible]. Some rooms are small. [illegible] on the floor would be welcome.

Open All year.
Rooms: 6 suites, 37 double, 29 single.
Facilities: Lift, bar, restaurant; [illegible] rooms.
Location: Central; valet parking.
Credit cards: All major ones accepted.
Terms: [illegible]

Hotel Florhof
Florhofgasse 4
8001 Zürich

Tel (01) 2[illegible] 24 [illegible]
Fax (01) 2[illegible] 24 [illegible]

This small family-run hotel, in a fine 16th-century house with Louis XV style, with [illegible] of fresh flat [illegible], stands on a quiet side street near the [illegible] (neoclassical, Venetian, and Impressionist and post-Impressionist collections). It has been called "cosy without being [illegible]" and has a terrace where you can eat or drink under huge shady trees. One visitor was "delighted with the room, the breakfast, the general helpfulness", but thought that the "cushions" were not really [illegible]. "Charming, [illegible] quiet." Typical Swiss, with a family feeling. In the bathroom a [illegible] of [illegible] gold-plated [illegible]. The new restaurant, Zum [illegible], features local specialities and wines. [illegible] thought it a bit [illegible]. [illegible] please.

Open All year except [illegible].
Rooms: 1 suite, 28 double, 6 single; some [illegible]. Air-conditioning [illegible].
Facilities: Lift, salon, bar, restaurant, [illegible] conference facilities; [illegible] garden.
Location: [illegible] central [illegible] parking.
Credit cards: All major cards accepted.
Terms: [illegible]

The heart of an innkeeper

Graeme Jameson

Graeme Jameson, mine host of the Wykeham Arms *in Winchester, won a 1996 César Award for his tripartite success in running under one roof a thriving city inn, a seriously esteemed restaurant and a welcoming small hotel. We asked him how he did it. This was his response.*

"You've gotta have heart, miles and miles of heart," runs an old song. It could serve as the opening to an address on the art of hotel-keeping. For a hotel without warmth and good humour provides a hollow welcome to the weary traveller. And heart alone will enable the innkeeper to transform the endless series of blind dates – for that is the nature of the initial relationship between a hotelier and his guest – into an encounter which can give satisfaction to both parties.

With his hotel set up and his heart full of pride, the hotelier awaits his guests. He rarely has much advance information about them. They all want certain basic comforts such as adequate heating and clean rooms, but they also have personal quirks and habits, to be adjusted to as quickly as possible. It is like a practical version of University Challenge, and it certainly makes the adrenalin run. With a certain amount of luck, the blind date can end in success. But understanding is needed on both sides. As a 50-year-old guide to hotels put it: "Hostelry keeping is a profession which, like medicine and unlike manufacturing, ministers to the mental and bodily welfare of its clients. Like the doctor, the good host trades in human beings. He tries to make them welcome, well-fed and comfortable. He knows that if he succeeds they will return, and there is a sporting chance they will tell their friends. But no one is infallible. The staff, though willing and loyal, may slip up occasionally. So there needs to be a little give and take."

It is a sad fact that hotel-keeping today is virtually monopolised by large conglomerates which have reduced the status of hotels to souped-up cuboid sleep shops. The trade is notorious for low pay and poor working conditions. It is not surprising that so many hotels fail. As long ago as 1850, Anthony Trollope wrote: "It is because we have put up with bad things that hotel-keepers continue to give them to us." There is one simple question that you should ask yourself as you take your leave. Does the hotelier run the business for his convenience – or mine?

Heart doesn't enter the lists as a prerequisite in the modern hotel, and trust, the hallmark of all good relationships, is equally missing. If you have any heart yourself, it will soon be strained as you heave your baggage to your room, or broken by the stuffy cheerless corridor on the way.

Hotel-keeping is a vocation. It calls for a gregarious nature, empathy, unfailing good humour, an iron constitution, and – most important – an ability to motivate the staff. I estimate that my guests come into contact with staff about 25 times a day – 25 opportunities to make the guest feel welcome or else wish that he had stayed somewhere else. I recently scanned the vacancies page of the biggest catering trade magazine. In six weeks I failed to spot a single advertisement that called for the ability to smile or the possession of a warm personality; they were all full of starchy business-school gobbledygook.

When I am not there, my staff are my ambassadors: they are the make-or-break link for the customer. Enthusiasm is a rare and wonderful quality, and it's contagious. Spread from the top it casts its influence throughout the building. My particular way of encouragement is to include a personal hand-written note with the weekly wages which always starts by saying "thank you" and which also tries to find something of note in an individual's performance. It takes three hours on a Sunday afternoon and is probably the most important thing I do all week.

As with all the best things in life, warm unfeigned hospitality cannot be bought. Neither can it be replaced by imposing portals, smart uniforms or daily dusted trinkets and antique furniture. Nor can it be confected. To those who practise hospitality, it is not an easy road to a quick buck – but done properly it can bring ample rewards and a glow of satisfaction as the guest squeezes your hand and assures you that he will be back. At that moment, the commitment, the heartache and the physical pain all dissolve. . . .

Entente Cordiale

As we mentioned in the Introduction, we are sharing some promotional activities this year with the Champagne House of Joseph Perrier. As a change from inspecting hotels, the Editor visited its venerable caves *at Châlons-en-Champagne. Here is his account of the visit.*

Good hotels come in different sizes, though the ones I like best tend to be small, personally run family affairs; the larger the hotel the more likely it is to be owned by a mega corporation. And the same is true of the champagne business. Nearly all the most celebrated houses have long since left private hands. So it was a pleasure to discover that Joseph Perrier should be small and family-owned for more than a century.

I have called Joseph Perrier small, and so it is by comparison with the best-known *marques*, each of which produces several million bottles every year. Joseph Perrier's production is a mere half-million, though when you visit its cellars – more than two miles of *caves* dug deep into the chalky hillside on the original workings which date back to Gallo-Roman days, with bottles stacked up 4 feet high on either side – 500,000 seems a spectacularly large figure.

Most of the great houses are concentrated around Épernay and Reims. Joseph Perrier is a maverick, since its *caves*, where the newly pressed wine is sent when the harvest is over, are 30 kilometres from champagne's epicentre in a town which used to be called Châlons-sur-Marne, but which gratifyingly honoured its one remaining Champagne House by changing its name at the end of 1995 to Châlons-en-Champagne.

One of the pleasures of visiting a famous wine business is to enjoy the contrast between tradition and modern technology. Joseph Perrier (or Joseph as it is known locally) lacks nothing in the way of hallowed atmosphere. The elegant reception room, where tastings are provided for visitors, is full of memorabilia: a handsome portrait of the founding father, a rather less sympathetic portrait of a sulky lady who may or may not be a later descendant, a document ordering supplies for Queen Victoria, followed by another requesting more of the same for her fun-loving son, the Prince of Wales, advice from Louis Pasteur concerning the use of yeast in fermentation, and early labels including one dated 1842 with a portrait of the Duke of Wellington looking uncommonly like the late Sir Anthony Blunt.

Outside the offices a different scene presents itself. Half-a-dozen men, dressed in their traditional royal blue overalls, are manning a hideously noisy bottling machine. As the bottles lurch off the line, they are taken away at speed on an electric trolley to the stacks in the cellars. We follow behind, watching our backs, to the long, dimly lit galleries. It is here that the process of *remuage* takes place: the meticulous repeated turning of every bottle over a three-month period until the wine is ready to be corked and labelled. *Chez* Joseph, this is still done by the *remueur*.

Most of the champagne from the house is a superior non-vintage *brut*, which will have matured for at least three years before reaching the market. But Joseph Perrier, like other major houses, also produces vintage *cuvées*, which have a higher percentage of chardonnay, are aged for five years before being marketed, and will steadily improve over the years. 1995 saw the production of a vintage *cuvée royale*, also a *brut rosé*, and still in demand among some show-business womenfolk, though no longer as glitzy as it was in, say, Toulouse-Lautrec's day; and, finally, a top-of-the-range prestige *Cuvée Joséphine*. There was another vintage *cuvée* in 1989, and there is likely to be an announcement of a *Millennium Cuvée* before the end of the decade. Perhaps you should start saving now. . . .

HILARY RUBINSTEIN

The voucher below enables you to purchase a case of Joseph Perrier's Cuvées (Non Vintage, 1989 Vintage, Rosé, or Josephine) at a 10% discount, from any of the following distributors and retail outlets: *Avon*: Great Western Wine Co, (01225) 446009; *Berks:* ISIS, (01628) 771199; *Cambs & Northants:* Wine Bin Ends Ltd, (01223) 568991; *Cheshire, Shrops & N Wales:* Tanners Wines Ltd, (01743) 232400; *Devon & Cornwall:* Wickham & Co Ltd (Jolly's Drinks), (01237) 473292; *Dorset, Wilts & Mail Order:* Hall Woodhouse Wines Ltd (retail shops); Hicks & Don, (01258) 452141; *E Anglia:* Hall Batson, (01603) 415115; Thos Peatling, (01284) 755948; *E Midlands:* Evingtons of Leicester, (0116) 254 2702; Weavers of Nottingham, (01159) 580922; *London & Lancs:* Francis Stickney Fine Wines (distributor), (0181) 201 9096; Army & Navy Stores; Balls Brothers; Fullers Wine Shops; Harvey Nichols; Holland Park Wine Co; New London Wine; Selfridges; The Wine Business; *Midlands:* John Frazier Ltd (retail shops), (0121) 704 3415; *Oxon:* The Oxford Wine Co, (01865) 820789; *Scotland:* Wine Importers of Edinburgh, (0131) 556 3601; *S Wales:* The Celtic Vintner Ltd, (01633) 430055; *Sussex:* King & Barnes Ltd, (01403) 270470; *West Country & Gloucs:* Edward Sheldon Ltd, (01608) 661409; *Yorks:* Great Northern Wine Co Leeds & Ripon, (01132) 461200. For further information, contact Joseph Perrier's UK Agent, Charles Hawkins, (01572) 823030.

THE GOOD HOTEL GUIDE 1997

This voucher entitles the bearer to purchase any case of Joseph Perrier's Cuvées at a discount of 10% off the normal retail price. Valid until 12th September, 1997.

Alphabetical list of hotels

England
Abbey Penzance 155
Abbey House Abbotsbury 5
Albright Hussey Shrewsbury 173
Alexandra Lyme Regis 136
Amberley Castle Amberley 6
Amerdale House Arncliffe 9
Angel Midhurst 142
Appletree Holme Farm Blawith 28
Archway Windermere 216
Ark Erpingham 79
Arundell Arms Lifton 119
Ashfield House Grassington 88
Ashwick House Dulverton 77
At the Sign of the Angel Lacock 110
Avondale Carlisle 53
Aynsome Manor Cartmel 53
Bailiffscourt Climping 64
Bales Mead West Porlock 209
Bank House Oakamoor 151
Basil Street London 123
Beaufort London 123
Beeches Norwich 151
Beechleas Wimborne Minster 213
Beetle and Wedge Moulsford-on-Thames 143
Berkeley House Lewes 119
Berkeley Square Bristol 42
Biggin Hall Biggin by Hartington 24
Bishopstrow House Warminster 201
Blackaller North Bovey 149
Blakeney Blakeney 26
Bond's Castle Cary 54
Borrowdale Gates Grange-in-Borrowdale 86
Boscundle Manor St Austell 165
Bourne Eau House Bourne 32
Bowerfield House Otley 151
Bowlish House Shepton Mallet 171
Bradfield House Bradfield Combust 34
Bradford Old Windmill Bradford-on-Avon 36
Breamish House Powburn 159
Bridge House Beaminster 20
Brockencote Hall Chaddesley Corbett 56
Brookdale House North Huish 150
Brookfield on Longhill Buxton 50
Buckland Manor Buckland 45
Budock Vean Budock Vean 46
Burgh Island Bigbury-on-Sea 23
Burghope Manor Bradford-on-Avon 36
Burgoyne Reeth 161
Cadogan London 124
Calcot Manor Tetbury 189
Callow Hall Ashbourne 9
Capital London 125
Carnethic House Fowey 83
Casterbridge Dorchester 74
Castle Taunton 187
Caterham House Stratford-upon-Avon 182
Cavendish Baslow 12
Chapel House Atherstone 10
Charingworth Manor Charingworth 58
Chedington Court Chedington 59
Chelwood House Chelwood 60
Chewton Glen New Milton 146
Chilvester Hill House Calne 50
Cleeve Hill Cleeve Hill 63
Cliveden Taplow 186
Coach House at Crookham Crookham 70
Cobwebs Leck 115
Cockle Warren Cottage Hayling Island 100
Cokerhurst Farm Bridgwater 40
Collin House Broadway 42
Congham Hall Grimston 91
Connaught London 125
Corse Lawn House Corse Lawn 66
Cotswold House Chipping Campden 61
Cotswold House Oxford 152
Cottage in the Wood Malvern Wells 139
Country Friends Dorrington 75
Cragwood Windermere 216
Crantock Bay Crantock 69
Crit Hall Benenden 22
Croft Great Longstone 90
Crosby Lodge Crosby-on-Eden 71
Cross Keys Cautley 55
Crossways Wilmington 212
Crown Southwold 178
Curdon Mill Vellow 199
D'Isney Place Lincoln 120
Danescombe Valley Calstock 51
Delbury Hall Diddlebury 73
Devonshire Arms Bolton Abbey 29
Diglis House Worcester 222
Dinham Hall Ludlow 135

Dove Brighton 41
Dukes Bath 13
Durrants London 126
Duxford Lodge Duxford 77
Eagle House Bathford 17
Eastbury Sherborne 172
Easton Court Chagford 56
Ees Wyke Near Sawrey 146
Egerton House London 126
Elmdon Lee Littlebury Green 122
Eslington Villa Gateshead 84
Evesham Evesham 81
Farlam Hall Brampton 38
Farthings Hatch Beauchamp 95
Feathers Woodstock 221
Fischer's Baslow Hall Baslow 13
42 The Calls Leeds 116
Frog Street Farm Beercrocombe 21
Frogg Manor Broxton 45
Gabriel Court Stoke Gabriel 181
Garrack St Ives 167
George and Dragon Kirkbymoorside 109
George Stamford 180
Gidleigh Park Chagford 57
Gilpin Lodge Windermere 216
Glewstone Court Glewstone 86
Goldhill Mill Tonbridge 191
Goring London 127
Grafton Manor Bromsgrove 44
Grange York 223
Gravetye Manor East Grinstead 79
Great House Lavenham 114
Greenway Shurdington 174
Grey Cottage Leonard Stanley 117
Grey Friar Lodge Ambleside 6
Haley's Leeds 117
Halkin London 128
Hambleton Hall Hambleton 93
Hancocks Farmhouse Cranbrook 68
Hartwell House Aylesbury 11
Haydon House Bath 14
Hazel Bank Rosthwaite 163
Hazelwood House Loddiswell 122
Hazlitt's London 128
Headlam Hall Headlam 101
Heddon's Gate Heddon's Mouth 101
Highbullen Chittlehamholt 62
Highfield House Hawkshead 97
Hintlesham Hall Hintlesham 103
Hipping Hall Cowan Bridge 67
Hobbits York 224
Hodgkinson's Matlock Bath 139
Hoe Hill Binbrook 24
Holbeck Ghyll Windermere 217
Holdfast Cottage Little Malvern 120
Hollington House Woolton Hill 221
Holly Lodge Bath 14
Homewood Park Hinton Charterhouse 104
Hooke Hall Uckfield 195
Hope End Ledbury 115
Hope House Tynemouth 195
Horn of Plenty Gulworthy 92
Horton Grange Newcastle upon Tyne 148
Hoste Arms Burnham Market 47
Hotel on the Park Cheltenham 60
Howtown Ullswater 196
Hunts Tor House Drewsteignton 76
Huntsham Court Huntsham 107
Inn at Whitewell Whitewell 210
Island Tresco 194
Ivy House Braithwaite 38
Jeake's House Rye 164
Knightsbridge Green London 129
Lake Isle Uppingham 199
Lamb Burford 47
Lamb Inn Shipton-under-Wychwood 172
Langar Hall Langar 111
Langley Castle Langley-on-Tyne 112
Langley House Langley Marsh 112
Langorf London 129
Langshott Manor Horley 106
Lansdowne Leamington Spa 114
Lastingham Grange Lastingham 113
Lea Hill Membury 140
Leeming House Watermillock 204
Leena's Guest House Salisbury 169
Leonard London 129
Leusdon Lodge Poundsgate 158
Lewtrenchard Manor Lewdown 118
Linden Hall Longhorsley 133
Lindeth Fell Bowness-on-Windermere 33
Linthwaite House Bowness-on-Windermere 33
Little Barwick House Barwick 11
Little Hemingfold Battle 18
Little Hodgeham Bethersden 22
Lodge Bathford 18
Look Out Branscombe 39
Lord Crewe Arms Blanchland 27
Lords of the Manor Upper Slaughter 198
Lovelady Shield Alston 5
Lower Pitt Restaurant East Buckland 78
Lower Slaughter Manor Lower Slaughter 135
Lydgate House Postbridge 157

Lygon Arms Broadway 43
Lynton House Holdenby 105
Mains Hall Little Singleton 121
Maison Talbooth Dedham 73
Mallory Court Bishop's Tachbrook 26
Manoir aux Quat'Saisons Great Milton 90
Manor Farm Crackington Haven 67
Mansion House Poole 156
Marlborough Ipswich 108
Marsh Eyton 81
McCoy's Staddlebridge 180
Michael's Nook Grasmere 87
Middlethorpe Hall York 224
Mill Mungrisdale 144
Mill at Harvington Harvington 94
Mill End Chagford 57
Miller Howe Windermere 218
Miller's House Middleham 141
Millstream Bosham 31
Mizzards Farm Rogate 162
Morston Hall Morston 143
Mortal Man Troutbeck 194
Mount Royale York 225
Mynd House Church Stretton 62
Nags Head Pickhill 156
Nanscawen House St Blazey 166
Nansloe Manor Helston 102
Nare Veryan 200
Netherfield Place Battle 19
New House Farm Lorton 134
New Inn Coln St Aldwyns 64
Newstead Grange Norton 150
Northcote Manor Langho 111
Northill House Horton 106
Northleigh House Hatton 95
Number Sixteen London 130
Nuthurst Grange Hockley Heath 104
Old Bank House Hayfield 99
Old Beams Waterhouses 204
Old Bell Malmesbury 138
Old Church Watermillock 205
Old Cloth Hall Cranbrook 69
Old Farmhouse Raskelf 161
Old House Wickham 211
Old Manor Cropredy 71
Old Millfloor Trebarwith Strand 193
Old Parsonage Frant 84
Old Parsonage Oxford 153
Old Parsonage West Dean 208
Old Rectory Campsea Ashe 52
Old Rectory Great Snoring 91
Old Rectory Hopesay 105
Old Rectory Lynton 137
Old Vicarage Rye 165
Old Vicarage Witherslack 219
Old Vicarage Worfield 222
On the Park Cheltenham 60
Ounce House Bury St Edmunds 48
Oxenham Arms South Zeal 178
Painswick Painswick 154
Park House South Molton 177
Parrock Head Slaidburn 175
Pear Tree at Purton Purton 160
Pembridge Court London 130
Penmere Manor Falmouth 82
Periton Park Middlecombe 141
Pheasant Seavington St Mary 171
Pickett Howe Buttermere 49
Pier at Harwich Harwich 95
Plumber Manor Sturminster Newton 183
Powder Mills Battle 19
Priory Bath 15
Priory Wareham 201
Priory Steps Bradford-on-Avon 37
Queensberry Bath 15
Ram Jam Inn Stretton 183
Rampsbeck Watermillock 206
Random Hall Slinfold 175
Red Lion Henley-on-Thames 103
Restaurant Nineteen Bradford 34
Rhydspence Inn Whitney-on-Wye 210
Richmond Lodge Mursley 145
Rising Sun Lynmouth 137
River House Thornton-le-Fylde 190
Romney Bay House New Romney 147
Rookery Hall Nantwich 145
Rose and Crown Romaldkirk 162
Roseland House Portscatho 157
Rothay Manor Ambleside 7
Rough Close Hawkshead 98
Royal Crescent Bath 16
St Petroc's House/Seaford Restaurant Padstow 153
Sandringham London 130
Seaford Restaurant and St Petroc's House Padstow 153
Seatoller House Borrowdale 30
Seaview Seaview 170
Sharrow Bay Ullswater 197
Sign of the Angel Lacock 110
Simonsbath House Simonsbath 174
Soar Mill Cove Soar Mill Cove 176
Somerset House Bath 16
South Lodge Lower Beeding 134
Star Castle St Mary's 168
Starr Great Dunmow 89
Steppes Ullingswick 196
Stock Hill House Gillingham 85

Ston Easton Park Ston Easton 182
Stone House Hawes 96
Stone House Rushlake Green 163
Stratford Lodge Salisbury 170
Stratton House Swaffham 184
Summer Lodge Evershot 80
Swan Southwold 179
Swinside Lodge Newlands 149
Swiss Cottage London 131
Talland Bay Talland-by-Looe 185
Tamhorn Park Farmhouse Fisherwick 83
Tanyard Boughton Monchelsea 31
Tarr Steps Hawkridge 97
Tavern House Willesley 211
Temple Sowerby House Temple Sowerby 188
Thomas Luny House Teignmouth 187
Thornbury Castle Thornbury 189
Tides Reach Salcombe 169
Tophams Ebury Court London 131
Topps Brighton 41
Trebrea Lodge Tintagel 191
Tregildry Gillan 85
Treglos Constantine Bay 65
Tregony House Tregony 193
Trengilly Wartha Constantine 65
Twelve Angel Hill Bury St Edmunds 49
22 Jermyn Street London 132
Underscar Manor Applethwaite 8
Uplands Cartmel 54
Upper Court Kemerton 109
Upper Green Farm Towersey 192
Victoria Bradford 35
Vin & Bistro Winchester 214
Vine House Paulerspury 154
Wallett's Court West Cliffe 208
Waltzing Weasel Birch Vale 25
Warren Downton 75
Wasdale Head Inn Wasdale Head 202
Water Yeat Guest House Water Yeat 203
Wateredge Ambleside 7
Waterford House Middleham 141
Waterside Inn Bray 40
Weaver's Haworth 99
Well House St Keyne 167
Wenlock Edge Inn Wenlock Edge 206
Wesley House Winchcombe 213
West Lodge Park Hadley Wood 93
Westerclose Country House Withypool 220
White House Charmouth 59
White House Williton 212
White House Manor and Restaurant Prestbury 159
White Moss House Grasmere 88
Whitechapel Manor South Molton 177
Whitehall Broxted 44
Whiteleaf at Croyde Croyde 72
Wilbraham London 132
Windrush House Hazleton 100
Winterbourne Bonchurch 29
Winteringham Fields Winteringham 218
Woodhayes Whimple 209
Woolley Grange Bradford-on-Avon 37
Woolpack Inn Beckington 20
Worsley Arms Hovingham 107
Wykeham Arms Winchester 215
Yalbury Cottage Dorchester 74
Ye Olde Salutation Inn Weobley 207

Wales

Bodysgallen Hall Llandudno 234
Carlton House Llanwrtyd Wells 238
Cnapan Newport 241
Conrah Country House Aberystwyth 228
Crown at Whitebrook Whitebrook 247
Dol-llyn-wydd Builth Wells 229
Egerton Grey Porthkerry 242
Fairyhill Reynoldston 244
Gilfach Goch Farmhouse Fishguard 231
Gliffaes Crickhowell 230
Hillcrest House Mumbles 240
Lake LLangammarch Wells 237
Llangoed Hall Llyswen 239
Llanwenarth House Govilon 232
Maes-y-Neuadd Talsarnau 245
Milebrook House Knighton 233
Minffordd Talyllyn 246
Old Rectory LLansanffraid 237
Parva Farmhouse Tintern 247
Pen-y-Gwryd Nantgwynant 240
Penbontbren Farm Glynarthen 231
Penmaenuchaf Hall Penmaenpool 242
Penyclawdd Court Llanfihangel Crucorney 236
Porth Tocyn Abersoch 227
Portmeirion Portmeirion 243
Riverside Abersoch 228
St Tudno Llandudno 235
Three Cocks Three Cocks 246

Ty-Isaf Farmhouse Llanfachreth 236
Ty-Mawr Brechfa 229
Tyddyn Llan Llandrillo 234
Ty'n Rhos Llanddeiniolen 233
Warpool Court St David's 244
Ynyshir Hall Eglwysfach 230

Scotland
Airds Port Appin 292
Allt-Chaorain House Crianlarich 264
Altnaharrie Ullapool 300
Apple Lodge Lochranza 286
Ardanaiseig Kilchrenan 280
Ardsheal House Kentallen 280
Ardvourlie Castle Ardvourlie 251
Arisaig House Arisaig 252
Auchendean Lodge Dulnain Bridge 266
Auchterarder House Auchterarder 254
Babbity Bowster Glasgow 274
Baile-na-Cille Timsgarry 299
Balbirnie House Markinch 286
Balcary Bay Auchencairn 253
Balfour Castle Shapinsay 295
Balgonie Country House Ballater 255
Ballathie House Kinclaven 284
Banchory Lodge Banchory 258
Brook Linn Callander 261
Busta House Busta 260
Castleton House Glamis 273
Ceilidh Place Ullapool 301
Clifton House Nairn 288
Collin House Auchencairn 253
Corriegour Lodge Spean Bridge 297
Coul House Contin 263
Creebridge House Newton Stewart 288
Crinan Crinan 264
Cringletie House Peebles 290
Crolinnhe Fort William 272
Cromlix House Kinbuck 283
Cross Kingussie 285
Culloden House Inverness 278
Darroch Learg Ballater 256
Dower House Muir of Ord 287
Druimard Country House Dervaig 265
Drummond House Edinburgh 268
Dryburgh Abbey St Boswells 295
Dunain Park Inverness 278
Dungallan House Oban 289
Eilean Iarmain Isle Ornsay 279
Enmore Dunoon 267
Factor's House Fort William 272
Farleyer House Aberfeldy 249
Glenelg Inn Glenelg 276
Glenfeochan House Kilmore 282
Grange House Whiting Bay 302
Harlosh House Dunvegan 268
Haven Plockton 291
Inverlochy Castle Fort William 273
Isle of Colonsay Colonsay 263
Isle of Eriska Eriska 270
Kilcamb Lodge Strontian 298
Kildrummy Castle Kildrummy 281
Killiecrankie Killiecrankie 282
Kinloch House Blairgowrie 259
Kinnaird Dunkeld 266
Kirkton House Cardross 262
Knockie Lodge Whitebridge 301
Knockinaam Lodge Portpatrick 293
Kylesku Kylesku 285
Lake Port of Menteith 292
Leachin House Tarbert 299
Ley Innerleithen 277
Loch Melfort Arduaine 251
Malmaison Edinburgh 269
Malmaison Glasgow 274
Maryculter House Maryculter 287
Minmore House Glenlivet 276
Monachyle Mhor Balquhidder 257
Old Manse of Marnoch Bridge of Marnoch 260
Old Mansion House Auchterhouse 255
One Devonshire Gardens Glasgow 275
Ossian Kincraig 284
Park Peebles 290
Pennyghael Pennyghael 291
Riverside Inn Canonbie 262
Roman Camp Callander 261
17 Abercromby Place Edinburgh 269
Shieldhill Quothquan 294
Sibbet House Edinburgh 270
Skirling House Skirling 297
Summer Isles Achiltibuie 250
Taychreggan Kilchrenan 281
Tigh an Eilean Shieldaig 296
Torbeag House Banavie 258
Town House Glasgow 275
Tullich Lodge Ballater 256
Viewfield House Portee 294
Wheatsheaf Swinton 298
Woodwick House Evie 271

Channel Islands
Atlantic St Brelade 304
Château La Chaire Rozel Bay 303
Frégate St Peter Port 305
Longueville Manor St Saviour 306

Petit Champ Sark 306
Sablonnerie Sark 307
St Brelade's Bay St Brelade 304
Stocks Sark 307

Northern Ireland
Ash-Rowan Belfast 309
Beech Hill House Derry 310
Killyhevlin Enniskillen 311
Tullylagan Country House Cookstown 310

Republic of Ireland
Aherne's Youghal 344
Ardagh Clifden 324
Ardnamona House Lough Eske 336
Ariel House Dublin 327
Assolas Country House Kanturk 331
Bailick Cottage Midleton 337
Ballycormac House Aglish 315
Ballylickey Manor Ballylickey 316
Ballymakeigh House Killeagh 332
Ballymaloe House Shanagarry 343
Ballynahinch Castle Recess 342
Bantry House Bantry 318
Beaufort House Beaufort 318
Belcamp Hutchinson Dublin 327
Bow Hall Castletownshend 323
Caragh Lodge Caragh Lake 320
Carnelly House Clarecastle 323
Cashel House Cashel 321
Castle Grove House Letterkenny 335
Cedar Lodge Carrigbyrne 321
Chestnut Lodge Monkstown 337
Clohamon House Bunclody 320
Coopershill Riverstown 342
Cromleach Lodge Castlebaldwin 322
Currarevagh House Oughterard 340
Delphi Lodge Leenane 334
Doyle's Townhouse Dingle 326
Dunraven Arms Adare 314
Enniscoe House Crossmolina 326
Flemingstown House Kilmallock 333
Grangebeg House Dunlavin 329
Grey Door Dublin 328
Hibernian Dublin 328
Hilton Park Clones 325
Hunter's Rathnew 341
Kingswood Country House Dublin 329
Kylenoe Ballinderry 315
Longueville Manor Mallow 336
Lotamore House Cork 325
Marlfield House Gorey 330
Milltown House Dingle 327
Muckross Park Muckross 338
Newport House Newport 339
Norman Villa Galway 330
Old Presbytery Kinsale 333
Old Rectory Wicklow 344
Park Hotel Kenmare Kenmare 331
Quay House Clifden 324
Rathmullan House Rathmullan 340
Rosleague Manor Letterfrack 335
Rosturk Woods Mulrany 339
Roundwood House Mountrath 337
Sea View House Ballylickey 316
Sheen Falls Lodge Kenmare 332
Temple House Ballymote 317
Tinakilly House Rathnew 341
Tulfarris House Blessington Lake 319
Tullanisk Birr 319
Zetland House Cashel 322

Austria
Altstadt Radisson Salzburg 358
Amadeus Vienna 361
Berggasthof Gschnitzerhof Gschnitz 354
Burg Bernstein Bernstein 350
Deim zum Goldener Hirschen Freistadt 352
Elefant Salzburg 358
Gams Bezau 351
Gschwandtner Bad Zell 350
Haus Senger Heiligenblut 355
Kaiserin Elisabeth Vienna 361
Kasererbräu Salzburg 358
König von Ungarn Vienna 362
Krone Schruns 359
Landgasthof Pritz Emmersdorf 352
Landhotel Erlhof Zell am See 363
Mader Steyr 360
Madrisa Gargellen 353
Nestroy Vienna 362
Nikolasch Millstatt am See 356
Panoramahotel Wagner Semmering 360
Parkhotel am See Gmunden am Traunsee 353
Parkhotel Tristachersee Lienz 356
Pension Nossek Vienna 362
Pension Pertschy Vienna 363
Peter St-Wolfgang 357
Romantik Hotel Gmachl Elixhausen 352
Romantik Hotel Minichmayr Steyr 360
Romantik Hotel Tennerhof Kitzbühel 355

Römischer Kaiser Vienna 363
Schloss Haunsperg Oberalm bei Hallein 357
Schlossberg Graz 354
Sporthotel Singer Berwang 351
Walkner Seeham 359
Weisses Kreuz Innsbruck 355

Belgium
Adornes Bruges 366
Agenda Brussels 370
Agter de Weyreldt Herselt 373
Anselmus Bruges 367
Aragon Bruges 367
Botaniek Bruges 368
Bryghia Bruges 368
Château d'Hassonville Marche-en-Famenne 375
Château de Palogne Vieuxville 377
Côte Vert Waterloo 377
Firean Antwerp 366
Grappe d'Or Torgny 376
Kasteel Solhof Aartselaar 365
Moulin de Lisogne Lisogne 373
Moulin Hideux Noirefontaine 375
Oud-huis Amsterdam Bruges 368
Prieuré de Conques Herbeumont 372
Rembrandt Brussels 370
Rosier Antwerp 366
Sanglier des Ardennes Durbuy 371
Scholteshof Hasselt-Stevoort 372
Shamrock Maarkedal 374
Snippe Bruges 369
Swaene Bruges 369
Ter Duinen Bruges 370
Trôs Marets Malmédy 374
Val d'Amblève Stavelot 376
Village Gastronomique Eddy Vandekerckhove Kortijk 373
Welcome Brussels 371

The Czech Republic
Adria Prague 381
Continental Plzeň 380
Harmony Prague 381
Hoffmeister Prague 382
Maximilian Prague 382
Obora Prague 382
Pařîž Prague 383
Pegas Brno 380
Pension U Raka Prague 383
Pension-Restaurant Belarie Český Krumlov 380
Pod Věží Prague 383
Škoda Plzeň 381
U Tří Pštrosů Prague 384

Denmark
Angleterre Copenhagen 385
Ascot Copenhagen 386
Dagmar Ribe 389
Falsled Kro Millinge 388
Hesselet Nyborg 389
Jørgensens Horsens 387
Marstal Marstal 388
Pension Bondehuset Fredensborg 386
Postgaarden Sorø 390
71 Nyhavn Copenhagen 386
Sønderho Kro Sønderho 390
Store Kro Fredensborg 387

France
À l'Orée du Bois Futeau 450
Abbaye Le Bec-Hellouin 406
Abbaye Paris 491
Abbaye Talloires 539
Abbaye de la Pommeraie Sélestat 535
Aigle d'Or Rimbach 510
Aigle Noir Fontainebleau 447
Aiguillons St-Martial-Viveyrols 524
Alain Chapel Mionnay 479
Alisiers Lapoutroie 469
Angleterre Châlons-en-Champagne 422
Angleterre Paris 492
Anne d'Anjou Saumur 533
Antiques St-Rémy-de-Provence 527
Arcades Aigues-Mortes 394
Arlatan Arles 398
Armoiries Valbonne 548
Artistes Lyon 473
Arverna Vichy 553
Arvor Dinan 441
Au Bon Coin du Lac Mimizan 478
Au Puits Enchanté St-Martin-en-Bresse 524
Aussois Semur-en-Auxois 536
Aux Armes de Champagne L'Épine 442
Aux Maronniers Encausse-les-Thermes 442
Aux Trois Roses La Petite-Pierre 500
Avenue Annot 397
Bas Rupts et Chalet Fleuri Gérardmer 452
Bastide de Tourtour Tourtour 544
Beatus Cambrai 417
Beau Lieu Forges-les-Eaux 449
Beau Rivage Condrieu 432
Beau Site Talloires 539

Beauséjour Calvinet 416
Belle Gasconne Poudenas 506
Belle-Isle sur Risle Pont-Audemer 503
Bellerive Rasteau 508
Bellevue Les Roches-de-Condrieu 513
Bellevue St-Florent 519
Belvédère St-Cyprien 516
Benvengudo Les Baux-de-Provence 405
Bérangère Les Deux-Alpes 439
Bérard La Cadière-d'Azure 415
Bergerie Rugy 515
Berges Illhaeusern 462
Bon Laboureur et Château Chenonceaux 426
Bonne Étape Château-Arnoux 424
Bories Gordes 456
Bories Marquay 474
Bosquet Pégomas 498
Bourgogne Cluny 429
Boyer Les Crayères Reims 509
Bradford Paris 492
Bretagne Questembert 507
Brises La Rochelle 512
Brittany Roscoff 514
Cagnard Haut-de-Cagnes 459
Calendal Arles 398
Carayon St-Sernin-sur-Rance 528
Caron de Beaumarchais Paris 493
Carrière Josselin 464
Castel Clara Belle-Ile-en-Mer 407
Castel Seurre 536
Cathédrale Strasbourg 537
Cazaudehore-La Forestière St-Germain-en-Laye 521
Central Peyrehorade 501
Chaîne d'Or Les Andelys 396
Chalet Coulandon 435
Champ des Oiseaux Troyes 546
Chapon Fin et Restaurant Paul Blanc Thoissey 542
Charpinière St-Galmier 520
Chartreuse du Val-St-Esprit 456
Chat Botté St-Clément-des-Baleines 516
Château d'Adoménil Lunéville 472
Château d'Ayres Meyrueis 477
Château d'Igé Igé 462
Château d'Urbilhac Lamastre 467
Château de Barive Ste-Preuve 530
Château de Beaulieu Joué-lès-Tours 464
Château de Bellefontaine Bayeux 405
Château de Boussac Target 541
Château de Courcelles Courcelles-sur-Vesle 436
Château de la Barge Crèches-sur-Saône 436
Château de la Chèvre d'Or Èze-Village 445
Château de la Gondelaine Contres 433
Château de la Poitevinière Huismes 461
Château de la Treyne Lacave 466
Château de la Vérie Challans 421
Château de Longueville Deux-Chaises 440
Château de Madières Madières 474
Château de Montreuil Montreuil 482
Château de Nieuil Nieuil 488
Château de Noizay Noizay 489
Château de Riell Molitg-les-Bains 480
Château de Rigny Gray 458
Château de Rochecotte St Patrice 526
Château de Sassangy Buxy 414
Château de Seignan St-Girons 521
Château de Vault-de-Lugny Avallon 401
Château des Monthairons Les Monthairons 481
Château du Plessis La Jaille-Yvon 463
Château St-Saturnin St-Saturnin-de-Lenne 528
Châtillon Paris 493
Cheval Blanc Bléré 409
Cheval Blanc Langres 468
Cimes St-Bonnet-le-Froid 515
Clairière Illhaeusern 463
Cléry Hesdin-l'Abbé 460
Clos Chablis 420
Clos des Délices Ottrott 490
Clos du Cher St-Aignan-sur-Cher 515
Clos Médicis Paris 494
Clos Saint-Martin Mellecey 475
Clos Saint Vincent Ribeauvillé 510
Club Vignemale Gavarnie 451
Colombier Forcalquier 448
Combe: Chez Michelon Aiguebelette-le-Lac 393
Commanderie St-Emilion 518
Commerce Mirepoix 479
Concasty Boisset 410
Conquérant Barfleur 403
Constantin Kaysersberg 465
Coq Hardi Verdun 550
Cordonant Cordon 434
Côte Bleue Bouzigues 411

Côte Saint-Jacques Joigny 463
Crillon le Brave Crillon-le-Brave 437
Crispol Vézelay 552
Crouesty Arzon 399
Cuq en Terrasses Cuq-le-Château 438
Daille Florimont-Gaumiers 447
Diderot Chinon 427
Dolce Vita Ajaccio 395
Domaine de Bassibé Ségos 534
Domaine de Clairefontaine Chonas l'Amballan 427
Domaine de Rochevilaine Muzillac 486
Domaine de St-Luc La Baume de Transit 404
Domaine du Breuil Cognac 430
Dragon Strasbourg 538
Ducs Duras 442
Eber Paris 494
Entraigues Uzès 547
Équipe Molines-en-Queyras 480
Escaou Courségoules 436
Espérance Vézelay 553
Esplanade Domme 441
Étrier Camarguais Les Stes-Maries-de-la-Mer 531
Europe Avignon 401
Falaises Gluges 455
Farandole Les Deux-Alpes 440
Faudé Lapoutroie 469
Ferme Avignon 402
Ferme de la Rançonnière Crépon 437
Ferme du Vert Wierre-Effroy 559
Fleuri Sars-Poteries 532
Flore Villefranche-sur-Mer 555
Florets Gigondas 453
Fontaine Accolay 392
France Loches 471
France/Restaurant des Fuchsias St-Vaast-la-Hougue 529
Frênes Montfavet 481
Froeningen Froeningen 449
Gabetière Estrablin 443
Georges Blanc Vonnas 558
Géraniums Le Barroux 403
Glycine Bénouville 408
Glycines Eyzies-de-Tayac 445
Grand Duc Gincla 454
Grand Écuyer Cordes 433
Grand Hôtel Cala Rossa Porto-Vecchio 505
Grand Hôtel de l'Europe Langres 468
Grand Hôtel de la Reine Nancy 487
Grand Hôtel du Commerce Pau 498
Grand Hôtel du Lion d'Or Romorantin-Lanthenay 514
Grand Hôtel Moderne et Pigeon Limoux 471
Grand Hôtel Pélisson Nontron 489
Grand Large Dolus d'Oléron 441
Grand Saint-Léonard St-Léonard-de-Noblat 523
Grand'Maison Mur-de-Bretagne 485
Grande Chaumière St-Florentin 520
Grands Hommes Paris 495
Grangette Velleron 550
Granitière St-Vaast-la-Hougue 529
Grau Espezel 443
Grenouillère Montreuil 483
Gué du Holme St-Quentin-sur-le-Homme 527
Guide Verteillac 551
Guilhem Montpellier 482
Gutenberg Strasbourg 538
Halle Givry 455
Hameau St-Paul-de-Vence 526
Hauts de Montreuil Montreuil 483
Hauts de Mourèze Mourèze 485
Hermitage Buzançais 414
Horizon Thionville 542
Hospitaliers Le Poët-Laval 501
Huchette Replonges 509
Husseren les Châteaux Husseren-les-Châteaux 461
Ile de la Lagune St-Cyprien-Sud 517
Ile de Sées Sées 534
Jabloire Florent-en-Argonne 447
Jardin des Arts Château-Gontier 425
Jean-Paul Jeunet Arbois 397
Jeu de Paume Paris 495
Kastelberg Andlau 396
Kastell Dinec'h Tréguier 545
Laborderie Tamniès 540
Lameloise Chagny 421
Lecoq-Gadby Rennes 509
Létraz Sévrier 536
Levernois Levernois 470
Lion d'Or Bayeux 405
Loges de l'Aubergade Puymirol 507
Logis des Remparts St-Emilion 518
Lou Calen Cotignac 435
Lozerette Cocurès 429
Lucarne aux Chouettes Villeneuve-sur-Yonne 556
Madone Peillon 499
Magnolias Meursault 476
Maison d'Or Monte Carlo 480
Maison de la Houve Audinghen 399

Maison des Chanoines Turenne 546
Maître Pannetier Vouvant 559
Manoir Aix-les-Bains 394
Manoir d'Hastings et Hôtel La Pommeraie Bénouville 408
Manoir d'Hautegente Coly 430
Manoir de la Fôret La Ville-aux-Clercs 554
Manoir du Lys Bagnoles-de-l'Orne 402
Maréchal Colmar 430
Marie d'Agoult Arpaillargues 398
Marine Carteret 418
Maritonnes Romanèche-Thorins 513
Maronne St-Martin-Valmeroux 524
Marronniers Paris 496
Mas d'Aigret Les Baux-de-Provence 404
Mas d'Entremont Celony 419
Mas du Langoustier Porquerolles 505
Mas du Pastre Eygalières 445
Mas du Terme Barjac 403
Meijette La Grave 458
Menez-Frost Bénodet 408
Mermoz Toulouse 543
Mésanges Uriage-les-Bains 547
Métropole Beaulieu-sur-Mer 405
Meunière Thannenkirch 541
Michel Bras Laguiole 466
Michel Chabran Pont-de-l'Isère 502
Midi et Restaurant Barattéro Lamastre 467
Midi-Papillon St-Jean-du-Bruel 523
Mistou Pontempeyrat 504
Monnaie La Rochelle 512
Montagne de Brancion Brancion 412
Montagnes Pailherols 491
Montalembert Paris 496
Montmirail Gigondes 454
Montrachet Puligny-Montrachet 506
Monts de Vaux Poligny 502
Mougins Mougins 484
Moulin de l'Abbaye Brantôme 412
Moulin de la Gorce La Roche-L'Abeille 511
Moulin de la Wantzenau La Wantzenau 559
Moulin de Lourmarin Lourmarin 472
Moulin de Villeray Villeray 556
Moulin du Roc Champagnac-de-Belair 423
Moulin du Vey Clécy 428
Moulin Flagy 446
Moulins de Paillas et Résidence Gigaro La Croix-Valmer 438
Navas "Les Hauts de Mourèze" Mourèze 485
Notre-Dame Paris 497
Ostellerie du Vieux Pérouges Pérouges 500
Oustal del Barry Najac 486
Panthéon Paris 497
Parc St-Hippolyte 522
Parc des Maréchaux Auxerre 400
Parc Victoria St-Jean-de-Luz 522
Passiflore Vergèze 551
Pavillon de la Reine Paris 497
Pen'Roc St-Didier 517
Pereria Guéthary 459
Pérouse Nice 487
Petit Castel et Auberge du Cochon d'Or Beuzeville 409
Petit Palais Nice 488
Plage Ste-Anne-la-Palud 530
Plage de Bestouan Cassis 419
Plaisance St-Emilion 518
Poids Public St-Félix-Lauragais 519
Pointe de Mousterlin Fouesnant 449
Pommeraie/Manoir d'Hastings Bénouville 408
Pont de l'Ouysse Lacave 465
Pont Romain Sommières 537
Port Yvoire 560
Poste et Champanne Brioude 413
Pré Bossu Moudeyres 484
Pré-Vert Rabastens 508
Prés d'Eugénie et Le Couvent des Herbes 444
Prés du Lac Talloires 540
Prieuré Chênehutte-les-Tuffeaux 425
Prieuré Villeneuve-lès-Avignon 555
Primavera St-Palais-sur-Mer 525
Pullman Grand Cabourg 415
Quatre Dauphins Aix-en-Provence 394
Radio Chamalières 422
Régalido Fontvieille 448
Régent Villers-Cotterets 557
Relais Christine Paris 494
Relais de Farrou Villefranche-de-Rouergue 554
Relais de la Magdeleine Gémenos 451
Relais du Bois St-Georges Saintes 531
Relais du Fréhel Fréhel 449
Relais du Louvre Paris 495

Relais du Soleil d'Or Montignac 482
Relais du Touron Carsac-Aillac 418
Relais du Val d'Orbieu Ornaisons 490
Relais Saint-Jean Troyes 546
Renaudière Chenonceaux 426
Résidence Le Val d'Ajol 548
Restaurant Pic Valence 548
Rimains et Maison de Bricourt Cancale 417
Rivage Gien 452
Roches Fleuries Cordon 434
Rohan Strasbourg 538
Romantik Hotel Beaucour Strasbourg 537
Romarins Gordes 456
Roseraie Vence 550
Rostaing Passenans 498
Royal Champagne Champillon 424
Royal-Lieu Compiègne 431
Saint-Antoine Albi 395
Saint Barthélémy Pernes-les-Fontaines 499
St Benoit Aniane 397
Saint-Germain Paris 497
St-Hubert Hallines 459
St-Jacques Cloyes-sur-le-Loir 428
Saint-James Bordeaux 410
Sainte-Foy Conques 432
7 Molles Sauveterre-de-Comminges 533
Signoria Calvi 416
Solognote Brinon-sur-Sauldre 413
Sud-Bretagne Pornichet 504
Table du Comtat Séguret 535
Taillard Goumois 457
Tamarissière Agde 393
Terminus Cahors 416
Terrasse Meyronne 477
Terrasse au Soleil Céret 420
Téthys St-Palais-sur-Mer 525
Thermes Bourbon-l'Archambault 411
Ti al Lannec Trébeurden 544
Tilleuls Vincelottes 558
Tirel-Guérin Gouesnière 457
Tour de Pacoret Grésy-sur-Isère 458
Tour du Roy Vervins 552
Tour Rose Lyon 473
Treizain Gassin 450
Troisgros Roanne 511
Truite d'Or Lods 471
Ursulines Autun 400
Val d'Or Mercurey 476
Val de Vienne Le Vigeant 554
Val-Suzon Val-Suzon 549
Valmarin St-Malo 523
Vert Mauroux 475
Verte Campagne Trelly 545
Vieux Logis Lestelle-Bétharram 470
Vieux Logis Thomery 543
Vieux Moulin Autun 400
Vieux Pérouges Pérouges 500
Vieux Pont Belcastel 406
Vieux Puits Pont-Audemer 503
Vignette St-Hippolyte 522
Villa Florentine Lyon 474
Villa Henri IV St-Cloud 516
Wilson Dijon 440

Germany

Abtei Hamburg 576
Admiral Wiesbaden 598
Alexander Wiesbaden 598
Altes Herrenhaus zum Bären Holzappel 578
Am Brühl Quedlinburg 590
Am Hohen Hahn Schwarzenberg 595
Am Markt Baden-Baden 564
An der Oper Munich 584
Anker Marktheidenfeld 582
Annas Hof Gohrisch 574
Backmulde Heidelberg 577
Belvedere Berlin 567
Berghotel Schlossanger Alp Pfronten 589
Bischofshof am Dom Regensburg 591
Brandenburger Hof Berlin 567
Brauereigasthof Aying Aying 563
Buchholz Cologne 569
Bülow Residenz Dresden 572
Burghotel Auf Schönburg Oberwesel 587
Christliches Hotel Amalienhof Weimar 597
Detmolder Hof Detmold 571
Deutschherrenhof Trier 595
Dittberner Berlin 567
Dorer Schönwald 593
Dornröschenschloss Sababurg Hofgeismar 578
Eisenhut Rothenburg ob der Tauber 591
Elephant Weimar 598
Englischer Garten Munich 583
Eurener Hof Trier 595
Franzen Rottach-Egern 592
Garni Hornburg Rothenburg ob der Tauber 592
Gastätte Grenzbaude Waltersdorf 597

Gold- und Landhaus Kampen Kampen 579
Goldener Anker Dinkelsbühl 571
Hanseatic Hamburg 576
Haus Lichtenhardt Hellenthal 577
Haus Lipmann Beilstein 566
Hecker's Berlin 568
Heiligenstein Neuweier 586
Historische Schlossmühle Horbruch im Hunsrück 579
Jagdhof Glashütte Bad Laasphe-Glashütte 564
Kaiserhof Lübeck 581
Krone Berchtesgaden 566
Landgasthof Michels Schalkenmehren 593
Landhaus Ammann Hannover 577
Landhotel Hirsch Tübingen 597
Landhotel Schindlerhof Nuremberg-Boxdorf 586
Löwen Meersburg 582
Martha Hospiz Dresden 572
Müler Schwangau 594
Münchner Hof Regensburg 591
Neumayr Munich 583
Pannonia Hotel am Schlosspark Gotha 575
Pesterwitzer Siegel Pesterwitz 588
Petrisberg Trier 596
Pflaums Posthotel Pegnitz Pegnitz 588
Residenz Berlin 568
Residenz Heinz Winkler Aschau im Chiemgau 562
Residenz Joop Magdeburg 581
Romantik Hotel Augsburger Hof Augsburg 563
Romantik Hotel Spielweg Münstertal 585
Romantik Hotel Waldhorn Ravensburg 590
Romantik Hotel Weinhaus Messerschmitt Bamberg 565
Sassenhof Hinterzarten 577
Schloss Cecilienhof Potsdam 589
Schlosshotel Kurfürstliches Amtshaus Daun 570
Schlosshotel und Villa Rheinfels St Goar 593
Schrenkhof Munich 584
Seehof Berlin 568
Seehotel Siber Konstanz 580
Sonne – Meier's Restaurant Johannesberg 579
Sonnenhof Königstein im Taunus 580
Sophien Eisenach 573
Strand-Hotel Schwerin 595
Uhland Munich 585
Villa Hügel Trier 596
Wald- und Schlosshotel Friedrichsruhe Friedrichsruhe 574
Waldhotel Eiche Burg 569
Waldhotel Sonnora Dreis 571
Waldhotel Stein Bayreuth-Seulbitz 565
Wasserturm Cologne 569
Westend Frankfurt am Main 573
Zum Ochsen Schönwald 594
Zum Schwanen Neckargemünd 585
Zur Rose Oberammergau 587
Zur Traube Grevenbroich 575

Greece

Adonis Mykonos 606
Akti Myrina Myrina 607
Amphitriti Chania 601
Amphora Chania 602
Byron Nafplion 608
Chromata Imerovigli 605
Chryssi Avgi Kastron 605
Elounda Mare Elounda 603
Hera Athens 601
Herodion Athens 601
Kalamitsi Kardamyli 605
Kivotos Clubhotel Mykonos 606
Orloff Hydra 604
Perrakis Gavrion 604
St Nicolas Bay Aghios Nikólaos 600
Skala Skala 608
Villa Andromeda Chania 602

Hungary

Alba Budapest 609
Beatrix Panzió Budapest 609
Budapest Hilton Budapest 611
Erzsébet Budapest 610
Gellért Budapest 610
Kastélyszálló Fertöd 612
Korona Eger 611
Senator-Ház Eger 612

Italy

Ala Venice 670
Albareta – Gualtiero Marchesi Erbusco 626
Antico Pozzo San Gimignano 658
Arathena Rocks Giardini-Naxos 634
Archimede Reggello 653
Bad Ratzes Siusi allo Scialar 663
Bandita Bettolle 618
Bastiglia Spello 664

Bel Soggiorno San Gimignano 659
Bellavista Francischiello Massa Lubrense 637
Bellevue Cogne 625
Belvedere Argegno 615
Belvedere Taormina 665
Borgo Paraelios Poggio Catino 648
Borgo Pretale Sovicille 664
Bosone Palace Gubbio 635
Buca di Michelangelo Caprese Michelangelo 623
Campo de' Fiori Rome 654
Cannero Cannero Riviera 622
Carrubella Park Hotel Monreale 640
Caruso Belvedere Ravello 652
Casalta Monteriggioni 641
Casetta delle Selve Pugnano 651
Castel San Gregorio San Gregorio 659
Certosa di Maggiano Siena 662
Cesàri Rome 655
Chiostro di Pienza Pienza 646
Chiusa Montefollonico 640
Claudio Bergeggi 618
Convento di San Francesco Cetona 624
Corona d'Oro Bologna 619
Country House Assisi 616
Diligenza – Da Rodolfo Borgo Pace 620
Dolada Pieve d'Alpago 647
Duchessa Isabella Ferrara 627
Eggwirt St Walburg in Ulten 661
Elefante Bressanone 621
Elimo Erice 627
Emilia Portonovo 650
Emmy Fié allo Sciliar 628
Europa Torri del Benaco 668
Fado 78 Mele 637
Faro Porto Conte 649
Fattoria Pieve a Salti Buonconvento 622
Flora Venice 670
Fonte della Galletta Alpe Faggeto 614
Fragsburg (Castel Verruca) Merano 638
Gabbia d'Oro Verona 672
Gattapone Spoleto 665
Giardinetto Pettenasco 646
Giardino – Da Felicin Monforte d'Alba 640
Giordano e Villa Maria Ravello 653
Grand Hotel Victoria Menaggio 638
Gregoriana Rome 655
Helvetia and Bristol Florence 629
Hermitage Florence 629
Internazionale Rome 656
Italia Urbino 669
Lac Bellagio 618
Lac Varenna 669
Leone Pomponesco 648
Loggiato dei Serviti Florence 630
Londra Palace Venice 671
Lord Byron Rome 656
Luna Convento Amalfi 615
Manzoni Milan 639
Margutta Rome 657
Miranda – Da Oreste Riva di Solto 654
Moderno Erice 627
Monaco e Grand Canal Venice 671
Monna Lisa Florence 631
Morandi alla Crocetta Florence 631
Nazionale Levanto 635
Nido di Fiascherino Tellaro di Lerici 666
Panoramica Loranzè 636
Park Hotel Paradiso Ghiffa 634
Pellicano Porto Ercole 649
Pensione Accademia Venice 669
Pensione Bencistà Fiesole 628
Pierre Milano Milan 639
Pitti Palace Florence 632
Porto Roca Monterosso al Mare 641
Portoghesi Rome 657
Principe Cuneo 626
Relais Ca' Masieri Trissino 668
Relais Fattoria Vignale Raddi in Chianti 651
Relais La Fattoria Castel Rigone 624
Relais Torre Pratesi Brisighella 621
Residence Castello di Gargonza Gargonza 633
Residenza di Campagna Santa Maria degli Ancillotti Assisi 617
Residenza Rome 657
Roma Bologna 619
Romantik Hotel J and J Florence 630
Romantik Hotel La Perla Corvara 625
Rosetta Perugia 646
St Veit Sesto 662
San Domenico Palace Taormina 666
San Michele Cortona 625
San Rocco Orta San Giulio 643
Santa Caterina Siena 663
Saracina Pienza 647
Saturnia e International Venice 671
Schloss Korb San Paolo 660
Sole Ranco 652
Sonia Santa Maria di Castellabate 661
Spadari al Duomo Milan 640

Stella d'Italia San Mamete 660
Su Gologone Oliena 642
Tenuta di Ricavo Castellina in Chianti 623
Titano San Marino 660
Torcolo Verona 672
Torino Parma 645
Tre Vaselle Torgiano 667
Umbra Assisi 617
Victoria Verona 673
Villa Campestri Vicchio 673
Villa Cipriani Asolo 616
Villa Crespi Orta San Giulio 642
Villa del Parco Rome 658
Villa del Quar Pedemonte 645
Villa di Monte Solare Fontignano 632
Villa Elisa Bordighera 620
Villa La Principessa Lucca 636
Villa Le Barone Panzano in Chianti 644
Villa Liberty Florence 630
Villa Nencini Volterra 673
Villa Ottone Ottone 643
Villa Rucellai Prato 650
Villa Sangiovese Panzano in Chianti 644
Villa Scacciapensieri 663
Villa Sirina Taormina 666
Vittoria Genoa 633

Luxembourg
Bel-Air Echternach 675
Grand Hôtel Cravat Luxembourg 676
Grunewald Luxembourg 676
Theis Bourscheid-Plage 675

Malta
Gillieru Harbour Hotel St Paul's Bay 679
Ta' Cenc Sannat 680

The Netherlands
Ambassade Amsterdam 682
Amsterdam Wiechmann Amsterdam 685
Canal House Amsterdam 683
Corona The Hague 686
Europe Amsterdam 683
Herberg Onder de Linden Aduard 681
Hoofdige Boer Almen 682
Huize den Treek Leusden 687
Jan Luyken Amsterdam 684
Kaatje bij de Sluis Blokzijl 685
Kasteel Wittem Wittem 688
Lapershoek Hilversum 687
Leeuwenbrug Delft 685
Roosterhoeve Roosteren 687
Tante Sien Vasse 688
Toro Amsterdam 684
Van Gaalen Heeze 686

Norway
Alexandra Loen 692
Augustin Bergen 690
Continental Oslo 693
Dr Holms Geilo 691
Fossheim Lom 692
Kvikne's Balestrand 689
Mølla Lillehammer 692
Mundal Fjærland 690
Trugstad Gård Holter 691
Utne Utne 694
Venabu Fjellhotell Ringebu 693

Portugal
Albatroz Cascais 697
Casa de San Tiago do Castelo Óbidos 705
Casa Miradouro Sintra 706
Estalagem Abrigo da Montanha Monchique 703
Estalagem do Caçador Macedo de Cavaleiros 702
Estalagem do Convento Óbidos 705
Horta da Moura Reguengos de Monsaraz 705
Infante de Sagres Porto 705
Lapa Lisbon 700
Mar Bravo Nazaré 704
Palace Buçaco 696
Palácio de Seteais Sintra 707
Pousada de Dom Dinis Vila Nova de Cerveira 707
Pousada de Santa Cristina Condeixa-a-Nova 698
Pousada de Santa Marinha Guimarães 700
Pousada de São Bento Caniçada 697
Pousada de São Gonçalo Amarante 696
Pousada de São Lourenço Manteigas 703
Pousada do Castelo Óbidos 704
Pousada dos Lóios Évora 698
Quinta da Capela Sintra 706
Quinta da Penha de França Funchal 699
Quinta do Pintor Évora 698
Reid's Funchal 699
Senhora do Monte Lisbon 701
Tivoli Jardim Lisbon 702
York House Lisbon 702

Slovenia
Austrotel Ljubljana 712
Grad Otočec Otočec Ob Krki 713
Grand Hotel Toplice Bled 710
Maestoso Lipica 712
Pavovc Bled 710
Pension Krona Kamna Gorica 711
Planika Ajdovščina 710
Pod Gorjanci Kostanjevica Na Krki 712
Tartini Piran 713
Urška Stranice 714
Vila Bled Bled 711

Spain
Abril Seville 744
Aigua Blava Bagur 720
Albucasis Córdoba 728
Almazara Toledo 749
Altamira Santillana del Mar 742
América Granada 731
Born Palma de Mallorca 738
Bosque Mar Reboredo 739
Bracamonte Ávila 719
Can Boix Peramola 738
Can Borrell Maranges 736
Casa Aloha Mijas-Costa 737
Casa de Carmona Carmona 725
Casas de la Judería Seville 745
Casona de Mestas Taranes 749
Colón Barcelona 721
Convento Arcos de la Frontera 718
Convento Santa Maria de Mave 742
Don Miguel Ronda 740
Doña María Seville 745
Es Molí Deyá 729
Finca La Mota Alhaurin el Grande 717
Finca Listonero Turre 751
Gernika Guernica 734
Halcón Palace Cofiño 727
Hospederia Convento de San Francisco Vejer de la Frontera 753
Hospederia del Real Monasterio Guadalupe 733
Hostal Carlos III Santander 742
Hostal del Cardenal Toledo 750
Infanta Isabel Segovia 743
Lancelot Arrecife 719
Mar i Vent Bañalbufar 720
Marina Camariñas 724
Marisa Córdoba 728
Molino del Santo Benaoján 722
Montico Tordesillas 750
Oso Pardo Cosgaya 728
Palacete Peñalba Figueras del Mar 730
Pampinot Fuenterrabía 730
Parador Alcázar del Rey Carmona 725
Parador Casa del Barón Pontevedra 739
Parador Casa del Corregidor Arcos de la Frontera 718
Parador Castillo de la Zuda Tortosa 750
Parador Conde de Gondomar Bayona 722
Parador Conde de la Gomera Gomera 731
Parador Condes de Villalba Villalba 753
Parador Condestable Dávalos Úbeda 752
Parador de Argómaniz Vitoria-Gasteiz 754
Parador de Bielsa Bielsa 723
Parador de Chinchón Chinchón 727
Parador de Guadalupe Guadalupe 733
Parador de Hondarribia Fuenterrabía 731
Parador de Jarandilla de la Vera Jarandilla de la Vera 735
Parador de la Concordia Alcañiz 717
Parador de Mérida Mérida 737
Parador de Nerja Nerja 737
Parador de Ronda Ronda 740
Parador de San Francisco Granada 732
Parador de San Marcos León 735
Parador de Santa Catalina Jaén 734
Parador de Santo Domingo Santo Domingo de la Calzada 743
Parador de Segovia Segovia 744
Parador de Sigüenza Sigüenza 746
Parador de Trujillo Trujillo 751
Parador de Tuy Tuy 752
Parador del Príncipe de Viana Olite 738
Parador Fernando de Aragón Sos del Rey Católico 747
Parador Hernán Cortés Zafra 754
Playa Ribadesella 740
Posada de Palacio Sanlúcar de Barrameda 741
Posada Gualchos 733
Posada Mies de Villa Somo 747
Pousada o Almacén Cervo 726
Prado Madrid 736
Rectoral Taramundi 748
Reina Christina Granada 732

Residencia Deyá 729
Residencia Rector Salamanca 741
San Marcus Sobrado de Los Monjes 746
Ses Rotges Cala Rajada 724
Tahona Besnes-Alles 723
Tamariu Tamariu 748
Villa Real Madrid 736

Sweden
Åby Gård Knivsta 756
Åkerblads Tällberg 759
Bentley's Stockholm 757
Buena Vista Båstad 755
FågelbroHus Värmdö 760
Fryksås Orsa 757
Grythyttans Gästgivaregård Grythyttan 756
Lady Hamilton Stockholm 758
Värdshuset Clas på Hörnet Stockholm 758
Victory Stockholm 758
Wallin Stockholm 759

Switzerland
Alpenrose Gstaad-Schönried 766
Alpenrose Wengen 774
Antares Zermatt 775
Aparthotel Castle Blitzingen 762
Armures Geneva 764
Beau Rivage Weggis 774
Belvedere Grindelwald 765
Bergsonne Rigi-Kaltbad 770
Bristol Zermatt 776
Caso Berno Ascona 762
Chalet du Lac Iseltwald 767
Chesa Mulin Pontresina 769
Cigogne Geneva 765
Eiger Wengen 775
Flüela Davos 763
Gare Le Noirmont 769
Golf Hotel René Capt Montreux 768
Haus Paradies Ftan 763
Landgasthof Alpenrose Hofstetten Bei Brienz 766
Landgasthof Ruedihaus Kandersteg 768
Metropol Zermatt 776
Park Hotel Beausite Wengen 775
Park-Hotel Sonnenhof Vaduz 772
Posthotel Engiadina Zuoz 778
Real Vaduz 772
Relais du Belvédère Champex 763
Rheinhotel Fischerzunft Schaffhausen 770
Riffelalp Zermatt 777
Romantik Hotel Schweizerhof Grindelwald 766
Rothorn Schwanden 771
Royal Hotel Bellevue Kandersteg 767
Soglina Soglio 772
Terrasse am See Vitznau 773
Tiefenau Zürich 779
Tourelle Vésenaz 773
Victoria Glion-sur-Montreux 765
Victoria Ritter Kandersteg 768
Villa Maria Vulpera 773
Walliserhof Zermatt 777
Zum Storchen Zürich 778

Maps

BRITISH ISLES

1 South-West England
including the Channel Islands

2 Southern England

3 Wales and the Cotswolds

4 The North of England and the Lake District

5 Scotland

6 Ireland

THE CONTINENT

7 Scandinavia

8 North-West France

9 Benelux and North-East France

10 West and Central France

11 The South of France

12 Eastern France and the Alps

13 Spain and Portugal
including Madeira and the Canary Islands

14 Germany and the Czech Republic

15 Switzerland

16 Austria

17 Northern Italy, Malta and Slovenia

18 Southern Italy

19 Hungary

20 Greece

British Isles maps

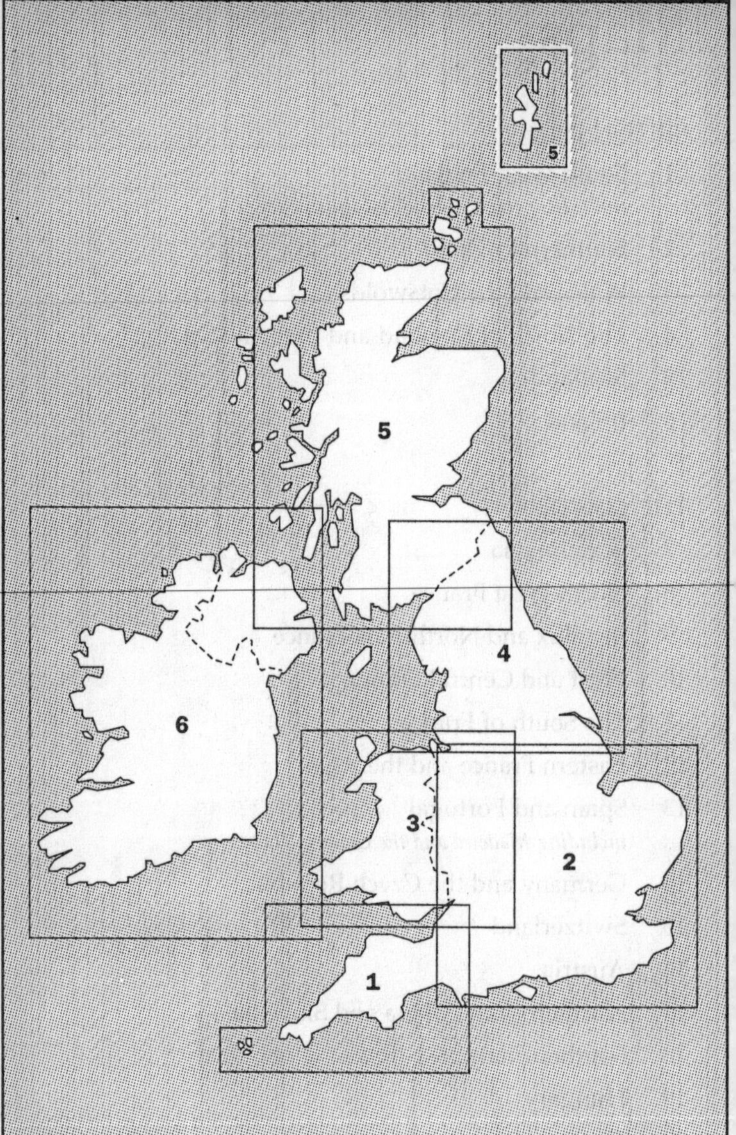

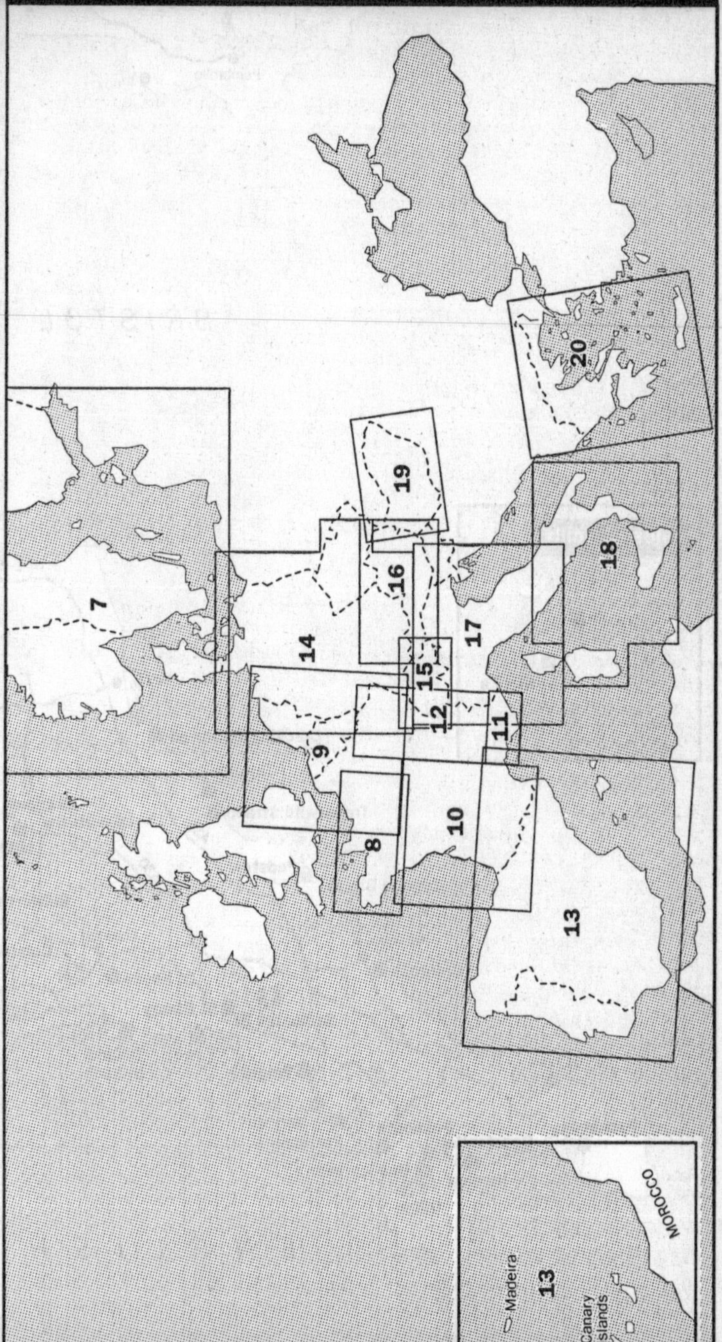
7
14
9
8
16
19
15
12
11
10
17
18
20
13
Madeira
13
Canary Islands
MOROCCO

1 South-West England

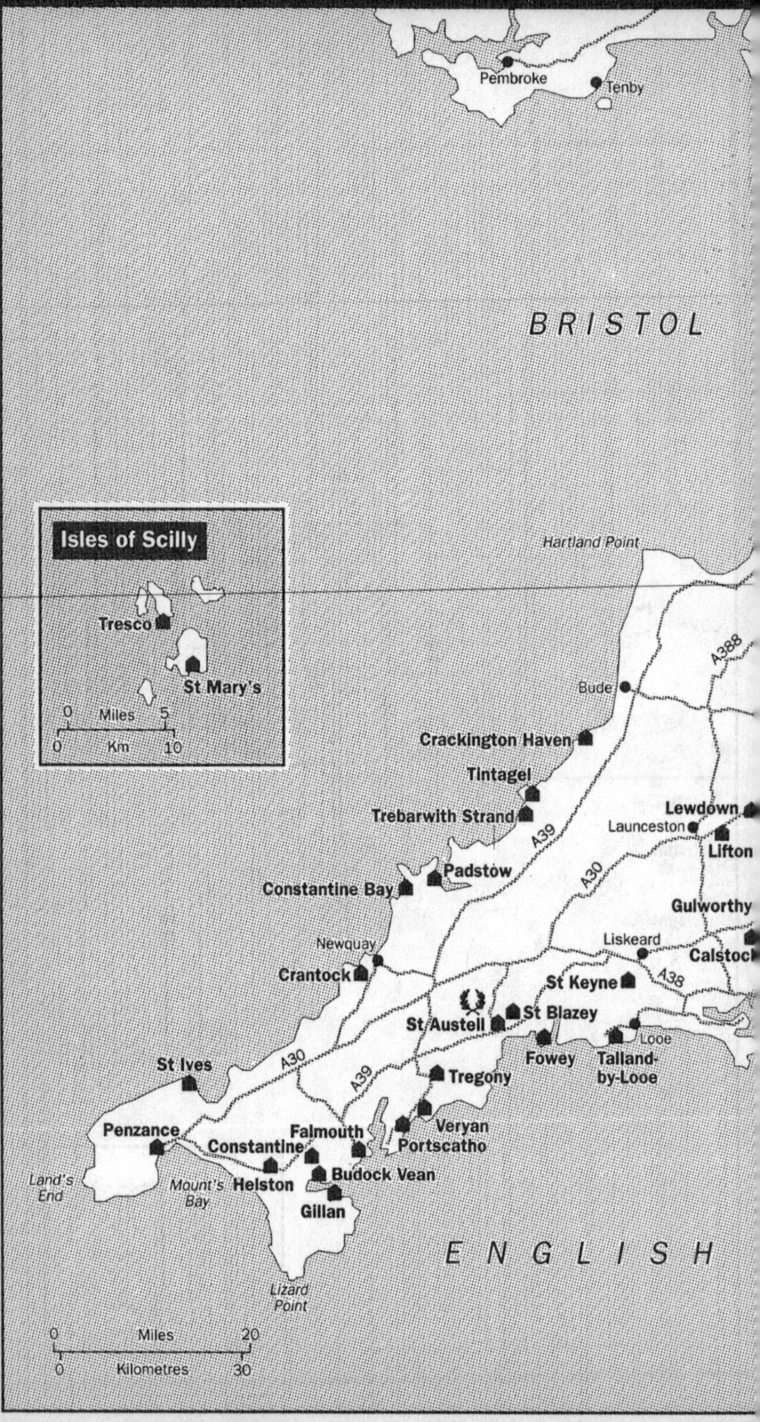
Pembroke
Tenby
BRISTOL
Isles of Scilly
Tresco
St Mary's
0 Miles 5
0 Km 10
Hartland Point
A388
Bude
Crackington Haven
Tintagel
Trebarwith Strand
Lewdown
Launceston
Lifton
A39
A30
Padstow
Constantine Bay
Gulworthy
Newquay
Liskeard
Calstock
Crantock
St Keyne
A38
St Blazey
St Austell
Looe
Fowey
Talland-by-Looe
St Ives
A30
A39
Tregony
Veryan
Penzance
Falmouth
Constantine
Portscatho
Land's End
Mount's Bay
Helston
Budock Vean
Gillan
ENGLISH
Lizard Point
0 Miles 20
0 Kilometres 30

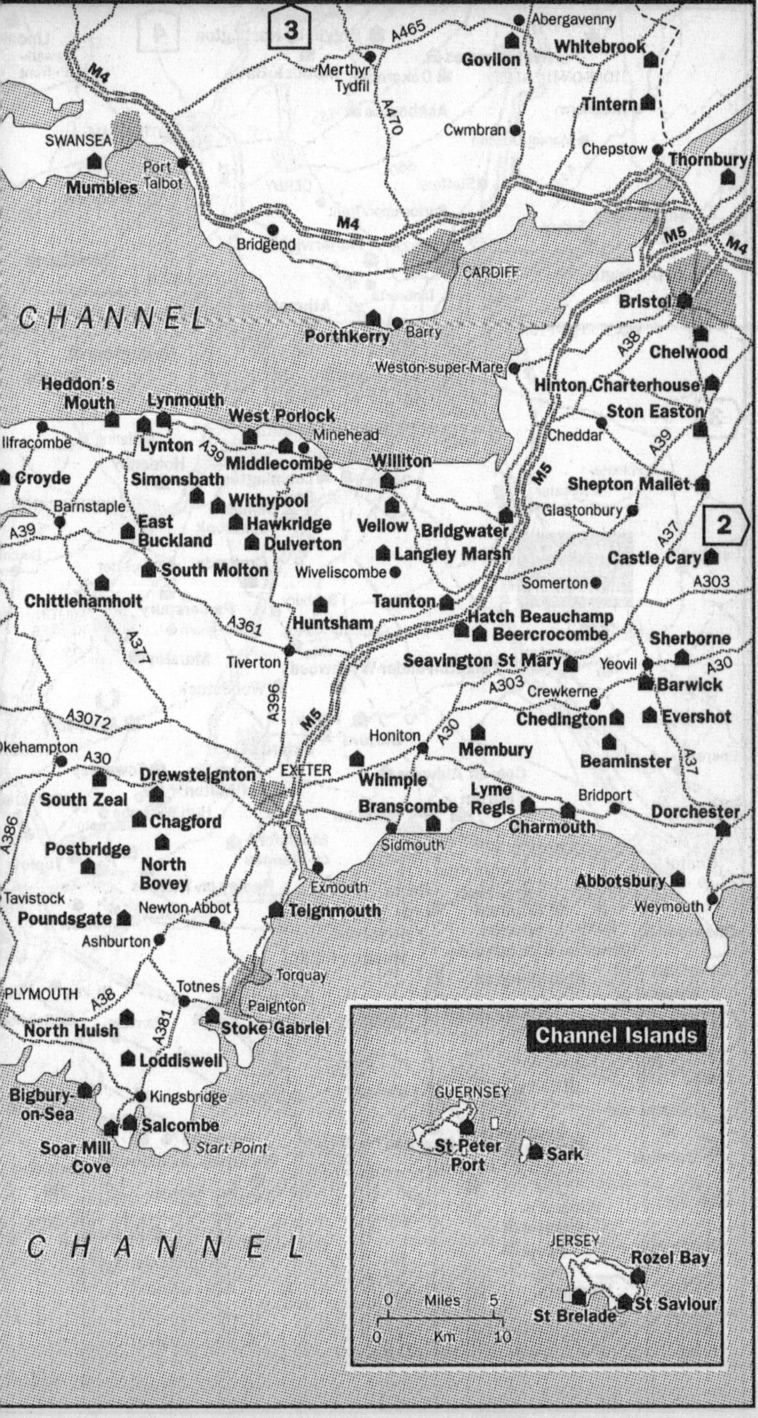
3
Abergavenny
Govilon
Whitebrook
A465
Merthyr Tydfil
A470
Tintern
Cwmbran
Chepstow
Thornbury
SWANSEA
Mumbles
Port Talbot
M4
Bridgend
CARDIFF
M5
Bristol
CHANNEL
Porthkerry
Barry
Weston-super-Mare
A38
Chelwood
Hinton Charterhouse
Ston Easton
Cheddar
A39
Heddon's Mouth
Lynmouth
West Porlock
Minehead
Ilfracombe
Lynton
Middlecombe
Williton
Croyde
Simonsbath
Withypool
Shepton Mallet
Barnstaple
Hawkridge
Vellow
Bridgwater
Glastonbury
2
East Buckland
Dulverton
Langley Marsh
A37
Castle Cary
South Molton
Wiveliscombe
Somerton
A303
Chittlehamholt
Taunton
A361
Huntsham
Hatch Beauchamp
Beercrocombe
Sherborne
A377
Tiverton
Seavington St Mary
Yeovil
A30
A396
Barwick
Crewkerne
A3072
Chedington
Evershot
Honiton
Okehampton
Membury
Beaminster
EXETER
Drewsteignton
Whimple
Lyme Regis
Bridport
South Zeal
Branscombe
Charmouth
Dorchester
Chagford
A386
Sidmouth
Postbridge
North Bovey
Exmouth
Abbotsbury
Tavistock
Newton Abbot
Weymouth
Poundsgate
Teignmouth
Ashburton
Torquay
PLYMOUTH
Totnes
Paignton
North Huish
A381
Stoke Gabriel
Loddiswell
Bigbury-on-Sea
Kingsbridge
Salcombe
Soar Mill Cove
Start Point
CHANNEL
Channel Islands
GUERNSEY
St Peter Port
Sark
JERSEY
Rozel Bay
St Brelade
St Saviour
0 Miles 5
0 Km 10

2 Southern England

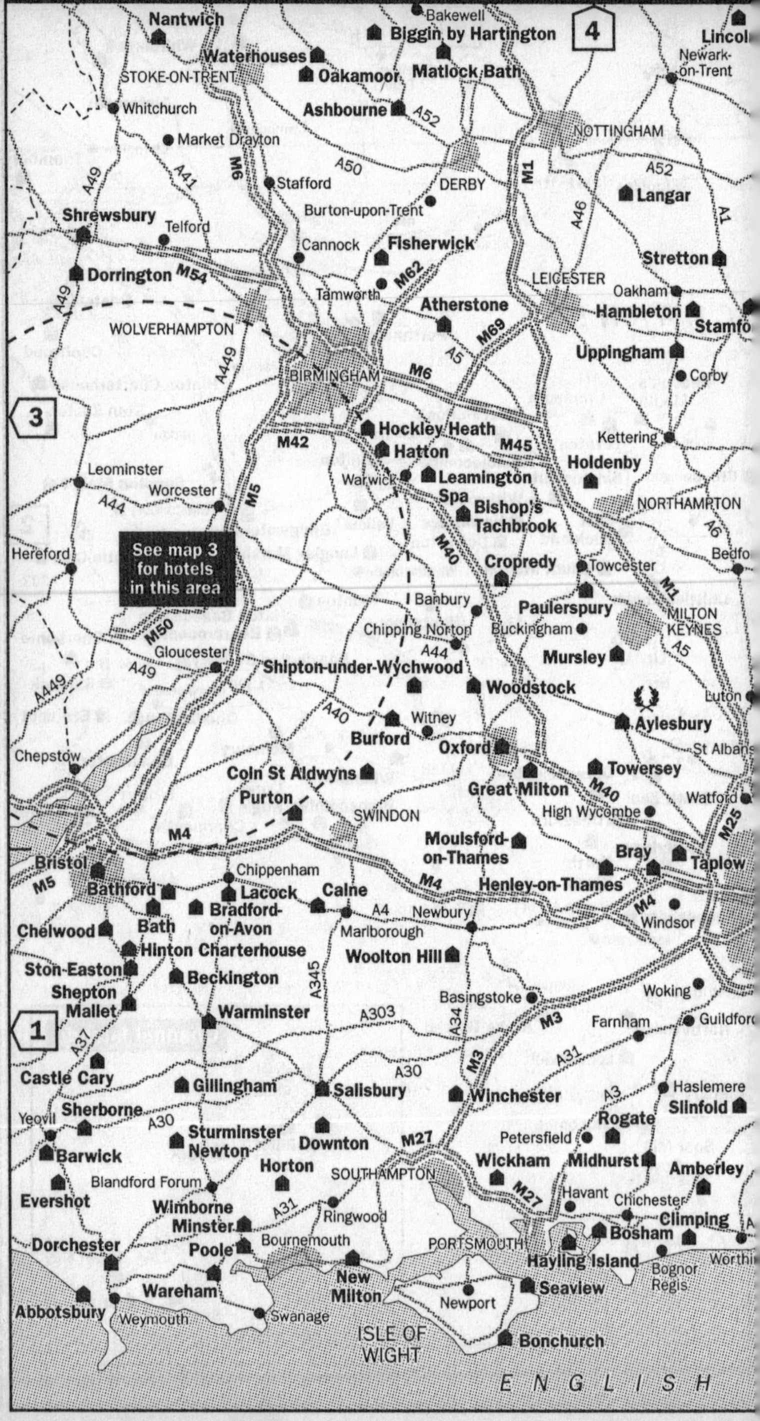

Southern England 2

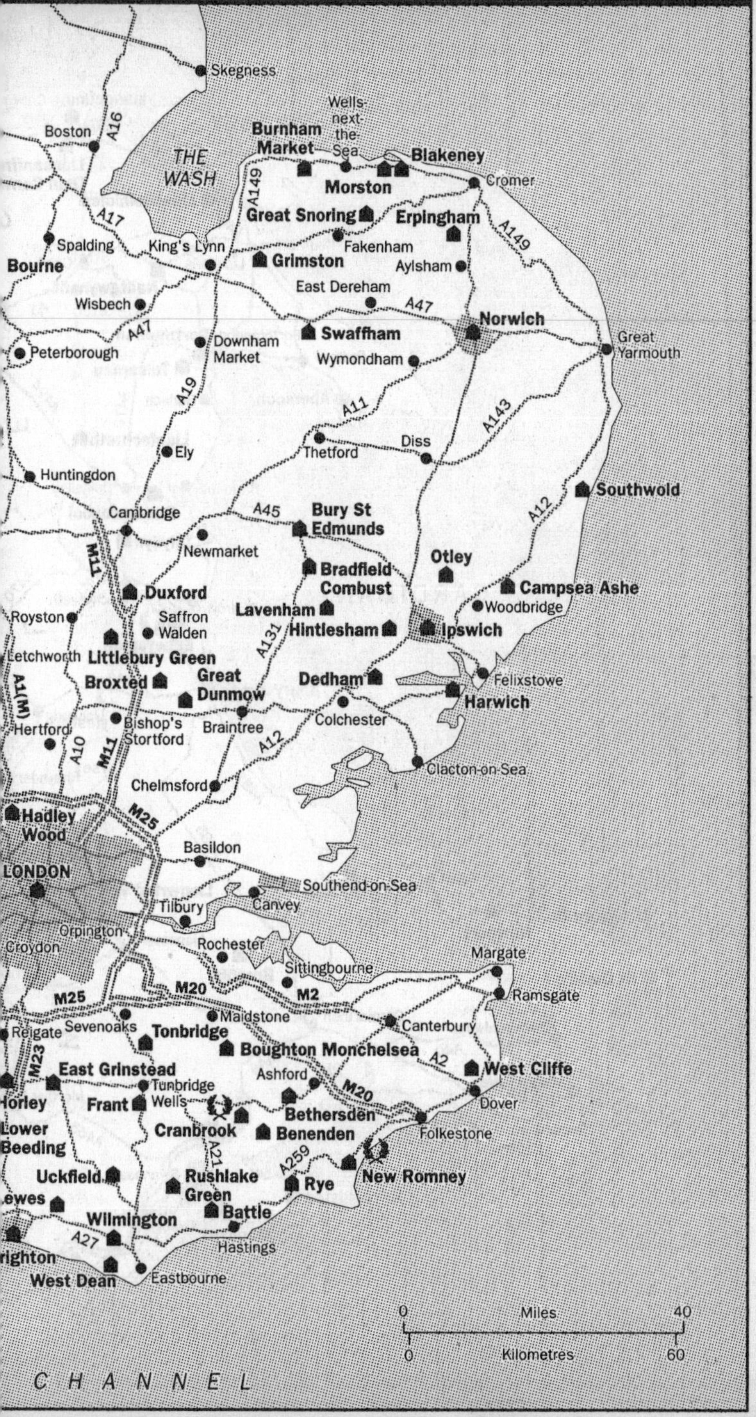

3 Wales and the Cotswolds

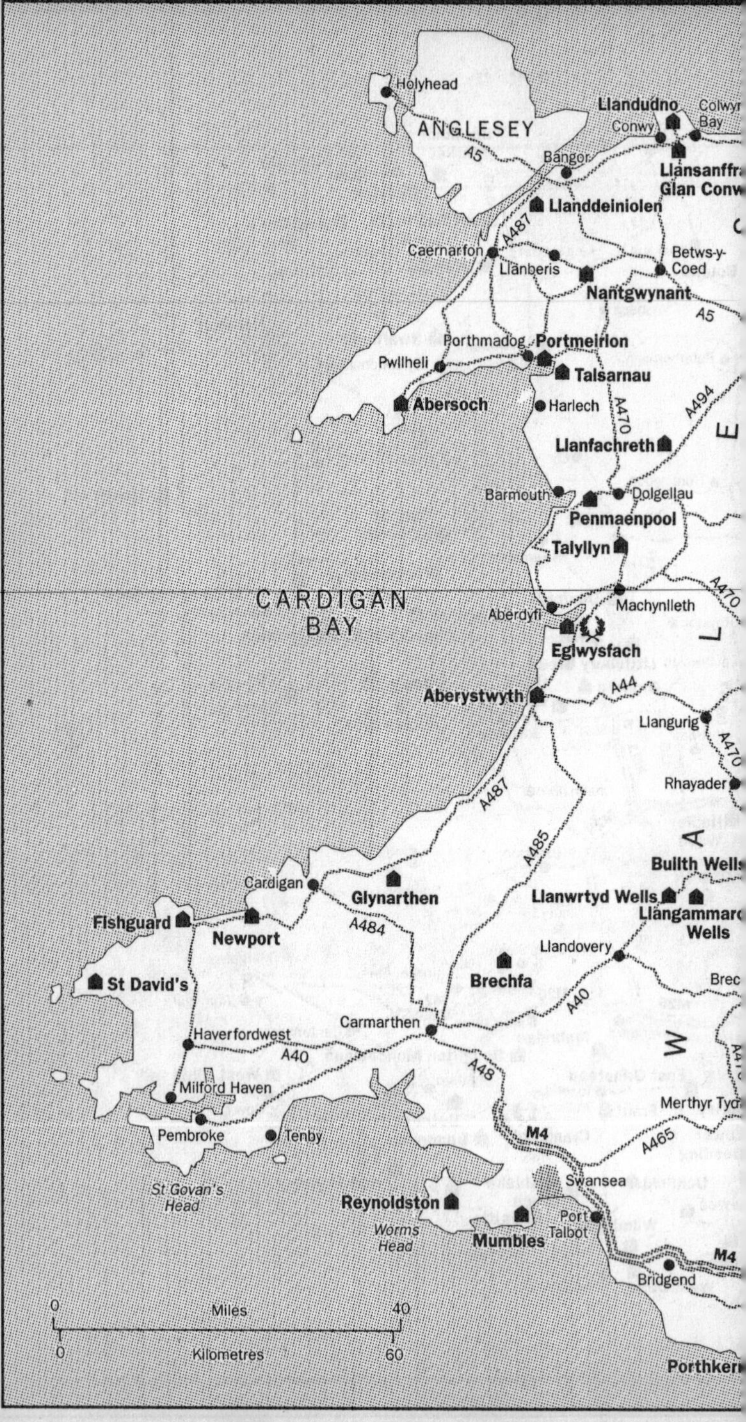

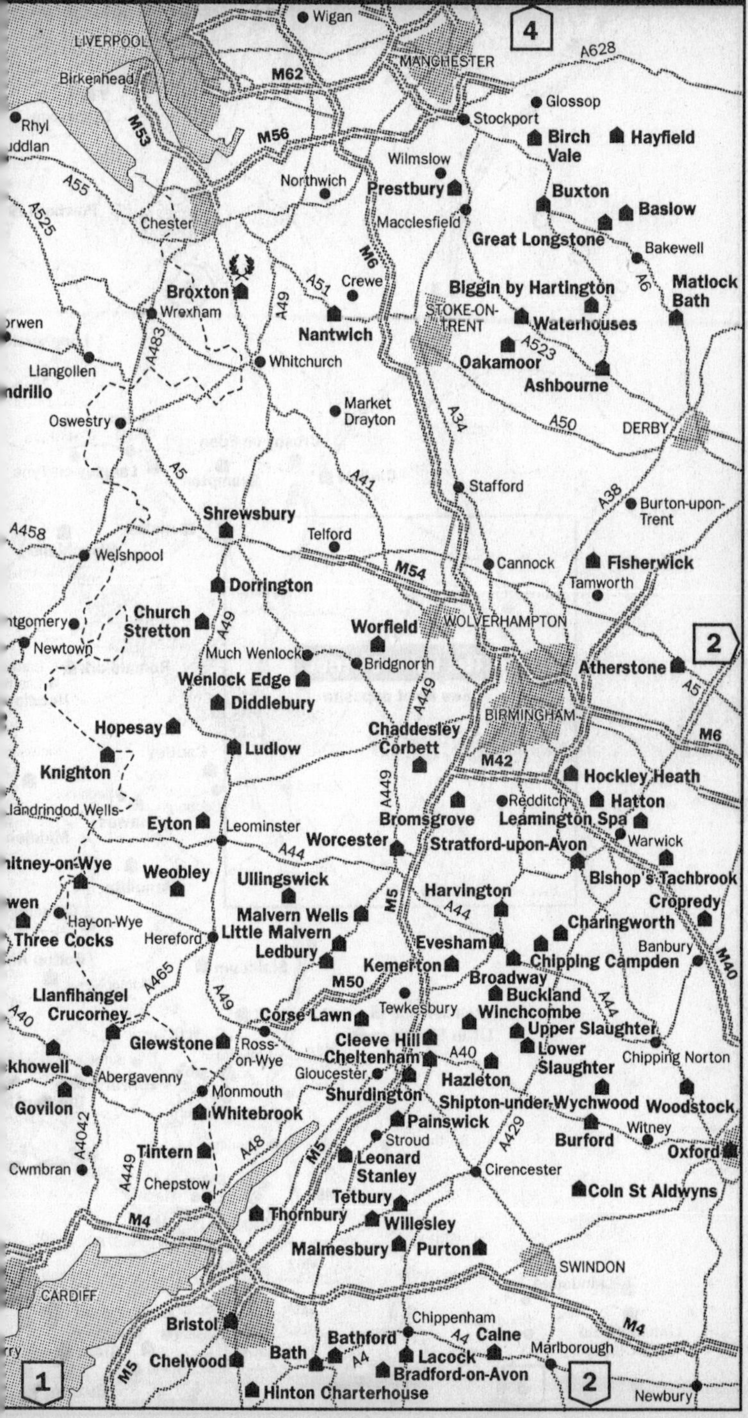
4
Wigan
LIVERPOOL
MANCHESTER
A628
Birkenhead
M62
Glossop
Rhyl
Stockport
Birch Vale
Hayfield
M53
M56
Wilmslow
Northwich
Prestbury
Buxton
Baslow
A55
Chester
Macclesfield
Great Longstone
Bakewell
A525
M6
Crewe
A51
Biggin by Hartington
Matlock Bath
A6
Broxton
Wrexham
A49
STOKE-ON-TRENT
Waterhouses
Nantwich
A523
Oakamoor
A483
Whitchurch
Llangollen
Ashbourne
Market Drayton
A34
Oswestry
A50
DERBY
A5
A41
Stafford
A38
Burton-upon-Trent
Shrewsbury
A458
Telford
Welshpool
M54
Cannock
Fisherwick
Dorrington
Tamworth
Church Stretton
A49
Worfield
WOLVERHAMPTON
Newtown
Much Wenlock
Bridgnorth
2
Atherstone
A5
Wenlock Edge
A449
Diddlebury
BIRMINGHAM
Hopesay
Chaddesley Corbett
M6
Ludlow
M42
Knighton
A449
Hockley Heath
Redditch
Hatton
Llandrindod Wells
Eyton
Leominster
Bromsgrove
Leamington Spa
Warwick
Worcester
Stratford-upon-Avon
A44
Bishop's Tachbrook
Ullingswick
Weobley
M5
Harvington
Cropredy
A44
Charingworth
Hay-on-Wye
Malvern Wells
Three Cocks
Hereford
Little Malvern
Evesham
Banbury
Ledbury
Chipping Campden
M40
Kemerton
A465
M50
Broadway
Buckland
Llanfihangel Crucorney
A49
Tewkesbury
A44
Corse Lawn
Winchcombe
A40
Upper Slaughter
Glewstone
Ross-on-Wye
Cleeve Hill
Lower Slaughter
A40
Cheltenham
Chipping Norton
Abergavenny
Gloucester
Hazleton
Shurdington
Monmouth
Shipton-under-Wychwood
Woodstock
Govilon
Whitebrook
Painswick
A429
Witney
Burford
A4042
Stroud
Oxford
Tintern
A48
M5
Leonard Stanley
Cwmbran
A449
Chepstow
Cirencester
Coln St Aldwyns
Tetbury
M4
Thornbury
Willesley
Malmesbury
Purton
SWINDON
CARDIFF
Chippenham
Bristol
M4
Calne
Bathford
A4
Bath
Lacock
Marlborough
Chelwood
A4
M5
Bradford-on-Avon
1
2
Hinton Charterhouse
Newbury

4 The North of England and the Lake District

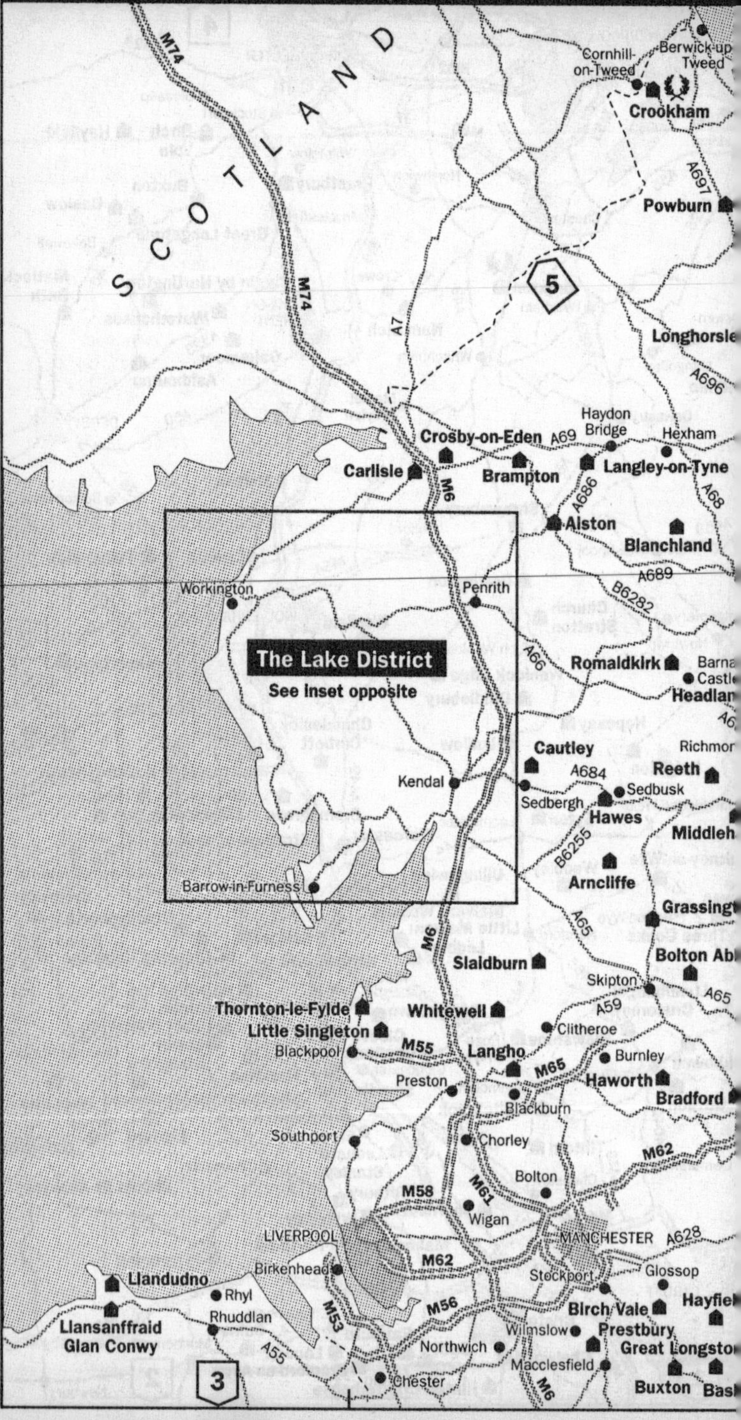
SCOTLAND
M74
A7
5
Cornhill-on-Tweed
Berwick-upon-Tweed
Crookham
A697
Powburn
Longhorsley
A696
Haydon Bridge
Hexham
Crosby-on-Eden
A69
Carlisle
Brampton
Langley-on-Tyne
M6
A686
A68
Alston
Blanchland
A689
B6282
Workington
Penrith
The Lake District
See inset opposite
A66
Romaldkirk
Barnard Castle
Headlam
Cautley
Richmond
Kendal
A684
Reeth
Sedbergh
Sedbusk
Hawes
Middleham
B6255
Arncliffe
Barrow-in-Furness
Grassington
A65
Bolton Abbey
Slaidburn
Skipton
Thornton-le-Fylde
Whitewell
A59
Little Singleton
Clitheroe
Blackpool
M55
Langho
Burnley
M65
Preston
Haworth
Bradford
Blackburn
Southport
Chorley
M62
Bolton
M58
M61
Wigan
LIVERPOOL
MANCHESTER
A628
Birkenhead
M62
Stockport
Glossop
Llandudno
Rhyl
M56
Birch Vale
Hayfield
Rhuddlan
M53
Wilmslow
Prestbury
Llansanffraid Glan Conwy
A55
Northwich
Great Longstone
Macclesfield
3
Chester
M6
Buxton
Baslow

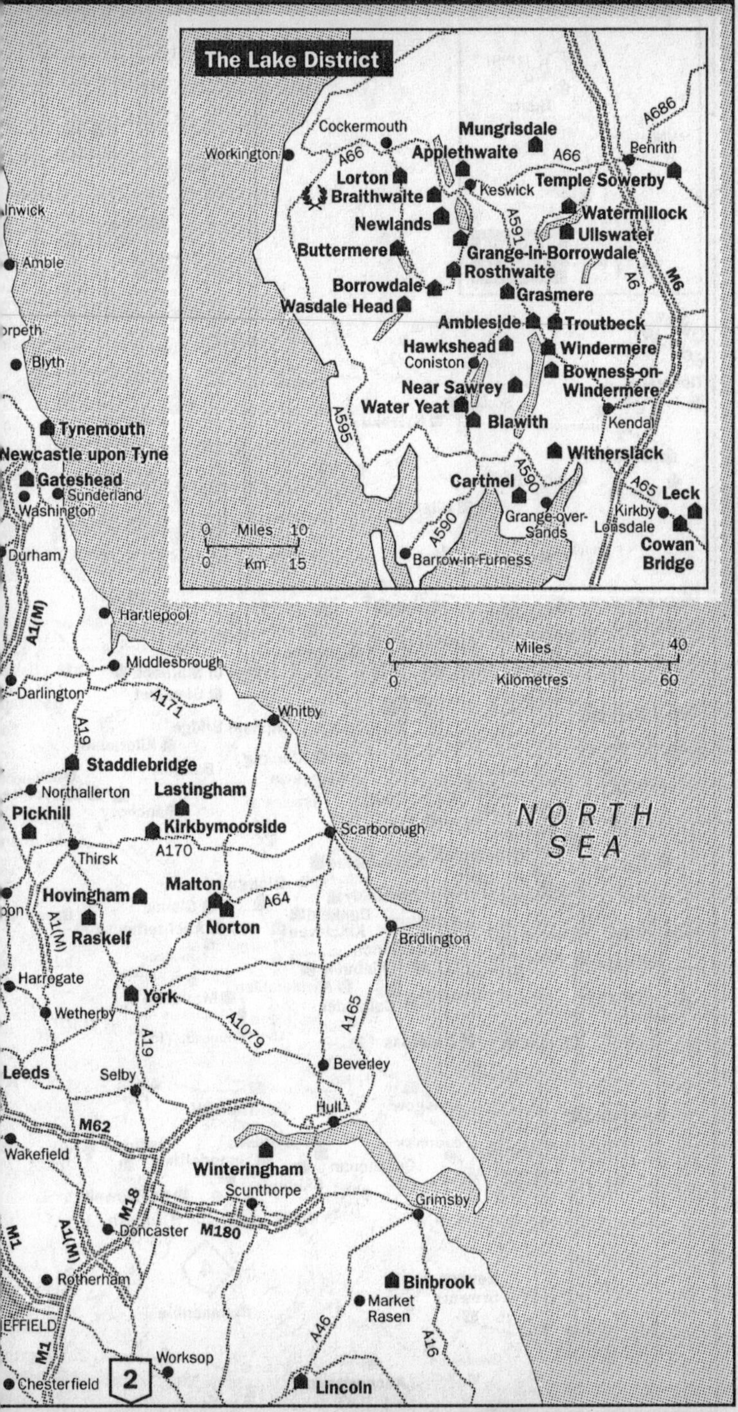
The Lake District
Cockermouth
Mungrisdale
Workington
A66
Applethwaite
A66
Penrith
A686
Lorton
Keswick
Temple Sowerby
Braithwaite
Newlands
A591
Watermillock
Ullswater
Buttermere
Grange-in-Borrowdale
Rosthwaite
A6
M6
Borrowdale
Grasmere
Wasdale Head
Ambleside
Troutbeck
Hawkshead
Windermere
Coniston
Bowness-on-Windermere
Near Sawrey
Water Yeat
Blawith
Kendal
A595
Witherslack
A590
Cartmel
A65
Leck
Kirkby Lonsdale
Grange-over-Sands
A590
Cowan Bridge
Barrow-in-Furness
0 Miles 10
0 Km 15
Alnwick
Amble
Morpeth
Blyth
Tynemouth
Newcastle upon Tyne
Gateshead
Sunderland
Washington
Durham
A1(M)
Hartlepool
Middlesbrough
0 Miles 40
0 Kilometres 60
Darlington
A171
Whitby
A19
Staddlebridge
Northallerton
Lastingham
Pickhill
Kirkbymoorside
Scarborough
NORTH SEA
Thirsk
A170
Malton
Hovingham
A64
A1(M)
Raskelf
Norton
Bridlington
Harrogate
York
Wetherby
A1079
A165
A19
Beverley
Leeds
Selby
Hull
M62
Wakefield
Winteringham
Scunthorpe
Grimsby
M18
M1
A1(M)
Doncaster
M180
Rotherham
Binbrook
Market Rasen
SHEFFIELD
A46
A16
M1
Worksop
Chesterfield
2
Lincoln

5 Scotland

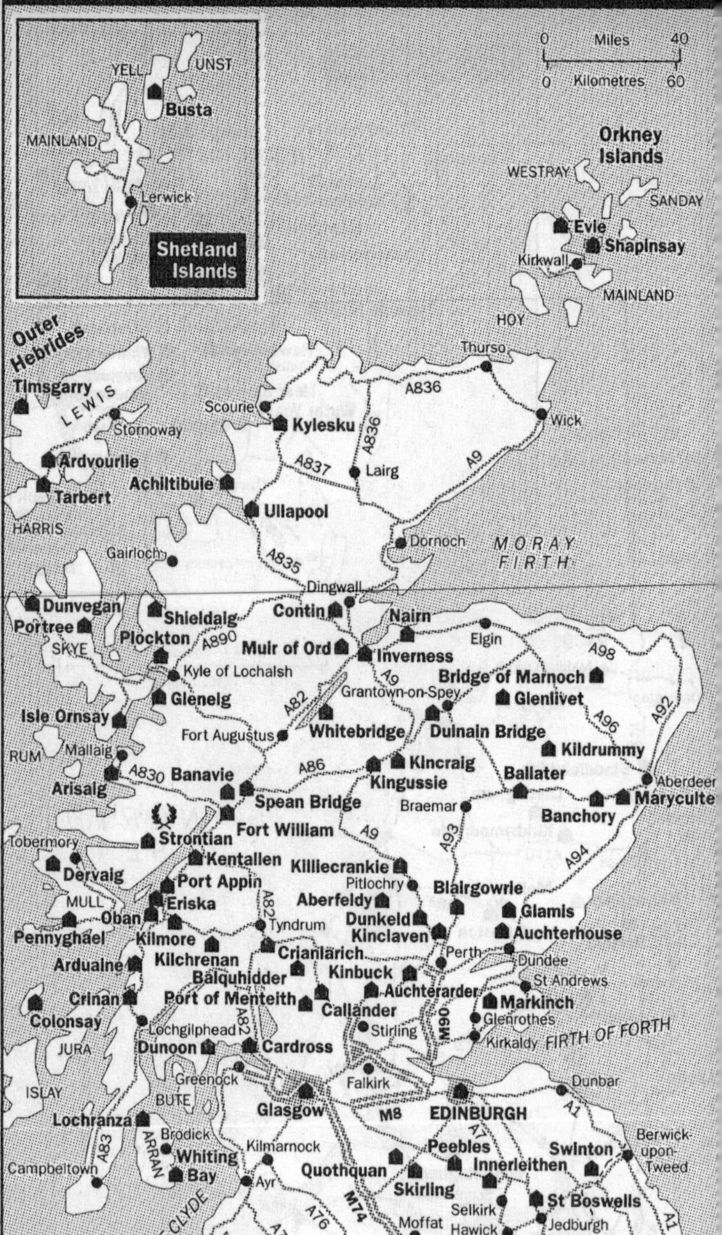

0 Miles 40
0 Kilometres 60
YELL
UNST
Busta
MAINLAND
Lerwick
Shetland Islands
Orkney Islands
WESTRAY
SANDAY
Evie
Shapinsay
Kirkwall
MAINLAND
HOY
Outer Hebrides
Timsgarry
LEWIS
Stornoway
Ardvourlie
Tarbert
HARRIS
Thurso
A836
Scourie
Kylesku
Wick
A837
Lairg
A9
Achiltibuie
Ullapool
Dornoch
MORAY FIRTH
Gairloch
A835
Dingwall
Dunvegan
Shieldaig
Contin
Nairn
Portree
Plockton
A890
Muir of Ord
Inverness
Elgin
A98
SKYE
Kyle of Lochalsh
A9
Grantown-on-Spey
Bridge of Marnoch
Glenelg
A82
Glenlivet
Isle Ornsay
Whitebridge
Fort Augustus
Dulnain Bridge
A96
A92
RUM
Mallaig
Kildrummy
A830
Banavie
A86
Kincraig
Ballater
Arisaig
Kingussie
Aberdeen
Spean Bridge
Braemar
Maryculter
Banchory
Fort William
Tobermory
Strontian
A9
A93
Kentallen
Killiecrankie
A94
Dervaig
Port Appin
Pitlochry
Blairgowrie
MULL
Eriska
Aberfeldy
A82
Glamis
Oban
Tyndrum
Dunkeld
Pennyghael
Kilmore
Kinclaven
Auchterhouse
Kilchrenan
Crianlarich
Perth
Ardual ne
Dundee
Balquhidder
Kinbuck
Auchterarder
St Andrews
Crinan
Port of Menteith
Callander
Markinch
Colonsay
A82
M90
Glenrothes
Lochgilphead
Stirling
JURA
Dunoon
Cardross
Kirkaldy
FIRTH OF FORTH
Greenock
Falkirk
ISLAY
BUTE
Glasgow
M8
EDINBURGH
Dunbar
Lochranza
A7
A1
Brodick
ARRAN
A83
Kilmarnock
Peebles
Berwick-upon-Tweed
Whiting Bay
Swinton
Campbeltown
Quothquan
Innerleithen
Ayr
Skirling
St Boswells
M74
Selkirk
A76
Moffat
Hawick
Jedburgh
A1
FIRTH OF CLYDE
A77
A713
4
A7
A696
Newton Stewart
Canonbie
Stranraer
A75
Dumfries
ENGLAND
Portpatrick
Gatehouse of Fleet
Auchencairn
Carlisle
M6

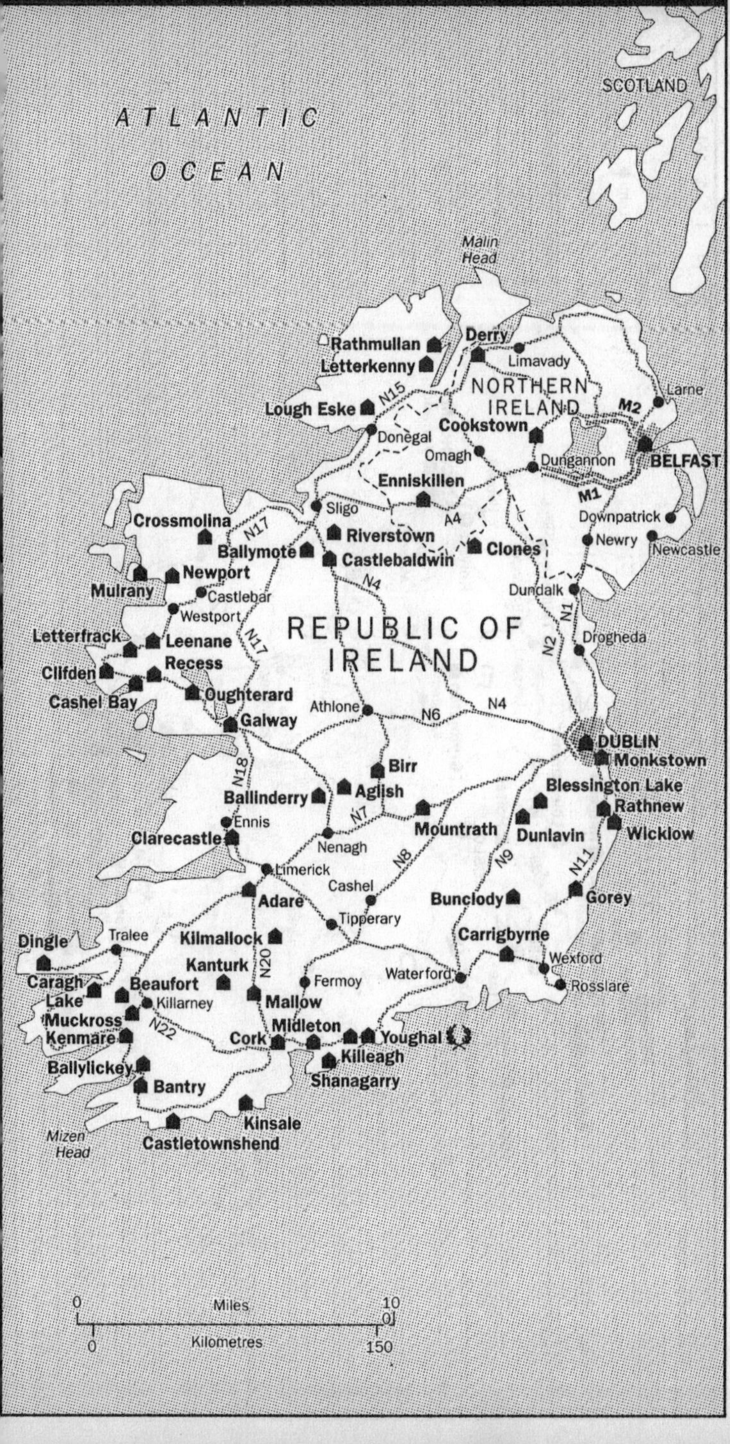
ATLANTIC
OCEAN
SCOTLAND
Malin Head
NORTHERN IRELAND
REPUBLIC OF IRELAND
Rathmullan
Letterkenny
Derry
Limavady
Larne
Lough Eske
N15
M2
Donegal
Cookstown
Omagh
BELFAST
Dungannon
Enniskillen
Sligo
A4
M1
Crossmolina
N17
Downpatrick
Riverstown
Newry
Newcastle
Ballymote
Castlebaldwin
Clones
Newport
Mulrany
Castlebar
N4
Dundalk
Westport
N1
Letterfrack
Leenane
N17
Drogheda
Recess
N2
Clifden
Oughterard
Cashel Bay
Athlone
N4
N6
Galway
DUBLIN
Monkstown
N18
Birr
Blessington Lake
Aglish
Ballinderry
Rathnew
N7
Ennis
Mountrath
Dunlavin
Wicklow
Clarecastle
Nenagh
N9
N11
N8
Limerick
Cashel
Adare
Bunclody
Gorey
Tipperary
Dingle
Tralee
Kilmallock
Carrigbyrne
N20
Kanturk
Wexford
Waterford
Caragh Lake
Beaufort
Fermoy
Rosslare
Killarney
Mallow
Muckross
N22
Midleton
Kenmare
Cork
Youghal
Killeagh
Ballylickey
Shanagarry
Bantry
Kinsale
Mizen Head
Castletownshend
0
Miles
100
0
Kilometres
150

7 Scandinavia

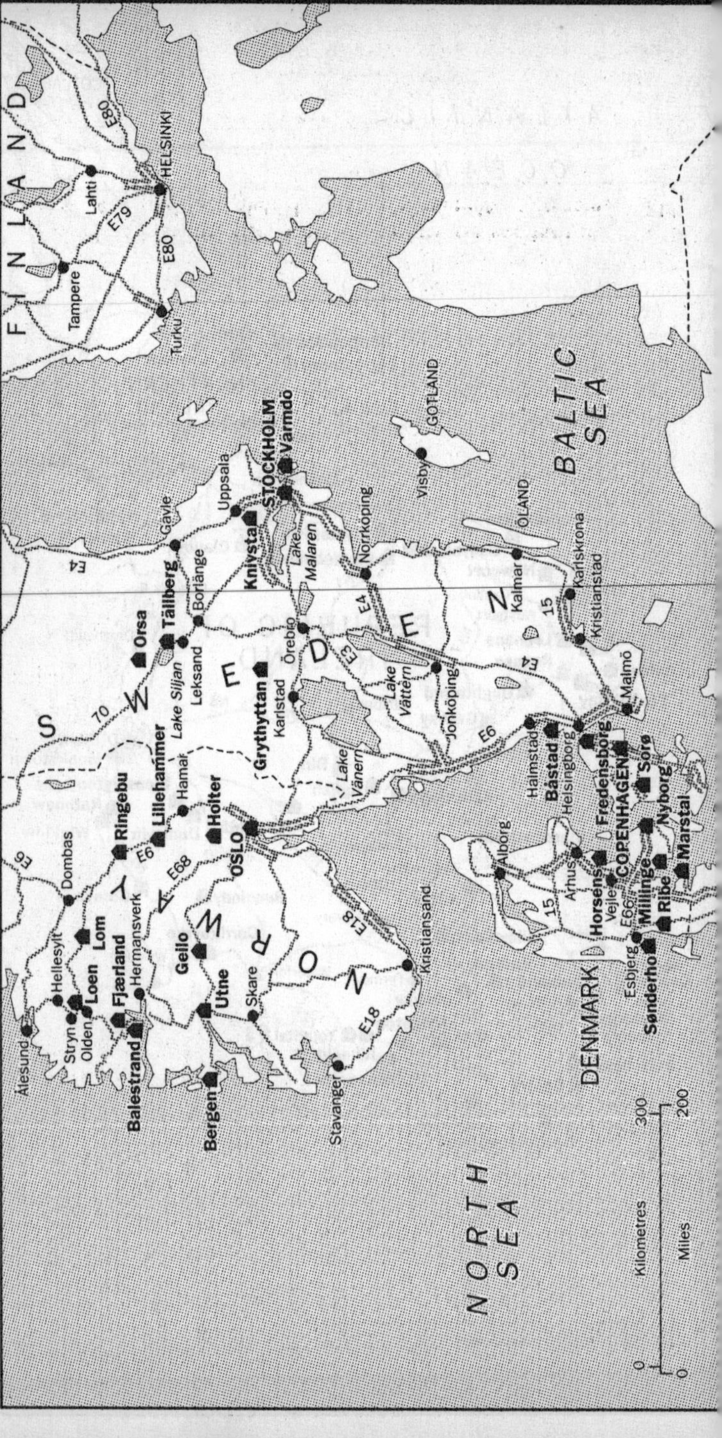

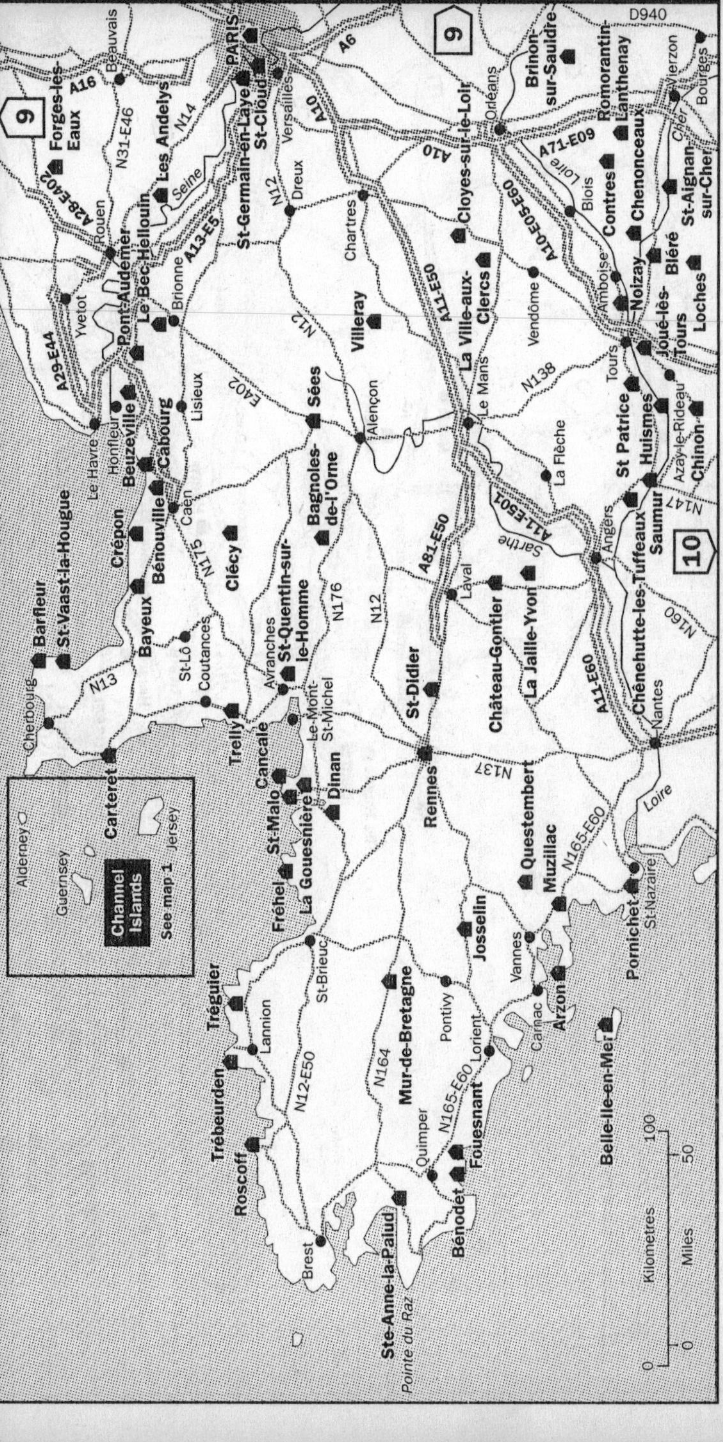
PARIS
St-Germain-en-Laye
St-Cloud
Versailles
Beauvais
Forges-les-Eaux
Les Andelys
Rouen
Le Bec-Hellouin
Pont-Audemer
Brionne
Yvetot
Le Havre
Honfleur
Beuzeville
Cabourg
Lisieux
Caen
Bénouville
Crépon
Bayeux
Barfleur
St-Vaast-la-Hougue
Cherbourg
Carteret
St-Lô
Coutances
Trelly
Avranches
St-Quentin-sur-le-Homme
Le-Mont-St-Michel
Cancale
St-Malo
Dinan
La Gouesnière
Fréhel
St-Brieuc
Tréguier
Lannion
Trébeurden
Roscoff
Brest
Ste-Anne-la-Palud
Pointe du Raz
Quimper
Bénodet
Fouesnant
Mur-de-Bretagne
Pontivy
Lorient
Carnac
Arzon
Vannes
Josselin
Belle-Ile-en-Mer
Muzillac
Questembert
Pornichet
St-Nazaire
Nantes
Rennes
St-Didier
Château-Gontier
La Jaille-Yvon
Laval
Angers
Chênehutte-les-Tuffeaux
Saumur
La Flèche
Le Mans
Alençon
Sées
Bagnoles-de-l'Orne
Clécy
Villeray
La Ville-aux-Clercs
Cloyes-sur-le-Loir
Chartres
Dreux
Vendôme
Tours
St Patrice
Huismes
Azay-le-Rideau
Chinon
Joué-lès-Tours
Loches
Amboise
Noizay
Bléré
Blois
Contres
Chenonceaux
St-Aignan-sur-Cher
Orléans
Romorantin-Lanthenay
Brinon-sur-Sauldre
Vierzon
Bourges
Seine
Loire
Cher
Sarthe
A16
A28-E402
A29-E44
A13-E5
N31-E46
N14
N12
A10
A6
A11-E50
A71-E09
A10-E05-E60
N138
E402
N175
N176
N13
N12-E50
N164
N165-E60
N137
A81-E50
A11-E501
A11-E60
N160
N147
D940
9
10
Channel Islands
See map 1
Alderney
Guernsey
Jersey
Kilometres
Miles
0
50
100

9 Benelux and North-East France

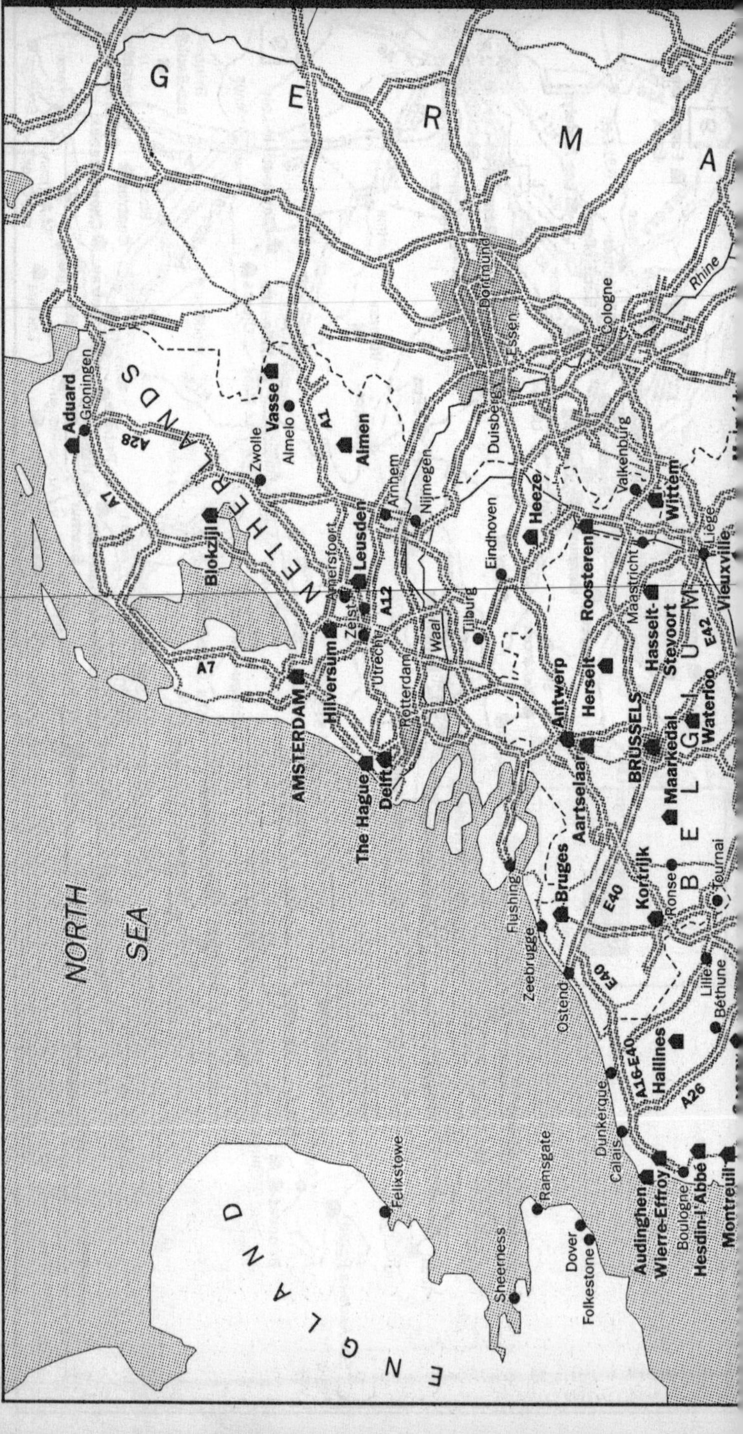

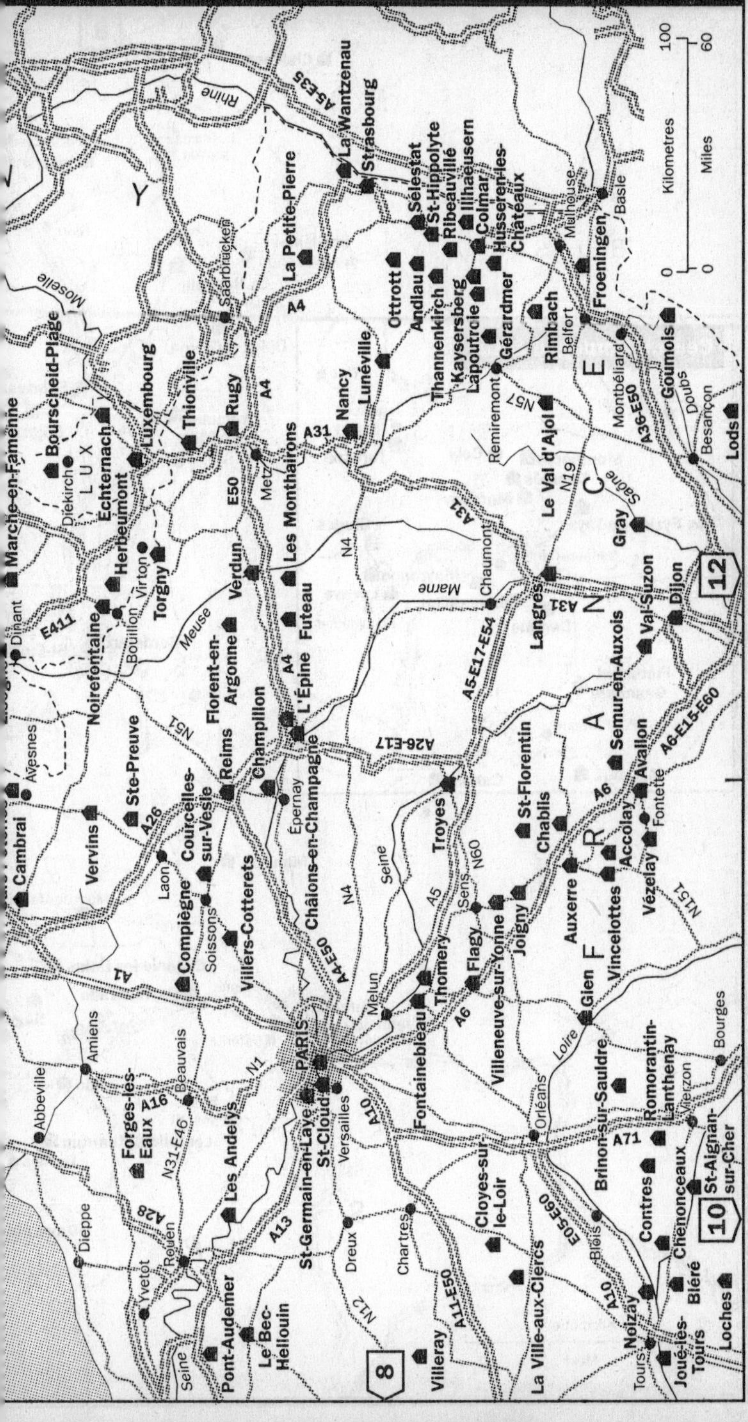
Cambrai
Vervins
Ste-Preuve
Avesnes
Noirefontaine
Dinant
E411
Bouillon
Marche-en-Famenne
Herbeumont
Virton
Torgny
Diekirch
LUX
Bourscheid-Plage
Echternach
Luxembourg
Moselle
Thionville
Rugy
Metz
Saarbrucken
La Petite-Pierre
Rhine
A5-E35
La Wantzenau
Strasbourg
Sélestat
St-Hippolyte
Ribeauvillé
Illhaeusern
Colmar
Husseren-les-Châteaux
Ottrott
Andlau
Thannenkirch
Kaysersberg
Lapoutroie
Gérardmer
Rimbach
Mulhouse
Basle
Froeningen
Belfort
Montbéliard
Goumois
Doubs
Besançon
Lods
A36-E50
Remiremont
N57
Le Val d'Ajol
N19
Saône
Gray
Langres
A31
Chaumont
Marne
A32
Nancy
Lunéville
A31
A4
E50
Verdun
Les Monthairons
Futeau
L'Épine
Châlons-en-Champagne
Florent-en-Argonne
Champillon
Épernay
Reims
Meuse
N51
A26
Laon
Courcelles-sur-Vesle
Soissons
Compiègne
Villers-Cotterets
A1
Amiens
Abbeville
Beauvais
Forges-les-Eaux
A16
A28
N31-E46
Dieppe
Yvetot
Rouen
Seine
Les Andelys
Pont-Audemer
Le Bec-Hellouin
N1
PARIS
St-Germain-en-Laye
St-Cloud
Versailles
A13
Dreux
N12
Chartres
A10
A11-E50
Villeray
8
Cloyes-sur-le-Loir
La Ville-aux-Clercs
E05-E60
Orléans
Blois
A10
Noizay
Tours
Joué-lès-Tours
Loches
Bléré
Chenonceaux
Contres
10
St-Aignan-sur-Cher
Brinon-sur-Sauldre
A71
Vierzon
Romorantin-Lanthenay
Bourges
Loire
Gien
Fontainebleau
Melun
Thomery
A6
Flagy
Villeneuve-sur-Yonne
A4-E50
N4
Seine
A5
Troyes
Sens
N60
Joigny
A26-E17
Auxerre
Vincelottes
Chablis
St-Florentin
A5-E17-E54
Accolay
Vézelay
Fontette
Avallon
Semur-en-Auxois
A6-E15-E60
Val-Suzon
Dijon
12
N151
F R A N C E
Kilometres
Miles
0
100
60

10 West and Central France

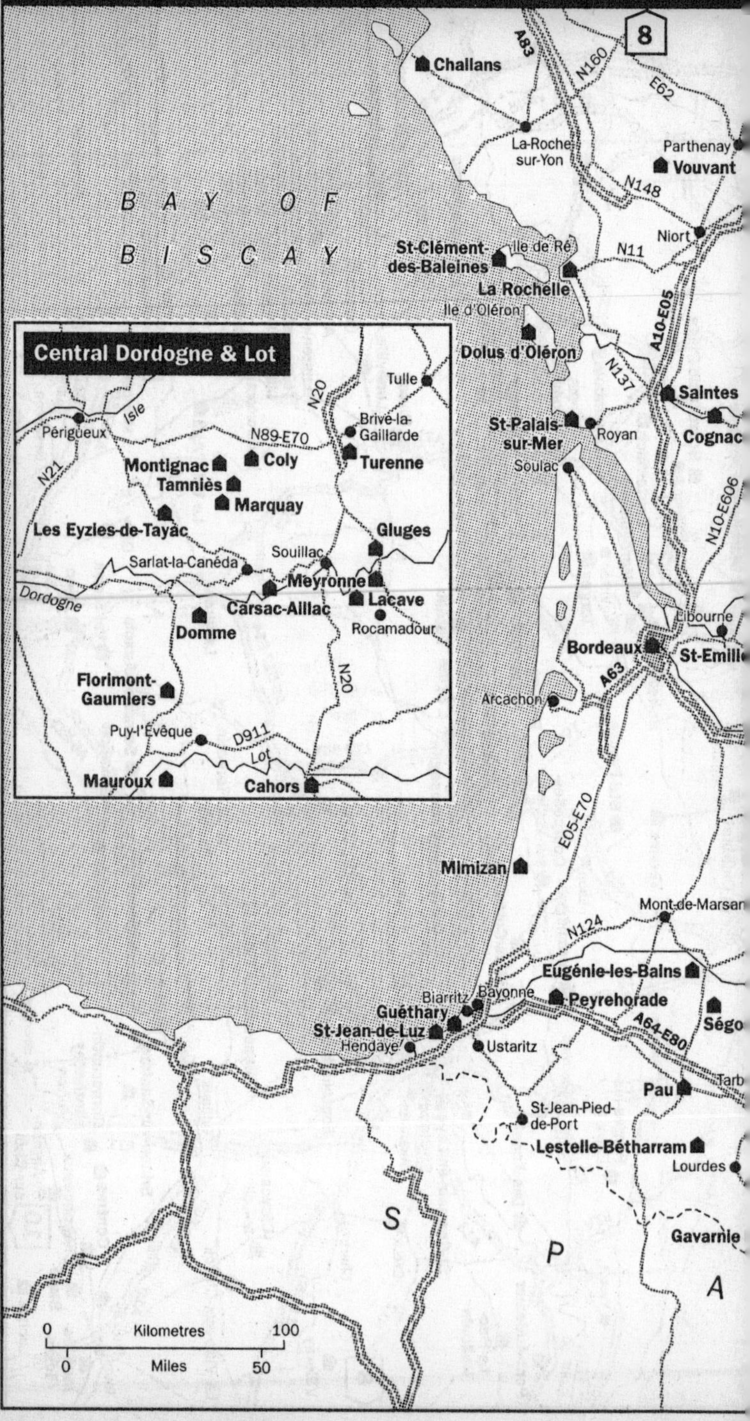

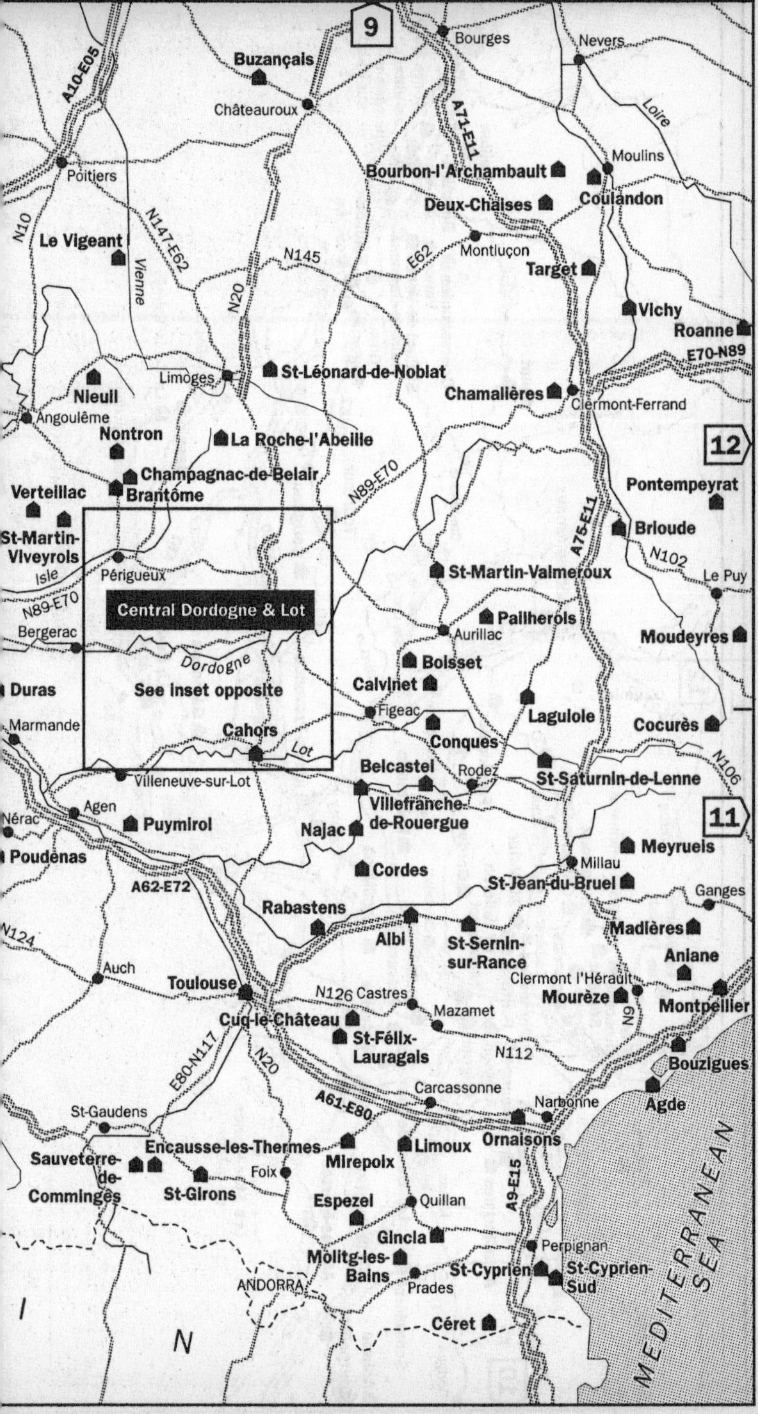
9
Bourges
Nevers
Buzançais
A10-E05
Châteauroux
A71-E11
Loire
Moulins
Poitiers
Bourbon-l'Archambault
Deux-Chaises
Coulandon
N10
Le Vigeant
N147-E62
Vienne
N145
E62
Montluçon
Target
N20
Vichy
Roanne
E70-N89
Limoges
St-Léonard-de-Noblat
Nieuil
Chamalières
Clermont-Ferrand
Angoulême
Nontron
La Roche-l'Abeille
12
Champagnac-de-Belair
N89-E70
Verteillac
Brantôme
Pontempeyrat
St-Martin-Viveyrols
A75-E11
Brioude
N102
Isle
Périgueux
St-Martin-Valmeroux
Le Puy
N89-E70
Central Dordogne & Lot
Pailherols
Bergerac
Aurillac
Moudeyres
Dordogne
Boisset
Duras
See inset opposite
Calvinet
Laguiole
Figeac
Marmande
Cahors
Conques
Cocurès
Lot
N106
Belcastel
Rodez
St-Saturnin-de-Lenne
Villeneuve-sur-Lot
Villefranche-de-Rouergue
11
Agen
Nérac
Puymirol
Najac
Meyruels
Poudenas
Millau
Cordes
A62-E72
St-Jean-du-Bruel
Ganges
Rabastens
Madières
N124
Albi
St-Sernin-sur-Rance
Aniane
Auch
Clermont l'Hérault
Toulouse
N126 Castres
Mourèze
Montpellier
Mazamet
N9
Cuq-le-Château
St-Félix-Lauragais
E80-N117
N20
N112
Bouzigues
Carcassonne
Agde
A61-E80
Narbonne
St-Gaudens
Ornaisons
Encausse-les-Thermes
Limoux
Mirepoix
Sauveterre-de-Comminges
Foix
St-Girons
A9-E15
MEDITERRANEAN SEA
Espezel
Quillan
Gincla
Perpignan
Molitg-les-Bains
St-Cyprien
St-Cyprien-Sud
ANDORRA
Prades
I
N
Céret

11 The South of France

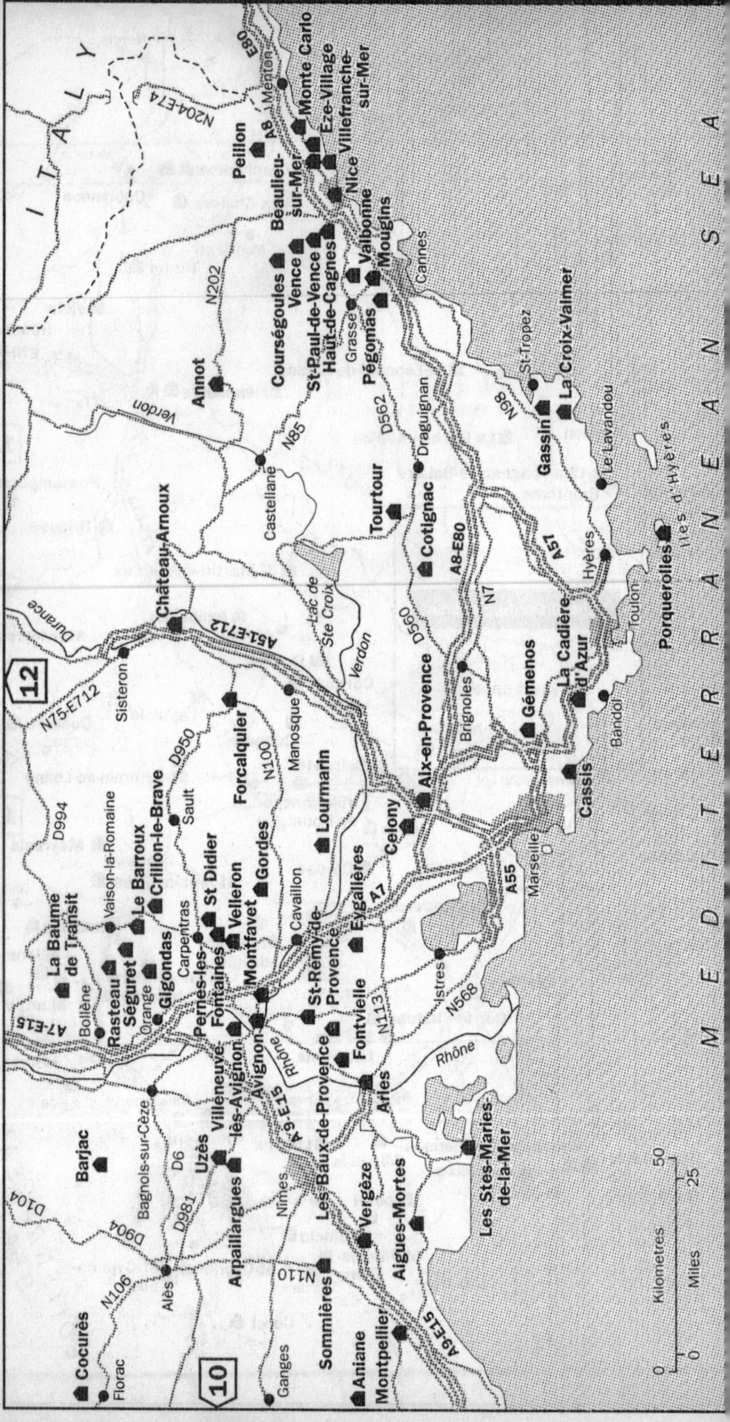

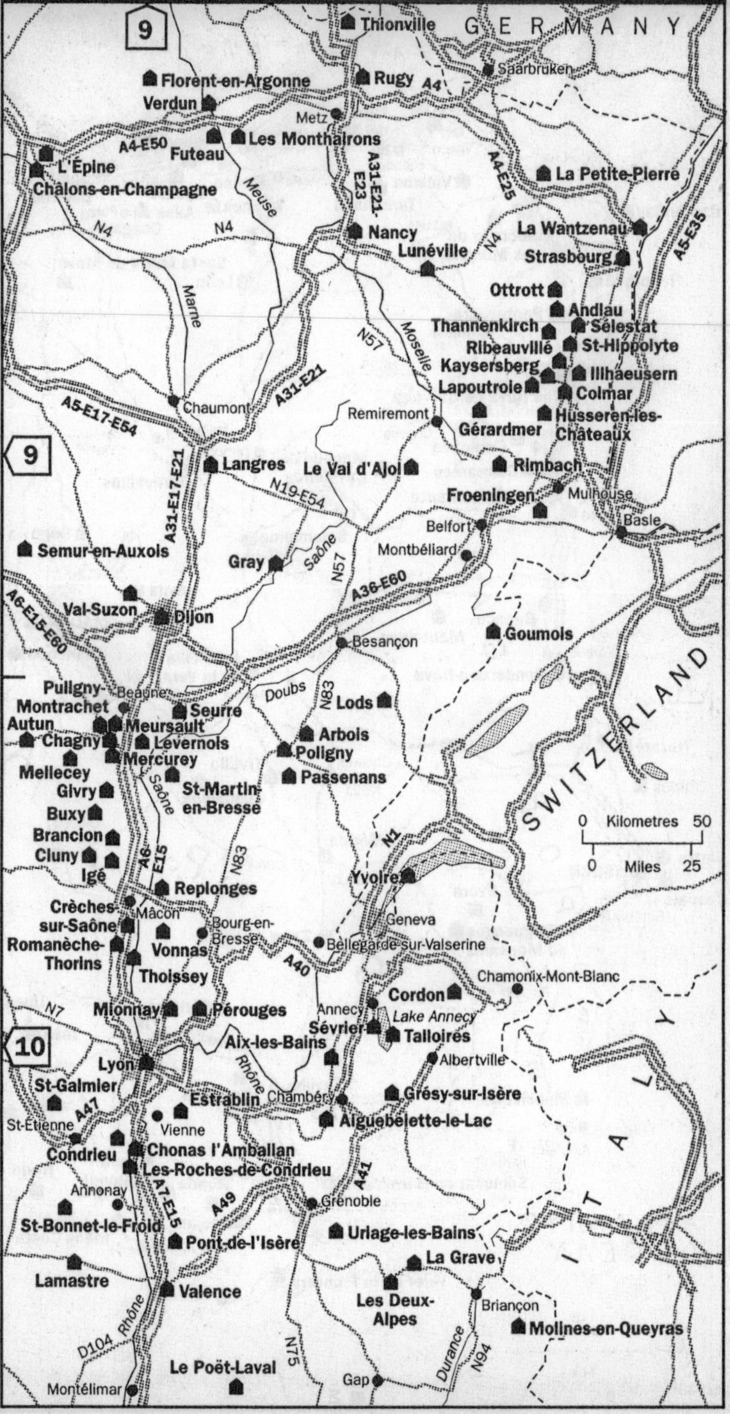
9
Thionville
GERMANY
Florent-en-Argonne
Rugy
Saarbruken
Verdun
A4
Metz
Les Monthairons
Futeau
A4-E50
L'Épine
Châlons-en-Champagne
A31-E21-E23
A4-E25
La Petite-Pierre
Meuse
N4
N4
Nancy
La Wantzenau
A5-E35
Lunéville
Strasbourg
N4
Marne
Ottrott
Andlau
Thannenkirch
Sélestat
N57
Moselle
Ribeauvillé
St-Hippolyte
Kaysersberg
Illhaeusern
A31-E21
Lapoutroie
Colmar
A5-E17-E54
Chaumont
Remiremont
Husseren-les-Châteaux
Gérardmer
9
Langres
Le Val d'Ajol
Rimbach
A31-E17-E21
N19-E54
Froeningen
Mulhouse
Belfort
Basle
Semur-en-Auxois
Gray
Saône
N57
Montbéliard
A36-E60
Val-Suzon
Dijon
A6-E15-E60
Goumois
Besançon
Puligny-Montrachet
Beaune
Doubs
N83
Lods
SWITZERLAND
Seurre
Autun
Meursault
Arbois
Chagny
Levernois
Poligny
Mercurey
Mellecey
Passenans
Givry
St-Martin-en-Bresse
Saône
Buxy
0 Kilometres 50
Brancion
N1
0 Miles 25
Cluny
A6
E15
N83
Igé
Yvoire
Replonges
Crèches-sur-Saône
Mâcon
Geneva
Bourg-en-Bresse
Vonnas
Bellegarde-sur-Valserine
Romanèche-Thorins
A40
Thoissey
Chamonix-Mont-Blanc
Cordon
N7
Mionnay
Pérouges
Annecy
Lake Annecy
Sévrier
Talloires
10
Aix-les-Bains
Lyon
Rhône
Albertville
St-Galmier
Estrablin
Chambéry
Grésy-sur-Isère
A47
St-Étienne
Vienne
Aiguebelette-le-Lac
ITALY
Condrieu
Chonas l'Amballan
Les-Roches-de-Condrieu
A41
Annonay
A7-E15
A49
Grenoble
St-Bonnet-le-Froid
Pont-de-l'Isère
Uriage-les-Bains
La Grave
Lamastre
Valence
Les Deux-Alpes
Briançon
Molines-en-Queyras
D104
Rhône
N75
Durance
N94
Le Poët-Laval
Montélimar
Gap

13 Spain and Portugal

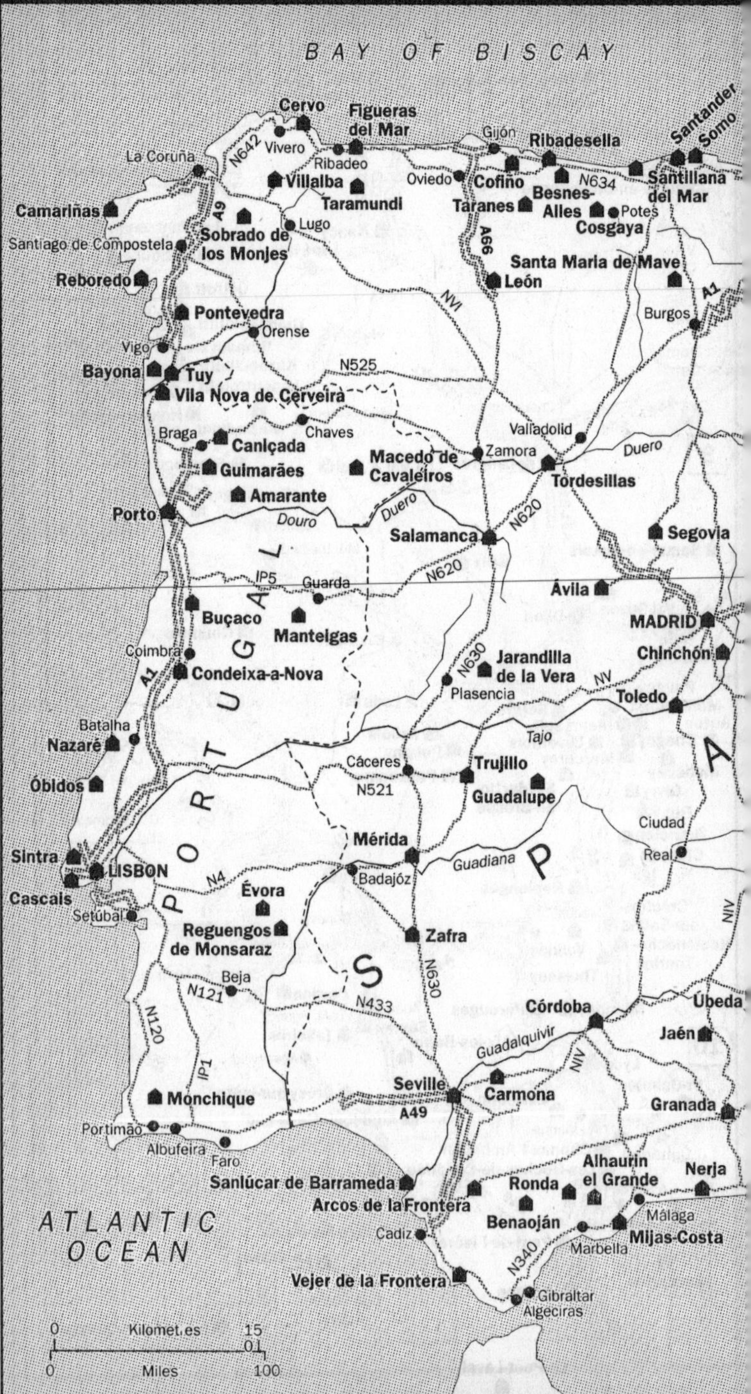

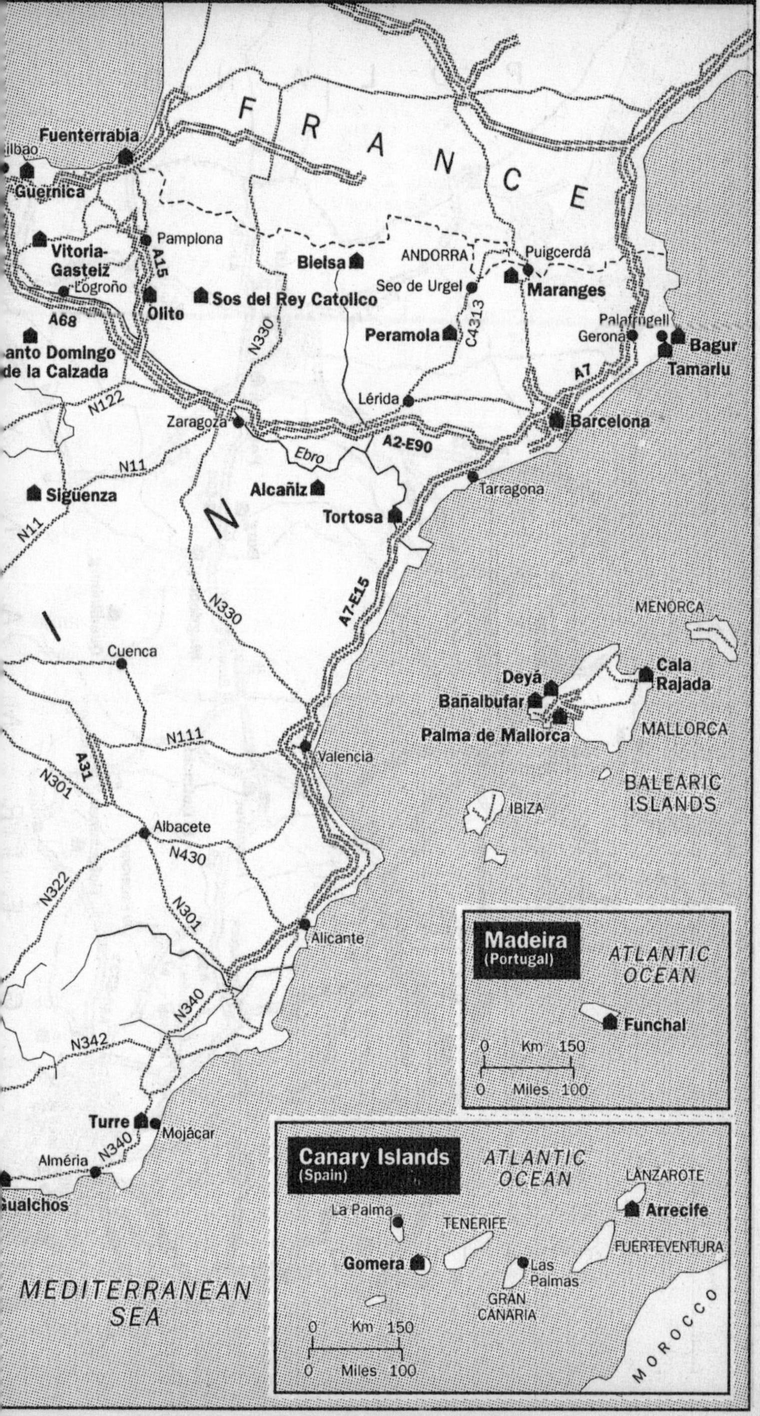
FRANCE
Fuenterrabia
Guernica
Vitoria-Gasteiz
Pamplona
A15
Logroño
A68
Olite
Sos del Rey Catolico
Bielsa
ANDORRA
Puigcerdá
Seo de Urgel
Maranges
C4313
Peramola
N330
Palafrugell
Gerona
Bagur
Tamariu
A7
Lérida
N122
Zaragoza
Barcelona
A2-E90
Ebro
N11
Sigüenza
Alcañiz
Tortosa
Tarragona
A7-E15
MENORCA
Cuenca
Deyá
Cala Rajada
Bañalbufar
Palma de Mallorca
MALLORCA
N111
Valencia
A31
N301
BALEARIC ISLANDS
IBIZA
Albacete
N430
N322
Alicante
N340
N342
Turre
Mojácar
Almeria
Gualchos
MEDITERRANEAN SEA
Madeira (Portugal)
ATLANTIC OCEAN
Funchal
0 Km 150
0 Miles 100
Canary Islands (Spain)
ATLANTIC OCEAN
LANZAROTE
La Palma
TENERIFE
Arrecife
FUERTEVENTURA
Gomera
Las Palmas
GRAN CANARIA
MOROCCO
0 Km 150
0 Miles 100

14 Germany and the Czech Republic

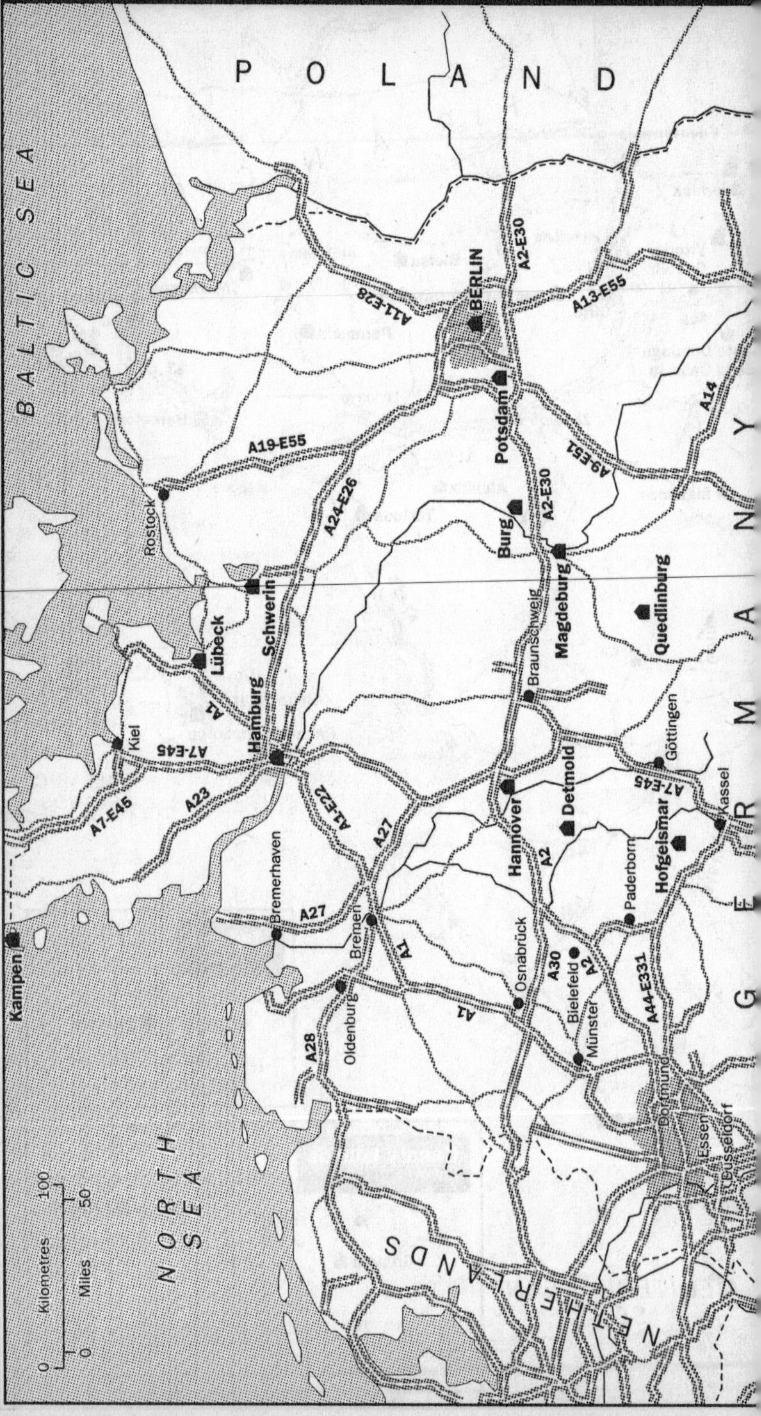

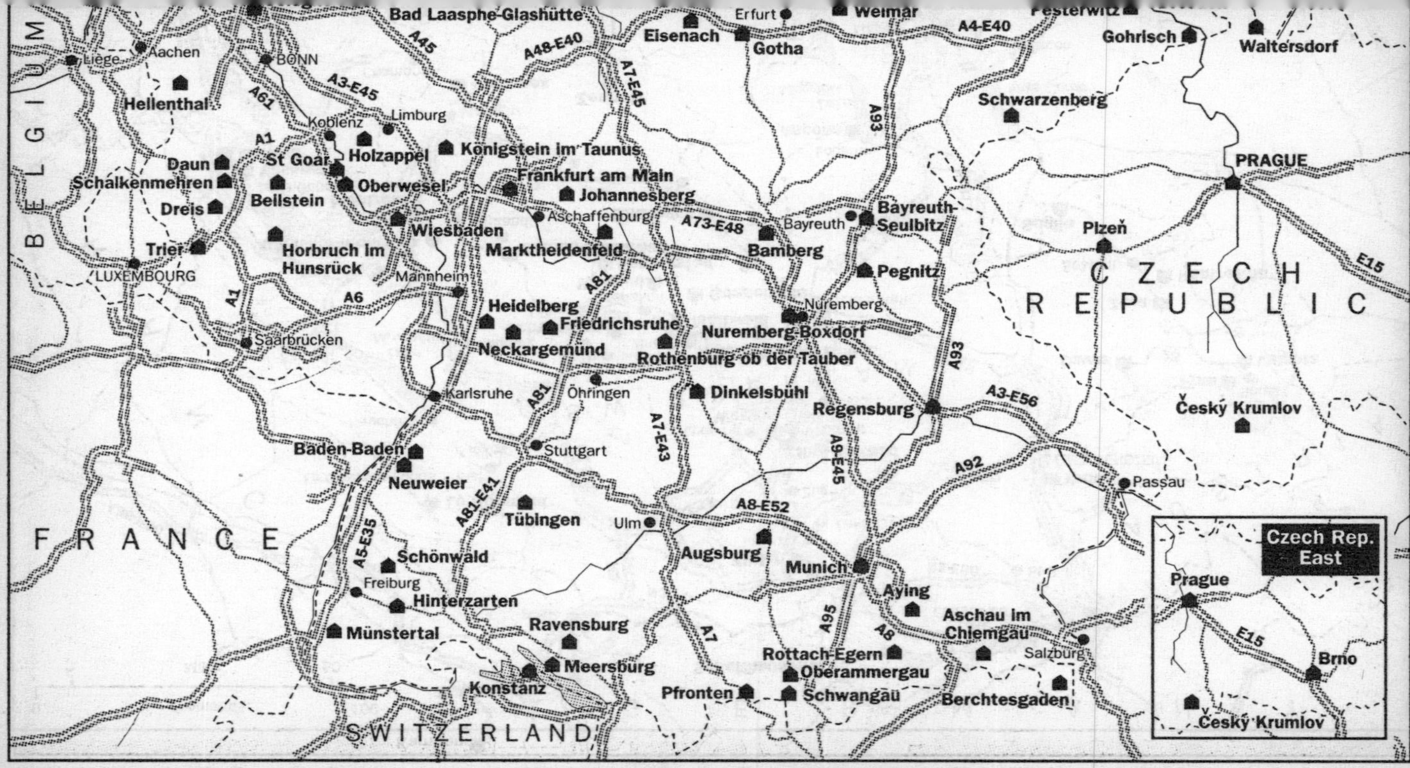
BELGIUM
Liège
Aachen
BONN
Hellenthal
A61
A3-E45
A45
Bad Laasphe-Glashütte
A48-E40
A7-E45
Eisenach
Erfurt
Gotha
Weimar
A4-E40
Gohrisch
Waltersdorf
Schwarzenberg
PRAGUE
Koblenz
Limburg
A1
Holzappel
Königstein im Taunus
Daun
St Goar
Frankfurt am Main
Schalkenmehren
Oberwesel
Johannesberg
Dreis
Bellstein
Aschaffenburg
Bayreuth-Seulbitz
Bayreuth
Wiesbaden
A73-E48
Plzeň
Trier
Horbruch im Hunsrück
Marktheidenfeld
Bamberg
LUXEMBOURG
Mannheim
A81
Pegnitz
CZECH REPUBLIC
E15
A6
Heidelberg
Nuremberg
Friedrichsruhe
Nuremberg-Boxdorf
Saarbrücken
Neckargemünd
Rothenburg ob der Tauber
A93
Karlsruhe
Öhringen
Dinkelsbühl
A3-E56
Regensburg
Český Krumlov
A7-E43
Baden-Baden
Stuttgart
A9-E45
A92
Neuweier
Passau
A81-E41
Tübingen
A8-E52
FRANCE
A5-E35
Ulm
Augsburg
Munich
Schönwald
Freiburg
Aying
Hinterzarten
A95
A8
Aschau im Chiemgau
Münstertal
Ravensburg
A7
Salzburg
Rottach-Egern
Meersburg
Oberammergau
Konstanz
Pfronten
Schwangau
Berchtesgaden
SWITZERLAND
Czech Rep. East
Prague
E15
Brno
Český Krumlov

15 Switzerland

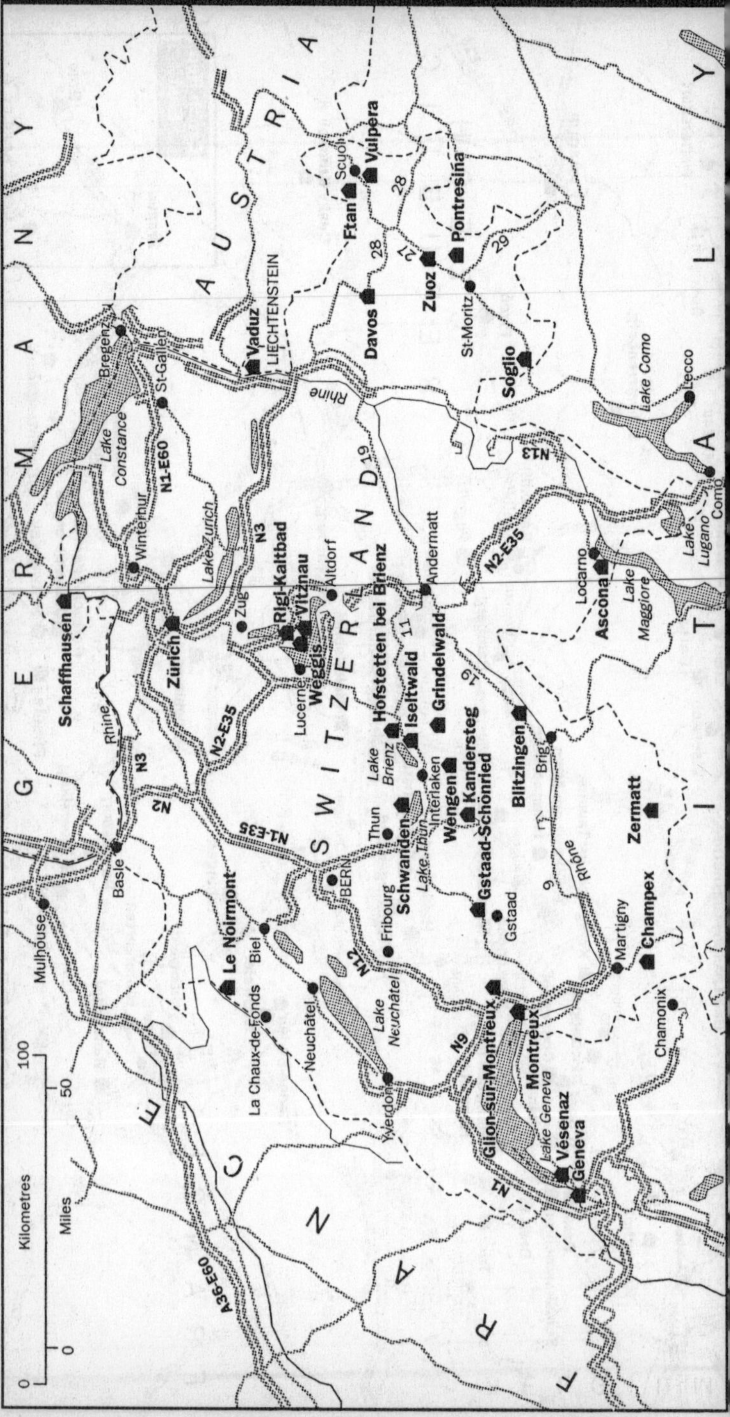

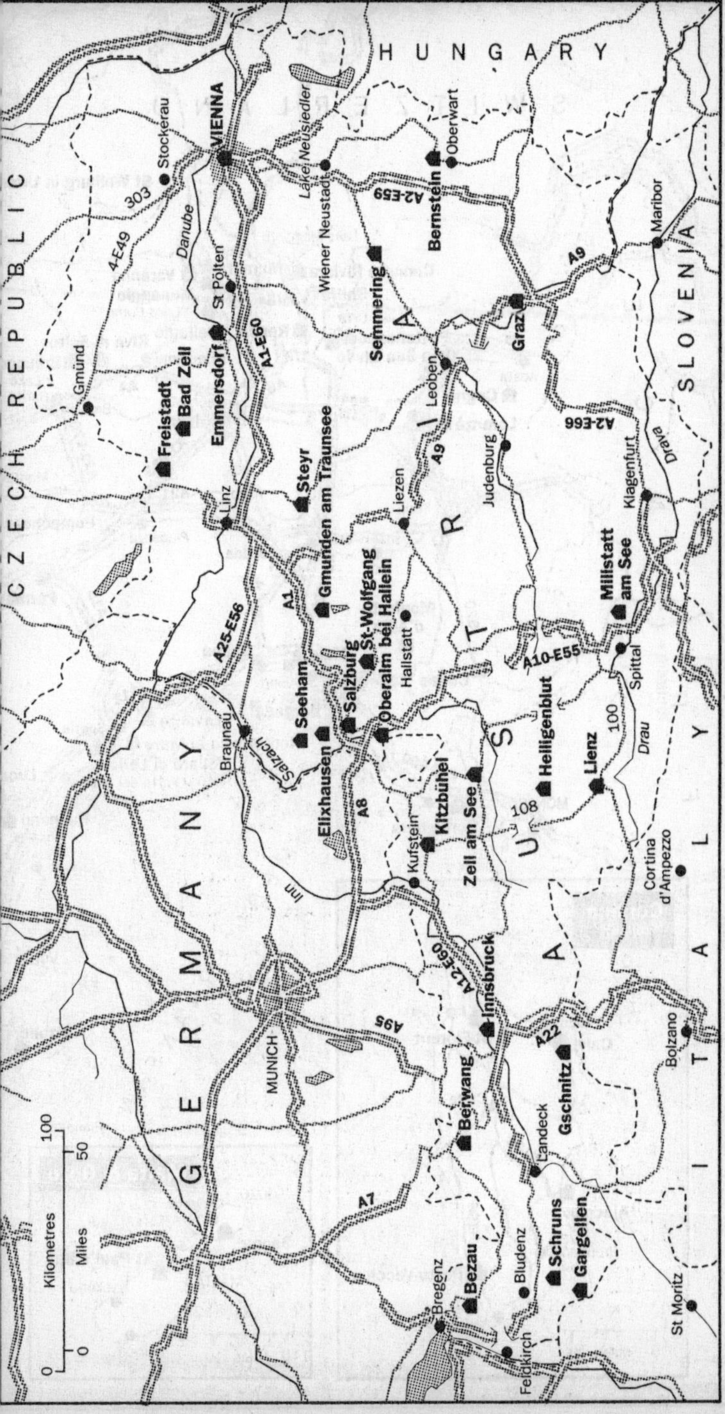
CZECH REPUBLIC
HUNGARY
GERMANY
AUSTRIA
SLOVENIA
ITALY
Kilometres
0
100
Miles
0
50
VIENNA
Stockerau
303
4-E49
Danube
Gmünd
Freistadt
Bad Zell
Emmersdorf
St Pölten
A1-E60
Linz
Steyr
Gmunden am Traunsee
A1
A25-E56
Braunau
Salzach
Seeham
Elixhausen
Salzburg
St-Wolfgang
Oberalm bei Hallein
Hallstatt
Liezen
Leoben
A9
Judenburg
Lake Neusiedler
Wiener Neustadt
Semmering
Bernstein
Oberwart
A2-E59
Graz
A2-E66
Maribor
Klagenfurt
Drava
Millstatt am See
Spittal
A10-E55
Heiligenblut
Lienz
100
Drau
108
Zell am See
Kitzbühel
Kufstein
A8
Inn
MUNICH
A95
A12-E60
Innsbruck
A22
Gschnitz
Landeck
Berwang
A7
Bregenz
Bezau
Bludenz
Schruns
Gargellen
Feldkirch
St Moritz
Bolzano
Cortina d'Ampezzo

17 Northern Italy, Malta and Slovenia

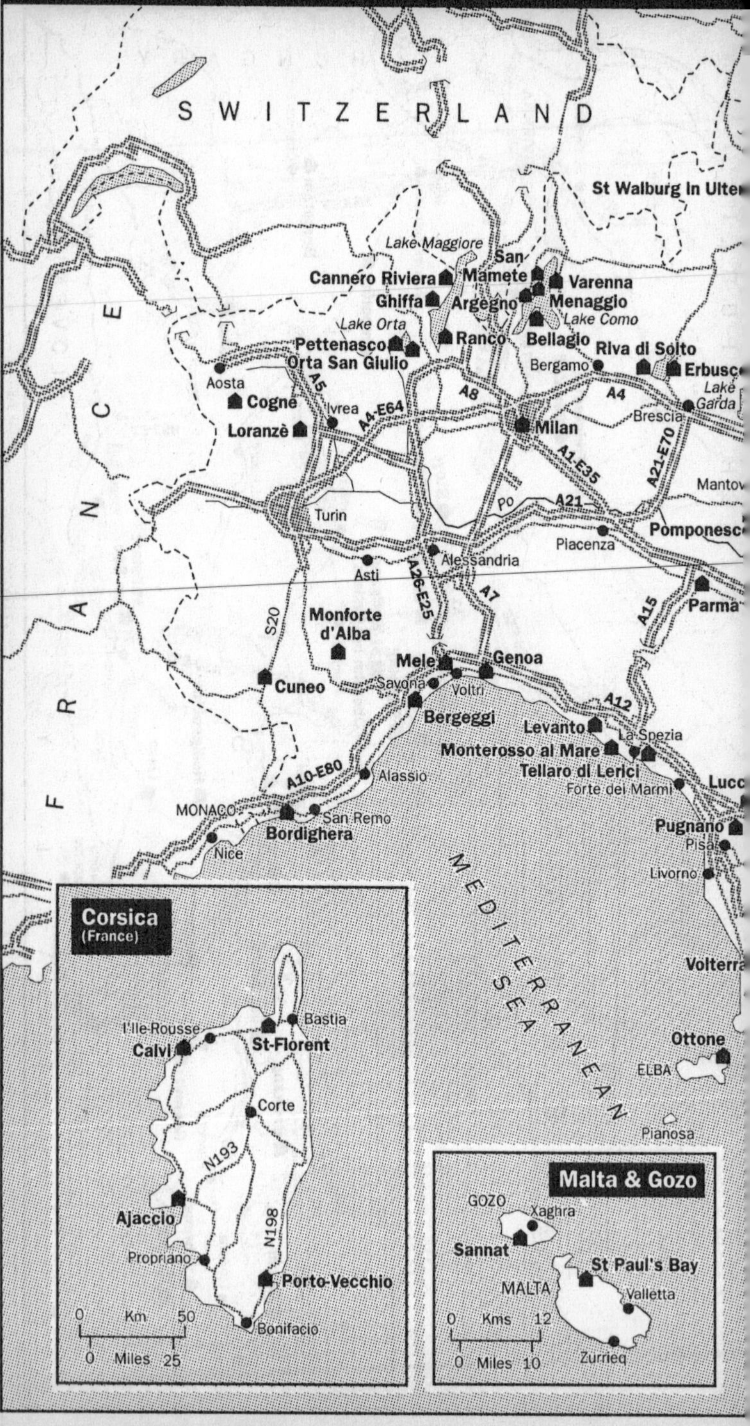

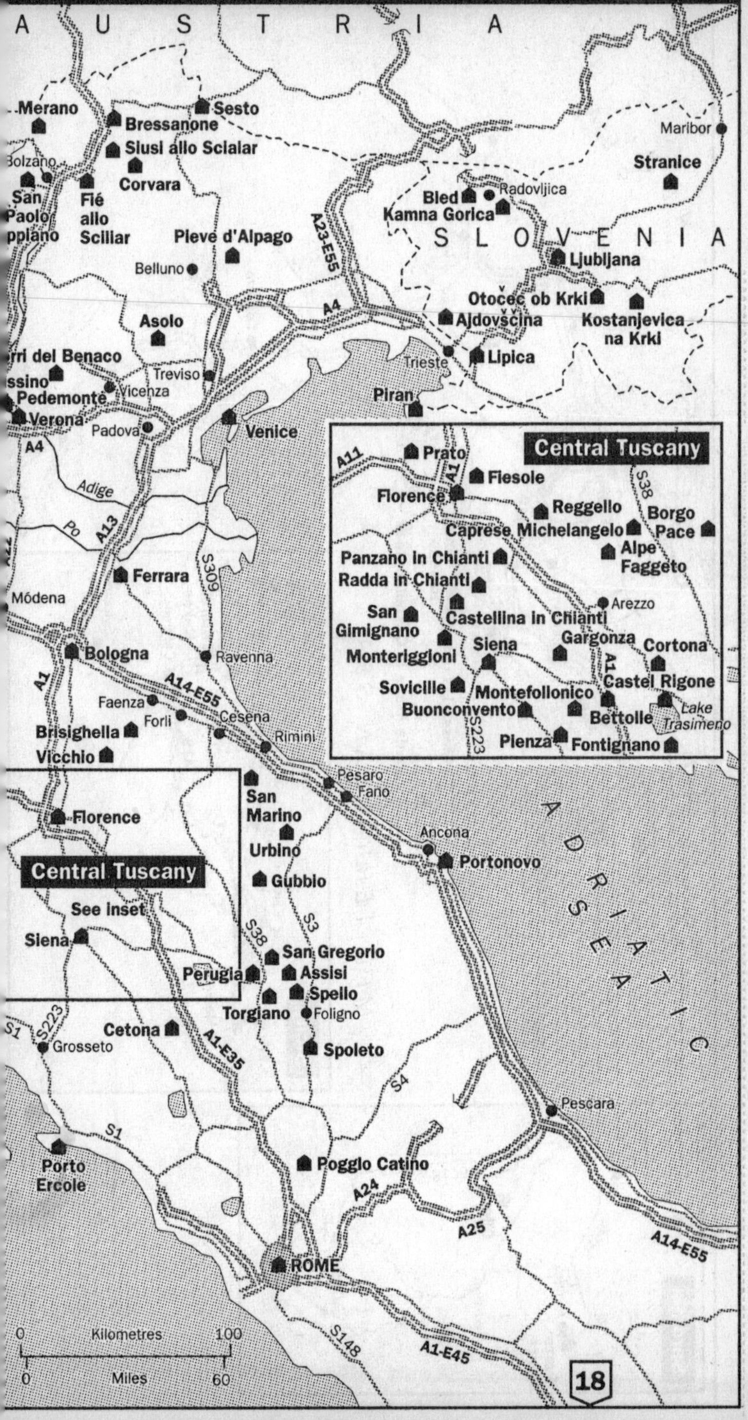
AUSTRIA
Merano
Sesto
Bressanone
Slusi allo Scialar
Bolzano
Corvara
San Paolo Appiano
Fié allo Sciliar
Pieve d'Alpago
Belluno
A23-E55
Maribor
Stranice
Bled
Radovljica
Kamna Gorica
SLOVENIA
Ljubljana
Otočec ob Krki
Kostanjevica na Krki
A4
Ajdovščina
Asolo
Trieste
Lipica
Treviso
Vicenza
Pedemonte
Verona
Padova
Piran
Venice
A4
Adige
Po
A13
S309
Ferrara
Módena
Bologna
Ravenna
A1
A14-E55
Faenza
Forli
Cesena
Rimini
Brisighella
Vicchio
Pesaro
Fano
San Marino
Urbino
Ancona
Portonovo
Florence
Central Tuscany
Gubbio
See inset
S3
S38
Siena
San Gregorio
Perugia
Assisi
Spello
Torgiano
Foligno
S223
S1
Grosseto
Cetona
A1-E35
Spoleto
S4
Pescara
S1
Porto Ercole
Poggio Catino
A24
A25
A14-E55
ROME
S148
A1-E45
0 Kilometres 100
0 Miles 60
18
ADRIATIC SEA
Central Tuscany
A11
Prato
A1
Fiesole
S38
Florence
Reggello
Borgo Pace
Caprese Michelangelo
Alpe Faggeto
Panzano in Chianti
Radda in Chianti
Arezzo
San Gimignano
Castellina in Chianti
Gargonza
Cortona
Monteriggioni
Siena
A1
Castel Rigone
Sovicille
Montefollonico
Lake Trasimeno
Buonconvento
Bettolle
S223
Pienza
Fontignano

18 Southern Italy

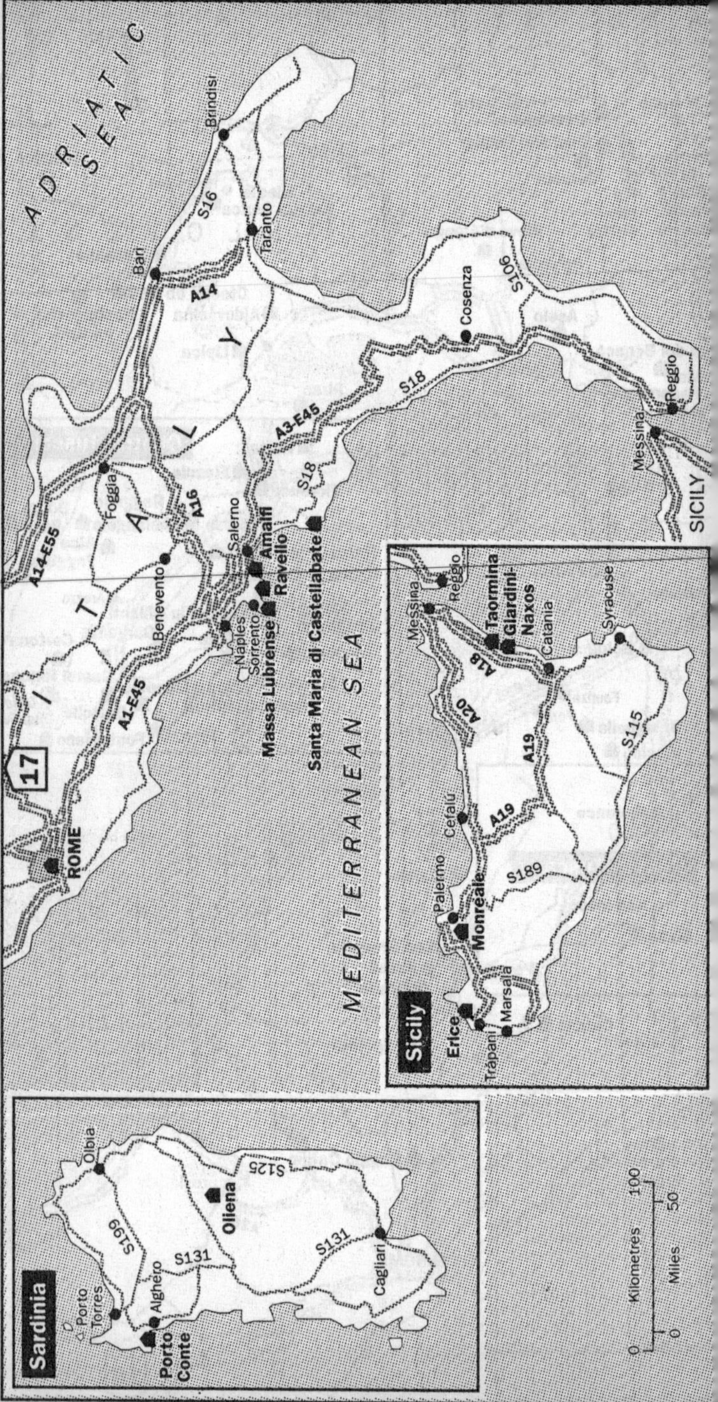

Hungary 19

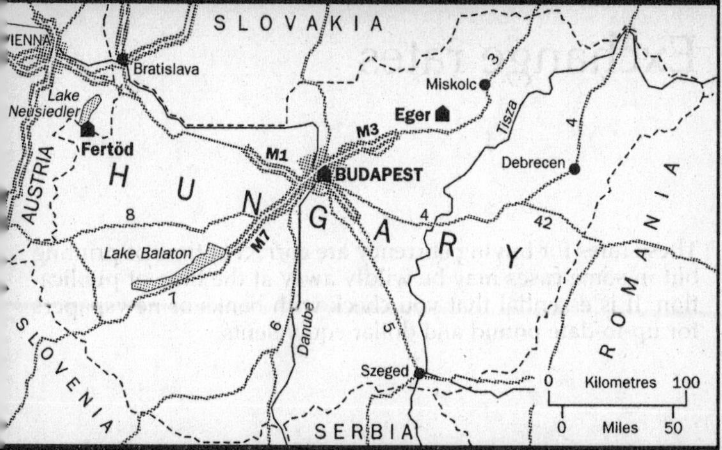

Greece 20

Exchange rates

These rates for buying currency are correct at time of printing but in some cases may be wildly awry at the time of publication. It is essential that you check with banks or newspapers for up-to-date pound and dollar equivalents.

	£1 sterling	US$1
Austria (Schilling: Sch)	16.6	10.7
Belgium (Belgian Franc: Bfrs)	48.7	31.4
Canada (Canadian Dollar: Can$)	2.12	1.37
Czech Republic (Koruna: Kč)	42	27.6
Denmark (Danish Krone: Dkr)	9.1	5.9
France (French Franc: frs)	8	5
Germany (Deutschmark: DM)	2.3	1.5
Greece (Drachma: drs)	374	241
Hungary (Forint: fts)	231	149
Ireland (Punt: £IR)	0.97	0.62
Italy (Lira: L)	2,398	1,547
Luxembourg (Luxembourg Franc: Lfrs)	48.7	31.4
Malta (Maltese Lira: LM)	0.56	0.36
Netherlands (Guilder: glds)	2.6	1.7
Norway (Norwegian Krone: Nkr)	10	6.5
Portugal, Madeira (Escudo: esc)	244	157
Slovenia (Tolar: SIT)	213	137
Spain, Balearics, Canaries (Peseta: pts)	199	128
Sweden (Swedish Krona: Skr)	10.4	6.7
Switzerland (Swiss Franc: Sfrs)	1.9	1.2

Champagne winners and hotel reports

The report forms on the following pages may be used to endorse or criticise an existing entry or to nominate a hotel that you feel deserves inclusion in the *Guide*. But it is not essential that you use our forms or restrict yourself to the space available. All reports (each on a separate piece of paper, please) should include your name and address, the name and location of the hotel, and the date and length of your stay. Please nominate only hotels you have visited in the past 12 months unless you are sure from friends that standards have been maintained. And please be as specific as possible, and critical where appropriate, about the character of the building, the public rooms and the bedrooms, the meals, the service, the nightlife, the grounds. We should also be grateful for some impression of the location as well as of the hotel, particularly in less familiar regions. Comments about worthwhile places to visit in the neighbourhood and, in the case of B&B hotels, recommendable restaurants would also be much appreciated.

Do not feel embarrassed about writing at length. We want the *Guide* to convey the special flavour of its hotels, so the more time and trouble you take in providing small details that will help to make a description come alive, the more valuable to others will be the published result. Many nominations just don't tell us enough. We mind having to pass up a potentially attractive hotel because the report is inadequate. You need not bother with prices or routine information about the number of rooms and facilities. We obtain such details direct from the hotels. We want readers to supply information that is not accessible elsewhere. And we should be extremely grateful, in the case of foreign hotels and new nominations, if you would include brochures whenever possible. Nominations for the 1998 edition, which will be printed in the UK in autumn 1997, should reach us not later than 25 May 1997. The latest date for comments on existing entries is 1 June 1997.

Please never tell a hotel that you intend to file a report. Anonymity is essential to objectivity.

Please let us know if you would like more report forms. Our address is: The Good Hotel Guide, Freepost, London W11 4BR, for UK correspondents (no stamp needed). Reports can also be faxed to us on (0171) 221 5291. Reports posted outside the UK should be addressed to: The Good Hotel Guide, 61 Clarendon Road, London W11 4JE, England, stamped normally.

As usual we have awarded a dozen bottles of champagne for the best reports of the year. This year Joseph Perrier have made it possible for us to reward the most generous and eloquent readers with a magnum. The winners are: Margaret Box of Sutton Coldfield, West Midlands; Alan and Margaret Clarke of Flore, Northants; Richard Creed of Malmesbury, Wilts; Jean Dundas of Kirriemuir, Scotland; Colin Eastaugh, Jeremy and Anthea Larken, and Claire Wrathall of London; Kay Hickman of Godstone, Surrey; Delia and Oliver Millar of Penn, Buckinghamshire; Braham Murray of Bramhall, Cheshire; Ruth and Derek Tilsley of Santa Monica, California; and Nick and Myriam Whalley of Woking, Surrey.

A further case will be on offer for 1998. No special entry form is required; everything we receive in the course of the year will qualify. A winner may be someone who nominates a new hotel or comments on an existing one. We award champagne to those whose reports are consistently useful, as well as to individually brilliant examples of the art of hotel criticism.

[1997]

To: *The Good Hotel Guide*, Freepost, London W11 4BR

NOTE: No stamps needed in UK, but letters posted outside the UK should be addressed to 61 Clarendon Road, London W11 4JE and stamped normally. Unless asked not to, we shall assume that we may publish your name if you are recommending a new hotel or supporting an existing entry. If you would like more report forms please tick ☐

Name of Hotel ______________________________

Address ______________________________

____

Date of most recent visit — Duration of visit

☐ New recommendation — ☐ Comment on existing entry

Report:

Please continue overleaf

I am not connected directly or indirectly with the management or proprietors

Signed ______________________________

Name and address (capitals please) ______________________________

____

[1997]

To: *The Good Hotel Guide*, Freepost, London W11 4BR

NOTE: No stamps needed in UK, but letters posted outside the UK should be addressed to 61 Clarendon Road, London W11 4JE and stamped normally. Unless asked not to, we shall assume that we may publish your name if you are recommending a new hotel or supporting an existing entry. If you would like more report forms please tick ☐

Name of Hotel ________________________________

Address ____________________________________

____

Date of most recent visit — Duration of visit

☐ New recommendation — ☐ Comment on existing entry

Report:

Please continue overleaf

I am not connected directly or indirectly with the management or proprietors

Signed ______________________________

Name and address (capitals please) ______________________________

____

[1997]

To: *The Good Hotel Guide,* Freepost, London W11 4BR

NOTE: No stamps needed in UK, but letters posted outside the UK should be addressed to 61 Clarendon Road, London W11 4JE and stamped normally. Unless asked not to, we shall assume that we may publish your name if you are recommending a new hotel or supporting an existing entry. If you would like more report forms please tick ☐

Name of Hotel ____________________________________

Address ____________________________________

____

Date of most recent visit

Duration of visit

☐ New recommendation

☐ Comment on existing entry

Report:

Please continue overleaf

I am not connected directly or indirectly with the management or proprietors

Signed ______________________________

Name and address (capitals please) ______________________

____

[1997]

To: *The Good Hotel Guide,* Freepost, London W11 4BR

NOTE: No stamps needed in UK, but letters posted outside the UK should be addressed to 61 Clarendon Road, London W11 4JE and stamped normally. Unless asked not to, we shall assume that we may publish your name if you are recommending a new hotel or supporting an existing entry. If you would like more report forms please tick ☐

Name of Hotel ________________________________

Address ____________________________________

____

Date of most recent visit | Duration of visit

☐ New recommendation | ☐ Comment on existing entry

Report:

Please continue overleaf

I am not connected directly or indirectly with the management or proprietors

Signed ____

Name and address (capitals please) ________________________

____

[1997]

To: *The Good Hotel Guide,* Freepost, London W11 4BR

NOTE: No stamps needed in UK, but letters posted outside the UK should be addressed to 61 Clarendon Road, London W11 4JE and stamped normally. Unless asked not to, we shall assume that we may publish your name if you are recommending a new hotel or supporting an existing entry. If you would like more report forms please tick ☐

Name of Hotel ______________________________

Address ______________________________

____

Date of most recent visit
☐ New recommendation
Duration of visit
☐ Comment on existing entry

Report:

Please continue overleaf

I am not connected directly or indirectly with the management or proprietors

Signed ____

Name and address (capitals please) ____________________

____

[1997]

To: *The Good Hotel Guide*, Freepost, London W11 4BR

NOTE: No stamps needed in UK, but letters posted outside the UK should be addressed to 61 Clarendon Road, London W11 4JE and stamped normally. Unless asked not to, we shall assume that we may publish your name if you are recommending a new hotel or supporting an existing entry. If you would like more report forms please tick ☐

Name of Hotel ________________________________

Address ____________________________________

____

Date of most recent visit

Duration of visit

☐ New recommendation

☐ Comment on existing entry

Report:

Please continue overleaf

I am not connected directly or indirectly with the management or proprietors

Signed ______________________________

Name and address (capitals please) ______________________________

____